ENCYCLOPEDIA OF CRIME AND JUSTICE

EDITORIAL BOARD

ENCYCLOPEDIA

OF

Crime and Justice

Sanford H. Kadish

EDITOR IN CHIEF

A. F. and May T. Morrison Professor of Law
University of California, Berkeley

VOLUME 2

THE FREE PRESS

A Division of Macmillan, Inc., New York

Collier Macmillan Publishers, London

THE FREE PRESS
A Division of Macmillan, Inc.
866 Third Avenue, New York, N. Y. 10022

Collier Macmillan Canada, Inc.

Printed in the United States of America

printing number

1 2 3 4 5 6 7 8 9 10

Library of Congress Cataloging in Publication Data
Main entry under title:

Encyclopedia of crime and justice.

  Includes bibliographies and index.
    1. Crime and criminals—Dictionaries. 2. Criminal
justice, Administration of—Dictionaries. I. Kadish,
Sanford H.
HV6017.E52 1983   364′.03′21   83–7156
ISBN 0–02–918110–0 (set)

C

(CONTINUED)

CRIMINALISTICS

Introduction

The term *criminalistics* refers to the profession and scientific discipline that undertakes the recognition, identification, individualization, and evaluation of physical evidence by applying the findings of the natural sciences to the law. The criminalist's work is premised on the idea that human action produces physical changes which, by means of scientific analysis, can be retrieved and used to specify the details of that action. For example, a burglary is reconstructed from the physical changes of broken glass, splintered wood, gouged metal, torn fabric, spilled blood, disturbed furniture, and broken cabinets, so that a picture is obtained of how the burglary was carried out and some characteristics of the burglar are established.

The criminalist's first step is to recognize the possibility that these physical changes constitute an interpretable pattern of burglary. With the second step, identification, the criminalist seeks to classify a physical change, for example, to determine that a stain is fecal matter, that a metal fragment is an alloy of zinc and copper, or that a hair is a rat hair. In identification, a standard scientific procedure of classification is used. In individualizing, the third step, the criminalist attempts to establish that a torn fragment of paper came from a given torn sheet, that a bullet recovered from a corpse was fired by a particular gun, or that a smear of paint on a shirt came from a specific freshly painted wall. In contrast to the usual scientific procedure of seeking a generality, empirical knowledge is used to seek a particular. The criminalist's fourth step, evaluation, requires him to interpret scientifically each physical change as part of a pattern of human action. From identification and individualization the criminalist derives a set of inferences describing the burglary and linking an individual to it. By scientific evaluation he converts the physical changes—a wood splinter found caught in the sweater of a suspect and the broken door of a bicycle shop—into a relationship, establishing the probability that the wood splinter is from the broken door. The inference that the suspect committed the burglary is then supported by the criminalist's evaluation.

Through the use of scientific knowledge, the criminalist thus aids in understanding how and by whom a crime was committed. Interestingly, the modern criminalist is a different person from his nineteenth-century counterpart. Criminalistics at first included systematized and empirical knowledge drawn from all fields relevant to the investigation of crime, the administration of the criminal justice system, and the adjudication of criminal activity. At that time the criminalist was the official legally responsible for preparing a public case. With the expansion of scientific knowledge, the term *criminalist* was redefined in the twentieth century to mean a specialist in empirical knowledge relating to crime. The earlier definition survives in the use of *criminalist* to describe the criminal law scholar specializing in crime and its prevention.

The historical antecedents of the concept of criminalistics include the increasing importance of secular judgment, the growing professionalization of science, and the technological needs of criminal investigation.

On these antecedents, Hans Gross (1847–1915) built the original concept of criminalistics and disseminated it worldwide. As criminal investigation became the province of the police, criminalistics was redefined in the mid-twentieth century. The principle basic to both definitions is that of the physical-evidence process, which premises an interrelationship of human action, physical change, and public policy: knowing part of a pattern allows inferences to be made about the remaining parts. From change, physical continuity—the extension of an object or person through time—is known with less error, leading to improved knowledge of related human action. Until physical evidence is recognized, the use of scientific knowledge is thwarted; hence this initial step is crucial to further criminalistic work. The final step, evaluation, moves the scientifically educated criminalist into the area of legal logic, where certainty, or at least finality, is sought. With justice as a goal, evaluation must attempt to integrate scientific facts into the fabric of social control.

Historical background

Secular judgment. Several historical events combined in the evolution of the concept of criminalistics. One was the evolution in jurisprudence of rational inquiry into the facts and circumstances of criminal conduct. Criminal procedure in the Western world progressed during the thirteenth century from trial by ordeal to the inquisitorial process of the European Continent and to the petit jury system of England. At the Fourth Lateran Council of 1215, Pope Innocent III prohibited the clergy from taking part in trial by ordeal, which set in motion changes in criminal procedure. The replacement of divine by human judgment necessitated new methods of proof.

In the inquisitorial process, circumstantial evidence such as the possession of a bloody weapon, although inadequate in itself for conviction and condemnation, could form part of the proof necessary to allow judicial torture in a case of murder. The circumstantial evidence was irrelevant if two eyewitnesses testified to the guilt of the accused, or if the accused confessed to the crime and explained the commission in detail. In the absence of the testimony of two eyewitnesses or a detailed confession, conviction could not be obtained under the Roman-canon law of proof. If there was one eyewitness to testify or circumstantial evidence sufficient for half-proof (determined by adding the weighted values for various types of circumstantial evidence), the accused could be examined under torture. Judicial torture was limited to those crimes involving the sanctions of death or extreme physical maiming.

The development of new sanctions—imprisonment and forced labor—in part explains the gradual decline of judicial torture (Langbein, p. 48). It was abolished by various nations in the late eighteenth and the nineteenth centuries. Before abolition, even if the circumstantial evidence amounted to less than half-proof or if the accused was tortured without confessing, imprisonment or forced labor could be imposed if the court believed that the accused was guilty. A system of "free judicial evaluation of the evidence" (Langbein, p. 56) emphasized circumstantial evidence in the conduct of a criminal investigation. Rational judgment was based on the evidence gathered by an official—a judge in earlier times.

In England, the petit jury originated during the reign of Henry II (1154–1189). The jury served as a means of settling disputes, particularly over land, although not in the manner of a modern trial. The jurors were expected to know or inform themselves as to the facts of the case before answering upon their oath. Twelve oaths in agreement decided the dispute. After the decree of the Fourth Lateran Council, the jury trial gradually became the accepted means of fact-finding in England. During the fourteenth and fifteenth centuries the roles of juror and witness separated: at first, persons who attested to documents served as jurors, but later it was required that documents be presented in open court, and finally a distinction was drawn between document witnesses and jurors. Still later other witnesses, including those with specialized knowledge, were distinguished from the jurors. A major change in the juror's role occurred in the sixteenth century, when the juror no longer gathered facts. As the trier of fact, the juror passively received information from the local justice of the peace, who performed the investigative and prosecutorial functions.

Professionalization of science. The second historical development in the rise of the concept of criminalistics was the professionalization of science. A change from an agrarian to an industrial basis for most occupations, which resulted from the interplay of the agricultural and industrial revolutions, affected science as well as other human institutions. It became at first possible and then probable that persons interested in science would find employment in it. Whereas before the nineteenth century science had been a gentlemanly avocation, it now became a vocation, and a scientific community arose, drawn more from the middle and lower classes. The scientific community began to grow exponentially as the small, relatively stable number of men engaged in science burgeoned during the nineteenth century into thousands of professionally trained and educated specialists.

Among the sources of income opening up to scientists was that of serving as an expert in consulting work and in civil and criminal trials. Indeed, "during the Victorian period the rising tide of litigation on chemical-industrial matters provided a substantial income for many chemists" (Fullmer, p. 2). The testimony of well-known chemists in the British case of *Severn v. Olive*, 129 Eng. Rep. 1209 (C.P. 1821) concerning a fire in a sugar refinery was a novelty. Within thirty years, such appearances were commonplace, and large fees could be earned from industrial consulting and litigation. Nor was scientific knowledge limited to use in civil matters. Mathieu Orfila, the founder of toxicology, was frequently called as an expert for criminal trials in France. The alleged arsenic poisoning by Louis Mercier and his wife of their son in 1839 was the first case in which Orfila applied the very sensitive Marsh test that had been devised by the English chemist James Marsh; Orfila then testified as an expert witness for the prosecution. François-Vincent Raspail, the founder of chemical microscopy, was the defense's expert. Earlier journal articles by both Orfila and Raspail point to an early manifestation of the problem of bias in expert witnesses. "Raspail was as eager to prove an impecunious defendant innocent as Orfila was bent on obtaining convictions" (Weiner, pp. 183, 187–189).

Criminal investigation technology. A third historical trend leading to the rise of the concept of criminalistics was the technological enhancement of criminal investigation. At the beginning of the nineteenth century, the investigation of criminal activity was largely a matter of setting a thief to catch a thief. The Bow Street Runners, established in 1750 by the novelist Henry Fielding when he was serving as an English justice of the peace, were a group of men knowledgeable about criminal habits and methods, often gained through personal experience, and reminiscent of the legendary Jonathan Wild, a private thief-taker and master fence. The French Sûreté was founded in 1810 on a similar basis by François Vidocq, who in his later career as a public official organized a force of former convicts to investigate and arrest criminals of all types. Such men as Vidocq were able to curb crime by maintaining constant association with the underworld and by collecting detailed records on known criminals.

For Europe and England, the eighteenth and nineteenth centuries brought complex changes in the human condition. Between 1750 and 1850, the popula-

tion more than doubled. Industrialization converted a rural life-style to an urban one for millions of people. Changes in the sphere of public administration included the French creation of the police as a means of controlling crime and violence. Although scholars debate the extent of crime and the direction of trends during this period, the growth in criminal records certainly placed an increasing strain on investigation. It was rapidly becoming impossible to retrieve a record for a specific individual by the late nineteenth century.

Two technological applications of scientific knowledge were used to deal with the retrieval problem. The first was the use of precise measurements of human body structure (anthropometry) in 1883 by Alphonse Bertillon, a clerk in the Paris Prefecture of Police. In the first year that he used his method, Bertillon was able to match his card collection against several hundred individuals otherwise unsuspected as prior criminals. This system, called bertillonage, was used by many police forces before being superseded by the second technological application, fingerprinting. Beginning in 1859, William Herschel used fingerprints in India to distinguish individuals. In 1880, Henry Faulds pointed out the investigational value of fingerprints taken at the scene of a crime. Herschel, on learning of Faulds's proposal, responded by claiming priority in the use of fingerprints. Francis Galton, acquainted with both bertillonage and fingerprinting, scientifically studied fingerprints and concluded that the ten fingerprints of an individual were unique to that individual. It remained for Juan Vucetich to devise a classification system for fingerprints in South America, and for Edward Henry to create in 1896 the fingerprinting system that came to be used worldwide.

Hans Gross and criminalistics

As an examining justice in Austria, Hans Gross quickly learned that his legal studies had left him deficient with regard to establishing the facts of a particular crime. In his town and the surrounding area, police forces were composed mostly of former soldiers adept at keeping the peace. Crime detection was a task for the examining magistrate. From the time he took up his post in 1869, Gross applied himself to learning everything that could conceivably contribute to determining the facts in a case. His appetite was eclectic and holistic, and he left no field of human knowledge of his time unnoticed. He explored both natural and social-science findings, which he combined with information gleaned from tradespeople and police officers.

He viewed a criminal investigation as a scientific problem that the judge was to solve by "research without suppositions" (Grassberger, p. 307). In 1883, Gross published his *Criminal Investigation,* a handbook for magistrates, police officers, and lawyers, which set out what he had learned about criminal investigation. He carefully discussed the characteristics of the successful investigator, giving great attention to the possibilities of error. Gross extensively covered the psychological aspects of interrogation and the evaluation of evidence obtained from it. He reviewed in detail all aspects of physical evidence, devoting particular attention to the use of experts by the criminal investigator. He emphasized that a successful investigator must understand the criminal's actions and the reasons behind them. The value of the book was shown by its rapid distribution. A second edition was published the next year, subsequent editions followed, and the book was translated into several foreign languages. In the third edition of 1899, Gross developed further his system with the help of his friend and colleague, the legal scholar Franz von Liszt. A subtitle to that edition described the work as "a system for criminalistics." To Gross,

the object of the book then is to show how crime is to be handled, investigated, and accounted for, to explain the motives at work and the objects to be attained . . . how the arson was accomplished, what means and assistance the incendiary had at his disposal, how its origin may be accounted for, the character of the criminal and—here comes in criminal psychology—the weight to be attached to the testimony of the witnesses, the consideration of errors in observation and deduction, to which judge, jury, and all who have to deal with crime are exposed—these things are part and parcel of our subject [1962, p. xxv].

In another seminal work, *Criminal Psychology,* Gross discussed the orientation of the criminal investigator, lawyer, or judge, *as a criminalist:*

The whole business of the criminalist is the study of causes. . . . The fact that we deal with the problem of cause brings us close to other sciences which have the same task in their own researches; and this is one of the reasons for the criminalist's necessary concern with other disciplines. . . . And we observe that the whole problem of method is grounded on causation. Whether empirically or aprioristically does not matter. We are concerned solely with causation. In certain directions our task is next to the historians' who aim to bring men and events into definite causal sequence [1968, pp. 117–118].

The task of the criminalist was to coordinate a criminal investigation, making use of specialists in various fields of scientific or unusual knowledge. The criminalist was required to have sufficient insight to know when a specialist was needed, what specialist was needed, and what the specialist should be asked. Gross did not see the criminalist himself as the expert.

In the first quarter of the twentieth century, various European countries established crime detection laboratories as government or university units; the laboratory founded in 1910 by Edmond Locard of the Lyons state police became the most prolific in making scientific contributions to criminalistics. Locard's exhaustive studies centered on his exchange principle (contact transfer) for physical evidence. Much of the European work in criminalistics was heavily influenced by forensic medicine, not surprisingly since the investigation of murder uses the services of both fields.

The works of Hans Gross attracted attention in the United States. John Henry Wigmore, the noted scholar in the fields of criminal law and criminology, convened a national conference of criminal law and criminology in 1909, at which he was elected president of the new American Institute of Criminal Law and Criminology. A presidential committee of the institute arranged for the translation of important foreign works on criminology, including Gross's *Criminal Psychology.* In the dedication of his *Principles of Judicial Proof,* Wigmore indicated his estimate of Gross's importance by hailing him as the "professor of criminal law . . . who has done more than any other man in modern times to encourage the application of science to judicial proof."

August Vollmer became the leader in the professionalization of police work in the United States. Elected marshal of Berkeley, California, in 1905 and appointed the town's police chief in 1909, Vollmer's interest in scientific crime detection was encouraged by a University of California biology professor, Jacques Loeb. Gross's works on criminal investigation and criminal psychology were recommended to Vollmer by Loeb. The qualities of the criminal investigator enumerated by Gross clearly affected the evolution of Vollmer's conception of the professional policeman.

Criminalistics redefined

During the nineteenth century the meaning of the term *science* shifted from systematized general knowledge to experimental knowledge of the physical world. By the end of the century it began to encompass any discipline employing the methodologies of the physical sciences, for example, the social sciences. With the expansion of the community there arose a new designation for the individual member, *scientist,* although it was debated fiercely in the mid-nineteenth century before winning general acceptance. The experimental criterion for scientific knowledge was shown as early as the 1820s by the creation of the laboratory for training, education, and investigation. With this shift, the basis was laid for the introduction of empirical science into criminal justice and for the redefinition of criminalistics.

The potential in criminal investigation for technological applications of scientific knowledge, especially of knowledge drawn from the natural sciences, increased dramatically in the early twentieth century. The use of scientific experts as independent consultants gradually began to change after World War I. Scientific experts now began to testify in their capacity as employees of crime detection laboratories. The preparation of criminal cases by the police for judicial review slowly became standard practice in European and Anglo-American procedure. Locard's laboratory was the first to be organized under police administration in Europe. In the United States, Vollmer reorganized the Los Angeles Police Department in 1924 to include a crime laboratory. By 1935, the London Metropolitan Police were provided with expanded crime laboratory services. A report to the British Home Office in 1938 concluded that the integration of scientific work with police work was vital to many criminal investigations and likely to be useful in almost any criminal investigation. In 1930, Wigmore was delighted to provide space for the Scientific Crime Detection Laboratory at the Northwestern University Law School. Economic conditions shattered Wigmore's dream although laboratory staff members went on to establish other midwestern and eastern crime laboratories.

As private consultants and public laboratories made increasing use in criminal cases of scientific knowledge from such fields as chemistry, physics, and biology, a term was needed to describe such specialists. By mid-century, *criminalist* was offered as a suitable term, principally in the United States. Use of the term was actively promoted by one of the leading American authorities in the field, Paul Kirk. Kirk had begun his academic career in 1929 at the University of California at Berkeley, teaching biochemistry. One of his students, Roger Greene, who had taken the first laboratory class offered by Kirk in microanalysis, was hired on graduation by the state of California to establish the first state-level crime detection laboratory in the United States.

Kirk's own interest in crime investigation was sparked by a 1935 dog-poisoning case. He had become aware of the police's interest in physical evidence through a colleague, Carl Schmidt. Vollmer had enlisted Schmidt's aid in establishing a technical component of the criminology program at the university. Kirk became the program's advisor in technical criminology in 1937 and worked closely with the Berkeley police chief John Holstrom to establish the university's School of Criminology in 1950. By that time, Kirk had earned an international reputation for the scientific analysis of physical evidence. Most of the research articles published in the leading criminological journal between 1932 and 1950 represented outgrowths of Kirk's program (Dillon, p. 206). At mid-century, Berkeley's was one of only two academic-degree programs in criminalistics in the United States, and students from around the world came to study with Kirk.

The Depression of the 1930s and World War II slowed the growth of police organizations and the progress of criminalistics, although wartime needs drew upon the expertise of specialists in physical-evidence examination in all countries. The criminalistic component of the criminology program at Berkeley was inactive between 1942 and 1945. With the return of peace, research and the education of criminalists again became Kirk's main concern. His educational efforts culminated in 1963, when his student Donald Nelson, of New Zealand, was awarded the University of California's first doctorate in criminology.

In 1955 the scientific staffs in California's crime detection laboratories formed the California Association of Criminalists and thereafter gradually evolved the current definition of criminalistics. The American Academy of Forensic Sciences, which had been organized in 1950, initially included a section for police science that later became the criminalistic section, with one of the largest memberships in the academy.

Public concern with the crime problem in the United States increased in the 1960s, as it had briefly in the 1930s. In 1965, Congress voted to apply substantial resources to the problem, and one area that received funding was the use of science and technology in law enforcement. A national symposium on this subject called for research into the applications of science to crime detection (Nicol). Continuing public concern resulted, in part, in more funds being provided for crime detection laboratory facilities and personnel; by 1975 the number of laboratories had more than doubled and staffs had increased to more than two thousand. In Great Britain, the importance of research on physical evidence was underscored when the Home Office Central Research Establishment, which had been proposed in the 1938 Home Office report, was created under the directorship of Alan Curry. This center has been eminently successful in conducting research and in supporting the scientific approach to criminal investigation. Since 1973, the Federal Bureau of Investigation's symposium on crime laboratory development has been an annual event, and the crime laboratory directors attending the first session organized the American Society of Crime Laboratory Directors. In 1980 construction of the Forensic Science Research and Training Center began with federal support. Such efforts in Great Britain and the United States are part of a worldwide interest in criminalistics. In 1978 there were eleven hundred crime detection laboratories in eighty-nine countries.

Criminalistics and the physical-evidence process

The premise that physical change, human action, and public policy interrelate to form an interpretable pattern underlies the criminalist's concern for physical evidence. Whether the problem is one of discovering how a man died, deciding how an injury occurred, crossing a street safely, or repairing a kitchen mixer, physical evidence is a powerful tool in reaching a solution. In each of these problems, physical change takes place. A set of physical changes is interrelated in a pattern, which is interpreted as a result—a homicidal death, an unsafe machine, a safe street crossing, or a working kitchen mixer. This process of recognizing physical changes, discovering a pattern, and from the pattern interpreting a result is called the construct of physical evidence. The process is not error-free.

To improve the chances of selecting a correct pattern and interpreting a correct result, close attention to physical change is necessary. Through insights into energy and substance, the natural sciences offer the means to know what *happened* physically from what *changed* physically. Take, for example, a floor on which glass pieces are found in a rough semicircle near a desk. Glass as a substance is known to break easily, and any object receives a jolt on falling. Thus, a broken object will scatter from the place of impact. These commonly known physical changes support a hypothesis that the observed pattern is one of a glass object that has fallen from the desk to the floor, where it broke and scattered. However, it could have been thrown rather than simply have fallen, so that two distinct patterns with the same result are possible. To the answers as to what changed physically can be added answers as to how the *physical* change occurred. A "throwing" pattern emerges when it is discovered that a glass object similar to the broken one bounces each time on falling from the desk height, but breaks if thrown onto the floor. Actually, it is only known that more energy is required for throwing than for falling from desk to floor, and that the substance, a glass object, requires some minimal amount of energy to break.

Another example is a colored shirt with white blotches on its front, found in a garage with freshly painted white walls. Close examination reveals that each blotched spot is a hard crust adhering to the shirt threads. It is known that painting is prone to cause spattering, that fresh paint drops form spots, and that paint on drying becomes a hard layer. It would be reasonable to guess that the shirt was spattered during the painting of the garage. Other distinct patterns with the same result are, however, possible. For example, the blotches could be something other than paint. To the previous questions about physical changes, two additional questions are, When did the physical change occur, and what is the substance involved in the physical change? If the paint on the garage wall is wet and the shirt blotches are dry, there is less confidence in supposing that the shirt was spattered during the painting of the garage. When tests on the substance forming a blotch show something other than paint, the guess becomes unreasonable and another pattern is sought.

The search for physical change provides answers that allow a criminalist to sort out the puzzle of physical continuity. This is done by taking all the possible patterns and comparing each to the answers obtained to the questions about physical change. The combination of physical processes detected in a search narrows attention to fine points in the possible patterns of human behavior, such as criminal activity. The difficulty in selecting the correct pattern shows that physical change is an *indirect* measure of specific behavior. At times, knowing what happened physically will enable the possible behavioral patterns to be ranked from "unlikely" to "likely." If several independent answers to what happened physically are found, a degree of probability attaches to the rank order, strengthening the inference that one pattern occurred. The inference can be further bolstered by comparing these physical changes with what is known to have happened.

As a product of human activity, physical evidence is a powerful tool in decision-making. Since physical change is an ever-present aspect of action, the answers to the question of what happened *physically* provide an indication of the physical continuity. Error is possible, but it can be reduced by careful attention in scientifically examining each physical change. In seeking answers to what happened behaviorally, a single, indirect indicator of physical change is very weak; the combination of different physical changes affords a stronger probability of valid answers. When a criminalist's analysis of physical changes is coupled with known behavioral facts, past human activity can be specified.

Physical-evidence recognition

Gross emphasized that investigation required "a provisional classification to guide inquiry" (1962, p. 5). The first step in criminalistic analysis, recognition, serves a gatekeeping function since, obviously, unrecognized physical evidence is information lost to an investigation. Two common approaches to the recognition of physical evidence are to classify by type of case or by type of object. The first classification follows the legal definitions—common-law, statutory, or administrative—of proscribed behavior, for example, homicide, arson, burglary, product misrepresentation, and traffic-accident and occupational-safety violations. Within each class, the definitional elements are specified for the evidence, and these become the framework for seeking physical change. The second classification uses evidence associated with human behavior, such as blood, handwriting, air pollutants, or skid marks. Physical change is noted by the presence of the particular substance.

These two approaches have proved useful in practice, but there are major problems with such "provisional classifications." One is that the recognition and preservation of physical change is usually delegated by criminalists to the investigator. Another problem is the degree of abstractness. A case approach infers an actual state of affairs, that is, a burglary took place or did not take place. The investigator is thus led to look for physical change specifically supporting either contention, but he does not consider that the "burglary" may be a fraud simulated for economic purposes. In the object approach, a subjective sense of probability directs the search for physical change since the list of possibilities is infinite. The investigator who has found fingerprints in many other cases looks for fingerprints and little else.

A minor problem with the two approaches is the interaction between classifications: the "burglary" investigation may concentrate on fingerprints and neglect the drop of blood on the windowsill if the investigator subjectively regards the possibility of blood being shed in burglaries as negligible. Another problem is that in both approaches the payoff is unknown. Although the importance of physical evidence is generally recognized, the relative importance of each type by crime categories is not known (Forst, Lucianovic, and Cox).

A desirable "provisional classification" would, in effect, freeze the moment under investigation. Given the preservation of sufficient detail from that moment, the physical state of the situation is known *now*. Once knowledge is gained of the physical state *before* the situation, it is possible by comparison to unravel the physical state *during* the situation. A physical pattern is then extracted from the physical changes. For example, a coin—a physical object—is the carrier of a pattern and the matrix of information. The simplest expression of pattern is position, or the manner in which a physical object is placed in relation to another physical object. A flipped coin landing on a rug has a space position (heads up relative to the rug) and a time position ("now" relative to "before"). With continued flipping of the coin, the successive positions form a pattern—the number of times heads appears and the number of times tails appears—that is a composite of multiple positions. The patterns of a single position and of multiple positions represent physical changes resulting from action, the application of energy to a physical object over time. For investigational purposes, a pattern of physical changes is a key that unlocks what has happened before by drawing comparisons to what is known now. Such patterns, faithfully recorded, yield the least abstracted record. For this reason photography, a record of minimal abstraction, is of great importance in criminal investigation.

It is desirable that all relevant physical changes be recognized. Since relevance is often unknown, all physical changes in an investigation need to be recognized. Indeed, even when relevance is known, it is a useful cross-check to treat it as unknown. Since human data processing is limited, a simple classification of six categories allows for the recognition of all physical changes. Physical objects in criminal investigation need only be considered as examples of position, breakage, dispersion, impression, transfer (the Locard principle), and substance.

A pattern can be found in each of these categories, and none of the six is exclusive of the others since all involve positional aspects. Position as the present location of a physical object is a consequence of energy. The next four categories also represent the effect of energy applied to a physical object. Breakage is the separation of a physical object into a few pieces—for example, snapping a pencil in two or ripping a piece of paper in fourths. With dispersion, a physical object is scattered into many pieces: a ceramic statuette falls to a hard floor and shatters into bits and pieces that are thrown in all directions. The fourth category, impression, results from the interaction of two physical objects, one of which is effectively harder than the other: for example, a truck passes over a muddy patch on the street. In the fifth category, transfer, three physical objects take part, one of the three changing its position from the second to the third object, as when butter is spread from a knife onto toast. All five categories produce physical changes that result from energy: a new location, torn paper, a scattered statuette, a tire print, and a piece of buttered toast.

The sixth category, substance, is the nature of a physical object. In substance, the attention is more on the object as a repository of energy, as opposed to the energy flows of the other five categories. A physical object represents a state of energy—built-in energy, so to speak. It is a group of atoms arranged in multiple positions forming substantive patterns, which are revealed by applying energy. Even the most sophisticated instruments used by the criminalist function by pattern retrieval from applied energy. Physical change as characterized by energy flows and repositories can be recognized with the aid of these six categories.

A criminal investigation can be likened to walking into a movie theater at the end of the film. The last few frames, a slice of time, remain as the "now" patterns, the physical traces of the past. These patterns are preserved by written reports, sketches, photographs, and collections. Photographing, sketching, and writing are done with little or no change of the patterns, whereas collecting does change them. A twisted piece of metal picked up from the floor and taken to a window for examination in a better light is a physical change that loses the information as to where the piece was and how it was oriented. The investigator can avoid such losses by considering each physical object present in terms of the six categories mentioned above. Obviously, position, including orientation, can be preserved through photographs, sketches, and report notes made before a physical collection. The handling of a broken object should not increase the breakage or damage the broken area. When an object has been dispersed, the possibility and desirability of reassembly may require a total collection. An impressed object will require protection of the physically changed area. In the event of a transfer, the recipient object is collected since the means by which a transferred object is attached to it may be important.

The structure of a physical object is a critical consideration in collection. Solids are least troublesome unless the size is awkward or the material fragile. Liquids present more difficulties. The container in which they are placed should not interact with them chemically or physically since this complicates analysis. Another difficulty is that a liquid may be unstable and undergo physical change continuously. The use of preservatives may slow such alterations. Gases present a major difficulty since they often dissipate quite rapidly.

The total preservation of "now" patterns would be a very time-consuming procedure, however desirable. A procedure of sampling is necessary. Although it is not easy, sampling offsets the time bind and makes the preservation of patterns manageable. One rule to follow in sampling is that the sample, a part, must be representative of the total situation, the whole. If this requirement is satisfied, the sampling will be adequate. The test of adequacy is a comparison between what is taken and the site from which it has been removed: can the "now" patterns be reproduced from the sampling? Errors will be made, but they can be detected by periodic reevaluation and monitoring by criminalists as the number of investigations increases.

Physical-evidence evaluation

The criminalist identifies and individualizes physical evidence by using techniques drawn from a multitude of empirical disciplines and specialties. This technical information permits connections to be made between different parts of the physical evidence. In his concluding step, that of evaluation—the reconstruction of physical continuity that establishes what happened and who did it—the criminalist makes his contribution to the administration of justice.

Each decision to make use of technical information where the law and science intersect requires a synthesis of these human systems that deal with social and physical realities. A challenging field of study is that of the operational logics employed by these human systems and the difficulties experienced in reaching a synthesis. The application of the law in a given situation basically entails the use of a two-variable logic, that is, guilt or innocence, negligence or nonnegligence, liability or nonliability, responsibility or nonresponsibility. This is not to deny that in applying the law a complex variety of intermingled values are involved, reflecting the economic, political, social, personal, and other aspects of human experience. They serve only to sharpen the focus on the *legal* action: a decision must be reached and a line must be drawn, now, on each particular matter.

In contrast, the *scientific* action employs a multivariable logic, arriving at such conclusions as a small chance of infection, a strong probability of rain, a four-in-ten chance of the occurrence of blood group A, or an estimate of 83 percent positive outcomes. Scientific fact-finding seeks to represent a range of possibilities and to determine the distribution of possibilities within that range. As the degree of correspondence between representation and that which is represented increases, the capability of explaining the past or predicting the future also increases. The degree of correspondence is found to be valid for purposes of explanation when the representation allows a greater number of facts from the past to fit its pattern; this is so for purposes of prediction, when the representation specifies details of a possible future that becomes reality. A multivariable logic allows validation to be expressed as a probability, thereby providing an estimate of possible error for science, a human invention.

At the operational intersection of science and the law, this multivariable logic of science is juxtaposed to the two-variable logic of the law. Equating the extremes is somewhat less difficult than contending with issues of degree. What Warren Weaver referred to as problems of simplicity suffer the least in translation from science to the law. These are problems in which a few variables are related to such a degree that knowing the measure of one variable allows a very accurate prediction for another. For example, the law may specify that possession of a particular drug is illegal. If a technical finding is made that a seized substance agrees by measurement with the known properties of a certain illegal drug, the legal status of the possessor is inferred routinely. Conflict between scientific and legal logics at this level may be illustrated by a situation in which the law specifies that no given pollutant can exist. To verify that none exists, scientific fact-finding would require that every molecule be measured in order to demonstrate the absence of the pollutant. When in practice the best means of detection require 1,000 molecules merely to indicate presence, the legal standard is unobtainable.

The seemingly obvious solution to the above difficulty would be to change the legal standard to set the detection limit at a given technical capability. This raises issues of degree that, in turn, involve Weaver's problems of disorganized and organized complexity. These are problems of either a multitude of variables behaving erratically and incomprehensibly for which average properties can be determined, or a multitude of variables behaving as a systemic entity. The multivariable logic of probability enables science to handle problems by statements of degree. The example of pollution within a specified detection limit would an-

swer the question as to the presence at or above that limit (a question of simplicity), but not the question as to whether the presence is harmful (a question of complexity). The latter question combines issues and attending degrees. Is there an amount below which human health is unaffected, how is that amount to be determined, and for whom is the determination to be made? How is the decision to be made between accepting a determined amount that is too high and one that is too low?

Scientific responses to such questions are given in probabilistic terms, sometimes stated as "on the one hand and on the other hand." In a hearing on the health effects of pollutants, a United States senator was prompted to call for "one-armed" scientists. Although respecting the senator's yearning for certainty, the scientific response must state its basis, namely, the operational logic and the *error in that operation.* Even the logic of arithmetic, which among all human inventions has been an extremely powerful means of learning, has not been proved consistent, that is, error-free. The measurements of science represent human constructs; each new construct or each new application of a previous construct must be validated. A necessary part of that validation is a statement of associated error. Moreover, there are questions to which the scientific response is silence: "Is it certain?" is one. The criminalist's professional opinion is based on the operational logic of the natural sciences, where confidence in the reliability of knowing has both objective and subjective components. It is important that the subjective component of personal belief not mask the objective component of scientific consensus as to the inherent error.

BRIAN PARKER

See also BURDEN OF PROOF; *both articles under* CRIMINAL PROCEDURE; *both articles under* EYEWITNESS IDENTIFICATION.

BIBLIOGRAPHY

CARTE, GENE E., and CARTE, ELAINE H. *Police Reform in the United States: The Era of August Vollmer, 1905–1932.* Berkeley: University of California Press, 1975.

DILLON, DUAYNE J. "A History of Criminalistics in the United States, 1850–1950." Ph.D. dissertation, University of California at Berkeley, 1977.

FORST, BRIAN; LUCIANOVIC, JUDITH; and COX, SARAH J. *What Happens after Arrest?: A Court Perspective of Police Operations in the District of Columbia.* Washington, D.C.: U.S. Department of Justice, Law Enforcement Assistance Administration, National Institute of Law Enforcement and Criminal Justice, 1978.

FULLMER, JUNE Z. "Technology, Chemistry, and the Law

in Early Nineteenth-century England." *Technology and Culture* 21 (1980): 1–28.

GALTON, FRANCIS. *Fingerprints* (1892). New introduction by Harold Cummins. New York: Da Capo, 1965.

GRASSBERGER, ROLAND. "Hans Gross, 1847–1915." *Pioneers in Criminology*. 2d ed., enlarged. Edited and introduced by Hermann Mannheim. Montclair, N.J.: Patterson Smith, 1972, pp. 305–317.

GROSS, HANS G. A. *Criminal Investigation: A Practical Textbook for Magistrates, Police Officers, and Lawyers* (1924). Adapted by John Adam and J. Collyer Adam from the *System der Kriminalistik*. 5th ed. Edited by Richard Leofric Jackson. London: Sweet & Maxwell, 1962.

———. *Criminal Psychology: A Manual for Judges, Practitioners, and Students* (1898). Translated from the 4th German edition by Horace M. Kallen. Introduction by Joseph Jastrow. Reprint. Montclair, N.J.: Patterson Smith, 1968.

HAQ, TALIB UL; ROCHE, GEORGE W.; and PARKER, BRIAN. "Theoretical Field Concepts in Forensic Science: Part I. Application to Recognition and Retrieval of Physical Evidence." *Journal of Forensic Sciences* 23 (1978): 212–217.

Home Office. *Report of the Departmental Committee on Detective Work and Procedure* (1938). Reprint. London: Her Majesty's Stationery Office, 1954.

KIND, STUART, and OVERMAN, MICHAEL. *Science against Crime*. London: Aldus Books, 1972.

KIRK, PAUL L. "The Standardization of Criminological Nomenclature." *Journal of Criminal Law, Criminology, and Police Science* 38 (1947): 165–167.

LANGBEIN, JOHN H. *Torture and the Law of Proof: Europe and England in the Ancien Régime*. University of Chicago Press, 1977.

LOCARD, EDMOND. *Traité de Criminalistique*. 6 vols. Lyons: J. Desvigne, 1931–1936.

MANNING, PETER K. *Police Work: The Social Organization of Policing*. Cambridge, Mass.: MIT Press, 1977.

MENDELSOHN, EVERETT. "The Emergence of Science as a Profession in Nineteenth-century Europe." *The Management of Scientists*. By Everett Mendelsohn, Anne Roe, Royden C. Saunders, Jr., Albert F. Siepert, Norman Kaplan, and Herbert A. Shepard. Boston: Beacon Press, 1964, pp. 3–48.

NICOL, JOSEPH D. "Present Status of Criminalistics." *Law Enforcement Science and Technology: Proceedings of the First National Symposium*, vol. 1. Edited by S. A. Yefsky. Washington, D.C.: Thompson Books, 1967, pp. 245–246.

O'HARA, CHARLES E., and OSTERBURG, JAMES W. *An Introduction to Criminalistics: The Application of the Physical Sciences to the Detection of Crime*. New York: Macmillan, 1949.

PARKER, BRIAN. "The Scientific Assessment of Physical Evidence from Criminal Conduct." *Handbook of Criminology*. Edited by Daniel Glaser. Chicago: Rand McNally, 1974, pp. 505–526.

PETERSON, JOSEPH L., ed. *Forensic Science: Scientific Investigation in Criminal Justice*. New York: AMS Press, 1975.

ROSS, SYDNEY. "Scientist: The Story of a Word." *Annals of Science* 18, no. 2 (1962): 65–85.

SAFERSTEIN, RICHARD. *Criminalistics: An Introduction to Forensic Science*. 2d ed. Englewood Cliffs, N.J.: Prentice-Hall, 1981.

THORWALD, JÜRGEN. *The Century of the Detective*. Translated by Richard and Clara Winston. New York: Harcourt, Brace & World, 1965.

———. *Crime and Science: The New Frontier in Criminology*. Translated by Richard and Clara Winston. New York: Harcourt, Brace & World, 1967.

WEAVER, WARREN. "Science and Complexity." *American Scientiest* 36 (1948): 536–544.

WEINER, DORA B. *Raspail: Scientist and Reformer*. New York: Columbia University Press, 1968.

WIGMORE, JOHN HENRY. *The Principles of Judicial Proof; or, The Process of Proof as Given by Logic, Psychology, and General Experience, and Illustrated in Judicial Trials*. 2d ed., rev. and rewritten. Boston: Little, Brown, 1931.

CRIMINALIZATION AND DECRIMINALIZATION

Introduction

The question of the proper scope of the criminal law—what to punish and why—is a continuing and difficult one. Since all criminal laws in the United States are created by statute, this question is primarily addressed to the legislature: What new criminal prohibitions should be enacted, and which existing prohibitions should be expanded, eliminated, or narrowed? However, when courts are called upon to interpret the scope of criminal statutes, they sometimes address similar questions, either as a matter of presumed legislative intent or as a matter of public policy.

How the criminal law has been used and abused. When most people think about "crime," they imagine such serious offenses as murder, rape, assault, robbery, burglary, and traditional forms of theft, that is, the stealing of tangible property. There have been relatively few changes in the scope of the criminal law in these areas, although major issues of criminalization occasionally arise, for example, the question of when appropriation of valuable secret information should be treated as theft. The focus of debate on the criminalization question tends to be elsewhere, involving a host of miscellaneous offenses designed to protect public morality, support government regulation of the economy, protect the environment, or generally promote the public welfare.

Despite efforts in many states to reform and recodify criminal codes, these various "morals" and "public welfare" offenses remain on the books, and new offenses of this type are continually being added. Indeed, there appears to be a unidirectional tendency to adopt new criminal laws, without repealing or substantially restricting old ones that are not even enforced. New statutes are enacted in reaction to the scandals or crises of the day, by legislators who are eager to do something about these problems or who wish to demonstrate their strong support for public morality and good order. Rarely does any effective lobbying group or other impetus compel legislators to repeal or restrict existing laws. Moreover, the scope of government regulation and welfare programs has expanded enormously since the late nineteenth century, and each new program has brought with it new penal laws. Criminal penalties have been applied to widely varied activities in the effort to end the killing of endangered species; to regulate automobile traffic; to discipline school officials who fail to use required textbooks; to regulate commerce in foods, drugs, and liquor; to uphold housing codes; and to regulate the economy through price control and rationing laws, antitrust laws, export controls, lending laws, and securities regulations (Allen, p. 3; Kadish, 1963, p. 424; 1967, pp. 158–159; Packer, pp. 130, 273).

In response to the ever-increasing number of criminal statutes, numerous proposals have been made to define more narrowly the scope of the criminal law and to decriminalize a large number of morals and public-welfare offenses. The laws most often proposed for repeal relate to public drunkenness, vagrancy, general "disorderly" conduct, homosexuality, sodomy, fornication, adultery, bigamy, incest, prostitution, obscenity, pornography, abortion, suicide, use or sale of drugs and liquor, gambling, violations of child-support orders, passing of worthless checks, economic regulatory violations, minor traffic offenses, and juvenile offenses that would not be criminal if the actor were an adult (Kadish, 1963, 1967; Allen; Schur; Packer; Morris and Hawkins; U.S. Department of Justice).

The authors of these proposals do not always reject the same offenses, nor do they all agree on a common rationale or criterion for decriminalization. However, there is considerable consensus that many of the laws proposed for repeal are either inappropriately invasive of individual freedom of action, hypocritical, unenforceable, or too costly to enforce. These authors also appear to agree that the scope of the criminal law can and should be defined by a single set of principles capable of efficient application to all types of offenses and should reflect general consensus among reasonable persons of widely differing moral and philosophical views. Such an approach has the advantage of avoiding narrow, subjective disputes about the wisdom of specific laws, although it also has the disadvantage inherent in any abstract, a priori schema. This article will describe the various criminalization criteria that have been proposed and will attempt to reconcile them and present a consensus of the consensus-seekers.

Definition of a "criminal" sanction. Before examining the wide variety of issues involved in the choice of the criminal sanction, it is useful to consider what it means to call something a crime and, in particular, how criminal prohibitions differ from various civil laws and regulations. Although criminal penalties tend to be more severe than civil and regulatory remedies, perhaps only the death penalty is unique to the criminal law. Property is taken by taxation, civil fines, and civil forfeitures; even individual liberty may be denied by such civil procedures as quarantine, civil commitment, and the military draft. Thus, what principally distinguishes the criminal sanction is its peculiar stigmatizing quality, even when sentence is suspended and no specific punishment follows conviction. Criminal sanctions have traditionally been viewed as expressing society's moral condemnation of the defendant's behavior and its "hatred, fear, or contempt for the convict" (Henry M. Hart, pp. 401–406). This is probably still true, despite the dilution of "moral" blame which has resulted from the continuing expansion of the criminal law.

A second distinguishing feature of the criminal law, which follows naturally from the special stigma and severe sanctions that may be imposed, is the strict procedure of adjudication required. As a matter of constitutional law, criminal defendants are entitled to proof beyond a reasonable doubt, the privilege against compelled self-incrimination, and numerous other Bill of Rights guarantees. Criminal statutes may also violate due process if they are unduly vague (*Papachristou v. City of Jacksonville*, 405 U.S. 156 (1972)); and they are traditionally construed narrowly, both as a matter of common-law public policy and as a means to avoid unconstitutional vagueness problems. A third distinguishing feature of the criminal law, which follows in part from the first two, is that it employs specialized agencies of enforcement: police, prosecutors, criminal courts, and correctional agencies focus their efforts largely or entirely on the criminal law.

The stigmatizing effect of criminal penalties is related to one of the traditional purposes of criminal sanctions: to exact retribution by imposing "deserved" punishment. Retribution is a nonutilitarian ethic that views punishment as being proper for its own sake, whether or not it has any effect on future wrongdoing by the offender or others. Various utilitarian theories, on the other hand, justify punishment because it discourages the offender from future wrongdoing (special deterrence), intimidates other would-be offenders (general deterrence), and strengthens behavioral standards in more indirect ways (the educative or moralizing function of punishment). Punishment also allegedly prevents further crime by the defendant through physical restraints on his liberty or privileges (incapacitation), or through education or other treatment aimed at changing underlying social, psychological, or physical causes of his criminal behavior (rehabilitation) (Packer, pp. 37–58; Zimring and Hawkins, pp. 74–89). Clearly, the extent to which the enactment and enforcement of criminal penalties actually achieve any of these purposes of punishment must be an important factor in deciding whether to employ criminal sanctions in a particular case.

How does the criminal law achieve these purposes? That is, what types of criminal sanctions are available? In addition to the punishments listed or implied above (death, imprisonment, fines, suspended sentence), defendants may be given a conditional prison sentence or fine. A conditional sentence is not carried out if the defendant complies with certain restrictions or requirements, such as periodic reports to a probation officer or other supervisor; limitations on travel, place of residence, or associates; abstinence from liquor or drugs; restitution to the victim; community-service work; participation in educational, counseling, or medical treatment programs; and refraining from further criminal behavior, particularly of the same type.

Persons convicted of crimes may also lose certain privileges or suffer other disabilities, either automatically or at the discretion of various officials. These include revocation or denial of a driver's license or other permit; ineligibility for government or private employment, programs, or contracts; loss of voting rights; forfeiture of property used to commit the crime; liability to greater penalties or less favorable procedures upon subsequent convictions; and loss of credibility as a witness, through rules permitting impeachment by prior convictions.

As suggested earlier, many of these sanctions can also be imposed by means of civil or regulatory procedures; indeed, civil sanctions are sometimes imposed through criminal procedures. In Minnesota, for example, most moving-traffic violations, violation of certain ordinances, and minor drug offenses are classified as petty misdemeanors, punishable by a fine of up to $100; they are declared by statute not to be "crimes"

(Minn. Stat. Ann. § 609.02 (4a) (1981 Supp.)). However, they are enforced by the police and criminal courts, and are governed by the code of criminal procedure (Minn. R. Crim. P. 1.01 (1981); cf. Model Penal Code, § 1.04 (5), which defines a similar hybrid offense classified as a "violation"). To some extent, the opposite may also be true: clearly criminal laws may be enforced by specialized police agencies, such as the Internal Revenue Service. The United States Supreme Court has had some difficulty in determining which of these various hybrids are subject to full constitutional criminal procedures. The Court has held that most of the Bill of Rights guarantees apply only to offenses which are labeled criminal or which involve "infamous" penalties, such as imprisonment. However, the privilege against compelled self-incrimination, as well as certain other protections (for example, the ex post facto clause and the Eighth Amendment ban on cruel and unusual punishments), apparently applies to any form of punishment—that is, any provision whose dominant purpose is to exact retribution for an offense or to deter or otherwise prevent future offenses of that type (Clark, pp. 382–385; Packer, p. 31).

How should one treat such civil and quasi-criminal penalties when approaching the criminalization problem? Although they all could be viewed as criminal laws, this article initially adopts a narrower approach and defines *criminal laws* as those that are generally labeled or regarded as criminal in a formal sense, are enforced by the police and other traditional criminal justice agencies, and are subject to constitutional and nonconstitutional rules of criminal procedure. However, it will be necessary to consider the various hybrids as well. In its broadest sense, the criminalization question thus becomes several questions: Should this behavior be prohibited or regulated by law? If so, should this be done by purely civil or administrative laws, quasi-criminal sanctions, or formal criminal penalties? Which agencies should enforce these prohibitions and sanctions?

A review and typology of criminalization arguments

It is useful at the outset to distinguish between two fundamentally different types of arguments for and against the use of the criminal law. Arguments of principle assert that as a matter of political or moral philosophy, it is proper (or improper) to prohibit certain conduct. The second category, that of arguments of practicality, is logically relevant only if it has been determined that society may legitimately prohibit the conduct in question; practical arguments assert that, although legitimate, certain prohibitions are unwise because in practice they cause more harm than good.

Arguments of principle. The broad question of whether, and to what extent, the law may enforce morality represents one of the classic debates in philosophical and criminal law literature. This debate has tended to focus on the use of formal criminal sanctions, and most of the arguments appear to make no distinction between criminal and noncriminal prohibitions. Of course, if the law may not legitimately interfere at all with certain behavior, then criminal sanctions may not be used. On the other hand, if the law may legitimately interfere, there is the further, largely unaddressed question of whether it is legitimate, necessary, or desirable to use criminal sanctions.

Arguments in favor of prohibition. Some writers have argued that society is permitted, and perhaps even obligated, to enforce morality by means of criminal or other legal sanctions. There are at least two distinct variations of this argument. What H. L. A. Hart calls the "conservative thesis" asserts that the majority in society have the right not only to follow their own moral convictions but to preserve their "moral environment" as a thing of value and to insist that all members of society abide by their moral convictions (1967, p. 2; Stephen, pp. 135–178). What Hart calls the "disintegration thesis" asserts that public morality is the "cement of society," which must be maintained to prevent social disintegration (1967, p. 1). A major proponent of this thesis was Patrick Devlin, who argued that the law should protect society's political and moral institutions and the "community of ideas" necessary for men to live together. Devlin wrote, "Society cannot ignore the morality of the individual any more than it can his loyalty; it flourishes on both and without either it dies" (p. 22).

Even if it is conceded that the legal enforcement of morality is legitimate, however, several practical difficulties arise: whose "morality" is to be enforced, and how much of it? Although the United States has a highly "moralistic" criminal law (Morris and Hawkins, p. 5), many types of behavior that would generally be considered "immoral" have never been considered criminal—for example, breach of contract (Packer, p. 264). The nineteenth-century jurist James Fitzjames Stephen suggested that the criminal law should be limited to "extreme cases . . . [of] gross acts of vice," that public opinion and common practice must "strenuously and unequivocally condemn" the conduct, and that "a moral majority must be overwhelming" (pp. 159, 162). Devlin, although he saw

no possibility of setting theoretical or a priori limits on the power of the law to enforce morality, conceded the need for "toleration of the maximum individual freedom that is consistent with the integrity of society"; only if the majority has "a real feeling of reprobation, intolerance, indignation and disgust" for the conduct may it be prohibited (pp. 16–17). But how are such judgments to be made, and by whom? Devlin answered that the standard should be that of the "reasonable" man or "the man in the jury box," because the "moral judgment of society must be something about which any twelve men or women drawn at random might after discussion be expected to be unanimous" (p. 15).

Although these formulations do suggest some limiting principles, they provide little concrete guidance to legislators. Moreover, in an increasingly secular, pluralist society there is less and less consensus about fundamental moral principles, and some doubt whether twelve persons "drawn at random" would be unanimous about anything. Finally, in deciding how much of morality to enforce with the law, there is no inconsistency in also considering the practical advantages and disadvantages of attempting to prohibit certain conduct. Indeed, Devlin accepted this, citing such practical considerations as the extent to which enforcement would be ineffective or would inevitably violate rights of privacy (pp. 18–22).

Moral arguments against criminalization. In sharp contrast to Devlin, other writers have argued that the law may not legitimately prohibit certain behavior. The classic statement of this position was made by the nineteenth-century English philosopher John Stuart Mill, who argued that society may interfere with the individual's freedom of action only "to prevent harm to others. His own good, either physical or moral, is not a sufficient warrant" (p. 15). Mill believed that the individual must be accorded the maximum degree of liberty and autonomy that is consistent with the rights of others. Although writers such as Devlin concede the importance of protecting individual liberty, Mill and his followers appear to give this factor much greater weight. They view the individual's freedom and self-determination as preeminent rights, which outweigh mere utilitarian considerations of "the greatest good for the greatest number" (Richards, 1979a, pp. 1222–1223).

To some extent, the United States Supreme Court and a few state courts have adopted this approach, holding that individual rights of privacy and free expression, implicit in the First, Fourth, and Ninth Amendments, prevent the state from prohibiting certain acts (*Stanley v. Georgia*, 394 U.S. 557 (1969) (possession of obscene material in the home); *Roe v. Wade*, 410 U.S. 113 (1973) (abortion during the first three months of pregnancy); *Ravin v. State*, 537 P.2d 494 (Alaska 1975) (possession of marijuana in the home); *Commonwealth v. Bonadio*, 490 Pa. 91, 415 A.2d 47 (1980) (sodomy between consenting adults in private)). On the other hand, the Supreme Court has also stated that broad deference should be given to legislative judgments about the wisdom of prohibiting certain conduct, even if those judgments are based on moral assessments. Thus, for example, the Court has upheld punishment of obscenity in a private theater to which access was limited to consenting adults (*Paris Adult Theater I v. Slaton*, 413 U.S. 49 (1973)).

Analysis of the earlier quotation from Mill reveals several distinguishable purposes of punishment: individuals might be punished for their own "moral" benefit, for their own "physical good," and to prevent "harm to others." Modern writers have tended to agree with Mill that the first purpose is clearly improper: as far as the law is concerned, the individual has "an inalienable right to go to hell in his own fashion, provided he does not directly injure the person or property of another on the way" (Morris and Hawkins, p. 2).

However, most modern writers do not share Mill's total opposition to prohibitions aimed at protecting the defendant's physical well-being. Mill apparently felt that paternalism was a rationale too easily abused (Richards, 1979b, p. 1424), but modern authors seem more willing to recognize some limited version of this rationale. Mill did approve of laws to protect children from their own lack of judgment (p. 15), and some modern writers have broadened this justification to include protection against exploitation and corruption of other especially vulnerable groups, including those "weak in body or mind, inexperienced, or in a state of special physical, official or economic dependence" (*The Wolfenden Report*, para. 13; Morris and Hawkins, p. 4; H. L. A. Hart, 1963, pp. 32–34). Other writers maintain that individuals must be given the maximum freedom to make choices which they may later regret; these writers would narrowly limit paternalism to cases of "extreme irrationality or non-rationality likely to harm irreparably serious human interests," such as rationality, freedom, or life itself (Richards, 1979b, pp. 1422, 1424).

As for Mill's third category, "harm to others," it is unclear whether he would have distinguished between tangible and intangible harms. If intangible harms include the weakening of "public morality," there is obviously little point to Mill's other limitations. A related problem involves the use of the criminal law for "verbal vindication of our morals" (Kadish, 1967, p. 162), with no effort actually to enforce the law. Since such symbolic legislation provides intangible benefits to "others," and does not directly inhibit the individual's freedom of action or punish him for his own moral benefit, how does it violate either the letter or the spirit of Mill's philosophy? Modern followers of Mill usually respond with practical arguments about the collateral disadvantages of unenforced law (for example, diminished respect for law), rather than with arguments of principle (Kadish, 1972, p. 720).

Also problematic is Mill's support for laws punishing offenses against public "decency" (Mill, p. 120; H. L. A. Hart, 1963, p. 45; Morris and Hawkins, p. 15; Richards, 1979a, p. 1274). The offense caused to the "victims" of public indecency seems different in degree, but not in principle, from the revulsion that such victims feel toward similar acts performed in private. Perhaps the distinction is that prohibition of public solicitation, nudity, and other "indecencies" does not totally eliminate the freedom of the individual to engage in such behavior in private, or with others who are not offended. Nevertheless, the result is to limit individual freedom for the sake of preventing an intangible harm to others.

Another intangible harm to others, recognized by at least one modern follower of Mill as a proper justification for punishment, is the breach of promises of marital fidelity (Richards, 1979a, p. 1273). Traditional laws prohibiting adultery, bigamy, and prostitution would seem to be justified on this basis, yet the same author opposes such laws, apparently on the ground that they are over- or underinclusive. That is, these laws purportedly cover some conduct which poses no threat to fidelity, yet they fail to punish other conduct which clearly does pose such a threat (p. 1274 n.).

A third category of harm which might be viewed as intangible, at least from the point of view of human beings, is that of cruelty to animals. Several modern followers of Mill's philosophy appear to support prohibitions against such cruelty (H. L. A. Hart, 1963, p. 34; Morris and Hawkins, p. 19), without considering whether these laws are consistent with the harm-to-others criterion.

As for more tangible harm to others, such as physical injury or property loss, there is widespread agreement with Mill's position that this is a proper basis for punishment. However, as Herbert Packer has pointed out, it is almost always possible to argue that a given form of conduct involves *some* risk of harm to the interests of others; the harm-to-others criterion is thus a matter of degree—"a prudential criterion rather than a hard and fast distinction of principle" (p. 266). Packer goes on to argue that the risk of harm to others must be "substantial" and unjustified by reasons of social utility. He also asserts that the harm should not be trivial in two senses: it should not be so minor that the imposition of any criminal punishment would be disproportionate to the social harm caused, nor should it be so minor that law enforcement and sentencing authorities are unwilling to enforce the law or to make regular use of "real criminal sanctions," such as imprisonment (pp. 271–273).

Other modern followers of Mill appear to recognize a much broader authority to "protect the citizen's person and property" (Morris and Hawkins, p. 4). Difficult problems of remoteness of harms are also posed by conduct that, if widely practiced, might cause serious social disorganization—for example, drug addiction. Thus, one court, while upholding the right to use marijuana in the home, implied that such use could be punished if it ever became so widespread that it might "significantly debilitate the fabric of our society" (Ravin, 509).

A strict application of the Mill philosophy thus poses a number of difficulties. As noted above, it is difficult to find a "pure case" of behavior that harms no one but the actor; clearly, however, the extent of harm to others, both in seriousness and probability, is an important factor to be considered in the criminalization decision. Second, depending on how broadly "harm to others" is defined and on how willing we are to recognize paternalistic legislation, the Mill principle may not be all that limiting, particularly if it is recognized that the legislature has at least some discretion to be both over- and underinclusive in pursuit of its goals. Third, to the extent that a strict interpretation of Mill's philosophy is based on an elaborate theory of the moral or "human" rights of the person (Richards, 1979b, pp. 1404–1414), this approach to criminalization may prove too vague or too subjective to command broad consensus and application. Fourth, Mill and his followers offer little guidance in the choice of various noncriminal sanctions; indeed, a strict reading of the Mill philosophy (pp. 123–125) would seem to invalidate not only civil and criminal penalties but any interference with individual "liberty of action," including, for example, excise taxes on alcoholic beverages! Finally, there is no reason why "moral" arguments against criminalization should preclude consideration of practical disadvantages as well, particularly since most of the moral arguments do not lend themselves to definitive, "bright line" distinctions.

Arguments of practicality. Although modern advocates of decriminalization have often cited Mill's philosophy in support of their arguments, they usually go on to argue that even if prohibition might be legitimate, it is unwise. Such arguments typically take one of two forms. One group of writers argues that all "victimless" crimes be repealed. A more complex approach attempts to catalog the specific practical difficulties and disadvantages of trying to prohibit certain behavior; it argues that, on balance, the total "costs" of criminalization outweigh the benefits.

Victimless crime. The concept of victimless crime is frequently suggested as a basis for decriminalization (Schur). The term itself is somewhat misleading, since it has been applied to offenses such as public drunkenness and adultery, which often have direct, readily identifiable "victims." Furthermore, it is arguable that most other so-called victimless crimes, such as drug offenses and prostitution, do have at least potential victims: the participants themselves, relatives, taxpayers, or society at large. The users of this term tend to stress the practical disadvantages of trying to enforce victimless crimes—for example, that the lack of complaining witnesses leads to the use of intrusive police practices, bribery, and discriminatory enforcement. However, many of these problems arise in the enforcement of penalties for crimes that have not been labeled as victimless or proposed for repeal (for example, carrying an unregistered weapon). The victimless crime concept may draw some of its rhetorical appeal from largely unarticulated philosophical premises: if a crime is truly victimless, efforts to enforce it may not only be difficult but illegitimate (Morris and Hawkins, p. 4). But whether the victimless crime criterion is best viewed as an argument of principle or one of practicality, the concept is of very limited utility in deciding the more difficult issues of criminalization. The criterion lacks a clear definition, fails to cover some of the offenses to which it has been applied, and applies equally well to other offenses that have not been proposed for repeal. The relative victimlessness of an offense is closely related to several important practical issues in the criminalization decision (discussed below). However, labeling a crime as victimless only begins what is, in most cases, a very difficult process of assessing complex empirical facts and fundamental value choices.

The cost-benefit approach. A more sophisticated (but less rhetorically effective) practical approach to the criminalization question seeks to identify the specific advantages and disadvantages of invoking the criminal law, in an effort to determine whether the total public and private "costs" of criminalization outweigh the benefits (Kadish, 1967). Strictly speaking, cost-benefit analysis involves the weighing of variables that are measurable in dollars or other quantitative units. The proponents of a cost-benefit approach to criminalization generally concede that there is little quantitative data in this area, but they argue that the approach is still a useful way of thinking about criminalization problems (Kadish, 1972, p. 722).

The costs of criminalization include public and private burdens, both tangible and intangible. Beginning with tangible public costs, it is necessary (but often difficult) to separate out the police, court, attorney, and correctional expenditures properly attributable *only* to the enforcement of a specific offense. Occasionally this "marginal" cost is fairly clear—the salaries and expenses of the police narcotic division, for example. In some cases, apparent costs may not disappear with decriminalization: many of the previous enforcement efforts (such as collecting and jailing public drunks) may have simply taken up the slack in police and jail resources that must still be maintained to handle peak loads. Moreover, decriminalization may require the police and other public officials to respond to the underlying behavioral problem in alternate ways that have their own costs: in the example above, removal of penalties for public drunkenness may lead to more arrests for disorderly conduct or may increase pressures on public and private medical facilities.

Private costs of criminalization include not only concrete items such as attorneys' fees and other litigation expenses, but also several factors that are harder to measure. These include the individual's loss of the freedom, pleasure, or other value that was a concomitant of engaging in the forbidden conduct (for example, having sex with a prostitute); the anxiety and social ostracism imposed upon offenders, whether or not they are detected and prosecuted; the reduction or elimination of the offender's economic earning power during the period of pretrial and trial proceedings, while sentence is being served, and perhaps for the rest of his life; the loss of freedom itself, before and after conviction; and the uncompensated costs and inconveniences imposed on witnesses and jurors.

An even less tangible cost, which may affect both public and private interests, is the tendency of criminalization to produce more, rather than less, socially undesirable behavior. Examples of illegal behavior that may result from criminalization are bribery of the police or other enforcement officials; extortion by officials of money or other favors in return for nonenforcement; private blackmail by threats to expose the offender; discriminatory enforcement of the law against unpopular groups or individuals, or in

favor of defendants with more political or social influence; and the use of illegal methods of obtaining evidence, such as searches, electronic surveillance, coercive interrogations, and entrapment. Indeed, some categories of crimes (for example, vagrancy and disorderly conduct) seem to have been specifically designed to undercut constitutional limitations on arrest, search, and interrogation (Kadish, 1967, p. 167).

Even where the methods of law enforcement are not clearly illegal, they may be so contrary to widely held feelings of privacy or fairness that they cause a lowering of public respect for the law, particularly among social groups already alienated from society, including ethnic minorities and the poor. Examples of such questionable tactics include selective enforcement in order to conserve resources; the use of undercover agents and decoy officers; the use of informers from the criminal milieu who are paid in money or leniency; arrests for purposes of harassment or to "clean the streets," with no effort to prosecute; "legal" searches, electronic surveillance, and intrusive physical surveillance (for example, peering through holes in the ceilings of public washrooms in order to observe possible homosexual or narcotic offenses). As may be noted, the problems listed above arise primarily when the behavior involves consenting parties and few, if any, witnesses. It is partly this relative invisibility of victimless crimes that makes their enforcement so costly.

Other costs of criminalization arise when the prohibited conduct involves goods, activities, or services that are in great demand, such as gambling, drugs, liquor, illegal weapons, abortion, commercial sex, and pornography. When there is high demand, prohibition tends to limit supply more than demand, thus driving up the black-market price and creating monopoly profits for those criminals who remain in business. Organized criminals tend to have advantages over less organized ones in exploiting illegal markets and coping with law enforcement pressures, and consequently, criminalization tends to foster the growth of sophisticated, well-organized, and powerful criminal groups. Once in existence, organized crime tends to diversify into other areas of crime. Its high profits provide ample funds for bribery of public officials, as well as capital for diversification.

Although higher prices tend to discourage some would-be participants in prohibited activities, the underlying high demand, combined with restricted supply, maintains both high prices and high participation rates. In extreme cases of high and inflexible demand (for example, heroin addiction), exorbitant prices force participants to commit other crimes to pay for the illegal goods or services they want. These are generally nonviolent property crimes, such as shoplifting, or other forms of vice, such as prostitution, gambling, or sale of drugs, but violent property crimes may also be encouraged. Finally, because the illegal goods or services are in great demand, a large number of otherwise law-abiding citizens are driven into association with the criminal elements who supply these goods and services. There is a danger that these citizens will come to view themselves as criminals, since society labels them as such; as members of the criminal subculture, they may lose respect for the law and are more likely to be drawn into other forms of crime.

A further concrete cost of criminalization is the barrier that the law erects between the criminal and important social services and protections. When the law forbids abortion and drug use, for example, consumers are forced to make use of medically unsound procedures and instruments, increasing the risk of death, injury, or infection. If harm occurs they are unwilling to seek the medical attention they need, for fear of exposing their criminal behavior. Laws against prostitution and homosexuality may have a similarly adverse effect: participants who contract a venereal disease are less likely to seek timely medical treatment. Moreover, although prostitution laws may seek to prevent the exploitation and physical abuse of female prostitutes by their pimps, the existence of criminal penalties and enforcement efforts probably makes women more likely to seek the support and protection of the pimp, while discouraging them from seeking legal protection from exploitation and abuse.

Other costs of criminalization include overloading the criminal justice system with a mass of petty cases; creating a law enforcement bureaucracy with a "vested interest in the status quo" (Packer, p. 333), thus thwarting efforts at reform or even research; and fostering the illusion that a social problem has been taken care of, thereby discouraging the development of more-effective alternative measures (Kadish, 1967, p. 159). Criminal laws may also violate principles of equal justice even if not intentionally enforced in a discriminatory manner. For example, poor or uneducated women are less likely to obtain a safe, although illegal, abortion and thus must either bear unwanted children or suffer the risk of death or severe medical complications. Efforts to enforce prostitution laws against "call girl" operations are costly and difficult, and therefore most arrests of prostitutes involve street solicitations by lower-class or minority-group women (Morris and Hawkins, pp. 14, 23). Finally, it can be argued that extending the criminal law to behavior which is widely believed to be morally neutral or which

is engaged in by the vast majority of citizens dilutes the stigmatizing quality of criminal sanctions generally, thus robbing them of their peculiar effectiveness in dealing with more serious conduct (Packer, pp. 262–263; Kadish, 1967, p. 160). Of course, lack of widespread moral condemnation may also make the law difficult or impossible to enforce, thus limiting the benefit of prohibition.

On the other side of the ledger, the benefits achieved by criminalization fall into several categories. To the extent that the criminal law is enforced with a view toward preventing specific social or individual harms, the likelihood of achieving such preventive benefits depends on the following factors:

1. The probability that the behavior defined as criminal will be observed or detected by anyone other than the immediate participants
2. The probability that various parties will invoke formal criminal processes: that witnesses or participants will report the crime to the police and support prosecution efforts, that the police will arrest or at least contact prosecuting authorities, that the authorities will approve and support formal prosecution, and that judges and juries will apply criminal sanctions
3. The probability of success in apprehending the suspect(s), effecting arrest and continued jurisdiction over the defendant, and establishing the defendant's guilt consistent with legal standards of proof and admissibility of evidence
4. The likelihood that conviction and sentence will reduce the future incidence of the behavior defined as criminal, either through general deterrence of other potential offenders, the "educative" effect of punishment, special deterrence or rehabilitation of the punished offender, or incapacitation of the punished offender
5. The likelihood that reducing the incidence of the behavior defined as criminal will reduce the more remote harm (if any) sought to be prevented, such as reducing helmetless motorcycle riding to reduce the seriousness of motorcycle accident injuries

Of course, to the extent that punishment of criminal behavior is considered proper for its own sake, the last two factors are irrelevant. From such a "retributive" point of view, the benefits of criminal law enforcement depend only upon the likelihood of obtaining convictions and the seriousness of the crime, discussed below.

Even if criminal prosecution is not successful or is not even attempted, the mere existence of criminal prohibitions might have some indirect effect on the incidence of the behavior defined as criminal and thus, even more indirectly, on any more remote harm to be prevented. The labeling of behavior as criminal represents a social judgment that it is morally wrong or at least undesirable, and this judgment may serve to reinforce similar feelings in the individual. As with actual enforcement efforts, the extent of this symbolic effect depends on the strength of the perceived relationship between the prohibited behavior and the more remote social harm, if any, sought to be prevented (for example, the relationship between euthanasia and the devaluation of human life). Another important set of considerations here involves attitudes about unenforced law; to the extent that most people believe that the law should either be enforced or repealed, unenforced law promotes cynicism and disrespect for the law, particularly the criminal law (Kadish, 1967, p. 160). Thus, legislative attempts to denounce certain behavior symbolically, with no intention or ability to enforce the law, probably do more harm than good.

Perhaps the most critical determinant of the total "benefit" of criminalization, whether by means of actual enforcement efforts or symbolic denunciation, is the importance of the social harm involved. In the case of heroin possession or sales, for example, it must be decided how seriously society views the *use* of heroin—and, in particular, the more remote but more serious harm of heroin *addiction*—in order to decide whether the costs of criminalizing heroin use and sale are worth bearing. A host of tangible and intangible factors must then be considered: the values of human rationality and full consciousness; the losses of life and health that are not attributable to prohibition itself; the potential loss of the economic productivity of users; and perhaps even the anguish that heavy use or addiction may impose on relatives and close friends of the user.

Even if the benefits of criminalization exceed the costs, proponents of the cost-benefit approach point out that various civil, administrative, or regulatory measures may be more effective than criminal sanctions, less costly, or both. Examples of such noncriminal alternatives include the zoning or licensing of pornography and prostitution (Richards, 1979a, pp. 1279–1284); civil detoxification or commitment of public drunks (Kadish, 1967, p. 166); medically supervised distribution of maintenance doses to heroin addicts (Morris and Hawkins, p. 9); and the use of civil fines for certain drug, traffic, and other minor violations. Presumably, such alternatives must also be subjected to a weighing of costs and benefits; whichever approach (criminalization or some alternative) pro-

duces the greatest excess of benefits over costs is the approach that should be followed, and if no approach produces a net benefit, then the ultimate alternative is to do nothing at all (Packer, p. 258).

There are several reasons why noncriminal measures may be more effective or less costly than criminal sanctions. As discussed earlier, the former may not be subject to the strict procedural requirements applied to criminal statutes, and the personnel who administer noncriminal sanctions may be less highly trained and paid. Another "solution" to the problems of proving guilt in criminal cases would be to redefine crimes in order to reduce or eliminate the traditional criminal law requirement of culpable mental state (mens rea) or the requirement of personal guilt, thus imposing "strict liability" without any culpable mental state, or "vicarious liability" for the acts or omissions of others. However, these alternatives create new problems of enforcement: to the extent that the prohibited behavior is not generally viewed by witnesses, police, prosecutors, judges, and juries as morally blameworthy, criminal penalties will not be fully enforced (Kadish, 1963, pp. 435–437), but civil penalties might be. Even where blame is attached, sympathy for the defendant (for example, the woman who seeks an illegal abortion) may similarly limit the willingness of jurors and other decision-makers to impose criminal penalties (Kadish, 1967, p. 163). Noncriminal sanctions, on the other hand, might be seen as an appropriate compromise between condemning and condoning the prohibited behavior. Finally, noncriminal procedures may be better adapted to controlling and regulating violations of a continuing nature: an injunction proceeding, for example, uses past misconduct to formulate a rule of behavior specifically tailored to the situation, and then makes use of rather summary contempt proceedings each time that rule is violated in the future.

On the other hand, noncriminal procedures are not always less costly or more effective than criminal penalties. As noted previously, courts have occasionally applied criminal law procedural requirements to violations labeled as civil, because of the penalties authorized, the punitive intent of the legislature, or other indexes of punishment. The decision in *Brown v. Multnomah County Dist. Ct.*, 280 Or. 95, 570 P.2d 52 (1977), for example, invalidated an attempt to decriminalize first-offense drunk driving and dispense with right-to-counsel and proof-beyond-a-reasonable-doubt guarantees. Even the requirements of civil due process may make enforcement difficult and costly. For example, *Heap v. Roulet*, 23 Cal. 3d 219, 590 P.2d 1 (1979) held that state constitutional due process requires proof beyond a reasonable doubt, as well as a unanimous jury in civil conservatorship and commitment proceedings; *United States v. One 1976 Mercedes Benz,* 618 F.2d 453 (7th Cir. 1980) held that the owner of a car subject to a narcotic-related forfeiture action has a Seventh Amendment right to a jury trial. Moreover, the abuses of discretion and other nonfinancial costs of criminal law enforcement are not necessarily avoided by the use of civil enforcement procedures: civil inspectors and regulators would seem just as likely to discriminate invidiously, take bribes, use intrusive means of detection, and the like. Indeed, to the extent that noncriminal alternatives are governed by lower standards of proof and procedure, one should expect the results to be less reliable and more subject to abuse, and one should also expect these less formal procedures to be invoked much more often. Past experience with informal measures such as the juvenile court and pretrial diversion suggests caution in abandoning the procedural protections of the criminal law (Allen, pp. 13–24; Morris, pp. 9–12).

In terms of the effectiveness of sanctions, there are undoubtedly certain types of behavior that cannot be adequately controlled without the use of the criminal law. Given its greater stigmatizing effect and more severe penalties, the criminal law is more likely, all things being equal, to prevent future offenses through deterrence (general and special) or incapacitation. Criminal penalties also have greater retributive impact. Moreover, even where the behavior in question (for example, nonpayment of support) can generally be prevented and controlled without the use of the most severe penalties, there is often a need to retain the criminal law to deal with aggravated cases or to encourage cooperation with lesser forms of regulation or treatment (Morris and Hawkins, p. 25). Although efforts can and should be made to define the scope of the criminal law as narrowly as possible in these areas, the traditional reliance on administrative discretion to tailor the penalties to the offense reflects, in part, the difficulty of specifying in advance precisely when criminal penalties and procedures are appropriate.

The last and perhaps the most important step in the cost-benefit analysis is to consider whether, in a world of limited law enforcement resources, the time and money spent attempting to control the behavior in question would be better spent elsewhere. A major criticism of attempts to prohibit such offenses as drunkenness, prostitution, and drug use is that these cases overload the police, courts, and correctional systems; thus, these offenses distract those systems from their more important task of preventing serious crimes against persons and property and reduce the quality of justice in serious and nonserious cases alike. Implicit in this criticism is the assumption that other offenses are more socially harmful, easier to detect and prosecute, or subject to fewer collateral costs (police corruption and the like); the assessment of priorities thus involves another level of cost-benefit analysis, focusing on the marginal benefit that would be achieved by shifting resources from one type of offense to others. This priorities analysis presumably applies to noncriminal as well as criminal sanctions, since the public resources available for both are likely to be limited; one must also consider whether it would be better to shift the resources completely away from law enforcement into other social uses, such as education and transportation.

To summarize, the cost-benefit approach first examines the various costs and benefits of using the criminal law to control the behavior or social harm in question. If the costs outweigh the benefits, criminal prohibition is rejected; even if the benefits of criminalization outweigh the costs, however, it is necessary to consider whether some noncriminal form of prohibition or regulation would produce not only a net benefit but a greater net benefit than criminalization. If neither criminalization nor a noncriminal alternative produces a net benefit, then the solution is to do nothing or leave the matter up to existing remedies and procedures—such as private civil damages actions—that exist for nonpunitive, nonregulatory reasons. If there is a net benefit, whichever form of prohibition yields the greatest net benefit must then be compared with the alternative uses of the resources involved, to see whether these resources would produce a still greater benefit if applied elsewhere.

Synthesis of criminalization theories

In theory, the cost-benefit approach described above covers all relevant considerations and has the further advantage of relying, as much as possible, on matters that are subject to empirical verification. However, it seems unlikely that one will ever obtain reliable data on most of the relevant variables, and the existing data on each variable may not be commensurate with that on other variables. How does one compare, for example, the cost of discriminatory enforcement of prostitution laws with the benefit of preventing a certain number of women from aggressively soliciting unwilling men on the street? Moreover, the cost-benefit calculus is too complex and too easily dominated by decisions to emphasize certain variables over others to provide much concrete assistance in thinking about specific criminalization problems. Finally, although practical problems of law enforcement are certainly very relevant considerations, they must not be allowed to overshadow the fundamental value choices that must be made: What purposes of prohibition are legitimate in a free, secular society? How much discretion should lawmakers have in defining prohibitions aimed at achieving concededly legitimate goals? How important are various social harms (such as drug addiction) and values (such as the ideal of marital fidelity)? How important are the various unquantifiable costs of criminalization (such as loss of privacy or the right to use drugs or possess weapons for self-defense)?

In light of these complexities, it is tempting to fall back on more simplistic criteria: the law may enforce morality with few, if any, a priori limitations (Devlin); the law may only seek to prevent "harm to others" (Mill); the law may not violate the "human rights of the person" (Richards); "victimless" crimes should be repealed; and so on. As this article has attempted to demonstrate, however, the search for a simple, bright-line criterion is illusory: both in matters of principle and of practicality, criminalization is almost always a question of degree, and seldom a matter of clear-cut alternatives.

How, then, should legislators proceed? How can the mass of interrelated, often conflicting criteria discussed above provide any concrete guidance in the choice of the criminal sanction? The list below attempts to synthesize the views of modern writers on this subject and poses a series of questions that hypothetical legislators (or their constituents) should ask themselves.

1. What is the specific social or individual harm that the law seeks to prevent or minimize, how important is it, and how likely is it to follow from the behavior sought to be prohibited? Although the law may on occasion seek to go beyond concrete "harm to others" to achieve paternalistic goals (such as the safeguarding of children) or to protect intangible interests (such as public "decency"), the dangers of abuse of individual rights increase the closer one comes to basing the law on public morality, intangible harms, or protection of the criminal "for his own sake." In particular, protection of the individual's private morality (especially in sexual matters) for no other reason than his own good would seldom, if ever, be justified in a secular society.

2. What are the major pros and cons of criminalization? Like the cost-benefit approach described earlier, this question addresses the practical difficulties of enforcing the law (because, for example, there are few civilian witnesses, or the prohibited behavior is highly desired by the participants) and the likely success of criminal penalties in preventing both the prohibited acts and any more remote social harms sought to be prevented. Even if the practical pros and cons cannot be quantified and rigorously compared with each other, their mere enumeration and description ensure that no relevant considerations are overlooked, and may signal the need for legislative caution.

3. Are any noncriminal methods of control more effective or less costly? Here again, the legislator must consider the major advantages and disadvantages of civil, administrative, or quasi-criminal forms of prohibition or regulation. Given the procedural complexities of the criminal law, its more severe stigma and sanctions, and the need to permit the agencies of the criminal law to concentrate their energies on the most serious social harms, noncriminal procedures are often preferable. In such cases, residual, "last resort" criminal penalties will sometimes be necessary, but they should be kept to a minimum, both to avoid problems of discretionary enforcement and to prevent interference with noncriminal procedures (for example, by discouraging prostitutes from registering or obtaining medical assistance). There are some cases, of course, for which the criminal law and its procedures are peculiarly appropriate, as in dealing with violent behavior. In other cases, only certain aspects of the criminal law may be needed (such as the arrest powers of the police), but not its severe stigma or sanctions. The opposite may also be true (as in tax fraud cases). Sometimes it may be administratively convenient to give the police, prosecutors, or other criminal justice agencies responsibility for enforcing a given noncriminal prohibition, for example, in the case of minor traffic offenses. Ultimately, the assessment of these practical advantages and disadvantages may not be possible without a willingness to experiment and evaluate carefully the actual results of switching to noncriminal modes of control.

4. In what ways does prohibition or regulation limit the freedom of action or self-determination of the individual, and how important is such freedom? Although this consideration is probably implicit in the criminal and noncriminal cost-benefit assessments envisioned above, the point deserves to be stated separately. Even if individual freedom (or "human rights") rarely provides an absolute, a priori limit on prohibition, it is a crucially important factor to be weighed along with the purposes of prohibition and the practical considerations. Once it has been determined which criminal or noncriminal prohibition is most beneficial, and the nature of the proposed curtailment of individual freedom thus clearly identified, the legislator should compare this curtailment with the harms that are the object of prohibition (step 1 above). In many cases the harm will not justify the loss of freedom, even assuming substantial effectiveness and the low cost of prohibition.

5. Would the resources devoted to criminal or noncriminal prohibition produce greater benefit if applied to other undesirable behavior, or to public and private purposes unrelated to law enforcement?

6. What would happen if all prohibitions or regulatory efforts were discontinued? The alternative of doing nothing is almost always the least expensive, although it is politically the most difficult. Legislators and their constituents like to believe they are "doing something" about social problems, even if this is an illusion, and the removal of all legal prohibitions may encourage the behavior in question, at least in the short run. As with the use of noncriminal alternatives, however, legislators must show a greater willingness to experiment with new approaches; this, after all, is one definition of leadership. Much guidance can be received from those jurisdictions that have pioneered deregulation, and of course, prohibition can be reinstated if the results of deregulation are unsatisfactory. The important point is simply that the existence of a criminal or noncriminal prohibition must not create any presumption of its own validity; the criminalization question is a continuing one and must be reexamined periodically, without preconditions, by the public and its elected officials. New prohibitions should not be casually added without careful consideration of the lessons of past criminalization efforts.

RICHARD S. FRASE

See also ABORTION; ADULTERY AND FORNICATION; ALCOHOL AND CRIME: LEGAL ASPECTS; DRUGS AND CRIME: LEGAL ASPECTS; GAMBLING; HOMOSEXUALITY AND CRIME; PROSTITUTION AND COMMERCIALIZED VICE: LEGAL ASPECTS; VAGRANCY AND DISORDERLY CONDUCT; VICTIMLESS CRIME.

BIBLIOGRAPHY

ALLEN, FRANCIS A. The Borderland of Criminal Justice: Essays in Law and Criminology. University of Chicago Press, 1964.

American Law Institute. Model Penal Code: Proposed Official Draft. Philadelphia: ALI, 1962.

CLARK, J. MORRIS. "Civil and Criminal Penalties and Forfeitures: A Framework for Constitutional Analysis." Minnesota Law Review 60 (1976): 379–500.

DEVLIN, PATRICK. The Enforcement of Morals. New York: Oxford University Press, 1965.

HART, H. L. A. Law, Liberty, and Morality. Stanford, Calif.: Stanford University Press, 1963.

——. "Social Solidarity and the Enforcement of Morality." University of Chicago Law Review 35 (1967): 1–13.

HART, HENRY M., JR. "The Aims of the Criminal Law." Law and Contemporary Problems 23 (1958): 401–441.

KADISH, SANFORD M. "The Crisis of Overcriminalization." Annals of the American Academy of Political and Social Science 374 (1967): 157–170.

——. "More on Overcriminalization: A Reply to Professor Junker." UCLA Law Review 19 (1972): 719–722.

——. "Some Observations on the Use of Criminal Sanctions in Enforcing Economic Regulations." University of Chicago Law Review 30 (1963): 423–449.

MILL, JOHN STUART. "On Liberty" (1859). On Liberty; Representative Government; The Subjection of Women: Three Essays. By John Stuart Mill. Introduction by Millicent Garrett Fawcett. London: Oxford University Press, 1946, pp. 5–141.

MORRIS, NORVAL. The Future of Imprisonment. University of Chicago Press, 1974.

——, and HAWKINS, GORDON J. The Honest Politician's Guide to Crime Control. University of Chicago Press, 1970.

PACKER, HERBERT L. The Limits of the Criminal Sanction. Stanford, Calif.: Stanford University Press, 1968.

RICHARDS, DAVID A. J. "Commercial Sex and the Rights of the Person: A Moral Argument for the Decriminalization of Prostitution." University of Pennsylvania Law Review 127 (1979a): 1195–1287.

——. "Human Rights and the Moral Foundations of the Substantive Criminal Law." Georgia Law Review 13 (1979b): 1395–1446.

SCHUR, EDWIN M. Crimes without Victims: Deviant Behavior and Public Policy—Abortion, Homosexuality, Drug Addiction. Englewood Cliffs, N.J.: Prentice-Hall, 1965.

STEPHEN, JAMES FITZJAMES. Liberty, Equality, Fraternity (1874). Edited with an introduction and notes by R. J. White. London: Cambridge University Press, 1967.

U.S. Department of Justice, Law Enforcement Assistance Administration, National Advisory Commission on Criminal Justice Standards and Goals. A National Strategy to Reduce Crime. Washington, D.C.: The Commission, 1973.

The Wolfenden Report: Report of the Committee on Homosexual Offenses and Prostitution. Authorized American edition. Introduction by Karl Menninger, M.D. New York: Stein & Day, 1963.

ZIMRING, FRANKLIN E., and HAWKINS, GORDON J. Deterrence: The Legal Threat in Crime Control. University of Chicago Press, 1973.

CRIMINAL JUSTICE RESEARCH

See CRIME STATISTICS: REPORTING SYSTEMS AND METHODS; CRIMINOLOGY: RESEARCH METHODS; RESEARCH IN CRIMINAL JUSTICE.

CRIMINAL JUSTICE SYSTEM

1.
OVERVIEW

Introduction

The criminal justice system may be considered from at least three perspectives. First, it can be considered a normative system, that is, a body of legal rules expressing social values through prohibitions backed by penal sanctions against conduct viewed as seriously wrong or harmful. Second, the criminal justice system can be regarded as an administrative system. This view comprehends the official apparatus for enforcing the criminal law, including the police and other front-line enforcement agencies, prosecutorial authorities, the judiciary, and penal and correctional facilities and services. A third view of criminal justice is that of a social system. In this perspective, defining and responding to criminal conduct involves all elements of society. This definition of criminal conduct includes not only the penal law enacted by the legislature but also the way in which these provisions are interpreted by the citizenry at all levels. For example, if particular communities do not regard simple assaults taking place within the family as fully criminal, those communities are unlikely to summon the police when one family member beats up another. So also, prosecutors generally do not pursue white-collar crime with the same intensity as they pursue violent crime, even if the actual harms are comparable, because the constituencies to which prosecutors generally respond are more concerned with violent crime. By taking into account such societal views of criminal behavior, it is possible to explain many apparent anomalies in the administration of criminal justice, for example, why many criminal provisions are in some degree "dead letters." Another example is the phenomenon of "acquittal of the guilty," that is, the fact that juries and judges often return findings of not guilty of accused persons with respect to whom the proof of technical guilt is clear and uncontroverted.

These three aspects of the criminal justice system may be integrated in examining particular phases of criminal justice and in interpreting the system as a whole. Hence, the arrest and prosecution of an of-fender for theft can be considered simultaneously as a manifestation of a legislative prohibition against knowingly taking another's property, as a response by the police, prosecutor, judiciary, and penal-correctional system to conduct that appears to be criminal, and as a community interpretation of the behavior in question. Criminal justice as a whole results from the interaction between legal rules, administrative practice, and societal attitudes and behavior.

Some caution is required in using the term *system* to refer to the myriad complexities contained in this framework. The term may imply a series of transactions that are arranged in a rational and efficient way to produce specified results within more or less consciously perceived constraints. The criminal justice system does indeed have a substantial degree of coherence in this sense. Thus, in the law of crimes itself the penalties for deliberate homicide are much more severe than the penalties for assault. This differential is rationally coherent if one assumes that the underlying value is protection of human life and that an attack resulting in death is a more serious impairment of that value than an attack which leaves the victim alive. Similarly, it is rational that adjudication of guilt by the court system should follow *after* investigation of an offense by the police, if the underlying value is that guilt should be determined on the basis of a disinterested weighing of evidence and not upon predisposition.

Nevertheless, it must be recognized that the criminal justice system is pervaded by anomalies and discontinuities. For example, although law and public opinion attach high value to human life, as expressed in the penalties for willful homicide, measures to control the distribution of weapons, particularly handguns, are modest to the point of being virtually nominal. So also, great efforts are made to control industrial pollutants at the same time that subsidies are provided for the production of tobacco, even though cigarette smoke probably has worse immediate effects on health than any other pollutant. Still another example of discontinuity is the phenomenon of street drunks being arrested, jailed overnight, and then released in a never-ending cycle, rather than being handled in some nonpenal way. When full account is taken of such anomalies, the criminal justice process is a "system" in only a limited sense. Although a comprehensive view of criminal justice can be projected only in terms of some conceptual system, it is important to remember that concepts are merely constructs for interpreting profoundly ambiguous and endlessly complex social events.

In the following analysis, attention will focus on

the penal law as a normative system and on the police, the prosecutor, the judiciary, and the penal agencies as constituting an administrative system. The system of criminal procedural law and the larger social system that envelops the whole are considered only incidentally.

The penal law

Common law. Taken together, the legislative provisions defining crimes and prescribing punishments are usually referred to as the penal law, although they are also called the criminal law. The penal law in virtually all states in the United States is legislative in origin. That is, conduct is not criminally punishable unless it has been proscribed by statute.

The situation was not always thus. In the original common law, which began its development with the Norman domination of England after 1066, crimes and civil wrongs were not clearly distinguished. Moreover, there was no systematic body of criminal prohibitions. Rather, the original common-law offenses consisted of the use of force by the offender in violation of the King's peace and could result in both punitive and compensatory sanctions. It was the use of violence as such, rather than the particular consequences of a violent act, that constituted the wrong. From this foundation, the common law of crimes evolved over the course of centuries. Development took place through judicial decisions interpreting and elaborating the concept of violence into such specific categories as homicide, robbery, arson, and assault. In the later years of the common law's development, particularly from the sixteenth century onward, enactments of Parliament added specific crimes to the array of common-law offenses.

There was, however, no penal code or official systemization of the law of crimes. Commentaries by jurists, such as Matthew Hale's *History of the Pleas of the Crown* and the fourth volume of William Blackstone's *Commentaries on the Laws of England*, undertook to group the array of offenses, common-law and statutory, into coherent order according to the nature of the harm inflicted and the intensity and severity of the violation. The law of crimes thus unofficially systematized was nevertheless essentially common law, that is, the pronouncements of courts defining conduct that constituted a crime. In the colonization of British North America, the common law of crimes was received and applied. With the rupture of sovereignty in the colonies at the time of the American Revolution, however, a strong movement arose to establish all law, including the criminal law, on the foundation of legislative enactment. Initially, this took the form of legislative enactments that simply declared the common law, including the common law of crimes, to be in effect except as displaced by particular statutory provisions. However, the principle was established in many states that the definition of crimes was the province of the legislature and not of the courts.

Legislation. The period of social and political upheaval after the American and French revolutions engendered, among many other legal changes, a strong movement toward legislative codification of law, particularly the criminal law. Reform efforts aimed both to order and clarify the law and to ameliorate its severity, for in English law by 1800 more than one hundred different kinds of offenses were punishable by death. A leading reformer was Jeremy Bentham, whose utilitarianism afforded a coherent basis for ordering the law of crimes according to the principle of degrees of social harm. Many reform efforts were launched in the United States, paralleling and to some extent inspired by those of Bentham, as a result of which the law of crimes in many states was recast into more or less coherent penal codes. At least since the late nineteenth century, the criminal law has been expressed in a penal code in all but a few American jurisdictions.

Today the paradigm of penal legislation, both in substance and format, is the Model Penal Code, promulgated by the American Law Institute in 1962. The Code is a comprehensive reformulation of the principles of criminal liability that is drawn from previous codes, decisional law, and scholarly commentary. It has been substantially adopted in many states and is the preeminent source of guidance in revision and reform of substantive criminal law in the United States.

The Model Penal Code establishes a hierarchy of substantive criminal proscriptions and a corresponding hierarchy of social values. It can be considered as having two dimensions. The first consists of the principles of criminal liability; the second, of the definition of various specific crimes.

Principles of liability. The principles of liability express the fundamental notion that an individual is responsible for conforming his behavior to the standards prescribed in the criminal law. Quite different fundamental conceptions of criminal responsibility might be imagined. An individual could be considered responsible under the criminal law, and hence subject to condemnation and punishment, for causing any kind of substantial injury to another person, even for an accidental act on his own part. Some offenses actually are defined in this way, so that a violator is subject to criminal penalties even though he did not intend the result or indeed made an effort to avoid it. A familiar example is that of parking violations, which are penalized without regard to the actor's intention and for the purpose of allocating the use of street parking. However, in American law, as in Western cultures generally, such strict liability under criminal law usually is limited to monetary penalties in various regulatory schemes governing business and financial transactions. Aside from these "regulatory" offenses—which in modern society are widespread—Anglo-American criminal law generally reflects the principle that criminal liability should depend on an intention to commit wrong, or at least an awareness that serious wrong will result from a course of action.

Closely related to the principle of intentionality is that of justification or excuse. The essential notion is that a serious harm to another is not criminally punishable if it resulted from conduct that was necessary to preserve some other equal or superior interest. The most obvious example is self-defense as a basis for avoiding liability for homicide or assault on another. Other defenses include protection of third persons, protection of property, and necessity in the carrying out of official responsibilities, for example, where a policeman uses physical force to subdue a person resisting arrest. The criminal law thus holds the individual responsible for the consequences of his intended acts, but it authorizes him in a limited way to exercise judgment to vindicate fundamental interests of social safety and order. However, popular sentiment—that is, the principles of criminal responsibility embedded in popular culture—is often more lenient. As a result, there is tension between the norms of responsibility expressed in the penal law and those shared by the ordinary citizenry. Where there is a serious discrepancy between the legal concept of responsibility and the common notions of responsibility, the result is often erratic enforcement. This tendency, in turn, compromises to some extent the legitimacy of the criminal law and therefore the legitimacy of the administration of criminal justice.

The principle of responsibility has a corollary concerning the effect of mental incapacity or immaturity on the individual's accountability. This aspect of the problem includes the endlessly debatable question of the "insanity defense." Fundamentally, the question is whether an individual under given circumstances "could but did not" control his behavior or "could not" control it. In extreme cases, everyone would recognize that a given individual is "really crazy"—that is, obviously demented. On the other hand, to excuse one who acted on the basis of impulse or passion

would be to say that crimes consist only of wrongs that were definitely premeditated and committed without emotion. A society could function with a criminal law of this limited scope, relying on communal control, persuasion, and inhibition to protect its members. But our society is inhospitable to communal control, for individual autonomy holds a high place in our values. Our system therefore relies on a combination of self-control and criminal penalties for breach of self-control. The conflicting tendencies of this policy are perhaps most fully revealed in the dilemma as to how intense and how pervasive must a mental or emotional disorder be before it excuses an actor from criminal responsibility for inflicting serious harm on another.

For similar reasons, intense conflict attends the question of immaturity as a basis for limiting or precluding criminal responsibility. The notion that a youth is not fully responsible for his acts is the basis of the law governing juvenile offenders. The law provides that juveniles below a very young age are not criminally responsible at all, for example, a five-year-old who kills a playmate. Above that age but below the level of adulthood, a youthful offender is treated as responsible but with less severity than an adult under the same circumstances. The central issues are the definition of immaturity, particularly the age below which prosecution as an adult is not permitted, and the degree to which sanction against a youthful offender should emphasize rehabilitation rather than punishment. In popular terminology, this conflict presents itself as the question of whether a youthful offender is "a kid" or "a young thug." Such conflicting epithets reveal both the importance of the concept of responsibility in the criminal law and the difficulties of giving specific legal definition to the concept. A legally specified age of responsibility is, at the margin, necessarily arbitrary, and it also necessarily contradicts some segments of popular opinion.

Specific offenses. On the foundation of these basic concepts of criminal liability, the penal law defines specific offenses. The crimes established in the law are enormous in number and variety. There is a classical distinction between fundamentally or intrinsically criminal types of misbehavior, and misbehavior that is only formally criminal. This distinction is expressed in the terms *malum in se* and *malum prohibitum:* wrongs in themselves, and wrongs that are such only because they have been so declared. In this classification, homicide, assault, and theft are *mala in se*—acts that would be regarded as serious wrongs in any legal system in any culture. In contrast, the crime of driving on the wrong side of the street can be regarded as *malum prohibitum;* with much less confidence the same can be said of the crimes of failing to conform to pollution control requirements and violating building and zoning codes. However, it is evident that many offenses in the latter category are designed to induce patterns of behavior that will in turn minimize risks of serious social harms. Traffic regulations are intended, among other things, to prevent death and injury from highway accidents, and pollution controls are intended to prevent the accretion of toxic substances to lethal or injurious levels. Although it is therefore possible loosely to classify criminal offenses as *mala in se* and *mala prohibita,* it is impossible to use such a distinction for refined classification.

Among serious crimes there is an ordering that reflects fundamental social values. At one time in Western cultures, treason headed the list of crimes. It may be inferred that this positioning expressed a strong sense of insecurity about the stability of government. In modern society the state is relatively stable except under extraordinary circumstances of turmoil or revolution, and the penal law of the modern state characteristically places homicide at the head of the list of crimes. Such is the arrangement of the Model Penal Code, which begins with homicide and then proceeds to other offenses against the person: assault, including threat of assault; kidnapping; and sexual offenses, including rape, sexual molestation of minors, and related offenses. The next general category encompasses offenses against property, including arson, burglary, robbery, various forms of theft, and forgery and other frauds committed by manipulation of documents. A third general category is that of offenses against public administration, including bribery and corruption, perjury, obstruction of justice, and abuse of office. There is also a category of offenses against the family, including incest and abortion. These offenses perhaps could better have been classified as offenses against the person, but they can be viewed as addressed to the protection of the family as a social institution. Finally comes the category of offenses against public order, such as riot, disorderly conduct, and violation of privacy. Within each category there are comparable gradations. Thus, the provisions dealing with homicide begin with willful murder and end with negligent homicide, and the offenses against property begin with arson, burglary, and robbery, all of which involve an element of threat to human safety, and proceed to simple theft of various forms, where that element is absent.

This classification expresses a system of values in which individual human life stands highest and public decorum stands relatively low. A rather different hier-archy of values can be conceived. Preservation of decorum, for example, could be given far greater relative weight. Some differences in value are conspicuous. American penal law places high value on human life as compared with protection from fraud; accordingly, the fact that an attacker has previously been defrauded by the person assaulted is not a justification for an assault. However, a penal code would be intelligible which provided that assault is excusable in these circumstances, since it would thus express a high societal value on integrity in exchange transactions as compared with the value of immunity from physical violence. In any event, the relative weight attached to these specific values as expressed in the penal code is not the relative value in which they are held by some members of society. Specifically, it seems probable that the poor more than the rich regard fraud as comparable in wrongfulness to assault, and perhaps even more wrongful.

The relative order of social values in the criminal law manifests itself in still another way. In some societies, and certainly in contemporary America, the resources available to enforce the criminal law fall considerably short of those required to suppress crime completely. The administration of criminal justice therefore entails allocating resources in such a way that suppression of some crimes is pursued intensely whereas other crimes are more or less ignored. Allocation of resources may take place at the micro level, as when a policeman on patrol decides, in response to an unfolding situation, whether to chase a purse-snatcher or to respond to a burglary alert. The process also occurs at the macro level, in the way in which police, prosecution, and other agencies are organized and deployed. Thus, all police departments apparently devote a great deal of effort to following up homicides—effort that is probably disproportionate to the actual effect on the incidence of homicide. Meanwhile, they give only sporadic attention to those norms whose systematic enforcing might substantially affect behavior, for example, the incidence of muggings. The deployment of criminal justice resources is a complex mixture of efficiency and symbolism. But both calculation of efficiency and projection of symbols are intelligible only by reference to the system of values that society seeks to realize.

The administrative system in general

Subsystems. The system of criminal justice can be considered as an administrative bureaucracy consisting of four principal subsystems: police, prosecution, judiciary, and corrections. Broadly speaking, the police are responsible for prevention of crime through patrol, and for detection of crime after it has taken place. The prosecution is responsible for assembling evidence gathered by the police, determining whether prosecution is warranted, and, where it is, presenting the evidence and the law to establish the accused person's guilt. The judiciary is responsible for deciding the questions of law and fact relevant to determination of guilt and imposition of sentence; and the correctional system provides imprisonment and monitoring of offenders who are released on probation or parole.

The functional divisions between these subsystems are not tidy. The police not only investigate crimes but may exercise considerable influence in the determination of which crimes are prosecuted. Prosecutorial policies influence police practices regarding patrol and detection. Judge-made law pervasively influences the whole criminal process and apparatus, and the judicial attitude toward sentencing affects dispositions at every point in the system. The capacity and competence of the correctional system to provide either incarceration or rehabilitation constrain the effectiveness of the criminal law as an instrument of deterrence and rehabilitation. As in all complex administrative systems, there is continuous intercommunication and influence among the components of the system and the people within them.

Influential constituencies. There are other groups, not officially part of the administrative system, who strongly interact with it. Among these is the legal profession, particularly the lawyers who regularly represent criminal defendants. They continually monitor and check the enforcement apparatus, influence the development of the law in the courts and legislatures, and mediate impressions of the system to various sectors of the general population. Another highly influential group is the news media. It is an ancient maxim that justice must not only be done, but must be seen to be done. The modern public sees the criminal justice system chiefly as the media present it, in what is published, ignored, or withheld. Another important influence in many communities, a semiofficial constituency, are the labor organizations of which police and corrections officers are members.

Also influencing the system are the accused persons themselves. Most criminal suspects are young, male, and relatively poor. They are disproportionately members of ethnic minorities. In some sense they are official participants in the criminal justice process, for their status as such is legally recognized and defined. They are permitted by law to express their attitudes and inclinations in certain key decisions by the system. Furthermore, although the resources of the prosecution are formidable when compared with those of an individual defendant, the criminal defendant group as a whole has resources that the administrative system cannot ignore. It is well recognized that the inmate population of a penal institution strongly influences the operation of the institution; similar influence operates, although in a less obvious manner, in the functions of the police, prosecution, and judiciary.

Other agencies. The exposition here focuses primarily on the ordinary criminal justice system as it exists at the state and local level. In addition to that system, there is a federal law enforcement apparatus, which includes such police agencies as the Federal Bureau of Investigation and the Customs Bureau; the prosecutorial authority of the attorney general of the United States and the local United States district attorneys; the United States courts, particularly the district courts that have trial jurisdiction and are located throughout the country; and the Federal Probation Service and the Federal Bureau of Prisons, constituting the federal correctional system.

In addition, at both the federal and state levels there are many specialized law enforcement agencies having important criminal responsibilities. These include the state police and motor-vehicle bureaus, revenue enforcement agencies such as the Internal Revenue Service at the federal level and tax commission agencies at the state and local level, and a myriad of specialized regulatory agencies having authority to investigate and prosecute violations of penal prohibitions governing health, safety, environment, and the like. The functions of these specialized agencies are not considered here. It may be noted, however, that the offenses with which these agencies deal generally are classified as white-collar offenses, for which the typically employed sanction is a monetary penalty rather than either imprisonment or probation.

System characteristics.

Mass production and discretion. Several general observations should be made about the administrative system. First, it is required to deal with a large and never-ending flow of cases. Even though the system attempts to individualize its response to each offender, and in theory is supposed to treat each case as though it stood alone under the law, the process is in fact one of mass production. This is not to say that the system was planned as a mass-production system. Quite the contrary, many difficulties with it arise from the discrepancy between the fact of mass production and the ideal that each case be considered on its own merit.

A second general observation is that the system is

pervaded by exercise of loosely controlled discretion, which is both systemic and particular. Systemically, discretion is exercised to mediate between the high incidence of crime and the modest resources available to respond to it. Decisions must be made as to the allocation of the system's resources. These decisions are made officially and to some degree publicly, but often they are not based upon open deliberation. Thus, for example, no legislative act or mayoral directive says that the police shall devote intensive effort to investigating crimes against police officers, or that they shall deal with rape only where the victim is willing to carry the prosecution all the way through, but such policies in fact exist in most communities. They are necessary simply so that the system may deal with the overload of demand that would exist if it attempted to enforce the criminal law across the board.

Exercise of discretion is particular in that subsystems and individual officials within the system have a high degree of autonomy in performing their functions. A policeman is assigned a beat, but the patrol of the beat is usually under minimal supervision from superior police officers; the patrolman's allocation of time and effort is not subject to anything like the direction given an ordinary office or production-line worker, for example. In prosecutor's offices, individual deputy prosecutors generally have considerable discretion in deciding on the types and quality of cases that should be fully prosecuted. This discretion results partly from loose administration and partly from the fact that the prosecuting staff consists of lawyers who regard themselves as having the right and duty to exercise professional judgment in the performance of their functions. At the judicial stage, judges are the principal officials and have broad professional discretion in the exercise of their functions, particularly in sentencing. Moreover, the courts are very loosely administered in most localities, so that individual judges have administrative autonomy to an important degree. So also in the correctional system, discretion is both formal and de facto. Broad official discretion is exercised with regard to whether imprisonment will be terminated and parole granted, whether "good time" allowance (resulting in the shortening of imprisonment) will be denied for violation of prison regulations, and so on. Lower-level, informal discretion is exercised by prison guards in responding to prisoner behavior of all kinds.

Taken as a whole, the system is subject to pervasive formal legal controls, but it is also characterized by the pervasive exercise of unsupervised discretion. There are dynamic relationships between these two phenomena: because legal rules so thoroughly govern

official action, it is assumed that the official actions are under control and that higher administrative controls are unnecessary; and the rigidity of legal controls creates incentives to seek waivers, a fact that in turn entails exercise of discretion.

Balkanization. The administrative structure of the criminal justice system is extremely decentralized. There are about forty thousand different public police forces in the United States, one for almost every city and for many villages, and usually a separate one in every county. In some large cities there are several different police agencies, such as transit police or housing police, in addition to the municipal police as such. In virtually all states, the prosecutorial function is centered at the county level in the office of the district attorney. Many large cities have a further division of prosecutorial authority in that municipal legal departments prosecute misdemeanors. The judiciary is usually organized along county lines, although in rural areas in most states the counties are grouped into judicial districts. In a few states the judiciary is organized on a statewide basis, but even there the daily operation of calendars and judicial assignments usually is handled separately in each courthouse. In any case, the work load of judges and supporting court staff is unbalanced and poorly managed in many jurisdictions.

The correctional system is sharply divided in almost all states between local authorities and state authorities. At the local level, except in very thinly populated rural areas, virtually all counties maintain a jail. All cities of substantial size have their own jails. Jails are used for temporary incarceration of persons awaiting prosecution and for punishment of offenders sentenced to short jail sentences. Also at the local level, but usually attached to the court system rather than the jail system, is the probation service, which performs essentially two functions. The first is investigating an offender's background immediately after conviction and before sentence for the purpose of providing information on which to base the sentence. The second is supervising offenders who are given a sentence of probation. The correctional system at the state level consists of the prison system, including institutions for the incarceration of juveniles, and the parole service. The parole service is usually attached to the state prison administration and provides supervision of offenders who have served a prison term and are released on parole.

The administrative autonomy of these various administrative organizations has two dimensions. First, each of the components—police, prosecution, judiciary, and corrections—generally is administratively autonomous from the others. (In a few states the courts and the prosecutor's office are under one administrative authority.) Second, the various local subdivisions of each of these functions are administratively separated from one another. Thus, police units of different cities, even those in a single metropolitan area, are subject to no common administrative control, although they often have various formal and informal working arrangements. The same is true of prosecutor's offices from one county to the other and, to a lesser extent, of courts and probation services.

The foregoing description if anything understates the lack of administrative coordination in criminal justice. A complete account would require describing the separation between various federal criminal justice agencies and their state counterparts, and between state-level criminal justice agencies, such as the state police and the state attorney general's office, and their local counterparts. It would also describe how these separations impede vital routines, such as controlling the flow of cases from one subsystem to another, coordinating allocation of resources, and using common terminology and comparable statistics. On the other hand, the fact that these organizations are not well orchestrated has certain important benefits. Most obvious is the maintenance of the independence of the judiciary, with the resulting governance of the functions of police, prosecution, and corrections by independent judicial review. This legal control of the criminal justice system is unparalleled anywhere else in the world. Moreover, the tensions arising between autonomous agencies result in public visibility of fundamental issues in criminal justice that otherwise would be submerged within a bureaucracy. For example, the fundamental issue of allocating police and prosecutorial resources is manifested in conflicts between police and prosecutorial agencies over priorities regarding specific crimes. Making the issues visible subjects them in some degree to resolution in accordance with public opinion, rather than simply with the preference of the agencies involved.

Another generalization is that the degree of professionalism and competence in the broadest sense varies considerably throughout the country. The variance is probably much less than it was around 1960, and certainly less than it was in 1930. The day of the bumpkin sheriff or of the judge who is law unto himself has virtually passed. Modern communication and interaction disseminate techniques and standards of performance despite administrative boundaries. Nevertheless, variance remains and has important consequences. "Professionalism" implies certain values, particularly impersonality, neutrality, and formal ra-

tionality in goals and techniques. The fact that professionalism is unevenly distributed among various elements in the system indicates, among other things, that there are corresponding differences of public opinion on the underlying issues of value. It seems fair to say, for example, that some communities prefer an "old boy" police force.

Police

Organization. Of the two basic police functions, prevention and detection, prevention—patrolling streets and other places where crime may happen—is the most visible.

Prevention and detection. Patrolling is a "proactive" technique, that is, it consists of planned anticipatory maneuvers which frustrate potential criminal activity. Detection consists of investigating crimes that already have taken place, and may be described as a reactive technique, in that it is mobilized after, and in response to, criminal activity initiated by an offender. In strategic terms, prevention and detection obviously reinforce each other. Effective prevention makes unnecessary the laborious process of identifying and prosecuting criminal offenders, whereas effective detection provides a deterrent to crime that would take place beyond the scrutiny of a preventive patrol.

From an organizational and tactical point of view, however, prevention and detection are generally fairly distinct. Characteristically, preventive police patrol is carried out by more or less widely dispersed police officers, operating individually or in pairs and patrolling on foot or in patrol cars. The number and distribution of patrols is worked out, mainly on the basis of continuous trial and error, with the aim of reducing crime in public spaces (such as street assaults), and in places accessible from public spaces (such as burglaries in residential districts). Police departments rarely patrol purely private locations, such as apartment houses or office buildings, partly because of legal limitations on such patrols and partly because responsibility for such locations is deemed a matter of private concern. Hence, there has been an enormous expansion of private policing of private locations through all kinds of guards and "security officers" in stores, office buildings, shopping areas, apartment houses, and residential areas, where private police forces are employed to supplement public patrol. The number of private police engaged in various forms of patrol is now substantially larger than the number of public police engaged in that function. Whether patrol is performed by public or private police, however, it is characteristically performed by low-ranking officers assigned to cruise a particular territory and to keep an eye out for criminal eventuality. In most urban localities it is very dangerous work.

Specialized squads. The detective function is usually performed by specialized squads. Many police departments have several detective squads dealing specifically with such crimes as homicide, burglary, rape, and narcotic trafficking. The detective function is so organized because detection essentially involves compiling and sifting through background information. For certain types of crime, particularly homicide, the useful information relates chiefly to the facts of the immediate crime and the identity of persons having a motive, since that crime typically involves people who have had a relationship with each other. With respect to other crimes, particularly burglary and robbery, the investigative task consists of comparing prior police records with what is known about the immediate offense to derive a suspect or set of suspects upon whom more intensive investigation may then focus. The key to any suspect is a pattern of repeated offenses, that is, his modus operandi (M/O). In either case, the detection focus is largely a historical investigation, dealing with records, photographs, fingerprints, and the like, whereas patrol is a face-to-face "action" interchange.

In general, detection is performed by police who are older, higher in rank, longer in service, and more knowledgeable about patterns of crime and the criminal process than are patrol officers. However, virtually all detectives are former patrolmen, a consequence of the fact that virtually all police forces hire at the patrolman rank and promote from within. The detection function is thus carried out by officers who have first established their ability to perform the more rough-and-ready functions of patrol. Few police departments directly recruit and train experts in detection, although in urban centers there are specialists in such fields as ballistics and fingerprint analysis. Few police departments have officers trained in detection of white-collar crime, a circumstance that contributes to relegating responsibility for controlling such crime to specialized administrative agencies.

Most urban police departments have specialized units that deal with victimless crimes, including narcotic violations, gambling, and prostitution. Characteristically, these offenses involve consensual participants, and hence no unwilling victims. For this reason, these offenses cannot be suppressed by either patrol or the usual detective function, since these methods presuppose either that the offense is directly observable by the police or that persons injured by the offense will cooperate in supplying information about the of-fender. In dealing with victimless crimes the police therefore must be both aggressive and surreptitious, using such methods as hidden surveillance and informers. Because concealment and deception necessarily must be used, this kind of police work is morally ambiguous and often crosses the border of legal restrictions on police search, interrogation, and entrapment. In addition, victimless crimes constitute a commerce often involving large sums of money, a circumstance which makes police operations directed against such crimes very vulnerable to corruption.

Police operations addressing crime, whether through patrol or detection, in fact occupy only a fraction of the effort and attention of police departments. Most police departments spend the bulk of their time in various helping services to the public, such as traffic control, crowd control, emergency ambulance and other health and safety care, physical rescue, and emergency taxi service. In addition, all police departments devote a substantial amount of effort to traffic offenses and to the routine arrest and temporary jailing of drunks, both motorists and pedestrians.

Arrest. The term *arrest* is ambiguous. Legally, an arrest includes a temporary involuntary interception of a person's otherwise intended movement, for example, stopping a pedestrian or motorist to ask a question. Arrest also means the more formal and complete act of taking a suspect into custody for purposes of detention and possible prosecution. Many of the legal rules defining police authority to make an arrest apply to both forms of arrest, although it is recognized that the threshold of suspicion sufficient for stopping and questioning is much lower than the threshold for taking a person into custody. Nevertheless, the basic law of arrest is founded on the premise that the involuntary suspension of a person's movements usually requires the same justification as a full-blown arrest and detention.

Probable cause. Authority to arrest depends upon the existence of "probable cause"—the existence of a substantial factual basis for supposing that an offense was committed and that the arrested person committed it. If such facts are evident to the police officer, an arrest may be made without a warrant. If the crime involved is a felony, the police officer need not have directly witnessed the required facts. The same rule generally applies to misdemeanors, but in some states a misdemeanor arrest is authorized only if the offense took place in the officer's presence. Alternatively, if the police have evidence constituting probable cause, they can seek a judicial warrant for arrest. If the court determines that probable cause exists, it issues the warrant, and the police arrest on the basis of the warrant. The judicial determination that probable cause exists constitutes a prior adjudication that there is sufficient evidentiary basis for arrest.

Most arrests made on police patrol are made without warrants, for the obvious reason that an encounter with crime on a patrol requires immediate response. Warrants for arrest therefore are more often used where the suspect is identified through detection, when emergency conditions have subsided. Arrest warrants are awkward to use with regard to victimless crime because successful prosecution usually requires that the offense actually has been committed, as distinct from being in preparation. Apart from the problem of maintaining secrecy, it is generally difficult to show that such a crime will probably be committed.

Search warrant. An arrest warrant must be distinguished from a search warrant. A warrant for arrest authorizes taking the person in question into custody. A search warrant authorizes the police to enter premises and to search for specified evidence of criminality such as weapons, stolen goods, or narcotics, and it requires a showing of reasonable cause to believe that the evidence will be found at the specified premises. Without a search warrant, the police may search a person, a vehicle, or premises only under very limited circumstances. Arrest without a warrant and search without a warrant are governed by rules developed by the United States Supreme Court under the Bill of Rights and the Fourteenth Amendment. The rules involve many fine distinctions and render the process of arrest and search a highly technical exercise except where an offense is committed in the presence of a policeman. This fact is a powerful inducement for police to assert that an offense was committed before their very eyes when this is not true—that is, to lie. The legal controls on arrest and search serve to protect individual rights, but they also carry the risk of morally corrupting the police.

An arrest in the course of patrol is usually made on the basis of the individual officer's judgment, but sometimes upon radio consultation with a supervisory officer. An arrest by detectives or upon warrant by definition is usually based on a decision by a higher authority. In either case, the arrested person is taken to a police facility, either a central jail or a precinct station. For some types of less serious offenses, a policeman who observes the offense is permitted, rather than making an arrest, to issue a citation requiring the offender to appear in court at a specified time. The procedure is adapted from, and is essentially similar to, the issuing of a "ticket" for a motor-vehicle violation.

Police follow-up.

Scope and criteria. Where an arrest has been made by a patrol officer, the question arises whether prosecution should be followed through. A chief issue is whether the evidence is sufficient to carry the case through to the prosecutor's office. From their continuous dealings with the prosecutor, the police know the standards of proof that the prosecutor will require to commence judicial proceedings, and if they believe that the standard of proof has been met, they forward the case to the prosecutor. After having made an arrest the police rarely presume to decide not to prosecute a case; discretion at this stage is reserved to the prosecutor and the judiciary. On the other hand, if the evidence does not meet the standard required by the prosecutor, the police have to decide whether further investigatory effort is justified. That decision will be based on the seriousness of the crime, whether a victim is willing to pursue the case, whether there appear to be sources of additional evidence, whether the offender has a prior record, and other circumstances. The additional investigation may be relatively intensive or virtually perfunctory. For example, the killing of a police officer will be pursued relentlessly even in the face of few promising leads. On the other hand, muggings not involving serious injury generally are given sufficient attention to placate the victim, thereby pacifying public opinion about the police, but are given no more attention unless the crime fits a pattern pointing to a specific suspect. The police have a realistic sense of the futility of trying to identify a snatch thief from the portfolio of hundreds of plausible suspects whose photographs are on file from previous arrests.

An essentially similar calculation is made in the detective units responsible for investigating crimes reported to the police. Serious offenses against the person receive relatively intensive pursuit, particularly if the victim actively participates and if serious injury was involved. On the other hand, routine cases of breaking and entering dwellings are pursued by reviewing files on past offenses for clues to a pattern associated with a particular offender.

Booking. A person who is taken into custody to be charged is "booked" by the police. In the era before tight legal restrictions were imposed on arrest, patrol officers confronted with doubtful cases could take a suspect into custody and leave it to the station officer to decide whether the accused should be booked or simply released. Now that a patrol arrest can have serious legal consequences, including possible civil litigation against the arresting officer, the police resolve doubtful cases on patrol in favor of releasing the suspect, subject to the possibility of follow-up investigation. Indeed, the patrol officer may simply let the suspect go or ignore the situation. These front-line decisions, made rapidly and according to the officer's personal judgment, often determine whether a suspect will be virtually untouched or will be caught up in the prosecutorial apparatus coming into play after an arrest.

Release pending prosecution.

Bail. An arrested suspect is generally entitled to release after booking. Where the charge is a misdemeanor, the suspect ordinarily becomes automatically eligible for release upon his promise to appear in court to answer the charge against him; sometimes he must also post bail. When the charge is a felony, the accused generally may obtain release from custody only by posting bail. Bail is a deposit of cash or a cash-equivalent asset, or the posting of bond. A bond is a written promise to pay the bail sum and is posted in lieu of bail by a person whose financial credit is recognized by the court, such as a professional bondsman. Until about 1960, bail typically was high, so that indigent suspects simply stayed in jail until their cases came before the court. A bail reform movement led to a radical reduction of bail, and by the early 1980s bail had been dramatically reduced except in serious offenses where there was a demonstrated risk that the offender would fail to appear for trial.

Preventive detention. The desuetude of bail has led to a search for alternatives. The underlying concern is not that the suspect will flee but that he will commit more offenses pending prosecution and conviction. To deal with this problem, the procedure of "preventive detention" has been widely proposed and in some places adopted. In preventive detention a judicial hearing is held to determine whether the suspect is likely to commit more offenses if released. Preventive detention procedure juxtaposes two fundamental but contradictory ideas. On the one hand, many suspects arrested in the modern criminal justice system have had repeated encounters with the police. They are almost certainly guilty of something and are quite possibly guilty of the offense for which they have been arrested; they may well commit other offenses if they are let go. At the same time, it is a principle of law that no person should be held in jail unless he has been convicted according to law. Preventive detention authorizes the court to estimate whether an arrested but legally innocent person is likely to commit another offense, and on the basis of such an estimate to order his detention. As a technique of public protection, preventive detention serves much the same function as high bail and has the additional merit of focusing

on the question of the accused's present dangerousness. Nevertheless, it has proved impossible to make very accurate estimates of dangerousness, and there is an inevitable tendency in actual administration to err on the side of caution. As a practical matter, suspects with a prior record are likely to be held if they are charged with a serious offense. In any event, the decision whether to insist on bail or preventive detention rests with the court rather than the police.

Aiding prosecution. After the police develop a case sufficiently for formal prosecution, they relinquish control of the matter to the prosecution and the courts. However, the police participate in the prosecution. Police officers are often important witnesses, particularly in cases encountered on patrol, and they usually have responsibility for conserving evidence and conducting such supplemental investigation as the prosecutor determines to be necessary. This division of authority between police and prosecution is not necessary in the nature of things. In other countries the police have substantial responsibility for prosecution: in some, the prosecuting attorney is essentially a legal representative of the police, and in others, the police are subject to administrative supervision by the prosecutor. The division of function between police and prosecution in the American criminal justice system means that there can be continuing unresolved conflict over enforcement policy and practice. Furthermore, there is often conflict between the police and the courts, the police perceiving that their cases disappear into the prosecutor's office and become ensnarled in judicial technicalities.

Prosecution and defense

Adversary system. A criminal proceeding moves along through the mechanism of the adversary system. In the adversary system the accused is presumed innocent until proved guilty, and under modern American criminal procedure he has a right to assistance of counsel from the point where he is arrested. The procedure for determining guilt is that of competitive presentations by the prosecuting attorney as legal representative of the state, countered by the defense counsel as representative of the defendant. Although only a small fraction of all charges originating from the police actually go to trial, the adversary process dominates criminal prosecutions from the point of arrest and even before that point. A criminal charge can become a conviction only through an adversary trial or by guilty plea on the part of the defendant. Although it may be said that the police function is administratively self-contained and operates by a system of quasi-military command, the prosecutorial function proceeds by a dialectic between the prosecuting attorney and the defense counsel. Hence, the most fundamental practical problem confronting a prosecution is whether the proceedings leading to trial, and trial itself, can be successfully sustained in face of challenge and resistance by the defendant through his legal counsel.

The adversary system may be contrasted with the inquisitorial, or investigatory, system of prosecution that prevails in most of Europe and in such countries as Japan, whose legal system is patterned on that of Western Europe. In the investigatory system, the prosecutor has more authority, but also more responsibility, for determining the charge and the evidence that will be presented to the court. In some versions of the European system the prosecutor is regarded as a member of the court. By contrast, in the adversary system, prosecutor and defense counsel stand as equals. However, even in the Anglo-American system the prosecutor is required to be not only advocate for the state but a guardian against unfair or unwarranted prosecution. This dual responsibility obliges a prosecutor continually to balance between overcoming the defendant's resistance to conviction, and terminating the prosecution if he himself is not satisfied that the defendant is legally guilty.

Prosecutor.

Office of the prosecutor. The prosecuting attorney is a full-time public official, except in very sparsely populated rural counties. In most jurisdictions he is chosen by election in the county in which he serves; in a few jurisdictions the prosecutor is appointed by a state-level authority. In urban areas the prosecutor has a supporting staff, which in large cities may run to hundreds of lawyers, along with paralegals, investigators, and clerical staff. The legal and paralegal staff is largely professionalized, in contrast to the patronage system once prevalent. In some states, members of the legal staff hold merit-rated positions, and a substantial percentage of the incumbents serve as such during their entire professional career. On the other hand, top-level deputies are often discretionary appointments and are often selected on political or patronage grounds. There is also a relatively high turnover at junior-level staff positions, with lawyers entering to gain rapid, intensive trial experience and then moving on to private practice. This pattern results in many cases being handled by deputy prosecutors who are young in years and limited in experience.

The prosecutor's office is responsible for a case from the point where it is received from the police through its termination by trial, guilty plea, or dismissal. The prosecutor is responsible for determining whether a formal charge should be lodged, and, if so, what specific crime should be charged; for conducting settlement negotiations where a plea of guilty may be in prospect; for deciding to abandon prosecutions that cannot be proved or settled; and for trying cases that go to trial. Particularly in the charging and negotiating processes, the prosecutor has very broad range of discretion.

Decision to charge. A complex set of factors is involved in the decision to charge. The single most important factor is the seriousness of the crime; if it is serious, only a dearth of evidence or extraordinary circumstances would warrant a prosecutor's refusing to proceed. The decision to charge is strongly influenced by the strength of the evidence available to the prosecutor. Where the offense is heinous but the evidence is weak, the prosecutor may be obliged to charge a lesser offense that can be proved. Another relevant factor is the defendant's criminal record. If he has a prior record, the prosecutor will be much more inclined to charge—and to charge the maximum offense that the evidence will permit—than if the accused has no prior record. The theory is simply that the accused with a criminal record deserves further punishment and is also more dangerous to the community.

Still another factor is the attitude of the victim. Victim attitude influences the availability of evidence, obviously so where a conviction can be obtained only if the victim will testify. But beyond this, the fact that the victim wants prosecution is morally and politically influential, for the prosecutor's office must sustain public confidence that it is seriously interested in vindicating the criminal law. On the other hand, if the accused has no criminal record and is a provably good citizen, if the crime was in some sense a response to provocation, or if the victim is a provably evil person, the prosecutor normally will be inclined to a lesser charge or, in some circumstances, will simply let the matter go without prosecution.

Alternatives to prosecution. Also relevant in formulating the charge is the possibility of redress outside the criminal justice system. For example, if an offense appears to have been the product of violent emotion, and if the accused has agreed to submit to psychological therapy or supervision, the prosecutor may suspend prosecution or moderate the charge. Prosecutions for possession or use of narcotics are often terminated in a disposition that involves voluntarily submitting to rehabilitative therapy. Where the offense involves actual harm to the victim, the fact that the defendant can make restitution is a relevant circumstance, particularly if restitution is made voluntarily. Basically, the charging decision consists of selecting the appropriate criminal component of a suitable overall resolution of the transaction. This reflects the fact that the conduct in question results from a complex transaction in which the involvement of a crime is only a part of the picture, although of course often the most important part.

This perspective reveals the practical importance of whether the accused has economic and social resources to commit in closing the transaction. Noncriminal redress is, up to a point, a substitute for criminal redress. In an extreme case, a wealthy offender may be able to buy off a victim. Less dramatically, the community, speaking through the prosecutor, may be propitiated by gestures of contrition and acts of redress outside criminal prosecution. These gestures and acts generally are more feasible for the relatively affluent and literate than for the poor and inarticulate. Hence, there is an inherently unequal capacity among the affluent and the poor to participate in the "closing" of a transaction involving a crime. The resulting tendency is that the poor submit to heavier criminal sanctions, or have their offenses treated on a lower moral plane, than do the affluent.

Constituencies. Serving to moderate and channel the prosecutor's discretion are influences from various constituencies to which the prosecutor must be responsive. These include (1) the courts, whose past decisions have to be taken into account and whose future decisions have to be anticipated; (2) the police, who in some sense are the prosecutor's clients and who certainly can influence the esteem in which the prosecutor's office is held by the general public; (3) the press; (4) victims, bystanders, neighbors, and other more or less proximately involved elements of the public; (5) other agencies of government, particularly mayors and city councilmen; and (6) the legal profession, of which the lawyers in the prosecutor's office are members. These cumulative surveillances place the charging decision in something of a goldfish bowl, so that its exercise is only in a formal sense ungoverned by outside controls. The prosecutor's decisions also are influenced by the limited resources available to deal with the steady flow of incoming cases.

Only a fraction of the cases booked by the police are charged at about the same offense level by the prosecutor. Many potential prosecutions are abandoned, and most others go forward on a reduced charge, which may be reduced still further through settlement or at trial.

Negotiation of pleas. A substantial majority of all prosecutions filed by the prosecutor's office are resolved by a negotiated plea of guilty. The prosecution agrees that the original charge will be reduced to a somewhat lesser offense, thus reducing the range of penalties that the judge may impose. In addition, or alternatively, the prosecutor may agree to make a specific recommendation to the court regarding the sentence. The defendant agrees in return to abandon resistance to the accusation and to plead guilty. Generally, and appropriately, this process is called plea bargaining.

Resource constraints. Plea bargaining is a practical necessity in the criminal justice system. The prosecution does not have the resources to develop evidence and conduct trials to convert every accusation into a conviction through a trial. Similar considerations constrain the defense. Where a defendant has retained his own counsel, the cost of conducting a defense is a relevant factor in all but those crimes for which the penalty is so severe that monetary considerations become irrelevant. The cost factor is particularly relevant if the state's evidence is strong, for then the probability of success in defense is correspondingly small. It would make little sense for a defendant to spend five or ten thousand dollars pursuing a one-in-fifty chance of acquittal when conviction means a probable prison sentence and a negotiated plea of guilty will result in probation. Where the defendant is represented by publicly employed counsel, for example, a public defender, these economic constraints still exist but fall directly on the lawyer rather than on the client. That is, a public defender's legal staff cannot afford to spend five or ten thousand dollars' worth of its resources on behalf of a defendant who is simply being stubborn, where the consequence is to reduce the assistance that could be provided to other defendants whose cases are more meritorious.

The guilty plea purports to be a voluntary concession of guilt by the defendant. Expressions of contrition are relevant in a moral calculation of the wrongfulness of an offender's conduct. This moral factor is a part of plea bargaining, for the prosecutor, the court, and public opinion are constrained to leniency toward a defendant who has, at least ostensibly, acknowledged his responsibility for wrong. This explains and justifies the fact, often officially denied, that courts on the average are less severe with defendants who plead guilty than with those who defend their innocence to the end. However, this tendency also vitiates to some degree the presumption of innocence, for it results in the imposition of heavier sentences on offenders who have insisted on their right to trial than on offenders who acquiesce in the accusation against them. Furthermore, the possibility of a plea bargain is an incentive for a person who sincerely believes himself innocent to acquiesce in a negotiated plea of guilty in order to eliminate the risk of a severe sentence that may result from conviction following a trial. The incentive is particularly strong where the flood of cases is so great that the system makes many mistakes. A system of plea bargaining therefore inevitably creates inducements for innocent persons to plead guilty. Furthermore, the exaction of disingenuous guilty pleas undermines the morality of contrition.

Guilty pleas and innocence. Plea bargaining also results in anomalous guilty pleas. For example, a case involving homicide may yield a negotiated plea to the offense of manslaughter when the facts of the killing show that it was almost certainly murder. Such a plea is perfectly intelligible where the evidence for the prosecution is sufficient to go to trial, but insufficient, in the prosecutor's estimation, to be clearly convincing to a jury. In such a situation, and especially if the defendant's prior record and personal situation warrant only a modest sentence, both parties have strong incentives to reach the plea bargain. The prosecution faces a serious risk of failure to obtain any conviction at all; the defense faces the risk that a trial will result in conviction of the much more serious crime of murder. Both parties agree to conviction of a lesser crime, even though that crime certainly did not occur. Negotiated pleas in such situations, and endless varieties of a less dramatic type, are a part of the routine of criminal justice administration. They violate the premises both of the substantive penal law, which attempts to apportion blame according to the nature of the offense, and of the rules of criminal procedure and evidence, which seek to ensure that criminal punishment will be imposed only on those who are proved guilty beyond a reasonable doubt.

Plea bargaining is perhaps the most controversial and disparaged aspect of modern criminal justice administration. Yet some process is necessary by which to discount a criminal charge to reflect the value of the evidence that supports it, for not all charges stand on the same quality of proof. The variability of proof in turn reflects several more fundamental propositions about criminal law: it can never be certain that an accused is guilty or innocent; the criminal law cannot be fully enforced because the state has limited resources to enforce it; defendants cannot insist on ultimate efforts to determine whether they are really innocent, again because of resource constraints; an accused person who acknowledges guilt is morally more worthy than one who attempts to escape responsibility before the law and should be treated with corresponding leniency; and it is morally outrageous that a person who is actually innocent should have to plead guilty in order to avoid the greater injustice of being wrongly convicted of a serious crime. All these propositions are both true and intractable.

It seems evident that charge discounting in some form has existed for as long as there has been a system of criminal justice, that is, a system where guilt is determined only in accordance with law and a standard of objective proof. The biblical story of King Solomon's threat to cut the baby in half can be interpreted as the use of a coercive method to obtain a guilty plea from the false mother, thus obviating a dismissal for lack of sufficient evidence. The fundamental question, then, is where and by whom the business of charge discounting is to be done. In many criminal justice systems, it is done at the police interrogation stage, with charges formulated after it is established how the defendant will respond to a particular accusation. In the present American system, it is conducted at the prosecution stage by lawyers on behalf of the state and the defense. Charge discounting goes on, overtly or tacitly, from the point the case arrives in the prosecutor's hands until trial, indeed until the matter is submitted for decision by the judge or jury.

Procedure.

Post-arrest stage. The prosecution stage begins at the transition between arrest and formal accusation. There are two basic pathways, depending on whether the defendant has been arrested upon a warrant or without a warrant. An arrest upon a warrant presupposes a hearing before a magistrate, who is a judge or a parajudicial officer, in order to obtain the warrant. Obtaining a warrant for arrest requires a charge and a showing of probable cause that a crime was committed and that the defendant committed it. A prosecutor ordinarily will not have sought an arrest warrant unless the evidence is also sufficient to carry through the prosecution, that is, unless the evidence easily meets the standard of probable cause. However, notwithstanding the fact that an arrest warrant was obtained, it may be open to the defendant to object that probable cause has not been established.

In most criminal cases the accused is arrested without a warrant. After an arrest, if the prosecutor is satisfied that the evidence is sufficient, a charge is filed against the offender. The technical purpose of the charge is to justify holding the accused in custody (subject to the right to bail) pending further proceedings. Custody is justified if there is probable cause to believe that a crime was committed and that the defendant committed it. Whether probable cause exists is determined by a judicial officer at a preliminary hearing. The preliminary hearing thus is functionally similar to a hearing on an application for an arrest warrant, but it takes place after the arrest rather than before.

The procedure in prosecutions beyond this point depends on whether the accusation is a felony or a misdemeanor, and whether a grand jury is involved. Where the crime charged is a misdemeanor, the charging document is denominated a complaint. If the defendant has been arrested, probable cause must be established at a preliminary hearing; if the defendant was not arrested, he will have been, or will be, summoned to answer. In either case, the defendant responds through a plea of guilty or not guilty. This simple form of procedure is used for lesser crimes and for petty offenses.

Preliminary hearing. In some jurisdictions, the preliminary hearing is a relatively superficial review of the evidence. In other jurisdictions, it is a "minitrial" where the prosecution's evidence is fully developed and the defendant's counsel may challenge the evidence through cross-examination. In either event, but particularly where the preliminary hearing is relatively extensive, prosecution and defense are able to assess their cases with greater realism, having seen how the evidence will come across in open court. The more realistic assessments may change the parties' positions, resulting in either a reduction or dismissal of the charge or an acceleration of a guilty plea.

Assuming that the prosecution sustains its burden of showing probable cause, the defendant is "bound over" on the charge. This means that he remains obligated to appear to respond to the charge and may be required to post bail.

Felony and misdemeanor. The procedure from this point forward depends on whether the charge is a felony or a lesser offense. Where the charge is a misdemeanor or petty offense, the defendant responds through a plea of guilty or not guilty, and the issue thus joined goes on the trial calendar. The procedure for charging a felony is more complicated. Under common-law procedure, a felony could be charged only by an indictment of a grand jury. The grand jury is a criminal investigation body composed of laymen selected under the auspices of the court in much the same way that an ordinary (petit) jury is assembled. In the earlier common law, before professional police had been established, community knowledge

of a crime was transformed by the grand jury into accusations that were then tried before judges riding on circuit. A vestige of this original function remains in the many states in which a felony accusation still requires a grand jury indictment. In these jurisdictions, after the police have investigated a crime and the prosecutor has been satisfied that sufficient evidence exists to justify prosecution, a presentation is made to the grand jury to obtain an indictment. The process usually is wholly routine, for in appearance, and to a considerable extent in fact, the grand jury is simply a rubber stamp for the prosecution. However, the grand jury serves as something of a check on the prosecutor's freedom to go forward with prosecution.

Grand jury. Grand juries nevertheless can exercise a very important investigative function. A grand jury has authority to subpoena witnesses and documents, a power that the prosecutor ordinarily does not have. Hence, where crime is involved that requires extensive investigation, particularly crimes involving conspiracy or the conduct of illegal businesses, the grand jury is a powerful investigative mechanism and its function as such is anything but routine.

Because the procedure for grand jury indictment is redundant in routine cases, many states provide an alternative method of accusation, known as the information. An information is an accusation made on the authority of the prosecutor; instead of a grand jury affirming its belief that the accused is guilty, the prosecutor himself does so. Abuse of the power to proceed by information is constrained by the right to a preliminary hearing and by the fact that in most jurisdictions the defendant can demand that there be a grand jury indictment instead.

After an indictment or information is filed, the defendant makes a further appearance, which is called the arraignment. The arraignment is simply a summoning of the defendant to respond formally to the charge. The defendant pleads guilty or not guilty. If he pleads guilty, the matter proceeds to the sentencing stage. If the defendant pleads not guilty, it proceeds to trial.

Trial.

Prosecution's case. A trial begins with the selection of the jury, unless a jury trial is waived. The charge is formally read by the judge, and a record is made of the fact that the defendant has pleaded not guilty. Thereupon the prosecution begins its presentation. The presentation commences with an opening statement, which is a narrative of the nature of the offense, the identity of the victim and the defendant, the facts and circumstances of the crime, and the evidence that will be offered. The defendant at this point is permitted, but not required, to make an opening statement corresponding in subject matter to that of the prosecution. However, the defendant may reserve making an opening statement until the conclusion of the prosecution's case.

The prosecution then presents the evidence constituting its "case in chief," that is, all of its case except what may later be added as a rebuttal of the defendant's evidence. This consists of testimonial evidence and may include real evidence such as a weapon, documents, and expert testimony. Upon completing its evidence, the prosecution rests.

Defense. When the prosecution has rested, the defendant may move for dismissal of the charge on the ground that the evidence does not establish proof of the crime beyond a reasonable doubt. The court may dismiss all or some of the charges, depending on its assessment of the evidence. If the matter is tried before a jury, the court's function is to determine whether the jury properly could find guilt beyond a reasonable doubt with respect to the various offenses charged. Charges not established by this quantum of evidence are dismissed by the court. The charges for which the required evidentiary standard has been met are open for consideration by the jury, subject to the right of the defendant to present his own contradicting evidence. In a case tried by the judge without a jury, the motion to dismiss may be treated as a request to find the defendant not guilty.

The defendant has the privilege of introducing contradictory evidence, but he may simply rest on the prosecution's evidence. Under the Fifth Amendment privilege against self-incrimination, the defendant is not required to testify but has a right to do so. He also has the right to offer evidence other than his own testimony. For example, in the case in which ballistics is the central issue, the defendant may have his own ballistics expert. After the defendant has presented his evidence, he rests. The prosecution then may introduce rebuttal evidence, limited to proof contradicting new matter offered by the defendant; the prosecution is not allowed simply to offer evidence additional to that initially presented.

After all the evidence has been received, counsel for each side may address the jury or, in a nonjury case, the judge. This address is called the final argument, or summation, and is an opportunity for the prosecution and defense in turn to review the evidence and argue its cogency and weight. At the conclusion of the summations, the judge instructs the jury as to the governing legal principles and may review and comment upon the evidence. A standard instruction in a jury case is that questions of fact, including questions of credibility and of the weight of the evidence, are for the jury to decide. The jury then retires for deliberation and a verdict. If the case is tried without a jury, the court simply takes the matter under deliberation.

Verdict and judgment. The verdict may be one of acquittal or conviction, or the jury may become deadlocked and reach no verdict. If the verdict is an acquittal, that is the end of the matter, for the state has no right of appeal from an acquittal. If a jury returns a verdict of guilty, the defendant may request a new trial on the ground either of procedural error during the trial or of the evidence being insufficient to sustain the conviction. If the jury is deadlocked, a mistrial is declared and a new trial may be held.

When the defendant has been found guilty, a judgment of conviction is entered. The defendant is thereupon sentenced. After sentence, the defendant may simply accept the disposition and proceed to serve whatever penalty is imposed, but he has the right of appeal. In modern procedure, where a defendant is provided with the assistance of publicly compensated counsel, appeals are routine where a prison sentence is imposed. Not infrequently, a court imposes a sentence of "time served" where the offense is not heinous and where the defendant has been compelled to stay in jail for want of bail during prosecution.

Courts

Court systems.

Federal and state systems. The American judiciary includes a system of federal courts and a separate system of courts in each state. The federal courts are organized on a nationwide basis. In each state there is a federal trial court, the United States District Court. Above the district courts in the federal hierarchy are the twelve United States courts of appeals, organized by geographical regions called circuits. At the apex of the federal court system is the United States Supreme Court, which has appellate jurisdiction over the lower federal courts and also authority to review issues of federal law that arise in state courts.

State courts. Each state has its own court system. The structure in most states is essentially similar to the federal court system—a trial court level, an intermediate appellate court, and a state supreme court. The trial courts in most states are organized along county lines, with a separate trial court in each county, although in some rural areas several counties are grouped together to form a trial court district. In most states the trial courts are in two divisions, an upper one of general jurisdiction and a lower one of limited authority. The trial court of general jurisdiction is variously called the district court, circuit court, or superior court; the court of limited jurisdiction had its origin in the justice-of-the-peace courts and municipal courts of an earlier era and is now called by various names. Generally speaking, felony prosecutions are conducted in the trial court of general jurisdiction, whereas the courts of limited jurisdiction conduct preliminary hearings in felony cases, and trials in cases involving misdemeanors and minor offenses.

Procedural standards.

Federal due process. All offenses against federal law are prosecuted in federal courts. All prosecutions for offenses against state law are prosecuted in state courts, with exceptions concerning offenses that involve federal activity. However, the federal courts have important supervisory authority with regard to the administration of criminal justice in the state courts. Since about 1930, the Supreme Court has been interpreting the due process clause of the Fourteenth Amendment to imply procedural requirements that state courts must observe in criminal prosecutions. These federally imposed procedural requirements now include (1) the right to jury trial in all serious offenses; (2) the right to assistance of counsel in any case in which a jail sentence may be imposed; (3) the privilege against self-incrimination, including the right not to testify against oneself and a prohibition against comment by the prosecution on the defendant's failure to testify; (4) a requirement that proof of guilt be established beyond a reasonable doubt; (5) the right to refuse to respond to police interrogation and the right to demand the presence of a lawyer during such interrogation; and (6) freedom from racial and sex discriminatory provisions in substantive and procedural criminal law.

These federally created procedural rights must be observed by the state courts. An accused who contends that he has been denied or improperly interpreted has a right to appeal through the state court system to the Supreme Court. Although this right of appeal to the Supreme Court is important in principle, its practical effect is limited because the Court is able to consider only a small fraction of state court cases involving federal questions. However, the Court has also developed doctrines protecting these federal rights through habeas corpus proceedings in the United States district courts. After a state court conviction has become final, the state prisoner petitions the federal court to determine whether the state court observed his federal procedural rights.

Although basic criminal procedure in state courts is prescribed by state law, procedural protections established by federal law amount to a supplemental code of criminal procedure. Enforcing these protections results in federal trial court review of the procedural regularity of criminal prosecutions that have already been reviewed by state appellate courts. The total effect of federal procedural protections has been virtually revolutionary. As late as 1950, state criminal process, except in unusually serious or complex cases, consisted of relatively free police investigation, charging based on the prosecutor's estimate of the sufficiency of the evidence, defense without the assistance of counsel in the case of indigents, and convictions that were rarely appealed. By the 1980s, police investigatory methods were stringently regulated, particularly concerning interrogation and search of premises; prosecution was restricted by the requirement that evidence be legally obtained and by the stricter enforcement of standards of proof; defense counsel was provided to the indigent; and conviction was almost routinely followed by appeal if a substantial sentence had been imposed. The proceeding as a whole became subject to the possibility of still additional review through federal habeas corpus proceedings.

Technical complexity. Criminal procedure has probably become more complicated and technical than any other body of procedural law. Additional complexity results from the fact that much of this law has evolved through case law decisions over time, rather than through comprehensive legislative enactment. As a result, at any given time it is often difficult to say what the law is, particularly since the Supreme Court has shifted its approach from time to time and because lower courts have inevitably overinterpreted or underinterpreted Supreme Court trends. In addition, a number of state supreme courts have themselves been very active in elaborating procedural rights for defendants. In some states, the procedural protections established by state courts are considerably more exacting than those established by the Supreme Court in interpretation of the federal Constitution. These developments have changed the whole tenor of criminal proceedings and have reduced the risk of unjust conviction, particularly the disproportionateness of the risks to which minorities are subject.

In modern criminal procedure the trial court judiciary is responsible for applying a highly complex body of procedural law to a very high volume of cases. Giving full-scale treatment to all cases is simply impossible. In heinous offenses, particularly ones that have attracted public attention, the full panoply of procedures unfolds, so that it can cost literally hundreds of thousands of dollars to try a major felony where the evidence is in serious dispute and the defendant is determined to seek acquittal. The criminal justice system adapts with shortcuts in routine cases, including waiver of various formalities, dispositions by stipulation, and postponement. These cases constitute virtually a system of consensual justice, in which prosecution goes forward on the basis of the defendants' acquiescence. The low-visibility cases that flow endlessly through the criminal justice system are resolved by "slow plea" and "delayed dismissal." The slow plea is a guilty plea to a relatively minor offense, elicited from the defendant through the persuasion of his own counsel in response to alternating threats and cajolery from the prosecution. A delayed dismissal is a dismissal obtained from the prosecutor by defense threats and cajolery but withheld for a time—perhaps three to six months—as a stern warning to the defendant and to allow the victim to be placated or at least reconciled to the fact that a severe sanction will not be forthcoming. Prosecutor and defense counsel work out the slow pleas and delayed dismissals while the lower courts record and monitor.

Juvenile courts. Brief mention should be made of the juvenile court system. In all states, offenders under a specified age, typically sixteen or eighteen, are proceeded against in juvenile courts, except in the most heinous offenses such as murder. The proceedings nominally are civil rather than criminal, the theory being that the respondent is to be rehabilitated rather than punished. However, the basis of the proceedings is an act which if committed by an adult would be a criminal offense. In some states, the juvenile court is a separate trial court; in others, it is a specialized branch of the regular trial court. In any event, juvenile court procedure roughly corresponds to criminal procedure; however, it is less formal and less technical and, in almost all jurisdictions, trials are held with a judge alone rather than with a jury. Until about 1960, juvenile court procedure was quite informal, intended to be mediatory and protective rather than accusatory and concerned with the question of guilt. Procedural changes, many of them required by Supreme Court interpretations of the due process requirement, have subsequently made juvenile court procedure quite formal. It is now required that there be a written accusation, proof beyond a reasonable doubt, and the assistance of counsel. The aim and character of juvenile courts nevertheless remain more amelioratory than is so in the criminal courts. However, as serious offenses have come to be committed by younger and younger persons, the case pattern in juvenile courts has come increasingly to resemble that of criminal courts. The cases include a high proportion of assaults and thefts by young males who are predominantly from poor families and ethnic minorities.

Sentencing and corrections

An offender who has been convicted, whether by trial or by plea of guilty, is subject to sentencing. Imposing sentence is the responsibility of the judge, except in a few jurisdictions where the jury is authorized to impose the penalty for felonies. Sentence may consist of confinement in jail or prison, release under supervision, a fine, or a combination of these sanctions. Every state has a cluster of penal facilities for the incarceration of offenders, and a cluster of agencies responsible for the supervision of convicted offenders.

Jails and prisons. The most familiar penal institution is the local jail. Jails are maintained in all urban communities, operated by cities or counties or both. A jail provides temporary custody for arrested persons pending prosecution, and a place of punishment for persons sentenced to short periods of confinement. In most urban communities the jail is part of a facility that also serves as police headquarters or subheadquarters. A jail is thus a police administration center, an intake facility, a holding place, and a facility for local punishment. Its inmate population at any given time commingles the legally innocent, the legally guilty, and people whose legal and life situation is in disarray. It is a population that is above all transient. Jails in large urban centers generally have a mildly chaotic atmosphere, stabilized by the facts that all inmates have an interest in getting out and that most have excellent prospects of doing so soon if they do not seriously misbehave. In general, urban jails are chronically overcrowded and have few services beyond preserving order and providing food, a bunk, and a common room with a television set. In all but very rural communities, separate facilities are provided for women and for juveniles. Generally, the level of services in juvenile detention centers is somewhat higher, but those facilities have the same characteristic atmosphere of transience and boredom.

All states operate penal institutions at the state level. These institutions include a state prison and a state juvenile training facility. Separate wings or facilities are provided for female adult prisoners and for female juveniles. For adult males, and sometimes for other categories of offenders, facilities are graduated according to tightness of security and rigor of regimen, ranging from maximum security to fairly liberal conditions. Most states, including all those with large populations, have a number of separate facilities graduated in this way. The total number of prison facilities in the country, excluding the federal system, exceeds five hundred. The total prison and jail population in 1981 was estimated at more than five hundred thousand.

Sentencing purposes.

Multiple purposes. Sentence to imprisonment is designed to fulfill a mixed set of objectives. The most immediate and popular purpose is punishment. Since about 1800, prisons have been a substitute in this respect for capital punishment, corporal punishment such as whipping or disfigurement, and enslavement or banishment, which were the forms of punishment used in earlier times. The will to punish is a strong one, animated by the outrage and desire for revenge that are aroused by the offenses for which offenders are typically given prison sentence—murder, rape, assault, and robbery. A second and rather different theory of imprisonment is that isolation in confinement provides occasion for an offender to reconsider his life and mend his ways. This theory is the origin of the term *penitentiary,* that is, a place in which to be penitent. It may be doubted whether there was ever much realistic possibility that convicts would undergo transformation through penitence, but there is little doubt that the prison experience brings home the lesson that committing crime can interfere with one's life. A third objective, also associated with prison reforms of the nineteenth century, is that a prison should be a place of rehabilitation, where the prisoner undergoes a change in outlook and acquires the capacity to live a law-abiding life through education and training provided in the institution. A fourth theory is that incarceration simply keeps the offender out of circulation, so that as long as he remains in prison he cannot do further injury to society. Finally, it is said that the foregoing consequences of imprisonment serve as examples to others and thus deter them from committing crime.

Conflict among purposes. It seems obvious, although it is not always recognized, that this set of purposes is internally inconsistent in several important ways. The purpose of punishment and deterrence is served by making prison as brutal and bleak an experience as possible; however, making prisons brutal and bleak has the effect of making them poor places in which to conduct moral education and technical training for the purposes of rehabilitation. The theory of penitence holds that an offender through his own will can come to understand and control himself; however, placing him involuntarily in custody presumes his inability to govern himself. Furthermore, if the prisoner really is meditating, it is inconsistent to punish him

for doing so. The rehabilitation of offenders would require that they be taught job skills through which they can earn a satisfactory living; however, given the typically low level of achievement and educability of most prison populations, attaining such an objective would entail creating an educational program far more extensive than is afforded to persons of similar background who are not in prison, resulting in an anomalous distribution of social benefits. At the same time, truly effective rehabilitation and training would require long periods of incarceration, although those who perform well in rehabilitation programs deserve to be released early. Finally, if the aim of prison is to keep the offender out of circulation, it is not clear why investment should be made in rehabilitation until shortly before he is ready for release.

These inconsistencies reflect a deeper contradiction in the attitude toward crime that seems always to have prevailed. This is the dilemma of whether to condemn an offender as an outlaw and treat him as absolutely or provisionally subhuman, or instead to regard him as an autonomous being who can be brought around to behave himself. This fundamental ambivalence seems unavoidable. If it is, inconsistency in the administration of penal policy is also unavoidable. At any rate, the contemporary prison system in the United States reflects these contradictions.

Prisons.

Conditions. Prisons are elaborate and expensive, but the number of places in prison is low compared to the demand. Hence at least since the 1960s prisons have been chronically overcrowded. For most prisoners in the United States, the prison term is nominally long but actually short through allowance for "good time" and parole. As a result, productive training programs are extremely difficult to manage. Physical brutality is prohibited but, particularly in the case of violence by inmates against other inmates, is inadequately controlled and sometimes unofficially condoned. Psychological brutality is pervasive. Rehabilitation programs are elaborate in ambition and are the subject of continuously reborn experimental and demonstration programs, but they are generally underfunded and often technically obsolete and pedagogically dispirited. The moral ambivalence and technical mediocrity that characterize modern American prisons help explain the state of demoralization and danger generally prevailing within them. The environment is literally vicious, involving pervasive use of drugs, physical exploitation between prisoners including rampant homosexuality, and a culture dominated by prisoners with long criminal records and serving long sentences. The overwhelming majority of prisoners in most American prisons are black or Hispanic, whereas the guards are white lower-level civil servants. The growing legal protection of prisoner rights has considerably restricted the extent to which prison authorities can use arbitrary administrative methods to control inmates. The improved legal status of prisoners has reduced the degree of official lawlessness in handling prisoners, but it may also have contributed to increased lawlessness among prisoners. As a result, life in modern prisons is subject to less discrimination and arbitrary official action, but it also seethes with repressed unrest that periodically bursts out in riots and rampage.

The condition of prisons is largely the result of a desire by governmental authorities, particularly at the state level, to have a criminal justice system that provides rigorous sanctions at low operating cost. The combination of growing rates of crime and growing incidence of prison sentences increases demand for prison places. Relentless inflation, higher building costs, and rising staff compensation rates increase the cost of each place. The transformation of the prison population from predominantly white to predominantly black reduces the empathy of the general population with the prison population. As a result, almost all prisons are overcrowded and understaffed but are subject to unremitting pressures to accept more inmates.

Federal legal intervention. Partly in response to this deterioration, the courts, and particularly the federal courts, have become actively involved in scrutinizing the administration of prisons. Expansion of prisoners' legal rights, a major legal development since the late 1960s, has taken place along two related lines. The first is procedural—the decision procedures used by prison authorities in such matters as imposing prison punishments or withholding good time, granting or refusing parole, and dealing with disputes between prisoners and prison personnel. In general, there has been expansion of rights to a hearing or at least to statements of the reason for official action. The other line of development has concerned prison programs and facilities. Under the rubric in the Bill of Rights forbidding "cruel and unusual punishments," the courts have prohibited the use of brutal corporal punishment, the unregulated use of solitary confinement, and the arbitrary restriction of outside communication. Affirmatively, the courts have regulated the availability and quality of medical care and access to legal services and law books. Taken as a whole, these legal standards, enforceable by proceedings in federal court, have considerably raised the legally required level of administration in prisons.

This improvement, welcome insofar as it has been given actual effect, results in two additional discrepancies in contemporary prison policy. The first is between the level of legally prescribed conditions in penal institutions, and the level of conditions that actually exist. In general, prisons are probably not much worse than they were in 1960, and many of them are considerably better. In the meantime, however, the legally prescribed standards have risen still farther, so that the gap between aspiration and fulfillment may have widened. This generates a legitimate sense of injustice among prisoners that is not conducive to their acceptance of their sentences. The second discrepancy concerns the theory of prison management. Both the old-style lockup prison and the reformed rehabilitative penal institution were administered on principles of hierarchical authority, in which prisoners were told what to do. This concept of management remains, but is now intersected by what amounts to management with the participation of prisoners, who use legal proceedings as leverage.

Probation and parole.

Probation policy. The alternative to jail or prison is release under supervision. Most persons convicted of crimes are sentenced neither to jail nor to prison but are released back into the community under obligation to report periodically to a probation officer charged with supervising their behavior. Probation is the most frequent disposition of a first offender convicted of anything but murder or murderous assault. The period of probation usually is proportional to the length of the prison sentence that would have been imposed for the crime in question. Since penalties of imprisonment average perhaps a nominal five years, and involve an actual term of something less than two years, probation usually is imposed for a period of one to three years. While on probation, the convicted person is required to stay out of trouble, to avoid association with previous companions in crime, to attempt to find a job, to avoid use of alcohol or narcotics, and to report periodically to the probation officer. Theoretically, the probation service provides psychological, social, and employment counseling. In idealized form the relationship between probation officer and offender is avuncular.

Probation practice. However, probation resources in manpower and auxiliary services generally are insufficient to live up to the stated aims. As a result, probation in fact generally consists merely of nominal supervision in which the probation officer keeps in occasional touch with the convicted person and becomes actively involved only when a new offense has been committed, which happens in a substantial fraction of cases. At that point, the offender's performance while on probation, so far as it can be established from information available to the probation service, will become a highly relevant factor in determining whether probation will be revoked and whether the offender will be prosecuted for his subsequent offense. Often a subsequent offense will result in a proceeding before the court at which revocation is threatened but where probation is actually continued. The records of many offenders, particularly those who avoid really heinous offenses, consist of a series of convictions, probation, brief revocations, and reprobation. All these determinations are made on the basis of proof falling considerably short of the standard required for conviction, but they result in treating the offender as a repeater. At some point along the line, if the pattern of behavior continues, prison will result. The hope, however, is that prison can be avoided, to spare the offender a harsh disposition and the system additional expense.

Some form of probation must always have existed in the criminal justice system. That is, offenders, particularly those who admitted their guilt, were simply let go on a promise to behave themselves. In the modern system, the probation decision is made by the judge on the basis of a presentence investigation conducted by the probation service. Theoretically, this investigation includes a full account of the circumstances surrounding the offense (including details not admissible in a trial), a biography of the offender, and a scientific psychological appraisal of his predisposition to further criminal behavior. In fact, the information provided the court generally falls short of this ideal, partly because diagnostic technique is very imperfect and partly because resources generally do not exist to permit a full professional workup of each case. Nevertheless, an attempt is made to provide the court with information so that it can formulate a sentence with regard not only to the offense but also to the offender.

An offender who has served a jail sentence is usually simply discharged at the conclusion of the specified period; one sentenced to prison is subject to a more complicated set of adjustments in his sentence. While in prison he is entitled to reduction of the nominal sentence on the basis of good time: for every interval in prison in which he avoids breaking rules, the offender receives a proportionate reduction in his sentence. An offender who maintains steady good time can shorten his sentence by about two-thirds. On top of this, the rules fixing eligibility for parole generally permit a person to be considered for parole at regular intervals after the commencement of his sentence.

If the prisoner is regarded as a safe bet for parole, he may be paroled ahead of the normal time, and this is frequently done in the case of persons without prior records.

Parole. Supervision on parole is essentially similar to probation supervision, except that the parole service is an agency of the state correctional system, whereas probation services are connected administratively to the court system. If a parolee violates parole, the consequences are the same as for violation of probation. Parole may be revoked, with the parolee returned to prison, or it may simply be continued with a warning. In general, violation of parole is more likely to lead to reimprisonment than is violation of probation, because the population that has found its way into parole by way of imprisonment is made up of persons with more serious criminal records.

Although the criminal justice system seeks at all points to consider each offender as an individual, it functions on the supposition that the best indicator of an offender's future behavior is his pattern of behavior in the past. This is no doubt a realistic supposition, although in practice if not in theory it contradicts the legal presumption of innocence.

GEOFFREY C. HAZARD, JR.

BIBLIOGRAPHY

American Bar Association. *Standards for Criminal Justice.* 2d ed. 4 vols. Prepared with the assistance of the American Bar Foundation. Boston: Little, Brown, 1980.

American Law Institute. *Model Penal Code: Proposed Official Draft.* Philadelphia: ALI, 1962.

BLACKSTONE, WILLIAM. *Commentaries on the Laws of England* (1765–1769). 4 vols. Reprint. University of Chicago Press, 1979.

Cleveland Foundation. *Survey of the Administration of Criminal Justice in Cleveland, Ohio.* Cleveland: The Foundation, 1922.

GOLDSTEIN, HERMAN. *Policing a Free Society.* Cambridge, Mass.: Ballinger, 1977.

HALE, MATTHEW. *The History of the Pleas of the Crown* (1685; first publication, 1736). 2 vols. Edited by W. A. Stokes and E. Ingersoll. Philadelphia: Small, 1847.

LaFAVE, WAYNE R. *Arrest: The Decision to Take a Suspect into Custody.* Edited by Frank J. Remington. Boston: Little, Brown, 1965.

McINTYRE, DONALD M. *Law Enforcement in the Metropolis: A Working Paper on the Criminal Law System in Detroit.* Chicago: American Bar Foundation, 1967.

MILLER, FRANK W. *Prosecution: The Decision to Charge a Suspect with a Crime.* Edited by Frank J. Remington. Boston: Little, Brown, 1970.

MORRIS, NORVAL. *The Future of Imprisonment.* University of Chicago Press, 1974.

PACKER, HERBERT L. *The Limits of the Criminal Sanction.* Stanford, Calif.: Stanford University Press, 1968.

President's Commission on Law Enforcement and Administration of Justice. *The Challenge of Crime in a Free Society.* Washington, D.C.: The Commission, 1967.

SILBERMAN, CHARLES E. *Criminal Violence, Criminal Justice.* New York: Random House, 1978.

THOMAS, WAYNE H. *Bail Reform in America.* Berkeley: University of California Press, 1976.

U.S. National Commission on Law Observance and Enforcement. *Report.* Washington, D.C.: The Commission, 1931.

WILSON, JAMES Q. *Varieties of Police Behavior: The Management of Law and Order in Eight Communities.* Cambridge, Mass.: Harvard University Press, 1968.

2.
SOCIAL DETERMINANTS

This article examines the principal social determinants of enforcement activity across three stages of the criminal justice system: arrest, prosecution, and sentencing. Research has clearly shown that the criminal justice system does not simply respond to the stimulus of criminal behavior but is selective both in its perception of lawbreaking and in its application of sentences. Indicators of social stratification, as well as characteristics of and relationships between the participants to a dispute, can explain observed variations in law enforcement activity.

Criminal justice activity is approached here from a microtheoretical perspective, which studies variations within and across different segments of a single criminal justice system rather than large-scale differences across entire legal systems. Although this is the perspective of most modern research in criminology and the sociology of law, it should be viewed in the light of a larger, macrotheoretical perspective on the study of legal life.

Historical background

Macroanalyses of legal systems. The study of legal systems as social phenomena can be traced back at least as far as Charles-Louis de Montesquieu's *L'Esprit des lois,* published in 1748. Notwithstanding such efforts, however, analyses of social determinants of legal evolution failed to blossom until the late nineteenth and early twentieth centuries, with the works of such sociological theorists as Emile Durkheim and Max Weber. Durkheim was concerned with the development of the division of labor, its relationship to social integration, and the impact of these structural features

of society on legal sanctions. Weber's interest centered on the procedures of legal decision-making and the rationalization of these procedures that culminated in industrialized capitalism. For each theorist, the nature and development of a legal system was neither an invariant nor an inherent property of social life. Instead, comparative and historical analyses led them to conclude that variations in dimensions of law were dependent upon such facets of social life as integration and rationalization.

In a similar vein, the work of Karl Marx (1818–1883) was also methodologically relevant. Marx studied the economic foundations of different societies throughout history and postulated that changes in social life resulted from changes in economic structures. Since he also viewed law as a product of a society's economic system, Marx paid scant attention to the subject. However, Marx's thesis had a significant impact on subsequent legal scholarship. For example, George Rusche and Otto Kirchheimer hypothesized in 1939 that variations in the types of punishment found in Western society were a function of the economic structure of a given society. Placing considerable emphasis on labor supplies in the preindustrial period and after the consolidation of industrial capitalism, they concluded that this structural change explained the shift from utilitarian to repressive incarceration.

Whereas scholarship on legal evolution and cross-cultural variations in criminal justice systems has continued in the tradition of Durkheim and Marx (Greenberg, 1977a), sociological research since 1960 has largely focused on issues of legal effectiveness and discrimination within particular segments of the criminal justice system.

Microanalyses of legal life: labeling and conflict perspectives. By the early 1960s, sociologists, in attempting to explain the causes of criminal behavior, began to shift attention from the motives or character of the criminals themselves to those individuals and agencies who identify others as criminal. Labeling theory viewed law violation as a routine occurrence and assumed that offenders were created through the invocation of social control rather than by an individual's specific law-violating actions. Examples of the concern with the selective identification of only a minority of all law violators is particularly evident in research on juveniles. Irving Piliavin and Scott Briar suggested, for example, that whether the police arrested a youth, as well as the manner in which they chose to dispose of him, was largely based on the youth's group affiliations, age, race, grooming, dress, and demeanor. Labeling theory also underscored the importance of the "interaction between those alleged to be engaged in wrong-doing and those making the allegations" (Becker, p. 3). As a result, scholars also began studying the informal networks of courtroom personnel and the negotiations involved in plea bargaining (Blumberg).

Conflict theory, which postulates that social life can best be understood by examining the respective positions of power and wealth held by certain groups in society, has also bolstered interest in the study of various components of the criminal justice system (Chambliss and Seidman). Within this framework, particular emphasis has been placed on the question of whether such extralegal factors as race, sex, and age can explain disparities in the sentences imposed on criminal defendants.

By shifting attention to the agencies of social control, both labeling and conflict theory generated a large body of research on deviance-processing systems. However, there has generally been little interest in relating the findings of these microstudies to variations in other areas of legal life. Instead, in discovering evidence of discrimination, the implication of these academic endeavors has been that the criminal justice system deviates from the master ideal of due process (Blumberg).

Patterns of criminal law enforcement

The rich empirical and ethnographic studies produced since the early 1960s have illuminated the social determinants of the criminal justice system. Utilizing the approach of such classical scholars as Durkheim and Weber, researchers are discovering what aspects of social life will predict the enforcement patterns emerging across three different stages of the criminal justice system. For example, it has been shown that the greater the degree of intimacy between complainant and suspect, the less likely it is that the police will make an arrest (Black, 1980, p. 104). These findings have led to questioning the relationship between intimacy and intervention in other segments of the criminal justice system, such as charging and sentence severity. Similarly, since police behavior differs considerably not only between a poor urban ghetto and a wealthy suburb, but also within each community according to the race of the officers and that of the citizens (Black, 1980, pp. 8–11, 108), one can question how judges' social statuses mesh with the community in which they serve (Levin). To the degree that the racial or economic status of criminal justice agents relative to their constituency predicts and explains the quantity and quality of adjudication in a community, at least one of the social determinants of the criminal justice system is stratification.

Thus, the discussion below seeks to isolate those variables that explain differences in American criminal justice systems. Nevertheless, the methodology applied can be extended both to variations in civil law and in legal evolution (Black, 1976).

The invocation of law: the police. The vast majority of police work is reactive: 87 percent of police time is spent responding to citizen requests for help or reports of victimization (Black, 1980, pp. 87–88). Consequently, one major determinant of criminal justice is who elects to call the police.

Reports to police. The National Criminal Justice Information and Statistics Service has revealed that in 1976 only 27 percent of all personal larceny and 47 percent of all assaults were reported to the police (U.S. Department of Justice, p. 13). Who calls the police, therefore, is not merely a function of whether a crime occurs.

A relatively consistent finding is that citizens victimized by strangers are more likely to call the police and report the event than are citizens victimized by relatives or intimates (Black, 1976, p. 42). This may be because related, acquainted, or intimate parties to a dispute do not perceive their hostilities as illegal or criminal, regardless of the actual conduct involved. Nevertheless, some of these disputes do invoke a request for police assistance, and at least one major determinant of this decision appears to be the social class of the parties involved. Donald Black (1980) analyzed 317 police encounters involving two or more acquainted or related individuals and found that the typical case involved a lower-class black woman complaining against a lower-class black man; middle-class citizens were underrepresented in these police-involved disputes. Black attributed this apparent class-related disparity to the hierarchical nature of middle-class households as contrasted with the more egalitarian nature of lower-class households: a middle-class white woman, in comparison to a lower-class black woman, is more likely to be economically dependent upon her husband and thereby subject to his authority (Black, 1980, pp. 124–128). One might also suggest that, as evidenced in other societies (Peattie, p. 60), requests for legal assistance may be a function of the degree to which alternative forms of conflict resolution are available (Black, 1976, p. 6). Members of the middle class have well-organized informal mechanisms of social control more readily available—

through the assistance of marriage counselors or psychologists—than do members of the lower class.

Police behavior. Since the police have the power to arrest and detain, citizens may view police notification as the most definitive way of resolving a dispute or calling attention to an illegal matter. However, the police utilize a variety of alternatives to writing an official report or making an arrest. They exercise therapeutic social control when they decide that an individual is exhibiting abnormal behavior and is in need of psychiatric care; they exercise conciliatory social control when they attempt to resolve a conflict without regard to who is right or wrong; and they may also exercise compensatory social control in requiring that restitution be made by one party to another (Black, 1980, pp. 130–131).

A number of factors predict penal control and the exercise of full enforcement. Relational distance, which is measured by the scope, frequency, and duration of interaction between people (Black, 1976, p. 41), has been shown to affect not only who calls the police but also the extent of enforcement action in which the police will engage. The police are less likely to write an official crime report if the parties are friends, neighbors, or acquaintances, and especially if they are family members (Black, 1980, p. 75). The same pattern appears for arrests, with the probability of arrest decreasing as the relational distance between the parties decreases (LaFave, pp. 199–123; Black, 1980, p. 104). In fact, the relationship between two parties to a dispute is far more important than the legal seriousness of their actions (Black, 1980, pp. 75–77).

The social class of both the complainant and the suspect also influences whether the police take official action. For example, Black's observational study of the police led him to conclude that police favor white-collar complainants and white-collar suspects (1980, pp. 142–147). Similarly, within the lower class, Richard Lundman (pp. 134, 137) found that the police are more likely to arrest "declassified citizens" or those on the fringes of the dominant culture than blue-collar offenders. In addition, if social class differs between the parties involved in a conflict, the police are more likely to comply with the request of the upper-status individual (Black, 1980, pp. 147–152).

The general respectability of both the complainant and the offender, as indicated by such facts as prior criminal convictions and employment stability, affects both how the police will handle a case and the nature of policing itself. The police are more likely to engage in full enforcement when a suspect has a prior record or is known to be a marginal member of the community. In fact, proactive policing—or police-initiated intervention in the lives of citizens—is concentrated primarily in those parts of a community that contain the least respectable element of the populace: skid-row (Bittner) areas with a high incidence of prostitution (LaFave, pp. 450–464). However, if the victim or complainant is also disreputable, the chances for full enforcement are slim (LaFave, pp. 123–124; Bittner, p. 711).

Finally, the complainant's preference for arrest or leniency and the demeanor of both the complainant and the suspect affect police behavior (LaFave, p. 112; Black, 1980, pp. 73–74, 77–80, 92–93). The police comply with most citizen requests regardless of whether a felony or misdemeanor is involved. However, the less respect a complainant offers the police, the less likely will his request be honored. Similarly, the less respect a suspect shows toward the police, the more likely it is that he will be arrested. Demeanor has also been offered as an explanation for race-based disparities in police behavior. It is argued that blacks fare worse than whites at the hands of police because they evidence little respect toward the police (Black, 1980, p. 105). The precise relationship between a suspect's race and police behavior has not been clarified (Sherman, pp. 79–81), but a valuable line of inquiry would be to examine the race of the police officer as well as that of the victim (Black, 1980, p. 108).

Social scientists are beginning to document differences in policing based on the race of an officer relative to his constituency. White officers working in white neighborhoods and black officers in black neighborhoods seem more likely to engage in full enforcement action; by contrast, white officers in black communities and black officers in white communities are far more lenient in exercising their arrest powers (Bayley and Mendelsohn, pp. 143–171). Scholars are also beginning to explore the associations between the percentage of nonwhite individuals in a community and arrest rates, police homicide rates, and even municipal policing expenditures (Jackson and Carroll). Although this research reveals little about the actual combination of races in encounters between complainant, suspect, and police, it does suggest that race may be a more important dimension of the invocation of criminal law than had previously been thought.

In summary, just as calls to the police are not distributed according to whether a criminal event or social disruption has taken place, police behavior is not merely a function of the degree to which a citizen complains or a suspect's actions meet legal prerequisites. Instead, the available data suggest that the respectability, relational distance, social class, and race of the complainant, the suspect, and the police officer all interact to determine how and whether the law will be enforced.

The confirmation of law: prosecution. Subsequent stages of the criminal justice system either support police action or negate it. The arrest charges brought against an individual may be dropped by the prosecutor; if the charges are not dropped, they may be either reduced or increased in the conviction process.

Who goes to court. Criminal prosecutors have virtually complete discretionary power to determine when and if a private dispute between a victim and a suspect will come before the court (Myers and Hagan, pp. 439–441). The factors that determine whether a defendant's case will be prosecuted are akin to those that influence whether a suspect will be arrested: the victim's preference, the defendant's economic status, and the respectability, relational distance, and race of both victim and defendant. For example, Frank Miller's qualitative analysis of prosecutorial discretion in three midwestern states revealed that assaults between blacks frequently resulted in the release of the offenders. It was further discovered that the official acceptance of nonprosecution of these offenders derived from the facts that the victim and offender were known to each other, that the victim was reluctant to testify, and that the victim was black (Miller, pp. 174–175).

A study by Martha Myers and John Hagan (pp. 446–447) provides further support for Miller's observations. Analyzing roughly one thousand felony cases disposed of in Indiana, they found that the probability of full prosecution decreased if the victim did not wish to prosecute the case and if the case involved a black intraracial event. They did not find, however, that acquainted and related parties were more likely to have their cases dismissed. In interpreting these findings, they suggested that the gravity of the offense with which the defendants were charged may have mediated prosecutorial discretion (p. 448). Since the severity of the offense also affects sentencing decisions (Clarke and Koch), this variable appears as an important determinant of criminal sanctions. However, notwithstanding the apparent impact of the offender's conduct on prosecution charges, such charges seem to be significantly influenced by the race, economic status, and respectability of both the defendant and the victim (Newman, pp. 114–125).

Seriousness of the offense. Not only is the severity of the offense charge mediated by the defendant's characteristics, but so also is the offense for which

he is convicted. Since the major form of adjudicating criminal defendants in the United States involves plea bargaining, the criminal behavior for which an individual is convicted is intimately tied to the plea negotiation process.

Plea bargaining can involve negotiations concerning recommendations for probation, sentence severity, or even habitual criminal status. However, the most frequent course of action involves dropping multiple charges or reducing a felony charge to a lesser included misdemeanor charge (Newman, pp. 78–90). The offense negotiated through this bargaining process depends upon which of a variety of "normal crimes" the public defender believes his client to typify. These "normal crimes" represent "knowledge of the typical manner in which offenses of given classes are committed, the social characteristics of the persons who regularly commit them, the features of the setting in which they occur, the types of victims often involved and the like" (Sudnow, p. 259). In addition, statistical analyses have revealed that the magnitude of charge reduction varies with the defendant's occupational status, sex, and race (Bernstein et al., pp. 375–377; Swigert and Farrell, p. 26).

Thus, the available data suggest that full prosecution and conviction vary directly with the seriousness of the infraction (Gottfredson and Hindelang, p. 16). However, the data also suggest that the "seriousness of the infraction" is a very flexible factor and, moreover, one that may be molded by the social status of the victim and defendant.

The relevance of the lawyer's status. Technically, the system of public defense was designed to provide all defendants with qualified legal representation. Nevertheless, the background, education, and resources of private attorneys place them in a higher social status than public defenders (Eisenstein, pp. 106–107). Some scholars have noted that this disparity produces dispositional disparities: private attorneys are more successful in obtaining favorable dispositions for their clients (Myers and Hagan, p. 446). However, since an intervening factor in this relationship is the operation of social class in the ability to retain private counsel (Swigert and Farrell, pp. 23–24), it appears that it is the combination of upper-class defendant and upper-class attorney that produces the advantage.

It should also be noted that, independently of the association between race and class, the races of the prosecutor, the defendant, and the victim may affect a criminal disposition. For example, in Miller's (p. 175 n.) analysis of prosecutorial discretion, an assistant prosecutor justified his relatively frequent nonaction in black intraracial offenses by referring to the lack of a moral code in the black community. In other words, this prosecutor clearly viewed the life-styles within the black community as distinct from his own and, consequently, as requiring different treatment. To be sure, this case only represents one prosecutor, but in conjunction with the above findings on social class, it suggests that the social characteristics of courtroom participants are relevant to a further understanding of variations in criminal adjudications.

The dispensation of law: sentencing. Alternatives in sentencing open to the court include fines, probation, county jail, split sentences, and commitment to state prison. Although the dispositional alternatives to probation and prison sentences are well known in the criminology literature, in most American jurisdictions they are primarily applied to misdemeanants. In the majority of felony cases, the sentencing judge's basic choice is between probation and prison (Levin, p. 91).

Who is granted probation. The decision to grant probation is significant in that it allows a convicted offender to retain freedom. The available research suggests that factors affecting the probability of a loss of freedom include the defendant's sex, race, economic status, and respectability. Males, low-income defendants, members of minority groups, and persons with a prior criminal record are more likely to be sentenced to prison (Pope; Clarke and Koch).

The association between sex and severity of disposition is not the result of gender per se but of a gender-related characteristic, economic dependency. Traditionally, women have lived off the incomes of others. As a result, their behavior has been more readily criticized and disciplined than that of economically self-sufficient persons (Black, 1976, p. 32). A woman who derives all her resources from her husband, no matter what the income level, will generally have less freedom and control in her household than the woman who is financially independent. She is not likely to call the police about her husband's treatment of her, even though it may involve violence, and the police, if summoned, are not likely to respond sympathetically (Black, 1980, p. 125). Moreover, just as the police are reluctant to intervene with the authority structure in such a household, so also is the judiciary: women who are economically dependent are sentenced less severely than their self-supporting counterparts (Kruttschnitt). Since legal control is least apparent when other forms of social control are operative (Black, 1976, pp. 107–111), one might expect a similar outcome for young boys and older men who are dependent on the income of others for their day-to-day necessities. Thus, it may be the status of economic dependency with its adjacent social control, rather than sex per se, that affects legal behavior.

Sentence severity. Not surprisingly, the variables that predict who is sent to prison also predict the length of a prison sentence. For example, males and poor or nonwhite defendants are likely to receive harsher sentences (Scott; Lizotte). However, there is considerable variation among the studies which find that either race or income explains sentence length. A lack of systematic attention to victim-relevant information and the inclusion of both legal and extralegal variables make the consistency of sentencing studies somewhat problematic. Additionally, those studies that have explored both the effect of the defendant's characteristics on earlier phases of case processing and the effect of these characteristics on the ability to obtain legal advantages, such as pretrial release, have had the most consistent results. These results, moreover, speak to previously noted adjudicatory patterns.

The relevance of judicial characteristics. Just as evidence is beginning to suggest that the backgrounds and social characteristics of police and attorneys affect the outcome of a criminal case, so also is evidence accumulating on the relevance of judicial characteristics. For example, A. Didrick Castberg measured the social distance between judiciary and defendants by ranking the difference in their respective ethnic backgrounds. He found that among defendants with only a few prior convictions, the greater the social distance between the judge and the offender, the more likely was the offender to receive a severe sentence (pp. 432–433). Similarly, data from Atlanta, Georgia, suggest that white judges sentence black defendants more harshly than white defendants and, conversely, that black judges give white defendants more severe sanctions (Greenberg, 1977b, p. 175).

The judiciary's social class background also appears to affect sentencing. Martin Levin's study of the sentencing patterns of judges in two cities found that, regardless of the defendant's race, judges with working-class backgrounds were particularly sympathetic and lenient to working-class defendants (pp. 136–156). Thus, not only do the social characteristics of defendants and their victims appear to underscore variations in sentencing, but so also do the social characteristics of the individuals handing down the sentences.

Summary

This article has attempted to suggest the relevance of the available disposition literature to an understanding of the variations within American criminal justice systems. The focus has been on isolating variables that have a notable impact on the legal decisions of victims, police, prosecutors, and judges. Although such variables as sex and race may be viewed merely as the individual attributes of disputing parties and their respective arbitrators, they should be set in a larger social context. Friedrich Engels (p. 320), for example, predicted that the inequality of women would be eliminated only when women were allowed to engage in economically productive activity. Thus, one might expect a reduction in the sex-based disparities noted in criminal justice dispositions as women increase their participation in the labor force. Nevertheless, the information gathered here has not been advanced as a set of propositions or assertions regarding the relationship between law and other aspects of social life. Sociological knowledge regarding some of the factors that influence both criminal and civil litigation has been set forth in propositional form for further examination and refinement (Black, 1976).

The considerable variation in the findings of disposition studies may to a large degree be attributed both to contextual and methodological variation. For example, studies conducted in southern states have consistently indicated the prevalence of racial bias in law enforcement activity. This may be caused by regional differences in discriminatory attitudes, but it may also result from some of the social determinants of law enforcement activity, for example, economic distinctions among regions based on their modes of production, or distinctions in levels of social integration because of the economies of different geographic areas.

Similarly, little is known about the factors influencing the style of conflict resolution employed by criminal justice agents. Black's work suggests that the race, household status, age, and intimacy of disputing parties predict police use of either penal control or, for example, therapeutic or conciliatory control (1980, pp. 135–157). To the degree that these social statuses also predict whether defendants are incarcerated or afforded psychiatric counseling, one can project the extent to which, and the direction in which, the arms of the criminal justice system will grow. Each of these problems is a fascinating field of study in itself. Nevertheless, a synthesis of discrete studies is necessary for the development of a comprehensive understanding of the social determinants of the criminal justice system.

CANDACE KRUTTSCHNITT

See also CLASS AND CRIME; CRIME CAUSATION, articles on POLITICAL THEORIES and SOCIOLOGICAL THEORIES; CRIMINAL JUSTICE SYSTEM: OVERVIEW; CRIMINOLOGY: MODERN CONTROVERSIES; ECOLOGY AND CRIME; FEAR OF CRIME; INFORMAL DISPOSITION.

BIBLIOGRAPHY

BAYLEY, DAVID H., and MENDELSOHN, HAROLD. Minorities and the Police: Confrontation in America. New York: Free Press, 1968.

BECKER, HOWARD S. "Labelling Theory Reconsidered." The Aldine Crime and Justice Annual, 1973. Edited by Sheldon Messinger et al. Chicago: Aldine, 1974, pp. 3–32.

BERNSTEIN, ILENE NAGEL; KICK, EDWARD; LEUNG, JAN T.; and SCHULZ, BARBARA. "Charge Reduction: An Intermediary Stage in the Process of Labelling Criminal Defendants." Social Forces 56 (1977): 362–384.

BITTNER, EGON. "The Police on Skid-Row: A Study of Peace Keeping." American Sociological Review 32 (1967): 699–715.

BLACK, DONALD. The Behavior of Law. New York: Academic Press, 1976.

———. The Manners and Customs of the Police. New York: Academic Press, 1980.

BLUMBERG, ABRAHAM S. "The Practice of Law as Confidence Game: Organizational Co-optation of a Profession." Law and Society Review 1, no. 2 (1967): 15–39.

CASTBERG, A. DIDRICK. "The Ethnic Factor in Criminal Sentencing." Western Political Quarterly 24 (1971): 425–437.

CHAMBLISS, WILLIAM J., and SEIDMAN, ROBERT B. Law, Order, and Power. Reading, Mass.: Addison-Wesley, 1971.

CLARKE, STEVENS H., and KOCH, GARY G. "The Influence of Income and Other Factors on Whether Criminal Defendants Go to Prison." Law and Society Review 11 (1976): 57–92.

DURKHEIM, EMILE. The Division of Labor in Society (1893). Translated by George Simpson. New York: Free Press, 1964.

EISENSTEIN, JAMES. Politics and the Legal Process. New York: Harper & Row, 1973.

ENGELS, FRIEDRICH. The Origin of the Family, Private Property, and the State in the Light of the Researches of Lewis H. Morgan. Translated by Alick West and Dana Torr. London: Lawrence & Wishart, 1943.

GOTTFREDSON, MICHAEL R., and HINDELANG, MICHAEL J. "A Study of the Behavior of Law." American Sociological Review 44 (1979): 3–18.

GREENBERG, DAVID F. "The Dynamics of Oscillatory Punishment Processes." Journal of Criminal Law and Criminology 68 (1977a): 643–651.

———. "Socioeconomic Status and Criminal Sentences: Is There an Association?" American Sociological Review 42 (1977b): 174–176.

JACKSON, PAMELA IRVING, and CARROLL, LEO. "Race and the War on Crime: The Sociopolitical Determinants of Municipal Police Expenditures in Ninety Non-southern U.S. Cities." American Sociological Review 46 (1981): 290–305.

KRUTTSCHNITT, CANDACE. "Women, Crime, and Dependency: An Application of the Theory of Law." Criminology 19 (1982): 495–513.

LaFave, Wayne R. *Arrest: The Decision to Take a Suspect into Custody.* Edited by Frank J. Remington. American Bar Foundation Administration of Criminal Justice Series. Boston: Little, Brown, 1965.

Levin, Martin A. *Urban Politics and the Criminal Courts.* University of Chicago Press, 1977.

Lizotte, Alan J. "Extra-legal Factors in Chicago's Criminal Courts: Testing the Conflict Model of Criminal Justice." *Social Problems* 25 (1978): 564–580.

Lundman, Richard J. "Routine Police Arrest Practices: A Commonweal Perspective." *Social Problems* 22 (1974): 127–141.

Miller, Frank. *Prosecution: The Decision to Charge a Suspect with a Crime.* Edited by Frank J. Remington. American Bar Foundation Administration of Criminal Justice Series. Boston: Little, Brown, 1970.

Montesquieu, Charles-Louis de Secondat, baron de la Brède et de. *The Spirit of the Laws* (1748). Translated by Thomas Nugent. Introduction by Franz Neumann. New York: Hafner, 1949.

Myers, Martha A., and Hagan, John. "Private and Public Trouble: Prosecutors and the Allocation of Court Resources." *Social Problems* 26 (1979): 439–451.

Newman, Donald J. *Conviction: The Determination of Guilt or Innocence without Trial.* Edited by Frank J. Remington. American Bar Foundation Administration of Criminal Justice Series. Boston: Little, Brown, 1966.

Peattie, Lisa Redfield. *The View from the Barrio.* Ann Arbor: University of Michigan Press, 1968.

Piliavin, Irving, and Briar, Scott. "Police Encounters with Juveniles." *American Journal of Sociology* 70 (1964): 206–214.

Pope, Carl E. "The Influence of Social and Legal Factors on Sentence Dispositions: A Preliminary Analysis of Offender-based Transaction Statistics." *Journal of Criminal Justice* 4 (1976): 203–221.

Rusche, George, and Kirchheimer, Otto. *Punishment and Social Structure.* Foreword by Thorsten Sellin. New York: Columbia University Press, 1939.

Scott, Joseph E. "The Use of Discretion in Determining the Severity of Punishment for Incarcerated Offenders." *Journal of Criminal Law and Criminology* 65 (1974): 214–224.

Sherman, Lawrence W. "Causes of Police Behavior: The Current State of Quantitative Research." *Journal of Research in Crime and Delinquency* 17 (1980): 69–100.

Sudnow, David. "Normal Crimes: Sociological Features of the Penal Code in a Public Defender Office." *Social Problems* 12 (1965): 255–276.

Swigert, Victoria Lynn, and Farrell, Ronald A. "Normal Homicides and the Law." *American Sociological Review* 42 (1977): 16–32.

U.S. Department of Justice, Law Enforcement Assistance Administration, National Criminal Justice Information and Statistics Service. *Criminal Victimization in the United States, 1976.* A National Crime Panel Survey Report. Washington, D.C.: NCJISS, 1979.

Weber, Max. *Max Weber on Law in Economy and Society* (1922). Edited with an introduction and annotations by Max Rheinstein. Translated by Edward Shils and Max Rheinstein. Cambridge, Mass.: Harvard University Press, 1954.

3.
PLANNING

The planning process

Planning is an analytic process in which an organization attempts systematically to make rational choices for the future. The emphasis is on the process by which those choices are made, rather than on the choices themselves.

The nature of rational choices. Choices made within the criminal justice system are "rational" in the sense that they address the objectives of this system, as opposed to other objectives that may well influence behavior in the criminal justice system—for example, the desire of political figures to be reelected and the desire of civil servants to preserve their jobs. Even though such objectives are real (and they are certainly rational from the perspective of the people who are concerned with them), rational planning in the criminal justice system involves concern for such questions as crime reduction, the enhancement of liberty, and reduction in the total social cost of crime control.

The future orientation. A primary characteristic of the planning process is its orientation toward the future, involving choices made in the present for implementation in a future—and therefore uncertain—world. The planning process must confront this uncertainty. In the criminal justice field, such uncertainty derives partly from an inability to predict the social and political changes that will influence criminal behavior and the operation of the criminal justice system itself. Chiefly, however, it derives from the difficulty of anticipating the effect on criminal behavior of the system's actions. Crime and the actions of the criminal justice system are mutually responsive, influencing each other in ways that are only minimally predictable; general changes in the political and socioeconomic climate will affect both crime and the criminal justice system in a similar manner.

Because of this uncertainty, techniques of statistical estimation must be employed wherever possible to anticipate critical aspects of the future, such as projected crime rates. However, the complexity of the criminal justice system necessitates the use of considerable nonstatistical judgment in obtaining and working with any such projections.

Creating choices to be made. Choices made in the planning process require a combination of forecasting, developing alternatives, predicting the impact of each alternative, and assessing the costs and benefits associated with each. Community estimates of the value and consequences of alternative courses of action are an important consideration.

Steps in the planning process

A planning process that "makes rational choices for the future" thus includes (1) description of the current system; (2) projection of the future environment; (3) development of alternatives among which to choose; (4) analysis of the impact of each alternative ("preevaluation"); (5) allocation of resources to, and implementation of, chosen alternatives; (6) evaluation of their impact ("postevaluation"); and (7) regular and continuing repetition of this process.

Description of the current system. Consideration of alternatives for the future must be firmly grounded in an understanding of the current system, including the nature of the present crime situation, how the current criminal justice system works, what resources are applied, where and how they are applied, and how budgetary allocations are distributed among the parts of the criminal justice system and among the various types of crime.

Projection of the future environment. This step involves forecasting anticipated crime rates, as well as projecting the future behavior of the criminal justice system. The projection of crime rates might be undertaken by a variety of means, including the simple assumption that current crime rates will persist into the future. Other possibilities include extrapolation from the previous few years of data, the use of more sophisticated time series analysis techniques, or the use of elaborate mathematical relationships involving projections of the crime rates for each demographic group (for example, according to age, race, and sex combinations), as well as census predictions of the size of each group. All of these methods have their virtues. The simpler ones are more readily understood and implemented, and the more elaborate ones impose a considerably greater demand for data and for computational power, which is sometimes matched by considerably greater predictive power.

For other features of the criminal justice system, it is desirable to choose measures that are reasonably stable over time. Thus, for example, the number of cases processed will vary from year to year, as will, accordingly, the number of dispositions of guilt or innocence. In most settings, however, the *proportion* found guilty is likely to be far more stable than the total number of guilty cases. Here again, the simplest projection is to assume that next year's disposition patterns, unit costs, and work load per case will be the same as this year's. If a longer time series for these various measures were available, one might project that time series in ways similar to the projection of crimes. In other cases, however, the introduction of new programs, new court decisions, or new legislation will force a qualitative change in some of those measures, and that change must be taken into account in the planning process. In some cases, empirical evidence from other jurisdictions can indicate the effects of a new program. In other cases, the best estimate is simply a judgmental guess.

Development of alternatives. Since the planning process involves choices, one must first define alternatives from among which to choose. The development of such alternatives is a creative process by which new ways of doing things are proposed by staff members of existing agencies (although loyalty to old methods does tend to interfere); by staff from planning agencies who consider innovations that have been employed successfully in other jurisdictions; or by means as diverse as citizens' suggestions and "brainstorming" sessions.

The preevaluation process. A preevaluation process is undertaken as a means of choosing among alternatives before they are implemented in local jurisdictions. Again, judgment is called for, but it is significantly enhanced by the use of appropriate analytic tools. Since preevaluation takes place prior to implementation and is an inherently analytic or abstract process, it must make use of mathematical models that represent abstractly the behavior of the criminal justice system.

One such model that has been used in a number of jurisdictions is known as JUSSIM (an acronym for Justice System Interactive Model). This model uses a computer in an "interactive" mode: a planner sits at a terminal, calling up a stored data base characterizing his criminal justice system, and he interacts in a conversational way with the computer program. No technical training or computer programming skills are required since the entire process is carried out in plain English. In the JUSSIM model, the criminal justice system is examined as a sequence of stages through which offenders "flow" and are "processed." The user at a terminal implements changes in policies or programs by changing the parameters that previously characterized this flow process; he can then examine the effects of those changes on flows, costs, or resource requirements.

The preevaluation process provides an initial assessment of the impact of a change both in the part of the criminal justice system to which it is directly applied, and in other parts of the system. Such an assessment should include not only the "downstream" parts (for example, the effect of a change in police arrest practices on court work loads), but also the "upstream" consequences (for example, the effect of increasing sentences for certain crimes on defendants' willingness to plead guilty to those crimes). Once a planning agency has made such an impact assessment, it will then allocate resources to new programs, taking into account the estimate of these impacts, as well as the more direct costs and benefits associated with alternative choices.

The postevaluation process. Having made the choice and implemented it on at least a pilot basis, or possibly throughout a jurisdiction, the planning process can then undertake an experimental postevaluation of its impact. This evaluation is modeled on the classic random, controlled experiment. But such experiments in the criminal justice system are limited by the difficulty of introducing randomization. Without randomization, the selective assignment of "subjects" to "treatments" confounds evaluation of any "treatment." Yet despite these problems, the evaluative information represents an important part of the planning process and provides information that will aid all the previous stages for the next planning cycle.

Planning for the criminal justice system

Even though planning for the future has characterized the operation of many of the separate functional agencies constituting the criminal justice system, the concept of comprehensive planning for the entire system is relatively new. This delay stems from a view of the criminal justice system as composed of entities in inherent conflict. Such conflict—between the police and the courts, for example—is intended to maintain the checks and balances that prevent each branch of government from assuming excessive power over any individual who comes within its reach. It is the courts, principally, that serve to limit the power and authority assumed by the police and correctional agencies.

The concept of criminal justice planning was a primary outgrowth of the work of the President's Commission on Law Enforcement and Administration of Justice in 1967. The commission noted that planning for disparate parts of the system confronted issues at an aggregate level, and that such planning need not interfere with the intended checks and balances, which operate at an individual level. Thus, even though the police, courts, and correctional agencies must operate at arm's length when they deal with individual cases, they need to understand the effects of their operations on other parts of the system, both "upstream" (for example, from courts to police) and "downstream" (from police to courts to corrections).

This concept was put into practice by the enactment on June 19, 1968, of the Omnibus Crime Control and Safe Streets Act of 1968, which mandated the creation in each state of a criminal justice planning agency to plan for the entire criminal justice system in the state (Pub. L. 90-351; 82 Stat. 197 (codified as amended in scattered sections of 5, 18, 28, 42, 47 U.S.C.)). In addition, the act provided for grants to be administered by these agencies for plan implementation.

The state planning agencies met with varying success; some of the worst abuses involved the use of this seemingly "free" money to buy such inappropriate items as armored vehicles, or to provide helicopters for favored public officials. Even in the well-meaning programs that constituted the large majority, the ability to plan for specific improvements was severely limited by the difficulty of estimating with any degree of accuracy the consequences of actions taken by the criminal justice system.

Program decisions in the state planning agencies were made by supervisory boards composed of senior government officials as well as citizens. The boards usually followed recommendations prepared by staff members. Especially because of perceived pressure to spend grant money, many decisions were dominated more by political than by rational considerations. The exercise was as much one of "cutting up the pie" as it was one of rational planning. A consequence of the disappointment that this process engendered was the termination of the federal Law Enforcement Assistance Administration (LEAA) in 1982 and the cutting off of the grant funds to the states. This led directly to the demise of a number of the planning agencies. In some states, their functions were absorbed elsewhere in the state government. Other agencies did survive, though, and many of them turned their primary attention to the problem of prison overcrowding—the most pressing state criminal justice crisis of the 1980s. The problem of prison overcrowding is particularly amenable to rational planning because prisons are the receptacles of decisions made elsewhere in the criminal justice system.

ALFRED BLUMSTEIN

See also CRIME COMMISSIONS; *articles under* CRIME PREVENTION; *articles under* CRIME STATISTICS; POLICE: ADMINISTRATION; PRISONS: PROBLEMS AND PROSPECTS; PUBLIC OPINION AND CRIME.

BIBLIOGRAPHY

BLUMSTEIN, ALFRED. "Planning Models for Analytical Evaluation." *Handbook of Criminal Justice Evaluation.* Edited by Malcolm W. Klein and Katherine S. Teilmann. Beverly Hills, Calif.: Sage, 1980, pp. 237–257.
FEELEY, MALCOLM M., and SARAT, AUSTIN D. *The Policy Dilemma: Federal Crime Policy and the Law Enforcement Assistance Administration, 1968–1978.* Minneapolis: University of Minnesota Press, 1980.
National Academy of Public Administration. *Criminal Justice Planning in the Governing Process: A Review of Nine States.* Prepared under a grant from the U.S. Department of Justice, Law Enforcement Assistance Administration. Washington, D.C.: The Academy, 1979.
President's Commission on Law Enforcement and Administration of Justice. *The Challenge of Crime in a Free Society.* Washington, D.C.: The Commission, 1967.
SHANAHAN, DONALD T., and WHISENAND, PAUL. *The Dimensions of Criminal Justice Planning.* Boston: Allyn & Bacon, 1980.
U.S. Department of Justice, Law Enforcement Assistance Administration, National Advisory Commission on Criminal Justice Standards and Goals. *Criminal Justice System.* Washington, D.C.: The Commission, 1973.

4.
MEASUREMENT OF PERFORMANCE

Introduction

Institutions are typically evaluated on the basis of an assessment of their net social contribution, or "performance." An integral part of this process is the systematic measurement of social contribution and cost in order to provide an objective basis for evaluating institutions and their policies.

Performance measurement is especially important for public-sector institutions such as the criminal justice system and its component agencies because the consumers of the services of these institutions rarely have the opportunity to select among alternatives, as they more commonly do in the private sector. Although members of the community at large may have strong opinions about how well they are served by the criminal justice system, these opinions generally have only an indirect and limited influence over the decisions and policies of the individual agencies that make up that system. In the absence of market mecha-

nisms for shaping the services of criminal justice agencies, it is necessary to shape those services through the political process. The attempt to measure performance accurately can, and often does, play an important role in this process.

Basic principles of performance measurement

Performance can be assessed only in relation to a set of standards or goals. Identifying the goals of an agency sets the context of performance measurement; analyzing data that relate to those goals provides the content. Indeed, one of the major benefits of performance measurement is its tendency to stimulate thought about agency and system goals.

Several primary goals can be identified for the criminal justice system as a whole. Herbert Packer has identified two objectives: due process and crime control. Fiscal realities dictate the acknowledgment of a third goal, that of cost containment. Celerity, or speed of case settlement, is yet another goal.

These basic goals are not mutually compatible. The due process model stresses the importance of constitutional protection of the innocent, which sometimes conflicts with the goals of reducing crime and speedy justice, also supported by the Constitution. Similarly, achieving either the due process or the crime control goal typically requires additional criminal justice resources. In setting bail, for example, the due process model holds that all persons charged with crimes are presumed innocent until proved guilty and that the detention of a suspect is justifiable only to ensure appearance at trial; detention is not justifiable under the due process model merely because the defendant may pose a serious threat to the community. The crime control model, on the other hand, holds that persons charged with crimes should be detained if they pose a danger to the community. The cost reduction model argues against expenditures for jail construction or maintenance that are often needed to ensure low rates of either flight or crime on bail. The goal of speedy trial, in the extreme, obviates the need for pretrial detention altogether; however, as case loads grow, speedy justice can produce errors that contravene both due process and crime control.

Incompatibility among these goals has been at the heart of much of the debate over criminal justice policy. The setting of policy and the exercise of discretion at each stage of the criminal process typically have consequences in terms of due process, crime control, the speed of justice, and the consumption of scarce resources; the assessment of policy can be facilitated by attempts to measure those consequences.

Although achievement of the due process goal is difficult to establish empirically, the goals of crime control, cost containment, and speed of justice do lend themselves more readily to quantitative assessment. Crime control is most often assessed on the basis of the crime rate, which in the United States is measured in two ways by federal agencies: from data on crimes reported to the police and assembled by the Federal Bureau of Investigation, and from victimization survey data collected by the Census Bureau, operating in conjunction with the Department of Justice. Each of these approaches to estimating the crime rate has it strengths and weaknesses.

Inaccurate measurement of crime is not, however, the primary barrier to use of the crime rate as a measure of performance. The crime rate is limited as an indicator of the ability of the criminal justice system to control crime primarily because it is extremely difficult to isolate the effect of criminal justice practices on crime from other factors that contribute to fluctuations in the crime rate. The crime rate has been found, for example, to vary with changes in the demographic characteristics of the population, especially age and race, and with social and economic conditions. The reported crime rate also varies with changes in the willingness of people to report crime. However, since the nature and strength of these effects are unclear, the effects of various changes in criminal justice policy on the crime rate—effects that can be difficult enough to separate from one another—have been virtually impossible to establish definitively.

Crime control is more easily monitored at the level of the individual offender than at a higher level of aggregation. Although it cannot usually be known precisely how many offenses an offender actually commits, the figure can be estimated either on the basis of offender surveys or from arrest records and knowledge of the rate at which various offenses result in arrest. Thus, policies related to bail, prosecutive targeting on certain classes of offenders, sentencing, and parole can be evaluated by comparing actual rates of rearrest under those policies with rates of rearrest that are projected under alternative policies. Such assessments can be extremely valuable, both for uncovering important factors that have been omitted from case-processing decisions, and for identifying factors that have been used in those decisions because they are incorrectly believed to be related to recidivism or other forms of misbehavior.

The goal of cost containment, like that of crime control, is more easily monitored than the due process goal, but it too is less than perfectly measurable. Fiscal costs of a criminal justice agency are usually a matter of public record. The costs of a particular policy implemented by that agency, however, are rarely a matter of record even with the office. Since the time spent by individuals within the office is typically not documented in terms of individual cases or activities, the cost implications of policies that affect those allocations tend to be unclear. Moreover, policies and procedures implemented by criminal justice agencies often impose or reduce costs on victims, witnesses, defendants, and others; the measurement of these costs invariably escapes the public record.

Tension between the inherent limitations in measuring performance and the need to hold public agencies accountable for their performance extends beyond the criminal justice system. The extremes in these two positions have been succinctly stated by two eminent scholars: (1) "If you can measure it, that ain't it . . ." (Kaplan, p. 206), and (2) ". . . if you cannot measure, measure anyhow!" (Knight, p. 166). The first proposition, advanced by the philosopher Abraham Kaplan, argues that measurement inevitably involves abstraction and error. Certain important characteristics of institutional performance are necessarily omitted in any quantitative description, and those characteristics that are included are often measured inaccurately, thus rendering the exercise of performance measurement virtually useless. The second viewpoint, offered by the economist Frank Knight, argues that the alternative of no quantitative assessment of performance at all is generally even worse than performance poorly measured. As with most controversies, each side has merit.

Measuring the performance of component agencies

Because criminal justice policies typically affect different components of the criminal justice system differently, and often apply directly only within an individual component agency, the measurement of performance of the criminal justice system can be viewed in terms of the components of the system rather than of the system as an entity. Before considering the assessment of performance within a component, it is useful to review briefly the exercise of discretion by the various agencies.

The law enforcement agency that is called upon to handle a given criminal episode typically decides whether to investigate and arrest. If an arrest is made, it then determines the proper jurisdiction for prosecution—for example, United States attorney, state attorney, county district attorney, or city prosecutor. The prosecutor then decides whether to accept or reject the case or to refer it to a prosecutor in another jurisdiction. If the prosecutor accepts the case, a public defender may be assigned by the court. The choice among alternative prosecution strategies (how to charge, whether to induce a plea, and so on) generally influences whether the defendant in the case is convicted; if he is, the judge must then decide whether to incarcerate. If imprisonment is chosen, the offender is classified and sent to an institution that has an appropriate level of security. Later, the parole board decides when to release the offender.

The measurement of the performance of each of these agencies is typically a matter of balancing its criminal justice functions with the other functions that it is expected to perform.

Law enforcement agencies. The police are the first line of response in the control of crime; crime control is generally regarded as the most important single goal of law enforcement agencies. (The goals of due process and cost containment are typically viewed as constraints that limit the ability of the police to control crime.) For reasons previously noted, and because other criminal justice agencies share in the responsibility to control crime, the police cannot be held solely accountable for the crime rate. They can be held more directly accountable for the performance of activities that may be *related* to the crime rate: maximizing the rate at which offenders are apprehended, maintaining a visible presence that deters crime, responding quickly to calls that result from criminal episodes, producing "convictable" arrests by obtaining tangible evidence and cooperative witnesses in cases brought to the prosecutor, and providing sufficient additional support to the prosecutor as it is needed, for example, testimony in trial.

Because the police are responsible for functions other than those that relate directly to crime control, such as traffic control, response to emergencies, crowd control, and provision of public information, an overall assessment of police performance cannot be restricted to the crime control functions. However, these other functions, like those relating to the control of crime, do not lend themselves readily to performance measurement. Moreover, it is difficult to weigh the relative importance of the crime control responsibility of the police against the importance of each of the other responsibilities. To the extent that police performance lends itself readily to measurement, it tends to be along several narrow dimensions, each of which provides only a partial assessment of policing. Assessment of performance also tends to be based on global measures that may be largely beyond the ability of the police to control, such as the crime rate and the level of citizen satisfaction.

Prosecution. The prosecutor screens arrests brought by the police, rejecting the weakest (in terms of strength of evidence and seriousness of offense) and filing charges with the court in the strongest. For the cases accepted, the prosecutor generally strives to obtain a conviction, either by way of a guilty plea or a guilty verdict in trial.

Prosecutors rarely hold themselves accountable for the crime rate, largely because the precise effects of their operations on crime are not known. They usually do hold themselves accountable for the conviction rate, defined narrowly as the ratio of convictions (guilty pleas and guilty verdicts) to the sum of guilty pleas and trials. A broader measure of the conviction rate—the ratio of convictions to arrests—is objectionable to most prosecutors because it includes cases that they believe are unworthy of prosecution. The narrowly defined conviction rate typically is about 90 percent, and the broader measure typically yields conviction rates approaching 50 percent. Both measures ignore the extent of reduction in charges from screening to conviction; neither measure tells much about the ability of the prosecutor to control crime through general deterrence, special deterrence, or incapacitation.

Police-prosecutor coordination. The chronic and widespread unwillingness of prosecutors to be held accountable for the arrests that they reject or drop—about half of all arrests—is approximately matched by a chronic and widespread unwillingness of the police to be held accountable for what happens after arrest. From the perspective of the entire criminal justice system, the dropping of so many arrests by prosecutors suggests the existence of a large number of arrests that should either not have been made by the police or not have been dropped by the prosecutor, or both. Yet each agency typically produces annual reports that present statistics indicating high levels of performance: the police report high rates of crime cleared by arrest, and the prosecutor reports high conviction rates. A prosecutor with a system-wide perspective might routinely provide information to police departments about the dispositions of all arrests and the reasons for rejections, and thereby expand the accountability of both police and prosecutor. Such practice is in fact rarely requested by the police or followed by prosecutors.

Pitfalls in performance measurement

The tendency of criminal justice agencies to produce mostly self-serving measures of performance is less a shortcoming of performance measurement per se than a defect in the common use of the measures. Pitfalls in performance measurement have been noted above: some goals are more easily measured than others; some goals are more accurately measured than others; and causal relationships between criminal justice policy and performance are difficult to establish empirically. Other problems related to performance measurement and its use have revealed themselves in much of the empirical research on the criminal justice system; several are described below.

The impossible standard. It has become common practice to criticize programs designed to "end the rise in crime" for their failure to do so. The Law Enforcement Assistance Administration (LEAA), for example, has been fair political game in national elections for its failure to end the rise in crime, which was a primary purpose of its creation in the late 1960s. Americans were told that the LEAA would stop increases in the crime rate, and because it did not, it would appear to have failed.

Using a more appropriate standard of performance, the LEAA may in fact have succeeded. Demographic and social trends in the 1970s, together with an increased willingness of people to report crimes to the police, may have made it virtually impossible for any federal program to have ended the rise in reported crime during that decade. The LEAA may even have contributed to people's willingness to report crimes. Without the LEAA it is probable that the true crime rate would have been higher ten years after the agency's creation—perhaps by an amount that would easily justify the cost of the LEAA. This, of course, is impossible to know for certain, which is a sufficient reason for not holding the LEAA accountable for its failure to reduce crime in the first place. It is nonetheless probable that future programs that are successful by reasonable standards will be regarded as failures for their inability to achieve unrealistic goals.

The shotgun or "catalog" approach. With the advent of advanced computer technology, an inconceivable variety of criminal justice statistics has been produced. National compendiums of criminal justice statistics and annual agency reports publish data on phenomena ranging from whether Democrats believe that abortions should be legal to the number of Coast Guard courts-martial held for the offense of sleeping while on duty. Such facts may be interesting and useful for certain purposes, but they are of limited value when presented without an explanation of how they relate to the goals of the criminal justice system or its component agencies.

The misleadingly precise estimate. Criminal justice data are known to be less than perfectly accurate. The policies and decisions that are sometimes supported by these data, on the other hand, typically are expressed in highly explicit and exact terms. Crim-

inal justice practitioners who make those policies and decisions are often uneasy with empirical inferences that are expressed with qualifications about measurement error—qualifications that characterize good research. As a result, those who provide estimates may be inclined to present them as numbers carried out to six significant digits. This suggests a level of precision that practitioners can feel more comfortable about, but that is also misleading. Even the first significant digit may, in fact, be incorrect.

For example, the following finding, reported by Isaac Ehrlich, was used by lawyers arguing for the effectiveness of the death penalty before the United States Supreme Court in *Gregg v. Georgia*, 428 U.S. 153 (1976): "In fact, the empirical analysis suggests that on the average the tradeoff between the execution of an offender and the lives of potential victims it might have saved was of the order of magnitude of 1 for 8 for the period 1933–67 in the United States" (Ehrlich, p. 398). One might infer from such a statement an actual number of between six and ten lives saved for each execution. In fact, a Nobel laureate who reanalyzed the same data believed it "unthinkable to base decisions on the use of the death penalty on (those) findings, as the Solicitor General of the United States has urged. They simply are not sufficiently powerful, robust, or tested at this stage to warrant use in such an important case. They are as fragile as the most tentative of econometric estimates of parameters" (Klein, Forst, and Filatov, p. 358). It is clear that the credibility of performance measurement is undermined by the presentation of precise estimates of the effectiveness of policies or agencies when such precision cannot be supported by the data.

Counting crimes, offenders, arrests, and victims. Measurement of the performance of criminal justice agencies and policies often involves the counting of criminal episodes, offenders, arrests, or victims. The assessment of performance can easily suffer from the misuse of such counts.

An example of the potential for misuse is in the area of assessing sentencing policy. Estimates of the number of crimes per offender have been used to support a sentencing strategy of incapacitation. Such estimates are often derived by dividing estimates of the number of crimes by estimates of the number of offenders. Difficulties in making each of these estimates are legion. Should each crime reported to the police count as a single offense, regardless of the number of victims or offenders? What adjustments should be made to account for unreported crimes? Should it be assumed that each person arrested really committed the offense for which the arrest was made? If estimates are based on "self-report data" obtained by interviewing prison inmates, should inmates be believed? Should estimates of the self-reported criminal behavior of a particular group of inmates be attributed to other offenders?

Estimating the number of offenses per offender involves other problems as well. For example, incapacitation estimates may overlook the tendency of juveniles to commit crimes in groups. Because of that tendency, the proportion of *offenders* that are juveniles is higher than the proportion of *crimes* that are committed by juveniles. It is probably incorrect to assume that the same amount of crime will be prevented by imprisoning four twenty-five-year-olds, each of whom committed a particular type of crime acting alone, as by imprisoning four juveniles who committed the same type of offense as a group. Removing a single juvenile from a group may leave unaffected the number of future crimes committed by the group. To assume that the same number of persons will be spared victimization by the incarceration of an active juvenile offender as by the incarceration of an active adult offender thus overlooks the tendency of juveniles to commit crimes in groups and ignores the biases that result. Other factors, such as differences in the rates at which juvenile and adult offenders avoid apprehension, may result in additional bias. The net effect of all such biases is not known with any precision.

Influence of the media in performance assessment

A prodigious share of the accountability of criminal justice agencies takes the form of news media reports of the most sensational individual cases that pass through those agencies. By itself, of course, this is not detrimental. The news media have strong incentives to report accurately, and they usually report events much more quickly than do scholars and other professional commentators. However, to the extent that the assessment of criminal justice agencies is perceived to be based primarily on the outcomes of sensational cases, the incentives of those agencies tend to shift away from the effective handling of the vast majority of cases, which are not covered by the media. It may not be mere coincidence that most of the sensational crimes are successfully resolved, whereas the vast majority of crimes committed do not end in arrest and the majority of arrests do not result in guilty verdicts or pleas.

With the advent of computer technology and the more systematic collection of data by each criminal justice agency, it is now possible to counteract the tendency for the police, prosecutors, and other criminal justice agents to overinvest in the sensational cases. Although the media are still inclined toward preoccupation with those cases, they do not hesitate also to report increases in the crime rate, in prison populations, in criminal justice costs, and in other measures that describe various aspects of the criminal justice system in aggregates.

BRIAN FORST

See also CRIME COMMISSIONS; *articles under* CRIME STATISTICS; CRIMINAL JUSTICE SYSTEM, *articles on* OVERVIEW *and* PLANNING; POLITICAL PROCESS AND CRIME.

BIBLIOGRAPHY

DORFMAN, ROBERT, ed. *Measuring Benefits of Government Investments: Papers Presented at a Conference of Experts Held November 7–9, 1963.* Washington, D.C.: Brookings Institution, 1965.

EHRLICH, ISAAC. "The Deterrent Effect of Capital Punishment: A Question of Life or Death." *American Economic Review* 65 (1975): 397–417.

KAPLAN, ABRAHAM. *The Conduct of Inquiry: Methodology for Behavioral Science.* San Francisco: Chandler, 1964.

KLEIN, LAWRENCE R.; FORST, BRIAN; and FILATOV, VICTOR. "The Deterrent Effect of Capital Punishment: An Assessment of the Estimates." *Deterrence and Incapacitation: Estimating the Effects of Criminal Sanctions on Crime Rates.* Edited by Alfred Blumstein, Jacqueline Cohen, and Daniel Nagin. Washington, D.C.: National Academy of Sciences, 1978, pp. 336–360.

KNIGHT, FRANK H. *On the History and Method of Economics: Selected Essays.* University of Chicago Press, 1956.

PACKER, HERBERT L. *The Limits of the Criminal Sanction.* Stanford, Calif.: Stanford University Press, 1968.

QUADE, EDWARD S. *Analysis for Public Decisions.* New York: Elsevier, 1975.

Urban Institute. *Measuring the Effectiveness of Basic Municipal Services: Initial Report.* Washington, D.C.: International City Management Association, 1974.

ZIMRING, FRANKLIN E. "Kids, Groups, and Crime: Some Implications of a Well-known Secret." *Journal of Criminal Law and Criminology* 72 (1981): 867–885.

CRIMINAL LAW REFORM

Dissatisfaction with the state of the criminal law has been typical in Western societies over the past several centuries, and efforts to reform the law have been a constant feature of the social response to crime. What kinds of changes seemed most important in particular eras? What factors made them seem so? What issues have tended to be recurrent? What has been the progress of change? What historical forces tended to inhibit it, and what forces accelerated it? These are some of the issues that make criminal law reform an important subject of study in its own right. The articles in this entry address the subject by presenting the development of law reform in three places: continental Europe, England, and the United States.

1. CONTINENTAL EUROPE   Hans-Heinrich Jescheck
2. ENGLAND   P. R. Glazebrook
3. HISTORICAL DEVELOPMENT IN THE
   UNITED STATES   Charles McClain
4. CURRENT ISSUES IN THE
   UNITED STATES   Louis B. Schwartz

1.
CONTINENTAL EUROPE

Criminal law reform as a common European movement

Continental criminal law rests upon Roman law, the dissemination of which began in the twelfth and thirteenth centuries, spreading out from the universities of Bologna, Pavia, and Padua, which were the centers of civil law study in medieval Europe. In contrast to the process of legal change in the largely judge-made Anglo-American common law, the reform of continental criminal law has always had a strongly academic foundation and has accompanied broader political movements against monarchical or authoritarian governments. For centuries, the basic principle of the proportionality of guilt and punishment has been the most far-reaching contribution of the Roman-law tradition to the development and reform of continental criminal law systems.

General reform efforts

The Enlightenment. The radical intellectual renewal in eighteenth-century Europe that was known as the Enlightenment provided the modern cause of legal reform with its essential political and philosophical principles: the rule of law, reason, liberty, and humanitarianism. In France, Montesquieu demanded that punishment correspond to the gravity of the deed and advocated the separation of powers in order to preserve judicial independence in the face of rulers' interference in individual trials. Appalled at the ancien régime's socially prejudiced judicial system, Voltaire vigorously opposed capital punishment and exhorted the criminal justice administration to concentrate on preventing crime rather than repressing it.

The most far-reaching influence was exerted by the Italian writer Cesare Beccaria (1738–1794), who laid the foundations of modern criminal policy in his opposition to the death penalty, corporal punishment, and maiming, in his support for the principle of proportionality between crime and punishment, and in his insistence that prevention be the primary objective. Enlightened monarchs whose laws reflected the reform ideals included Frederick the Great of Prussia, Joseph II and Leopold II of Austria, and Gustavus III of Sweden.

The codification movement. The philosophy of the Enlightenment found concrete expression in the legislation of the codification movement—legislation that has shaped the history of continental criminal law since the early nineteenth century. These codes represented the first reform of the old European law. The first important codes were the Austrian criminal code of 1803, the French Code Pénal of 1810, and the Bavarian criminal code of 1813. Subsequent significant legislative reforms included the codifications in Spain (1822), Greece (1834), Norway (1842), Prussia (1851), Portugal (1852), Sweden (1864), Belgium (1867), the German Empire (1871), the Netherlands (1881), and Italy (1889). Late fruits of the nineteenth-century codification movement included the Polish criminal code of 1932, the Rumanian criminal code of 1936, and the Swiss criminal code of 1937.

Penitentiary reform. The greatest practical achievement of the reform movement during the Enlightenment and the nineteenth century was the improvement of prisons, which, under the ancien régime, were both few and infamous for their cruel mistreatment of the incarcerated. As early as 1595, the first penitentiary in the modern sense of an institution for the moral improvement of prisoners was founded in Amsterdam. It was imitated in other European countries, culminating in 1775 with the establishment of the Ghent penitentiary, which provided prisoners with individual treatment.

The construction of prisons and the nineteenth-century system of imprisonment were strongly influenced by Anglo-American models, but European academic penology made an equally strong contribution to prison reform on the Continent. The most important landmarks of the reform movement were the founding of the Ecole Pénitentiaire by Charles Lucas and Bonneville de Marsagny, the establishment of the Société des Prisons (1877) in France, and the exemplary penitentiary reform carried out under Eduard Ducpétiaux and Adolphe Prins in Belgium. The first of a series of international prison conferences was held in 1846 in Frankfurt under the chairmanship of the liberal jurist Karl J. A. Mittermaier. At the 1878 Stockholm Congress, the International Penal and Penitentiary Commission was founded, with its headquarters in Bern; until its functions were assumed by the United Nations in 1950, it encouraged significant contributions to the theory and practice of imprisonment. The Geneva International Penal and Penitentiary Foundation continues some of the commission's work.

Modern reform efforts. With the rise of anthropology and sociology in the second half of the nineteenth century, the philosophical outlook known as positivism came to dominate the reform movement in continental criminal law. The leading European criminologists were the Italians Cesare Lombroso, Enrico Ferri, and Raffaele Garofalo. In Germany, Franz von Liszt, departing from the Kantian idealist notion of justice, developed social rationales justifying criminal law sanctions. Taking positivism to its logical extreme, Pedro Dorado Montero in Spain designed his reforms in criminal law to protect the criminal instead of society.

Organizations for penal law reform. The driving force of the modern penal law reform movement was the International Union of Penal Law, formed in 1889 by von Liszt, Prins, and the Dutchman Gérard van Hamel; its work has been continued since 1924 by the International Association of Penal Law, which was founded on Belgian and French initiative. The reform demands of these organizations included the introduction of probation, the abolition of short-term imprisonment, the long-term incarceration of professional criminals, the creation of a special criminal law for juveniles, and the substitution of other sanctions for deprivation of liberty. Many of these proposals have been realized in legislation.

The social-defense movement. Arising as a reaction to the spiritual and material devastation of World War II, the social-defense movement sought to combine the ideals of humanitarianism and effectiveness within the framework of the rule of law. The International Society for Social Defense, founded in 1949, was first led by the Italian Filippo Gramatica, who wished simultaneously to replace criminal law with nonpenal methods of resocializing antisocial persons and to change the structures of state and society. The moderate school of the French comparative-law scholar and criminologist Marc Ancel has taken a more flexible view, which has had considerable influence on the legislation of various European countries.

The crisis in criminal law reform. As was the case in the United States and Great Britain, the cause of criminal law reform on the Continent entered a crisis in the early 1960s from which it has yet to emerge. Modern penal and recidivism research has deeply shaken the belief that criminals can be resocialized through suitable treatment in institutions. Far-reaching attitudinal changes as to the proper means of combating crime have become apparent, particularly in Sweden, Norway, and the United States, where criminal law had become most closely intertwined with social therapy. The long-term, indeterminate sentence, with nonjudicial boards deciding upon the release date, is losing ground to the determinate sentence. New forms of imprisonment have been devised that attempt to avoid grave injury to the social fabric by using such strategies as work release, weekend imprisonment, and open institutions. Alternatives to the deprivation of liberty, such as community service, are being developed.

Criminal law reform in continental Europe

Continental criminal law reform has rested on shared principles. Nonetheless, the specific expression and embodiments of the reform effort have differed from one country to another, especially among legal systems reflecting disparate historical and cultural development.

The Germanic countries.

The Federal Republic of Germany. After the original codification of law in nineteenth-century Germany, further reform efforts culminated in 1975 with the revision of the General Part of the criminal code. Both an official and a private draft were prepared; the final law incorporated the theoretical concepts of the official draft and the private draft's punishment system. Outmoded criminal provisions have been abolished, particularly in the area of moral offenses. The criminality of various acts and the definition of individual offenses are still being revised.

Reform efforts have also been directed to punishments and such related measures as preventive detention. As a result of a legislatively expressed preference for fines, sentences of imprisonment have declined markedly, falling from more than one-third of all convictions to 17 percent. The older system of lump-sum fines has been replaced by the Scandinavian day-fine system, under which the fine is calculated by multiplying a certain number of days reflecting the crime's gravity by a daily sum based on the guilty person's available income. More than half of all sentences of imprisonment are suspended; and despite the much shorter prison sentences given by German judges, in one-third of the sentences served the prisoner is paroled. Even in the case of sentences of life imprisonment, parole after fifteen years is possible.

The traditional philosophical foundation of German criminal law—namely, that punishment should correspond strictly to individual responsibility—has been continued. The degree of guilt determines not only the finding of liability but also the measure of punishment that is to be inflicted. As a logical corollary to its emphasis on subjective guilt, German criminal law retains a dual system of subjectively earned punishments and measures for the protection of society. Particularly important in this respect are the new measures providing for confinement in social therapeutic institutions of criminals with serious personality abnormalities and for extended social help in the form of post-incarceration supervision of recidivists combined with effective control. Prison conditions have improved significantly since the mid-1950s, and in 1976 the terms and requisites for the carrying out of sentences were removed from administrative discretion. They are now governed by federal law.

Austria. In close cooperation with West Germany, Austria also revised its criminal code in 1975, adopting many provisions that parallel the new German legislation, including the day-fine system, a preference for fines over imprisonment, extensive decriminalization of sexual offenses and abortion, and such preventive measures as separate institutions for mentally disturbed criminals and dangerous recidivists. Today, about 75 percent of all sentences require fines and about 25 percent call for imprisonment.

Switzerland. The core of the Swiss criminal code of 1937 continues to be accepted. Swiss law, like German law, adheres to the principle that the convicted person's degree of guilt determines his punishment, and it retains both criminal penalties and preventive measures. There is neither a priority clause favoring fines over imprisonment nor provision for a day-fine system. The chief sanction remains the short prison sentence, which, however, is commonly suspended. Reform efforts now seek to reduce the number of offenses and to modify the punishment system by providing for new forms of imprisonment.

The Netherlands. Here, in the birthplace of modern imprisonment, the Germanic and Romance legal traditions meet. The French Code Pénal was imposed on the Dutch in 1811 and remained in force until 1886; its influence did not end when it was superseded by the Dutch criminal code of 1881. Nevertheless, the new Dutch code was an independent creation, blending elements of German and French criminal law. The most characteristic features of the code were the restriction of sanctions to prison, detention, and fines, the existence of preventive measures for the mentally ill and insane, and the participation of private organizations in the care of prisoners and released convicts.

The most noteworthy consequence of the Netherlands' criminal policy is the country's extremely low number of prisoners, despite a crime rate equal to that of other Western countries. This results from the possibility of out-of-court settlement with the police or prosecution, from an extensive use of nolo contendere pleas, and from a preference for fines in lieu of imprisonment. In the Netherlands only 27 percent of convictions include prison sentences, of which considerably more than 50 percent are suspended. The modern prison system of the Netherlands has served as a model for other Western countries.

The Romance countries.

France. In France, the Code Pénal of 1810 is still substantially in force. French criminal law reform has been achieved through many partial revisions of the code, most notably the introduction of mitigating circumstances in 1832, of parole in 1885, and of suspended sentences for first offenders in 1891. In contrast to these progressive measures, however, French law has long retained a severe side. The chief penalty remains incarceration; deportation to Devil's Island ceased only in 1938, and the death penalty was not abolished until 1981. Periods of conservative or right-wing rule in France have usually been marked by a preference for harsh sanctions, which have been partially reversed when parties of the Left came to power.

The first effort completely to reform the Code Pénal, a draft of 1934, failed amid the polarization of left- and right-wing forces at the time. The prison system was modernized after 1944, and it has been regulated by statute since 1959. Other progressive developments of the postwar years have included the introduction of parole officers, the extension of suspended sentences in 1959, and the introduction of alternatives to imprisonment in 1975 that permitted courts to impose a guilty verdict with delayed sentencing and to employ as the chief punishment such secondary penalties as deprivation of a driver's license. In 1978 an official preliminary draft for a reformed code was presented, but it was withdrawn from legislative consideration in 1980. In February 1981, highly controversial legislation was enacted that responded with extreme severity to an upsurge in violent crime. However, the election of a socialist government later that year led to the abolition of the death penalty and was expected to advance criminal law policies inspired by modern social defense.

Italy. While the Fascist government was transforming the entire Italian legal system to accommodate the authoritarian state, the country's scholars were working to reform the liberal criminal code of 1889. Although the resulting criminal code of 1930 is a technical masterpiece, the harshness of many of its provisions betrays the dominant ideology of its time.

Since the fall of Fascism, there has been no complete revision of Italian criminal law, although partial reforms have been achieved through legislation and decisions of the Constitutional Court. The death penalty was abolished in 1944, and the constitution of 1948 incorporated such basic principles of modern criminal policy as personal criminal responsibility and the reeducative goals of imprisonment. Parole was introduced in 1962. In 1975, new legislation on corrections was enacted that gave social workers responsibility for supervising convicts under probation schemes and work-release programs, under which prisoners work on the outside during the day, returning to the prison at night and on weekends. Subsequently the Constitutional Court declared that imprisonment for nonpayment of fines constituted discrimination against indigent persons, thus forcing the legislature to reexamine the law governing this entire sector of criminal policy. In addition, the Italian legislature has introduced, by way of replacement of default imprisonment, both substitute labor and controlled liberty.

By the late 1970s, terrorism, an increase in violent crime, and a prolonged economic and political crisis helped block the realization of further reforms, including a revision of the criminal code, for which there have been numerous drafts. Legislation since 1974 has tended to increase the severity of existing law.

Spain. Initiated in 1975 immediately after the restoration of democracy, criminal law reform is still under way in Spain. Criminal laws designed to maintain the authoritarian state, and other outdated provisions, have been repealed. Nevertheless, the criminal code of 1944 in its amended 1973 version remains in force; in its structure and especially in its system of penalties, the Spanish code resembles its forerunner of 1848.

There are six different kinds of deprivation of liberty, which can be shortened by as much as half their duration through parole or time-credit earned by labor. In addition to deprivation of liberty, Spanish law provides for three types of restriction of liberty, of which banishment is the most severe, and for a variety of security measures. A 1970 law allowing detention of up to five years for vagrancy or petty mischief is still in force.

The 1978 constitution abolished the death penalty and affirmed that all deprivations of liberty, whether punishments or security measures, must strive to reintegrate the convict into society. The 1980 draft code seeks a radical reform expressly incorporating the principle that the degree of guilt determines the amount of punishment, and it provides only for fines, imprisonment for definite periods, and the deprivation of civil rights. The minimum continuous incarceration is six months, although shorter sentences are possible in the form of imprisonment for up to twenty-four weekends. The day fine is to be employed in calculating monetary penalties, and various supplementary measures complement the penalties. Status-based preventive measures prior to the commission of a crime have been abolished. Serious prison riots have prompted penitentiary reform.

The Scandinavian countries.

Sweden. The modern criminal policy of Sweden has been a model for the rest of Europe. Significant early reforms of the criminal code of 1864 included the abolition of the death penalty in 1921, the introduction of the day-fine system in 1931 on the initiative of Johan Thyrén, who in turn was indebted to a Finnish measure of 1921, and the adoption of Anglo-American probation in 1939. The progressive 1962 criminal code designed by Karl Schlyter has realized that famous reformer's 1934 exhortation to "depopulate the prisons," but it still puts its trust in the resocializing effect of treatment during indeterminate imprisonment. The code has replaced the duality of criminal penalties and preventive measures with a unitary approach allowing the judge to choose the sanction on the basis of individual prevention alone, without primary regard to subjective guilt.

The general crisis in criminal policy has caused Sweden to reconsider the rehabilitative ideal. In 1980, juvenile institutions employing indeterminate imprisonment were abolished. Even the indeterminate incarceration of dangerous professional and habitual criminals came under sharp attack and has been repealed. Sweden has thus returned to the definite sentence as the sole sanction that involves deprivation of liberty. Such imprisonment, however, is to be imposed only rarely and for the shortest possible term; conditional release is possible after three months. Public opinion favors the complete abolition of deprivation of liberty. Guilt findings without the imposition of sentence; protective supervision sometimes combined with fines; and mandatory care for juvenile, alcoholic, or mentally ill criminals are alternatives to imprisonment.

Sweden has the world's most modern penitentiary system, structured according to a law passed in 1974.

The goal of imprisonment is the convict's preparation for release, an aim to be achieved through education, vocational training, work release, leaves of absence, vacations, and assistance in finding a job and an apartment. Prisons are of optimal size: regional institutions contain from 20 to 60 inmates, and national institutions that offer vocational education programs and psychiatric care are designed for 60 to 100 prisoners. The Council on Crime Prevention was founded in 1974 as a body that advises parliament and the government.

Norway. As a consequence of close Scandinavian cooperation in criminal policy, Norway has followed the lead of Sweden in reforming its criminal law. Norwegian practices, however, retain distinctive traits.

Bernard Getz's 1902 criminal code, still in force although substantially amended, was strongly influenced by the International Union of Penal Law. The code provides for imprisonment for terms of determinate duration, particularly for drunk driving, and for lump-sum fines that are not, however, calculated according to the day-fine system. Life imprisonment is possible, although it is rarely employed. Conditional judgments—sentences whose execution is at first suspended—may be imposed, as well as probation.

Norwegian criminal law rests on the idea that the degree of guilt determines the amount of punishment, and that related considerations of proportionality limit the measure of punishment, which is otherwise determined by the goal of general prevention. The once strongly held belief in the possibility of rehabilitation by penal institutions has been shaken. Measures of indeterminate duration are on the wane; the special measures providing for education of juvenile delinquents in workhouses were abolished in 1975; and forced labor for alcoholics and vagrants ceased in 1970. Protective custody for mentally ill offenders and preventive detention for habitual criminals have been reduced to a minimum. In the future more reliance will probably be placed on handling the convict in the community, including assistance by the social-welfare administration, if necessary. Imprisonment is increasingly viewed as an exceptional measure, and, in direct contrast to the rehabilitative theory, as a burden on the prisoner rather than a benefit to him.

The modern Norwegian penitentiary system, based on a 1958 law, is highly advanced. The Criminal Legislation Council, a standing body, advises parliament and the government in matters of criminal policy.

The socialist countries. The criminal law of the socialist states is based on Marxist-Leninist principles, which include the optimistic view that man is inherently good, corrupted only by presocialist influences.

The law is viewed as an instrument for the building of socialism and the protection of the power of the working class, represented by the Communist party. Crime, it is believed, will disappear with the coming of a fully developed communist society.

After the initial imposition of Soviet practices after World War II, revised criminal codes were enacted throughout Eastern Europe in the 1960s. Soviet criminal law is everywhere the predominant model, although the degree of Soviet influence varies considerably. It is, for example, quite strong in the German Democratic Republic, which in adopting a new socialist criminal code in 1968 cut the last links with the legal tradition it had shared with the Federal Republic of Germany. Soviet influence is considerably weaker in the criminal law of Poland, despite the adoption of a new criminal code in 1969 that replaced the code drafted by Juliusz Makarewicz in 1932.

The establishment of socialist societies in Eastern Europe has entailed broad changes in the criminal law and in the punishment of convicted persons. A primary principle holds that any action must be shown to be socially dangerous before it can be made criminally punishable. In applying the criminal law, a distinction is drawn between ideological opponents and merely "misled" workers. Supreme courts are authorized to issue regulations for the entire criminal justice system. In the German Democratic Republic, prison administrators have broad discretion, so that there are great differences in the manner in which penalties are inflicted. Political opponents and recidivists of all types are dealt with most severely. The death penalty is imposed for a few of the most serious crimes. Penalties involving deprivation of liberty include incarceration (for life or for definite periods) and short-term arrest; there are also provisions for parole. Despite a significantly lower crime rate than in Western Europe, the number of prisoners per capita is three to five times higher, according to unofficial estimates. Penalties without imprisonment include probation, fines, and public reprimands. "Comrades' courts" have jurisdiction over minor offenses, and workers' collectives share with state agencies the responsibility for reintegrating convicted persons into society. Recidivism is combated by the imposition of significantly increased penalties on second offenders and by a variety of social-control measures, such as extremely close police supervision (as in the German Democratic Republic) and a sentence of up to five years of reeducation in a social-adaptation center after release from prison (as in Poland).

Some socialist countries have begun abandoning ideologically determined sanctions, reforming their systems along lines somewhat resembling Western European practices. For example, the concept of "socialist reeducation" has gained some prominence in the German Democratic Republic, and in Poland innovative "restrictions of freedom" have been adopted as penalties, including restriction to the place of residence, compulsory community service, and (most commonly) a salary reduction of 10 percent to 25 percent. In addition to a number of security measures directed against juvenile and insane offenders and against dangerous criminals, Polish law provides for probation, parole, judicial determination of guilt without sentence, nolo contendere pleas, and extraordinary mitigation of punishment. In implementing parole or probation policies, social organizations and workers' collectives are expected to assist in aiding reintegration into society. The complete reform of Polish criminal law, begun in 1980, was interrupted by the military coup of December 1981.

The unification of criminal law in Western Europe

For the past two centuries, constant academic interchange has resulted in strong reciprocal influences across national boundaries. German and French criminal law set the pattern for legal reform in other continental countries during the nineteenth century; since World War II the progressive criminal policies of the Scandinavian countries and Anglo-American criminology have been the most influential models for reform. The common European legal heritage now finds new expression in the activities of the transnational institutions associated with the European Economic Community (Common Market) and the Council of Europe, as well as in the close cooperation on criminal matters of the Western European countries, whose crime rates and attitudes toward fighting crime are broadly similar.

In 1950 the European Human Rights Convention was promulgated, under which the European Commission and the European Court of Human Rights were established. The decisions of these bodies have had considerable influence on the legislation of the thirteen countries that have submitted to their jurisdiction, and the convention has exerted an enduring impact in stimulating reform of substantive criminal law and especially of criminal procedure. The resolutions of the Council of Europe's committee of ministers have similarly influenced member states' legislation in such spheres as traffic laws, narcotic violations, criminal sanctions, and prison systems. For example, the European version of the United Nations' Standard Minimum Rules for the Treatment of Prisoners was promulgated by the Council of Europe in this manner.

As early as 1927 the International Association of Penal Law began working for greater uniformity in European legal systems, although without success at the time. Since World War II the European Consultative Assembly has proposed drafting a uniform criminal law that would be similar to the American Model Penal Code of 1962. It is, however, unrealistic to expect the rise of a genuine European criminal law in the foreseeable future, as long as Europe remains a community of sovereign nations, each with its own legal system.

HANS-HEINRICH JESCHECK

See also ADVERSARY SYSTEM; CRIMINAL PROCEDURE: COMPARATIVE ASPECTS; TORTURE.

BIBLIOGRAPHY

American Law Institute. *Model Penal Code: Proposed Official Draft.* Philadelphia: ALI, 1962.

ANCEL, MARC. *Social Defence: A Modern Approach to Criminal Problems.* Translated by J. Wilson. Foreword by Leon Radzinowicz. London: Routledge, 1965.

ARZT, GUNTHER. "Responses to the Growth of Crime in the United States and West Germany: A Comparison of Changes in Criminal Law and Societal Attitudes." *Cornell International Law Journal* 12 (1979): 43–64.

Association of American Law Schools. "Symposium: The New German Penal Code." Foreword by J. Hall and W. J. Wagner. *American Journal of Comparative Law* 24 (1976): 589–778.

DARBY, JOSEPH J., trans. *Alternative Draft of a Penal Code for the Federal Republic of Germany.* Introduction by Joseph J. Darby. Commentary by Jürgen Baumann. American Series of Foreign Penal Codes, 21. South Hackensack, N.J.: Rothman, 1977.

FLETCHER, GEORGE P. *Rethinking Criminal Law.* Boston: Little, Brown, 1978.

GRÜNHUT, MAX. *Penal Reform: A Comparative Study.* Oxford: Clarendon Press, 1948.

JESCHECK, HANS-HEINRICH. "The Influence of the Union Internationale de Droit Pénal and of the Association Internationale de Droit Pénal on the International Development of Modern Criminal Policy." *Association Internationale de Droit Pénal: XIIᵉ Congrès International de Droit Pénal— Actes du Congrès.* Edited by H.-H. Jescheck. Baden-Baden: Nomos, 1980, pp. 44–60.

———. "Modern Criminal Policy in the Federal Republic of Germany and the German Democratic Republic." *Crime, Criminology, and Public Policy: Essays in Honour of Sir Leon Radzinowicz.* Edited by Roger Hood. New York: Free Press, 1974, pp. 509–525.

LOLIS, NICHOLAS B., trans. *The Greek Penal Code.* Introduction by Giorgios Mangakis. American Series of Foreign Penal Codes, 18. South Hackensack, N.J.: Rothman, 1973.

MANNHEIM, HERMANN, ed. *Pioneers in Criminology.* Introduction by Hermann Mannheim. Library of Criminology, no. 1. London: Stevens, 1960.

MOREAU, JEAN F., and MUELLER, GERHARD O. W., trans. *The French Penal Code.* Introduction by Marc Ancel. American Series of Foreign Penal Codes, 1. South Hackensack, N.J.: Rothman, 1960.

MUELLER GERHARD O. W., ed. *Essays in Criminal Science.* South Hackensack, N.J.: Rothman, 1961. Includes contributions on French and German criminal law reform.

———, and WISE, EDWARD M., eds. *Studies in Comparative Criminal Law.* Springfield, Ill.: Thomas, 1975. Includes contributions on Italian, Polish, and German criminal law reform.

NELSON, ALVAR. *Responses to Crime: An Introduction to Swedish Criminal Law and Administration.* Translated by Jerome L. Getz. Introduction by Warren E. Burger. Criminal Law Education and Research Center Monograph Series, vol. 6. South Hackensack, N.J.: Rothman, 1972.

"The Politics of Criminal Law Reform." *American Journal of Comparative Law* 21 (1973): 201–317. Articles dealing with the United States, England, Japan, France, Germany, Sweden, and Eastern Europe.

ROSS, NEVILLE, trans. *The German Draft Penal Code, E 1962.* Introduction by Eduard Dreher. American Series of Foreign Penal Codes, 11. South Hackensack, N.J.: Rothman, 1966.

SCHJOLDAGER, HARALD, and BACKER, FINN, trans. *The Norwegian Penal Code.* Introduction by Johannes Andenaes. American Series of Foreign Penal Codes, 3. South Hackensack, N.J.: Rothman, 1961.

SELLIN, THORSTEN, and GETZ, JEROME, trans. *The Penal Code of Sweden as Amended January 1st, 1972.* Introduction by Lennart Geijer. American Series of Foreign Penal Codes, 17. South Hackensack, N.J.: Rothman, 1972.

WISE, EDWARD M., and MAITLIN, ALLEN, trans. *The Italian Penal Code.* Introduction by Edward M. Wise. American Series of Foreign Penal Codes, 23. Littleton, Colo.: Rothman, 1978.

2.

ENGLAND

Introduction

English criminal law, like almost every other English legal, political, religious, educational, and social institution, has undergone substantial reform since the second quarter of the nineteenth century; but reform has taken place piecemeal and very slowly. At no point has there been any decisive break with the past such as has occurred in many European countries with the promulgation of a penal code and code of criminal procedure. Not only is England still without either but dozens of reforms cogently urged by publicists, parliamentary committees, and royal commissions in the first half of the nineteenth century have had to wait until the second half of the twentieth to be implemented. Some, like the complete abolition of common-law offenses, as well as codification itself, still await completion.

Two factors have combined to make the pace of reform of the criminal law even slower than that of the reform of most other English institutions. The first has been the influential presence in both houses of Parliament of considerable numbers of lawyers; many of the most senior judges, as well as other lawyers, sit in the House of Lords, and many magistrates and practicing lawyers are members of the House of Commons. The second is the British parliamentary practice that permits the scrutiny and debate of the detail, and not just the principle, of proposed legislation. This combination of factors has made it impossible to effect any substantial reform to which either the judiciary or the practicing profession (or, in the nineteenth century, if not the twentieth, the magistracy) is strongly opposed.

In 1786 the lord chancellor, Lord Loughborough, said that any proposal for changing the criminal law should either originate from the judges or be approved by them before being submitted to Parliament, and this convention has generally been followed (at least by governments) ever since. Lawyers form a notoriously conservative profession. This, together with the fact that many of the reforms would have the effect of curtailing the powers and discretion of the judiciary (the wide extent of which has always been one of the most striking characteristics of English criminal law), has meant that judicial and professional opposition to reform has been the rule, and support of reform the exception. Moreover, the breadth of this judicial discretion, coupled with both the absence of any rule or machinery compelling the prosecution of known offenders, and the uncontrollable liberty of juries to acquit in the teeth of the evidence, has often made it possible for the worst of the law's defects to be palliated in response to public opinion. It could therefore frequently be argued that in practice the law was nowhere near as objectionable as it was in theory, and that reforming legislation was, accordingly, unnecessary and might well result in unforeseen harm. At least two generations (a period long enough for the desirability of a change in the law to become universally recognized, and for law students to become judges) have therefore commonly elapsed between the proposal and the enactment of a reform.

Furthermore, the amount of parliamentary time likely to be consumed in considering any comprehensive legislation has constantly deterred the promotion of those reforms of the substantive law that even the legal profession has come to recognize as—in principle—desirable.

The unreformed law

In 1818 the youthful Thomas Macaulay described English criminal law as "a penal code at once too sanguinary and too lenient, half written in blood like Draco's, and half undefined and loose as the common law of a tribe of savages . . . the curse and disgrace of the country" (Cross, p. 520). He did not exaggerate. The law had been growing haphazardly for more than five centuries. Much had been added, often under the influence of temporary alarms. Very little had been taken away. As a result the criminal law was seriously defective both in substance and in form, and many aspects of the procedure under which it was applied were equally unsatisfactory.

Substantive law. For over a century and a half before Macaulay wrote his description of English criminal law, Parliament had sought to compensate for the absence of any adequate nationwide machinery for enforcing law and order (such as police forces would later provide) by threatening the severest penalty for those relatively few offenders unlucky enough to be caught. In 1818 there were more than two hundred statutes in force imposing the death penalty for a wide variety of offenses, both serious and trivial. These offenses ranged from treason and murder to forgery and even to criminal damage and petty theft when committed in a host of specified circumstances, as well as to several sex offenses, including sodomy. There was, however, no question of implementing all the death sentences that the judges were required by this undiscriminating legislation to pass whenever a prosecutor with the necessary nerve (or malice) found a jury willing to convict. Capital sentences were carried out, in 1810, in less than one case in twenty, although as might be expected the proportion varied greatly from crime to crime. Fewer than one convicted person in twenty was executed for theft unaccompanied by personal violence, but about one in six was put to death for the more serious offenses, including murder, rape, arson, counterfeiting, forgery, and attempted murder.

Whether or not the convicted defendant was reprieved largely depended on the trial judge, although in cases tried in London his recommendations were reviewed by the Privy Council. His discretion was affected, but not controlled, by public opinion, professional expectations, and the influence of persons in high places. The judge did not have to give any reasons for his decision, which was as likely to be determined by matters irrelevant to the defendant's guilt and to the jury's verdict as by anything that the defendant himself had actually done: the defendant's past record, the reputed prevalence of his offense in the locality, the extent of the perjury committed by witnesses called on his behalf, and the number of other defendants sentenced to death at the same assizes. But although the trial judge had a wide (or, as many critics said, an arbitrary) discretion to decide whether a defendant convicted of a capital offense should die, he had no discretion as to what should happen to the defendant if he was allowed to live.

The alternatives to the death penalty were whipping, a short term of imprisonment, or transportation—after 1787, usually to an Australian colony (the American ones being no longer available for this purpose) for a fixed period, which was usually seven years, but for some offenses fourteen years, and for a few, life. However, by no means all the defendants who had been sentenced to death and then reprieved on condition of being transported left English shores. Whether a convict was in fact transported or merely served a short (two- or three-year) period in an English prison hulk before being released depended not on the nature of the offense, but on purely administrative and practical considerations with which the judges were not concerned—the Australian demand for convict labor, and the availability of the requisite shipping.

The law governing these capital offenses was thus inefficient, as well as cruel and capricious. The chances of an offender actually suffering the extreme penalty with which the law threatened him were small, and its deterrent effect was therefore slight. Yet the chance that he *might* suffer the death penalty deterred many victims from prosecuting, many witnesses from giving evidence, and many juries from convicting.

The form of the law was chaotic and extremely obscure. In 1821 it was estimated that there were 750 acts of Parliament concerning the criminal law in force, together with another 400 relating to proceedings before magistrates. These statutes were the product of three centuries of parliamentary activity, and not only had almost all been enacted without regard to any of the others, but they also presupposed the "unwritten" common law of crime, without a knowledge of which the statutes themselves were more often than not quite unintelligible. Such matters as the definitions of the basic offenses (murder, rape, robbery, burglary, theft, forgery, and assault), the rules of secondary (accomplice) liability, and general defenses were a matter of judicial tradition sustained by three seventeenth- and eighteenth-century books of authority—Edward Coke's *Third Institute;* Matthew Hale's *History of the Pleas of the Crown,* first published in 1736; and William Hawkins's *Pleas of the Crown.* These were supplemented by a very small amount of reported case law. Although the judges recognized that either immemorial custom or an act of Parliament was required to make conduct a felony and a capital offense, they exercised a wide power to declare an act criminal as a misdemeanor, and to punish with the pillory, whipping, imprisonment, or a fine, any conduct which they happened to consider immoral or antisocial.

Trial procedure (and also powers of arrest and ancillary liability) was determined by whether the offense with which a defendant was charged was a treason, a felony, or a misdemeanor, although with the shifts and changes in the law that had occurred over the years these distinctions had become more than a little arbitrary. Theft, for example, was a felony, however small the amount stolen, but obtaining by false pretenses was a misdemeanor, however valuable the property obtained. (All capital offenses were either treasons or felonies, but not all felonies were capital—either because a statute had so provided, or because of the perversion of the medieval jurisdictional rule known as benefit of clergy. This could, unless a statute otherwise provided, be invoked by every felon the first time he was convicted, in effect giving him a conditional discharge.) Accordingly, a defendant could not be tried simultaneously for a felony and a misdemeanor, however closely related in point of fact the two charges might be (as, for example, the inchoate offense to the completed offense). Indeed, only one felony could be tried at a time.

Most importantly, at a felony trial the defendant's counsel could only examine witnesses and argue points of law: he was not allowed to address the jury, although he might do so at treason or misdemeanor trials. A defendant was not entitled to any prior notice of the case against him beyond the information provided by the indictment itself; and since it was a general rule that neither a party to the proceedings nor anyone who had any pecuniary interest in the result of a trial could give evidence at it, not only the defendant but frequently also the victim was excluded from the witness stand. (Defendants were, however, usually allowed to make a statement at the very end of the trial, when it was difficult for anyone to test its correctness.)

There were no special procedures for youthful offenders. Everyone over the age of seven was subject to the same law, modes of trial, and penalties; and even though children were very rarely hanged, they were sentenced to death and imprisoned. This reflected the fact that the common law knew only one form of criminal trial, trial by jury. Statutes had in specific instances given to magistrates, sitting singly or in small groups, the power to try persons charged with certain statutory offenses (for example, under the game laws and the revenue legislation), but there was no general provision for the summary trial of offenses of a minor character. There was, finally, no system of criminal appeals, either on the facts, on account of the judge's misdirection of the jury, or from a sentence in those cases in which the judge had discretion. Only a very limited and rarely invoked remedy existed for the review of procedural and similar technical errors.

Movements for reform

The literary movement for the reform of English criminal law began in 1771 with the publication of William Eden's *Principles of Penal Law.* The parliamentary movement was initiated in 1810 by Samuel Romilly's (unsuccessful) attempt to make three forms of petty theft noncapital crimes, and by the establishment in 1819, on the motion of James Mackintosh, of a select committee of the House of Commons "to consider so much of the criminal laws as relates to capital punishment in felonies, and to report their observations and opinions upon the same" (Cornish). Both Romilly and Mackintosh were the friends as well as the disciples of the philosopher Jeremy Bentham (1748–1832), whose ideas and writings (published and unpublished) pervaded every proposal for the reform not only of the criminal law but of most other legal and political institutions for more than half a century.

William Blackstone (1723–1780) had not been uncritical of several aspects of the criminal law in the fourth volume of his *Commentaries on the Laws of England;* but Eden's book, published when the author was only twenty-six, and strongly inspired by Montesquieu and Beccaria, was the first attempt at a critical examination of the criminal law's structure and principles. It also represented the first effort to evolve a comprehensive plan for its reform. Although he favored retaining the death penalty for a substantial number of offenses (including maiming, rape, sodomy, arson, and burglary), Eden argued that the severity of penal laws should be controlled first by "natural justice" and second by "public utility," and that punishments should bear some relation to the gravity of offenses. He accordingly identified scores of offenses that in his view should no longer be capital—a bold suggestion to make at a time when Parliament was still readily adding to the number of capital offenses. Eden disapproved of transportation, on the ground that if it did not kill the convict, it often conferred a benefit on him. He also disapproved of imprisonment, which he considered a dead loss to everyone. On the other hand, he favored flogging, fines, and compulsory labor in public works. Finally, he proposed the outright repeal of all obsolete statutes, and the consolidation of those that were to remain. Nearly all of Eden's reforms (with the exception, of course, of the disuse of imprisonment) were ultimately implemented by Parliament, but the process took more than seventy years.

In 1808, Romilly sought the repeal of a statute imposing the death penalty—one dating from 1565, for stealing "privately" from the person (that is, pickpocketing)—but it was his speech in the House of Commons on February 9, 1810 (printed, with additions, as *Observations on the Criminal Law of England as It Relates to Capital Punishments, and on the Mode in Which It Is Administered*), that reopened public debate on the state of the criminal law. Romilly's argument was a masterly exposure (still well worth reading) of the fallacies of the orthodox justifications for the law's indiscriminate threats, but relatively infrequent and largely arbitrary imposition, of the death penalty. Since the three statutes whose repeal he unsuccessfully sought covered a considerable proportion of all nonviolent offenses against property, Romilly's proposed reform was a substantial one going to the heart of the existing law.

Mackintosh's committee of 1819 made the first official large-scale investigation into the criminal law and its effects ever attempted, and its report, with detailed statistical returns of convictions and executions, as well as a chronological review of the statute law, served as a model for official reports on the criminal law for the rest of the nineteenth century. The committee recommended (1) that twelve obsolete statutes be repealed and fifteen others amended; (2) that Romilly's proposed reform of 1810 (for the repeal of three capital theft offenses) be carried out; (3) that the statute law of forgery be consolidated; and (4) that all forgery offenses other than the actual forging of Bank of England notes, as well as a second conviction for uttering forged notes, should cease to be capital. The fourth of these reforms was strongly supported by bankers and businessmen, who found it virtually impossible to obtain convictions while the offenses remained capital. Although the committee's recommendations met with determined opposition

and were at first rejected by Parliament, they were implemented during the 1820s, after Home Secretary Robert Peel had in 1823 committed the government to an extensive review of the criminal law.

Legislation, 1823–1849

The review promised by Peel resulted in very substantial improvements in the form of the law, but only in relatively minor reductions in its severity and arbitrariness. Peel was accordingly able to secure the support of the judiciary in carrying a considerable body of legislation through Parliament. Three hundred and sixteen acts of Parliament were consolidated in four statutes, which covered nearly four-fifths of all offenses (the Larceny Act, 1827, 7 & 8 Geo. 4, c. 29, consolidating 92 statutes; the Malicious Injuries to Property Act, 1827, 7 & 8 Geo. 4, c. 30, consolidating 48 statutes; the Offences against the Person Act, 1828, 9 Geo. 4, c. 31, consolidating 56 statutes; and the Forgery Act, 1830, 11 Geo. 4 & 1 Will. 4, c. 66, consolidating 120 statutes). Peel's acts also totally repealed obsolete statutes, filled small gaps in the law, and made other minor amendments; but being merely consolidating statutes, they did not incorporate the common-law rules. Thus, his Larceny Act contained no definition of larceny (which was not provided until 1916); his Forgery Act, no definition of forgery (not provided until 1913); and his Offences against the Person Act, no definitions of murder, manslaughter, assault, or rape (only rape has since been defined, and then only in 1976). This legislation did not therefore amount to codification, as Bentham and his followers would have wished, and as Edward Livingston was contemporaneously projecting for Louisiana. Nor did it do much to mitigate the severity and arbitrariness of the law relating to capital punishment. Even in 1830 Peel, against the wishes of the banking and commercial community, favored retention of the death sentence for forgery, although no one was in fact executed for this offense after that date.

Only four reforms were effected in the substance, as opposed to the form, of the law under Peel's leadership. First, in 1823, two of the three capital offenses of theft that Romilly had singled out in 1810 were repealed, as well as another eight whose abolition had been proposed by Mackintosh's committee. Four more were repealed in 1825, and two others (larceny in booths and larceny in churches), in 1827. Second, another statute of 1823 provided that death sentences should not be pronounced if the judge intended to recommend a reprieve. This meant that the judge had to decide openly for, rather than privately against, the carrying out of the death sentence. This statute thus increased the number of cases in which the death penalty was commuted. Third, in 1827 Parliament abolished the technicalities of benefit of clergy and the distinction between grand and petty larceny, with the result that a second conviction for the theft of more than twelvepence was no longer capital. The practical consequence was not any reduction in the number of death sentences carried out but rather that such thefts became triable at quarter sessions, which was much more convenient for prosecutors than trial at assizes. Fourth, many changes were introduced in the scale of punishments for lesser offenses, which had the same effect.

The formation of Earl Grey's Whig reform ministry in November 1830 made possible more radical changes. In 1832 William Eden's son, George Eden, president of the board of trade and master of the mint, successfully sponsored the Coinage Offences Act, 1832, 2 & 3 Will. 4, c. 34 (repealed), which not only consolidated the existing law but also carried through the drastic reform of abolishing the death penalty for all counterfeiting offenses. During the next two years, and in the face of opposition from Peel and the judges, the death sentence was abolished for several forms of four offenses (larceny, housebreaking, forgery, and robbery), being replaced by mandatory sentences of transportation, either for life or for not less than seven years.

In 1835 the appointment as home secretary of Lord John Russell, a disciple of Romilly and a member of Mackintosh's committee, stimulated further reform. Between April and July of 1837, Russell carried ten reforming bills through Parliament, seven of them directly concerned with the death penalty. The total number of capital offenses was thereby reduced from thirty-seven to sixteen, nearly all of these involving some element of violence against the person. The principle that no offense against property alone should be punishable by death, for which the reformers had long contended, was at last implemented. In the same year a motion in the House of Commons seeking the abolition of the death penalty for all crimes "save those of actual murder" failed by a single vote. By 1839 the only offenses still subject to the death penalty were treason, riot, arson of naval ships and of naval and military stores, murder and other offenses involving attempts on or risks to life, rape, buggery, sexual intercourse with girls under ten years of age, and robbery and burglary when accompanied by personal violence—much the same list as that proposed by Eden in 1771. Rape ceased to be a capital crime in 1840.

The opposition of twelve of the fifteen judges notwithstanding, Russell also carried in 1836 a bill that allowed counsel or an attorney representing a defendant charged with a felony to address the jury on his behalf. The law and practice governing proceedings before magistrates (both committal proceedings and summary trial), however, remained in its unreformed state until John Jervis, as attorney general, took the matter in hand, piloting through Parliament in 1848 and 1849 three statutes that laid down basic procedures and procedural standards for those jurisdictions. This reform made it politically possible to increase the number of minor offenses that might be tried summarily (a process inaugurated by the Criminal Justice Act, 1855, 18 & 19 Vict., c. 126), and, as a consequence, the number of offenders who were in fact prosecuted. And in 1847 the first step was taken toward creating a separate jurisdiction for young offenders, when it was provided that children under fourteen (after 1850, under sixteen) charged with simple larceny could be tried summarily with their parents' consent. This procedure was extended to all offenses, other than homicide, in 1879, but it was not until 1908 that juvenile courts, held at different times from those for adults, were established.

The criminal law commissioners, 1833–1849

In 1833 Lord Brougham, lord chancellor in Earl Grey's ministry, and another of Bentham's friends and disciples, had initiated what proved to be the first of three projects for the codification of English criminal law. (The second, initiated by James Fitzjames Stephen, was to come before Parliament between 1877 and 1881; the third, initiated by the Law Commission in 1967, is still continuing.) A royal commission, composed of five practicing lawyers, was appointed "to digest into one statute all the enactments concerning crimes, their trial and punishment, and to digest into another statute all the provisions of the Common Law touching the same; and to enquire and report how far it might be expedient to combine both these statutes into one body of the Criminal Law, repealing all other statutory provisions; or how far it might be expedient to pass into law the first mentioned of these two statutes." This was a mammoth assignment, but it was completed in a little over ten years, although the commissioners' work on their principal task was interrupted by requests from Lord John Russell to consider and report on the special question of the right of counsel for a prisoner to address the jury in felony cases. He also asked the commissioners to consider which offenses should continue to incur capital punishment (*Second Report* [1836], which formed the basis for Russell's legislation on these matters), and procedures for the trial of juvenile offenders (*Third Report* [1837], which was applied, as noted above, to charges of simple larceny in 1847, but not to all other offenses until 1879). The commission's *First Report* (1834) considered the need for codification and the best way of achieving it. It contained a draft digest, with a commentary, of the law of theft—as complicated and difficult a subject as any in the criminal law.

As a result of their first report, the commissioners' terms of reference were widened to include recommendations as to "what partial alterations may be necessary or expedient for more simply and completely defining crimes and punishments and for the more effective administration of criminal justice." That is, the commissioners were authorized to make recommendations for the reform, as well as the restatement, of the criminal law. In the ensuing years they accordingly reported (with draft legislation) on homicide, offenses against the person, theft, fraud, and criminal damage (*Fourth Report* [1839]); on burglary, offenses against the executive power and the administration of justice, forgery, and offenses against the public peace (*Fifth Report* [1840]); on treason and other offenses against the state and religion, libel, coinage offenses, and offenses against the revenue (*Sixth Report* [1841]); and on the general principles of criminal responsibility (*Seventh Report* [1843]). The *Seventh Report* also contained a complete draft code of the substantive criminal law, revising the digests contained in previous reports, and was complemented in the *Eighth Report* (1845) by a draft code of criminal procedure.

The royal commission's eight reports contain the most thorough and principled examination of English criminal law that has ever been made by an official body. The commissioners recommended many reforms that were ultimately to reach the statute book, even if the abolition of the felony-murder rule (under which a death accidentally caused while committing a felony amounted to murder) and of the distinction between a felony and a misdemeanor was not accomplished for more than a hundred years—in 1957 and 1967, respectively. They succeeded in producing codes that combined in legislative form the rules of both the common- and the statutory law of crime. These codes would, therefore, have ended the judges' freedom to extend the criminal law to include any conduct of which they disapproved. Equally importantly, the commissioners followed Livingston's example and offered a classification of offenses that sought to reflect their relative heinousness in an elaborate

scheme of graduated penalties. Had it been accepted, this classification would have considerably reduced judicial discretion in sentencing. The mixture of rigidity and arbitrariness that had characterized the eighteenth-century law had given way to chaos, largely as a result of the shifts and compromises that occurred when the death penalty was removed from different offenses. In an appendix to the *Fourth Report* (1839), the commissioners demonstrated that, leaving aside death and various obsolete penalties, forty different penalties were provided for felonies and ninety-six for misdemeanors. In the commission's *Seventh Report* (1843), only forty-five classes of punishment were specified. The number was reduced to thirteen by the revising commissioners (see below) in their *Second Report* (1846); it rose to thirty-one in their *Third Report* (1847), but finally dropped to eighteen in their *Fourth Report* (1849).

The draft code of substantive criminal law was introduced as a bill in the House of Lords by Lord Brougham in 1844, but it was withdrawn when the lord chancellor, Lord Lyndhurst, announced the appointment of a new royal commission to reconsider and revise the draft. This commission, which included three of the five 1833 commissioners, published five reports between 1845 and 1849 that recommended further reforms and revisions—but no radical alterations—in their predecessors' draft code. The revised code of substantive law, which was published in the *Fourth Report* (1848), was introduced into the House of Lords in the same year by Lord Brougham, and referred to a select committee. As a result of the latter's report, it was decided that the draft code should be split up and submitted to Parliament piecemeal. The Criminal Law Amendment (No. 1) Bill, dealing with the general principles of liability, defenses, homicide, and offenses against the person, was accordingly prepared and given a second reading by the House of Lords in 1853. A second bill, dealing with larceny and other offenses of dishonesty, was also tabled. Lord Cranworth, who had recently become lord chancellor, circulated these bills to the judges, seeking their comments. He asked in particular whether the policy of bringing the whole of the criminal law—statutory and common law—into one statute (that is, codification, not merely consolidation) was likely to be beneficial to the administration of criminal justice. The judges' replies showed that although they were ready to concede the advantages of further consolidation, they were unanimously opposed to reducing the common law to statutory form. As one judge expressed it, "to reduce unwritten law to statute is to discard one of the great blessings we have for ages enjoyed in rules capable of flexible application"; according to another, it was "inadvisable to lose the advantage of the power of applying the principles of the common law to new offences, and combinations of circumstances, arising from time to time."

In the face of this adverse judicial reaction, the bills were not reintroduced. It was decided that the draftsman (C. S. Greaves, Q.C.) should confine himself to producing consolidating statutes that would replace Peel's acts, which were now obsolescent as a result, first, of the removal of the death penalty for many offenses in the 1830s, and second, of the abolition—by the Penal Servitude Act, 1857, 20 & 21 Vict., c. 3—of the sentences of transportation that had taken the place of capital punishment. The latter reform had been urged by Eden in 1771, as well as by many subsequent publicists, and had been strongly recommended by Molesworth's Select Committee in 1838. Six of these consolidating statutes were enacted in 1861 (Accessories and Abettors Act, Larceny Act, Malicious Damage Act, Forgery Act, Coinage Offences Act, and Offences against the Person Act, 24 & 25 Vict., cc. 94, 96, 97, 98, 99, 100, respectively). Since the 1840s only murderers had been executed (and by no means all of them), so this legislation provided the opportunity for bringing the law into line with practice. The death penalty was retained only for murder, treason, and arson of naval vessels. Seven years later, public executions came to an end, when the Capital Punishment Amendment Act of 1868 provided that executions should take place within the prison in which the prisoner was confined (31 & 32 Vict., c. 24).

Substantial parts of the first two of the 1861 acts still remain in force. The other four lasted well into the twentieth century: the Larceny Act until 1916, the Malicious Damage Act until 1971, the Forgery Act until 1913, and the Coinage Offences Act until 1936. Sexual offenses, many of which had been included among the crimes covered by the Offences against the Person Act, were not consolidated again until 1956. In some of these twentieth-century statutes the draftsman was at last allowed to incorporate statutory formulations of some of the common-law rules without provoking a howl of protest from the judiciary. Most notably, he was able to incorporate definitions of the offenses in the Larceny Act, 1916, 6 & 7 Geo. 5, c. 50; the Forgery Act, 1913, 3 & 4 Geo. 5, c. 27; and the Perjury Act, 1911, 1 & 2 Geo. 5, c. 6. However, other statutes, such as the Sexual Offences Act of 1956 (4 & 5 Eliz. 2, c. 69), were merely consolidating statutes that presupposed, but did not state, the common-law rules. This legislation, although a small step forward, was still, therefore, a long way from the codification recommended by the criminal law commissioners in 1834.

The Indian Penal Code, 1835–1860

While the criminal law commissioners were at work on a code for England, Macaulay, who had gone to India in 1834 to be the law member of the governor-general's council, was drafting a penal code that was intended to apply to the entire population—native and expatriate—of British India. Instructions were issued to four commissioners in June 1835, but because of the illnesses and absences of the others, Macaulay was virtually the sole author of the draft code that he submitted in October 1837 to the governor-general, Lord Auckland. The governor-general maintained the Eden family's interest in the criminal law that he had already demonstrated when promoting the Coinage Offences Bill in England in 1832. Macaulay's code was an extremely able piece of drafting, "the first specimen," as Stephen said, "of an entirely new and original method of legislative expression" (1883, p. 299). The work of a master of English prose, the code was concise, lucid, and free of legal jargon. It paid careful attention to the degree of fault required for each offense, and was accompanied by a well-argued introduction and set of notes. Influenced by the thinking of Bentham and John Austin (1790–1859), as well as by the *First Report* (1834) of the English commissioners (in which they had outlined their program for codification), the substance, but not the language, of Macaulay's code was to a large extent an improved version of the English law of the 1830s. He also, however, drew on Edward Livingston's code for Louisiana and on the French Code Pénal, for he was not under the restraints that forced the English commissioners to restate as closely as possible the existing law, and to justify any departure from it.

Despite, or because of, its virtues, Macaulay's draft had a very hostile reception from the contemporary Indian judiciary (which was composed of English lawyers doing a tour of duty abroad). It was not enacted until 1860, coming into force in 1862 in the aftermath of the Indian Mutiny of 1857, with amendments that were by no means all improvements. The code worked well, and is still in force, in India, Pakistan, and Sri Lanka, as well as in the Sudan and Northern Nigeria, where it was adopted while these territories were under the jurisdiction or influence of the British Colonial Office. It also strongly influenced the second attempt—Stephen's—to provide England with a code of criminal law.

Stephen's codes, 1877–1883

Stephen served in India as law member of the governor-general's council from 1869 to 1872. In this capacity he had been involved in the revision of the Criminal Procedure Code and the passing of the Indian Evidence Act of 1872 and the Indian Contract Act of the same year. He was much impressed by the Penal Code. "To compare [it] to English criminal law," he wrote on his return, "is like comparing cosmos with chaos." Shortly afterward, Stephen joined in the drafting of the Homicide Law Amendment Bill, which offered a statutory definition of murder, abolished the felony-murder rule, and made infanticide a lesser offense than murder. This bill was introduced in Parliament in August 1872. It was reintroduced in May 1874 and referred to a select committee, where it was to founder. Although the committee agreed that a redefinition of murder was "urgently needed," it found the judiciary very critical of the bill.

In particular, the Lord Chief Justice, Alexander Cockburn, although professing himself a strong supporter of codification (and, if so, the first chief justice of whom this could be said), argued that the "partial and imperfect codification" of the bill, which included clauses dealing with the insanity defense, necessity, and the presumption of intention, applying only to homicide cases, would be fatal to the prospects of a complete code (Stephen, 1877, p. v). Stephen responded to this challenge by publishing in 1877 *A Digest of the Criminal Law (Crimes and Punishments)*, in which he showed the form that a complete code might take. As a result, Lord Cairns, the lord chancellor, later that year instructed Stephen to draft two bills: one a penal code, the other a code of criminal procedure. The first was introduced into Parliament as the Criminal Code (Indictable Offences) Bill in May 1878, and was sufficiently well received to be referred to a royal commission composed of three judges (two English and one Irish) and Stephen himself. The commission was to consider and report on the bill and also to suggest any other alterations in the existing law or procedure that seemed desirable, it being recognized that Parliament itself could not give the bill the detailed technical legal scrutiny required.

The commission sat daily from November 1878 to May 1879, discussing, according to Stephen, "every line of and nearly every word of each section" of the two bills. Although it added 127 sections to Stephen's draft (in particular, detailed provisions concerning the use of force in self-defense, defense of property, and the prevention of crime), the royal commission agreed to recommend to Parliament both the principle of codification and a revised bill. This was a considerable achievement, especially since the commission's chairman, Lord Blackburn, the most eminent judge of the day, had previously been opposed to codification.

The Criminal Code Bill had its first two readings in the House of Commons in April and May 1879, but no third reading that session. It was reintroduced in February 1880, but there was a change of government in April of that year, and although the part of the code dealing with criminal procedure was announced as a government measure in the Queen's Speech in both 1882 and 1883, Parliament's time and attention were dominated by the struggle for Irish home rule. Consequently, nothing further was done to secure the code's enactment. Since it not only consolidated and codified the existing law but also included a considerable number of reforms, its passage through Parliament would almost certainly have been controverted and, therefore, time-consuming.

The fact that Lord Chief Justice Cockburn was again highly critical (on the ground that even this code was incomplete, because it omitted some obsolescent statutory offenses, as well as all summary ones) inevitably cast a shadow. However, Cockburn's objections were easily answered by Stephen, and they need not have proved fatal to the code if parliamentary time had been made available for its consideration. More significantly, perhaps, the Statute Law Committee, which had been established in 1868 to promote statutory consolidation and revision, favored a more gradual program of reform and consolidation. In addition, doubts came to be felt about the quality of Stephen's drafting, and comparisons (not to Stephen's advantage) were drawn with the code that R. S. Wright had drafted for the colony of Jamaica between 1874 and 1877 to be a model, or so the Colonial Office hoped, for the rest of the Empire.

Among the changes envisaged by Stephen's code that had to wait many years before they were finally effected were (1) abolition of the felony/misdemeanor distinction (first recommended in 1839 but implemented only in 1967); (2) abolition of the felony-murder rule (recommended in 1839 and implemented in 1957); (3) allowing words as well as acts to constitute provocation, reducing an intentional killing from murder to manslaughter (implemented in 1957); (4) the coalescence of larceny and the other offenses of dishonest appropriation in a single offense of theft (achieved in 1968); (5) abolition of the defense of marital coercion (still surviving); (6) allowing the defendant always to be a competent witness at his own trial (implemented in 1898); and (7) establishment of a court of criminal appeal (a bill for which was first introduced in 1844 and which was finally implemented in 1907, after a protracted public campaign).

The public debate over Stephen's code showed that the judges were no longer opposed to codification in principle, as they had been in the 1850s. But the fact that the project was allowed to lapse reveals how little concerned the judges or the profession were that the law should, as Cockburn had put it, "be suffered to remain in its present state of confusion, arising from its being partly unwritten and partly in statutes so imperfectly drawn as to be almost worse than unwritten law" (Stephen, 1877, p. v). In 1901 Courtney Ilbert, the principal government draftsman, lamented that "it was impossible to view . . . without a certain degree of humiliation, the entire cessation during recent years of any effort to improve the form of English Law, and the apathy with which that cessation has been regarded" (p. 162). He observed that the lack of a criminal code and a code of criminal procedure "produces practical and substantial inconveniences." Revised versions of Stephen's code were, however, adopted in Canada, New Zealand, Queensland, Western Australia, many of the British territories in East and West Africa, Cyprus, and Palestine, and proved quite satisfactory.

Royal commissions and departmental and select committees, 1900–1960

The first half of the twentieth century saw extraordinarily few reforms in the criminal law. Such attention as was given to problems of criminal justice centered on the conditions and effects of—and alternatives to—imprisonment, and especially on ways of dealing with young and first offenders. As far as the criminal law itself was concerned, apart from the already-mentioned revisions of the 1861 acts and the consolidation of statutory offenses of perjury (which, being misdemeanors, had not previously been undertaken), the most important pieces of legislation were the act that established the Court of Criminal Appeal in 1907 (Criminal Appeal Act, 1907, 7 Edw. 7, c. 23 (repealed)) and the Indictments Act, 1915, 5 & 6 Geo. 5, c. 90 (repealed in part). The latter effected a very substantial simplification in the form of indictments. All these statutes were sponsored by the reforming Liberal government which took office in 1906. The principal reforms of that government were, however, directed at other aspects of English life, politics, and law. For the rest, royal commissions and departmental and select committees were from time to time established to consider particular matters. Their recommendations were rarely implemented, and then only after considerable delay.

Among the chief of these bodies was the Departmental Committee on Insanity and Crime (1922), whose report was put aside after ten of the twelve King's Bench judges said they were opposed to its proposals. Others were the Select Committee on Insanity and Crime (1930), the Departmental Committee on Sexual Offences against Young Persons (1925), and the Interdepartmental Committee on Abortion (1939). The Royal Commission on Betting, Lotteries and Gaming (1951) resulted in the Betting, Gaming and Lotteries Act, 1963, c. 2; the Royal Commission on Capital Punishment (1953), in the Homicide Act, 1957, 5 & 6 Eliz. 2, c. 11; the Select Committee on Obscenity (1958), in the Obscene Publications Act, 1959, 7 & 8 Eliz. 2, c. 66; and the Departmental Committee on Homosexual Offences and Prostitution (1957), in the Sexual Offences Act, 1967, c. 60, and the Street Offences Act, 1959, 7 & 8 Eliz. 2, c. 57.

This list shows that in the 1950s, after the interruptions and dislocations caused by two world wars and a major economic recession, there was a long-overdue revival of public interest in the need to reform the criminal law so that it would be less out of accord with contemporary standards and expectations. (Another sign was the foundation in 1957 of JUSTICE, the British section of the International Commission of Jurists, which has produced a valuable series of reports drawing attention to defects in criminal law and procedure, and proposed many reforms.) But all this interest was confined to very specific matters. The concern shown by the nineteenth-century reformers for the principles that should govern the criminal law, and for its overall structure, was absent.

Thus, when the Royal Commission on Capital Punishment returned to problems that had occupied the criminal law commissioners in the 1830s and the royal commission of 1866, its terms of reference were limited to considering ways in which the incidence of capital punishment might be restricted: it was not asked to say whether capital punishment should be retained. The commission accordingly recommended (and the Homicide Act of 1957 implemented) the abolition of the felony-murder rule, the widening of the defense of provocation to include provocative words, and the creation of two new forms of manslaughter in cases where the intentional killer was mentally disordered (but not insane) or had acted in pursuance of a suicide pact. The commission recommended that degrees of murder (of which only the first would carry the death penalty) should not be introduced, but this recommendation was rejected by the Conservative government, which, in an attempt to stymie the campaign for the total abolition of capital punishment, distinguished in the 1957 act between capital and noncapital murders. This distinction quickly proved to be so unacceptable that it was discarded in 1965, when the death penalty for murder was suspended for an experimental period of five years, a suspension made permanent in 1970. The Homicide Act of 1957 did not, however, include a statutory definition of murder (or any other homicidal offense). There was, consequently, the extraordinary spectacle of the definition of murder, still a matter of common law, being the subject of no less than three appeals to the House of Lords within the next twenty-five years (*Director of Public Prosecutions v. Smith,* [1961] A.C. 290; *Hyam v. Director of Public Prosecutions,* [1975] A.C. 55; *Regina v. Cunningham,* [1981] 2 All E.R. 863 (H.L.)).

The Criminal Law Revision Committee, 1959—

The most important manifestation of the revival of interest in criminal law reform during the 1950s was the establishment in 1959 (by Home Secretary R. A. Butler, largely at the instigation of Glanville Williams, the leading academic writer on English criminal law) of the standing Criminal Law Revision Committee. This committee was "to examine such aspects of the criminal law of England and Wales as the Home Secretary may from time to time refer to the Committee, to consider whether the law requires revision and to make recommendations" (*First Report,* Cmd. 835, 1959, p. 3). (The standing Law Revision Committee, first appointed by the lord chancellor in 1934 and reconstituted as the Law Reform Committee in 1952, has never considered any aspect of criminal law.)

The Criminal Law Revision Committee always includes three or four senior judges, one or two circuit judges, the chief London stipendary magistrate, and the director of public prosecutions, as well as several practicing and one or two academic lawyers. It thus maintains the convention, promulgated in the eighteenth century, that the government should sponsor only those reforms in the criminal law which have the support of the judiciary. The committee has produced fourteen reports on specific matters, of which the most important have been the seventh (Cmnd. 2659, 1965), recommending the abolition of the felony/misdemeanor distinction (implemented in 1967); the eighth (Cmnd. 2977, 1966), on theft and related offenses (implemented in 1968); the eleventh (Cmnd.

4991, 1972), proposing many important changes in the law of evidence; and the fourteenth (Cmnd. 7844, 1980), on offenses against the person, including homicide.

As might be expected from its composition and sponsoring department, the committee has adopted a very pragmatic approach to its work. It has eschewed all interest not only in codification but in restating the common law in statutory form, its reports showing a readiness to retain common-law rules whose vagueness and uncertainty ("flexibility") has been their chief attraction. The Home Office has, as a result, readily and promptly promoted legislation to give effect to most of the committee's proposals. But it quickly lost interest in the committee's only report (its eleventh, on the law of evidence in criminal cases) that made any radical proposals for rationalization and reform, after just one of its many recommendations had attracted a great deal of (ill-informed) public criticism.

The Law Commission, 1965—

Codification has, however, been one of the professed aims of the Law Commission. This is a permanent governmental agency, composed of five lawyer commissioners (one of whom, in practice the chairman, must be a judge), which was established at the instigation of Lord Gardiner, lord chancellor in the Labor government that came to office in 1964. Lord Gardiner was convinced that by then too much of the law was in need of reform for the task to be left to commissions and committees appointed ad hoc. The Law Commissions Act, 1965, c. 22 (there is another commission for Scotland) places the commissioners under a duty "to take and keep under review all the law . . . with a view to its systematic development and reform, including in particular the codification of such law." In 1967, after Home Secretary Roy Jenkins had stated that in the government's view there was a pressing need for codification of the criminal law to begin, the commission included in its second program of law reform "a comprehensive examination of the Criminal Law with a view to its codification."

Since the commission has a responsibility to keep "all the law" (not just the criminal law) under review, it has been able to devote only a small proportion of its attention and staff to this work. Between 1967 and 1973 a working party (subcommittee) investigated the general principles governing criminal liability. It published several working papers (discussion documents) on particular matters, including the mental element in crime, inchoate and secondary liability, and defenses. These working papers, which were to a considerable extent modeled on, and influenced by, the tentative drafts prepared for the American Law Institute's Model Penal Code between 1952 and 1962, set out not so much to restate the existing law in statutory form, as to consider what the best rule on each point would be. This proved, however, to be too ambitious a project, and it was discontinued.

The commission has nonetheless published a series of reports recommending legislation on both the general principles of liability and the definitions of particular offenses. These include reports on the mental element in crime (1978), the inchoate offenses of conspiracy (1976) and attempt (1980), defenses of general application (1977), and the law's territorial extent (1978), as well as on the offenses of criminal damage (1970), forgery and counterfeiting (1973), and interfering with the course of justice (1979). There has, as a result, been legislation on conspiracy (1977), attempt (1981), criminal damage (1971), and forgery and counterfeiting (1981). These proposals and legislation, although piecemeal and poorly coordinated (both with one another and with the contemporaneous work of the Criminal Law Revision Committee), will undoubtedly ease the work of codification, for which the elimination of the remaining common-law offenses and the statutory statement of the general part of the criminal law are essential prerequisites. In 1981, in order to give fresh impetus to its codification program, the Law Commission appointed a team of four academic lawyers "(1) to consider and make proposals in relation to—(a) the aims and objects of a criminal code; (b) its nature and scope; (c) its content, structure and the interrelation of its parts; (d) the method and style of its drafting; and (2) to formulate, in a manner appropriate to such a code—(a) the general principles which should govern liability under it; (b) a standard terminology to be used in it; (c) the rules which should govern its interpretation" (*Sixteenth Annual Report*, 1980–1981, p. 4).

But for the foreseeable future, responsibility for considering proposals for criminal law reform in England (whether they emanate from pressure groups or are simply prompted by inconvenient or unjust decisions and practices of the courts) is likely to continue to be divided. The Criminal Law Revision Committee will concentrate on areas where forensic and law enforcement considerations are paramount. The Law Commission will concern itself with the general principles of liability, the less important common-law offenses, and codification, and ad hoc royal commissions and departmental committees will be appointed

when the issues are controversial and the government wishes to distance itself from them. Examples have been those that studied official secrets (1972), contempt of court (1974), abortion (1974), obscenity (1979), and pretrial criminal procedure (1981). There will certainly be more than enough work to keep everyone busy.

P. R. GLAZEBROOK

See also CRIMINAL LAW REFORM, *articles on* CURRENT ISSUES IN THE UNITED STATES *and* HISTORICAL DEVELOPMENT IN THE UNITED STATES.

BIBLIOGRAPHY

BLACKSTONE, WILLIAM. *Commentaries on the Laws of England* (1765–1769), vol. 4. Reprint. University of Chicago Press, 1979.

COKE, EDWARD. *The Third Part of the Institutes of the Laws of England: Concerning High Treason, and Other Pleas of the Crown, and Criminal Causes* (1641). London: E. & R. Brooke, 1797.

CORNISH, WILLIAM R. et al. *Crime and Law in Nineteenth Century Britain.* Introduction by P. Ford and G. Ford. Dublin: Irish University Press, 1978. Contains full bibliographic information concerning parliamentary and governmental reports and papers referred to in this article.

Criminal Law Revision Committee. *Reports.* London: Her Majesty's Stationery Office, 1959–1980. Fourteen reports were issued by the committee during this period; the most important of them are described in this article.

CROSS, RUPERT. "The Making of English Law: Macaulay." *Criminal Law Review* (1978): 519–528.

———. "The Making of English Law: Sir James Fitzjames Stephen." *Criminal Law Review* (1978): 652–661.

EDEN, WILLIAM. *Principles of Penal Law.* London: White, 1771.

FARRAR, JOHN J. *Law Reform and the Law Commission.* London: Sweet & Maxwell, 1974.

FRIEDLAND, M. L. "R. S. Wright's Model Criminal Code." *Oxford Journal of Legal Studies* 1 (1981): 307–346.

GARDINER, GERALD, and CURTIS-RALEIGH, NIGEL. "The Judicial Attitude to Penal Reform." *Law Quarterly Review* 65 (1949): 196–219.

GLAZEBROOK, P. R., ed. *Reshaping the Criminal Law: Essays in Honour of Glanville Williams.* London: Stevens, 1978. The essays by Cross, Hodgson, and Spencer are especially relevant.

HALE, MATTHEW. *The History of the Pleas of the Crown* (1685; first publication, 1736). 2 vols. Edited by W. A. Stokes and E. Ingersoll. Philadelphia: Small, 1847.

HAWKINS, WILLIAM. *Pleas of the Crown* (1716–1721). 8th ed. Edited by J. Curwood. London: Butterworth, 1824.

ILBERT, C. P. *Legislative Methods and Forms.* Oxford: Oxford University Press, Clarendon Press, 1901.

JUSTICE (Society). *Annual Report.* London: The Society, annually.

KADISH, SANFORD H. "Codifiers of the Criminal Law:

Wechsler's Predecessors." *Columbia Law Review* 78 (1978): 1098–1144.

Law Commission. *Annual Report.* London: Her Majesty's Stationery Office, annually.

PHILLIPSON, COLEMAN. *Three Criminal Law Reformers: Beccaria, Bentham, Romilly.* New York: Dutton, 1923.

RADZINOWICZ, LEON. *A History of English Criminal Law and Its Administration from 1750,* vols. 1 and 4. London: Stevens, 1948, 1968.

ROMILLY, SAMUEL. *Observations on the Criminal Law of England as It Relates to Capital Punishments, and on the Mode in Which It Is Administered.* 3d ed. London: Cadell & Davies, 1813.

STEPHEN, JAMES FITZJAMES. *A History of the Criminal Law of England,* vol. 3. London: Macmillan, 1883.

———. "Introduction." *A Digest of the Criminal Law (Crimes and Punishments).* London: Macmillan, 1877. This introduction is absent from later editions.

WILLIAMS, GLANVILLE. "The Reform of the Criminal Law and of Its Administration." *Journal of the Society of Public Teachers of Law* 4 (1958): 217–230.

———. "The Work of Criminal Law Reform." *Journal of the Society of Public Teachers of Law* 13 (1975): 183–198.

———, ed. *The Reform of the Law.* London: Gollancz, 1951.

3.
HISTORICAL DEVELOPMENT IN THE UNITED STATES

Introduction

It is an incontrovertible fact that the law of crimes has historically suffered from a kind of malign neglect in America. In other branches of the law, from the beginning there has been a tradition of willingness, if not eagerness, on the part of judges, legislators, and legal commentators to examine basic premises and to promote doctrinal change if they thought society required it. But the dominant attitude of the American legal profession toward the penal law seems in general to have been that if it needed improvement, it would somehow improve itself. It is not surprising, therefore, that the criminal law long remained one of the least developed, most confused, and, in a sense, most primitive bodies of American law.

There are, to be sure, several significant exceptions to this general rule of neglect. From time to time in American history there have been bursts of interest in criminal jurisprudence, and reformers have arisen who have sought in one way or another to humanize the criminal law, to modernize it, or perhaps only to introduce a measure of clarity into it. These efforts have varied enormously in inspiration, in scope, and in caliber, and they have had varying impacts on the

course of legal developments. But they have all represented a recognition of the crucial importance of the law of crimes and a readiness to come to grips with at least some of its inherent problems. As such, they stand out as bright landmarks in what is otherwise a rather gray landscape.

This article surveys the checkered history of criminal law reform in America. The principal emphasis is on the substantive penal law, by which is meant also the law governing the treatment of criminal offenders. However, there are some observations as well on attempts that have been made to reform criminal procedure and the administration of justice.

The colonial period

The New England colonies. It is appropriate to begin a discussion of the history of criminal law reform with the colonial period since that era witnessed the first efforts at improvement. All of the American colonies drew principally on the jurisprudence and laws of the mother country in fashioning their criminal law. Obviously, small bands of colonial settlers, few of them with any legal training, do not fabricate criminal codes out of nothing, but from the beginning, the colonists displayed a willingness to experiment with alterations in the English inheritance if their own values seemed to call for them. In the very first body of laws promulgated in British North America, the Plymouth Code of 1636, a notable divergence from the English model in the punishment of serious crimes was already apparent. Although the list of capital offenses in England was long and comprehended almost all serious misdeeds, the death penalty in Plymouth was limited to treason, murder, arson, and several morals offenses. One should not attach too much importance to this document, since it was a rudimentary code of laws in many respects and Plymouth was a tiny settlement that was destined soon to fade into insignificance. Still, its modifications in the criminal law signaled a trend that was later to be followed by other colonies.

A much more sophisticated document than the Plymouth Code, *The Laws and Liberties of Massachusetts* (1648), embodied in addition major changes in the common and statutory criminal law of the mother country. It, too, reduced the number of capital offenses, and in general prescribed more lenient penalties for noncapital offenses than did English law. Its general prohibition against "cruel and barbarous" punishments was itself an innovation. The inspiration for the whole code came as much from the Old Testament as from the English common law. Deuteronomy and other parts of the Pentateuch were repeatedly cited in justification of penal provisions, and this reliance on the Bible had the net effect of making the code less sanguinary than it might have been. Only those offenses for which Scripture clearly prescribed death were made capital offenses. The code included several significant improvements in criminal procedure as well. Conviction of a capital crime required the testimony of two witnesses (this requirement, too, was rooted in Scripture), and appeal was a matter of right in all capital cases.

Besides the inspiration of Scripture, *The Laws and Liberties of Massachusetts* was pervaded by a spirit of rationality and a healthy distaste for the many accidental features of English criminal jurisprudence. The device of benefit of clergy, for example, was perceived—accurately—as a result of historical accident, having no foundation in Scripture or reason, and as such was excluded from the code.

The significance of these New England criminal codes, especially that of Massachusetts Bay, lies as much in the fact that they were codes as it does in the modifications which they made in individual provisions of English penal law. Underlying the codes was the strong belief that the criminal law of a community was too important to be allowed to grow up piecemeal, as, in the opinion of many of these Puritan settlers, had been the case with the English common law. Rather, it was something that ought to be crafted systematically and with deliberation to reflect the deepest moral sense of the community and to further the social purposes for which the community existed. This insight was unfortunately lost sight of in later years.

The Pennsylvania experiment. Although the criminal law of the American colonies was in general less sanguinary than that of the mother country, it was certainly no less retributive, and was very harsh by any modern standards. Crime and sin were virtually identical in the colonial mind. The criminal was seen as a free moral agent, and punishment was justified as a kind of social revenge or a species of divinely ordained, if humanly implemented, retribution. Schedules of punishments were little more than crude attempts to proportion the penalty to the sinfulness of the offense, and virtually no attention was paid to the individual circumstances of the offender. Exhibiting a very different spirit, however, were the penal laws enacted by Pennsylvania colony in the closing decades of the seventeenth century. There, between 1682 and 1718, a most remarkable experiment in criminal law reform was undertaken under the aegis of William Penn and other Quaker notables. Although

it came to an unhappy end, it planted seeds that were later to bear fruit.

One year after it was established by William Penn under a royal charter, Pennsylvania enacted a complete code of criminal laws—part of a larger codification known as the Great Law of 1682—that was quite unlike anything that had gone before it. The Quaker founders of the colony were opposed in principle to cruelty, to gratuitous bloodshed, and, barring the most unusual conditions, to the taking of human life. They were repelled by the existing English system of penal sanctions and felt compelled to look for alternatives. The alternative they found was the prison. In their code, imprisonment at hard labor or imprisonment coupled with a fine was the prescribed penalty for all crimes save willful and premeditated murder, the length of imprisonment varying according to the offense and the circumstances surrounding its commission. The terms of confinement were in general not severe. Thus, burglary was punishable by three months' imprisonment and quadruple restitution to the victim. Arson merited a year at hard labor and corporal punishment (usually whipping) according to the discretion of the court. Assault on a magistrate was punishable by a month's confinement. Common assault and battery, as well as manslaughter, were to be punished according to the nature and circumstances of the acts in question. In contrast to the rather mild sanctions accruing to these crimes, sex offenses were sternly dealt with in the Quaker code. Bigamy, for example, was punishable by life imprisonment upon first commission, and rape, upon second conviction.

Another remarkable feature of the Pennsylvania code was its approach to religious offenses—a popular category of offense in the criminal law of most jurisdictions. These kinds of crimes were completely abolished, and full freedom of conscience was assured to all inhabitants.

The Pennsylvania code of 1682 represented Quaker criminal jurisprudence at its purest. In the next three decades the colony's criminal law was modified by a series of legislative enactments and became somewhat severer. More offenses were made punishable by imprisonment, prison terms became longer, and harsh corporal punishments such as branding were introduced for certain crimes. Yet even after these alterations, Pennsylvania's criminal law remained a model of enlightenment and humanity in comparison with that of its neighbors. In 1718, however, the Quaker experiment came to an abrupt end. The colony had for some time been pressing the Crown to allow Quakers to testify on affirmation rather than on oath, and the Crown had been seeking to bring the colony's criminal law into closer conformity with that of the mother country. A bargain was struck under which Quakers received recognition for affirmation in exchange for the colony's agreement to substitute the English criminal law for its own.

The Revolution and its aftermath

The American Revolution stimulated several forays in the direction of criminal law reform, all of them interesting for the new attitudes toward punishment that they revealed, although only one produced any long-term results. In the aftermath of the break with Great Britain, the newly independent colonies all faced the question of how much of the mother country's law they wished to retain. Some patriots urged that American criminal law was in particular need of change. Its harsh provisions, they argued, reflected a British rather than an American ethos. These arguments struck a responsive chord in certain state capitals. In New Hampshire, the first state constitution (promulgated in 1784) exhorted the legislature to do something about the sanguinary penal laws with which the state was saddled. It opined that it was not wise to affix the same punishment to crimes as diverse as forgery and murder, "the true design of all punishments being to reform, not to exterminate, mankind" (art. 1, § 18). Regrettably, the legislature refused to respond to the invitation, and the state's penal law changed in no significant respect. There were parallel developments in Virginia.

Jefferson's proposed reform of the penal law of Virginia. A few weeks after the signing of the Declaration of Independence, the General Assembly of Virginia passed An act for the revision of the Laws (ch. 9 (1776), Hening's Virginia Statutes at Large 175 (Richmond, Va., 1821)), with a view to bringing the state's laws into greater harmony with the spirit of republicanism. The committee that was entrusted with the task of revision included George Mason and Thomas Jefferson. As part of the revision effort, Jefferson prepared a draft of a bill for a new system of criminal sanctions. This draft was the product of an exhaustive survey of theoretical writings on punishment and on the history of the treatment of criminal offenders from ancient to modern times. The footnoted version of the bill that appears in Jefferson's papers includes citations, in the original language, from the laws of the Anglo-Saxons. It is widely regarded as a model of literary draftsmanship (Boyd, p. 594).

Among the theorists Jefferson read, none had so great an impact on him as the great Italian criminologist Cesare Beccaria, whose essay *On Crimes and Punishments* (1764) was stimulating lively discussion in educated colonial circles. Beccaria urged a thoroughly utilitarian approach to the criminal law, and the influence of his ideals permeated the whole of Jefferson's penology. Jefferson's guiding principles were (1) that the only goal of the penal law was the deterrence of crime; (2) that sanguinary laws were self-defeating because men recoiled at the idea of enforcing them to the full and thus left many crimes unpunished; (3) that if punishments were proportioned to the crime, men would be more likely to see that the laws were observed; and (4) that the reform of criminals was an object worthy of the law's promotion. Finally, Jefferson's criminal jurisprudence reflected a fascination for the theory of analogical punishments, which stated that punishments ought to be symbolic reflections of the offenses to which they were affixed, so that crimes and their consequences would be inextricably linked in the minds of citizens. This curious theory had first been suggested by Beccaria and had an enormous impact on the course of penological thought in the late eighteenth and early nineteenth centuries.

These principles combined to produce a proposed system of punishments that in general was mild and enlightened but that was marred by some rather bizarre features. Jefferson cut drastically the long catalogue of offenses punishable by death under the prevailing law, limiting them to treason and murder, and prescribed much milder sanctions for most of these traditionally capital crimes. But the penalties designated for some offenses had, because of what might almost be called an obsession with analogy and proportionality, a somewhat ghoulish hue. Thus, the punishment for treason was burial alive. Murder by poison was punished by poisoning, rape by castration, and mayhem by maiming the offender. Jefferson's proposals were seriously debated in the Virginia legislature but eventually were defeated.

Pennsylvania and the degrees of murder. The first state in which the new advocates of penal law reform were able to translate theory into reality was Pennsylvania, which had earlier experimented with large-scale changes in its penal regime. The ground may have been rendered even more fertile by the fact that during the Revolution many Pennsylvania political offices fell into the hands of a coalition of populist farmers and Philadelphia radicals. In any event, in 1776 the state approved a constitution that included provisions concerning the reform of the criminal law very similar to those later included in the New Hampshire Constitution of 1784. (New Hampshire may well have taken some of its language from the Pennsylvania document.) The difference was that Pennsylvania commanded, rather than exhorted, its legislature to reform the penal laws of the state and to make punishments more proportional to crimes. Echoing a favorite theme of the new generation of reformers, the constitution also articulated the view that crime was more effectively deterred by visible punishments of long duration—that is, by imprisonment—than by intense, bloody, but brief sanctions (Pa. Const. of 1776, §§ 38–39).

The first step toward the reform of the penal law was taken by the Pennsylvania legislature ten years later, when it eliminated the death penalty for robbery, burglary, and sodomy (Act of Sept. 15, 1786). In 1791 a statute was passed abolishing capital punishment for witchcraft and ending the barbarous practice of branding for adultery and fornication (Act of Sept. 23, 1791, §§ 5, 8). Notwithstanding these developments, there were signs in the early 1790s that the momentum which had been generated during the Revolution in favor of fundamental and wide-scale reform of the criminal law was beginning to slow down. For example, a new Pennsylvania constitution, promulgated in 1790, failed even to mention the subject. Perhaps with this in mind, a number of very eminent Pennsylvanians began now to speak out publicly and vigorously on behalf of the reformist cause.

In 1790, James Wilson, the first professor of law at the University of Pennsylvania, a signer of the Declaration of Independence, and a co-drafter of the United States Constitution, delivered a series of lectures in Philadelphia on crime and punishment. Citing with approval the views of Beccaria and that other great eighteenth-century legal theorist, Montesquieu, Wilson argued forcefully that prevention was the sole end of punishment and that anything more severe than the minimum punishment necessary to deter crime ill became a civilized nation. In 1792, Benjamin Rush, professor of medicine at the same university, published a widely disseminated essay entitled "Considerations on the Injustice and Impolicy of Punishing Murder by Death," in which he argued that capital punishment was "contrary to reason and to the order and happiness of society." That same year, William Bradford, justice of the Pennsylvania Supreme Court, entered the fray. In a report on the death penalty as a deterrent to crime, prepared at the instance of Governor Thomas Mifflin, Bradford argued that the supreme penalty was totally unnecessary and adduced statistics to show that the penalty of imprisonment, provided by the act of 1786, had proved just as effective in deterring burglary, robbery, and sodomy as had the earlier punishment of death.

Governor Mifflin, taking his cue from Bradford's memorandum, proposed to the Pennsylvania legislature that further mitigations in the penal regime seemed warranted and urged it to consider implementing additional reforms. The legislature's response was ambivalent. It was quite unwilling to go the full distance down the path that Bradford, Wilson, and others were urging it to go, but it did agree that the punishment of death ought to be inflicted only when it was absolutely necessary to ensure the public safety. In light of this philosophy, it prepared a bill that for the first time in Anglo-American legal history divided the crime of murder into two degrees. The first degree, punishable by death, referred to homicides perpetrated by lying in wait or by poison, or to any other kind of willful, deliberate, and premeditated killing. (There were echoes here of the act of 1682.) All other kinds of murder were classified as murder in the second degree, punishable by imprisonment at hard labor or in solitary confinement or both for a term not to exceed twenty-one years. This bill was duly passed by the legislature in 1794 with the addition of felony murder to the category of the first degree (Act of April 22, 1794, § 2).

The division of murder into two degrees proved to be Pennsylvania's most lasting contribution to the general criminal jurisprudence of the United States. In 1796, Virginia enacted a similar law, to be followed in 1824 by Ohio, in 1835 by Missouri, in 1846 by Michigan, and eventually by the vast majority of American jurisdictions.

The antebellum period

The passage of the statute on the degrees of murder took much of the wind out of the sails of the Pennsylvania movement for the complete abolition of capital punishment. The movement remained quiescent for several decades but was to revive again in the 1820s as part of a larger anti-capital-punishment crusade that flourished on the national scene roughly between 1820 and 1850. This discussion will be resumed below, but attention must now be shifted to the state of Louisiana and to the work of the most fertile and imaginative of all nineteenth-century penal law reformers, Edward Livingston.

Livingston. Edward Livingston (1764–1836), born in New York State, had a distinguished political career before turning to the work of criminal law reform. He served as a member of the House of Representatives, as United States attorney, and finally as mayor of New York City. Livingston left New York in 1804 and moved to New Orleans, where he opened a law practice and quickly became involved in Louisiana politics. At the same time he continued to cultivate a long-standing interest in jurisprudence and the reform of the law.

In 1820, Livingston was elected to the Louisiana legislature and in the same year was instrumental in the passing of an act that authorized the preparation of a code of criminal law "founded on one principle, viz., the prevention of crime" (Livingston, vol. 1, pp. 1–2). The following year, he was appointed to direct the effort.

Livingston read all the available materials on criminal jurisprudence and conducted a wide correspondence with jurists and legal practitioners in other states and abroad in order to draw on their ideas and experience. In 1826, he finally laid before the General Assembly of the state of Louisiana a finished product.

The Livingston Code consisted of four separate parts: a code of crimes and punishments, a code of procedure, a code of evidence, and a code of reform and prison discipline. Each code was accompanied by an introductory report that described its background and explained its underlying philosophy. There were in addition two lengthy reports in which Livingston set forth his general views on criminal jurisprudence. In one of them he made it clear that he thought his code to be the first real attempt, at least in the Anglo-American world, to place the criminal law on a sound, scientific basis. He compared the previous criminal law to pieces of fretwork, the product of caprice, fear, and carelessness, which by reason of cruel or disproportionate punishment and inconsistent provisions endangered the lives and liberties of the people (Livingston, vol. 1, p. 11).

The theorist to whom Livingston owed his greatest intellectual debt—one he freely acknowledged—was the English utilitarian philosopher Jeremy Bentham, and the whole structure of the code rests solidly on Benthamite principles. There is first a commitment to the principle that the content of the laws should be fully accessible to all educated citizens. "Penal laws should be written in plain language, clearly and unequivocally expressed, that they may neither be misunderstood nor perverted," Livingston wrote (vol. 1, p. 5). It is remarkable how little of that technical jargon of which lawyers are so fond appears in the code. It is one of the few pieces of legislation of which it can truly be said that it is a delight to read.

Consistent with Benthamite philosophy, the code is also permeated with a deep distrust of judges and a thorough aversion to any species of judicial lawmaking. The code of crimes and punishments forbade the punishment of any acts not expressly made criminal by statute, and judges were forbidden to punish anything not made criminal by the letter of the law under the pretense that the act in question came within the law's spirit (vol. 2, p. 15). Livingston wished to leave no room for judges to infuse their own moral beliefs into the penal law.

Finally, again in the interest of the involvement of the ordinary citizen in the law's process, the code sought to make transparent the rationale for its specific provisions. Thus, individual prohibitions on types of conduct were often accompanied by illustrations and by explanations why they had been included. It was Livingston's view that if people saw that the laws were rational and were framed on the great principle of utility, they would be more disposed to obey them.

Livingston's code in general represented a major consolidation and clarification of the existing penal laws and the pruning away of much of its weedlike overgrowth; he believed firmly that there were too many crimes and that the criminal sanction was most unwisely used when the civil sanction would suffice. In addition, however, many particular substantive provisions of the code were quite innovative. This was especially true in the areas of civil liberties and of privacy. To open a letter addressed to another was made criminal (vol. 2, p. 166), and it was a misdemeanor to interfere with the exercise of anyone's right of free speech or free assembly (vol. 2, p. 69). Homosexuality was removed from the list of criminal offenses on the grounds that to describe such offenses in a code was potentially corrupting to youthful readers and, further, that making sexual deviance criminal was an invitation to blackmail (vol. 1, p. 27).

Of all the innovations in Livingston's code, the most striking was the abolition of the death penalty (vol. 1, pp. 185–224). Livingston devoted a large part of his "Introductory Report to the Code of Crimes and Punishments" to a defense of this proposal. His chief argument was that the state was justified in taking life only if it could demonstrate that this was absolutely necessary. But, he averred, it could be shown by logic and by experience that lesser penalties would suffice for the prevention of great crimes. He also pointed to the corrupting effect that public executions had on social morals, to the not infrequent instances of courts incorrectly convicting defendants, and to the impossibility of remedying these errors under a system that allowed capital punishment. In a part of his discussion that has been relatively unnoticed by commentators, Livingston also argued that capital punishment was insufficient for the deterrence of serious offenses. The fear of death was simply not enough to offset in the minds of potential offenders the powerful passions that drove them to commit their crimes. The rapacious spendthrift, he suggested, might risk the momentary, if intense, pain of death to promote his interest in a life of idleness and debauchery, whereas the prospect of a life spent under a hard prison regime might be sufficient to cool his thievish instincts (vol. 1, pp. 37–40).

The system that Livingston wished to introduce for the treatment of social deviance had never been proposed before. He recognized that conditions of poverty and idleness led to crime, and so his code of reform and prison discipline provided for a house of refuge, which would give employment to those who could not find work, and a house of industry for those who refused to work in the house of refuge. The latter institution would also offer employment to recently discharged convicts. For the treatment of genuinely criminal offenses he offered an exquisitely gradated schedule of penalties, ranging from fines to imprisonment. The conditions of imprisonment were themselves graded according to the nature of the offense. The purpose of imprisonment was both to rehabilitate the offender and to deter crime by means of example.

Livingston's code of reform and prison discipline was in most respects far in advance of its time. It forbade any mistreatment of inmates and prescribed that they be adequately clothed and fed. It also prescribed strict standards of training and behavior for prison personnel. But it had its less pleasing side as well, incorporating as it did rather crude techniques of psychological manipulation, both of the offender and of the members of the public who were to be deterred by his example. Murderers, for example, were for the remainder of their lives to have no contact with persons from the outside world other than official visitors, and little contact with their fellow prisoners. Their cell walls were to be painted black, and on the outside of the cells an inscription was to be hung affirming that the inhabitants were dead in all but body; their bodily existence was being prolonged solely in order that they might remember their crimes and repent of them, and in order that their tribulations might serve as an example to others (vol. 2, p. 573).

Livingston argued passionately in the legislature for the adoption of his penal law, but it was not to the liking of that body and was never enacted. It was,

in retrospect, an odd growth in the regressive, slaveholding society that was antebellum Louisiana.

The movement to abolish the death penalty. As noted earlier, a movement to abolish capital punishment came to life and flourished on the national scene in the second half of the antebellum period. Beginning in New England and in Pennsylvania, it spread quickly to other states and soon comprised a national constituency. By the 1840s there were well-organized anti–capital punishment societies in eleven states, and in 1845 a national society was launched with George Dallas, the vice-president of the United States, as its first president. Quakers and others who opposed the death penalty on grounds of Christian humanitarianism were in the forefront of the movement, but also prominent were those who took their inspiration from the tradition of enlightened rationalism and utilitarianism. These opponents, many of them lawyers, often drew on the penological theories of Edward Livingston in making their arguments.

The advocates were called abolitionists—a well-chosen word, for there was significant overlap between the antislavery crusade and the death-penalty movement. Wendell Phillips, for example, was one of the founders of the Massachusetts society. The abolitionists were especially active on the floors of state legislatures. Their strategy was usually to engineer inquiries by legislative or outside consultative committees into the efficacy and necessity of capital punishment. These inquiries led to varying results.

In 1836, Governor Edward Everett of Massachusetts appointed a committee headed by Robert Rantoul, the great Jacksonian lawyer and advocate of codification, to look into the question of whether capital punishment might be eliminated for all crimes save murder. The committee issued a report that quickly became a classic in the movement, intermixing utilitarian arguments with appeals to Scripture in calling for abolition. Rantoul did not persuade the legislature to adopt his views, but in 1839 the body did abolish the death penalty for burglary and highway robbery (Act of April 8, 1839). In New York, too, there was legislative agitation for reform.

Abolition of the death penalty repeatedly came up for debate on the floor of the New York Assembly during the 1830s and was the subject of several committee inquiries during that decade. Occasionally the results of these deliberations proved disappointing to the antagonists of capital punishment. Thus, in 1838 an assembly committee rejected the Livingstonian argument that prison was a more effective deterrent than death, contending instead that since most criminals were paupers, the prospect of free lodging and board in prison would be positively attractive to them.

The most signal success of the anti–capital punishment movement occurred in 1846, when the Michigan legislature voted to abandon the death penalty for all crimes except treason (Mich. Rev. Stat. tit. 30, chs. 152–153, 658 (1846)). Rhode Island followed suit in 1852, and Wisconsin, in 1853. The movement crested with these events, however, and then began to lose vigor. By the eve of the Civil War it had ceased to have much impact on the national consciousness.

Much later, during the Progressive Era, the anti–capital punishment movement enjoyed a brief renascence, and a half-dozen states were persuaded to abolish the death penalty. Some of these triumphs were short-lived, however, as popular pressure forced most of these states to reintroduce the death penalty within a few years of abolition.

The postbellum period

The second half of the nineteenth century was not marked by any great ferment in the field of substantive penal law reform. American lawyers and legislators were by and large preoccupied with other matters during this era of industrialization and commercial expansion. One notable exception to the rule, however, was the effort mounted in New York and presided over by David Dudley Field to completely reshape the state's criminal law.

Field's reforms in New York State. David Dudley Field (1805–1894) was one of the towering figures of the nineteenth-century American bar, and by the Civil War he had become the leading advocate of codification in the United States. His efforts on behalf of penal-law reform were part of his larger codification project. In 1846 a New York constitutional convention, convoked in large measure because of successful lobbying by Field and other Jacksonian Democrats, passed a resolution directing the New York legislature to reduce into a written and systematic code the whole body of the state's laws. A pathbreaking code of civil procedure was prepared by Field and other members of a specially appointed commission and enacted by the New York legislature before the Civil War (1849 N.Y. Laws, ch. 438), but work on the other codes was not to be completed until after the war.

In 1857 a new commission, with Field again a member, was established and given the responsibility of preparing a civil code, a political code, and a penal code. Field played a predominant role in drafting the first two documents, but he had no professional or scholarly expertise in the criminal law, and the bulk of the work on the last code, which was presented to the New York legislature in 1865, was done by Field's two co-commissioners, Curtis Noyes and B. V. Abbot. Nonetheless, Field participated in the drafting to a limited extent, and, inasmuch as he was the guiding spirit behind the whole New York codification effort, it is fitting that the penal code, like all the other New York codes, has always borne his name.

The stated objectives of the drafters of the Field Penal Code were, first, to bring within the compass of a single volume the whole body of the state's criminal law. The drafters noted that the state's penal provisions were scattered helter-skelter through the collected statutes and that many acts were criminal by virtue of judicial decision only; if made criminal by statute, they could be defined solely by recourse to common-law decisions. All this, they said, caused uncertainty to pervade New York's criminal jurisprudence. Second, the drafters intended to rectify deficiencies and correct errors in existing definitions of crimes. Third, they aimed to eliminate inequalities and disparities in punishments, and finally, they wished to criminalize acts that should be criminal but were not (New York State Commissioners of the Code, pp. iii–vi).

It was a comprehensive and bold agenda, and there seemed instinct in it at least the possibility of a searching, critical reexamination of the fundamental principles of American criminal jurisprudence, a task that had not been undertaken by anyone save Livingston. But the finished product that the commissioners delivered was in this respect a profoundly disappointing document. Field and his colleagues seem to have felt that their reform agenda was completed when the scattered parts of the state's penal law had been pulled together and a semblance of order introduced into this collection of provisions. Nowhere in the document is there any evidence of a desire to clarify or reformulate any of the confused or archaic common-law concepts that lay at the base of Anglo-American criminal law, or to simplify or consolidate the enormous corpus of statutory crimes and regulatory offenses that had been added to the state's criminal law since the Revolution. This "reformist" code thus left the status quo quite unaltered.

What the Field Code did achieve in full was its objective of bringing all of the criminal law within the compass of a single volume. Every instance in which criminal penalties were imposed for any action was included in the code's provisions. Nothing was left outside, nor was there any attempt to consolidate. Thus there are separate, specific provisions on "the refilling of mineral bottles" (§ 417), on "omitting to mark packages of hay" (§ 449), and on "throwing gas tar into public waters" (§ 434). Four kinds of arson are described, ranging from maliciously burning an inhabited building at night to burning an uninhabited building in the daytime—each covered by a separate provision (§§ 531–539). In perhaps the most ludicrous example of overspecificity, separate provisions cover, respectively, malicious mischief to railroads, to public highways or bridges, to toll houses or turnpikes, to mile markers and guideposts, and to telegraph lines (§§ 690–695).

Notwithstanding these limitations, the Field Code proved extremely popular. It was eventually enacted by the New York legislature in 1881 (1881 N.Y. Laws, ch. 676), it was adopted almost in its entirety by California and the Dakotas, and it had significant influence on the penal law of several other western states, including Arizona, Idaho, Montana, Oregon, Utah, and Wyoming.

Progressivism and its fruits

In the last decade of the nineteenth century and the first decades of the twentieth, a dynamic, complex social reform movement known as Progressivism swept through the middle and upper sectors of American society. The Progressives were a varied lot, and they had a varied political and social agenda. But among their chief aims were the elimination of corruption from politics, the introduction of efficiency and scientific technique into the governmental process, the uplifting of the underprivileged, and the assimilation into society's mainstream of the immigrant masses who were then pouring into the United States in record numbers. The whole Progressive program rested solidly on two fundamental principles: faith in the perfectability of man, and implicit trust in the state's ability to promote individual well-being. The major reforms in the treatment of criminal offenders—probation, parole, and the juvenile court—that were either introduced or came into vogue during this era may be seen as manifestations of the Progressive spirit.

Probation. Probation, whose philosophy is that at least some criminal offenders are more likely to be rehabilitated by being placed in the community under the supervision of a trained official than by being incarcerated, is an American invention and has its origins in the work done in Boston in the 1840s and 1850s by the shoemaker John Augustus. With the permission of the courts, Augustus had for almost two decades taken into his care persons convicted of (usually minor) criminal offenses, with a view to rehabilitating them. Augustus accumulated a rather impressive record, but his arrangement with the Boston courts remained entirely informal, and his example inspired no imitators elsewhere. The modern system of probation dates in actuality from 1878, when Massachusetts enacted a statute authorizing the mayor of Boston to appoint a paid probation officer, and in 1880 this authority was extended to all cities and towns in the state (Mass. Probation Act of 1880, 1880 Mass. Acts, ch. 129). Other states toyed with the idea of introducing similar reforms but hesitated because of doubts about the constitutional propriety of the scheme. For many, this cloud was removed in 1894 when the highest court of New York ruled that a state law authorizing judges to suspend sentence, a necessary prerequisite to any system of probation, was not an unconstitutional infringement on the executive power of pardon (*People ex rel. Forsyth v. Court of Sessions*, 141 N.Y. 288, 36 N.E. 386 (1894)). Between 1900 and 1905, twelve states adopted probation for juvenile offenders; the number grew to twenty-three by 1911. By 1925, all forty-eight states permitted the probation of juveniles. Adult probation proceeded at a somewhat slower pace, but it too made steady strides during the Progressive Era.

Parole. Probation emphasized the individualized treatment of the malefactor by professionals: criminals were now seen as ill and in need of therapy, rather than as evil and deserving of retribution. As such, it was in harmony with the deep-seated Progressive belief in the educability of all through the use of scientific method. The same was true of parole. Parole and the other reform with which it usually went hand in hand—the indeterminate sentence—were first implemented in New York's Elmira Reformatory, which began admitting youthful offenders in 1877. The reformatory was to detain its inmates so long as was necessary to rehabilitate them, and then was to turn them over to trained professionals for further noncustodial supervision or treatment in the outside world. New York passed a general indeterminate sentencing law in 1889 (1889 N.Y. Laws, ch. 382, § 74), and by 1891 eight other states had enacted some form of indeterminate-sentence or parole legislation.

The juvenile court. Of all the criminal justice reforms promoted by progressives, the most emblematic was the juvenile court. Progressivism was a child-centered movement, and child welfare was a major focus of Progressive activity. Before the advent of juvenile court, jurisdictions had often devised ways of sparing youthful offenders the full rigors of the legal process, but, as has been pointed out, what was missing was the conception that a young person who ran afoul of the law was to be dealt with *from the outset* "not as a criminal, but as a person needing care, education and protection" (Warner and Cabot, p. 600). During the 1890s a wide spectrum of enlightened professionals, including members of the bar and representatives of the emerging behavioral sciences, pressed for the removal of juvenile offenders from the adult criminal process and the introduction of a separate system for their treatment. Illinois was the first state to respond favorably to these appeals, in 1899 enacting a law that created a juvenile court for Chicago (1899 Ill. Laws, ch. 131). The statute had been drafted by a committee of the Chicago Bar Association, and it established the court essentially as a court of equity with corresponding administrative powers. The plan was that the court should, when circumstances so warranted, assume guardianship over wayward or neglected youths with a view to giving them the care, custody, and discipline that a good parent would give his own children. The court, in sum, was to be thrust into the role of *parens patriae*, a role not unknown to equity courts. The juvenile court was to operate under relatively relaxed, nonadversarial procedures, with the role of counsel reduced, and its role was to be seen as remedial rather than punitive. The question before the court would not be whether the accused juvenile was guilty of a crime, but whether he was "delinquent" and thus in need of the state's care and education.

After the passage of the Illinois statute, the juvenile court movement acquired some of the features of a crusade. Proponents of the reform pushed vigorously in other states for its adoption. In addition to theoretical arguments, they now had a practical example to offer in support of their proposals, and in the personnel of the Chicago juvenile court they found eager and willing allies. For example, Timothy Hurley, the court's chief administrator, published the monthly *Juvenile Court Record*, which detailed the success of his institution and recorded the progress of the movement. The proponents encountered little or no opposition, and state after state rushed to imitate the Chicago model. To be sure, a few did raise the question of whether the loose, informal procedure that characterized juvenile court, and the immense discretion of the juvenile magistrate, adequately protected youths from arbitrary deprivation of liberty. But these voices were drowned out by the rising chorus of approbation. By 1920, all but three states had created juvenile courts.

Twentieth-century developments

By the 1920s, attention had shifted from improving the techniques of rehabilitating the individual offender to the control of criminal behavior in the aggregate. This was the period of the great national experiment of Prohibition, with its attendant rise in illegalities of all sorts. Citizens across the land, but especially in large cities, became increasingly agitated at what they perceived to be an alarming increase in crime and the seeming inability of the criminal justice system to deal with it. Some charged that the corruption of government officials by the criminal element was the root cause of the problem—and indeed, there were many instances of political corruption during the period. Others insisted that the system of criminal justice was itself at fault and was desperately in need of overhaul. There was a widespread demand for some kind of action.

The Cleveland survey. The city of Cleveland was the first to attempt to address the problem in systematic fashion. It had for several years been suffering from a rising crime rate, and a pall of distrust hung over the municipal criminal justice apparatus. Matters came to a head in the spring of 1920, when the chief judge of the city's municipal court was forced to resign because of complicity in an atrocious crime. A number of civic organizations, headed by the Cleveland bar, persuaded the Cleveland Foundation, a private philanthropic organization, to sponsor a survey of criminal justice in the city. A staff of investigators headed by Roscoe Pound, then dean of the Harvard Law School, and by Felix Frankfurter of the Harvard law faculty, was assembled. After two years of empirical observation and the accumulation of masses of statistics, they delivered a lengthy report on the criminal justice process in Cleveland. It was the most comprehensive, detailed, and accurate portrait of the problems of urban law enforcement that had ever been produced. Every nook and cranny of the machinery of criminal justice was explored, from police administration to the criminal courts and the city's correctional facilities. There was even a section on legal education in Cleveland and its impact on the criminal justice process.

The report highlighted many flaws in the existing machinery of criminal justice and made recommendations for change. However, these recommendations were ameliorative rather than revolutionary. The report proposed no radical redesign of the existing system, but rather the streamlining and modernization of its operation. The emphasis was on the introduction of greater efficiency into all phases of the criminal justice process. Much space was devoted, for example, to explaining how prosecutorial staffs and courts could process more smoothly and expeditiously the large criminal case loads with which they were confronted. The report also emphasized the need for the full professionalization of criminal justice staffs and for the elevation of the status of the criminal law practitioner.

The example of the Cleveland crime survey stimulated the establishment in other jurisdictions of crime commissions charged with similar responsibilities. Georgia in 1924, Minnesota and Missouri in 1926, Memphis in 1928, and Illinois and New York State in 1929 all launched investigations of their own into the conditions of local law enforcement. However, they were in general pale imitations of the original.

The Wickersham Commission. At this time, the national government itself decided to enter the picture. In 1929, President Herbert Hoover appointed the National Commission of Law Observance and Enforcement, under the chairmanship of United States Attorney General George Wickersham. The Wickersham Commission, as it came to be known, was originally charged only with the responsibility of looking into problems of law enforcement under the Eighteenth Amendment, but it soon expanded its scope to include the entire field of criminal justice. Over the next two years it undertook a sweeping investigation into crime and law enforcement in America and published fourteen volumes of reports on all phases of the process. Its findings and recommendations in many ways paralleled those of the Cleveland survey, but it broke important new ground as well. Its report on police practices, for example, exposed patterns of police abuse of suspects and stressed the need for the elimination of these practices. An entire volume, *The Causes of Crime*, took a broad sociological view of criminal behavior and suggested methods for attacking the conditions that, according to the commission, bred crime.

The focus of the great crime surveys of the 1920s was almost entirely procedural, but Pound, the guiding spirit of the Cleveland survey, had on several occasions pointed to the enormous inconsistencies and anachronisms embedded in the American substantive law of crimes and had emphasized how these stood in the way of erecting a truly modern and efficient system of criminal justice. The Wickersham Commission as well called attention to the deplorable, chaotic state of the federal substantive criminal law. Furthermore, ever since the turn of the century and continuing into the 1920s, scholars in criminal law, in the behavioral sciences, and in the nascent field of crimi-

nology had been leveling broadsides at the theoretical foundations of the criminal law. They challenged the scientific soundness of such fundamental notions as "criminal intent," "deliberation," and "premeditation," and questioned the purpose served by the subtle and often bizarre definitional distinctions that had grown up over the centuries in the common law of crimes.

To be sure, some of these critiques were seriously marred by a naive determinism—a few went so far as to say that science had totally vitiated the concept of free will or was on the verge of identifying the biological and psychological types that inevitably led to criminal behavior. But the majority were far more subtle and tentative, and there can be no caviling with the point, made by all, that there was much that was amiss in the existing criminal law.

The Model Penal Code. The American Law Institute, an organization of lawyers, judges, and legal scholars, was founded in 1923 for the purpose of clarifying and improving the law. One of the major causes that had led to its establishment was dissatisfaction with the state of the criminal law, and thus it is no surprise that criminal law reform occupied a high place on its agenda from the outset. However, it proved difficult to translate this concern into action. The institute was quick to decide that the method of restatement which seemed the appropriate way to proceed in other fields of law was inappropriate for the law of crime. As Herbert Wechsler, a leading theorist of penal jurisprudence, later explained, "The need . . . was less for a description and reaffirmation of existing law than for a guide to long delayed reform" (1974, p. 421). A proposal for a model penal code was advanced in 1931, but the project was large in scope, and the funding to carry it out was not forthcoming during the Depression years.

In 1950 the infusion of a large grant from the Rockefeller Foundation stirred the model penal code project to life again. An advisory committee, made up of distinguished scholars in the field of criminal law, was assembled by the American Law Institute. Wechsler was appointed chief reporter of the enterprise, and Louis Schwartz, another eminent authority in the field, was named co-reporter.

Early in the project's life, Wechsler made it clear that he and his colleagues were confronting a task of immense magnitude. In Wechsler's view, American society had entered the twentieth century without having ever rationally articulated "the law on which men placed their ultimate reliance for protection against all the deepest injuries that human conduct can inflict on individuals and institutions" (1974, p. 420). Instead, the penal law of the various states was a hopelessly disorganized and internally inconsistent mass of common and statute law—with the statutes often more important in their gloss than in their text—less the product of informed, deliberate choice than of accident, chance, and unreflecting imitation. As Wechsler put it, American penal law was "a combination of the old and the new that only history explains" (1955, p. 526).

From beginning to end, Wechsler was the code project's guiding spirit, and he deserves most of the credit for leading the enterprise to successful completion. But the drafting of the Model Penal Code was no solo performance by Wechsler. It was very much a collaborative effort, drawing on the talents of virtually the whole of the academic criminal law establishment, of a goodly number of judges, and of a handful of practitioners. It was also an effort that proceeded carefully and deliberately. The writing of the Code took ten years, from 1952 to 1962, during which time thirteen tentative drafts were circulated for general discussion and comment after debate in the project's advisory committee and on the floor of the American Law Institute.

In 1962 the institute's Proposed Official Draft of the Model Penal Code was promulgated, the greatest attempt since Livingston's time to put the house of penal jurisprudence into some kind of rational order. In truth, the Proposed Official Draft was in many respects a very Livingstonian document. This was seen particularly in its commitment to the principle that the sole purpose of the criminal law was the control of harmful conduct, and in its adherence to the notion that clarity of concept and expression were essential to that purpose's fulfillment. The draft was wholly lacking, however, in that ideological smugness and imperiousness which at times had tarnished the work of Livingston and of his mentor, Bentham. As befitted a product of the mid-twentieth-century American mind, the draft was suffused with a spirit of pragmatism, albeit a pragmatism tempered by principle.

The Code was divided into four parts: general provisions, definitions of specific crimes, treatment and correction, and organization of correction. Each contained significant innovations with respect to existing law. In keeping with the principle that the criminal law's only purpose was to deter blameworthy, harmful conduct, and the converse principle that faultless conduct should be shielded from punishment, new standards of criminal liability were established in the Code's general provisions. In the area of inchoate crimes, for example, the law of attempt was rewritten to sweep away all questions as to factual impossibility

and to focus attention on the actor's perception of the circumstances surrounding the commission of his act (§ 5.01). In conspiracy, on the other hand, the traditional common-law rule that made every member of the conspiracy liable for any reasonably foreseeable crime committed by any other member of the conspiracy was rejected. Instead, an accomplice's liability was limited to those crimes of the principal that the accomplice intended to assist or encourage (§ 5.03). Thus too, in the interest of protecting faultless conduct, the use of defensive force was declared justifiable in cases of apparent, as opposed to actual, necessity (§ 3.04). Reasonable mistake of fact was affirmed as a defense in crimes such as bigamy (§ 230.1). In addition, a limited defense of *ignorantia legis* was made available to defendants who harbored good faith beliefs regarding the innocence of their conduct as a result of reliance on official opinion or as a result of the unavailability to them of the enactment they were accused of violating (§§ 2.02, 2.04).

The most striking provisions in the Code's general part were those that sought to articulate a new definition of the mental element in crime. The common law used a bewildering variety of terms to designate the mental blameworthiness (mens rea) that had to be present if a person were to be convicted of a criminal offense. For this profusion of terms the Code drafters substituted four modes of acting with respect to the material elements of offenses—purposely, knowingly, recklessly, and negligently—one of which would have to be present for criminal liability to attach (§ 2.02). The Code achieved a creative compromise in the area of strict liability, allowing for the possibility of such offenses by classifying them as violations punishable only by fines.

In addition to attempting to order and rationalize the general, underlying principles of criminal liability, the Model Penal Code wrought numerous innovations in the definitions of specific offenses. Perhaps the most signal achievement in this regard was its substitution of a unified law of theft for the potpourri of common-law offenses that went under the names of larceny, larceny by trick, false pretenses, and embezzlement. It sought, too, to bring greater rationality and fairness to the sentencing of those convicted of crimes. It proposed a scheme of determinate sentencing, under which all felonies were classified into three punishment categories and all misdemeanors into two. Upper and lower limits of sentences were set out for each category, with the determination of the exact length left to the discretion of the judge (§§ 6.06, 6.08). Extended terms were authorized for persistent offenders and professional criminals (§§ 7.03, 7.04).

The American Law Institute neither expected nor intended that its Model Penal Code would be adopted in toto anywhere, or that it would lead to the establishment of a uniform national penal law. Diversity of political history and of population makeup in the various states made that kind of expectation quite unrealistic. Rather, the institute hoped that the Code would spark a fresh and systematic reevaluation of the penal law in many jurisdictions and that its provisions would be liberally drawn on. The institute was not to be disappointed in this hope. By 1980, in large part owing to the Model Penal Code's example, some thirty states had adopted revised criminal codes, and another nine had code revisions either under way or completed and awaiting enactment. It is no exaggeration to say, as did Sanford Kadish, that within three decades of the time when Code drafts began to be circulated, the Model Penal Code had "permeated and transformed" American substantive law (p. 1144).

A final salutary impact of the Model Penal Code must be mentioned, namely, the impetus that it gave to the effort to codify—for the first time in the true sense of the word—the federal penal law. In 1962, when the Code's Proposed Official Draft was promulgated, the federal criminal law was in a sorrier condition than that of most of the states. It had grown up in an unsystematic, piecemeal fashion since the beginnings of the republic, and the several efforts that had been previously undertaken to place it on a more rational basis had not come to very much. In 1866 Congress, alarmed at the uncontrolled manner in which the corpus of federal criminal law seemed to have been growing since 1800, had impaneled a commission to introduce some order into the confusion. The work of this commission led to the passage of a body of revised statutes, which at least had the virtue of arranging federal penal provisions into some sort of coherent order (U.S. Congress). In 1897 and later in 1909, revisions and rearrangements of federal penal statutes were again undertaken (Appropriations Act of June 4, 1897, ch. 2, 30 Stat. 11; Act of March 4, 1909, ch. 321, 35 Stat. 1088 (codified in scattered sections of 18 U.S.C.)). Finally, in 1948, after eight years of work by another commission, Congress enacted Title 18 of the United States Code, which purported to be the first codification of the federal criminal law. If it was a codification, it was one in the Fieldian rather than the Benthamite-Livingstonian sense—and even that may be a charitable overstatement.

In 1966 Congress established the National Commission on Reform of Federal Criminal Laws to examine the state of the federal penal law and to propose a reformulation. The action was in part taken to appease an anxious public which was insisting that Congress do something about dramatically escalating crime rates, but it was motivated as well by an authentic desire to reform and improve the law. Congress left no doubt that it wished to see a thorough rethinking of the federal law of crimes, and its mandate was heeded. In due course the commission produced a thorough revision of the federal substantive law of crimes, and several bills were promptly introduced for the enactment of some version of it into law.

The middle decades of the twentieth century, thanks in part to the work of Wechsler and his colleagues, witnessed a widespread quickening of interest in the field of criminal justice, as well as considerable activity aimed at the reformation of the criminal law. Whether this signaled the reversal of past patterns of inattention and the beginning of a new, long-term trend or whether it was merely another episode of flirtation with the subject, only the future can determine.

CHARLES McCLAIN

See also CAPITAL PUNISHMENT; CRIME COMMISSIONS; JUVENILE JUSTICE: HISTORY AND PHILOSOPHY; PRISONS: HISTORY.

BIBLIOGRAPHY

American Law Institute. *Model Penal Code: Proposed Official Draft*. Philadelphia: ALI, 1962.

BARNES, HARRY ELMER. *The Evolution of Penology in Pennsylvania: A Study in American Social History* (1927). Reprint. Montclair, N.J.: Patterson Smith, 1968.

BECCARIA, CESARE. *On Crimes and Punishments* (1764). Translated with an introduction by Henry Paolucci. Indianapolis: Bobbs-Merrill, 1963.

BOYD, JULIAN P., ed. *The Papers of Thomas Jefferson*, vol. 2. Princeton, N.J.: Princeton University Press, 1950.

"Colony of New Plymouth: Laws of 1636." *The Compact with the Charter and Laws of the Colony of New Plymouth*. Edited by William Brigham. Boston: Dutton & Wentworth, 1836, pp. 35–57.

"Constitution of Pennsylvania, 1790." *The Federal and State Constitutions, Colonial Charters, and Other Organic Laws of the States, Territories, and Colonies Now or Heretofore Forming the United States of America*, vol. 5. Edited by Francis Newton Thorpe. Washington, D.C.: Government Printing Office, 1909, pp. 3092–3103.

DAVIS, DAVID BRION. "The Movement to Abolish Capital Punishment in America, 1798–1861." *American Historical Review* 63 (1957): 23–46.

DRESSLER, DAVID. *Practice and Theory of Probation and Parole*. New York: Columbia University Press, 1959.

GOEBEL, JULIUS, JR., and NAUGHTON, T. RAYMOND. *Law En-*

forcement in Colonial New York: A Study in Criminal Procedure (1664–1776) (1944). Reprint. Montclair, N.J.: Patterson Smith, 1970.

HALL, JEROME. "Edward Livingston and His Louisiana Penal Code." American Bar Association Journal 22 (1936): 191–196.

HALL, LIVINGSTON. "The Substantive Law of Crimes: 1887–1936." Harvard Law Review 50 (1937): 616–653.

HARNO, ALBERT J. "Some Significant Developments in Criminal Law and Procedure in the Last Century." Journal of Criminal Law, Criminology, and Police Science 42 (1951): 427–467.

KADISH, SANFORD H. "Codifiers of the Criminal Law: Wechsler's Predecessors." Columbia Law Review 78 (1978): 1098–1144.

KEEDY, EDWIN R. "History of the Pennsylvania Statute Creating Degrees of Murder." University of Pennsylvania Law Review 97 (1949): 759–777.

The Laws and Liberties of Massachusetts. Reprinted from the copy of the 1648 edition in the Henry E. Huntington Library. Introduction by Max Farrand. Cambridge, Mass.: Harvard University Press, 1929.

LIVINGSTON, EDWARD. The Complete Works of Edward Livingston on Criminal Jurisprudence, Consisting of Systems of Penal Law for the State of Louisiana and for the United States of America (1873). 2 vols. Introduction by Salmon P. Chase. Reprint. Montclair, N.J.: Patterson Smith, 1968.

NELSON, WILLIAM E. The Americanization of the Common Law: The Impact of Legal Change on Massachusetts Society, 1760–1830. Cambridge, Mass.: Harvard University Press, 1975.

New York State Commissioners of the Code. Draft of a Penal Code for the State of New York. Albany: Weed, Parsons, 1864.

POUND, ROSCOE. Criminal Justice in America (1930). Reprint. New York: Da Capo Press, 1972.

———, and FRANKFURTER, FELIX, eds. Criminal Justice in Cleveland: Reports of the Cleveland Foundation Survey of the Administration of Criminal Justice in Cleveland, Ohio. Cleveland Foundation, 1922.

ROTHMAN, DAVID J. The Discovery of the Asylum: Social Order and Disorder in the New Republic. Boston: Little, Brown, 1971.

SAYRE, FRANCIS. "Public Welfare Offenses." Columbia Law Review 33 (1933): 55–88.

U.S. Congress. "Title LXX." Revised Statutes of the United States. 2d ed. 43d Cong., 2d sess., 1873–1874. Washington, D.C.: Government Printing Office, 1878, pp. 1035–1075.

WALKER, SAMUEL E. Popular Justice: A History of American Criminal Justice. New York: Oxford University Press, 1980.

WARNER, SAM B., and CABOT, HENRY B. "Changes in the Administration of Criminal Justice during the Past Fifty Years." Harvard Law Review 50 (1937): 583–615.

WECHSLER, HERBERT. "American Law Institute: II. A Thoughtful Code of Substantive Law." Journal of Criminal Law, Criminology, and Police Science 45 (1955): 524–530.

———. "The Model Penal Code and the Codification of American Criminal Law." Crime, Criminology, and Public Policy: Essays in Honor of Sir Leon Radzinowicz. Edited by Roger G. Hood. New York: Free Press, 1974, pp. 419–468.

———, and Michael, Jerome. "A Rationale of the Law of Homicide." Columbia Law Review 37 (1937): 701–761, 1261–1325.

4.

CURRENT ISSUES IN THE UNITED STATES

Introduction

This article focuses on major developments in criminal law reform in the United States during the second half of the twentieth century. The most important reform projects of this period were the Model Penal Code of the American Law Institute (ALI), upon which numerous state reforms were modeled, and the Proposed New Federal Criminal Code of the National Commission on Reform of Federal Criminal Laws. The nature, objectives, and strategies of criminal law reform will be examined below, and important and recurrent issues will be cataloged.

Around the middle of the twentieth century, a coalescence of forces produced a powerful movement to reform American criminal law. Prominent among them were (1) a peaking in public sensitivity to "crime waves" and "organized crime"; (2) urbanization and vast internal migrations, which disrupted the normal socializing effect of family, religion, and other nonlegal influences, exacerbated racial tensions, and increased alienation among youths, minorities, and the poor; (3) the rising influence of the social sciences and their powerful apparatus for criticizing existing institutions; (4) the growing prestige of academic lawyers and their tendency to iconoclasm, especially as jurisprudential style shifted from the analytic and pseudoscientific to the functional and realistic; (5) the sexual revolution created or revealed by Alfred Kinsey's studies of human sexual behavior, rendering ludicrous much Victorian penal legislation in this area; and (6) the research and influence of the ALI.

The ALI is a private association of eminent lawyers, judges, and professors, committed to improvement of the law. It enjoyed generous financial support from major philanthropic foundations. Initial ALI projects focused on "Restatements" of the common law (that is, judge-made and nonlegislative law) in such fields as torts, contracts, and property law. Extensive research and preliminary drafting were carried out under the direction of "Reporters," usually leading law professors, who summarized the fields and submitted proposed formulations for the ALI's approval. Although the early restatements purported to be clarifications rather than reforms, it soon developed that the ragbag of judicial decisions offered enough examples of inconsistency to give the reporters ample opportunity to choose preferred positions. It was a short way from this to outright legislation, and soon the ALI began to address itself to model codes as well as restatements. The proposed official draft of the Model Penal Code, for which Herbert Wechsler of the Columbia University School of Law and Louis Schwartz of the University of Pennsylvania Law School were co-reporters, was published in 1962. Commentaries had been published with earlier tentative drafts; but definitive updated commentaries were not published until 1980, and then only with respect to Part II of the Code, in which specific offenses were defined. As of that date, thirty-four state codifications or revisions had drawn on the Model Penal Code, and ten more were pending.

The crime phobia of the 1960s and reform of federal criminal laws. The saga of federal criminal law reform in the 1970s is instructive. In the 1960s, reported crime rates and public anxiety about "crime in the streets" and "organized crime" reached new heights. There was much agitation over the "softness on crime" attributed to the United States Supreme Court (the "Warren Court") and manifested in a series of decisions by the Court that vindicated the rights of suspects and accused persons. These decisions banned the use of evidence obtained by such illegal police practices as baseless search or arrest, coercive secret interrogation, entrapment, or illicit wiretapping. The popular press and conservative politicians linked the Court's decisions to the increasing crime rate, although it was obvious that the minuscule fraction of guilty persons who escaped as a result of police violations of legal restraints could have no discernible effect on deterrence of crime. Any such effect would be lost in the vast numbers of culprits who were never apprehended because of police ineptitude or police compliance with constitutional standards, or where prosecution failed owing to the operation of such unchallenged constitutional protections as the right to counsel and the necessity of proving guilt beyond reasonable doubt.

Besides the Supreme Court's "softness," the leniency of sentencing judges and parole boards was much touted as a cause of crime. The public was understandably provoked by recurrent reports of scoundrels and thugs sentenced to probation rather than prison, or released on parole after short imprisonment, only to commit new offenses. There were real grounds for concern here, but newspapers, maga-

zines, and broadcasters irresponsibly failed to communicate the true nature of the problem. Any system employing discretion in sentencing *must* "fail" in some fraction of its cases. The only way completely to prevent commission of new offenses by some probationers and parolees would be to abolish probation and parole. The alternative to accepting some errors in discretionary judicial sentencing is to eliminate judicial discretion, for example, by statutory prescription of flat sentences for each offense regardless of mitigating or aggravating circumstances. Since few favor such nondiscretionary alternatives, the real problems (discussed in detail below) are how to get good people appointed to discretionary posts, and how to guide, limit, and review their exercise of discretion.

The anxieties of the 1960s about crime, exacerbated no doubt by such other political thorns as the Vietnam War, the "youth rebellion," and the assassination of President John Kennedy, gave impetus to a number of investigations, preeminently that of the President's Commission on Law Enforcement and Administration of Justice. The report of that commission, entitled *The Challenge of Crime in a Free Society,* and the excellent separate task force reports on every phase of the criminal justice system, are essential to an understanding of the crime and law enforcement problems of that era. The work of the President's Commission was paralleled and supplemented by the American Bar Association's Project on Standards for Criminal Justice, which produced in the same decade a superb series of studies and recommendations, mostly on issues of procedure and sentencing. In academia, the ferment was expressed in such key publications as Francis Allen's *The Borderland of Criminal Justice,* Herbert Packer's *The Limits of the Criminal Sanction,* and Norval Morris and Gordon Hawkins's *The Honest Politician's Guide to Crime Control.*

The National Commission on Reform of Federal Criminal Laws. The stage was set for national action. Congress was already enacting hard-line statutes on organized crime, drugs, gambling, wiretapping, and confessions (Omnibus Crime Control and Safe Streets Act of 1968, Pub. L. No. 90-351, 82 Stat. 197 (codified as amended in scattered sections of 5, 18, 18 App., 28, 40, 42, 47 U.S.C.)). The Johnson Administration, committed to protection of civil rights, including the rights of accused persons, was on the defensive, but it had to show its own concern for dealing with crime. Accordingly, it sponsored the Act to establish a National Commission on Reform of Federal Criminal Laws, Pub. L. No. 89-801, 80 Stat. 1516 (1966). The commission was given a limitless mandate to "improve the federal system of criminal justice" and paricularly to propose a revision and recodification of the criminal laws. It comprised three senators, three congressmen, three federal judges, and three presidential nominees, one of whom, designated as chairman, was Edmund ("Pat") Brown, who had served as a district attorney, as attorney general of California, and as governor of that state. The political balance was approximately seven to five in favor of the liberals, but ominously for them the conservatives included three senators who dominated the Senate Judiciary Committee, which would shape the legislative consideration of the commission's proposed code.

The congressional struggle. The report of the National Commission on Reform of Federal Criminal Laws went, as required by the statute, to President Richard Nixon and both houses of Congress. The conservative senators of the Judiciary Committee took the lead in preparing a revised version of the code, which became the first Senate bill of the Ninety-third Congress and was thus designated S. 1. This bill followed the general plan of the National Commission's proposed code of substantive criminal law and even some of the liberal innovations, but it introduced harsh changes and additions. The general level of sentences was increased, some prison sentences were made mandatory, and parole was narrowly constrained. Appeals from sentence were permitted, but to the prosecution as well as the defendant, and the appellate court was authorized to increase any sentence appealed. The defense of insanity was abolished. Disobedience to a policeman's order made during a riot was to be punishable by a jail sentence. S. 1 rejected the National Commission's policy declaration of preference for nonprison sanctions unless the judge believed that a prison sentence was more appropriate. The Senate committee's decision to expand the reform to cover procedure as well as substance doubled the length of the bill to more than six hundred pages. It also vastly increased the targets of criticism since the codified procedures included wiretapping and other recently enacted controversial enforcement practices which were anathema to civil liberties groups that could not tolerate even a reaffirmation of existing law in these areas. But above all, so far as the press was concerned, S. 1 was unacceptable because it contained provisions penalizing information "leaks" from the bureaucracy. This feature of S. 1, dubbed "the Official Secrets Act," became the focus of opposition so bitter that in debate over successive reform proposals in subsequent congresses far better bills could be seriously jeopardized by characterizing them as "Son of S. 1" or "Grandson of S. 1."

The role of the American Civil Liberties Union. A more serious consequence of the S. 1 controversy was that it crystallized the resistance of the American Civil Liberties Union (ACLU). The union developed a rigid opposition to any bill that did not satisfy the whole civil liberties agenda. Thus, legislative compromise became impossible, and the "best" became enemy of the good. When Senator Edward Kennedy's federal criminal law reform bill in the Ninety-fifth Congress, S. 1437, passed the Senate by a vote of seventy-two to fifteen, with the support of virtually every liberal senator, the ACLU would be found in opposition along with the small band of right-wing senators who thought the bill far too liberal and "soft." The ACLU must take credit or blame for preserving intact, through the 1970s and beyond, an obsolete and oppressive federal criminal law. The advent of a conservative national administration ensured that any penal code which might be enacted would regress toward the harshness of S. 1. The ACLU succeeded in blocking reform not because it possessed political power in the conventional sense but because—happily for freedom in most cases—it has the ear of the press, which loves alarums, and because it enjoys the implicit confidence of many liberal congressmen as the authentic protector of the Bill of Rights. Those congressmen, unfortunately including some members of the National Commission influential in the House Judiciary Committee, were immobilized by doubt and pressure, even if not convinced of the validity or prudence of the ACLU's opposition.

Nature of criminal law reform. Reform of the criminal law is a never-ending enterprise. The point must be stressed because otherwise the true nature and goals of the activity will be misunderstood, reform effort will be misdirected and wasted, and the reform movement will be obstructed by well-meaning groups who insist on unrealistic demands to achieve the ideal—to correct at once all perceived shortcomings in existing law. There is no "ideal" penal code. A penal code, especially in a democracy, must reflect the perpetual dynamic flux of political, social, philosophic, and moral ideas out of which the law grows.

Realistically, the goals of a reform code must be the relatively modest ones of eliminating the manifest injustices, irrationalities, and inconsistencies that accumulate in aggregations of old statutes; filling obvious gaps; and making such advances in theory and practice as can command a consensus in the community. This does not mean that a reform should faithfully mirror contemporary biases and the passions of the "man on the street" or even of uninformed legislators. The process of drafting the code should itself become an opportunity to educate the public and all those more immediately engaged in the process as to the nature of the problem, the available alternatives, and the "state of the art" of criminal law, criminology, and penology. However, reliance on these social sciences should not be carried so far as to defer legal reforms until one has determined the "causes of crime" or the cure. Centuries of experience demonstrate that agreement or reasonable certainty as to causes and cure are not achievable. Thus common sense, illuminated if possible by contemporary social science, must be the guide in identifying the manifest injustices that should dominate the agenda of a reform movement.

If at any moment an ideal code could be invented and become effective on Day One, it would begin to become obsolete on Day Two because of changes in the infrastructure. This is illustrated by dramatic instances where reformers drafted provisions that were regarded at the time as exceedingly "liberal," but that shortly thereafter were declared to be unconstitutionally restrictive. This happened to the abortion provisions of the ALI's Model Penal Code of 1962. There, overcoming conservative resistance, the reformers proposed to decriminalize abortion in the first trimester of pregnancy if the mother's life or health was threatened by continuance of the pregnancy, if the pregnancy resulted from rape or incest, or if continued pregnancy would result in the birth of defective offspring. Only a decade later, the Supreme Court held, in *Roe v. Wade*, 410 U.S. 113 (1973), that a woman's right to terminate an early pregnancy could not be so circumscribed.

The perennial issues of penal reform

Substantive criminal law and criminal procedure. This article deals with the reform of substantive criminal law, as distinct from that of criminal procedure. Substantive criminal law defines the misbehavior that will be subject to punishment and specifies penalties for such misbehavior. Procedural law regulates the activities of officials involved in law enforcement, for example, the police in investigating, arresting, and searching for evidence; the prosecuting attorney in dealing with witnesses and screening complaints; and the judge in making decisions about the admissibility of evidence, instructing the jury, and determining whether the prosecution's evidence is sufficient to warrant submitting the case to a jury. Procedure and substance are closely interrelated, so that provisions which are analytically procedural will be found in substantive codes, and vice versa. For exam-

ple, when a substantive code specifies the type of hearing to which the accused is entitled with respect to sentencing, or the kind of appeal he may take against an allegedly excessive sentence, these are procedural matters. Despite the interrelation of substance and procedure, procedural reforms have generally been separate enterprises.

Why codify? Criminal law is constantly undergoing reform through daily enactments by legislatures and continuous reinterpretation by judges. Major reform projects, on the other hand, are proposed in the form of integrated codes in which legislatures or private groups synthesize the accumulating decisions, impose order on the chaos of inconsistent statutes, and give effect to modern perceptions of dangerous antisocial activity, penology, sociology, and individual freedom. A reasonable initial question for legislators to ask is why one should undertake the formidable task of rewriting the whole of the criminal law in a single code rather than proceeding by a series of amendments dealing with particular subjects.

Without suggesting that total recodification is, under all political circumstances, to be preferred, the arguments favoring such an enterprise once every generation may be summarized as follows. The penal code is a system all of whose parts should fit together. One cannot specify maximum terms for specific offenses without considering how the discretion of sentencing judges and parole authority will be exercised, whether the law is to authorize expanded maxima for "specially dangerous offenders," and whether multiple offenses may be unlimitedly matched by multiple cumulative sentences. One does not know how to define specific offenses until one knows whether there are to be other provisions dealing broadly with attempt, conspiracy, and solicitation. For example, should espionage be defined to include these inchoate offenses—to be punishable equally with, or less severely than, the completed offense—or should there be a uniform approach to inchoateness in relation to all offenses? In defining particular offenses, may one rely on the existence elsewhere of provisions specifying circumstances under which generally forbidden activity may be justified: self-defense, defenses of property, coercion, and the like? The definition of particular offenses involves the use of terms describing the psychological components of guilt, such as malice, intent, purpose, recklessness, or mistake; it would seem only prudent that there be a limited number of such terms and that they be given standardized meanings for the whole code.

An especially sticky issue for American legislatures seems to be whether to codify justifications, excuses, and other defenses. The Model Penal Code and the National Commission's code did include general legislative provisions on these subjects. They seem to go to the heart of the subject matter. To ban assaults and other aggressions without specifying the circumstances under which policemen or private citizens may employ force defensively or to carry out the purposes of the law seems to leave matters up in the air: "This is forbidden—except in circumstances where the courts say it is not forbidden." Nevertheless, the embattled federal codifiers of the 1970s eventually dropped the sections on justification, which proved difficult to draft in a way that would enlist consensus support. Yet, on democratic principles, the legislature rather than the judiciary is the proper institution to decide such crucial issues as when a policeman may employ lethal force to capture a suspect, when a subordinate official may justify an action on the ground that a superior has ordered it, or when a person charged with bigamy may successfully defend on the ground that he or she acted on the advice of counsel that a prior marriage was terminated by a valid divorce.

Postulating the goals of a penal system. One might expect a penal reformer to start by listing a set of goals. It is easy to enumerate such goals, which have been articulated in centuries of philosophic reflection and penological debate. The usual ones are deterrence of crime, rehabilitation of offenders, retribution, and isolation of dangerous persons to incapacitate them from committing further crimes. Unfortunately, it turns out that these goals are to some degree unattainable and are frequently inconsistent.

Obviously, no penal system could deter or repress all crime. Some types of crime are so dominated by passion or psychopathy that no threat of punishment, however certain and drastic, would prevent their commission. It may even be that the risk of punishment entices some to commit crime. This is very far from saying that the penal code does not serve as a potent and useful discouragement of crime. Introspection tells us that anticipation of unpleasant consequences influences our behavior, just as anticipation of profit or reward is an incentive to socially useful endeavor. Moreover, the penal code informs and intensifies such nonpenal restraints on misbehavior as education, religion, parental control, and press attitudes. Some philosophers assert that only retribution—giving the culprit what he deserves—justifies punishment, and that it is immoral to inflict pain on one who by hypothesis does not deserve it, merely to serve society's purpose to deter others from misbehavior.

Rehabilitation of offenders is obviously a worthy

aspiration, especially since much crime is committed by previous offenders. Crime would be reduced, therefore, if first offenders could be educated, reoriented, or inspired to reform themselves. However, although rehabilitation undoubtedly occurs, even in prison conditions, its feasibility has been seriously impugned by studies of recidivism under such supposedly rehabilitative regimes as probation, parole, and juvenile court supervision. Be that as it may, it is clear that the goals of retribution and deterrence are likely to point in opposite directions. Deterrence might call for severe punishment, which could actually embitter the offender and make him more likely to engage in further crimes. Rehabilitating a member of a violent slum gang might call for transplanting him to a pleasant suburb where his reeducation might proceed in a setting comparable to that of a select private school. The clash of this vision with deterrent and retributive goals, to say nothing of the immense economic cost, is manifest. Modern commentators have been especially disenchanted with the notion that imprisonment might be ordered or prolonged with a view to rehabilitation, thus subjecting the convict "for his own good" to more punishment than he "deserves."

Isolation or incapacitation of dangerous individuals would seem to be an essential ingredient of penal policy. Yet it too has its problems of feasibility and contradiction of other goals. Our ability to diagnose dangerousness is distinctly limited; our ability to determine when a once-dangerous person has ceased to be so is doubtful. Thoughtful people undoubtedly are apprehensive about entrusting such judgments to sentencing officials who, under political and media pressure, have to play the cautious game of releasing very few people when these people, presumably multiple offenders and recidivists, must be certified as presently "safe." The dilemma of incapacitation is illustrated by the problem of dealing with career petty criminals. What is to be done with an individual who is a lifetime pickpocket and has accumulated scores of arrests and short-term jail sentences? Sentence him finally to life imprisonment as incorrigible, for his seventy-seventh pinch yielding ten dollars? Should the social cost of maintaining him in prison be weighed against the social cost of his continued peculations?

Retribution—sentencing the convict to "what he deserves"—is probably the most popular goal of the criminal law. Most people cannot comfortably accept the notion that a culprit should be treated worse than he deserves in order to serve some public purpose. The world seems equally out of kilter if the culprit is punished less than he deserves, thus "getting away" with something. But "just deserts" are hard to measure, and the penal system always inflicts some pain on innocents, for example, the deprived family of the imprisoned convict. A retributive criterion of punishment must frequently clash with the goal of rehabilitation. Where deterrence would be adequately served by milder measures, deterrence and retribution clash as goals. There is the additional difficulty that we, the punishers, could not stomach the sort of punishment that some crimes could be said to deserve. We abjure torture, capital punishment, mutilation, and flogging. The modes of punishment, in short, reflect the mores of the punishers more than the deserts of the punished.

Retribution is disapproved by some as the equivalent of vengeance, a base passion that calls for inflicting pain whether or not it serves a utilitarian purpose. On the other hand, James Stephen, the famous nineteenth-century historian of the criminal law, remarked that the criminal law stands to the passion of vengeance in much the same relation as marriage to the sexual appetite, that is, a legitimate outlet for a universal drive. More broadly, retribution may be seen as utilitarian insofar as it substitutes a restrained public punishment for the fury and chaos of private vengefulness. Minimally, retribution can serve to set an outer limit to imprisonment that might otherwise be cruelly prolonged in the name of deterrence, rehabilitation, or incapacitation.

If the affirmative goals of the penal system are thus beset with doubt and contradiction, it seems nevertheless useful to state these goals in the penal code. Judges, prosecutors, and other officials are thus warned against headlong and idiosyncratic pursuit of a single goal at the expense of other goals highly regarded in this pluralist community. A statement of purposes enshrined in the code is similarly useful to the legislature itself as it deliberates upon criminal law proposals. In this connection it will be useful to have the list include not only aims we seek to accomplish, but also some hazards we seek to avoid. The National Commission, for example, had declared its purpose "to safeguard conduct that is without guilt from condemnation as criminal," a counsel of prudence that was dropped from S. 1.

Regulating the exercise of discretion in sentencing. The overriding issue in any system of criminal justice is how to control the exercise of discretion in sentencing. A tyrant would have no need for a penal code, which could be expressed in a single sentence: "Misbehavior will be punished as I deem appropriate." No need to define misbehavior; no need to classify offenses into categories to which different levels of maximum punishment are assigned. Even in a tyranny, however, the tyrant, compelled to employ judges and other officials to carry out his policies, will need to define his policies: to tell the officials what he regards as misbehavior and what punishments he deems appropriate. In a democracy with a developed legal and constitutional tradition, this becomes all the more necessary. Democracy is skeptical about officials and wants them curbed more firmly than would an absolute monarch. It insists that nothing be punishable which has not been publicly prohibited prior to the alleged misbehavior. The democratic society insists also that the fallible human beings who, with their various biases and shortcomings of intellect and character, become judges shall not have delegated to them the tyrant's limitless discretion to punish. American federal and state constitutions assert this principle by banning "cruel and unusual" punishment, a doctrine that has increasingly been applied to require "proportionality" of punishment to the heinousness of the offense and to the general scale of punishments authorized for other offenses. In *Coker v. Georgia*, 433 U.S. 584 (1977), for example, capital punishment for rape was precluded.

Classifying offenses and punishments. A first step in any reform project is to select a set of categories into which all crimes will be classified. Crimes may be divided, as anciently, into simply two categories—felony and misdemeanor—or, as in modern codes, into approximately half a dozen categories. These may include three levels, or "degrees," of felony, two or three levels of misdemeanor, and a submisdemeanor class of "infraction." The corresponding ranges of maximum imprisonment might be as follows:

1. First-degree felony: life imprisonment (or thirty years)
2. Second-degree felony: fifteen years
3. Third-degree felony: five years
4. First-degree misdemeanor: one year
5. Second-degree misdemeanor: sixty days
6. Infraction: five days (or fine only)

The necessity of classifying offenses and matching penalties manifested itself first in the ancient distinction between felonies and misdemeanors. Felonies were subject to capital punishment; misdemeanors were punishable by imprisonment at the discretion of the judge (or, in some American states, by the jury). In time, as the legislatures circumscribed the use of capital punishment, made more felonies subject to imprisonment for specified maximum terms of years, and discriminated among misdemeanors with respect to the maximum sentence that might be imposed, the old distinction between felony and misdemeanor lost its critical significance. In modern usage the distinction survives only in the idea that felonies are more serious. In the federal system and some state systems, all offenses punishable by more than one year are designated felonies, with certain consequences regarding procedure, place of imprisonment, and collateral consequences of conviction.

Important issues are at stake in selecting a classification system. The number of categories should be few enough to lend some structure to the system. Without such legislative restraint there is little to stop the lawmakers from assigning a unique sentence maximum for every offense, resulting in confusion and inconsistency. Moreover, it becomes increasingly difficult to pretend that there is a rational relationship between sentence and the goals of punishment. It defies belief that sentence maxima for different offenses set at two, three, five, seven, or eight years, and so forth, correspond to equally heterogeneous needs for deterrence, rehabilitation, incapacitation, and the like. What is most probably represented by such a patternless scheme is the transient retributive evaluations of particular legislatures passing successive statutes outside the discipline of an organized penal code. A code that merely assembled such discrete legislative judgments might give the impression of being "fine tuned"; but no such fine tuning is possible where, as in a statute, one must dispose wholesale of innumerable varieties of offense and offender within any single type of crime, for example, theft.

A major task for the reformer is to select the appropriate ladder of punishment to correspond with the classification system. There are two main difficulties: to identify principles governing the punishment categories, and to face up to the fact, if it be so, that a principled use of imprisonment might result in discontinuous ranges of sentencing discretion—a ladder with missing rungs. As to principles, consideration may begin by noting that the most frequently observed pattern of imprisonment is strongly linked to astronomical or anatomical phenomena plainly unrelated to the goals of punishment. A typical pattern will set maxima at thirty days (the lunar month), one year (the duration of the earth's revolution about the sun), five years (the number of fingers on one hand), ten years (the number on two hands), and twenty years (the number of fingers plus toes). It makes more sense to try to relate the framework of sentencing to the plausible purposes sought to be accomplished by short, medium, and long sentences. Pursuit of this line of thought reveals that the general purposes enumerated in the penal code may be blended in different proportions at various levels of punishment and various stages of the criminal process.

The duration of short sentences must surely be determined with reference to deterrence. Not even the staunchest advocate of rehabilitation would pretend that a sentence of five, fifteen, fifty, or ninety days affords enough time for a program of vocational or moral retraining. Retribution has little role to play in this realm of minor violations of driving rules or other prophylactic regulations. Incapacitation is irrelevant since the culprit will in any event soon be returned to freedom. If, then, deterrence is our aim, one must ask how much imprisonment is needed for that purpose. Least is best. Short-term jail sentences mean crowded, wretched confinement in idleness. There is reason to believe that the greatest impact of the indignity of a short jail sentence is the sharp shock of the initial clanging shut of the steel cage door. There is no evidence that increments of detention beyond the initial week or so add to deterrence. The burden of proof is therefore heavily on those who would authorize short-term imprisonment beyond that.

Long sentences can be rationalized only as serving the goals of retribution and incapacitation. It is an axiom of penology that prolonged incarceration is counterproductive so far as rehabilitation is concerned: the prisoner degenerates, becoming more and more difficult to reintegrate in freedom. As for deterrence, it defies belief that a would-be rapist or robber, not put off by the prospect of ten years' imprisonment, would be restrained if the limit of imprisonment were extended to twenty or thirty years. When very long sentences are in prospect, deterrence becomes a function of the likelihood of being caught and convicted rather than speculation on the actual length of sentence.

The length of intermediate sentences should reflect predominantly the goals of rehabilitation and retribution, although deterrence and incapacitation will also be served. One is on treacherous ground here, but it would be plausible to adopt four years as the ordinary maximum for efforts to educate and reorient prisoners. This is by analogy to the typical four-year program of education in high schools and colleges. Rapid progress by the prisoner would enable him to "graduate" earlier. Within the limit set by the criteria of retribution and incapacitation, an intermediate sentence might be longer than four years, for example, up to six or eight, for special classes of convicts: recidivists, professionals, and others found to be "specifically dangerous." A rehabilitative sentence might reasonably be for a minimum corresponding to an academic year; that much time would be required to mount a substantial program and to appraise the results.

If short deterrent sentences last only a few weeks and intermediate sentences dominated by rehabilitative considerations have a minimum in the neighborhood of one year, it will strike many as strange that sentences between one and twelve months are precluded. A similar gap presents itself between the intermediate and the very long sentences, dominated by the goals of retribution and incapacitation. A discontinuous scale of punishments violates the canon of "just deserts," since blameworthiness varies continuously. On the other hand, if we seek to justify our punishments on utilitarian grounds, some rungs on the ladder of punishments may have to be removed as ill-suited to our goals.

Locus of discretion in sentencing. Classification of offenses, with an appropriate array of sentence maxima, is an exercise of legislative control over the disposition of offenders. A critical feature of any criminal code is the system it adopts for regulating the exercise of discretion *within* the limits set by the statute. The principal options are as follows:

1. The sentencing judge may be authorized to sentence to a definite number of years (any number within the statutory maximum) or to no imprisonment at all ("probation"). This vests the discretion entirely in the sentencing judge.
2. The judge may be required to impose an "indeterminate" sentence, for example, five to ten years, leaving it to a parole board subsequently to determine when, within the limits of the indefinite sentence, the prisoner shall be released.
3. The legislature may impose additional constraints on the exercise of judicial discretion, for example, by limiting the imposition of consecutive sentences, mandating the imposition of specified minimum terms, reserving the upper ranges of the statutory maxima for persons found to be especially dangerous, or creating presumptions against imprisonment as against alternative sanctions.
4. The legislature may create a new agency, a "guidelines commission," whose regulations will constrain or guide the sentencing authorities in exercising their functions.
5. The legislature may authorize appeal from sentence, thus subjecting the trial court's sentencing discretion to check by higher authority.

The first option set forth above, definite sentences at the discretion of the judge, without parole or judi-

cial review, is an unacceptable relic of the past. The second option, indeterminate sentence and parole, came into the law in modern times as a great reform. It was designed to moderate the excessive harshness of some judicial sentences, to reduce the scandalous disparity of sentences handed out by different judges or even by the same judge at different times, and to give play to the idea of rehabilitation, inasmuch as a prisoner who gave evidence of reform, or at least submitted to a regimen of rehabilitation, would be released early. Following the usual cycle of human affairs, this great reform of the past became a principal target of later reform movements. As abuses manifested themselves in parole and as faith in rehabilitation faded, it was proposed to reemphasize the judicial sentence, but now with tighter controls on judicial discretion, formulated either by the legislature (option 3) or by the "guidelines commission" (option 4). Judicial review of sentencing (option 5) is coming on the scene as an alternative or supplement to other methods of rationalizing the exercise of sentencing discretion. The Model Penal Code and the National Commission code expanded legislative constraints on judicial discretion, retained parole, and espoused appellate review of sentence. The federal reform bills of the Ninety-sixth Congress proposed option 4, the guidelines commission, and virtual abolition of parole.

Parole. Under option 2, indeterminate sentence and parole, the judge's discretion as to the outside limit of detention is bounded only by the legislatively set maximum for the relevant category of offense. The legislatures commonly provide that the lower limit of an indeterminate sentence may not exceed one-third or one-half of the upper limit. This is to protect against judges' evading the legislative purpose to give the parole board a substantial share of discretion, as would be the case if the judge could impose an "indefinite" sentence in which the minimum was very close to the maximum, for example, nineteen to twenty years. The greater the range between minimum and maximum in the judge's sentence, the more discretion is entrusted to the parole board. Although the statutes ordinarily prevent the judge from setting a disproportionately high maximum, he is usually free to set as low a minimum as he pleases. A very low minimum means that the judge has delegated much of his sentencing discretion to the parole board, which might, for example, release the prisoner soon after he begins serving his indeterminate sentence.

The case that has been made against the system of indeterminate sentence and parole is as follows. Parole, at least as it too often has operated in the ast, is arbitrary, with baneful effects on prisoner morale. The prisoner was allowed a perfunctory hearing or none, and was given no reason for denials. Behavior in prison was the chief basis on which parole decisions seemed to be made. This made submissiveness in confinement the test for reliability in freedom, a poor criterion that played into the hands of prison-wise convicts and sycophants. Uncertainty and recurrent disappointment with regard to date of release embittered the prison population and contributed to riots. Moreover, the credibility of parole-board forecasting of prisoner success after release has been seriously impugned, not only by the inevitable and much-publicized commission of violent crimes by some parolees, but also by demonstration that many of the factors purportedly relied on by parole boards have no statistical correlation with success on parole. The few factors that can be correlated with success—for example, nature of the crime, stabilizing links with family or employer, and first offense or not—turn out to be ascertainable at the time of the judicial sentence. If no helpful information can be counted on to emerge hereafter while the convict is in prison, the theoretical basis for putting off the definitive decision as to release is undermined.

To these arguments, it is responded that parole boards, under pressure of judicial and academic criticism, have ameliorated their procedures, improved their hearings, given reasons for their decisions, and alleviated uncertainties by setting tentative release dates soon after imprisonment begins. Parole boards have also begun to publish and follow their own guidelines, thus introducing more consistency of decision. Additionally, it is said that even under close regulation by guidelines, enough discretion will remain in the hands of judges to warrant centralized effort to minimize disparity. Another line of thought sees parole as facilitating an inevitable and benign hypocrisy of the criminal law: the populace craves heavy sentences at trial, but is tolerant of subsequent remission.

Guidelines prescribed by legislature. Two kinds of guidelines are identified in options 3 and 4 above—those declared in the code itself and those that may be formulated by a guidelines commission. Until the establishment of guidelines commissions, such guidelines as are provided will be found in the statute or will gradually be evolved on a case-by-case basis in the decisions of appellate courts as review of sentence is accepted into the law. Possibly some guidelines should continue to be statutory even after the guidelines commission goes into operation. These would probably be in the nature of prohibitions directed either to the courts or to the guidelines commission, such as the following. "Do not sentence consecutively for a crime and conspiracy to commit that crime." "Do not sentence a nonviolent first offender to prison if a nonprison sanction will adequately protect the public interest." "Do not grant probation to a narcotic trafficker or 'racketeer.' "

Other controversial issues relating to guidelines will be discussed below. Here, as we comment on the general distinction between guidelines specified by the legislature and guidelines formulated by an administrative body acting under general standards laid down by the legislature, it is worth observing that pushing the idea of the guidelines commission to its logical ultimate would imply the disappearance of legislative guidelines from the penal code, including even the grading of offenses into degrees, as in first-, second-, or third-degree rape, or three degrees of theft differentiated largely according to the amount stolen. The circumstances of aggravation which warrant the degree distinctions are precisely those that a sophisticated set of guidelines would take into account. In guidelines, however, these circumstances would be blended with many other factors relating to the offender as well as the offense, to yield an appropriate range of permissible sentences.

It is difficult to draft statutory provisions on grading that reflect the endless variations in the circumstances of the offense itself, to say nothing of variations in the character and status of the offender. The federal reform projects illustrate this in the grading of theft. There, although grading was in principle based on the amount stolen, numerous qualifications had to be grafted onto the underlying principle. Stealing small amounts was treated as more serious if the object of the theft was something that might be used to carry out a major theft, such as a vehicle, a gun, drugs, mail, or a key. Stealing small amounts was treated as more serious if the thief was a public employee or other fiduciary betraying his trust, or if the thief obtained the property by force or intimidation.

The decision whether to incorporate a guideline in the statute itself or to leave the matter within the discretion of the guidelines commission has important consequences. Statutory guidelines are likely to be mandatory; a sentence which disregards them is illegal and can therefore be reversed on appeal even in a jurisdiction that does not allow discretionary sentences to be appealed. They are less likely to fit neatly into a general rationalization of sentencing, and somewhat more likely to reflect the popular preference for retribution. Statutory guidelines are, of course, harder to change than administrative guidelines.

The distinction suggested above between mandatory guidelines in the statute and more flexible administrative guidelines should not be overdrawn. Penal codes that authorize courts to treat the offenses of youths either in the ordinary fashion or under the special procedures and lenient sanctions of the juvenile court and youth-offender laws are essentially suggestions rather than mandates. Moreover, a statutory sentencing guideline may go no farther than to call upon the sentencing authority to "consider" certain factors as mitigating or aggravating. Administrative guidelines, on the other hand, are more than mere suggestions. Typically, the reform projects require the sentencing judge to articulate his reasons for not staying within the guidelines, and they authorize appeal from sentences that do not conform.

Guidelines formulated by the guidelines commission. If an agency other than the legislature itself is to formulate guidelines for sentencing, it becomes important to the legislature and the public how that agency is constituted and how much control the legislature retains over the process. Unquestionably, the judiciary must be well represented on the guidelines commission, because the judges have long experience with sentencing and will have to carry out the new policies, which must be comprehensible and acceptable to them. Moreover, reformers should not ignore the hard political fact that judges, whose sentencing discretion is to be constrained, have great influence with the legislatures. Their concerns about loss of power must be assuaged.

A central issue, then, is whether the formulation of guidelines should be left wholly to the judiciary. In the Ninety-sixth Congress, the House bill (H.R. 6915) to reform the federal penal code delegated the guidelines function to the Judicial Conference of the United States, advised by a sentencing committee consisting predominantly of judges. A Senate bill (S. 1722) created an independent guidelines commission with seven members appointed by the President. Three would be federal judges, nominated by the Federal Judicial Council. Other members would be the attorney general of the United States, a federal prosecutor, and an experienced defense attorney. The House bill obviously entrusted the formulation of guidelines almost completely to the judges, whereas the Senate bill delegated the guidelines function to a body that was much more representative of the interests involved.

The extent to which judicial power is preserved under a guidelines system depends not only on the structure of the guidelines commission but also on how stringently the sentencing judges are held to the guidelines. The House bill instructed the sentencing judge to follow the guidelines "unless [the judge] finds that an aggravating or mitigating circumstance should result in another sentence." The Senate bill instructed the sentencing judge to follow the guidelines unless the aggravating or mitigating circumstances were "not adequately taken into consideration . . . in formulating the guidelines." Clearly, the Senate bill reined in the judges more tightly. Both bills provided a six-month waiting period before the guidelines became effective, so as to provide an opportunity for Congress to intervene.

Other reform issues

The following survey of issues debated in modern criminal law reform projects is necessarily limited to a sampling. Many questions relating to sentencing have been discussed above. Some important issues evoking basic philosophical and political controversy, such as capital punishment, gun control, abortion, entrapment, wiretapping, and other law enforcement practices, are reviewed in other articles. Topics have been selected for discussion here to give an idea of the range and flavor of the controversies.

Sex offenses. By the third quarter of the twentieth century, the main target of modern reform in this area had been achieved; there was general acceptance of the principle that consensual sexual practices of adults in private should not be penalized. Thus, the laws on sodomy, homosexuality, adultery, and fornication were being wiped from the books. This was not so much a product of "permissiveness" as a pragmatic judgment that more harm than good resulted from making criminal law applicable here. As so often in social evolution, practice had preceded formal articulation of principle. The police departments and prosecutors had virtually abandoned enforcement of these laws. It came to be realized that prosecution was feasible only in a tiny fraction of transactions in which both parties participate willingly in private. Thus the criminal law was ineffectual as a deterrent. The rarity of complaint meant that accusations were likely to be arbitrary, perhaps made for blackmail purposes. A genuine effort to enforce the old sex laws would have required police intrusion with surveillance devices into bedrooms. The unsavory practice of using police decoys to entice homosexual overtures was offensive to many. Many practical law enforcement officials believed that it was a misallocation of police resources to assign officers to the sex beat who could otherwise be detecting and arresting rapists, robbers, and burglars, the real source of public concern about crime. This pragmatic base for "decriminalization" made it possible for people who were hostile to illicit sexuality on religious or moral grounds to join the decriminalization movement. Others joined on the principle of respecting individual autonomy with regard to behavior entailing no manifest harm to non-participants, a principle for which constitutional support has been found in "the right of privacy" and the First Amendment guarantee against government support of particular religious views.

Acceptance of the principle leaves open, however, a number of questions of application. For example, what is to be done about open commerce in sex or about "nuisance" solicitations? Who is an "adult" where decriminalization draws the line against sexual engagement with children? As to commerce, the laws, including most reform proposals, continue to penalize the operation of houses of prostitution and call-girl enterprises; indeed, engaging in these businesses on a substantial scale is subject to especially severe penalties under current legislation against organized crime or racketeering. The dominant attitude seems to be that supplying sexual services, with the incidental consequence of creating incentives to promote such activities, is a legitimate target of *economic* regulation, however disinclined the community may be to penalize the patron. A similar distinction has been made between patrons and those who make a living by exploiting the public appetite for gambling or for illicit alcoholic beverages.

All criminal codes penalize, in one form or another, "disorderly conduct," including the public nuisance of offensive or harassing public solicitation of sexual relations. Two distinct problems arise. One has to do with the right of a person to be let alone: the right of a man or woman to walk the public way without enduring persistent unwelcome advances. The other might be described as a matter of aesthetics: the right to enjoy a public park with one's children or to use a public lavatory without being affronted by what is perceived as an outrageous and annoying encounter with the sexual enterprises of others, such as indecent exposure of genitals or actual copulation. The reform codes do not fail to protect the psychological interests of the uninvolved spectator, but controversy easily arises over some loose definitions of the offense. For example, the Model Penal Code offense of "loiter[ing] in or near any public place for the purpose of soliciting or being solicited" for sexual purposes (§ 251.3) has been held unconstitutional (*People*

v. Gibson, 184 Colo. 444, 521, P.2d 774 (1974)) because it proscribes the vague "loitering" without requiring proof of any particular act of solicitation, much less harassment. The official comments to Section 251.3 point, with scarcely concealed embarrassment, to another difficulty: "public place" would seem to include so-called gay bars, which are frequented by homosexuals precisely for the purpose of sexual encounter.

The question of who is an adult under statutes that decriminalize consensual sexual activity among adults while retaining penal sanctions against sexual relations with willing children leads to a discussion of statutory rape. The archetypal common-law felony of forcible rape had over the course of time been interpreted to include sexual intercourse with unconscious, insane, or drugged females. In such cases there was no force, but no valid consent either. This line of development was easily extended by nineteenth-century legislation raising the age of consent to fourteen, sixteen, eighteen, or even twenty-one. Although the original notion was to deter seduction of young girls by mature men, the conventional statutory rape law took no account of the fact that a boy, who might be younger than the girl and possibly the target rather than the perpetrator of the seduction, could be the accused. The result was that innumerable juvenile sexual encounters were made felonious for one of the partners. Such an arrangement was not defensible under reform projects that were decriminalizing adult consensual sex.

The reform codes cautiously ameliorated the older law. The age of consent (for males in homosexual encounters, as well as for females) would not be higher than sixteen, and—consistent with the rationale that statutory rape was penalized to deter exploitation of children by mature partners—the offense could be committed only by a person four or more years older than the "victim." The offense was also drastically downgraded to distinguish it from forcible rape. There are a number of indications that this modest reform has fallen behind evolving social attitudes. Considering that female puberty usually occurs at twelve or earlier, that sex education and tolerance for teenage sexual activity are widespread, and that prosecution of youths for this offense is so rare as to be aberrant (notwithstanding millions of illegitimate births to youngsters), broadened decriminalization appears to be in order.

Notable debate over the scope of a modern rape law revolves around feminist demands that husbands not be immune from prosecution for this offense, that cross-examination of complaining witnesses be circumscribed, and that a complainant's testimony should not have to be corroborated. Few would disagree that husbands should not be entitled to force sex on wives. Whether such misbehavior should be subject to the dire penalties of rape is another matter. Physical violence by a husband is, in any event, punishable as assault; this supplies the useful peg on which police intervention to protect battered wives can be rested. Beyond that, the concept of intrafamily coercion is so difficult to define as to make one hesitate to authorize extreme sanctions. Police experience with charges of assault against spouses is that the complainant rarely carries through; reconciliation and dropping of the charges is far more likely and far preferable socially, but it is surely precluded if one spouse succeeds in jailing the other. A notorious case of successful prosecution of a husband for rape in Oregon blew up in laughter when complainant and convict reestablished marital relations.

Cross-examination of complaining witnesses had been the scandal of some state penal systems, subjecting the complainant to the indignity of a full review of her prior "chastity," to degrading suggestions that she was promiscuous, and to baseless innuendos that she had provoked her ravisher. On the other hand, where there is a real issue whether the sexual relations were consensual, it is difficult, in fairness to the defendant, totally to bar such inquiries as whether the complainant had on previous occasions copulated voluntarily with the accused, whether on the occasion in question she had voluntarily permitted precoital sexual play, or whether on this occasion she had voluntarily engaged in relations with several partners.

As to corroboration of complaining witnesses, it does indeed strike one initially as strange that in a proceeding where guilt must in any event be proved beyond a reasonable doubt, there should be additional requirements of corroboration. The requirement is not quite so anomalous as it seems when one remembers that corroboration is required in the proof of certain other offenses. For example, the Constitution itself contains a requirement of corroboration in prosecutions for treason. Moreover, in prosecutions for perjury, where the question of the defendant's guilt often turns on whether the jury believes the defendant or his accuser, a requirement of corroboration is not uncommon. It may be that, as in the case of abusive cross-examination, the problem is not so much with the law as with the competence and character of the judges chosen to administer it. Where a plausible defense of consent has been of-

fered, as in the case of alleged rape by a social companion of the complainant who may previously have had consensual sexual relations with her, a sensitive judge might well wish to suggest to the jury that it ought not to convict of a serious felony where it is merely a matter of her word against the defendant's. But a mechanical requirement of supporting testimony (witnesses are, after all, unlikely to have been present) is inappropriate, as are other arbitrary evidentiary requirements formerly encountered, such as "prompt outcry" or "resistance to the uttermost."

Conspiracy and organized crime. Multiparty crime and continuing organization for crime have always been regarded as especially serious. The participants evince a settled antisocial propensity; they shore up each other's resolve to defy the law, impairing its deterrent efficacy; the harm of which they are capable is more extensive; the victims are less able to defend themselves; and the police force itself may be intimidated or corrupted by a large-scale criminal organization. Accordingly, more severe punishment seems to be appropriate, and society is willing to intervene well before the harm has materialized. The agreement itself is made criminal; conspiracy law, therefore, like the law of attempt, is an "inchoate" crime.

Critics of conspiracy law point to a number of abuses and argue that all the evils of multiparty crime can be handled without resort to a special offense called conspiracy. As to abuses, it is pointed out that although the alleged dangers of multiparty crime would arise only from the involvement of substantial numbers, the usual definition of conspiracy embraces every case in which merely two persons agree to commit an offense. Every crime in which there is an accomplice thus supports prosecution for conspiracy as well as the underlying offense. Moreover, charging scores or even hundreds of people as participants in a conspiracy, when nearly all of them had menial roles in small fractions of the enterprise, forces each of them to defend against charges of misconduct by all the others, known or unknown to the particular defendant, wherever the conspiracy may have taken place, perhaps thousands of miles from the scene of that defendant's activities, over a long period of years perhaps antedating the defendant's association with the enterprise. The simultaneous trial of scores of defendants means that the trial will last many months, resulting in heavy legal expense and other hardships to each accused, and in probable confusion of the jury. Unfairness arises also because a conspiracy is punishable wherever it was in force or any part of it was carried out; an accused who was never outside Maine may therefore find himself being tried in Hawaii, notwithstanding the general constitutional principle that trials for crime should take place where the crime was committed.

As regards the inchoate aspect of conspiracy, critics focus on the fact that the offense is regarded as complete the moment that two people arrive at an understanding that a crime (which may be a political crime, such as advocating overthrow of the government, or defying a military draft) will be committed. The conspirators need do no further act. Even in states where the conspiracy statute calls for an "overt act," that requirement can be satisfied by the most trifling behavior far removed from consummation, for example, the holding of another meeting to discuss the affair. Thus conspiracy is far more comprehensive than attempt, the classic inchoate crime, which is not committed until the activity comes "dangerously close" to consummation.

The criminal law would suffice for all reasonable needs without a conspiracy offense, the critics argue. All persons who collaborate in the actual commission of a substantive offense or an attempt may be prosecuted for that offense as accessories. The long maximum sentences typically authorized for serious substantive offenses give adequate range for discretionary sentences to take account of the aggravating circumstance of multiparty criminal alliance. The law of attempt permits preconsummation arrests with necessary safeguards against premature social intervention.

The most radical reform proposal would simply abolish the offense of conspiracy. Less drastic solutions would (1) require proof of a substantial act designed to carry out the alleged conspiracy; (2) allow a defense of withdrawal from the conspiracy prior to consummation; (3) prevent cumulative sentencing for conspiracy and the substantive offense; and (4) broaden the discretion of trial judges to split oppressively comprehensive conspiracy trials into separate proceedings. The conspiracy offense might well be trimmed back closer to its original rationale of greater danger from concerted crime by limiting the concept to ongoing enterprises involving at least five or ten accomplices.

At this point conspiracy and the concept of organized crime converge. Hard-line reformers of the 1960s and 1970s gave effect to the concept by providing for "extended" sentences for managers of criminal syndicates. Other reformers accepted the principle but fitted it into a general scheme that reserves the upper ranges of the maximum authorized sentences for "especially dangerous" offenders, among whom would be numbered the leaders of organized crime.

Corporate crime. Ordinary criminal law, with its focus on personal guilt and human behavior, is ill-adapted to the misbehavior of corporations and other groups. Since a corporation can act only through human agents, it may be argued that punishment of the human guilty actors is all that is necessary. However, this often seems inadequate because the immediate actors may be underlings, whereas the really responsible officials—who failed to supervise adequately or whose continual pressure on the underlings for profits explains their misdeeds—escape punishment. A corporation cannot be imprisoned, and although in a sense it can be executed by cancellation of the corporate charter, this is hardly a satisfying sanction since the same entrepreneurs can immediately form another corporation to carry on the business. Fining the corporation seems to put the real onus on innocent parties, namely, the stockholders.

Under these circumstances, reformers are looking for some adaptation of criminal law to group behavior. To bring responsibility home to senior corporate officials, it has been proposed to make them responsible for offenses by "wilful default in supervision . . . which contributes to the occurrence of that offense" (U.S. National Commission, 1971, § 403(4)). The proposal did not survive the opposition of business interests. Another proposal, designed to bring the reprobation of the criminal law down upon the corporate entity as well as on the human participants, was to require the convicted corporation to advertise its own derelictions (§ 3007). The theory here was that higher corporate officials and their public relations advisers are so sensitive to adverse reflections on the "corporate image" that this sanction would encourage more effective anticrime supervision.

Regulatory offenses. One of the most chaotic realms of existing criminal law is the penalty structure for violating the myriad statutory and administrative regulations relating to such matters as operating vehicles, practicing trades and professions, fire protection, health protection, handling of dangerous substances, and sale of alcoholic beverages. Often, violation is penalized without regard to criminal intent or even negligence; so-called strict liability is deemed necessary to spare the prosecutor the onerous task of proving culpability. The penalties prescribed in the numerous statutes vary from fines only to substantial jail sentences, evincing no consistent policy. The National Commission, in Section 1006 of its proposed code, sought to articulate a defensible scheme of punishment for regulatory offenses. Nonculpable violations would not carry jail penalties. Willful violation would be subject to brief imprisonment. Flouting regulatory authority by willful and persistent disobedience would entail imprisonment of up to one year. However, the resistance of both bureaucrats and businessmen to disturbance of the hard-fought compromises in each of the separate regulatory regimes blocked this advance.

"Real offense" sentencing. A final illustration of controversies on the front line of modern penal reform has to do with the extent to which sentences should reflect information that a defendant has committed other crimes in addition to those on which he stands convicted. The question is presented in acute form by the practice of plea bargaining, where a prosecutor may, in exchange for a plea of guilty, reduce a number of charges to one. In the review of the plea bargain by the judge, the defendant's guilt of the dropped charges may be manifest or even conceded. Or the prosecutor may be happy to settle for a plea of guilty to second-degree theft, although the value of the property clearly exceeded that required to constitute first-degree theft. Or a presentence report to the judge may disclose, perhaps largely on the basis of hearsay, that the defendant has never been gainfully employed but has lived off crime. Should the judge take those circumstances into account in selecting the particular sentence to be imposed on the guilty plea? There is little question that judges do in fact respond to information as to the real scope of the defendant's criminality. Some critics contend that they should not do so—and perhaps even cannot do so constitutionally—since the "real offense" has not been proved beyond a reasonable doubt. In response, it is pointed out that the sentence *is* for a proved offense; only its discretionary length is in question. Curiously, the question was passed over in the federal reform bills of the Ninety-sixth Congress, although certain considerations that were there explicitly approved would lead almost inevitably to recognition of real-offense sentencing. For example, those bills provided for consideration of the defendant's history of prior delinquency, his "pattern" of criminal behavior, or the undue risk of further criminal behavior. What seems principally needed as a safeguard is that the defendant be apprised of this basis for sentencing him and given an opportunity to rebut.

Conclusion

The foregoing limited sampling of the areas of controversy in penal law reform has sought to provide some sense of the variety of continuing issues, of the perplexities involved, and of the need for recurrent and systematic reconsideration of the penal law. This is not so much because reform is likely to reduce the crime rate or flatten the current "crime wave," but in order that we, the punishers, can believe that we are rendering justice as well as possible and that our system is worthy of our own respect.

LOUIS B. SCHWARTZ

See also CRIMINAL LAW REFORM: HISTORICAL DEVELOPMENT IN THE UNITED STATES; POLITICAL PROCESS AND CRIME.

BIBLIOGRAPHY

ALLEN, FRANCIS A. *The Borderland of Criminal Justice.* University of Chicago Press, 1964.

————. *The Decline of the Rehabilitative Ideal: Penal Policy and Social Purpose.* New Haven: Yale University Press, 1981.

American Bar Association. *Standards for Criminal Justice.* 2d ed. 4 vols. Prepared with the assistance of the American Bar Foundation. Boston: Little, Brown, 1980.

American Law Institute. *Model Penal Code and Commentaries: Official Draft and Revised Comments.* Philadelphia: ALI, 1980.

————. *Model Penal Code: Proposed Official Draft.* Philadelphia: ALI, 1962.

FRANKEL, MARVIN E. *Criminal Sentences: Law without Order.* New York: Hill & Wang, 1973.

LANG, MAURICE E. *Codification in the British Empire and America.* Amsterdam: H. J. Paris, 1924.

MORRIS, NORVAL, and HAWKINS, GORDON. *The Honest Politician's Guide to Crime Control.* University of Chicago Press, 1970.

National Commission on Reform of Federal Criminal Laws. *Final Report: A Proposed New Federal Criminal Code (Title 18, United States Code).* Washington, D.C.: The Commission, 1971.

————. *Working Papers.* Washington, D.C.: The Commission, 1970.

PACKER, HERBERT L. *The Limits of the Criminal Sanction.* Stanford, Calif.: Stanford University Press, 1968.

President's Commission on Law Enforcement and Administration of Justice. *The Challenge of Crime in a Free Society.* Washington, D.C.: The Commission, 1967.

Royal Commission on Capital Punishment, 1949–1953. *Minutes of Evidence, August 4/5, 1949–December 6, 1951.* London: His Majesty's Stationery Office, n.d.

SCHWARTZ, LOUIS B. "Options in Constructing a Sentencing System: Sentencing Guidelines under Legislative or Judicial Hegemony." *Virginia Law Review* 67 (1981): 637–698.

————. "Reform of the Federal Criminal Laws: Issues, Tactics, and Prospects." *Law and Contemporary Problems* 41 (1977): 1–62.

U.S. Department of Justice, Law Enforcement Assistance Administration, National Advisory Commission on Criminal Justice Standards and Goals. *Community Crime Prevention: Report.* Washington, D.C.: The Commission, 1973.

———. *Corrections.* Washington, D.C.: The Commission, 1973.

———. *Courts.* Washington, D.C.: The Commission, 1973.

———. *The Criminal Justice System.* Washington, D.C.: The Commission, 1973.

———. *Police: A Report.* Washington, D.C.: The Commission, 1973.

WECHSLER, HERBERT. "The Challenge of a Model Penal Code." *Harvard Law Review* 65 (1952): 1097–1133.

The Wolfenden Report: Report of the Committee on Homosexual Offenses and Prostitution. Authorized American edition. Introduction by Karl Menninger, M.D. New York: Stein & Day, 1963.

WOLFGANG, MARVIN. *National Survey of Crime Severity.* Washington, D.C.: U.S. Department of Justice, Bureau of Justice Statistics. Forthcoming publication.

ZIMRING, FRANKLIN E., and HAWKINS, GORDON J. *Deterrence: The Legal Threat in Crime Control.* University of Chicago Press, 1973.

CRIMINALLY INSANE

See DIMINISHED CAPACITY; EXCUSE: INSANITY; MENTAL HEALTH EXPERT, ROLE OF THE; PSYCHOPATHY.

CRIMINAL PROCEDURE

1. CONSTITUTIONAL ASPECTS   John E. Nowak
2. COMPARATIVE ASPECTS   Thomas Weigend

1.
CONSTITUTIONAL ASPECTS

Introduction

The term *criminal procedure* refers broadly to the process of investigation, prosecution, and punishment of those activities that society defines as criminal. This discussion of the constitutionalization of criminal procedure will examine the extent to which the actions of the participants in that process are controlled by the United States Constitution. The basic inquiry is why American society, more than any other in the Western world, has the major components of its criminal justice system defined by nonelected judges.

The importance of the role of the judiciary, and particularly the Supreme Court, in the American criminal justice process is undisputed. Not only does the Supreme Court, like the judicial branches of some other governments, dictate the procedure to be used in civil and criminal trials, but it also sets standards for the investigating of crime, charging of the accused, the scope and process of sentencing, and the carrying out of sentences. Even in the determination of proper in-court procedures, the Supreme Court's role differs from that of high courts in most other countries because the Supreme Court can be reversed only by constitutional amendment. Although Supreme Court decisions have been modified by constitutional amendments to introduce the income tax and to protect state governments from federal suits, the Constitution has never been amended to reverse a criminal procedure decision of the Supreme Court.

The criminal procedure rulings of the Supreme Court divide into four discrete historical eras: (1) pre-1937, (2) 1937–1960, (3) 1961–1969, and (4) post-1969. In American constitutional and social history these periods represent, respectively: (1) the adjustment of the Court and the nation to the industrial revolution and the New Deal era; (2) the search for the appropriate role of government in the post–World War II era; (3) the "liberal" attempt to solve large and small problems by means of the federal government; and (4) the changing role of the federal government in tailoring goals to preserve individual liberties in the face of scarce economic resources. As shall be seen, in each era the Supreme Court has closely mirrored prevailing attitudes of society, government leaders, and prominent scholars.

Throughout each of the four eras, the Court has confronted three basic tasks: ensuring the accuracy and fairness of the factual process by which guilt or innocence is determined, ascertaining the degree of respect for individual dignity that the government must accord an accused person, and resolving the problem of federalism as to the degree of freedom to be allowed local and state governments in solving their own problems and experimenting with alternative procedural systems. As the Justices have dealt with these problems in each era, much of their discussion has involved the concept of the "incorporation" of the Bill of Rights into the Fourteenth Amendment.

The Constitution initially contained few safeguards for individual rights. However, during the ratification debate many members of state conventions argued for explicit recognition of individual rights and their protection from encroachment by the new federal government. Because of this concern, Congress submitted a list of proposed amendments to the states for ratification, and the ten that were approved became known as the Bill of Rights. In the early nineteenth century, however, when the Supreme Court was confronted with the issue of whether the Bill of

Rights provisions were protections against state governments as well as the federal government, Chief Justice John Marshall held that the Bill of Rights did not apply to state governments.

Section 1 of the Fourteenth Amendment, adopted after the Civil War, established the right of national citizenship for persons born or naturalized in the United States. The second sentence of Section 1, perhaps the most important in the Constitution, declares that "no State shall make or enforce any law which shall abridge the privileges or immunities of citizens of the United States; nor shall any State deprive any person of life, liberty, or property, without due process of law; nor deny to any person within its jurisdiction the equal protection of the laws." The amendment's equal protection clause prohibited improper classifications of persons under civil or criminal laws, and its due process clause required fair treatment in the criminal justice process.

Whether the amendment went further and made the Bill of Rights guarantees applicable against state governments was crucial in the area of criminal procedure, for much of the Bill of Rights restricts the power of government in obtaining evidence in criminal cases and in its manner of prosecution. Those Justices in favor of incorporating the Bill of Rights into the Fourteenth Amendment would make these specific guarantees applicable to state and local governments so that a state court case involving a Bill of Rights provision would be decided by examining the history and purpose of that provision. Those opposing incorporation have instead focused solely on the concept of due process and would approve any state or local practice that is not "fundamentally unfair" or a deprivation of life, liberty, or property without due process. Under the latter view, a practice that might violate a specific provision of the Bill of Rights if it had been engaged in by the federal government may, nevertheless, satisfy the demands of due process.

The history of criminal procedure decisions by the Supreme Court is the history not only of the concept of incorporation but also of due process methodology. Whether the Court is deciding an issue under the due process clause or under a more specific Bill of Rights provision, it should be concerned with the fairness of the procedure. Before labeling this methodology a due process methodology, one must examine in each case the nature of the constitutional value implicated by the government's action and the defendant's claim; the degree to which that value is perceived to be an essential part of American society's history and goals; the degree to which that value is impaired by the government practice; and the need

of government and society to redefine these values over time in order to adjust to new problems in the criminal justice system. Although this methodology may not always be expressed by Supreme Court Justices, it raises questions that should be asked in any evaluation of Supreme Court rulings on incorporation—or any other criminal procedure issue—in each historical era.

Pre-1937 decisions

There were only a limited number of Supreme Court criminal procedure rulings of consequence prior to 1937. The Court's inactivity was partly a result of the fact that until the late nineteenth century few opportunities for Supreme Court intervention in criminal justice issues were presented. Although the Supreme Court had been empowered to review final decisions of state courts in criminal cases since the first federal jurisdictional act, there had been no federal issue presented by such cases, since the Bill of Rights did not apply to the states. Even after the passage of the Fourteenth Amendment, the Court showed little interest in using it to examine criminal cases. This was true although Congress had provided further means to examine such issues by passing statutes that permitted the removal of certain state criminal cases to federal courts and, in 1867, extending the remedy of habeas corpus to prisoners held in state or local custody "in violation of the Constitution."

In 1873 the Supreme Court, in the course of ruling that a state was free to determine who could engage in certain professions within the state, held that the Fourteenth Amendment did not authorize federal judges to review state laws strictly (*Slaughter-House Cases*, 83 U.S. (16 Wall.) 36 (1873)). The relevance of the case to criminal procedure decisions was the Court's opinion that the privileges and immunities clause of the Fourteenth Amendment did not protect citizens from denial of state rights, but only from deprivation of such fundamental rights of "national citizenship" as the right to interstate travel. For the remainder of the nineteenth century and into the twentieth century, the Court held to this analysis of the meaning of the Fourteenth Amendment in criminal procedure cases.

The Court's reluctance to interfere with a state's control over individual rights arose from its historical respect for the principles of federalism. Prior to 1937, a majority of the Justices felt committed to maintaining a balance of power that guaranteed a meaningful role for state and local governments. The Supreme Court's view of the federal system was manifested in the Court's refusal to make criminal procedure provisions of the Bill of Rights applicable to state governments. The Court held that only those rights it deemed "fundamental" to national citizenship would be incorporated into the Fourteenth Amendment and made applicable to the states, and it did not find any Bill of Rights provisions relating to the criminal process to be so applicable. But in each case that found a Bill of Rights provision inapplicable to state proceedings, the Court nevertheless noted that if the state adopted a procedure unfair to the defendant and indefensible as a legitimate state interest, it might be held to violate due process.

Although the Court rejected the concept of incorporation, its expression of concern for the rights of individual defendants had laid the groundwork for federal court review of state criminal cases. In 1914 and 1915 the Court held that the due process clause of the Fourteenth Amendment required that statutes which made conduct criminal must be sufficiently clear so that a person could know the standards they set and understand what actions he need take to avoid criminal sanctions. The Court's concern with individual criminal cases was also demonstrated in *Frank v. Magnum*, 237 U.S. 309 (1915), upholding a murder conviction despite the defendant's claim that disorder in the courtroom resulted in his unjust conviction. The importance of the case is that for the first time the Court examined the facts of a state criminal conviction in detail to determine whether the adjudicatory process had been so fundamentally unfair as to violate due process. Although the state procedures were found to protect the defendant's rights sufficiently, the majority stated that interference with the course of justice by outsiders would be "a departure from due process of law in the proper sense of that term."

Employing the *Frank* principle eight years later, the Court for the first time overturned a state court decision on the ground that it violated due process (*Moore v. Dempsey*, 261 U.S. 86 (1923)). The Court, having broken with its deferential stance to state courts that had precluded realistic review, began to set precedents in developing the meaning of due process. The case of *Powell v. Alabama*, 287 U.S. 45 (1932) involved the nationally famous trial of the "Scottsboro boys," young black men accused of raping a white woman in a classic case of "small-town justice." The young men were unable to afford counsel, the trial court refused to appoint counsel, and they had no real opportunity to present their defense at trial. The Supreme Court held that in some instances due process required the appointment of counsel for indigent defendants even though the Sixth Amendment's right-to-counsel provision did not apply to the states. Thus, for the first time the Court required the states to take an affirmative step to ensure fair treatment of defendants. In 1936 the Court invalidated a state criminal conviction because it rested primarily upon a confession that police had obtained by torturing the defendant (*Brown v. Mississippi*, 297 U.S. 278 (1936)). Although the Fifth Amendment did not apply to the states, the extraction of involuntary testimony from a defendant by force violated the principle of fundamental fairness inherent in the due process clause.

By 1936, the Supreme Court had taken significant steps in its protection of individual rights. Even apart from the criminal justice process, the Court had established the principle that if a Bill of Rights provision was so fundamental a right that it was necessary to any fair system of justice, such a right would apply to the states. Thus, the First Amendment freedoms of speech and press applied to the states. Although the Court had not made the Bill of Rights criminal procedure provisions applicable to the states, it had declared that a fundamentally unfair procedure could not be used to deprive a defendant of his life, liberty, or property. This change in attitude can in part be traced to a natural development of both the Court and society. The "age of big business," still booming at the turn of the century, inspired little sentiment among the legal or public communities for protecting individual rights in other than the economic sphere. During the next several decades, however, the Justices, along with other government and social leaders, began to consider the plight of those individuals unable to defend themselves in either the legal or economic arenas. The onset of the Depression magnified the social problems of the poor, and even though the Court in the early 1930s invalidated several New Deal measures designed to aid the poor, the Justices were not insensitive to the existing social conditions. Francis Allen has noted that the Court's change in attitude toward individual liberties coincided with the rise of fascism in Europe, suggesting that the Justices, just as other Americans, were becoming increasingly concerned that their own system of government treat individuals fairly so as to prevent the adoption of the immoral attributes of a fascist system (1959, p. 213).

1937–1960: a search for constitutional values

The year 1937 marked perhaps the most dramatic change in the course of Supreme Court rulings in American history. In that year the Court altered its position regarding the constitutional restrictions on federal commercial legislation and the authority of state governments to regulate the activities of private persons in the economic sphere. No longer would the Court invalidate federal commercial regulation as intruding upon subjects of local concern. Additionally, the Justices decided that state and federal "economic and social welfare" regulations would not be subject to careful review under Fifth or Fourteenth Amendment due process clauses. Thus began the modern era of Supreme Court rulings. Turning its attention to other constitutional issues, the Court went through a period of evolution from 1937 to 1960 as it tested the suitability of due process and equal protection principles in granting individual rights to preserve free speech, freedom from racial discrimination, and fairness in criminal proceedings.

The Supreme Court rulings on civil liberties issues during this period reflected contemporary attitudes toward these issues. During the 1940s and 1950s, national political leaders brought about the supremacy of the federal government in both economic regulation and individual rights. For the first time since the post–Civil War era, civil rights issues came before national political conventions and received congressional attention. Although the Court may have been a leader in the developing interest in civil rights, it was not out of step with the attitudes prevailing in the nation.

The Court did rule on the application of specific Bill of Rights provisions to federal prosecutions during this period, but the majority of its criminal justice rulings developed due process principles governing state criminal investigations and prosecutions. The Justices now attempted to develop a due process formulation that would allow them, as well as federal judges ruling on habeas corpus petitions, to protect individual rights without unnecessary interference with state systems. The Court began by reviewing state proceedings to ensure that the procedures used at trial were not so unfair or arbitrary that they were likely to result in the conviction of innocent persons, thus making use of the fundamental fairness standard formulated in the pre-1937 cases. As time passed, however, the Court went beyond the concern for merely technically correct decision-making and increasingly emphasized the obligation of the states to grant every accused person a fair procedure that accorded a certain respect for the dignity of the individual.

Near the close of this era, Sanford Kadish analyzed the Court's development of due process principles during this evolutionary period, noting how the Court had vacillated between formulations of "fixed and flexible" concepts of due process (p. 319). The "fixed" concept of due process was embraced by those Justices who believed that any process acceptable at common law, prior to the adoption of the Fifth and Fourteenth Amendments, would be acceptable today, and that any practice deviating from the common-law tradition would violate constitutional values. Such an approach proved to be unworkable for the majority of Justices, since it failed to address the constitutional values of fairness and respect for life, liberty, and property inherent in the due process clauses. The concept of "flexible" due process gained favor with the Court because it allowed the Justices to analyze the dangers to individual rights and constitutional values presented by certain prosecutorial or investigatory practices, and to weigh those constitutional values against the legitimate needs of state and local governments to operate a criminal justice system efficiently.

The Supreme Court's position on the applicability of the Bill of Rights to state governments did not materially change during this period, since the Court protected only those rights "fundamental" to an ordered system of justice. The Court during this period refused to apply the Fifth Amendment double jeopardy and self-incrimination clauses to the states, although these cases aroused strong dissent: an example was *Adamson v. California*, 332 U.S. 46 (1947), with Justices Hugo Black, William Douglas, Frank Murphy, and Wiley Rutledge dissenting. Thus, the majority adopted a position of selective incorporation, allowing the Justices to apply those provisions fundamental to any system of justice rather than to apply the Bill of Rights wholesale to the states.

The Supreme Court first engaged in meaningful incorporation in 1948, when it held that the concept of due process in the Fourteenth Amendment mirrored the Sixth Amendment requirements that an accused be given notice of the charges brought against him and that trials be public. The most dramatic shift, however, came in *Wolf v. Colorado*, 338 U.S. 25 (1949), where the Court found that arbitrary intrusions into a person's privacy by state or local police would violate the due process clause of the Fourteenth Amendment, just as similar intrusions by federal agents would violate the Fourth Amendment. The Court thus made the Fourth Amendment applicable to the states, but only to the extent that it would give each person a constitutionally guaranteed right to privacy. However, the exclusionary rule, whereby evidence gained in violation of an individual's right to privacy could not be admitted against him at trial, was not a part of the fundamental principles of the Fourth Amendment that would apply to the states. Thus, when state or local police violated an individual's right to privacy, they were violating the Fourth Amendment as applied to the states, but evidence gained from the violation would not be suppressed unless it was gained in a manner which violated concepts of fundamental fairness so that the Court would find its use at trial violating the due process clause. Accordingly, only those police practices "shocking to the conscience" (for example, use of a stomach pump to obtain evidence) would result in the exclusion of evidence from state proceedings (*Rochin v. California*, 342 U.S. 165 (1952)).

As in the pre-1937 period, the Justices found it easiest to examine cases involving claims of unfair adversary proceedings, since such claims, if supported by evidence, indicated that the states were not properly using their criminal justice system to ensure conviction of the guilty and acquittal of the innocent. Now the Justices also held that states were required to ensure that no arbitrary barriers restricted a defendant's ability to appeal. In *Griffin v. Illinois*, 351 U.S. 12 (1956), the Court held that the due process and equal protection clauses of the Fourteenth Amendment required the states to furnish a transcript of court proceedings to those defendants convicted of felonies and unable to pay for a transcript. Although a state need not create an appellate system to comport with due process, it may not create a system that conditions the right to appeal on the furnishing of a transcript or the payment of a fee.

The question of when the government was required to furnish an attorney to those unable to afford counsel demonstrates both the distinction between state and federal cases under the selective incorporation rule, and the evolution of the due process concept as a significant restraint on state proceedings. In the 1930s the Court found that the Sixth Amendment required that in federal prosecutions, defendants unable to obtain attorneys have an attorney appointed for them unless they "intentionally and competently" waived their right. Yet the Court refused to make this Sixth Amendment rule applicable to the states until 1963. During the intervening period the Court formally used the "special circumstances rule" of *Betts v. Brady*, 316 U.S. 455 (1942). In that case, the Court held that the due process clause did not make the Sixth Amendment right to counsel applicable to the states because the right to have one's defense presented by an attorney was not a fundamental aspect of an ordered system of justice. Nevertheless, the Court recognized that in many instances the defendant could not receive a fair hearing without the assistance of counsel. Thus, a state was required to provide an attorney whenever the complexity of the charge or defense, or the defendant's limited abilities, indicated that the defendant could not receive a fair trial without the assistance of counsel.

The *Betts* rule proved difficult to enforce, since it required federal courts in habeas corpus cases and the Supreme Court in reviewing appeals to second-guess the judgment of every state court which had refused to find that counsel was necessary in an individual case. In the 1940s the Court ruled that counsel was required in any capital case since there might be many technical ways for an attorney to assist the defendant in avoiding the death penalty. However, the results of other cases decided under the "special circumstances rule" were unpredictable. As time passed, the Justices were less influenced by considerations of federalism and were more likely to review state court proceedings carefully. In fact, after 1950 the Justices required the appointment of counsel for indigents in all but the most minor cases, although they retained the special circumstances rule.

Challenges to the use of confessions confronted the Court with problems that seemed almost insoluble in terms of the due process test. Because the Fifth Amendment privilege against self-incrimination did not apply to state proceedings, the Court attempted to determine whether the confession was "voluntary," since the use of involuntary confessions would violate the due process clause. The Court initially overturned the use of confessions deemed "untrustworthy" because they had been extracted from prisoners by means of physical abuse. When there was no evidence of physical coercion, the Justices considered whether the length of interrogation and the surrounding circumstances had resulted in coercion of the defendant. The trustworthiness explanation did not account for the Court's exclusion of confessions when the trustworthiness of the confession had been verified by other evidence but the confession had been the product of coercion. In these cases the Court indicated that the due process voluntariness test would prohibit the use of confessions gained through police procedures that violated society's beliefs as to the proper prosecutorial procedure and as to the respect an individual must be accorded by the government. By the late 1950s, the Court was in fact applying two different tests to determine whether confessions were admissible. First, the confession had to be voluntary, in that it was gained by means not likely to produce a confession from an innocent person. Second, the means used must not be "shocking to the conscience" in terms of the respect due the individual.

Some defendants raised claims that use of their confession violated due process because they were interrogated without having consulted with an attorney after they had requested one. Because the Sixth Amendment was not applicable to the states, the Court used a "fundamental fairness test" to determine whether questioning of a defendant after denying him the ability to consult counsel violated due process. If there was no evidence of coercion, the Court normally allowed the use of the defendant's confession because the Justices did not find the denial of counsel to be fundamentally unfair. Summarizing the Court's position on involuntary confessions at the end of this era, Chief Justice Earl Warren stated in *Spano v. New York*, 360 U.S. 315, 320–321 (1959): "The abhorrence of society to the use of involuntary confessions does not turn alone on their inherent untrustworthiness. It also turns on the deep-rooted feeling that police must obey the law while enforcing the law; that in the end life and liberty can be as much endangered from illegal methods used to convict those thought to be criminals as from the actual criminals themselves." Some concurring Justices went further and declared that once the adversary process had been started by his indictment, a defendant had the right not to be questioned in the absence of his attorney. The case exemplifies the position of the Court at the end of this era: the majority strictly enforced the due process restrictions on state criminal proceedings, whereas others suggested a role for the Bill of Rights provisions in controlling the investigatory techniques of local police.

The 1960s: era of incorporation

The 1960s witnessed a dramatic shift as the nation left behind older notions of federalism and looked to the federal government alone for solutions to economic and social problems. For the first time in almost a century there was widespread popular support for protecting the civil liberties of individuals, particularly members of racial minorities. In the mid-1960s Congress passed the first important civil rights legislation since the Reconstruction era. It was a period of unprecedented federal intervention in state government through both the direct regulation of state activities and the awarding of federal monies based on performance conditions. In this era of popular faith in federal power and concern for individual rights, it is not surprising that the Supreme Court imposed significant restraints on state criminal justice systems and fashioned clear-cut rules that would allow the federal judiciary to monitor those systems.

It was in the 1960s that the term "Warren Court" became popular in referring to the Court's reliance on "liberal" (in the modern American sense) political philosophy in evaluating constitutional issues. However, the Justices were not seeking to alter society in ways antithetical to the will of the populace or the elected branches of the government. Rather, by applying such a political philosophy the Justices merely showed that they were men of their times, reacting to the social problems presented to them much as did members of the legislative and executive branches of the federal government.

In deciding which Bill of Rights provisions should apply to the states, the Court considered not whether a provision was fundamental to a system of ordered liberty but whether it had historically been perceived as fundamental to the Anglo-American system of justice. But the Court used this formulation to incorporate almost all of the Bill of Rights. Prior to the 1960s, all of the First Amendment freedoms and the Fourth Amendment had been made applicable to the states. During that decade, the Court found that the Fifth Amendment's double jeopardy and self-incrimination clauses both applied to the states. The notice and public-trial provisions of the Sixth Amendment had been incorporated in the 1940s; the Court now applied to the states the Sixth Amendment requirements of a speedy trial by jury and of the rights to confront witnesses, to have compulsory process to produce witnesses for the defendant, and to have the assistance of counsel. The Court also explicitly applied the cruel and unusual punishment clause of the Eighth Amendment to the actions of state and local governments, and readily assumed that the prohibition on excessive bail in that amendment also applied to the states. By 1969 all the Bill of Rights provisions governing criminal procedure had been made applicable to the states, with the exception of the grand jury clause of the Fifth Amendment, which has never been applied to them.

Some of the Justices believed that even if the Bill of Rights were to apply to the states, its provisions need not be interpreted as strictly when reviewing state proceedings as when reviewing federal proceedings. However, the majority rejected this view and has consistently held that a Bill of Rights provision incorporated into the Fourteenth Amendment applies to state and local proceedings in the same manner as it does to federal actions. Since the primary purpose of incorporation was to provide the Court with a vehicle for the rigorous scrutiny of state court proceedings, it would have been pointless to incorporate the Bill of Rights while setting different standards for state governments.

The Warren Court's imposition of control over state criminal justice systems is demonstrated most clearly by the Fourth Amendment search and seizure rulings. In *Mapp v. Ohio*, 367 U.S. 643 (1961), the Court held that the exclusionary rule which prohibited the use of evidence gained in violation of the Fourth Amendment in federal trials was applicable to state cases. Since the Court's previous rulings applying the Fourth Amendment to the states without the sanction of the exclusionary rule had not resulted in all states honoring the commands of the amendment, the exclusionary rule was found necessary to protect the individual against intrusions by state or local officers.

Three key decisional areas regarding search and seizure are of importance in evaluating the Warren Court's development of control over state proceedings: the expansion of privacy rights protected by the Fourth Amendment, the limitation of searches conducted without a warrant, and the allowance of certain "stop and frisk" practices. First, during the 1960s the Court interpreted the Fourth Amendment more strictly in determining the existence of probable cause and the reasonableness of searches and arrests. The process culminated in the Court's redefinition of the areas and interests protected by the Fourth Amendment in *Katz v. United States*, 389 U.S. 347 (1967). In *Katz*, the Court held that Fourth Amendment requirements applied to electronic surveillance even when there was no physical intrusion into property occupied by the defendant. The Court found that the Fourth Amendment gave each person a reasonable expectation of privacy which the government could not violate without complying with the restrictions of the amendment. Second, the Warren Court required police to refrain from searching for evidence until they had obtained a search warrant, except in emergency circumstances. Finally, in 1968, the Court held that the police could stop a person whenever they had a reasonable suspicion (less than probable cause to arrest) that criminal activity might be afoot, and that they could frisk him for weapons whenever they had a reasonable suspicion that the situation was dangerous. The Court's conclusion resulted from balancing the privacy interests of persons on the street against the legitimate need to provide an efficient system of criminal investigation. The balancing process demonstrated the Justices' realization that they could not control the details of the criminal justice system from the top of the judicial pyramid.

No discussion of Warren Court decisions would be complete without mention of the Court's rulings on the individual's right to an attorney and on the restrictions placed on police interrogations of suspects. In *Gideon v. Wainwright*, 372 U.S. 335 (1963), the Court incorporated the Sixth Amendment right to counsel into the Fourteenth Amendment and applied it to the states. Although *Gideon* did not state whether appointed counsel for indigent defendants would be required in all cases or in only the most serious ones, the Court notably rejected the case-by-case special circumstances rule.

In *Douglas v. California*, 372 U.S. 353 (1963), the Court found that although a state was not required to provide an appellate process, it could not create one and then deny it to those who could not afford an attorney to present their arguments to the appellate court. The Court's decision in *Douglas* made reference to due process methodology by indicating that appeal was not truly meaningful without the assistance of counsel, and the Justices held that defendants unable to employ counsel could not be denied access to this basic aspect of fair judicial process. However, the opinion's focus on the equal protection principle rather than due process complicated later attempts to determine the scope of the right to counsel.

The Warren Court also extended the Sixth Amendment right to counsel to police interrogations. The Court held that after the adversary process had begun, normally by indictment, the police could not elicit information from a defendant in the absence of his retained or appointed counsel (*Massiah v. United States*, 377 U.S. 201 (1964)). The ruling was based neither on a belief that obtaining statements from the defendant in this way was fundamentally unfair, nor on a belief that the defendant was somehow forced to incriminate himself in such situations. It was designed to prevent not police misconduct toward the defendant, but rather the subversion of the attorney's role in the adversary process. In the same year, the Supreme Court held that police interrogation of a defendant even before the initiation of adversary proceedings violated the Sixth Amendment when the police refused to allow the defendant to seek the advice of his lawyer upon the defendant's request (*Escobedo v. Illinois*, 378 U.S. 478 (1964)).

The Sixth Amendment restrictions on police interrogations were largely forgotten in the 1960s, although they would again become important in the late 1970s and the early 1980s. During the intervening period, the Sixth Amendment was eclipsed by the Court's focus on the Fifth Amendment. In *Miranda v. Arizona*, 384 U.S. 436 (1966), the Supreme Court, in an opinion written by Chief Justice Warren, excluded from evidence in criminal cases voluntary statements made by defendants under certain circumstances. The Chief Justice found that when someone was "taken into custody or otherwise deprived of his freedom of action in any significant way" and questioned by agents of the government, there was an inherent coercive pressure to give interrogators the answer they sought. Additionally, the Court found that there was no realistic means for courts to discover whether police had engaged in psychologically coercive tactics, even though the absence of physical coercion had been proved. To prevent the destruction of the Fifth Amendment principle that only voluntary confessions be used, and of the Sixth Amendment principle guaranteeing the defendant the assistance of counsel during an interrogation, the Court created a rule requiring that a defendant be informed of those rights and that no statement be accepted as evidence unless the defendant had waived his Fifth and Sixth Amendment rights.

The adverse public reaction to the *Miranda* decision typifies the relationship between the Warren Court and the nation. As Francis Allen has noted, the Court enjoyed its greatest success when its opinions and principles appealed to the basic ethical consensus in society (1975 b, p. 518). Thus, there was no real objection to granting counsel to indigent defendants at trial or to attempts to end the "third degree." But public ire was aroused when it appeared that the Court was creating technical rules about police conduct which might free persons who had committed serious crimes. Perhaps if the Court had based more of its rulings on due process considerations, it would have transmitted its concern with the fairness of the adversary process to the public and gained more support.

The post-1969 era: post-incorporation problem-solving

During the modern era, the Court appears to have abandoned due process methodology and the search for fair procedures in all but a few cases. In the late 1950s, Sanford Kadish explained that incorporation of the Bill of Rights into the Fourteenth Amendment would not necessarily expand the rights of individual defendants or protect against improper governmental action. Incorporation might instead merely shift the formal focus of the Justices' inquiry from the fairness of the procedure to the interpretation of specific Bill of Rights provisions. Thus, in interpreting a Bill of Rights provision in a given case, one Justice could assert that the provision did not restrict governmental action or protect a defendant without examining the fairness of the procedure in question.

Kadish's prophecy was realized in the 1970s and 1980s. Although the Justices have not overturned the more liberal Warren Court decisions, they have refused to extend them, simply by determining that the Bill of Rights provision involved in each case did not require additional procedural safeguards. Perhaps this was to be expected, for in the 1970s and 1980s American society and its political leaders backed away from the faith in federal power and concern for equality and civil rights that had provided the impetus for the Warren Court rulings. Although the shift in concern from the values of equality and dignity to the value of federalism may have been foreseeable for a Court operating in the current societal climate, it is unfortunate that the Justices replaced due process methodology with simple assertions as to the scope of Bill of Rights provisions. The failure of the Warren Court and the Burger Court to focus on the fairness of proceedings has contributed to the public perception of the criminal justice system as nothing more than a highly technical adversary contest between attorneys, and not a system for fairly separating the guilty from the innocent and fairly imposing sanctions upon the guilty.

The right-to-counsel decisions of the Supreme Court in the modern era have abandoned due process methodology and any attempt to determine whether the failure to provide indigent defendants with counsel has resulted in unfair convictions. In cases that happened to involve post-indictment lineups, the Warren Court had required that counsel be provided for a defendant at the lineup so as to ensure effective cross-examination at trial. But the Burger Court found that the Sixth Amendment would come into play only after the initiation of adversary proceedings, refusing to require counsel at identifications taking place before the defendant was formally charged with the offense.

The modern Court has so limited the Warren Court rulings on the right to appointed counsel that indigents today might be better off if the Warren Court had kept the special circumstances rule of *Betts* and not incorporated the Sixth Amendment. The right to counsel for all indigents seemed assured at the beginning of the 1960s, for the Justices unanimously held that the government must provide an attorney for any indigent defendant who was to be incarcerated after a finding of guilt. This attitude did not last, however, as the philosophy of the new Court took shape. In *Scott v. Illinois*, 440 U.S. 367 (1979), the Court held that counsel need not be appointed for an indigent defendant under any circumstances if he was not sentenced to imprisonment. Thus, defendants without means to retain counsel and of marginal ability to defend themselves became subject to serious sanction by fine, loss of license, or other nonincarceration punishments. Some have expressed hope that in the future the Court will give more attention to due process principles and find that even in these "minor" cases, counsel should be appointed when special circumstances show that the proceeding was not fairly conducted without the presence of an attorney. However, nothing in the language of the decisions of the modern Court gives much substance to that hope.

Even while remaining the focus of public interest and anger, the *Miranda* rules have continued throughout the modern era, although the Burger Court has refused to build upon them. For example, the Court has held that after a defendant invokes his right to remain silent, police can ask him again if he chooses to waive his rights, so long as there is sufficient time between their requests to allow him to make a knowing and intelligent decision whether to waive his Fifth Amendment right. A majority of Justices on the modern Court have indicated their belief that the rule does not relate to principles of fairness in the criminal process, but serves only as a minor deterrent to certain police activities designed to subvert a defendant's Fifth Amendment rights. Thus, the Court has upheld the use of statements gained in violation of *Miranda* for the purpose of cross-examining a defendant at trial, on the belief that initially denying the prosecution the opportunity to submit such statements as evidence constitutes a sufficient deterrent on improper police activity.

The Justices of the modern era have expanded the defendant's right to be free from government interrogation after the initiation of adversary proceedings against him. Government agents are forbidden to elicit information from a defendant who has been charged with a crime unless the defendant explicitly waives his right to have an attorney present. Apparently placing a high value on the adversary aspect of the criminal justice process, the Court has decided that the government is to deal with the defendant only through his attorney, once that process has been initiated. Although this rule engenders surprise, coming as it does from a Court notably unsympathetic toward defendants and their procedural rights, it is consistent with the attitude of a Court more "libertarian" than "liberal." The Justices are not concerned with the fairness of the criminal justice system, but require that each participant in the adversary process must play according to precise rules.

The Fourth Amendment rulings in the modern era have demonstrated a high degree of respect for the concept of federalism and little respect for the interests of privacy. The Justices determined that the leniency of federal judges in habeas corpus cases toward Fourth Amendment claims caused unnecessary continued litigation over whether state police had violated the amendment. The Court therefore held that Fourth Amendment objections to the admission of evidence in state proceedings could not be reviewed in a federal court habeas corpus proceeding so long as the state had given the defendant a fair opportunity to litigate the Fourth Amendment issues in his state trial or appellate proceedings.

The Court has found that only those who have a clear expectation of privacy in an area subject to search may raise an objection to police activities which produce evidence from that area. Thus, a passenger in an automobile has no right to object to the illegal search of the vehicle even though the police turn up evidence in the search that will be used against him. Nor does a visitor to a house have a basis for objecting to an illegal police search in that house.

The Supreme Court has given some consideration to due process values in the modern era, in requiring procedural safeguards to ensure that defendants are convicted by proof beyond a reasonable doubt. During the 1960s, the Warren Court established the principle that to incarcerate a person guilty of a criminal offense, due process required the prosecution to prove its case beyond a reasonable doubt. The Court respected this principle when it allowed a defendant convicted in a state trial to bring before a federal court, in a habeas corpus proceeding, the question of whether there was sufficient evidence at trial to justify the conviction. The majority used due process methodology to evaluate the historic and practical value of the reasonable doubt standard and the ability of the modern federal judicial system to enforce that standard on a case-by-case basis. The Court concluded that it would be intolerable to preclude defendants from federal review of whether they had been proved guilty of the crime for which they were punished.

The Supreme Court's due process decisions on the proper standard of proof in criminal cases stand in stark contrast to its decisions limiting the guarantees of the Bill of Rights. Perhaps this contrast demonstrates that the Justices in all cases consider the functional and historic values inherent in the due process clauses but simply fail to explore those issues in their opinions in Bill of Rights cases. Yet, the decision-making process of the Court as reflected in its opinions may be more important than the rules it adopts in a given year. Specific rulings are subject to review and limitation by future Courts, particularly if the opinions appear to be based more on fiat than on reasoning. Use of due process methodology rather than assertions regarding the meaning of the Bill of Rights tends to focus the attention of the Court and the public on the judicial duty to define constitutional values of individual dignity and fairness in the criminal justice process. It can only be hoped that the Justices appreciate this point and that they will return to using a due process methodology.

Some commentators have claimed that the Supreme Court "follows the ballot box," and some of the Court's history detailed here would support such a cynical thesis. However, there is no evidence that the Court has ever changed a single ruling, much less its entire attitude toward a constitutional issue, on the basis of what the Justices believe is politically acceptable at a given moment. Rather, changes in Supreme Court directions occur for precisely the same reasons that changes occur in the elected branches of government. American society does, indeed, have an ethical consensus at different points in its history, and American governmental leaders operate against the backdrop of the consensus. It would be unrealistic to expect Justices, despite their removal from the political process, not to reflect the values of society in general. It is no surprise that today the Justices are "libertarian" and concerned with restricting the power of the federal government, including that of the federal judiciary. This concern is neither more nor less justifiable than was the concern of the Court in the 1960s with the expansion of federal power, or the pre-1937 Court's concern with the principles of federalism. Yet although the Justices of the Supreme Court cannot be expected to remove themselves from their historical context, it is distressing when they appear to forget their basic function in the criminal justice area: to ensure that society provides a fundamentally fair means of determining who is deserving of sanctions for violating criminal laws. No specific set of Justices may be more or less "right" than others, but they can be honestly and fairly graded in terms of whether they have adequately explained their decisions based on these values.

JOHN E. NOWAK

See also ARREST AND STOP; BURDEN OF PROOF; CONFESSIONS; COUNSEL: RIGHT TO COUNSEL; DISCOVERY; DOUBLE JEOPARDY; EXCLUSIONARY RULES; EYEWITNESS IDENTIFICATION: CONSTITUTIONAL ASPECTS; HABEAS CORPUS; JURY: JURY TRIAL; PRISONERS, LEGAL RIGHTS OF; PROBATION AND PAROLE: PROCEDURAL PROTECTION; PUBLICITY IN CRIMINAL CASES; SEARCH AND SEIZURE; SENTENCING: PROCEDURAL PROTECTION; SPEEDY TRIAL; TRIAL, CRIMINAL; WIRETAPPING AND EAVESDROPPING.

BIBLIOGRAPHY

ALLEN, FRANCIS A. "Federalism and the Fourth Amendment: A Requiem for Wolf." *Supreme Court Review, 1961.* Edited by Philip B. Kurland. University of Chicago Press, 1961, pp. 1–48.

———. "Foreword: Quiescence and Ferment—The 1974 Term in the Supreme Court." *Journal of Criminal Law and Criminology* 66 (1975a): 391–399.

———. "The Judicial Quest for Penal Justice: The Warren Court and the Criminal Cases." *University of Illinois Law Forum* (1975b): 518–542.

———. "The Supreme Court, Federalism, and State Systems of Criminal Justice." *DePaul Law Review* 8 (1959): 213–255.

FAIRMAN, CHARLES. "Does the Fourteenth Amendment Incorporate the Bill of Rights?: The Original Understanding." *Stanford Law Review* 2 (1949): 5–139.

FRIENDLY, HENRY J. "The Bill of Rights as a Code of Criminal Procedure." *California Law Review* 53 (1965): 929–956.

ISRAEL, JEROLD H. "Criminal Procedure, the Burger Court, and the Legacy of the Warren Court." *Michigan Law Review* 75 (1977): 1319–1425.

KADISH, SANFORD H. "Methodology and Criteria in Due Process Adjudication: A Survey and Criticism." *Yale Law Journal* 66 (1957): 319–363.

KAMISAR, YALE. *Police Interrogation and Confessions: Essays in Law and Policy.* Ann Arbor: University of Michigan Press, 1980.

———; LAFAVE, WAYNE R.; and ISRAEL, JEROLD H. *Modern Criminal Procedure: Cases, Comments, and Questions.* 5th ed. St. Paul: West, 1980.

KAPLAN, JOHN. "The Limits of the Exclusionary Rule." *Stanford Law Review* 26 (1974): 1027–1055.

LAFAVE, WAYNE R. *Search and Seizure: A Treatise on the Fourth Amendment.* 3 vols. St. Paul: West, 1978.

NOWAK, JOHN E. "Foreword: Due Process Methodology in the Postincorporation World." *Journal of Criminal Law and Criminology* 70 (1979): 397–423.

———. "Foreword: Evaluating the Work of the New Libertarian Supreme Court." *Hastings Constitutional Law Quarterly* 7 (1980): 263–314.

———; ROTUNDA, RONALD; and YOUNG, J. NELSON. *Handbook on Constitutional Law.* St. Paul: West, 1978 (plus annual supplements).

SCHAEFER, WALTER V. "Federalism and State Criminal Procedure." *Harvard Law Review* 70 (1956): 1–26.

———. *The Suspect and Society: Criminal Procedure and Converging Constitutional Doctrines.* Evanston, Ill.: Northwestern University Press, 1967.

STONE, GEOFFREY. "The Miranda Doctrine in the Burger Court." *Supreme Court Review, 1977.* Edited by Philip B. Kurland and Gerhard Casper. University of Chicago Press, 1978, pp. 99–169.

WELLINGTON, HARRY H. "Common Law Rules and Constitutional Double Standards: Some Notes on Adjudication." *Yale Law Journal* 83 (1973): 221–311.

2.
COMPARATIVE ASPECTS

Purposes and problems

Knowledge of foreign ways of solving procedural problems generates a pool of ideas for law reform at home. That insight has led American proceduralists to study foreign procedural systems. Traditionally, the English and other common-law systems were the models for domestic reform. Since the 1970s, however, dissatisfaction with the realities of Anglo-American criminal procedure has become so intense that radically different models have been sought. The criminal process of countries belonging to the civil law family, especially France, West Germany, and Italy, has attracted growing interest.

Although potentially valuable as a reform tool, comparison must be conducted with great caution. A few major pitfalls should be mentioned. First, areas of comparison can be defined too dogmatically. A researcher may look in vain for the equivalent of a particular procedural institution; yet it may be that another arrangement of procedural or even substantive law, appearing in a totally different context, has similar effects. Second, adaptation of foreign solutions creates its own problems. A procedural device that works excellently in its original environment may be ineffectual or even counterproductive as a transplant severed from its roots. Particular attention must be paid to the attitudes of judges and lawyers toward imports from foreign systems: lawyers have a tendency to digest concepts imposed on them by "integrating" them into the old mold and thus preventing substantive change. Finally, comparativists must beware of merely comparing the laws on the books. Especially in the field of criminal procedure, practice can be radically different from the letter of the law, and institutions may be quite unlike what they seem on paper.

This article explores areas in which the comparison of foreign procedural systems may be relevant to American law. Legal systems included are those of France, West Germany, Spain, and Japan. West Germany, and especially France, represent the approach typical of the inquisitorial model of the criminal process. The pretrial investigation is conducted by a magistrate or an impartial state's attorney; at the trial, the presiding judge examines the evidence and interrogates witnesses, and the attorneys for the state and the accused play only supplementary roles. That mode of proceeding is diametrically opposed to the adversary system of the common-law countries, where the parties collect the evidence and present it in a trial that often assumes the form of a combat. Spain and Japan represent intermediate solutions. In Spain, the investigation is conducted by an independent magistrate, but at the trial the evidence is presented by the parties. In Japan, the police investigate the case under the supervision of the state's attorney, but an adversary trial takes place that includes presentation and cross-examination of witnesses by the parties.

The contrast between the inquisitorial and the adversary modes of proceeding has long been the cornerstone of scholarly comparison of criminal procedure. Its practical importance has been greatly overrated, however, as the existence of a variety of eclectic systems demonstrates. In fact, every modern system of criminal procedure includes at least some inquisitorial as well as adversary features; procedural functions are distributed in some way or other between the representatives of the parties and the detached representatives of the state. The inquisitorial as well as the adversary models thus are no more than ideal types that refer back to differing styles of allocating political authority (Damaška, 1975).

Investigation

Investigation in criminal matters is in all procedural systems a function of the police, even though the law often confers investigatory authority on a magistrate, as in France (Code de Procédure Pénale [CPP], arts. 80, 81) and Spain (Ley de Enjuiciamiento Criminal [LEC] promulgada por R.D. de 14 de septiembre de 1882, Gaceta 1882, nos. 260 and 283, art. 306), or on the state's attorney, as in West Germany (Strafprozessordnung [StPO] vom 7. Januar 1975, Bundesgesetzblatt 1975 I, p. 129, § 160). These officials regularly delegate routine matters to police or other nonlegal personnel but retain the right to investigate important or sensitive cases. Express judicial authorization of acts interfering with the liberty or privacy of citizens is required in all systems, but exceptions for urgent cases are provided with varying liberality.

Detention, arrest, search, and seizure. Pretrial detention can be ordered only by a magistrate (CPP, art. 146; StPO, § 114; LEC, art. 502; Japanese Keiji Soshoho [KS] of July 10, 1948, Law No. 131, § 60). No judicial warrant is necessary, however, for arrest and brief (one to three days') detention by the police if the suspect is apprehended while committing the crime or shortly thereafter, or under circumstances creating strong suspicion (CPP, arts. 62, 73; LEC, arts. 490, 492; KS, § 212). In West Germany, the police can arrest and detain a suspect for up to forty-eight hours if there is good reason to believe that he might flee or destroy evidence (StPO, § 127, para. 2). Article 33 of the Japanese Constitution of 1946 permits arrest without warrant only when the offender is caught in the act, but Section 210 of the Code of Criminal Procedure of Japan authorizes police to arrest the suspect first and seek a judicial warrant later in urgent cases of serious crime (cf. Dando, pp. 316–317).

Similarly, searches and seizures must on principle be ordered by a magistrate, but they can be conducted without such authorization if required by exigent circumstances (CPP, art. 56; StPO, §§ 105, 111e; KS, § 220). Standards of suspicion authorizing police to conduct searches and to make arrests tend to be somewhat lower in civil law countries than the exacting probable cause requirement imposed by American law. Because the law accords the individual less extensive protection against invasions of his privacy in the course of a criminal investigation, the problem of controlling police behavior plays a lesser role in civil law countries. Nevertheless, conflicts between the interests of vigorous law enforcement and the rights of the individual do arise, and everywhere citizens need protection from overzealous police.

Control of police. The conflict between law enforcement and the individual's privacy does not lend itself to simple solutions, since both interests are valued highly in free societies. American law has adopted an indirect approach designed to give maximum protection to the individual. Evidence obtained in violation of the suspect's rights cannot be used in court to support a conviction (*Mapp v. Ohio*, 367 U.S 643 (1961)). Proponents of that rule, assuming that police have a professional interest in the conviction of criminals, expect it to have a deterrent effect on illegal police behavior.

In other systems, comparable but less sweeping rules apply. In West Germany and Japan, confessions obtained by force, deception, or other illegal means cannot be introduced as evidence (StPO, § 136a; KS, § 319). Other violations, however, such as an illegally prolonged period of detention (Abe, pp. 71–72) or a failure to warn the defendant of his right to remain silent (cf. Judgment of the German High Court of Appeals of May 31, 1968, 4 StR 19/68, 22 Entscheidungen des Bundesgerichtshofes in Strafsachen [BGHSt] 170 (1969)), do not render a confession inadmissible. In France, confessions made without proper warnings of the right to remain silent and of the right to obtain the assistance of an attorney are stricken from the record; however, this rule applies only to statements made before an investigating magistrate (CPP, arts. 114, 118, 170, 174). Police violations of procedural rights remain without sanction unless the court finds that they have fundamentally vitiated the fact-finding process (Merle and Vitu, pp. 320–322). Contraband obtained through illegal searches or seizures is generally treated as valid evidence in West Germany and Japan, but it is excluded in cases of serious crime in France (CPP, arts. 59, para. 3; 171).

Because indirect control of the police through the exclusion of tainted evidence is severely limited in civil law countries, one would expect to find other control mechanisms. Such alternatives exist, but their practical efficacy is questionable, to say the least. The criminal and civil liability of police officers may check outright brutality, but it provides only a fragmentary and notoriously ineffectual remedy for violations of procedural law. Nor do organizational arrangements necessarily prevent police misconduct. In West Germany, police in criminal matters are formally regarded as auxiliaries of the state's attorney and subject to his orders and supervision (Gerichtsverfassungsgesetz [GVG] vom 9. Mai 1975, Bundesgesetzblatt 1975 I, p. 1077, § 152); in France and Japan, "judicial police" are similarly subordinated to the prosecutor (CPP, arts. 12, 13; KS, § 193). When police are regarded as the extended arm of other authorities formally in charge, unlawful investigatory behavior can conceivably be prevented in two different ways: either by requiring a prior judicial order for each step in the investigation (cf. LEC, arts. 286–296) or by according special disciplinary authority to the supervising magistrate or prosecutor (cf. CPP, arts. 224–230; KS, § 194).

The latter method has not gained much practical importance as a check on police misconduct in the countries whose statutes make it available (Merle and Vitu, p. 899). This is hardly surprising, since formal disciplinary proceedings, especially if initiated by an external agency, appear disproportionate with respect to routine violations and should be reserved for the most egregious offenses.

The idea of entrusting to an impartial magistrate rather than to the police the conducting of essential portions of the investigation has been recommended for adoption in the United States (Weinreb). The institution of the investigating magistrate is characteristic of continental criminal procedure, but its practical importance may have been overestimated. Whereas France, Italy, and Spain still retain the investigating magistrate, West Germany abolished that office in 1975 because it was no longer regarded as necessary. In France and Italy the investigating magistrate is often bypassed or reduced to token activity (Goldstein and Marcus, pp. 246–259). A Spanish statute requires that the investigating magistrate be informed within twenty-four hours of all acts of investigation performed by the police and that he collect transcripts of police protocols. In practice he does little else. Even the interrogation of the suspect and of witnesses, which is the magistrate's sole domain under Spanish law (LEC, arts. 385, 410), is in minor cases often delegated to supporting personnel (Volkmann-Schluck, p. 19). Whatever the statutory arrangement, it appears inevitable that the prime responsibility for conducting the investigation resides with the police. It would be unrealistic to expect that a magistrate or state's attorney could single-handedly conduct or even control the investigation as long as the police monopolize the requisite manpower, equipment, and experience. The "myth of judicial supervision" (Goldstein and Marcus) created by the theoretical omnipotence of the investigating magistrate may indeed have the effect of shielding the police from effective control.

External supervision of police conduct is unlikely to succeed for yet another reason: violations of procedural rights often occur in one-to-one encounters between a police officer and a citizen, and therefore are difficult to prove. Moreover, police tend to perceive hostile attitudes in magistrates, prosecutors, or judges reviewing their actions, and to close ranks against searching intrusions from the outside. Thus, control of police by police remains the only effective means of ensuring lawful police conduct. Internal control through strict supervision and disciplinary procedures works well within the hierarchical police structures of West Germany and Japan. In both countries, a traditional sense of discipline and a strong esprit de corps on the part of individual police officers constitute the psychological basis for efficient self-policing (Bayley, chap. 4). In Japan, the Human Rights Bureau of the Ministry of Justice acts as a police ombudsman, accepting and investigating complaints of police misconduct and urging police to discipline officers when allegations are found to be true (Bayley, pp. 68–69). Civilian review boards can be effective even if they lack enforcement powers, but they are dependent on police acceptance and cooperation.

Prosecution

Prosecutorial discretion. The virtually uncontrolled power of the American prosecutor to dismiss cases even when conviction is probable has been criticized by American scholars (cf. Davis, Busck et al.) on the ground that it permits arbitrariness and unequal treatment. Since American law by and large prevents private citizens from filing criminal charges, absolute prosecutorial discretion creates the further danger of frustrating the legitimate interests of victims.

Foreign systems offer alternatives to unfettered prosecutorial discretion. Three methods of limiting or controlling discretion can be distinguished, each of which is employed by at least one of the four countries under consideration: (1) the statute can impose a duty to prosecute if, given the evidence available, conviction is probable; (2) a mechanism of independent review of dismissals can be provided; and (3) the complainant (or any citizen) can be given the right to file criminal charges directly with the court.

Spain is one of several European countries in which the prosecutor cannot legally decline to prosecute cases if there is enough evidence to convict (LEC, art. 105). In Germany the same principle applies, but only with respect to serious felonies (StPO, § 152, para. 2). Observers of Spanish practice, however, report that many Spanish prosecutors only pay lip service to the law: they move for dismissal of a considerable number of convictable minor cases but disguise that exercise of discretion by claiming insufficiency of the evidence (Volkmann-Schluck, pp. 44–45). That phenomenon can also be found in other countries that rely on the principle of mandatory prosecution. Prosecutorial discretion, it seems, cannot be abolished by legislative fiat: since the function of the prosecutor in all systems is to weed out cases lacking a reasonable prospect of conviction, he has (and exercises) the actual power to dismiss provable but trifling cases along with unsubstantiated ones. All participants tacitly accept this arrogation of discretion not conferred by the law. The screening of cases that do not merit the court's time is recognized as an appropriate task for the prosecutor. Systems of mandatory prosecution provide the prosecutor with a clear guideline but are incapable of eliminating discretion.

West Germany and, to a limited extent, Japan provide for external review of the prosecutor's decision to dismiss. When a West German prosecutor closes a case because he deems the evidence insufficient for conviction, he must notify the private complainant and state his reasons. A victim not satisfied with the disposition can complain to the supervising state's attorney, and if the original dismissal is upheld, the victim can file an appeal with the state appellate court. The court, if it concludes that the victim's claim is well founded, orders the prosecutor to file charges. The victim then has the right to join the proceedings as a "supplementary prosecutor" (StPO, §§ 171–175, 395). German victims have recourse to the appellate courts only in a minuscule number of all cases dismissed by the prosecutor, but the fact that the option is available serves as a check on prosecutorial arbitrariness. German prosecutors can dismiss cases of lesser seriousness, even if a conviction at trial is probable, whenever there is minor guilt on the part of the accused and no public interest in prosecution (StPO, § 153). In these cases the victim cannot appeal the prosecutor's decision outside the prosecutorial hierarchy, but the dismissal must be approved initially by the magistrate unless only a minor property offense is involved.

Japanese law similarly permits the private complainant to appeal the dismissal of his case but limits that possibility to certain offenses involving misconduct of public officials (KS, § 262). Other cases can be presented to an inquest commission consisting of eleven citizens selected by lot (Dando, p. 342). This independent commission investigates cases in which the public prosecutor has refused to file charges. It is not empowered to direct the prosecutor to change his position but is limited to giving advice and making recommendations. Statistics for the years 1967 through 1971 show that the prosecutor followed the commission's recommendation to bring charges in only 15 percent to 28 percent of the cases in which such recommendations were made (Kühne, p. 1093). The inquest commission, which was modeled after the grand jury and was introduced in 1948, thus appears to be of limited efficacy.

A third way of confining prosecutorial discretion is to permit criminal prosecution by private citizens. English law relies almost exclusively on private prosecution; many other countries provide for it in cases when public prosecution is denied. In France, anyone who suffers harm, material or otherwise, as a result of a criminal act can initiate an action for damages before the criminal court, and the public prosecutor must then join that action by filing criminal charges (CPP, art. 1, para. 2). Spanish law goes even further: not only the victim but any citizen can file a criminal complaint (LEC, arts. 101, 270). This right is guaranteed by Article 125 of the Spanish Constitution of 1978. Upon receipt of a citizen's complaint, the investigating magistrate is obliged to conduct a regular preliminary investigation. The court cannot dismiss charges preferred by a private complainant unless it finds that the act in question does not constitute a crime (LEC, art. 645). In West Germany, private accusation is limited to certain minor offenses typically committed among neighbors and acquaintances, for example, libel, slander, trespass, destruction of property, and assault (StPO, § 374). With respect to these

crimes, the law confers upon the wronged party primary responsibility for prosecution, but the state's attorney can take over if the public interest so requires (StPO, §§ 376, 377).

In practice, neither in Spain nor in West Germany does private prosecution play a significant role. Under Spanish law the public prosecutor has an unqualified duty to prosecute all cases of crime, so that little scope is left for private initiative (cf. Volkmann-Schluck, pp. 46–47). The West German system requires the private complainant to prepare the case for litigation without the help of the police or other state agencies—a task that most private individuals are ill-equipped to undertake. Moreover, courts often dismiss private complaints because of the defendant's "minor guilt" (StPO, § 383, para. 2), which leaves the complainant with the bill for his own as well as his adversary's expenses. That practice is not likely to increase the enthusiasm of crime victims for private prosecution.

In France, by contrast, private action (*action civile*) is quite popular (Grebing, p. 36). The secret of its success lies in the combination of criminal prosecution and redress for harm suffered by the complainant. Many victims avail themselves of the speedy, inexpensive, and efficient course of seeking damages through criminal proceedings, rather than suing in civil court. *Action civile* not only serves pecuniary interests but also constitutes the victim's tool for achieving retribution in spite of the public prosecutor's unwillingness to act. Courts have admitted organizations representing certain classes of crime victims as private prosecutors, and although these organizations claim only symbolic damages, they have a strong interest in the criminal conviction of the offender (Stéfani, Levasseur, and Bouloc, pp. 160–172, 207–208).

The French system provides a most effective check on the prosecutor's decision not to file charges in instances of crime in which the victim is an individual. This check may even go too far in that it subjects the prosecutor to the judgment of the individual victim: if the victim initiates an *action civile*, the public prosecutor is bound to follow suit. The West German system offers a more balanced solution: if a conflict arises between the prosecutor and the victim, a neutral judge decides whether criminal prosecution is warranted. This system should, however, be extended to decisions based not on the sufficiency of the evidence but on other, discretionary reasons for nonprosecution. If the prosecutor's estimate of the chances of conviction can be submitted to judicial review, the victim should a fortiori have the right to obtain an objective reassessment of the prosecutor's discretionary decision to drop a case in which he regards conviction as probable. The examples of West Germany and Japan demonstrate that the efficacy of judicial supervision does not depend on a large number of cases actually being appealed. The mere possibility of external review forces the prosecutor to formulate and adhere to rational standards of decision-making.

Diversion. To the extent that the law permits dismissal of cases in which convictions could have been obtained, it enables the prosecutor to divert presumably guilty suspects from the criminal process. In some systems, the power to impose informal sanctions is added to the prosecutor's authority to divert. This is true, for example, in Japan, where the prosecutor can make dismissal contingent on the fulfillment of certain conditions. The defendant can be sent to a classification center, and restrictions can be imposed upon his life style for a period of several months (Kühne, pp. 1090–1091). All these measures are based on the formal consent of the defendant; yet his submission can hardly be called voluntary if the alternative is criminal prosecution.

West German law also provides for prosecutorial diversion. If the defendant is suspected of having committed an offense of lesser seriousness and if his guilt was minor, the prosecutor, with the consent of the court, can offer to dismiss the case on the condition that the defendant pay a sum of money to the victim, to a charitable organization, or to the state (StPO, § 153a). The defendant can refuse to accept that arrangement, but he risks conviction in the criminal court if he does.

Such diversionary practices are popular because they save time and money and at the same time allow marginal offenders to avoid the stigma of criminal conviction. Yet critics point to a number of drawbacks: sanctioning authority is effectively shifted from the judge to the prosecutor; there is a lack of standards of eligibility for diversion, which may lead to unequal treatment; innocent defendants may be psychologically coerced into accepting diversionary sanctions rather than risking conviction; and the availability of diversionary measures may enlarge rather than reduce the overall scope of state control over individuals' lives. In spite of these objections, most of which come from academics, a further growth of diversion can be expected. Its practical advantages commend it to prosecutors, court administrators, and defense counsel alike, and it is beneficial to the great majority of defendants.

However, it is important to develop proper safeguards for the fair and equitable application of diversionary measures. Eligibility standards should be regulated by explicit guidelines; diversion should be possible only after a thorough investigation has established with reasonable accuracy the criminal liability of the defendant; there should be a requirement that diversionary sanctions be approved by a neutral magistrate; and it should be guaranteed that a defendant who refuses diversion is not penalized for that refusal. The introduction of these safeguards would reduce to some extent the informality of diversion and would assimilate it to a simplified form of adjudication. That might make it less attractive to prosecutors, as the West German experience with a fairly formalized variant of prosecutorial diversion indicates (Zipf, p. 146). Yet a prosecutor who imposes serious sanctions and thus fulfills functions of a judge should accept at least some of the procedural restrictions applicable to judicial adjudication and sentencing.

Adjudication

Adversary and inquisitorial styles of trial. One of the most commonly noted differences between Anglo-American and continental procedural systems lies in the allocation of functions at the criminal trial. On the Continent, the trial is typically dominated by the presiding judge, who determines the order in which evidence is taken and who examines witnesses and experts; by contrast, in the Anglo-American system the presentation of evidence is generally the task of the parties. Whatever the advantages and disadvantages of either method of proof-taking, it would be quite unrealistic to expect that either system voluntarily adopt the style of the other. Modes of proceeding at trial are much too deeply entrenched in the traditions of each country and too intimately connected with the legal education and role concepts of legal personnel to be changed merely upon recognition of the superiority of a differing approach. The following survey of four procedural systems shows, however, that there is room for a wide variety of modifications in either model.

French criminal procedure is closest to the prototype of the inquisitorial model. It confers central responsibility for finding the truth upon the presiding judge, who sits with two associate judges in regular cases, and with two associate judges and nine lay assessors in the most serious cases. When the formal document of accusation is filed with the court, the presiding judge reviews the evidence gathered by the investigating magistrate and instructs him to undertake additional investigations if necessary (CPP, art. 283). Both parties submit lists of witnesses to be heard at the trial, but the presiding judge can call additional witnesses and have any other evidence produced, including transcripts of earlier statements of witnesses who do not testify at trial; furthermore, he can appoint experts and direct the court to view the scene of the crime (Merle and Vitu, pp. 709–710). Article 310 of the French criminal code gives the presiding judge discretionary authority to take all measures he deems useful to discover the truth. He interrogates all witnesses and the defendant; the parties and their representatives can suggest additional questions but may not themselves examine witnesses (CPP, art. 312). At the end of the trial the representatives of the parties deliver closing statements. The presiding judge does not sum up the evidence or instruct the lay judges in open court (art. 347, para. 2), but as he participates in the deliberations of the court he has ample opportunity to explain the law and advise on the evidence behind closed doors. French judges are not bound by any formal rules in the evaluation of the evidence but are to decide on the basis of their "internal conviction" (*intime conviction*) (art. 427). If the court sits with lay assessors, a majority of eight votes is needed to convict (art. 359). The votes are cast in a secret ballot (art. 357).

In West Germany, trial courts consist of professional judges and laymen in all but the most petty cases, which are decided by a professional judge sitting alone. The court is responsible for having all relevant evidence available at the trial. Thus, witnesses and experts are usually called by the court, either upon a motion by one of the parties or upon the court's own initiative. However, either party has a right to call its own witnesses and experts, whom the court is obliged to hear unless the facts about which they are to testify are irrelevant or duplicative (StPO, § 245, para. 2). The defendant (if he wishes to testify) and all witnesses and experts are examined by the presiding judge, but all other judges and the parties have the right to ask additional questions. Witnesses testify in narrative form (§ 69), but in practice the judge usually guides them with questions and confronts them with statements they had made earlier. For that purpose, he makes liberal use of the dossier of the pretrial investigation, to which professional (but not lay) judges have access.

Section 239 of the West German code permits the examination and cross-examination of witnesses by the parties upon the request of both parties; the judge is then limited to asking additional questions. This provision is almost never used in practice. German attorneys are not trained in the art of examining witnesses and gladly leave that task to the judge. Except in extraordinary cases, parties make sparing use even of their right to ask additional questions; some attor-

neys fear to antagonize the judge by probing further when he deems the examination of a witness complete. The presiding judge can reject irrelevant and inappropriate questions (§ 241, para. 2). The state's attorney and defense counsel each sum up their positions at the end of the trial, and the defendant has the opportunity to speak last. As in France, professional and lay judges deliberate and decide together; a two-thirds majority is required for conviction (§ 263).

Both the French and the German systems are committed to the principle of substantive truth. The court, which is responsible for finding the facts and applying the law, must seek to determine what has actually happened. It is not bound by contentions, stipulations, and admissions of the parties. The court must determine the credibility of each piece of evidence without being guided by any legal rules in that respect. The same principles apply in the Japanese and Spanish systems, even though evidence is presented by the parties.

Japanese criminal procedure law originally followed the model of the French and German codes, but after World War II, American procedural principles were superimposed on its inquisitorial structure. The Japanese Constitution, in force since 1946, guarantees every accused person the right to counsel and to a speedy trial as well as the right to use compulsory process for obtaining witnesses and the right to examine all witnesses (art. 37). Article 38 of the Constitution contains the privilege against self-incrimination and a requirement that confessions be corroborated by independent evidence. The ensuing structure has been called adversary in form but investigatory in substance (Dando, pp. 82, 173).

In Japan, most criminal matters are decided by a single professional judge; only very serious cases are adjudicated by a court consisting of three professional judges. There are no jurors or other lay judges in Japanese procedure. The judge has no prior knowledge of the results of the pretrial investigation conducted by the police. At the beginning of the trial, the prosecutor reads the formal accusation. The defendant is then asked whether he declares himself guilty as charged. If he does, the trial is conducted in simplified form. If the defendant denies guilt, the evidence as proposed by the parties is examined. The judge can also introduce evidence on his own motion (KS, § 298, para. 2). According to the Japanese code, the judge is to interrogate each witness first, and the parties then have an opportunity to examine and to cross-examine him (§ 304). In practice, the order is almost always reversed. The defendant is heard last, and if written evidence of a confession is admissible, it is read into the record at the end of the trial (§ 301). Hearsay evidence is generally excluded, but there are liberal exceptions to this rule.

The principle of party determination, typical of the adversary process, is satisfied in that the prosecutor's formal accusation defines the factual and legal contentions at issue. But the court can, in the course of the trial, order the counts altered or supplemented even without the consent of the parties (§ 312, para. 2). Japanese courts have given narrow interpretations to two other American implants: the defendant's right to have witnesses subpoenaed has been made dependent on a discretionary decision of the court (Dando, p. 282), and an exception to the requirement that confessions must be corroborated has been recognized for confessions made in open court (Dando, p. 226, n. 3). Thus, it seems that in many instances the inquisitorial heritage of Japanese criminal procedure shines through its adversary disguise.

A similar phenomenon has been described with respect to the Spanish criminal process (Volkmann-Schluck). When the Spanish Code of Criminal Procedure was drafted in the nineteenth century, its authors intended to reform the traditional inquisitorial process by introducing rules they found in English procedural law, in particular the principle of party determination and presentation of evidence. Thus, the Spanish code requires the parties to define in advance the contested issues and to submit to the court lists containing the evidence they wish to introduce. Article 728 of the Spanish code expressly forbids the court to examine any other evidence. In practice, however, Spanish courts care little about that restriction but call witnesses on their own motion and even go beyond the issues defined by the parties, relying on the fact that the taking of additional proof cannot be raised successfully on appeal (Volkmann-Schluck, pp. 75–76).

The Spanish Code of Criminal Procedure prescribes examination and cross-examination by the parties as the primary method of taking oral testimony and restricts the presiding judge to asking additional questions (LEC, art. 708). Judges also have the right to reject irrelevant questions, and they often use that right to limit questioning by defense counsel to issues already explored in the course of pretrial investigation (Volkmann-Schluck, pp. 92–93). If the judge calls a witness not named by one of the parties, the rule of party interrogation does not apply, and it is the judge who asks the questions. But even where the law's demand for party presentation of oral testimony is honored, the spectacle of examination and cross-examina-

tion often lacks practical relevance: the facts have been developed thoroughly by the investigating magistrate before trial, and the court can (and frequently does) rely on the dossier of the pretrial investigation, especially if a witness's oral testimony deviates from his earlier statements (LEC, art. 714). Since there are no lay judges, strict adherence to rules of evidence is regarded as unnecessary, and since the court is familiar with the transcript of the pretrial investigation, it can—at least informally—consider the information gathered before trial as though it were competent evidence (Volkmann-Schluck, p. 85).

The examples of Spain and Japan demonstrate how resistant the inquisitorial heritage is to efforts to inoculate it with elements of a foreign system; they also show to what extent procedural practice is shaped by the traditions and attitudes of the lawyers involved rather than by the letter of the law. Attempts to implement wholesale change in the mode of trial simply by legislation are therefore bound to fail. On the other hand, this survey of procedural systems that are in continuous use in countries generally regarded as civilized shows that inquisitorial principles of criminal adjudication do not necessarily involve the rack and the screw but are compatible with the presumption of innocence and with an attitude of respect for the civil rights of the accused. Reforms that are suggested within the common-law system, such as giving the trial judge a more active role in the fact-finding process, should therefore not be discredited merely because of their affinity to the continental system.

Trial and sentencing. In common-law countries, trial and sentencing are kept strictly separate. Sentencing becomes an issue only if the trial has led to a verdict of guilty. Sentencing hearings take place a few days or weeks after the trial, sentencing decisions are in most cases made by the judge alone and not by the jury, and the rules of evidence are somewhat relaxed when the trial itself is over. However, different procedures prevail in the countries belonging to the civil law family. In France, West Germany, Spain, and Japan a single trial is held, at which the issues of both guilt and sentence are argued and decided upon. No distinction is made between evidence relevant to guilt and evidence relevant to sentencing; even the most sensitive information, such as the prior record of the defendant, is admissible at the trial insofar as it has an impact on sentencing. The judgment proclaimed at the end of the session includes both the finding on the issue of guilt and, except in the event of acquittal, the sentence.

The main argument in favor of this arrangement is that it saves time. But, viewed in comparison with the separation of the issues as practiced in Anglo-American law, the unitary trial creates at least three major problems. First, since evidence relevant to sentencing is freely admissible, there is no restriction against material prejudicial to the defendant on the issue of guilt; second, since the emphasis of the trial is on the determination of guilt or innocence, the rehabilitative and protective aspects of sentencing are often not sufficiently explored; and third, in his closing statement, defense counsel is constrained to argue for acquittal and simultaneously for lenient punishment of the defendant. For these reasons, West German academics have long favored the Anglo-American practice of holding separate hearings (Herrmann), and experiments with that model have been conducted, with some success, in German courts since the late 1970s.

Lay judges. Trial by a jury of one's peers was one of the great demands of liberal reformers of the criminal process in the nineteenth century. Each of the four countries considered in this article adopted trial by jury, often citing English procedure as a model; but none of them has retained the jury system. In France, the jury was introduced in 1791 and merged into a court consisting of professional and lay judges in 1941. In Germany, the Code of Criminal Procedure of 1877 (Strafprozessordnung vom 1. Februar 1877, Reichsgesetzblatt 1877, p. 253) established juries for the most serious offenses; they were abolished as independent fact-finders in 1924, but lay judges were retained to serve together with professional judges on mixed panels (cf. Langbein, 1981). Spain introduced the jury system in 1888 but abolished it in 1923 and, after a brief interlude during the period of the Second Republic, abolished it again in 1936. Article 125 of the Spanish Constitution of 1978 guarantees every Spanish citizen the right to participate in the administration of criminal justice as a juror, but the mandate to change the procedural laws has not yet been carried out. Japanese law provided for criminal juries only from 1928 to 1943. The institution was so alien to the Japanese legal tradition that it was not revived after World War II.

Historically, the demand for a jury system was rooted in the liberal reformers' distrust of professional judges selected and controlled by the sovereign. As the judiciary gained increasing independence, the original justification for the existence of courts consisting exclusively of laymen disappeared. At the same time, dissatisfaction with the performance of juries was growing: as the law and the factual background of many offenses became increasingly complicated, jurors lost their ability fully to comprehend the issues and rendered capricious judgments. Moreover, the jury system turned out to be rather expensive, which made it a favorite target for abolition in times of war or economic crisis. Those countries wishing to retain a lay element in criminal jurisprudence, for example, France and West Germany, have introduced systems of mixed courts, in which lay judges selected from the general population hear and decide the case together with professional judges. In the French court of assizes and in German courts dealing with less serious crimes, the lay judges have a majority; in Germany, three professional and two lay judges decide the most serious cases. In this system of lay participation, the freshness of judgment and worldly experience of nonlawyers are combined with the sophistication of judges educated in the law.

American law, bound by the Constitution, has preferred to retain the independent jury. It has paid a heavy price in so doing. Because jurors deliberate without the guidance of a lawyer, the law of evidence must be shaped so as to minimize confusion and error on the part of lay persons. This, in the context of the adversary system, has led to the formulation of highly complicated and technical rules of evidence based on questionable assumptions about the psychology of the average juror. Moreover, the attempt to make difficult issues of fact or law palatable to the juror tends to protract trials. As jury trials become costly and unmanageable, the parties' desire to avoid them increases. The result is a trial rate of less than 10 percent in many American cities. The experience with mixed panels abroad might encourage American courts to experiment with such panels in cases in which the defendant waives his right to a jury trial; if such experiments prove successful, the mode of lay participation in the administration of criminal justice may be reconsidered.

Adjudication of uncontested cases. The common law makes a sharp distinction between contested and uncontested criminal cases. Regular criminal trials are reserved for the former, whereas the latter are adjudicated solely on the basis of the defendant's plea of guilty. Although this system avoids wasteful proceedings in clear-cut cases, it lends itself to abuse; pressure can be (and often is) exerted upon the defendant to forego his procedural rights and to refrain from contesting the state's case.

Most civil law countries do not provide for distinctive modes of processing cooperative and uncooperative defendants. The inquisitorial ideal requires a full investigation of the facts even if the defendant confesses guilt. In France, West Germany, and Japan, cases of serious crime are therefore always adjudicated by holding a complete trial; however, credible admissions made by the defendant may reduce the amount of extrinsic evidence necessary to establish the truth.

A proceeding similar to the taking of a guilty plea exists in Spanish law. When the preliminary investigation is completed, the prosecutor files a statement listing the offenses allegedly committed by the defendant and demanding a specified penalty. If the defendant acquiesces in the proposed disposition he is convicted and sentenced without trial; the penalty demanded by the prosecutor constitutes the upper limit for sentencing by the court (LEC, arts. 655, 694). Contrary to what one might expect, this procedural arrangement does not lead to a practice of plea bargaining. The principle of mandatory prosecution prevents the Spanish prosecutor from dropping individual charges; the facts cannot be "adjusted" because they have been established by a thorough pretrial investigation; and sentencing is largely predetermined by statutory schedules. Therefore, the Spanish guilty plea is used in only 15 percent of the cases, usually as a device for assigned counsel to avoid trial work (Volkmann-Schluck, pp. 131–132).

If the accused makes a confession in a case of lesser seriousness, the structure of the process may not change, but practical adjustments can be expected. In Japan, the trial can be simplified if the defendant does not contest the charges concerning a crime of lesser seriousness (KS, § 291-2). In that case, the formal rules of evidence do not apply. Most importantly, the court receives the dossier of the pretrial investigation and can proceed on the basis of it. The defendant's confession must, however, still be corroborated, and the court can acquit the defendant if it is not convinced of his guilt (Dando, pp. 377–379).

In France, minor offenses are tried before a court of three professional judges; formalities are reduced and rules of evidence relaxed. Oral testimony of witnesses can be replaced by the record of their interrogation by the police, and closing statements are often limited to a few perfunctory remarks. Moreover, in 1976 more than 20 percent of the cases in lower courts were disposed of by a conviction by default. Petty offenses punishable only by fines can be adjudicated in a simplified written procedure (CPP, arts. 524–528-2). In these cases, the judge receives the prosecutor's file of the investigation and issues a penal order (*ordonnance pénale*) comprising a brief statement of the facts, a recitation of the applicable law, a finding of guilt, and the sentence. The penal order can also contain an acquittal. Both the prosecutor and the defendant have the right to appeal the order and to demand

a regular trial; if neither party appeals, the penal order is enforceable like any regular judgment.

Similar procedures exist in Japan (KS, §§ 461–470) and West Germany (StPO, §§ 407–412). In neither country can imprisonment be imposed by penal order; nevertheless, penal orders have a wide range of application since the great majority of all offenders receive only fines and supplementary punishments, for example, revocation of the driver's license. In 1979, German prosecutors applied for a penal order and for a trial in 42 percent and 58 percent of all criminal cases, respectively. The great majority of penal orders in Germany are accepted by defendants; in 1979, only 22 percent demanded a regular trial.

Although the general idea of the penal order is the same in France, West Germany, and Japan, there are slight variations in detail. In Japan, the accused must consent to the written proceeding before the prosecutor can apply for a penal order; yet the defendant can still appeal the penal order if he is not satisfied with the sentence. In West Germany, it is the prosecutor who drafts the penal order including the penalty; the judge has the choice between signing it as submitted and ordering a trial.

Penal orders, although similar to the guilty plea in some respects, are not usually subject to bargaining between the parties. There is no evidence that defendants are penalized for appealing a penal order and demanding a full trial (Felstiner, p. 314). The penal order thus provides a speedy and inexpensive method of dealing with routine cases of nonserious crime. Whether it would function equally well in an adversary context remains an open question, however; the habit of bargaining for justice is so deeply ingrained in the American tradition that it might quickly infect a transplanted penal-order system.

Agenda for comparative research

American scholars have largely concentrated on overall comparison between the adversary and the inquisitorial models. Such inquiries are of some theoretical interest but have little practical application. In the future, research might profitably be directed toward studying solutions found abroad for problems arising in similar ways in every procedural system. Such solutions, although often tied closely to their procedural environments, may lend themselves to transfer more easily than complete procedural structures. Areas where large-scale comparative research has not yet been conducted but may prove fruitful include the system of pretrial detention and bail, pretrial discovery, the reduction of delay in criminal proceedings, the system of appeals in criminal matters, the organization of defense services, the possibility of restitution in the criminal process, and the conflict between the integrity of court proceedings and the rights of the press.

THOMAS WEIGEND

See also ADVERSARY SYSTEM; COMPARATIVE CRIMINAL LAW AND ENFORCEMENT, articles on CHINA and SOVIET UNION; CRIMINAL LAW REFORM; CRIMINAL PROCEDURE: CONSTITUTIONAL ASPECTS; MILITARY JUSTICE: COMPARATIVE ASPECTS; PROSECUTION: COMPARATIVE ASPECTS.

BIBLIOGRAPHY

ABE, HARUO. "Police Interrogation Privileges and Limitations under Foreign Law: An International Symposium—Japan." *Journal of Criminal Law, Criminology, and Police Science* 52 (1961): 67–72.

BAYLEY, DAVID H. *Forces of Order: Police Behavior in Japan and the United States.* Berkeley and Los Angeles: University of California Press, 1976.

CASPER, GERHARD, and ZEISEL, HANS. "Lay Judges in the German Criminal Courts." *Journal of Legal Studies* 1 (1972): 135–191.

Code de procédure pénale. 21st ed. Petits Codes Dalloz. Paris: Dalloz, 1979–1980. Translated as *The French Code of Criminal Procedure.* Translated by Gerald L. Koch. American Series of Foreign Penal Codes 7. South Hackensack, N.J.: Rothman, 1964.

Code of Criminal Procedure of Japan. Rev. ed. EHS Law Bulletin Series. Tokyo: Eibun-Horei-Sha, 1975.

DAMAŠKA, MIRJAN. "Evidentiary Barriers to Conviction and Two Models of Criminal Procedure: A Comparative Study." *University of Pennsylvania Law Review* 121 (1973): 506–589.

———. "Structures of Authority and Comparative Criminal Procedure." *Yale Law Journal* 84 (1975): 480–544.

DANDO, SHIGEMITSU. *The Japanese Law of Criminal Procedure.* Translated by B. J. George, Jr. South Hackensack, N.J.: Rothman, 1965.

DAVIS, KENNETH C.; BUSCK, LARS et al. *Discretionary Justice in Europe and America.* Urbana: University of Illinois Press, 1976.

FELSTINER, WILLIAM L. F. "Plea Contracts in West Germany." *Law and Society Review* 13 (1979): 309–325.

GOLDSTEIN, ABRAHAM S., and MARCUS, MARTIN. "The Myth of Judicial Supervision in Three 'Inquisitorial' Systems: France, Italy, and Germany." *Yale Law Journal* 87 (1977): 240–283.

GREBING, GERHARDT. "Staatsanwaltschaft und Strafverfolgungspraxis in Frankreich." *Funktion und Tätigkeit der Anklagebehörde im ausländischen Recht.* Edited by Hans-Heinrich Jescheck and Rudolf Leibinger, with the assistance of J. Driendl et al. Baden-Baden, Federal Republic of Germany: Nomos, 1979, pp. 13–81.

HERRMANN, JOACHIM. *Die Reform der deutschen Hauptverhandlung nach dem Vorbild des anglo-amerikanischen Strafverfahrens.* Bonn, Federal Republic of Germany: Röhrscheid, 1971.

KÜHNE, HANS-HEINER. "Opportunität und quasi-richterliche Tätigkeit des japanischen Staatsanwalts." *Zeitschrift für die gesamte Strafrechtswissenschaft* 85 (1973): 1079–1101.

LANGBEIN, JOHN H. *Comparative Criminal Procedure: Germany.* St. Paul: West, 1977.

———. "Mixed Court and Jury Court: Could the Continental Alternative Fill the American Need?" *American Bar Foundation Research Journal* (1981): 195–219.

MERLE, ROGER, and VITU, ANDRÉ. *Procédure pénale.* Traité de droit criminel, vol. 2. 3d ed. Paris: Editions Cujas, 1979.

STÉFANI, GASTON; LEVASSEUR, GEORGES; and BOULOC, BERNARD. *Procédure pénale.* 11th ed. Paris: Dalloz, 1980.

VOLKMANN-SCHLUCK, THOMAS. *Der spanische Strafprozess zwischen Inquisitions- und Parteiverfahren.* Baden-Baden, Federal Republic of Germany: Nomos, 1979.

WEIGEND, THOMAS. "Continental Cures for American Ailments: European Criminal Procedure as a Model for Law Reform." *Crime and Justice: An Annual Review of Research,* vol. 2. Edited by Norval Morris and Michael Tonry. University of Chicago Press, 1980, pp. 381–428.

WEINREB, LLOYD L. *Denial of Justice: Criminal Process in the United States.* New York: Free Press, 1977.

ZIPF, HEINZ. *Kriminalpolitik.* 2d ed. Heidelberg and Karlsruhe, Federal Republic of Germany: C. F. Müller, 1980.

CRIMINAL SUBCULTURES

See CRIME CAUSATION: SOCIOLOGICAL THEORIES; DELINQUENT AND CRIMINAL SUBCULTURES; PRISONS: PRISON SUBCULTURE.

CRIMINAL SYNDICALISM

See SEDITION.

CRIMINOLOGY

The study of crime has probably existed almost as long as lawbreaking. It is traced from prehistoric to modern times in INTELLECTUAL HISTORY, *which has an international perspective. The article* MODERN CONTROVERSIES *discusses in detail current issues in criminology, with special focus on the English-speaking world. The third article,* RESEARCH METHODS, *analyzes a series of strategies for studying crime, each method designed to minimize some types of errors but also having limitations in coping with other types of errors, either in feasibility or in the ethical problems that it creates.*

1. INTELLECTUAL HISTORY	Israel Drapkin
2. MODERN CONTROVERSIES	James F. Short, Jr.
3. RESEARCH METHODS	Alden D. Miller

1.
INTELLECTUAL HISTORY

Prehistoric times. It is generally presumed that the earliest form of punishment was private revenge. Retaliation for an inflicted injury was the personal affair of the victim or his surviving next of kin, and the community did not interfere. Private revenge often escalated into blood feuds between the family, clan, or tribe of the victim and those of the offender. The resulting losses of life and property became so great that the communities to which feuding families belonged started, very slowly, to impose trials and official penalties on offenders and to restrict private vengeance. However, feuds between dominant families of different communities were prominent in the primordial origins of war.

Religious leaders were early moderators of conflicts and punishers of offenders. They threatened criminals with divine revenge at a time when, owing to the fear of gods and supernatural forces, magic and religion were effective sociopolitical tools. Acts adversely affecting the well-being of the community or its members were considered affronts to the deities, who might express their anger through plagues, earthquakes, or other desolation. Punishment of the wrongdoer was thought to lessen the gods' fury if there was a proper correspondence between the injury and the chastisement. This was the remote origin of *lex talionis* ("an eye for an eye and a tooth for a tooth") and the point at which the concepts of crime and sin began to overlap.

Finally, there was state revenge. It was believed that antipersonal or antisocial behaviors not only offended the gods, but affected the political stability and the welfare of the social group. The state acted independently of the temple in punishing the wrongdoer, and this state revenge is the origin of modern justice—the victim has to ask for redress from the proper authorities for the suffered wrong.

Earliest codes of law. The Sumerian system of written law dates from the very beginning of writing (c. 3100 B.C.), and transactions were inscribed on clay tablets, the first known legal documents, as early as 2500 B.C. The oldest known fragments of a code of law are associated with the Sumerian ruler Ur-Nammu (c. 2050 B.C.). The code consisted of a prologue, the text, and an epilogue. The prologue explained how Ur-Nammu was selected by the gods as their earthly representative to rule over Sumer and Ur. The body of the text was so badly damaged that only five of the laws have been interpreted with any degree of certainty: one refers to a trial by some kind of water

ordeal, and a second to the returning of a slave to his rightful owner; the other three establish pecuniary compensation for injuries. The epilogue prescribes blessings for those who honor the code and curses for those who desecrate it.

The Sumerian Laws of Eshnunna (c. 1760 B.C.) include five groups of delicts: offenses against persons and property, abduction of married or betrothed women, sexual offenses, and damage caused by animals. Delicts always called forth penalties, mostly of a pecuniary nature, but the more serious offenses were punishable by death.

The Code of Hammurabi. Dating from about 1750 B.C. and inscribed in stone, the Code of Hammurabi was also divided into the traditional three sections. It is apparent that the prologue and epilogue were copied from earlier texts, but there is no evidence that its legal provisions were borrowed from other codes. The 282 extant clauses are in the general style of older codes, but there are some modifications: the code has more purely secular provisions, sanctions are largely based upon a new retributive principle, the arrangement of subjects is more systematic, and the language is perfectly clear.

The code covered offenses committed during a trial, regulation of patrimonial rights, family laws and inheritance, bodily injuries, rights and obligations of special classes of society, and offenses relating to prices and salaries and to slaves. In at least twenty-seven clauses capital punishment was prescribed for a variety of offenses. Other clauses referred to retributive sanctions, and severe corporal punishment was introduced. Homicide was a capital crime with no possibility of settlement by pecuniary compensation, and even an unintentional killer was held responsible in order to satisfy the victim's family. The basic legal principle was a life for a life. Differences among social classes were well established, and the nature and severity of the punishment imposed were related to the victim's and the perpetrator's respective social positions. The law of retribution, which made its first appearance in the Code of Hammurabi and became a fundamental principle in all subsequent codes of law, replaced the pecuniary penalties of earlier systems. It in turn was gradually superseded by other forms of punishment.

The Hebrews. Hebrew society was the first to separate executive and judicial power. There were three types of courts: the first consisted of three judges who dealt with private conflicts and a few delicts; the second had twenty-three judges who dealt mainly with cases in which the life of the accused was at stake; and the final court, the Sanhedrin, was made up of seventy-one judges who sat in the Temple and were charged with interpretation of the law. Judicial procedure demanded more than one witness, and false testimony was punished with great severity. The most serious delict was idolatry, for which the punishment was death by stoning. A distinction was drawn between intentional homicide, always a capital offense, and unintentional homicide, in which the slayer had the right to leave the city and seek sanctuary elsewhere. The local court could, after hearing the case, pardon or acquit the accused. The chief places of refuge were the temples, and the right of sanctuary was intended to deter violent revenge by the victim's next of kin. Sodomy was a capital crime, as was cursing or striking a father or mother. Corporal and pecuniary sanctions were also imposed. The famous *lex talionis*, which has been criticized as excessively cruel and barbaric, was actually only a concise expression of the retributive concept of the Code of Hammurabi. Properly read as "no more than an eye for an eye . . . ," the dictum marked a significant advance in limiting the excesses of private revenge.

India. Brahmanic India, one of history's most absolute theocracies, produced the Laws, or Code, of Manu, generally thought to date from between the thirteenth and ninth centuries B.C. It specified that part of the judge's function was to probe the heart of the accused and the witnesses by studying their posture, mien, and changes in voice and eyes. Thus, this was the first code of law to take account of judicial psychology.

According to the code, litigants were entitled to present witnesses, who were selected from among the middle castes. Women could testify only in matters related to women, and untouchables only in matters that concerned themselves; slaves were outside the system. Individuals normally not permitted to serve as witnesses, beginning with the king, were required to testify if they were eyewitnesses to a homicide, and in the absence of witnesses, the judge was obliged to discover the truth by means of oaths or ordeals.

Killing a Brahman or stealing his gold, drinking alcoholic beverages, and incest were capital crimes. Punishments for lesser offenses included mutilation, restriction of liberty, banishment, corporal punishment, and fines.

China. Ancient Chinese law was secular, entirely indigenous, and political in intent. Rather than upholding religious values or protecting private property, the law was designed to impose tighter controls upon a society that was losing its old cultural values before new ones had appeared. The first Chinese imperial code, although promulgated only in the third century B.C., was based on laws dating from at least three centuries earlier.

The Confucians, who considered that government by law was secondary to government by moral precepts and example, at first opposed the new law, but eventually they accepted it reluctantly as a necessity. The legalists, ardent advocates of the law, were tough-minded men of affairs with no regard for "human rights." Although not power-hungry, unscrupulous politicians, they believed that only through total methods could peace and unity be brought to their war-torn world. The imperial codes of China were based on four major principles: (1) prescribing punishment to fit the crime; (2) differentiating by social status, that is, distinguishing among officials, commoners, and slaves; (3) differentiating among eight privileged groups, the first including members of the imperial family and the last the mass of commoners; and (4) differentiating within the family according to sex, seniority, and degree of kinship. Confucianism attached great importance to filial piety, and close relatives were permitted to conceal the crime of a family member without legal penalty. Death sentences in imperial China had to be confirmed by the highest judicial body, even by the emperor himself, before being carried out. Confucian humanitarianism was expressed in special exemptions and lesser sentences for the aged, the young, and the physically or mentally infirm.

Classical Greece. Little is known about the primitive laws of Greece. The exiguous remains of the early-seventh-century B.C. Draconian Code in Athens and the Gortyn Code of Crete, dating from the mid-fourth century B.C., could be considered as the transition between the primitive and later codes. Greek law was never systematized. There were originally only two kinds of crime: an offense committed by a stranger against a member of the clan, which was subject to revenge, and one committed by a clan member against a victim belonging to the same clan, which was not. The distinction between the two eventually disappeared, but for a long time homicide remained a matter for private revenge. The Greek philosophers never considered law a serious subject for study, but they did deal with the definition and classification of crime, as well as with its causes and dynamics.

For Plato (429?–347 B.C.), the basis of law was the prevailing morality, and every action against that morality constituted a crime. In his *Republic* and *Laws* he delineated four types of offenses: (1) against religion (theft within a temple, impiety, or disrespect); (2) against the state (treason); (3) against persons (poisoning, use of drugs, witchcraft, sorcery, infliction of injury); and (4) against private property (killing a thief caught stealing at night was not punishable). The Greeks were convinced that "fate" was the main cause of crime, with different consequences determined by the gods, and even Plato accepted the prevailing fatalism, although he considered crime the product of a faulty education.

Aristotle (384–322 B.C.) based his ideas on observation of facts, not on moral concepts. Man was for him a synthesis of a body and a soul, endowed with intelligence, emotion, and desire. In his *Nicomachean Ethics*, Aristotle defined crime as the act not of a sick individual, but of one who acted of his own volition, stimulated by his own desires. Thus children, idiots, the mentally ill, and individuals in a state of ecstasy were absolved from criminal responsibility.

According to Aristotle, the social reaction to crime could be preventive or repressive. His concept of a preventive reaction included three elements: (1) eugenic (he distinguished between children who should be nurtured and educated, and those who should be abandoned and left to die because of some deformity); (2) demographic (the number of births should be limited, and unnecessary pregnancies should be terminated); and (3) deterrent (intelligent punishment was designed primarily to intimidate the offender and deter the onlookers). Repressive punishment was originally limited to private revenge, but it became progressively more humane and was extended to include such measures as noxal abandonment (turning the offender over to the victim's family) and atimy (perpetual banishment).

As early as the time of the Draconian Code, Greek law drew a distinction between premeditated and involuntary homicide. Plato described four kinds of crime: voluntary, involuntary, accidental, and mixed, the last taking place when passion exceeded reason and led to violence. The severity of the imposed punishment was a function of the degree of culpability and was retributive in nature. Plato also introduced the idea of "social utility": a criminal is a sick individual who must be cured, and if he cannot be cured he must be disposed of.

Rome. Rome was the source of the world's most powerful legal influences. The Twelve Tables are considered to be the basis of all Roman law, public and private, and it is thought that they were promulgated about 450 B.C. The tables were secular laws, clearly different from religious or moral rules, and included some forty clauses.

The Eighth Table was similar to a body of criminal law and detailed crimes and their punishments. Intentional homicide, setting fire to a dwelling or harvested crop, treason, and parricide were all capital crimes.

One who inflicted an injury was subject to a pecuniary sanction or retributive penalty if he did not pay the agreed compensation. Punishments for theft were also prescribed, varying between compensation equal to double the value of the stolen goods and the death penalty for the thief caught in the act. If the thief was a free man, he could be given to his victim as a slave. Death sentences were also imposed on judges or arbitrators caught taking bribes and on witnesses giving false testimony. However, the sentences could only be carried out with the consent of the whole assembly of citizens, and citizens of Rome were rarely put to death. After the second century A.D., exile and banishment became common punishments. The institution of slavery decisively influenced the evolution of the penal system in Rome because the special and very severe sanctions devised for slaves were later extended to the entire population, with the exception of a limited number of privileged and wealthy citizens. When the population of Rome reached one million, during the second century A.D., permanent tribunals were established, composed of thirty or more jurors presided over by a praetor. At first the jurors had to be of the senatorial class, but gentlemen, wealthy citizens, and soldiers later became eligible. These tribunals were empowered to deal with cases of treason, homicide, parricide, adultery, corruption, and kidnapping, and there was no appeal from their decisions.

The Middle Ages. The acceptance of Christianity altered the concept of crime in Europe. New offenses, such as infanticide, abortion, homosexuality, blasphemy, sacrilege, and witchcraft, were punished, but celibacy, a serious offense in Roman times, was no longer considered a crime. Demonology explained crime and aberrant behavior as resulting from possession, and exorcism was one of the accepted treatments. Punishments were primitive and cruel. Trial by ordeal or combat was the norm; torture was common, becoming more refined and sadistic as time went on; and executions were public and were very well attended. On the other hand, the Middle Ages saw the beginnings of trial by jury and extended the concept of sanctuary in churches and monasteries.

The scholastics, who taught that as a result of original sin man is born evil, considered positive law as real law only when it was the written version of the natural law decreed by God. Maimonides, the great twelfth-century Jewish philosopher and physician, did not accept the idea of natural law, holding that moral principles are not based on reason and cannot be demonstrated.

St. Thomas Aquinas (1225–1274) interpreted the doctrine of the fall to mean that men live in suffering and pain as a result of it. Crime is only one manifestation of the fall, and is regarded as a sin. This duality of crime and sin had a major conceptual consequence because it followed that only the man who committed the sin had to be punished, not members of his family. St. Thomas regarded human passions and misery as criminogenic factors, and he offered an impassioned defense of *furtus famelicus,* or stealing out of extreme misery.

Early modern criminology. The end of the Middle Ages brought the demise of supernatural explanations and initiated the search for natural explanations of the phenomenon called crime. The Renaissance was the great age of the humanists, who were interested in man, his character and personality, his society, and his politics. Especially prominent among the humanists of the fifteenth to seventeenth centuries were the utopian writers, whose name derives from the *Utopia* of Thomas More. The *Utopia* purports to describe a strange land where men were uncorrupted; where reason, love, and law worked in harmony to make a perfect society, pervaded by a sense of brotherhood among all educated people; where everyone worked and no one was idle; and where justice was designed to eliminate vice rather than to destroy the criminal. In the *Utopia,* More criticized economic conditions in England, discussed their relationship with criminality, and decried the extreme harshness of English justice under Henry VIII. Erasmus, author of *The Praise of Folly,* exposed the foolishness and absurdity of human behavior and may also be considered a utopian. One of the earliest advocates of the experimental method, Francis Bacon, described in *New Atlantis* an imaginary island inhabited by happy people and free of crime. Tomasso Campanella, who spent twenty-seven years in prison, there wrote *The City of the Sun,* depicting an ideal city without classes or private property, which he called the sources of egoism and crime. The great religious reformer Martin Luther was perhaps the first thinker to distinguish between rural and urban criminality. Thomas Hobbes, in *Leviathan,* portrayed a primeval state in which man preys upon man, where there is no distinction between just and unjust, and where deceit, violence, and crime reign supreme.

The eighteenth-century social-contract writers, whose name derives from *The Social Contract* of Jean-Jacques Rousseau, were a group of thinkers opposed to the enforced social order of the ancien régime and to the penal practices of the day. In *The Spirit of the Laws,* Montesquieu insisted that prevention of crime was better than punishment of the criminal, and that punishment merely for its own sake was evil. Voltaire became the leader of a movement against the arbitrariness of the French criminal justice system and the prevailing barbaric treatment of prisoners. He advocated rehabilitation and suggested employing prison inmates in dangerous public works as an alternative to enforced idleness. Rousseau himself was convinced that poverty was the source of most criminal transgressions and that the institution of property caused most criminality. He strongly opposed the existing penal system and successfully fought scholasticism, declaring that man is basically good and that only untenable social conditions transform him into a criminal.

The utopian and social-contract writers led the struggle against unnecessary cruelty in the punishment of offenders, and the French Revolution, despite all its violence, was a milestone in the effort to achieve human rights, including those of the criminal offender.

In his *Introduction to the Principles of Morals and Legislation,* published in 1780, Jeremy Bentham presented the doctrine of utilitarianism, which holds that the state should provide the greatest possible happiness to the greatest number of citizens. He favored prevention over punishment and insisted that when punishment was imposed it had to be corrective. In his *Panopticon, or the Inspection House,* Bentham proposed a new type of prison, constructed to enable a guard in the center of its circular courtyard to see simultaneously all the inmates of his floor. The design was a remarkable success and is still to be found in many prisons worldwide.

Beccaria and the classical school of penal law. At the beginning of the eighteenth century there were two active and mutually antagonistic intellectual trends in Europe. On one side stood the Roman Catholic Church, with its fundamental insistence on man's fall from an original state of grace and innocence and on his will being a psychological reality governing his behavior. According to this doctrine, man had freedom to choose and thus was responsible for his own actions. Fear of physical pain was the best deterrent to wrongdoing, and the threat of severe punishment created fear and thus resulted in proper behavior. Society had the right to punish, and for practical reasons that right was transferred to the state.

In direct confrontation with this view stood the advocates of the new rationalism and the critics of the prevailing human and social conditions, the utopian and social-contract writers. Their protest movement against the abuses of judges, prosecutors, and jailers in the treatment of offenders evolved into the classical school of criminal justice, whose most outstanding representative was Cesare Beccaria.

Beccaria first became aware of judicial abuses and prison conditions after one of his friends became Protector of Prisoners in Milan, and in 1764 he published *On Crimes and Punishments,* which urgently advocated sweeping reforms. Beccaria's ideas about penal law rested on seven basic concepts, as follows:

1. The legislature must dictate the nature of punishment, a judge cannot impose a punishment not established by law, and it is improper to apply analogy in the interpretation of the law.
2. The judge's function should be limited to establishing guilt or innocence, and trials must be public and speedy.
3. Any act of authority not grounded in law is tyrannical.
4. Prevention of crime is more important than punishment, and the certainty and celerity with which a sentence is carried out has a greater preventive effect than its severity. Capital punishment should be abolished, and prisons should be improved, with inmates segregated on the basis of age, sex, and type of crime.
5. There should be a fixed legal scale of crimes and punishments, and acts not listed should not be crimes and may not incur punishment.
6. Punishment should be uniform and public and should depend solely on the nature of the crime, not on the social status of the offender.
7. The act and not the intent should be the measure of the injury, because the intention does not alter the nature of the crime.

The classical school did not deal with the causes of crime. Questions related to motive, intent, and various possible consequences were deliberately ignored, and no distinctions were drawn between first offenders and recidivists, the sane and insane, or minors and adults. The French Criminal Code of 1791, based on the ideas of Beccaria, proved unenforceable and was eventually modified, evolving into the 1810 and 1819 codes that incorporated the basic concepts of the neoclassical school of penal law.

The neoclassical school retained the essential principles of the classical school, but modified the concept of "the same punishment for the same crime." The two new codes allowed judges some degree of discretion and individualization, and the particular circumstances of each case were taken into account. The neoclassicists recognized that an individual's freedom of will could be affected by pathology as well as by other factors. They introduced the concept of premeditation, admitted the validity of physical, environmental, and psychological mitigating circumstances as bases for attributing only partial responsibility, and accepted expert testimony as to whether an accused was capable of distinguishing and choosing between right and wrong. These basic principles remained dominant until they were superseded by the tenets of the positive school of penal law.

The pre-Lombrosian period. In the search for the causes of crime, the pre-Lombrosian period, lasting from the mid-sixteenth century to 1875, encompassed the work of physiognomists, phrenologists, early psychiatrists, and prison physicians. Gianbattista della Porta published his *Physiognomy* in 1586, and Johan Gaspar Lavater produced his four-volume *Physiognomic Fragments* in 1775. Franz Joseph Gall claimed to have discovered the "organs" for homicide, alcoholism, and theft. His student Johan Gaspar Spurzheim took Gall's ideas to America, with little success. However, one American follower, Charles Caldwell, did subsequently publish *Elements of Phrenology* in 1824.

Among the eighteenth- and nineteenth-century psychiatrists and prison physicians, Phillipe Pinel unchained mental patients and undertook one of the first studies of the mentality of the criminally insane. Jean-Etienne Esquirol added statistics to his clinical studies and introduced the concept of monomania, the predominance of one insane idea in an otherwise normal mind. He also insisted that the criminally insane are not legally responsible for their actions and therefore should not be punished. Similar ideas were developed by James Prichard with the name of moral insanity. Prosper Lucas drew attention to the relationship between criminality, heredity, and atavism, and Benedict Morel introduced the concept of "degeneration," a hereditary entity with physical, mental, and moral stigmata that were common among criminals and the mentally ill.

Charles Darwin (1809–1882) never dealt with problems of crime, but his theory of evolution served as one of the main bases for criminal anthropology, which began its development in the nineteenth century. J. Bruce Thomson conducted studies on the height and weight of 5,432 inmates of Perth prison. Identifying crime with mental illness, Henry Maudsley described the two as being at opposite ends of a continuum. Within this continuum, crime was sometimes a manifestation and sometimes a cause of mental illness, but external factors counted for much in causing crime. The father of criminal pyschology, Prosper Despine, hypothesized that an abnormally formed brain could cause crime and madness, and Paul Broca, author of the theory of cerebral localization, examined the skulls of criminals and concluded that their criminality had a pathological basis. Each of the foregoing researchers contributed in one way or another to the subsequent development of Lombroso's theory of the born criminal.

Cesare Lombroso and the positive school of penal law. Cesare Lombroso (1835–1909) studied medicine at the University of Pavia, where he earned a medical degree, and psychology and psychiatry at the University of Vienna. In 1871 he examined 400 criminally insane subjects, and among them were the two who became the starting points for his theory of the born criminal. The first was a certain Vilella, a highwayman who died in prison. At the postmortem, Lombroso discovered that the skull's occipital crest, on the internal side of the bone, was missing and that there was instead a third, or median, fossa. This deviant feature, being an anthropoid characteristic, led him to conclude that the criminal is an atavistic creature, a "throwback" to an earlier stage of man's evolution. The discovery of a second physiologically similar subject, Vincenzo Verzeni, who had raped, strangled, and dismembered women, convinced Lombroso that the hypotheses of moral insanity and atavism were valid. In 1878, while testifying as an expert witness at the trial of a soldier who had suddenly killed eight of his comrades, Lombroso concluded that the offender had epileptic characteristics, and thereafter he added epilepsy as a basic element of his theory.

In 1876, Lombroso published his principal work, *The Criminal Man,* considered to be the starting point of all scientific criminology. Only in 1899 did he add some socioeconomic considerations to his basic theories, but they never assumed much importance in his overall outlook. In 1885, together with Enrico Ferri and Raffaele Garofalo, Lombroso organized the First International Congress of Criminal Anthropology, at which his basic concepts predominated. However, beginning around 1886 he encountered opposition to his theory of the born criminal, and this opposition increased steadily until his death in 1909.

Over the years, Lombroso had espoused several theories of criminal anthropology. The first was his universal approach, which maintained that crime is not only a human condition but also exists among animals and plants. He soon abandoned this broad concept, and compared the criminal to primitive man, ignoring the fact that crime was very rare in primitive societies. Once more he had to change his position, and for a brief time he expounded an ontogenetic viewpoint, comparing the criminal to the child who shows moral abnormalities and criminal drives at a very early age.

After these abortive attempts at theorizing, Lombroso developed his theory of the born criminal, which states that the criminal is born with many degenerative traits, as well as a tendency toward epilepsy. The criminal is similar to the morally insane individual, and heredity and atavism explain his characteristics. He is, in fact, a new species of *Homo sapiens—homo delinquens.* Lombroso classified criminals into three main categories: born criminals, encompassing a third of all offenders; insane criminals, constituting about a tenth of the total; and criminaloids, just over half of the total, who lack psychosomatic stigmata but suffer from more subtle defects and who, under given circumstances, would be capable of engaging in criminal behavior. Occasional offenders were not included in his classification, because he considered them only pseudodelinquents.

Lombroso insisted that punishment made no impression on the born criminal, that the insane needed treatment rather than punishment, and that criminaloids were best reformed through a prison regimen that included fasting and cold showers, followed by probation. He opposed short-term imprisonment on the ground that it would not allow enough time for proper treatment. Notwithstanding the negative aspects of his monumental work, Lombroso was persistent in his determinist approach. He was a master of observation, scrupulously honest in his work, and often aware of some of his many weaknesses. A controversial figure who has been "buried" more than once, Lombroso still exerts an influence and occupies a prominent place in the annals of criminology.

Enrico Ferri. Although partially accepting Lombroso's ideas on the biological bases of crime, Enrico Ferri (1856–1929) emphasized the role of socioeconomic and political factors. He presented his own classification of offenders, enlarging upon the Lombrosian definition: the born criminal, conditioned by heredity and biology; the insane criminal, an extreme case of the born type; the occasional or chance criminal, who is involved in crime by accident, temptation, or error; the professional criminal, who pursues a criminal career; and the passional criminal (a distinctive category of the occasional criminal), who is moved by irresistible impulses resulting from anger, jealousy, or shame.

According to Ferri, crime is based on three kinds of factors: physical (climate, geographic location, seasonal effects, and temperature), anthropological (race, heredity, sex, age, and physiological and psychological conditions), and sociological (density of population, customs, religion, type of government, and economic and industrial characteristics). His *Law of Criminal Saturation,* based on statistical research, asserted that in a given social setting with a certain population under certain physical conditions, the same number of crimes would be committed every year.

Ferri favored preventive measures over penalties and advocated such economic and social reforms as free trade, abolition of monopolies, inexpensive housing for workers, public savings banks, better street lighting, birth control, freedom of marriage and divorce, state control over the manufacture and sale of weapons, marriage for clergymen, and public recreation areas. He accepted the death penalty, but wanted to limit its use to cases in which the accused was absolutely incapable of leading a normal life. Ferri became the undisputed leader of the positive school, the one that succeeded the previous classical school, headed by Francesco Carrara (1805–1888).

Raffaele Garofalo. A magistrate and professor of criminal law at the University of Naples, Raffaele Garofalo (1852–1934) attempted to formulate a sociological and universal definition of crime, referring specifically to acts that any civilized society would define as criminal—acts that violate the fundamental sensitivities of probity (respect for the rights of others) and pity (opposition to those who cause others to suffer). As a magistrate he was primarily concerned with reforms in criminal procedure that would provide practical assistance to offenders. Garofalo classified criminals into four categories: (1) murderers, who are egoists with no altruism or pity; (2) violent offenders guilty of such endemic crimes as vendettas in Naples or terrorism in czarist Russia; (3) criminals with deficient probity, who engage mainly in crimes against property; and (4) lascivious individuals and sex perverts.

Garofalo accepted capital punishment in cases where rehabilitation was a total impossibility, advocated life imprisonment and transport to penal colonies for hardened criminals, recommended periods of work in agricultural colonies for young and potentially reformable offenders, and endorsed reparation by those who committed crimes under exceptional circumstances, such as accident, temptation, or error. He was convinced that these penalties would satisfy the public demand for punishment, would be sufficiently intimidating to deter crime, and would eventually eliminate the inveterate criminal element from society.

The anti-Lombrosian reaction. Among the salient objections to Lombroso's theories were the argument that the stigmata he dwelt upon were not found only in criminals and that cranial and facial asymmetries were the rule rather than the exception in normal human beings. It was also pointed out that mentally ill, psychopathic, and other abnormal individuals could have degenerate traits without displaying criminal tendencies, and that normal people could evidence the same stigmata and lead honest, even successful, lives.

Charles Goring was opposed not so much to Lombroso's concepts as to his methodology. In 1913 he published the results of an eight-year statistical study that examined alleged differences between criminals and noncriminals, and concluded that there is no such thing as a physical criminal type. On the other hand, Goring did observe that the criminals he studied were consistently smaller in stature and lower in weight than noncriminals, and he decided that heredity does create a predisposition for deviant behavior.

Earnest Hooton in 1939 tried unsuccessfully to undermine the general acceptance of Goring's work with highly publicized research that challenged Goring's methods. However, Hooton's claims that the prison inmates he measured were physically inferior were rejected by critics because his comparison group of noncriminals consisted disproportionately of firemen and national guardsmen selected for their physical superiority. Moreover, the height distinctions that, Hooton claimed, differentiated various types of criminals were not statistically significant.

Among the German psychiatrists prominent in the development of criminology were Emil Kraepelin, who stressed the need for the indeterminate sentence; Ernst Kretschmer, with his human typology based on constitutional factors; Kurt Schneider, who developed a typology of constitutional psychopaths; and Johannes Lange and Heinrich Kranz, who pioneered in the study of criminal twins.

The founder of the Austrian school of criminology was Hans Gross, who developed the discipline of judicial psychology and established the basic rules for interrogating suspects. Gross was followed by several other important scholars, including Adolf Lenz and Ernest Seelig, who both had a strong biopsychological viewpoint and were convinced that an understanding of the human personality required a knowledge of man's physical as well as psychological aspects. Lenz and Seelig believed that heredity and bodily stigmata might facilitate antisocial behaviors and that although social environment is of limited importance compared with heredity factors, an adverse environment can promote criminal behavior.

Sociological research. Crime has always been ascribed at least partially to poverty, but it was not until the sixteenth century that records were kept in various countries of Europe that could test the validity of this relationship. France established a very high standard for official crime registration in its *General Report of the Administration of Criminal Justice in France*, first published in 1825. In 1833, André Guerry brought out the final version of his *Essay on the Moral Statistics of France*, in which he used maps with different colors and shades to show the incidence of crime in certain geographic areas. In 1835, Adolphe Quételet, a Belgian mathematician, published *Social Physics*. The work analyzed criminal statistics in France, Belgium, Luxembourg, and Holland, concluding that society is responsible for criminal behavior and that the offender is merely the individual committing the criminal offense.

Auguste Comte, the nineteenth-century French positivist philosopher who coined the word *sociology*, denied freedom of will and demanded that science and law be totally divorced from morality. In the realm of criminology, positivism asserted that only scientific methods should be employed in the study of crime and criminals, that prevention is more important than punishment, and that the protection of society is more important than the exaction of retribution.

Emile Durkheim, one of the pioneers of the French sociological school of criminology, was convinced that the explanation for crime is to be found in the very nature of society. In his *Rules of Sociological Method* (1895) he asserted that crime is normal to society and that it is thus utterly impossible to conceive of a social group without it. Punishment is not imposed to rehabilitate the offender but to define the boundaries of permissible conduct for the rest of society. When social norms change too rapidly, fostering anomie (normlessness), suicide and crime rates rise; with orderly social change, there is much less criminality.

Gabriel Tarde, one of the principal anti-Lombrosians of the same period, presented his basic ideas in three books: *Comparative Criminality, Penal Philosophy*, and *The Laws of Imitation*. In the first he stated that social factors are far more important determinants of criminal behavior than are anthropological characteristics. In the second, he developed this concept further, and in the third he dealt with the importance of repetitive patterns in human behavior. For Tarde, crime was an antisocial phenomenon based on psychological and social factors, but with social factors predominating. Tarde stressed the differences between the basically cunning nature of urban crime and the violent nature of rural criminality. In his opinion, criminal responsibility was related to concepts of personal identity and social attachment. The first was psychological in nature and related to temporary mental disturbances that interfere with normal behavior. The second was sociological and a function

of an individual's integration into his own society.

The eclectic phase. Both classicists and positivists were excessively insistent on their positions regarding free will and determinism, and it became clear that neither side was totally correct. Although it is certainly a serious mistake to consider the individual criminal apart from his society, the converse view that society is totally responsible is also clearly untrue. Compromise between the two schools of thought was necessary and inevitable.

Perhaps the most important movement in the eclectic period, which began at the turn of the twentieth century, was the French, or Lyons, school, headed by Alexandre Lacassagne. As a physician, Lacassagne was well aware of the importance of the individual, even as he stressed what he considered to be the fundamental issue, the social milieu. In 1885 he opposed Lombroso's theory by comparing a criminal to a microbe. Each will become dangerous, he said, only within its proper milieu: the microbe in a bacteriological culture, and the criminal in his social environment. Lacassagne also declared that "societies have the criminals they deserve," and compared propensity for crime to a loaded gun: the predisposing factor is the gun itself, the determining factor is the bullet, and the precipitating cause is the act of pulling the trigger.

The Marburg school, led by Franz von Liszt (1851–1919), stressed the revolutionary idea that criminal anthropology, penology, sociology, psychology, and statistics all had to be included in any basic course in criminal law. He was convinced that a "synthetic combination" of the individual disposition and the social environment was the root cause of crime. According to von Liszt, crime was the result of exogenous and endogenous factors, and knowing these factors would permit the creation of conditions to solve the problem of crime. In 1889, together with Adolphe Prins and Gerard van Hamel, von Liszt established the International Union of Penal Law, dedicated to cooperative scientific study of the anthropological and sociological features of crime and to the establishment of the best possible preventive programs. Even in Italy, Lombroso's ideas were not universally accepted. By the end of the nineteenth century, the third, or critical, school diametrically opposed von Liszt by advocating the complete independence of criminology from criminal law.

Social defense, a European criminological movement led by Marc Ancel that began after World War II, was opposed to typological classification on the ground that humanity is not subject to categorization. Believing in moral values, its adherents tried to establish a balance between society and the criminal. For

Ancel, criminal policy was both a science and an art—the source of the principles of positive law that would be developed from the results of criminological studies.

Practical achievements during the eclectic period, which lasted from the 1890s to World War I, included the organization of international congresses, the establishment of the first prison centers for the clinical study of offenders, the creation of international scientific societies to deal with the problem of crime, and the development of criminology as an academic subject. Yet, because of the excessive polemics and intransigence among European criminologists, by the mid-twentieth century, American criminology came to the fore.

There was a clearly apparent need, expressed by many scholars, for a permanent international forum to deal with penological problems. In 1872 the American penologist Enoch Wines, together with a number of colleagues, organized in London the First International Penal and Penitentiary Congress, and in 1875 the International Penal and Penitentiary Commission was established to organize future congresses. The commission functioned until 1950, when it transferred its responsibility for arranging congresses to the United Nations, under whose auspices meetings are held every five years.

The International Penal and Penitentiary Commission, now the International Penal and Penitentiary Foundation, organizes periodic seminars and similar meetings, holding a general assembly every five years. In 1924 the International Union of Penal Law was replaced by the International Association of Penal Law, which holds international congresses every five years. The International Society of Criminology was founded in 1935, and the International Society of Social Defense, soon after World War II.

There are chairs of criminology in many important universities in the United States, Europe, Latin America, and the Far East; they function in different academic frameworks that indicate the emphasis of their respective programs. In the English-speaking countries, criminology is generally taught in the department of sociology; in Europe and Latin America, in the faculty of law; and in Japan, in the faculty of medicine.

American criminology. As discussed above, when European criminology lost its initial impetus and began to decline, the discipline aroused interest in the United States. In June 1909, Northwestern University organized the National Conference in Criminal Law and Criminology, which gave impetus to the founding of a number of institutions, among them the American Institute of Criminal Law and Criminology. The *Journal of Criminal Law and Criminology*, established in 1909, is still published. A committee on translations was created by the institute to make the most important foreign-language treatises on criminology accessible in English, and the committee published nine very influential volumes between 1911 and 1917, introducing American criminologists to Lombroso, Ferri, Garofalo, and others.

Discarding the biological considerations so important to the European criminologist, American criminology developed a system based on the sociological aspect of criminality, building on the pioneering work of Durkheim and Tarde. Thorsten Sellin at the University of Pennsylvania, Ernest Burgess at the University of Chicago, and Edwin Sutherland at the universities of Chicago and Indiana created major research centers in criminology. Today, American criminology leads the world in both theoretical and empirical criminological research.

ISRAEL DRAPKIN

See also CRIME STATISTICS: HISTORICAL TRENDS IN WESTERN SOCIETY; JUVENILE JUSTICE: HISTORY AND PHILOSOPHY; POLICE: HISTORY; PRISONS: HISTORY; PUNISHMENT; VICTIMOLOGY.

BIBLIOGRAPHY

BECCARIA, CESARE. *On Crimes and Punishments* (1764). Translated and with an introduction by Henry Paolucci. Indianapolis: Bobbs-Merrill, 1963.

BODDE, DERK, and MORRIS, CLARENCE. *Law in Imperial China: Exemplified by 190 Ch'ing Dynasty Cases, Translated from the Hsing-an hui-lan. With Historical, Social, and Juridical Commentaries.* Cambridge, Mass.: Harvard University Press, 1967.

BONGER, WILLEM A. *Race and Crime.* Translated by Margaret Mathews Hordyk. New York: Columbia University Press, 1943.

BULFERETTI, LUIGI. *Cesare Lombroso.* Turin, Italy: Unione Tipografico-Editrice Torinese, 1975.

DIAMOND, ARTHUR S. *Primitive Law, Past and Present.* London: Methuen, 1971.

DURKHEIM, EMILE, *The Rules of Sociological Method* (1895). 8th ed. Translated by Sarah A. Solovay and John H. Mueller. Edited by George E. G. Catlin. Reprint. New York: Free Press, 1964.

GORING, CHARLES B., ed. *The English Convict: A Statistical Study.* London: His Majesty's Stationery Office, 1913.

HOOTON, EARNEST A. *The American Criminal: An Anthropological Study.* Cambridge, Mass.: Harvard University Press, 1939.

International Society of Criminology. *The University Teaching of Social Sciences: Criminology.* Paris: UNESCO, 1957.

"Jerusalem." *Encyclopedia Judaica*, vol. 9. New York: Macmillan, 1971, pp. 1378–1594.

KRAMER, SAMUEL NOAH. *The Sumerians: Their History, Culture, and Character.* University of Chicago Press, 1963.

KRETSCHMER, ERNST. *Physique and Character: An Investigation of the Nature of Constitution and of the Theory of Temperament* (1936). 2d ed., rev. Translated from the 2d revised and enlarged edition by W. J. H. Sprott. Reprint. New York: Cooper Square, 1970.

LANGE, JOHANNES. *Crime and Destiny: A Study of Criminal Twins.* Translated by Charlotte Haldane. New York: Boni, 1930.

LOMBROSO, CESARE. *Crime: Its Causes and Remedies* (1876). Translated by Henry P. Horton. Introduction by Maurice Parmelee. Boston: Little, Brown, 1911.

MANNHEIM, HERMANN, ed. *Pioneers in Criminology.* London: Stevens, 1960.

PARMELEE, MAURICE. *Criminology.* New York: Macmillan, 1926.

SCHAFER, STEPHEN. *Theories in Criminology: Past and Present Philosophies of the Crime Problem.* New York: Random House, 1969.

SCHNEIDER, KURT. *Psychopathic Personalities.* Translated by M. W. Hamilton. Foreword by E. W. Anderson. Springfield, Ill.: Thomas, 1958.

VOLD, GEORGE B. *Theoretical Criminology.* New York: Oxford University Press, 1958.

YARON, REUVEN. *The Laws of Eshnunna.* Jerusalem: Hebrew University, Magnes Press, 1969.

ZILBOORG, GREGORY, and HENRY, GEORGE W. *A History of Medical Psychology.* New York: Norton, 1941.

2.
MODERN CONTROVERSIES

Introduction

The very concept of crime, as well as its nature, is controversial. Most would agree that crime is behavior lawfully punishable by the state, but even this basic definition is debated. "White-collar crime" is "crime" although it is subject to civil as well as criminal law, Edwin Sutherland insisted, and Paul Tappan argued that *crime* should refer only to behavior for which conviction in a criminal court has been obtained. Some contend that the definition should be extended to all violations of human rights, or at least to those that harm the interests of the working class (Greenberg). Beyond such definitional concerns, controversy is virtually endemic to criminology, with future as well as present consequences.

Problems of definition

For a variety of reasons, radical criminology's definition of crime as "all human rights violations" has attracted few supporters. Karl Marx himself, the major

intellectual forebear of those who are dissatisfied with definitions bound by the laws of states, rejected such a definition. It is recognized, furthermore, that a legal definition does not preclude—indeed, that it invites—historical and comparative studies of the conditions of lawmaking. Moreover, a human rights definition makes even more ambiguous a field of inquiry that is already vague and hard to delimit, and the upholding of human rights values does not distinguish the advocates of such a definition from traditional criminologists. Indeed, use of a legal definition tends to restrain any overtly political use of the criminal law process.

The term *white-collar crime,* on the other hand, remains an ambiguous one, and alternative concepts have been proposed. Some are subsets of the original, such as corporate crime (Clinard and Yeager) and organizational crime (Schrager and Short). Others are generic, for example, Gilbert Geis's use of the term *avocational crime* and the concept of white-collar violations deriving from Sutherland's research strategy, which included behavior punishable by the state under administrative and civil, as well as criminal, statutes (Reiss and Biderman).

Other elements of definition are implied in the uses to which the term *crime* is put. Thus, Daniel Glaser has referred to crime as "a legal classification of behavior made by judges or juries in ruling on specific cases" (1974, p. 46). This usage emphasizes the position of "sociological jurisprudence," namely, that the life of the law resides in experience—that of police, judges, and other functionaries of the justice system, as well as of complainants, defendants, and legal counsel. Although the basic premise of this approach is widely granted, its chief weakness, as Philip Selznick noted, has been its failure to develop "a theory of the distinctively legal" (p. 51).

All of this places a heavy burden on the sociology of law, with which, some assert, criminology begins. Sutherland's classic definition of criminology as "the body of knowledge regarding . . . crime as a social phenomenon" specifically included "the processes of making laws, of breaking laws, and of reacting toward the breaking of laws" (1924, p. 3). Controversy remains, however. Is criminology an "integrative" but independent discipline, as Marvin Wolfgang and Franco Ferracuti have argued, or is it necessarily a dependent discipline (Cressey, 1968)? Is it restricted to the canons of science, or must it be normative, as the "new criminology" insists (Taylor, Walton, and Young)?

An equally controversial matter is the relationship of criminology to other disciplines and professions.

Concern with the limited scope of academic criminal justice programs has prompted Richard Myren to call for an even broader discipline of "justiciology." There is much resistance to such expansion, however, and disagreement over the content, standards, and objectives of criminology and criminal justice education is widespread.

Criminology as science and as politics. "New criminologists" have sought to discredit positivist, mainstream criminology on political as well as theoretical grounds. As Donald Cressey (1979) has noted, however, the nineteenth-century positivists who focused on crime, such as Cesare Lombroso and Adolphe Quételet, were involved in political as well as scientific history. Their research, and much of that which followed in the twentieth century, questioned "the efficacy of coercive crime control" and thus attacked the power of the state (p. 457). Debate on such issues remains virulent: some, such as Greenberg, argue that Marxist criminology is committed to a scientific approach, but others deny that possibility. For Richard Quinney and others, criminology is socialist revolutionary advocacy, whereas Austin Turk insists that conflict analyses of crime be nonpartisan.

Measurement

Measurement, which is critical to any science, has been in a state of disarray in criminology for much of its history. After the prodigious achievement of the Uniform Crime Report system of the Federal Bureau of Investigation, which is based on reports collected from thousands of police departments operating under different state and local statutes and customs, questions were raised about the reliability and validity of such reports (Sellin and Wolfgang). Polarities in the controversy are represented by John Kitsuse and Aaron Cicourel, who argue that official statistics reflect *only* the workings of official agencies, and by Robert Gordon, who maintains that the "court record criterion" represents "a lower bound for the degree of severity that defines 'delinquent' in a manner with which it is profitable for society (and hence social science) to concern itself" (p. 270). Controversy over possible biases of official statistics and case processing is likely to continue, both because definitive evidence is lacking and because of the political nature of the issues—for example, the extent to which they bear on racial and feminist issues (Harris and Hill).

Several alternatives to official data for epidemiologic and etiologic research have developed, principally self-reports of delinquent behavior and surveys of criminal victimization. Both have been critically reviewed (Hindelang, Hirschi, and Weis; Gottfredson and Hindelang). Methodological and substantive questions remain, and none of the three methods is satisfactory for studying white-collar offenses. Lack of standardized methods, offenses, and continuity have plagued self-report studies, although the work of Delbert Elliott, Brian Knowles, and Rachelle Canter represents an exception. Victimization surveys reveal the social distribution of some types of crime, but they add little to knowledge of white-collar or "victimless" offenses. Improvements in these methods are likely to continue, but a nagging problem remains: how to capture in generalizable form the richness of oral history (Bennett) and of observational studies focusing on specially targeted populations, such as that of Francis Ianni on organized crime, of Bettylou Valentine on ghetto life and crime, or of Joan Moore and her associates on crime in Los Angeles barrios and in prison.

Evaluation of the *seriousness* of crime has produced persistent controversy over technical problems of measurement, but the issue of greatest relevance to criminology is the universality of such evaluations. Peter Rossi and Patrick Henry review both types of controversies and conclude, with reservations, that seriousness offers promise as "a measure for all purposes" (p. 489). However, Herman and Julia Schwendinger argue that failure to incorporate social conditions associated with a criminal act renders these measures relatively meaningless. It seems probable that both the theoretical and the applied significance of seriousness measures will be enhanced by future studies. Already it is apparent that the conventional wisdom which views white-collar crime as less serious than ordinary crime (Wilson) is contradicted by more carefully conceived studies (Braithwaite, 1979).

Characteristics of criminals and the social distribution of crime

Despite methodological advances, the most elementary "facts" about crime remain controversial. Examples include the incidence, prevalence, patterning, and trends of crime and delinquency among males and females and among persons who differ in age, place of residence, social class, race, ethnicity, and level of intelligence. Expansion of the empirical base has proceeded more rapidly than has theoretical advance with respect to these issues.

Whether, how, and why rates of female crime and delinquency may have changed are matters of theoretical and empirical debate (Harris and Hill; Steffensmeier). Age influences the sex distribution of crime and delinquency, but precisely how much and why remains unknown. Disputes as to the social-class distribution of delinquent behavior were fueled in the 1950s by early self-report studies that found few differences in reported delinquent behavior among young people in different social classes. John Braithwaite's assessment of the evidence (1979), together with the suggestion by Michael Hindelang, Travis Hirschi, and Joseph Weis, that earlier studies did not find a social-class–delinquency association because they failed to study serious crimes, have revitalized the argument.

The racial distribution of crime and delinquency has been disputed on grounds similar to those attending social class. Self-reports generally have failed to reveal the large racial differences found in official statistics. Victimization studies, however, have confirmed higher rates of offending (and of victimization) among blacks. Methodological research suggests that self-reports are not equally valid among all categories. Young black males who have been officially defined as delinquents appear less likely than others to report offenses known to the police (Hindelang, Hirschi, and Weis).

The relationship of intelligence quotient (IQ) to crime and delinquency is tied to other characteristics, including race. In the early heyday of the idea that feeblemindedness is a cause of crime, the intelligence factor was a casualty of poor measurement and research design. However, new attention is being given to measured intelligence as an element in delinquency owing to research on relevant evidence conducted by Gordon and by Hirschi and Hindelang. Dispute on the meaning of measured intelligence has not been stilled by research, and until that question can be answered definitively, the mechanisms or processes by which intelligence contributes to behavior are also likely to remain in dispute.

Theories of causation

The major theoretical controversies in criminology have concerned the hegemony of one or another parent discipline and, within disciplines, the relative importance of different perspectives, such as strain versus control. Much of what has been happening since the mid-1900s may be characterized as "normal science," elaborating and carrying to completion earlier work, both theoretically and empirically (Harris and Hill). Sutherland's broad principle of "differential association" (Sutherland and Cressey) has been modified by several scholars, based on learning theories developed in psychology (see, for example, Albert

Bandura). Sutherland's principle, as well as Robert Merton's seminal idea in "Social Structure and Anomie," was also extended by Albert Cohen and by Richard Cloward and Lloyd Ohlin, among others. Social-control theory, brought back into prominence by Albert Reiss (1951), has been elaborated by Hirschi and others. Labeling theory and symbolic interactionist thought have undergone transformation as well. Since the mid-1970s, innovative applications of econometric models to data analysis and of human-capital economics theory to crime (Gary Becker) have led to both challenge and emulation. This scholarly activity has been facilitated by expansion of the empirical base and by increasingly sophisticated quantitative techniques of data analysis.

Controversies over the relative importance of one or another perspective often result from addressing different levels of explanation. The problem has been posed in a number of ways. Alex Inkeles suggests that sociologists have ignored *personality* in the equation involving social structure, culture, and behavior; they need to add consideration of *group process* (Short). Harold Finestone maintains that "the dichotomization of theoretical approaches" between social organization and structure, on the one hand, and social psychology, on the other, requires "transitive concepts" that might help bridge these levels of explanation.

Many attempts to assess the relative significance of various partial theories have not been notably successful, and some have argued that integration is not desirable because it might destroy the healthy theoretical ferment which has characterized criminology. Yet the many voices with which criminologists speak are confusing to policymakers and the public—not to say themselves. Failure to pursue integration will surely contribute to those problems and prevent full exploitation of the "partial insights" of various formulations.

Attempts to explain delinquency and crime often become embroiled in controversy over what is to be explained. Suggestions that legal descriptions of offenses are of limited value for theories of causation have led to numerous efforts to interpret police contact and arrest records in a manner that would permit their use for etiologic purposes. These include simple comparisons of officially defined delinquents with those who are not so defined, the familiar combinations of crimes against property and against persons, and "victimless" offenses, transformations based on seriousness ratings (Sellin and Wolfgang), and elaborate statistical combinations of official charges. Other scholarly studies have focused solely on officially classified behaviors that seem to satisfy theoretical needs.

Controversies over what is being explained are based upon both methodological and theoretical criteria. A major theoretical dispute centers on whether criminal or delinquent *acts* or *persons* are to be explained and, if the latter, how a delinquent person should be defined. Some have rejected the act as a proper focus of attention on the ground that sustained patterns of behavior, social roles, or personal identity are the foremost areas requiring explanation (Cloward and Ohlin; Howard Becker). Even crudely identified official criminals have occasionally proved to be useful for theoretical purposes, however, as in studies of the self-identity and "criminal choice" of black and white prisoners (Harris and Hill).

Typological definitions of crime and delinquency seek to bring empirical and theoretical order out of the vastly heterogeneous behaviors included under these rubrics. Most such attempts have been guided by some theoretical purpose, but they have been no more successful, statistically, in explaining behavior than have theories that seek explanations of delinquency or crime *in general.* Future typological advances may indeed be more successful, but even the most ardent supporters of typologies have come to question their efficacy (Gibbons).

Theories purporting to explain crime or delinquency in general are of a quite different order than those that seek to explain particular forms of these phenomena. In setting forth the theory of differential association, for example, Sutherland's aim was akin to Darwin's in advancing the theory of evolution, for it was concerned with explaining "the conditions which produce" crime, rather than with "short-range predictions of behavior" (Cressey, 1979, p. 462). The point also applies to general social-control theories and to such broad theoretical frameworks as "strain theory," since they all require extension, refinement, and empirical investigation. Extensions are not always recognized as such, however. Cressey notes that "labeling a person as a delinquent or criminal can be a behavior pattern favorable to crime" (1979, p. 465), a point seldom associated with the labeling perspective.

Howard Becker has observed that the labeling perspective is not theory in a formal sense, nor is it "focused so exclusively on the act of labeling as some have thought" (p. 81). However that may be, a review of the social psychology of deviance suggests that the labeling perspective has been the dominant object of empirical and theoretical inquiry since the early 1960s (Harris and Hill). The review also suggests that the perspective has not fared particularly well as a result of these inquiries. Indeed, its authors conclude that labeling has diverted attention from important and valuable sociological concerns, such as the dynamics and impacts of social change, the social and material costs of crime and deviance, and issues related to social control. The paradox in this observation is found in Becker's assessment that labeling is "a perspective whose value will appear, if at all, in increased understanding of things formerly obscure" (p. 81).

Among the many theoretical controversies in criminology, two broad areas of inquiry warrant additional comment. First, the challenge posed by the several varieties of "conflict theory" and the "new criminology" has both political and scientific implications, and the two are difficult to disentangle. Second, the challenge to social-science approaches to criminology posed by *biological* research has political overtones as well, insofar as biological determinism carries overtones of racism. Political controversy in both areas may be muted somewhat—although certainly not stilled—by scholarly efforts stimulated by scientific controversies. The irony of linking these two areas of controversy lies in the fact that one of the aims of the new criminology was to break with individual (including biological) explanations of crime.

Revisionist historiography and criminology. The work of revisionist historians has had a major impact on traditional, as well as on conflict and Marxist, criminologists (Hay). The "operation of the law as ideology" is, as Richard Sparks (p. 200) notes, an important insight for mainstream, conflict, and Marxist criminologists alike. Similarly, critical social histories of prisons and punishment, although initially well received, have generated controversy even among those who have dealt with these subjects. Michael Ignatieff has challenged revisionist histories of prisons and, by implication, revisionist histories of the juvenile court and other institutions of the modern welfare state. Although his challenge focuses on specific works, including his own, its implications are more general. Declaring himself a "counter-revisionist," Ignatieff challenges revisionist historians and classical theorists of social organization alike, including Max Weber. Thus, he charges that too much emphasis has been placed on the state's monopoly over legitimate use of violence, on locating "the binding sources of social order" in the moral authority and power of the state, and on superordinate and subordinate social relations (pp. 156–157). The implications of scholarly inquiry in these areas extend to the most fundamental questions about social order.

Biology and crime. Biological determinism has not fared well in criminology despite a venerable history.

Social scientists quite justifiably rejected simplistic earlier theories regarding biological contributions to delinquency and crime, but they subsequently neglected important contributions, at times on the basis of criteria which, if applied to social factors, would reject these as well.

The importance of biological factors *in interaction* with social factors in the causation of crime is supported by many studies. Although still generating controversy, some research of the 1970s may bridge the gap between theories stressing social and biological processes. Thus, the discovery of mechanisms and processes by which biological and biologically related factors (such as intelligence) influence behavior defined as criminal or delinquent offers the hope—if not the promise—that long-standing etiological controversies may be resolved. The suggestion that the connection between intelligence and delinquent behavior is mediated by poor school performance (Hirschi and Hindelang) is compatible with a biosocial theory of antisocial behavior. Even if these theoretical puzzles are solved, controversy seems certain to continue concerning the social policy implications of such work.

Controversies related to social policy

Most debates over social policy relate not to crime causation theory but to theory in social organization and control, in law, in political and economic systems, and occasionally, in social psychology.

Discretion. Several important controversies in criminology relate to the exercise of discretion in juvenile and criminal justice: How much should there be, and of what types? Much of the debate is misguided in that it portrays a choice between discretion and nondiscretion, and ignores the fundamental role played by citizens. As Reiss (1974) has noted, in societies that limit "police access to places where crimes occur . . . by institutions of privacy," citizens "have discretionary control over knowledge of crimes committed in private places" (p. 682). Because local law enforcement tends strongly to be reactive rather than proactive, discretion in criminal justice begins with citizen choice. Citizens also exercise discretion regarding cooperation with authorities and defense attorneys. Additionally, some have argued that the entire system of criminal justice depends crucially upon the exercise of discretion in "doing justice." The extent and the nature of "discretionary justice" have been the subject of increased political debate, legislative action, justice system reaction, and intellectual inquiry.

Police roles and functions. Focus on discretion has changed the study of the police role and has generated still more disagreement in an always controversial field. Viewed initially as the incidental and regrettable result of ambiguities in law and in enforcement policies (Joseph Goldstein), discretion came soon to be interpreted as essential and unavoidable. Coupled with another "discovery"—that of the helping and peacekeeping functions of police work—acknowledgment that the police make choices in every work situation led to important empirical and theoretical elaboration of both discoveries. Some legal commentators, such as Sanford Kadish, tended to see discretion as requiring control through new rules and procedures. Social scientists have analyzed competing, and often conflicting, role expectations of police, often in terms of the maintenance of order versus law enforcement. Jerome Skolnick, for example, has suggested that "law and order" frequently are in opposition, "because law implies rational restraint upon the rules and procedures utilized to achieve order" (p. 9). The President's Commission on Law Enforcement and Administration of Justice challenged this position and asked for increased resources and more effective administrative control over police behavior.

Research and commentary on such issues by criminologists have been political as well as analytical. Rubén Rumbaut and Egon Bittner are convinced that efforts at police reform since the release of the commission's report lack policy direction and attenuate "the aims of substantive political justice, including those of police accountability, local community review, and control of police discretionary policymaking powers" (p. 239). The controversy has been joined by professional police organizations, which have challenged the findings of experiments calling into question such traditional police practices as preventive patrol and field interrogation. Criticism, Rumbaut and Bittner note, has tended to alienate and polarize the police and to stimulate organizational efforts to protect police interests. Even police community-relations projects, designed ostensibly to promote police-community accord and to bring police policies and practices under effective community review, have been attacked on the grounds that they obfuscate "the contradictions of policing" (Manning, p. 362).

Because it looms so large in the public consciousness, the role of force in police work requires special comment. Most discussions of police functions (American Bar Association, 1980) have tended to ignore the role of force or its threat. Bittner's influential analysis, however, characterizes the police as "a mechanism for the distribution of situationally justified force in society" (1970, p. 39). Richard Sykes has challenged this position, noting that the police use force infrequently and as a last resort. Sykes defines policing theoretically as "intervention by an objective third party in the domain of problems of person-position interaction . . . a basic and permanent regulatory activity of every human group" (p. 255). The fact that such intervention may require "the use of force at the point of . . . [its] occurrence" (Bittner, 1970, p. 44), however, appears to be what distinguishes police work from other sorts of regulatory activity. This critical factor is often ignored in debates over the "crime fighter versus social worker" roles of the police.

Police "brutality" and "deadly force" have become public issues primarily as a result of civil rights concerns. Conflicting interpretations of police reaction to public demonstrations, such as the one that took place in Chicago at the 1968 Democratic National Convention, sparked public and scholarly interest alike. Social scientists entered these controversies by undertaking careful field observation and analysis of police records, and by bringing to bear concepts of organizational analyses (Sherman, 1980).

Criminological interest in police *corruption*, long a matter of public and political concern, also is quite recent. Traditionally approached as a problem of individual cupidity and greed, analyses stressing organizational properties and behavior have proven more fruitful, both theoretically and in terms of "practical" implications (Herman Goldstein; Sherman, 1978).

Plea bargaining and sentencing disparity. Arthur Rosett and Cressey observe that just as police reform has failed to produce the judicious police officer, technically oriented efforts to prevent court abuses through restrictions on plea bargaining and mandated sentences have failed to produce justice in the processing of criminal cases. There has been long-standing controversy over pleas "negotiated" between prosecutors and defense attorneys, with the judge often involved as well. Sentencing disparities have been another source of controversy. Alaska banned plea bargaining in 1975 without the expected consequences of court overload and delay, but efforts to abolish the practice elsewhere have encountered much successful resistance.

Judicial and administrative discretion in sentencing have been the subject of much dispute. Variation within and between states in available sanctions for similar offenses, and discrepancies in the relationship of sanctions to severity of offense, have been characterized by the American Bar Association as "utterly without any rational basis" (1967, p. 49). Similar disparities between judges in actual sentencing have

been subject to equally scathing comments. Proposed solutions have taken the form of model statutes designed to bring greater uniformity in sanctioning for broadly similar offenses, and of frequent legislative attempts to restrict discretion on the part of judges and administrative boards.

Rosett and Cressey conclude that "the exercise of discretion is a response to a fundamental need for flexibility, for procedures that are fair because they avoid formal rules" (p. 170). Yet, as Stephen Morse notes, in an adversarial system designed to equalize the power of the individual vis-à-vis the state, the exercise of discretion compromises that goal in the interest of making the system work. Ernest Van den Haag has argued against discretion at any point in the criminal justice system because he believes deterrence will be maximized by punishments that are mandated by law (with little discretion left to the courts), that are determinate, and that are not reducible by prison administrators or parole boards. The uniqueness of crimes and of criminals, he believes, renders it impossible to do justice by imposing individualized punishments.

It is not likely that any version of these arguments will win the day entirely, for the questions and the options are as much political as they are empirical or theoretical. Empirical studies strongly suggest that discretionary adjustments will occur within the criminal justice system, regardless of how restrictive the laws may become. Criminologists clearly have much work to do in determining the conditions under which various purposes are served by policies related to discretion at all points in justice systems.

The "nothing works" approach. A 1975 study by Douglas Lipton, Robert Martinson, and Judith Wilks surveyed more than two decades (1945 to 1967) of correctional program evaluations and confirmed what many had long suspected: there was little evidence that any of the programs evaluated had succeeded in preventing recidivism. Widely interpreted to mean that "nothing works," the survey stirred up a controversy that seems certain to continue. Subsequent evaluative studies have failed to find convincing evidence of program success, but the debate has become more sophisticated, politically as well as scientifically.

The conclusion that "nothing works" has been taken by some to suggest that evaluation of experimental programs, when badly done, may be exploited politically and may discourage innovation by giving aid to outdated ideas and entrenched programs. Challenges to the survey's conclusions and interpretations began to appear almost immediately. Some have found, for example, that deinstitutionalization and diversion programs have not been effectively implemented and that they have often been confused. Competent evaluations, moreover, have been rare.

Most correctional programs ignore theoretically fundamental principles of crime causation, and when they do not, the manner in which theoretical concepts have been studied and measured has been suspect. Even relatively successful programs that have been carefully evaluated often undergo changes which alter the principles crucial to initial success when they are expanded beyond small, experimental populations.

It seems clear that the "nothing works" conclusion is erroneous. Martinson, who had publicized the Lipton study, apparently had subsequent doubts concerning both its conclusion and the validity of the research upon which it was based. Devastating critiques of correctional programs and evaluations—of which the Lipton study was only one—may have had a stultifying effect on theoretically based correctional programming, prompting policymakers to retreat to simplistic notions of deterrence, retribution, or "just deserts." These critiques have, on the other hand, stimulated critical thought in an area previously characterized by the absence of theory and by naive applications and research.

Deterrence. The deterrent effect of legal sanctions, long dismissed by criminologists as "an archaic theoretical construct associated with Bentham, Beccaria, and other somewhat naive scholars from the distant past" (Cook, p. 212), has emerged as a major point of controversy among social scientists, philosophers, and policymakers. Survey research has brought the public as well into the debate, first, by providing new and more objective information on evaluation of the seriousness of crimes, and second, by bringing to bear more systematic information on public knowledge, concern, and opinion regarding correctional policy. Public evaluations and opinions are being introduced into scholarly debate as factors relevant to arguments concerning seriousness, just deserts, the death penalty, and other social policies.

The major questions debated, however, revolve around matters of "criminal choice," that is, the effects of sanctions on the choices individuals make with regard to their participation in criminal activity. The debate has centered on a model of behavior advanced by human capital economists, such as Gary Becker. The general hypothesis, as presented by its most persistent advocate, Isaac Ehrlich, is that "all potential offenders—even the perpetrators of 'crimes of passion'—on the whole respond to costs and gains, prices and rewards, in much the same way, although not

necessarily to the same extent, as do individuals who pursue legitimate or socially approved activities" (p. 27). From this general perspective it has been deduced that, other things being equal, an increase in the probability or severity of punishment for crime will reduce the crime rate.

Alfred Blumstein, Jacqueline Cohen, and Daniel Nagin found much evidence suggestive of the deterrent effects of legal threats and punishments, but they concluded that methodological flaws and lacks in the existing knowledge base made it impossible to draw firm and specific conclusions concerning the nature of those effects. It seems fair to say that, despite charges and countercharges, evidence of a deterrent effect is plentiful but inconsistent, and that philosophical and scientific questions alike remain to be answered.

Philip Cook's attempt to "lay the groundwork for the second decade" of research in criminal deterrence focuses on models of individual choice to commit a criminal act. Cook rejects the "Ehrlich paradigm," which dominated the debate during the 1970s, on the ground that "the quest for a single set of universally applicable estimates of deterrence effects is hopeless, given the nature of available data and the complexity of the underlying process which generates crime rates and sanction threats" (p. 262). Cook's suggestions for further research promise to offer ample means for resolving some controversies and generating others. Of fundamental interest in this regard is the suggestion, made by Anthony Harris and Gary Hill, that the "political economy" of deviance (in this case, crime) involves values placed on status and "the boundaries of moral order," as well as traditional economic values.

Just deserts. Encouraged by the absence of convincing evidence that the criminal justice system either corrects or deters, retribution has reemerged in scholarly debate and policy discussion. A retributive position holds that justice requires that criminals receive the punishment they deserve and that punishment is deserved because the person who violates rules has gained unfair advantage over those who abide by them. The function of punishment, therefore, is to restore the balance of effort and advantage that is entailed in citizenship.

The just-deserts argument has been challenged on philosophical, legal, ethical, moral, and social-science grounds. Justice norms differ considerably among various segments of the population, and lower-class offenders are unfairly disadvantaged in terms of available options.

Braithwaite (1982) argues that insisting on just deserts would necessarily result in less equitable and just policies than would adherence to the utilitarian principles upon which correctional policies have come to be based. His argument joins the issue of achieving justice with respect to white-collar, as opposed to ordinary, crime. He holds that it is impossible either to achieve or to restore an equilibrium of benefits or burdens shared by *individuals* and *organizations*. He then notes that white-collar crimes are committed on an extremely large (but not precisely known) scale and that the public considers many white-collar crimes to be more serious, and deserving of more severe punishment, than most forms of common crime. Therefore, the economic costs of enforcing a just-deserts policy to control white-collar crime would be prohibitive. In addition, the complexity of fixing organizational responsibility and assessing objective harm, the necessity of compromising just deserts in the interest of such other values as protecting public health, and the regulatory and educative functions of white-collar crime control all make it impossible effectively to implement a just-deserts model.

Like so many other issues bearing on social-policy considerations, the relevance of the just-deserts position as a criminological issue is as much political as it is scientific. So long as social science was concerned only with "root causes," its relevance to crime control was extremely tenuous because of the compelling need to "do something" about crime. The relevance of social science to social policy has been greatly enhanced by the emergence of a strong applied dimension in each of the social sciences. Although controversies abound, there has been a considerable increase in the theoretical and empirical sophistication of evaluative research, policy analysis, and the assessment of public knowledge, concern, and opinion regarding crime and crime control. Indeed, an important future controversy is likely to revolve around the relevance of applied research—as opposed to basic research and theory—to crime control and justice. The technical achievements of applied social science are impressive. When joined with basic research concerns, they can be expected to contribute to knowledge on an unprecedented scale. Most criminologists would probably agree that crime causation theory that is derived from the most relevant abstract behavioral science theory, that is formalized and continually made explicit, and that is rigorously tested both by practical application and theoretically designed test cases remains the best hope for increasing valid and useful knowledge of how to promote justice and cope with lawbreaking (Glaser, 1979, p. 231).

Conclusion

The resolution of controversies in criminology has resulted primarily from an expansion of what is empirically known about crime, or from experimentation that had practical, rather than theoretical, objectives. To some extent this merely indicates normal scientific activity—the filling-in that occurs when empirical questions are raised by major theoretical positions. It also reflects the failure of the field to generate theory, or to explain the relevance of theory, for the "practical" problems that the criminal and juvenile justice systems face. The field has in some respects become more self-consciously experimental—for example, with respect to police patrol and bail policies—perhaps *because* persuasive theory is lacking. It has also benefited from quasi-experimental analysis of the consequences of major changes in policy, for example, the release of incarcerated juvenile delinquents in Massachusetts that was assessed by Lloyd Ohlin, Alden Miller, and Robert Coates. When rigorous experimentation takes place, theoretical advance sometimes ensues, depending on the skills and imagination of the investigators.

On dependence and the erosion of trust: criminology's ultimate controversy? As societies become more complex and knowledge more specialized, dependence on expertise is increasingly necessary. The cost of such dependence, Bittner (1981) argues, is twofold: in terms of the erosion of self-reliance, and of an increase in the regulatory control of individuals' lives. These problems are most evident in the search for solutions to such highly technical problems as those associated with nuclear energy and genetic engineering. Even these problems are ultimately social, political, and economic in nature, as are efforts to cope with "the vexations of ordinary life." Dependence on expertise and the accompanying increase in behavioral regulation, Bittner suggests, "threaten to change our lives from [the] relatively independent, if somewhat chaotic, condition which has characterized most of human history, to a smooth-running, scientifically rationalized consumer function" (p. 3).

Cressey's (1978) thoughtful analysis of the increasing bureaucratization of research and of crime control efforts is also pertinent. He notes that in the 1970s, the "freedom of criminal justice personnel to be wise, compassionate, judicious, and even innovative" has increasingly been abridged by legislative mandates restricting discretionary action by the "experts" of the system—police, judges, and parole boards. This change he interprets as a shift from the principle of the performance contract to that of the behavioral contract, noting that the element of *trust* implied by the performance contract is lacking in the specificity of behavior required under the terms of behavioral contracts.

Cressey has identified four factors that are responsible for the shift from performance to behavioral criteria in criminal law and its administration, all of them both more general than the crime problem and specific to it. First, bureaucracy has grown as society has become more complex, resulting in the ever-closer regulation of citizen-to-citizen and citizen-to-government relationships. Second, suspicion and disdain of governmental procedures, which are perceived to favor the rich and powerful and to discriminate against the poor and weak, have led to increasingly detailed and restrictive legal requirements. Paradoxically, these formal requirements often result in even more deviation by—and favorable treatment of—the affluent and powerful. Third, the growth of economic rationality in the management of governmental functions has meant ever-more restrictive regulations and tighter controls. Fourth, a "fear of crime and criminals" has encouraged an emphasis on the closer monitoring of citizens and has caused the abandonment of "intervention in the crime-producing process" (p. 44). This combination of factors produces an increasingly stringent bureaucratic regulation of criminal justice policy, and limits the freedom of action of criminal justice personnel at every level.

Underlying the trend toward limiting expert professional discretion is the erosion of *trust.* Perhaps this is the ultimate challenge, not only to criminology and criminologists, but to all who would understand the nature of the social fabric—its strengths and its weaknesses. For beyond the conflicting visions of the technocrat at one extreme, and of the libertarian at the other, lie fundamental questions of trust. Who is to be trusted, and under what conditions? Who *must* be trusted to advise or to make decisions in fateful matters so technical as to preclude knowledge by any except a specialized few? What are the boundaries between technical knowledge and wisdom, compassion, and judiciousness? What is the nature of the social compact between those who possess special knowledge and those whose lives may depend on that knowledge? Is it possible to maintain—even strengthen—self-reliance, rather than weakening it by reliance upon those possessed of special knowledge, perhaps by developing a better-educated and more aware and self-confident citizenry? Sociologists will recognize in such questions the Durkheimian quest for organic, as opposed to mechanical, solidarity, a problem that today seems infinitely more complex and fraught with danger than was the case in Durkheim's day. These questions extend beyond the province of criminology, suggesting the ultimate convergence of the concerns of criminology with those of other disciplines.

JAMES F. SHORT, JR.

See also CRIME: CONCEPT OF CRIME; CRIME CAUSATION; CRIME STATISTICS: REPORTING SYSTEMS AND METHODS; DETERRENCE; PREDICTION OF CRIME AND RECIDIVISM; PRISONS: PROBLEMS AND PROSPECTS; RACE AND CRIME; REHABILITATION; WOMEN AND CRIME.

BIBLIOGRAPHY

American Bar Association. *Sentencing Alternatives and Procedures.* Chicago: ABA, 1967.
———. "The Urban Police Function." *Standards for Criminal Justice,* vol. 1. 2d ed. Prepared with the assistance of the American Bar Foundation. Boston: Little, Brown, 1980, chap. 1.
BANDURA, ALBERT. *Principles of Behavior Modification.* New York: Holt, Rinehart & Winston, 1969.
BECKER, GARY S. *The Economic Approach to Human Behavior.* University of Chicago Press, 1976.
BECKER, HOWARD S. *Outsiders: Studies in the Sociology of Deviance.* Reprint. New York: Free Press, 1973.
BENNETT, JAMES. *Oral History and Delinquency: The Rhetoric of Criminology.* University of Chicago Press, 1981.
BITTNER, EGON. "Autonomy and Technique: How Far May We Go before Professional Solutions for All Problems Will Begin to Diminish Human Life?" *SSSP Newsletter* 12, no. 4 (1981): 2–3.
———. *The Functions of the Police in Modern Society: A Review of Background Factors, Current Practices, and Possible Role Models.* Chevy Chase, Md.: National Institute of Mental Health, Center for Studies of Crime and Delinquency, 1970.
BLUMSTEIN, ALFRED; COHEN, JACQUELINE; and NAGIN, DANIEL, eds. *Deterrence and Incapacitation: Estimating the Effects of Criminal Sanctions on Crime Rates.* Washington, D.C.: National Academy of Sciences, 1978.
BRAITHWAITE, JOHN. "Challenging Just Deserts: Punishing White-collar Criminals." *Journal of Criminal Law and Criminology* 73, no. 2 (1982): 723–763.
———. *Inequality, Crime, and Public Policy.* Boston: Routledge & Kegan Paul, 1979.
CLINARD, MARSHALL B., and YEAGER, PETER C. "Corporate Crime: Issues in Research." *Criminology* 16 (1978): 255–272.
CLOWARD, RICHARD A., and OHLIN, LLOYD E. *Delinquency and Opportunity: A Theory of Delinquent Gangs.* New York: Free Press, 1960.
COHEN, ALBERT K. *Delinquent Boys: The Culture of the Gang.* New York: Free Press, 1955.
COOK, PHILIP J. "Research in Criminal Deterrence: Laying the Groundwork for the Second Decade." *Crime and Jus-

tice: An Annual Review of Research, vol. 2. Edited by Norval Morris and Michael Tonry. University of Chicago Press, 1980, pp. 211–268.

CRESSEY, DONALD R. "Crime: I. Causes of Crime." *International Encyclopedia of the Social Sciences*, vol. 3. New York: Macmillan and Free Press, 1968, pp. 471–476.

———. "Crime, Science, and Bureaucratic Rule." *Center Magazine* 11, no. 4 (1978): 40–48.

———. "Fifty Years of Criminology: From Sociological Theory to Political Control." *Pacific Sociological Review* 22 (1979): 457–480.

DURKHEIM, EMILE. *The Division of Labor in Society* (1893). Translated by George Simpson. Reprint. New York: Free Press, 1947.

EHRLICH, ISAAC. "The Economic Approach to Crime: A Preliminary Assessment." *Criminology Review Yearbook*, vol. 1. Edited by Sheldon Messinger and Egon Bittner. Beverly Hills, Calif.: Sage, 1979, pp. 25–60.

ELLIOTT, DELBERT S.; KNOWLES, BRIAN A.; and CANTER, RACHELLE J. *The Epidemiology of Delinquent Behavior and Drug Use among American Adolescents*. Boulder, Colo.: Behavioral Research Institute, 1981.

Federal Bureau of Investigation. *Crime in the United States*. Uniform Crime Reports for the United States. Washington, D.C.: U.S. Department of Justice, FBI, annually.

FINESTONE, HAROLD. "The Delinquent and Society: The Shaw and McKay Tradition." *Delinquency, Crime, and Society*. Edited by James F. Short, Jr. University of Chicago Press, 1976, pp. 23–49.

GEIS, GILBERT. "Avocational Crime." *Handbook of Criminology*. Edited by Daniel Glaser. Chicago: Rand McNally, 1974, pp. 273–298.

GIBBONS, DON C. "Offender Typologies—Two Decades Later." *British Journal of Criminology* 15 (1975): 140–156.

GLASER, DANIEL. "The Classification of Offenses and Offenders." *Handbook of Criminology*. Edited by Daniel Glaser. Chicago: Rand McNally, 1974, pp. 45–83.

———. "A Review of Crime-Causation Theory and Its Application." *Crime and Justice: An Annual Review of Research*, vol. 1. Edited by Norval Morris and Michael Tonry. University of Chicago Press, 1979, pp. 203–237.

GOLDSTEIN, HERMAN. *Policing a Free Society*. Cambridge, Mass.: Ballinger, 1977.

GOLDSTEIN, JOSEPH. "Police Discretion Not to Invoke the Criminal Process: Low-visibility Decisions in the Administration of Justice." *Yale Law Journal* 69 (1960): 543–594.

GORDON, ROBERT A. "Prevalence: The Rare Datum in Delinquency Measurement and Its Implications for the Theory of Delinquency." *The Juvenile Justice System*. Edited by Malcolm W. Klein. Beverly Hills, Calif.: Sage, 1976, pp. 201–284.

GOTTFREDSON, MICHAEL R., and HINDELANG, MICHAEL J. "Sociological Aspects of Criminal Victimization." *Annual Review of Sociology*, vol. 7. Edited by Ralph H. Turner and James F. Short, Jr. Palo Alto, Calif.: Annual Reviews, 1981, pp. 107–128.

GREENBERG, DAVID F., ed. *Crime and Capitalism: Readings in Marxist Criminology*. Palo Alto, Calif.: Mayfield, 1981.

HARRIS, ANTHONY R., and HILL, GARY D. "The Social Psychology of Deviance: Toward a Reconciliation with Social Structure." *Annual Review of Sociology*, vol. 8. Edited by Ralph H. Turner and James F. Short, Jr. Palo Alto, Calif.: Annual Reviews, 1982, pp. 161–186.

HAY, DOUGLAS. "Crime and Justice in Eighteenth- and Nineteenth-century England." *Crime and Justice: An Annual Review of Research*, vol. 2. Edited by Norval Morris and Michael Tonry. University of Chicago Press, 1980, pp. 45–84.

HINDELANG, MICHAEL J.; HIRSCHI, TRAVIS; and WEIS, JOSEPH. *Measuring Delinquency*. Beverly Hills, Calif.: Sage, 1981.

HIRSCHI, TRAVIS. *Causes of Delinquency*. Berkeley: University of California Press, 1969.

———, and Hindelang, Michael J. "Intelligence and Delinquency: A Revisionist Review." *American Sociological Review* 42 (1977): 571–587.

IANNI, FRANCIS A. J., with REUSS-IANNI, ELIZABETH. *A Family Business: Kinship and Social Control in Organized Crime*. New York: Russell Sage, 1972.

IGNATIEFF, MICHAEL. "State, Civil Society, and Total Institutions: A Critique of Recent Social Histories of Punishment." *Crime and Justice: An Annual Review of Research*, vol. 3. Edited by Norval Morris and Michael Tonry. University of Chicago Press, 1981, pp. 153–192.

INKELES, ALEX. "Personality and Social Structure." *Sociology Today: Problems and Prospects*, vol. 2. Edited by Robert K. Merton, Leonard Bloom, and Leonard S. Cottrell, Jr. Reprint. New York: Harper Torchbooks, 1965, pp. 249–276.

KADISH, SANFORD H. "Legal Norm and Discretion in the Police and Sentencing Process." *Harvard Law Review* 75 (1962): 904–931.

KITSUSE, JOHN I., and CICOUREL, AARON V. "A Note on the Uses of Official Statistics." *Social Problems* 11 (1963): 131–139.

LIPTON, DOUGLAS; MARTINSON, ROBERT; and WILKS, JUDITH. *The Effectiveness of Correctional Treatment: A Survey of Treatment Evaluation Studies*. New York: Praeger, 1975.

MANNING, PETER K. *Police Work: Essays on the Social Organization of Policing*. Cambridge, Mass.: MIT Press, 1977.

MERTON, ROBERT K. "Social Structure and Anomie." *American Sociological Review* 3 (1938): 672–682.

MOORE, JOAN W., with GARCIA, ROBERT; CARDA, LUIS; and VALENCIA, FRANK. *Homeboys: Gangs, Drugs, and Prison in the Barrios of Los Angeles*. Philadelphia: Temple University Press, 1978.

MORSE, STEPHEN J. "Understanding Adversary Process and Conflict in Criminal Justice." *Handbook of Criminal Justice Evaluation*. Edited by Malcolm W. Klein and Katherine S. Teilmann. Beverly Hills, Calif.: Sage, 1980, pp. 331–356.

MYREN, RICHARD A. " 'Justiciology': An Idea Whose Time Has Come." *Justice Reporter* 1, no. 1 (1980): 1–7.

OHLIN, LLOYD E.; MILLER, ALDEN D.; and COATES, ROBERT B. *Juvenile Correctional Reform in Massachusetts: A Preliminary Report of the Center for Criminal Justice of the Harvard Law*

School. Washington, D.C.: U.S. Department of Justice, Law Enforcement Assistance Administration, Office of Juvenile Justice and Delinquency Prevention, National Institute for Juvenile Justice and Delinquency, 1977.

President's Commission on Law Enforcement and Administration of Justice. *The Challenge of Crime in a Free Society.* Washington, D.C.: The Commission, 1967.

QUINNEY, RICHARD. *Class, State, and Crime: On the Theory and Practice of Criminal Justice.* New York: McKay, 1977.

REISS, ALBERT J., JR. "Delinquency as the Failure of Personal and Social Controls." *American Sociological Review* 16 (1951): 196–207.

———. "Discretionary Justice." *Handbook of Criminology.* Edited by Daniel Glaser. Chicago: Rand McNally, 1974, pp. 679–699.

———, and BIDERMAN, ALBERT D. *Data Sources on White-collar Law-breaking.* Washington, D.C.: U.S. Department of Justice, National Institute of Justice, 1980.

ROSETT, ARTHUR I., and CRESSEY, DONALD R. *Justice by Consent: Plea Bargains in the American Courthouse.* Philadelphia: Lippincott, 1976.

ROSSI, PETER H., and HENRY, J. PATRICK. "Seriousness: A Measure for All Purposes?" *Handbook of Criminal Justice Evaluation.* Edited by Malcolm W. Klein and Katherine S. Teilmann. Beverly Hills, Calif.: Sage, 1980, pp. 489–505.

RUMBAUT, RUBÉN G., and BITTNER, EGON. "Changing Conceptions of the Police Role: A Sociological Review." *Crime and Justice: An Annual Review of Research,* vol. 1. Edited by Norval Morris and Michael Tonry. University of Chicago Press, 1979, pp. 239–288.

SCHRAGER, LAURA SHILL, and SHORT, JAMES F., JR. "Toward a Sociology of Organizational Crime." *Social Problems* 25 (1978): 407–419.

SCHWENDINGER, HERMAN, and SCHWENDINGER, JULIA. "Defenders of Order or Guardians of Human Rights?" Reprint. *Critical Criminology.* Edited by Ian R. Taylor, Paul Walton, and Jock Young. Boston: Routledge & Kegan Paul, 1975, pp. 113–146.

SELLIN, THORSTEN, and WOLFGANG, MARVIN E. *The Measurement of Delinquency.* New York: Wiley, 1964.

SELZNICK, PHILIP. "Law: I. The Sociology of Law." *International Encyclopedia of the Social Sciences,* vol. 9. New York: Macmillan and Free Press, 1968, pp. 50–59.

SHERMAN, LAWRENCE W. *Scandal and Reform: Controlling Police Corruption.* Berkeley: University of California Press, 1978.

———, ed. *The Police and Violence.* Annals of the American Academy of Political and Social Science, vol. 452, 1980.

SHORT, JAMES F., JR. "Social Structure and Group Processes in Explanations of Gang Delinquency." *Problems of Youth: Transition to Adulthood in a Changing World.* Edited by Muzafer Sherif and Carolyn W. Sherif. Chicago: Aldine, 1965, pp. 165–188.

SKOLNICK, JEROME. *Justice without Trial: Law Enforcement in Democratic Society.* 2d ed. New York: Wiley, 1975.

SPARKS, RICHARD F. "A Critique of Marxist Criminology." *Crime and Justice: An Annual Review of Research,* vol. 2. Edited

by Norval Morris and Michael Tonry. University of Chicago Press, 1980, pp. 159–210.

STEFFENSMEIER, DARRELL J. "Sex Differences in Patterns of Adult Crime, 1965–1977: A Review and Assessment." *Social Forces* 58 (1980): 1080–1108.

SUTHERLAND, EDWIN H. "Is 'White Collar Crime' Crime?" *American Sociological Review* 10 (1945): 132–139.

———, and CRESSEY, DONALD R. *Criminology* (1924). 10th ed. Philadelphia: Lippincott, 1978.

SYKES, RICHARD E. "A Regulatory Theory of Policing: A Preliminary Statement." *Police and Society.* Edited by David Bailey. Beverly Hills, Calif.: Sage, 1977, pp. 237–256.

TAPPAN, PAUL W. *Crime, Justice, and Correction.* New York: McGraw-Hill, 1960.

TAYLOR, IAN; WALTON, PAUL; and YOUNG, JOCK. *The New Criminology: For a Social Theory of Deviance.* Boston: Routledge & Kegan Paul, 1973.

TURK, AUSTIN T. "Analyzing Official Deviance: For Nonpartisan Conflict Analyses in Criminology." *Radical Criminology: The Coming Crises.* Edited by James A. Inciardi. Beverly Hills, Calif.: Sage, 1980, pp. 78–91.

VALENTINE, BETTYLOU. *Hustling and Other Hard Work: Lifestyles in the Ghetto.* New York: Free Press, 1978.

VAN DEN HAAG, ERNEST. *Punishing Criminals: Concerning a Very Old and Painful Question.* New York: Basic Books, 1975.

WEBER, MAX. *Economy and Society: An Outline of Interpretive Sociology* (1922). 2 vols. Edited by Guenther Roth and Claus Wittich. Reprint. Berkeley: University of California Press, 1978.

WILSON, JAMES Q. *Thinking about Crime.* New York: Basic Books, 1975.

WOLFGANG, MARVIN E., and FERRACUTI, FRANCO. *The Subculture of Violence: Towards an Integrated Theory in Criminology.* Translated from the Italian. London: Tavistock, 1967.

3.
RESEARCH METHODS

Research methodology is the study of the choices necessary in planning a research project. Most of the choices aim either at minimizing or at neutralizing the effects of different kinds of errors.

The researcher's first choice is of an overall strategy—a way of conceptualizing the research problem, its explanation, and possible error. Second, within the selected strategy, a design (a specific way of analyzing data within that strategy) must be chosen, given the problem of error. Third, having chosen a design, the researcher must decide whether to involve time in that design, again with an eye to the effect of error. Fourth, having reached this point, he must make a choice on the definition of variables. It is here that controversies about the special nature of social science and criminology, as opposed to the natural sciences, are most influential. The fifth choice is of a means of data collection, including such considerations as sampling, observation, and use of records. Finally, there are issues of ethics, which arise because of the possibility of harm to the people being studied, invasion of privacy, and lack of informed consent.

There is much in this succession of choices that is technical, but these technical considerations provide an alternative to impressionistic conjecture in a field that is charged with strong feeling. Attention to methodology can reconcile the results of apparently conflicting studies and permit policies to be based on informed analysis of experience. Knowledge does not exist apart from the methods that produce it. An understanding of the methodological issues is essential for confidence about what is learned.

Error

In research, mistakes frequently take place, such as employing a bad research design or using an inappropriate statistical technique. Mistakes evoke severe criticism. One may also make errors. Errors are the things that go wrong when the researcher made the right methodological choices. One kind of error is simply failure to measure all causes of the problem to be explained. If one is examining the effect of poverty on crime rates, and measures only poverty and crime, then all other causes of crime besides poverty will contribute to the error, that is, to variations in crime rates that are not explainable by poverty.

A second kind of error is measurement error. Since most offenders try to avoid discovery, it is obviously difficult to measure crime rates accurately, and therefore these measurements are often inexact. Similarly, since poor people are more likely to be miscounted in the census, estimates of poverty may also be inaccurate. If, instead, attitudes are measured, the difficulty of defining the attitude in a precise, fixed way would cause errors in measurement. Or, when asked how many children the family has, some interviewees forget to count the new baby, producing measurement error.

A third kind of error is specification error, or error in stating the dimensions of the problem. When looking for an explanation of a problem, such as crime, some practical limits are usually set on what is looked for. For example, in conducting a survey based on interviewing many people, only a limited number of relevant variables can be measured, and the relationship among only a smaller number of these variables can be examined intensively. Even in an observational study, in which people's actions are observed and writ-

ten down, there are limits to what can be seen. Thus, in studying a community, state government effects such as those of legislative decisions on the community might be overlooked. In this way an error may be made in the specific dimensions chosen for study.

A fourth type of error is sampling error—the failure of a sample to be representative. Seldom can all relevant instances of the phenomenon of interest be examined. The instances looked at constitute the sample. Sometimes this sample consists of whatever instances can be recorded, in which case the sampling error is of unknown proportions, since one cannot know all the ways in which the instances sampled differ from those not sampled. Sometimes a method of choosing randomly is used, in the simplest case making sure that every instance has an equal chance of being selected into the sample. Then the statistical probabilities of different amounts of sampling error in the results can be estimated by the mathematical laws of probability. For example, if a random sample of the population is interviewed about poverty and crime, estimates of the prevalence of crime and poverty, as well as estimates of the degree to which one explains the other, may be in error to the degree that an atypical group of people has been interviewed. The error, however, will probably fall within specifiable limits.

According to their different strategies, researchers cope with these four types of error in various ways.

Strategies: first level of choice

Analytic induction. The strategy of analytic induction allows the explanation to emerge progressively from the facts observed and to have no error at all. The researcher must constantly revise conceptualization and measurements. In practice, this strategy is likely to entail informal, probing interviews, observation, or participant observations—those in which the observer joins the group he is watching. A provisional explanation of the phenomenon to be studied is formulated, and the researcher tries to find cases that do not fit this explanation. In a study of drug addiction, for example, he would seek drug addicts who became addicts in some way other than that which the provisional explanation suggested (cf. Cressey). The explanation is then revised to cover the negative cases, or the definition of the phenomenon itself is narrowed to exclude them. These steps are repeated until no negative cases are found. An important characteristic of this approach is the rule that one explanation must account for every instance of the same phenomenon. Thus the researcher may end either with very general explanations or with very narrowly defined phenomena to be explained, one or both of which may be unsatisfactory. However, the four types of error have been eliminated.

General multicausal model. In the general multicausal model, which is basic to most research, the researcher presumes that the phenomenon to be explained may have many causes, some among those aspects he has measured and some among those he has not. Different instances of the phenomenon may be accounted for by different combinations of these many causal factors. The model may be used with virtually any form of data collection, ranging from survey interviews and official records to observation or content analysis of the media. Error resulting from unmeasured causes of the event to be explained, measurement error, specification error, and sampling error are all expected to be problems. Research designs within this strategy focus on ways to prevent such errors from causing faulty results.

Multicausal model with finite number of causes. This model falls between analytic induction and the general multicausal model in its approach to error. Where analytic induction tries to eliminate error, and the general multicausal model tries to live with all kinds of error, this model eliminates error resulting from unmeasured causes of the thing to be explained. However, it tries to tolerate the other three kinds of error: measurement error, specification error, and sampling error. Unlike analytic induction, this strategy depends more on logic than on successive approximation.

A logically exhaustive list of factors that might account for a phenomenon is drawn up—the finite number of causes in terms of which the problem is formulated. Each cause in the list is necessarily abstract. Indicators are then selected for measuring each cause. By logical definition of the problem no causes are missing, but each cause may be measured incorrectly. Much that in the general multicausal model would be regarded as error owing to unmeasured causes would in this approach be treated as measurement error. The practical consequence is that efforts to improve explanation by this approach focus on improving conceptualization and measurement, rather than on seeking additional, previously unthought-of abstract factors. This kind of model has been used to analyze power and correctional reform (Miller, Ohlin, and Coates).

Unique case analysis. In unique case analyses there is at first glance no error; there is simply the account of a person's life history, or of a social movement's development. A historical analysis of the use

of force by police might be narrated, or the distribution of different types of crime in a city during different decades might be mapped. If wrong, the researcher himself is blamed for mistakes more often than the results are attributed to error in his methods.

Yet frequently the matter is not so simple. A case analysis requires breaking the case into multiple observations, or subcases. For example, a study of a youth gang may involve an analysis of the gang members. Or the analysis of the gang over a period of time may seek to establish regularities of cause and effect, such as an effect of increasing unemployment on gang activity. In such situations there is within the case analysis a study of multiple cases, and one probably uses analytic induction, the general multicausal model, or the multicausal model with a finite number of causes. The case analysis may function as a kind of exploratory study that leads to larger analyses of many cases, again using one of the other strategies. William Whyte used this method in his study of an Italian slum.

Simulation. Although simulation is actually a theoretical analysis, not an approach to research, it can be related to research in such a way as to determine how the research is carried out.

A simulation is a mathematical model, or set of equations, such that if an initial state of affairs is specified, the simulation can project what will follow, according to the theory on which it is based. Some simulations project the movement of individuals through a system, such as the criminal justice system. Some project how changes in causal factors will produce changes in a particular variable of interest, such as fear of crime. Certain simulations make precise predictions of how each variable will change in time, whereas others present probability distributions of all possible changes at successive points in time.

Simulations become research strategies in several ways. Sometimes the simulations are themselves empirically based, in which case the research problem is to make empirical estimates of the causal effects described by the simulation. Such research can involve any or all of the strategies discussed above. However it is derived, the simulation is a theoretical statement that may be tested against data. The discovery of error in this process is somewhat complicated. The simulation itself, as a theoretical conceptualization, may be wrong. The data against which it is tested may involve all four types of error: unmeasured causes, measurement error, specification error, and sampling error. If the simulation is empirically based, the empirical analysis that lies behind it may also be subject to all four kinds of error.

Designs within the general multicausal strategy: second level of choice

Most research either follows the general multicausal strategy or draws upon it within some larger strategy, such as a unique case analysis. Designs within that strategy represent different ways of dealing with all four kinds of error. The choice of strategy is a choice of a way to define the problem—not simply in terms of what is sought, but in terms of how a solution is pursued. The choice of a design within a strategy takes that process of choice one step farther.

Cross-tabulation. Perhaps the simplest design is the cross-tabulation. It is begun by identifying cases. They may be individuals characterized by such variables as frequency of criminal behavior, amount of income, and sex. A case may be a single individual observed at successive points in time, or the cases may be neighborhoods in a city, characterized by varying crime rates, housing characteristics, and population compositions. A case might also be a youth gang observed at successive points in time and characterized by its social organization, relation to adults, and degree of criminal involvement at each time.

When the cases have been identified, they are sorted into categories by one of the characteristics, or variables. Thus, individuals might be sorted into high- and low-income categories. Within each category of income the frequency of crime is tabulated, so that the crime rates of the two income categories can be compared. If it is thought that sex might be related to income and also to crime, that could cause a problem. Suppose that the lower-income category had proportionately more females than the higher-income category, and that the females engaged in less crime. This would result in the lower-income crime rate being lower and the higher-income crime rate being higher than if sex were not a factor. The solution is to sort by sex, and then repeat the analysis (tabulating crime by income category) separately within each category of sex. Crime rates can also be associated with sex categories within income categories. The problem is that the income categories "high" and "low" still include much variation in income, so that income is not completely "controlled" in the analysis and can still interfere with estimates of the relationship of sex to crime.

Extension of this problem to a consideration of unmeasured causes of crime in place of sex leads to an understanding of this design's assumption about error resulting from unmeasured causes. Clearly, if only income and crime were measured, and sex remained unmeasured, the sex variable would have caused error. Underlying this design is the assumption that unmeasured causes of the dependent variable (crime) are unrelated to the measured causes included in the analysis.

The effects of measurement error are also evident. Income crudely divided into "higher" and "lower" is a very rough measure that can cause difficulty, particularly when observing the effects of such other factors as sex while controlling by the variable with measurement error (such as income crudely divided into high and low). Thus, this design presupposes the absence of measurement error, especially in control variables.

Cross-tabulation is obviously dependent on the assumption that the right variables were selected (that the analysis is specified properly). Specification decisions require not only the inclusion of the right variables, but also allowance for the right complexities of relationship. If income is dichotomized, it cannot be known whether income had a curvilinear relationship to crime—that is, it cannot be known whether the highest crime rates are at both the high and the low extremes of income and whether the lowest crime rates are at middle-income levels. Finally, cross-tabulation is clearly susceptible to sampling error. Whether findings from the sample can be generalized to a large population depends on whether the sample can be assumed to be a random one.

This design appears to be most appropriate when all the variables of interest fall naturally into homogeneous categories, and when one can reasonably assume that unmeasured causes of the dependent variable are unrelated to the measured ones.

Ordinary least squares regression. Ordinary least squares regression is similar in its treatment of error to cross-tabulation, but it is a more sophisticated and more flexible research design. It requires greater effort to learn and understand because it involves more mathematical manipulations. The method is worth the trouble, however, because it allows a researcher to shape and focus his research with greater precision.

With this type of research design, variables do not have to be categorized, and the analysis can be designed to detect specific types of patterns while ignoring others. For example, it can record the number of crimes each subject is reported to commit per year, the person's income, and the person's sex, with only sex being categorized; crime rates or income need not be divided into high and low categories. If crime is represented as Y, income as X, and sex as W, a simple regression equation can be written:

$$Y = a + bX + cW + e$$

W, the sex variable, might be scored one if female, and zero if male. The Y, X, and W are the known data for each subject, and the a, b, c, and e are the unknowns. Leaving aside for the moment how computers solve for the unknowns, consider what they mean. The a in the equation is the average value of Y (crime) when income is zero and when sex is zero (male). The b is the change in Y when income is increased by one dollar, the c is the change in income when sex is changed from male to female, and the e is measurement error and error resulting from unmeasured causes of crime. If the data are from a random sample, probability laws permit computations of the probable sampling error for b and c. However, there is no measurement for specification error, which sometimes, but not always, will make the e larger.

The equation as specified shows that a unit increase in a causal variable always makes the same average difference in the crime rate, regardless of the values of other variables. If this is doubted, terms could be added to the equation to represent curvilinear effects where a unit increase in the causal variable has a different effect on the dependent variable, depending on the starting point of the change in the causal variable. Or terms could be added to make the effects of one variable conditional on the value of another variable. The fact that these choices can be made is an advance over cross-tabulation, which is compelled to present conditional effects (such as separate analyses of income and crime for each sex) and curvilinearity to the extent that there are enough categories in each variable to chart it. The regression design thus allows specification of simplifications, and hence easily procured summary measures.

This design is obviously appropriate when one has continuous variables (information would be lost by categorizing them) and when one can assume that the error is unrelated to the causal variables. Its use is controversial where the dependent variable is a dichotomy—for example, if crime is measured as simply occurring or not occurring rather than as a rate. Like cross-tabulation, this design is impaired by measurement error, especially in the causal variables.

Interdependent systems. Cross-tabulations and ordinary least squares regression both assume that error is unrelated to the causal variables in the analysis. Hidden in that general assumption is the more specific assumption that there are no feedback loops—that the dependent variable (crime in the example) does not affect income or sex as well as being affected by them. While it might well be argued that such an assumption is reasonable regarding sex, it might be questionable regarding income. That would be to question the appropriateness of the cross-tabulation and ordinary least squares research designs for this problem. Interdependent-systems designs, as their name implies, include a variety of computational procedures that allow some of the variables in the analysis to be reciprocally related to one another. Examples of these procedures are two-stage least squares, instrumental variables, and confirmatory factor analysis.

Experiment. A special instance of interdependent systems is the experiment, which introduces a randomized manipulation. For example, in order to measure the impact of guaranteed minimum income aid on crime, an experimental policymaker could randomly decide which of several communities to provide with such income, and which communities to leave on their own. This assumes that except for chance, there is no difference between the randomly chosen experimental and control communities in unmeasured causes of crime. It also assumes that the experimental actions do not affect crime except through their effects on income. The randomization procedure can provide great confidence in the first assumption, but not necessarily in the second. The analysis usually consists simply of comparing the outcome scores (here, crime rates) of the randomly selected experimental and control groups (here, the communities selected randomly for minimum income guarantees and those randomly selected for no aid). The resulting measures are generally expressed in terms of the probability that there was some effect. However, the impact of the experimental intervention can also be calculated by more complex regression and interdependent-systems methods.

Many people regard the experiment as the first choice among research designs for causal inference. It is appropriate where a manipulation can be carried out without violating people's rights or otherwise endangering them, as well as where the result has enough correspondence to the natural world to be illuminating. The latter point is one of considerable controversy. Policymakers want to know if an intervention would work in the real world, with all its programmatic and political complexities. Experiments require stable conditions in that nothing happens to the manipulated group which would make it different from the control group—except for the experiment itself. A carefully controlled and sheltered experiment is like a political backwater, and testing a program idea in such a setting is a little like testing an ocean-going tanker in a sheltered harbor.

Because experiments are the most commonly understood case of interdependent systems, many researchers have based their reasoning about nonexperimental studies on the experimental model instead of on the general cases of interdependent systems, ordinary least squares regression, and cross-tabulation. Hence one frequently encounters the term *quasi-experiment* in discussions of nonexperimental designs (Campbell and Stanley).

Qualitative analysis. Qualitative analysis is simply an informal version of one or more of the research designs described above. The researcher, working with verbal rather than quantitative reports, makes comparisons that are usually much like cross-tabulation or a crude version of interdependent systems, somewhat like experiments without the randomization. The comparisons are usually informal and verbal. They introduce no new principles, however.

The term *qualitative analysis* is occasionally also used to refer to any analysis of qualitative or categorized variables, even when highly mathematical analyses using the other designs or using numerical measurement models are employed. Thus, in the example, sex is categorized into "male" and "female." If income were categorized into "high" and "low" and crime into "some" and "none," any analysis that was done using any of the research designs could be called a qualitative analysis.

Longitudinal analysis

The third level of choice, after strategy and design, is whether to involve time, and if so, how its variations would be relevant to any of the research designs described above.

The two most familiar ways of involving time are time series analysis and panel analysis. A time series might measure the three variables (crime, income, and sex) at many successive points in time for a single case, such as a person or a community. These points in time, each characterized by the three variables (and any others needed to complete the analysis, such as local economic conditions or income maintenance), are treated as separate observations and can be analyzed by the general causal or other models.

Panels are slightly different in conception. Variables are measured to characterize each of a large number of cases (people or communities) at several, perhaps two or three, points in time. The people or communities are the cases. Instead of the three variables (income, sex, and crime) of the example, there are six variables in the instance of two points in time, nine with three points in time, and so on. Income, crime, and sex are measured separately at the different points in time, and each measurement at a different time

is regarded as a new variable. Thus, an analysis might be done to distinguish the effects of current income on crime from the effects of income one or two time periods ago. Whether the effects of current income on crime are the same now as they were a period or two ago could also be investigated. Again, any additional variables needed, such as local economic conditions, can be added to complete a viable design.

Alternatives to time series and panel analysis as described above are special techniques of time series analysis that seek to isolate and analyze identifiable trends and wave forms, or cycles, in the data, as well as sharp breaks or changes in these patterns that might reflect the effect of an intervention.

Assumptions about error are essentially the same when time is involved as when it is not. However, the implications of those assumptions can be more devastating. Measurement error becomes even more important than in analyses without time. If a variable has measurement error at two successive points in time, it may well appear to have changed when actually it has not, or when it has changed in the opposite direction.

A more complicated, but crucial, point is that the error arising from unmeasured causes of the dependent variable—crime in the example—may be related to itself over time. This is called autocorrelated error. Suppose that the unmeasured causes include access to a criminal subculture. These unmeasured causes of crime at an earlier time affect crime at the earlier period. If crime then affects income while simultaneously the unmeasured factors at the later time again affect crime, then there is a spurious relationship between income at the earlier time and crime at the later time. This spurious relationship reflects the autocorrelation of the error of not measuring some causes of crime and the effect of crime on income. Yet it can appear that only the effect of prior income on current crime is observed. Not all that looks convincing is real.

Procedures for coping with autocorrelated error are not totally satisfactory, but there are some things that can be done. Interdependent-systems methods offer some complex solutions. A new variable unrelated to the error, such as local economic conditions, is measured as before, and if that variable was selected correctly, the autocorrelation of the error will not bias the analysis. Another method is to introduce a series of additional terms into the regression equation to measure the error. This is accomplished by including among the independent variables additional variables that consist of original ones, measured one time period earlier. A third possibility is to conduct panel analysis with special assumptions, for example, that the effect of income in time one on crime in time two is the same as the effect of income in time two on crime in time three.

It may be noted that no research design that has been mentioned will give answers about causal effect without assumptions. It is in fact easily proved mathematically that this reliance on assumptions is characteristic of all possible research designs. There is no "free lunch," and there are no absolute answers about cause and effect.

Variable definition: conceptualization and measurement as givens, as data, or as analysis

The fourth level of choices a researcher must make concerns the ways variables come to be defined and measured. The researcher may take the variables as givens, for example, he may assume that "crime" is the number of crimes in police records and that "income" refers to the top line of the income-tax form. The variable of "sex" is obvious. These definitions are perhaps treated as givens because the data were already collected and there were no resources for obtaining more data.

One alternative would be to have the definitions generated as part of the data. Many proponents of qualitative analysis prefer this method. They go out and discover what people think of as crime, how they define their income, and how they identify their sex. The conceptualization of variables then reflects the views and perspectives of the population on which the research is being conducted. Some researchers insist that this is the key to an important difference between research on people and research on other natural phenomena. Rocks cannot tell you how to measure them; people can.

A second alternative is to treat conceptualization and measurement as part of the analysis. Variables are tried out in the analysis and then revised in the attempt to make them and the analysis work better. The process is long and involved, and it can be considerably speeded up by resorting to the use of mathematical simulation between stages of data analysis. One quickly learns, for example, that for a variable to serve a given function in a model or theory, it must have certain characteristics. If one thinks of income as the intervening link between ethnic identity and crime, one must conceptualize and measure income in such a way that it can in fact logically serve as that link. If ethnicity has eight categories and crime five, a two-category version of income can do little

to connect ethnicity and crime in the analysis, no matter how true it may be that in society, income accounts for any relationship between ethnicity and crime. An inventor working on a new machine assumes that it will be necessary to keep redesigning the parts of the machine, as well as the way they are put together, as the machine is improved and finally made to work. The criminologist building a model of society may find it necessary to do the same. The process becomes somewhat like analytic induction, but with many causal variables and with allowance for error terms.

The choices involved here, and the modifications that may be made in conceptualization, go far beyond refinements in the detail of measurement. One may fundamentally alter one's notions of what crime is, perhaps going from crime as the breaking of a rule to crime as an act that is censured. One can even interchange cases and variables. Suppose that the crime, income, and sex of five hundred people are measured at ten points in time. The people can be regarded as the cases, or observations, and each can be characterized by income, crime, and sex, with time treated as in a time series. That would mean regarding each person in each time period as a case, with a total of five thousand cases. Or the matter could be conceptualized as a panel analysis, and each person regarded as a case, characterized by thirty variables. There would then be five hundred cases. Or time periods could be regarded as cases, and numbers of people with certain crime, income, and sex characteristics as variables, producing ten cases. Finally, people could be aggregated by some other characteristic, such as neighborhood, and the neighborhoods characterized at given time periods by proportions of people involved in crime, having large incomes, and being of a given sex. The point is that the possibilities are endless, and the researcher may find it profitable to shake off any notion that there is one obvious way to define cases and variables.

Data sources and collection techniques

Data sources and collection techniques come in countless variations. Most data in criminology are taken from official records of criminal justice agencies, interviews, observations, or content analyses of media and documents. However, there are also physiological data from the laboratory, such as galvanic skin responses, and surveys of genetic material from large populations. Census data, population-register data, and vital statistics have also been used. How this fifth level of choice, the choice of data, is exercised depends largely on convention and the accidents of the researcher's individual training. However, the choice is relevant to the issue of error.

Interviews may be conducted conversationally and informally in an effort to probe to the truth, or they may be carried out in a highly standardized manner in order to ensure that all respondents are answering the same questions. Observation may be done in natural settings by strangers to minimize contamination of what is being studied by the social influence of the data collector, or it may be conducted in very structured, artificial laboratory settings in order to increase its reliability and to maximize the possibility that the observers will not miss anything. Or it may be done by observers who participate in the group being observed, in order to obtain an insider's view. Records may be used, in spite of the fact that they are generally created for management and public-relations purposes and may be badly biased for research purposes. The researcher may use them simply because they are all that is available, or because he wants to know what the officials are saying. This perspective redefines what might be called error as itself the object of study.

Sometimes a researcher's concerns with error change as he moves through the stages of a study. He may at first be most concerned about errors of basic understanding as to what people are thinking and doing, and may opt for participant observation. After being satisfied that he knows basically what the dimensions of the research problem should be, he may then begin to shift toward standardized survey interviews of large random samples of people to minimize sampling error.

For many years the objective in measurement was to come as closely as possible to eliminating all error. In the late 1960s, social scientists began to pay more attention to the effects of specific types of error on specific analyses. That change in approach led to analysis strategies designed to cope with specific patterns of random error, and to the view that error in a measurement is acceptable if the source of that error is not related to the wrong things. For example, random measurement error in the dependent variable (crime in the above example of crime, income, and sex) is not related to the independent variables (income and sex in the example) and hence is not much of a problem. Measurement error in income would contribute to a relationship between the error term of the equation and the independent variables, and is a problem. An interdependent-systems solution might solve the problem. Confirmatory factor analysis is particularly popular for this kind of work. Frequently, when measurement error is the only problem and no reciprocal causation is involved, a researcher will use a different indicator of income as an instrumental variable. For example, a different measure of income will have its own measurement error, but will not be related to the measurement error in the principal measure of income, will be related to true income, and will be related to crime only through its relation to true income, which can be taken into account by computations.

Ethics

The sixth level of choice is a matter of ethics. The researcher must choose among methods that have different possible consequences for the people he studies. Two basic dimensions of concern are prominent. Most obvious is the issue of whether the people who are studied will be harmed. In criminological research a pervasive cause of possible harm is the disclosure of criminal acts previously unknown to the authorities, thus exposing the perpetrator to prosecution. Therefore much criminological research is arranged with elaborate precautions to protect confidentiality. The other dimension of concern relates to informed consent. Both issues are much affected by the federal guidelines that accompany federal funding and that may even affect nonfederally funded research in institutions that have some federal funding.

The choices regarding harm relate primarily to designing the research so that data can be collected anonymously. Truly anonymous data collection is probably possible only in cross-sectional research, that is, research that collects all data at only one time. When the researcher has to return for future interviews, respondents' names and addresses must be preserved. They are usually separated from the data itself and connected by a secret code. Thus if an intruder gained access to the data, the identity of the respondents would still be secret, and what they said in the interviews could not be connected by the intruder to their names.

Still another technique for guarding confidentiality is the introduction of random error of known amounts into the recording of the responses. With this method it cannot be known with certainty exactly which question the respondent was actually answering, although the relationships among aggregate frequencies of each response possibility can be recovered with close approximation for the sample as a whole. This technique has the added advantage of protecting the respondent's privacy even from the interviewer. Finally, another method is to caution the respondent not to mention specific times and places of criminal acts:

times and places are needed for indictment. In addition, some federal funding agencies have legal provisions that protect data in projects they fund from being subpoenaed.

Informed consent may be thought of as part of the harm issue, but it is sometimes considered separately. The idea is that human subjects involved in research projects should know that they are being studied and should first give their consent. However, absolute adherence to such a rule would eliminate much research, and opinions vary considerably on how absolutely informed consent should be required. The most likely areas of research to be readily exempted involve the observation of public behavior. But many other studies also require some deception of the respondent in order to obtain meaningful data. For example, subjects are unlikely to behave naturally after they have just been told that the researcher wants to find out whether they have authoritarian personalities.

These choices, then, can have much to do with how a research project is shaped. In making the choices, the researcher is guided by a concern for ethics combined with the practical concern that respondents must not be alienated if there is to be more research in the future. He is also aware of the bureaucratic reality that the university or other responsible research organization, as well as the federal government, may not allow him to make his decisions with a free hand.

Conclusion

The foregoing analysis may help to make better sense of common labels attached to studies. For example, to say that a study is a case study tells little, other than a bit about strategy, and leaves completely open the questions of design, presence or absence of time in the analysis, variable definition, data collection, and ethics. To identify a study as a sample survey describes the data collection but leaves open the design and strategy. To call a study a cohort study, wherein a group of people with something in common are followed over a period of time, indicates that time is involved, but leaves open nearly all the other choices. Historical studies, archival or records studies, and cross-cultural or comparative studies are all partially identified in terms of the data collection. A historical study will use historical documents of one sort or another; archival or record studies will use official records and collections of documents that were probably assembled for a quite different purpose; and comparative or cross-cultural studies will use data relating to more than one society.

Clearly, the common labels tell something, but not very much. Going beyond the common labels and examining the six choices described above is necessary to understand how a study came to its conclusion, and thus how to interpret and make use of that conclusion. Therefore, from the point of view of the reader of research reports, understanding the choices taken in producing knowledge is crucial to knowing anything.

Looking at the matter from the researcher's point of view, awareness of the choices is a matter of both discipline and liberation. There are no formulas for the "right" research methodology, although some choices may be clearly wrong or unproductive. The study of methodology should open up infinite possibilities of variation in research methods, and hence infinite possibilities for knowing, rather than forcing everyone onto the same narrow road.

ALDEN D. MILLER

See also CRIME STATISTICS: REPORTING SYSTEMS AND METHODS; PREDICTION OF CRIME AND RECIDIVISM; PUBLICATIONS IN CRIMINOLOGY; RESEARCH IN CRIMINAL JUSTICE.

BIBLIOGRAPHY

BLALOCK, HUBERT M., JR., and BLALOCK, ANN B., eds. *Methodology in Social Research*. New York: McGraw-Hill, 1968.

BORGATTA, EDGAR F., ed. *Sociological Methodology*. Official Publication of the American Sociological Association. San Francisco: Jossey-Bass, annually.

CAMPBELL, DONALD T., and STANLEY, JULIAN C. *Experimental and Quasi-experimental Designs for Research*. Chicago: Rand McNally, 1963.

CRESSEY, DONALD R. *Other People's Money: A Study in the Social Psychology of Embezzlement* (1953). Reprint, with a new introduction by the author. Montclair, N.J.: Patterson Smith, 1973.

DENZIN, NORMAN K. *The Research Act: A Theoretical Introduction to Sociological Methods*. Chicago: Aldine, 1970.

——. *Sociological Methods: A Sourcebook*. Chicago: Aldine, 1970.

DILLMAN, DON A. *Mail and Telephone Surveys: The Total Design Method*. New York: Wiley, 1978.

DUNCAN, OTIS DUDLEY. *Introduction to Structural Equation Models*. New York: Academic Press, 1975.

EMPEY, LAMAR T., and LUBECK, STEPHEN G. *The Silverlake Experiment: Testing Delinquency Theory and Community Intervention*. Chicago: Aldine, 1971.

HAYS, WILLIAM L. *Statistics for Psychologists*. New York: Holt, Rinehart & Winston, 1963.

KAHN, ROBERT L., and CANNELL, CHARLES F. *The Dynamics of Interviewing: Theory, Technique, and Cases*. New York: Wiley, 1957.

KRISHNAN NAMBOODRI, N.; CARTER, LEWIS F.; and BLALOCK, HUBERT M., JR. *Applied Multi-variate Analysis and Experimental Design*. New York: McGraw-Hill, 1975.

MILLER, ALDEN D.; OHLIN, LLOYD E.; and COATES, ROBERT B. *A Theory of Social Reform: Correctional Change Processes in Two States.* Cambridge, Mass.: Ballinger, 1977.

NEJELSKI, PAUL, and LERMAN, LINDSEY MILLER. "A Researcher-Subject Testimonial Privilege: What to Do before the Subpoena Arrives." *Wisconsin Law Review* (1971): 1085–1148.

WEISS, CAROL H. *Evaluation Research: Methods for Assessing Program Effectiveness.* Englewood Cliffs, N.J.: Prentice-Hall, 1972.

WHYTE, WILLIAM FOOTE. *Street Corner Society: The Social Structure of an Italian Slum.* 2d ed., enlarged. University of Chicago Press, 1955.

WINKLER, ROBERT L., and HAYS, WILLIAM L. *Statistics: Probability, Inference, and Decision.* 2d ed. New York: Holt, Rinehart & Winston, 1975.

WOLFGANG, MARVIN E.; FIGLIO, ROBERT M; and SELLIN, THORSTEN. *Delinquency in a Birth Cohort.* University of Chicago Press, 1972.

WONNACOTT, RONALD J., and WONNACOTT, THOMAS H. *Econometrics.* 2d ed. New York: Wiley, 1979.

CROSS-EXAMINATION

See CRIMINAL PROCEDURE: CONSTITUTIONAL ASPECTS; TRIAL, CRIMINAL.

CRUEL AND UNUSUAL PUNISHMENT

Introduction

The Eighth Amendment to the United States Constitution prohibits the infliction of "cruel and unusual punishments." This language was taken directly from the Virginia Declaration of Rights of 1776, which in turn had adopted the language of the English Bill of Rights, 1 Wm. & Mary, Sess. 2, c. 2 (1688) and 2 Wm. & Mary, Sess. 1, c. 1 (1689). The constitutions of many American states contain similar provisions, although the wording varies. Sometimes the prohibition is against cruel *or* unusual punishments, a variation which may have some significance for a punishment such as the death penalty, which is allegedly cruel but widely enacted. In *District Attorney v. Watson,* 411 N.E.2d 1274 (Mass. 1980), it was held that the death penalty violates the Massachusetts constitutional provision forbidding cruel *or* unusual punishment.

Little is known about which punishments the framers of the American Bill of Rights had in mind. One congressman objected to the clause because it might be construed to prohibit such cruel but "necessary" punishments as hanging, whipping, and ear-cropping. On the other hand, some prominent Americans from Virginia and Massachusetts who had called for inclusion of a bill of rights in the Constitution were apparently concerned that Congress might enact some of the barbarous penalties provided at the time by the laws of England and other European countries. For example, in England a traitor could be dragged to the place of execution behind a cart, hanged until nearly dead, disemboweled alive, and his head cut off and his body quartered. Women convicted of treason could be burned alive until 1790. Some Americans also worried that Congress might authorize the use of torture to extract confessions.

If late-eighteenth-century Americans meant to forbid torture and other barbaric punishments altogether, however, this was apparently not the intention of the Englishmen who used the same language in the English Bill of Rights. There is no evidence that this bill meant to forbid atrocious penalties for atrocious crimes, and indeed the infliction of such penalties as drawing and quartering continued into the nineteenth century. The makers of England's Glorious Revolution believed in horrifying punishments, just as their predecessors did. In prohibiting both "excessive fines" and "cruel and unusual punishments," the authors of the 1689 bill may have meant simply to incorporate the common-law tradition forbidding penalties disproportionate to the offense. Parliament probably had in mind the extraordinary penalties of life imprisonment, huge fines, whippings, pillorying four times a year, and defrocking that were inflicted on Titus Oates for the perjury he committed in connection with the alleged Popish Plot of 1678–1679. No statute or precedent had authorized this unusual sentence, and the House of Commons declared it invalid in 1688. (Unlike its American counterpart, the English Bill of Rights is not part of a written constitution: English courts have never had the power to declare an act of Parliament unconstitutional.)

The history of the clause provides no conclusive answer to the recurring question of whether its American authors meant only to bar certain barbarous punishments altogether or whether they also meant to ban penalties, not unlawful per se, that are disproportionate to the crime. With the arguable exception of the death penalty, American law has never stipulated on any widespread basis the kind of torturous penalties that the framers of the Bill of Rights may have had in mind. If the clause prohibits only punishments that would be considered "cruel" no matter what the crime, its contemporary impact is far less than it would be if it also refers to punishments that are disproportionate to the crime committed.

Application and analysis

In the decisions of the United States Supreme Court, the clause has had important application in a number of areas.

Conditions of confinement. During the nineteenth century, the clause seemed to some commentators to be as obsolete as the barbaric penalties against which it had seemingly been directed. But in 1910 the Supreme Court revived the clause in *Weems v. United States*, 217 U.S. 349 (1910). Weems was a minor public official in the Philippines who had been convicted of falsifying an entry in a public document at a time when the islands were under American rule. The minimum penalty for the offense under local law was twelve years of *cadena temporal*—a Hispanic punishment which required that the convict during the period of confinement "always carry a chain at the ankle, hanging from the wrists," that he be employed at "hard and painful labor," and that he receive "no assistance whatsoever from without the institution" (*Weems*, 364). A series of extraordinary accessory penalties included lifelong surveillance, perpetual disqualification from the right to vote or hold office, loss of retirement pay, and "civil interdiction" (loss of parental and marital authority and of the right to inter vivos disposition of property).

The Supreme Court held that the imposition of these punishments violated the clause, which by statute had been made applicable to Philippine laws. The Court suggested that such an exotic and vindictive penalty would be unconstitutional even for serious crimes, but it also relied on the disproportionate nature of the penalty for a relatively minor offense. *Weems* may thus be said to stand for two propositions: that the effect of the clause is not limited to those cruel punishments that the framers presumably had in mind; and that a penalty may be cruel and unusual because it is disproportionate to the offense, even if the same penalty might be constitutional for a more heinous crime.

No statutes in the United States specify that prisoners must wear chains, or require them to perform "painful" labor. The principle of the *Weems* case has nonetheless been invoked against prison conditions which are inhumane because of such factors as overcrowding, inadequate diet and medical care, brutality by guards, insufficient protection of inmates from abuse by other inmates, and the use of "strip cells"

or punishment units where recalcitrant inmates are consigned to live in filth and darkness on a restricted diet. Some prisons and jails have all of these characteristics, and many have some of them.

Conditions in the notorious prisons of Arkansas were described in *Holt v. Sarver*, 309 F. Supp. 362 (E.D. Ark. 1970), *aff'd. and remanded*, 442 F.2d 304 (8th Cir. 1971). The Arkansas prisons had all the above unsatisfactory features, as well as others that stemmed from the state government's attitude that prisons should be entirely or mainly self-supporting. As a consequence, the prisoners were required to work long hours at agricultural labor in all weather conditions and without pay. Control was almost entirely in the hands of inmate "trusty" guards who brutalized their fellow convicts at will, and housing was in dormitory units, facilitating assaults and other atrocities.

The district court concluded that the conditions in Arkansas prisons were excessively cruel. They were doubtless also unusual, although conditions in many other state prisons and local jails were only marginally less deplorable. When a federal court intervenes to correct what seem to be outrageous conditions, however, serious problems arise as to the scope and manner of the remedy. Severe overcrowding may make conditions of confinement unconstitutional, but how much space does the Constitution require each inmate to have? If adequate medical care is considered a necessity and not a luxury, how much medical care must the prison provide when poor people who are *not* in prison may have difficulty obtaining adequate care? How are prisoners to be protected from assaults, sexual and otherwise, by other prisoners? Can the authority of the guards be preserved if they may not impose swift, certain, and severe punishments? Above all, there is the question of funding by the state or local government. The best prison administrator in the world cannot do much to improve an intolerable situation without adequate funding. Can a court supersede the judgment of elected officials and order a tax increase or a diversion of money from other governmental activities to support the prison system?

Despite these difficulties, federal courts have on occasion intervened to require significant changes in state prisons or jails, although the Supreme Court itself exerted a conservative influence in *Bell v. Wolfish*, 441 U.S. 520 (1979). The Court directed lower federal courts to defer to the "expert judgment" of local correctional officials, an admonition that presumably does not require them to tolerate extremely degrading or life-threatening conditions. The decision in *Rhodes v. Chapman*, 452 U.S. 337 (1981) held that the "double-celling" of prisoners is not necessarily unconstitutional.

Prison disciplinary measures are subject to Eighth Amendment review because they are part of the total punishment for a crime, but punishments outside the criminal setting are not necessarily so limited. In *Ingraham v. Wright*, 430 U.S. 651 (1977), a bare majority of the Supreme Court held that corporal punishment of schoolchildren does not come within the clause. In contrast, a federal appeals court ruled in *Jackson v. Bishop*, 404 F.2d 571 (8th Cir. 1968) that the beating of a prisoner with a strap violates the Eighth Amendment.

Loss of citizenship. In *Trop v. Dulles*, 356 U.S. 86 (1958), the Supreme Court overturned a statute which provided that persons convicted by court-martial for wartime desertion lose their nationality. The Court was closely divided, and there was no majority opinion. Chief Justice Earl Warren, writing for the plurality, stated as an alternative ground of decision that loss of citizenship was cruel and unusual when imposed as a punishment. The point is surprising, since desertion in wartime has always been a capital crime. It is surely better to be without a country rather than without a life. However, the Chief Justice declared that "the existence of the death penalty is not a license to the Government to devise any punishment short of death within the limit of its imagination" and that the Eighth Amendment is not static in its interpretation but "must draw its meaning from the evolving standards of decency that mark the progress of a maturing society" (*Trop*, 101). The opinion went on to hold that denaturalization is a punishment more primitive than torture because it destroys an individual's political existence. Despite this opinion's shaky status as a precedent, its language is often quoted to justify an expansive interpretation of the amendment.

Punishment for disease or status. A California statute made it a misdemeanor (with a minimum ninety-day jail term) to "be addicted to the use of narcotics." In *Robinson v. California*, 370 U.S. 660 (1962), the Supreme Court invalidated this statute on the ground that it is cruel and unusual to punish a person for the status or "disease" of narcotic addiction. The majority opinion likened addiction to insanity, leprosy, and venereal disease, remarking:

A State might determine that the general health and welfare require that the victims of these and other human afflictions be dealt with by compulsory treatment, involving quarantine, confinement, or sequestration. But, in the light of contemporary human knowledge, a law which made a criminal offense of such a disease would doubtless be universally thought to be an infliction of cruel and unusual punishment in violation of the Eighth and Fourteenth Amendments [*Robinson*, 666].

The decision in *Robinson* was pregnant with possibilities. It expressly acknowledged that a state may punish addiction-related behavior such as the sale, purchase, and possession of narcotics, and that a state may implement compulsory treatment programs for addicts which involve a confinement not easily distinguished from imprisonment. If *Robinson* were interpreted as being limited to these proportions, the case would stand only for matters of formality—the states would be free to impose criminal penalties against drug addicts as long as they were careful about their labels.

But a much broader reading based on other language of the opinion is equally plausible. *Robinson* was one of those decisions in which the Court launches a principle capable of almost indefinite expansion, but then limits it carefully so as to keep all options open for the future. The majority opinion by Justice Potter Stewart had observed that "even one day in prison would be a cruel and unusual punishment for the 'crime' of having a common cold" (667). It seems to follow that it would be no less cruel and unusual to impose punishment for sneezing. If we may not punish the insane for being insane, neither may we punish them for acts that they are helpless to prevent because of their insanity. Punishment for the "symptom" is indirect punishment for the disease itself. The concepts of status, disease, symptom, and involuntariness could thus be extended to bar punishment for such disease-related acts as narcotic sales or armed robbery perpetrated to support a narcotic habit. If alcoholism is also a "disease," then public drunkenness, drunk driving, and even alcohol-related assaults may be considered to be caused by the condition rather than by any evil intention of the alcoholic, and consequently immunity from punishment must follow. But if either a broad or a restrictive interpretation of the holding in *Robinson* is permissible, how can one determine which is preferable?

It may be helpful to understand the *Robinson* case in the context of its times. Liberal opinion around 1960 was hospitable to the idea that punishment for crime is a relic of barbarism and should be gradually supplanted by the more humane concepts of treatment and rehabilitation. Perhaps the high-water mark of this approach was the famous *Durham* decision of 1954 (*Durham v. United States*, 214 F.2d 862 (D.C. Cir. 1954)). *Durham* held that a criminal defendant was not guilty if his acts "were the product of a mental disease or defect," a formulation designed to give the widest possible scope to expert testimony about a defendant's mental condition. It also permitted an indefinite expansion of the concept of legal insanity insofar as psychiatrists were able to increase their knowledge of the extent to which criminal acts are "caused" by a mental condition rather than by free will.

Robinson stated a similar expandable proposition in constitutional terms. As knowledge of the causes of human behavior increases, more forms of antisocial behavior may be seen as symptoms of an involuntarily acquired disease or status, and the regime of prisons must increasingly give way to a new and enlightened system of hospitals and treatment centers. On the other hand, the narrow holding of *Robinson* was so carefully limited that the Court was not committed to anything if further reflection should indicate that a more conservative approach was advisable.

The Supreme Court opted for the conservative alternative in 1968 when it determined the constitutionality of punishment for public intoxication in *Powell v. Texas*, 392 U.S. 514 (1968). A closely divided Court held that it is not unconstitutional to punish a chronic alcoholic for appearing in public while intoxicated. Although the state trial judge had found the defendant guilty, he had obligingly made findings that uncritically incorporated the conclusions of the defendant's expert witness that "chronic alcoholism is a disease which destroys the afflicted person's will power to resist the constant, excessive consumption of alcohol" and that "a chronic alcoholic does not appear in public by his own volition but under a compulsion symptomatic of the disease of chronic alcoholism." The five Justices who voted to affirm were unimpressed. New constitutional principles should not be dictated by a trial judge's offhand endorsement of the claims of a defense witness regarding highly controversial medical and philosophical concepts. Looking to sources outside the record, the plurality opinion asserted that medical authorities label alcoholism as a "disease" merely because the medical profession has concluded that it should attempt to treat those who have drinking problems. The label does not necessarily mean that the doctors know what causes the "disease," or how to cure it. Nor does the label help define the elusive concepts of volition and free will.

The plurality in *Powell* emphasized the limits of the Supreme Court's power to coerce the states and localities into reforming their methods of dealing with the problem of public intoxication. Requiring the states to "commit" addicts rather than "convict" them does not guarantee more humane treatment; indeed, it may invite a longer period of confinement, since sentences for petty crimes are usually short and civil commitments may last indefinitely. Beyond this evident practical point, the plurality was reluctant to adopt a broad reading of the *Robinson* doctrine because it could not see how to limit it. Drunk driving, assault, and even robbery or murder might be a part of an alcoholic's compulsive behavior.

Duration of confinement. If the Eighth Amendment forbids punishment disproportionate to the crime, it may have important applications in a wide range of criminal sentencing problems. Laws of many American jurisdictions permit sentences of up to life imprisonment for nonviolent sexual offenses, for selling or giving away small amounts of narcotics, and for thefts or forgeries involving small amounts of money where there are prior convictions. These harsh penalties are not necessarily relics of a more primitive age: some have been enacted even in the 1970s, and they are not infrequently imposed.

The issue is made difficult by the absence of any standard to guide and limit judicial review of legislatively authorized sentences. Criminal sentencing is governed by a variety of conflicting principles. There is no generally accepted basis for assessing the relative culpability of the habitual thief, the situational murderer who will probably never offend again, the seller of narcotics, and the child molester. Moreover, there is the excruciating problem of drawing lines. If life imprisonment is too much, what about twenty years, or ten? Is a life sentence with a possibility of parole after ten years more severe than a twenty-year sentence with no parole? If the courts begin to review legislatively authorized sentences on constitutional grounds, it is not easy to see where they are to stop.

Nevertheless, a number of decisions in the state and lower federal courts before 1980 held various state prison sentences unconstitutional as disproportionate to the offense. The most frequently cited case was *Hart v. Coiner*, 483 F.2d 136 (4th Cir. 1973). Holding a life sentence unconstitutional for a third offender convicted of perjury, the court identified four factors to be considered: the gravity of the underlying offenses; whether the presumed legislative purpose of the punishment could have been served by imposing a lesser penalty; a comparison with the penalty that the defendant could have received in other states; and a comparison with the penalties for other offenses within the jurisdiction.

Further development of Eighth Amendment law in this area was checked, however, by the Supreme Court's decision in *Rummel v. Estelle*, 445 U.S. 263 (1980). In that case a bare majority of the Court upheld a life sentence (with eligibility for parole after twelve years) for a man convicted of stealing $120 after prior convictions for forgery and credit card theft. The opinion by Justice William Rehnquist held that the habitual criminal statute had a rational basis because of the state's interest in dealing more harshly with recidivists, and that considerations of federalism and judicial restraint required allowing the state to determine the appropriate term of imprisonment free of federal judicial oversight. The dissenting judges urged an approach similar to that taken in *Hart*. Of course, state courts may still invoke their own constitutions to strike down prison sentences of excessive length, and some state constitutional provisions have long been held to require that sentences be proportionate to the gravity of the crime.

The death penalty. Many people today consider the death penalty to be one of those "barbarous" punishments that the "cruel and unusual punishments" clause forbids. However, it is not easy to reconcile this judgment with the constitutional language. Plainly, the framers of the Bill of Rights had no intention of abolishing capital punishment. Its legitimacy was unquestioned in 1789, and the Fifth Amendment refers explicitly to "capital" crimes and forbids the taking of *"life,* liberty, or property" (italics added) only if "due process of law" is not observed. A constitutional argument that the cruelty of the death penalty itself establishes its unconstitutionality thus finds no basis in the original understanding of the Bill of Rights. Many resourceful advocates have struggled to overcome this difficulty. Their arguments tend to fall into four main categories, as follows.

Evolving standards of decency. This phrase from Chief Justice Warren's opinion in *Trop* invokes a concept of moral evolution under which enlightened opinion gradually comes to reject a penalty that was acceptable to the cruder standards of an earlier age. The concept seemed plausible in an era when some states were repealing death penalty statutes and when executions were generally becoming far less frequent. Thus, the Supreme Court would only be anticipating an eventual public demand by holding that the Eighth Amendment forbids society to punish crime with death. In *Furman v. Georgia*, 408 U.S. 238, 257 (1972), Justice William Brennan found evidence of such a developing consensus in the increased unwillingness of juries to impose the supreme penalty in any but a small number of eligible cases. Justice Brennan conceded that legislatures continued to authorize death sentences and that public opinion polls and referendum votes continued to show substantial public support. However, he argued that this approval of capital punishment in the abstract was less significant than society's reluctance to impose the penalty in individual cases. Although the Justices in *Furman* could not agree on a rationale, a majority did agree to hold all the particular death statutes at issue unconstitutional. But after this decision was handed down, public support for capital punishment seemed actually to increase. Thirty-five states and the federal government promptly reenacted death penalty statutes, and juries regularly voted to impose the penalty.

When the issue came before the Court again in 1976, most of the Justices accepted this public reaction as a decisive refutation of the "evolving standards" argument. In his dissenting opinion in *Gregg v. Georgia*, 428 U.S. 153, 231 (1976), Justice Thurgood Marshall reiterated an argument he had made in *Furman* to the effect that evidence of overwhelming public and legislative support for the death penalty does not establish its acceptability to contemporary society, since it is the views of "an informed citizenry" that are crucial, and not the views of uninformed voters who know little about the issues. Distinguishing enlightened from unenlightened opinion is a notoriously subjective process, however, and this explicitly elitist argument has attracted little support.

Gratuitous and unnecessary cruelty. This argument begins with the premise that the Eighth Amendment forbids the infliction of unnecessary suffering, and then maintains that the death penalty is unnecessary because a life sentence to prison would be equally effective in deterring crime and incapacitating a dangerous individual. There has been a vigorous dispute over whether the death penalty has a deterrent effect. Evidence from empirical studies is inherently inconclusive because of the impossibility of a controlled experiment. It is therefore unlikely that the state could successfully carry the burden of showing that the death penalty is a greater deterrent than a life sentence. But even assuming that the death penalty is not necessary to deter the commission of capital crimes or to protect society from dangerous individuals, why can the state not punish a criminal simply because he deserves it? The plurality opinion in *Gregg* stated that retribution itself is a permissible goal of criminal punishment, whether or not some utilitarian objective is served. Justice Marshall replied on the contrary that "the taking of life 'because the wrongdoer deserves it' surely must fall, for such a punishment has as its very basis the total denial of the wrongdoer's dignity and worth" (*Gregg*, 240–241).

The connection between a penalty's lack of utilitarian justification and its tendency to deny human worth and dignity is obscure. On Kantian principles, punishment for purely retributive purposes is most clearly consistent with human dignity, because it does not involve using a human being as an instrument to further a social goal. Torture obviously violates human dignity, but not because it is ineffective: often it is very effective. Torture destroys human dignity because it tends to make a human being behave as an animal, to lose all courage and self-respect and beg for mercy. Yet innumerable persons have faced death with dignity, and all of us must come to terms with it in the end. A lengthy prison sentence may be far more likely to reduce a human being to a bestial level than would the prospect of a prompt and relatively painless death. In other words, the fact that immediate death is more dreaded than imprisonment does not necessarily mean that it is more degrading.

Utilitarian arguments against capital punishment tend to assume that imprisonment is a reasonably economical and effective alternative. There is an enormous literature today, however, which asserts that prisons are extremely expensive to maintain and ineffective in rehabilitating prisoners or reducing crime. If prison is such a costly failure, it may be difficult to say with confidence that capital punishment has no advantages. When so little is known, the balancing of costs and benefits is a slippery and even circular process. Judges who doubt the morality of judicial killing may hamper executions by imposing cumbersome procedural obstacles and by reversing sentences and convictions on the slightest pretext, and consequently the process will be expensive, ineffective, and arbitrary. Imposing death sentences may have a positive or a negative effect on public respect for the law, depending upon the attitude the public can be persuaded to take toward the death penalty. It is likely that the utilitarian arguments serve primarily as rationalizations for moral intuitions which resist logical explanation.

Capriciousness and discrimination. Even if death is not inherently an unconstitutional punishment, it can be argued that our fallible prosecutorial and judicial systems are not capable of administering it fairly. Judges and juries may impose the penalty capriciously upon only a small number of eligible cases or, worse, with outright prejudice against racial minorities or the poor and deprived. To a degree this argument is also applicable to imprisonment (most convicts are from deprived backgrounds), but arguably a discriminatory or arbitrary effect is more objectionable when the penalty is the supreme one. Even the elaborate structure of appellate review that is necessary to guard against unfairness adds to the psychological cruelty of the penalty, for executions are repeatedly postponed and rescheduled.

The arguments from arbitrariness and discrimination have had some success in the Supreme Court, although they have not led to a holding that the penalty is inherently unconstitutional. The Court has, however, required that death-penalty statutes provide guidelines to the jury or judge which adequately protect against arbitrary or capricious death sentences and which permit the trier of fact to consider all possible mitigating circumstances (*Lockett v. Ohio*, 438 U.S. 586 (1978)). Thus the argument of the abolitionists that the death penalty is different from other punishments and must be justified on unusually stringent criteria has been accepted to the extent that protective procedures which would not be required for other sentencing decisions are constitutionally mandated in death cases.

Proportionality. The death penalty is most frequently imposed for murder, but many statutes also prescribe it for some cases of rape, robbery, kidnapping, or airplane hijacking. In *Coker v. Georgia*, 433 U.S. 584 (1977), a plurality held that a sentence of death for the rape of an adult woman was grossly disproportionate and excessive punishment under the Eighth Amendment. The defendant in *Coker* had committed the rape at knifepoint after escaping from a state prison, where he had been serving sentences for murder, rape, kidnapping, and aggravated assault. The decision may thus be cited for the proposition that the Eighth Amendment requires proportionality between the punishment and the crime, regardless of the offender's past record of incorrigibility. This approach contrasts strikingly with the majority reasoning in *Rummel.* It is not uncommon for judges in a death case to be swayed by arguments that they would reject in any other context.

Conclusion

The "cruel and unusual punishments" clause of the Eighth Amendment has been a relatively minor factor in American constitutional jurisprudence. In other than death cases, the courts have been far less concerned with questions of penalty than with issues involving police investigative techniques and adversarial procedures at trial. Yet the determination of penalty is the most important question in most criminal cases, and the subjects discussed in this article involve some of the most disquieting features of our criminal justice system. Few would deny that prison sentences are often unreasonably long and that conditions of confinement are frequently unhealthy and brutalizing. On the other hand, such defects are not easily corrected through the invocation of constitutional guarantees.

The standards of the Eighth Amendment are unavoidably subjective, and the problems of designing remedies are formidable. In the hands of an activist court willing to defy these difficulties, the clause could have an enormous effect. Although some lower courts have occasionally applied the clause in this way, the Supreme Court's approach to it has consistently been one of judicial restraint.

PHILLIP E. JOHNSON

See also CAPITAL PUNISHMENT; CORPORAL PUNISHMENT; PRISONERS, LEGAL RIGHTS OF; PUNISHMENT; TORTURE.

BIBLIOGRAPHY

BLACK, CHARLES L. *Capital Punishment: The Inevitability of Caprice and Mistake.* New York: Norton, 1974.

GRANUCCI, ANTHONY F. " 'Nor Cruel and Unusual Punishments Inflicted': The Original Meaning." *California Law Review* 57 (1969): 839–865.

Note. "Complex Enforcement: Unconstitutional Prison Conditions." *Harvard Law Review* 94 (1981): 626–646.

Note. "The Cruel and Unusual Punishment Clause and the Substantive Criminal Law." *Harvard Law Review* 79 (1966): 635–655.

ROBBINS, IRA P. "The Cry of *Wolfish* in the Federal Courts: The Future of Federal Judicial Intervention in Prison Administration." *Journal of Criminal Law and Criminology* 71 (1980): 211–225.

SCHWARTZ, CHARLES WALTER. "Eighth Amendment Proportionality Analysis and the Compelling Case of William Rummel." *Journal of Criminal Law and Criminology* 71 (1980): 378–420.

CULPABILITY

See CRIME: CONCEPT OF CRIME; GUILT; PUNISHMENT; *both articles under* STRICT LIABILITY.

CUSTODY

See ARREST AND STOP.

D

DANGEROUSNESS

See PREDICTION OF CRIME AND RECIDIVISM; VIOLENCE.

DEADLY FORCE

See ARREST AND STOP; HOMICIDE: LEGAL ASPECTS; *articles under* JUSTIFICATION.

DEATH PENALTY

See CAPITAL PUNISHMENT.

DECRIMINALIZATION

See CRIMINALIZATION AND DECRIMINALIZATION.

DEFENSE COUNSEL

See both articles under COUNSEL.

DEFENSE OF OTHERS

See JUSTIFICATION, *articles on* LAW ENFORCEMENT *and* SELF-DEFENSE.

DEFENSE OF PROPERTY

See JUSTIFICATION, *articles on* LAW ENFORCEMENT *and* SELF-DEFENSE.

DELINQUENCY, JUVENILE

Juvenile delinquency refers to conduct by children or youths that is either violative of the prohibitions of the criminal law or is otherwise regarded as deviant and inappropriate. The subject is treated in a variety of entries and articles. The juvenile justice system as an alternative to the criminal justice system for juveniles is dealt with in the three articles under the entry JUVENILE JUSTICE—HISTORY AND PHILOSOPHY, JUVENILE COURT DISPOSITION, *and* ORGANIZATION AND PROCESS. CHILDREN, CRIMINAL ACTIVITIES OF *discusses the criminal activities of prepubescent juveniles.* CONTRIBUTING TO THE DELINQUENCY OF MINORS *concerns the pattern of criminal prohibitions against adults for exposing minors to harmful influences.* CRIME PREVENTION: JUVENILES AS POTENTIAL OFFENDERS *sets forth what is known about predicting future serious offenders on the basis of patterns of juvenile delinquency.* DELINQUENT AND CRIMINAL SUBCULTURES *describes the theory of subcultures as an explanation of criminal behavior generally, including juvenile crime.* EDUCATION AND CRIME *discusses the close relationship between school experiences and criminality, particularly among juveniles.* EXCUSE: INFANCY *traces the early and modern laws that excuse children below a certain age from criminal responsibility.* FAMILY RELATIONSHIPS AND CRIME *focuses on the data and theories supporting the importance of family relationships in leading to delinquent acts by juveniles.* JUVENILE STATUS OFFENDERS *describes the forms of behavior that are wrongful for minors but not for adults.* POLICE: HANDLING OF JUVENILES *focuses on those duties of urban police which involve them in dealing with juveniles.* PRISONS: CORRECTIONAL INSTITUTIONS FOR DELINQUENT YOUTHS *focuses on the history, nature, and functioning of institutions especially designed for juvenile delinquents.* SCHOOLS, CRIME IN THE *is directed to the various forms of crime and other misbehavior engaged in by juveniles in school settings.* YOUTH GANGS AND GROUPS *describes what is known about the effect upon patterns of criminality of juveniles organizing in the form of gangs and other groups.*

DELINQUENT AND CRIMINAL SUBCULTURES

A subculture is a set of conduct norms which cluster together in such a way that they can be differentiated from the broader culture of which they are a part. Thus, if some of the rules of behavior for the working class are different from those for the middle class, it is proper to speak of working-class and middle-class subcultures, even though there are so many identical rules of conduct in these two social classes that it is reasonable to consider the two as belonging to the same overall culture. Similarly, if some rules of conduct are in opposition to, and inspire violation of, a society's laws against stealing—these rules indicating that it is "all right" to steal under certain conditions—it is proper to speak of the rules as a "stealing subculture" or, more generally, as a "criminal subculture" or a "delinquent subculture." Indeed, some authorities refer to such countervailing norms as "contracultures" or "countercultures."

Pervasiveness

Subcultural delinquency and crime is committed by persons who follow prescriptive and proscriptive subcultural norms, which include values, ideologies, attitudes, beliefs, and other behavior patterns. However, such subcultural behavior is analytically distinct from the conduct norms on which it is based. At law, persons who are so mentally disturbed that they do not follow subcultural rules of conduct when they perpetrate harmful acts are said to be insane and, therefore, not guilty of violating the law. However, all persons properly adjudicated as violators of criminal law have been guided by conduct norms that are in conflict with those specified in criminal law. Thus, criminals and juvenile offenders are in trouble with the law because they have conformed to rules of conduct that were in existence long before they were born. As they followed these countervailing norms, they participated in a delinquent or criminal subculture and perpetrated subcultural delinquency or subcultural crime, whether acting alone or in concert with others.

Origins

Little is known about the conditions under which delinquent and criminal subcultures were invented. Emile Durkheim, Karl Marx, Max Weber, and Robert Merton, among others, noted that changes in social structure—that is, in the patterned sets of relationships between people—stimulate invention of new rules of conduct. Weber, for example, showed that as the economic structure of societies changed, new rules for religious conduct were invented. Similarly, Durkheim, Marx, and Merton explored the conditions under which general conduct norms condoning delinquency and criminality originated. Still needed are studies documenting the historical origins of rules condoning specific crimes, such as robbery, theft, burglary, forgery, assault, embezzlement, restraint of trade, and misrepresentation in advertising.

Social reforms as experiments. Casual observations about the origin of rules favorable to crime and delinquency are made whenever people propose that social reforms be instituted as a means of eradicating the crime problem. The unstated assumption of such proposals has two components: that behavioral change follows structural change, and that contemporary structural change will modify delinquent and criminal behavior based on subcultural rules which were produced by social changes occurring in some earlier historical period. Some reformers acknowledge the importance of subcultural delinquency and crime but concentrate their efforts on preventing subcultural values from spreading from one person to another, as youth-club workers try to do. Other reformers attack the rules for delinquency and crime themselves, as legislators do when they increase penalties, thus ostensibly bolstering the contention that following subcultural rules does not pay. Still a third set of reformers explicitly or implicitly advocate that the social structure be modified in such a way that rules for delinquency and crime will wither away or that rules for antidelinquency or anticrime will replace the deviant rules. For example, Marxists and others argue that if social inequality were eradicated, delinquency and crime would disappear because the subcultures supporting them would disappear. If, then, social inequality actually were eliminated and the predicted results occurred, it could be reasonably concluded that creation of the structure of inequality at some time in the past had led to invention of the rules for delinquency and crime.

Origins versus maintenance. Significantly enough, however, drawing such a conclusion from an experiment in social reform might be in error. Even if the experiment produced the predicted results, observers would still have to determine whether the conditions of social inequality led to the invention of the subcultural conduct norms, or merely lent themselves to maintaining rules whose invention had been stimulated earlier by some other structural condition. Subculture theorists avoid this issue when they discuss the "origin and maintenance" of deviant subcultures as though they were one process.

Many types of delinquent and criminal subcultures have long been present in industrialized societies. For this reason, no juvenile gang, criminal organization, neighborhood group, ethnic group, or social class needs to invent such a subculture in order to take on a high rate of criminality. Most apparent inventions of norms making delinquency and criminality acceptable, even if illegal, are merely variations on themes invented long ago.

It is obvious, however, that all delinquent and criminal subcultures have not been in existence for equal lengths of time. Accordingly, studies of the origins of some of them need not go very far back in history. For example, since the 1960s an increasing number of persons have followed rules which insist that it is both desirable and proper to use and to sell illegal drugs. In modern criminology, influenced by subcultural considerations, the first and most important question about this behavior is, What are the conditions under which the rules were invented? The second, but subsidiary, question is, What accounts for the differential distribution of these rules? Variants of this subsidiary question include the following: Why are the rules followed more frequently in New York than in London or Salt Lake City? Why are they followed by males more frequently than by females, and by young people more than by their elders? Why are they more frequently followed by members of the working class than by those of the middle class? How does it happen that a young man follows the rules, but his brother does not? The "cultural-transmission school" of criminology has directed its attention to this subsidiary question rather than to the question of origins.

Behavioral theory

The idea that the values, ideologies, and other behavior patterns comprising delinquent and criminal subcultures are transmitted from person to person has become a fundamental principle of criminology. This principle was derived in turn from one of the two major kinds of theory used by behavioral scientists to describe the relationship between personality and behavior, on the one hand, and social organization, culture, and subcultures, on the other.

Psychologists and sociologists at one pole think of infants as naturally autonomous. They consistently view people's lifelong interactions with the rules and regulations of a society, of groups, and of other organizations as *submission,* and personality as an outgrowth of the effects that social restrictions have on the individual's expression of basic drives and urges.

At the opposite pole are those behavioral scientists who think that infants become persons, and thus obtain their essence, not from restriction but from *participation* in customs based on the myriad rules which surround them. To them, there is no war between the individual and society; social organization and personality are considered two facets of the same thing. All persons are held to behave according to the rules (which are sometimes contradictory) of the many organizations in which they participate; they cannot behave in any other way.

Certainly, the two theories about the relationship between personality and culture are more complex than these simple statements suggest, and few behavioral scientists maintain one or the other exclusively and with no qualifications. Nevertheless, criminological theory tends to be divided into the same two sets. Consistent with restriction or submission theory is the idea that delinquent or criminal behavior is a trait of the person exhibiting it. Consistent with participation theory is the idea that delinquent or criminal behavior is subcultural and thus is behavior which the person in question has learned while participating in social relationships.

Differential association

Edwin Sutherland's principle of differential association, first published in the 1939 edition of his *Principles of Criminology* and later presented in Sutherland and Donald Cressey's *Criminology,* is a variant of participation theory. A basic point of this principle is that delinquent and criminal behavior—like other actions, attitudes, beliefs, and values which people exhibit—is owned by groups, not by individuals. Just as a collectivity owns the English language, people sharing subcultural norms own delinquent and criminal behavior patterns. Some individuals are surrounded by persons who define the legal codes as rules to be observed, and are thus taught to be noncriminal, even anticriminal. Others are surrounded by persons whose definitions are favorable to the violation of legal codes, and thus in both subtle and manifest ways are taught to act criminally. As individuals conform to a group's expectations, they exhibit the group's behavior patterns—legal or illegal, conformist or deviant.

But most persons are simultaneously surrounded by definitions both unfavorable and favorable to law violation. Sutherland's principle holds that whether they become criminals or not depends upon the ratio of these two kinds of behavior patterns in their life experiences. For example, most American children are likely to learn that "honesty is the best policy," but they also are likely to learn, in an extraordinarily complex and subtle process, that this moral axiom has many loopholes—that "it is all right to steal if you are hungry," "it's a dog-eat-dog world," "honesty is for suckers," "business is business," and so on. Whether a given child will grow up to be a criminal, then, depends on the balance of participation in these two kinds of behavioral directives, one coming from the dominant culture and the other from a criminalistic subculture.

Symbolic interaction. Participation in behavioral directives or, more generally, in social relationships and social organization is, of course, the subject matter of all anthropology, sociology, and social psychology. The mechanism making participation possible is language, as George Herbert Mead, the father of modern symbolic interaction theory, observed in the early twentieth century. Following Mead, subcultural theories of delinquency and criminality note that the rules making up cultures and subcultures are embedded in words. The meaning of words makes it proper to behave in a certain way toward an object designated as "cat" and improper to behave in the same way toward an object designated as "table."

Rationalizations and ideologies. At the ideological level, words and their meanings also make it wrong or illegal to behave in certain ways, and right or legal to behave in others. Most significantly, words—in the form of subcultural rules for delinquency and crime—make it acceptable to behave in a manner that is wrong and illegal. For this reason, such rules are called rationalizations, a usage which is quite different from that employed in psychoanalysis. As Cressey showed in his study of embezzlers, a rationalization is not merely an ex post facto justification for delinquent or criminal behavior that has been prompted by some deeply hidden psychological motive. It is itself a motive, a set of words that is formulated before the deviant act takes place and that constitutes the person's reasons for acting. These motives are not invented by criminals on the spur of the moment. Rather, criminals' rationalizations are reflections of cultural ideologies pertaining to the propriety of committing crime under certain circumstances. They exist as group definitions in which crime is either appropriate or somehow permissible. They are the most relevant components of delinquent and criminal subcultures.

Among some American groups, criminal and delinquent behavior is common because persons apply to their own conduct some variation of the ideology that "it is not wrong to steal a loaf of bread when you are starving." In a group in which such ideologies exist—and such groups are very extensive—the individual using them has a sense of support and sanction. If individuals have learned that "all people steal when they get into a tight spot," it will not be surprising to find them stealing when they get into what they define as a tight spot. People who use such rationalizations are not deterred by cultural prohibitions and admonitions about committing delinquencies or crimes, for participation in a delinquent or criminal subculture has convinced them that their behavior is not really crime. In *An Introduction to Cultural Anthropology*, the noted anthropologist Robert Lowie illustrated this point as follows: "The Burmese are Buddhist, hence must not take the life of animals. Fishermen are threatened with dire punishment for their murderous occupation, but they find a loophole by not literally killing the fish. 'These are merely put on the bank to dry, after their long soaking in the river, and if they are foolish and ill-judged enough to die while undergoing the process, it is their own fault.' . . . When so convenient a theory had once been expounded, it naturally became an apology of the whole guild of fishermen" (p. 379).

Normative conflict and industrialization

Similar deviant, delinquent, and criminal ideologies thrive in all societies, but there are variations from time to time and from place to place. In modern industrialized nations such as the United States, the moral influences surrounding most persons are dramatically inconsistent. All children are confronted with alternative ways of behaving even within the home, for parents themselves display alternative behavior patterns. And, of course, standards of conduct among groups outside the home are often in conflict with those within it. As Thorsten Sellin pointed out in his pioneering *Culture Conflict and Crime*, "The more complex a culture becomes, the more likely it is that the number of normative groups which affect a person will be large, and the greater is the chance that the norms of these groups will fail to agree, no matter how much they may overlap as a result of common acceptance of certain norms" (p. 30).

The condition of normative conflict identified by Sellin suggests that modern societies do not possess a broad consensus with respect to social goals or else do not possess consensus regarding the proper means for individuals to achieve personal goals. Consequently, individuals are confronted with alternative goals or means, or live under conditions in which the norms of some members of the society are unknown to others. So far as delinquency and crime are concerned, such a mixture of norms in a society means that both a delinquent or criminal subculture and an antidelinquent or anticriminal subculture have developed. The society has become organized in such a way that a premium is placed both on refraining from crime and on perpetrating it.

Under conditions of normative conflict, the significance of criminal laws becomes relative. Some are obeyed and some are not, depending on whether one "believes in" them. According to Durkheim and Merton, this is a price paid for industrialization, for in the attempt to locate and train the most talented persons to occupy technical roles, industrial societies maintain that personal, material success is available to all, regardless of social origins. By asserting that achievement of such success is a sign of moral worth and by asserting that great economic success is available to all, an optimum number of persons can be motivated to compete for the rewards. However, as Merton long ago pointed out, the structure of industrialized societies is not necessarily consistent with the idea that economic success is available to everyone. In industrialized societies the social structure effectively blocks access to success goals for some parts of the population. One result is the invention of delinquent and criminal subcultures and of norms that make it appropriate, even if illegal, to achieve success by routes other than the standard ones. Normative conflict arises, and both individuals and groups then have an opportunity to learn illegitimate, as well as legitimate, means for achieving personal success. In this kind of social arrangement, multiple moralities abound.

The behavior of organizations

In addition to studying how criminalistic ideologies come to be invented, as well as the processes by which individuals learn them, criminologists have tried to account for the behavior of delinquent gangs and criminal organizations. The task here is not to discover the circumstances under which Lowie's guild of fishermen invented its ideology, which Lowie called both a "theory" and an "apology." Neither is it to stipulate the process by which a youngster learns that it is all right, even if illegal, to catch fish and let them die. Rather, it is to determine why the guild of fishermen behaves as it does.

The problem of accounting for the criminal behavior of collectivities was introduced to modern criminology by Richard Cloward and Lloyd Ohlin, and it has subsequently been studied with reference to organized crime and white-collar crime as well as to other delinquent and criminal organizations. Cloward and Ohlin observed that the leading criminological theory used to explain why individual delinquents and criminals behave as they do (differential association) also can be used to explain why groups such as guilds of Burmese fishermen, gangs, and criminal organizations behave as they do. According to the differential association principle, persons become criminals because they experience more behavior patterns favorable to following rules that condone crime than behavior patterns unfavorable to crime. This does not mean, of course, that individuals become totally corrupt. For example, a person may learn to be highly anticriminal with reference to burglary or robbery but highly procriminal with reference to tax evasion. Subcultural definitions of appropriate behavior pertain to very specific kinds of offenses rather than to crime in general. A boy who participates in the subcultural rationalizations shared by members of a delinquent gang learns the delinquent ways of that gang and will exhibit those ways if not inhibited by lack of opportunity or by countervailing rules. By the same token, Cloward and Ohlin pointed out, the conduct of the gang as a whole is determined by its participation in specific aspects of the broader culture and social organization.

Classification of activities. As the first step in a three-step process, Cloward and Ohlin classified delinquent gangs according to the activities involved, rather than beginning, as had been customary, with a classification according to structure. They started with function, specifying that the slums of large American cities contain gangs of lower-class boys variously oriented toward theft and other property offenses, toward conflict and violence, and toward drug use.

In all three types of gangs, the members are committed to an ideology that neutralizes the antidelinquent ideology held by some groups in the larger society. For this reason, their delinquencies are subcultural. Gangs organized primarily for pursuit of material gain by theft, fraud, and extortion have adopted a status system based on values that regard the members of conventional society as "suckers," businesses as rackets, and politics as graft. However, lower-class boys have problems of status as well as problems of economic acquisition. Accordingly, in "conflict" gangs the role model is the "bopper," who follows rules of conduct also followed by the courageous hero and the successful warrior. In "retreatist" gangs, participants learn that to be important they must follow rules of conduct stressing the desirability of detachment from the life-style and everyday activities of the masses.

Structure of the gang. In the second step, Cloward and Ohlin noted that the structure of the gang—its status system, its degree of integration, and its age hierarchy—is related to one or another of the three principal kinds of delinquent subculture they identified. The structure of a gang oriented toward theft is not the same as the structure of a gang oriented toward violence, which in turn differs from the structure of a retreatist gang. For example, a conflict gang is more likely than a retreatist gang to be organized hierarchically, and a gang oriented toward theft is more age-structured than is either a conflict gang or a retreatist gang.

Distribution of norms. In the third step, Cloward and Ohlin proposed that a society's culture and subcultures shape the specific activities which delinquent gangs and criminal organizations display. Accordingly, as Irving Spergel later demonstrated, the behavior of delinquent gangs is predictable, just as is the behavior of individual delinquents.

The differential association principle makes sense of gang behavior as well as of individual behavior. Thus, a gang or other organization, like a person, takes a delinquent or criminal course of action rather than a nondelinquent or noncriminal course of action because a delinquent or criminal subculture—in the form of values, ideologies, attitudes, and beliefs—is more readily available to it than are antidelinquent norms. Walter Miller's studies have shown that lower-class urban boys' gangs are delinquent because their members are trying to achieve standards of value as they are defined in lower-class urban areas; they try to do what everyone around them tries to do. Referring to individuals, not gangs, Cloward and Ohlin restated the differential association principle as follows: "The individual must have access to appropriate environments for the acquisition of values and skills associated with the performance of a particular role; and he must be supported in the performance of the role once he has learned it" (p. 148).

Age structure. If a delinquent or criminal subculture is to persist, there must be devices for passing the rules for delinquency or crime along to newcomers, whether these newcomers are children or immigrants from an area where the subculture does not exist. For example, the theft subculture described by Cloward and Ohlin is rather stable, and one source of this stability is the network of bonds existing between age levels. Children are linked with adolescent delinquents and share their norms; adolescent delinquents are in turn linked with young adult offenders, who are linked with adult criminals. On the other hand, Cloward and Ohlin's conflict subculture is less stable, probably because the devices for socializing

persons into it have not developed to the same degree. Although any newcomer must learn the norms of this subculture, the norms are those of adolescents, not of children and adults. Accordingly, participants do not proceed through a set of age-graded patterns; they tend to be guided by other norms when they reach young adulthood, rather than moving on to an "adult" or "mature" form of violence.

Cloward, Ohlin, and others extended these observations to delinquent gangs and criminal organizations. It became clear that organizations oriented toward stealing do not develop where the stealing subculture is not readily available, that organizations oriented toward violence do not appear where values favorable to violence are scarce, and that organizations oriented toward drug use do not develop in locations where drugs and knowledge of their pleasing effects are rare. Stated positively, the evidence is that gangs, cliques, and criminal organizations oriented toward theft develop in social areas where access to legitimate channels for success are denied to youngsters, and where the criminality of adults makes readily available to youngsters both the rules favorable to theft and the opportunities for adopting these rules. Similarly, gangs oriented toward conflict or retreatism arise only in areas where rules in support of violent action or retreatism are available.

Location data

Because delinquent and criminal subcultures are not distributed uniformly in a society, they are not equally available for adoption by all segments of the population. For example, working-class persons living in large American cities have available for adoption a different kind of criminal subculture than do business executives and upper-class persons. Accordingly, high rates of larceny, burglary, automobile theft, antitrust violation, and so on are "location data"; that is, they direct attention to the problem of determining the origin and continuation of the specific kinds of delinquent and criminal subcultures thriving at different points in the social structure.

Albert Cohen produced one of the best studies using location data as a stimulus to exploration of the characteristics of a delinquent subculture. Cohen examined "nonutilitarian delinquency." Statistical data indicate that a destructive kind of "hell-raising" vandalism is more prevalent among working-class boys than among either middle-class boys or working-class girls. Following leads provided by Durkheim and Merton, Cohen determined the existence of a vandalism subculture. The theory he developed to account for its presence maintains that the subculture arose in response to a conflict between the aspirations inspired by middle-class values and the ability and opportunity that working-class boys have for fulfilling these aspirations.

Middle-class values have been incorporated into the criminal law and into other general codes of legitimate and moral conduct—codes that prescribe proper conduct for everyone. At the same time, however, working-class persons who follow these codes cannot achieve some of the goals assigned to everyone, specifically, personal success of the kind that comes from rational, honest labor; careful long-range planning; and deferral of immediate gratification. In response to this conflict, Cohen concluded, rules have developed for achieving personal success by turning middle-class values upside down. Once this subculture had arisen, boys could, for example, achieve social status either by doing well in school or by vandalizing the school at night.

Cohen's theory, like other subcultural theories, does not attempt to account for the delinquency or nondelinquency of individuals. It explains the distribution of vandalism by accounting for the distribution of a delinquent subculture. Because the rules for nonutilitarian delinquency thrive in working-class locations, they are more readily available for learning by working-class youths. Further, because they arose in connection with conflicts between culturally defined aspirations regarding success, on the one hand, and opportunities for achieving success, on the other, they are more readily available for learning by boys than by girls.

Limits of structural frustration

On the individual level, both Cohen's and Cloward and Ohlin's stress on relationships between social structure and norms made it clear that frustration arising from poverty or limited legitimate opportunities does not alone produce delinquency or criminality. Even in societies disproportionately stressing goals of individual success to such a degree that delinquent subcultures have been invented, most persons do not use illegitimate means for achieving approved ends. This is because they do not experience normative conflict, even if they live in a geographic or social area where a delinquent or criminal subculture thrives. For example, a young man frustrated by poverty may relieve his tension by adopting a nondelinquent solution, such as renouncing all worldly things and be-

coming a hermit, or moving into the political arena to effect economic reforms. Alternatively, he may simply work harder, holding down two jobs at the same time. He becomes a criminal only if he solves the problem by adopting one or more criminal solutions such as engaging in burglary, shoplifting, robbery, extortion, bookmaking, embezzlement, or white-collar crime. Which, if any, criminal solution is adopted by the young man depends upon its availability. Similarly, as already noted, whether a gang moves in the direction of a particular kind of delinquency depends upon the availability of directives for action and of training for action.

Double failure

In addition to applying the differential association principle to organizational behavior, Cloward and Ohlin formulated the now-standard double-failure hypothesis about motivation to delinquency. This proposition suggests that conflict gangs are composed of young men who have not been able to achieve success legitimately and also have not been able either to achieve success by theft or to explain away their failure. They are thus ripe for adoption of what Gresham Sykes and David Matza called "techniques of neutralization"—that is, rationalizations which make delinquencies and crimes acceptable. Similarly, members of retreatist gangs were said by Cloward and Ohlin to have failed in the use of both legitimate and illegitimate means for achieving success.

However, it has been repeatedly shown that conflict and retreatism are only two of the many possible personal reactions to double failure. Indeed, in a study of Chicago gangs, James Short and Fred Strodtbeck showed that retreatist gangs are quite rare, probably because in the United States the rules for retreating to drug use are not as clearly formulated or widely dispersed as the rules for violence. When the drug-use reaction to double failure occurs, it does so in locales where behavior patterns favorable to drug use are widespread, and where the opportunities for obtaining and learning how to use drugs are present. Both are parts of the drug-addiction subculture.

Thus, the activities of delinquent cliques, gangs, and criminal organizations, as well as of individual offenders, are consistent with specific rules provided by delinquent and criminal subcultures. Because of inconsistencies in social structure, certain forms of delinquent and criminal activity have become substitutes for legitimate means of gaining status. This kind of activity is subcultural, and the rules for delinquency or for criminality that underlie it constitute a subculture. However, as noted earlier, an explanation of the process by which such rules come into existence, develop, and change is different from an explanation of the behavior of individual delinquents and criminals, whether these persons perform their illegal acts alone or in gangs or other collectivities.

Subcultural traditions

Delinquent gangs are, above all, important agencies for diffusion of the values that make up delinquent subcultures. Acts of delinquency having the support of a group are likely to recur with great frequency, for delinquent behavior can be used to achieve acceptance and status in the group. Further, participation in gang or other organizational delinquent or criminal activities makes a delinquent or criminal difficult to change, since the participant's behavior belongs to an explicit network of expectations and obligations. Delinquent gangs and criminal organizations thus provide alternative opportunities for gaining and maintaining social status and symbols of status. Whether these opportunities are or are not present in a social area depends on the traditions of the people in the area—traditions of beliefs, attitudes, values, ideologies, and other rules of conduct that are integrated closely enough so that they can be called a subculture. The behavior of delinquent gangs and criminal organizations, like the behavior of individual delinquents and criminals, is based on an extension of the behavioral rules followed by nondelinquents and noncriminals.

DONALD R. CRESSEY

See also CRIME CAUSATION: SOCIOLOGICAL THEORIES; *both articles under* CRIMINAL CAREERS; DEVIANCE; ORGANIZED CRIME: OVERVIEW; *both articles under* PROFESSIONAL CRIMINAL; PROSTITUTION AND COMMERCIALIZED VICE: SOCIAL AND ORGANIZATIONAL ASPECTS; YOUTH GANGS AND GROUPS.

BIBLIOGRAPHY

CLOWARD, RICHARD A., and OHLIN, LLOYD E. *Delinquency and Opportunity: A Theory of Delinquent Gangs.* New York: Free Press, 1960.

COHEN, ALBERT K. *Delinquent Boys: The Culture of the Gang.* New York: Free Press, 1955.

CRESSEY, DONALD R. *Other People's Money: A Study of the Social Psychology of Embezzlement.* New York: Free Press, 1953.

DURKHEIM, EMILE. *Suicide: A Study in Sociology* (1899). Translated by John A. Spaulding and George Simpson. Edited, with an introduction, by George Simpson. New York: Free Press, 1951.

LOWIE, ROBERT H. *An Introduction to Cultural Anthropology.* New and enlarged ed. New York: Farrar & Rinehart, 1940.

MEAD, GEORGE HERBERT. *Mind, Self, and Society from the Standpoint of a Social Behaviorist.* Edited, with an introduction, by Charles W. Morris. University of Chicago Press, 1934.

MERTON, ROBERT K. "Social Structure and Anomie." *American Sociological Review* 3 (1938): 672–682.

MILLER, WALTER B. "Lower Class Culture as a Generating Milieu of Gang Delinquency." *Journal of Social Issues* 14, no. 3 (1958): 5–19.

SELLIN, THORSTEN. *Culture Conflict and Crime: A Report of the Subcommittee on Delinquency of the Committee on Personality and Culture.* Bulletin 41. New York: Social Science Research Council, 1938.

SHORT, JAMES F., JR., and STRODTBECK, FRED L. *Group Process and Gang Delinquency.* University of Chicago Press, 1965.

SPERGEL, IRVING. *Racketville, Slumtown, Haulburg: An Exploratory Study of Delinquent Subcultures.* Foreword by Lloyd E. Ohlin. University of Chicago Press, 1964.

SUTHERLAND, EDWIN H., and CRESSEY, DONALD R. *Criminology* (1924). 10th ed. Philadelphia: Lippincott, 1978.

SYKES, GRESHAM M., and MATZA, DAVID. "Techniques of Neutralization: A Theory of Delinquency." *American Sociological Review* 22 (1957): 664–670.

WEBER, MAX. *The Protestant Ethic and the Spirit of Capitalism* (1904). Translated by Talcott Parsons. With a foreword by R. H. Tawney. New York: Scribner, 1958.

DEMOGRAPHY AND CRIME

See AGE AND CRIME; CLASS AND CRIME; CRIME STATISTICS: HISTORICAL TRENDS IN WESTERN SOCIETY; RACE AND CRIME; WOMEN AND CRIME.

DEPORTATION

See BANISHMENT AND EXILE; PENAL COLONIES.

DETENTION

See ARREST AND STOP.

DETENTION, PRETRIAL

See both articles under BAIL; CRIMINAL COURTS: LOWER CRIMINAL COURTS; JAILS; SPEEDY TRIAL.

DETERMINATE SENTENCING

See SENTENCING: DETERMINATE SENTENCING.

DETERMINISM

See CRIMINOLOGY, *articles on* INTELLECTUAL HISTORY *and* MODERN CONTROVERSIES; EXCUSE: THEORY; GUILT; PSYCHOPATHY; PUNISHMENT.

DETERRENCE

The concept

The narrow sense: fear of punishment. In a narrow sense, *deterrence* can be defined as the prevention of socially undesirable behavior by fear of punishment. A person who might otherwise have committed a crime is restrained by the thought of the unpleasant consequences of detection, trial, conviction, and sentence. A distinction is often made between *general deterrence*, which signifies the deterrent effect of the threat of punishment, and *special deterrence* (or *individual deterrence*), which signifies the effect of actual punishment on the offender.

The distinction may be of some value for analysis but should not be given too much importance. The basic phenomenon is the fear of punishment. This fear may be influenced by the experience of punishment. When an offender has been punished his motivation is more complex than before. He now knows what it is like to be prosecuted and punished, and this may strengthen his fear of the law. The experience may, however, work the other way. It is conceivable that the offender previously had exaggerated ideas of the consequences of being caught but now draws the conclusion that it was not as bad as he had imagined. In this case, the special deterrent effect of the punishment is negative. More important, probably, a person who has been convicted of a somewhat more serious crime, and especially one who was sentenced to imprisonment, will have less to fear from a new conviction, since his reputation is already tarnished. In practice, it will be difficult or impossible to isolate the deterrent effects of the prison experience from other effects of the stay in prison. What we can measure is how offenders perform after punishment, expressed in figures of recidivism.

The broad sense: the moral effects of criminal law. In a broad sense, *deterrence* is taken to include not only the effect of fear on the potential offender but also other influences produced by the threat and imposition of punishment. Criminal law is not only a price tariff but also an expression of society's disapproval of forbidden behavior, a fact influencing citizens in various ways. Most people have a certain respect for formal law as such. Moreover, the criminalization of a certain type of behavior may work as a moral eye-opener, making people realize the socially harmful character of the act ("the law as a teacher of right and wrong"). The moral condemnation expressed through the criminal law may also affect the moral attitudes of the individual in a less reflective way. Various labels are used to characterize these effects: the moral, the educative, the socializing, the attitude-shaping, or the norm-strengthening influence of the law. Opinions vary with regard to the importance of this component; it may also be of varying importance in different cultural settings. Nevertheless, few, if any, would disregard it altogether. From the legislator's perspective, the creation of moral inhibitions is of greater value than mere deterrence, because the former may work even in situations in which a person need not fear detection and punishment.

The consideration of the moral effects of criminal law calls for a long-term perspective, or, as it has been stated, the legislation of one generation may become the morality of the next (Walker, p. 214).

General deterrence and general prevention. In continental literature *general prevention* is used as a technical term that denotes both the effect of fear and the moral effect of the criminal law. This is equivalent to *general deterrence* in the broad sense. Most research papers on deterrence do not mention the question of definition but do in fact work with the broad concept, since they are concerned with all effects on crime rates of the system of criminal justice and make no effort to exclude effects produced through mechanisms other than fear.

Habituative effects of criminal law. Much law-abiding conduct is habitual, and the threat of punishment plays a role in this habit formation. It is sufficient to mention the response of drivers to traffic signals. In a broad sense *deterrence* can be taken to include also the habituative effects of the law. Habit formation is, however, a secondary phenomenon. For a habit to be established, there must first be compliance based on other sources, which may include fear and respect for the law. The habit is eventually formed through repetition of the law-abiding conduct.

A historical perspective

Historically, deterrence has been, along with retribution, the primary purpose of punishment. The deterrent purpose has often led to penalties that, to contemporary minds, seem cruel and inhuman. Capital punishment and corporal punishment were the backbone of the systems of criminal justice up to the late eighteenth century. Executions were made public spectacles, and cruel methods of execution were often invented in order to enhance the deterrent effect.

In the eighteenth century the writers of the classical school of criminal justice—notably Cesare Beccaria in Italy, Jeremy Bentham in England, and P. J. A.

von Feuerbach in Germany—based their theory of criminal law on general deterrence. The central idea was that the threat of punishment should be specified so that in the mind of the potential lawbreaker the fear of punishment would outweigh the temptation to commit the crime. The penalty should be fixed by law in proportion to the gravity of the offense. The certainty of punishment was considered as more important than the severity of the punishment. According to the classical theory, the penalty in the individual case had as its primary function to make the threat of the law credible. Only occasionally did these writers mention the moral effects of the criminal law.

In the late nineteenth century and the first half of the twentieth century the idea of deterrence lost ground to the idea of treatment and rehabilitation. Criminologists and penologists voiced the view that the most important aim of punishment was to correct the offender and, if this proved impossible, to incapacitate him. Therefore, the penalty had to be adjusted to the needs of the individual offender. In the United States the indeterminate sentence was introduced. The idea of the indeterminate sentence is based on an analogy to medical treatment in a hospital. The offender should be kept as long as necessary in order to cure him, no shorter, no longer; and just as with a stay in a hospital, the duration should not be decided in advance but on the basis of the observation of progress. On the European continent, measures of safety and reform for certain categories of offenders were introduced, based on similar ideas. The idea of deterrence was often ridiculed as fictitious, outmoded, and the cause of much unnecessary suffering. The saying "Punishment does not deter crime" was often accepted as established truth.

Although these ideas were dominant in the professional literature up to the 1950s, legislators, prosecutors, and judges continued to have faith in deterrence. From the early 1960s a change in criminological thought began to take place and gradually gained momentum. Research into the differential effects of various sanctions led to great skepticism with regard to society's ability to rehabilitate offenders. It appeared that choice of sanction had very little effect when compared to the personality and background of the offender and to the social environment he went back to after his encounter with the machinery of justice. Moreover, it seemed that no one was able to tell when to release the offender in order to maximize his chances of a law-abiding life in the future. At least for the overwhelming majority of offenders, the hospital analogy does not work.

Two tendencies have emerged: a movement in favor of fixed sentences in proportion to the gravity of the offense, as demanded by the classical school of criminal law ("neoclassicism"); and a revival of interest in deterrence. When faith is lost in the idea of treatment and rehabilitation as the basis for a system of criminal sanctions, other aims of punishment come into focus. Up to 1965 the only empirical research in deterrence consisted of a few papers on the death penalty. Since the mid-1960s a series of books and a stream of research papers have been published on the subject, mainly in the United States, Canada, and Great Britain, but also in Germany, the Netherlands, and Scandinavia (see Beyleveld). Most research has been undertaken by either sociologists or economists. The economists look upon the risk of punishment as a cost of crime and apply econometric methods to find out how a change in the price affects the rate of crime.

Empirical and ethical questions

In discussing deterrence one is confronted with two categories of questions. One category consists of empirical or factual questions: Does deterrence work, and if so, how well, in which fields, and under what circumstances? Another category consists of ethical questions: To what extent is the purpose of deterrence a valid moral basis for lawmaking, sentencing, and the execution of sentences? A penalty may be effective as a deterrent yet unacceptable because it is felt to be unjust or inhumane. The position on such questions as capital punishment, corporal punishment, and the length of prison sentences is dependent not only on views on efficacy but also on moral feelings. Even if it were possible to prove that cutting off the hands of thieves would effectively prevent theft, proposals for such a practice would scarcely win many adherents in the Western world today. Much of the discussion on deterrence has been of an emotional nature and has not separated the empirical questions from the value questions. Often people have let their views on empirical questions be heavily colored by their value preferences instead of basing them on a dispassionate scrutiny of the available evidence (Andenaes, 1974, pp. 41–44).

General deterrence: myth or reality?

The strongest basis for the belief in deterrence is the eminent plausibility of the theory from the viewpoint of common sense. That the foresight of unpleasant consequences is a strong motivating factor is a familiar experience of everyday life. It would be a bold statement that this well-known mechanism of motivation is of no importance in the decision to commit or not commit an offense. This position must presuppose that offenders are a special breed of people who do not react to the prospect of negative consequences in a normal way or that they are in a special situation which excludes normal motivation. Such cases no doubt exist. However, modern research into unreported criminality has shown that violation of criminal law is a much more widespread phenomenon than previously realized. Most offenders, and even more so most potential offenders, are within the borders of psychological normalcy. There is no prima facie reason to assume that they are insensitive to negative inducements.

Historical experiences from police strikes and similar situations show that even a short breakdown of criminal justice leads to great increases in offenses such as burglary and robbery (Andenaes, 1974, pp. 16–18, 50–51). By introspection many know that the risk of detection and negative sanctions plays a role for their own compliance with rules about taxation, customs, drinking and driving, and other traffic offenses. It seems to be a universal experience that police regulations which are not enforced gradually cease to be taken seriously. Paradoxically, the consequences of police corruption can be mentioned as a demonstration of the deterrent impact that the criminal law has when the machinery of justice is working normally and properly (Andenaes, 1975, pp. 360–361). All available data indicate that organized crime flourishes most where the local police have been corrupted. Police corruption paralyzes enforcement and gives professional criminals a feeling of immunity from punishment. That crime flourishes when the criminal justice system is paralyzed through corruption is another way of stating that a criminal justice system which works normally does deter crime, or at least some forms of crime, to some degree.

It seems safe to conclude that criminal law and law enforcement play an indispensable role in the functioning of a modern, complex society. However, from a practical point of view, this insight is of limited value. Policymakers are not confronted with the choice of retaining or abolishing the whole system of criminal justice. The choices are of a much more narrow kind. The legislator sometimes has the choice between criminalization or decriminalization of a certain type of behavior, such as homosexual conduct, abortion, pornography, or blasphemy. More often the choice is between a somewhat stricter or milder penalty or between somewhat higher or lower appropriations for the police or other control agencies. For the police,

the prosecutor, the judge, and the prison administrator the choices are still more limited. The questions of practical importance do not refer to the total effects of criminal law but to the marginal effects of this or that change in the level of punishment or the allotment of resources (Zimring and Hawkins, pp. 7–8). These effects are difficult to foresee. Decisions on whether to change or not to change are often made on the basis of overly simplistic assumptions.

Factors in deterrence

Severity and credibility of the threat. According to common sense, the motivating force of the threat of punishment will normally increase with the severity of the penalty and the risk of detection and conviction. It is a fair assumption that most offenses would not have been committed if the potential offender foresaw a 50 percent risk of being detected and receiving a severe prison sentence. Even in this situation there would, of course, be exceptions: cases of psychopathological crime, crime under extreme emotional stress, certain political crimes, and so on.

Since Beccaria it has been generally accepted that certainty of punishment is more important than severity, and research gives some support for this assumption. Such a simple formula needs qualifications. For example, in the field of white-collar crime a fine may be considered merely a business expense, whereas a prison sentence, through its stigmatizing character, may act as a strong deterrent. But if the level of penalties is already very high, it seems probable that further increases in severity will yield diminishing returns. Moreover, excessively severe penalties may be counterproductive by reducing the risk of conviction. When the penalties are not reasonably attuned to the gravity of the violation, the public is less inclined to inform the police, the prosecuting authorities are less disposed to prosecute, and juries are less apt to convict. Thus, Frederick Beutel, by comparing the enforcement and effects of bad-check laws in Nebraska and Colorado, found that the strict laws of Nebraska were only spottily enforced and that bad checks were rarer in Colorado, where the law was milder but enforcement more uniform and effective (p. 366).

The problem of communication. The motivating effect of criminal law does not depend on the objective realities of law and law enforcement but on the subjective perception of these realities in the mind of the citizen. A change that is not noticed can have no effect. If we intend, for example, to increase the deterrent effect in a certain field by more severe sentences or increased police activity, a crucial question will be whether people will become aware of the change. This aspect did not attract much attention in the classical theory of deterrence. It seemed to be tacitly assumed that there would be an accord between objective facts and subjective perceptions. Survey research into public beliefs and attitudes has demonstrated that this is far from the case. Smaller changes tend to go unnoticed whether they tend toward increased severity or leniency. It seems that most people overestimate the risk of detection and apprehension for criminal acts. It therefore may be doubtful whether perfect information maximizes deterrence. If people were better informed this might reduce their fear of the law.

Types of offenses. The importance of deterrence is likely to vary substantially, depending on the character of the norm being protected by the threat of punishment. Common sense tells one that the threat of punishment does not play the same role in offenses as different as murder, incest, tax fraud, shoplifting, and illegal parking. One distinction of importance is between actions that are immoral in their own right, *mala per se,* and actions that are morally neutral if they were not prohibited by law, *mala quia prohibita.* In the case of *mala per se,* the law supports the moral codes of society. If the threat of legal punishment were removed, moral feelings and the fear of public judgment would remain as powerful crime-prevention forces. In the case of *mala quia prohibita* the law stands alone; without effective legal sanctions the prohibition would soon be empty words. There are, however, great variations within each of the two groups. As Leslie Wilkins stated, "The average normal housewife does not need to be deterred from poisoning her husband, but possibly does need a deterrent from shoplifting" (p. 322).

Another distinction that has been made is between expressive and instrumental acts (Chambliss, pp. 712–719). Expressive acts are committed because they are pleasurable in and of themselves, whereas instrumental acts are committed because they are a means to some other goal. Drug use and murder are mentioned as examples of expressive acts, and parking violations and shoplifting, as examples of instrumental acts. According to Chambliss, the available research suggests that expressive acts are resistant to punishment as a deterrent, whereas instrumental acts are more likely to be influenced by the threat or imposition of punishment. Other authors have found the analytical value of this distinction doubtful (Andenaes, 1974, pp. 85–86; Beyleveld, pp. xxxii–xxxv). In any case, all such generalizations are of limited practical usefulness. A realistic appraisal of the role of deterrence demands a thorough study of the specific offense and the typical motivation of violators.

Differences among persons. People are not equally responsive to legal threats. Some are easily deterred, but others may lack the intellectual or emotional ability to adjust their behavior to the demands of the law. Children, the insane, and the mentally deficient are for this reason poor objects of deterrence. The same holds true for people who lack the willpower to resist the desires and impulses of the moment, even when realizing that they may have to pay dearly for their self-indulgence. Individuals who are well integrated into the social fabric have more to lose by conviction than those on the margin of society. When experts and political decision-makers discuss the deterrent impact of the threat of punishment, there is always a risk that they may draw unjustified conclusions on the basis of experience limited to their own social groups.

Conflicting group norms. The motivating influence of the criminal law may become more or less neutralized by group norms working in the opposite direction. One may think of religious groups opposing compulsory military service, organized labor fighting against a prohibition of strikes, or a racial minority fighting against oppressive legislation. In such cases there is a conflict between the formalized laws of the state and the norms of the group. Against the moral influence of criminal law stands the moral influence of the group; against the fear of legal sanction stands the fear of group sanction, which may range from the loss of social status to economic boycott, violence, and even homicide. Experience shows that the force of the group norm often prevails. In an atmosphere of alienation and antagonism, any attempt at law enforcement, even a well-justified and lawful arrest, may be the signal for an outbreak of violence and disorder, as was the case with the Watts riot of 1965 (President's Commission, pp. 119–120).

Methods of research

In spite of the great importance accorded deterrence in considerations in lawmaking and sentencing, deterrence remained a neglected field of research until about 1970, in part because of ideology and in part because of great methodological difficulties. In subsequent years research activity has been intense. Most of the research falls under the following categories.

Comparison over time. The most straightforward method of exploring the effects of a change in legislation or enforcement on the rate of crime is before-and-after research. The great difficulty in such research is to identify the impact of the change among all the other factors that have been involved at the same time. Only abrupt and major changes can be expected to give clear statistical evidence of the effects. Changes introduced in the system may be accompanied by changes in the tendency of the victims to report the crime or by changes in the practice of crime registration, so that the statistics are not comparable. These difficulties can, to some degree, be overcome by victimization studies undertaken both before and after the reform. Another complicating factor that is often overlooked is the phenomenon of regression to mean. A change in legislation or enforcement can be made as a response to a rising crime rate. If the crime rate decreases after the change in policy, this is easily attributed to the change, whereas the study of a longer time period may suggest that what really happened was the return to a more normal rate, which might have happened anyway.

Perhaps the most important and best-known example of before-and-after research was conducted in connection with the Road Safety Act, 1967, c. 30 (Great Britain), which made it an offense to drive with a blood alcohol concentration of 0.08 percent or more. The penalty is normally a fine and loss of license for one year on the first offense. From the day the new legislation went into effect, there was a considerable drop in highway casualties as compared with previous years. For the first three months casualties were 16 percent lower than in the preceding year, and deaths were down by 23 percent. For the night hours casualties were reduced by about 40 percent. Unfortunately, it seems that most of the effect has gradually been lost. As time passed it became increasingly difficult to isolate the effects of the law, but H. Laurence Ross's conclusion seems well founded: the benefits produced by the legislation had largely been canceled by the end of 1970 (p. 77). Strong support for this conclusion is found in the proportion of drivers killed in road accidents who were found to have more than the prescribed limit of blood alcohol. Before the law this proportion was 25 percent. After the law the figure dropped to 15 percent, but by 1971 it had returned to the earlier level and has continued to increase.

According to Ross, the explanation of this declining effect lies in a lack of enforcement. The publicity accompanying the law had given the public exaggerated and quite unrealistic ideas about the risk of apprehension and conviction, but little effort was made to enforce the law. The police did not perceive the law as defining an important task, and gradually the public learned that it had overestimated the risk. Thus, the experiences with the British drinking-and-driving law

have demonstrated that it is possible, at least in some fields, to change behavior by the threat of punishment, and also that an initial success will not endure if there is not sufficient enforcement to make the threat credible.

Comparison between geographic areas. A second method is to compare areas with differences in legislation, in sentencing, or in law enforcement, to see whether these differences are reflected in crime rates. This method was used in research on capital punishment as early as the 1920s, by comparing murder rates in retentionist and abolitionist states. Beginning in the late 1960s the method of geographical comparison has been widely used for different types of crime, by both sociologists and economists, who have used various statistical techniques in order to discover the effects of differences in certainty and severity of sanction. The great bulk of American research in deterrence from the late 1960s consists of such cross-sectional studies. Most of the studies use the individual states as units of comparison, base themselves on official statistics, and are limited to the seven index crimes (homicide, assault, sex offenses, robbery, burglary, larceny, and auto theft, as enumerated by the Federal Bureau of Investigation).

The research has almost invariably found an inverse relationship between certainty of punishment (or rather certainty of imprisonment) and crime rates. Some, but not all, of the researchers have found a similar but mostly lower relationship between severity of punishment (normally measured in length of prison sentences) and crime rates. The findings are, however, difficult to interpret. A few points should be mentioned:

1. Most of the studies do not try to distinguish between effects of deterrence and effects of incapacitation. The effects they ascribe to deterrence may in fact be a result of the incapacitation of offenders sentenced to prison.
2. A correlation between crime rates and severity and certainty of sanction does not in itself say anything about the direction of causality. Crime rates may influence severity or certainty of sanction as well as the other way around. The correlation may also be the result of a third factor, for example, the normative climate in a society. Few of the studies tackle these problems in a wholly satisfactory way.
3. The statistical equations have certain built-in assumptions that are not necessarily true.
4. If a study does not find a correlation between crime rates and severity or certainty of sanction, this does not prove that the differences in severity or cer-

tainty are without effect but only that in the given sample the effect is not of a sufficient magnitude to be statistically demonstrable.

For these and other reasons the comparative research should not be accepted uncritically. The highly technical character of such research also constitutes a barrier against practical application until a high degree of agreement among researchers is reached.

Survey research. Survey research can be of interest to the theory of deterrence in many ways. The simplest form of such research consists in collecting data on public knowledge and beliefs about the system of criminal justice. Studies have generally found that such knowledge is low and haphazard. Comparisons over time or between geographical areas of such surveys can be used to explore how perceptions of severity and certainty of punishment vary with actual severity and certainty.

Another type of survey research compares the subjective perceptions of severity and certainty of punishment with rates of self-reported crime. The findings are similar to those of the comparative research based on objective measures of severity and certainty.

The survey method seems especially suitable for research into the moral effects of criminal law. Attitude surveys in England before and after introduction of the blood-alcohol limit (Sheppard) showed that the new statute and the accompanying publicity did not have any tangible effect on the attitudes to drinking and driving. In contrast, a survey study from Norway, where similar but stricter legislation had been in force for forty years, indicated that the law had been successful in reaching the citizens with its message (Hauge). Thus, the two studies taken together give some confirmation to the view that the moral effect of the law depends on a longtime process.

Limits of research

The stream of research papers and the accompanying theoretical discussions have above all clarified the methodological problems and illustrated the limitations of different research methods. The research has produced fragments of knowledge that can be of use to check and supplement commonsense reasoning, which will have to be relied on for a long time to come. There is a long way to go before research can give quantitative forecasts about the effect on crime rates of contemplated changes in the system. Some researchers have tried to quantify their findings. The best-known example is Isaac Ehrlich's controversial work on the effects of capital punishment on the murder rate. According to Ehrlich, statistics on the use of capital punishment in the United States in the years from 1933 to 1969 indicated that each execution in this period had prevented seven to eight murders. Such quantitative assessments seem clearly premature.

It may be asked how far the problems of deterrence are at all researchable. The long-term moral effects of criminal law and law enforcement are especially hard to isolate and quantify. Some categories of crime are so intimately related to specific social situations that generalizations of a quantitative kind are impossible. One may think of race riots, corruption among politicians and public employees, and many types of white-collar crime. An inescapable fact is that research will always lag behind actual developments. When new forms of crime come into existence, such as hijacking of aircraft or terrorist acts against officers of the law, there cannot possibly be a body of research ready as a basis for the decisions that have to be taken. Common sense and trial by error have to give the answers.

JOHANNES ANDENAES

See also CAPITAL PUNISHMENT; CRIMINOLOGY: MODERN CONTROVERSIES; PUNISHMENT; SENTENCING: JUDICIAL FUNCTION.

BIBLIOGRAPHY

ANDENAES, JOHANNES. "General Prevention Revisited: Research and Policy Implications." *Journal of Criminal Law and Criminology* 66 (1975): 338–365.

———. *Punishment and Deterrence.* Foreword by Norval Morris. Ann Arbor: University of Michigan Press, 1974.

BEUTEL, FREDERICK KEATING. *Some Potentialities of Experimental Jurisprudence as a New Branch of Social Science.* Lincoln: University of Nebraska Press, 1957.

BEYLEVELD, DERYCK. *A Bibliography on General Deterrence.* Aldershot, Hampshire, England: Saxon House, 1980. The bibliography also gives summaries of and useful comments to the included studies.

BLUMSTEIN, ALFRED; COHEN, JACQUELINE; and NAGIN, DANIEL, eds. *Deterrence and Incapacitation: Estimating the Effects of Criminal Sanctions on Crime Rates.* Washington, D.C.: National Academy of Sciences, 1978.

CHAMBLISS, WILLIAM J. "Types of Deviance and the Effectiveness of Legal Sanctions." *Wisconsin Law Review* (1967): 703–719.

EHRLICH, ISAAC. "The Deterrent Effect of Capital Punishment: A Question of Life and Death." *American Economic Review* 65 (1975): 397–417. For full references and commentaries to the controversy, see Beyleveld, pp. 184–201, 382–385.

GIBBS, JACK P. *Crime, Punishment, and Deterrence.* New York: Elsevier, 1975.

HAUGE, RAGNAR. "Drinking-and-Driving: Biochemistry, Law, and Morality." *Scandinavian Studies in Criminology* 6 (1978): 61–68. Oslo: Scandinavian University Books, Universitetsforlaget.

President's Commission on Law Enforcement and Administration of Justice, Task Force on Assessment of Crime. *Task Force Report: Crime and Its Impact—An Assessment.* Washington, D.C.: The Commission, 1967.

ROSS, H. LAURENCE. "Law, Science, and Accidents: The British Road Safety Act of 1967." *Journal of Legal Studies* 2 (1973): 1–78.

SHEPPARD, D. *The 1967 Drink-and-Driving Campaign: A Survey among Drivers.* Road Research Laboratory Report LR230. Crowthorne, Berkshire, England: Ministry of Transport, 1968.

WALKER, NIGEL. "Morality and the Criminal Law." *Howard Journal* 11 (1964): 209–219.

WILKINS, LESLIE T. "Criminology: An Operational Research Approach." *Society: Problems and Methods of Study.* Edited by A. T. Welford. London: Routledge & Kegan Paul, 1962, pp. 311–337.

ZIMRING, FRANKLIN E., and HAWKINS, GORDON J. *Deterrence: The Legal Threat in Crime Control.* Foreword by James Vorenberg. University of Chicago Press, 1973.

DEVELOPING COUNTRIES, CRIME IN

Many different social, economic, and technological changes are encompassed by the concept of "development," and ideological and value judgments are often implicit in it. The United Nations, for example, considers as "underdeveloped," "less developed," or "developing" nations not those that lag in their cultural progress but rather those that have failed to achieve an adequate standard of living.

One of the most striking aspects of the developmental process has been a sharp increase in crime. This increase is closely associated with—and results from—such factors as urbanization and industrialization, migration and the ensuing growth of city slums, increased availability of consumer goods, and marked changes in normative behavior standards. Despite some uncertainties about the adequacy of statistical reports gathered from the developing countries, findings almost unanimously indicate that crime in general, and property crime in particular, is rising and fast becoming a major problem in these countries. In fact, crime rates in most developing countries are rising more rapidly than are those of the developed countries. Although they do not always reflect the true extent of crime, the reported figures represent a basic minimum figure. If the actual total amount of crime were known, reported increases would undoubtedly be far greater.

As a result of these marked increases in crime in the developing countries, scarce developmental resources must be diverted to crime control. Additional manpower, transportation, special equipment, and buildings must be provided for police, courts, and prisons. In some instances, for example, street lighting is being improved, largely to guarantee more adequate security.

Urbanization and crime

A dominant characteristic of developing countries is their greatly accelerated rate of urbanization—a rate exceeding that encountered in developed countries. Urban populations in developing countries are growing at a rate of two or three times the corresponding national average, and urban living patterns are rapidly replacing those typical of traditional village life. In their drive for sustained economic growth, developing countries may allow vital resources to concentrate in a single "primate city," or at most in two or three such centers, which hold out the hope of a better life and hence attract burgeoning populations from the countryside. Concurrently, rapidly rising rural populations force the young to seek alternate ways of living in the large urban centers. It is in these cities that crime becomes increasingly concentrated: they generate the motivation and the means to commit crime, and they lower the risk of detection.

Urban life in developing and developed societies alike is marked by heterogeneity, anonymity, rapid social change, materialism, and competitive individualism. In the less developed countries, urban areas often exert a relatively greater influence on the society as a whole than do their counterparts in the developed world. They become the focal points of foreign investment and increasingly visible material wealth, which in turn create enhanced opportunities for committing crime, particularly property offenses. Potential offenders in these settings also have greater contact with experienced criminals and with the "fences" who can dispose of stolen goods. Consequently, such huge cities as Bombay, Calcutta, Bangkok, Seoul, Manila, Caracas, Bogotá, Mexico City, Cairo, Lagos, Abidjan, and Nairobi experience far higher—and more sharply rising—crime rates than their respective countries' national averages. Modernization, in short, maximizes the capacity of urbanization to generate crime in developing countries.

Migrants. Constantly exposed to urban values and necessities, migrants to developing countries' cities face the difficult choice of accepting the urban way of life or trying to sustain some semblance of their former, more traditional way of life in an unfamiliar, even hostile setting. Their sense of community, belonging, and self-importance is usually undermined, if not completely lost, in making the transition from village to city. It is true that many migrants do not commit themselves fully to the city; some return to their villages if they succeed in achieving their economic goals. For others, contacts with relatives or friends who have already settled in the urban area can lessen the impact of radically changed social environments. But as these familiar associates succumb to the city's anonymity, the help they can extend to newcomers diminishes.

Moreover, most migrants who remain in the city find many impediments to a successful life there: work is hard to find, and by the time migrants do find employment they may well have exhausted whatever financial resources they had. Over time, many of them shed their intimate ties and are enveloped in impersonality and anonymity. Those who become permanent city dwellers fall into new social alignments based on the urban criteria of status and importance. Under these circumstances, both the internal psychological and the external social checks on criminal behavior tend to disappear. Migrants who are ultimately drawn into some type of criminal activity are more likely to lack supportive contacts with relatives or friends who might have better prepared them for an urban life that would not be dependent on crime (Clinard and Abbott, 1973, p. 127).

Slums. Population density forces many urban migrants in developing countries to settle in slum neighborhoods with which they have little affinity. In developing and developed countries alike, the slum is the main locus of crime. Not all slums, however, have high crime rates, and such factors as physical condition, socioeconomic status, or population stability do not in themselves predict the incidence of slum crime. Slum communities with low crime rates appear to have a greater degree of unity, more participation in local organizations, broader friendship patterns, and greater stability in family relationships (Clinard and Abbott, 1976). Largely as a result of cultural homogeneity and emphasis on both kin and tribal ties, members of some slum communities manage to escape the high crime rates of more heterogeneous, anonymous, and impersonal communities. Strong primary group bonds within a slum neighborhood appear to lessen the tendency to steal from neighbors and make it more difficult for a stranger to enter the area to commit a crime. Older slum residents help maintain unity within the neighborhood and also help enforce compliance with community rules.

Poverty, differential opportunity, and crime. By definition, developing countries are the poorest (although many Arab countries are exceptions), but this does not explain their generally high crime rates. On the contrary, the increase in economic development and per capita wealth in developing countries has been accompanied by continued increases in the crime rates. Similarly, the high crime rates of many industrialized countries negate the hypothesis that a rising standard of living diminishes crime. In both developing and developed countries, high crime rates are the result not of poverty or bad housing but rather of the subculture that develops within slum areas (Clinard, 1966). Some observers believe that the poverty of the lower classes in developing countries prevents them from using such legitimate means as education to achieve financial security, thus leaving no alternative to illegitimate activities. However, when this differential opportunity theory was tested in a large African city, it was found that economic or educational deprivation did not distinguish offenders from nonoffenders; approximately similar proportions of both groups were unemployed or had little education (Clinard and Abbott, 1973, pp. 176–187). The poverty of the developing countries is thus too simplistic an explanation for the complex process of socialization into criminal norms.

Types of crime

Property crime, which constitutes the bulk of the crimes committed in any city in any country, shows a sharp increase with modernization, a consequence of greater opportunities for theft and of the rising prestige of material possessions as status symbols. Even the simplest object—a used shirt, an iron pipe, a light bulb—can mean money to its possessor because the potential market for any stolen goods is far greater than in most developed countries. Special markets are often readily available in the cities for the disposal of stolen goods. Difficulties in adequately protecting property, and the widespread absence of even the simplest security measures, also present greater opportunities for thieves.

Auto theft generally takes place less frequently in developing countries, where automobiles are scarce and many persons cannot operate them. Quite common, however, is the theft of vehicle wheels, tires, parts, and accessories, all of which have large resale markets, particularly where imports are restricted. Auto thieves often use highly sophisticated techniques to thwart protective devices and to dispose of the vehicles—in many cases by taking them across national borders. Joyriding and vandalism by youths are far less common than in developed countries, but these offenses, as well as check forgery, embezzlement, and the use of stolen credit cards, will probably increase with further modernization.

Robbery with violence or the threat of violence also increases as a country develops. Armed attacks involving robbery of homes as well as trains and highway buses are a growing problem, the latter accompanying the spread of industrial, banking, and commercial enterprises requiring the transport of large sums of money, generally with few guards. The rising incidence of armed robbery is in part a reflection of the more sophisticated criminal techniques that offenders learn while incarcerated in developing countries' growing prison systems.

In both rural and urban areas, many developing countries report rates of violent crimes such as homicide and assault that are much higher than those of developed countries, and this gap may be even larger in view of the underreporting of these crimes that is probably common in less developed societies. Throughout the world, many subcultures encourage violence as a means of settling disputes or as part of their value system, for example, the emphasis on "machismo" in Latin America, and the violent tribal customs of certain African peoples. But as in developed countries, most violent acts originate in disputes between relatives, friends, or acquaintances, and the most frequent offenders appear to be young males, usually in their early twenties.

Interrelated corruption in business and government increases as a country becomes modernized, and it seems most prevalent during the intense phases of industrialization. Such corruption, tending to divert to private use funds that could be channeled into national development, is typical of the transition from a traditional to a rapidly modernizing society, in which nepotistic family and village loyalties continue to take precedence over considerations of national welfare. Observers generally agree that political corruption is an acute problem in most Asian, Latin American, and African countries, with many functionaries and their families amassing large fortunes while in office.

Some common crimes committed by businessmen in developing countries include embezzlement and violations of income tax laws and of import, export, and currency control regulations. Every aspect of governmental activity, even small purchases by official agencies, is often accompanied by an elaborate series of kickbacks, and the granting of licenses and privileges produces much graft. Foreign interests, notably large multinational corporations seeking concessions for purchases of raw materials or sales of their products, become linked to the large-scale corruption of high officials throughout the developing world (Clinard and Yeager, pp. 168–180).

Developing countries have higher rates than developed countries for such offenses as the use of children for illegal purposes. Children are used by adults in stealing, begging, and prostitution, as well as for transporting illicit alcohol or illicit rationed items. Because relatively cheap labor costs permit persons of even moderate means to hire servants, thefts by domestic employees are more commonly recorded. It is impossible to say whether the employees of commercial firms steal more frequently in developed or developing countries. Other offenses that take place more frequently in developing countries include the adulteration of foodstuffs, begging, cattle theft, black marketeering in currency, rioting in times of food shortages, and fighting between villagers or between religious, tribal, and caste groups. Crimes against the political system are also commonly encountered. Some of these offenses may decline with further modernization.

Since it is largely an urban phenomenon, prostitution is probably less common overall in developing countries, which remain predominantly rural. On the other hand, prostitution is generally encountered more frequently in the developing countries' primate cities, with their abnormal sex distribution and scarcity of economic opportunities for unattached women, who are often exposed to prostitution practices. Prostitutes in different developing countries vary by marital status and motives for entering prostitution, although everywhere large percentages of them are migrants from the countryside. By comparison to the situation in developed countries, urban prostitutes in developing countries carry less stigma, and the institution is both more open and less organized.

Most crime in the developing countries is committed by groups, although they vary by organization, size, and behavior. Gangs and other criminal groups provide alternate sources of support for a family unit that has often been severely disrupted by the effects of urbanization. The importance of companions and youth gang membership in the cities of the less developed countries, as in the developed ones, has been indicated in numerous studies. For example, in a study of youth offenders in Accra, Ghana, most of whom were migrants, it was shown that those "who became delinquents were exposed and susceptible to the influence of delinquent associates. Whether manifested in stealing or in prostitution, delinquency is learned predominantly from association with other delinquents" (Weinberg, p. 480).

Responses to crime

Overall planning. The developing countries must recognize that one price for development will probably be a marked increase in crime. They may be able to avoid some impending problems by including crime control policy in their overall development planning, anticipating potential measures at least five to ten years in advance. Developed countries owe part of their chronic problem of high crime rates to the lack of prior long-term planning for crime control. Unfortunately, most developing countries neglect such planning in the widespread but erroneous belief that improvements in general socioeconomic conditions will almost automatically eliminate crime.

Control of urban migration. Most developing countries have had virtually no control over migration from rural areas to cities; this has resulted in a disruption of planned development, overurbanization, and an inability to meet problems of urban life, including crime. The best answers to continued population concentration in primate cities might well be the encouragement of small-scale and cottage industries in the countryside, the development of new, smaller cities, and the dispersion into rural areas of industrial, commercial, and governmental programs. However, the forces impelling urban migration—particularly the attractions of large cities to young people—are so great that the primate cities will continue to grow despite efforts to decentralize and create better employment opportunities elsewhere.

Slum areas. Slum communities ought to become the focal point of efforts to combat crime and other deviant behavior in urban areas (Clinard, 1972). Programs aimed at improving community relations and crime control should be instituted, and slum dwellers must be encouraged to gain a better understanding of what crime means to them and to their communities. They must learn to reduce the use of violence in settling disputes, to help unattached young migrants adjust to urban life without resorting to crime, and to help others understand the role of the police and other agencies of social control. A community services department of small political units or wards (each embracing one to five thousand persons) can set up slum organizations, in which some degree of local leadership, initiative, and organization can be expected. Slum residents willing to help combat crime can always be found. Improvement of slum conditions de-

pends largely on the motivation and interest generated by indigenous community leaders, who must therefore be allowed to assume direct responsibility for initiating change (Clinard, 1966, pp. 166–187).

Education. The less developed countries must recognize the inverse relationship that exists between education, on the one hand, and urban drift and criminality, on the other. Educational programs must offer vocational training and must be geared toward employment opportunities. They should emphasize mechanical and agricultural skills, so that youth in the countryside may participate in small-scale rural development. Alone, such programs may not be effective in controlling the criminal behavior of young people: there must also be more direct education in traditional social values, in problems of regional, clan, and tribal relationships, and in understanding national objectives. Unfortunately, education in developing countries has often followed the formal Western model, generally ignoring problems of acculturation and seldom preparing students for the specific demands of modernization. However, several less developed countries have established youth service programs to absorb the large numbers of unemployed youth and to channel surplus labor into public works and rural settlement projects.

Preventing corruption. Although an integral part of the developmental process, corruption can be controlled through strong preventive measures. Concerted efforts can be made to promote more resistance to corruption among civil servants. It is difficult to eradicate corruption in any rapidly developing country, but civil servants do become less corruptible if they are well indoctrinated and disciplined and if they are provided with opportunity to advance in salary and status. Leaders, particularly cabinet ministers, must play an especially vital role in recognizing the dangers posed by political corruption and in guiding the behavior of their subordinates.

Crime prevention and law enforcement. Adoption of security measures that are commonplace in developed countries may have a great impact on crime rates in less developed countries. Such precautionary measures as the wider use of checks, and improved security in transporting company payrolls or large sums of currency to and from banks, would prevent many crimes. Although check usage might cause increased forgery, the losses would not be nearly so great as those from currency theft. Banks could be more widely used for holding cash funds now secreted in houses, and as repositories for such convertible wealth as jewelry. Business firms should install more burglar alarms and other protective systems. The homes of the poor need simple locks, and business concerns, as well as the houses of wealthy persons, should have greater protection through the use of night watchmen (either privately or jointly), watchdogs, barred windows, and improved lighting. To prevent shoplifting in supermarkets, greater control should be exercised over displays of valuable goods, more shop assistants hired, and closed-circuit television considered. Automobiles should be outfitted with security devices such as steering-wheel locks.

Well-trained police forces equipped with patrol cars and radios can serve an important role in developing countries. Although their primary function may still, as in colonial days, be one of maintaining order and enforcing the law, police can also contribute in more active ways: educating the public in simple techniques of crime prevention, and promoting community organization, particularly in high-crime slums. Great emphasis must be placed on the role of police forces in national development.

Prisons. Most developing countries rely heavily on imprisonment, a method of punishment and deterrence inherited from colonial times. Prisons, if effectively run, are extremely costly, and they should be used only for serious, habitual offenders for whom no alternatives are feasible. Some developing countries have initiated compulsory work programs, under which prisoners pay their debt to society by participating in industrial or agricultural projects. Such programs contribute to general development, and some countries even seek to extract a profit from them, which, of course, should not be their primary purpose. Other alternatives to imprisonment include fines, victim restitution, probation, community service, and partial confinement in the local community. All of these alternatives are relatively inexpensive, and some (particularly compulsory work and community service) may actually promote developmental objectives.

MARSHALL B. CLINARD

See also COMPARATIVE CRIMINAL LAW AND ENFORCEMENT, *articles on* CHINA, ISLAM, *and* PRELITERATE SOCIETIES; CRIME CAUSATION, *articles on* POLITICAL THEORIES *and* SOCIOLOGICAL THEORIES; CRIME STATISTICS: HISTORICAL TRENDS IN WESTERN SOCIETY.

BIBLIOGRAPHY

BAYLEY, DAVID H. *The Police and Political Development in India.* Princeton, N.J.: Princeton University Press, 1969.

BILES, DAVID, ed. *Crime in Papua New Guinea.* Canberra: Australian Institute of Criminology, 1976.

CLIFFORD, WILLIAM. *An Introduction to African Criminology.* Nairobi, Kenya: Oxford University Press, 1974.

CLINARD, MARSHALL B. *Slums and Community Development.* New York: Free Press, 1966.

———. "Urban Planning for Crime and Delinquency Prevention." *A Policy Approach to Planning in Social Defence.* United Nations, Department of Economic and Social Affairs. New York: United Nations, 1972, pp. 32–65.

———, and ABBOTT, DANIEL J. "Community Organization and Property Crime: A Comparative Study of Social Control in the Slums of an African City." *Delinquency, Crime, and Society: Symposium on Juvenile Delinquency.* Edited by James F. Short, Jr. University of Chicago Press, 1976, pp. 186–206.

———. *Crime in Developing Countries: A Comparative Perspective.* New York: Wiley, 1973.

CLINARD, MARSHALL B., and YEAGER, PETER C. *Corporate Crime.* With the collaboration of Ruth Blackburn Clinard. New York: Free Press, 1980.

HEIDENHEIMER, ARNOLD J. *Political Corruption: Readings in Comparative Analysis.* New York: Holt, Rinehart & Winston, 1970.

LÓPEZ-REY, MANUEL. *Crime: An Analytical Appraisal.* New York: Praeger, 1970.

MILNER, ALAN, ed. *African Penal Systems.* New York: Praeger, 1969.

TIBAMANYA MWENE MUSHANGA. *Crime and Deviance: An Introduction to Criminology.* Kampala, Uganda: East African Literature Bureau, 1976.

United Nations, Department of Economic and Social Affairs. *A Policy Approach to Planning in Social Defence.* New York: United Nations, 1972.

United Nations, Secretariat. *Report of the Sixth United Nations Congress on Prevention of Crime and the Treatment of Offenders, Caracas, Venezuela, 25 August–5 September 1980.* Documents A/CONF/87/14 Rev./ and A/CONF/87/14/Add. 1. New York: United Nations, 1980.

WEINBERG, S. KIRSON. "Juvenile Delinquency in Ghana: A Comparative Analysis of Delinquents and Non-delinquents." *Journal of Criminal Law, Criminology, and Police Science* 55 (1964): 471–481.

WEITZ, RAANAN, ed. *Urbanization and the Developing Countries: Report on the Sixth Rehovot [Israel] Conference.* New York: Praeger, 1973.

DEVIANCE

The term *deviance* came into common use among social scientists in the early 1950s to designate what may broadly be called social problems. Although the study of social problems was closely intertwined with the early development of sociology in the United States and Great Britain, the two fields eventually separated as mainstream sociologists became more sensitive to the possible influence of value judgments on their work and as they grew self-conscious about methodology. Social problems were at first conceived of in terms of conditions or situations believed to be socially harmful and in need of ameliorative action by a substantial number of people. This view was consistent with democratic philosophy and American pragmatism, but it ran counter to the pretensions of those seeking to make the study of social problems scientific.

Social pathology

A somewhat more scientifically tenable conception of social problems was that of social pathology. This perspective drew heavily upon the theory of evolution, and it identified social pathology with individual failures to adjust or adapt to the evolving institutions of society. Social pathologists, as they came to be called, focused on such problems as crime, delinquency, alcoholism, mental disorders, physical handicaps, and illness, but they also included among pathologies phenomena that were less obviously individual: unemployment, divorce, illegitimacy, and child neglect. The perspective of social pathology remained viable so long as social change continued to be equated with social progress and so long as the evolutionary theory of institutional change prevailed.

The conception of social pathology helped to organize thought and discussion about social problems, but it did not produce any well-articulated theory from which hypotheses could be drawn for systematic testing. The format for the discussion of social problems was laid down in college textbooks in the synthetic tradition of Herbert Spencer (1820–1903), embracing a variety of loosely collated information about these problems' causes, effects, and proposed solutions. A more systematic application of the pathology metaphor came in social work, which in its early years of growth was closely allied with sociology. Practitioners in the field applied schemes for the study, diagnosis, and treatment of individual maladjustments, especially those of children. These epitomized what subsequently came to be referred to as the medical model of deviance, a conception still having advocates, especially in the study of alcoholism, drug addiction, and mental disorders.

Conceiving of social problems and deviance as individual pathologies became less tenable as the idea of evolution lost favor in the 1920s and as anthropologists challenged the presumed superiority of Western institutions with detailed ethnographic studies of primitive cultures and functional interpretations of moral practices. Repercussions from the events of the 1930s, including totalitarian revolutions abroad and the Great Depression, further weakened the hold of social pathology on sociologists. Massive increases in unemployment within a few short years, for example, could scarcely be attributed to individual failures of adjustment.

Social disorganization

Although by 1940 social pathologists had begun to write about the pathologies of institutions, the theoretical preferences of most sociologists shifted to the perspective of social disorganization. This shift emphasized "dyssensus," uneven change, conflict, and inconsistencies between culture and emerging science and technology as sources of social problems. Much of what now is called deviance was then conceived of as symptoms of the underlying dilapidation of institutions and the failure of societies to achieve integrated change.

Social-disorganization theory derived from the writings of Charles Cooley on the consequences of changed means of communication and transportation for modern social organization and from the work of W. I. Thomas and Florian Znaniecki on problems attending foreign immigration to American cities after the turn of the twentieth century. The theory gained empirical substance from the lively development of ecological research by University of Chicago sociologists. They borrowed directly from plant and animal ecology to create a methodology for demarcating areas of a city according to socioeconomic characteristics, including various "indices of social disorganization": crime, delinquency, mental disorders, and drug addiction. These were seen as products of natural processes, such as competition and accommodation, which in some areas led to the breakdown of social control and the growth of deviance. The theory stated that deviance sometimes becomes organized into subcultures and behavior systems, such as professional theft. This contrapuntal tendency, when conjoined with findings from ethnographic research on vice and crime in the Italian slums of eastern cities, made it problematic whether patterns of deviance in ethnic areas were signs of social disorganization or merely differentiated but organized ways of living, integrated through accommodations with the dominant social organization of the city. In any case, the social disorganization perspective on deviance was weakened by the uncertainty of its distinction between social and personal disorganization and by the difficulty of separating social organization, social disorganization, and social reorganization.

Functionalism

The 1940s and 1950s saw the rise to eminence of functionalist conceptions of deviance, which broke sharply with the dichotomy between the pathological and the normal, holding that deviant as well as conforming behavior contributed positively to the stability and perpetuation of social systems. Much of the analysis in this vein bore a strong affinity with Emile Durkheim's version of society as a system in which the punishment of criminals, for example, was a ritual reaffirmation of the central values (collective representations) that provided the basis for conformity and social integration.

Functional analysis was an artful way of interpreting the seeming anomaly by which historically old forms of deviance persist in the face of social disapproval and efforts at their elimination. Prostitution, for example, was shown to serve biological, psychological, and social needs, ultimately reinforcing the values of family life. Functional analysis was applied also to jealousy, poverty, vice, gambling, graft, and political corruption. The last two were stated to have positive latent functions, as opposed to their more obvious effect of encouraging crime and social problems. Through financial and other support, organized crime thus made possible the existence of political parties, without which the constitutionally separated branches of American government would not have had the necessary unity to govern. Organized crime also provided alternative channels of upward mobility for economically underprivileged and educationally handicapped members of ethnic groups.

A narrower, middle-level type of functional interpretation was applied to the role of deviant individuals within groups. This interpretation held that, contrary to the impression that groups summarily eject deviants, they cherish and sustain such persons as a means of clarifying group norms, of establishing group boundaries, and of providing a base point for distinguishing and rewarding degrees of individual compliance with these norms. An extension of this line of analysis held that the amount of crime in a community tends to be constant but that the portion of it which is selected out, defined as such, and punished varies with the degree to which community values are threatened.

The logical and methodological difficulties of functional analysis in general are well known (Davis). Demonstrating that a particular pattern of behavior is necessary or contrary to the working of society is not easily done, particularly when it takes place only once or occasionally. The only real test of functional necessity is whether or not members of a society can get along without the pattern in question. Whether, as Durkheim contended, the amount of crime in a society is a measure of its health and whether a society of saints would invent or create deviance if none existed, must remain hypothetical questions, not readily testable if at all.

Functionalist thought concludes that both conformity to norms and deviance promote societal integration, which has prompted the comment that the functionalists "would have it both ways" (Davis). At best, functionalism calls attention to the positive values that otherwise socially disapproved actions may have under certain circumstances. Conversely, dysfunctional consequences of conventional behavior can be shown to contribute to the genesis of deviance. But this changes the basis of discourse to social criticism and ideological controversy, for functionalist theory has no viable way of dealing with value conflict. Functionalism leaves untouched the question of how human beings recognize and organize actions concerning which there is no value consensus.

In other words, the functionalist perspective on deviance does not provide for choice. Although values have their place in the scheme of functionalism, active evaluation in the sense of weighing, deliberating, and choosing among alternative courses of individual and collective action does not. Values for functionalists become a kind of script specifying actions that flow mainly from the social system to the individual actor. Under such conditions, social control of action becomes reactive and mechanistic, made plausible by the assumption of a consensus of values in the system.

However, a different conception of social control is required if the analysis of deviance recognizes the pluralist and dynamic proliferation of values characteristic of modern industrial societies. Harmful forms of behavior must be perceived as such by persons or groups in power before social control can be applied to those responsible. How this happens requires a complex understanding of social dynamics, which involve the interaction of groups, the aggregation of values, and actual forms of behavior. The important question is not whether social control is reactive or proactive, but rather how it works with other factors to produce a particular type of deviance.

In small groups, signs of "trouble" or a "problem" may be explained and justified as normal, or perceived as deviance to be accommodated. But this may or may not lead to effective social control. Moreover, the effect of these control measures—whether the deviant is sustained, kept within the group through accommodation, or ejected and ostracized—may prove either favorable or unfavorable to increasing group integration. The structure and morale of groups may be strengthened or weakened by accommodations with deviants, as well as by their removal. The probability of either outcome is best explored by an analysis of group processes, extended sufficiently through time to have a historical dimension.

Carefully studied, Durkheim's functionalism proves to be less distinctive and consistent than it has been represented. His conclusion that crime is "normal," universal, and no more than the differentiation of individuals defined as criminal by the collective conscience has much in common with labeling theory. Opposed to this was his conception of suicide as abnormal and "pathological," not created by the collective conscience. It indicated a "morbid disturbance" in society manifested by an increase in collective sadness and melancholy expressed in philosophy and revolutionary ideologies. This "morbidity" in turn resulted from accelerated evolution, which uprooted established institutions without putting anything in their place.

Durkheim's theory that the attenuated bonds between the individual and society are the sources of suicide is not too far removed, when closely scrutinized, from the social-disorganization theories of Thomas and Znaniecki and of Cooley. The resemblance is strongest in the work of the first two writers, who defined social disorganization as a decline in the influence of rules of behavior over individual members of the group. In contrast to Durkheim, however, these writers gave attention to the differential effects of declining social control by interposing personality types with differing reactions to disorganization.

Social structure, anomie, and deviance

An effort to combine functionalism with social disorganization theory appeared in Robert Merton's 1938 essay "Social Structure and Anomie," whose argument subsequently became generalized in the literature as a strain theory of deviance. Merton sought to account for differences in the rates of deviance among societies and among different strata within the same society. In this formulation (which stimulated a large amount of research), strain derived from discontinuity between a cultural structure that inculcated mass-based achievement goals and a social (class) structure that for some portions of the population limited access to institutionally prescribed means for their attainment. The various responses to anomie were called modes of adaptation, depending on the special relationship of ends to means. For example,

crime and delinquency were classified as innovation in that the cultural goals were accepted but illegal means were developed to reach them, in contrast to other possible modes, such as withdrawal, ritual conformity, or rebellion.

Merton's scheme for showing how blocked opportunities for upward mobility produced high crime rates in lower social classes distantly resembles the Marxist theory of crime and deviance, but without any reference to concerted exploitation by a privileged class. The rebellion mode in his model, involving the rejection of established goals and means and the creation of new ones, implied conflict, but at an individual rather than a collective level. Moreover, the theory explicitly rejected the simple idea that poverty was a cause of crime; lack of privilege had to be accompanied by rising material aspirations in order to generate anomie and innovative deviance as modes of adaptation.

It is difficult to set aside entirely the notion that structurally induced strain plays some part in the causation of crime, but research efforts to demonstrate the relationship have proved to be inconclusive. The theory for the most part foundered on the difficulties of finding empirical indicators for anomie and empirical distinctions between ends and means. Futhermore, strain theory ignored the long-standing concern of sociologists with groups, culture, and subculture as influences in the production of crime and delinquency. Finally, there is little in anomie theory that considers the variable meanings which socially structured situations may have for different individuals. The theory leaps broadly from a generally described social structure to individuals, with faint regard for the possible complexities of their motivations.

Although externally produced strain, frustration, and lack of economic opportunity are not without importance in understanding how crime and delinquency emerge, they are by no means simple, unidimensional influences. Rather, they frequently occur in a context of multiple conflicting claims made by other persons and groups of varying significance to the individual affected. Whether rigidities of overall social structure are actually the chief source of such conflict or strain is not easy to demonstrate. As Raymond Firth showed in his 1961 study of Polynesian suicides, conflicting obligations without tenable solutions produce the risk of deviance but do not specify the form that the outcome of the conflict situation takes. An explanatory model that focuses on the assessment and taking of risks, already applied in some interpretations of suicide, may have more general use for other forms of deviance as a way to make the connection between social structures, symbolic meanings, and acts. Such a theory has been applied, for example, to explain certain forms of check forgery.

Labeling theory

Although Merton's structural theory of anomie and deviance lived on in an uneasy alliance with social-disorganization theory, it was eclipsed in the 1950s by the meteoric rise of what is commonly referred to as labeling theory. The origins of the new theory were somewhat diverse, but generally it is understood to be the collective result of essays and research by sociologists variously known as the Neo-Chicagoans, the West Coast School, or the Pacific Seminar. The common thread running through their work derived from social behaviorism or the perspective of symbolic interaction as formulated by George Mead. This perspective led to a primary emphasis on understanding the process of becoming deviant rather than on the identification of the causes of deviance. The Neo-Chicagoans departed more sharply than the functionalists from the concept of social pathology primarily because they insisted on a full appreciation and naturalistic description of deviance that included the subjective viewpoint of persons labeled as deviant. To a large extent the labeling perspective shifted the focus of analysis away from the attributes of individuals as causes of deviance and toward the ways in which persons were typified as deviant and subjected to social penalties, corrections, treatment, and welfare ministrations. When such social control was depicted as a process, perceived subjectively from the retrospective positons of the participants, it took on new and different meanings often drawn from the vocabularies of the deviants themselves and recast by the sociologist. The discourse of labeling theory was liberally colored with irony and studded with paradoxes as contrasts were drawn between the benign purposes and pretensions of social control and its consequences as revealed in detailed ethnographies of deviance.

Secondary deviance. One of the more provocative concepts linked with labeling theory is that of secondary deviance, which calls attention to the way in which criminal corrections, welfare services, or psychiatric treatment may actually exacerbate the deviance they seek to change or eliminate. Older antecedents of the notion of secondary deviance lay in the dilemma of welfare, in which the giving of charity perpetuated the status or condition of dependency that it was designed to alleviate. Scattered observations in the nineteenth-century psychiatric literature noted how placing emotionally disturbed persons in asylums often converted transitory symptoms of insanity into permanent conditions. Ample corroboration of this untoward consequence of "treatment" can be found in the history of military psychiatry. Psychologists have also contributed evidence that a psychophysical basis exists for certain kinds of circular maladaptive responses in individuals that fit the concept of secondary deviance; and they have shown how "bad habits" such as alcoholism can be activated by the very means that individuals adopt in an effort to prevent the recurrence of their drinking. Clinical psychologists working in the area of speech correction have developed theories of stuttering that favor a process interpretation over a causal one. This process explanation focuses on the way negative reactions by parents and others to normal speech variation in small children generate anxiety that disrupts their speech rhythms.

Still other evidence for the validity of the secondary deviance concept is found in the phenomena of opiate addiction and alcoholism, most dramatically in cases of the former. Unless the individual has a large income, the heavy use of heroin necessarily alters his whole life-style under the urgent necessity of securing a supply of the drug, made extremely costly by legal prohibition of its use. Whatever problems originally motivated the drug's use are now replaced by the individual's need to support his habit. Typically, this means turning to crime by male users and to prostitution by females. The addict's participation in a specific subculture, the constant threat of arrest, and the ever-present imminence of painful withdrawal symptoms combine to produce a highly distinctive pattern to this kind of deviance.

Whether delinquency and crime in general change from primary to secondary deviance is less clear. Arrest and juvenile court statistics have not been conclusive in showing that labeling youths as delinquent produces further delinquency. Quite possibly, negative findings in such research do little more than document that mere contact with control agencies does not necessarily have a significant impact on youths if it does not in itself create problems requiring adaptive changes. Indeed, in some instances the experiences may have a deterrent effect on the further commission of delinquent acts. However, lengthy incarceration, continued surveillance by police and probation officers, and community rejection obviously pose secondary problems for youths, such as educational retardation and a sense of injustice. Yet even when a youth becomes a labeled and self-defined juvenile delinquent, he still may mature or phase out of his delinquency. Why some delinquents persist in a pattern leading to adult crime is not well understood, but the probability that the effects of punitive social control play a part in such transitions is not easily dismissed.

Criticisms of labeling theory. The labeling theory of deviance has provoked a variety of criticisms, some valid and some spurious. Criminologists in the positivist tradition understandably were affronted by its disregard of individual attributes as a cause of crime, as well as by the labeling assumption that "hidden" delinquency and crime occurs substantially among nondelinquents as well as among those arrested and processed by courts. From the labeling perspective, law enforcement thus becomes arbitrary, with arrests and court convictions for crime seen to be more influenced by extralegal factors than by due process of law.

A closely related criticism of labeling theory is that it discounts or ignores the importance of the behavior or the etiology of acts that result in deviance. More generally, the theory is faulted for its cultural relativism—its insistence that it is the sociocultural meaning of acts rather than the acts per se, as they are defined by the penal code, that produces deviance. Positivists have tried to settle this issue by holding that certain kinds of acts, such as robbery and homicide, have been defined as crimes throughout recorded history and that all people so regard them. This revives an old controversy going back to attempts to demonstrate the cross-cultural reality of crime by showing how it violates universally held sentiments.

But efforts of this sort have not been successful. About the only thing that crimes can be shown to have in common is that they are violations of law. When viewed in the context of different societies, the social-defining process by which crime emerges is quite clearly culturally based, although the ideas or conceptions of crime may resemble one another among societies. When closely scrutinized, tremendous variations can be found in the circumstances of actions that are reacted to as crime, the persons involved, the particular acts, the kinds of values threatened or destroyed by the acts, and the means and motivations for their social control. The variation is sufficiently diverse to render any universal categories of crime of small value in predicting action to apprehend and punish wrongdoers.

The theoretical stand of the positivists of course can still be adopted at the level of single societies by assuming approximate consensus and acceptance of state definitions of criminal deviance as well as comparative uniformity in the administration of justice. The acts or attributes of arrestees ipso facto can be treated as independent variables in the production of deviance. A reflection of the importance attached to this issue is evident in research on the correspondence between official crime reports and self-reports of criminal offenses. Some findings indicate similarities between the two measures insofar as serious offenses are concerned. There are also some preliminary indications from research that the attrition of cases in the criminal justice process is more affected by the amount and nature of evidence than by extralegal factors. However, conclusions from such investigations must remain tentative since labeling theorists and their opponents are known to draw different conclusions from the same data. Thus it can be held with equal facility that legal "evidence" is socially constituted or, conversely, the product of technical proof of facts.

The concept of process and deviance

To the extent that they have discussed the matter, partisans of labeling theory protest that requiring the theory to prove itself by the traditional methods of science is inappropriate since the theory assumes that deviance is an emergent quality of acts resulting from symbolic interaction in the social affairs of everyday life. This stance turns attention to the meaning of the terms *interaction, emergence,* and *process* and to the particular ways in which they have been employed in writing and research. More precise queries can be raised as to where process analysis begins, what forms process takes, what kind of time span it embraces, and whether processes can be described in universalistic terms apart from their cultural content. Needless to say, a great deal of confusion and inconsistency clouds such questions, a condition aggravated by the failure of the authors of many deviance studies to give the location in time and their geographic locale.

An early version of the labeling process was described by Frank Tannenbaum in 1938 as the "dramatization of evil," in which petty intrusions by children, such as playing ball in city streets or "pinching" fruit from stands, were elaborated into official delinquency by progressive conflict between the children and the police. In the course of this interaction, new issues entered—disrespect for authority and justice—which then transformed minor irritations into evil acts. In retrospect, Tannenbaum's figurative statement has to be understood as a historian's critique of American penal practices, which he saw as an anachronistic survival of scapegoating based on ancient Hebraic absolutist morality. Tannenbaum's ideas did not initiate labeling theory; they lay fallow in the literature for several decades, to be rediscovered after the theory appeared.

Although Mead's writings are ordinarily credited with fostering the perspective to which labeling theorists give their allegiance, there is little to be found in his works dealing with deviance. This is understandable because his social psychology, in contrast to the French-inspired collective psychology that it replaced, did not oppose the individual to the group. Nor did it perpetuate the dichotomy between social and antisocial behavior, normal and pathological, that is inherent in the conception of the processes of social life as associative and dissociative. Self and society for Mead were simply aspects of a unitary, or reciprocal, process, whether the self's behavior was moral or immoral, conventional or criminal.

Mead's one contribution to criminology (on the psychology of punitive justice), like Tannenbaum's discussion of the dramatization of evil, was written as a critical commentary on the archaic nature of contemporary criminal justice, which through intransigent stigmatization of the "jailbird" made his rehabilitation unlikely. Mead called this process the "modern organization of taboo" and as counterpoint noted with approval the emerging ideology of individualized justice exemplified by the then newly established juvenile court.

A number of writers credit Edwin Lemert with originating the theory of labeling, although the recurring emphasis in his work was on the societal reaction to deviance rather than on labeling per se. Lemert's *Social Pathology* reflected the dominant influence of University of Chicago sociology of the time, including the ideas of Mead, but it was also informed by the Thomas-Znaniecki view that individuals in disorganized environments respond creatively as well as pathologically. This approach, when joined with Lemert's comparative anthropological perspective, allowed that deviant persons could, under specific conditions, adapt reasonably well to their problems. Accordingly, definitions of deviance had to be understood not simply in interactional terms but also in their historical and cultural contexts.

There are several themes in Lemert's ideas, not all consistent, having their sources in behaviorism, topological psychology, and the legal realist school of jurisprudence. Although stating that analysis should begin with social differentiation, he recognized the existence of deviance from accepted modes of behavior, a deviance to which society or the community reacted with moral disapproval and various kinds of social control. However, in addition to this "substantive" deviance there was putative deviance—social disapproval, penalties, segregation, and stigmatization of persons, without the prerequisite of deviation from accepted behavior. In a rough way the two alternative processes were brought together in the concept of secondary deviance, which left the door open for causal research into deviation while shifting the interpretation to process in the analysis of the experiences of deviant persons, with a completely noncausal process explanation of deviance—for example, in stuttering and witchcraft.

Labeling theory received its most explicit statement in the writings of Howard Becker, apparently undertaken at the behest of his mentor, Everett Hughes. An interest in the social psychology of occupations led Becker to study dance band musicians and to conceive of them as a deviant group. In an article on the process of becoming a marijuana smoker, Becker followed Mead by depicting the process as essentially symbolic learning, in which the neophyte smoker's physiological sensations and reactions are explained and defined in interaction with other smokers. In Becker's formal exposition of labeling theory, process was conceived of as the creation of rules by a group, which invoked them to impose the status of "outsider" on any individual not in the group. In developing the theory, Becker devised a fourfold table showing possible combinations of rule-breaking and labeling. These included "secret deviance"—rule-breaking without labeling—which was inconsistent with his postulate that deviance is constituted by labeling. Becker's table also introduces something other than the point of view of the deviant as a source of data for the study of deviance. Making rule-breaking a prior condition of becoming deviant also raised the nagging question of whether labeling theory, so stated, did not betray affinities with more traditional positivist theories of deviance.

Erving Goffman's work, which did much to popularize the interactionist perspective on deviance, drew directly from Mead's conception of socialization as a form of dramatic play and gaming. Dramaturgic analysis, as elaborated by Goffman, portrayed deviant life as a theater in which individuals striving to present the self in the best possible light resort to a variety of adaptive devices in order to avoid or minimize the invidious implications of physical stigma and moral blemish. One of Goffman's more insightful contributions to the study of process likened becoming a mental patient to a "moral career" made up of unforeseen situations confronting the individual and degrading his status as he moved from prepatient to ex-patient. Although Goffman, like Becker, wrote from the perspective of the deviant "underdog" individual, in the seldom-cited article "The Insanity of Place" he reversed his view to detail how the mentally disturbed person disrupts the private order of the family system.

David Matza made a sustained effort to deal with process issues in *Becoming Deviant,* which addressed underlying epistemological questions and strongly urged social scientists to shift to a naturalist view of the subject. Positivism is replaced by what Matza called "soft determinism." He proceeded to redefine and incorporate the idea of differentiating attributes of individuals in a naturalistic scheme. In order for deviance to occur, there has to be an *affinity* for some acts, *affiliation* with other persons engaging in deviance, and *signification* by which definitions of the acts are applied to others. Full appreciation of Matza's thinking should not overlook his innovative interpretation of the dynamics of delinquent subcultures, which stands almost alone as an attempt to account for the phasing-out process that appears to be commonplace among delinquents.

The common sense of deviance—ethnomethodology. In some ways, ethnomethodology mounted a stronger revolt against positivism than did the Neo-Chicagoans, but it clung to a concern with social structures or patterns of deviance and social control, primarily to account for the processes by which they come into existence. The originator of the school, Harold Garfinkel, appears to have searched for some kind of synthesis of structural analysis and symbolic interactionism. Works by ethnomethodologists assert that the reality of deviance is socially constructed by aggregating what people say and mean about human actions or situations. The method of inquiry is to observe and depict how those involved go about their "work" of creating deviance through the use of commonsense language in everyday activities. The data are indexical expressions—habitual, routine, or proverbial characterizations by which people sort out and respond to the living tasks with which they are confronted. A frequently cited example of the method outlines the conditions of successful degradation ceremonies (Garfinkel), in which a person is denounced and morally separated from his group by a number of staged maneuvers that redefine the feelings and attitudes of its members toward the deviant.

Ethnomethodologists hold to a commonsense conception of the deviance process and in their own fashion follow the bent of labeling theorists in exposing the way professional specialists go about constructing their assessments of problematic situations that they must define. This they have done with studies of the coding of clinical records, determinations of suicide in death certificates, jury deliberations, and diagnoses by military psychiatrists. In the last case it has been shown how particular situations and expectations in war and combat lead to commonsense decisions by psychiatrists that are divergent from, if not at odds with, their official or professional diagnostic procedures.

Ethnomethodologists have also paid attention to the problem of how patterns of action are maintained. Their contribution here is largely technical. It involves deliberate or systematic disruption of routine activities in order to discover how they are "really" or subculturally organized by taken-for-granted preconceptions of what should take place ordinarily in these activities. In actuality these devices reveal the way in which conventional, rather than deviant, patterns are maintained. Whether these methods are more informative than simple ethnographic observations—for example, observations made of deviant, otherworldly groups—may be debatable. The methods may be more useful for studying social control than for studying deviance.

Ethnomethodology goes beyond the mere presumption of pluralism implicit in labeling theory, for it assumes that manifest social reality is by nature fluid, contingent, and even without meaning, or "absurd," on its face. Substantive rules are discounted as predictors of human action and as the basis for understanding social definitions of deviance. However, ethnomethodology is more than sociology of the happenstance, for it recognizes "rules behind the rules" in the form of background expectancies; these are "deeper" or interpretative rules of a relational nature. They are like rules of the game in determining, for changing situations, such matters as who goes first, who follows, and what choices of action are available.

The micropolitics of trouble. A summary of the oversights of labeling theory includes its neglect of the informal processes leading to deviance and of the reciprocal relationships between informal processes and formal social control. One way of dealing with these questions is to place them in a framework of micropolitics, in which "trouble" rather than rule-breaking initiates the deviance process. This assumes that troubles, large or small, fleeting or persistent, emerge more or less ambiguously in any social setting and that deviance is elaborated by stages, often from quite prosaic beginnings. Such troubles and their remedies may be confined to a personal matter or may involve others. Ordinarily they are "remedied" by normalization or accommodations, in which redefinitions of relationships occur. At a more advanced stage, troubles lead to complaints and the intervention of third parties who are "trouble specialists." Professional ideologies, as well as situational and pragmatic considerations, influence whether troubles are defined as deviance or as conflict. There is no intimation that interaction necessarily moves from trouble to deviance in a unilinear way, nor that coercive or punitive social control will ensue.

This kind of process analysis seems best suited to the study of deviance that involves mental disturbances, misadventures of children, domestic quarrels, assaults, shoplifting, and possibly some rapes. Casting the police in the role of interveners between two aggrieved parties scarcely applies in most instances of burglary, robbery, and murder, in which complaints are made directly to the police and no prior interaction takes place between the victim and the "troublemaker."

Macrocosmic analysis of deviance

During the 1970s the interest of sociologists in deviance turned away from the microanalysis of deviant socialization and the processing of deviants by agencies, toward a greater concern with the dynamics of the societal reaction. It had become obvious that the application of labeling theory too often produced research studies that were astructural and ahistorical. To this was added a critical appreciation that the symbolic interactionist perspective, so useful in studying deviance, did not provide as strong a theoretical basis for the study of social control—perhaps because Mead's social behaviorism could not transcend its focus on the point of contact between the individual and society.

Parenthetically, however, it should be noted that societal-reaction and labeling theories, although not rich in collective theory, were by no means barren in this respect. The first directed attention to the interaction of groups making up the societal reaction and to the spurious quality of reform movements aimed at prostitution and other vices. Labeling theory as well offered an interpretation of the larger process by which the rules defining deviance were created. Such rules were the work of moral entrepreneurs—a special class of righteous people motivated to impose their absolutist moral views on others. They were primarily interested in ends rather than means, and in time they tended to become professional reformers. Becker's conception of the source of new moral ideas, derived from his study of marijuana legislation in the United States, had a good deal in common with Joseph Gusfield's conception of symbolic crusades, which emerged from his study of the American temperance movement. Gusfield described the leaders of this movement and their supporters as a class of people whose absolutist values were threatened by social change and who saw in the Prohibition movement a means of maintaining or reestablishing the dominance of their values.

Although the notion of symbolic politics, under which Becker's and Gusfield's theories are best subsumed, was useful for the study of changing moral ideas, its specifics and limits remained to be worked out. On their face, Gusfield's and Becker's theories are reductionist in the sense that they assign personality traits, common motivations, and similar psychological needs to a class of people who then become the generating force for movements of moral reform. An alternative approach, more suited to understanding moral and legal reform movements in modern pluralist society, stresses the various special purposes served by reform for groups with quite different values.

Thus, an unresolved question is whether symbolic crusades or symbolic politics actually achieve their avowed purposes by the rules and laws they bring about. A plausible interpretation is that legal reforms and their administration often result in negotiations and compromises between coalitions of groups in conflict that reflect the values and purposes of neither side. In some instances only token rules and ritual social control are produced.

The shifting of sociologists' attention to the processes by which deviance definitions change and new ones come to the fore revived interest in older historical studies of legal change, such as the investigation of theft and the law in the changing society of eighteenth-century England, and the emergence of sexual-psychopath laws in twentieth-century America. During the 1960s a number of historical case studies of changing moral and legal conceptions appeared, covering vagrancy laws, the asylum, mental illness, housemaid legislation, the child-saving movement, and marijuana legislation.

The most challenging perspectives on deviance to appear during the 1970s were those of the New Criminology and of conflict theory. The first was an outgrowth of conferences on deviance held in Great Britain. It can best be characterized as a loose merger of labeling theory with Marxist class analysis, English style. The New Criminology more or less ran aground on the question of whether criminal deviants were passive victims of a predatory system of social control or potential recruits for revolutionary action. One consequence of raising this issue was to renew interest in the nature and significance of the deviant act.

American conflict theorists have faulted labeling theory for its undue preoccupation with the effect on deviants of the activities of middle-echelon agents of social control, and for its concentration on the more visible and readily identifiable forms of individual or group deviance. These are held to be relatively insignificant in relation to the destructive actions of persons and groups in positions of power, whose forms of deviance are designated as exploitation, racism, sexism, genocide, and imperialism. Thus, the conflict perspective repudiates the state definition of crime and substitutes an ideological basis for defining deviance and crime by otherwise unspecified groups or institutions. Much of the conflict theory of deviance is called critical sociology, and is given over to the demystification of law and social control. Some of its advocates attempt to clarify the criteria by which deviance is defined in capitalist society through reference to actions that threaten the interests of those holding power in the system. Conflict theory stresses the apparently rational adaptation of means of social control to the narrowly organized materialist purposes of the capitalist class, but it also concludes that such efforts are ultimately defeated by the untoward results, or "contradictions," produced by that control.

It is ironic that some of the most telling criticism of the conflict theory of deviance has come from English Marxists of the so-called Warrick group. Particularly important are the deeply probing historical inquiries into the factors at work in the establishment of the ideology of the law in eighteenth-century England by E. P. Thompson, Douglas Hay, and others. These authors carefully examined the nature of crimes, as well as the growth and administration of the criminal law, seeking to explain specific rather than general features: an increase in crime and an increase in the number of crimes made capital offenses, coupled with comparatively few executions. They concluded that the law was something more than a mere instrument of control in the hands of a landowning class. The ideology of the law contained its own inherent ethic, constraining the actions of landowners, judges, and prosecutors, as well as of offenders, and manifesting itself in distinctive features of the law in action: dramatization (majesty), justice, and mercy.

The politicization of deviance. When attention is given to the background of the law, it becomes apparent that the interest in social control of deviance depends on the extent to which issues in its various areas appear to be settled or unsettled. That is, concern with social control grows as the status of deviants becomes politicized. This concern flourished in the 1960s and 1970s, when a number of social movements were organized to advocate the "rights" and "libera-tion" of various stigmatized populations: homosexuals, prostitutes, welfare recipients, squatters, physically handicapped persons, juvenile delinquents, and prison inmates. The more exuberant radical sociologists urged in general terms that the context of deviance was becoming politicized in that deviants were rejecting the welfare ideology and the rehabilitative or assimilationist ideal. They were described as organizing into alliances for struggle with powerful groups to secure equality with the rest of the population.

Some of the new criminologists and those of the conflict school went on to "disavow" deviance and argue that, given the imminent abolition of the capitalist system, it would no longer be necessary to criminalize deviance. The only true deviants left would be the sick and the handicapped. Other sociologists, more libertarian than radical, asserted that deviance was disappearing and resolving into nothing more than different life-styles. At most, this leaves a residual field of the politics of deviance.

A difficulty in pursuing this line of thought is that the concept of politicization has never been systematically clarified. Critics have pointed out that distinguishing between political and nonpolitical behavior requires a determination of the intent of the actor. It is open to question whether some transcendent moral or political purpose lies behind the manifest deviance and whether the participants are aware of the consequences of their actions. This reproduces all the problems of determining the mens rea accompanying the criminal act. The diversity of participants in radical movements and the unsubstantial nature of their motives are well known to their leaders, a phenomenon that has been discussed elsewhere in connection with "true believers" (Lauderdale). Criminals also are known to have preempted radical movements for their own purposes.

Fully applied, the concept of politicization recognizes how issues of deviance become settled as well as unsettled. Although some forms of behavior may become criminalized, concurrently other forms may be decriminalized. Thus, the status offenses of juveniles—running away, behaving incorrigibly, and playing truant—have been decriminalized to a considerable extent in the United States. At the same time, offenses committed by older juveniles have been increasingly criminalized. It is also true that the opposing processes of decriminalization and criminalization have varied considerably in different jurisdictions. Finally, it must be noted that even though deviant behavior is decriminalized, it may become subject to other forms of restrictive social control.

Conclusion

Although one strand of thinking about the collective dynamics of deviance puts it into the context of politics, another moves it back into the ambit of social problems. But however formulated, thinking about deviance or social problems continues to have a strong psychological and sociological bias.

Criticism of the concept of politicization as reductionist is justified. It is also doubtful whether the emergence of particular social definitions of deviance can be explained by concepts such as hegemony, which convey the extent to which "a way of life and thought" and "its spirit" become institutionalized and morally dominant throughout society. A similar "sociologized" notion is that of "a culture of public problems," which revolves around the rhetoric, fiction, and dramatization of such public concerns as drunken driving. It highlights the monopoly of such problems by authoritative experts and the way their selective perceptions of those problems are built into legal procedures for their control.

Malcolm Spector and John Kitsuse, who are among the chief revisionists of labeling theory, more or less merge the study of deviance into a broader concern with the dynamics of community problems. The sociologist's task, as they see it, is to explain and account for the claims-making activities of individuals and groups with respect to some putative condition. Spector and Kitsuse contend that the process by which social problems are created is exclusively social, and they explicitly reject any need to consider objective conditions which may underlie or help generate the process (p. 74).

The preoccupation of sociologists with perceptions, symbolic representations, and the social creation of the reality of deviance reflects the highly contrived nature of modern society, only parts of which can be known directly. Lacking theoretical models for the inclusion of remote social, economic, physical, and biological factors in their explanations, many sociologists ignore their possible influence, and some even make a virtue of this. As long as deviance studies remain in a limited time frame with cross-sectional rather than longitudinal data, it is possible to ignore what else is happening other than symbolic interaction or the social creation of immediate reality: for example, the daily maintenance of police transportation and communications, the relation of prison populations to bed space, or the availability of foster homes in relation to dispositions of juvenile court cases. When researchers turn to the changing context of deviance, it becomes clear that something other than ideas, culture, and symbolic representations must be taken into account. Granted that individuals and groups impute the objective conditions of social problems and deviance, it does not follow that the imputation is always necessarily social. Furthermore, individuals and groups take heed of the consequences and results of their imputations as gauged by the feedback of information from the objective world (Lemert, 1981).

EDWIN M. LEMERT

See also CRIME CAUSATION: SOCIOLOGICAL THEORIES; CRIMINOLOGY: MODERN CONTROVERSIES; DELINQUENT AND CRIMINAL SUBCULTURES.

BIBLIOGRAPHY

BECKER, HOWARD S. *Outsiders: Studies in the Sociology of Deviance.* New York: Free Press, 1963.

COOLEY, CHARLES H. *Social Organization: A Study of the Larger Mind.* New York: Scribner, 1924.

DAVIS, NANETTE J. *Sociological Constructions of Deviance: Perspectives and Issues in the Field.* 2d ed. Dubuque, Iowa: Brown, 1980.

DURKHEIM, EMILE. *The Rules of Sociological Method* (1895). 8th ed. Translated by Sarah A. Solovay and John H. Mueller. Edited by G. E. G. Catlin. New York: Free Press, 1964.

FIRTH, RAYMOND. "Suicide and Risk-taking in Tikopia Society." *Psychiatry* 24 (1961): 1–17.

GARFINKEL, HAROLD. "Conditions of Successful Degradation Ceremonies." *American Journal of Sociology* 61 (1956): 420–424.

GOFFMAN, ERVING. "The Insanity of Place." *Psychiatry* 32 (1969): 357–388.

GUSFIELD, JOSEPH. *Symbolic Crusade: Status Politics and the American Temperance Movement.* Urbana: University of Illinois Press, 1963.

HAY, DOUGLAS. "Property, Authority, and the Criminal Law." *Albion's Fatal Tree: Crime and Society in Eighteenth-Century England.* By Douglas Hay, Peter Linebaugh, John G. Rule, E. P. Thompson, and Cal Winslow. New York: Pantheon Books, 1975, pp. 17–63.

LAUDERDALE, PAT. "A Power and Process Approach to the Definition of Deviance." *A Political Analysis of Deviance.* Edited by Pat Lauderdale. Minneapolis: University of Minnesota Press, 1980, pp. 3–14.

LEMERT, EDWIN M. "Issues in the Study of Deviance." *Sociological Quarterly* 22 (1981): 285–305.

——. *Social Pathology: A Systematic Approach to the Theory of Sociopathic Behavior.* New York: McGraw-Hill, 1951.

MATZA, DAVID. *Becoming Deviant.* Englewood Cliffs, N.J.: Prentice-Hall, 1969.

MEAD, GEORGE H. "The Psychology of Punitive Justice." *American Journal of Sociology* 23 (1918): 577–602.

MERTON, ROBERT K. "Social Structure and Anomie." *American Sociological Review* 3 (1938): 672–682.

SPECTOR, MALCOLM, and KITSUSE, JOHN I. *Constructing Social Problems.* Menlo Park, Calif.: Cummings, 1977.

TANNENBAUM, FRANK. *Crime and the Community.* Boston: Ginn, 1938.

THOMAS, WILLIAM I., and ZNANIECKI, FLORIAN. *The Polish Peasant in Europe and America* (1918–1920). Reprint. New York: Dover, 1958.

DIFFERENTIAL ASSOCIATION

See CRIME CAUSATION, *articles on* PSYCHOLOGICAL THEORIES *and* SOCIOLOGICAL THEORIES; CRIMINOLOGY: MODERN CONTROVERSIES; DELINQUENT AND CRIMINAL SUBCULTURES.

DIMINISHED CAPACITY

Introduction

For centuries, the criminal law has struggled with the question of how to treat evidence of mental abnormality that does not establish the offender's legal insanity in homicide prosecutions. Regardless of how criminal responsibility standards are defined, there will always be mentally disabled but legally sane defendants who frustrate the criminal law's attempt to draw a sharp line between the "mad" nonresponsible actor and the "bad" culpable offender who merits full punishment. To avoid the apparent injustice of punishing a mentally disabled but sane offender with the same severity as the "normal" killer whose mental capacities were unimpaired at the time of the crime, many jurisdictions have adopted the "diminished capacity" defense to provide a new basis for grading degrees of liability in homicide offenses. Unlike the insanity defense, which, if successful, absolves the defendant of all criminal liability, diminished capacity is only a partial defense. In many jurisdictions, the defense is used to reduce first-degree murder to second-degree murder. A small minority of these jurisdictions also employ the defense to reduce intentional homicide to manslaughter.

Unfortunately, defining what constitutes "diminished capacity" is not a simple task. Courts have fostered considerable doctrinal confusion by using the label to describe two very different principles. In some jurisdictions, the defense authorizes the admissibility of evidence of mental abnormality whenever it is relevant to prove that the defendant did not entertain the mens rea element of the crime charged. A successful "mens rea" defense results in the reduction of the offense to a lesser one that does not require proof of the mental element at issue. While this defense is generally applicable to other crimes, it is raised most frequently in homicide prosecutions. In other jurisdictions, diminished capacity refers to a partial defense of diminished responsibility that usually applies only to homicide crimes. The diminished responsibility defense permits the jury to reduce a first-degree murder charge, whose formal elements (including mens rea) are proven, to second-degree murder or manslaughter whenever the jury believes that the defendant's mental disability reduced his culpability. This article examines whether either version of the diminished capacity doctrine provides an appropriate basis for making grading distinctions among homicide crimes in cases involving mentally abnormal but sane offenders.

The diminished responsibility model: the true diminished capacity defense

The historical roots of the diminished capacity defense can be traced back to the Scottish courts' recognition of a "partial insanity" defense in the mid-nineteenth century. To avoid executing a mentally disabled but sane defendant charged with a capital offense, the Scottish courts used this defense to reduce the punishment of the "partially insane" from murder to culpable homicide, a noncapital offense. In 1957 the British Parliament adopted a modern version of this defense by passing the Homicide Act, 1957, 5 & 6 Eliz. 2, c. 11 (Great Britain), which empowered the fact finder to find the defendant guilty of manslaughter instead of murder if he was suffering from an "abnormality of mind" which "substantially impaired his mental responsibility" for his conduct. The defense permits the jury to return a verdict for manslaughter instead of murder in cases in which it believes that the mentally abnormal but sane defendant is less culpable than his normal counterpart who commits the same crime.

Despite its simplicity, the diminished responsibility defense raises perplexing theoretical, moral, and practical questions. Several of these questions can best be illuminated by examining the doctrine's connection to criminal responsibility theory.

Diminished responsibility and insanity. To understand the doctrinal justifications for the diminished responsibility defense, one must explore the basic premises and limits of the insanity defense. The criminal law presumes that most individuals are capable of conforming their conduct to its minimal dictates. This presumption of "free will" underlying all tests for criminal responsibility is not empirically based; instead, it embodies a normative judgment that most people should be treated as legally responsible for their conduct because they have the minimal capacity for voluntary choice required for criminal responsibility. Accordingly, most criminals are viewed as "culpable" or "blameworthy" because they could have chosen to abide by the law's dictates.

To support this legal expectation of personal accountability, the insanity defense attempts to identify those few severely disabled defendants who lack the minimal capacity for rational and voluntary choice upon which the law's expectation of responsibility is predicated. Such offenders are labeled "insane" because their incapacity to comply with the law negates their culpability and demonstrates the futility, as well as the injustice, of applying criminal sanctions to their conduct. Social control and rehabilitation are better served by confining the dangerously insane in a secure hospital setting. Retribution is inappropriate because the insane person is not deserving of punishment. Specific deterrence of the severely disabled offender appears unlikely, and, arguably, general deterrence is ill served by the application of the criminal sanction to a "crazy" individual with whom law-abiding citizens cannot identify.

Since the insanity defense is designed to protect the law's expectation of accountability, the defense's criteria for exculpation must ensure that the defense can only be raised successfully in those exceptional cases in which the actor's mental disability has stripped him of the minimal mental capacity required for criminal responsibility. Thus, regardless of how the insanity test is formulated, it will not apply to many criminal defendants who are legally accountable for their acts but whose range of options and understanding were substantially diminished because of mental illness. While the criminal law holds these defendants criminally responsible for their acts and deserving of punishment, our intuition suggests that such disabled defendants are less culpable than the "normal" offender whose capacity for self-control and rationality has not been so impaired.

Recognizing that reduced culpability may warrant reduced punishment, the criminal law has permitted the sentencing authority to consider a sane offender's mental disability as a mitigating factor at sentencing. However, mitigation at sentencing may not be possible in jurisdictions whose most serious homicide offenses carry mandatory penalties such as the death penalty or life imprisonment. The diminished responsibility defense alleviates this problem by giving the jury de facto sentencing power to reduce the defen-

dant's punishment in homicide prosecutions. Whether the jury should be given such power is a separate question.

Justifications for a diminished responsibility defense. Proponents of the defense have advanced three separate but related rationales for its adoption by the criminal law.

Prevention of the execution of a mentally disabled but sane killer. As indicated earlier, the diminished responsibility defense was originally designed to alleviate the absence of any express sentencing discretion to consider the defendant's mental abnormality in capital offenses carrying the death penalty. However, critics of the defense have argued that a more straightforward solution would be to give the sentencing authority express discretion to consider mitigating and aggravating factors before making its sentencing decision in capital cases. This legislative solution has been constitutionalized in the United States in a series of Supreme Court decisions that have interpreted the Eighth Amendment to require such individualized sentencing discretion for most capital offenses.

Amelioration of defects in the insanity defense. A jurisdiction can ameliorate defects in its insanity test by giving mitigating effect to evidence of mental abnormality that does not satisfy the insanity test's criteria. This rationale applies with greatest force to *M'Naghten* jurisdictions (*M'Naghten's Case,* 8 Eng. Rep. 718 (1843)) because the diminished responsibility defense permits juries to consider evidence of a defendant's impaired volitional controls that theoretically cannot be used to demonstrate his insanity. However, such defects could be corrected directly by adopting an insanity test that exculpates defendants whose volitional controls were substantially impaired by mental illness. Indeed, a majority of American jurisdictions presently employ insanity tests that explicitly include a volitional component.

Improvement of the jury's capacity to make more refined culpability judgments in homicide prosecutions. The most compelling justification for the diminished responsibility defense is its recognition that a mentally abnormal but sane defendant may be less culpable than the unimpaired offender who commits the same crime. The defense enhances the jury's capacity to make more individualized culpability judgments by authorizing a far broader inquiry into the defendant's mental status at the time of the crime than that permitted by narrowly drawn statutory mental elements such as premeditation and deliberation or malice.

This justification for the diminished responsibility defense rests on two basic assumptions whose validity is subject to serious question. The first assumption is that the jury will be able to make more sophisticated culpability judgments in distinguishing between grades of homicide offenses when it considers evidence of a sane defendant's mental abnormality. Proponents of the defense insist that it requires the jury to make a commonsense moral judgment about whether the particular defendant was sufficiently impaired to warrant reduced punishment. However, when one examines this inquiry in the specific context of homicide crimes, its "commonsense" nature becomes more questionable. If the jury is being asked to decide whether the particular defendant is less culpable than the "normal" killer, one assumes that a realistic comparison is being made. But, apart from the professional hired gun, who is the "normal," fully culpable killer who maturely and meaningfully contemplates the gravity of his act before killing? Even if one assumes the jury is capable of making such distinctions, its inquiry will not be aided by the testimony of mental health experts because their elastic definition of mental abnormality easily encompasses anyone who kills without justification or excuse. At least in the homicide context, it can be argued that the diminished responsibility defense implicitly asks the jury to distinguish among sane killers by considering evidence from experts who cannot provide any factual basis for making such comparative culpability judgments.

The second assumption made by the diminished responsibility defense is that a showing of reduced culpability *automatically mandates* a reduction in criminal liability to a less serious homicide offense. The validity of this assumption depends upon the model of punishment that the legislature is using to grade the seriousness of an offense and its punishment. The diminished responsibility defense relies on a "just deserts" model of punishment, which correlates grades of criminal liability to the actor's degree of culpability. The just-deserts model embraces a subjective theory of criminal liability which requires, at the very least, that the maximum level of punishment for any crime be tied to the individual offender's degree of culpability.

However, most legislative schemes for the gradation of offenses and formulation of defenses rely on a more *mixed* model of punishment that considers other factors (such as incapacitation of the dangerous offender and deterrence) besides culpability. Legislative use of a mixed model of punishment reflects the conflicting policy objectives served by a criminal justice system that must balance its concern for the actor's culpability with the criminal law's social control function. Despite its subjective-sounding rhetoric, the criminal law is generally unwilling to vary legal norms in order to accommodate a particular individual's capacity to meet the standards they prescribe. Thus, the vast majority of complete and partial defenses reflect the criminal law's delicate balancing act between these competing concerns because they do not rely exclusively on the individual offender's culpability as the sole criterion for negating or reducing his degree of punishment. Instead, they are qualified by objective conditions that require the jury to determine whether a reasonable person endowed with the characteristics believed necessary to serve the criminal law's function of social control would have acted as the defendant did. Since the diminished responsibility defense authorizes the jury to reduce a defendant's punishment without ever considering whether he might be more dangerous than the "normal," unimpaired killer, proponents of the mixed model of punishment reject the defense out of hand.

Finally, even some advocates of the just-deserts model of punishment have rejected the defense's basic premise that a showing of reduced culpability *automatically* mandates a reduction in criminal liability. Relying on evidence suggesting that most mentally abnormal individuals are capable of controlling their antisocial impulses and usually do so, these commentators reject the diminished responsibility defense because they see no reason why the criminal law should give special consideration to mentally abnormal offenders who are criminally responsible for their acts. They insist that an individual who has the mental capacity for voluntary and rational choice required for criminal responsibility is fully culpable for his failure to comply with the minimal standards of conduct prescribed in the criminal law. While conceding that such offenders may be less culpable than a normal offender who commits the same crime, they conclude that evidence of diminished culpability should only be considered at sentencing.

The mens rea model

The pure model: a rule of evidence. Despite the simplicity of the diminished responsibility model, no American jurisdiction has *explicitly* adopted this variant of the diminished capacity defense. Instead, American courts have embraced the mens rea model because it seems to offer a logical way of relating medical data about the accused's personality to preestablished legislative gradations of criminal liability.

Judicial descriptions of the mens rea approach as a variant of the diminished capacity defense are, however, misleading because the "model" simply restates the basic proposition that evidence tending to confirm or negate the existence of a material element of the crime should be considered by the jury. Since the prosecution must prove all the elements of the crime charged beyond a reasonable doubt, the defendant must be given the opportunity to show that the state has not met its constitutional burden of proof. Viewed in this light, the pure mens rea model embodies no special legal theory or new defense; it is simply a restatement of a constitutionally grounded rule of evidence.

Although the pure mens rea model is not a special partial defense, some American courts have treated it as if it were. These courts have restricted its application to "specific intent" crimes to ensure that this "partial defense" does not lead to outright acquittal. In most American jurisdictions, a successful mens rea defense results in the reduction of the offense to one that carries a lesser maximum penalty and does not require proof of the specific intent at issue. Such an arbitrary (and probably unconstitutional) restriction to specific-intent crimes is inconsistent with the rule's underlying rationale that the jury must consider relevant evidence of mental abnormality which disputes the existence of any statutory mental element.

While doctrinally sound, the pure mens rea model does not resolve the problem of how the criminal law should treat mentally abnormal but sane offenders charged with homicide offenses. In practice, defendants use the mens rea defense to show how their mental abnormality at the time of the crime prevented them from premeditating, from entertaining malice, or from possessing an intent to kill. However, their evidence of mental abnormality will rarely dispute the presence of these statutory mental elements because most psychological descriptions of the defendant's mental status have little to do with the criminal law's concept of intent.

Consider the following hypothetical case: Ms. Fanatic believes that God has ordered her to kill her neighbor because he is an agent of the devil. Fanatic buys a gun and ammunition, invites her neighbor over for tea, and calmly blows his brains out. Psychiatrists testify that Fanatic was suffering from paranoid schizophrenia, as evidenced by her delusion that God had ordered the killing. In those jurisdictions that employ the Model Penal Code's insanity test, Fanatic would be exculpated because she lacked substantial capacity to conform her conduct to the law's dictates. Yet, the same evidence of mental abnormality would not refute the existence of either the specific intent to kill or premeditation and deliberation. Fanatic certainly intended to kill, and her objective acts clearly evidenced a preconceived design to effectuate that intent in a calm, deliberate manner.

Is this an illogical result? How can the defendant be insane and therefore entitled to a complete defense, and yet not qualify for what is considered a partial defense? The simple answer is that there is no necessary connection between a judgment about the defendant's criminal responsibility and his mental capacity to entertain the state of mind required by the crime. Since the criminal law's concept of mens rea requires minimal intelligence and cognitive capacity, it is perfectly plausible that the defendant entertained the specific mental state but was still insane. In fact, most mentally abnormal offenders are fully capable of thinking about their criminal act before they commit it, turning it over in their minds, planning the act, and then performing it in accordance with their preconceived plan. Evidence of how Fanatic's mental abnormality impaired her behavior controls or made it difficult for her to appreciate the act's gravity does not negate the existence of the required mental states; it merely explains them. Such psychiatric explanations of a defendant's deviant behavior, which do not dispute the presence of conscious intent, should not be admissible evidence under the pure mens rea model. Consequently, if courts administer the pure mens rea model honestly by only admitting evidence of mental abnormality that disputes the existence of the requisite mental state, abnormal but sane defendants will rarely benefit from this defense.

From "mens rea" to "diminished responsibility": California's experience

Since the pure mens rea model does not permit the jury to mitigate the punishment of most mentally abnormal but sane offenders, a few American courts have broadened the nature of the inquiry into the offender's mental condition authorized by the defense. Instead of focusing on whether the defendant's mental abnormality prevented him *in fact* from entertaining the requisite mens rea, these courts use the defense to authorize the admission of any evidence suggesting that the defendant's *mental capacity* to entertain the intent was diminished owing to mental illness.

The California diminished capacity cases provided the most striking and extreme illustration of this shift in focus. In cases in which the evidence clearly established that the defendant did in fact entertain the requisite intent, the California Supreme Court required the jury to make a qualitative assessment about the manner in which the defendant thought about his criminal act as compared with the normal offender. For example, the court redefined the traditional concept of "premeditation and deliberation" required for first-degree murder by asking the jury to consider whether the defendant's mental disability prevented him from reflecting upon his contemplated act in a mature and meaningful fashion. By shifting the focus of the mens rea inquiry from assessing whether a defendant has possessed the requisite intent to evaluating why and how he had entertained it, the California cases required the jury to determine whether the defendant's mental abnormality destroyed the normal culpable significance attached to the presence of these statutory mental elements. While maintaining the fiction that the defendant's evidence of mental abnormality correlated to statutory mental elements, the court's redefinition of those elements converted the mens rea defense into a covert diminished responsibility defense.

The California Supreme Court's refusal to acknowledge in theory what it had done in practice fostered several unfortunate side effects. Since the court insisted that evidence of mental abnormality was admitted to dispute proof of statutory mental elements, it was forced to articulate different qualitative standards for assessing each distinct mental element in homicide crimes. The court's attempts to do so required juries to make some exceedingly subtle, if not impossible, distinctions between diminished capacity evidence that negated one element but not another. More important, the court's perpetuation of a legal fiction impaired the jury's capacity to make a rational decision on the actual question of mitigation presented to it. Unsurprisingly, juries acted in an erratic manner when asked to decide whether the defendant premeditated the killing in cases in which it was obvious from the facts that he did so. Finally, by refusing to admit that it was redefining statutory mental elements, the court never addressed the basic question of its authority to interfere with the legislature's gradation of homicide offenses.

In 1981, the California legislature abolished the diminished capacity defense. The legislature explicitly repudiated the court's redefinition of "premeditation" and "malice," and it prohibited the admission of mental abnormality evidence to negate the defendant's *capacity* to entertain these statutory mental elements. In effect, the California legislature reaffirmed the pure mens rea model because it authorized the admission of mental abnormality evidence for the sole purpose of establishing whether the defendant in fact entertained the requisite criminal intent.

Conclusion

California's experience with the diminished capacity doctrine suggests that neither the mens rea model nor the diminished responsibility model of the defense provides a satisfactory response to the problem of how the criminal law should treat mentally disabled but sane offenders charged with homicide offenses. By definition, the mens rea model does not provide a new basis for grading degrees of liability in homicide prosecutions. Since evidence of the defendant's mental abnormality will usually not dispute the existence of the statutory mental element, the mens rea model will rarely have any significant effect on the jury's verdict. In contrast, the diminished responsibility model does give the jury de facto sentencing power to mitigate the punishment of mentally disabled offenders because of the offenders' reduced culpability. However, the courts arguably lack the authority to adopt such a defense because it provides a basis for grading homicide offenses which may conflict with the legislature's grading scheme. Finally, there is no compelling reason why the legislature should give the jury de facto sentencing power to reduce the defendant's degree of criminal liability simply because he may be less culpable than other offenders who commit the same offense.

PETER ARENELLA

See also EXCUSE, *articles on* INSANITY, INTOXICATION, *and* THEORY; MENTALLY DISORDERED OFFENDERS.

BIBLIOGRAPHY

American Law Institute. *Model Penal Code and Commentaries: Official Draft and Revised Comments.* Philadelphia: ALI, 1980.
ARENELLA, PETER. "The Diminished Capacity and Diminished Responsibility Defenses: Two Children of a Doomed Marriage." *Columbia Law Review* 77 (1977): 827–865.
————. Review of *Mental Disabilities and Criminal Responsibility* by Herbert Fingarette and Ann Fingarette Hasse. *Columbia Law Review* 80 (1980): 420–434.
DIX, GEORGE E. "Psychological Abnormality as a Factor in Grading Criminal Liability: Diminished Capacity, Diminished Responsibility, and the Like." *Journal of Criminal Law and Criminology* 62 (1971): 313–334.
FINGARETTE, HERBERT, and HASSE, ANN FINGARETTE. *Mental Disabilities and Criminal Responsibility.* Berkeley: University of California Press, 1979.
LAFAVE, WAYNE R., and SCOTT, AUSTIN W., JR. *Handbook on Criminal Law.* St. Paul: West, 1972.
LEWIN, TRAVIS H. D. "Psychiatric Evidence in Criminal Cases for Purposes Other than the Defense of Insanity." *Syracuse Law Review* 26 (1975): 1051–1115.

MORSE, STEPHEN J. "Diminished Capacity: A Moral and Legal Conundrum." *International Journal of Law and Psychiatry* 2 (1979): 271–298.

SPARKS, RICHARD F. "Diminished Responsibility in Theory and Practice." *Modern Law Review* 27 (1964): 9–34.

WOOTTON, BARBARA. "Diminished Responsibility: A Layman's View." *Law Quarterly Review* 76 (1960): 224–239.

DISABILITIES, CIVIL

See CONVICTION: CIVIL DISABILITIES.

DISCOVERY

The rationale for discovery

Definition. Discovery is the exchange of information by the parties to a proceeding, such as the prosecutor and the defendant in a criminal case. In every case each party has reason to want to know the evidence and the theories of an opponent or even of a person with similar interests—for example, a codefendant. Such knowledge can help the parties plan responses to opposing litigation strategies and strengthen their own strategies.

The adversary system and discovery. The adversary system, especially as it has been developed in American courts, depends upon the parties to bring cases before courts, to develop their own theories of cases, to gather evidence, to present evidence, and to raise proper objections to others' presentations. The judge will resolve disputes about the parties' respective rights and duties only if such disputes are raised by the parties. One rationale for an adversary system is that parties who have a personal stake in litigation have unique incentives to hone their theories, to find evidence, to present it persuasively, and to object or reply to opposing evidence.

Discovery seeks to assure that the adversary system does not give one party an unfair advantage over another. Thus, discovery sometimes prevents a party with evidence from denying another party, who may need the evidence to present a case, access to that evidence. Moreover, discovery helps to prevent a party who has gathered evidence from surprising an opponent with it in a way that makes the evidence appear more powerful than it really is. Discovery is limited, however, so that one party cannot depend on another to do all the evidence-gathering.

Even if there were no limits on discovery, many parties would never trust an opponent to gather evidence when the very process of gathering it might mold the evidence in a way that could influence the outcome of litigation. For example, it is well known that a party who takes the statement of a witness has an opportunity to influence the statement by asking questions in a particular way. Thus, litigants always have some incentive to conduct investigations and to prepare on their own even if they have access to the work of opponents. American jurisdictions presume, however, that a greater incentive is needed and that with unfettered discovery some litigants would ride the coattails of others and would unduly benefit from others' work. Hence, for better or worse, discovery is limited.

Civil versus criminal cases. In American courts discovery is more routine, accepted, and liberalized in civil than in criminal cases. Standard civil discovery devices often are not available in criminal proceedings. This results from traditional negative attitudes toward criminal defendants on the part of prosecutors, police, legislators, and many judicial officers. Whereas civil disputants are regarded as ordinary citizens seeking to do what society encourages them to do—that is, to take their disputes to court when they cannot resolve them through private bargaining, rather than to use force in attempting to win a dispute—criminal defendants are viewed less favorably.

Discovery by the criminal defendant

Before examining particular aspects of discovery and how they are restricted in many jurisdictions, it is helpful to examine the attitudes toward criminal defendants that account for the restrictions and to consider some of the problems that these attitudes present. Generally, prosecutors would welcome more discovery for themselves, but they do not seek it because to do so might produce greater opportunities for defense discovery.

Arguments against discovery by the defendant. *The balance of advantage.* The view is often expressed that criminal defendants receive too many protections and that additional protections ought to be resisted lest the system become further imbalanced. If the scales already are heavily weighted in the defendant's favor, it is understandable that there would be resistance to creating additional defense rights. There are, however, reasons to question whether any imbalance exists and, if it does, whether it justifies reduced discovery.

Undoubtedly, the procedural rights guaranteed by federal and state constitutional provisions and by many statutes and court rules require the government to justify interference with a citizen's liberty. No one has demonstrated that the standards under which law enforcement officials act are either too burdensome on law enforcement or too lax to protect citizens, and it is possible that this could not be demonstrated empirically. Yet, American law traditionally has not permitted the government to act whenever it wishes against whomever it wishes for whatever purpose it wishes, and there is little reason to believe that there would be popular support for giving it such discretion. Constitutional standards and other rules that regulate interferences with liberty help to ensure that the government does not act prematurely or arbitrarily. These protections exist in large part because government cannot differentiate the guilty from the innocent in any satisfactory way early in an investigation.

Even more importantly, many of the rights afforded defendants or suspects in no way impair the government's ability to legitimately prevail at trial. Many rights afford protections against interference with liberty, not advantages in litigation. Of those protections that do relate to trial matters, some are designed to ensure that trials are fair. This is why, for example, the Supreme Court has ruled that when a person stands to lose liberty, he must have the opportunity to retain counsel, either at his own or the state's expense.

Some rules, such as those placing on the prosecutor the burden of proof beyond a reasonable doubt as to essential elements of a crime, and denying the prosecutor the opportunity to call the defendant as witness, do make the government's task more difficult. Each rule serves an important societal interest, however. Thus, the heavy burden of persuasion that a prosecutor bears is a deliberate allocation of the risk of error between government and individual in a way that favors the individual. The government bears the principal risk of a mistake because the system recognizes no higher value than the importance of convicting only the truly guilty, never the innocent. This respect for the sanctity of the individual is also evident in the privilege against self-incrimination that protects the defendant from being used as a witness for the prosecution without his consent. It hardly follows that a system so structured would readily accept limits on discovery that might increase the risk of innocent persons being tried and convicted.

The special nature of criminal proceedings. Some have argued that in a civil trial both sides search for the truth, whereas in a criminal trial only the prosecution searches for the truth while the defendant resists the search. This is little more, it turns out, than a restatement of the argument that the prosecutor bears a heavy burden of persuasion and cannot force the defendant to testify when trying to satisfy the burden. The judges who supervise trials seek the truth as much in criminal as in civil cases, as do the juries that are sometimes used to decide the merits of both civil and criminal controversies. It may be that certain of the rules excluding evidence in criminal cases have no counterpart in civil litigation. If this is the case, it is not because the goal of criminal litigation is to reach something other than the truth. Rather, it is because certain constitutional rights have been held to require exclusionary remedies if they are to be meaningful, and these rights extend only to criminal matters.

The perjury problem. Another argument against defense discovery is that the criminal will procure perjured testimony and distort the search for the truth if he has advance knowledge of the information in the government's hands. This argument assumes that all defendants either are guilty or are so corrupt that, whether guilty or not, they will encourage perjury or perhaps commit perjury themselves. It assumes also that they can find accomplices to help them and that the process of cross-examination of witnesses at trial cannot satisfactorily deal with problems of perjury. It assumes too that civil litigants with their reputations or lifetime earnings at stake in litigation will act properly, but that any criminal defendant who has anything to lose will not. In addition, it assumes that all government evidence can be matched with perjured testimony—certainly a doubtful assumption with respect to much physical evidence and to many statements by observers of events. It may even assume that defense counsel are so corrupt as to tolerate perjury. These assumptions, which one must make in order to accept the argument, are all suspect.

Protection of witnesses. Some prosecutors and police fear that defendants with knowledge of the government's case will threaten witnesses, will attempt to deter citizens from cooperating with prosecutions, or will try to destroy physical evidence. Such fears lead to a conclusion that the less the defendant knows about the witnesses and the evidence that the government possesses, the less danger there is to people and tangible objects.

Some defendants would undoubtedly pose a threat to witnesses or to evidence, but it is unclear whether the number of such defendants is large. One possible response would be to limit discovery in certain kinds of cases thought to involve especially dangerous defendants, or in particular cases where it can be shown that a defendant has threatened witnesses in the past or has indicated an intent to do so if the witnesses can be found. Some witnesses—professional police, for example—are unlikely to be intimidated in any event. Moreover, much evidence can be disclosed in such a way that it can be secured and protected. Frightened witnesses can be kept under the watchful eye of law enforcement personnel, and trials may be advanced on the docket to reduce the waiting period for witnesses to testify. When jurisdictions with more liberal discovery are compared to jurisdictions with restrictive discovery, it is difficult to ascertain that witnesses in the former jurisdictions are less cooperative or more likely to refrain from assisting the government than those in the latter jurisdictions.

Substitutes for prosecution discovery. Prosecutors have substitutes for discovery which enable them to obtain information in ways that are unavailable to defendants. The availability of substitutes helps to explain why prosecutors are willing to limit defense discovery even if it means foregoing prosecutorial discovery from the defense.

Perhaps the most formidable discovery device available to a prosecutor is the grand jury. Through the grand jury and its subpoena power the prosecutor can call witnesses and require them to appear with documents and other evidence. If a witness refuses to testify on self-incrimination grounds, some form of immunity from prosecution or from having immunized testimony used against him can be granted so that he must tell the grand jury what he knows.

In addition, prosecutors can obtain help from the police in gathering evidence. Even though citizens may not be required by law to talk to police, they are far more likely to be cooperative when questioned by law enforcement officers than by a criminal defendant charged with violating the law. Furthermore, police can obtain search warrants permitting them to seize any evidence in which they demonstrate sufficient interest. Other governmental agencies, such as the Internal Revenue Service, also may keep records that provide assistance to prosecutors.

Substitutes for defense discovery. Compared to prosecutors, defense lawyers and their clients clearly have limited alternatives to discovery. They cannot impanel grand juries, create police forces with legal authority to act in the name of the state, or use government agencies to gather evidence for them. It is for these reasons that a common practice has developed whereby defense counsel make a variety of pretrial motions, ostensibly for legitimate nondiscovery purposes, but often to "smoke out" the government's case. Motions for suppression of evidence, for the quashing of identifications, for severance of trial when a number of defendants are charged together, and

for pretrial rulings on evidence questions may be used as discovery mechanisms as well as means of enforcing other defense rights. Thus, the denial of discovery rights results in pressure for information elsewhere in the criminal justice system. Recently, freedom of information acts have been the basis of some defense requests to gather information that is in the hands of the government. This highlights the fact that defendants want to prepare prior to trial or bargaining. They want information and will use available avenues to obtain it.

Informal discovery. The system of informal discovery looms large in everyday criminal practice. Some prosecutors have adopted a policy of sharing almost everything that comes into their hands with defendants, except in particular cases where there is some special reason to fear for the safety of witnesses or for the security of evidence. Many other prosecutors have no uniform policy; they will share more or less information with a defendant, depending on how they feel about him and about his willingness to be cooperative. Trading information on an informal basis is so common that it is difficult to determine accurately how much discovery is taking place in a jurisdiction at any given time.

Informal discovery is not a perfect substitute for defense discovery rights. Since the prosecutor has broad discretion, he can exercise it to limit or to prevent informal discovery in all or in a few cases, and courts will not interfere with his discretion to do so.

Specifics of defense discovery. Recognition of the informational needs of defendants preparing for trial or contemplating pleas of guilty has led some jurisdictions to expand formal discovery rights for defendants. There remain, however, significant limitations in most parts of the United States. Considered below are some of the familiar aspects of discovery, with an indication as to how limited they are likely to be in typical American jurisdictions.

Grand jury transcript. The grand jury is a powerful investigative body that is able to gather extensive evidence. It is standard practice to make grand jury proceedings secret and, by statutes or rules, to bar most participants in grand jury proceedings from revealing the jurors' work prior to the filing of a charge. Secrecy enables the grand jury to gather evidence without disclosing to suspects the fact that they are under investigation, which, if known, might lead to destruction of evidence. In some cases secrecy allows a charge to be made and an arrest carried out before a suspect has notice that the law is after him and thus has an opportunity to flee. Witnesses who testify before the grand jury remain protected by secrecy, and if charges are not made, persons who were investigated will have no reason to harbor a grudge against those who testified. Secrecy also permits a person who is not charged to remain completely untainted, since the public will not know that any investigation was undertaken.

Once a charge and arrest are made, the reasons for secrecy largely evaporate. One concern remains: that witnesses might be fearful if the fact that they testified is known to a defendant. But all witnesses share this concern, and at some point it is probable that these witnesses will testify at trial. The kind of defendant who poses a threat to witnesses is unlikely to be viewed as less dangerous during their testimony than before it. Moreover, as noted above, in many cases there is no perceived danger to witnesses. The absence of persuasive reasons to compel secrecy after a charge is filed has caused some jurisdictions to provide the defendant with a grand jury transcript. But most jurisdictions do not do so.

Preliminary hearing. Another potentially useful discovery device is the preliminary hearing, which is a screening mechanism employed in some cases, usually those involving felonies. In most jurisdictions such a hearing will not be held after a defendant is indicted. It might be held, however, if the defendant is awaiting grand jury action. Usually it will be held if the defendant is to be charged not by a grand jury but by the prosecutor himself, who will file either an "information" or a complaint that is the equivalent of a grand jury indictment.

In the preliminary hearing the prosecutor must disclose enough evidence to show that there is probable cause to believe the defendant committed a crime. Some jurisdictions make the hearing a discovery device as well as a protection for the defendant against unfounded charges. But the prosecutor usually is not forced to reveal all his evidence, and the defendant thus discovers only that which the prosecutor chooses to present in an effort to establish reasonable cause to take the defendant to trial. Although in many other jurisdictions the preliminary hearing is not a discovery device at all, defendants attempt to use it as best they can for discovery. This often is difficult, though, since the prosecutor may be allowed to present only a few witnesses to summarize a case, and most of the names of the other witnesses and their evidence will remain undisclosed.

Bill of particulars. If the defendant does not obtain grand jury testimony and has no effective preliminary hearing discovery, he may seek a bill of particulars, which is a judicial order that the prosecutor tell the defendant more about the charges than is found in an indictment, information, or complaint. Due process of law requires that the defendant have adequate notice of the charges against him so that he can understand what he must defend against and can protect himself against being charged more than once for the same offense. Courts are reluctant to grant bills of particulars, and if a bill is granted, the prosecutor must provide fuller information about the offense charged rather than the proof to be offered in support of the charge.

Government witnesses. There are several kinds of information that a defendant would like to obtain through discovery. One of the most important is who will testify for the government. If possible, defense counsel will talk with the witnesses to see whether their testimony will be damaging and whether it may be shaken if the defense is properly prepared. The defense will want to gather opposing evidence to meet the testimony of government witnesses. In addition, the defense will want to have any pretrial statements that witnesses have given to the government. Not only might such statements help the defense to prepare by foreshadowing the likely trial testimony for the government, but they might also help the defense to look for inconsistencies between pretrial statements and trial testimony that might be used to attack the credibility of government witnesses.

A few jurisdictions require that the names and addresses of all witnesses known to the prosecutor be supplied to the defendant; more require that the names and addresses of witnesses who testified before the grand jury be listed on the indictment. Most jurisdictions do not require that the names of witnesses be disclosed. Although trial judges in many jurisdictions might have the power to order discovery unless a statute or court rule prohibits it, few order reluctant prosecutors to provide defendants with witness lists. Where names of witnesses are not provided, pretrial statements of witnesses are not provided either, lest the identities of the witnesses be disclosed.

If witnesses' names are disclosed, or if they are discovered by a defendant, the defendant still may be unable to induce them to speak with the defense. Witnesses need not talk informally unless they wish to, and most jurisdictions do not permit them to be deposed, that is, questioned under oath. This limitation on discovery protects witnesses from one extra testimonial burden and eliminates work for prosecutors. Its justification is cost, not danger. It would be possible to reduce the costs of such discovery by limiting depositions to cases in which no full preliminary hearing is held and the prosecutor is unwilling or unable to provide the defense with grand jury testimony of witnesses. But prosecutors do not seem to suffer from being unable to take depositions, and courts do not seem anxious to expand this form of discovery.

Once the witnesses testify at trial, their relationship to the case is obvious. In federal courts, the Jencks Act, 18 U.S.C § 3500 (1976) provides that recorded or transcribed statements of witnesses must be turned over to the defense after the witnesses testify. At this point disclosure no longer presents any perceptible danger to the witnesses, and the need of the defense to test the earlier statements against the trial testimony is recognized. Not all states provide for automatic disclosure of statements. Statements of witnesses might not be disclosed unless a special need is shown.

Defendants' statements. The one "witness" whose statements seemingly ought to be discoverable without question is the defendant himself. If he has given statements to the police or to prosecutors, most courts will require that his statements be disclosed to him. It might be thought that there is no reason for disclosure because the defendant should know what he said. The question, however, may be precisely what he did say. Any inconsistency between a defendant's pretrial statement and his trial testimony may be important. The only reason to deny a defendant access to his own statement would be to discourage perjury, but this argument hardly seems persuasive, since the prosecutor has the pretrial statement and can use it against the defendant.

Documents and tangible objects. It is more likely that documents and tangible objects the government possesses and plans to use at trial, or that the defense wants to see because they are or might be material to the case, will be made available for inspection. For some reason, fears about possible perjury do not stand in the way of this discovery, even though it would seem that perjurers could mold testimony to respond to some physical evidence as well as to witnesses. This might suggest either that protecting and alleviating burdens on witnesses accounts for most of the limitations on defense access to evidence previously discussed, or that prosecutors do not want to suffer delays at trial while defendants inspect physical evidence for the first time.

Medical and scientific evidence. This last explanation probably clarifies why reports of medical examinations and scientific tests in the government's hands that the government will use at trial, or that might be used by the defense, are likely to be disclosed before trial. Almost certainly there would have to be a continuance at trial if this information were revealed there for the first time. Courts are likely to assume that a defendant can be ready to cross-examine a witness immediately after the witness testifies. But courts are not nearly as likely to assume that a defendant is capable of responding to technical or expert evidence without having some time to develop the necessary expertise.

Work product. One aspect of the prosecutor's work that is insulated from discovery is what is known as a lawyer's work product. The legal theories, conclusions, and opinions of the prosecutor are likely to be immune from discovery everywhere. This is consistent with the rationale for the adversary system—that each party should prepare its own case. Although the work product concept is familiar, its scope is not the same in all jurisdictions. Some jurisdictions make police reports part of work product; others limit the concept to legal work by the prosecutor and his staff.

Constitutionally required disclosure. Most choices with respect to how much discovery the defense will have are left to each jurisdiction to make for itself. There are, however, several United States Supreme Court decisions that require prosecutors to disclose some of their information. In *Mooney v. Holohan*, 294 U.S. 103 (1935), the Court found that it was a denial of due process for a prosecutor to present perjured testimony and to fail to disclose evidence that would have impeached the testimony. Another landmark case was *Brady v. Maryland*, 373 U.S. 83 (1963), in which the Court indicated that suppression of evidence required by, and possibly useful to, the defense was unconstitutional. But in *Moore v. Illinois*, 408 U.S. 786 (1972), the Court took a narrow view of what evidence was important enough to come within the compulsory disclosure rule.

Later, in *United States v. Agurs*, 427 U.S. 97 (1976), the Court noted that when the prosecutor has been specifically asked for identifiable evidence and has suppressed it, or when the prosecutor has knowingly used perjured testimony, courts are likely to reverse any conviction affected by the prosecutor's misconduct. But where a defendant has made no specific request for exculpatory evidence or has made only a general request, and later discovers that exculpatory evidence was concealed, he must bear a heavy burden of showing that the evidence was so important that a different verdict would have been rendered if the evidence had been disclosed. Since the defendant usually does not know what evidence the prosecutor has before discovery takes place, general or no-request cases are common, and *Agurs* suggests that suppression of evidence, even knowingly, by a prosecutor will not necessarily require reversal of a conviction. Nevertheless, prosecutors still have an ethical duty to disclose, and courts assume that this duty will be met.

Discovery by motion or automatically. Some jurisdictions provide that prosecutors must disclose certain information to defendants upon request; others require that defendants move for discovery in court. A trend toward establishing discovery rights upon request exists because avoiding routine motions saves court time and establishes some uniformity in discovery. Even if discovery upon request is specified by statute or court rule, in some cases prosecutors may be able to obtain a special protective order to prevent discovery so as to protect witnesses or evidence. In jurisdictions which provide that defendants must formally move for discovery in court, prosecutors can oppose these requests, and trial judges make the final determinations as to what discovery should be permitted.

Discovery by the prosecution

Reciprocal and nonreciprocal discovery. In some jurisdictions prosecutors can only obtain discovery if defendants ask for it first. Apparently, the reciprocal statutes reflect two ideas. First, it is believed that if defendants are willing to fend for themselves, prosecutors should do so also. But this is a questionable assertion in view of the special burden placed on prosecutors to prove guilt beyond a reasonable doubt. Second, there is some fear that giving prosecutors a right to discovery independent of defense requests might violate the privilege against self-incrimination. The problem here is that if the privilege is violated by discovery, it probably is violated whether or not discovery is reciprocal, since even under a reciprocal discovery system, defendants who want discovery are coerced into responding to government discovery requests. Even in systems that give prosecutors an independent right to discovery, prosecutors may not force defendants to provide testimonial evidence; only evidence falling outside the scope of the privilege against self-incrimination may be sought.

One aspect of reciprocity is constitutionally mandated. In *Wardius v. Oregon*, 412 U.S. 470 (1973), the Supreme Court indicated that a statute or rule may not require defendants to provide disclosure of information when prosecutors keep secret their information on the same subject. If the defendant is forced to disclose, the prosecutor must also disclose.

Specifics of prosecution discovery.

Documents and scientific evidence. It is common for prosecutors to seek discovery of documents, tangible objects, and reports of examinations and tests that defendants plan to use at trial. The rationale for discovery is that the prosecution needs time to prepare a response to scientific or technical matters.

This rationale also explains why some jurisdictions require that a defendant give notice of an intent to raise an insanity or mental defect defense. Failure to give proper notice may result in loss of these defenses at trial, for prosecutors want to have time to gather the medical evidence necessary to respond to such defenses. Continuances of trial for medical or psychiatric examinations are not very feasible, since these examinations sometimes take a great deal of time.

Notice of alibi. More controversial is the notice of alibi requirement that some jurisdictions impose upon defendants. If the defendant plans to raise an alibi defense he must, upon pain of losing the defense, notify the government of his intent and state where he claims to have been and the names and addresses of the witnesses he plans to call.

Some critics of the notice requirement claim that it violates the privilege against self-incrimination. The Supreme Court rejected this claim in *Williams v. Florida*, 399 U.S. 78 (1970). Other critics observe that it is difficult to see why the argument for prosecutorial discovery of alibi witnesses is any stronger than the argument for defense discovery of witnesses in nonalibi cases. If prosecutors need to know the names of witnesses in order to be prepared to meet an alibi defense, critics suggest that this is a strong indication that defendants really do need to know about prosecution witnesses in order to prepare for trials generally. The argument is appealing, but it has not been widely accepted, even in jurisdictions that use notice of alibi rules.

Work product. Like prosecutors, defendants are able to protect a lawyer's work product that is generated in preparation for trial. The scope of the protection differs throughout the United States. Any statements by defendants to their lawyers are also protected by the attorney-client privilege.

In 1980, Rule 26.2 was added to the Federal Rules of Criminal Procedure. This rule provides that when witnesses are called by the defense and finish testifying, any recorded statements made by the witnesses in the hands of the defense must be revealed to the government. This, in effect, is a reverse version of the Jencks Act. It is likely to be popular and to be adopted in many states. Both the Jencks Act and the new federal rule provide for full disclosure of prior recorded statements in order to promote fair evaluation of witness testimony. If they diminish parties' incentives to gather pretrial statements, the reduction is one that American courts tolerate in order to promote better fact-finding at trial.

Discovery by motion or automatically. If jurisdictions encourage discovery by defendants upon request without formal motion, they also are likely to encourage discovery by prosecutors upon request. Similarly, if motions by defendants are required, they are likely to be required of prosecutors.

STEPHEN A. SALTZBURG

See also COUNSEL: ROLE OF COUNSEL; CRIMINAL PROCEDURE: CONSTITUTIONAL ASPECTS; GRAND JURY; PRELIMINARY HEARING.

BIBLIOGRAPHY

American Bar Association, Project on Standards for Criminal Justice. *Standards Relating to Discovery and Procedure before Trial.* New York: ABA, 1970.

American Bar Association, Standing Committee on Association Standards for Criminal Justice. "Discovery and Procedure before Trial." *Standards for Criminal Justice,* vol. 2. 2d ed. Prepared with the assistance of the American Bar Foundation. Boston: Little, Brown, 1980, chap. 11.

American Law Institute. *A Model Code of Pre-arraignment Procedure.* Washington, D.C.: ALI, 1975.

BRENNAN, WILLIAM J., JR. "The Criminal Prosecution: Sporting Event or Quest for Truth?" *Washington University Law Quarterly* (1963): 279–295.

FLETCHER, ROBERT L. "Pretrial Discovery in State Criminal Cases." *Stanford Law Review* 12 (1960): 293–322.

GOLDSTEIN, ABRAHAM S. "The State and the Accused: Balance of Advantage in Criminal Procedure." *Yale Law Journal* 69 (1960): 1149–1199.

KAMISAR, YALE; LAFAVE, WAYNE R.; and ISRAEL, JEROLD H. *Modern Criminal Procedure: Cases, Comments, Questions.* 5th ed. St. Paul: West, 1980.

LANGBEIN, JOHN H. *Comparative Criminal Procedure: Germany.* St. Paul: West, 1977.

LOUISELL, DAVID W. "Criminal Discovery: Dilemma Real or Apparent?" *California Law Review* 49 (1961): 56–103.

MUELLER, GERHARD, and LE POOLE-GRIFFITHS, FRÉ. *Comparative Criminal Procedure.* New York University Press, 1969.

NAKELL, BARRY. "Criminal Discovery for the Defense and the Prosecution: The Developing Constitutional Considerations." *North Carolina Law Review* 50 (1972): 437–516.

National Conference of Commissioners on Uniform State Laws. *Special Commission on Uniform Rules of Criminal Procedure.* St. Paul: West, 1973.

SALTZBURG, STEPHEN A. *American Criminal Procedure.* St. Paul: West, 1980.

U.S. Department of Justice, Law Enforcement Assistance Administration, National Advisory Commission on Criminal Justice Standards and Goals. *Courts.* Washington, D.C.: The Commission, 1973.

WEINREB, LLOYD L. *Denial of Justice: Criminal Process in the United States.* New York: Free Press, 1977.

WRIGHT, CHARLES ALAN. *Federal Practice and Procedure,* vol. 1. St. Paul: West, 1969.

DISCRETION

See CRIMINAL JUSTICE SYSTEM: OVERVIEW; INFORMAL DISPOSITION; *articles under* JUVENILE JUSTICE; *articles under* POLICE; *articles under* PROBATION AND PAROLE; *articles under* PROSECUTION; *articles under* SENTENCING.

DISORDERLY CONDUCT

See articles under RIOTS; VAGRANCY AND DISORDERLY CONDUCT.

DISPARITY IN SENTENCING

See SENTENCING: DISPARITY.

DISPUTE RESOLUTION PROGRAMS

America's courts have experienced many difficulties in handling minor criminal and civil cases. Typical problems documented in research studies include extensive delays, high costs, assembly-line procedures, and citizen dissatisfaction with the quality of justice rendered. Minor criminal cases constitute a substantial portion of many courts' case loads and include such common problems as assault and harassment cases among neighbors, relatives, and acquaintances. In response to the courts' problems in handling such cases, a wide variety of dispute resolution programs have been developed in the United States. These programs provide opportunities for citizens to have their case mediated by trained hearing officers. The hearing officers are typically not empowered to impose a settlement upon the case, but rather simply attempt to help the disputing parties develop their own resolution to the problem. This article discusses the origins of such programs, reviews the major types of dispute resolution programs, and notes research findings regarding their impact.

Historical perspective

Every society develops mechanisms for the processing of disputes among its citizens. Some societies, such as the United States, rely quite heavily upon the courts for the handling of disputes: for example, American courts handle more than ten times as many cases per capita as do the courts in some Scandinavian nations (McGillis and Mullen). In contrast, other societies have highly developed methods for processing disputes outside the courts; Jerome Cohen has documented the use of such procedures in the People's Republic of China. Patterns of dispute settlement are not firmly set in any society, however, and a number of legal scholars have noted a tendency for societies to alternate between a stress on highly formal justice mechanisms and more informal approaches to the resolution of disputes (Pound).

During the late 1960s and early 1970s, growing concern with the justice system's problems in handling minor criminal and civil cases led to experimentation with the mediation of such cases outside the courts. The earliest such dispute resolution programs appear to have been developed by prosecutors and court officials. The Philadelphia Municipal Court Arbitration Tribunal was established in 1969 and the Columbus City Attorney's Night Prosecutor Program was developed in Ohio in 1970. Both programs handled a wide variety of minor criminal cases and gave disputants the opportunity to discuss their conflict and attempt to resolve the problem. The Columbus program's mediators were law students from a local university who were trained in mediation skills. The program grew rapidly and was designated an exemplary project by a board of United States Department of Justice officials in 1974. The Justice Department developed extensive documentation on the project and sponsored seminars throughout the United States to encourage adoption of the program elsewhere. The Columbus program and other projects in New York City, San Francisco, Boston, and elsewhere were replicated extensively across the nation during the late 1970s. By 1980, programs were in operation in approximately 140 cities in more than thirty states.

Program characteristics

The dispute resolution programs have many local names, including "citizen dispute settlement center," "neighborhood justice center," "community mediation center," "community board program," and "urban court project." Program structures and procedures vary considerably; major differences in program sponsorship, case criteria, referral sources, dispute resolution techniques, and hearing officer characteristics are noted below.

Program sponsorship. Dispute resolution programs are sponsored by a wide variety of organiza-

tions. Common variations include (1) public sponsorship; (2) private sponsorship with close ties to the justice system; and (3) private sponsorship with a community orientation. Public sponsors include the courts (as in the Miami Citizen Dispute Settlement Program), prosecutors' offices (the Columbus Night Prosecutor Program), and city or county government agencies (the Portland, Oregon, Neighborhood Mediation Project). A number of projects have been sponsored by private organizations in conjunction with the local justice system. For example, the Orlando, Florida, Citizen Dispute Settlement Project is sponsored by the local bar association, and the Rochester Community Dispute Services Project is operated by the American Arbitration Association. Such programs typically rely on local justice system agencies for case referrals. Projects also have been developed under the sponsorship of local private organizations, which rely primarily upon community control of operations and the referral of cases directly from the community, with only limited referrals from the justice system. For example, the San Francisco Community Board Program is sponsored by a local nonprofit corporation and stresses community control and operation rather than justice system linkages.

Case criteria. Programs vary considerably with regard to case criteria. Some programs handle a diverse array of minor criminal and civil cases. Typical minor criminal cases include those involving assault and harassment, and the programs tend to handle primarily cases among persons with an ongoing relationship—neighbors, relatives, acquaintances, and the like. Common minor civil cases include landlord-tenant, merchant-consumer, and employer-employee conflicts. A number of programs have sought to mediate felonies taking place among acquaintances, but this approach is not common, and most programs deal only with misdemeanors. Some mediation programs specialize in certain types of cases, such as landlord-tenant matters and domestic disputes, and have titles indicating such specialization, for example, "housing mediation center" or "divorce mediation center."

Referral sources. Dispute resolution programs receive referrals from many sources, including the police, prosecutors, the courts, social-service agencies, and individual citizens. Some programs accept referrals from a variety of sources, whereas others receive most of their referrals from a single source: the bench (Boston), the court clerk (Rochester), the prosecutor (Columbus), and the police (Orlando).

Dispute resolution techniques. Many projects attempt to settle disputes through conciliation before scheduling a formal mediation session. In conciliation attempts, the disputants are contacted by telephone or by mail. In mediation, a neutral third party seeks to settle a dispute through discussion and mutual agreements. A mediator does not have the power to resolve a dispute unilaterally, but instead encourages the disputants to resolve the matter themselves. Other programs offer arbitration. In such programs the disputants must agree in writing to participate in the arbitration session, and the arbitrators have the authority to develop a binding agreement enforceable in the civil courts if the disputants fail to reach an agreement. The majority of states have modern arbitration legislation and can support projects using either mediation or arbitration. In practice, mediation projects are far more common. Hearings range in length from thirty minutes to more than two hours, and programs vary in the number of mediators used, from one to as many as five.

Hearing officer characteristics. The most common types of mediators used in dispute resolution programs are lay citizens trained by the programs in mediation skills. Programs typically select persons representative of the community in terms of age, sex, and race, and they often attempt to match mediator demographic characteristics to those of disputants. Some programs employ mediators with specialized training, such as law students (Columbus), lawyers (Orlando), and social workers or clinical psychologists (Miami).

Dispute resolution program accomplishments

A number of research studies have investigated the accomplishments of dispute resolution programs and have sought to determine their strengths and weaknesses. The most extensive such study was conducted by Royer Cook, Janice Roehl, and David Sheppard and was funded by the Department of Justice. The researchers studied neighborhood justice center projects in Atlanta, Kansas City, and Los Angeles. The programs were funded by the Justice Department's National Institute of Justice and were developed at the direction of Attorney General Griffin Bell.

The researchers found that citizens viewed the programs very favorably. Composite data from the program evaluation indicated that 84 percent of the more than one thousand disputants interviewed at the three neighborhood justice centers were satisfied with the mediation process, 88 percent expressed satisfaction with the mediator, 88 percent were pleased with the overall experience at the mediation programs, and 73 percent said that they would return to the neighborhood justice center for similar problems in the future. These data are difficult to interpret without comparable data from other dispute processing fo-

rums, such as the courts, but they do suggest high absolute levels of satisfaction.

In addition to citizen satisfaction, studies have also indicated that the programs tend to process cases much more rapidly than the courts, typically scheduling hearings within seven to fifteen days of referral (Florida Supreme Court). Court processing of comparable cases is often found to require ten weeks or longer. Programs are also reported to improve access to justice since they do not charge for services, do not require lawyers, and hold hearings at times convenient to all parties.

Much remains to be learned about the effectiveness of dispute resolution programs; little information is available regarding the impact of mediation hearings on the actual longevity of dispute settlement. Proponents of the programs argue that since mediation gives disputants the opportunity to explore the underlying causes for disputes, the resulting settlements should be more durable than court settlements. Craig McEwen and Richard Maiman have conducted a detailed study of small-claims case mediation in the Maine district courts and reported that mediated settlements were more likely to result in full payments by defendants. McEwen and Maiman surveyed persons who had participated in either mediation sessions or court hearings on small-claims matters, and found in addition that defendants in such cases felt a greater legal and moral obligation to pay their settlement after mediation than after court judgments. This finding does not seem to result from self-selection by defendants into the mediation sample as opposed to the court sample since persons in the survey were often directly assigned to mediation. The mediation and court case samples in the Maine study were carefully matched, and comparably sophisticated research is needed regarding the impact of mediation on minor criminal cases.

Additional data are also needed on the comparative costs of mediation and court case processing. Present studies suggest that mediation costs vary widely across the nation, depending primarily upon the size of the specific program's case load (McGillis and Mullen). Detailed data on the costs of processing comparable cases through the courts are very difficult to gather because of the uncertainties regarding how far such cases would proceed in the courts. Additional information is also needed on the determinants of mediation program case load sizes. Some programs (primarily those operated by the justice system) have substantial case loads. For example, the Columbus Night Prosecutor Program handles more than ten thousand mediation cases per year, and it holds many additional administrative hearings on other matters as well. Some other programs have experienced considerable difficulty in developing adequate case loads. Programs have found it particularly difficult to encourage "walk in" referrals directly from citizens.

Prospects for the future

Dispute resolution programs have been developed widely throughout the United States. As in the case of all social programs, they face challenges in receiving reliable funding. Many programs have been successfully institutionalized into the budgets of courts and prosecutors' offices. Other programs will inevitably be closed as a result of fiscal cutbacks.

Regardless of the short-term prospects for individual dispute processing projects, it appears that the widespread support for alternatives to the courts may herald a major shift in American jurisprudence. Lon Fuller and Frank Sander have written compellingly on the limits of adjudication for the handling of certain matters. Their concerns appear to have been validated nationally with the development of mediation centers. The detailed jurisprudence is yet to be written. The continuing experimentation across the country may point the way to the development of a more highly differentiated and coordinated justice system, with different forums and procedures suited to different types of human conflict.

DANIEL McGILLIS

See also CRIME PREVENTION: COMMUNITY PROGRAMS; FAMILY RELATIONSHIPS AND CRIME; INFORMAL DISPOSITION; PRETRIAL DIVERSION; *articles under* VIOLENCE IN THE FAMILY.

BIBLIOGRAPHY

COHEN, JEROME A. "Chinese Mediation on the Eve of Modernization." *California Law Review* 54 (1966): 1201–1226.
COOK, ROYER F.; ROEHL, JANICE A.; and SHEPPARD, DAVID I. *Neighborhood Justice Centers Field Test: Final Evaluation Report.* Washington, D.C.: U.S. Department of Justice, National Institute of Justice, Office of Program Evaluation, 1980.
Florida Supreme Court. *The Citizens Dispute Settlement Process in Florida: A Study of Five Programs.* Tallahassee: Office of the State Court Administrator, 1979.
FULLER, LON L. "The Forms and Limits of Adjudication." *Harvard Law Review* 92 (1978): 353–409.
McEWEN, CRAIG A., and MAIMAN, RICHARD J. "Small Claims Mediation in Maine: An Empirical Assessment." *Maine Law Journal* 33 (1981): 237–268.
McGILLIS, DANIEL, and MULLEN, JOAN. *Neighborhood Justice Centers: An Analysis of Potential Models.* Washington, D.C.: U.S. Department of Justice, Law Enforcement Assistance Administration, National Institute of Law Enforcement and Criminal Justice, 1977.
POUND, ROSCOE. *An Introduction to the Philosophy of Law* (1922). Rev. ed. New Haven: Yale University Press, 1954.
SANDER, FRANK E. A. "Varieties of Dispute Processing." *Federal Rules Decisions*, vol. 70. St. Paul: West, 1976, pp. 111–134.

DIVERSION

See DISPUTE RESOLUTION PROGRAMS; INFORMAL DISPOSITION; PRETRIAL DIVERSION.

DOUBLE JEOPARDY

The history of double jeopardy protection

The principle that a defendant may not be tried twice for the same offense has been described as "one of the oldest ideas found in western civilization," with roots traceable to early Greek, Roman, and canon law (*Bartkus v. Illinois*, 359 U.S. 121, 151–155 (1959) (Justice Black dissenting)).

England. William Blackstone recognized it as a "universal maxim of the common law of England that no man is to be brought into jeopardy of his life, more than once for the same offence" (* 335). The exact origins of the "universal maxim," however, are not clear. A controversy in the twelfth century between Henry II and Archbishop of Canterbury Thomas à Becket over the trial and punishment of clerks in both ecclesiastical and King's courts may have influenced the adoption of the doctrine. It is also possible that the double jeopardy principles were not native to England and were taken from the Continent through canon law (Sigler, pp. 1–37; Friedland, pp. 5–15).

The development of double jeopardy protection in England was strongly influenced by the political environment and by changes in criminal law and procedure. The tensions between church and state during the twelfth century caused sporadic application of the protection against punishment in both the ecclesiastical and King's courts.

Within the King's courts, criminal procedure of the period permitted a penal proceeding to be initiated either by a private person (an appellor) or by the king or his agent. In the thirteenth century, the courts established that a suit by an appellor that resulted in either an acquittal or a conviction of the defendant was a bar to another suit by the same appellor. An indictment by the king was subject to the same limitation. A suit by an appellor, however, did not bar an indictment by the king. Further, double jeopardy limitations applied to capital offenses only.

Not until the second half of the seventeenth century did the "universal maxim" receive more serious attention in English law. It was then held that a trial in another jurisdiction would bar further proceedings (*Rex v. Thomas*, 83 Eng. Rep. 1180 (K.B. 1664)). The Court of King's Bench ruled that reprosecution should be barred after an acquittal (*Rex v. Read*, 83 Eng. Rep. 271 (K.B. 1660)). In addition, the courts attempted to end the practice of discharging the jury when it appeared that a defendant would be acquitted, a practice instituted so that the prosecution could bring another action after improving the evidence.

The United States. The movement in seventeenth-century England toward increased protection was not enough for some American jurisdictions, and therefore the double jeopardy doctrine was further expanded in the colonial period. For example, the doctrine was extended, first by Massachusetts and eventually by other colonies, to all offenses, capital and otherwise.

Double jeopardy protection was generally not included in the first colonial constitutions, but the doctrine did appear in the case law. In 1789, the prohibition of double jeopardy was included in the Bill of Rights: the Fifth Amendment provides that no person shall "be subject for the same offense to be twice put in jeopardy of life or limb." These words, although simple, did little to clarify the meaning and scope of the protection.

States formulated their own protection against double jeopardy, and many adopted standards different from those of the federal government. In 1969, however, the Supreme Court held that the Fifth Amendment double jeopardy clause applied to the states and that the same constitutional standards of double jeopardy restricted both state and federal governments (*Benton v. Maryland*, 395 U.S. 784, 793–796 (1969)).

Functions of double jeopardy protection

The classic summary of the purposes served by the double jeopardy guarantee is found in *Green v. United States*, 355 U.S. 184 (1957): "The underlying idea . . . is that the State with all its resources and power should not be allowed to make repeated attempts to convict an individual for an alleged offense, thereby subjecting him to embarrassment, expense and ordeal and compelling him to live in a continuing state of anxiety and insecurity, as well as enhancing the possibility that even though innocent he may be found guilty" (187–188).

This concise statement contains a number of different and partially inconsistent notions. An important, although largely implicit, idea is that of finality, or res judicata. The notion is that once a matter has been fully and fairly litigated, the decision rendered should put the matter to rest once and for all. The idea of finality reflects notions of fairness to the prevailing party, the importance to society of establishing a sense of repose, and the need for efficient administration of the judicial process. These concerns apply in all litigation, civil and criminal, and accordingly, the doctrine of res judicata generally bars the reopening of any dispute once the matter has been resolved in a fully litigated case.

The concerns identified by the Supreme Court in *Green* go beyond these notions of finality and give the double jeopardy clause its distinctive significance in criminal cases. When an initial prosecution is terminated before a verdict is reached, finality notions would not bar further proceedings, but a second prosecution will nonetheless subject the accused to further "embarrassment, expense and ordeal." Thus, double jeopardy concerns arise even though the first proceeding has not led to a decision on the merits of the case. When the initial prosecution leads to an acquittal, ordinary finality principles would not bar an appeal and subsequent relitigation if the first proceeding was found to be tainted by error. But because the state has vastly greater resources than the ordinary criminal defendant, such a retrial can create an unacceptable risk that an innocent defendant will ultimately be convicted. Because of this, double jeopardy principles often suggest denying the usual process of appellate review when the decision at trial has been favorable to the accused. The concern for protecting the innocent is reinforced by the traditional notion that the jury is entitled to discharge the accused even when guilt is clear.

The double jeopardy principle thus serves a number of distinct purposes, and its concern for protecting the individual facing the great power of the state often requires safeguards that defeat the goal of accurate, efficient resolution of disputes by full and fair litigation. The difficulty of ascertaining the proper reach of these competing goals undoubtedly has complicated the task of determining precise double jeopardy requirements in different procedural settings.

The scope of double jeopardy protection

The Supreme Court has summarized the double jeopardy protection as threefold: a protection against reprosecution for the same offense after acquittal; a protection against reprosecution for the same offense after conviction; and a protection against multiple punishment for the same offense (*North Carolina v. Pearce*, 395 U.S. 711, 717 (1969)). But these constitutional protections are not self-explanatory, and their scope is not clearly indicated by the history and purposes of the double jeopardy concept. To understand the nature of the double jeopardy guarantee, it will be necessary to discuss (1) the kinds of proceedings regarded as involving an initial jeopardy (or, as the courts put it, the situations in which jeopardy "attaches"); (2) the legal consequences of terminating that initial proceeding by mistrial, acquittal, or conviction; (3) the government's right to appeal adverse decisions made in the initial proceeding; (4) the kinds of subsequent charges regarded as involving the same offense; (5) the circumstances in which different but related offenses must be prosecuted in the same proceeding (the problem of joinder); (6) the circumstances in which a factual dispute resolved in the initial proceeding can be reopened in a subsequent prosecution for a different offense (the problem of collateral estoppel); and (7) the application of double jeopardy principles to successive prosecutions by different governmental units (the problem of dual sovereignty).

The attachment of jeopardy. Logically, a defendant must have undergone initial jeopardy before he can complain of another prosecution for the same offense. It is therefore necessary to identify the point in the criminal proceedings at which jeopardy attaches. The Supreme Court has held that in a jury trial, jeopardy attaches when the jury is impaneled and sworn (*Crist v. Bretz*, 437 U.S. 28, 37 (1978)). In a trial without a jury, jeopardy does not attach until the judge receives the first evidence (*Serfass v. United States*, 420 U.S. 377, 388 (1975)). In consequence, a defendant is not considered to be in jeopardy when arrested, when arraigned, or even when formally indicted and ordered to stand trial. Nor is a defendant considered to be in jeopardy when motions are presented and argued prior to trial, even though formal hearings may be held and witnesses called to testify. Criminal proceedings can be terminated at any of these pretrial stages and then reopened without violating the prohibition against double jeopardy.

Termination of proceedings after jeopardy attaches. The possibility of reprosecution after termination of a trial depends on the circumstances of the termination. Different rules apply according to whether the trial ends in mistrial, acquittal, or conviction.

Mistrial. Once a criminal trial is under way, circumstances sometimes suggest the desirability of terminating the proceedings prior to a formal verdict of guilt or acquittal. For example, the death or serious incapacitation of several jurors usually would warrant interrupting the proceedings and beginning the trial again before an entirely new jury. In such a situation the judge typically will declare a "mistrial"; this is in effect a declaration that the merits of the case cannot fairly be resolved one way or the other and that a new trial may be initiated if the prosecution chooses to do so. The Supreme Court has held that if the declaration of mistrial is appropriate under the circumstances, the defendant may be retried without violating double jeopardy requirements (*United States v. Perez*, 22 U.S. (9 Wheat.) 579 (1824)). However, if the trial judge acted improperly in declaring the mistrial (that is, if the initial trial should have been pursued to completion), a subsequent trial will be viewed as imposing double jeopardy, in violation of the constitutional command (*Downum v. United States*, 372 U.S. 734 (1963)).

Under what circumstances can a judge properly declare a mistrial? In *Perez* (580), the Supreme Court ruled that mistrial is proper when "there is a manifest necessity for the act, or the ends of public justice would otherwise be defeated." Subsequent decisions have attempted to clarify this "manifest necessity" test and its application to the many diverse problems that arise during trials (Schulhofer). The precise content of the manifest necessity requirement nonetheless remains somewhat unpredictable. Since 1973, Supreme Court decisions have tended to require considerable deference to the trial judge's initial conclusion about the necessity for declaring a mistrial (*Arizona v. Washington*, 434 U.S. 497 (1978); *Illinois v. Somerville*, 410 U.S. 458 (1973)).

Acquittal. An acquittal acts as an absolute bar to further prosecution even if the acquittal is clearly erroneous (*United States v. Ball*, 163 U.S. 662, 670 (1896)). This principle is considered fundamental to double jeopardy jurisprudence. "To permit a second trial after an acquittal, however mistaken the acquittal may have been, would present an unacceptably high risk that the Government, with its vastly superior resources, might wear down the defendant so that 'even though innocent, he may be found guilty' " (*United States v. Scott*, 437 U.S. 82, 91 (1978), quoting *Green*, 188).

The definition of *acquittal* has often shifted, and remains controversial. In the view of the Supreme Court in the 1970s, a judgment constituted an acquittal only if it was a determination of the factual innocence of the defendant—"a resolution . . . of some or all of the factual elements of the offense charged" (*Scott*, quoting *United States v. Martin Linen Supply Co.*, 430 U.S. 564, 571 (1977)). A discharge of the defendant at his request based on a procedural issue unrelated to innocence did not constitute an acquittal for double jeopardy purposes.

One clear example of acquittal is a jury verdict of not guilty or a judgment of not guilty rendered by a judge in a bench trial. The determination of what constitutes an acquittal is more difficult when the judge discharges a defendant during the trial but before a verdict is returned. An appellate court faced with a double jeopardy claim must review the trial court's reasons for discharge and decide whether they are related to the factual innocence of the defendant.

The distinction between a discharge based on a purely procedural defect and one based on a finding of factual innocence is not always obvious, and the Court in *Scott* did not provide clear tests for distinguishing between the two. The Court did say that a discharge on the basis of defenses such as insanity and entrapment would constitute an acquittal. A discharge based on a finding that the defendant was prejudiced by preindictment delay would not constitute an acquittal, however, even though the determination of prejudice requires some consideration of the strength of the evidence of guilt. If the judge holds testimony inadmissible under the rules of evidence and then finds the remaining evidence insufficient to establish guilt, the insufficiency ruling is considered an acquittal, even though it depends solely on the application of rules of evidence unrelated to factual innocence (*Sanabria v. United States,* 437 U.S. 54 (1978)).

Conviction. In principle, a defendant convicted and sentenced after trial may not be retried or resentenced for the same offense. However, sometimes a conviction is reversed by an appellate court, and in these circumstances both reprosecution and resentencing are permitted, with certain exceptions.

With respect to reprosecution, the governing rule is similar to the one applicable to acquittals. If the reversal is based on an error in the proceedings leading to conviction, reprosecution is allowed (*Ball,* 662). But if the reversal is based on the appellate court's view that there was insufficient evidence to convict, further prosecution will be barred (*Burks v. United States,* 437 U.S. 1 (1978)). This type of reversal is essentially the same as an acquittal: it represents a finding that there is at least a reasonable doubt regarding the factual innocence of the defendant.

The double jeopardy clause does not ordinarily restrict the sentence that may be imposed after a conviction has been set aside and the defendant has been reprosecuted and reconvicted. The second sentence may be more severe than the one originally imposed, but any time that the defendant served in prison on the original charge must be credited toward the new sentence (*Pearce*).

The exception to this general rule is a sentence imposed under a procedure closely resembling a formal trial (*Bullington v. Missouri,* 451 U.S. 430 (1981)). In *Bullington,* the jury participated in a sentencing hearing designed to determine whether the defendant should receive the death penalty or life imprisonment. The Supreme Court held that this special setting was closely analogous to a trial on the merits, and that once life imprisonment had been imposed at the initial sentencing proceeding, the initial sentence could be viewed as an acquittal on the prosecution's demand for the harsher penalty of death. Thus, double jeopardy protection came into play after the implied acquittal.

The government's right to appeal. The defendant's right to appeal from an unfavorable judgment is long-standing, but in federal prosecutions the government's right to appeal was long governed by narrow statutory limitations. In 1970, Congress passed a new criminal appeals act, designed to remove statutory barriers to prosecutorial appeal in federal cases. The act provided that the government may appeal from a district court dismissal of one or more counts of the indictment or information "except that no appeal shall lie where the double jeopardy clause of the United States Constitution prohibits further prosecution" (Omnibus Crime Control and Safe Streets Act of 1968 (part), as amended, 18 U.S.C. § 3731 (1976)). The act allowed the Supreme Court to focus on the constitutional, rather than the statutory, boundaries of the government's right to appeal.

It had been well established by 1970 that a jury verdict of not guilty, or an acquittal in a nonjury trial, would bar government appeal and reprosecution (*Ball*). More difficult questions arise when a judge terminates the proceedings prior to a definitive verdict on the question of guilt. In this connection, two different kinds of termination orders must be distinguished. If the judge declares a mistrial, the order itself contemplates new proceedings, and reprosecution is therefore permissible unless the defendant succeeds in challenging the propriety of the mistrial (*Abney v. United States,* 431 U.S. 651 (1977)). In contrast, if the judge grants an acquittal or dismisses the charges for any reason, the decision stands as a barrier to reprosecution unless the government can win a reversal of the decision from an appellate court.

In 1975, the Supreme Court held that the Fifth Amendment guarantee would be violated by a government appeal if jeopardy had attached and if the appeal would cause further proceedings on the question of the defendant's guilt (*United States v. Jenkins*, 420 U.S. 358, 370 (1975)). Thus, any mid-trial discharge favorable to the defendant (whether or not amounting to an acquittal on the merits) would bar government appeal, because a successful appeal would require additional proceedings.

Three years after the adoption of the "further proceedings" test, the Supreme Court abandoned it. In *Scott*, the Court held that when a judge discharges a defendant at his request before a verdict is handed down, the government may appeal unless the discharge constitutes an acquittal. Thus, when a mid-trial dismissal is not based on findings concerning the factual elements of the offense charged, the prosecution may appeal the ruling; if the appeal is successful, a second prosecution will be permissible.

A similar rule applies to a government appeal on the question of punishment. In many jurisdictions, local law prohibits any appellate review of sentences, and some states allow appellate review only at the request of the defense. But where statutes permit the prosecution to challenge the trial judge's sentencing decision as too lenient, the double jeopardy clause will bar the appeal only if the original sentence is deemed an implied acquittal of any greater sentence (*Bullington*).

In most cases, imposition of a relatively lenient sentence will not be deemed an implied acquittal of any greater sentence (*United States v. DiFrancesco*, 449 U.S. 117 (1980)). Ordinarily the sentencing decision is left to the broad discretion of the trial judge, under relatively informal procedures and a relaxed standard of proof. In *DiFrancesco*, the Supreme Court viewed these factors as sufficient to distinguish most sentencing procedures from a trial on the merits. This difference nevertheless is somewhat formalistic: the double jeopardy clause has been held to bar reprosecution for first-degree murder if the judge or jury convicts only for the second-degree offense (*Green*), but the clause does not bar appeal and resentencing to the statutory maximum sentence, even when the judge or jury has rejected such a punishment at trial.

The same offense. The protection against double jeopardy is a protection against multiple prosecutions for the same offense. The proliferation of technically different offenses encompassed in a single instance of criminal behavior has increased the importance of defining the scope of the offense that controls for purposes of the double jeopardy guarantee.

Distinct statutory provisions will be treated as involving separate offenses for double jeopardy purposes only if "each provision requires proof of an additional fact which the other does not" (*Blockburger v. United States*, 284 U.S. 299, 304 (1932)). Where the same evidence suffices to prove both crimes, they are the same for double jeopardy purposes, and the clause forbids successive trials and cumulative punishments for the two crimes. The offenses must be joined in one indictment and tried together unless the defendant requests that they be tried separately (*Jeffers v. United States*, 432 U.S. 137 (1977)).

Under the *Blockburger* test, two offenses are the same not only when both crimes require proof of the same facts, but also when one offense is a "lesser included offense" of the other. For example, the offense of joyriding, or taking a car temporarily, is a lesser included offense of auto theft, that is, taking a car with intent to deprive the owner permanently of possession (*Brown v. Ohio*, 432 U.S. 161 (1977)). Thus, a defendant could not be separately prosecuted or punished for joyriding and auto theft. The rule against separate prosecutions may, however, be inapplicable when the state, for good cause, is unable to proceed on the more serious charge at the outset.

The "same evidence" test does not preclude multiple prosecutions and cumulative punishments when a criminal act causes harm to several victims. For example, if a robber takes money from a group of six poker players, the robbery of each person is a separate offense because separate evidence is required to prove the harm done to each person.

The same-evidence test has been criticized as giving the prosecution multiple opportunities to perfect its case and obtain a conviction (*Ashe v. Swenson*, 397 U.S. 436, 451 (1970)). A minority of jurisdictions has adopted a broader test requiring that the prosecution join all charges against a defendant that grow out of a "single criminal act, occurrence, episode or transaction" (*Ashe*, 453–454). Under this "same transaction" test, the alleged robber of the poker players could not be prosecuted separately for robbing each of the six men because the robberies all arose out of a single criminal episode. The American Law Institute also recommended adoption of the same-transaction test. The Institute's Model Penal Code requires joinder of separate offenses arising from a single criminal episode whenever the offenses are known to the prosecuting officer at the start of the first trial, and when the offenses are within the jurisdiction of a single court. However, the trial court would have the authority to order separate trials when justice requires (§ 1.07(2), (3)).

Collateral estoppel. The doctrine of collateral estoppel means that "when an issue of ultimate fact has once been determined by a valid and final judgment, that issue cannot be litigated between the same parties in any future lawsuit" (*Ashe*, 443). The Supreme Court has held that this doctrine is embodied in the guarantee against double jeopardy (*Ashe*, 445). Thus, when an issue of fact has been settled in a prosecution for one offense, the double jeopardy clause forbids relitigation of that issue even in a prosecution for a different offense.

The effect of the collateral estoppel doctrine may best be understood by an illustration. In *Ashe*, six men playing poker were robbed by armed intruders who also stole a car. Ashe and three other defendants were charged with armed robbery of each of the six victims and with theft of the car. However, Ashe was first tried for the armed robbery of one of the men. The evidence that a robbery had occurred was unquestionable, but there was doubt about whether Ashe was one of the robbers. The jury found him "not guilty due to insufficient evidence."

Ashe was then brought to trial for the robbery of one of the other poker players. The Supreme Court concluded that the jury in the first trial must have found that Ashe was not one of the robbers, or that there was at least a reasonable doubt on this issue. The prosecution was therefore barred from relitigating this question, and further prosecution of Ashe for robbing any of the other poker players was precluded.

When a jury submits a general verdict—that is, a conclusion of guilty or not guilty without specific findings of fact—it may be difficult to determine what factual conclusions the jury reached, and therefore difficult to decide whether any factual issues should be considered settled for purposes of further prosecution. The Supreme Court has ruled that when a defendant seeks to invoke the collateral estoppel doctrine, the reviewing court must examine the record of the previous trial and other relevant material to determine "whether a rational jury could have grounded its verdict upon an issue other than that which the defendant seeks to foreclose from consideration" (*Ashe*, 444). When a defendant has essentially raised but one defense, as when Ashe claimed he was not one of the robbers, this "rational jury" test will often permit the reviewing court to conclude that the jury must have accepted the defense, and the collateral estoppel doctrine will be available. But perhaps more frequently, a defendant will raise a variety of alternative defenses, and a general verdict of not guilty might rest on any one of several factual conclusions. In this frequently occurring situation, the collateral estoppel doctrine will seldom afford a defendant protection against successive prosecutions for related but technically separate offenses.

Dual sovereignty. The principle of dual sovereignty is a significant limitation on double jeopardy protection. Separate prosecution and punishment has been held not to violate the double jeopardy clause if a criminal act violates both state and federal laws (*Bartkus; Abbate v. United States*, 359 U.S. 187 (1959)).

The dual sovereignty rule appears to contradict the policy against using government power to try people twice for the same conduct. In defense of the rule, the Supreme Court has argued that any other rule would hinder either state or federal law enforcement. Frequently, a defendant's acts impinge more seriously on either a state or a federal interest. Allowing only one sovereign to prosecute would prevent the other from vindicating its perhaps greater interest (*Abbate*, 195).

In practice, the state and federal governments are not eager to duplicate prosecutions for the same criminal act. Department of Justice policy forbids federal prosecution after state prosecution on the same charges except when necessary to advance a compelling interest of federal law enforcement, and then only with explicit approval of the appropriate assistant attorney general (*Petite v. United States*, 361 U.S. 529, 530–531 (1960); *Rinaldi v. United States*, 434 U.S. 22 (1977)).

About half of the states have adopted legislation that bars a subsequent state prosecution under certain circumstances. The state rules vary considerably in the breadth and nature of the prohibition against multiple prosecutions.

The dual sovereignty principle does not extend to successive prosecutions by a state and by a municipality within the state. For purposes of double jeopardy doctrine, municipalities are considered subordinate to state authority (*Waller v. Florida*, 397 U.S. 387 (1970)). However, Indian tribes that have retained their sovereign power to punish offenders are considered separate sovereigns. Thus, tribal and federal prosecutions for the same criminal act are not barred by the double jeopardy clause (*United States v. Wheeler*, 435 U.S. 313 (1978)).

Conclusion

The Supreme Court has struggled to develop principles that are consistent with the history and purposes of the double jeopardy clause. The doctrines that have emerged often seem inconsistent and difficult to reconcile with the values that double jeopardy protection should serve (Westen and Drubel). It may be suggested that, technical complexities aside, much of the difficulty stems from the Court's continuing ambivalence about whether double jeopardy requirements should serve primarily to promote finality and related values of efficient judicial administration, or whether the rules should also serve to protect the accused from some of the normal consequences of "full and fair litigation" against a vastly more powerful adversary.

STEPHEN J. SCHULHOFER

See also APPEAL; CRIMINAL PROCEDURE: CONSTITUTIONAL ASPECTS.

BIBLIOGRAPHY

American Law Institute. *Model Penal Code: Proposed Official Draft.* Philadelphia: ALI, 1962.
BLACKSTONE, WILLIAM. *Commentaries on the Laws of England* (1765–1769), vol. 4. Reprint. University of Chicago Press, 1979.
FRIEDLAND, MARTIN L. *Double Jeopardy.* Oxford: Clarendon Press, 1969.
SCHULHOFER, STEPHEN J. "Jeopardy and Mistrials." *University of Pennsylvania Law Review* 125 (1977): 449–539.
SIGLER, JAY A. *Double Jeopardy: The Development of a Legal and Social Policy.* Ithaca, N.Y.: Cornell University Press, 1969.
WESTEN, PETER, and DRUBEL, RICHARD. "Toward a General Theory of Double Jeopardy." *The Supreme Court Review 1978.* Edited by Philip B. Kurland and Gerhard Casper. University of Chicago Press, 1979, pp. 81–169.

DRINKING AND DRIVING

The social problem of drinking and driving

Drinking and driving is a leading cause of death and injury in all societies highly dependent on the automobile. The problem is relatively greater in those mature societies in which the automobile is frequently used and in which highway engineering and vehicle safety measures have made it less likely that road or vehicle defects will cause crashes. In the United States, for example, traffic crashes are the leading cause of violent death, and between one-third and two-thirds of drivers in fatal crashes are found to have been drinking.

The problem of crashes caused by drivers influenced by alcohol has preoccupied public opinion and the law ever since the invention of the automobile in the late nineteenth century, although the subsequent accumulation of knowledge and experience has led to important changes in both the definition of the problem and the official reaction to it. At first it was simply felt that gross, clinically manifest drunkenness caused crashes, and the law accordingly forbade driving while drunk. Since the mid-twentieth century, however, authorities have tended to favor a subtler definition of the problem, in which crashes are statistically correlated to the alcohol in the driver's blood. It has been found that a correlation between drinking and crashes exists even when alcoholic influence is not clinically evident. Therefore, the law now prohibits driving with blood alcohol concentrations in excess of a stated standard.

Research on drinking and driving. The early view that drunkenness produced crashes rested on commonsense observation. It was evident that alcohol taken in large amounts interfered with the perceptual and motor skills necessary to drive a vehicle, and thus led to crashes. The newer view rests on research employing scientific measurements of blood alcohol concentrations. Techniques for making these measurements were developed in the 1920s and yielded two general lines of research, comprehensively reviewed by Ralph Jones and Kent Joscelyn.

In the first line of research, laboratory studies and limited field experiments were made to discover the effect of various blood alcohol concentrations on driving-related skills and abilities. It was found that moderate blood alcohol concentrations, well below those associated with clinically observable alcohol influence, could cause hazardous driving behavior. Blood alcohol concentration at all levels was shown to vary in direct proportion to the deterioration of perceptual and motor skills.

The second line of research investigated more broadly the blood alcohol concentrations of drivers involved in crashes, which were compared to the blood alcohol concentrations in control samples of drivers who had not crashed. The first large-scale work of this type, which has remained definitive, was that of Robert Borkenstein and his colleagues in Grand Rapids, Michigan, in the 1960s. The Grand Rapids study demonstrated that the risk of crash involvement increased significantly with the concentration of alcohol in the blood, at least above a very low threshold. Subsequent research in the United States and abroad has confirmed this hypothesis. The risk of a crash appears to rise importantly as concentration levels exceed .08 percent, a level that might occur in a typical male who consumes four drinks in an hour on an empty stomach. This research has also demonstrated that alcohol plays a considerably greater role in causing serious crashes (those involving injury or death) than in minor accidents, and that drinking is a particularly significant factor in nighttime and single-vehicle crashes.

The legal response to drinking and driving. Changing assessments of the nature of the drinking-and-driving problem have modified the legal approach to its control. Vehicle codes initially forbade driving "while under the influence of intoxicating liquor," driving in an "intoxicated condition," or simply "drunk driving." These "classical" laws were directed against obviously blameworthy conduct and prescribed traditional criminal penalties and procedures. However, frequent changes in the definition of the behavior forbidden under these laws suggested that their imprecision was causing dissatisfaction. It was also apparent that convictions were difficult to obtain under the classical laws, even in the case of grossly impaired drivers, if no crash had resulted from the impairment. Popular and official dissatisfaction with the classical laws was reinforced by the new research that was being conducted. Laboratory findings challenged the limitation of alcoholic influence to overt drunkenness, and field research revealed that where the classical laws prevailed, up to half of all fatal crashes were the result of drinking and driving.

A new legal approach to drinking and driving, which has been called *Scandinavian-type law*, emerged in response to widespread dissatisfaction with existing provisions. The first instance of such an approach was a Norwegian law of 1936, a somewhat modified version of which was enacted in Sweden in 1941. These Scandinavian innovations were not the result of advanced understanding of the drinking-and-driving problem (the new research had barely begun to yield results) but rather reflected temperance sentiments in Scandinavian politics (Andenaes). The Scandinavian-type laws prohibited driving with blood alcohol concentrations exceeding specific levels relative to body weight: .05 percent in the original Norwegian law and .08 percent in Sweden. Enforcement required chemical tests: a preliminary breath test that could be demanded by a policeman who suspected a driver of committing the offense, and an evidentiary quantitative blood test for those failing the first test. Penalties for violating the laws included license suspension and confinement in prison; the latter was made mandatory for a blood alcohol concentration exceeding .05 percent in Norway and .15 percent in Sweden. In short, the Scandinavian laws introduced objective, nonclinical definitions of the drinking-and-driving offense, employing novel scientific criminal procedures

and severe penalties. After World War II these laws were widely adopted throughout the developed, automobile-dependent world.

Scandinavian-type laws and deterrence

Comparison with the deterrence model. The theory of deterrence holds that the threat of punishment will curtail prohibited behavior to the extent that swift and severe application is perceived to be likely (Gibbs). Drinking-and-driving laws of the Scandinavian type correspond much more closely than do the classical laws to prescriptions derived from deterrence theory. The severity of penalties in Scandinavia is obvious. It is less clear that an objective definition of the offense, and scientific procedures for its investigation, may alter potential offenders' perception of the likelihood of punishment. Although Scandinavian-type laws did not render prosecution completely efficient, they did eliminate many of the problems inherent in subjectively detecting prohibited conduct, including the determination of whether a driver was under the influence of alcohol and of whether his driving was indeed impaired at the time of arrest. The Scandinavian experience offers less conclusive evidence as to consequences of swift punishment, but because prosecution procedures are comparatively simple it is likely that punishment follows relatively quickly upon accusation.

After World War II the provisions of Swedish and Norwegian law were widely adopted elsewhere. Although sanctions as severe as mandatory prison sentences for first offenses were uncommon, the measures that were introduced to increase the impression of swift and certain punishment frequently exceeded those of the Scandinavian models. For example, the Road Safety Act, 1967, c. 30 (Great Britain) provided that police constables could, without prior suspicion of alcoholic influence, demand screening tests for alcohol in the event of a traffic infraction or a crash. A French law of 1978 provided for breath testing of all drivers at arbitrarily erected roadblocks, similarly requiring no suspicion of the use of alcohol.

Evaluation of Scandinavian-type laws. At the time of their enactment, the Norwegian and Swedish laws were not accompanied by attempts at evaluation in the modern sense. Since then, vigorous efforts have been made to show their effectiveness as deterrents, but the evidence is almost entirely impressionistic and anecdotal. One attempt to analyze historical data (Ross, 1975) found no evidence that either the Norwegian or the Swedish law affected drinking and driving, as measured by changes in the rates of total crashes and of fatal crashes in the years preceding and following the enactment of these laws. However, these negative results have been offset by several factors: gaps in the data, the possible effects of cataclysmic historical events (the Swedish law was introduced during World War II), and, above all, the relatively little publicity that accompanied the enactment of these laws, which were part of a general effort to increase the deterrent effect of legal measures in the two countries.

However, the adoption of Scandinavian-type laws in other countries has been accompanied by more reliable evaluations of their effectiveness in preventing infractions. The adoption of well-publicized measures appears to heighten perceptions of the likelihood of apprehension, conviction, and punishment of drinking drivers. The best example has been the British Road Safety Act of 1967, referred to above, which introduced a blood alcohol concentration limit of .08 percent and which permitted testing the breath of drivers involved in crashes and serious traffic law violations without the police officer's prior suspicion of alcohol. In addition to being well publicized officially, the law was frequently and vigorously debated in the media for months before its enactment and for years afterward. A statistically significant change was noted in the levels both of all crashes and of serious ones involving fatal or serious injuries. Serious crashes on weekend nights, when alcohol was quite likely to be involved, were cut in half immediately after the law went into effect, whereas crashes occurring during commuting hours, when alcohol would rarely be a factor, showed no change. It is highly probable that this law initially was an effective deterrent (Ross, 1973).

Similar conclusions emerged from an analysis of the French law of 1978, using the quasi-experimental technique of interrupted time-series analysis (Ross, 1981). Deterrent effectiveness has also been claimed in two independent evaluations of a Canadian federal drinking-and-driving law of 1969 (Carr, Goldberg, and Farbar; Chambers, Roberts, and Voeller), even though this law was introduced with relatively little publicity and its apparent effect on the frequency of crashes was therefore much smaller. An evaluation of a Dutch drinking-and-driving law of 1974 claimed to prove a reduction of serious crashes by more than one-third (Noordzij).

Studies of the deterrent value of Scandinavian-type laws have also suggested, however, that the effect eventually dissipates. In France, vehicle crashes returned to earlier levels within a few months of the passage of the 1978 law, and both Canadian investigating groups concluded that their country's law had a deterrent effect for only about one year. In the Netherlands the incidence of drivers having an elevated blood alcohol concentration had largely reverted to previous levels a year after the law's enactment. Even in Great Britain, where the Road Safety Act at first was remarkably effective in reducing the number of weekend crashes, the law's effect was only half as strong a few months later, and thereafter a clear trend back to the former frequency of crashes became apparent. Two years after the act was passed, the proportion of illegal blood alcohol concentrations found among drivers killed in crashes, which had confirmed the act's initial deterrent effect, returned to and even exceeded the levels of the period just before its enactment.

Enforcement campaigns. Several jurisdictions that had passed Scandinavian-type laws conducted enforcement campaigns designed to increase public awareness of the probability that intoxicated drivers would be punished. Notable examples of such campaigns were the Cheshire "blitz" of 1975 in England (Ross, 1977) and similar efforts in New Zealand in 1978 (Hurst and Wright) and Melbourne, Australia, in 1977 and 1978 (Cameron, Strang, and Vulcan). The United States Department of Transportation conducted several similar campaigns, called Alcohol Safety Action Projects. Although studies of these campaigns varied in quality, it was significant that all found that declines in the incidence of drinking and driving were limited to the period of the campaigns.

Punishment campaigns. Attempts have also been made to increase penalties for drinking and driving without raising the actual or perceived likelihood of apprehension. Examples of informal innovations include the traffic court's crackdown on drinking drivers in Chicago in 1970 (Robertson, Rich, and Ross) and the "Traffictown" magistrate's campaign in Australia (Misner and Ward). A more formal innovation in Finland involved great increases in the length of prison terms to which drinking drivers could be sentenced; in 1957, Finland doubled what were already the world's most stringent penalties for this offense.

The results of these efforts differ considerably from those of the enforcement campaigns discussed above. Neither in Chicago nor in "Traffictown" was there any sign that increasing the severity of penalties reduced drinking and driving, nor did the augmented Finnish penalties produce significant favorable results (Ross, 1975, pp. 303–308). Rather, it appears that such plans to increase the severity of penalties may often be inadequately implemented and that unintended and undesired consequences may ensue elsewhere in the legal system. For example, the reporting of violations may be distorted, causing a decline in convictions and thereby reducing the likelihood that violators will receive any punishment at all.

Conclusion

Implications for criminology. Innovations in drinking-and-driving law provide useful tests of deterrence theory (Ross, 1982). An increased public perception of the likelihood of punishment does deter drinking and driving, as research has shown. Well-publicized replacements of classical drinking-and-driving laws by Scandinavian-type laws have brought about decreases in indexes of drinking and driving, especially in rates of serious crashes. The eventual rise of these rates back to previous levels can be interpreted as evidence that *actual* increases in the likelihood of punishment did not correspond to the increases that the public had been led to expect by the publicity and controversy surrounding the new laws' enactment. In the United States, for example, the actual chances of a drinking driver being apprehended under a Scandinavian-type law have been estimated at between 1 in 200 and 1 in 2,000 (Beitel, Sharp, and Glauz; Borkenstein). Similar estimates have been made in other countries, for example, Sweden (Persson). It is reasonable to conclude that drivers who drink soon gain a realistic and accurate idea of the risk of being caught. The chances of detection and punishment achieved in measures to date appear to be insufficient to deter drinking and driving over the long term.

Announced increases in severity of punishment have produced no measurable deterrence of drinking and driving. Common sense suggests that this is at least in part a consequence of a low probability of any punishment at all. If punishment is unlikely, it is doubtful that increasing the severity of penalties will have notable success. Indeed, it could be said that one risk of drinking and driving is capital punishment in the form of death in a crash, yet some people seem willing to assume the risk.

Little data exist concerning swiftness of punishment, the third variable of the simple deterrence theory. This variable has not been clearly and independently tested.

Implications for policy. The deterrent effect on drinking and driving that is apparently achieved by the adoption and enforcement of Scandinavian-type laws affords some encouragement to those who advocate deterrence as a means of dealing with this problem. However, the universal experience of a declining and vanishing deterrent effect suggests the need for great caution. In the future, policies using deterrence to control drinking and driving might aim at increasing the genuine likelihood of punishment to such an extent that important and permanent changes in public perception are achieved. As yet, however, there is no reason to believe that it would be financially and politically feasible to do this, particularly in view of the increased intrusion of the police into citizens' lives that would be necessary.

Since previous attempts to control drinking and driving have been unavailing, policymakers ought to consider alternatives to deterrence. For example, broader attacks on alcohol abuse might be made by raising the price of alcohol by taxation, thereby reducing its consumption, or by using selective prohibition to eliminate the distribution of alcohol in roadhouses and other places that must be reached by car. Such measures may have some appeal because they transcend the issue of highway safety and address other social problems related to alcohol. It might also be beneficial to control the consequences, rather than the commission, of driver error—for example, by removing roadside hazards or by installing passive restraints in automobiles that minimize injuries associated with crashes. Such efforts would have broader consequences by diminishing the effects of driver error, whether resulting from inattention, heart attack, or many other human factors resulting in crashes, in addition to drinking.

H. LAURENCE ROSS

See also ALCOHOL AND CRIME, *articles on* BEHAVIORAL ASPECTS *and* TREATMENT AND REHABILITATION; POLICE: STATE POLICE; TRAFFIC OFFENSES.

BIBLIOGRAPHY

ANDENAES, JOHANNES. "The Effects of Scandinavia's Drinking-and-driving Laws: Facts and Hypotheses." *Scandinavian Studies in Criminology* 6 (1978): 35–53.

BEITEL, GEORGE A.; SHARP, MICHAEL C.; and GLAUZ, WILLIAM D. "Probability of Arrest while Driving under the Influence of Alcohol." *Journal of Studies of Alcohol* 36 (1975): 109–116.

BORKENSTEIN, ROBERT F. "Problems of Enforcement, Adjudication, and Sanctioning." *Alcohol, Drugs, and Traffic Safety.* Edited by S. Israelstam and S. Lambert. Toronto: Addiction Research Foundation of Ontario, 1975, pp. 655–662.

———; CROWTHER, R. F.; SHUMATE, R. P.; ZIEL, W. B.; and ZYLMAN, R. *The Role of the Drinking Driver in Traffic Accidents.* Edited by Allen Dale. Bloomington: Indiana University, Department of Police Administration, 1969.

CAMERON, M. H.; STRANG, P. M.; and VULCAN, A. P. "Evaluation of Random Breath Testing in Victoria, Australia." Paper read at Eighth International Conference on Alcohol, Drugs, and Traffic Safety, Stockholm, 1980.

CARR, B. R.; GOLDBERG, H.; and FARBAR, C. M. L. *The Breathaliser Legislation: An Inferential Evaluation.* Ottawa: Ministry of Transport, 1974.

CHAMBERS, L.; ROBERTS, R.; and VOELLER, C. "The Epidemiology of Traffic Accidents and the Effect of the 1969 Breathaliser Amendment in Canada." *Accident Analysis and Prevention* 8 (1976): 201–206.

GIBBS, JACK P. *Crime, Punishment, and Deterrence.* New York: Elsevier, 1975.

HURST, PAUL M., and WRIGHT, PHYLLIS G. "Deterrence at Last: The Ministry of Transport's Alcohol Blitzes." Paper read at Eighth International Conference on Alcohol, Drugs, and Traffic Safety, Stockholm, 1980.

JONES, RALPH K., and JOSCELYN, KENT B. *Alcohol and Highway Safety 1978: A Review of the State of Knowledge,* summary volume. National Highway Traffic Safety Administration Technical Report DOT HS-803 764. Washington, D.C.: NHTSA, 1978.

MISNER, ROBERT L., and WARD, PAUL G. "Severe Penalties for Driving Offenses: A Deterrence Analysis." *Arizona State Law Journal,* no. 4 (1975): 677–713.

NOORDZIJ, P. C. "The Introduction of a Statutory BAC Limit of 50 mg./100 ml. and Its Effect on Drinking and Driving Habits and Traffic Accidents." Paper read at Seventh International Conference on Alcohol, Drugs, and Traffic Safety, Melbourne, 1977.

PERSSON, LEIF G. W. "Actual Drunken Driving in Sweden." *Scandinavian Studies in Criminology* 6 (1978): 101–112.

ROBERTSON, LEON S.; RICH, ROBERT F.; and ROSS, H. LAURENCE. "Jail Sentences for Driving while Intoxicated in Chicago: A Judicial Policy that Failed." *Law and Society Review* 8, no. 1 (1973): 55–67.

ROSS, H. LAURENCE. *Deterrence of the Drinking Driver: An International Survey.* National Highway Traffic Safety Administration Technical Report DOT HS-805 820. Washington, D.C.: NHTSA, 1981.

———. "Deterrence Regained: The Cheshire Constabulary's 'Breathalyser Blitz.'" *Journal of Legal Studies* 6 (1977): 241–249.

———. *Deterring the Drinking Driver: Legal Policy and Social Control.* Lexington, Mass.: Heath, Lexington Books, 1982.

———. "Law, Science, and Accidents: The British Road Safety Act of 1967." *Journal of Legal Studies* 2 (1973): 1–78.

———. "The Scandinavian Myth: The Effectiveness of Drinking–Driving Legislation in Sweden and Norway." *Journal of Legal Studies* 4 (1975): 285–310.

TAKALA, HANNU. "Drinking and Driving in Scandinavia: Finland." *Scandinavian Studies in Criminology* 6 (1978): 11–19.

U.S. Department of Transportation. *Alcohol Safety Action Projects Evaluation of Operations: Data, Tables of Results, and Formulation.* Washington, D.C.: National Highway Traffic Safety Administration, 1979.

DRUGS AND CRIME

1.
BEHAVIORAL ASPECTS

This article is dedicated to the late William H. McGlothlin (1924–1980) and is based extensively on his works.

Introduction

The extent to which crime is related to drug use remains a controversial issue. Opinions in the literature on the possible relationships are varied and contradictory. The presumption of a causal link between the two played a significant part in the passage of the Harrison Act of 1914, ch. 1, 38 Stat. 785, the first major federal legislation regulating the distribution and use of opiates and cocaine. In the late 1960s, negative public reaction to the use of marijuana, LSD, and other hallucinogens by large numbers of middle-class youths led to the development of more punitive social policies toward all illicit drug use. As mores regarding the use of marijuana, LSD, and cocaine subsequently changed, social policy became fragmented, ambivalent, and contradictory. Decriminalization for marijuana and other "soft" drugs was proposed, as well as increased penalties for heroin possession and all forms of drug trafficking. During several presidential administrations national attention focused on drug abuse, and federal intervention and treatment policy has been based on the assumed causal link between drugs and crime. The creation of the Special Action Office for Drug Abuse Prevention in 1971 and of the National Institute on Drug Abuse in 1974 was predicated on the assumption that a decrease in crime would naturally follow a decrease in drug abuse.

Massive infusions of money, time, and expertise have resulted in a substantial increase in information on drugs, drug abuse, and drug-related effects on criminal behavior. As with all complex behavioral and social phenomena, however, the increased information has not suggested any simple, immediate solutions. Rather, studies have pointed out that people use drugs for many reasons and in varied contexts, with results dependent on culture, person, place, setting, and expectation.

The question of the relationship between drug use and crime has been most frequently approached by way of three hypotheses, which are not mutually exclusive: (1) drug use causes or leads to crime; (2) crime leads to drug use; and (3) both drug use and crime are the result of other factors. Such general statements, however, are of limited use. They do not, for example, specify qualifying or conditional circumstances that limit or enhance the proposed relationship. At the very least, it is necessary to identify the type of drug and the context of use. Drugs in common use differ greatly in their pharmacological effects. Differences in cultural and social acceptance are also of prime importance in determining the consequences of using certain drugs. For example, the supply reduction policies that have been adopted by most nations result in greatly inflated costs of opiates. Such policies may contribute to the amount of income-generating crime among users. Thus, the use of a particular drug may be related to crime in some societies but not in others.

When considering more specific causal hypotheses concerning drug use and crime, it is necessary to distinguish between theories relating to direct pharmacological effects and those relating to indirect effects. Often included among the former are the disinhibition theories, which argue that the use of certain drugs results in impulsive behaviors that would normally be under personal or social control. Disinhibition theories are often found in discussions of alcohol and violence and, beginning about 1975, of phencyclidine (PCP) and violence. Although intuitively appealing, this idea of disinhibition, or loss of control, is closely related to the sensationalism of the "reefer and cocaine madness" of the 1930s, and other explanatory mechanisms have replaced the rather complex set of assumptions implied by disinhibition theories (Collins).

More reasonably, acute drug-induced paranoia or psychosis and the cumulative effects of chronic use (brain atrophy, sleep deprivation, and hypoglycemia) might produce physiological changes related to criminal violence. Additionally, the impairment of perceptual and cognitive functioning caused by acute drug use may, in certain social settings, cause interacting participants to focus only on the most obvious behavioral and verbal cues to the exclusion of other moderating cues, and therefore often to misinterpret their meaning. If the misconstruing individual initiates aggressive behavior, which is reciprocated by other participants (who may also be drug-involved), successive exchanges may escalate and culminate in a violent act (Pernanen). Crimes of negligence, such as those resulting from driver-impaired performance, would also be classified as caused directly by drug effects. Finally, there are references to persons utilizing drugs as a means of fortifying themselves to engage in planned criminal activities (Tinklenberg).

Hypotheses as to how drug use may indirectly cause or lead to crime are numerous (Research Triangle Institute). It is often argued that participation in one illicit behavior, drug use, facilitates other deviant activities through associations and opportunity. A sociological labeling theory approach would posit, for example, that once an individual is labeled deviant in one respect, he is likely to further modify his behavior to fit this description in other respects. In any case, the necessity of obtaining a drug from illicit sources often exposes the user to persons involved in various deviant behaviors, and may also expose that person to more addictive and expensive drugs whose use may be more closely related to income-generating crime. The high rate of homicides among drug users involved in drug trafficking signifies that violence, as well as property crime, is associated with the illegal market. Although all of these may contribute to a relationship between drug use and crime, the issues of major concern in the United States are the question of income-generating crime among individuals with expensive drug habits, and the extent to which the crime is directly caused by the drug costs.

Other common hypotheses are that drug use leads to crime through drug-induced personality changes or reduced economic opportunities. Drug use may directly affect attitudes, beliefs, and values; and it may possibly act as a catalyst, making the individual more susceptible to the influence of others in a deviant subculture. To the extent that drug use interferes with school or work, it may contribute to economic dislocation through the closure of normal job opportunities.

This article will focus only on non-narcotic drugs (primarily marijuana) and narcotics (primarily heroin). These two drugs have provoked the greatest social concern, as well as the bulk of research efforts. Research findings and their implications will be discussed in three sections. The first will treat the relatively limited material dealing with evidence that drug use contributes to crime as a direct result of pharmacological effects. The second and third sections will discuss the literature on the possible indirect relation of non-narcotic drug use and crime and of narcotic drug use and crime.

Direct pharmacological effects

Alcohol is the only drug for which there are sufficient statistical data to establish a causal effect, and the evidence clearly shows a relationship between acute effects and crimes of negligence (Pernanen). Alcohol use has been correlated with crimes of property and violence, but the mechanism of action depends on personality, type of crime and social context, as well as the nature of the relationship in question and the immediate interaction between those involved.

Jared Tinklenberg has reviewed the various classes of other drugs and concludes that barbiturates seem to be the most likely to induce criminal behavior. Interestingly, these are the drugs most pharmacologically similar to alcohol. Tinklenberg has also conducted a study of adolescent offenders that tends to support the thesis of a link between barbiturates and assaultive behavior. Alcohol was the drug most commonly associated with such behavior, but barbiturates, used either alone or in combination with alcohol, were the next most common. In addition, those using barbiturates reported that these drugs were the most likely to enhance assaultive tendencies. Marijuana, psychotogens, and opiates were reported as decreasing assaultiveness.

Amphetamines and cocaine are stimulants whose chronic use in high doses can produce paranoid reactions. Although one might expect these characteristics to be related to crime, there is relatively little evidence for such a relationship in the literature. A number of case histories have reported on persons who had committed homicides while intoxicated with amphetamines (Research Triangle Institute). Most conclude that paranoid delusions resulting from the amphetamine use and a long-term solitary life-style were factors in several of the homicides.

Marijuana and the stronger hallucinogens are also capable of occasionally producing psychotic reactions, and there are several references in the literature to violent behavior during these episodes. Reports of cannabis-related psychosis and violent behavior appear most often in the older foreign literature, possibly as a result of the high doses used in some countries. Western descriptions of cannabis psychosis have occasionally commented on the presence of aggres-

sive behavior. Overall, the amount of crime resulting from marijuana- and hallucinogen-related psychosis is minimal. Psychotic reactions are relatively rare, and a very small percentage of such cases result in criminal behavior (Commission of Inquiry into the Non-medical Use of Drugs).

Opiates produce a reliable sedating reaction without the increased emotional lability and aggressive behavior often accompanying alcohol and barbiturate use. There is also little or no tendency for opiates to produce psychosis or paranoid reactions. One would expect the direct pharmacological properties to decrease rather than induce criminal behavior, and this is generally consistent with the available evidence (McGlothlin). Acquisitive crimes committed while undergoing withdrawal symptoms might be considered a direct pharmacological effect of opiate use.

In sum, although there is evidence that some drug use contributes to crime directly, the overall amount of crime attributable to direct pharmacological effects seems minor. The exception to this is when drug use contributes directly to crimes of negligence through impaired functioning.

Indirect effects: non-narcotic drugs

Non-narcotic drug use and crime. Pre-1965 studies, primarily of marijuana users, were not able to assess the relative prevalence of criminal behavior among drug users and nonusers. Users for the most part showed a number of deviant behaviors and social adjustment problems, but there was little evidence that use per se was associated with violence or major crime (Commission of Inquiry into the Non-medical Use of Drugs). The advent of the middle-class drug epidemic was quickly followed by drug-use surveys, some of which contained self-report data on crimes and arrests.

The most significant cross-sectional survey of this type was reported by John O'Donnell and his colleagues on a representative sample of 2,500 American males, aged between twenty and thirty years, during 1974 and 1975. The data show a clear relationship between drug use and crime. If the sample is divided on the basis of those having used marijuana (55 percent) and those never having used it (45 percent), the relation to self-reported crime is as follows: breaking and entering, 18 percent and 6 percent; shoplifting, 56 percent and 29 percent; and armed robbery, 2 percent and less than 0.5 percent. There is also a positive relationship between crime and amount of drug use. For example, 10 percent of experimental or light marijuana users reported breaking and entering, as compared to 27 percent of heavy users. Further analyses of these data showed a positive correlation between crime and type of drug use. For example, only 1 percent of those who restricted their use to marijuana reported committing an armed robbery, compared to 11 percent of those having used heroin. On the other hand, even those using only marijuana showed more minor criminality than those not using it. To cite an example, 47 percent of users had been involved in shoplifting, as opposed to 28 percent of nonusers.

Similar relationships existed between arrests and heavy use of marijuana. Eighteen percent of the nonuser group had been arrested for a nontraffic offense, compared to 55 percent of those classified as heavy users. Other studies examining the relationship between drug use and crime have yielded similar results (McGlothlin).

The question of causality. It is of interest to note that the data reported by O'Donnell and his colleagues show that the relationship between alcohol use and crime is not substantially different from that for marijuana and crime. The rates for the light and heaviest categories of alcohol use are as follows: breaking and entering, 6 percent and 18 percent; shoplifting, 31 percent and 56 percent; and armed robbery, 1 percent and 2 percent. The corresponding rates for no marijuana use and heavy use are 6 percent and 27 percent, 29 percent and 64 percent, and less than 0.5 percent and 4 percent. The O'Donnell study clearly shows a positive association between non-narcotic drug use (including alcohol) and crime. The question remains whether there exists a causal relationship.

One means of investigating the hypothesis that drug use leads to crime is to examine the temporal order of the two phenomena. Several studies have indicated that other forms of criminal deviance generally precede the beginning of non-narcotic drug use (Gandossy et al.). However, there are some problems in interpreting these and other data on the temporal relationship between drug use and crime. For example, the order of occurrence may be strongly dependent on the opportunity to use drugs and on the age at which individuals typically engage in various types of deviance. Two sequential national youth surveys provide some aggregate data that are less subject to problems of method and interpretation. A 1972 survey showed significantly less delinquency among male and female youths than was found in a similar survey conducted in 1967. Since the prevalence of non-narcotic drug use increased severalfold during this period, the results argue against a causal relation-

ship between drug use and delinquency (McGlothlin).

Although the available data on individual temporal sequence of drug use and crime are difficult to interpret, a number of longitudinal studies provide convincing evidence that individuals who subsequently become users of marijuana and other drugs can be predicted on the basis of personality and behavioral measures. As one would expect, such individuals are less conventional and conforming prior to initial use. Future marijuana users among high-school students are more alienated and socially critical, show more tolerance of deviance and are themselves more deviant, are less religious, and are more influenced by friends than by parents (U.S. National Commission on Marihuana and Drug Abuse). These results may be interpreted in terms of degree of socialization, with early-to-intermediate users at the low end of the scale and late users and nonusers at the high end. These studies were not designed to treat drug use and crime per se, but they do show that adolescent drug users demonstrate pre-use personality and behavioral patterns of nonconformity that clearly differentiate them from nonusers. These patterns tend to support the hypothesis that both drug use and other forms of delinquency result from a common set of variables.

Clearly, there is a relationship between crime and even modest use of illicit drugs; however, one would expect any direct causal relation to be largely restricted to those individuals for whom drug use has a major impact. Such individuals are relatively few compared to the overall population of users, and they have been shown to have preexisting personality traits differing from those of persons who are less drug-involved. Involvement in a subculture focused on obtaining, using, and selling drugs seems to be a more important predictor of crime involvement than drug use per se. Drug use may be a behavior necessary for acceptance within such a subcultural group. However, after having gained entry, the individual is influenced by the attitudes, values, norms, and behaviors of the group. Crime and other types of antisocial behavior are often more common within such subcultures. Thus, drug use is merely one deviant aspect (although a salient one) among many within the subculture, all of which increase the probability of criminal acts.

In 1972, the Canadian Commission of Inquiry into the Non-medical Use of Drugs concluded that "there is no scientific evidence that cannabis use, itself, is significantly responsible for the commission of other forms of criminal behavior. . . . A causal relationship between the use of the drug and other illegal behavior has not been established" (p. 110). Later studies have not invalidated that opinion, and other nonaddictive drug use may be included as well. In sum, it is reasonable to conclude that nonaddictive drug use does not directly lead to crime in more than a small percentage of users.

Indirect effects: narcotic drug use and crime

In contrast to the availability of data on non-narcotic drug use, there are no adequate general-population probability sample studies of narcotic addiction. Thus, data are restricted to those obtained from available populations, primarily persons entering the criminal justice system and treatment programs. Differences in the characteristics of the various samples undoubtedly account in part for some of the lack of agreement among studies. In addition, findings are not necessarily representative of the overall population of narcotic addicts. Nonetheless, several conclusions can tentatively be drawn from the existing literature.

Pre- and post-addiction criminality.

Pre-addiction criminality in early and later studies. In 1974, Stephanie Greenberg and Freda Adler compiled a comprehensive review of the changes in addicts' pre-addiction criminality patterns since the 1920s. Most of the studies of individuals first addicted between 1920 and 1950 concluded that criminal behavior was minimal prior to addiction. For example, of about one thousand male addicts at the Public Health Service Hospital in Lexington, Kentucky, only 25 percent had arrests prior to addiction, and these were mostly for misdemeanors. Conversely, studies of persons first addicted after 1950 show that the majority had a history of pre-addiction criminality. Policies of increasing criminalization of drug use were undoubtedly important factors. As drug use came to be generally considered a severely antisocial behavior, only more deviant individuals within a subculture providing access to narcotics initiated and maintained use.

Changes in criminality after addiction. The early study of Lexington addicts cited by Greenberg and Adler is of interest because the majority were not involved in crime prior to addiction. The proportion of males with recorded nondrug offenses increased from 30 percent before addiction to 47 percent after addiction. Since the median age of the onset of addiction was around thirty years, the increase in criminality took place during a period when it would normally be declining. Increases occurred for property crimes, but not for crimes against persons. Of those obtaining their narcotics through a physician, only 9 percent were arrested subsequent to addiction.

Studies of samples more typical of the 1970s addict population also generally show an increase in the amount of crime committed after addiction, especially for income-generating crimes. Although the bulk of the evidence indicates an increase in overall nondrug arrests and self-reported criminality after addiction, some investigators have reported a corresponding decrease in assaults and other violent crimes against persons, as might be expected from the pharmacological effects of narcotics (McGlothlin).

Male and female criminality patterns. The limited literature on criminal behavior among female addicts indicates that arrest and incarceration rates are generally lower than those for males, both before and after addiction. Fewer female treatment clients report committing illegal acts prior to the first use of heroin. After addiction, approximately one-third report a need for money to purchase drugs as the reason for their first illegal act. Male addicts give this reason half as often. Additionally, in several studies of female addicts in treatment, a majority have never been arrested. Subsequent data indicate that although female addict arrests are fewer than half those of males prior to addiction, the total arrest rate after addiction converges over time with that for males. However, the rates for more serious crimes remain at about one-third of those for males.

Prostitution is a major source of support for female addicts, and estimates of involvement have ranged from 30 percent to 70 percent. Several reports reveal that about half of all female addicts indicate that prostitution was the primary means of support at some time during their addiction careers (McGlothlin).

Types of crime committed after addiction. Self-report and arrest data used to examine the types of crimes committed by narcotic addicts have shown that shoplifting and other forms of petty larceny are the most frequent nondrug offenses, followed by burglary. Forgery, auto theft, and robbery are less frequent. Since minor theft offenses are less likely to result in arrest than are more serious crimes, the self-report data typically indicate a higher percentage of minor crimes than do the arrest statistics.

Most studies of arrestee and incarcerated populations are quite consistent in showing that (1) the proportion of nondrug arrests and sentences for robbery and property crimes is higher for heroin users than for nondrug users; and that (2) the proportion of arrests and sentences for violent crimes against persons is lower for heroin users than for nondrug users.

The question of causality. In many respects, the criminogenic role of narcotic use is not in dispute, at least for addicts in the United States. Many addicts engage in income-generating crime and use most of the money obtained to purchase drugs. Numerous self-report studies have recorded the types and frequency of crimes committed primarily to obtain money to purchase drugs. Other ethnographic studies have described the various types of addict "hustles" and life-styles in considerable detail. Finally, some of the arrestee studies have shown that an exceptionally high proportion of certain types of crime are committed by addicts (McGlothlin).

In research conducted on addict samples in the United Kingdom, Joy Mott concludes that "all the evidence so far available suggests . . . that addiction and criminal histories tend to run a parallel course. . . . For males, the number convicted . . . has not been found to exceed the number for the general male population of similar age and number of previous convictions. Thus, apart from drug offenses, and allowing for their criminal histories before coming to notice, addicts are no more likely to be convicted of offenses than are non-addicts" (p. 447). These findings demonstrate the importance of culture and national social policies toward drug use as factors that influence the relationship of drug use and crime. In the United Kingdom, where registered narcotic addicts are legally maintained on heroin or other opiates, research supports the hypothesis that drug use and crime are the result of other factors and that, apart from drug offenses, they are not necessarily linked in a causal manner.

Does crime lead to narcotic drug use? As O'Donnell has observed, traffic in illicit drugs is controlled by the criminal element of the population, and some prior contact with criminality is thus a necessary condition of addiction for most addicts. One study, cited by McGlothlin, demonstrated this relationship among black males. Youths with records of delinquency were far more likely to become addicted to heroin than a comparative nondelinquent group. Isidor Chein and his colleagues found that neighborhoods with high narcotic usage also had very high delinquency rates; however, there were also high-delinquency areas with relatively low drug usage, the latter areas being less socially and economically deprived than those with both high delinquency and high drug usage. Chein also found that youths who were delinquent prior to narcotic use tended to become social users as part of an overall delinquency pattern, and that those who were not delinquent prior to drug use tended to be more psychologically disturbed. In general, Chein concluded that both narcotic use and crime are largely the result of social and economic deprivation. However, as discussed earlier, delinquency precedes addic-

tion in the majority of cases and, for many, results in the contacts necessary to initiate narcotic use.

Does criminality increase after addiction? It is useful to go beyond the overall statistics and examine the direct relation between the cost of narcotics and the methods of obtaining the funds to buy them. First, it should be emphasized that in the United States, actual addiction is typically an intermittent phenomenon. Addicted periods are often interrupted by incarceration, brief periods of treatment, illness, lack of an adequate heroin supply, or the inability to obtain funds to purchase heroin. Studies that have covered extensive periods of addict careers show that even during the period of active addiction (prior to permanent discontinuation), the rate at which an addict is using heroin daily when not incarcerated is typically no more than 50 percent to 60 percent. The need for income-generating crime to purchase narcotics is not a major factor during periods of irregular heroin use: the nonaddicted heroin user typically injects no more than two or three times a week, whereas the addicted user often injects heroin several times a day.

Another aspect that needs to be considered is the percentage of addicts who purchase drugs with legitimately obtained funds, or who obtain the needed funds through drug selling. Overall, approximately one-fourth have reported supporting their use primarily by working, and another one-third through some form of participation in the drug distribution network. Fewer than half relied primarily on other illicit activities. Various studies have reported that between 20 percent and 70 percent obtain funds to purchase narcotics through other than criminal activities. Female addicts tend to report lower involvement in criminal activities than males, but this is partly because many are supported by illicit funds provided by addict spouses. McGlothlin and his colleagues found that during periods of daily narcotic use, 19 percent of male addicts' income derived from employment or other legitimate sources, 57 percent from street crime, and 24 percent from drug dealing. Since these data are primarily taken from arrest and treatment samples, they probably overestimate the criminal involvement of the undetected portion of the heroin-using population.

The self-report data thus show a substantial reliance on street crime to support narcotic use; however, the initiation of regular narcotic use does not ensure involvement in these activities. Much of the heroin users' nonincarcerated time involves less-than-daily use, which is relatively inexpensive, and much of the money for narcotics is obtained through drug sales or legitimate sources. As discussed earlier, virtually all of the pre- and post-addiction criminality studies show an increase in arrests and self-reported crimes after the onset of addiction. On balance, it would appear that narcotic addiction causes an increase in crime that would not otherwise have taken place. It should be remembered, however, that this relationship exists in the context of social policies directed at the suppression of drug supplies, resulting in an increased cost of narcotics in the illicit marketplace. As noted earlier, this causal relationship does not seem to hold for opiate addicts in the United Kingdom (Mott).

Does criminality decrease after the cessation of addiction? A few investigators have attempted to relate changes in heroin use to community crime rates. A National Institute on Drug Abuse panel on drug-related criminal behavior cited data on property crime before and after the 1972 East Coast heroin shortage (McGlothlin). There was some evidence for a reduction in heroin use as reflected in the serum hepatitis rates, as well as a decline in property crime rates in the areas affected by the heroin shortage.

Although it has been suggested that a reduction in heroin addiction results in decreased property crime, there are other explanations for the decrease. In particular, increased enforcement efforts may have been responsible for reducing nonaddict as well as addict crime. In general, studies of trends in the aggregate amount of crime and heroin addiction are unlikely to provide more than suggestive evidence of a causal relation because of the inability to control other relevant variables.

More direct evidence is provided by the large literature on the effects of various treatment programs. In 1973 the United States National Commission on Marihuana and Drug Abuse reviewed the available studies and concluded that the evidence did not show a treatment-related reduction in criminal behavior, a conclusion resulting more from deficiencies in the available research methodology than from the existence of definitive negative findings. Other reviews have arrived at the opposite conclusion (McGlothlin); however, even if it is agreed that there is no acceptable evidence of an overall treatment-related reduction in crime, the treatment studies may still be useful in examining the question of a causal relation between narcotic addiction and crime. The question should be posed in two parts: (1) does treatment at least temporarily reduce daily narcotic use; and (2) if there are at least temporary reductions in daily narcotic use, does this result in reduced criminal behavior during these periods? Although the post-treatment effectiveness of methadone maintenance may be in doubt, there is no serious dispute that while in treatment the percentage of time patients use heroin, and the level of use, are greatly reduced. With regard to the narrower question of whether these reductions in use are accompanied by decreased criminal behavior, a large number of methadone maintenance studies have reported reduced criminality during treatment (McGlothlin).

The final evidence on the relationship between cessation of addiction and crime is provided by three studies of addiction careers. The first involved a follow-up of 242 Puerto Rican residents who were admitted to Lexington Hospital between 1935 and 1962 (Ball and Snarr), and especially a subsample of 53 males for whom both personal interview histories and Federal Bureau of Investigation arrest records were available. Of a total of 850 person-years from onset of addiction to interview, 31 percent were spent incarcerated, 50 percent addicted, and 19 percent not addicted. The arrest rate while addicted was five times that when not addicted.

The second study, by McGlothlin and his colleagues, examined arrest rates and self-reported criminal behavior as a function of frequency of narcotic use during the addiction careers (first daily use to last daily use) of a sample of 690 admissions to the California Civil Addict Program. Thirty-five percent of the addiction-career nonincarcerated time involved less-than-daily or no narcotic use. During these periods arrest rates for property crimes, as well as self-reported criminal behavior, were significantly lower than for periods of daily use.

A third study, conducted by John Ball and his colleagues, obtained data from 243 Baltimore opiate addicts randomly selected from police records. Results replicate those of McGlothlin. An extremely high rate of property crime was reported overall; two-thirds of the addicts had from 100 to 365 crime-days per year for each nonincarcerated year of their entire addiction career. Crime-days when addicted (248 per year) were six times the number when abstinent (41 per year). Ball suggested that opiate use itself, and the degree of that use, are the principal causes of high crime rates among addicts.

In sum, career history studies, together with methadone maintenance results and the earlier findings of increased criminality after the onset of addiction, provide fairly strong evidence that, because of high illicit market costs, narcotic addiction causes an increase in the amount of income-generating crime.

Conclusions

The following conclusions briefly summarize the research findings on drug use and crime.

1. There is some evidence that the use of drugs other than alcohol causes crimes directly as a result of such factors as impaired functioning, paranoia, and negligence. However, the overall contribution is quite small relative to that for alcohol use.

2. There exists a relation between crime and even modest use of illicit nonaddictive drugs. (A similar relation also exists for alcohol.) However, prospective follow-up longitudinal studies have found no evidence that nonaddictive drug use leads to crime; rather, both appear to result from the interaction of multiple factors. The available data do not preclude the possibility that heavy involvement may contribute to crime for some individuals.

3. For contemporaneous samples of narcotic addicts, criminality generally precedes narcotic use and typically increases after the onset of addiction.

4. There is strong evidence that narcotic addiction results in an increase in the amount of income-generating crime. Criminality is reduced during periods of less-than-daily use and during periods of methadone maintenance treatment.

M. Douglas Anglin

See also Alcohol and Crime: behavioral aspects; Drugs and Crime, *articles on* legal aspects *and* treatment and rehabilitation.

BIBLIOGRAPHY

Ball, John C.; Rosen, Lawrence; Flueck, John A.; and Nurco, David N. "The Criminality of Heroin Addicts: When Addicted and When Off Narcotics." *The Drugs-Crime Connection.* Edited by James A. Inciardi. Beverly Hills, Calif.: Sage, 1981, pp. 39–65.

Ball, John C., and Snarr, Richard W. "A Test of the Maturation Hypothesis with Respect to Opiate Addiction." *Bulletin on Narcotics* 21 (1969): 9–13.

Chein, Isidor; Gerard, Donald L.; Lee, Robert S.; and Rosenfeld, Eva. *The Road to H: Narcotics, Delinquency, and Social Policy.* New York: Basic Books, 1964.

Collins, James J., ed. *Drinking and Crime: Perspectives on the Relationships between Alcohol Consumption and Criminal Behavior.* New York: Guilford Press, 1981.

Commission of Inquiry into the Non-medical Use of Drugs. *Cannabis.* Ottawa: Information Canada, 1972.

Gandossy, Robert P.; Williams, Jay R.; Cohen, Jo; and Harwood, Henrick J. *Drugs and Crime: A Survey and Analysis of the Literature.* Washington, D.C.: U.S. Department of Justice, Law Enforcement Assistance Administration, National Institute of Justice, 1980.

Greenberg, Stephanie W., and Adler, Freda. "Crime and Addiction: An Empirical Analysis of the Literature, 1920–1973." *Contemporary Drug Problems* 3 (1974): 221–270.

McGlothlin, William H. "The Etiologic Relationship between Drug Use and Criminality." *Research Advances in Alcohol and Drug Problems,* vol. 4. Edited by Yedy Israel, Frederick B. Glaser, Harold Kalant, Robert E. Popham, Wolfgang Schmidt, and Reginald G. Smart. New York: Plenum Press, 1978, pp. 367–394.

Mott, Joy. "Opium Use and Crime in the United Kingdom." *Contemporary Drug Problems* 9 (1980): 437–451.

O'Donnell, John A. "Narcotic Addiction and Crime." *Social Problems* 13 (1966): 374–385.

———; Voss, Harwin L.; Clayton, Richard R.; Slatin, Gerald T.; and Room, Robin G. W. *Young Men and Drugs: A Nationwide Survey.* Rockville, Md.: U.S. Department of Health, Education, and Welfare, National Institute on Drug Abuse, 1976.

Pernanen, Kai. "Alcohol and Crimes of Violence." *Social Aspects of Alcoholism.* Edited by Benjamin Kissin and Henri Begleiter. The Biology of Alcoholism, vol. 4. New York: Plenum Press, 1976, pp. 351–444.

Research Triangle Institute. *Drug Use and Crime.* Springfield, Va.: U.S. Department of Commerce, National Technical Information Service, 1976.

Tinklenberg, Jared R. "Drugs and Crime." *Drug Use in America: Problem in Perspective,* Appendix, vol. 1. Washington, D.C.: U.S. National Commission on Marihuana and Drug Abuse, 1973, pp. 242–299.

U.S. National Commission on Marihuana and Drug Abuse. *Drug Use in America: The Problem in Perspective.* Washington, D.C.: The Commission, 1973.

2.
LEGAL ASPECTS

Introduction

Pharmacologists define a drug as a substance that, when taken into the body, alters the structure or function of any part of the organism. Although this is a very broad definition, it is important to avoid too narrow a focus—otherwise one may incorporate into the definition concepts of medical harmfulness or social unacceptability that may unduly narrow perspectives.

Social concern with drug use arises because of the awareness that such an activity may damage either the user or others. The overwhelming danger in drug use is usually felt to be the danger to the user himself. The number of homicides committed under the influence of alcohol is dwarfed by the death rate of drinkers from cirrhosis and other alcoholism-related diseases. The dangers of tobacco to smokers in terms of lung cancer, emphysema, and various circulatory diseases far outweigh the damage done by smoking-caused fires. Even heroin, harmful as it is to society, is arguably more destructive to its users than to others, at least so long as it is illegal, expensive, and impure.

The use of a drug in such a way as to damage the

user's physical or mental health or his adjustment in society is called drug abuse. One must be wary of confusing the concept of drug abuse with the control mechanisms that the legislature has adopted to lessen the harm that a drug does. The illegal drugs are not always terribly dangerous, and the legal drugs are by no means always perfectly safe. It is true, of course, that some drugs have a much greater potential for abuse than others, in that they injure a higher percentage of their users or because the injuries they cause are regarded as especially serious. But an injury produced by drug abuse is typically the result of a complex interaction involving the drug itself, the way it is used, the disposition of the person using it, and the reaction of the surrounding society to the user. Some people, for example, apparently can take heroin for a long period without becoming addicted or otherwise harming themselves, whereas others injure themselves with coffee, the most "legal" of legal drugs.

Models of drug control

Although the criminal law is a major instrument of drug control, it is by no means the only legal device for reducing drug abuse. To better understand the variety of legal controls on drug use, it is instructive to note the various models that society has adopted to control different types of drugs.

Coffee, tobacco, and alcohol. Coffee may be sold and used in all nations, although in some places its use was once punishable by imprisonment or death. In many countries it bears taxes that are disproportionate to those on other imported items of consumption, but in the United States no legal effort is aimed at discouraging its use. The fact that it is a drug which injures at least some of its users seems to be reflected solely in nonlegal social controls—for example, the sight of an eight-year-old having a cup of coffee is sufficiently remarkable to be remembered for some time.

The regulations on tobacco are more onerous than those on coffee. Tobacco is taxed far more heavily than most other consumables, its advertising is restricted, and its sale to minors is nominally forbidden. In the United States, moreover, cigarette manufacturers are required to put a notice on their packages stating that "The Surgeon General Has Determined that Cigarette Smoking Is Dangerous to Your Health." Finally, considerable amounts of government money are spent to convince users of the harmfulness of this drug, although they do not remotely approach either the revenues taken in through tobacco taxes or the amounts spent by the cigarette industry to promote sales.

Alcohol is a drug that causes enormous social damage and endangers a fairly sizable proportion of its users. To prevent its use altogether, the United States and several other Western nations have, for brief periods, tried prohibition, which made the manufacture and sale (and in some states the use) of alcoholic beverages a crime. This type of control, however, has almost everywhere been abandoned, except in certain Muslim countries, where it is supported by a strong religious taboo. Methods of control in the United States are less ambitious but are generally regarded as more successful. The drug is sold either through a government monopoly or by license, which is restricted to those found to be of good moral character; it is heavily taxed; and there are prohibitions on its sale to those under a certain age, ranging from eighteen to twenty-one, depending on the state. Its advertising is restricted, and its sale is forbidden in areas close to schools or churches. Several states have "rationing" systems and others have "posting" laws, whereby a public official can determine that an individual is abusing alcohol and can make it illegal for anyone to give or sell it to him. Finally, some government funds are spent to warn the public against the dangers of alcohol abuse.

The medical model. The next type of drug-control model—the medical model—is used for a wide range of drugs, from antibiotics to the major tranquilizers. This model seems to be the preferred one for drugs having medical uses, in that, when taken under the direction of a physician, their value outweighs their danger. Under the medical model, the medical profession is given control of the legal right to obtain the drug. The ordinary citizen can purchase it only if he has the permission of a physician, who is given almost uncontrolled discretion in permitting use of the drug. The physician's prescription allows the user to buy the specified quantity and form of the prescribed drug from a licensed pharmacist.

The vice model. Usually the medical model is combined with what has been called the vice model to restrict transactions that are not part of medical treatment. Under the vice model, a user who does not have a prescription but can still get someone to sell him the drug commits no crime, but the seller is guilty of a criminal offense. Punishment of the seller is not restricted to the criminal law. If the seller is a pharmacist, he may lose his license—perhaps a more serious penalty than the criminal sentence that might be imposed upon him.

The vice model is so called because it is the type

of legal regulation generally applied to such vices as gambling and prostitution. To restrict these illegal commodities or vices, which it is felt may injure their user, the seller is made guilty of a crime. However, because there are typically far more buyers, the law does not undertake the much more costly process of attempting to apply the criminal sanction to them. The vice model is also used in a large variety of situations, many of which could not be called vices. It protects drivers and passengers from injury caused by automobiles that lack seat belts or padded dashboards by making the sale of such vehicles illegal. It is further used to protect diet-soda drinkers from cancer of the bladder, which, it is believed, may be caused by dietetic soft drinks containing cyclamates. In addition, it is often used to protect users from the abuse of drugs obtained outside medical channels.

Prohibition. Finally, there are drugs for which it is felt that none of the previous models exert sufficient control. Some of these drugs, for example, heroin, have no recognized medical use, and hence the medical model cannot be applied to legalize some use under a physician's prescription. But all are considered so dangerous that the law must act against the user as well as the seller, and therefore the vice model is felt to be insufficient. As a result, whatever use takes place outside of medical channels is subject to complete prohibition of both sale and use, and such drugs are legally possessed (if at all) only for research purposes.

Drug-control law. The basic federal law on drug control was laid down in the Comprehensive Drug Abuse Prevention and Control Act of 1970, as amended (part), 21 U.S.C. §§ 801–965 *passim* (1976 & Supp. IV 1980). The statutory scheme is somewhat complex, but in essence it divides the drugs to be controlled into five major categories, or schedules, of which only two have major bearing on the criminal justice system. Schedule I includes the most strictly regulated drugs and includes, among many other lesser-known substances, heroin, marijuana, and such hallucinogens as LSD and mescaline. These drugs are regarded as having, in the words of the statute, "a high potential for abuse" and "no currently accepted medical use in treatment in the United States." Drugs in this category are not available through prescription, and any trafficking or illegal possession of them is severely punished.

Schedule II includes drugs that are similarly believed to have "a high potential for abuse" but that also have some accepted medical uses. The principal members of this group are opium, morphine, and cocaine, which, because of their medical usefulness, may be made available by prescription, although under considerable restrictions. Trafficking in or possession of these drugs outside medical channels is punished with penalties similar to those for Schedule I drugs. Schedules III, IV, and V cover those drugs whose potential for abuse is considered to be less than that for the drugs in Schedules I and II, and for the most part, these drugs are felt to create no great social problem.

A solid majority of the states have passed the Uniform Controlled Substances Act (National Conference), which mirrors the federal statute. State law often provides even higher penalties for violation than does federal law, but a number of states have markedly lower penalties for some marijuana offenses.

Problems of drug control

The practical effects of American drug-control laws vary, depending upon the drug involved: some drugs raise no problems, whereas others impose considerable law enforcement and other costs upon society. The three drugs that have received the most publicity and law enforcement attention are heroin, cocaine, and marijuana. Although from the viewpoint of drug control these drugs create quite similar problems, they are in many ways very different. Heroin is a narcotic, cocaine is a stimulant, and marijuana is sui generis, although it is sometimes classified as a mild hallucinogen. Cocaine, which has medical uses, is listed on Schedule II of the federal law, whereas heroin, which is used medically in Great Britain, is felt to have no medical use in the United States and, along with marijuana, is listed in Schedule I. All three of these drugs, however, are widely used. Estimates of heroin addicts run to about five hundred thousand, and there are about as many nonaddicted users. Cocaine is used by about three times as many people, and marijuana by about twenty million, with twice that number in the "having tried" category.

Sources of supply. Each of these drugs is, for the most part, produced outside the United States and smuggled in. So far as is known, all the heroin and cocaine used in the United States is imported, as is about 85 percent of the marijuana. Although trade routes shift depending upon the convenience of smuggling syndicates and law enforcement pressure, it is thought that most of the heroin consumed in the United States is imported from Mexico, the Near East, Pakistan, and the "Golden Triangle" of Thailand, Laos, and Burma. Most of the cocaine comes from the Andes region by way of Colombia, and most of the marijuana consumed in the United States is produced in Mexico, the Caribbean, and Colombia—although an expanding proportion is being produced domestically in urban closets and attics and on "pot plantations" in inaccessible rural areas.

Although it would seem that it should be easy to spray crop-killing chemicals on the opium poppies, coca bushes, and marijuana plants that produce the raw materials for heroin, cocaine, and marijuana, respectively, the problem is that the sovereign nations in which these plants are grown are generally unwilling to have defoliants sprayed on their land and people. To be sure, some countries have cooperated fully with the United States in destroying their drug crops. The Mexican government has made use of American technical assistance—planes and defoliants—to wipe out many of its illegal poppy and marijuana fields. However, most of the nations in which the opium poppies, coca plants, or marijuana grow do not think of their drugs as constituting a problem, in contrast to their genuinely urgent problems, such as those involving health, education, industrial development, and sometimes insurgency.

Growing such plants is usually not crucial to the overall economy of these countries, but cultivation is often quite important to the farmers in some regions, both as a cash crop and for their own use. Frequently, the central government can bring little force to bear on these relatively inaccessible areas, and it worries about risking insurgency by alienating the growers, who can be quite numerous.

In Turkey, for example, an estimated 40 percent of farmers raised the poppy in 1971. The disproportion between American and Turkish interests in the suppression of opium cultivation was such that Turkish cooperation had to be purchased by the United States with various forms of persuasion and inducement (costing some $35 million in one year), and at that it was only temporary.

Smuggling. Not only is it difficult to prevent the production of heroin, cocaine, and marijuana abroad, but it is also hard to prevent the smuggling of these drugs into the United States. There is a major difference between heroin and cocaine on the one hand, and marijuana on the other. Small doses of the first two are far more powerful; the total United States consumption of heroin is estimated at less than ten tons, and that of cocaine, less than twenty tons. Compared to the yearly total of more than a hundred million tons of freight brought into the United States and to the 250 million individual crossings of the American border, the magnitude of the task of preventing the smuggling of such a small amount becomes clear. The problem is somewhat different with respect to marijuana. Here the amount smuggled in is estimated to be on the order of fifteen thousand tons. This drug is so bulky that smugglers more often do not attempt to use the usual channels of commerce to conceal shipments. Rather, a great amount of marijuana is brought in each year by private airplanes that illegally cross the American borders, landing at out-of-the-way airstrips, and by fishing boats and launches that deliver their cargo to deserted beaches.

It is estimated that less than 10 percent of the heroin, cocaine, and marijuana entering the United States is seized at the borders. Worse yet, improving this performance greatly would threaten to cause intolerable inconvenience to persons legitimately crossing the borders and would incur a sizable bill for the vast increase in technology and manpower that would have to be devoted to preventing smuggling.

Domestic law enforcement. Although efforts in other countries and at the borders are aimed at reducing the supplies of heroin in the United States, law enforcement within the United States has a somewhat different effect. It does reduce the total amount consumed, but its more important effect is to determine the structure of the drug market and to control which potential customers have access to illegal drugs.

Federal, state, and local agencies. Any detailed picture of the way law enforcement acts to accomplish this task is necessarily quite complex, since various enforcement agencies with overlapping jurisdictions work independently of one another and sometimes at cross-purposes. Federal enforcement officials function not only within the United States but also abroad and at the borders, and often their domestic investigations result from leads developed in foreign countries or during a border search. Theoretically, they concentrate on major traffickers, but in many cases small-time operators are swept into their net. State enforcement agents may be employed by a division of the state police or a statewide drug enforcement agency, whereas local enforcement officers may be either members of the drug squad or simply policemen on a beat.

Each of these police agencies regards itself as having some specific mission and expertise in an area of narcotic enforcement, although considerable overlap and rivalry may develop among them, and the particular interest of an agency may change over time. Generally speaking, federal agents consider their specialty to be the mounting of lengthy undercover investigations in an effort to suppress relatively high-level dealing and to put whole organizations out of business. At the other end of the spectrum, the beat patrolman is more likely to be concerned with not letting drug sales get too far out of hand and too visible in his area.

Constraints on police. In their effort to escape punishment, traffickers are aided by two major constraints on the police: the constitutional protections accorded to the privacy of the citizen, and the shortage of police resources. Actually, these two police problems are connected, because observance of the constitutional protections greatly increases the amount of time and effort the police must expend in developing their cases.

Although, as the large volume of search and seizure cases indicates, the police often break the rules, they seldom ignore them entirely. As a result, some drug suppliers will inevitably be so careful or lucky that the constitutional protections of their (and of law-abiding citizens') privacy will make it impossible for the police to catch them. It may be that the escape of a certain percentage of drug suppliers is simply part of the price that American society pays for the constitutional rules under which it lives—but that does not make the job of law enforcement any easier.

For the most part, however, the constitutional protections do not insulate drug suppliers from the law, but merely require the police to expend resources by building their cases through time-consuming, difficult investigations. Unfortunately, the police often lack the manpower and equipment to do this. At the higher levels, investigations can be enormously expensive and protracted; and at the lower levels, where cases are much easier to make, there are so many suppliers that the police cannot arrest them fast enough.

Limits to deterrence. Part of the problem is that far more resources would have to be devoted to law enforcement in order to make either deterrence or isolation, the two chief mechanisms by which the criminal law acts directly to repress crime, work at all well in the area of drug trafficking. So far as deterrence is concerned, law enforcement cannot make the chances of apprehension great enough so that rational criminals would not undertake trafficking in drugs.

At the higher levels of trade, the profits are simply too large. For example, in 1981 the price of heroin outside the United States was about $20,000 per kilogram; smuggled into the United States, it was worth $180,000 per kilogram; and after dilution and passage through three or four more hands it retailed for the equivalent of $2 million per kilogram. Thus, a smuggler could have turned a quick profit of one and a half million dollars on a suitcaseful, and a wholesaler could earn even more on the same amount. The figures are not very different for cocaine. Moreover, al-though marijuana is so bulky that the amounts trafficked must be several hundred times as great, the return on invested capital is of a similar order of magnitude.

Even if the chances of apprehension and severe punishment were sufficient to frighten the majority of citizens away from the drug trade, many people find the profits too tempting. They may regard the rewards in money, excitement, and life-style as worth the risk. In addition, some are especially reckless and optimistic about their cleverness and resourcefulness in escaping detection.

Moreover, as law enforcement drives more competitors out of the market and makes the drug scarcer, both the price of the drug and the profits from dealing in it rise. Thus, each imprisonment of a trafficker acts not only to deter others but also to increase the rewards for those entering the business.

The other major utilitarian justification for the criminal law is isolation. This is premised on the common-sense view that society is made safer by apprehending and imprisoning individuals who have committed crimes, so that they cannot do further harm. If it required a rare skill or organizational talent to go into the drug supply business, it might be that enough suppliers could be isolated to make a difference. Apparently, however, there is more than enough talent to go around, and for each dealer arrested there are usually several able to step into his place. Moreover, the failure of deterrence guarantees that the risk involved will not cause a shortage of those willing to try.

In theory, if one arrested an entire organization, including the lieutenants and "Mr. Big" himself, it would not be able to recover. In actuality this does not happen very often, since it is extremely difficult to put simultaneously out of action all the members of any large organization. Since there are usually enough members left with enough knowledge to carry on, damaged organizations have a way of rebuilding themselves quite quickly.

Costs. Law enforcement against the drug supply is not only difficult but also expensive. Resources are scarce at all stages of the criminal process. In urban areas, the trial system is so overburdened that it is unable successfully to deal with violent crime, let alone the far higher number of burglaries and larcenies that swamp it. Courts, prosecutors, and public defenders are all so grossly understaffed that the system can process its case load only by offering concessions and otherwise pressuring defendants into pleading guilty in about 90 percent of cases. Without more resources, the addition of more drug offenders will further overcrowd the courts, requiring more tempting plea bargains to be offered to others awaiting trial.

Finally, the correctional system is also grossly overcrowded. The county jails, the state prisons, and other correctional institutions are so crammed that many prisoners must be held under conditions which, if they were better known, would no more be tolerated than cutting off the hands of thieves or blinding assaulters. The probation and parole offices, moreover, stagger under such a case load that they must ignore both the social needs and the subsequent criminality of those in their jurisdiction.

Even police resources are badly stretched. It has often been pointed out that law enforcement is at its best when it is alerted by the victim of a crime, as in a robbery or rape, or where tangible evidence of the crime remains behind for examination and study, as in embezzlement or homicide. Where all the parties to a transaction not only make no effort to report it to the police but do all they can to hinder investigation, the police are at a particular disadvantage. Indeed, the problems of enforcing the drug laws are typical of those engendered in victimless, or consensual, crime, where the police seem singularly ineffective at preventing illegal transactions between willing buyers and sellers.

Effectiveness of law enforcement. On the other hand, even within the constraints of resources and constitutional guarantees, law enforcement can have major effects on the market for illegal drugs. Police efforts can drive drug dealing underground. Aside from marijuana sellers, who often operate openly at rock concerts, drug dealers in most areas do not generally sell openly on the streets. Nor do they generally sell from accessible, publicized locations, for the obvious reason that they may be observed by the police and arrested.

The law thus forces the dealers to move into back apartments, hallways, and other areas that tend to be free of police presence. Here, they run a severe risk from predators. Illegal drugs are extremely valuable commodities, and since the seller is unable to complain to the police that his stock-in-trade was stolen, he becomes fair game for the numerous "rip-off artists" and "musclemen" who populate the drug culture.

The drug dealer is vulnerable to losing his profits and working capital as well as his inventory. Although he may be in a somewhat better position to complain to the police if he is robbed of money rather than of an illegal drug, the disadvantages of attracting police attention and having to answer embarrassing questions about the source and purposes of his money are generally enough to deter his complaint.

The loss of his property in a robbery is not all that the drug dealer must fear. He may be robbed by an acquaintance or by someone whom he can identify—one of the most dangerous kinds of robbery known, since the robber realizes that some kind of retaliation will follow unless he prevents it. As a result, such robberies are often accompanied by murder, and are a major factor in the surge of what is commonly called drug-related killings. Nor is the risk of violence to the drug seller confined to robbery and its aftermath. In certain circumstances he may be subjected to the violent efforts of competitors to gain a larger market share by putting him out of business.

Admittedly, there is a rough analogy between the risks of theft of goods or of violence in the legal marketplace, and the risks in the chain of heroin distribution. After all, the hijacking of legal liquor, cigarettes, or jewelry is hardly unknown, and sometimes competition in legal industries becomes overvigorous. Nonetheless, the difficulties of complaining to the police or other enforcement agencies by both buyers and sellers, the necessity of doing business in places where the police cannot intervene directly, the impossibility of making long-term enforceable supply or sales contracts, the many disputes caused by the constant disruption of the market, and the fact that most of the participants in the activity must be constantly armed and alert all escalate both the costs of physical protection and the risks to life and property far more with respect to supplying illegal drugs.

In addition to the expensive precautions that those at all levels of drug marketing must take against the constant risk of violence, participants in the drug business must incur great expense in minimizing the danger of police apprehension. Every dealer, whatever his level, must try to guard against the possibility that his customer may be an undercover police agent or a "flipped" informer whom the police have already caught and "turned" to help them make cases. Suppliers must take precautions against their telephones being tapped or their conversations bugged, and they are forced into what may be expensive and difficult methods of hiding their wares from police searches. All of these precautions, which make detection more difficult, both raise the supplier's cost of doing business and make it more difficult for him to find and be found by possible customers.

These costs, together with the higher profit necessary to compensate for the dangers of illegal violence and police apprehension, are the factors chiefly responsible for raising the price of drugs far above their production costs. Obviously there are certain advantages to increasing the selling price of illegal drugs. Inasmuch as the demand for them is not completely inelastic, higher prices mean less consumption. On the other hand, higher prices for illegal drugs impose disadvantages upon society as well. To the extent that the demand of some users for a drug is relatively inelastic—as is often said of heroin demand by addicts—increases in price require that the drug users must raise more money to support their use. If, as seems to be the case, heroin addicts often finance their habit by committing property crimes, increasing the price to them results in society's having to bear a higher level of criminality.

In addition, the high prices of drugs cause the drug trade to be immensely profitable. As has been noted, this greatly complicates the efforts of the law to deter trafficking; it also offers many young people the role model of the flashy, exciting, and fabulously wealthy drug dealer. For many, it may be demoralizing to work at regular jobs or to engage in demanding studies while knowing that others can lead the life—even temporarily—of the millionaire playboy on the artificially high profits gained from dealing in drugs. The segment of the population to whom this life-style is attractive and glamorous is obviously far larger than that which would actually engage in such activities. Nonetheless, the existence of such career paths through law violation cannot but have a corrosive effect upon the aspirations and values of many youths.

Corruption in law enforcement. Finally, the large profits derived from dealing in drugs and the way the drug laws are enforced—through informers and undercover agents—have led to staggering levels of police corruption. Police departments have reacted to this problem by enacting a whole series of rules, such as those requiring police supervisors to be present when large seizures of drugs or of the proceeds of drug sales are to be made. The object of such regulations, of course, is to make it more difficult for any officer or small group of officers to form partnerships with drug dealers and suppliers. Often, however, it turns out that one officer may "unexpectedly" seize a sizable amount of heroin, cocaine, or even marijuana, and then, as it were, go into business with one of his informants. On other occasions, one or several officers will simply accept bribes for not making certain seizures or arrests, or for eliminating their client's competition.

The full extent of corruption in drug enforcement is not, of course, known. It is sometimes alleged that the corruption in heroin enforcement is far greater than in the enforcement of the cocaine and marijuana laws, although there is little evidence for such a proposition. In any event, some observers have estimated that the problem of corruption impinges on about one-third of narcotic officers. For example, about half of the federal narcotic agents in New York were indicted or discharged on grounds of corruption around 1970, and the Knapp Commission investigation into the New York City police indicated that corruption in that department was even more of a problem.

As long as the profits in drug dealing remain so high and the means of enforcing the law do not change, there will be no way to guarantee the honesty of the officers enforcing the drug laws. On the other hand, the effort of higher police authorities to keep their officers honest does interfere with narcotic enforcement. Many police departments insist on transferring their narcotic officers out of that specialty after two years, to prevent the buildup of contacts leading to corruption. One result, of course, is that a great deal of expertise and information is lost to law enforcement.

Although efforts have been made to induce narcotic officers to share their informants and to write down the information that they have received so that these valuable aids to enforcement are not lost, the tradition in narcotic enforcement is strongly to the contrary. Not only do agents generally resist the bureaucratization of their employment, but in particular they zealously guard the identity of their informants. Partly this occurs out of a sense of rivalry among agents for the best source of information, and partly it is because they regard their advancement as determined by their production of arrests, seizures, and information, which in turn is a result of the information they can glean from their informants. In addition, narcotic officers consider it necessary to encourage their informants by offering them protection against their identity being revealed, either by other agents or through court subpoena of police records.

Of course, the interference with narcotic enforcement caused by corruption is not the most serious cost of this kind of police misconduct. When awareness of such widespread corruption surfaces from newspaper reports of periodic scandals or simply from knowledge "on the street," the effect on public attitudes toward the police is devastating.

Constitutional values. A final cost of drug enforcement, over and above that in terms of law enforcement resources and corruption, is the moral cost of compromising constitutional values. Those against whom police techniques are directed are entitled to the constitutional rights of citizens, and the violation of their rights must remain a matter of concern in a society based upon law. This is not merely a question of abstract principle. As has been learned from the numerous narcotic raids on people who turned out to be completely innocent of any drug involvement, police methods in this area are an ever-present threat to the rights of the innocent as well as of the guilty.

One problem is that many of the law enforcement techniques used to enforce the drug laws often lead to violations of the constitutional rights of the individual. The stopping and questioning of suspected street-level pushers by beat patrolmen may easily become arrests and searches without the probable cause required by the Fourth Amendment. Wiretapping and police raids to seize narcotics without—and sometimes even with—search warrants often transcend constitutional limits, and the use of undercover narcotic officers to purchase drugs from suppliers may overstep the line and become illegal entrapment.

Even when these police methods are technically legal, they often come quite close to the borderline. Proper street questioning of suspects, legal searches made pursuant to a search warrant, and legally authorized wiretapping may be within the rights of the police, but they are nonetheless intrusive methods of investigation. Even when the pressure placed upon informants is legal, it engenders in the police habits that compromise the dignity of the individual and raise serious problems as to the role of the police in a free society. Legal or not, such tactics are much resented by those against whom they are used. Persons who are caught on a minor charge and pressured into working as a police informant keenly feel the degradation of being forced to turn in their friends and associates, even when these are drug suppliers.

It is not only the guilty who may suffer from these tactics. The police's use of informants means that all persons can be just that much less secure and trusting in their personal relationships. Allowing the police to give leniency in exchange for "work" compromises the idea of fair punishment for the informant's original crime, and officers' treatment of drug abusers, who are in no position to complain about police misconduct, develops in the police habits of casualness toward the law itself.

Overall effects. Probably the best summary, then, of the effect of drug-control policies is that with respect to those drugs for which no considerable demand exists, and perhaps also with respect to those that may be in significant demand but for which the technology of production or distribution is easy to interdict, the laws have an effect in reducing abuse and do not impose great costs on society. In the case of drugs that are in demand, the effect of the law is usually to make them far more expensive, less available, and perhaps, for society as a whole, less harmful. (With regard to heroin this may be disputed because of the catastrophic effects of the greatly increased price of the drug upon the sizable number of its compulsive users.)

It must be remembered that without the efforts of the law, many of the illegal drugs would become more widely and cheaply available. It could be said that the illegal drugs, because of adulterants and unreliable supply, are more harmful to their users than legal ones, a proposition that seems true with respect to heroin, marijuana, and alcohol under Prohibition, but that is probably not true of cocaine. On the other hand, newly legalized drugs might cause even more social damage by producing a lesser degree of impairment in a vastly greater number of users. However, since lowering the use of, and the damage caused by, the illegal drugs is sometimes bought at a very high price, a number of measures have been proposed to improve the balance of costs and benefits in the area of drug control.

Proposed changes in drug control

More efficient enforcement. Many suggestions have been made to render the law enforcement system more efficient with respect to drugs. Since 1960 the Federal Bureau of Narcotics has been reorganized several times, and in 1982 its successor, the Drug Enforcement Administration, was placed under the jurisdiction of the Federal Bureau of Investigation—all in furtherance of this aim. It is not clear whether or to what extent these reorganizations have produced their intended results, but since at least the early 1960s, the cry has been heard to reduce competition among agencies, to go after the bigger traffickers, to expend more time and resources on complex financial investigations, to raise the penalties for drug trafficking, to extend the rights of the police to conduct search and seizure operations, and to take many greater or lesser steps toward mounting a more powerful law enforcement threat to the drug supply.

Legalization of supply. It has been questioned whether certain drugs may have been misclassified. Probably the strongest arguments have been made for two changes: reclassifying marijuana from an illegal drug to a legally approved social intoxicant (such as alcohol), and allowing the use of heroin in the medical treatment of addiction, either through private physicians or through clinics set up for that purpose.

A powerful argument can be made for licensing the sale of marijuana as the sale of alcohol is licensed. It would be educationally valuable to broadcast the message that both marijuana and alcohol are drugs that involve significant health dangers. Moreover, an unenforceable prohibition of sale prevents the use of the many controls that a licensing scheme can apply. Although less stringent than the threat of the criminal law, these controls may in some ways be more effective. Thus, a licensing scheme could provide for control of potency, so that users would not risk inadvertent overdose; for control of quality, so that no harmful adulterant would be mixed in with the marijuana; for dissemination to users of information about the known hazards, as is now done on cigarette packages; and for taxation, which would enable the bulk of the profits on marijuana trading to be used by the government for combating the casualties of drug abuse and for educational purposes.

Probably most important, the licensed sale of marijuana would attenuate the link between marijuana and the more dangerous drugs. For many years a major (at various time *the* major) argument for making all involvement with marijuana illegal was that marijuana acts as "a stepping-stone" to the use of harder drugs. It is now admitted by almost all authorities that there is no pharmacological reason why marijuana should cause a user to go on to other drugs, any more than alcohol does. It is true that most heroin addicts had previously used marijuana, but they tend to have sniffed gasoline, smoked tobacco, and become drunk on alcohol even earlier. If marijuana use in any way does cause heavier drug use, it is probably because, by making the sale of marijuana illegal, a monopoly on this very popular product has been given to drug pushers. Since they will be severely punished if they are caught selling marijuana, they have little to lose by selling more dangerous drugs as well; and by selling marijuana they have acquired a clientele accustomed to using an illegal drug and reliant upon its suppliers for information about drugs. Thus, the marijuana dealer can readily become a conduit for higher-profit and more dangerous drugs.

On the other hand, it is clear to most observers that the licensed, legal sale of marijuana will lead to an increased use of the drug. One's view of what increase will occur, of the damage that this increased use will do to the users and to society, and of the magnitude of the costs of the present attempts at law enforcement, will help determine one's attitude toward this change in legal treatment.

Similarly, arguments have been made that heroin maintenance should be adopted and that addicts should be given the drug of their choice by private physicians or at special addiction clinics. There are obvious advantages to this, in better health for the addicts and, presumably, in a lowered number of property crimes attributable to a lessened need to support an expensive heroin habit. Advocates of such an arrangement, however, have not worked out the serious problem caused by the fact that heroin is a short-acting drug that the addict must use every four to six hours.

As a result, there are serious disadvantages to an on-the-premises maintenance system that would require the addict to inject his heroin under supervision in a clinic or doctor's office. The addict, who would have to appear at the clinic three or four times a day, would find it hard to hold any legal employment, and the difficulties of journeying to the maintenance office might be so great that many addicts simply would not put up with them. On the other hand, there are serious problems inherent in any prescription system that attempts to eliminate the inconvenience of an on-the-premises system by allowing an addict to receive heroin for later use. In all probability, heroin will remain an extremely valuable commodity. To expect heroin addicts—who, as a class, are probably among society's less law-abiding people—not to take advantage of this fact is perhaps too much to ask. If an addict had a specific ascertainable and invariant need for heroin, the problem would not cause much difficulty, but unfortunately, addicts can vary their doses over a large range, and it is exceedingly difficult to verify their needs. As a result, under a prescription heroin maintenance system, addicts will probably sell a considerable quantity of the drug prescribed for them to occasional users or to anyone willing to try it, thus adding, perhaps greatly, to the number of new addicts.

Greater stringency. Not all drug-control suggestions have been in the direction of a more lenient classification of drugs. Thus, it has been argued that stricter regulation of alcohol is needed—short of prohibition, of course, but involving higher taxes and lessened availability—to reduce the harm that this drug causes. Similar but less detailed suggestions have been made in an attempt to limit the damage caused by tobacco. Efforts have been undertaken to raise the taxes on the drug, to increase consumer awareness of its health dangers, and to restrict smoking in public, in the hope of lowering the inconvenience that tobacco use causes others. It has also been argued that the minor tranquilizers, such as diazepam (Valium), should be subject to more stringent controls, again short of criminalization. These drugs, which have medical uses of considerable importance, are also very widely abused.

Decriminalization of use. Finally, dispute has raged both on jurisprudential and practical grounds over whether the prohibition of small-scale possession and use of drugs is an appropriate means of drug control. On jurisprudential grounds, the arguments are that the drug user should be seen as a victim rather than as a criminal, and that punishing someone for risking injury to himself is too great an interference by the state with the autonomy of the individual.

On practical grounds, it has been argued that because far more users than suppliers are in fact arrested, laws punishing the user impose much higher law enforcement and other costs upon society than they are worth. It does appear, from research conducted in those states which have accepted these arguments with respect to marijuana, that whether or not the individual user of a drug is made a criminal has little, if any, effect upon the total amount of use or abuse of the drug. In any event, approximately one-third of the nation's population has subjected marijuana to the vice model, or "decriminalized" it by not criminally punishing the possession of small amounts. Moreover, even in states where the law penalizes such activity, the police very commonly ignore the offenses. There is, however, as yet little public support for the view that the vice model is more appropriate than complete prohibition in controlling cocaine and heroin.

JOHN KAPLAN

See also ALCOHOL AND CRIME: LEGAL ASPECTS; CRIMINALIZATION AND DECRIMINALIZATION; EXCUSE: INTOXICATION; VICTIMLESS CRIME.

BIBLIOGRAPHY

BRECHER, EDWARD M. et al. *Licit and Illicit Drugs: The Consumers Union Report on Narcotics, Stimulants, Depressants, Inhalants, Hallucinogens, and Marijuana, including Caffeine, Nicotine, and Alcohol.* Boston: Little, Brown, 1972.

Drug Abuse Survey Project. *Dealing with Drug Abuse: A Report to the Ford Foundation.* Foreword by McGeorge Bundy. New York: Praeger, 1972.

DUPONT, ROBERT I.; GOLDSTEIN, AVRAM; and O'DONNELL, JOHN, eds. *Handbook on Drug Abuse.* Washington, D.C.: U.S. Department of Health, Education, and Welfare, National Institute on Drug Abuse, 1979.

INCIARDI, JAMES A., ed. *The Drugs-Crime Connection.* Sage Annual Review on Drug and Alcohol Abuse, vol. 5. Beverly Hills, Calif.: Sage, 1981.

KAPLAN, JOHN. *Marijuana: The New Prohibition.* New York: World, 1970.

———, and Skolnick, Jerome H. *Criminal Justice: Introductory Cases and Materials.* 3d ed. Mineola, N.Y.: Foundation Press, 1982.

The Knapp Commission Report on Police Corruption. Report of the New York City Commission to Investigate Allegations of Police Corruption and the City's Anti-corruption Procedures. Foreword by Michael Armstrong. New York: Braziller, 1972.

MUSTO, DAVID F. *The American Disease: Origins of Narcotic Control.* New Haven: Yale University Press, 1973.

National Conference of Commissioners on Uniform State Laws. "Uniform Controlled Substances Act" (1970). Reprint. *Uniform Laws Annotated*, vol. 9. Master ed. St. Paul: West, 1979, pp. 187–640.

SILBERMAN, CHARLES E. *Criminal Violence, Criminal Justice.* New York: Random House, 1978.

U.S. General Accounting Office. *Gains Made in Controlling Illegal Drugs, yet the Drug Trade Flourishes.* Report to the Congress of the United States by the Comptroller General. Washington, D.C.: The Office, 1979.

WIKLER, ABRAHAM. *Opioid Dependence: Mechanisms and Treatment.* New York: Plenum Press, 1980.

3.
TREATMENT AND REHABILITATION

Introduction

For more than two centuries, narcotic addiction has been viewed in the United States as a problem with moral overtones. Prior to World War I the distribution of opiate drugs was regulated mainly by state laws, and opiates were available in a variety of over-the-counter preparations, as well as by physicians' prescriptions. Many individuals became addicted in this way, and physicians frequently maintained addicted patients on narcotics legally by prescriptions. However, moralistic attitudes prevailed and crimes and immorality were increasingly blamed on the use of narcotics.

The first attempt at federal control was the Harrison Act of 1914, ch. 1, 38 Stat. 785, which required every dealer in narcotics to register and keep records, and made possession by a consumer illegal without a valid prescription. However, it was not until 1919 that the United States Supreme Court ruled that it was illegal to maintain an addict by prescription if the addict had no illness other than addiction (*Webb v. United States*, 249 U.S. 96 (1919); *United States v. Doremus*, 249 U.S. 86 (1919)). Accordingly, forty-odd heroin maintenance clinics scattered across the country were closed. In 1929, as the federal prisons were becoming crowded with Harrison Act violators, many of whom were addicts, two federal narcotic hospitals (known as narcotic farms) were created under the Public Health Service, in Lexington, Kentucky, and Fort Worth, Texas. These were operated under psychiatric direction until the mid-1960s.

With the creation of the Federal Bureau of Narcotics in 1930, the thirty-two-year tenure of Commissioner Harry Anslinger began—a period of relentless enforcement effort. Increasingly severe penalties followed the postwar upsurge in addiction among ghetto youth in such large metropolitan areas as New York and Chicago. According to David Musto (Lowinson and Ruiz, pp. 3–18), "this was the peak of punitive legislation against drug addiction in the United States" (p. 14).

Along with many individuals and groups, both the American Bar Association and the American Medical Association eventually became disenchanted with the wisdom of mandatory minimum sentences and their underlying punitive philosophy. The pendulum began to swing toward treatment at about the same time that Anslinger retired in 1962. New state and federal legislation provided for civil commitment as an alternative to prison and set the stage for massive treatment program efforts in the 1970s and 1980s.

In the United States, large-scale federal funding of treatment programs for drug abusers was initiated in the early 1970s, and the most adequate evaluative studies extant were carried out for these programs. Initially intended for narcotic addicts, they subsequently expanded to include abusers of other illicit drugs. The federal strategy at that time was to combat the epidemic spread of heroin addiction and incidentally to control crime associated with narcotic addiction. Treatment of addicts, in conjunction with some efforts at primary prevention, represented the demand side of this strategy. On the supply side, the government launched a worldwide program to curtail the flow of heroin to the United States and created the Drug Enforcement Administration to expand federal drug law enforcement. Peter Bourne (Lowinson and Ruiz, pp. 35–42) estimated that there were about one-half million active heroin addicts in the United States when these programs were initiated.

Since 1970, the prevalence of use of narcotic drugs has fluctuated, primarily with variations in supply, reflecting both the success of interdiction efforts and the ingenuity of suppliers in developing other sources. Heroin use is believed to have declined somewhat in the late 1970s and early 1980s, but the use of marijuana, with more than 9 million users in 1977, and of cocaine, with 1.2 million users in 1977 (Richards),

has escalated dramatically. So has the use of hallucinogens and other illicit drugs, as well as the nonmedical use of over-the-counter and prescription drugs. According to William McGlothlin and James Weissman, the association of drug use and criminal behavior was confined mainly to opiates, as of the time of their studies. However, non-narcotic drug-related crime seems to have increased in the early 1980s.

In 1980, some 254,000 clients were admitted to federally supported drug treatment programs, and of these, 114,000 (45 percent) reported at least daily opiate use and could be considered addicts. Around 94,000 (37 percent) reported their primary drug as heroin, and the remaining 20,000 (8 percent) reported their primary drug of abuse as "other opiates" (U.S. Department of Health and Human Services). There were subtle differences between these two groups. The heroin addicts who entered treatment in 1980 were predominantly older, socially marginal adults, who had started opiate use at an earlier age and had used the drug longer than the "other opiate" addicts. The latter included higher percentages of whites, high-school graduates, and individuals who had married or lived for a prolonged period with a person of the other sex. Ten years earlier, an even higher percentage of the opiate addicts entering treatment were black or Hispanic males who used heroin as their drug of addiction. It is not yet clear whether the "other opiate" addiction pattern is a new, predominantly white phenomenon, or a transitional pattern, as new cohorts embrace this life-style.

The major crime involved in all drug abuse is that of illicit trafficking and distribution. Crime at the level of the individual user mainly involves income-generating activities to maintain the addictive use of narcotics (Greenberg; McGlothlin in Dupont et al.; Weissman). The available information concerning these crimes is based primarily on data for individuals caught in the criminal justice system and those in treatment. Thus it is not necessarily representative of the total population of narcotic users, but only of those whose behavior has attracted official attention.

Treatment approaches for narcotic addicts

Treatment here refers broadly to all intervention approaches focused on the addict, other than penal confinement. A major distinction is made between approaches undertaken under correctional auspices and those undertaken under medical-health system auspices. Programs in the correctional system are generally described as compulsory and involuntary, and those in the medical-health system, as voluntary. Superficially and legally, these labels appear to fit, but it is probably closer to the truth to say that almost every individual who enters treatment for drug addiction does so under some degree of coercion—if not by court order or plea bargain, then by real or perceived social pressure or threat. At the same time, effective treatment, in both systems, appears to involve some degree of discipline and a high degree of positive affect between clients and staff, with both the presence and absence of these factors abundantly observable in each system.

Evaluation of the effectiveness of any treatment is complex. It requires consideration not only of treatment goals but also of a myriad of variables relating to the program structure, the clients (or patients, as they are called in medical settings), the staff, the immediate treatment environment, the surrounding community environment, aspects of the enveloping society (such as epidemiological trends, the political situation, and the economy), and the outcome measures. Research design issues, such as methods of demonstrating causal influence of treatment on outcomes, as opposed to the attribution of all client change from admission to post-treatment to the effects of treatment, are of utmost importance. Independence of the evaluation is also a major concern (S. B. Sells in Dupont et al., pp. 105–118; in Lowinson and Ruiz, pp. 783–800).

Unfortunately, scientifically acceptable, large-scale field studies that meet reasonable design criteria are not available for most of the approaches reviewed here. However, all but the major modalities and the civil commitment programs (discussed below), for which acceptable evaluation studies have been completed, have for the most part involved relatively few addicts. These are described and evaluated, based on available information, in recent compendiums (Dupont, Goldstein, and O'Donnell; Lowinson and Ruiz).

Approaches in the correctional system. Leon Brill (Lowinson and Ruiz, pp. 517–531) considers "rational authority" as the common denominator for a variety of treatment approaches undertaken under correctional auspices. Most of those described here were initiated in the 1960s, whereas the medical approaches described subsequently came mainly in the 1970s. However, the shift appears to reflect more a change of attitude than a rational decision based on hard evaluative data.

Parole supervision. In New York State, one of the early efforts to control narcotic use was the Special Narcotics Project initiated by the Division of Parole in 1956. It provided close supervision and support for some six hundred addict parolees. Meyer Diskind described this program in terms of the role of the professional parole officer using the authoritative casework approach, with a small case load and the flexibility to tailor authority and support to the needs of individual parolees. He reported that after six years, 27 percent of 695 parolees (with a median length of supervision of sixteen months) made a fully satisfactory adjustment, that is, they never relapsed or were guilty of any delinquent behavior. An additional 13 percent used drugs on only isolated occasions, bringing the success rate to 40 percent. No formal report on this program is available for critical review, but it appears to have been an effective program in a system that neglected evaluation.

Civil commitment. This approach was begun in the 1960s by the federal government and the states of California and New York. Civil commitment programs were viewed initially as advances over the previous incarceration, parole supervision, or hospitalization of prisoners, methods that lacked aftercare services to facilitate return to community living.

The federal program was established under the Narcotic Addict Rehabilitation Act [NARA] of 1966, Pub. L. No. 89-793, 80 Stat. 1438 (codified as amended in scattered sections of 18, 28, 42 U.S.C.). NARA authorized (1) pretrial civil commitment to treatment, in lieu of prosecution, for addicts charged with certain federal crimes; (2) voluntary civil commitment for addicts not under criminal charges (Titles I and III, administered by the National Institute of Mental Health [NIMH]); and (3) sentencing of addicts convicted for certain federal crimes to commitment for treatment (Title II, administered by the Bureau of Prisons). Potential clients were required to petition a United States attorney for determination of status as an addict and of the probability of rehabilitation. If qualified, they were committed to inpatient care for a period not over six months, to be followed by outpatient care for up to three years, with discharge from the program requiring court proceedings. For clients in the NIMH program, inpatient care was provided at the Lexington and Fort Worth hospitals (renamed clinical research centers), and outpatient care was given at contract facilities, usually in the client's city of residence. Bureau of Prisons clients were treated in selected prisons and could then be paroled to outpatient care in the community (Brill in Lowinson and Ruiz). Title IV of NARA authorized grants for community treatment programs for addicts.

The California program provided civil commitment for treatment and a mandatory aftercare program, with reduced case loads, testing for narcotic use, and authorization for a halfway house, as well as a mandate for research on the rehabilitation of narcotic addicts. Commitment for addicts convicted of misdemeanors or felonies was for seven years, and for volunteers, thirty months. The first six months involved inpatient treatment at the California Rehabilitation Center at Corona, followed by assignment to an outpatient unit. A client who abstained from narcotic use for three years could be discharged from his commitment and the criminal charges against him dropped (McGlothlin, Anglin, and Wilson).

The New York program, authorized by legislation in 1966, provided for (1) commitment of persons convicted of crimes, on proof of addiction, to a *compulsory* program of rehabilitation and treatment; (2) narcotic rehabilitation centers and aftercare with close supervision in state-operated or private contract programs; and (3) a central agency (the Narcotic Addict Control Commission [NACC]) to conduct an anti-addiction program, including treatment, rehabilitation, education, training, aftercare, research, and evaluation. The law provided for civil certification to NACC for up to thirty-six months for both nonarrested and arrested addicts, and for criminal certification of convicted addicts. For arrested and convicted addicts, certification required NACC consent. According to Brill and Charles Winick, the choice between treatment and prosecution was a forerunner of the court diversion and Treatment Alternatives to Street Crime (TASC) programs developed in the 1970s.

Evaluation of the NARA program. The NIMH part of this program began in 1967, and by mid-1971 some ten thousand persons had applied for admission. The peak year of admissions was 1970; subsequently the program declined. The Bureau of Prisons program started more slowly but continued to grow; by 1979 it had twenty-three NARA units in operation. NIMH encountered problems with the district courts and the assistant United States attorneys, as well as in locating and training qualified aftercare contractors. At the same time, community treatment programs were being established under Title IV, and dependence on NARA programs decreased. As of 1972, there were 20,576 clients in treatment at sixty-eight operating community treatment programs, and the cumulative number of community treatment clients was 44,723—four times as great as the total number ever served by the NARA civil commitment program (Lindblad and Besteman).

No evaluation data are available on the Bureau of Prisons program. Evaluation of the NIMH program by Wallace Mandell and Zili Amsel showed that about 50 percent of the addicts who applied were rejected as not suitable for treatment. Of the remainder admitted for treatment, 35 percent never reached aftercare. Only 25 percent of the applicants completed the inpatient treatment and one year of aftercare. This study claimed that the NARA program administered by the NIMH failed to use the authority inherent in its mandate, and hence was a quasi-voluntary program rather than a true civil commitment program. The NIMH found the program unwieldy and expensive compared with the expanding community treatment alternatives, and eventually abandoned it. Nevertheless, Richard Lindblad and Karst Besteman considered the emphasis on aftercare in the client's home community an important innovation. They concluded that the seeds planted by the NARA program had germinated into a national community-based treatment network, many of the original NARA aftercare contract programs having grown into major treatment programs.

Evaluation of the California program. McGlothlin, M. Douglas Anglin, and Bruce Wilson interviewed and investigated 756 former admittees to the California Rehabilitation Center, five to twelve years after admission. They compared 225 persons admitted in 1964 with a matched comparison subgroup of 214 persons admitted in 1962–1963 who received early discharge during the initial stage of inpatient treatment by writs of habeas corpus. Essentially this was similar to comparison of a treated and a nontreated group. For the period during commitment (admission plus seven years), the 1964 treated group had fewer arrests than the 1962–1963 nontreated group (.8 nondrug arrests per year, in contrast to 1.18). The two groups were alike with respect to time incarcerated (51 percent in both cases). The treated group spent less time dealing drugs (28 percent versus 38 percent of the time), more time employed (62 percent versus 49 percent), less time in self-reported criminal activities (29 percent versus 43 percent), and less time using narcotics daily (31 percent versus 48 percent).

There were also some benefits observed during the period from seven years after admission to the time of interview: nondrug arrests (.72 versus .90 per person), time incarcerated (25 percent versus 32 percent), involvement in drug dealing (18 percent versus 25 percent), percentage employed (61 percent versus 53 percent), involvement in criminal activities (21 percent versus 31 percent), and percentage using narcotics daily (21 percent versus 28 percent). On a composite measure, reflecting the percentage of time alive, not incarcerated, and not using narcotics daily, the results were: during commitment, 36 percent versus 28 percent; post-commitment 57 percent versus 46 percent. According to the authors, the combination of close monitoring for narcotic use and short-term incarceration for the 1964 group appears to have been more effective than a pattern, in the 1962–1963 group, of less supervision but long-term sentences when apprehended.

The authors also studied 251 admissions in 1970, when methadone maintenance was made available in the program. For the first three years after admission, the 1970 group performed worse than the 1964 group for the comparable period. Afterward, their behavior was equal to or better than that of the 1964 group, and this improvement was attributed in part to the increasing enrollment in methadone maintenance. Although emphasis on close supervision is a distinctive feature of the California civil commitment approach, the contribution of methadone maintenance during a period when supervision was reportedly more lenient was an unexpected finding.

Evaluation of the New York program. As in the NARA program, the New York State program struggled to begin operations after its authorization in 1966. Problems arose in recruiting, mobilizing, and training both residential and aftercare staff and in almost every phase of the entire program. According to Brill and Winick, over the life of NACC there was a steady decline in the percentage of arrested or convicted addicts referred to the program, from more than 50 percent during the first three years to a trickle by 1976. Apparently, arrested addicts learned that crowded court calendars and plea bargaining, with resulting quick return to the streets, was preferable to a compulsory three-year treatment commitment. The authors also noted that the decline in the state facilities' census was materially affected by the large-scale implementation of community methadone maintenance programs that took place during much of the life of the civil commitment program.

Brill and Winick summarized the available empirical and outcome studies of this program. A follow-up study by Dan Waldorf of 375 residents of five facilities, interviewed in 1968 and again thirteen months later, indicated that 26 percent had "good" outcomes, 29 percent "intermediate" outcomes (in treatment after return from aftercare or escape), and 27 percent "bad" outcomes (escaped, absconded, or in prison). The remaining 18 percent were still in treatment or discharged, or no information about them was available. Dean Babst and Sharon Diamond found that of 17,401 cases registered in August 1972, 12 percent were in residential facilities, 42 percent were in aftercare, and 40 percent had absconded. In 1970, New York's Office of Drug Abuse Services conducted a three-year follow-up study of clients who had been treated for three years and discharged from its custody. Regrettably, the sample did not include any of the 40 percent said to be abscondees. The results indicated, over the three years, a sharp decline in heroin use (from 83 percent to 24 percent) and cocaine use (from 38 percent to 20 percent). Almost half (47 percent) of the sample had engaged in some kind of criminal activity in the first year, but only 26 percent in the third year. There was only a slight improvement in amount of time spent employed (from a mean of 8.3 months to 9.6 months annually), but the three-year annual mean for nondrug users was 10 months, compared to 5 months for heavy drug users.

It is difficult to compare the studies by Waldorf and by the Office of Drug Abuse Services with other research because of differences in samples and methodology; nevertheless, considering all factors, it could be estimated that between 10 percent and 20 percent of the clients admitted showed favorable outcomes, despite the shortcomings in the program disclosed by various audits and investigations. For example, according to Brill and Winick, the New York State Commission of Investigation called for a sweeping top-to-bottom review of the program after an investigation in 1976, and subsequently the residential part of the program was abandoned, even though the laws remained. Brill and Winick were critical of the fact that the reports by Waldorf, Babst and Diamond, and others were not published and that there was no evaluation of this program during the first three years. As a result of this, rumor and rhetoric about the program became widespread, to its detriment.

Diversion and referral to treatment in lieu of prosecution. The growth of the national system of community-based treatment programs funded by the NIMH under Title IV of NARA and by the National Institute on Drug Abuse (NIDA), successor to NIMH in the drug abuse area, gave rise to practices in the courts of referring addicts to treatment, often by plea bargaining. In 1972, through the efforts of the Special Action Office for Drug Abuse Prevention (in the Executive Office of the President), the recruitment of addicts to treatment was further advanced by the referral of addict-defendants to community-based treatment in lieu of prosecution. This program was called Treatment Alternatives to Street Crime (TASC) and used criminal justice pressure to move addicts into treatment and hold them there. When arrested, the suspect could be evaluated by a diagnostic unit and held pending transfer to a treatment program. Dropping out of treatment or other noncompliance was treated by the courts as violation of the conditions of release. According to Brill, TASC focused initially on pretrial intervention, but after this approach was resisted by prosecutors in many areas, it was broadened to adapt to local preferences. In 1974, each locality was allowed to decide whether screening was to be mandatory or voluntary and to determine eligibility standards, points of referral, choice of treatment modality, and criteria of success.

No overall evaluation of the impact of TASC and other diversion programs is available. However, they are believed to have performed the treatment outreach function successfully: for example, 50 percent of the referrals entered treatment for the first time, 10 percent were rearrested on new charges while in treatment, and 30 percent were classified as dropouts or failures. According to Brill, Winick asserted that "by providing an alternative to criminal justice dispositions [these programs] have pro tem resolved the dilemma of how to deal with the heroin addict who is chronically involved in minor property crimes" (Lowinson and Ruiz, p. 527).

Nevertheless, court referral has received much criticism from the treatment community. Diversion procedures are claimed to impede needed law reform; reliance on court referrals is said to have altered the basic role of the treatment program as viewed by the community; and it is charged that treatment programs can become formal extensions of the court and thus agents of social control. Furthermore, critics hold that the treatment agency might shift responsibility from the client to the court, and that treatment goals might be altered to fit the needs of the court rather than of the client (Brill in Lowinson and Ruiz).

Treatment approaches within the medical-health system. The major treatment approaches in the NIDA program have been methadone maintenance (MM), therapeutic communities (TC), outpatient drug-free programs (DF), and detoxification (DT). All these programs operate in community settings. Detoxification from heroin and other narcotics has also been utilized as an initial phase of treatment in drug-free TC and DF programs, and should be considered separately from detoxification from methadone, which may be included as a late phase of MM treatment. The use of opiate antagonists to avoid relapse after maintenance treatment has been studied experimentally. Among the treatments and treatment components that have been attempted and described in the literature are psychotherapy and psychoanalytic therapy, acupuncture, various religious approaches and programs, family therapy, vocational rehabilitation, behavior modification, and transcendental meditation (Lowinson and Ruiz).

Maintenance. Maintenance on opiates involves providing a drug (such as heroin, morphine, opium, or methadone) under supervision on a daily basis, with a dosage that prevents craving and withdrawal. Such maintenance was provided by private physicians and clinics prior to 1920. According to Alfred Lindesmith (Lowinson and Ruiz, pp. 339–343), maintenance arrangements have on occasion been made for some prominent and highly privileged addicts despite the law, and some physicians have practiced sub-rosa morphine maintenance for certain addicted patients for years. Although such maintenance has apparently been successful (for example, John O'Donnell found that only five of forty-five such patients had ever been sentenced in a court of law after they became addicted), the available evidence is mainly anecdotal and relates for the most part to practices of an earlier era and away from large urban centers with large-scale, illegal drug traffic. Public and official attitudes have continued to frown on this approach.

Nevertheless, the heroin epidemic of the late 1960s and the growing desperation over the apparently uncontrolled spread of heroin-related crime led to the widespread adoption of methadone maintenance (MM). The pioneering research of Vincent Dole and Marie Nyswander (1965) and a series of demonstration projects in New York, Philadelphia, and Washington, D.C., convinced the Bureau of Narcotics and Dangerous Drugs and the Food and Drug Administration to approve the use of methadone as an investigational drug for experimental maintenance programs. However, although the treatment designed by Dole and Nyswander (1976; cf. Joyce Lowinson in Lowinson and Ruiz, pp. 344–354) was oriented toward rehabilitation, both the government and the public embraced it as a panacea for the eradication of addiction and crime.

MM treatment, usually on an outpatient basis, involves the controlled substitution of methadone, an addictive synthetic opioid that satisfies the craving but lacks the euphoric psychological effects, or "high," of heroin. Methadone is combined with rehabilitation-oriented individual and group therapy and such other services as vocational training and placement, remedial education, family therapy, and housing assistance. The treatment aims at enabling the individual to return to conforming and productive community living. Many methadone advocates, including Dole, believe that detoxification (and abstinence) is not a realistic goal for most addicts and that many thousands of hard-core addicts can be restored to responsible citizenship only by long-term maintenance, which proponents liken to the maintenance of diabetics on insulin. Others, however, believe that the goal of treatment should be abstinence, and they include a detoxification phase (methadone to abstinence) toward the end of treatment. Their treatment program frequently includes efforts to change the value-orientation of the client through a blend of MM and change-oriented group dynamics, as in the therapeutic community (discussed below), as well as to teach social and vocational skills.

As federal support of MM programs enlarged, funding for ancillary rehabilitative services generally became inadequate, although these were in some instances provided through local funds. Under federal guidelines, clients assigned to MM must have a documented addiction history and must have been previously treated.

After extensive research beginning in the early 1970s, a long-acting substitute for methadone, known as LAAM (levo-alpha Acetylmethadol), was developed and made available on an experimental basis. According to Walter Ling and Jack Blaine (Dupont, Goldstein, and O'Donnell, pp. 87–96), this research has "established LAAM as a safe and effective maintenance treatment agent for chronic opiate addiction. It is an acceptable alternative to methadone and has certain advantages over the latter because of its longer duration of action" (p. 95). The use of LAAM would reduce the number of clinic visits from seven to three per week and would eliminate the need for take-home doses of methadone, provided to enable patients to avoid daily clinic visits. At the same time, it would remove the temptation to sell or give away part of the take-home medication, which has been a vexing problem with methadone.

Opiate antagonists. Maintenance treatment protects the addict patient, but does not contribute to shortening the period of physical dependence on the drug. After detoxification and treatment, relapse often occurs in the presence of other addicts or in surroundings associated with narcotic use, as though by a conditioned response. A group of drugs known as opiate antagonists (for example, cyclazocine and naltrexone) have received extensive study because of properties they have that prevent such relapse. These drugs are not in themselves addicting, but according to Charles O'Brien and Robert Greenstein (Lowinson and Ruiz, pp. 403–407), "if an individual maintained on an antagonist experiences craving or withdrawal and administers an opiate, the effects are blocked. With this protection, the patient can be exposed to conditions where relapse is possible without the danger of readdiction" (p. 403).

The most promising antagonist for routine clinical use is naltrexone, which is still under investigation.

O'Brien and Greenstein reported that in a large multimodal treatment program, 5 percent to 10 percent of opiate addicts showed an interest in naltrexone and 30 percent to 40 percent of those who took it for three months were opiate-free (abstinent) six months after stopping treatment. There was a high drop-out rate, but even those who dropped out early often showed improvement. It appears that compared to maintenance, treatment with opiate antagonists is unlikely to become popular among addicts since it provides little or no reinforcement that is intrinsic to methadone and other opiates. Nevertheless, advocates of antagonists consider it the "logical choice" for patients who are determined to remain opiate-free.

Therapeutic communities. The term *therapeutic community* was popularized in the mental health field by Maxwell Jones and colleagues, and the concept of such a community was actualized as a distinctive method for the treatment of narcotic addiction in the Synanon community in 1958 (David Deitch and Joan Zweben in Lowinson and Ruiz, pp. 289–302). However, despite the charismatic influence of the first practitioner of the Synanon model, Charles Dederich, and the impressive stories of its accomplishments, subsequent developments in this approach departed from the methods used in the original program. Significant differences included (1) endorsement of re-entry to the outside community after treatment rather than permanent membership in the therapeutic community, as in Synanon; (2) no payment of an entrance fee, as contrasted to a $1,000 fee in Synanon; (3) acceptance of government funds; (4) participation and leadership of physicians and other professionals in program direction; and (5) research and evaluation, which were vehemently opposed in Synanon. Nevertheless, the essential therapeutic approach of a surrogate family, with communal support to combat alienation and mental and physical dysfunction in a full-time residential setting, was profoundly influenced by the Synanon model.

Subsequent TC programs (such as Daytop Village, Phoenix House, and Gateway House) included encounter-group therapy, tutorial learning sessions, remedial- and formal-education classes, residential job duties, and, in later stages, conventional occupations for live-in–work-out clients (William O'Brien and D. Vincent Biase in Lowinson and Ruiz, pp. 303–315). This therapy involves a highly demanding twenty-four-hour-a-day social setting, with patient government and group pressures to socialize the individual into accepting more adaptive attitudes, as well as patterns of mature, productive behavior. Among the TC programs, the planned duration of treatment varied from two months to a year or longer, although in the latter case the actual time in treatment was much shorter.

Outpatient drug-free treatment. This broad category includes a wide variety of outpatient nonmaintenance programs that in the early 1970s catered mainly to youthful nonopiate users, offering individual and group therapies and other services according to the needs of those served. The DF programs varied widely, ranging from highly demanding daytime TCs to relaxed programs that featured "rap" sessions, recreational activities, and help with individual problems. Subsequently, however, almost as many opiate addicts have entered DF as MM programs, and DF programs that have a predominance of addicts have adapted their approaches to these clients. Herbert Kleber and Frank Slobetz (Lowinson and Ruiz, pp. 31–38) point out that DF treatments have something to offer several types of clients, such as younger addicts seeking their first treatment experience, and addicts who are not eligible for MM, who have successfully completed other treatments, who have relapsed after other treatments, or who require treatment after a prison or hospital stay. Although usually short-term and limited in resources, DF programs have developed referral linkages with community agencies for health, mental health, education, vocational, legal, housing, financial, family, and other required services.

Detoxification. According to Kleber (Lowinson and Ruiz, pp. 317–338), the purposes of detoxification are (1) to rid the body of the acute physiological dependence experienced in the daily use of narcotics; (2) to relieve the pain and discomfort that can occur during withdrawal, especially when it is abrupt; (3) to provide a safe and humane treatment to help the individual over the initial hurdle in stopping narcotic use; and (4) to provide an environment conducive to making a commitment to long-term treatment and a means of referral to such treatment. The most common DT method involves a gradually decreasing dosage of methadone over a period of five to twelve days; this can be done in an inpatient, a residential, or an outpatient setting. Some DT units function only as definitive treatment services, whereas others also provide detoxification for clients entering drug-free treatments. Robert Newman (Dupont, Goldstein, and O'Donnell, pp. 21–30) used the experience of the Ambulatory Detoxification Program in New York City (where detoxification has been in tremendous demand) to justify this method, which, when compared

to illicit narcotic use, has resulted in tremendous savings in lives, property, and suffering.

Evaluation of NIDA community treatment programs. From the very outset of the federal community treatment program, arrangements were made for independent evaluation of treatment effectiveness as a basis for policy guidance. This involved a large-scale client reporting system, the Drug Abuse Reporting Program (DARP), operated with federal funding by the Institute of Behavioral Research (IBR) at Texas Christian University. DARP began receiving reports from six treatment programs in June 1969 and from forty-six additional programs that were added over a four-year period, until the reporting of new admissions was discontinued in March 1973. Until 1972, the DARP included a majority of the NIDA-supported treatment programs, which eventually numbered over two hundred. The final computerized DARP file included 43,943 clients from fifty-two programs located throughout the United States and in Puerto Rico. Most of these programs continue to operate and are represented in the extensive during-treatment and post-treatment follow-up studies conducted by the IBR.

For purposes of the research, admission (case history) and bimonthly status reports up to termination of treatment were collected on the DARP population, and were the source of extensive during-treatment outcome studies, replicated successively in different admission cohorts. This research took into account client characteristics and background, treatment environment and experience, and outcomes—drug and alcohol use, criminality, employment, marital status, and living arrangements during time "at risk," that is, not incarcerated (Sells; Sells and Simpson, 1976, 1980; Sells, Demaree, Simpson et al.).

The major results of the during-treatment evaluation studies were as follows:

1. Substantial changes in the composition of the treatment population could be observed over time, as reflected in comparison of the three cohorts. The shift was in the direction of increased proportions of females, youths, whites, and nonopioid drug users. At the same time, the proportion of addicts in MM (but not the absolute number) decreased and the proportion in DF increased.

2. Planned, as well as actual, duration of TC and DF treatments became shorter. MM treatment, despite the belief in indefinite maintenance held by many practitioners, also decreased in average time. The median time in treatment for all DARP clients was more than twelve months in MM, between three and four months in TC and DF, and less than half a month in DT. The most frequent category of termination in all treatments was "quit," which was highest in DT but also high in TC and DF. In all treatments, length of stay and favorable termination (completed or referred to other treatment) correlated significantly with the quality of behavioral outcomes.

3. Generally favorable performance during treatment was observed in all groups in all treatments. Favorable outcomes were correlated with age (older), with ethnic group (white), and with favorable baseline levels on the outcome measures. Thus, it appeared as though those who needed treatment least did best, and vice versa, a phenomenon familiar in schools and other social institutions. Unlike the other treatments, in MM, where methadone was substituted for street heroin, impressive reduction in opiate use and criminality was observed in most addict clients as soon as they were stabilized on methadone.

4. Early favorable reports on most outcome measures (on the first bimonthly status report) for a majority of clients suggested the existence of a compliance factor, reflecting the response to coercion associated with treatment entry and perceived surveillance of their behavior while in treatment. However, continued improvement over time, particularly in MM, suggested a therapeutic change factor as well. Since residential TC clients were not at risk during most of their stay in treatment, and since the duration of DT was very brief, comparable evaluation of during-treatment change was not observable in those programs.

Post-treatment follow-up studies, extending the existing data files with information obtained by interview with samples of DARP clients, were initiated in 1974, and the third cycle of these began in 1982 (a twelve-year follow-up). The follow-up of Cohorts 1 and 2 was reported by S. B. Sells, Robert Demaree, and Christopher Hornick, and of Cohort 3, by D. Dwayne Simpson, L. James Savage, and Sells. Together, these studies included interviews with 4,627 clients (Simpson and Sells).

Conceptually, the DARP research is based on a prospective data acquisition process. It also reflects a nonintrusive, naturalistic approach in the assessment of service delivery, in that the routine operating procedures of the constituent programs were respected. This is contrary to traditional experimental procedures that alter the treatment process in the field by requiring random assignment of clients to treatments. It is believed that the opportunity for clients to express a choice of treatment alternatives is integral to the treatment process, and indeed, this was insisted upon by the participating programs. As a result, there

were no "control" groups, in the traditional experimental-design sense, but the advantages of realism and the use of rigorous analytic procedures justified the decision.

In the follow-up studies, data were analyzed separately for active addicts, who had used heroin daily during the two-month period prior to admission, and for former addicts, who had used opioids and frequently other drugs during that two-month period, but not heroin (or other opioids) daily. The former addicts were younger, more often white, and more frequently in TC and DF than in MM, compared to the active addicts.

In a series of follow-up studies, results were examined for the first month after leaving DARP treatment, for the first year, and for the first three years. The results consistently showed that significantly favorable outcomes with respect to opiate use, other drug use, time in jail or prison, and employment were obtained in MM, TC, and DF treatment, but not in DT (Sells and Simpson, 1980).

To provide a clear idea of the changes from pre-DARP (admission) to post-DARP levels with respect to outcome measures, figures were compiled by Simpson and Sells (see Table 1) from a subsample of 2,099 black and white male addicts: 895 in MM, 582 in TC, 256 in DF, 214 in DT, and 152, comprising a no-treatment comparison group (called IO, for intake only), who were admitted but never reported for treatment.

Analysis of the DARP follow-up data revealed that (1) the results of treatment were pronounced with respect to reduction of opiate use and criminality indicators; (2) the results were more pronounced for MM, TC, and DF than for DT and IO; (3) the results became more favorable over time, thereby reducing the differences between MM, TC, and DF, compared to DT and IO; and (4) substantial percentages of all groups enrolled in subsequent treatment. Both marijuana and alcohol use (moderate and heavy) showed increases from pre-DARP to each of the three years after DARP. Other nonopioid use showed a modest decline.

For composite outcomes, in the first year post-DARP, 27 percent of the MM, 28 percent of the TC, and 24 percent of the DF clients used no illicit drugs and had no arrests or time in jail or prison, as compared to 15 percent and 14 percent, respectively, of the DT and IO clients. These results are impressive, considering the severity of this criterion. At a somewhat less severe standard (moderately favorable) of no daily use of any illicit drugs and no major criminality—that is, not over thirty days in jail or prison and

TABLE 1. *Changes on three outcome measures, from before treatment (pre-DARP) to one year after and three years after treatment, for black and white male addicts in MM, TC, DF, DT, and the IO (intake only—no treatment) comparison group*

Outcome measures	Treatment group	Pre-DARP (percent)	After one year (percent)	After three years (percent)
	MM	100	36	24
	TC	100	39	26
Used opiates daily	DF	100	44	28
	DT	100	64	37
	IO	100	53	41
	MM	50	28	30
	TC	62	33	32
Spent time incarcerated	DF	51	34	36
	DT	48	35	34
	IO	43	41	38
	MM	88	27	20
	TC	95	33	23
Had been arrested	DF	87	34	22
	DT	83	38	25
	IO	86	39	23

SOURCE: Simpson and Sells.

no arrests for crimes against persons or crimes of profit—the corresponding figures were MM, 41 percent; TC, 40 percent; and DF, 33 percent; as compared to DT, 25 percent; and IO, 27 percent. The treatments evaluated were in every case a single treatment episode in the DARP system, but the effects of subsequent, post-DARP treatment were reflected in these outcome measures. Some further treatment did take place in the first post-DARP year, but generally those clients who showed the best outcomes did not return to treatment.

In agreement with other research, such as that of McGlothlin, Anglin, and Wilson, the DARP studies found that clients who remained in treatment longer and who demonstrated more favorable performance during treatment tended to have more favorable post-treatment outcomes. There also appeared to be a minimum time in treatment for any favorable results: clients in MM, TC, and DF who remained less than ninety days had relatively poor outcomes, comparable with those in the DT and IO groups, regardless of the reason for termination.

Finally, no significant predictors were found, based on client background variables, that would justify differential matching of clients with particular treatments to maximize outcome. As in the during-treatment studies, pre-DARP measures on each outcome variable were correlated with post-DARP measures on the same variable, in all treatments. For example, those who were employed before treatment tended to be employed after treatment. The highest correlation of this sort was for criminality, and those with extensive criminal histories tended to do most poorly in treatment, showing high further criminality, as well as high opiate use and avoidance of legitimate employment. If there has been one area in which the entire treatment effort has been unsuccessful, it has been in the failure to cope effectively with the hard-core criminal addict.

Conclusion

There is ample evidence, both in the community treatment programs and in the civil commitment programs, that for substantial percentages of addict clients, treatment has been followed by favorable outcomes with regard to opiate use and criminality for up to at least four years. Within the DARP research on community treatment programs, these percentages varied between 25 percent and 50 percent (in different samples) for MM, TC, and DF treatment, depending on the manner in which "favorable outcome" was defined. Although the outcome measures were not comparable, similar claims would appear reasonable in the research on the California Civil Commitment Program (McGlothlin, Anglin, and Wilson) and perhaps also in other treatments mentioned. Whether such results should be attributed directly to specific treatment processes is doubtful. It seems clear, however, that the results do represent the interactions of clients motivated to engage in the treatment process vis-à-vis the staffs, environments, and regimens of the various programs. Clients with negative attitudes toward treatment, such as the hard-core criminal addicts mentioned above, have usually not responded favorably to any treatments studied thus far.

To a great extent, these results exceed the expectations of many who have been critical of the treatment approach without the benefit of the research data. It is known that the NARA and other civil commitment programs were assembled hastily, under crisis conditions, and that the funding and administration of publicly supported programs have been subject to political influence. In many instances, the legislative rhetoric spoke in terms of rehabilitation, whereas the budgets and the regulatory provisions appeared to focus on control. Much credit is due to the dedicated professional and paraprofessional staffs throughout the treatment community for the impressive results achieved.

Any realistic appraisal of drug treatment must also take account of the during-treatment results, because even residential treatment in therapeutic community programs is highly cost-effective, compared to incarceration for equal periods. During treatment, the most spectacular results were obtained in the MM programs, where addicts who were stabilized on methadone used virtually no other opiates and engaged in very little illegal behavior. Unfortunately, many addicts who have taken opiates for years and who have adapted to the routines of the street life cannot lose their craving for narcotics, even after detoxification and treatment. For them, continued maintenance may be a realistic alternative, but this would require a change of attitude on the part of legislators and the general public. In the present system, many addict clients must go through numerous treatment episodes—or, alternatively, punitive confinement—before they finally retire or disappear.

A reasonable position appears to be that expressed by James Maddux and David Desmond:

Methadone maintenance has become a legal method for providing an opioid drug to persons dependent on illegal opioids. It apparently reduces criminal behavior, but as presently practiced it attracts and retains only part of the population of opioid users. It would probably retain more if the programs had fewer restrictions with respect to dispensing hours, urine testing, and take-home methadone. Allowing more methadone to be taken home for self-administration would increase the hazard of use by others, some of whom would become new compulsive users [p. 210].

The latter hazard would be greatly reduced by the use of LAAM, as noted earlier.

Perhaps a more definitive solution to the addiction problem will emerge eventually from the research on the biology of opiates. For example, Eric Simon (Lowinson and Ruiz, pp. 45–56) has noted recent work that suggests the existence in the nervous system of several different opiate receptors:

Preliminary evidence suggests that one of the receptors is primarily concerned with the analgesic function of opiates and opioid peptides, whereas another receptor may be responsible for their addiction liability. If this proves correct, molecules could be tailor-made to fit one, but not the other receptor. Such an approach would provide a rational basis for the hitherto empirical search for analgesics of low addiction liability and for drugs useful in the treatment of addicts. The day when drug addiction can be either prevented or treated in a rational manner may not yet be around the corner, but the enormous research activity that the recent discoveries have given rise to in the opiate field augurs well. If and when the molecular basis of the addictive process is understood for opiates, it may well serve as a model for the elucidation of the mechanism of addiction to alcohol, nicotine, and other substances currently abused in this country and elsewhere [p. 54].

S. B. SELLS

See also ALCOHOL AND CRIME: TREATMENT AND REHABILITATION.

BIBLIOGRAPHY

BABST, DEAN V., and DIAMOND, SHARON. Abscondence Trends for NACC Certified Clients. New York: Narcotic Addiction Control Commission, 1972.

BRILL, LEON, and WINICK, CHARLES. "The New York Civil Commitment Program." The Compulsory Treatment of Opiate Dependence. Edited by William H. McGlothlin and M. Douglas Anglin. Forthcoming publication.

DISKIND, MEYER H. "The Role of the Parole Officer or the Use of the Authoritative Casework Approach." Rehabilitating the Narcotic Addict. Edited by S. B. Sells. Washington, D.C.: U.S. Department of Health, Education, and Welfare, Vocational Rehabilitation Administration, 1967, pp. 285–292.

DOLE, VINCENT P., and NYSWANDER, MARIE E. "A Medical Treatment for Diacetylmorphine (Heroin) Addiction: A Clinical Trial with Methadone Hydrochloride." Journal of the American Medical Association 193 (1965): 646–650.

———. "Methadone Maintenance Treatment: A Ten-year Perspective." *Journal of the American Medical Association* 235 (1976): 2117–2119.

DUPONT, ROBERT L.; GOLDSTEIN, AVRAM; and O'DONNELL, JOHN, eds. *Handbook on Drug Abuse.* Rockville, Md.: U.S. Department of Health and Human Services, National Institute on Drug Abuse, 1979.

GREENBERG, STEPHANIE W. "The Relationship between Crime and Amphetamine Abuse: An Empirical Review of the Literature." *Contemporary Drug Problems* 5 (1976): 101–130.

JONES, MAXWELL et al. *The Therapeutic Community: A New Treatment Method in Psychiatry.* Foreword by Goodwin Watson. New York: Basic Books, 1953.

LINDBLAD, RICHARD A., and BESTEMAN, KARST J. "Implementation of the Narcotic Addict Rehabilitation Act of 1966." *The Compulsory Treatment of Opiate Dependence.* Edited by William H. McGlothlin and M. Douglas Anglin. Forthcoming publication.

LOWINSON, JOYCE H., and RUIZ, PEDRO, eds. *Substance Abuse: Clinical Problems and Perspectives.* Baltimore: Williams & Wilkins, 1981.

MADDUX, JAMES F., and DESMOND, DAVID P. *Careers of Opioid Users.* New York: Holt, Rinehart & Winston, 1981.

MANDELL, WALLACE, and AMSEL, ZILI. *Status of Addicts Treated under the NARA Program.* Baltimore: Johns Hopkins University, Department of Mental Hygiene and Public Health, 1973.

McGLOTHLIN, WILLIAM H.; ANGLIN, M. DOUGLAS; and WILSON, BRUCE D. *An Evaluation of the California Civil Addict Program.* Rockville, Md.: U.S. Department of Health and Human Services, National Institute on Drug Abuse, 1977.

O'DONNELL, JOHN A. *Narcotic Addicts in Kentucky.* Chevy Chase, Md.: U.S. Department of Health, Education, and Welfare, National Institute of Mental Health, 1969.

New York State Office of Drug Abuse Services. *Three Years Later: A Followup of Decertified ODAS Clients.* New York: ODAS, 1976.

RICHARDS, LOUISE G., ed. *Demographic Trends and Drug Abuse, 1980–1995.* Rockville, Md.: U.S. Department of Health and Human Services, National Institute on Drug Abuse, 1981.

SELLS, S. B., ed. *Evaluation of Treatments.* The Effectiveness of Drug Abuse Treatment, vols. 1–2. Cambridge, Mass.: Ballinger, 1974.

———; DEMAREE, ROBERT G.; and HORNICK, CHRISTOPHER W. *The Comparative Effectiveness of Methadone Maintenance, Therapeutic Community, Outpatient Drug-free, and Outpatient Detoxification Treatments for Drug Users in the DARP: Cohort 1–2 Followup Study.* Rockville, Md.: U.S. Department of Health and Human Services, National Institute on Drug Abuse, 1979.

SELLS, S. B.; DEMAREE, ROBERT G.; SIMPSON, D. DWAYNE; JOE, GEORGE W.; and GORSUCH, RICHARD. "Issues in the Evaluation of Drug Abuse Treatment." *Professional Psychology* 8 (1977): 609–640.

SELLS, S. B., and SIMPSON, D. DWAYNE. "The Case for Drug Abuse Treatment Effectiveness, Based on the DARP Research Program." *British Journal of Addiction* 75 (1980): 117–131.

———, eds. *The Effectiveness of Drug Abuse Treatment,* vols. 3–5. Cambridge, Mass.: Ballinger, 1976.

SIMPSON, D. DWAYNE; SAVAGE, L. JAMES; and SELLS, S. B. *Evaluation of Outcomes for the First Year after Drug Abuse Treatment: A Replication Study Based on 1972–1973 Admissions.* Fort Worth: Texas Christian University, Institute of Behavioral Research, 1980.

SIMPSON, D. DWAYNE, and SELLS, S. B. *Evaluation of Drug Abuse Treatment Effectiveness: Summary of the DARP Followup Research.* Rockville, Md.: U.S. Department of Health and Human Services, National Institute on Drug Abuse, 1982.

U.S. Department of Health and Human Services, National Institute on Drug Abuse. *National Institute on Drug Abuse Statistical Series: Annual Data, 1980.* Rockville, Md.: NIDA, 1981.

WALDORF, DAN. *New York's Candy Coated Penitentiaries.* New York: Urban Resources, 1970.

WEISSMAN, JAMES C. "Understanding the Drugs and Crime Connection: A Systematic Examination of Drugs and Crime Relationships." *Journal of Psychedelic Drugs* 10 (1978): 171–192.

DRUNK DRIVING

See DRINKING AND DRIVING; TRAFFIC OFFENSES.

DRUNKENNESS

See articles under ALCOHOL AND CRIME; DRINKING AND DRIVING; EXCUSE: INTOXICATION.

DUE PROCESS

See APPEAL; CRIMINAL PROCEDURE: CONSTITUTIONAL ASPECTS.

DURESS

See EXCUSE, *articles on* DURESS *and* SUPERIOR ORDERS.

EAVESDROPPING

See WIRETAPPING AND EAVESDROPPING.

ECOLOGY OF CRIME

The ecology of crime studies how illegal activities relate to the larger human and nonhuman environment. Looking beyond offenders and criminal justice officials, such an inquiry considers how the basic sustenance patterns of a society, through daily patterns of community life, engender criminal inclinations and provide the opportunity to translate such inclinations into action. The ecology of crime is part of a larger field of scientific research known as human ecology, which in turn is linked to the biological subfield of ecology (Hawley).

Ecology studies the relationship of organisms or groups of organisms to their environment. Human ecology examines how people use technology and organization to adapt to their larger nonhuman environment, as well as of how different human communities adapt to one another. The ecology of crime examines the ways illegal activity carves its niche into the larger structure of legal activity. Rather than studying why certain individuals violate laws, it asks how community structure facilitates such violations by providing a population with key opportunities.

Fundamentals of the ecology of crime. Some illegal acts are purely parasitic, adding nothing to community sustenance. Other crime provides real goods and services that some of the public wishes to consume, such as prostitution and illegal drugs. Still other crime permits the evasion of impractical restrictions on productivity that are built into the law, such as outmoded or overly stringent building codes. In any case, crime must feed upon the larger community to survive. The basic ecological theorem of crime is that society provides a variety of facilities, equipment, and supplies for legal activities that people also use in violating laws or in preventing others from doing so. To understand this process, one needs to examine how technology and the organization of legal activities offer such opportunities. Legal activities take place in space and time and thus set the stage for spatial and temporal patterns of crime as well. Certain parts of cities, regions, nations, hours of the day, days of the week, and months of the year have a much higher crime incidence than others. Such patterns in space and time are structured in part by the settings and rhythms of legal activities. Because technological and organizational changes influence the patterns of daily life, crime patterns and rates might be expected to change accordingly.

Ecological analysis distinguishes four types of criminal offenses in terms of the form of human interdependence they entail: competitive, exploitative, mutualistic, and individualistic. In competitive crime, different offenders act illegally so that gain by one means loss to another: examples include fights over desired property, esteem, sexual activity, or the control of illegal business or territory. In contrast, exploitative crime involves persons acting in different roles, in which one illegally seizes or tries to seize control over the person or property of another. Many larcenies, robberies, rapes, and burglaries fit in this category. Mutualistic crime includes so-called victimless offenses, in which two or more persons cooperate to violate the law, playing different roles in the process. A gambler and gambling house or a prostitute and client serve as good examples. Individualistic crime includes suicide, solo drug abuse, or any other violation by lone individuals that is contingent upon the absence of interference by others.

Both competitive and exploitative offenses may entail a struggle among people for property, safety, territorial hegemony, sexual outlet, physical control, or sometimes survival itself. Yet the difference between the two remains important because the first category may involve completely innocent victims, whereas the second pertains to individuals struggling illegally with one another. The two types of offenses may draw participants from different segments of the population and evoke different responses from the legal system. The central challenge to the ecologist of crime is to catalog key participants in crime and justice, to reveal their interdependence, and to discover how this links them to the larger system of activities—no easy task, since potential offenders, victims, law enforcement personnel, and other participants interact in a complex fashion.

Specific circumstances. Crime and crime control consist of practical tasks in the tangible world, where individuals and groups gain or lose materially in the process. Illegal acts draw their participants, facilities, equipment, and supplies from a larger environment. Even unplanned lawbreaking may depend upon specific circumstances that influence the probability of occurrence. Research reveals dramatic differences in the probability that various tangible situations will engender criminal acts (Cohen and Felson). Such findings, many derived from victimization research, provide an important source of information linking criminal opportunities to community life.

Mutualistic offenses generally have at least a producer and a consumer of illegal goods or services, as well as whatever licit or illicit paraphernalia, facilities, or goods are involved in these illegal acts. Competitive violations generally take place in situations that produce and escalate aggression, typically involving young males, the use of alcohol or other drugs, and the absence of older adults. In general, a situation tends to be violence-prone if it includes likely combatants, objects of competition, provocateurs, and the absence of potential peacemakers. Individualistic offenses require at least the absence of inhibitors.

Exploitative criminal acts generally involve, at a minimum, a likely offender, a suitable target, and the absence of someone capable of preventing an offense. A likely offender may be anyone with appreciable incli-

nation to commit either a certain kind of offense or offenses in general. Any person or thing evoking criminal inclinations may be a suitable target, its suitability reflecting such factors as its value or desirability for offenders, including the monetary or symbolic value of property or whatever personal characteristics attract offenders. A target's suitability may also be influenced by its visibility to offenders or their informants, by legal or illegal access to it and ease of escape from its site, by the portability or mobility of objects sought by offenders, or by the physical strength or other capacities—relative to those of a potential offender—of would-be personal targets.

The absence of capable guardians is an important variable in the ecology of crime, and it does not mainly refer to the quantity or quality of policing. Indeed, most evidence indicates that police are unlikely to be present at or near the scene of criminal offenses. Rather, the prime potential guardians against crime are average citizens going about their daily life, often unaware that they may be performing this function.

In general, the various participants in crime play their roles through direct physical contact or physical separation. Hence, a criminogenic circumstance normally requires the physical convergence of likely participants and the absence of likely inhibitors. This general principle links crime to the larger community, which affords such a convergence. Indeed, in the ebb and flow of ordinary life, undaring offenders can find either more or less opportunity to carry out exploitative offenses, and circumstances arise that are favorable or unfavorable for illegal competitions or mutualistic offenses. A fundamental theorem of the ecology of crime is that the necessary features of a direct-contact violation must converge in space and time for direct-contact crimes to occur. The vast majority of criminal acts in fact require direct physical contact between exploiter and victim, between producer and consumer of illegal services, or among illegal combatants, or they result from the absence of contact with guardians or inhibitors of crime. Consequently, any features of community life influencing such contact become important for understanding crime.

Early studies. In 1796, Patrick Colquhoun presented a lucid account of a serious crime wave in London at the end of the eighteenth century. His explanation pointed to a great increase in the assembling and transporting of valuable goods through London ports and terminals. Although the language of human ecology had not yet been invented, Colquhoun adopted the ecological perspective long before most criminologists of the twentieth century. Subsequently, many early studies in several nations showed that known criminal activity was distributed very unevenly over space. André Michel Guerry's demonstration of this in 1833 preceded by almost a century the work of such American ecologists as Clifford Shaw, who mapped delinquent activities and correlated them with the attributes of area residents.

Like the study of human ecology in general, the study of the ecology of crime began with spatial generalizations. For example, much research demonstrated that crime varied systematically between urban and rural areas, from central cities to their outer rings, and among regions. These studies used various units of area, such as neighborhoods, suburbs, cities, metropolitan areas, states, provinces, and nations. The different generalizations that emerged from such comparisons have been summarized by Judith Wilks. One of the most consistent relationships found is the excess of urban over rural crime rates. Yet even this finding has been accompanied by weaker relationships for violent crimes and by evidence that homicide is sometimes an exception to the rule.

Great spatial variations in crime rates are repeatedly observed within cities, towns, and metropolitan areas. For much of the twentieth century, higher crime rates in most North American cities were found in deteriorating areas near the urban core, decreasing as one proceeded, often outward, to areas of higher socioeconomic status and lower rates of family disruption. Ecologists called high-crime districts near the center "zones of transition," noting that their character often persisted after population composition had changed. Thus, the highest crime rate areas of many North American cities were populated mainly by persons of Irish ancestry around 1900, by those of Italian or Polish descent around 1920, by blacks around 1950, and by Hispanics around 1980. This observation has sometimes justified the policy recommendation that physical renovation or even demolition of these areas would itself reduce crime, an outcome that has not been substantiated. To be sure, a positive correlation exists between urban crime and neighborhood deterioration at a given time. Yet trends toward better living conditions and lower urban population density in the United States after World War II did not result in lower crime rates—if anything, quite the opposite. This realization prompted students of the ecology of crime to examine some new ideas.

Metropolitan crime in an automotive era. Urban ecology developed in large part prior to World War II, when the automobile was a luxury and when residential areas usually provided for most needs of urban residents: work, school, and leisure facilities were located nearby, and work was concentrated in or around a central business district. With the coming of the automotive age, homes, jobs, and stores spread over a wider metropolitan space. A metropolitan patchwork quilt emerged during the decades after World War II in the United States and certain other industrial nations. Since automobiles could cross neighborhood boundaries quickly, traditional notions of the delinquency area began to lose their utility, particularly once the adolescent population had gained access to autos. The urban-rural distinction also lost its clarity with the spread of suburbs, whose moderate population densities differed from both urban and rural patterns of the past. Telecommunications further blurred the boundary between urban and rural life. Compared to those of the past, the crime patterns of such a society became much more complex. Crime ecologists began to develop a more elaborate ecology of crime for a fast-moving population living here, working there, matriculating elsewhere, and finding leisure in still other places. Crime began to reflect new patterns of human intermingling and hourly shifts—often at high automotive speeds—of activities and populations.

Attention to the daily movement of lawbreakers was not new. As early as 1930, Andrew Lind studied the location of both the offender's residence and the scene of delinquency. This distinction was followed up by Clyde White, Terence Morris, and Sarah Boggs, although it was often neglected by others. Advances in victimization research during the 1970s enriched such research by providing more information on the specific circumstances of criminal acts and their occurrence. These studies repeatedly found common crime victimization to be more probable for adolescents and young adults than for older persons, for working people than for retired persons or homemakers, for unmarried persons (including widowed and divorced individuals) than for those with an intact marriage, for those living in single adult households as opposed to members of households consisting of two or more adults, and for those living nearer to centers of cities rather than in outlying or rural areas (Hindelang, Gottfredson, and Garofalo). Such evidence indicated that a far greater risk of both personal and property victimization was incurred by engaging in activities away from family and household settings: even an automobile was found to be much more exposed to theft when it belonged to persons who were often away from home. Any social trends that draw people away from home thus became important for crime rate analysis.

Crime opportunity in an automotive age. Major shifts in patterns of activity and contact, as well as in the technology and organization of American society, occurred between 1950 and 1980 (Felson and Cohen). Such changes included a shift of activities away from family and household, owing to the suburbanization of work, school, and leisure; a growing tendency for women to hold jobs away from home; an increase of single-adult households; rising college enrollments; a greater reliance on automobiles; and the production of lighter or wheeled durable goods with significant values per movable pound. Considering the importance of such changes for common offenses, Cohen and Felson were able to show that these factors could account for most of the increases in reported crime during the period from 1950 to 1980. Changes in routine activities and resources apparently altered the probability that likely offenders would come into contact with unguarded targets for crime. Working women, single adults, college students, and others often engaging in nonfamily and nonhousehold activities would more often find themselves in settings where they and their property were subject to illegal attack, where they were more likely to blunder into competitive struggles, and where their collaboration in victimless crimes would escape unfavorable notice. Thus, ecological analysis has shown that a crime wave does not depend on increased motivation to engage in crime, providing that there is greater opportunity to act upon existing motivations.

Although it generally takes motivations for granted, ecology may still be useful for putting knowledge about motivations and their control into a tangible perspective. For example, by ensuring more success in crime, community life may reinforce its motivation. Such motivation may be more likely learned or less likely controlled in certain activities or settings, such as among young peers with adults. Hence, any activities that bring together peers in the absence of adults might tend to enhance criminal motivation or hinder its informal control. During the period from 1950 to 1980 in the United States, adolescents' increased automobile use and their concentration in large schools, adults' preoccupation with other activities, the decline of two-parent households, the increase of the adolescent population, and a general increase in prosperity all made it easier for adolescent groups to gain autonomy in an urban or suburban setting.

Interdependence between crime and the public. One conception of the ecology of crime might begin with a population of law enforcers pursuing a population of offenders, who in turn pursue the general public or its property. This naive model neglects the symbiotic interdependence, as well as the population overlap, of offenders, officials, and the general public. The interplay and overlap of these three populations renders crime analysis more subtle and yet offers a better understanding of how criminal activity grows or atrophies.

The interdependence of the general public and the offending population is multifaceted. Various social ties between the two populations may nurture crime and social control simultaneously. From the generally law-abiding public come victim and receiver of stolen goods; the guardian of the victim from the offender, or of the offender from the police; peacemaker and provocateur; the outraged citizen and the purchaser of illegal benefits; the informant for the police or for the offender; the resident of a community that crime destroys or of one that crime nurtures; the occasional lawmaker or lawbreaker; those who stigmatize offenders or acquiesce in their behavior; and those who cut offenders off or tie them into normal interaction. This population provides the moral turpitude, innocence, outrage, action, and apathy that influence the manner in which crime influences the larger system of activities.

Ironically, this overlap and interaction of the law-abiding and lawbreaking populations forms a web of interdependence that both impairs and facilitates law enforcement and the informal social control of crime. Respectable citizens who secretly consume illegal services may make excellent informers for the police, once they are discovered in compromising situations. Law-abiding friends and relatives of offenders can, perhaps reluctantly, provide officials with needed information about offenders. Such personal ties may also be activated to ensure informal social control. Law-abiding persons symbiotically tied to lawbreakers help sustain both crime and policing, even while providing offenders with suitable targets for criminal predation, customers for mutualistic crime, or recruits to the population of frequent offenders. The public may also take an aggressive role in attacking offenders caught in the act, causing them to attempt escape, and sometimes impelling them to commit more serious offenses or to use lethal weapons. Nor should one neglect the importance of activities bringing likely offenders into direct contact with suitable targets in the absence of capable guardians against crime.

Interdependence with law enforcement. The law enforcement population is itself drawn from the larger population and, occasionally, from the criminal population. It must live in the larger society and is itself subject to controls. Law enforcement aims at upsetting the ecological balance by keeping the population of frequent offenders from gaining membership in, and benefits from, the population of usual nonoffenders, while using the latter to gain information about, and to control, the former.

The law enforcement process depends largely upon the organization of the community. Detecting offenses, reaching the scene of a crime, finding witnesses, building a case, and carrying it through to conviction—all of these activities involve coordination and contact. It becomes more difficult for victims, witnesses, prosecutors, and police to cooperate if they are strangers and have greater distances to travel. A dispersion of activities away from family and household would tend to impair the efforts of the criminal justice system to find witnesses or to secure their continued cooperation in a prosecution. Such a dispersion would tend to place victims outside their community at the time of victimization, making it more difficult to draw assistance from others in punishing offenders.

Because they are the most direct agents of daily crime control, the police are more exposed than others to community change. Beyond their role in protecting innocent victims, law enforcement personnel gain their livelihood and risk their lives by stalking offenders or appearing to do so. Such "predatory" acts by officers of the law may include legally suppressing illegal activity, harassing such activity to keep it within bounds, or taking illegal bribes from offenders in return for allowing their continued activity. The police are viewed as predators by exploitative offenders and by both parties in mutualistic and competitive violations. The parties committing competitive violations, such as criminal organizations, may attempt to use the police against their competition; but whether they arrange it or not, any police failure to control one group's competitors in crime might easily destroy that group's criminal habitat.

This is not obvious until one considers that, if crime were allowed to overwhelm a community, offenders dependent upon finding victims or customers would find the very activities destroyed that provide their sustenance, much as an underhunted species would find its own population explosion destructive of its food supply and ultimately contrary to survival. For example, if street crime took over an entire area, it would drive out legal activity and destroy the influx of income from other activities that support such crime. Purveyors of drugs, prostitution, and other illegal goods and services often oppose the decriminalization of vices because they rely upon law enforcers to keep supplies restricted and prices high enough to sustain their illicit business. Some crime control strategies argue for the legalization or decriminalization of drugs, prostitution, or gambling precisely in order to remove a criminal niche and the secondary lawbreaking it presumably generates. Ironically, by keeping illegal predation from dominating the ecosystem, law enforcers make possible the continuation

of legal activities upon which a healthy population of offenders can routinely prey. The ecologist considers such results, regardless of anyone's intentions or awareness of his role in the criminal ecosystem.

When their niche is destroyed or impoverished, one might expect frequent lawbreakers to behave like any other population, turning to new types of crime, migrating to new locations, or shifting to legal sources of sustenance. This process might create some unanticipated consequences. Some offenders might abandon larceny and take up robbery or otherwise become more daring and aggressive. Others might place new burdens on public aid or pose new criminal threats to nearby areas where crime control activity has not proceeded at a similar pace. Such potential displacements illustrate the complexity of crime control considered from an ecological viewpoint. The greatest challenge to public policy is to determine how to control those illegal activities that are so deeply enmeshed in a larger system of legal activity.

Policy implications. Authorities on the ecology of crime offer a policy perspective that is at odds with much of nineteenth- and twentieth-century criminology. Rather than suggesting how criminal justice officials can reduce crime and protect law-abiding citizens from offenders, crime ecologists look upon citizens and officials as populations whose sustenance is intricately linked to crime, however innocent their intentions. This linkage, then, makes crime control a matter of comprehensive planning, not of isolated action by criminal justice agencies. Such planning must consider how to reduce the opportunities for crime offered by the routine activities of daily life. The shaping of public policy becomes very difficult when one considers the extent to which crime control depends not on ridding society of poverty and sloth, but rather on controlling prosperity and freedom of movement. The same opportunities that help people enjoy life may also expose them to encounters with criminals, give criminals access to potential recruits, and render more difficult the apprehension and prosecution of offenders.

Indeed, one policy implication of this perspective is hardly pleasant. Instead of the criminal population alone having to pay the price for diminishing crime, the general public might have to bear the major cost. If the public's prosperity and freedom of movement are too dear to sacrifice, then high crime rates may have to be accepted lest adequate crime control paralyze modern life.

If feasible policies emerge from this perspective, they will probably be implemented by agencies that are not usually responsible for criminal justice. For example, government policy concerning highway expansion and suburban sprawl, zoning, driver licensing, school size or age groupings, and housing for the aged may be more significant for crime reduction or expansion than the actions of criminal justice agencies. Rather than trying to influence offenders with punishment or rehabilitation, policy might be oriented toward preventing them from coming into direct contact with unguarded targets or toward reducing their recruits by keeping schools small and adolescents preoccupied with legal pursuits within their residential locales. However, smaller schools may increase social control only at the expense of reducing curricular variety, and raising the driving age would inconvenience parents and limit youths' work and school opportunities. Providing separate housing for the aged may protect them from young offenders, yet it would also segregate them from pleasant contacts with nonoffending youths. Not much is known yet about such policies, but they would surely interfere with routine legal as well as illegal activities.

The ecology of crime covers but a limited range of topics. For those who want to know why offenders break laws, the ecologist only points out the circumstances in which lawbreaking is most frequent. For those seeking causes, the ecologist points out the unanticipated consequences of social structure. For those pursuing deep meaning or broad purpose in crime trends, the ecologist offers a compendium of discrete events, linked only by conditional probabilities. For those in search of a direct and simple policy to control crime, the ecologist offers indirectness and the sacrifice of other social benefits. Yet the ecology of crime is systematic and simple, explaining many facts with a few clear principles.

MARCUS FELSON

See also CRIME CAUSATION: SOCIOLOGICAL THEORIES; CRIME PREVENTION: ENVIRONMENTAL AND TECHNOLOGICAL STRATEGIES; RURAL CRIME; URBAN CRIME.

BIBLIOGRAPHY

BOGGS, SARAH L. "Urban Crime Patterns." *American Sociological Review* 30 (1965): 899–908.
COHEN, LAWRENCE E., and FELSON, MARCUS. "Social Change and Crime Rate Trends: A Routine Activity Approach." *American Sociological Review* 44 (1979): 588–608.
COLQUHOUN, PATRICK. *A Treatise on the Police of the Metropolis, Containing a Detail of the Various Crimes and Misdemeanors by Which Public and Private Property Are, at Present, Injured and Endangered; and Suggesting Remedies for Their Prevention* (1796). 6th ed., corrected and enlarged. London: Mawman, 1800.
FELSON, MARCUS, and COHEN, LAWRENCE E. "Human Ecology and Crime: A Routine Activity Approach." *Human Ecology* 8 (1980): 389–406.
GUERRY, ANDRÉ MICHEL. *Essai sur la statistique morale de la France; précédé d'un rapport à l'Académie de Sciences, par MM. Lacroix, Silvestre, et Girard.* Paris: Crochard, 1833.
HAWLEY, AMOS H. *Human Ecology: A Theory of Community Structure.* New York: Ronald Press, 1950.
HINDELANG, MICHAEL; GOTTFREDSON, MICHAEL; and GAROFALO, JAMES. *Victims of Personal Crime: An Empirical Foundation for a Theory of Personal Victimization.* Cambridge, Mass.: Ballinger, 1978.
LIND, ANDREW W. "Some Ecological Patterns of Community Disorganization in Honolulu." *American Journal of Sociology* 36 (1930): 206–220.
MORRIS, TERENCE. *The Criminal Area: A Study in Social Ecology.* Foreword by Hermann Mannheim. New York: Humanities Press, 1958.
SHAW, CLIFFORD R.; MCKAY, HENRY D.; ZORBAUGH, FREDERICK M.; and COTTRELL, LEONARD S. *Delinquency Areas.* University of Chicago Press, 1929.
WHITE, R. CLYDE. "The Relation of Felonies to Environmental Factors in Indianapolis." *Social Forces* 10 (1932): 498–509.
WILKS, JUDITH A. "Ecological Correlates of Crime and Delinquency." *Task Force Report: Crime and Its Impact—An Assessment.* President's Commission on Law Enforcement and Administration of Justice, Task Force on Assessment of Crime. Washington, D.C.: The Commission, 1967, pp. 138–156.

ECONOMIC CRIME

The topic of economic crime, although referred to in a number of entries, is discussed most fully in three articles. The article on THEORY *addresses the topic broadly and delineates not only the purposes of criminal sanctions in the field, but also the characteristic difficulties and dilemmas encountered in such uses of the criminal law. The other two articles focus directly on specific areas of public policy.* ANTITRUST OFFENSES *traces the use of criminal sanctions in an important area of government policy, and notes the modern tendency toward increased resort to the criminal law as an enforcement device.* TAX OFFENSES *deals with the threat and use of criminal punishment in the exercise of the government's revenue powers and the problems encountered by individual taxpayers defending against criminal charges in this area.*

1. THEORY — Edmund W. Kitch
2. ANTITRUST OFFENSES — Kevin A. Russell
3. TAX OFFENSES — Steven Duke

1.
THEORY

Introduction

There is no generally accepted definition of the term *economic crime* and no distinct body of literature on the theory and practice of economic crime (Stearns; Elliott and Willingham, pp. 227–261). Economic crime might, for instance, be defined as crime undertaken for economic motives. So defined, it would sweep broadly across the field of crime from misdemeanor larceny to vast financial crimes, and from crimes of stealth to crimes of violence. The only crimes excluded by this definition are crimes undertaken for darker motives with no hope of economic gain. Such a definition would have its uses, for economic gain is doubtless an important motive in much criminal activity. It would tend, however, to make the discussion here nearly congruent with the subject of crime. For the purposes of this article, *economic crime* is defined as criminal activity with significant similarities to the economic activity of normal, noncriminal business.

There are two major styles of economic crime. The first consists of crimes committed by businessmen as an adjunct to their regular business activities. Businessmen's responsibilities give them the opportunity, for example, to commit embezzlement, to violate regulations directed at their area of business activity, or to evade the payment of taxes. This style of economic crime is often called white-collar crime. The second style of economic crime is the provision of illegal goods and services or the provision of goods and services in an illegal manner. Illegal provision of goods and services requires coordinated economic activity similar to that of normal business, but all of those engaged in it are involved in crime. The madam operating a brothel has many concerns identical to the manager of a resort hotel, and the distributor of marijuana must worry about the efficiency and reliability of his distribution system just as does a distributor of any other product. This type of economic crime is often called organized crime because the necessity of economic coordination outside the law leads to the formation of criminal groups with elaborate organizational customs and practices (Nelli).

Economic crime has three features that make it of special interest. First, the economic criminal adopts methods of operation that are difficult to distinguish from normal commercial behavior. Second, economic crime may involve the participation of economically successful individuals of otherwise upright community standing. Third, many economic crimes present special challenges to prosecutors, to the criminal justice system, and to civil liberties.

Some economic crimes are stunning in their size, complexity, and daring, and are accompanied by high living and a veneer of glamour. The intrigues and adventures of the large-scale economic criminal, often accompanied by spectacular financial collapses, are recounted at length in the nation's newspapers (Dunn; Moffitt).

The most important economic crime is the organized appropriation of goods and property by stealth or fraud. Organized theft of goods from businesses requires elaborate organization for the conversion of those goods into cash. Such organized-theft rings can present a far larger threat to legitimate business than occasional and nonsystematic theft, because of the potentially large losses involved. Aside from the usual penalties for the conversion of property, the law attempts to control this activity by regulating the resale market for used property. Pawnshops are subject to licensing and inspection. The organized receiving of stolen property is itself a crime (Model Penal Code § 223.6).

Fraud crimes depend upon the perpetrator's persuading his victim that his objectives are normal and legitimate. Such frauds impose costs on all businesses, because they increase the amount of resources that investors and customers must devote to the activity of detecting and preventing fraud.

Another type of economic crime supports tax or regulatory objectives of the government. Thus, the government uses the threat of criminal punishment to reduce the gains from tax evasion, sale of illegal services or commodities, avoidance of restrictive licensing regimes, or entry into illegal business arrangements.

Economic crimes are often committed by individuals of high social and economic standing. This is the phenomenon of white-collar crime. At first blush, it may seem surprising because such individuals have advantageous alternative opportunities. Why do they engage in crime when they are already well paid and respected? The phenomenon is the result of several interacting factors.

First, individuals with a background in productive enterprise have a large comparative advantage in the commission of certain kinds of economic crime. In order to evade taxes, embezzle funds, or commit an antitrust violation, one must have the opportunity to pay taxes, handle funds, or make business decisions. Many kinds of theft are facilitated by detailed knowledge of business practices and procedures that can be learned only through advanced education and participation in business affairs.

Second, government regulatory or tax regimes often create conditions that make their violation extraordinarily profitable. If the tax rate is high or the government is attempting to suppress a commodity or service in strong demand, the economic gains from thwarting the law become very large. The magnitude of this temptation may overcome normal inhibitions.

Third, the criminal conduct may be difficult to distinguish morally from legal activity. The sale of a commodity that is illegal may seem to the criminal little different from the sale of a legal commodity. Tax evasion may seem little different from tax avoidance. Finally, the frequency of detection and punishment of some economic crimes is low.

Types of economic crime

There are three major types of economic crime: property crimes, regulatory crimes, and tax crimes, the most complex of which are regulatory crimes.

Property crimes. Property crimes are acts that threaten property held by private persons or by the state. Theft statutes, which make criminal the taking of property, are the paradigm. The modern integrated theft offense was formulated and recommended by the American Law Institute in Article 223 of the Model Penal Code. The law previously made distinctions between numerous theft offenses according to the manner in which the property was taken and the nature of the property taken.

The integrated theft article of the Model Penal Code is supplemented by Article 224 on forgery and fraudulent practices, the scope of which suggests the range of stratagems available to the modern economic criminal. It prohibits forgery; the fraudulent destruction, removal, or concealment of recordable instruments; tampering with records; the passing of bad checks; the use of stolen or canceled credit cards; deceptive business practices; commercial bribery; the rigging of contests; the defrauding of secured creditors; fraud in insolvency; the receiving of deposits in a failing financial institution; the misapplication of entrusted property; and securing the execution of documents by deception.

Regulatory crimes. Regulatory crimes are actions that violate government regulations. One type of regulation limits the sale of certain kinds of services or commodities. This can be further subdivided into prohibition of the activity altogether, as in the ban on the sale of prostitution services or marijuana, and sub-

jection of the activity to government licensing, as in the regulation of the sale of pharmaceutical drugs. Activities are chosen for licensing because they are thought to represent a special threat to the community at large if not properly conducted. By requiring licensing, the government, usually through an administrative agency, hopes to monitor and control the service or commodity being sold.

For example, the Securities Act of 1933, as amended, 15 U.S.C. §§ 77 a–77 aa (1976 & Supp. IV 1980) requires that public interstate securities issues be registered with the Securities and Exchange Commission (SEC) and that specified procedures be followed prior to their sale. The act reflects a congressional judgment that the issuance of securities is an activity particularly prone to large-scale fraud and that a system of licensing securities issues can reduce the incidence of fraud. Failure to comply with the statutory procedures is a crime. In the Securities Exchange Act of 1934, as amended, 15 U.S.C. §§ 77 b–e, j, k, m, o, s, and 78 a–kk (1976 & Supp. IV 1980), Congress extended this approach to the licensing of brokers and dealers in securities, and made engaging in these activities without SEC approval a crime. Congress hoped thereby to reduce the level of fraudulent activity by brokers and dealers in securities. However, although licensing statutes sometimes serve legitimate purposes, all too often they are passed and administered in order to protect the interests of those in a given business from the competition of newcomers.

Another type of regulatory crime is the violation of regulatory reporting statutes. In order to make regulation effective, the statutes require the regulated firms to provide extensive information to the regulatory officials. Failure to provide these reports, or the submission of false reports, is usually a crime.

Other regulatory statutes make criminal the operation of a commercial enterprise in a way that creates unreasonable risks to workers or consumers. The operation of an inherently unsafe workplace and the sale of adulterated foods are both made criminal in order to reduce the incidence of these harmful activities. In the United States, the prominent examples are the Federal Food, Drug and Cosmetic Act of 1938, as amended, 21 U.S.C. §§ 301–392 (1976 & Supp. IV 1980) and the Occupational Safety and Health Act of 1970, as amended (part), 29 U.S.C. §§ 651–678 (1976 & Supp. IV 1980).

Finally, regulatory crime may consist of the creation of private arrangements in violation of legal standards established by statute. Thus, the Sherman Antitrust Act of 1890, as amended, 15 U.S.C. §§ 1–7 (1976) makes the private organization of cartels a crime, and the National Labor Relations Act of 1935, as amended, 29 U.S.C. §§ 151–169 (1976 & Supp. IV 1980) makes certain behavior by union or management officials criminal. Statutes such as the Federal Election Campaign Act of 1971, as amended (part), 2 U.S.C. §§ 431–441, 451–456, 490 a, b, and c (1976 & Supp. IV 1980), which regulates political activity, make certain kinds of political activity or political contributions a crime. Article 240 of the Model Penal Code deals with the criminal offenses of bribery and corrupt influence.

Tax crimes. Tax crimes are violations of the liability or reporting requirements of the tax laws. These acts are made criminal in order to counteract the powerful incentives not to admit tax liabilities or pay taxes owed. They extend to all taxes, for instance, federal income tax, federal customs duties, state sales taxes, and local property taxes.

Alternatives to criminalization

The role of the criminal law in the area of economic crime cannot be properly assessed without consideration of the alternative enforcement strategies available. A theft of property is in the first instance a matter between two individuals. The law may impose civil liability on the wrongdoer but not make his conduct criminal. Most torts and breaches of contract are handled in this fashion. The individual who drives negligently or breaks a promise may have to pay large damages to those he injures, but he is not subject to criminal punishment.

Civil remedies have many advantages. They are activated by private individuals and do not require significant administrative and investigative resources. The state need only provide (1) a judicial system in which the person harmed can make and prove his claim, and (2) procedures for enforcing the decisions of the judges. Second, if the private parties involved do not feel that a remedy is required, they can decide not to seek it, reducing the possibility that the law will be put in the position of punishing conduct that is not harmful (Landes).

Civil remedies also have limitations. If the injured individual is unable to identify or locate the person who has harmed him, he will be unable to activate the remedial process. The potential gain to the injured individual is only the amount of his harm, which may not be sufficient incentive for him to bring a private action. A person who repeatedly harms others but is only occasionally sued and forced to pay damages will profit from the activity. In the case of large-scale, organized criminal activity, an occasional civil

judgment could easily be absorbed as a "cost of doing business."

There is an important intermediate area between the civil and criminal penalties. The incentives for the private civil plaintiff can be strengthened by providing for the recovery of attorney's fees or some amount larger than the damages the plaintiff has suffered. In American law the most prominent example of this enforcement strategy has been the provision in the antitrust laws for private recovery of treble damages. Congress extended this approach to other crimes in the Racketeer Influenced and Corrupt Organizations Act (RICO) of 1970, as amended, 18 U.S.C. §§ 1961–1968 (1976 & Supp. IV 1980) (Title IX of the Organized Crime Control Act of 1970).

Even where there is no private victim of the crime to pursue a civil remedy, statutes can provide for civil fines payable to the government. For example, the penal code of the Federal Republic of Germany makes provision for a class of "regulatory violations" that are enforced by administrative fine (Kadish, p. 448). Taxes can often be more easily collected by suit for the taxes due, fraud penalties, and government levy upon the taxpayer's assets than by invocation of criminal procedures. The SEC can sanction conduct of its regulatees by threatening to revoke or suspend their licenses. These administrative remedies may often be more effective and less difficult to pursue than the criminal alternative.

Problems of the criminal remedy

Complexities of proof. The criminal remedy for economic crime must be administered within the traditional procedural rules of the criminal law, including a high burden of proof. Economic-crime cases present special problems of proof because they often involve many transactions and involved dealings.

Consider the prosecution of an embezzler who with the aid of confederates has created dummy firms to bill his employer for nonexistent supplies, analyzed and rendered ineffective the employer's procedures for verifying the regularity of bills, collected the payments, and diverted them to himself and his confederates. By analyzing the extensive and apparently regular commercial documentation and comparing it to the actual deliveries made to the employer, it would be possible to demonstrate that payments were made for goods not delivered. That proof would suffice in a civil action by the firm for return of the erroneous payments.

To prove a criminal case, the prosecutor would have to show that the defendants were the ones who purposefully manipulated the employer's payment system and submitted the erroneous bills for their own gain. This might require tedious proof of extensive commercial dealing and require the jury to make inferences from unfamiliar material. The defendants could argue that they believed the bills were legitimate and that they were as dismayed as the employer to discover that a mistake had been made.

In an antitrust case, the government might argue that a series of trade meetings occurring over a period of years, when considered together with the pricing and production actions of the industry, show a criminal price-fixing conspiracy. The defendants might argue that the meetings were simply social events bringing together businessmen with similar interests and that the industry's pricing and production actions were dictated by economic forces, such as the price of raw materials and the preferences of customers.

The burden on the prosecutor. The prosecutor will face special problems in economic-crime cases, because he will have to prove complex allegations against a defendant who may be well financed and capable of hiring skilled counsel. Prosecutors' offices, with heavy work loads and limited budgets, may be unable to dedicate sufficient legal talent to a case to analyze and explain effectively to the trial court the significance of a mass of facts. These forces may cause a prosecutor eager for a good conviction record to choose not to pursue economic crime cases vigorously. If an economic-crime prosecution is pursued, the prosecutor has to give up the opportunity to obtain many more convictions in simpler cases. The prosecutor who nonetheless continues to pursue economic crime may find that his staff, after obtaining expertise in cases of this kind, will then depart for private employment, the demand for their talents having been generated by the prosecutor's own program of vigorous enforcement. In the 1970s in the United States, concern about these problems has led to special programs designed to enhance the ability of prosecutors and their staffs to deal with the prosecution of economic crimes (Miller).

The impact on procedural protections. The presence in the criminal justice system of a class of defendants with large resources creates pressures for the curtailment or abrogation of civil liberties. For example, it has been argued that federal judges should be authorized to deny bail for persons charged with large drug transactions, because these persons are so wealthy that they will not hesitate to forfeit any bail that is put up. Yet, a no-bail rule does violence to the principles that a defendant is presumed innocent until proved guilty and that personal freedom

should not be lost until after conviction. More generally, procedural protections that on the whole work well where defendants have state-provided counsel or limited private resources, may become insuperable barriers to the conviction of guilty defendants in the hands of defense counsel with unlimited resources. This in turn creates pressures to limit those procedural protections.

Pressures on the definition of criminal conduct. The fact that the criminal remedy is being used creates special but conflicting pressures on the definition of *criminal activity*. On the one hand, notions of criminality carry with them the idea that the activity prohibited must be intentionally wrongful to justify the use of such a severe sanction. Thus, a criminal penalty may import into a regulatory area standards of conscious wrongfulness that warp and disrupt the regulatory purpose. It has been argued, for example, that the prosecutorial focus of the SEC diverts the commission's attention from the need to provide a framework that will support efficient capital markets (Karmel). The fact that the Sherman Antitrust Act is a criminal statute has caused courts to emphasize issues of intent and purpose more than the economic effects of business relationships in construing the statute.

Conversely, the problems of proof in criminal actions create pressures to reduce the standards of liability in order to make the sanction effective, a pressure that has been particularly apparent in the emergence of modern doctrines of strict criminal liability and criminal liability for corporate or conspiratorial acts.

Strict liability. A rare and unusual form of criminal liability that appears most often in the area of economic regulatory crimes is the imposition of liability on individuals for unanticipated consequences of their acts. Criminal liability is generally imposed for conduct that was "intentional." However, some statutes are construed to impose liability—called "strict" or "absolute" liability—without regard for intent. This is justified on the ground that the imposition of such liability will cause individuals to try harder to avoid liability under the statute by anticipating the consequences of their actions.

The courts have looked askance at the creation of criminal offenses not requiring proof of intent, and have held that the omission of an express intent requirement from a criminal statute does not mean that the offense is a strict-liability one. In *Morissette v. United States*, 342 U.S. 246 (1952), the United States Supreme Court held that a statute making it a crime to steal government property required proof that the defendant intended the offense. Justice Robert Jackson observed: "The contention that an injury can amount to a crime only when inflicted by intention is no provincial or transient notion. It is as universal and persistent in mature systems of law as belief in freedom of the human will and a consequent ability and duty of the normal individual to choose between good and evil" (250). The Supreme Court followed *Morissette* in *United States v. United States Gypsum Co.,* 438 U.S. 422 (1978) when it held that proof of a criminal offense under the Sherman Antitrust Act required proof of an intent to cause the proscribed harm.

Justice Jackson went on in *Morissette* to note the rise of modern offenses

which disregard any ingredient of intent. The industrial revolution multiplied the number of workmen exposed to injury from increasingly powerful and complex mechanisms, driven by freshly discovered sources of energy, requiring higher precautions by employers. Traffic of velocities, volumes and varieties unheard of came to subject the wayfarer to intolerable casualty risks if owners and drivers were not to observe new cares and uniformities of conduct. Congestion of cities and crowding of quarters called for health and welfare regulations undreamed of in simpler times. Wide distribution of goods became an instrument of wide distribution of harm when those who dispersed food, drink, drugs and even securities, did not comply with reasonable standards of quality, integrity, disclosure and care. Such dangers have engendered increasingly numerous and detailed regulations which heighten the duties of those in control of particular industries, trades, properties or activities that affect public health, safety or welfare [253–254].

In the United States, strict criminal liability has been imposed under the Federal Food, Drug and Cosmetic Act, 21 U.S.C. § 333(a); *United States v. Dotterweich,* 320 U.S. 277 (1943); *United States v. Park,* 421 U.S. 658 (1975); the so-called Refuse Act of 1899, 33 U.S.C. § 411 (1976); and *United States v. United States Steel Corp.,* 328 F. Supp. 354 (N.D. Ind. 1970), *aff'd,* 482 F.2d 439 (7th Cir. 1973). Both the food and refuse statutes are designed to protect large populations from risks to their health and safety. The Supreme Court held, however, that the liability of a corporate officer under the Food, Drug and Cosmetic Act did not extend to actions that it would have been impossible for him to correct (*Park,* 673).

Corporate crime. Many economic crimes are necessarily committed by large and complex economic organizations. Within these organizations, it may be difficult to locate any single individual who is responsible for the combination of acts and omissions that constitute the crime. Yet, it will be clear that the crime has been committed. Strict liability is one response

to this problem. Another response has been to impose criminal liability not on an individual but upon the organization or corporation itself. Courts have regularly and with little difficulty accepted the argument that corporations are just as capable of committing crimes as people are.

Courts have commonly imposed criminal liability on corporations by analogy from the master-servant law that makes a corporation civilly liable for the acts of its employees. Under the majority American rule, a corporation is criminally liable for the criminal acts of an employee if the employee commits a crime within the scope of his employment and with the intent to benefit the corporation.

Section 2.07 of the Model Penal Code, which has been influential, provides three different ways in which a corporation may be criminally liable for the acts of its employees. The first applies to crimes of intent where no "legislative purpose to impose liability on corporations plainly appears." A corporation can be held liable for these crimes only if the offense was performed, authorized, or recklessly tolerated by the board of directors or a high corporate officer. The second applies to crimes where the legislature intended to impose corporate criminal liability. A corporation is liable for these crimes if the acts fall within the master-servant rules. The third applies to strict-liability crimes where the corporation is liable without regard to whether there was any intent to benefit the corporation (Developments in the Law, pp. 1246–1258).

The sentencing dilemma. The convicted economic criminal presents the court with a serious problem of sentencing policy. He may appear before the court as a man of culture and means who has threatened no one with physical harm. He will profess regret and offer to use his means and talent for the benefit of the community. On the other hand, the potential profits of his criminal activity may have been so high, and the difficulties of detection and successful prosecution so great, that no one would be deterred from pursuing similar opportunities in the future unless very large and severe punishments were imposed. Yet, it may be obvious to the sentencing judge that the man before him is, in a fundamental sense, far less evil than the killer whom the judge has just sent to prison.

In the academic literature, the debate over sentencing has focused on whether a fine or imprisonment offers the best approach to deterrence. It has been argued that because many economic criminals have property, their cases present a particularly propitious area for the imposing of a fine. Simply by making the fine large enough to offset the potential gains from the criminal activity, the crime can be deterred. A fine avoids all the deadweight loss of imprisonment: the direct costs of imprisonment itself and the loss of the defendant's own productive potential (Posner). On the other hand, it has been argued that only by imprisonment, an expression of society's strong disapproval of the defendant's conduct, can the full weight of the criminal law be brought to bear on that conduct (Coffee). To fine the economic criminal but to imprison the pathetic, violent misfit is to condone implicitly the activities of the economic criminal.

The problem of prison administration. The economic criminal who is imprisoned may present special problems for the prison administrator. Without a taste or talent for violence, he is unlikely to attempt escape. With abilities and possibly wealth, he has strong incentives to return to society. Because of the differences between the economic criminal and the rest of the prison population, incarceration may actually threaten his safety and health. These factors create pressures on prison administrators to provide alternative confinement facilities for their "model" prisoners both because such facilities can be provided more cheaply and because they avoid the problems involved in mixing the different populations. Such "country club" prisons are the common abode of convicted economic criminals; the most famous in the United States is the minimum-security prison located at Allentown, Pennsylvania.

The absence or complicity of the victim. In many economic crimes either there will be no identifiable victim or the victim will have actively cooperated in the crime. Laws that prohibit the provision of goods or services are violated with the cooperation of people who want to buy those goods and services, who usually know they are being provided illegally, and who often assist the violator in the perpetration of the crime. The only way that violators can be found and detected may be for investigative agencies to use undercover agents to offer suspects an opportunity to commit the crime. In many fraud cases, the victim is induced into the fraud by appeals to his greed. Only when the fraud turns out badly for him does he become unhappy. A modicum of care and attention would have prevented the crime. Why should a prosecutor use his limited resources to protect those so unwilling to protect themselves?

Even the corporation victimized by management fraud may fail to take essential precautions to prevent abuse of office (Elliott and Willingham). In the Foreign Corrupt Practices Act of 1977 (part), 15 U.S.C.

§ 78 m (Supp. IV 1980), Congress required publicly held American corporations to maintain a system of internal accounting controls sufficient to provide reasonable assurance that transactions are recorded so that all assets can be accounted for.

The political overtones. Many economic-crime prosecutions have political overtones. This is most dramatically evident in cases brought against incumbent public officials for bribery or abuse of office, but the overtones are heard in almost any substantial prosecution for economic crime. These overtones further complicate the task of prosecutor, trial court, and prison administrator in seeking to administer the law in a fair and evenhanded way.

Because the number of prosecutions for economic crimes is small in relation to the number of such crimes actually committed—or so it is believed—even if the defendant is indisputably guilty, the further question arises of why this defendant in particular was singled out for investigation and prosecution. Even if the criminal acts have been recorded on videotape, that does not answer the question of what process led the investigative agency to expend substantial resources to target the particular defendants. Was it an impartial process of following investigative leads, or was it a process shaped by other forces? Even if the investigative agency has proceeded impartially, who gave the agency the leads that initiated the inquiry? The agency, claiming the need to protect its investigative sources, is not likely to explain.

Even when the defendant in an economic-crime case is not a political figure, he may be viewed by many as representative of a class of persons. For some, the indicted corporate official may be a symbol of the failures of an entire class, while his fellows may be muttering to themselves, "There, but for the grace of God, go I." To the extent that the defendant in an economic-crime case is viewed as representative of a larger and politically powerful class, the case inevitably takes on political overtones. Public and corporate officials may outwardly decry corruption, but they may be able to muster little real enthusiasm and support for the prosecutor who has made the vigorous investigation and prosecution of economic crime his hallmark. Conversely, so many prosecutors have ridden into high political office on the publicity generated by sensational prosecutions of the rich or powerful that the defendants in such cases can persuasively argue that they have been chosen for persecution simply to advance the career of the prosecutor.

Whatever the facts of a particular case, their overtones make the fair and impartial administration of these criminal laws especially difficult. The prosecutor and judge cannot rely on unanimous social condemnation of the defendant. The social commitment to the criminal law being enforced may be ambivalent. The society that makes the sale and consumption of liquor or drugs a crime but simultaneously supports a large illegal industry cannot be expected to unite in support of vigorous criminal enforcement. The complexity and difficulty of prosecution justifies a large area of prosecutorial discretion. Yet, the existence of that discretion leaves open the suspicion that it is being used for inappropriate ends.

The variable-response enforcement strategy

A pervasive feature of economic crime is that prosecutors do not attempt to pursue a policy of seeking criminal convictions in all cases that come to their attention. Instead, they follow a highly selective enforcement policy in which the decision to prosecute is determined by a number of interacting variables. These include (1) whether or not the victim is complaining; (2) whether or not the victim has been made whole for any loss; (3) the availability and efficacy of civil remedies available to the victim; (4) the extent to which the prosecutor's resources are equal to the complexity of the prosecution and the likely resources of the defense; (5) the degree of social harm the prosecutor thinks is caused by the criminal conduct; and (6) the impact a criminal conviction may have on the efficacy of the government's overall enforcement strategy.

The resulting pattern of variable criminal enforcement is further complicated by the fact that whether or not a violation comes to a prosecutor's attention may be determined by others. In the case of a theft crime such as shoplifting, a prosecutor may learn of violations only if the store chooses to pursue a policy of criminal prosecution rather than one of civil reimbursement. Under statutes with independent administrative enforcement officials, such as the federal securities acts or health and safety inspection laws, the relevant administrative officials make an initial decision whether to pursue violations civilly or to report the conduct to a prosecutor.

The result of these variable enforcement strategies is that people displaying conduct identical under the statute will be differentially treated. Most tax evaders who are caught will reach a civil settlement with the government. A few will be chosen for criminal prosecution, perhaps because their prominence (or perhaps even their political views) makes them effective exam-

ples. Prostitution in one part of a town will be ignored, whereas in another it will be dealt with harshly.

Prosecutorial policies of this sort raise obvious problems of fairness for the criminal law, and may also distort the associated civil procedures. A defendant who enters into a civil consent decree to avoid the risks of criminal prosecution may surrender rights or concede administrative jurisdiction that is not supported by the law. A zealous and dedicated enforcement agency such as the SEC can use this process to broaden its statutory powers (Kripke).

These well-known problems associated with economic crimes have led to repeated calls in the literature for de-emphasis of the criminal penalty in economic regulation and for a general reduction in the reach and ambition of the criminal law (Morris and Hawkins; Kadish; Bator). These calls have fallen on deaf legislative ears, and the scope and reach of regulatory crimes have continued to expand.

The evolution of economic crime

The evolution of economic crime illustrates the quasi-private character of the crime. Criminal penalties for economic crimes seem to emerge only as social experience demonstrates the need for a criminal sanction to reinforce civil duties. Over time, the definition of *criminal theft* has been expanded to include new forms of economically valuable property as they emerge (Hall). Illustrations from the 1970s are the criminalization of trade-secret theft and increased use of the criminal penalties against copyright infringement. The first is a response to the increased value in modern society of technological information, and the second, a response to the ease with which copyrights can be infringed by using modern copying technologies. However, the ambivalence of the legislators in these marginal areas is illustrated by the fact that neither trademark nor patent infringement is criminal.

The elaborate regulatory crimes of the twentieth century are not simply a product of the increased complexity of the modern economy; they also reflect the sophistication and resources of the modern state. When the reach and effectiveness of the King's justice was uncertain at best, it seemed absurd to entrust the protection of private property to the King rather than to the care and attention of its owner. However, the development of modern bureaucratic organizations supported by effective tax systems has made it possible for the state to assume a more ambitious role—to undertake not only to protect private property but to define and defend many more subtle and complex economic expectancies such as safety, health, and freedom from fraud.

Economic crime in the socialist state

The discussion of economic crime here has been confined to the practice of such crime in the capitalist state. It should be noted, however, that the problems of economic crime are different in a state where the role of private property is limited. Where there is no private property, there are no private incentives to protect that property. Every offense that interferes with the production and distribution of economic goods is an offense only against the state. Thus, the state must rely exclusively upon its own administrative and criminal process to protect that property. Because state prosecution becomes the first and only line of defense, its vigorous and successful pursuit becomes a matter of far greater social importance. Consequently, in socialist states economic crimes are treated far more harshly than in capitalist states, sometimes even resulting in capital punishment.

Conclusion

There is a sharp contrast between the academic writing on economic crime, which tends to call for uniform enforcement of economic-crime statutes and reduction of the scope of criminal liability, and the practice of legislatures and prosecutors, who proscribe broadly and disregard frequently. The system in practice is untidy, but it permits the officials of the criminal justice system to respond in practical ways to the fact that the statutes often reach conduct that should not be criminal, and ensnare individuals who can reasonably be described as innocent. Unfortunately, the discretion thus conferred is also capable of great abuse with little remedy.

The scholars who have grappled with these problems have tried to treat economic crime as a unity. That is probably the ultimate artificiality, for economic crime is as diverse and varied as man's economic activities. Too much of the criminal scholarship in this area discusses the criminal aspect of the problem without attention to the underlying regulatory substance. On the other hand, the scholarship that addresses particular substantive areas, such as antitrust issues, securities regulation, and housing-code enforcement, has tended to ignore the criminal aspect of economic regulation.

EDMUND W. KITCH

See also CONSUMER FRAUD; CORPORATE CRIMINAL RESPONSIBILITY; CRIME CAUSATION: ECONOMIC THEORIES; CRIMINALIZATION AND DECRIMINALIZATION; *other articles under* ECONOMIC CRIME; MAIL: FEDERAL MAIL FRAUD ACT; ORGANIZED CRIME: OVERVIEW; *both articles under* STRICT LIABILITY; VICARIOUS LIABILITY; WHITE-COLLAR CRIME: HISTORY OF AN IDEA.

BIBLIOGRAPHY

AMERICAN LAW INSTITUTE. *Model Penal Code: Proposed Official Draft.* Philadelphia: ALI, 1962.

BATOR, PAUL M. "An Essay on the International Trade in Art." *Stanford Law Review* 34 (1982): 275–384.

COFFEE, JOHN C., JR. "Corporate Crime and Punishment: A Non-Chicago View of the Economics of Criminal Sanctions." *American Criminal Law Review* 17 (1980): 419–476.

DEVELOPMENTS IN THE LAW. "Corporate Crime: Regulating Corporate Behavior through Criminal Sanctions." *Harvard Law Review* 92 (1979): 1227–1375.

DUNN, DONALD H. *Ponzi!: The Boston Swindler.* New York: McGraw-Hill, 1975.

ELLIOTT, ROBERT K., and WILLINGHAM, JOHN J. *Management Fraud: Detection and Deterrence.* New York: Petrocelli, 1980.

HALL, JEROME. *Theft, Law, and Society.* 2d ed. Indianapolis: Bobbs-Merrill, 1952.

KADISH, SANFORD H. "Some Observations on the Use of Criminal Sanctions in Enforcing Economic Regulations." *University of Chicago Law Review* 30 (1963): 423–449.

KARMEL, ROBERTA S. *Regulation by Prosecution: The Securities and Exchange Commission vs. Corporate America.* New York: Simon & Schuster, 1982.

KRIPKE, HOMER. *The SEC and Corporate Disclosure: Regulation in Search of a Purpose.* New York: Law & Business, 1979.

LANDES, WILLIAM M., and POSNER, RICHARD A. "The Private Enforcement of Law." *Journal of Legal Studies* 4 (1975): 1–46.

MILLER, CHARLES A. *Economic Crime: A Prosecutor's Hornbook.* A special edition of the Economic Crime Project Center's monthly newsletter. Washington, D.C.: National District Attorneys Association Economic Crime Project Center, 1974.

MOFFITT, DONALD, ed. *Swindled!: Classic Business Frauds of the Seventies.* Princeton, N.J.: Dow Jones Books, 1976.

MORRIS, NORVAL, and HAWKINS, GORDON. *The Honest Politician's Guide to Crime Control.* University of Chicago Press, 1970.

NELLI, HUMBERT S. *The Business of Crime: Italians and Syndicate Crime in the United States.* New York: Oxford University Press, 1976.

NOTE. "Increasing Community Control over Corporate Crime: A Problem in the Law of Sanctions." *Yale Law Journal* 71 (1961): 280–306.

POSNER, RICHARD A. "Optimal Sentences for White-collar Criminals." *American Criminal Law Review* 17 (1980): 409–418.

STEARNS, LISA. "Economic Crime: A Bibliography." Mimeographed. Stockholm: Scandinavian Research Council for Criminology, 1976.

2.
ANTITRUST OFFENSES

Since 1890 the Sherman Act, 15 U.S.C. §§ 1–7 (1976) has been the main weapon in the arsenal of the Antitrust Division of the United States Department of Justice. Yet the first eighty years of criminal enforcement under the act resulted in the imprisonment of only twenty-six antitrust violators. Most of these violators served brief sentences. As a result, obviously criminal but highly profitable antitrust violations showed no signs of letting up. This article examines efforts by Congress and the Justice Department to increase the deterrence of antitrust violations by stiffening these traditionally lenient criminal sentences.

The Sherman Act

Section 1: the general proscription and judicial and administrative refinements. The quarter-century after the end of the Civil War was a period of unprecedented industrial expansion and concentration in the United States. Railroads crisscrossed the nation, small businesses evolved into mass-producing industries, and aggressive enterprises exploited plentiful natural resources. Yet the abundance of wealth that arose from this productive explosion settled inequitably upon the American working population: unfortunate businessmen and investors were sacrificed in the panics of 1873 and 1887; the businessmen who managed to survive were often forced to sell out to larger business combinations or face cutthroat competition; and farmers were strangled by strongly declining prices for their goods, by high and discriminatory rates charged by railroads and grain elevators, and by tight credit with high interest charges offered by eastern lending institutions. The problem, as explained by Senator John Sherman, was "the inequality of condition, of wealth, and opportunity that has grown within a single generation out of the concentration of capital into vast combinations to control production and trade and to break down competition" (U.S. Congress). The popular discontent and political opposition voiced by these victims of industrial concentration led to the passage of the Sherman Act.

In Section 1 of the act, Congress sought to curb anticompetitive practices and to exalt free market competition by proscribing "every contract, combination . . . or conspiracy, in restraint of trade." Of course, Section 1 could not be interpreted literally because every contract, however innocuous, restrains to some extent the future commercial behavior of every buyer and seller. Congress intended to proscribe the excesses—not the everyday workings—of the marketplace. The Supreme Court, which has called the Sherman Act a "charter of freedom" with "generality and adaptability comparable to that found to be desirable in constitutional provisions" (*Appalachian Coals, Inc. v. United States*, 288 U.S. 344, 359–360 (1933)), remedied this interpretative difficulty in *Standard Oil of New Jersey v. United States*, 221 U.S. 1, 59 (1911). In a classic opinion, Chief Justice Edward White construed Section 1 as an "all-embracing enumeration to make sure that no form of contract or combination" by which "undue" restraint was achieved "could escape condemnation." This so-called rule of reason permits courts to determine the legality of commercial behavior on the basis of whether it is significantly and unreasonably anticompetitive in character or effect.

The Supreme Court also recognized that some conduct is by nature significantly anticompetitive and totally devoid of redeeming virtue. It deemed such conduct "per se illegal," or violative of Section 1 without analysis of its reasonableness. Hard-core price-fixing, which may be described simply as a secret agreement among competitors to avoid competition by fixing one price for their common product, is the most common per se offense. Other per se offenses include bid-rigging, which consists of several competitors agreeing to bid much higher for a contract so that one of their number may win the bid at an artificially inflated price, and market allocation, which consists of several competitors agreeing not to compete for customers within each other's territory.

A second interpretative difficulty with Section 1 of the Sherman Act is that, although it is a criminal statute, it fails to identify with any degree of specificity what conduct it makes illegal. The due process clauses of the Fifth and Fourteenth Amendments require criminal statutes to provide specific notice of what conduct they make illegal. The judicial refinements to Section 1 reflected in the rule of reason and the per se doctrine arguably provide businessmen—that is, potential criminal defendants—with adequate notice of what conduct is illegal under the Sherman Act. In this view, criminal charges could be filed in all antitrust cases.

In eighty years of practice, however, the Antitrust

Division of the Justice Department filed criminal charges against few antitrust defendants. The Justice Department originally viewed the Sherman Act as primarily a civil statute. It filed criminal charges only in some labor cases in which violence was involved. From 1938 to 1943, however, Thurman Arnold led the Antitrust Division and stood this view of the act on its head: 220 of the 330 cases he brought under Section 1 included criminal charges. Arnold justified his view in utilitarian terms: "As a deterrent, criminal prosecution is the only effective instrument under existing statutes" (p. 16). His indiscriminate branding of businessmen as criminals would not, it is certain, meet modern standards of due process.

Today, to meet the constitutional requirement of notice while imaginatively applying the act's broad proscription, the Justice Department draws the criminal-civil boundary basically along the per se–rule of reason line. In other words, it treats Section 1 as two statutes. One is a criminal statute dealing with such conduct as hard-core price-fixing. The other is a civil statute of great flexibility and an invitation to the judiciary to develop remedies to meet ever-changing restraints of trade. The department limits the criminal Section 1 even further by refusing to file criminal charges even in hard-core cases if special facts indicate confusion of the law, novel issues of law or fact, confusion among the defendants caused by past prosecutorial actions or inactions, or lack of appreciation on the part of the defendants of the consequence of their actions.

Lenient sentencing under the Sherman Act. Even those few defendants who were convicted of criminal antitrust charges received lenient sentences. The first half-century of lenient criminal sentencing set a pattern that has been followed, despite the unrestrained criminal enforcement of the Arnold era and the more carefully considered prosecutions since 1940. From 1890 to 1940 only 24 of the 252 criminal prosecutions resulted in prison sentences. Most of these sentences were suspended. From 1940 to 1955, prison sentences were imposed in only 11 Sherman Act criminal cases; in almost all of those cases, the sentences were suspended.

A new era in antitrust sentencing was predicted during the period from 1960 to 1966 on the strength of the so-called Electrical Equipment cases, *United States v. Westinghouse Electric Corp.*, [1960] Trade Cas. (CCH) ¶ 69, 699 (E.D. Pa. May 13, 1960), in which forty-five individuals and twenty-nine corporations were indicted and for which seven officials actually served thirty-day sentences. Such reports of the de-

mise of lenient criminal antitrust sentencing were greatly exaggerated, for from 1966 to 1974 only eighteen cases resulted in prison sentences or probation; in only seven cases were prison sentences actually served (Elzinga and Breit, p. 31).

This failure to imprison antitrust violators is traditionally explained in several ways. Judges may be unwilling to imprison antitrust violators whom they believe to be "decision-implementers" rather than "decision-makers." A judge who is unable to pinpoint the source of an illegal act may be unwilling to sentence criminally the individual who is, in reality, carrying out the commands of another corporate official. More generally, though, antitrust violators may escape imprisonment because they are respectable executives with an established position in their community. As such, they do not need to be rehabilitated. Society does not fear them and, thus, does not demand their isolation. In fact, some feel that the stigma of indictment, with or without conviction, is real and perhaps even sufficient punishment for these criminals.

Significant, too, is the fact that the imprisonment of antitrust violators disrupts the management of their corporations. Under the Sherman Act, imprisonment is only an alternative to fines. According to prominent antitrust economists, a sentencing policy based on fines would be a greater deterrent to violations and a more efficient allocation of resources. Such concerns also may have contributed to the failure of judges to imprison antitrust violators.

Responses to lenient sentencing

The lenient sentencing of antitrust violators had a profound effect on the practices and views of American businessmen. They treated fines as "license fees"—that is, simply as one of the costs of doing business—and considered such per se antitrust violations as price-fixing to be "technical" violations that need not be taken seriously. In other words, they continued to fix prices.

Congress and the Department of Justice responded, respectively, to this state of affairs by enacting the Antitrust Procedures and Penalties Act of 1974, Pub. L. No. 93-528, 88 Stat. 1706 (codified in scattered sections of 15, 47, 49 U.S.C.) (APPA), and by promulgating the "Guidelines for Sentencing Recommendations in Felony Cases under the Sherman Act." Section 3 of the APPA substantially increased the maximum individual fine (from $5,000 to $100,000), the maximum corporate fine (from $50,000 to $1 million), and the maximum prison sentence (from one year to three years) for Sherman Act violations. The "Guidelines for Sentencing" recommended that violators be imprisoned for a base sentence of eighteen months (adjusted on the basis of aggravating or mitigating circumstances) rather than fined.

The Antitrust Procedures and Penalties Act. The twofold purpose of the increased maximum criminal sentence in the APPA was to provide a punishment commensurate with the severity of antitrust violations such as price-fixing and to deter such violations. The first purpose responded to the notion that price-fixing was a "technical" violation. Businessmen, as well as the public, undoubtedly had this notion not only because of the lenient sentences received by price-fixers but also because price-fixing's moral reprehensibility was not immediately apparent. After all, it was "not criminal under traditional categories of crime" and it closely resembled "acceptable aggressive business behavior" (Ball and Friedman, p. 210). By making possible a three-year prison term for price-fixers, Congress hoped to impress upon both businessmen and the public that price-fixing was a crime and that price-fixers were criminals.

Congress also increased the maximum criminal sentence to deter antitrust violations. Its reasoning undoubtedly was that, all other things being equal, just as the increase in the price of a product reduces the public demand for that product, so an increase in the punishment for a crime reduces the number of people who will commit that crime. The analogy seems apt. Price-fixing is neither happenstance nor a crime of passion. Rather, it is a rational decision to risk punishment in order to reap monopoly profits, which will redound to the individual violator's benefit in the form of a promotion, a raise, or a greater share of the profits. Such rational decisions are more easily deterred by "threats" of increased punishment.

Moreover, although threats of punishment are communicated imperfectly in the American criminal justice system, the communications of the APPA's increased maximum criminal sentence to potential price-fixers should be very complete and unusually effective. Businessmen read newspapers and have lawyers. "Personalized" threats delivered directly by lawyers usually prove to be effective deterrents. Besides, "increased penalties are probably more or less significant depending on the size of the penalty increase relative to the size of the base penalty" (Zimring and Hawkins, p. 202), and a 200 percent increase at this low range of punishment would probably be of great significance to businessmen.

The costs, and thus the deterrent effect, of a potential increased prison sentence are greater in this situation chiefly because of the success that potential price-fixers have attained. They have the means to satisfy most of their material desires. Their futures are bright. By increasing the maximum criminal sentence for price-fixing, Congress intensified the loss these individuals would suffer if convicted and sentenced to prison.

The APPA may lack credibility, however, because of the tradition that price-fixers are not imprisoned. Congress increased the maximum penalties, but it did not set a mandatory minimum sentence. Potential price-fixers could reasonably assume that the few price-fixers who would be imprisoned under the APPA would receive somewhat longer sentences but that the overwhelming majority of convicted price-fixers would continue to be fined rather than imprisoned.

In addition, even if the length of prison sentences were tripled, the "social stigmatization" suffered by the price-fixer would probably not be tripled. Social stigmatization, one of the most potent elements in the threat of punishment, is comprised of reduction in a criminal's status and exclusion from his peer group. Once again, potential price-fixers could reasonably assume that few price-fixers would be imprisoned and suffer the stigmatization felt by prisoners. These few price-fixers would more likely suffer a total destruction of reputation on the basis of the old sentences, however, so the increased deterrent effect of the APPA, in this important regard, would be minimal.

The "Guidelines for Sentencing Recommendations." Rule 32 of the Federal Rules of Criminal Procedure gives the government attorney his opportunity to "speak to the Court" on sentencing. In 1977 the Justice Department seized this opportunity to interpret the APPA for the courts by combining the congressional goal of deterrence with its goal of sentencing consistency in the "Guidelines for Sentencing Recommendations."

The introduction to the "Guidelines for Sentencing Recommendations" notes that by increasing the maximum criminal sentence, Congress indicated "a judgment that imprisonment should play an important role in punishing antitrust crime" and that prison sentences for antitrust violators are "uniquely effective" deterrents. From these premises the Justice Department reached the conclusion that all price-fixers ought to be imprisoned for a base period of eighteen months.

This base sentence was to be adjusted up or down "in accordance with the aggravating or mitigating factors present in a particular case." The Justice Department listed such aggravating factors as conspiracies that involved over $50 million in any one year, lasted for more than one year, or included predatory conduct. It also listed such mitigating factors as cooperation with the government and personal, family, or business hardship.

Criminal sentencing under the APPA

The criminal sentences served by antitrust violators under the APPA suggest that Congress and the Justice Department have had mixed success in realizing their common objective of increasing the deterrence of antitrust violations. A look at the absolute number of antitrust cases in which criminal charges were filed indicates that criminal prosecutions were actively sought in the early 1960s (the era of the Electrical Equipment cases), disfavored from 1965 to 1972, and then with the enactment of—and somewhat in anticipation of—the APPA, once again actively sought since about 1973. Since 1974, the percentage of antitrust cases including criminal charges has also been higher than during any other period except the Thurman Arnold era.

This resurgence in criminal prosecutions has, predictably, led to many more antitrust violators being convicted. Still, it was not until 1977 and the promulgation of the "Guidelines for Sentencing Recommendations" that a significant number of these individuals actually served prison sentences. Indeed, judges imprisoned no more than eight antitrust violators in a single year until they imprisoned twenty-six in 1977. Apparently some sentencing judges have accepted the Justice Department's interpretation of the APPA's increased maximum criminal sentence as "a judgment that imprisonment should play an important role in punishing antitrust claims."

Justice Department personnel reporting these developments have spoken optimistically of "brisk" sentencing and an "upward trend" that would presumably continue until price-fixing was adequately deterred. Such optimistic reports may be premature. After all, since 1974, fewer than two antitrust violators per month have actually been imprisoned. These violators have been required to serve, on the average, only two months of the nine-month sentences they have received. Judges, in sum, are suspending the great part of the infrequent criminal sentences they impose.

In addition, the sentences served by antitrust violators continue to lag far behind those served by other white-collar criminals. Although all white-collar criminals commit surreptitious breaches of trust for their own economic gain, in 1978 the felony sentences served by antitrust violators (average: 2.4 months) simply cannot be compared with those served by violators of the securities laws (average: 38.6 months) or the tax laws (average: 22.3 months).

Yet another cause for concern among those who seek to increase the deterrence of antitrust violators has been the increasing and highly inconsistent imposition of probation and "community service." The classic example of such sentencing is the "Paper Label Case," Case Nos. 2372–2374, 2388, U.S. Antitrust Case Summaries 1970–1979. There, Judge Charles Renfrew fined the antitrust conspirators, gave them suspended prison sentences, and put them on probation. During probation each conspirator was required to "make an oral presentation before twelve (12) business, civic or other groups about the circumstances of this case and his participation therein" and to "submit a written report to the Court given each such appearance, the composition of the group, the import of the presentation, and the response thereto" (*United States v. Blankenheim*, Judgment and Order of Probation and Fine, No. CR-74-182-CBR (N.D. Cal., filed Nov. 1, 1974)). It has been argued that such sentencing is insufficiently unpleasant and stigmatizing and may even reinforce the notion that antitrust violations are just technical violations.

The APPA and the "Guidelines for Sentencing Recommendations" are not the last words on the subject of the criminal enforcement of the antitrust laws. The Justice Department has noted that antitrust conspiracies frequently involve the use of the mails or the filing of false affidavits and that such activity may give rise to liability under mail fraud, false statements, and antiracketeering statutes. It has begun to prosecute these offenses in conjunction with antitrust violations in an effort to increase the criminal sentences imposed on and served by antitrust violators. Its effort has been successful: of the sixteen antitrust violators who served at least three months in prison between 1976 and 1979, six were concurrently convicted of mail fraud, and indictments of four others who pleaded nolo contendere (no contest) included allegations of mail fraud. This prosecutorial action indicates that the battle to enforce criminally the antitrust laws, which competing forces have waged since the late nineteenth century, will continue to be fought on new and imaginative fronts into the foreseeable future.

KEVIN A. RUSSELL

See also CORPORATE CRIMINAL RESPONSIBILITY; ECONOMIC CRIME: THEORY; FEDERAL CRIMINAL LAW ENFORCEMENT; WHITE-COLLAR CRIME: HISTORY OF AN IDEA.

BIBLIOGRAPHY

ANDENAES, JOHANNES. "Deterrence and Specific Offenses." *University of Chicago Law Review* 38 (1971): 537–553.

ARNOLD, THURMAN. "Antitrust Law Enforcement, Past and Future." *Law and Contemporary Problems* 7 (1940): 5–23.

BAKER, DONALD I.; REEVES, BARBARA A.; DERSHOWITZ, ALAN M.; LINMAN, ARTHUR L.; and WHEELER, STANTON. "The Paper Label Sentences: Critiques." *Yale Law Journal* 86 (1977): 619–644.

BALL, HARRY V., and FRIEDMAN, LAWRENCE M. "The Use of Criminal Sanctions in the Enforcement of Economic Legislation: A Sociological View." *Stanford Law Review* 17 (1965): 197–223.

BERGE, WENDELL. "Some Problems in the Enforcement of the Antitrust Laws." *Michigan Law Review* 38 (1940): 462–478.

CLABAULT, JAMES M., and BLOCK, MICHAEL K. *Sherman Act Indictments, 1955–1980.* New York: Federal Legal Publications, 1981.

COFFEE, JOHN C., JR. " 'No Soul to Damn: No Body to Kick': An Unscandalized Inquiry into the Problem of Corporate Punishment." *Michigan Law Review* 79 (1981): 386–459.

ELZINGA, KENNETH G., and BREIT, WILLIAM. *The Antitrust Penalties: A Study in Law and Economics.* New Haven: Yale University Press, 1976.

KADISH, SANFORD H. "Some Observations of the Use of Criminal Sanctions in Enforcing Economic Regulations." *University of Chicago Law Review* 30 (1963): 423–449.

PACKER, HERBERT L. *The Limits of the Criminal Sanction.* Stanford, Calif.: Stanford University Press, 1968.

POSNER, RICHARD A. "A Statistical Study of Antitrust Enforcement." *Journal of Law and Economics* 13 (1970): 365–419.

RENFREW, CHARLES B. "The Paper Label Sentences: An Evaluation." *Yale Law Journal* 86 (1977): 590–618.

SULLIVAN, LAWRENCE ANTHONY. *Handbook of the Law of Antitrust.* St. Paul: West, 1977.

U.S. Congress, Senate, *Congressional Record,* 51st Cong., 1st sess., 1890, 21, pt. 3: 2460.

U.S. Department of Justice, Antitrust Division. "Guidelines for Sentencing Recommendations in Felony Cases under the Sherman Act." Memo from Donald I. Baker, Assistant Attorney General, February 24, 1977.

ZIMRING, FRANKLIN E., and HAWKINS, GORDON J. *Deterrence: The Legal Threat in Crime Control.* Foreword by James Vorenberg. University of Chicago Press, 1973.

3.

TAX OFFENSES

Dimensions of the problem. The United States government collects approximately $500 billion annually in various taxes. More than half of this sum is received in the form of individual income taxes, another 15 percent in corporate income taxes, and about one-fourth in employment taxes. Although income and employment taxes are withheld on wages, the withheld amounts must be refunded if they exceed an individual's tax liability. Thus, in the main, the receipt of tax revenue by the government depends on the filing by taxpayers of tax returns that acknowledge the obligation. This is referred to as a "self-assessment" system, in contrast to systems that rely on gross income or gross receipts withheld or collected by government agents at the source.

The Internal Revenue Service, the branch of the Treasury Department in charge of tax administration, receives approximately 150 million tax returns annually. Apart from verification of mathematical computations, not more than 2 percent of the returns are actually "examined," that is, checked, at least to some degree, in order to verify the matters reported. Hence, tax evasion, especially income-tax evasion, is in many cases a very low-risk, high-profit economic crime.

The American system of "voluntary" self-assessment of taxes is widely regarded throughout the world as a marvel of compliance and efficiency. In many Latin American and some European countries, tax evasion is rampant; little effort is made at enforcement, and criminal punishment is rare. In the United States, on the other hand, the traditional official stance of the government has been that tax evasion is uncommon (Long, pp. 389, 397–398). In the late 1970s, the official line came under attack by the popular press, which asserted that compliance was rapidly deteriorating ("How Tax Cheaters Get Away with Billions," p. 102). Such claims persisted into the 1980s (Maital, p. 74).

A study of taxpayer compliance released in August 1979 was the IRS's first effort to measure unreported income. It tended to support press assertions about noncompliance. This study of 1976 returns estimated that from 6 percent to 8 percent of reportable individual income went unreported. In those categories where no tax was withheld, compliance was much lower: only 60 percent to 64 percent of self-employment income was reported, and only 50 percent to 65 percent of rents and royalties. Of income from illegal sources (principally drugs and gambling), the study estimated that only 10 percent to 15 percent was reported; the rest, $25 billion to $35 billion, went untaxed (U.S. Department of the Treasury, 1979, pp. 8, 17, 133). Based on that study and on follow-ups, the IRS in 1982 estimated that nearly $100 billion in taxes was not being paid. Thus, the government was collecting only about four dollars in five of tax revenues (Wiener, p. 43).

Role of criminal sanctions. The relative importance of criminal sanctions and levels of enforcement in promoting tax compliance in the American system is problematic. Virtually all agree, however, that *some* criminal sanctions and *some* enforcement are essential. The limited function of criminal penalties is demonstrated by the statistics: never, since the income tax was enacted in 1913, have as many as 2,500 taxpayers been charged with tax crimes in a single year. In 1979, the number was 1,820 (U.S. Department of the Treasury, 1980, p. 20). The average number over the previous thirty years was well under 1,000 per year (Duke, pp. 35–36, 70–71). Thus, only about 1 tax return in 75,000 ever becomes the subject of a criminal prosecution.

Criminal prosecutions perform a limited, if vital, role in tax enforcement, for myriad reasons. Many noncriminal monetary sanctions are available that can be assessed and collected administratively, with much less cost to the government, and can directly produce additional revenue. The most extreme civil sanction is applicable to persons required to collect and pay over taxes, for example, an employer required to withhold taxes from an employee's wages: the penalty for willful noncompliance is 100 percent of the tax (I.R.C. § 6672 (1982)). Anyone else whose underpayment in whole or *in part* is "due to fraud" may be compelled to pay a penalty of 50 percent of the underpayment (§ 6653(b)). One who fails to file a return without reasonable cause can be penalized up to 25 percent of the tax due (§ 6651(a)(1)). All these penalties are in addition to the tax and interest thereon.

The civil penalties are not in lieu of criminal penalties. Both can be imposed on the same taxpayer for the same conduct (*Helvering v. Mitchell*, 303 U.S. 391 (1938)). Indeed, if a taxpayer is successfully prosecuted for a tax offense, civil penalties are routinely imposed thereafter, and the taxpayer is estopped to contest any issue, such as fraud, found against him in the criminal prosecution (*Moore v. United States*, 360 F.2d 353 (4th Cir. 1965)). Civil penalties are assessed in thousands of cases every year, and over a billion dollars in penalties are collected (U.S. Department of the Treasury, 1980, p. 67). In addition to civil monetary penalties, the IRS has numerous devices to make noncompliance costly, including embarrassing, time-consuming audits, arbitrary assessments, and liens on bank accounts and other property.

The essential contributions of the criminal sanctions to tax compliance are probably as follows, in order of importance:

1. Like all other criminal sanctions, the criminal penalty ceremonializes and solidifies the community's sense of the immorality of proscribed conduct and affirms the morality of compliance.
2. The risk of a criminal sanction is a potent factor in the calculus of many prospective tax evaders, especially since they are often of relatively high status and have much to lose by the stigma of prosecution, conviction, and imprisonment.
3. The implicit threat of criminal sanctions provides powerful leverage to the government in its negotiations with taxpayers over claimed delinquencies; it facilitates investigations and contributes to compromise.

The criteria employed to select targets for criminal tax prosecution are—beyond vague generalities—protected by governmental secrecy. Moreover, no single agency of government makes the decisions or develops the criteria. Most recommendations for criminal tax prosecution originate in the IRS. But after passing through several filters in the IRS hierarchy, a recommendation for prosecution is turned over to the Justice Department for further scrutiny. A recommendation that survives the central review function in the Justice Department is then transmitted to the United States attorney in the appropriate federal district. There, it undergoes further review before being submitted to a grand jury (Duke, p. 57; Chommie, p. 107). In 1979, the Criminal Investigation Division of the IRS proposed more than 3,000 prosecutions. The Office of Chief Counsel of the IRS declined prosecution in 376 cases, the Justice Department declined in 424, and United States attorneys declined in another 425; only about 1,800 survived (U.S. Department of the Treasury, 1980, p. 35).

More significant than the criteria employed to screen cases for prosecution are those used to select returns for audit, since only if a return is among the 2 percent or fewer that are audited is there a serious possibility of prosecution. (It is, however, possible that a criminal investigation by another branch of the government will incidentally disclose tax evasion, in which event tax charges may be added to other charges.) The criteria for audit are also substantially secret. They are arrived at primarily, however, by an intensive audit of 50,000 scientifically and randomly selected individual tax returns every three years. Levels and trends in taxpayer compliance are then measured, and a computerized scoring formula is developed that is applied to every tax return ("Income Taxes," p. 46). Guidelines thus created—for example, relationships between reported income and business or charitable deductions—are employed to screen new returns for analysis and possible audit.

Criteria for selecting returns for audit, and for prosecution of apparent tax evaders, are difficult to formulate because of the immense complexity of the criminogenics of tax evasion and the uncertain role of criminal sanctions in influencing these causes. Among the more important correlates with tax compliance or evasion (in addition to the threat or deterrent effect of sanctions) are, probably, the following:

1. *Taxpayer attitudes toward the federal government.* Is it "wasting too much money"? Is it spending money on the wrong things? Is it becoming "too big"? Is it "strangling business" and "killing initiative"? Is it "taking away cherished freedoms"? The rhetoric of much political discourse on such themes does not promote a desire to pay taxes. Indeed, some of its most extreme forms assert that tax evasion is a patriotic duty.

2. *Taxpayer perceptions of the fairness of relative tax burdens.* Middle-income taxpayers are responsible for the bulk of income-tax revenues. Their sense of moral obligation will deteriorate if they perceive that others receive such tax advantages as "write-offs," "tax shelters," "loopholes," deductions, credits, and exemptions which are unfair; that the "rich" or "the corporations" or "the politicians" are taxed at rates that are too low; or that other taxpayers, by virtue of having clever accountants and lawyers or improper influence, are obtaining some other unfair advantage.

3. *Taxpayer attitudes about the IRS.* If taxpayers have acquired resentments toward the IRS, based either on personal experience or on what they have heard or read about "high-handed," "cutthroat," or "illegal" tactics, or even if they have sought IRS assistance and were rebuffed or disappointed, their resentment is likely to affect their sense of obligation to pay taxes.

4. *Taxpayer perceptions of the prevailing norms of compliance and evasion.* If a taxpayer believes that most others whose circumstances are similar to his are reporting and paying what they owe, he is more likely to do so, for two reasons: (1) he feels more morally obliged to do so (Fried); and (2) he feels that if he cheats he is more likely to be detected and punished because his behavior will be more aberrant.

5. *Burdens of compliance.* The more burdensome it is, financially, to surrender the taxes one owes, the greater the temptation to evade. Thus, tax evasion may be expected to increase with growth in overall tax burdens or with reductions in disposable income. When taxes are substantially withheld, as they are from wages, the financial burden is not felt as severely as when the taxpayer actually has a choice to make, and pays only such taxes as he feels obliged to pay— as on income from self-employment. Similarly, as tax law becomes more complicated (it is now virtually incomprehensible), the financial, intellectual, and psychic burdens of compliance may contribute to evasion.

6. *Fears by taxpayers that compliance will be prejudicial to other interests.* A taxpayer who earns his living unlawfully will be tempted to risk tax evasion rather than reporting the source of his illegal income and opening himself to other criminal punishment or loss of livelihood. A normally law-abiding taxpayer who has stolen or embezzled money will be deterred from reporting it. A taxpayer who anticipates a bitter divorce action may "hide" part of his income from his spouse by omitting it from his tax returns. A taxpayer whose income may be entirely lawful may omit information, or evade tax, because he fears that disclosure on his tax return may be embarrassing.

The effect that criminal prosecution can have on many of the aforementioned variables is minimal. Patterns of prosecution may also reduce one cause of tax evasion only to exacerbate another. For example, undue emphasis on the prosecution of drug dealers or gamblers may convey a message to ordinary taxpayers that *they* have nothing to fear as long as they stay away from drugs and racetracks. It may also suggest that tax evasion is more common or flagrant than it would otherwise appear to be (Schwartz and Orleans, pp. 274, 276). A stepped-up program of criminal prosecution of "ordinary" taxpayers may produce resentments against the IRS in the populace at large, adversely affecting not only tax compliance but also the willingness of juries to convict. If too great a proportion of politicians or public figures is included among the criminal targets, taxpayers may perceive that tax sanctions are being employed as political weapons. This may produce resentments, as well as perceptions that one can commit tax evasion with relative impunity, provided one maintains a low public profile. On the other hand, prosecution of prominent people— politicians, entertainers, and gangsters—can provide enormous free publicity for the enforcement program, conveying the message that tax evaders are vigorously prosecuted, no matter how powerful they may be or how high their social position. The publicity value of one such prosecution may be the equivalent of hundreds of prosecutions of rank-and-file taxpayers.

Further compounding the difficulties of decision-makers in selecting targets for prosecution is the fact that producing tax compliance is not—and never has been—the sole objective of criminal tax enforcement. Throughout most of the twentieth century, criminal tax enforcement has been employed not merely for raising revenue but, as one commissioner of internal revenue put it, for "rooting out of our society certain undesirables" (Duke, p. 74). Tax prosecutions were a potent weapon in the government's arsenal during Prohibition—the aim was not to collect revenue but to prevent the unlawful production and sale of liquor—and they continue to be a powerful tool in the war against organized crime and corrupt politicians (Long, pp. 406–410; Chommie, pp. 98–116; Irey; Surface, pp. 15, 120–137).

Sometimes tax sanctions have been employed merely to harass or embarrass persons who were viewed as a threat to the administration. President Richard Nixon, for example, had an "enemies list" of scholars, politicians, political organizations, and reporters whom he directed the IRS to investigate (Lukas, pp. 22–26; White, pp. 151–153).

When limited resources are employed for purposes other than maximizing revenue, tax compliance will suffer. But beyond that, interlarded with and compounding problems of assessing the pragmatic effects of enforcement decisions on tax compliance and non-tax behavior (such as illegal activities), are some moral and legal issues. It is at least a plausible philosophical position to assert that in selecting targets for audit or sanctions the use of any criteria other than those related to tax compliance is morally wrong. Some even assert that it is immoral to place emphasis on taxpayers who earn their incomes illegally (Freedman, pp. 1030, 1034). It is also arguable that, despite its potent publicity value, no weight should legitimately be given to the public prominence of a taxpayer, because to do so is to punish the taxpayer for the activities that produced the prominence. Often, those actions—political activities and the exercise of the rights of freedom of speech and of the press—are constitutionally protected, and to take them into account may chill or burden the constitutionally protected activity. Taxpayers who have been singled out for investigation or prosecution because of their profession (*United States v. Swanson*, 509 F.2d 1205, 1208 (8th Cir. 1975)), their public prominence (*United States v. Peskin*, 527 F.2d 71, 86 (7th Cir. 1975)), or their tax protests (*United States v. Scott*, 521 F.2d 1188, 1195 (9th Cir. 1975); *United States v. Ojala*, 544 F.2d 940, 943 (8th Cir. 1976)) have failed in their challenges to the prosecutions. This does not resolve the moral issues, however, nor finally close the door to similar legal challenges (cf. *Lenske v. United States*, 383 F.2d 20, 27 (9th Cir. 1967) and *United States v. Steele*, 461 F.2d 1148 (9th Cir. 1972)).

As with most other modes of human behavior, little is actually known, in a scientific sense, about the varia-

bles affecting tax compliance, or the role of criminal sanctions in shaping or controlling those variables. A number of experiments have been conducted that have produced suggestive hypotheses (Schwartz and Orleans; Maital). It is impossible, however, to draw any firm or refined conclusions from experimental studies that do not involve actual taxpayers, actual tax returns, and sophisticated controls. Only the IRS is in a position to engage in meaningful manipulation and measurement of variables, and the task, even for that agency, is monumental.

Major tax offenses. The most serious offender against federal revenues is one who "willfully attempts in any manner to evade or defeat any tax . . . or the payment thereof" (I.R.C. § 7201 (1982)). This crime carries a maximum penalty of five years in prison and a $10,000 fine. To commit the offense, one must engage in an act constituting an "attempt," must do so "willfully" (that is, intending thereby to "evade or defeat" assessment or payment of a federal tax), and must actually have an unsatisfied tax obligation (*Sansone v. United States*, 380 U.S. 343 (1965)). Unlike most other criminal offenses, attempted tax evasion requires knowledge of the law. One cannot commit the offense unless he believes that he is legally obliged to pay a tax and that his "attempt" will evade or defeat that tax. Thus, it is not attempted tax evasion to omit taxable income from a return or to take an unlawful deduction if the taxpayer was unaware that his act was contrary to the tax law (Duke, pp. 4–5; *United States v. Garber*, 607 F.2d 92 (5th Cir. 1979)).

One "evades or defeats" a "tax or payment thereof" if he merely delays beyond the due date the assessment or payment of the tax. Hence, it is no defense that the taxpayer who willfully filed a false income-tax return intended thereby merely to delay payment and, when his finances improved, to file a correct return and pay the tax. The offense is complete when the false return is filed (*Sansone*).

Another novel feature of the tax crime is that it preserves to some extent the now largely discarded defense of factual impossibility. Since an actual tax deficiency is an element of the crime, it is a defense that the accused, although he believed he was evading his taxes, was mistaken. If a taxpayer omits income from his return and, years later, even after he is indicted, discovers an offsetting deduction, he is not guilty of the offense (cf. *Willingham v. United States*, 289 F.2d 283 (5th Cir. 1961)).

The typical method of "attempting" tax evasion is the filing of a false tax return. However, one who files a correct return but fails to pay all the tax due thereon, or who fails to file a required return, may commit the offense if he has engaged in any affirmative act "the likely effect of which would be to mislead or conceal" his income or assets, and if "tax evasion plays any part in such conduct" (*Spies v. United States*, 317 U.S. 492 (1943)). Thus, if a taxpayer, aware of an outstanding tax obligation and desiring thereby to "evade or defeat" it, lies to the IRS about his income or assets, he commits the offense (*United States v. Beacon Brass Co.*, 344 U.S. 43 (1952)). The crime may also be committed by "keeping a double set of books, making false entries or alterations or false invoices or documents, destruction of books or records, concealment of assets," or any other deceptive conduct (*Spies*, 499).

Ordinarily, a taxpayer who engages in a series of fraudulent acts, such as filing a false return, submitting false records to the IRS when audited, and lying repeatedly about income, assets, or both, will be charged with only one offense of attempt for each year's tax obligation that he has tried to evade. All of the affirmative acts will be regarded as integrated steps in a single attempt. In one case, however, a taxpayer was held to have committed two separate attempts to evade the same year's tax. He first filed a false return, for which he was convicted and sent to prison. After his release, he attempted to evade payment of the still-outstanding tax obligation by concealing assets. He was again convicted and was returned to prison, the court concluding that he had first, by the false return, attempted to evade the tax, and later, having failed at that, attempted to evade payment of the tax (*Cohen v. United States*, 297 F.2d 760 (9th Cir. 1962)). The implications of this decision for more common patterns of tax evasion are unclear, and the rationale is rarely advanced.

A number of lesser felonies can be committed by one whose conduct lacks all the elements of attempted tax evasion. Sections 7206 and 7207 of the Internal Revenue Code punish as felonies the presentation to the IRS of materially false returns or other documents. A general section of the federal criminal code (18 U.S.C. § 1001 (1976)) also reaches such documents, as well as false oral statements (*United States v. McCue*, 301 F.2d 452 (2d Cir. 1962)). It is unnecessary under any of these provisions that the offender actually have a tax deficiency. Nor must the false statement be made with intent to "evade or defeat" a tax or payment thereof (Balter, §§ 11.03, 11.04).

Willful failure to file a required tax return or willful failure to pay a tax, in the absence of deceptive conduct, is a misdemeanor only, punishable by imprisonment up to one year and a fine of $10,000 (I.R.C. § 7203 (1982); *Alessi v. United States*, 628 F.2d 1133

(2d Cir. 1980)). It is often argued that willful failure to file a return, that is, failure to file with knowledge of the obligation to do so, is as serious and flagrant an offense as attempts to evade, and ought to be elevated to felony status. However, many nonfilers cannot easily be equated with tax evaders. Their mental states often include elements of ignorance, pathological passivity, and even serious mental illness. To treat their intentional omissions as the equivalent, in all cases, of a calculated act designed to deceive and to evade assessment of one's tax obligations would conflict with fundamental distinctions in the criminal law between commissions and omissions (*Spies*).

Sentencing. The sentencing of persons convicted of federal tax offenses is a matter of perpetual controversy and disquieting disparity (Long, pp. 401–406). The IRS and the Department of Justice traditionally take the position that all persons convicted of such offenses should receive at least a substantial jail or prison sentence in order to deter tax evasion and to signify the seriousness of the dereliction (*Heidrich v. United States*, 373 F.2d 540 (5th Cir. 1967)). Many tax evaders, however, are otherwise law-abiding and pose no threat of recidivism. The prosecution and conviction themselves are degrading and traumatic. Accordingly, judges who are not comfortable with a general-deterrent justification for sentencing often impose probationary sentences (Andenaes, pp. 129–148).

STEVEN DUKE

See also FEDERAL CRIMINAL JURISDICTION; FEDERAL CRIMINAL LAW ENFORCEMENT; *both articles under* ORGANIZED CRIME; WHITE-COLLAR CRIME: HISTORY OF AN IDEA.

BIBLIOGRAPHY

ANDENAES, JOHANNES. *Punishment and Deterrence*. Foreword by Norval Morris. Ann Arbor: University of Michigan Press, 1974.

BALTER, HARRY G. *Tax Fraud and Evasion: A Guide to Civil and Criminal Practice under Federal Law*. 4th ed. Boston: Warren, Gorham, and Lamont, 1976.

CHOMMIE, JOHN C. *The Internal Revenue Service*. New York: Praeger, 1970.

DUKE, STEVEN. "Prosecutions for Attempts to Evade Income Tax: A Discordant View of a Procedural Hybrid." *Yale Law Journal* 76 (1966): 1–76.

FREEDMAN, MONROE H. "The Professional Responsibility of the Prosecuting Attorney." *Georgetown Law Journal* 55 (1967): 1030–1047.

FRIED, CHARLES. "Moral Causation." *Harvard Law Review* 77 (1964): 1258–1270.

"How Tax Cheaters Get Away with Billions." *U.S. News and World Report*, 27 March 1978, pp. 102–105.

"Income Taxes: Interview with Roscoe L. Egger, Jr., Com-

missioner of Internal Revenue." *U.S. News and World Report,* 19 April 1982, pp. 46–47.
IREY, ELMER L. *The Tax Dodgers: The Inside Story of the T-Men's War with America's Political and Underworld Hoodlums, as Told to William J. Slocum.* New York: Greenberg, 1948.
LONG, H. ALAN. *The Use of Criminal Sanctions for Tax Violations.* 12th Annual Tax Institute. New Orleans: Hauser, 1963.
LUKAS, J. ANTHONY. *Nightmare: The Underside of the Nixon Years.* New York: Viking Press, 1976.
MAITAL, SHLOMO. "The Tax-evasion Virus." *Psychology Today,* March 1982, pp. 74–78.
SCHWARTZ, RICHARD D., and ORLEANS, SONYA. "On Legal Sanctions." *University of Chicago Law Review* 34 (1967): 274–300.
SURFACE, WILLIAM. *Inside Internal Revenue.* New York: Coward-McCann, 1967.
U.S. Department of the Treasury, Commissioner of Internal Revenue. *Annual Report, 1979.* Washington, D.C.: Bureau of Internal Revenue, 1980.
U.S. Department of the Treasury, Internal Revenue Service. *Estimates of Income Unreported on Individual Income Tax Returns.* Washington, D.C.: IRS, 1979.
WHITE, THEODORE. *Breach of Faith: The Fall of Richard Nixon.* New York: Atheneum, 1975.
WIENER, LEONARD. "Income Taxes—New Crackdown by IRS?" *U.S. News and World Report,* 19 April 1982, pp. 43–45.

ECONOMICS AND CRIME

See CRIME CAUSATION: ECONOMIC THEORIES; CRIME STATISTICS: COSTS OF CRIME.

ECONOMIC STATUS AND CRIME

See CLASS AND CRIME; CRIME CAUSATION: ECONOMIC THEORIES; UNEMPLOYMENT AND CRIME; WHITE-COLLAR CRIME: HISTORY OF AN IDEA.

EDUCATIONAL PROGRAMS IN CRIMINAL JUSTICE

Education in criminal justice is a highly complex subject. Although some predominant patterns have crystallized, there is no general consensus regarding even the most basic issues. Diverse historical developments continue to exert a powerful impact on modern educational policies. Vested academic interests further complicate a situation in which there are genuine differences of opinion about the essence of the crime problem, varying interpretations of the etiology of criminal and delinquent behavior, and divergent views as to what crime-control policies should be. These viewpoints are often anchored in different political, social, and economic ideologies, and they affect educational policies with regard to subject matter; types, levels, and goals of educational programs; and research objectives.

Historical background

The status of criminal justice education in the United States cannot be properly understood without an awareness of its historical background. Crime has been studied as a social phenomenon only since the mid-nineteenth century. Prior to that time, crime was almost invariably approached in terms of the free-will world view, which maintained that punishment was the proper means for achieving justice and for effectively controlling and preventing crime.

The beginnings of criminology. Around the mid-nineteenth century, the budding empirical social and behavioral sciences advanced the proposition that criminal behavior, like all human behavior, was not so much a matter of free will as a phenomenon that had reasons or causes, and that the rational way of dealing with the crime problem was to eliminate its causes. Such reasoning obviously led to the need to understand these causes and to develop means of eliminating them. The scientific discipline proposed for this task was termed *criminology* by Cesare Lombroso in the early 1870s. From that time onward, universities began to introduce the teaching of criminology, and soon there was a student body that had chosen criminology either as their academic specialization or as one of their subjects of study.

Criminology in Europe. The development of the empirical social science of criminal behavior followed different paths in different countries and academic settings. On the Continent it was generally the faculty of law that offered a home for the emerging discipline, usually through the establishment of a chair of criminal law. The professor of criminal law often created an institute of criminology, whose staff included psychologists, psychiatrists and other members of the faculty of medicine, anthropologists, economists, and statisticians. Many of these scholars worked in the institute of criminology on a part-time basis, retaining their primary affiliation to their home discipline. Others gradually shifted their academic affiliation entirely to the institutes of criminology, and in some cases became leaders in the field through their research, writing, and teaching. Usually, however, these scholars—originally psychologists, physicians, or psychiatrists—adopted the legal perspectives and interests of criminal law and criminal procedure.

Some of the best-known institutes of criminology were located in the faculties of medicine, particularly in Italy. Most of the institutes of criminology in France, Germany, and the Netherlands, however, were affiliated with the faculties of law, and the criminology student in Europe has typically been a law student. To a large extent this pattern prevails in Latin America, the Arab world, and in other areas where the impact of continental European culture is strong. It has also had some influence in the United States.

Criminology in the United States. The development of American criminology followed an entirely different path. Criminology was introduced in the United States at about the same time as sociology, that is, around the turn of the twentieth century. American sociology rapidly demonstrated a remarkable viability and developed much more extensively than its European counterpart, so that almost every American university of any standing soon had a sociology department. Originally oriented toward practical social problems, sociology departments provided an academic niche for criminology; from about 1900 to 1960 criminology in the United States had an almost exclusively sociological focus and was studied by sociology students. To be sure, American psychologists, psychiatrists, psychoanalysts, anthropologists, and economists made important contributions to the study of criminal justice and delinquent behavior, but they did so more as the result of individual interests than of any organizational plan. Perhaps the most striking characteristic of American sociological criminology during that period was its separation from the law schools and the study of criminal law. This long remained the chief difference between European and American criminology.

The role of the social and behavioral sciences. A serious deficiency in criminological studies was the tendency of the social- and behavioral-science disciplines to colonize the study of crime primarily in their own interests. Having developed earlier than criminology (perhaps because the phenomenon of crime was formerly within the domain of criminal law, with its normative approach, and was not considered a proper subject of empirical studies), the disciplines of psychology, sociology, psychiatry, and economics readily turned to the popular and important area of crime, which attracted many students and guaranteed financial support. In their "empire building" endeavors, scholars in these fields opposed the development of an independent discipline of criminology.

The social- and behavioral-science disciplines undoubtedly contributed greatly in the United States to the growing body of scientific knowledge about crime. Of course, they did not deal with crime in its totality, but only from the perspective of a specific discipline and by means of research methodology germane to it. It became apparent that the body of knowledge and theory which was to serve as the foundation for a full understanding of criminal and delinquent behavior, and for the means of effectively dealing with it, could not depend upon a single traditional social-science discipline. This gradual realization was one reason for the efforts made in the 1970s to unify crime and delinquency studies under the rubric of criminal justice studies.

Career paths. Prior to the development of educational programs for an integrated field of criminal justice, there were three major and several lesser educational avenues leading to a professional career in criminology. The three major avenues were the law schools, the departments of sociology, and the schools of social work, each of which offered narrowly specialized and nonintegrated preparation.

The American law school provides, among other things, education in substantive criminal law and criminal procedure. Although such training is of crucial importance for lawyers, it does not ensure the acquisition of formalized knowledge of a social- or behavioral-science nature about the criminal, his motivation, or methods for preventing his criminal deeds. Thus, lawyers occupying positions in criminal justice agencies often face problems which (except for the purely legal aspects) they have not been trained to deal with.

Students of criminology in sociology departments study intensively the etiology of criminal and delinquent behavior, typologies of criminal offenders, careers in crime, and corrections, or methods of "making noncriminals out of criminals"—that is, removing the causes and motivations of criminal behavior. The graduates of sociology departments were as a rule far removed from criminal reality during their studies, and no formal channels led to employment in the criminal justice field. Thus, individuals with the maximum available theoretical knowledge about criminality had no opportunities to use their knowledge in dealing with the crime problem, and, moreover, were frequently termed "ivory-tower criminologists."

Schools of social work generally do not provide courses dealing specifically with crime and criminals. Rather, they believe in studying the problems of people in need of help in general, and the ways in which such help should be offered. Yet despite this approach, schools of social work maintain channels through which their graduates can enter the probation and parole service or can become prison counselors.

Thus, prior to the 1970s, an unusual educational setting served as the underpinning for theory and action directed toward the crime problem. The teaching of law, sociological criminology, and social work was not integrated, nor was it linked with the operational agencies. Law schools did not study criminal reality and the criminal offender, but only the legal aspects of crime. Nevertheless, the lawyers had the most direct access to legislation, policymaking, and the highest level of criminal justice administration, although they had to rely mainly on common sense and practical experience rather than on formal education. Sociological criminologists, on the other hand, learned much about crime and the criminal as social and behavioral phenomena, but they lacked access to the practical areas of prevention and control. Federal, state, and local governments employed few, if any, sociologists in crime-related positions. The schools of social work seldom taught criminology or criminal justice, but they did place their graduates in specific criminal justice occupations.

Criminal justice education

The term *criminal justice* in its broad sense emerged in the United States at the end of the 1960s. It refers to any legal matter, governmental activity, educational program, or research that deals with or is related to crime and juvenile delinquency, as well as their control and prevention. This use of the term is indicative of a far-reaching reorientation of crime-related policies, which had a crucial impact on educational policies in the field as well. Such an all-encompassing term was adopted to reflect an outlook, as it crystallized in the late 1960s, that emphasized viewing the nation's crime control agencies as a system, thus encouraging them to integrate their pursuit of common goals and objectives with thorough awareness of one another's activities. An understanding of the reasons for criminal and delinquent behavior is firmly anchored in the social and behavioral sciences, which, accordingly, in their study of the etiology of criminal behavior, clearly constitute part of the total crime control and prevention program. At the same time, the so-called labeling theories of criminal behavior, which assert that the actions of the law enforcement agencies themselves can be a criminogenic factor, gave further impetus to eliminating the earlier separation between criminological interests and those of the law enforcement agencies. Thus the integration of heretofore distinct inquiries into seemingly unrelated aspects of the crime problem became a reality.

College- and university-level educational policies and programs in criminal justice are the result of developments that began in the late 1960s. They were a response to an unprecedented national concern about the crime problem, mounting evidence of a steady and rapid increase in the amount and seriousness of adult criminality and juvenile delinquency, and resulting federal action. The government became involved in funding and policy development not only for operational activities in the field of criminal justice in general, but also specifically for education and research.

The impact of the Law Enforcement Assistance Administration. An important step in the government's involvement with the crime problem was Congress's establishment of the Law Enforcement Assistance Administration (LEAA) within the United States Department of Justice. Authorized in June 1968, this agency remained in existence until April 1982. At the peak of its activities it had an annual budget of close to $900 million, and overall, the support provided by LEAA to the criminal justice field is usually estimated at about $10 billion. The impact of this massive and manifold federal program was uneven, but in many respects it was singularly important. Perhaps the impact was felt most strongly in the area of criminal justice education. In this connection, LEAA very early adopted a certain set of conceptualizations regarding criminal justice. Moreover, it made funding conditional on acceptance of these policies by recipients, who were required to plan their activities in accordance with them. Receipt of block grants by states for improving their criminal justice agencies and facilities had to be justified by budgets developed in terms of a total system of criminal justice, so that all subsystems would receive proper financial support. This total system included the states' educational needs in the area of criminal justice.

A major part of LEAA's activities, the Law Enforcement Education Program (LEEP), provided tuition for students in criminal justice, in some years amounting to more than $40 million a year for as many as one hundred thousand students. To qualify for LEEP support, criminal justice programs in colleges were expected to provide instruction in all the major elements of the field, rather than concentrating on only one subsystem or one social-science discipline.

The extent of this "education explosion" in the area of criminal justice may best be judged from the following figures. In 1965 there were 95 academic programs in criminal justice in the United States: 65 at the associate's-degree level, 21 at the bachelor's level, and 9 at graduate levels. In 1975 there were

1,348 programs: 740 at the associate's level, 423 at the bachelor's level, and 185 at graduate levels. That same year an additional 408 programs were in the final planning stages: 200 at the associate's level, 150 at the bachelor's level, and 58 at graduate levels (Lejins; Kobetz). Thus, over a period of ten years the total number of programs in operation increased by a factor of fourteen, and if one adds programs in final stages of planning, of eighteen; for bachelor's-level programs, the corresponding figures increased by a factor of twenty and of twenty-seven, respectively. It should be noted, however, that not all criminology and criminal justice programs applied for LEEP support, and thus are not included in these statistics.

The status of criminal justice education in the United States. As a result of the above developments, education in schools, institutes, and departments of criminal justice in the United States is readily available and grants degrees on four academic levels: associate of arts, bachelor's, master's, and doctoral. The educational programs are free of rigid uniformity, and prescriptive curricula, although occasionally proposed, are generally not used. Indeed, it is feared that such strictures would place undesirable limitations on this still-developing and experimental field. Attempts at standard-setting and accreditation had not achieved success by the early 1980s. By and large, however, the programs have shown a substantial overall similarity, although emphases and specializations have differed. There is an obvious effort on all levels to treat criminal justice as a unified field and a valid academic discipline. Basic introductory courses covering all major segments of the field and encompassing the contributions of all appropriate disciplines are usually offered, and often required, on all academic levels, as are more sophisticated and specialized courses.

By now there are a number of academic programs that deal with the integrated field of criminal justice and offer bachelor's, master's, and doctoral degrees. Notable among these are the School of Criminal Justice at the State University of New York at Albany, the School of Criminal Justice at Rutgers University, the Institute of Criminal Justice and Criminology at the University of Maryland, the Criminal Justice Center at Sam Houston State University in Texas, and the School of Criminology at Florida State University. In some of these programs the faculties have more than twenty members of professorial rank, and all have strong research components. These schools epitomize the effort to achieve educational integration of the field and the establishment of a professional discipline in its own right. Their impact is increasingly felt not only in the area of education and in the crimi-

nal justice operational agencies, but also in the development of a specialized social-science discipline that deals with the phenomenon of crime in all its ramifications.

There are two principal academic organizations in the area of criminal justice. The Academy of Criminal Justice Sciences is the academic and professional organization uniting individuals teaching, studying, conducting research, and employed in the field. The American Association of Doctoral Programs in Criminal Justice and Criminology numbered ten universities in its membership as of 1982.

In spite of the emergence and rapid growth of an educational system designed specifically for the field of criminal justice, this system does not have the unanimous endorsement of all those involved in the study of crime. Social scientists in academic departments that were heavily committed to teaching and research in criminology have tended to support their own programs as they were developed prior to the 1970s. These scholars have opposed fusion with programs dealing with operational aspects of crime control such as the police, prosecution, the courts and corrections. The former police science and law enforcement programs have displayed greater willingness to accept the new concept of an integrated criminal justice field, even though some of their representatives are reluctant to allot appropriate recognition to courses on the etiology of criminal and delinquent behavior. Thus, it remains possible in the United States to study crime without enrolling in a criminal justice program, as this term was understood in the 1970s.

During that decade, many academic departments and other academic units in the social and behavioral sciences transferred their courses and staff members focusing on criminal justice and criminology to the new academic units created specifically for the unified field of criminal justice. Nevertheless, other departments of sociology, psychology, economics, political science, and public administration, as well as departments of psychiatry and psychoanalysis in schools of medicine, continue to teach and to sponsor research on aspects of criminology and criminal justice. Study in such departments represents another type of criminal justice education available in the United States, in addition to the specialized criminal justice programs.

PETER P. LEJINS

See also articles under CAREERS IN CRIMINAL JUSTICE; CRIMINOLOGY: RESEARCH METHODS; PUBLICATIONS IN CRIMINAL LAW; PUBLICATIONS IN CRIMINOLOGY; RESEARCH IN CRIMINAL JUSTICE.

BIBLIOGRAPHY

International Conference on Doctoral-level Education in Criminal Justice and Criminology, July 7–10, 1976: Proceedings. College Park: University of Maryland, Institute of Criminal Justice and Criminology, 1976.

KOBETZ, RICHARD W. *Law Enforcement and Criminal Justice Education Directory, 1975–76.* Gaithersburg, Md.: International Association of Chiefs of Police, 1975.

LEJINS, PETER P. *Criminal Justice in the United States, 1970–1975: An Overview of Developments in Criminal Justice.* Prepared for the Fifth United Nations Congress on the Prevention of Crime and Treatment of Offenders, Geneva, Switzerland, September 1975. College Park, Md.: American Correctional Association, 1976.

PIVEN, HERMAN, and ALCABES, ABRAHAM. *Education, Training, and Manpower in Corrections and Law Enforcement—A Digest of Data: Source Book.* Washington, D.C.: U.S. Department of Health, Education, and Welfare, Welfare Administration, Office of Juvenile Delinquency and Youth Development, 1966.

SHERMAN, LAWRENCE W. *The Quality of Police Education.* Prepared with the National Advisory Commission on Higher Education for Police Officers. San Francisco: Jossey-Bass, 1978.

U.S. Department of Justice, Law Enforcement Assistance Administration, National Institute of Law Enforcement and Criminal Justice. *Criminal Justice Education and Training.* The National Manpower Survey of the Criminal Justice System, vol. 5. Washington, D.C.: The Institute, 1978.

EDUCATION AND CRIME

Introduction

Few of the findings that have emerged in the study of crime and delinquency can rival in consistency and importance the relationship between schooling and law violation. Over many decades there has been persistent evidence that the school is a major factor in explaining offense behavior. Whether analysis focuses on children and adolescents or on persons observed at a much later point in the life cycle, such as prison inmates or adult parole violators, schooling looms large in both the prediction and the explanation of deviant careers. So uniform has this finding been that most analysis long ago shifted from investigating whether schooling is related to offense behavior and toward asking how and why schooling plays such a significant role. However, since school is central in the daily life of young persons, most studies on education and crime are concerned more with the school's contribution to the development of juvenile delinquency than with its relationship to adult criminal careers.

The individual level of analysis

One research tradition has concentrated on what can be termed the individual level of analysis. Here there is an attempt to explain the importance of schooling in terms of psychological or biological traits that account for an individual's behavior in the school setting. An illustration of this tradition concerns the relationship observed between intelligence quotient (IQ), schooling, and juvenile delinquency. Those who score low on IQ tests are likely both to have high levels of delinquency and to do poorly in school. The reasoning that some researchers derive from this evidence ultimately tends to downplay the significance of the school, however, since they see the individual attribute, the IQ, as the cause of both the delinquency and the school behavior. In other words, the connection between schooling and deviant behavior is alleged to be a spurious by-product of the more fundamental psychological causal factor, the IQ, and of its relationship to deviance. Schooling by itself is relatively unimportant, then, and could be dropped from the explanatory argument.

Such arguments are regarded scientifically as at best unproved and, more likely, untenable. Debate within the social-science disciplines about IQ and its measurement has been heated. Significant questions have emerged that remain unanswered by those who would argue for the causal importance of intelligence. Well-documented methodological flaws result in uncontrolled race and class biases that confound any use of IQ tests. Further, many studies have reported that even minimal training or instruction can bring about dramatic increases in measured scores of intelligence. The operational measure of aptitude represented by the IQ score thus hopelessly entangles the effects of individual ability with those of other influences on learning, such as school, race, and class variables.

Because of such flaws, the search for an explanation regarding the importance of schooling on delinquency should probably be aimed in some other direction. In general, it can be stated that in hundreds of attempts to trace causal paths between this and other biological and psychological variables and offense behavior, little positive support emerges (Gibbons).

The social psychological, or interactional, level of analysis

A potentially more significant mode of analysis is at the social psychological level and focuses on interpersonal relationships within the school. These analyses tend to be concerned with the different kinds of social interactions among students and others in the school setting, and they derive much of their impetus from *labeling perspectives* on deviance. For example, teachers play an important role in categorizing some students as "misfits" or "outsiders." As the students themselves come to accept these definitions, self-fulfilling prophecies of continued trouble and deviance are created. Guidance counselors and administrators also contribute to this labeling and status reinforcement process. Counselors, in particular, are able to draw upon school and police records, other community agency data, and their own observations to make decisions that can be critical in shaping student careers, both in terms of academic placement and of the development of deviant or misfit roles (Kelly; Cicourel and Kitsuse).

Another significant domain of interactional behavior concerns relationships with peers. One focus here has been on the role that gangs play in the school and delinquency. Much early sociological attention was given to the way in which those cast in the role of failure or outsider might as a result seek and find social support in delinquent gangs. However, subsequent research has tended to show that formalized participation in structured gangs is not an important aspect of delinquency, at least in terms of explaining the link between school experiences and delinquency. More promising has been the study of the degree to which failure in school inclines the student to develop loosely defined contacts and friendships with other unsuccessful peers. These collective interactions then lead to social encounters that in critical situations place the group in conflict with conventional authorities and norms.

The organizational, or social structural, level of analysis

A further level of analysis of the impact of schooling on delinquency—the social structural level—focuses on how major organizational procedures or institutional arrangements contribute to the development of rebellious or delinquent behavior.

The grading system. One central aspect of the school as an organization consists of its evaluation and grading of students. Low grades are a persistent and strong predictor of delinquency. Unlike some other variables, such as social class and ethnicity, these findings apply to both official and self-report delinquent behavior. The importance of grades holds up even when social class and other relevant factors are controlled. Both middle- and working-class students doing poorly in school are likely to have higher levels of law-violating behavior; those doing well in school will be alike in showing low violation rates. Successful academic performance thus insulates students from delinquency. Caution should be exercised with the interpretation of these findings, however, since a consistently strong relationship simultaneously exists between social class and school performance. This suggests a causal chain that runs from social class to school performance and thence to delinquency. Social class thereby remains in the analysis, because of its indirect effects on delinquency.

The tracking system. A second aspect of school organization that contributes to an understanding of delinquency is the presence within the school of "tracks" (called "streams" in Great Britain), whereby students are placed in homogeneous groups for instructional purposes. In the United States, this takes the form of distinctions at the high school level between students who are enrolled in college preparatory courses, and non-college-oriented students. Both in America and Great Britain, tracking has been found to be a consistent and good predictor of delinquency, with higher levels of delinquency reported in the lower tracks. These findings have been found to hold even when class, ethnicity, and measured "ability" are controlled (Polk and Schafer; Rosenbaum; Hargreaves).

The social dimension: extracurricular activities. Schools provide a third set of experiences that are often understated in terms of importance. Through its range of extracurricular activities, the school provides a variety of experiences that help create commitment to either conformity or deviance. Clubs, organizations, school government, athletics, and other activities both occupy the time of the successful student and permit adults to monitor the leisure time of adolescents. Since these activities are often the exclusive province of successful students, they are likely to add to the building of strong peer grouping among the successful, creating an additional layer of peer involvement and support for conventional behavior. The student who is unsuccessful in academic or official extracurricular activities, however, is cut off from these experiences, from adult-monitored events, and from successful and committed fellow students. For successful adolescents, in other words, the school is a conduit to involvement with legitimate activities and adults, but this pathway is closed to the unsuccessful. As a result, these students become outsiders with little recourse but to turn to their friends—also, as a rule, unsuccessful—for companionship, support, and fun. Such involvements do not always lead to delinquency; rather, these outsider peer groups lack the clear commitment to success and conformity that serves to tie the successful student more closely to conventional behavior. This creates a greater possibility that the unsuccessful students may drift together into occasional encounters with delinquency.

Dropping out. Numerous investigations have found that school dropouts show high levels of law-violating behavior. Careful analysis of the sequence of events over time suggests, however, that the highest levels of delinquency are found while the students are in school, with the law-violating behavior decreasing significantly after withdrawal from school. This dramatic decline has been interpreted as supporting the argument that initial academic failure creates forms of alienation and the seeking out of unsuccessful and unconventional peers, who in turn become involved in rebellious and delinquent activities. Such involvement itself then becomes a further source of alienation in the school and at home. Failure and delinquency come to interact, so that the delinquency in its own right becomes a cause of friction within the school setting. These mutually reinforcing pressures ease when the individual drops out of school, and the delinquency appears to recede as a result (Elliott and Voss).

The economic order, employment, and schooling. A final social structural concern is the linkage of delinquency, the school, and changing labor market conditions for young persons that results from modern technological development. The massive economic changes of the twentieth century, especially since World War II, have fundamentally altered both the nature of work and the way in which one is recruited and prepared for that work. Previously a much greater percentage of the labor force was unskilled, and in fact made up of adolescents and even children. The expansion of capital-intensive technology, with its emphasis on machines and productivity, has produced changes whereby in contemporary times (1) a relatively small percentage of the labor force is made up of young persons; and (2) those young persons who attempt to enter the labor force without needed skills experience unusually high levels of unemployment. The young, in other words, have become part

of not simply a surplus, but of a superfluous, labor force.

These trends in the workplace have had several effects on schools, especially in terms of alienation. To some degree all students in the segregated setting of the school are removed from experiences with work, which, in providing an income, creates some independence in decisions on where to live, what to eat, what to wear, and how to spend leisure time. Work also provides a sense of self-worth and self-importance, which derives from the fact that a worker is viewed as an individual of substance, deserving of respect. Virtually all young people today are subjected to an increasingly long period of time during which they are in school and dependent, and during which they must accommodate themselves to a situation of considerable isolation, aimlessness, and powerlessness. For some, however, the organizational routines of the school at least hold out a promise of future reward. Those in the college-bound track and those who are receiving good grades can balance the present alienation with the promise of a bright future.

The student at the bottom in academic achievement, however, has a double problem. To these general forces of alienation are added the pain and stigma that result from failure in school. Such individuals find themselves unwanted in the school but lack any viable employment prospects if they withdraw from the school. Failure "hurts" not only because of its immediate meaning in the life of the student, but also in terms of limited or denied access to work and income. The contemporary young person doing poorly in school not only lacks access to a positive work experience outside school, but has few places to turn for positive support and companionship other than a peer world of trouble, alienation, and delinquency. Thus, there is an economic basis for the linkage between delinquency and such school processes as tracking (Pearl; Pearl, Grant, and Wenk).

Safe schools: the issue of vandalism and violence. There has been much interest over the years in those characteristics of schools that are conducive to low rates of vandalism or violence. Vandalism is lower in smaller, close-knit schools in which parents support school discipline policies, where there is a general sense of cooperation among students, teachers, and administrators, and where the surrounding area is one with low crime rates. Violence seems to be lower in schools that are smaller and are located in areas with little crime. Discipline in these schools is consistently maintained and seen by the students as fair; the students consider grades to be important and plan to go on to college. Paradoxically, some of the characteristics associated with low levels of vandalism are associated with high levels of violence. For example, schools placing a high emphasis on grades report high levels of attacks on school property but low levels of attacks on either fellow students or teachers. This suggests that schools which emphasize good grades but make them hard to achieve generate a frustration which is expressed through attacks on school property, since the school is perceived as the source of that frustration (National Institute of Education).

Perspectives on the school and delinquency

Strain theory. A variety of theoretical perspectives have attempted to explain the contribution of the school to delinquency. Among the first was that of the "strain" theory, which argues that delinquency is primarily a working-class phenomenon produced by the response of working-class boys to school failure. This failure is seen as frustrating since, as its consequence, status aspirations must be significantly lowered. Delinquency results because some of the students who share this problem come together and strike back at the middle-class system that they view as responsible for their failure. Such an interpretation explicitly acknowledges the competitive nature of success, the consequences of failure, the relationship of the school to competing class interests and values in society, and the peer structures that are part of the delinquent response. A basic problem with such a view is that delinquency is not a unique working-class phenomenon; middle-class delinquency not only exists but also seems to be tied to school failure.

Control theory. An alternative perspective on the importance of the school derives from what has been called "control" theory, which focuses on conventional behavior and asks why some persons seem to be more strongly committed to such behavior. Its answer is that strong involvements and attachments to the school and the home develop strong bonds to the conventional order. Control theory thus takes into account the wealth of social and psychological processes through which the school and family insulate some persons against lawbreaking. Its weaknesses are that it provides no explanation why the school is especially important in the lives of adolescents; nor does it deal with the sequencing or relative importance of family, school, and peer influences.

The labeling perspective. In its more common forms, the "labeling perspective" is concerned with the way in which negative labeling experiences with the police or juvenile court authorities create visible and public identities for young persons that in turn change the perceptions and actions of adults. This shifts the primary focus of analysis from characteristics of the individual delinquent to the way young persons are viewed as a consequence of initial labeling. To be useful in considering the link between school experiences and delinquency, the discussion must be expanded beyond the common treatment of justice system labels to include those labels that arise in the school setting. This is no small shift. Justice system labels (police, court, training school) are fundamentally different from those encountered in the school, in that justice labels have a basically negative character. An arrest, for example, can be crucially harmful to a potential career if it produces the negative label of arrestee. Alternatively, if the misconduct is ignored and the arrestee released, there may be no label. The school can be viewed as having two influential labels, either negative (failure) or positive (success). The major focus of much of the available theory and research is on the interaction between those labeling and those being labeled. Thus, the central questions are: How is it that some persons are selected for labels? How do those so labeled respond? One of the contributions which labeling theory can make is that of directing attention to the way economic forces impinge upon the school, resulting in the evolution of such selection devices as grading and tracking; these create the phenomena of positive and negative labeling within which adolescent identities are forged. The school can be viewed as operating with only a limited number of positive labels to give, failure consequently being inevitable for at least some.

Labor market theory. There is a place, already discussed, for examining the school and delinquency in a framework of general economic and labor market trends. Although less well established in the delinquency literature, such perspectives explicitly place the school in a context of wider economic and political institutional networks. The weakness of a purely economic explanation for the relationship between schooling and delinquency is that it neglects the question of how particular experiences within the school create the distinctive patterns of peer behavior that are part of delinquency.

An integrated theory. Each of the above perspectives highlights particular features of the school that might affect delinquency. Labor market and strain theories place the school inside the framework of wider institutional forces. These wider forces, such as the labor market, create the basic framework for the tracking systems, which develop the major school labels that define student roles. From the labeling experiences, various peer groupings emerge. Taken together, institutional and peer experiences establish the network of social bonds that results in either stronger or weaker ties to conformity. Spanning all these perspectives, an integrated theory may explain why the school seems to be so important in adolescent life, why it is that such selection procedures as tracking and grading have their power in the prediction of delinquency, and how these school processes interact with distinctive peer groupings to create trouble, rebellion, and delinquency (Empey; Jensen and Rojek; Gibbons; Elliott, Ageton, and Canter).

The question of public policy

Given the importance of schooling in the lives of adolescents generally, and its specific importance in predicting delinquency, it is to be expected that schools would be important arenas for crime prevention and control efforts. Fortunately, considerable evidence is available on the impact of these programs, and some assessment of potentially productive avenues for future efforts can be presented.

Segregated schools for failing students. Perhaps the most commonly attempted program is one that identifies certain students as alienated failures or misfits and provides a segregated school setting for them. Such a program tends to be based on remedial instruction, low-level vocational training, and counseling. Despite their popularity, it would be difficult to conceive of programs more likely to produce, not prevent, delinquency. The remedial and vocational work worsens the competitive position of the students within the tracking system of the school at large, at the same time making their labels as school rejects even more visible by virtue of their physical separation. This segregation virtually ensures that the only peer contacts readily available will be with other misfits, that is, exactly those who are likely to reinforce delinquency. Research evidence suggests that such programs do not increase the educational performance of the students and that they foster more delinquency.

Counseling and youth service bureaus. A second common form of school-oriented delinquency prevention program involves counseling and remediation on either an individual or small-group basis, often with the cooperation of an outside community agency such as a youth service bureau. These programs tend to view failure and truancy as individual "adjustment problems" which can be resolved by treating the individual difficulties that are the sources of the maladjustment, with the support of secondary remedial efforts such as tutoring. Research has consistently shown that these and other counseling-type programs have little

or no effect in solving either the school problems or delinquency. Rather, such programs add to the already powerful labeling that has taken place earlier and fail to come to grips with the major dynamics of tracking and grading that serve to lock the participants in these programs into low status roles within the school.

Behavior modification. A third type of program seeks to improve such basic skills as reading and mathematics. These programs have been shown under limited conditions to be effective in the teaching of some academic skills, even for individuals with well-developed delinquent careers. At the same time, such efforts have little impact on their delinquency rates, since the skills learned are too few and are acquired too late to have much influence on the school career. A student who has been identified for several years as a low achiever is very rarely able to escape the noncollege track, and indeed, few ever do. However important reading or mathematical skills may be, learning them late in a school career marked by failure seldom means that several years of prerequisites can be made up and that the individual will be able to move into a more success-oriented track. The "success" of behavior modification techniques then becomes irrelevant, because these highly focused and limited programs leave untouched the wider systems of tracking and labeling.

Early identification. A fourth form of school programming that enjoys periodic popularity consists of attempts at early identification. Common sense is responsible for some of the support for early identification, since it would seem reasonable that a problem isolated early could be "nipped in the bud." Further, there is a common belief among teachers that they "know" very early in the school career which children are likely to end up in trouble. The problem here is that even if it were possible to identify a group of potential delinquents, there is no known form of treatment or early intervention that would be effective in changing the shape of their school careers. Counseling programs have a dismal record of failure in hundreds of trials, and even when the program is able to improve performance in specific academic skills at the preschool level, there is clear evidence that these effects diminish as the school career progresses. At least two kinds of factors will probably doom these early-identification programs. First, it is not clear whether the harmful effects of the program's stigma may be balanced with any positive educational gains that might be produced. Second, early-identification programs leave the whole system of selection and tracking untouched, and it is probable that the status distinction which these create in the late years of the school career are of primary importance in the development of delinquency.

Positive youth action programs. A final type of program policy is termed "positive youth action." This type of program deals with the deep and pervasive effects of tracking and grading by creating new learning settings, involving a mix of work and schooling, that generate a different quality of learning experience. Older youths with a background similar to that of younger failing students may be hired as tutors. Thus, their basic relationship to the school and teachers is changed: they become defined as part of the professional staff and therefore part of the school. Their experience in helping to teach the younger children makes them feel competent and helpful; at the same time, this experience improves their own knowledge of such skills as reading or basic computation—that is, whatever skills are demanded for the tutoring. Further, such training can be integrated into courses for the tutors at the high-school level, with grades and credit that can be defined as part of the college-bound curriculum. These programs may also recruit the older youths in group efforts to cope with such community issues as employment planning, development of recreation programs for younger children, development of a drug education program for young children, and oral-history programs, to name but a few.

A second major feature of positive youth action programs is that they mix all types of students, so that the endemic problem of isolation of the unsuccessful students is avoided. Thus, both successful and failing students are equally able to provide valued and rewarded service for some younger students or for other persons. Segregation of failing students is avoided, and positive peer groupings form that are likely to generate wider support for conventional activities and values (Gibbons; Jensen and Rojek; Polk and Kobrin; Pearl, Grant, and Wenk).

A note on adults

The focus of this discussion has been on schooling and delinquency, but research evidence suggests that education affects adult criminal behavior as well. For example, prison inmates generally have much lower levels of school attainment than those of the general population. Educational status also tends to be predictive of recidivism; for example, parole violation has been found to be related to lower educational attainment.

Despite such findings, it is also true that as individuals move into adulthood, the school setting from which they have departed comes to have less importance in their daily life. Although the effects of schooling greatly influence the kinds of work careers that adults achieve, the work situation itself progressively helps to determine the life patterns of adults. Thus, it is through work that education affects adult crime. Persons with criminal records are likely to have low levels of educational attainment, but because of their deficient schooling their work careers tend to be marginal as well.

In attempting to formulate educational policies for adults, especially to prevent crime, it is important that educational and employment programs be planned so that they are carried out together. Individuals who are older than their early twenties are likely to have obligations to spouses or others that make it difficult or impossible to regain, in a traditional school setting, what they lost during several years of earlier poor performance. A viable alternative might be a program that teaches skills needed in growing fields of employment. To combat crime, such a program must permit adults to start at the bottom and, by a combination of school training and work experience, to accumulate high levels of occupational standing over time. The program must be able to provide an adequate income while enabling its participants to achieve an acceptable level in relation to the educational attainments of their more successful age peers (Pearl and Riessman).

Conclusion

Dramatic shifts occurring since the mid-twentieth century have radically altered the nature of work and have consequently increased the influence of the school in the life of youths. The school has come to play a major part in forming the patterns of adolescent identity, including the patterns of failure that lead to delinquency. Changes in schools to reduce delinquency must provide new academic involvements that will enable young persons doing poorly in educational pursuits to gain competence and to mingle with successful students. Schools will clearly continue to play a fundamental role in shaping the lives of young people, and any public policy aimed at delinquency prevention or control must emphasize education.

KENNETH POLK

See also CLASS AND CRIME; CRIME CAUSATION: SOCIOLOGICAL THEORIES; FAMILY RELATIONSHIPS AND CRIME; INTELLIGENCE AND CRIME; SCHOOLS, CRIME IN THE; YOUTH GANGS AND GROUPS.

BIBLIOGRAPHY

CICOUREL, AARON V., and KITSUSE, JOHN I. *The Educational Decision-makers.* Indianapolis: Bobbs-Merrill, 1963.

ELLIOTT, DELBERT S.; AGETON, SUZANNE S.; and CANTER, RACHELLE J. "An Integrated Theoretical Perspective on Delinquent Behavior." *Journal of Research in Crime and Delinquency* 16 (1979): 3–27.

ELLIOTT, DELBERT S., and VOSS, HARWIN L. *Delinquency and Dropout.* Lexington, Mass.: Heath, Lexington Books, 1974.

EMPEY, LAMAR T. *American Delinquency: Its Meaning and Construction.* Homewood, Ill.: Dorsey Press, 1978.

GIBBONS, DON C. *Delinquent Behavior.* 3d ed. Englewood Cliffs, N.J.: Prentice-Hall, 1980.

HARGREAVES, DAVID H. *Social Relations in a Secondary School.* New York: Humanities Press, 1967.

JENSEN, GARY F., and ROJEK, DEAN G. *Delinquency: A Sociological View.* Lexington, Mass.: Heath, 1980.

KELLY, DELOS H. *How the School Manufactures "Misfits."* South Pasadena, Calif.: Newcal Publications, 1978.

National Institute of Education. *Violent Schools—Safe Schools: The Safe School Study Report to the Congress.* Washington, D.C.: U.S. Department of Health, Education, and Welfare, NIE, 1978.

PEARL, ARTHUR. *The Atrocity of Education.* St. Louis: New Critics Press, 1972.

———; GRANT, DOUGLAS; and WENK, ERNST A., eds. *The Value of Youth.* Davis, Calif.: International Dialogue Press, 1978.

PEARL, ARTHUR, and RIESSMAN, FRANK. *New Careers for the Poor: The Nonprofessional in Human Service.* New York: Free Press, 1965.

POLK, KENNETH, and KOBRIN, SOLOMON. *Delinquency Prevention through Youth Development.* Washington, D.C.: U.S. Department of Health, Education, and Welfare, Youth Development and Delinquency Prevention Administration, 1972.

POLK, KENNETH, and SCHAFER, WALTER E. *Schools and Delinquency.* Englewood Cliffs, N.J.: Prentice-Hall, 1972.

ROSENBAUM, JAMES E. *Making Inequality: The Hidden Curriculum of High School Tracking.* New York: Wiley, 1976.

ELDERLY, ABUSE OF THE

See VIOLENCE IN THE FAMILY: ABUSE OF THE ELDERLY.

ELEMENTS OF CRIME

See CRIME: DEFINITION OF CRIME.

EMBEZZLEMENT

See both articles under EMPLOYEE THEFT; THEFT; WHITE-COLLAR CRIME: HISTORY OF AN IDEA.

EMPLOYEE THEFT

1. BEHAVIORAL ASPECTS	Donald N. M. Horning
2. LEGAL ASPECTS	Donald N. M. Horning

1.
BEHAVIORAL ASPECTS

Ancient or modern problem?

Many regard theft by employees as a relatively new phenomenon that has emerged with impersonal bureaucratic organizations, technologically advanced systems of production, and a work force that has substituted permissive, situational ethics for the nonpermissive, absolute ethics of the past. But employee theft is neither a new problem nor one limited to modern systems of organization, technology, or values, as can be seen by examining the ancient Code of Hammurabi, promulgated in the eighteenth century B.C. and considered one of the most comprehensive of the extant ancient legal codes. The 288 laws of the code contain at least eight specific references to employer-employee and consigner-consignee relations that apply to what is today called employee theft. For example, the 265th law states: "If a shepherd to whom oxen or sheep have been given to pasture become unfaithful, alter the brand, or sell them, they shall convict him and he shall restore tenfold to their owner the oxen and sheep he has stolen" (Luckenbill).

What makes the problem of employee theft appear modern or of recent origin, rather than linked to the past, are the significant social changes that contemporary social organization represents. These changes have yielded new organizational structures, new relationships between employer and employee, new configurations of matériel and products, new victims for theft (including such abstract entities as corporate stockholders), new configurations of work norms regulating employee behavior, new structures and modes for handling employee theft, and a separation of property ownership from property control in the modern organization.

Terms used to describe employee theft

A sociolinguistic analysis of the terms used by the employee-perpetrator and the employer-victim to describe acts of employee theft reveals significant differences in the way these acts are perceived. Whereas the employee leans toward neutral terms that lie well within the work group's normative boundaries, the employer prefers terms that point directly to a conception of the act as a violation of norms. For example, the perpetrator is more likely to use such terms as *making well, salvaging, compensating, fringing, payback, borrowing, loaning, dipping, fiddling, converting, doing homework, scrounging, doing government work, brown-bagging,* and *leveling.* On the other hand, the victim or those officially representing him are more likely to refer to the behavior with such words as *theft, pilfering, poaching, stealing, heisting, peculating, embezzling,* and *filching.* Although each is referring to the same act, each is revealing a differing perception of it. Hence, what is a clear case of theft to an employer may be perceived by an employee as a form of compensation for some presumed injustice, as a form of "salvaging," in which damaged materials or scrap are appropriated for personal use, or as a fringe benefit of his job. Although employer and employee alike agree that the theft of company property is wrong, both may fail to recognize that they may be referring to different classes of acts or categories of matériel. It is not uncommon for workers to decry employee theft as reprehensible while regarding their own removal of property as legitimate or as not involving company property (Horning; Altheide et al.; Hair, Bush, and Busch).

Characteristics of the employee-thief

Empirical data on employee theft reveal that it is the rare employee who does not pilfer something during his work career. What differs for all but that rare employee, however, is the frequency of theft and the value of the goods taken: some steal often, whereas others almost never steal; some steal goods having considerable value, and others confine their theft to goods of little or no value. Although any given episode of employee theft may involve seemingly insignificant amounts, the cumulative effect for all employees at any given time or for each employee over time may be considerable. In 1980, *Industry Week* reported the annual cost of pilfering to be $75 billion. Averaged over a work force of 100 million, this placed the annual cost of theft per employee at $750.

Numerous attempts have been made to describe the typical employee-thief. Many experts in security management have developed profiles that describe him as male, either young or older (competing data support either conclusion), and having a financial problem stemming from gambling, drinking, or other equally costly excesses, such as an expensive hobby

or poor financial management (Green and Farber; Goldsmith). Although this description may apply to a particular segment of the workers who steal, it is not especially useful when one considers that only a few workers (normally less than 5 percent) steal with the intent of converting the goods to money. Most workers steal for personal use (Horning).

Non-work-related correlates. Many of the standard demographic variables, such as age, sex, race, education, religious affiliation, religiosity, residential mobility, number of dependents, size of community, marital stability, and home ownership, which play an important role in differentiating behavior in other forms of crime, do not appear to have much predictive value in the case of employee theft (Horning). The evidence is often contradictory. However, some non-work-related correlates, such as erratic personal and job histories, poor credit ratings resulting from financial mismanagement, difficulty in getting along with others, and alcohol or drug abuse, do appear to be strongly associated with a high risk of employee theft. When all of the evidence is considered, one must conclude that in general, most non-work-related factors, taken separately, are not particularly useful in predicting either the incidence of employee theft or the amount that employees will steal (Horning; Altheide et al.).

Work-related correlates. Many factors in the work setting may have a bearing on the incidence of employee theft, among them the following.

Type of work system. Although all work systems have some elements in common, each provides a unique configuration of matériel that is available to the potential employee-thief. Offices, mines, mills, factories, farms, hospitals, warehouses, retail stores, food processing plants, and foundries, for example, have many elements in common, but more notable are the differences that dictate what is pilferable from each. The great variability that exists within similar work systems may result from differences in scale, organizational structure, managerial philosophy, level of technology, production methods, and security systems, as well as from such intangible elements of the work subculture as formal and informal norms and behavior systems that have evolved over time and that play an important role in setting the parameters within which theft normally takes place. Additionally, in seemingly similar work organizations, such as two branches of a local supermarket chain, dissimilar intangible elements within each work subculture may yield strikingly dissimilar patterns of employee theft.

Thus, to fully understand employee theft, it is necessary first to acknowledge the importance of variations in different types of work systems, and second, to recognize the role that individual work subcultures play in defining the boundaries of approved behavior.

Job classification and job skills. A national survey of internal company theft, reported in 1982, revealed that whereas executive-level employees committed only 15 percent of the thefts, they were responsible for 85 percent of the total dollar loss. On the other hand, 85 percent of the thefts, which represented only 15 percent of the total dollar loss, were traced to such employees as clerks, deliverymen, warehouse and sales personnel, and assembly workers (Porter).

Although the type of job one has is obviously related to what one can and will steal, such variables as skill, vocational interest, ability to manipulate the system, security control, and access also play a role. Normally, the higher one moves up the organizational hierarchy, the greater the trust accorded to the occupational role and the less the monitoring of the property to which one has access.

Length of service with the employer. There does not seem to be a close correlation between theft and length of service with an employer. Although research suggests that length of service is neither as important a deterrent as some think nor as great a stimulus as others contend, the longer a worker is affiliated with a company, the greater is his awareness of theft throughout the work system, of the modus operandi, and of the work group's norms regarding theft. These, in turn, have a close relationship to the incidence of employee theft (Horning).

Level of satisfaction. Many authorities contend that a satisfied employee is less likely to steal than a dissatisfied one. Although this generally appears to be true, there are many varieties of satisfaction, and these seem to have a differential effect. For example, dissatisfaction with one's job or supervisor does not appear to significantly affect the level of one's theft; dissatisfaction with the work organization does. Generally, the greater the satisfaction with the work organization, the lower the level of employee theft (Horning; Altheide et al.; Zeitlin).

Attitudes toward employee theft

Workers' attitudes about property, and their perception of what constitutes a victim, appear to be closely related to their propensity to steal. In all but the simplest work systems, there are three forms of property—company property, personal property, and property of uncertain ownership—and two possible victims. The company is the victim in the loss of company property, and the individual is the victim in the loss of personal property. The theft of property of uncertain ownership has no readily identifiable victim.

Almost all workers report negative feelings about the theft of personal property, and in most systems it has all the elements of a taboo. The theft of such property has a victim, and even when unknown, the victim has a symbolic presence in the form of a generalized "other" with whom workers can identify. Most workers also report negative feelings about the theft of company property. This, however, appears to involve a lesser sense of a victim, for often the victim is an abstract construct, and more a reflection of generalized attitudes about theft. Few workers hold negative attitudes about taking property of uncertain ownership. Since by their definition it is property without an owner, its theft is victimless, and appropriating it is not viewed as true theft.

The taking of company and personal property are acts of theft, and any worker who engages in them has to grapple with feelings of guilt. Since the taking of property of uncertain ownership is not perceived as theft, guilt is generally minimal or is readily neutralized (Horning; Altheide et al.).

Modus operandi

Most employee theft is solitary behavior and does not require special equipment, procedures, or accomplices. The pilfered items are generally hidden on the person or carried in a purse, lunch pail, or briefcase. A pilferer may occasionally employ a more elaborate scheme, but this may force him to adopt a new rationale or to define his behavior as theft, something most employees assiduously avoid. The few workers who pilfer in volume often resort to schemes that are designed to circumvent normal security procedures, ranging from a relatively simple modus operandi, such as shipping matériel to themselves, to complex arrangements that may involve the complicity of people both within and outside the organization.

Conclusion

Employee theft does not follow expected patterns, and few of the standard demographic variables have any predictive value. What is important are the workplace values and norms that define the limits of acceptable behavior for all employees. Further, researchers in the field tend to limit their studies to blue-collar workers, who commit 85 percent of the acts of theft; they ignore the executive-level employees who, although responsible for only 15 percent of the incidence of theft, account for 85 percent of the total dollar loss. To comprehend employee theft fully, the full spectrum of the work force must be studied.

DONALD N. M. HORNING

See also COMPUTER CRIME; CRIME PREVENTION: ENVIRONMENTAL AND TECHNOLOGICAL STRATEGIES; EMPLOYEE THEFT: LEGAL ASPECTS; POLICE: PRIVATE POLICE AND SECURITY FORCES; SECURITY, INDUSTRIAL; THEFT.

BIBLIOGRAPHY

ALTHEIDE, DAVID; ADLER, PATRICIA A.; ADLER, PETER; and ALTHEIDE, DUANE A. "The Social Meanings of Employee Theft." *Crime at the Top: Deviance in Business and the Professions.* Edited by John M. Johnson and Jack D. Douglas. Philadelphia: Lippincott, 1978, pp. 90–124.

BRYANT, CLIFTON D. *Deviant Behavior: Occupational and Organizational Bases.* Chicago: Rand McNally, 1974.

GOLDSMITH, REGINALD. "When There's Money to Burn." *Security Problems in a Modern Society.* Edited by Sheryl Strauss. Woburn, Mass.: Butterworth, 1980, pp. 170–173.

GREEN, GION, and FARBER, RAYMOND. *Introduction to Security: Principles and Practices.* Los Angeles: Security World, 1978.

HAIR, JOSEPH F., JR.; BUSH, RONALD F.; and BUSCH, PAUL. "Employee Theft: Views from Two Sides." *Business Horizons* 19, no. 6 (1976): 25–29.

HENRY, STUART, and MARS, GERALD. "Crime at Work: The Social Construction of Amateur Property Theft." *Sociology* 12 (1978): 245–263.

HORNING, DONALD N. M. "Blue Collar Theft: Conceptions of Property, Attitudes toward Pilfering, and Work Group Norms in a Modern Industrial Plant." *Crimes against Bureaucracy.* Edited by Erwin O. Smigel and H. Laurence Ross. New York: Van Nostrand-Reinhold, 1970, pp. 46–64.

JOHNSON, MICHAEL. "How Many Criminals Do You Employ?" *Industry Week,* 22 September 1975, pp. 22–30.

LUCKENBILL, DANIEL D., trans. "The Code of Hammurabi." Edited by Edward Chiera. *The Origin and History of Hebrew Law* (1931). Edited by John M. Powis Smith. Reprint. University of Chicago Press, 1960.

PORTER, SYLVIA. "Shockers on Stealing from the Boss." *New York Daily News,* 19 March 1982.

TAYLOR, WILLIAM L., and CANGEMI, JOSEPH P. "Employee Theft and Organizational Climate." *Personnel Journal* 58 (1979): 686–688, 714.

"Theft Costs Firms 75 Billion Annually." *Industry Week,* 9 June 1980, pp. 32–34.

ZEITLIN, LAURENCE R. "A Little Larceny Can Do a Lot for Employee Morale." *Psychology Today,* June 1971, pp. 22–26, 64.

2.

LEGAL ASPECTS

The cost and distribution of employee theft

Virtually every society, every type of economy, every enterprise, and every occupation has a variant of employee pilfering. While it is most clearly manifest within bureaucratic organizations, such as supermarkets, department stores, large factories, and government offices, employee theft is found in all work organizations. In work systems where security is paramount, such as those of defense and banking, employee theft is constricted and largely limited to items normally used in the course of work. Where security is not paramount, as is the case in most work situations and occupations, employees pilfer a wide range of goods and services, using diverse techniques and rationales. Indeed, there are work systems, such as construction and cartage, in which employee theft has long been endemic. On the other hand, in some new industries, such as electronics and pharmaceuticals, pilfering has become epidemic.

Estimates of cost. Each year, millions of workers pilfer billions of dollars' worth of goods and services from the businesses and organizations where they work. Estimates of amounts pilfered annually in the United States range from less than $1 billion to more than $75 billion. A leading business magazine placed the cost of employee theft in 1978 at $40 billion and estimated that this amount increased at a compound rate of 15 percent annually, doubling every five years. An often-used benchmark places the value of employee pilfering at 2 percent of the gross national product. It has also been reported that the cost of employee pilfering exceeds the losses from all other forms of burglary and robbery throughout the United States. Estimates of the proportion of workers involved in employee theft range from 5 percent to 75 percent. According to the United States Chamber of Commerce, 50 percent of those who work in plants and offices pilfer; 5 percent to 8 percent pilfer in volume. Available data suggest that the total amount spent annually on the prevention and control of employee theft exceeds the amount lost through such theft.

Difficulties in estimating cost and incidence. As with other forms of criminal activity, many problems are encountered in efforts to estimate the incidence of employee theft. First, there is the very real problem of obtaining accurate data. Employee theft is, in the main, an activity that is hidden and generally undetected and that, when detected, is rarely reported or prosecuted. Further, it is often officially concealed because to admit to the problem is to risk a charge of poor management.

Second, employee pilfering is not an exclusive category in occupational crime: it overlaps with other forms of employee deviance, such as fraud, embezzlement, and sabotage, and it is often treated as if it were coterminous with other forms of crime, such as shoplifting, in which the organization is victimized by outsiders. One of the most common errors in the literature is the treatment of pilfering and shoplifting as though they were one and the same.

Third, it is not always clear what is included in the estimates. Some estimates cover only the value of the pilfered goods and services. Others add to direct costs some or all of the indirect costs, including cost of security personnel and security hardware, theft insurance, management time, theft investigation, loss of trained employees, training of employee replacements, production losses, losses from lowered morale, and legal fees.

Fourth, numerous legal questions complicate attempts to estimate the cost of employee theft, for in some work settings many illegal acts have evolved into quasi-legal, covert "job rights," whereby workers view their pilfering as a natural concomitant of their job, and management, either explicitly or tacitly, tolerates the behavior.

Fifth, the incidence and cost of employee theft is obscured by accounting practices that do not isolate the various means through which inventory shrinkage may occur. Thus, losses from spoilage, supplier skimming, breakage, sabotage, shoplifting, and waste are often included in estimates of employee theft.

Hence, the estimates of employee theft vary greatly, depending upon the manner in which the above factors are considered. At best, estimates of its incidence and cost are based upon data of uncertain accuracy and completeness. Often they are but crude indicators of an apparently growing problem.

Problems of enforcement and control

Legal status of employee theft. An important factor in the enforcement and control of employee theft is that its unambiguous legal status as a violation of the criminal law is coupled with its ambiguous social status as an activity that has been somewhat legitimated through subcultural norms. From a sociolegalistic perspective, employee theft is grossly underdetected and underreported relative to its incidence. It has unusually high immunity from prosecution, in that most victims seek solutions other than through legal procedures; termination of employment is the most common resolution. It involves numerous violations of the criminal law that, if pursued through the legal system, would be judged nonprosecutable because of the victim's tacit acceptance of the activity. It often results in civil arrangements between the offender and the employer to avoid prosecution (this, in itself, may be a crime in that it is an arrangement to conceal a crime). Finally, it is an activity that is viewed by most participants in the work system as legitimate or quasi-legitimate and, hence, one that does not cause the perpetrator to regard himself as a criminal.

Conceptions of property. Legally, there are only two types of property in any work system: corporate property, which belongs to the enterprise, and personal property, which belongs to specific workers. Workers acknowledge the existence of both of these, as well as of a third type—namely, "property of uncertain ownership." The last type has no official status; however, it is perceived by the work subculture to be very real. Property of uncertain ownership is comprised of countless items such as pencils, paper clips, tools, samples, damaged goods, and scrap, which are found in every work organization. It has the following general characteristics, among others: it numbers in the thousands; it is system-specific, in that every work system has its own distinctive configuration of property of uncertain ownership; it generally includes items that are used up in the course of work or are the by-products of work; it consists, in large part, of items for which no accounting is thought necessary or possible; it includes items for which control has been relinquished to those who use them in the course of their work; and it has been converted, in verbal designation and everyday thought, from owned property to property of uncertain ownership.

Through this process of thought there emerges a continuum of certainty of ownership. In legal theory, all property in the work system, both corporate and personal, originates with high certainty of ownership. In practice, through popular conventions of thought, some property drifts along the continuum toward low certainty of ownership. Ultimately, this yields a distribution of property that embraces the full length of the continuum from high certainty to low or no certainty of ownership.

Employee norms and employee theft. In time, every work organization and all of its subunits develop both formal and informal norms. The formal norms are official policies, procedures, rules, and definitions; the informal norms emerge as the workers seek to adapt the formal norms to their own particular situation. These customs of the workplace tend to produce important divergences from the formal norms. This is apparent in employee theft. Because the formal norms are legalistic, they ordinarily acknowledge only legal forms of property. The informal norms, being reality-based, reflect the full range of property conceptions described above. The formal norms ordinarily proscribe any form of employee theft or, in a few instances, provide a limited "take home" or "purchase at cost" policy for employees wanting company property. The informal norms define acceptable behaviors involving theft of property from the workplace. In general, informal norms are characterized by the following:

1. The work-group norms relative to theft develop uniquely in each workplace and are situationally specific; those found in one setting may differ significantly from those in another.
2. The norms of pilfering are passed from one worker to the next through the process of socialization at work, with precept and folklore the prime elements in the transmission of those norms.
3. Although necessarily vague, these norms define the boundaries within which "legitimate" employee theft may occur.
4. "Legitimated" employee theft is bounded by prescriptive and proscriptive definitions of property, modus operandi, the value of pilfered goods, and the legitimating rationales.
5. An important element in the boundary-establishing process is tolerant collusion by management, as well as management's own informal norms as to what is an economically rational limit to theft; the customary allowance for theft becomes an element in management's operational calculus.
6. Those who operate within these customarily accepted boundaries adopt suitable modes of action; legitimating vocabularies of justification and hence standards for judging their behavior and themselves; and strategies for coping with their guilt.
7. Those who operate within the parameters established by the norms receive the support of the work group, but those who operate in violation of the informal norms—for example, those who pilfer excessively—are viewed as a threat to the "collusive tolerance" of management and hence as a threat to the informal normative system. Thus, they are not accorded the support of the work group.
8. Those who inform on pilferers do so at considerable risk to their support by the work group.

Control strategies. Many techniques to control employee theft have been used over the years with varying degrees of success. Probably the original method was that of close supervision. Many of the most sophisticated techniques in use are merely variants of that very old approach. Contemporary control methods fall within two general classes, physical control and psychological control.

Physical control devices and strategies. Means of external physical control include fences, window barriers, gates, lighting, electronic surveillance, vehicle control, patrol guards, and canine units. Among methods of internal theft control are property "branding," electronic surveillance, controlled access to areas, surprise audits and inventory checks, package and personal-property control, surprise inspections of desks or lockers, surveillance mirrors, and scrap control.

Psychological control devices and strategies. Although the techniques described above have a psychologically deterrent quality of their own, here the focus is primarily psychological in nature and begins with a psychological premise. Psychological devices and strategies encompass pre-employment fingerprinting, pre-employment and periodic lie detector tests, staged episodes of theft to give credence to the formal proscriptions, pre-employment sworn statements, and periodic publication of the organization's formal policy on theft.

Assessment of strategies. Each control strategy has both positive and negative qualities. While some strategies are all but indispensable to the maintenance of the general security in the work organization, a few, especially those designed to induce fear, are introduced at considerable risk to employee morale. It is generally assumed that there is a strong relationship between pilfering and the organizational climate in the work organization: the more unhealthy the climate, the greater the likelihood of employee pilfering.

Most of the emphasis in the security field is on physical and psychological control strategies. It is obvious that these have not stopped employee theft; they may even stimulate employee theft by presenting new obstacles in a game. There is, in addition, a real risk that they may contribute to an unhealthy organizational climate. More attention needs to be given to sociological control strategies—that is, to the social relationships and norms prevalent in work-group and management subcultures. Each has its own strategies, definitions, rules, rationales, and parameters relative to pilfering. Eventually a basis may be established for a system of negotiated limits, with employees assuming a key role in the maintenance of those defined boundaries.

DONALD N. M. HORNING

See also COMPUTER CRIME; THEFT; WHITE-COLLAR CRIME: HISTORY OF AN IDEA.

BIBLIOGRAPHY

ALTHEIDE, DAVID; ADLER, PATRICIA A.; ADLER, PETER; and ALTHEIDE, DUANE A. "The Social Meaning of Employee Theft." *Crime at the Top: Deviance in Business and the Professions.* Edited by John M. Johnson and Jack D. Douglas. Philadelphia: Lippincott, 1978, pp. 90–124.

Chamber of Commerce of the United States of America. *A Handbook on White Collar Crime: Everyone's Problem, Everyone's Loss.* Washington D.C.: Chamber of Commerce, 1974.

DITTON, JASON. *Becoming a 'Fiddler': Some Steps in the Moral Career of a Naive Bread Salesman.* Working Papers in Sociology No. 6. Durham, England: University of Durham, Department of Sociology and Social Administration, 1975.

GREEN, GION, and FARBER, RAYMOND. *Introduction to Security: Principles and Practices.* Los Angeles: Security World Publishing Co., 1978.

HEMPHILL, CHARLES F., JR. *Management's Role in Loss Prevention.* New York: American Management Association, AMACOM, 1976.

HENRY, STUART, and MARS, GERALD. "Crime at Work: The Social Construction of Amateur Property Theft." *Sociology* 12 (1978): 245–263.

HORNING, DONALD N. M. "Blue Collar Theft: Conceptions of Property, Attitudes toward Pilfering, and Work Group Norms in a Modern Industrial Plant." *Crimes against Bureaucracy.* Edited by Erwin O. Smigel and H. Laurence Ross. New York: Van Nostrand-Reinhold, 1970, pp. 46–64.

HOROSZOWSKI, PAWEL. *Economic Special-opportunity Conduct and Crime.* Lexington, Mass.: Heath, Lexington Books, 1980.

ROBIN, GERALD D. "The Corporate and Judicial Disposition of Employee Thieves." *Crimes against Bureaucracy.* Edited by Erwin O. Smigel and H. Laurence Ross. New York: Van Nostrand-Reinhold, 1970, pp. 119–142.

———. "White Collar Crime and Employee Theft." *Crime and Delinquency* 20 (1974): 251–262.

ENGLISH LAW

See CRIMINAL LAW REFORM: ENGLAND; CRIMINAL PROCEDURE: COMPARATIVE ASPECTS; PROSECUTION: COMPARATIVE ASPECTS.

ENTRAPMENT

The nature of the entrapment defense. Entrapment is a defense based on a claim that police agents induced the accused to commit the crime charged. The defense arises most often in cases in which the accused is charged with the sale of contraband or with a crime such as counterfeiting, prostitution, or bribery. In order to detect these crimes, it is necessary to use undercover officers and informers, and often these agents must request the commission of a criminal act. For example, to make a case against a drug dealer, it is usually necessary for an undercover officer or informer to ask the dealer to sell him drugs.

Some requests for criminal acts are completely innocuous. An agent who asks for a drink in a speakeasy does not create any danger of corrupting the innocent. However, because persons engaged in crime are wary of strangers, agents must often do more than meet a suspect and make a simple request. They must cultivate trust and use persuasion. When the means of persuasion become excessive, the defense of entrapment may be available.

There is disagreement among courts and commentators about what constitutes excessive inducement, but most would agree that the following inducements go too far:

1. A female undercover agent offers sexual favors to a suspect if he will sell her marijuana (cf. *Spencer v. State*, 263 So. 2d 282 (Fla. App. 1972)).

2. After arresting a suspect for murder, a police officer offers to release him and drop charges if the suspect will pay a bribe. The officer's aim is to charge the suspect with bribery as well as murder (cf. *Ossen v. Commonwealth*, 187 Va. 902, 48 S.E.2d 204 (1948)).

3. A revenue agent asks former moonshiners to set up a still. The moonshiners refuse, saying that there is too much danger of being caught. The agent tells them they will be safe because he will purchase all the output and furnish all the necessary equipment and supplies (cf. *Greene v. United States*, 454 F.2d 783 (9th Cir. 1971)).

4. An undercover agent approaches a suspect known to be a user of heroin and offers him twice the going rate for a day's supply. Enticed by this unusual offer, the suspect sells the agent his own personal supply and is subsequently prosecuted for the sale.

5. An undercover agent approaches a heroin addict and asks to buy heroin. The addict refuses. The agent then says that his girl friend is sick from withdrawal symptoms and will leave him unless he can obtain heroin for her. The addict sells his personal supply to the agent (cf. *People v. Turner*, 390 Mich. 7, 210 N.W.2d 336 (1973)).

6. An agent offers a bribe to a public official, who refuses to take it. The agent continues to harass the public official and finally threatens to retaliate against her family unless she relents.

7. A revenue agent investigating moonshine whiskey decides to make a purchase from a suspect. The

agent assumes the guise of a traveling salesman and obtains an introduction. After some friendly conversation at the suspect's home, the agent asks for moonshine. The suspect refuses, saying he has none. The agent then continues to make small talk. After learning that both served in the same regiment in World War I, the agent reminisces about the war. Then he makes several more requests for moonshine, appealing to the suspect as a fellow veteran of the regiment. The suspect finally agrees, leaves to purchase moonshine from a neighbor, and resells it at the same price to the agent (cf. *Sorrells v. United States*, 287 U.S. 435 (1932)).

8. An informer cooperating with police meets a suspect in the office of a doctor who has been treating the suspect for heroin addiction. The informer tells the suspect that he (the informer) cannot shake the addiction and asks the suspect to supply him with some heroin. After several requests the suspect agrees and buys heroin with the informer's money. The informer and the suspect share the heroin (cf. *Sherman v. United States*, 356 U.S. 369 (1958)).

9. An agent tells a suspect that laws prohibiting the sale of certain firearms are a violation of the constitutional right to bear arms, and eventually convinces the suspect to sell him some illegal firearms (Model Penal Code, 1962, § 2.13(1)(a)).

The entrapment defense is often the last resort of a defendant who has indisputably committed a prohibited act. Normally, the defendant's claim of entrapping conduct is disputed by the prosecution at trial, and the defendant is placed in the unenviable position of both admitting a criminal act and hoping that the tribunal will believe his account of the events that caused him to commit the act. Moreover, even when a defendant is able to produce convincing evidence of inducement by police agents, he still faces the danger that the tribunal will decide that the inducements were not substantial enough to cause a normally law-abiding person to go astray. Consequently, the prosecution wins an overwhelming majority of entrapment cases.

Subjective and objective approaches. Despite its limited effect on the outcome of cases, the entrapment defense has drawn an abundance of commentary from judges and scholars. Most of this commentary has been devoted to the question of whether an "objective" approach to entrapment is better than the prevailing "subjective" approach.

Under the subjective approach, the entrapment defense is not available to a defendant who was ready and willing to commit the offense charged prior to inducement by police agents. In such a case, the defense will fail even if police agents used unduly persuasive inducements.

Under the objective, or "hypothetical person," approach, the defense is available whenever police agents have used overreaching inducements, regardless of whether the actual defendant was predisposed to commit the offense. The conduct of police agents is assessed by predicting its effect on a hypothetical law-abiding person, not on the actual target. If the agents used inducements that might have caused such a person to commit the offense, the defendant is entitled to acquittal, whether or not he himself was ready and willing to commit the offense.

Proponents of this approach view it as a way to prevent improper police conduct (Donnelly). To enhance its preventive effect, they urge acquittal of defendants who have been subjected to improper inducements, regardless of individual culpability. The approach's effectiveness in deterring misconduct by officers and informers is, however, open to serious question (Park).

The principal purpose of the subjective defense is protection of defendants, not deterrence of misconduct by the police. Nevertheless, the defense does not apply unless a police agent (an officer or someone cooperating with the police) induced the crime. A defendant who was corrupted by some other person is not entitled to acquittal. Critics of the subjective test contend that such a defendant is no more blameworthy than one corrupted by the police, and that it is therefore illogical to pretend that the defense is concerned with the defendant's culpability (Model Penal Code, 1959, commentaries on §§ 14–24; Donnelly). This argument fails to take into account the possibility that the subjective test has dual goals—protection of innocent defendants and condemnation of improper police conduct—and that the scales do not tip for acquittal unless both goals are served simultaneously. Alternatively, the failure of the subjective defense to cover inducements by private persons could be the result of an unstated judicial fear of encouraging collusive defenses. There would be a danger, for example, that in a multidefendant case one of the accomplices might be persuaded to take all the blame and to concoct an entrapment defense for the others by testifying falsely that he led them astray.

In four leading cases, a narrow majority of the United States Supreme Court endorsed the subjective approach to entrapment (*Hampton v. United States*, 425 U.S. 484 (1976); *United States v. Russell*, 411 U.S. 423 (1973); *Sherman; Sorrells*). A strong majority of commentators and law reformers disagree and favor the objective approach, which was endorsed by the drafters of the Model Penal Code and those of the Brown Commission's proposed federal criminal code (U.S. National Commission, 1970a, § 702(2)). A substantial minority of state jurisdictions have adopted the objective approach (*People v. Barraza*, 23 Cal. 3d 675, 591 P.2d 947 (1979), and authorities cited therein).

The choice of approaches also has consequences in terms of procedures followed at trial. Jurisdictions following the subjective test place the burden of persuading the tribunal on the prosecution, although the burden of initially producing evidence that police agents offered inducements rests on the defendant. Once the defendant has produced such evidence, the prosecution must prove beyond a reasonable doubt that the defendant was predisposed to commit the offense.

By contrast, objective-test jurisdictions tend to place the burden of persuasion on the defendant, who is generally required to prove by a preponderance of the evidence that police agents used inducements which might have caused a normally law-abiding person to commit the offense. This difference in allocation of the burden of persuasion probably stems from a belief, under the objective approach, that it is fair to place the burden on a defendant who is taking advantage of a defense that permits him to obtain acquittal even if he was ready and willing to commit the crime.

A second and very important procedural difference between the two approaches relates to the admissibility of evidence at trial. Under the subjective test, the predisposition of the accused is the ultimate issue, and evidence about prior crimes and bad acts is freely admissible to show predisposition. For example, in a case involving the sale of illicit drugs, the prosecution can introduce testimony that the accused sold drugs on other occasions, whether or not those sales led to arrest or conviction (*United States v. Owens*, 346 F.2d 329 (7th Cir. 1965); Fed. R. Evid. 405(b)). Testimony that the accused had the reputation of being a drug dealer would also be admissible because a trait of the defendant's character (his propensity to sell drugs) would be an ultimate issue (Fed. R. Evid. 405(b); Cleary et al., § 187). Moreover, to aid the prosecution in proving prior crimes, some courts have even admitted hearsay evidence that would otherwise not be admissible at trial, on the apparent theory that anything showing predisposition is admissible in an entrapment case (*United States v. McKinley*, 493 F.2d 547 (5th Cir. 1974)). Contrary holdings were reached in *United States v. Johnston*, 426 F.2d 112 (7th Cir. 1970) and *United States v. Catanzaro*, 407 F.2d 998 (3d Cir. 1969).

Under the objective test, predisposition is not an ultimate issue, and the rules concerning evidence of the defendant's character are therefore more restrictive. Character evidence in the form of testimony about the defendant's bad reputation will ordinarily be admissible only if the defendant opens the door by producing character witnesses himself (Fed. R. Evid. 404(a); Cleary et al., § 191). If the defendant testifies, the prosecution could attack his credibility as a witness by presenting evidence of certain prior convictions. Generally, however, evidence about prior bad acts not resulting in conviction is not admissible merely because the defendant has taken the witness stand (Fed. R. Evid. 608–609; Cleary et al., §§ 42–44). If the defendant neither testifies nor produces character witnesses, evidence about his prior convictions and bad acts is normally excluded completely.

In certain situations, however, evidence of prior criminal activity by the accused might be relevant to the question of whether the agent used an overreaching inducement. Suppose that an agent has reliable information that a target is a drug dealer. The agent approaches the target, who refuses to sell drugs. Because of the target's reputation, the agent assumes that the refusal is based solely on suspicion. Therefore, the agent makes a special effort to win the target's friendship and trust. The agent finds it necessary to make several requests before the target sells the drugs. In assessing the propriety of the agent's conduct, it might be appropriate, even in an objective-test jurisdiction, to take into account what the agent knew about the target's ongoing criminal activity. Inducements that would be improper when trying to purchase drugs from an addict might be appropriate when purchasing from a large-scale drug dealer (Park).

Opponents of the subjective test often point to its consequence of admitting evidence harmful to the defendant as a reason for switching to the objective test (Orfield; *Russell*, 443 (Justice Stewart dissenting)). However, if that is the main objection to the subjective approach, the proper solution is perhaps to change the rules of evidence instead of changing the definition of entrapment.

Another possible procedural difference between the two approaches involves the division of decision-making power between judge and jury. Under the subjective test, the defendant has a right to have the jury decide whether he was entrapped. This rule stems from the view that the defense is based upon the diminished culpability of the accused. Like other questions of guilt and innocence, the defense goes to the jury unless the defendant waives his right to jury trial.

Reformers who support the objective test have generally favored making the defense of entrapment a matter solely for the judge to decide. They view the defense as a preventive measure, and consider the judge better equipped to evaluate the ultimate effect of a particular decision on future police conduct. The jury, in contrast, is likely to be more concerned with doing justice to the individual defendant. However, despite the preference of academic law reformers for requiring that the judge rule on the objective defense, most of the states that have adopted it provide that the defendant may choose to put the entrapment defense to the jury.

Quasi-entrapment defenses. Although a defendant is not entitled to avail himself of the defense labeled "entrapment" in a subjective-test jurisdiction if the prosecution can demonstrate that he was predisposed, some subjective-test courts will allow predisposed defendants to use similar defenses that have other names.

If a predisposed defendant was subjected to a form of enticement that was shocking and outrageous, he can argue that the due process clause requires a judgment of acquittal. The Supreme Court alluded to the possibility of such a defense in *Russell*, in which an undercover agent had provided the defendant with an essential ingredient for manufacturing amphetamines. The defendant was clearly predisposed to commit the crime, and therefore his defense did not fall within the traditional confines of entrapment doctrine. Nevertheless, the Ninth Circuit Court of Appeals overturned his conviction on the ground that providing the ingredient constituted "an intolerable degree of governmental participation in the criminal enterprise." The Supreme Court disagreed and upheld the conviction. It indicated that the entrapment defense was not intended to give the federal judiciary untrammeled and discretionary veto over law enforcement practices of which it did not approve. However, the Court did not completely close the door on the possibility that in other cases a predisposed defendant might be entitled to acquittal. It indicated that in some circumstances police conduct might be so outrageous that the due process clause would bar conviction even if the defendant was predisposed.

The *Russell* opinion did not describe the types of instigation that might be prohibited by due process. It simply repeated familiar formulas, saying that government conduct would be unconstitutional if it violated "fundamental fairness" and was "shocking to the universal sense of justice."

One can only speculate about the dimensions of this due process defense in cases in which the police encouraged the defendant. Inducements involving a threat of physical violence probably fall within the scope of the defense. The due process clause could also be construed to prohibit conviction when the plan for ensnaring the target involved commission of crimes that posed a danger to other persons or to the criminal justice system (*United States v. Archer*, 486 F.2d 670, 676–677 (2d Cir. 1973) (dictum)). A defendant might also prevail when concern for overreaching government inducement overlaps with concern for First Amendment freedoms, as when the government sends provocateurs into political organizations to suggest the commission of crimes.

The due process defense is also likely to be raised when agents have played a substantial role in leading or organizing a criminal enterprise. For example, in one of the political corruption cases arising from the Abscam investigation, certain agents had played the role of wealthy Arabs with money to invest. Other agents told targeted public officials that the Arab investors wanted to make monetary gifts to the officials and that it was part of the "Arab way of doing business" to give gifts to people with power and influence. The agents indicated that if the supposed Arabs could not make friends in this fashion, they might not invest in the community at all. In granting a judgment of acquittal, the trial judge relied in part on the due process defense, indicating that conviction would be fundamentally unfair in light of the high sums offered, the lack of any demand for specific reciprocal acts by the officials, and the appeal to civic duty involved in the suggestion that taking the bribes would help the community (*United States v. Jannotti*, 501 F. Supp. 1182, 1204 (E.D. Pa. 1980) (alternative holding)). By comparison, *United States v. Myers*, 527 F. Supp. 1206 (E.D.N.Y. 1981), held that the absence of agents' prior cause to suspect targets of corruption, and the offering of generous bribes, were not sufficient reasons to constitute violation of due process.

In the 1960s and 1970s, a few lower federal courts adopted a per se rule against inducing offenses by supplying a target with contraband. For example, if a police agent supplied the drugs which a target later sold, these courts determined that the target was entitled to acquittal under what might be called the "furnishing contraband" defense (*United States v. Bueno*, 447 F.2d 903, 906 (5th Cir. 1971)).

For the federal courts, the furnishing-contraband defense was eradicated in 1976 by *Hampton*. Hampton had been convicted of two counts of distributing heroin. He conceded predisposition, but claimed that his conviction should nevertheless be reversed because the trial judge had refused to instruct the jury to consider the furnishing-contraband defense. In a 5–3 decision, the Court affirmed, ruling that even if the defendant had received the drugs from a government informer, he was not entitled to acquittal.

The case elicited three separate opinions, none joined by a majority of the Court. In his plurality opinion, Justice William Rehnquist, joined by Justices Warren Burger and Byron White, rejected both the furnishing-contraband defense and the broader proposition that government inducements might in some cases be sufficiently outrageous to justify acquittal of a predisposed defendant on due process grounds.

Justice Lewis Powell's concurring opinion, in which he was joined by Justice Harry Blackmun, also rejected the defendant's argument that furnishing contraband was in itself a sufficient ground for acquittal. However, Powell criticized the plurality's view that due process should never bar conviction of a predisposed defendant. He pointed out that the facts before the Court did not require it to consider that issue.

In dissent, Justice William Brennan, joined by Justices Thurgood Marshall and Potter Stewart, reiterated his preference for an objective approach to entrapment. He also stated that even under the subjective approach, the conviction should have been reversed because of the trial judge's refusal to instruct the jury that the defendant should be acquitted if the government supplied the contraband that was the basis for the charge.

Although the *Hampton* Court rejected the defendant's arguments by a 5–3 majority, only three of the Justices rejected the concept of a due process defense in cases in which police encouraged a criminal act. The only proposition that *Hampton* clearly established was that furnishing of contraband is not by itself sufficient to justify acquittal. The lower federal courts are free to hold that when the furnishing of contraband is accompanied by outrageous and excessive activity, even a predisposed defendant is entitled to acquittal, as seen, for example, in *United States v. Twigg*, 588 F.2d 373 (3d Cir. 1978). State courts have additional leeway. The *Hampton* decision was merely an interpretation of the federal due process clause. Nothing in it prohibits state courts from endorsing a per se furnishing-contraband defense, either as a common-law defense or as an interpretation of state due process clauses.

Conclusions. In all American jurisdictions, a defendant is entitled to acquittal on grounds of entrapment if (1) police agents used excessive inducements, and if (2) the defendant was not predisposed to commit the offense. When one of these two elements is missing, various jurisdictions can be expected to reach different results.

If a defendant who was not previously ready and willing to commit the type of crime with which he is charged nevertheless yielded to inoffensive inducements, he is entitled to acquittal under the subjective, but not the objective, test. Obversely, if he was ready and willing to commit the crime but was subjected to improper inducements, the result should be conviction under the subjective test and acquittal under the objective test. However, some subjective-test jurisdictions would hold that when police conduct was so improper that it was utterly outrageous, even a predisposed defendant is entitled to acquittal—not because of the entrapment defense, but because the police conduct violated due process.

ROGER PARK

See also POLICE, *articles on* MISCONDUCT, UNDERCOVER TACTICS, *and* VICE SQUAD; PROSTITUTION AND COMMERCIALIZED VICE: LEGAL ASPECTS.

BIBLIOGRAPHY

American Law Institute. *Model Penal Code: Official Draft.* Philadelphia: ALI, 1962.

——. *Model Penal Code: Tentative Draft No. 9.* Philadelphia: ALI, 1959.

CLEARY, EDWARD W. et al. *McCormick's Handbook of the Law of Evidence.* 2d ed. St. Paul: West, 1972.

DONNELLY, RICHARD C. "Judicial Control of Informants, Spies, Stool Pigeons, and Agents Provocateurs." *Yale Law Journal* 60 (1951): 1091–1113.

LAFAVE, WAYNE R., and SCOTT, AUSTIN W., JR. *Handbook on Criminal Law.* St. Paul: West, 1972.

ORFIELD, LESTER B. "The Defense of Entrapment in the Federal Courts." *Duke Law Journal* (1967): 39–71.

PARK, ROGER C. "The Entrapment Controversy." *Minnesota Law Review* 60 (1976): 163–274.

ROTENBERG, DANIEL L. "The Police Detection Practice of Encouragement." *Virginia Law Review* 49 (1963): 871–903.

TIFFANY, LAWRENCE P.; MCINTYRE, DONALD M.; and ROTENBERG, DANIEL L. *Detection of Crime: Stopping and Questioning, Search and Seizure, Encouragement and Entrapment.* Boston: Little, Brown, 1967.

U.S. National Commission on Reform of Federal Laws. *A Proposed New Federal Criminal Code.* Washington, D.C.: The Commission, 1970a.

——. *Working Papers.* Washington, D.C.: The Commission, 1970.

ENVIRONMENT AND CRIME

See CRIME PREVENTION: ENVIRONMENTAL AND TECHNOLOGICAL STRATEGIES; ECOLOGY OF CRIME.

EQUAL PROTECTION

See APPEAL; CRIMINAL PROCEDURE: CONSTITUTIONAL ASPECTS.

ESPIONAGE

See FEDERAL BUREAU OF INVESTIGATION: HISTORY; SEDITION.

ETHICS, LEGAL

See COUNSEL: ROLE OF COUNSEL; TRIAL, CRIMINAL.

ETHNIC GROUPS AND CRIME

See RACE AND CRIME.

EUROPEAN LAW

See CRIMINAL LAW REFORM: CONTINENTAL EUROPE; CRIMINAL PROCEDURE: COMPARATIVE ASPECTS; PROSECUTION: COMPARATIVE ASPECTS; TORTURE.

EUTHANASIA

The translation of the Greek word *euthanasia*—"easy death"—contains an ambiguity. It connotes that the means responsible for death are painless, so that the death is an easy one. But it also suggests that the death sought would be a relief from a distressing or intolerable condition of living (or dying), so that death, and not merely the means through which it is achieved, is good or right in itself. Usually, both aspects are intended when the term *euthanasia* is used; but when that is not the case, there can be consequences in legal analysis. The term is sometimes used to describe a program of painless killing carried out for the alleged benefit of the state (such as the Nazi program), but the present discussion is limited to single acts thought to be justified on grounds of beneficence to the subject (Foot, pp. 84–85).

Occasionally, criminal charges have been brought for an act described by the prosecutor as euthanasia; conversely, the term has been used by defendants to justify or excuse an act. There are, however, very few examples of convictions in circumstances where euthanasia has been established, and in any event, it is not actually a category in the criminal law, comparable to larceny or assault. Nevertheless, the term is used so loosely that it has been raised in numerous criminal cases; moreover, with modern medical technology capable of keeping dying patients alive for long periods, a form of euthanasia is widely thought to be practiced in many hospitals (Crane, p. 206).

Conceptual analysis

Euthanasia can be analyzed in several different ways. One of the most widely accepted views is to divide euthanasia four ways, by the intersection of two sets of variables: voluntary or nonvoluntary, and active or passive. The first of these distinctions may refer either to the act taken to bring about death or to the result itself; in most situations, the term *voluntary* or *nonvoluntary* must refer to the result in order to make sense. The second distinction rests more on the act or means employed.

Voluntary versus nonvoluntary. The term *voluntary* is used here simply to denote that the act or result proceeds from the will of the act's subject, or at least with his consent. It does not resolve the question of whether the subject was free from all sense of coercion by the circumstances or the wishes of others—in other words, whether the choice of euthanasia was an instance of unconstrained self-determination. If voluntariness in the latter sense is important to the ethical or legal licitness of a particular instance of euthanasia, it will require full exploration. *Voluntary* euthanasia is merely meant as a contrast with *nonvoluntary* euthanasia, in which the act or result is not grounded on the wish or consent of the subject.

Active versus passive. The distinction between active and passive euthanasia (sometimes phrased as "commission" versus "omission") is also useful in making a first division of the subject, but like the previous distinction, it may conceal as much as it reveals. Euthanasia is said to be *passive* when death occurs because a treatment that could hold off a life-threatening condition is omitted, and *active* when a human intervention directly causes or accelerates death in a person who would otherwise not die at that time from other causes. The distinction is usually advanced to support the view that the passive form is permissible even when direct killing would usually not be acceptable, since in passive euthanasia a human act is not the immediate cause of death (Joseph Fletcher). Indeed, in an attempt to avoid entirely the pejorative connotations of the term *euthanasia*, other descriptions have been coined for this category, such as *allowing to die* and (by transposing the Greek term into Latin) *benemortesia*.

Problems with the active/passive categorization

arise on both the descriptive and the ethical level. Descriptively, it is difficult to know how certain behavior should be characterized. For example, the claim that disconnecting a mechanical respirator is "passive" (because those who are treating the patient are merely stepping aside and allowing nature to take its course) is challenged on the ground that a physical act—"pulling the plug"—is required. For the people involved, there may be a psychological or emotional distinction between stopping treatment and not starting it, but it has little to offer analytically.

Further, it is usually recognized that not every act of withdrawing medical care can be termed passive if that word is meant to signify moral acceptability. For example, although it might be descriptively accurate to say that death would occur passively if normal sustenance were withdrawn from a newborn (in contrast to a baby who is poisoned), passive euthanasia's usual connotation of moral acceptability would not necessarily apply. The characterization of an action as active or passive requires a moral, as well as a purely descriptive, appraisal of the situation because it relates to distinct virtues or duties (Foot, p. 92). That moral evaluation is continually made more complicated by medical developments which do not always translate easily into traditional categories. For example, in what sense is the withdrawal of a tracheotomy tube providing the oxygen necessary for a patient's survival more or less "passive" than the withdrawal of a similar tube providing liquid nutriment?

The moral problems with the active/passive distinction go beyond the difficulty of knowing how to characterize a particular act. The whole grounding of the argument is challenged by the claim that in many circumstances the justification for ceasing treatment is not merely that it is futile but that the patient ought not to have to suffer any longer. Yet in some situations, the mere withdrawal of treatment will not ensure a patient a quick and painless death; an incurable illness can be life-threatening without meaning that death will occur within hours or even days once treatment is stopped. If the suffering of the patient provides a moral justification for passive euthanasia, it is argued that this also justifies active euthanasia, or "mercy killing" for a suffering patient who lacks the "blessing" of a disease that will kill rapidly once treatment is withdrawn (Rachels). Whatever the persuasive value of this argument in ethical theory, it overlooks the medical fact that in only a few cases is it not possible to relieve the pain of a dying patient. Nor has it been accepted in the law, which continues to exclude active killing from the category of the legally permissible.

Basic categories. For all the difficulty in applying these sets of distinctions, the four-way categorization they create provides a basic understanding of the subject. *Active, voluntary* euthanasia is the taking of a person's life directly by himself or by another on his instruction in a way that is painless and that provides a relief from a painful or debilitating condition, typically one that has been diagnosed as a terminal disease. *Passive, voluntary* euthanasia is the intentional foregoing of life-sustaining treatment by a person himself or by another who would otherwise provide such treatment when nontreatment will bring about or accelerate death from other (usually natural) causes. Although often accompanied by medical, psychological, or spiritual attention intended to make dying as easy as possible, this type of death is called "easy" because it represents a release from the suffering imposed by further treatment rather than because it is necessarily painless. Although clearly very different, these two categories of euthanasia share the important characteristic that both are premised on the choice of the patient. Given the importance of voluntariness in both Judeo-Christian ethical theory and Anglo-American law, this characteristic is clearly of great significance. Of course, voluntariness does not in itself paint a full picture morally or legally. The active taking of one's own life, for example, is disapproved in most moral and legal systems, although there is a tendency to make only the act of aiding and abetting, and not suicide itself, a felony. The more willful the act, the less likely it is to be acceptable; those who take their own lives under great duress or under the pressures of mental illness are less likely to be blamed. Similarly, under extreme circumstances taking another person's life may be ethically acceptable—for example, finishing off a gravely wounded comrade-in-arms whose condition precludes his being taken along by a retreating army and who begs not to be left to the mercies of a brutal enemy.

Passive, nonvoluntary euthanasia is the intentional foregoing of life-sustaining treatment by someone who would otherwise provide it, so that death is brought about or accelerated from other (usually natural) causes. It occurs most commonly in the decision-making of family and physicians with regard to dying patients who are unconscious or otherwise unable to participate in deciding about their own treatment. Nonvoluntariness in this case merely means that the deceased cannot be said to have *directed* that treatment be withdrawn or not commenced. The category is not, however, that of *involuntary* cessation of treatment, in the sense of actions done contrary to the will of the patient. *Active, nonvoluntary* euthanasia is the direct taking of a person's life by another acting without explicit instructions from the person, in a way that is painless and that provides relief from an unsatisfactory situation, usually one involving terminal disease.

It is useful to keep these four categories in mind; otherwise, it is very easy for two people discussing euthanasia to be talking about very different subjects. But the clarity of the concepts is far from blinding. Indeed, the law on the entire subject is noticeably unclear. Although it has been asserted that "euthanasia, whether voluntary or involuntary, whether by affirmative act or by omission, is a violation of existing criminal law" (Gurney), the law is actually less definite in both theory and practice.

Active taking of life

One point that at first appears clear is that an affirmative act to terminate a human life is murder, usually in the first degree (Morris). If an accused attempts to defend himself on the ground that the act was a "mercy killing," he has on the face of it chosen a weak argument, for four reasons.

First, such a killing, done to relieve the victim's suffering, is usually done only after careful thought. Such deliberateness would be more than enough to establish the premeditation that is an element of first-degree murder. Second, the fact that the victim requested—or even pleaded—to be killed does not defeat the charge. Unlike the civil law, the criminal law does not usually recognize the consent of the victim as a defense. Homicide, in particular, is not a victimless crime. Furthermore, consent will often be difficult to ascertain, and a rule of law that excused homicides on this ground would be in great danger of abuse (Kamisar).

Third, in objecting to a charge of murder on the ground that he had actually committed euthanasia, the heart of a defendant's plea would be that his motive for killing was beneficent, not venal. The common law, however, long ago gave a special meaning to "malice aforethought" in homicide law; it merely means to kill intentionally (George Fletcher). As important as compassionate motives may be to a layman's evaluation of the rightness or wrongness of an act, they play no part in the law's definition of whether a crime has been committed.

A fourth factor that is often present in cases of mercy killing—the imminence of death from the underlying disease or injury—is similarly of no merit in defeating a charge of murder. Courts have repeatedly held that any active shortening of life constitutes homicide, no matter how brief a time the victim would have lived if the defendant had not acted. To excuse a killing of a person with ten minutes left to live opens the door to excusing a killing when the victim would have lived an hour, or a day, and so forth.

The practical objections to the argument of imminent death are perhaps even stronger. Medicine is at best an uncertain science; even a definitive diagnosis does not ensure an accurate prognosis. In addition, there is always the chance of a new medical development that could alter a bleak picture and offer hope of recovery or at least a longer period of survival (Kamisar).

Moreover, the imminence of death is a double-edged sword for advocates of active euthanasia. The less time a person has to live (according to the best medical prognosis), the less need there would be to take his life. If the prognosis is correct, death will come quickly; if it turns out to be mistaken, an act to terminate life would have been taken on a false premise.

Double effect. Of course, the remaining period of life may be burdened by great pain. This factor is at the heart of most arguments in favor of mercy killing. As an empirical matter, however, it is doubtful that many such cases would occur if medicine's ability to relieve pain were carefully applied (John Fletcher, p. 305). To be sure, being free of pain does not necessarily mean that one's existence is good and that one has his full physical and mental powers. The goal of relieving suffering is receiving increasing attention by health professionals, and informal strictures against the use of certain analgesics (on the ground, for example, that they are addictive) are being discarded as irrelevant in the care of dying patients.

It is a well-known fact, however, that the use of potent painkillers (especially opiates) can accelerate the moment of death, typically by depressing respiration or interfering with the gag reflex. Might the use of such means to relieve pain themselves constitute active euthanasia—and, hence, amount to first-degree murder? Roman Catholic theologians and others who steadfastly oppose active killing nonetheless do not label as homicide those cases in which patients cease breathing while receiving progressively higher doses of analgesics (Sacred Congregation, p. 9). Under the "principle of double effect," the physician's intent is said to be one of ministering to the patient's suffering; in so doing, the physician may cause the second effect of bringing about the patient's demise, but that is not the physician's objective. In other words, death is a foreseen but unintended consequence of a medical act sufficiently justified by its other benefits to the patient (Sullivan, pp. 38–39). Although the law usually holds people accountable for the consequences of their acts that are reasonably foreseeable, the absence of prosecutions of physicians for providing necessary painkillers to dying patients indicates an apparent acceptance of this theoretically tenuous distinction between a goal and a consequence.

The law in practice. As the double-effect doctrine suggests, the law on active euthanasia does not look the same in practice as it does in theory with regard to any of the four points discussed above. Actions taken after conscientious deliberation to end the life of a patient who begged to be relieved of suffering when the medical prognosis was bleak usually result in nonprosecution or acquittal or, if conviction occurs, in lenient treatment. This is not to say that mercy killing is not murder, but merely that there are wide variations in the law's application (Sanders).

What may well constitute the greatest difference between theory and practice—the exercise of prosecutorial discretion not to bring charges—is the hardest to document. In light of the difficulty that prosecutors have in convicting accused mercy killers, it would not be surprising if one were to discover that they often elect not to prosecute. This is so especially when the killing takes the form of an assisted suicide, in which the dying person is not merely a voluntary participant but also an active agent in causing the death.

Acquittal. The trend in public opinion and in medical practice toward regarding mercy killing as acceptable in certain circumstances—for example, in the case of terminal patients in great pain without hope of relief or recovery—is reflected in the acquittal of some defendants in the teeth of what otherwise would be regarded as confessions of guilt. In the two American cases in which physicians were accused of giving dying patients lethal injections, the juries acquitted because the prosecution had not proved beyond a reasonable doubt that the deceased was alive at the moment the injections took effect (Meyers, p. 53). Some commentators regard this as a strength of Anglo-American jurisprudence; the jurors can give a merciful acquittal in breach of their oaths when they find it warranted by the totality of the circumstances (Kamisar, pp. 971–972). Acquittals by judges have also taken place in American as well as continental cases (Maguire, pp. 24, 40). It is sometimes noted, in defense of this result, that defendants in these cases are unlikely to be recidivists.

Defendants who are relatives of the deceased are more likely to be found not guilty on grounds of insanity than on factual grounds. Typically, the jury's finding of insanity is not based on psychiatric testimony,

and it is followed immediately by the judge's determination that the defendant is no longer insane and can be released.

Sentencing. In sentencing defendants convicted of mercy killing, judges often take into account factors that the law nominally excludes in determining criminality—the deceased's wishes, the closeness of a painful death, and the agony the defendant has already experienced. In some countries, the penal code makes explicit provision for punishment to be mitigated when the defendant acted out of "honorable motives" (Silving). As with the variations in prosecution and conviction, one can see the sentencing system as either wonderfully flexible or dangerously arbitrary. It is indisputable that essentially similar acts of mercy killing have been punished very differently (Sanders, pp. 355–357). The further consequences of conviction—such as whether mercy killing is a crime involving "moral turpitude," as homicide otherwise would be—are also uncertain (*Repouille v. United States*, 165 F.2d 152 (2d Cir. 1947)).

Foregoing treatment

The question of whether criminal homicide has occurred when a patient dies after a possibly life-prolonging treatment has been foregone has not been accorded a clear answer by Anglo-American law. As late as the mid-1960s, the answer might have been decided on the basis of the distinction between acts and omissions, meaning that if ceasing treatment were deemed an act, it would be that of first-degree murder (George Fletcher). This view is still held by some public officials (Paris and McCormick). But the trend is toward asking instead (1) whether the defendant had a duty to treat, and (2) whether the deceased did not want treatment instituted or continued.

Duty to treat. There are two main sources of a duty to treat whose omission may be criminal. The first grows out of family obligations, particularly the duties owed by parents to their children to provide sustenance and care. These duties are imposed by the law; their violation exposes not only parents, but those who aid them or who, bound by additional responsibilities, fail to correct the parents' wrong, to liability for child neglect and abuse, as well as for homicide. The few reported instances of successful prosecution did not, however, arise as cases of euthanasia but merely from parents' failure to seek or utilize reasonable medical care that would probably have saved their child's life (Robertson). The second duty is more contingent; it is the obligation of physicians and other health professionals to provide care to a patient when a physician-patient relationship exists or a patient has a reasonable expectation that the physician will render aid.

When, in light of the burgeoning ability of medicine to resuscitate patients and to prolong biological functioning, is an omission of care punishable because it breaches one of these duties? Plainly, maximum care need not be provided in every case. Ethicists have analyzed this issue with respect to ordinary and extraordinary treatments—the former denominating care that is obligatory; the latter, that which is optional. Although these terms have recently come into use by the courts, the more familiar formulation is to ask whether the conduct in question, that is, foregoing treatment in a particular instance, was reasonable. This points to several criteria of decision.

First, it is clearly reasonable to forego treatment that will be futile in curing the illness, restoring the patient's ability to function, or prolonging life for more than a brief period. Equally clearly, these will be factual questions that may engender considerable disagreement in each case. Moreover, the final issue is conceptually uncertain: How long must a treatment be capable of sustaining bodily functioning—although it will neither cure the patient nor restore his ability to function independently—in order for it not to be regarded as futile?

The second set of criteria turns on the notion of proportionality (McCormick). This is the gist of the idea behind the ordinary/extraordinary distinction. Although those terms may suggest that the reference point is the novelty, prevalence, artificiality, or expense of a treatment, the proportionality concept is less sociological than individual. That is, the issue becomes one of balancing the gains of treatment against its costs. The primary measure is the patient's own well-being, psychological as well as physical. For example, kidney dialysis would seem to be a reasonable treatment for a person with renal failure who is otherwise healthy, but it would not seem unreasonable to forego it if renal failure occurs in a cancer patient who has lapsed into a permanent coma. Similarly, the suffering a patient will endure under a particular regimen must be considered in the balance, including the distress felt by the patient because of any limitations on his ability to interact with others or because of the burdens placed on relatives. It has also been suggested that it is legitimate to take directly into account the burdens and suffering imposed on close relatives by continued treatment (Williams, 1958, pp. 1–2).

Refusals of treatment. The second ground on which a decision about the culpability of nontreatment

resulting in death will often turn is whether the treatment was opposed by the patient. In certain circumstances, a patient may object to the treatment itself, as when a Jehovah's Witness refuses blood transfusions. These are not really instances of euthanasia at all, although the judicial decisions in such cases may be found to apply to those in which a patient refuses treatment because he finds his condition intolerable and would rather be dead than continue treatment that "prolongs dying."

At one time American courts, in contrast to both secular and religious ethicists, tended to regard refusals of life-sustaining treatment as akin to suicide (*In re President and Directors of Georgetown College, Inc.,* 331 F.2d 1000 (D.C. Cir. 1964)). It is now generally recognized that a competent patient's refusal of treatment does not expose the patient or those involved in implementing his decision to liability, criminal or civil. An issue remains, however, about the circumstances in which treatment of an incompetent patient, such as a child or someone incapacitated by illness, may be omitted on the instructions of someone else, for example, the next of kin. This problem has been addressed by courts and legislatures.

Judicial decisions. Although prosecutions have been threatened in cases in which nontreatment of an incompetent person led to death, actual judicial decisions are limited to cases in which injunctions or declaratory judgments were sought in order to obtain prospective judicial determination of the legality of a certain course of conduct. In deciding these cases, the courts have agreed neither on the grounds for their conclusions nor on the procedures that must be followed for a decision to be legally acceptable. In the landmark decision *In re Quinlan,* 70 N.J. 10, 355 A.2d 647 (1976), the New Jersey Supreme Court held that a constitutional right of privacy protects a patient's right to refuse even life-sustaining treatment and that this right is not extinguished by the patient's inability to exercise it personally. When the attending physician concludes that further treatment will not return a patient to cognitive existence, the next of kin may order treatment ceased. The decision need not be reviewed by a judge but should be concurred in by a hospital "ethics committee," which is actually charged with verifying the accuracy of the physician's prognosis. Since there can be no breach of a duty to forego a treatment that the patient may properly refuse by proxy, the New Jersey court explicitly held that those participating in or implementing such a decision would not be guilty of homicide.

The Supreme Judicial Court of Massachusetts, in another leading case, *Superintendent of Belchertown State*

School v. Saikewicz, 373 Mass. 728, 370 N.E.2d. 417 (1977), also approved treatment termination for an incompetent patient, but it insisted that such decisions were acceptable only if first approved by a court of competent jurisdiction. In subsequent opinions, the court has backed away from this absolute position and recognized that many medical decisions which might be fatal for a patient, such as an order not to resuscitate if a dying patient experiences a cardiac arrest, can be reached without prior judicial approval.

A substantive rule that would open up a much broader range of conduct to criminal prosecution was adopted by the New York Court of Appeals in *Matter of Storar*, 52 N.Y.2d 363, 420 N.E.2d 64 (1981). The court held that the treatment of a presently incapacitated patient could be terminated only if there was clear evidence that the patient had stated when competent that he would want treatment terminated under the circumstances. Consequently, treatment may not be ceased for those patients, such as children and the permanently mentally impaired, who were never competent decision-makers—as well as for formerly competent persons who have simply failed to make their views clear.

Legislation. In the wake of Karen Quinlan's tragedy, the wide attention paid to the plight of patients who become permanently unconscious or otherwise hopeless generated legislative action beginning in the late 1970s. Usually called "natural death acts" after the first statute adopted in 1976 in California (Cal. Health & Safety Code §§ 7185–7195 (1982 Supp.)), the statutes were originally intended simply to give the force of law to so-called living wills, by which a person places limitations on the life-prolonging care to which he wishes to be subjected when there is no reasonable chance of recovery. Such advance directions have been criticized because of the inherent limitations in anyone's ability to anticipate how he would feel under such circumstances in the future. It is also noted, however, that the pain and treatment that are often part of terminal illness make it risky to rely on decisions made as the end nears, because the patient may then no longer be of sound mind (Kamisar).

The attempt to transform living wills from moral advice to legally binding directions met with many problems because the legislative desire "to permit the natural process of dying" could not easily be reconciled with the concern not "to condone, authorize or approve mercy killing" (Kan. Stat. Ann. § 65-28. 109 (1980)). It is doubtful whether the natural-death acts have actually changed the law in the way their sponsors intended (Capron). If they are effective, they have two consequences for the criminal law: first, no

action taken pursuant to a valid directive would constitute homicide or suicide (or the aiding thereof); and second, intentional disobedience to a directive is, under most of the statutes, a criminal violation of varying gravity.

Despite the confusion that has attended both judicial decisions and legislation, it is apparent that decisions are regularly made to cease, or not to commence, treatment for incompetent as well as competent dying patients, and that prosecutions in such cases are infrequently brought. Injunctions are sometimes sought where the health-care providers disagree with the decision of the next of kin or where a representative of the state, such as a prosecutor or child welfare official, believes that the action planned by the health providers with the family's concurrence would violate the law. However, reported criminal convictions for nonvoluntary, passive euthanasia are virtually nonexistent. The continuing threat of liability may nonetheless help ensure that decision-making is cautious and protects life whenever treatment will be reasonably efficacious (Burt).

ALEXANDER MORGAN CAPRON

See also HOMICIDE: LEGAL ASPECTS; JUSTIFICATION: NECESSITY; SUICIDE: LEGAL ASPECTS; VICTIMLESS CRIME.

BIBLIOGRAPHY

BURT, ROBERT A. *Taking Care of Strangers: The Rule of Law in Doctor-Patient Relations.* New York: Free Press, 1979.

CAPRON, ALEXANDER M. "The Development of Law on Human Death." *Annals of the New York Academy of Sciences* 315 (1978): 45–61.

CRANE, DIANA. *The Sanctity of Social Life: Physicians' Treatment of Critically Ill Patients.* New York: Russell Sage, 1975.

FLETCHER, GEORGE P. "Prolonging Life." *Washington Law Review* 42 (1967): 999–1016.

FLETCHER, JOHN C. "Is Euthanasia Ever Justifiable?" *Controversies in Oncology.* Edited by Peter H. Wiernik. New York: Wiley, 1982, pp. 297–321.

FLETCHER, JOSEPH F. *Morals and Medicine—The Moral Problems of: The Patient's Right to Know the Truth, Contraception, Artificial Insemination, Sterilization, Euthanasia.* Foreword by Karl Menninger. Princeton, N.J.: Princeton University Press, 1954.

FOOT, PHILIPPA. "Euthanasia." *Philosophy and Public Affairs* 6 (1977): 85–112.

GURNEY, EDWARD J. "Is There a Right to Die?: A Study of the Law of Euthanasia." *Cumberland-Samford Law Review* 3 (1972): 235–261.

KAMISAR, YALE. "Some Non-religious Views against Proposed 'Mercy-killing' Legislation." *Minnesota Law Review* 42 (1958): 969–1042. A leading account of the pragmatic, largely utilitarian objections to active euthanasia.

MAGUIRE, DANIEL C. *Death by Choice.* Garden City, N.Y.; Doubleday, 1974. A Catholic theologian's forceful argument for a change in law and social attitudes toward death and dying, including provision for active taking of life under certain circumstances.

McCormick, Richard A. *Ambiguity in Moral Choice*. Milwaukee, Wis.: Marquette University Press, 1973.

Meyers, David W. "The Legal Aspects of Voluntary Medical Euthanasia." *The Dilemmas of Euthanasia*. Edited by John A. Behnke and Sissela Bok. Garden City, N.Y.: Doubleday, Anchor Books, pp. 51–67.

Morris, Arval A. "Voluntary Euthanasia." *Washington Law Review* 45 (1970): 239–271. Contrasts existing law with arguments in favor of permitting free choice to have painless, dignified death.

Paris, John J., and McCormick, Richard A. "Living-will Legislation, Reconsidered." *America* 145 (1981): 86–89.

Rachels, James. "Active and Passive Euthanasia." *New England Journal of Medicine* 292 (1975): 78–80.

Robertson, John A. "Involuntary Euthanasia of Defective Newborns: A Legal Analysis." *Stanford Law Review* 27 (1975): 213–269.

Sacred Congregation for the Doctrine of the Faith. *Declaration on Euthanasia*. Vatican City, 1980.

Sanders, Joseph. "Euthanasia: None Dare Call It Murder." *Journal of Criminal Law, Criminology, and Police Science* 60 (1969): 351–359. Demonstrates the diversity of treatment received by "mercy killing" defendants.

Silving, Helen. "Euthanasia: A Study in Comparative Criminal Law." *University of Pennsylvania Law Review* 103 (1954): 350–389.

Sullivan, Joseph V. *The Morality of Mercy Killing*. Foreword by Francis J. Connell. Westminster, Md.: Newman, 1950.

Veatch, Robert M. *Death, Dying, and the Biological Revolution: Our Last Quest for Responsibility*. New Haven: Yale University Press, 1976.

Williams, Glanville. " 'Mercy Killing' Legislation: A Rejoinder." *Minnesota Law Review* 43 (1958): 1–12.

———. *The Sanctity of Life and the Criminal Law*. Foreword by William C. Warren. New York: Knopf, 1957.

EVIDENCE

See Adversary System; Corpus Delicti; Criminal Procedure: constitutional aspects; Discovery; Exclusionary Rules.

EXCLUSIONARY RULES

An "exclusionary rule" is a rule that generally operates to exclude from admission at a criminal trial evidence obtained as a result of unlawful activity by law enforcement officers or their agents. The purpose of such a rule is to keep the judiciary from acquiescing in police misconduct and to deter the police from participating in unlawful activity. The rule is most commonly used to deter violations of the Constitution's Fourth Amendment restrictions on "unreasonable searches and seizures" and Fifth Amendment restrictions on police interrogation. The Fifth Amendment requires, as a result of Supreme Court rulings, that an arrested individual not be questioned before being given the "*Miranda* warnings," a brief recitation of applicable constitutional rights.

Origins of the exclusionary rule

The Supreme Court decision usually credited with establishing the use of an exclusionary rule is *Weeks v. United States*, 232 U.S. 383 (1914). In *Weeks*, police officers searched Weeks's room and seized a number of his papers and possessions for later use as evidence in a criminal trial against him. Since the search was undertaken without a search warrant or other legal justification and thus was unconstitutional, the Supreme Court ruled that the evidence seized should not be admitted at trial. The Court reasoned:

The tendency of those who execute the criminal laws of the country to obtain conviction by means of unlawful seizures and enforced confessions, the latter often obtained after subjecting accused persons to unwarranted practices destructive of rights secured by the Federal Constitution, should find no sanction in the judgments of the courts which are charged at all times with the support of the Constitution and to which people of all conditions have a right to appeal for the maintenance of such fundamental rights [*Weeks*, 392].

The *Weeks* decision only established an exclusionary rule in federal courts; it was nearly half a century later before an exclusionary rule was applied by the Supreme Court to state court proceedings. Indeed, for many years federal law enforcement authorities avoided the effect of the federal rule by obtaining evidence unconstitutionally and turning it over to state authorities "on a silver platter" for use in those states where there was no counterpart to the federal exclusionary rule, but in 1960 this practice was held to be unconstitutional (*Elkins v. United States*, 364 U.S. 206 (1960)). A year later, the Court held, in its landmark decision in *Mapp v. Ohio*, 367 U.S. 643 (1961), that the exclusionary rule also applied to state court proceedings.

The facts in *Mapp* graphically illustrate why the Supreme Court determined that an exclusionary rule was vitally necessary to protect and preserve constitutional rights from destruction through police misconduct. Three Cleveland police officers had attempted to gain entrance to Mapp's house because they claimed to have obtained information from an un-named source that she was concealing a fugitive, as well as evidence of illegal gambling. After being re-fused entrance by Mapp, the officers waited outside the house for several hours before finally forcing their way in by breaking down the back door. Although Mapp's attorney had arrived at the scene by this time, other police officers denied him admission to the home to consult with his client. As for Mapp herself, she demanded to see a search warrant as the police officers broke in, and when one of the officers flour-ished a piece of paper in response, she immediately grabbed it and placed it inside her dress. At this point a vigorous struggle ensued, as a result of which the officers recovered the paper from Mapp's clothing (no warrant was ever offered into evidence and proba-bly never existed) and handcuffed her to restrain her further. She was then forced to accompany the officers as they searched her house from top to bottom, pur-portedly looking for the fugitive and the gambling materials, neither of which was ever found. The police did, however, find "obscene materials" in the course of their search of the house, and Mapp was tried and convicted in the Ohio courts for possessing them.

As the Supreme Court explained in *Mapp*, it really had no choice but to impose an exclusionary rule in these circumstances:

Were it otherwise, then just as without the *Weeks* rule the assurance against unreasonable federal searches and sei-zures would be "a form of words," valueless and undeserv-ing of mention in a perpetual charter of inestimable human liberties, so too, without that rule the freedom from state invasions of privacy would be so ephemeral and so neatly severed from its conceptual nexus with the freedom from all brutish means of coercing evidence as not to merit this Court's high regard as a freedom "implicit in the concept of ordered liberty" [655].

Five years later, in *Miranda v. Arizona*, 384 U.S. 436 (1966), the Supreme Court also permitted application of an exclusionary rule to assure protection of Fifth Amendment rights when an individual is interrogated by the police while in police custody without having first received warnings about his constitutional rights.

State and statutory exclusionary rules

A number of states had adopted exclusionary rules prior to the *Mapp* decision. In some, they were enacted by the legislature, but in most instances, they resulted from judicial interpretation of state constitutional law, judicially declared rules of evidence, or exercise of the "supervisory powers" authority that state supreme courts traditionally or constitutionally possess to su-pervise lower courts. Since the *Mapp* decision in 1961, other state courts have concluded that an exclusionary rule is required as a matter of state law as well. As a result, even if the Supreme Court were to overrule *Mapp*, many states would still have an exclusionary rule in force as a matter of settled state law.

There are also exclusionary rules established by leg-islative action, as in Title III of the Omnibus Crime Control and Safe Streets Act of 1968, 18 U.S.C. §§ 2510–2520 (1976 & Supp. III 1979). Title III is a comprehensive statute that bars private wiretapping and other forms of electronic surveillance and strictly regulates such activity on the part of law enforcement officers. In Section 2518(10)(a) of Title III, Congress provided that any person who was harmed by a viola-tion of that act had the statutory right to an exclusion-ary remedy with respect to evidence seized as a result of that violation. Even if there were no judicially estab-lished exclusionary rules in existence, legislative rules such as this one would continue to apply unless, and until, they were repealed by the legislative bodies that enacted them.

Scope of the rules

The exclusionary rule that the Supreme Court fash-ioned in *Weeks* and *Mapp* is only applicable in carefully limited and narrowly defined settings. Indeed, some commentators have argued that the Supreme Court has in effect destroyed any possible deterrent effect on police misconduct which the rule might possibly have by systematically narrowing the range of its ap-plication.

Unconstitutional acts by the government. The exclusionary rule only applies to unconstitutional acts performed by employees of a governmental body, usually law enforcement officers. This is known as the "state action" requirement. However, there are exceptions. For example, if the person who committed the act in question was an "agent" of a government employee, the exclusionary rule does apply, in order to deter the employee from engaging in such conduct, albeit at second hand. Similarly, if the police perform an unconstitutional act jointly with private citizens, the exclusionary rule applies, no matter which party actually procured the evidence in question.

Some states have modified or eliminated this state-action requirement as a matter of state law. The Mon-tana Supreme Court, for example, has concluded that the individual privacy protections in the Montana Constitution are so strong that they mandate use of an exclusionary rule to deter private illegal actions, such as that of the person who trespasses in his neighbor's yard and discovers marijuana, which he then turns over to the police. Certain other jurisdictions have extended an exclusionary rule to illegal searches by private security guards.

The exclusionary rule applies only if the conduct in question was unconstitutional, whether or not it was performed by a government employee. As for acts that are constitutionally permissible but are sometimes prohibited by statute or administrative regulation (for example, surreptitiously monitoring a conversation by concealing a transmitter on a police agent without court approval), some states apply their own exclusionary rules more broadly to deter such acts.

Criminal proceedings. The exclusionary rule is not available to defendants in all judicial proceedings. This is because "the application of the rule has been restricted to those areas where its remedial objectives are thought most efficaciously served" (*United States v. Calandra*, 414 U.S. 338, 348 (1974)).

The Supreme Court in *Calandra* ruled that someone called upon to testify before a grand jury investigating criminal activity had no right to avoid being questioned on the basis of unconstitutionally seized evidence, because the exclusionary rule simply did not apply in that setting. The Court reasoned:

Whatever deterrence of police misconduct may result from the exclusion of illegally seized evidence from criminal trials, it is unrealistic to assume that application of the rule to grand jury proceedings would significantly further that goal. . . .

In the context of a grand jury proceeding, . . . the damage to that institution from the unprecedented extension of the exclusionary rule . . . outweighs the benefit of any possible incremental deterrent effect [351, 354].

The Supreme Court's conclusion that application of the exclusionary rule would not have a significant enough deterrent effect to warrant its use in settings other than criminal trials has been extended beyond the grand jury room. In *United States v. Janis*, 428 U.S. 433 (1976), for example, the Court permitted evidence seized illegally by the Los Angeles police to be used in a civil proceeding for back taxes brought in federal court by the Internal Revenue Service. The Court reasoned that use of the exclusionary rule in such cases does not provide "a sufficient likelihood of deterring the conduct of the state police so that it outweighs the societal costs imposed by the exclusion" (454). The Court did not have occasion to answer the more significant question of whether the exclusionary rule would apply if state police improperly seized evidence later used in state civil proceedings, or if federal police improperly seized evidence later used in federal civil proceedings.

In another significant decision, the Supreme Court also refused to allow the exclusionary rule to be applied in a different noncriminal trial setting. In *Stone v. Powell*, 428 U.S. 465 (1976), the Court ruled that the Fourth Amendment exclusionary rule was not available to a federal habeas corpus petitioner after a state court had allowed the petitioner, already convicted in state court, a "full and fair" opportunity for a hearing on his Fourth Amendment claims. In such a collateral, post-conviction setting, a majority of the Supreme Court concluded that application of the exclusionary rule was unnecessary in the interest of deterrence: "There is no reason to believe . . . that the overall educative effect of the exclusionary rule would be appreciably diminished if search-and-seizure claims could not be raised in federal habeas corpus review of state convictions" (*Stone*, 493).

In short, the Supreme Court has devised a calculus by which the applicability of the exclusionary rule in a given noncriminal or nontrial setting is determined by assessing whether use of the rule in such a setting adds more than slightly to the rule's deterrent effect on police misconduct. Some critics argue, however, that this approach ignores the cumulative effect of the many exceptions to the rule which it permits, that police officers may have "learned" that there are so many possibilities for subsequent use of illegally seized evidence (even though each of these uses is unlikely in and of itself) that the exclusionary rule's supposed educative effect is compromised.

There remain a few noncriminal areas in which the exclusionary rule may still be applied. In *One 1958 Plymouth Sedan v. Pennsylvania*, 380 U.S. 693 (1965), for example, the Supreme Court permitted use of the exclusionary rule in a "quasi-criminal" proceeding for forfeiture of a car used in violation of the criminal law. Whether this 1965 decision would withstand reconsideration by the Court under its "additional deterrent effect" test is an open question.

Standing. To be entitled to an exclusionary remedy, a criminal defendant must possess "standing" to complain about the constitutional violation. Such standing exists only if the defendant seeks to remedy a violation of his personal rights as opposed to a "vicarious" assertion of another's rights. As the Supreme Court has concluded in the Fourth Amendment setting:

Since the exclusionary rule is an attempt to effectuate the guarantees of the Fourth Amendment, . . . it is proper to permit only defendants whose Fourth Amendment rights have been violated to benefit from the rule's protections.

. . . There is no reason to think that a party whose rights have been infringed will not, if evidence is used against him, have ample motivation to move to suppress it. . . . Even if such a person is not a defendant in the action he may be able to recover damages for the violation of his Fourth Amendment rights . . . or seek redress under state law for invasion of privacy or trespass [*Rakas v. Illinois*, 439 U.S. 128, 134 (1978)].

A criminal defendant's constitutional rights are breached in a manner sufficient to establish standing if the constitutional harm is done to that defendant personally, or at a place (for example, his home) or to something (for example, his briefcase) where he has a "legitimate expectation of privacy."

Although this Supreme Court view became firmly established in the late 1970s, there are states that have adopted a contrary view. California, for example, has rejected a standing requirement in Fourth Amendment cases. As the California Supreme Court explained:

If law enforcement officers are allowed to evade the exclusionary rule by obtaining evidence in violation of the rights of third parties, its deterrent effect is to that extent nullified. . . . such a limitation virtually invites law enforcement officers to violate the rights of third parties and to trade the escape of a criminal whose rights are violated for the conviction of others by the use of the evidence illegally obtained against them [*People v. Martin*, 45 Cal. 2d 755, 290 P.2d 855, 857 (1955)].

Derivative evidence. Evidence that is "derived" from the government's unconstitutional acts is inadmissible in criminal proceedings under the exclusionary rule even when it has been obtained as an indirect, rather than a direct, result of the constitutional breach. For example, if the police search someone's home illegally and seize his diary, thereby obtaining information that leads them to search someone else's home to look for evidence, whatever evidence they find at the second home is "derivative" of the initial misconduct and is therefore, in Justice Felix Frankfurter's colorful phrase, "fruit of the poisonous tree." Such "fruits" are inadmissible under the exclusionary rule, at least in a criminal trial against a defendant such as the diarist in the preceding example, who has standing to raise the issue.

There are exceptions to this rule. As the Supreme Court held in *Wong Sun v. United States*, 371 U.S. 471, 488 (1963), the "question . . . is 'whether, granting establishment of the primary illegality, the evidence to which instant objection is made has been come at by exploitation of that illegality or instead by means sufficiently distinguishable to be purged of the primary taint.' " In *Wong Sun*, the Supreme Court, apply-

ing this test, ruled that an illegally arrested defendant nonetheless gave a subsequent statement to the police which was not subject to the exclusionary rule. The reason the statement was admissible was that the defendant had been released for several days before he voluntarily returned to the police station to talk. In such an instance the statement was not "the fruit" of the earlier illegal arrest, since "the connection between the arrest and the statement had 'become so attenuated as to dissipate the taint' " (491).

The Supreme Court has been careful, however, not to apply the *Wong Sun* test too broadly. In a 1975 case, for example, the Court concluded that when police officers give an illegally arrested defendant *Miranda* warnings, that act is not, in and of itself, sufficient "to purge the taint" of, or to "attenuate," the prior police misconduct. Accordingly, a statement made under such circumstances may be suppressed (*Brown v. Illinois*, 422 U.S. 590 (1975)).

Furthermore, although "verbal evidence" (for example, a defendant's statement) may be "the fruit of the poisonous tree," the same rules do not hold true when a defendant seeks to exclude the testimony of witnesses who were illegally discovered by the police. The Supreme Court has concluded that "the greater the willingness of the witness to freely testify, the greater the likelihood that he or she will be discovered by legal means and, concomitantly, the smaller the incentive to conduct an illegal search to discover the witness." Since there is therefore less deterrent necessity to exclude such testimony, "a closer, more direct link between the illegality and [live-witness] testimony is required" before the exclusionary rule may be applied (*United States v. Ceccolini*, 435 U.S. 268, 276, 278 (1978)).

Impeachment.

Testimonial evidence. Statements made by a defendant that may be suppressed at trial because they were obtained illegally for failure to give *Miranda* warnings may, however, become admissible at that same trial if the defendant takes the stand and testifies in a way which contradicts those excluded statements. The use of illegally seized statements in this fashion is termed "impeachment," since the purpose of allowing the statements in evidence is strictly to impeach the defendant's credibility; the statements are not permitted to be a part of the prosecution's direct proof of the defendant's guilt (its so-called case in chief). As the Supreme Court has reasoned:

The impeachment process [provides] valuable aid to the jury in assessing [the defendant's] credibility, and the benefits of this process should not be lost, in our view, because of the speculative possibility that impermissible police conduct will be encouraged thereby. Assuming that the exclusionary rule has a deterrent effect on proscribed police conduct, sufficient deterrence flows when the evidence in question is made unavailable to the prosecution in its case in chief [*Harris v. New York*, 401 U.S. 222, 225 (1971)].

The *Harris* decision proved controversial and has been rejected by some states that, as a matter of state law, have declined to allow a defendant to be impeached on the basis of statements obtained in violation of *Miranda*. Many of these state decisions reflect the critical reasoning of Justice William Brennan, who argued, in his *Harris* dissent, that the decision undermined the deterrent purposes of the exclusionary rule by telling "the police that they may freely interrogate an accused incommunicado and without counsel and know that although any statement they obtain in violation of *Miranda* cannot be used on the State's direct case, it may be introduced if the defendant has the temerity to testify in his own defense" (232).

Physical evidence. Despite Justice Brennan's fears—which are shared by other judges and critics—a majority of the Supreme Court has reaffirmed its *Harris* ruling in the related context of impeachment based on physical evidence obtained as the result of police misconduct under the Fourth Amendment. In *United States v. Havens*, 446 U.S. 620 (1980), the defendant's trial testimony that he did not own certain incriminating items of clothing was, in the Court's view, properly impeached by the prosecution, which gained admission of illegally seized clothing to contradict the defendant's testimony. As the Court reasoned: "We have repeatedly insisted that when defendants testify, they must testify truthfully or suffer the consequences. . . . the ends of the exclusionary rules [are] adequately implemented by denying the government the use of the challenged evidence to make out its case in chief" (626, 627).

Criticisms of the exclusionary rule

General. The adoption of an exclusionary rule by the Supreme Court has attracted some heated judicial reaction. Perhaps the most frequently repeated criticism of the rule is Justice (then New York Court of Appeals Chief Judge) Benjamin Cardozo's pithy comment on the rule's illogicality as a remedial device: "The criminal is to go free because the constable has blundered" (*People v. Defore*, 242 N.Y. 13, 21, 150 N.E. 585, 587 (1926)). Four Supreme Court Justices (not a majority) expanded upon this criticism in 1954: "Rejection of the evidence does nothing to punish the wrong-doing official, while it may, and likely will, re-

lease the wrong-doing defendant. It deprives society of its remedy against one lawbreaker because he has been pursued by another. It protects one against whom incriminating evidence is discovered, but does nothing to protect innocent persons who are the victims of illegal but fruitless searches" (*Irvine v. California*, 347 U.S. 128, 136 (1954)).

Beginning in the early 1970s, the most vocal and visible critic of the exclusionary rule was Chief Justice Warren Burger. In a widely discussed dissenting opinion delivered in 1971, he commented:

I do not question the need for some remedy to give meaning and teeth to the constitutional guarantees against unlawful conduct by government officials. . . . But the hope that this objective could be accomplished by the exclusion of reliable evidence from criminal trials was hardly more than a wistful dream. Although I would hesitate to abandon it until some meaningful substitute is developed, the history of the suppression doctrine demonstrates that it is both conceptually sterile and practically ineffective in accomplishing its stated objective [*Bivens v. Six Unknown Named Agents of Federal Bureau of Narcotics*, 403 U.S. 388, 415 (1971) (Chief Justice Burger dissenting)].

Five years later, the Chief Justice declared: "With the passage of time, it now appears that the continued existence of the rule, as presently implemented, inhibits the development of rational alternatives. The reason is quite simple: Incentives for developing new procedures or remedies will remain minimal or nonexistent so long as the exclusionary rule is retained in its present form" (*Stone*, 500 (Chief Justice Burger concurring)).

Other Supreme Court Justices rose to the rule's defense in the face of the Chief Justice's strident criticisms. Justice Brennan, discussing the issue in 1975, expressed his fear that the exclusionary rule in Fourth Amendment cases was being covertly undercut by many of the Supreme Court's opinions and that this development might forecast "the complete demise of the exclusionary rule as fashioned by this court in over 61 years of Fourth Amendment jurisprudence." Such a result, Justice Brennan continued, would be disastrous:

Even its opponents concede that the great service of the exclusionary rule has been its usefulness in forcing judges to enlighten our understanding of Fourth Amendment guarantees. "It is . . . imperative to have a practical procedure by which courts can review alleged violations of constitutional rights and articulate the meaning of those rights. The advantage of the exclusionary rule—entirely apart from any direct deterrent effect—is that it provides an occasion for judicial review, and it gives credibility to the constitutional guarantees. By demonstrating that society will attach serious consequences to the violation of constitutional rights, the exclusionary rule invokes and magnifies the moral and educative force of the law" [*United States v. Peltier,* 422 U.S. 531, 554 (1975) (Justice Brennan dissenting)].

The deterrence question. A number of Supreme Court cases decided in the 1970s made the point that, at least in the unconstitutional search and seizure setting, where the exclusionary rule is applied most often, deterrence is the primary—if not the only—justification for utilizing the rule as a "remedy" for police misconduct. As the Supreme Court cogently declared in 1974, the "rule's prime purpose is to deter future unlawful police conduct and thereby effectuate the guarantee of the Fourth Amendment against unreasonable search and seizure" (*Calandra,* 347). The point of the exclusionary rule, in short, is educative: to the extent that police officers are made aware that certain forms of misconduct will lead to suppression of evidence, the expectation is that they will be deterred from engaging in it.

The question has often been raised, however, whether or not the exclusionary rule in actual practice has any real educative or deterrent effect on police misconduct. Chief Justice Burger has argued that the rule fails as a deterrent because it simply "does not apply any direct sanction to the individual official whose illegal conduct results in the exclusion of evidence in a criminal trial" (*Bivens,* 416). Moreover, Burger observed, "Whatever educational effect the rule conceivably might have in theory is greatly diminished in fact by the realities of law enforcement work. Policemen do not have the time, inclination, or training to read and grasp the nuances of the appellate opinions that ultimately define the standards of conduct they are to follow" (*Bivens,* 417).

Although Chief Justice Burger's analysis might be viewed as condescending in that it implicitly denigrates both the ability and the inclination of police officers to learn and follow the law, some studies appear to lend support to this viewpoint. In his now-classic analysis of the question, for example, Dallin Oaks surveyed the available data and concluded that the empirical evidence "contains little support for the proposition that the exclusionary rule discourages illegal searches." But Oaks's view was far from unequivocal. He also observed that the available empirical evidence "falls short of establishing that [the rule] does not [deter]" (p. 667).

Later scholars, for example, Steven Schlesinger, have performed their own studies of the issue and argue that at the very least, it is doubtful that the exclusionary rule effectively deters police misconduct.

Other researchers argue a contrary conclusion. A study by Stephen Wasby concluded that many—although certainly not all—police officers are both knowledgeable and concerned about the import, the effect, and particularly the "tone" of Supreme Court exclusionary rule decisions.

Perhaps most convincing of all is the view of a number of scholars who have simply cast doubt on the validity of any empirical studies that purport to demonstrate the unequivocal absence of a deterrent effect. As Bradley Canon (1979) has concluded, "Existing data at the present time make it impossible to establish empirically a universal 'yes, it works' or a 'no, it doesn't work' conclusion—or even anything approximating such a conclusion" (p. 403). The Supreme Court reached a similar "nonconclusion" in 1976: "Although scholars have attempted to determine whether the exclusionary rule in fact does have any deterrent effect, each empirical study on the subject, in its own way, appears to be flawed." As a result, the Court concluded that on the basis of available information, "we find ourselves, therefore, in no better position [in assessing deterrent efficacy] than the Court was in 1960" (*Janis,* 449–450, 453).

The rule as a constitutional requirement. The Supreme Court in *Mapp,* which established that the exclusionary rule applies in state court proceedings, concluded that "the exclusionary rule is an essential part of both the Fourth and Fourteenth Amendments" (657). However, the Court in the 1970s made it clear that the exclusionary rule was not a necessary part of either the Constitution or constitutional law. As the Court declared, "The rule is a judicially created remedy" (*Calandra,* 348).

This is a significant point. There are, to be sure, Supreme Court Justices, judges, lawyers, and legal scholars who argue to the contrary that the exclusionary rule is of constitutional weight; nonetheless, to the extent that the Supreme Court does not currently accept this view, other, nonexclusionary, remedies might be substituted or approved by the Court, as long as those other remedies adequately serve to protect against (or to deter) the breach of constitutional rights by the police.

Alternative remedies as a substitute for the rule. The Supreme Court in *Mapp* had concluded that the reason an exclusionary rule was necessary to protect constitutional guarantees against unreasonable searches and seizures was "the obvious futility of relegating the Fourth Amendment to the protection of other remedies. . . . that such other remedies have been worthless and futile is buttressed by . . . experience" (652). Nonetheless, some have argued that other effective remedies are conceivable. Chief Justice Burger commented in his *Bivens* dissent, discussed above, "Reasonable and effective substitutes [for the exclusionary rule] can be formulated if Congress would take the lead" (421).

What other effective remedies are there for police misconduct? One obvious remedy would appear to be a civil suit for damages against the offending police officers. However, although such lawsuits are theoretically available, they are difficult to pursue and generally unavailing, since the police officer's reasonable "good faith" in undertaking the conduct in question is a defense in such a lawsuit even though the officer's actions may have been unconstitutional. Moreover, the local governmental unit that employed the police officer whose activities are in question is not subject to liability for the officer's unconstitutional acts unless those acts represented "official policy" or official inaction where action was necessary. Further, the federal government, in a case involving federal officers, may be immune from many such lawsuits. As a result, since few police officers have sufficient assets to justify bringing such a difficult and lengthy lawsuit against them individually, and since it is difficult to establish liability, few wronged individuals even make the attempt. In short, the theoretical availability of civil lawsuits to redress police misconduct provides little or no incentive for police officers to avoid unconstitutional activity.

There are other theoretically—if not realistically—available remedies. Increased and more effective use of police disciplinary proceedings, for example, might create a viable deterrent to police misconduct. Experience has demonstrated, however, that such proceedings do not, and perhaps cannot be expected to, operate effectively to discipline police officers in all instances of unconstitutional activity. Injunctions are also occasionally available to restrain police misconduct. However, because of difficulties in the nature of the necessary legal showing, an injunction is rarely obtained and has no effect whatever on misconduct that occurred prior to the time it is issued.

The potential substitute for the exclusionary rule that has received the greatest amount of attention is some sort of administrative or quasi-judicial proceeding created specifically to handle complaints about police misconduct and to afford compensation to those whose rights have been violated. Chief Justice Burger in his *Bivens* dissent outlined the structure and duties of an administrative tribunal that he believed would, if created by Congress, suffice as an effective substitute for the exclusionary rule. The Chief Justice observed that "such a statutory scheme would have

the added advantage of providing some remedy to the completely innocent persons who are sometimes the victims of illegal police conduct—something that the suppression doctrine, of course, can never accomplish" (422).

Chief Justice Burger's suggested approach has been criticized, however, as unworkable. Anthony Amsterdam, for example, has commented that the Chief Justice's proposal was simply "pie in the sky":

Where are the lawyers going to come from to handle these cases for the plaintiffs [in Chief Justice Burger's proposed tribunal]? . . . what on earth would possess a lawyer to file a claim for damages before the special tribunal in an ordinary search-and-seizure case? The prospect of a share in the substantial damages to be expected? The chance to earn a reputation as a police-hating lawyer, so that he can no longer count on straight testimony concerning the length of skid marks in his personal injury cases? The gratitude of his client when his filing of the claim causes the prosecutor to refuse a lesser-included-offense plea or to charge priors [the commission of prior offenses in order to increase the sentence] or pile on "cover" charges? . . .

Police cases are an unadulterated investigative and litigative nightmare. Taking on the police in any tribunal involves a commitment to the most frustrating and thankless legal work I know. And the idea that an unrepresented, inarticulate, prosecution-vulnerable citizen can make a case against a team of professional investigators and testifiers in any tribunal beggars belief [p. 430].

It is possible that effective alternative remedies for the breach of constitutional rights by police officers will be developed and will, therefore, suffice to allow the courts to abandon or revise the exclusionary rule. However, at the present time, as the Supreme Court declared in 1978, " 'Self-scrutiny is a lofty ideal, but its exaltation reaches new heights if we expect a District Attorney to prosecute himself or his associates for well-meaning violations of the search and seizure clause during a raid the District Attorney or his associates have ordered.' . . . [Moreover,] the alternative sanctions of perjury prosecution, administrative discipline, contempt, or a civil suit are not likely to fill the gap. *Mapp v. Ohio* implicitly rejected the adequacy of these alternatives" (*Franks v. Delaware*, 438 U.S. 154, 169 (1978); quoting *Mapp*, 670).

The judicial integrity issue. Some critics have argued that the Supreme Court has relied too much on the rationale of deterrence and not enough on the rationale of judicial integrity, in assessing both the value of an exclusionary rule in and of itself, and the desirable scope of its application. Certainly the Court in *Mapp* forthrightly acknowledged the merits of the latter rationale as a justification for adopting an exclusionary remedy: " 'There is another consideration [in deciding to apply the exclusionary rule]—the imperative of judicial integrity.' . . . The criminal goes free, if he must, but it is the law that sets him free. Nothing can destroy a government more quickly than its failure to observe its own laws, or worse, its disregard of the charter of its own existence" (659; quoting *Elkins*, 222).

However, as previously noted, the Supreme Court in the 1970s often stated that deterrence of police misconduct is the primary rationale for the exclusionary rule, and that judicial integrity is merely a "subordinate factor." As a 1976 Supreme Court decision put it:

The primary meaning of "judicial integrity" in the context of evidentiary rules is that the courts must not commit or encourage violations of the Constitution. In the Fourth Amendment area, however, the evidence is unquestionably accurate, and the violation is complete by the time the evidence is presented to the court. . . . The focus therefore must be on the question whether the admission of the evidence encourages violations of Fourth Amendment rights. . . . This inquiry is essentially the same as the inquiry into whether exclusion would serve a deterrent purpose [*Janis*, 458, 459 n. 35].

Later, however, the Supreme Court acknowledged, as in *Mapp*, that the Fourth Amendment exclusionary rule "serves the 'twofold' purpose of deterring illegality and protecting judicial integrity. . . . [It] is applied in part 'to protect the integrity of the *court*, rather than to vindicate the constitutional rights of the defendant'" (*United States v. Payner*, 447 U.S. 727, 735 n. 8 (1980)). To some judges and commentators, such a conclusion means that the integrity rationale for the exclusionary rule is substantially different from the deterrence rationale:

If [a law enforcement agency] is permitted to obtain a conviction in federal court based almost entirely on . . . illegally obtained evidence and its fruits, then the judiciary has given full effect to the deliberate wrongdoings of the Government. The . . . court . . . become[s] the accomplice of the Government law-breaker, an accessory after the fact, for without judicial use of the evidence the "caper" would have been for nought. Such a pollution of the federal courts should not be permitted [*Payner*, 747–748 (Justice Marshall dissenting)].

This controversy over the viability and weight of the judicial integrity rationale is more than academic; it affects dramatically the scope of the exclusionary rule's application. If deterrence of police misconduct is the only rationale for the rule, then, as the Supreme Court argued in the 1970s, the rule should only be applied in those instances where deterrent efficacy is significantly furthered. If, however, judicial integrity is also a viable and independent reason for the rule's existence, it makes little difference whether application of the rule in a newly debated setting adds to the cumulative deterrent effect on police misconduct, since the integrity of the judicial process is compromised whenever illegally seized evidence is admitted.

Suggested revisions of the exclusionary rule

Given the high costs of the exclusionary rule, it is understandable that a number of revisions have been suggested which seek to retain the essence of the rule while mitigating its dire effects in cases of so-called technical or minor violations of constitutional law. The American Law Institute's Model Code of Pre-arraignment Procedure, a proposed model code for the states, contains a provision, for example, that permits suppression of evidence only when the constitutional violation by the police is either covered expressly in the constitutional text or is "substantial." A violation is deemed substantial, the Code continues, when "it was gross, wilful and prejudicial to the accused" without regard to "the good faith of the individual officer if it appears to be part of the practice of the law enforcement agency or was authorized by a high authority within it." Similarly, Chief Justice Burger urged in 1977 that given the flaws he sees in the exclusionary rule, "so serious an infringement of the crucial truth-seeking function of a criminal prosecution should be allowed only when imperative to safeguard constitutional rights. An important factor in this amalgam is whether the violation at issue may properly be classed as 'egregious' " (*Brewer v. Williams*, 430 U.S. 387, 422 (1977) (Chief Justice Burger dissenting)).

Neither the Code's "substantial violation" test nor Chief Justice Burger's "egregious violation" test have been adopted by a majority of the Supreme Court or any other court. To the extent that one believes either that the exclusionary rule is itself of constitutional dimension or that no alternative remedy currently exists that would serve to effectively remedy (or deter) police misconduct, such tests may be seen as of questionable constitutionality. Moreover, it can also be argued that there is, simply by definition, no such thing as a minor or technical violation of one's constitutional rights. Any breach of an individual's constitutional rights by the government, however small it may appear in "the big picture," may be immensely significant to the individual affected and, indeed, significant to everyone to the extent that the courts are subsequently called upon to "validate" police misconduct by convicting upon the basis of illegally seized evidence.

Another suggested revision of the exclusionary rule has gained some modest judicial and legislative currency, that is, the "good faith exception," or "good faith corollary," to the exclusionary rule. The good faith exception would except unconstitutional police conduct from application of the exclusionary rule in those instances where the police officers whose misconduct is in question acted reasonably and in good faith.

The reason such an exception is appropriate, its supporters argue, is that since deterrence is the prime rationale behind the exclusionary rule, it is both foolish and counterproductive to apply a remedy which presupposes that a police officer's unintended (that is, good faith) misconduct can realistically be deterred. As Justice Byron White, one of several Supreme Court Justices who have individually made the point, has argued:

When law enforcement personnel have acted mistakenly, but in good faith and on reasonable grounds, and yet the evidence they have seized is later excluded, the exclusion can have no deterrent effect. The officers, if they do their duty, will act in similar fashion in similar circumstances in the future; and the only consequence of the rule as presently administered is that unimpeachable and probative evidence is kept from the trier of fact and the truth-finding function of proceedings is substantially impaired or a trial totally aborted [*Stone*, 540 (Justice White dissenting)].

One of the strongest criticisms of the proposed good faith exception is that such an approach misconceives the very deterrence rationale which it purports to follow. As Justice Brennan has argued:

Deterrence can operate in several ways. The simplest is special deterrence—punishing an individual so that *he* will not repeat the same behavior. But "[t]he exclusionary rule is not aimed at special deterrence since it does not impose any direct punishment on a law enforcement official who has broken the rule. . . . The exclusionary rule is aimed at affecting the wider audience of all law enforcement officials and society at large. It is meant to discourage individuals who have never experienced any sanction for them" [*Peltier*, 556 (Justice Brennan dissenting)].

Despite Justice Brennan's—and other commentators'—critical arguments, a few state and federal courts have adopted one variant or another of the good faith exception to the exclusionary rule. Similarly, legislation has been introduced in Congress and a handful of state legislatures seeking to enact a good faith exception into law. The ultimate constitutionality of these judicial and legislative efforts remains to be determined.

JOHN M. BURKOFF

See also CONFESSIONS; CRIMINAL PROCEDURE: CONSTITUTIONAL ASPECTS; SEARCH AND SEIZURE; WIRETAPPING AND EAVESDROPPING.

BIBLIOGRAPHY

American Law Institute. *A Model Code of Pre-arraignment Procedure: Proposed Official Draft. Complete Text and Commentary.* Philadelphia: ALI, 1975.

AMSTERDAM, ANTHONY G. "Perspectives on the Fourth Amendment." *Minnesota Law Review* 58 (1974): 349–477.

BALL, EDNA F. "Good Faith and the Fourth Amendment: The 'Reasonable' Exception to the Exclusionary Rule." *Journal of Criminal Law and Criminology* 69 (1978): 635–657.

BURKOFF, JOHN M. "The Court that Devoured the Fourth Amendment: The Triumph of an Inconsistent Exclusionary Doctrine." *Oregon Law Review* 58 (1979): 151–192.

CANON, BRADLEY C. "The Exclusionary Rule: Have Critics Proven that It Doesn't Deter Police?" *Judicature* 62 (1979): 398–409.

———. "Testing the Effectiveness of Civil Liberties Policies at the State and Federal Levels: The Case of the Exclusionary Rule." *American Politics Quarterly* 5 (1977): 57–82.

DERSHOWITZ, ALAN M., and ELY, JOHN HART. "*Harris v. New York:* Some Anxious Observations on the Candor and Logic of the Emerging Nixon Majority." *Yale Law Journal* 80 (1971): 1198–1227.

GELLER, WILLIAM. "Enforcing the Fourth Amendment: The Exclusionary Rule and Its Alternatives." *Washington University Law Quarterly* (1975): 621–722.

———. "Is the Evidence In on the Exclusionary Rule?" *American Bar Association Journal* 67 (1981): 1642–1645.

KAMISAR, YALE. "The Exclusionary Rule in Historical Perspective: The Struggle to Make the Fourth Amendment More than 'An Empty Blessing.'" *Judicature* 62 (1979): 336–350.

———. "Is the Exclusionary Rule an 'Illogical' or 'Unnatural' Interpretation of the Fourth Amendment?" *Judicature* 62 (1978): 66–84.

———. "The Search and Seizure of America: The Case for Keeping the Exclusionary Rule." *Human Rights* 10 (1982): 14–17, 46–47.

KAPLAN, JOHN. "The Limits of the Exclusionary Rule." *Stanford Law Review* 26 (1974): 1027–1055.

LaFAVE, WAYNE R. "The Fourth Amendment in an Imperfect World: On Drawing 'Bright Lines' and 'Good Faith.'" *University of Pittsburgh Law Review* 43 (1982): 307–361.

———. *Search and Seizure: A Treatise on the Fourth Amendment.* St. Paul: West, 1978.

OAKS, DALLIN H. "Studying the Exclusionary Rule in Search and Seizure." *University of Chicago Law Review* 37 (1970): 665–757.

SCHLESINGER, STEVEN R. *Exclusionary Injustice: The Problem of Illegally Obtained Evidence.* New York: Dekker, 1977.

SCHROCK, THOMAS S., and WELSH, ROBERT C. "Up from

Calandra: The Exclusionary Rule as a Constitutional Requirement." *Minnesota Law Review* 59 (1974): 251–383.

SPIOTTO, JAMES E. "Search and Seizure: An Empirical Study of the Exclusionary Rule and Its Alternatives." *Journal of Legal Studies* 2 (1973): 243–278.

TRAYNOR, ROGER J. "*Mapp v. Ohio* at Large in the Fifty States." *Duke Law Journal* (1962): 319–343.

WASBY, STEPHEN L. *Small Town Police and the Supreme Court: Hearing the Word.* Lexington, Mass.: Heath, Lexington Books, 1976.

WILKEY, MALCOLM R. "A Call for Alternatives to the Exclusionary Rule: Let Congress and the Trial Courts Speak." *Judicature* 62 (1979): 351–356.

———. "The Exclusionary Rule: Why Suppress Valid Evidence?" *Judicature* 62 (1978): 214–232.

WRIGHT, CHARLES A. "Must the Criminal Go Free if the Constable Blunders?" *Texas Law Review* 50 (1972): 736–745.

YARBROUGH, TINSLEY E. "The Flexible Exclusionary Rule and the Crime Rate." *American Journal of Criminal Law* 6 (1978): 1–23.

EXCULPATION

See articles under EXCUSE; *articles under* JUSTIFICATION; MISTAKE.

EXCUSE

1. THEORY   George P. Fletcher
2. DURESS   Martin Lyon Levine
3. INFANCY   Martin Lyon Levine
4. INSANITY   Abraham S. Goldstein
5. INTOXICATION   Herbert Fingarette
                         Ann Fingarette Hasse
6. SUPERIOR ORDERS   Steven Duke

1.
THEORY

To approach the theory of excuse, one needs first to understand how excuses relate to other components of punishable, criminal conduct. Excuses become relevant only after proof that the actor has committed an unjustified act in violation of a criminal statute. Acts that fall outside the scope of the criminal law require no excuse; nor do nominal but justified violations of the law. If the actor has committed a criminal wrong (an unjustified violation of the statute), excuses speak to the question whether the actor is personally accountable for the wrongful act. This factor of personal accountability goes by many different names, including *culpability, blameworthiness, fault,* and *mens rea.* These overlapping terms have in common their logical incompatibility with excuses. A valid excuse implies that the actor is not to blame (not culpable, not at fault, without mens rea in the normative sense) for the wrongful act.

The range of excuses

Western legal systems have recognized, in varying degrees, a range of possible excusing circumstances. The paradigmatic excuse is that of insanity. Although definitions of *insanity* differ, all Western legal systems recognize that actors who, because of psychological incapacity, either do not realize they are doing wrong or cannot prevent themselves from doing wrong cannot be blamed for their wrongful violations of the law.

The claim of involuntary intoxication invites an analogy with insanity. If the intoxication is sufficiently acute and if it arises without the actor's voluntary choice, then the circumstances of the actor's incapacity closely resemble insanity. Indeed, West German law integrates acute intoxication into the framework of insanity (German (Federal Republic) Penal Code § 20). American law recognizes involuntary intoxication as a distinct excuse.

The claim of duress arises if another person threatens the actor with death or other serious harm if the actor does not commit a specific criminal act. Surrendering to the threat generates a possible excuse for the criminal act. As compared with insanity, however, claims of duress receive highly differential treatment. First, some legal systems, such as the Soviet system, do not recognize duress based on threats as an excuse, although some cases might fall under the justification of lesser evils. Second, even in systems recognizing duress as an excuse, considerable controversy attends the range of crimes that may be excused. German law recognizes the availability of duress in homicide cases. In English and American law, however, there is considerable resistance to recognizing duress as an excuse in homicide cases. Third, in legal systems recognizing duress as a distinct defense to at least some offenses, some scholars argue that the defense is grounded in a theory of justification rather than excuse (LaFave and Scott, pp. 378–379). The argument for this view is that the threat to the actor creates a conflict of interests: if the threat is sufficiently great and outweighs the interest sacrificed in committing the crime, the actor's submission to the threats will be justified on grounds of lesser evils. The more common interpretation of duress is that the threats do not justify the crime, but merely excuse the actor's having surrendered to the intimidating threats.

Even more controversial than the status of duress is the analogous situation of the actor committing an offense in response to the pressure of natural circumstances. The typical cases are those of stealing to avoid starvation or, as the issue was posed in *Regina v. Dudley and Stephens*, 14 Q.B.D. 273 (1884), killing and committing cannibalism in order to fend off starvation on the high seas. This case held that natural circumstances could neither excuse nor justify homicide, and the influential opinion even ruled out starvation as an excuse for theft. Although this case still influences the course of English and American law, both French and German law would endorse starvation and other natural circumstances as excuses even for homicide (French Penal Code art. 64; German (Federal Republic) Penal Code § 35). Hereafter, this article will refer to this possible excuse as "personal necessity."

An important middle ground between duress and personal necessity arises in cases of prison escapes to avoid threatened violence. The situation resembles duress in that the actor responds to a human threat. Yet, in his response, the actor seeks to avoid the threat rather than to comply with it. American courts have responded to this problem on the assumption that avoiding threatened violence falls outside the scope of duress. With personal necessity not recognized as an excuse in American law, the courts have had considerable difficulty recognizing a defense based on intolerable prison conditions. Since 1974, however, a number of courts have moved in that direction (*People v. Lovercamp*, 43 Cal. App. 3d 823, 118 Cal. Rptr. 110 (1974); *People v. Harmon*, 53 Mich. App. 482, 220 N.W.2d 212 (1974)). Although the rationale for this new defense remains uncertain, the argument seems to be one of excuse rather than of justification.

The prison-break situation illustrates why it is important to distinguish between claims of excuse and of justification. The distinction bears upon the question whether prison guards, fully aware of the reasons for the attempted escape, may use force to thwart the attempt. One should think of the guards' use of force as potentially privileged law enforcement. The guards may use reasonable and necessary force to uphold the order of the prison, but only against unlawful or wrongful challenges to that order. They could not, for example, use force against a lawful order to transfer specific prisoners to another facility. The question, then, is whether the attempted escape poses a lawful or unlawful challenge to the order of the prison.

If the escape were deemed justified, one would be inclined to think of the attempted escape as lawful (or, at least, not unlawful). After all, a valid claim of justification renders conduct right and proper. If the escape is not unlawful, the guards have no right to resist. Not so with an excuse: an excuse does not challenge the wrongfulness or unlawfulness of the conduct, but merely denies the personal accountability of the actor for the wrongful act. The guards retain the right to resist escapes excused on grounds of insanity, voluntary intoxication, duress, or personal necessity.

Some theorists might wish to argue that under certain circumstances—say when a fire threatens the lives of the inmates—the guards should not have the right to resist attempted escapes. In most cases of escape, however, the consensus would probably be that the guards have not only the right, but the duty, to protect society by resisting prisoners seeking to escape even from dire conditions. If this is the normative judgment, logic requires that conditions prompting escape be treated as a basis for excuse rather than justification.

In the period of the early common law, the courts clearly recognized an excuse of personal necessity in homicide cases. The excuse, called *se defendendo*, was limited to cases of self-preservation against a combatant. When the actor had no choice but to kill or be killed, he could excuse killing his opponent on the ground of *se defendendo*. The courts refused to expand this excuse to encompass cases such as *Dudley and Stephens*. Eventually, the statutory justification of self-defense supplanted *se defendendo* and became the standard for assessing liability in cases of killing aggressors or other combatants.

It is difficult to distinguish, in principle, between duress and personal necessity. Since the enactment of its first criminal code in 1871, German law has clearly recognized both excuses. Indeed, the 1975 code unites duress and personal necessity in one overarching provision (§ 35). It follows that in *Dudley and Stephens*, German courts would have considered the possibility of excusing the homicide. Despite some signs to the contrary (namely, in the prison-break cases), Anglo-American courts persist in distinguishing between duress, which they recognize, and personal necessity, which they have yet to recognize as an excuse.

Anglo-American ambivalence about personal necessity as an excuse corresponds to skepticism about another excuse well-recognized in German law: mistake of law. This claim arises if the actor violates the law without knowing it and under circumstances where it would have been unfair to expect him to have better informed himself of his legal obligations—for example, because the law is vague or imposes an obligation that bears no relation to conventional moral sentiments. Section 2.04(2) of the Model Penal Code recognizes a defense in cases in which the actor relies on an authoritative statement of the law that proves to be false. This limited defense is of no avail in cases in which the actor simply has no knowledge, and no basis for suspecting, that his conduct runs afoul of a prohibition in the criminal code. In *Lambert v. California*, 355 U.S. 225 (1957), Lambert was convicted for violating an ordinance requiring her, as a convicted felon, to register with the Los Angeles police within five days of entering the city. Her failure to register derived from understandable, potentially excusable ignorance of the ordinance. It is widely believed that her conviction under these circumstances was unjust. Yet the Model Penal Code's recommendation would have provided no relief, for Lambert had not relied on an authoritative statement of the law. Although the United States Supreme Court did not address the problem explicitly as an excusable mistake of law, it declared the conviction unconstitutional, holding that the government violated the due process clause by failing to provide sufficient notice of the obligation to register.

The rationale of excuses

The range of excuses remains in flux. The psychological sensitivity of the twentieth century generates claims for novel, as-yet-unrecognized excuses. Some people argue that prolonged social deprivation should excuse criminal behavior. Others maintain that conscientious civil disobedience should excuse acts of political protest. Those with determinist leanings would excuse all criminal acts; indeed, if genes, upbringing, and circumstances determine criminal conduct, there is no rational basis for blaming individuals for violating the criminal law. Carried to this extreme, excuses would engulf the entire criminal law. The practice of blame and punishment would then give way to institutions of social control that focused entirely on the suspect's predicted danger to social interests.

The ongoing controversy about excusing wrongdoers invites attention to the rationale for recognizing and rejecting excuses. The place to begin is with divergent attitudes toward punishment.

Retributive theory. A retributive theory of punishment insists that the actor deserves punishment only if he is personally accountable for violating the law.

The assumption is that no one is accountable for unavoidable acts, and excuses argue that the actor could not have avoided committing the criminal act. This standard of "avoidability" should be interpreted normatively. The question always is whether it would be fair under the circumstances to expect the actor to resist the pressures of the situation and abstain from the criminal act. If it would not be fair to expect avoidance of the act, then it cannot be fair to blame and punish the actor for succumbing to the pressures driving him toward the act.

This rationale of excuses rests on the assumption that either internal pressures (insanity, intoxication) or external pressures (duress, natural circumstances) might so intrude upon the actor's freedom of choice that the act committed under pressure no longer appears to be his doing. The act is attributable more to the pressure than to the actor's free choice. If the act is not his, he cannot be blamed for having committed it.

This model of excusing, based as it is on the model of overwhelming pressure, fails to encompass mistake and ignorance of law. In cases such as *Lambert*, the actor does not succumb to pressure; rather, she chooses to commit an act that, given knowledge of the criminal prohibition, she would presumably not choose to commit. In this sense, an act committed through ignorance fails to qualify as voluntary. In cases of mistake and ignorance of law, the actor does not choose to do wrong. Although the case differs from the model of overwhelming pressure, the wrongful act committed through ignorance ought to be excused, precisely as is the act done under pressure.

This retributive rationale of excuses presupposes that the actor is not accountable for the occurrence of the circumstances generating the excuse. If the actor has voluntarily induced his own intoxication, he cannot rely on intoxication to excuse his conduct. If she has been on a hunger strike, she can hardly claim starvation as an excuse for stealing. Similarly, if he could easily have informed himself of his obligations and had some reason to do so, he cannot plausibly claim mistake of law as an excuse. The antecedent culpability precludes a successful claim that the actor is not accountable at the time of committing the wrongful act.

In cases of insanity, intoxication, duress, and personal necessity, two normative questions envelop the analysis of the asserted excuse: whether the actor could fairly have resisted the pressure impelling him toward the act, and whether the actor is accountable for the circumstances generating the pressure. In cases of mistake or ignorance of law, there is only one normative question: whether the actor is accountable for his state of ignorance. So far as legal systems recognize these excuses, the trier of fact (in Anglo-American law, usually the jury) must assess these normative questions in making a judgment of criminal responsibility.

Utilitarian theory. Beginning with Jeremy Bentham (1748–1832), utilitarians have sought to account for recognized excuses by the following argument: As a measure causing pain, punishment should never be imposed when it is pointless. The purpose of punishment is to deter socially undesirable behavior. Punishment is pointless with regard to classes of actors, such as the insane, who are not deterrable. Therefore, nondeterrables should be excused from punishment for their criminal acts.

H. L. A. Hart was among the first to point out that this argument rests on a "spectacular non-sequitur" (p. 19). Bentham's reasoning assumes that the range of potential deterrables is defined by the precise characteristics of the defendant. He did not consider the possibility that punishing an insane or otherwise excused actor might have a deterrent effect on a whole range of potential criminals defined by broader characteristics. Punishing the insane might deter homicide generally; the utilitarian cannot simply assume that punishing excused actors would be pointless.

Utilitarian arguments are often invoked to justify disregarding possible excuses, such as duress, personal necessity, and mistake of law. By disregarding excuses and holding liable those who have unjustifiably violated the law, the criminal sanction arguably serves to induce higher standards of behavior. Disregarding excuses, therefore, may inflict a negative cost on those punished, but the gains to the many might outweigh the costs to the few.

The recognition of excuses expresses tolerance for human weakness, both weakness in succumbing to pressure and a weak resolve to keep abreast of one's legal duties. By rejecting human weakness as a defense, the criminal law takes a stand in favor of ideal human behavior. The law thus becomes our moral teacher. Those otherwise excused might be punished, but only in the name of bringing everyone to a higher standard of behavior.

The refutation of this utilitarian argument requires a shift of attention away from creating a better society toward the imperative of doing justice in the particular case. In *Director of Public Prosecutions v. Lynch,* [1975] A.C. 653, the majority of five judges in the House of Lords expressed this orientation by holding duress available as an excuse in a homicide case, at least in a situation in which the accused merely drove the car to the scene of the murder. Lord Morris rejected the utilitarian view that the law's standard should be higher than the average man can fairly be expected to attain: "The law would be censorious and inhumane which did not recognize the appalling plight of a person who perhaps suddenly finds his life in jeopardy unless he submits and obeys" (671). In *Lovercamp,* the leading case recognizing a defense in cases of escaping prison to avoid a threatened rape, the court reasoned with similar emphasis: "In a humane society some attention must be given to the individual dilemma" (827; 112). These arguments express compassion for the situation of the accused.

Justification and excuse: similarities and differences

Claims of excuse and of justification have some features in common. In cases of duress or personal necessity, the actor must be aware of the circumstances excusing his conduct; otherwise, it could hardly be said that the circumstances influenced that conduct. Further, these two excuses apply only if the actor responds to an imminent risk of harm. Again, this requirement finds its warrant in the principle that only circumstances overwhelming the actor's freedom of choice should generate excuses. These same requirements appear in justificatory claims, such as those of self-defense and lesser evils, but in that context they express different rationales for limiting the respective defenses.

Three distinctions between claims of justification and of excuse warrant emphasis. First, claims of justification are universal. They extend to anyone aware of the circumstances that justify the nominal violation of the law. If the threatened victim may justifiably defend himself against unlawful aggression, then others in a position to do so may justifiably intervene on his behalf. This feature of universality follows from the justification's rendering the violation right and proper. Excuses, in contrast, are personal and limited to the specific individual caught in the maelstrom of circumstances. This limitation derives from the required element of involuntariness in excused conduct. Sometimes excuses are defined so as to permit intervention on behalf of "relatives or other people close to the actor" who are threatened with imminent harm (German (Federal Republic) Penal Code § 35). The actor's intervening on behalf of this limited circle of endangered people might well be sufficiently involuntary to warrant excuse. Intervention on behalf of strangers is thought to be freely chosen and therefore not subject to excuse.

Second, claims of justification rest, to varying degrees, on a balancing of interests and the judgment that the justified conduct furthers the greater good (or lesser evil). Excuses do not ostensibly call for a balancing of interests. Inflicting harm far greater than that threatened to the actor might well be excused. Yet, indirectly, an assessment of the relation between the harm done and harm avoided might inform our judgment whether the wrongful conduct is sufficiently involuntary to be excused. Committing perjury to avoid great bodily harm would probably be excused, but committing mayhem on several people to avoid minor personal injuries would probably not be. As the gap between the conflicting interests widens, the assessment of the actor's surrendering to external pressures becomes more stringent. This covert attention to the conflicting interests elucidates the normative basis for finding conduct "involuntary."

Third, claims of justification and of excuse derive from different types of norms in the criminal law. Claims of justification rest on norms, directed to the public at large, that create exceptions to the prohibitions of the criminal law. Excuses are different. Excuses derive from norms directed not to the public, but rather to legal officials, judges, and juries, who assess the accountability of those who unjustifiably violate the law. Excusing a particular violation does not alter the legal prohibition. Recognizing mistake of law as an excuse does not change the law; if the excused, mistaken party were to leave the courthouse and commit the violation again, he would clearly be guilty. Neither does recognizing insanity, involuntary intoxication, duress, or personal necessity alter the prohibition against the acts excused on the basis of these circumstances. If someone relies upon the expectation of an excuse in violating the law (say, his ignorance of the law or his being subject to threats), his very reliance creates a good argument against excusing him for the violation. The expectation of an excuse conflicts with the supposed involuntariness of excused conduct.

Identifying excuses

In any given legal system, researchers might encounter difficulty enumerating the recognized excuses. At a certain period of history, certain circumstances might function as an excuse; at a later period the same considerations might be conceptualized as a denial that the act itself is criminal. The fate of the common-law excuses *se defendendo* (self-defense) and *per infortunium* (inevitable accident) illustrates this process. In the common law of homicide, both of these defenses generated the exemption from punishment known as "excusable homicide" (Blackstone, *182–187; Cal. Penal Code § 195.). Treating these claims as excuses reflected the assumption that any killing

of another human being was criminal or wrongful. The excuse did not negate this wrongfulness but rather, in the idiom of civil pleading, merely "confessed" the wrong and sought to "avoid" the consequences.

Today both of these claims are treated as denials that the act is criminal. As noted above, the excuse of *se defendendo* has given way to the statutory justification of self-defense. The excuse of *per infortunium* has undergone a reconceptualization, and functions now in the form of a denial that the killing was either intentional or negligent. Because it is now assumed that a wrongful killing must be either intentional or grossly negligent, the claim of accident challenges the wrongfulness of the killing.

If these excuses have been absorbed into the analysis of wrongfulness, other claims, properly regarded as justificatory, are occasionally treated as excuses. A good example is the claim of *respondeat superior,* or superior orders. This claim arises if a soldier or citizen executes "an order of his superior . . . which he does not know to be unlawful" (Model Penal Code § 2.10). If the order is lawful, then presumably the execution would also be regarded as lawful. A lawful act does not raise a question of excusability. However, if the order is unlawful, the actor's ignorance of the legal quality of the order and of his execution might excuse him by analogy with mistake of law. The Model Penal Code formulation encompasses both of these variations in one provision and locates the section in its chapter devoted primarily to claims of excuse rather than justification. The implicit analogy with duress in Section 2.09 of the Code stresses the coercive, rather than the legitimating, aspect of superior military orders.

Although the distinction between claims of justification and of excuse remains defensible in principle, Anglo-American legal thought has yet to achieve consensus regarding the exact nature not only of superior orders but of duress, personal necessity, and mistake of law.

GEORGE P. FLETCHER

See also ACTUS REUS; JUSTIFICATION: THEORY; MENS REA; MISTAKE; *both articles under* STRICT LIABILITY.

BIBLIOGRAPHY

AMERICAN LAW INSTITUTE. *Model Penal Code: Proposed Official Draft.* Philadelphia: ALI, 1962.
ARZT, GUNTHER. "Ignorance or Mistake of Law." *American Journal of Comparative Law* 24 (1976): 646–679.
BLACKSTONE, WILLIAM. *Commentaries on the Laws of England* (1765–1769), vol. 4. Reprint. University of Chicago Press, 1979.

Brandt, Richard B. "A Utilitarian Theory of Excuses." *Philosophical Review* 78 (1969): 337–361.

Fletcher, George P. "Commentary: Should Intolerable Conditions Generate an Excuse or Justification for Escape?" *UCLA Law Review* 26 (1979): 1355–1369.

———. "The Individualization of Excusing Conditions." *Southern California Law Reveiw* 47 (1974): 1269–1309.

———. *Rethinking Criminal Law.* Boston: Little, Brown, 1978.

Glover, Jonathan. *Responsibility.* New York: Humanities Press, 1970.

Gross, Hyman. *A Theory of Criminal Justice.* New York: Oxford University Press, 1979.

Hart, H. L. A. *Punishment and Responsibility: Essays in the Philosophy of Law.* Oxford: Oxford University Press, Clarendon Press, 1968.

Kadish, Sanford H. "The Decline of Innocence." *Cambridge Law Journal* 26 (1968): 273–290.

LaFave, Wayne R., and Scott, Austin W., Jr. *Handbook on Criminal Law.* St. Paul: West, 1972.

Lyons, David. "On Sanctioning Excuses." *Journal of Philosophy* 66 (1969): 646–660.

2.

DURESS

Duress is a defense available in some form throughout the common-law and civil law jurisdictions. It is said to excuse where an unlawful threat of imminent death or serious bodily injury causes the actor to engage in criminal conduct (*United States v. Bailey*, 444 U.S. 394, 409 (1980)). Traditionally, the coercion must have its source in another person rather than in the forces of nature; the conduct must be at the command of that person; the fear must be well grounded, and the threat must be one with which a person of ordinary firmness would comply; the actor must not kill an innocent person; he must take advantage of any reasonably available legal alternative; and the threat must be present, imminent, and impending. Although the actor has a defense, the one who threatened him is guilty of the crime.

Compulsion, coercion, and *necessity* are sometimes used as synonyms for *duress,* but useful distinctions can be drawn between these terms. In cases of physical compulsion, actual force is used on the defendant's body; the movements of his limbs are regarded as involuntary and not the defendant's actions at all. Coercion was a defense, now obsolete, to most crimes, historically available to wives who acted in their husband's presence. Unless it were proved that she took the initiative, it was presumed that the wife acted under his domination. (In Charles Dickens's *Oliver Twist,* it was this rule that prompted Mr. Bumble, with his domestic experience to the contrary, to say that "if the law supposes that, the law is a ass, a idiot.") The defense of necessity involves forces of nature that pose a choice between the commission of a crime and the occurrence of another harm, the defendant's choice of the lesser of the two evils, and the claim of justification, not merely an excuse. Most commentators distinguish duress from necessity on all three of these points, although others regard duress by another person as an aspect of the necessity doctrine. In *Bailey* the Supreme Court said that "modern cases have tended to blur the distinction between duress and necessity" (410).

History

"Hardly any branch of the law," observed James Fitzjames Stephen, "is more meagre or less satisfactory than the law on duress" (p. 105). Cases during the fourteenth and fifteenth centuries held that one had a defense to a charge of treason if one's acts were done in response to commands, backed by threats of force, that were issued by rebels or an invading army. Matthew Hale wrote that the defense was available only in time of war, not in peace, and that it was not applicable to murder (pp. 49–51). William Blackstone treated it as a well-established defense to a number of crimes, equally available during peacetime (*30). Nevertheless, Lord Denman, the English chief justice in 1838, instructed a jury that apprehension of personal danger does not furnish an excuse for crime (*Regina v. Tyler,* 173 Eng. Rep. 643 (1838)). Stephen noted that the courts in his day never accepted the defense in practice, and urged that it be abolished (pp. 107–108). In contemporary times, however, courts and law reform bodies have suggested new extensions for the defense.

Rationale

Four rationales of the duress defense have been offered. The "no intent" rationale asserts that no crime has occurred, because the actor lacked the state of mind required as part of its definition. The "choice of evils" rationale states that no crime has occurred, because the actor's behavior was the proper choice under the circumstances. The "nondeterrability" rationale concludes that punishment is inappropriate for crime-control purposes of the criminal law. The "reasonable man" rationale holds that punishment is unjust, given the moral purposes of the criminal law.

Blackstone regarded compulsion as a species of "defect of will," in which a man is urged to do something that his judgment disapproves and that his will (if left to itself) would reject (*27–30). Some have regarded the defendant's attempt to save his own life as literally compelled by human nature and thus beyond his control. Cases such as *Rex v. Bourne*, 36 Crim. App. 125 (1952) speak of absence of the intent, or mens rea, required to constitute a crime. In a 1971 English case, the court suggested that the rationale of duress is that the will of the accused is "overborne" or "neutralized" or "destroyed," so that the behavior is "no longer the voluntary act of the accused" (*Regina v. Hudson*, [1971] 2 Q.B. 202 (C.A.)). Such reasoning leads to the conclusion that the defendant has not exhibited the mental state required as one of the constitutive elements of the crime charged.

Critics of this argument have pointed out that one acting under duress acts voluntarily and intentionally, and sometimes even coolly and deliberately, showing great will. The critics, however, misunderstand the argument. Blackstone did not think that the will was "destroyed," and *Hudson* recognized that the actor must "make up his mind." In duress, the actor's intention conflicts with his wish, a circumstance called *coactus volui* (Williams, p. 751). The law takes account of the psychological conflict of wishes of one under duress, although elsewhere it dismisses such conflict as an irrelevancy, labeling it as involving merely "motives." In more modern language, one would not speak of duress as creating a defect of will but rather as reducing the defendant's range of choice.

Stephen viewed the actor under duress as faced with a choice of evils: subjected to motives at once powerful and terrible, the actor either commits the act or faces the likelihood that the threat will be carried out (p. 102). To some, if the harm threatened is more grave than the act required, then the actor chooses properly in complying with the command (Packer, p. 115). Thus, some commentators treat duress as a justification rather than merely an excuse (Williams, p. 755; LaFave and Scott, p. 374). Other authorities, however, follow Blackstone (*27–30) in sharply distinguishing the defenses of duress and choice of evils: only the latter defense provides a justification, and it is traditionally limited to situations created by natural forces. The Model Penal Code recognizes both these defenses (§§ 2.09, 3.02) and extends the choice-of-evils defense to include responses to human threats as well as to forces of nature.

Some argue that sanctions should be applied only to the extent useful to deter crime. For those under duress, the law's deterrent threat is said to be ineffective compared with the other person's threat of immediate and certain harm. The individual under duress will think, " 'If I do it not, I die presently [immediately]; if I do it, I die afterwards; therefore by doing it, there is time of life gained.' Nature thereof compels him to the fact" (Hobbes, p. 142). The class of persons under duress is thus regarded as undeterrable; it is concluded that there is no use in punishing any member of this class. One must add that the conclusion of nondeterrability is made within the limit of the punishment thought appropriate to that crime. Additionally, one must argue that none of the other mechanisms useful for crime control—specific deterrence, reformation, or isolation—are applicable, because the inducing cause of the prohibited act was external to the actor, and there is thus no reason to think that he is more likely than others to commit a similar act again.

Stephen supplied an answer to this argument: "Criminal law is itself a system of compulsion. . . . The law says to a man intending to commit murder, If you do it I will hang you. Is the law to withdraw its threat if some one else says, If you do not do it I will shoot you?" (p. 107). Stephen argued further, within the crime-control perspective, that to recognize the defense makes easier the work of those who issue the threats. It provides a charter, so to speak, to terrorists, gang leaders, and kidnappers, enabling them to confer on others an immunity from the criminal law by threatening them (*Director of Public Prosecutions v. Lynch*, [1975] A.C. 653). Furthermore, Jerome Hall argued that a substantial percentage of persons faced with duress are nevertheless deterrable, and also subject to the influence of morals. It is unproved, he said, that they feel an overpowering instinct to preserve their own lives if it would require killing another (pp. 436–448).

A different line of argument supporting the defense of duress is based on a moral theory of the criminal law: it is unjust for society to punish people when they could not reasonably be expected to resist. This is the Model Penal Code's approach to duress in Section 2.03. If an ordinary or reasonable man would behave in a similar way—even though the lawmaker might well prefer otherwise—to punish the actor for failing to be a hero would be unfair, or, as Herbert Packer put it, simply hypocritical and therefore wrong (p. 1181). England's Law Commission regards the defense as essentially a concession to human frailty. A similar rationale is found by George Fletcher to exist in German and French law: it is a question of fair social demands, and the standard is whether under the circumstances the defendant could fairly be expected to resist (pp. 829–835). In such views, duress doctrine may still use a balancing analysis or may recognize that the actor faces a "terrible agonizing choice of evils," as Lord Morris said (*Lynch*, 919). The issue, however, is not phrased as whether the actor is justified—as in the choice-of-evils rationale; the issue is seen instead as a moral one requiring judgment about the culpability of the actor's surrender to external pressure. The whole rationale of duress, said Lord Simon, is that the act is morally innocent (*Lynch*, 932). As the solicitor general conceded (*Bailey*, 425), it "has always been accepted" that punishment is inappropriate in duress situations because the actor "cannot fairly be blamed." Herbert Fingarette, in his essay "Victimization as an Excuse," argues that the key element in duress is that the defendant's act was *wrongfully* made the reasonable thing to do.

Controversies

There are controversies surrounding almost every aspect of the law of duress, which was called by Lord Simon an "extremely vague and elusive" juristic concept governed by a "narrow, arbitrary and anomalous" rule (*Lynch*, 931–932).

Murder. The traditional understanding of duress was that it was not available as a defense to a charge of murder, a rule that dates back to Hale and that "for hundreds of years has never been doubted" (*Abbott v. Regina*, [1976] 3 W.L.R. 462, [1976] 3 All E.R. 141, 146 (P.C.)). Rollin Perkins regards it as central to duress doctrine that it is an "inexcusable choice" for the actor intentionally to kill an obviously innocent and unoffending person to save his own life (p. 403).

Under the choice-of-evils rationale, however, in principle the defense of duress should be available when the killing of an innocent person is necessary to prevent the killing of many innocent people. From the crime-control perspective also, the defense should be available to murder charges, because the actor who is himself threatened with death is assumed to be undeterrable. From the moral perspective, Blackstone's reason for not allowing duress as a defense to murder—that murder is a violation of the law of God (*30)—no longer seems sufficient; the reasonable man under some circumstances could be coerced to assist in a killing. Nevertheless, some argue that the law should serve the moral function of declaring norms and helping shape character by requiring more than ordinary behavior. The Privy Council, as part of its reasoning in *Abbott*, rejected on moral grounds the thought that a duress doctrine could lead to acquittal of those who committed horrible crimes such as war atrocities, claiming superior orders and fear for their own lives.

The traditional murder exception has been abolished in some jurisdictions, such as New York (N.Y. Penal Law (McKinney) § 40.00 (1975)); elsewhere, as in Minnesota, duress is a mitigating circumstance reducing murder to manslaughter (Minn. Stat. Ann. § 609.20 (1964 & 1982 Supp.)). The House of Lords, by a split vote, allowed a defense of duress in *Lynch* to an accomplice who drove the car of the actual terrorist killer, whereas the Privy Council, by a split vote, denied the defense in *Abbott* to one who took an active part in a killing. The Law Commission would extend the defense even to the actual killer.

Target. Traditionally, for a defense of duress to be available, the threat must have been directed at the actor himself; modern statutes often continue this requirement. The contemporary case law, however, "leaves entirely uncertain" whether the threat must still be of harm to the actor himself, or whether it extends to threats to the immediate family of the actor or to any person (*Lynch*, 686). Extension of the defense is justifiable under the choice-of-evils theory. Similarly, under the reasonable-man rationale, when a third person's life is at stake, "even the path of heroism is obscure" (Wechsler and Michael, p. 738). Extension of the defense would be more limited under the nondeterrability theory.

Reasonableness. There is also controversy as to whether the issue in duress is subjective (relating to the actual state of mind of the defendant) or objective (relating to what a reasonable person would have believed or done).

With regard to the existence of the threat, the case law seems to assume that it is sufficient that the actor believed the threat to have existed. In some jurisdictions, however (Oklahoma, for example), the situation must have been that the actor was actually threatened (Okla. Stat. tit. 21, § 155 (1958 & 1981–1982 Supp.)).

With regard to the actor's compliance with the threat, the traditional law was that it must have been reasonable. Section 2.09(1) of the Model Penal Code provides that the threat must have been one that "a person of reasonable firmness in his situation would have been unable to resist." The Law Commission recommends that in deciding whether nonresistance is reasonable, the jury should consider all relevant subjective elements—not only the particular threats and action involved, but also the weakness or immaturity of the defendant.

An objective rule is in accord with the reasonable-man and choice-of-evils theories, but not with the nondeterrability theory. "It is arguable that the test should be purely subjective, and that it is contrary to principle to require the fear to be a reasonable one," said Lord Simon (*Lynch*, 686).

Gravity of the threat. Some early cases and some statutes require the threat to be of death, but most regard the threat of serious bodily harm as sufficient. "The law leaves it also quite uncertain" whether threatened loss of liberty suffices (*Lynch*, 686). Many cases say that threat of injury to property is not enough; cases have held the defense unavailable when the threat was of destruction of property, economic coercion, blackmail, or the like. The Law Commission would extend the defense to threat of mental as well as physical injury, such as that of administering damaging drugs.

"Nobody would dispute" that the greater the heinousness of the crime, the greater must be the pressure, said Lord Wilberforce (*Lynch*, 927). Under a choice-of-evils theory, the defense should be available if a small threat has coerced a still smaller crime; the reasonable-man and nondeterrability theories suggest a similar result.

Time frame. Traditionally, the threat must have been one made in the present to be implemented immediately, since only such a threat was thought to deprive the actor of opportunity to avoid it. The issue was reconsidered, however, in *Hudson*, which involved two young girls who committed perjury while the person who had previously threatened them sat in the courtroom. The court held that the threat of future injury could suffice. In general, it remains the law that one loses the defense if he has failed—between threat and action—to take advantage of an opportunity, without risk of harm to himself, to use a safe avenue of escape, to prevent the threatened harm, or to obtain the help of the authorities. *Bailey* held that in a crime where the prohibited behavior continues for a period (such as upon an escape) the actor must cease the crime as soon as feasible.

The defense is also not available to one who, before the threat, put himself into a situation in which he knew it likely that he would be commanded to commit crimes. For example, one who joined a terrorist group could not invoke the defense if its leaders thereafter required him to commit crimes. A reasonable man would not make the choice to be in that situation; the choice is itself morally culpable because of the risk to society that crimes will ensue; and because the risk was foreseeable at the time of joining the group, the law can deter the ultimate crime by deterring the act of joining.

Related defenses

Prison escapes. Prisoners prosecuted for escape have in several cases claimed they left prison to avoid intolerable conditions, such as being subjected to beatings and homosexual rapes. Their situation is not covered by traditional duress doctrine. The fellow prisoners who made the threats did not command the actors to escape; the time frame was not immediate; and the actors, at least when out of prison, could turn to the authorities. The case of *People v. Harmon*, 53 Mich. App. 482, 220 N.W.2d 212 (1974) nevertheless recognized a duress defense. Judge J. Skelly Wright, in *United States v. Bailey*, 585 F.2d 1087 (D.C. Cir. 1978), *rev'd* 444 U.S. 394 (1980), would have allowed the jury to consider the defense that the defendant's intent was only to avoid the danger to him, not to avoid confinement. The Supreme Court recognized a limited defense of "duress or necessity" to escape charges (*Bailey*, 413), provided the defendant surrenders to the authorities as soon as the duress or necessity has lost its coercive force.

Coercive persuasion. Another defense akin to duress has been invoked by defendants who claimed they were brainwashed while prisoners of war or captives of terrorists, and were thus caused to commit crimes thereafter. Traditional duress doctrine does not provide them a defense because, by the time of the commission of the prohibited act, the defendant may have passed up safe opportunities to escape, the threat may then no longer be present and immediate, and the defendant by then may have come to will the crime. Brainwashing as a basis for a duress defense has not yet been accepted by a court, but it was recognized in a working paper published by the United States National Commission on Reform of Federal Criminal Laws (p. 277).

Other related doctrines. A soldier who commits a prohibited act under military command (superior orders) has a defense, but only if the order is legal or, as some put it, if it is not obviously illegal. Entrapment, misleading legal advice given by a government official, the insanity defense (particularly its "irresistible impulse" version), and claims by drug addicts of "pharmacological duress" (discussed by Judge Wright in *Castle v. United States*, 347 F.2d 492 (D.C. Cir. 1964)) all bear a family resemblance to duress, but are generally analyzed under other rationales.

Conclusion

The Model Penal Code recognizes two doctrines covering duress situations: (1) when the actor has chosen the lesser of two evils, he is justified; and (2) as long as he has acted as a reasonable person would have under the circumstances, he is at least excused. In some circumstances, the judgment is that the actor has done the right thing. In other circumstances, the judge or lawmaker, when imaginatively identifying with one under duress, feels no guilt. At the least, as Lord Morris said, the judge must pay heed to the actor's "appalling" or "miserable and agonizing" plight (*Lynch*, 917–918). Contemporary law reform bodies and appellate courts have breathed new life into the law on duress. In years ahead, duress or defenses akin to it are likely to be further extended by courts and legislatures beyond traditional restrictions.

MARTIN LYON LEVINE

See also ACTUS REUS; EXCUSE: THEORY; JUSTIFICATION: NECESSITY.

BIBLIOGRAPHY

American Law Institute. *Model Penal Code: Proposed Official Draft.* Philadelphia: ALI, 1962.

Annotation. "Coercion, Compulsion, or Duress as Defense to Criminal Prosecution." *American Law Reports*, vol. 40. 2d series. Rochester, N.Y.: Lawyers Co-operative, 1955, pp. 908–919.

BLACKSTONE, WILLIAM. *Commentaries on the Laws of England* (1765–1769), vol. 4. Reprint. University of Chicago Press, 1979.

CROSS, RUPERT. "Murder under Duress." *University of Toronto Law Journal* 28 (1978): 369–380.

DELGADO, RICHARD. "Ascription of Criminal State of Mind: Toward a Defense Theory for the Coercively Persuaded (Brainwashed) Defendant." *Minnesota Law Review* 63 (1978): 1–33.

FINGARETTE, HERBERT. "Victimization as an Excuse." Unpublished manuscript, University of California at Santa Barbara, 1981.

FLETCHER, GEORGE P. *Rethinking Criminal Law.* Boston: Little, Brown, 1978.

GARDNER, MARTIN R. "The Defense of Necessity and the Right to Escape from Prison: A Step towards Incarceration Free from Sexual Assault." *Southern California Law Review* 49 (1975): 110–152.

HALE, MATTHEW. *The History of the Pleas of the Crown* (1685; first publication, 1736), vol. 1. Edited by W. A. Stokes and E. Ingersoll. Philadelphia: Small, 1847.

HALL, JEROME. *General Principles of the Criminal Law.* 2d ed. Indianapolis: Bobbs-Merrill, 1960.

HOBBES, THOMAS. *Leviathan; or The Matter, Forme, and Power of a Commonwealth, Ecclesiastical and Civil* (1651). Great Books of the Western World, vol. 23. Chicago: Encyclopaedia Britannica, 1952.

LaFAVE, WAYNE R., and SCOTT, AUSTIN W., JR. *Handbook on Criminal Law.* St. Paul: West, 1972.

Law Commission. *Criminal Law: Report on Defences of General Application.* London: Her Majesty's Stationery Office, 1977.

LUNDE, DONALD T., and WILSON, THOMAS E. "Brainwashing as a Defense to Criminal Liability: Patty Hearst Revisited." *Criminal Law Bulletin* 13 (1977): 341–382.

NEWMAN, LAWRENCE, and WEITZER, LAWRENCE. "Duress, Free Will, and the Criminal Law." *Southern California Law Review* 30 (1957): 313–334.

PACKER, HERBERT L. *The Limits of the Criminal Sanction.* Stanford, Calif.: Stanford University Press, 1968.

PERKINS, ROLLIN M. "Impelled Perpetration Restated." *Hastings Law Journal* 33 (1981): 403–425.

STEPHEN, JAMES FITZJAMES. *History of the Criminal Law of England*, vol. 2. London: Macmillan, 1883.

U.S. National Commission on Reform of Federal Criminal Laws. *Working Papers*, vol. 1. Washington, D.C.: The Commission, 1970.

WECHSLER, HERBERT, and MICHAEL, JEROME. "A Rationale of the Law of Homicide." *Columbia Law Review* 37 (1937): 701–761, 1261–1325.

WILLIAMS, GLANVILLE. *Criminal Law: The General Part.* 2d ed. London: Stevens, 1961.

3.
INFANCY

At common law, infancy was a defense: children under seven were deemed to lack the capacity to commit a crime, and those between seven and fourteen were rebuttably presumed incapable. Youths over fourteen were liable as adults.

History. Children received special treatment in the criminal law of the ancient Hebrews, Romans, and Chinese, and of the medieval Christians and Jews. In preconquest England, discretionary pardons for children were common and by the fourteenth century became routine; by the next century, judges at their discretion could dismiss such cases, and thereafter infancy was recognized as a defense. During the seventeenth century, fixed age lines became part of the defense of infancy, perhaps because rules came to be generally preferred over discretion, or because birth records were becoming available.

For children between seven and fourteen, there were different views on exactly what had to be proved to rebut the presumption of incapacity (*dolus incapax*). Many cases required proof that the child knew the difference between good and evil or right and wrong. Others held that what had to be proved was intelligent design, intention, consciousness of the wrongfulness of the act, or revenge and cunning, on the theory that "malice makes up for lack of age" (*malitia supplet aetatem*). The weight of the presumption decreased with age—the closer the child was to fourteen, the easier it was to overcome the presumption of incapacity. For children over fourteen, some authorities held the presumption of criminal capacity to be rebuttable, but most treated adolescents conclusively as adults.

Some specific crimes required a minimum age of capacity higher than seven. For example, no person under fourteen could be liable for rape, supposedly because of physical inability. Moreover, youth sometimes served as a mitigation when not a complete excuse, in order to bar imposition of the death penalty (*Eddings v. Oklahoma*, 102 S. Ct. 869 (1982)).

Modern status. Modern legislation often raises the minimum age of criminal responsibility from seven to anywhere from eight to sixteen. The modern English statute sets the age at ten (Children and Young Persons Act, 1963, c. 37, s. 16 (Great Britain)). The infancy defense has, however, been largely supplanted in function by juvenile delinquency laws. In the United States, about half the states allocate exclusive jurisdiction for all persons under sixteen to the juvenile court, deemed a noncriminal tribunal, in effect raising the minimum age of criminal capacity from seven to sixteen. Criminal court jurisdiction is sometimes retained for persons under sixteen for capital crimes or for minor offenses.

Most juvenile courts have not recognized the infancy defense, on the theory that the defense is only applicable to criminal proceedings and that juvenile court proceedings are designed only to aid the young. Some juvenile courts, however, have recognized the defense when the commission of a crime by the child was statutorily required for the child to be adjudicated a ward of the court (*In re Gladys R.*, 1 Cal. 3d 855, 863–864, 464 P.2d 127, 134 (1970)).

The common-law presumption for an intermediate age (seven to fourteen) has also been largely supplanted in function by rules permitting a waiver or transfer hearing for offenders aged sixteen to seventeen or eighteen, to determine whether they should be proceeded against in the criminal or the juvenile court. Major modern reform proposals retain exclusive juvenile court jurisdiction for all offenders under a certain age, either eighteen or sixteen, in effect setting that age as the minimum for criminal culpability. Several modern proposals also retain an explicit minimum age of capacity, usually ten rather than the traditional seven.

Legal rationale. The infancy rule's rationale has been disputed. One classic theory held that children were unable to have mens rea, understood as a "vicious will" and thought to be the shared mental element required to constitute all crimes. A similar modern theory posits that the infancy rule is an overriding defense dealing with what kind of person the actor is and whether he possesses the general ability to understand what the law requires and to conform to its requirements. Another classic theory held that children are unable to have mens rea, understood differently as the diverse mental elements required by the definitions of particular crimes, for example, to "intend" committing an act. To some scholars, extreme youth in principle merely evidences that inability. The infancy rule, however, excuses children from liability even for crimes requiring no mental element. Glanville Williams thus regarded the rule as an independent doctrine of substantive law.

A theory adopted by the Model Penal Code and by some states is cast in terms of the jurisdiction of the court rather than the capacity of the offender or the substantive criminal law. Under the jurisdictional theory, lack of age becomes a nonwaivable bar to prosecution, without overtones suggesting that children's misbehavior is free of moral fault and culpability.

Psychological and social bases. The infancy defense may alternatively be explained as based on common assumptions about the characteristics of children, or as derived from an adult-child interaction (that is, our feelings about children) and supported by its psychological value for adults.

The rule seems to reflect beliefs that there are stages of child development requiring different legal treatment. The general concept of child developmental stages is supported by the study of children's mental functioning by psychoanalysts such as Anna Freud and Erik Erikson, and by the examination of children's moral growth by scholars such as Jean Piaget and Lawrence Kohlberg. The research does not justify, however, the rule's reliance on chronological age, its fixed age lines, or its selection of particular ages, which are inexact proxies for a judgment on the complexities of individual cognitive and moral development.

Some emphasize the moral purposes of the criminal law in explaining the defense. The rule is thought to reflect a common intuition that children have not yet developed a capacity for moral judgment. Similarly, the tests for the intermediate age group reflect moral intuitions as to the prerequisites of blame, paralleling formulations of the insanity rule. Some emphasize instead the consequential purposes of criminal law in reducing the incidence of undesired behavior. They regard criminal sanctions as inappropriate for children because they believe that reform will be better achieved by the family or by the normal process of child development, without state intervention and stigmatization.

However, the rejection of proposals that the infancy rule consider mental age instead of chronological age suggests that the rule is not totally based on the child's characteristics. Another explanation for the infancy rule may be sought in the psychology of adult-child interaction. Adult criminals are punished in part because we identify with them, unconsciously seeking to condemn and restrain criminal urges within ourselves. Perhaps adults do not have that kind of identification with juvenile offenders. Juvenile offenders may remind adults primarily of the children they know most intimately—themselves when young—awakening their own childhood need for protection and forgiveness.

Alternatively, adults may transfer to juvenile offenders their sentiments toward those other juveniles they know so well, their own children. The actions of children sometimes stimulate in adults feelings of anger that may reach murderous intensity and about which adults are likely to feel guilty. The attitude of protecting and guiding the young rather than punishing them may be an innate biological characteristic required for the evolutionary survival of *Homo sapiens,* whose young are so long helpless. There may commonly exist a partial psychological blindness to the gravity of children's wrongdoing, comparable to the psychological denial of children's sexuality, that helps adults control their own urges to retaliate against children. The infancy rule may have a similar role as a societal denial of children's criminality.

The modern law's extension to juvenile delinquents of an equivalent of the infancy rule perhaps reflects society's granting of a psychosocial moratorium from adult responsibilities, under which the child may try even a criminal role without permanent labeling. Nevertheless, when youths are perceived as being a significant danger and resistant to reform, adult reaction can outweigh such attitudes and provoke use of the harsh standard of the criminal law against the young.

The infancy rule in many ways resembles the insanity rule, which early contained an explicit analogy to children. As an exception to liability to punishment, the rule can help us understand why others are punished.

MARTIN LYON LEVINE

See also AGE AND CRIME; CHILDREN, CRIMINAL ACTIVITIES OF; EXCUSE: THEORY; JUVENILE JUSTICE: HISTORY AND PHILOSOPHY.

BIBLIOGRAPHY

American Law Institute. *Model Penal Code: Proposed Official Draft.* Philadelphia: ALI, 1962.
ERIKSON, ERIK H. *Childhood and Society.* 2d ed., rev. and enl. New York: Norton, 1964.
FREUD, ANNA. *Normality and Pathology in Childhood: Assessments of Development.* New York: International Universities Press, 1965.
KEAN, A. W. G. "The History of the Criminal Liability of Children." *Law Quarterly Review* 53 (1937): 364–370.
KOHLBERG, LAWRENCE. *The Philosophy of Moral Development: Moral Stages and the Idea of Justice.* San Francisco: Harper & Row, 1981.
LEVINE, MARTIN. "The Current Status of Juvenile Law." *Juvenile Justice Management.* Edited by Gary B. Adams, Robert M. Carter, John D. Gerletti, Don. G. Pursuit, and Percy G. Rogers. Springfield, Ill.: Thomas, 1971, pp. 547–606.
LUDWIG, FREDERICK J. "Rationale of Responsibility for Young Offenders." *Nebraska Law Review* 29 (1950): 521–546.
PIAGET, JEAN et al. *The Moral Judgment of the Child* (1932). Translated by Marjorie Gabain. New York: Free Press, 1965.
PLATT, ANTHONY, and DIAMOND, BERNARD L. "The Origins of the 'Right and Wrong' Test of Criminal Responsibility and Its Subsequent Development in the United States: An Historical Survey." *California Law Review* 54 (1966): 1227–1260.
WILLIAMS, GLANVILLE. "The Criminal Responsibility of Children." *Criminal Law Review* (1954): 493–500.
WOODBRIDGE, FREDERICK. "Physical and Mental Infancy in the Criminal Law." *University of Pennsylvania Law Review* 87 (1939): 426–454.

4.
INSANITY

The insanity defense in American criminal law defines the extent to which persons accused of a crime may be relieved of responsibility because they were suffering from mental disease when the crime occurred. Despite its prominence in legal literature and in the media, the defense is rarely asserted, because a successful defense does not bring freedom with it. Instead, it results in temporary commitment to a mental hospital for the purpose of deciding whether the "acquitted" defendant should be committed until such time as he is no longer dangerous. A defendant is likely to plead the defense, therefore, only in a capital case or in one carrying a very heavy sentence. Even then, he will if possible elect an alternative defense that will allow the admission of evidence of mental illness—for example, that his act was involuntary or that he had only "partial responsibility" or "diminished capacity"—and that offers the prospect of a reduced sentence or freedom rather than indeterminate detention.

Competing processes further reduce the frequency with which the insanity defense is raised. For example, it may be raised only by persons who are mentally competent to stand trial. If they are incompetent, they are committed to a mental hospital and the defense may be lost; detention and release are then determined in accordance with procedures peculiar to the issue of competency to stand trial (*Jackson v. Indiana*, 406 U.S. 715 (1972)). If they are competent, they may abandon the defense in order to gain the advantage attaching to a criminal conviction, with its plea bargains and relatively determinate sentences and parole possibilities. Finally, through the exercise of police and prosecutorial discretion and through the use of civil commitment procedures, mentally disordered offenders may be dealt with by society without being formally regarded as criminals at all.

Much of the controversy surrounding the insanity defense traces to conflicting views of the objectives of criminal law and the ways those objectives are served by one or the other of the insanity rules that have competed for favor over the years. Under a retributive theory, the offender is said to owe a measure of suffering comparable to that which he has inflicted on the victim. Under a deterrence theory, criminal law is regarded as effective only for persons who can understand the signals directed at them by a criminal code, who can respond to its warnings, and who can feel the significance of its sanctions. The rehabilitation theory treats the defense as a way to divert the offender from a harsh and punitive criminal process to treatment in a mental hospital.

The constant element in these approaches is the concept of blame. Punishment of an insane offender is said not to advance any of the criminal law's objectives because the offender is so obviously different from most people that he cannot fairly be blamed. His conviction is not needed as an example to others because it is apparent that he was unable to heed the warnings of the criminal code, and his condition plainly marks him as someone who should be in a hospital rather than a prison. Yet the typical criminal trial makes only a limited effort to assess in detail the blameworthiness of the accused. Instead, the law presumes that all persons are sane and that they intend the natural and probable consequences of their acts. If an individual's acts mark him as a criminal by the standards of reasonable conduct, it may ordinarily be inferred that he acted culpably. Any evidence regarding his mental faculties—which may make him less capable of complying with the law than most—is ordinarily barred. Only through the insanity defense is an accused given free rein to rebut the presumptions and shift the focus to a subjective examination of his mental condition. By drawing more fully on his life history—his school problems, his prior aberrational behavior, and his experience with psychiatric clinics and mental hospitals—he is given greater latitude to demonstrate that his acts do not accurately portray his ability to have had the thoughts the law attributes to him at the time of the crime.

The insanity rules

The precise terms of the insanity defense are found in the instructions presented by the trial judge to the jury at the close of a case. Until the 1950s these were cast in a majority of the United States and in England in the language of the *M'Naghten* rule, which in many states was supplemented by a "control" rule. Today, *M'Naghten* remains the exclusive test in England and in a substantial minority of the United States. But a majority of the states and the federal courts now use the rule recommended by the American Law Institute in its Model Penal Code.

The *M'Naghten* rule. The *M'Naghten* rule (*M'Naghten's Case*, 8 Eng. Rep. 718 (1843)), formulated by the English House of Lords in 1843, tells jurors simply "that every man is to be presumed to be sane, and . . . that to establish a defense on the ground of insanity, it must be clearly proved that, at the time of the committing of the act, the party accused was laboring under such a defect of reason, from disease of the mind, as not to know the nature and quality of the act he was doing; or if he did know it, that he did not know he was doing what was wrong" (*M'Naghten*, 722).

The rule emphasizes knowledge of the sanctions threatened by the criminal code but says nothing about self-control. The tacit assumption is that powers of self-control are strengthened by knowledge of sanctions and that any injustices which might result to those who were nevertheless unable to control their conduct are less important than exerting the maximum possible pressure toward conformity with the law.

The key words of the rule have had remarkably little interpretation by the courts. "Disease of the mind," for example, is usually presented with little or no explanation as part of the charge to the jury. If expert witnesses testify that the offending conduct was attributable to something they characterize as a mental disease, the issue will generally be passed to the jury. The disease named most often is some form of psychosis; it has been assumed—more by expert witnesses than by the courts—that psychopathy and other nonpsychotic illnesses would not suffice. What little law has developed on the matter has emerged from cases involving marginal mental conditions, such as intoxication, which have been said not to qualify.

The phrase "nature and quality of the act" is sometimes omitted completely from the charge to the jury. When included, it is treated as though it adds little to the requirement that the accused knew his act was wrong, for if the accused did not know the nature and quality of his act, he may be said to be incapable of knowing it was wrong. There has, however, been a conflict of views as to whether *wrong* means moral or legal wrong. One group of American courts holds that an offender is sane if he knew the act was prohibited by law. The other group takes the position that *wrong* means moral wrong, according to generally accepted standards. Under this view, a defendant who thought it morally right that he should kill (for example, because he was ordered to do so by God) but knew it was legally wrong would be classed as insane.

It is the word *know* that has been at the center of the controversy surrounding *M'Naghten*. Most critics read it as referring to formal cognition or intellectual awareness alone. They distinguish this, the "law's" meaning, from what they describe as the "psychiatric" meaning, which they take to connote a fuller, deeper knowledge, involving emotional as well as intellectual awareness. This fuller knowledge can exist only when the accused is able to evaluate his conduct in terms of its actual impact upon himself and others and when he is able to appreciate the total setting in which he is acting. According to the critics, the law's type of knowledge is to be found even in the most serious psychosis. The consequences, the argument continues, are that *M'Naghten* directs jurors to hold many persons responsible who are seriously disturbed and that it makes a successful assertion of the insanity defense virtually impossible.

The assertion that *know* is narrowly defined has been made so often and so insistently that it comes as a surprise to find that very few appellate courts have imposed the restrictive interpretation. In several of the states that use *M'Naghten* as the sole test of insanity, the jury is told that an accused "knows" only if he "understands" enough to enable him to judge "the nature, character and consequence of the act charged against him" or if he has the "capacity to appreciate the character and to comprehend the probable or possible consequences of his act." In the remaining *M'Naghten* jurisdictions, jurors are given the words of the rule without explanation and left to find the "commonsense" meaning from their own backgrounds or from the materials presented to them at trial.

The rules may have a constraining effect, not when the jury is instructed on the law but at other stages of the process, as when evidence of mental illness is offered or when experts seek to explain the facts of mental disease. But in fact, there is very little support for the view that *M'Naghten* is responsible for inhibiting the flow of testimony on insanity and depriving the jury of the "insights of modern psychology." Virtually any evidence probative of the defendant's mental condition is admitted without regard to the supposed restrictions of the test used to define insanity for the jury. Even evidence relating to self-control rather than cognition has been admitted, and psychiatrists are regularly permitted to explain their interpretation of the words of the rule. As a result, if the case is properly tried, jurors hear both a narrow and a broad construction of the test from the experts if not from the judge.

The control rules. In a substantial number of states, juries considering the insanity defense are charged first in the words of *M'Naghten* and then in the words of what is commonly referred to as the "irresistible impulse" rule. The phrase is really little more than a text writer's caption that has been used uncritically to describe a group of "control" tests. Most courts do not use it in instructing jurors. Instead, they tell the jury to acquit by reason of insanity if it finds the defendant had a mental disease that kept him from controlling his conduct, even if he knew he was doing something wrong. The lineage of these rules is at least as old as that of *M'Naghten*, with which they have often competed for acceptance. They rest on the assumptions that there are mental diseases which impair volition or self-control even while cognition remains unimpaired and that persons suffering from such diseases would not be acquitted under *M'Naghten*. They enjoyed a considerable renaissance during the 1920s, when psychoanalysts turned to criminal law, found *M'Naghten* too rationalistic, and offered the control rules as a banner of reform.

Despite the fact that "irresistible impulse" is a misnomer, the words may have been the principal reason for finding the control rules inadequate. They were often said to limit the defense to impulsive behavior. Yet the cases do not sustain the view that a planned act cannot qualify. Evidence of mental condition is freely admitted; experts may explain what they mean by the words of the control tests; and the jury is rarely told that there must be proof of sudden, unplanned action. The situation in the control jurisdictions was strikingly similar to what was found in the analysis of *M'Naghten*. While the law did not impose the requirement that an action must have been sudden and unplanned, the principal actors in the trial may have been doing so.

The control rules inquire broadly into the capacity of the accused to control his conduct. They reach impaired control as well as impaired cognition, and they make sense to the average person. But they, too, have been branded as unsatisfactory by most commentators. Some regard the control tests as unnecessary if *M'Naghten* is properly construed, arguing that the personality is integrated and that any case of impaired volition will be marked by the failure of knowledge demanded by *M'Naghten*. Others are unhappy with the degree to which the *M'Naghten* and control rules imply that it is possible to separate the cognitive and emotional elements of the personality. A third group argues that since it is impossible to determine which acts were uncontrollable, the defense is available to psychopaths, neurotics, and perhaps to all who commit crime, and reduces the deterrent impact of the criminal law.

The criticisms are not very persuasive. Those who would rely entirely on *M'Naghten* place exaggerated demands on the word *know* and do not say why the law should not speak directly to the control issue. Those who see the defense as too narrow or too broad overlook the limited role of the defense as a standard for decision by a lay jury. While the issues raised by the control tests are hardly precise, they are not so very different from the questions of degree that arise throughout the law. Finally, it is not true that legions of defendants are rushing to assert the insanity defense. If anything, the problem is that too few are doing so because they fear the stigma of insanity or commitment to a mental hospital or the prospect of indeterminate detention.

The *Durham* rule. The pressure to "solve" the *M'Naghten* problem declined during the period surrounding World War II, but it revived soon afterward. In 1953 the British Royal Commission on Capital Punishment issued a report based on extensive hearings in which most medical witnesses agreed that the mind functions as an integrated whole and that it is impossible to isolate the separate functions of cognition and control. Nevertheless, most of the witnesses recommended that the *M'Naghten* rule be retained, either because no better rule could be found or because the rule was being given a broad interpretation in practice. The commission concluded, however, that the rule should be "abrogated" and the jury left "to determine whether at the time of the act the accused was suffering from disease of the mind (or mental deficiency) to such degree that he ought not to be held responsible" (Royal Commission, p. 116).

As an alternative, the commission suggested a rule that, in essence, combined *M'Naghten* and a control test. Three dissenting members described the first proposal as not a rule at all. They insisted that a standard of responsibility was necessary to limit arbitrariness on the part of the jury, to promote uniformity of decision, and to aid the jury in deciding between the conflicting testimony of the experts. The recommendations of the Royal Commission were not adopted in England, but they played a large role in the development of new rules in the United States. Most importantly, they tended to fix the debate on the insanity defense along lines that found *M'Naghten* and "irresistible impulse" both narrow and at odds with modern theories of how the mind worked.

The influence of the Royal Commission report is evident in *Durham v. United States*, 214 F.2d 862 (D.C. Cir. 1954). Written by Judge David L. Bazelon, the opinion drew upon the report again and again as it set forth the premises that were, in its view, forcing it to abandon the jurisdiction's blend of *M'Naghten* and the control test. The court took as its basic premise that the mind of man was a functional unit. It followed, therefore, that if the defendant had a mental disease, his mind could not be expected to respond properly to threats of sanction, he was not a "fit" object of anger and blame, and he belonged in a hospital rather than a prison. It would be a mistake, the court reasoned, to try to identify types of malfunctioning or groups of symptoms that would disable a person from complying with the criminal law, because an "integrated personality" could not be only partially diseased and because tests that focused on symptoms would tend to freeze the law in conventional patterns and make it difficult for psychiatric witnesses to appraise new clusters of symptoms that might be equally disabling. The test of insanity should, therefore, be a simple one, patterned on a rule adopted in New Hampshire in 1869 (*State v. Pike*, 49 N.H. 399 (1869)). In Judge Bazelon's words, "An accused is not criminally responsible if his unlawful act was the product of mental disease or mental defect." Psychiatrists would now be able to "inform the jury of the character of [the defendant's] mental disease" and juries would be "guided by wider horizons of knowledge concerning mental life." Only Maine and the Virgin Islands adopted the *Durham* rule, for a short period. Nevertheless, *Durham* had a tremendous and continuing impact upon the course of the debate.

The principal criticism of *Durham* was that it, like the Royal Commission's first proposal, was really a nonrule. It was said to provide the jury with no standard by which to judge the evidence or direct it to pathological factors relevant to the law's concerns—the impairment of reason and control. The jury was left entirely dependent upon the expert's classification of conduct as the product of mental disease. The court's tacit assumption was that the concept of mental disease would provide a better framework for expert testimony than the earlier tests. It left *mental disease* almost undefined so that the courtroom controversy might shift from the words of the insanity rule to the nature of the particular disease and its relation to the crime.

At the very time *Durham* was decided, the concept of mental disease was being subjected to devastating attack. It emerged as a concept whose content is often affected by the ends for which a diagnosis is made. As a result, when questions arose as to whether psychopathy or neurosis or narcotics addiction were mental diseases, the disputes were strikingly reminiscent of those which had previously characterized trials under *M'Naghten*. Psychiatrists for the prosecution classified a given defendant's behavior as not psychotic and, for that reason, not the product of a mental disease. Those testifying for the defense urged that it was psychotic or the product of a lesser mental disorder which nevertheless qualified as mental disease.

By 1962, the District of Columbia court concluded that it was necessary for trial judges to inform juries that mental disease or defect "includes any abnormal condition of the mind which substantially affects mental or emotional processes and substantially impairs behavior controls" (*McDonald v. United States*, 312 F.2d 847 (D.C. Cir. 1962)). *Durham* had thus traveled a circuitous path toward the conclusion that the jury needed guidance as to the effects of disease which were relevant to compliance with the criminal law. Those effects were very much like the ones which were central to the broadened *M'Naghten* and control tests. In *United States v. Brawner*, 471 F.2d 969 (D.C. Cir. 1972), the court abandoned *Durham* for a rule that would require expert evidence to be framed in a way more meaningful to a lay jury. This rule was the one proposed by the American Law Institute (ALI) in its Model Penal Code.

The ALI rule. The rule in the Model Penal Code that is known as the ALI rule is a modernized and improved rendition of the *M'Naghten* and control rules. It provides the following:

(1) A person is not responsible for criminal conduct if at the time of such conduct as a result of mental disease or defect he lacks substantial capacity either to appreciate the criminality of his conduct or to conform his conduct to the requirements of the law.

(2) As used in this Article, the terms "mental disease or defect" do not include an abnormality manifested only by repeated criminal or otherwise antisocial conduct [§ 4.01].

By substituting *appreciate* for *know*, the rule expresses a preference for the broader construction of *M'Naghten*, an interpretation which holds that a sane offender must be emotionally, as well as intellectually, aware of the significance of his conduct. By using the word *conform*, the rule tries to divest itself of historical baggage and avoids any implication of "irresistible impulse." By requiring only "substantial" incapacity, it eliminates the risk implicit in the older cases, which sometimes suggested that "complete" or "total" destruction of the defendant's mental capacity was required.

The principal criticisms that have been made of the ALI rule have been directed at its Section 2. Some have felt that the rule represents an inadvisable effort to bar psychopaths from the insanity defense. The drafters of the Code, on the other hand, believed that the effort was essential in order to keep the defense from swallowing up the whole of criminal liability, as it might if recidivists could qualify for the defense merely by being labeled psychopaths. It is probable, however, that the effort has not been entirely successful, since psychopathy is never manifested only by repeated criminal conduct. Psychiatrists would invariably testify that a psychopath always shows symptoms other than antisocial conduct.

There have been other objections to the ALI rule. Some have attacked it because it continues to rely on functional impairments, thereby ignoring the view that the mind cannot be separated into compartments. These critics would resume the search for a standard that puts medically correct questions to the jury. Others complain that the rule relies too heavily on a "medical model" of insanity. They would abandon the search for "correct" questions and simply tell the jury to acquit an offender who, because of a mental, emotional, or behavioral impairment, "cannot be justly held responsible for his act." Those who hold the first point of view ignore *Durham's* history, which teaches that functional definitions are needed to provide courts and juries with standards by which to evaluate evidence of mental illness. Advocates of the second position recognize that the defense is closely tied to the social objectives served by the criminal law, but they would instruct the jury in language that only explains why the law wants to relieve people of responsibility; they would not provide a standard for judging who should be relieved.

The criticisms swing from the extreme of wanting to give the matter almost entirely to the psychiatrists to the extreme of giving it entirely to the jury. The ALI rule strikes a sensible balance between the two extremes and probably achieves an optimal blend of medical science and social purpose. It solves most of the problems associated with the older rules yet represents the same line of historical development. As a result, it is now the dominant insanity rule in the United States.

Commitment and release

In most states, the trial judge (or jury) must determine whether a defendant acquitted by reason of insanity is presently in need of commitment. In discharging this function, the judge may commit the defendant for a limited period of observation and diagnosis. The jurors are usually told nothing about the prospect of commitment or release, just as they are told nothing about the sentences that may follow upon a guilty verdict. Yet the issue is unquestionably more troublesome with the insanity defense because jurors may think they are being asked to "acquit" and release a person who has established both his incapacity and his dangerousness. Only in a small number of jurisdictions is the trial judge required, or permitted in his discretion, to eliminate the ambiguity and tell the jury considering the defense that there will be a commitment and release process administered by court and mental hospital.

Several justifications are offered for some form of commitment procedure. The acquitted defendant has either demonstrated his inability to conform or has left doubts about whether he will be able to conform in the future. The fact that mental disease may have caused the misconduct raises some hope that the cause can be eliminated by treating and curing the disease. Two other justifications are sometimes offered, more often in the public forum than in the courts: that the risk of commitment may deter spurious claims of insanity, and that a bit of punishment (in the form of commitment) might not be such a bad thing even for an insane offender.

The critical issue, however, is not so much commitment as release. The applicable statutes are remarkably spare in the guidance they provide. They usually permit detention to continue until the patient has "recovered," is no longer mentally ill, is no longer dangerous, or some combination thereof. In virtually all jurisdictions, the patient who wishes to challenge his detention has the burden of persuading the court that he should be released. He must ordinarily prove that he is sane or will pose no threat to the community. In theory, this burden should not be encumbered at all by considerations of blame. Some courts follow the theory, imposing no heavier burden than they would upon any mentally ill patient. But a surprisingly large number treat persons acquitted by reason of insanity as members of a dangerous and "exceptional class," requiring stricter standards for release than the general run of mental patients. The class is sometimes said to be made up of "guilty persons" who should not "go unwhipped of justice."

The power to detain indefinitely is unquestionably the most important issue associated with the insanity defense. It is a device for preventive detention that is especially troublesome when it may continue beyond the limits fixed by the criminal code for the offending conduct. Two solutions to the problem have emerged. One would limit detention to the maximum sentence the offender would have served if he had not been acquitted by reason of insanity; to hold him beyond that limit, the state would have to initiate new commitment proceedings (Conn. Gen. Stat. Ann. § 53(a)–47(b) (1972)). A second would require the state, at the time of acquittal, to initiate civil commitment proceedings. Both approaches depend ultimately on the assumption that the civil commitment process has developed standards for release. Unfortunately, the substantive law of civil commitment has not advanced very far in dealing with the issue of probable danger. Nevertheless, it places the burden of proof squarely on the state to show that detention is necessary, not upon the patient to show that it is not necessary. Since the question of sanity or dangerousness is often close factually and ambiguous legally, the location of the burden of proof may make the critical difference between confinement and release. Moreover, statutes and judicial decisions increasingly require the state to apply periodically to a court or board for renewal of the commitment, with the patient represented by counsel and with findings on sanity or danger based on his current condition rather than on his condition at the time of the crime.

Abolition and modification

Dissatisfaction with the insanity defense has led, from time to time, to proposals to abolish or modify it. The abolition proposals have taken two principal forms: the first would truly abolish the defense; the second would abolish it in the sense of treating it as unnecessary if the mens rea requirement were properly understood.

The first approach is most often associated with the names of Enrico Ferri and Barbara Wootton. It is concerned not with "blame" but with objective danger and would ask the court to decide only whether the offending conduct had occurred. The offender's mental condition would be taken into account in a sentencing and treatment stage, during which measures to reduce or eliminate the danger would be prescribed. There are serious objections to this proposal. The effort to separate the offending act from the mental state of the offender has been singularly unsuccessful. For example, California's two-step trial, which tried to separate the issue of "guilt" from that of insanity, foundered on the difficulty of removing mens rea entirely from the guilt-finding portion of the criminal trial (Louisell and Hazard, p. 805). Further, two statutory attempts to eliminate both the mens rea requirement and the insanity defense were held to deny defendants due process of law. They deprived defendants of defenses that had "always" been passed on by the jury and that were too intrinsic to the concept of crime to be removed by legislation (*State v. Strasburg*, 60 Wash. 106, 110 P. 1020 (1910); *Sinclair v. State*, 161 Miss. 142, 132 So. 581 (1931)). The proposal would have the effect of sweeping toward sentencing and treatment large numbers of "offenders" who now go free because they lack mens rea. Finally, eliminating the insanity defense would remove from the criminal trial and the public conscience a vitally important distinction between illness and evil or would tuck it away in an administrative process, overlooking the role of a concept of individual responsibility in the complex of cultural forces that keep alive the moral lessons essential to a law-abiding society.

The second proposal would not so much abolish the defense as extend it. Its proponents argue that the mens rea requirement already compels the government to prove the defendant is sane, and that he should be permitted to show he lacked sanity (and mens rea) by allowing him to introduce the fullest possible evidence of how his mind works. If he prevails, he should be acquitted entirely and not subjected to preventive detention in a process that has not shown him to be currently dangerous. In short, the proposal would permit mental disorder to be used generally to negate the mental element required for any crime, whether it be intent, recklessness, or negligence. But unlike the insanity defense or the partial defenses, this form of "abolition" could lead to releasing defendants entirely. It is probable that to avoid that risk, jurors would nullify the law and convict rather than acquit a defendant who has demonstrated that he is less able than most to refrain from criminal conduct. In addition, the proposal would probably lead prosecutors to invoke civil commitment procedures more regularly in order to detain persons who are dangerous.

The two abolition proposals represent only one facet of a debate about the insanity defense that continues even as the ALI rule is winning the support of courts and legislatures. Several more modest proposals deserve notice. One, adopted in several states, would resurrect a brief English experiment that substituted the verdict "guilty but insane" or "guilty but not criminally responsible" to make it clear to the public that insane offenders do not go free. The problem is that this proposal condemns as "guilty" many persons who, lacking mental capacity, could not be said to have possessed mens rea at the time of the crime. A second proposal, enacted in Michigan, treats "guilty but insane" as a form of special verdict that supplements the insanity defense by directing guilty but mentally ill offenders to a treatment facility rather than to prison (Mich. Comp. Laws Ann. ch. 768 (1968 & 1968–1981 Supp.)). A third would treat the defense as established only if "the defendant, as a result of mental disease or defect, lacked the state of mind required as an element of the offense charged" (Proposed Criminal Code Reform Act, S. 1400, § 501, 93d Cong., 1st sess., 119 Cong. Rec. 9655 (1973)). Unfortunately, those words lend themselves to diametrically opposed constructions: one that sees insanity as it was viewed in *Durham*, with no functional criteria as to the kinds of "mental disease" and "results" which would qualify, and one that sees it as limiting the defense to crimes of specific intent, on the assumption that persons can act intentionally, recklessly, or negligently even when they have a mental disease.

The special virtue of the *Durham* debate and the ALI rule was the degree to which they had quieted some classic controversies. It had become evident by 1970 that the insanity defense, asserted occasionally in a contested criminal trial, could not be equated with the larger problem of the mentally ill offender. Attention turned for a while from the defense to its administration by counsel and experts as well as by judges, to the problem of indeterminate detention, and to whether the insanity defense (and the commitment associated with it) should be the exclusive vehicle for pursuing an entirely subjective approach to criminal liability. The persistence of the debate—about the words of the defense, its consequences, and whether it should even be retained—reminds us that the public finds the issues involved too fascinating to treat them as settled for very long by any insanity rule.

ABRAHAM S. GOLDSTEIN

See also DIMINISHED CAPACITY; EXCUSE: THEORY; MENS REA; MENTAL HEALTH EXPERT, ROLE OF THE; MENTALLY DISORDERED OFFENDERS; PSYCHOPATHY.

BIBLIOGRAPHY

AMERICAN LAW INSTITUTE. *Model Penal Code: Proposed Official Draft.* Philadelphia: ALI, 1962.

ARENELLA, PETER. "The Diminished Capacity and Diminished Responsibility Defenses: Two Children of a Doomed Marriage." *Columbia Law Review* 77 (1977): 827–865.

BRAKEL, SAMUEL J., and ROCK, RONALD S., eds. *The Mentally Disabled and the Law.* Rev. ed. University of Chicago Press, 1971.

BROOKS, ALEXANDER D. *Law, Psychiatry, and the Mental Health System.* Boston: Little, Brown, 1974.

FINGARETTE, HERBERT M. *The Meaning of Criminal Insanity.* Berkeley: University of California Press, 1972.

GOLDSTEIN, ABRAHAM S. *The Insanity Defense.* New Haven: Yale University Press, 1967.

GOLDSTEIN, JOSEPH, and KATZ, JAY. "Abolish the 'Insanity Defense': Why Not?" *Yale Law Journal* 72 (1963): 853–876.

KADISH, SANFORD H. "The Decline of Innocence." *Cambridge Law Journal* 26 (1968): 273–290.

LAFAVE, WAYNE R., and SCOTT, AUSTIN W., JR. *Handbook on Criminal Law.* St. Paul: West, 1972.

LOUISELL, DAVID, and HAZARD, GEOFFREY C., JR. "Insanity as a Defense: The Bifurcated Trial." *California Law Review* 49 (1961): 805–830.

MORRIS, GRANT H. *The Insanity Defense: A Blueprint for Legislative Reform.* Lexington, Mass.: Heath, Lexington Books, 1975.

PACKER, HERBERT L. *The Limits of the Criminal Sanction.* Stanford University Press, 1968.

ROYAL COMMISSION ON CAPITAL PUNISHMENT 1949–1953. *Report.* London: Her Majesty's Stationery Office, 1953.

SELLIN, THORSTEN. "Pioneers in Criminology XV: Enrico Ferri (1856–1929)." *Journal of Criminal Law, Criminology, and Police Science* 48 (1958): 481–492.

WAELDER, ROBERT. "Psychiatry and the Problem of Criminal Responsibility." *University of Pennsylvania Law Review* 101 (1952): 378–390.

WECHSLER, HERBERT. "The Criteria of Criminal Responsibility." *University of Chicago Law Review* 22 (1955): 367–376.

WOOTTON, BARBARA. *Crime and the Criminal Law: Reflections of a Magistrate and Social Scientist.* London: Stevens, 1963.

5.

INTOXICATION

The effect of intoxication upon criminal liability depends on whether the intoxication is voluntary or involuntary. Voluntary intoxication is the usual case and will be considered first.

Voluntary intoxication

It is a maxim of the common law that "intoxication is no excuse." Taken in a strict sense, the phrase as applied to voluntary intoxication is true. Since the mid-nineteenth century, however, both English and American courts have developed doctrine that, in its practical effect, allows intoxication to serve as a partial defense. Around 1850, British and American judges began to instruct juries that evidence of drunkenness could be considered in deciding whether some specific mental state essential to constitute the charged crime had in fact been absent. For example, in the early English murder case of *Regina v. Monkhouse*, [1849] 4 Cox, Crim. Law Cas. 55 (London 1851), evidence of intoxication was admitted to show that when the defendant shot the decedent he did not specifically intend to kill him. Since the legal definition of murder required the intent to kill, in the absence of such intent the defendant would not be guilty of murder. Thus intoxication was not in itself an excuse; judges believed they were merely reaffirming the fundamental principle that there could be no conviction for a crime unless all the essential elements of that crime were proved to be present, and the defendant was merely being allowed to present whatever evidence was pertinent to show that a specific mental element was absent.

As intended, the practical result in *Monkhouse* was that the defendant was found guilty of a "lesser included" offense, the crime of "doing grievous bodily harm," which is a less grave crime than murder and one that does not require an intent to kill.

Judges realized, however, that the defendant might claim to have been so drunk as not only to have lacked the intent to kill but also to have lacked awareness of assaulting the victim. Since such awareness was legally required to convict the defendant of doing grievous bodily harm, the success of such a defense would result in complete acquittal, a result judges have always strongly resisted on the ground that it would be bad public policy. This dilemma has been central to the development of the law on voluntary intoxication; the constant judicial quest has been to find ways of allowing for the abnormal state and consequent reduced responsibility of the intoxicated offender, and yet at the same time to prevent complete acquittal.

In response to this dilemma, there emerged in both England and the United States toward the end of the nineteenth century a legal doctrine now frequently referred to as the doctrine of specific intent or as the specific-intent exception. The seed had been planted when courts first admitted evidence of intoxication to show that some "specific intention" was absent; in using that phrase, however, judges were simply referring to whatever particular state of mind was required for the crime that had been charged (England: *Regina v. Cruse*, 173 Eng. Rep. 610 (1838); United States: *Pigman v. State*, 14 Ohio 555 (1846)). In the attempt to assure that defendants would not go completely free, the courts began to limit the meaning of the phrase "specific intention" to certain mental states only; they gave it a new, technical, and narrower meaning and then contrasted it with what they called "general intent."

For example, the new legal doctrine continued to permit evidence of voluntary intoxication to be used to show that there had not been a specific intent to kill the victim. But under the doctrine, evidence of intoxication could not be used in defense against the charge of the lesser included crime of manslaughter, because manslaughter was held to be a crime of general intent and the doctrine forbade use of evidence of intoxication to show absence of general intent. This distinction may have achieved a certain degree of plausibility in the context of murder-manslaughter because conviction for manslaughter can be based on the defendant's behavior as judged by an "objective" standard of "reasonableness." The reasonableness standard asks how a hypothetical "reasonable man" would have responded in the circumstances, rather than asking about the individual defendant's state of mind. Thus, a particular defendant's intoxicated state of mind is logically irrelevant.

The specific-intent doctrine received its classic English formulation in *Director of Public Prosecutions v. Beard*, [1920] A.C. 479. In 1977 the House of Lords, England's highest court, reaffirmed the doctrine, although it explicitly recognized that the specific-intent concept posed serious problems of definition and of logic. In spite of this, the judges believed that it was sound public policy to continue use of the doctrine in order to assure that intoxicated offenders would not go unpunished (*Director of Public Prosecutions v. Majewski*, [1977] A.C. 443).

An analogous development took place in the American law of homicide. By 1881, evidence of voluntary intoxication was admissible in defense against a charge of first-degree murder to show absence of the specific mental elements legally required for first-degree murder, "deliberation" and "premeditation" (*Hopt v. People*, 104 U.S. 631 (1882)). But such evidence could not be used in defense against lesser included charges of criminal homicide requiring only general intent. By the end of the nineteenth century, the concepts of specific and general intent had been generalized to apply to crimes other than murder (*O'Grady v. State*, 54 N.W. 556 (Neb. 1893)), and are now well entrenched (*Atkins v. State*, 105 S.W. 353 (Tenn. 1907); *United States v. Meeker*, 527 F.2d 12 (9th Cir. 1975)).

Most commentators agree that judges have been right in recognizing the lesser responsibility of some voluntarily intoxicated offenders, while preventing complete acquittal. On the other hand, it is also widely recognized that the specific-intent doctrine in all its variants has important defects. One major criticism is that the doctrine conflicts with the legal principle that all essential elements of a crime must be proved before a defendant can be found guilty. The problem arises because intoxication may, as a matter of psychological reality, result in absence of any intent, even a general intent, to commit an act. But the doctrine forbids the defendant to present such evidence. Thus, a defendant can be convicted of crimes requiring a general intent even if in fact the defendant did not have any intent and so did not commit the crime as legally defined.

A second problem is that the specific-intent doctrine does not guarantee the result that it had been intended to achieve for purposes of public policy, that is, to assure that the voluntarily intoxicated offender will at least be punished for a crime of general intent. This is because there are specific-intent crimes, such as theft, for which there are no suitable lesser included general-intent offenses. In such cases, the defendant who lacked the requisite specific intent because of voluntary intoxication may go unpunished.

Finally, the distinction between specific and general intent is itself obscure. It had seemed clear in the early cases, but the necessity of applying it to an ever-growing range of crimes revealed its inadequacy. For example, in *People v. Hood*, 1 Cal. 3d 444, 462 P.2d 370 (1969), the California Supreme Court had to decide whether assault was a crime of specific or general intent. The court could find no logical way to decide between the two views. As a matter of public policy, however, the court did not want to permit acquittals in a crime so frequently committed by intoxicated persons. The court therefore declared that assault was a general-intent crime and invoked the doctrine to justify excluding evidence of intoxication in cases of assault. This foreshadowed the similar reasoning in the English case of *Majewski*. Indeed, it has been widely remarked in England and America, by both high courts and legal scholars, that the distinction is "chimerical," "illogical," and "impossible to make sense of" (*Hood,* 457; *Majewski,* opinions of Lord Salmond and of Lord Edmund-Davies; Williams, p. 429).

In response to these problems there have emerged proposals to abandon the various specific-intent doctrines and to introduce other approaches. Recommendation 56 of the *Report of the Committee on Mentally Abnormal Offenders* (Home Office) proposed establishing a single statutory offense of being dangerously drunk: the defendant would be found guilty of this new crime if, because of voluntary intoxication, he lacked some mental element required for the original crime charged. Thus, some punishment would be assured. Another recommendation, reported in the Criminal Law Revision Committee's report *Offences against the Person,* ¶¶ 262–263, is based on the principle of establishing a set of special and separate voluntary-intoxication offenses; for each crime to which absence of a mental element can serve as a defense, there would be a parallel voluntary-intoxication crime with identical punishment. A third proposal would allow evidence of voluntary intoxication to be used as a defense to show absence of intent of any kind; however, evidence of intoxication could not serve as a defense where recklessness rather than intent was the issue (Model Penal Code § 2.08(2); Criminal Law Revision Committee, ¶ 279).

All these proposals avoid the obscurities and arbitrariness of the specific-intent limitation by abandoning it. The first and third proposals, which focus on the theme of dangerousness and recklessness, are more realistic psychologically. On the other hand, all the proposals present new problems of their own; no generally accepted alternative has emerged, and the admittedly unsatisfactory specific-intent doctrine remains generally in force.

Potentially more unsettling to the stability of the law than the problems discussed above is the growing body of new evidence that increasingly tends to undermine certain traditional beliefs about the effects of alcohol (MacAndrew and Edgerton; University of California at Berkeley). It is well substantiated that alcohol can impair thought processes, perception, and motor coordination; however, evidence from a variety of scientific disciplines contradicts the widely held view that alcohol also acts on the brain to weaken sexual, aggressive, and other moral and social "inhibitions." It appears that the expectations aroused by the social setting, and the individual's expectations about the effects of alcohol, not the direct chemical effects of alcohol itself, are what primarily determine conduct in these respects. But because the belief that alcohol chemically loosens one's inhibitions is so widespread, drinking has become a socially recognized ritual that often legitimizes excusing the drinker, at least to some extent, from certain social responsibilities. If, however, the belief that alcohol has a chemically disinhibitory effect is unsound, this basis for at least partly excusing uninhibited behavior, implicit in legal doctrine, loses much of its force.

Involuntary intoxication

In general, intoxication is considered involuntary if the intoxicant is introduced into one's body as a result of coercion or compulsion or if one did not know that the substance was intoxicating and this ignorance was not one's own fault.

The concept of involuntary intoxication as an excuse has had an uncertain history; it has long been recognized in theory as a defense, but until the mid-twentieth century it was not clearly recognized in practice. Since then, however, the availability of a bewildering array of chemical intoxicants has made the defense a more practicable option.

Involuntary intoxication has been claimed in connection with the following sorts of circumstances:

1. Pathological intoxication. Medically labeled "alcohol idiosyncratic intoxication," this condition seems very rare and may be associated with brain pathology (*Diagnostic and Statistical Manual of Mental Disorders,* § 291.40). It is caused by an amount of alcohol that would not normally be enough to intoxicate, and it manifests itself in aggressive behavior not normally characteristic of the person. If the offender did not know beforehand that he possessed this rare and little-known susceptibility, the intoxication would probably be found legally involuntary (Model Penal Code § 2.08(5)(c); *Kane v. United States,* 399 F.2d 730 (9th Cir. 1968)).

2. Ignorance, mistake, or deception. There are a great many ways in which people may unknowingly introduce into their bodies substances that may produce intoxication. For example, a potent drug may be mistaken for an innocuous substance such as aspirin, either because of deception (*Torres v. State,* 585 S.W.2d 746 (Tex. Crim. App. 1979)) or innocent mistake (*People v. Murray,* 56 Cal. Rptr. 21, 247 Cal. App. 2d 730 (1967)). Or a defendant may have been ignorant of the intoxicating side effects of a medically prescribed drug (*City of Minneapolis v. Altimus,* 306 Minn. 462, 238 N.W.2d 851 (1976)).

3. Coerced or physically compelled intoxication. Although cases actually decided on this point are almost nonexistent, it is generally acknowledged that such intoxication would be clearly involuntary (*State v. Palacio*, 221 Kan. 394, 559 P.2d 804 (1977)).

A defense based on involuntary intoxication usually amounts in American law to a variant of the insanity plea. Almost all legal definitions of insanity require either a defect of understanding or of self-control at the time of the offense, and they all require that these defects, or else the criminal act itself, be the result of a mental disease. In order to allow for a defense based on involuntary intoxication, courts and legislatures in the United States have increasingly made explicit provision for a defendant to use, in effect, the insanity defense by substituting "involuntary intoxication" for "mental disease" (*Prather v. Commonwealth*, 287 S.W. 559 (Ky. 1926); *People v. Koch*, 250 App. Div. 623, 294 N.Y.S. 987 (1937); *Altimus; Torres*). In England the law on the issue is for practical purposes much as in the United States, although it is less clearly established and is formulated in slightly different terms (*Regina v. Quick*, [1973] Q.B. 910, 3 All E.R. 347).

The defense based on involuntary intoxication should not be confused with defenses based on some other mental disorder. For example, long-term heavy intoxication can, in some individuals, result in a psychosis such as delirium tremens; or intoxication may be a result or side effect of a distinct preexisting psychosis or brain pathology. In such cases it is the psychosis or brain pathology, not the intoxication, that constitutes the mental disease legally requisite to an insanity defense.

It has also been argued, at times with success, that "alcoholism" and "addiction" are diseases and that this makes both the intoxication and some of the behavior that results from the intoxication involuntary. What is in question here, however, is the existence of certain persistent patterns of behavior and other chronic conditions rather than the state of intoxication itself (Fingarette and Hasse, chaps. 9–12).

An initial survey of the excusing role of intoxication in both its voluntary and involuntary forms might give the impression that the law in this area is reasonably well settled. But a deeper study presents a different picture: the specific-intent doctrine is under wide and persistent attack. Moreover, the rapid growth of scientific understanding of alcohol-related behavior has raised serious questions about the voluntariness or involuntariness of such behavior.

HERBERT FINGARETTE
ANN FINGARETTE HASSE

See also articles under ALCOHOL AND CRIME; DIMINISHED CAPACITY; DRINKING AND DRIVING; MENS REA.

BIBLIOGRAPHY

American Law Institute. *Model Penal Code: Proposed Official Draft.* "Voluntary Intoxication," § 2.08(2). "Pathological Intoxication," § 2.08(5)(c). Philadelphia: ALI, 1962.

BENTON, EDWARD HENRY et al. "Special Project: Drugs and Criminal Responsibility." *Vanderbilt Law Review* 33, no. 4 (1980): 1145–1218.

Criminal Law Revision Committee. *Fourteenth Report: Offences against the Person.* Cmnd. 7844. London: Her Majesty's Stationery Office, 1980.

Diagnostic and Statistical Manual of Mental Disorders. 3d ed. Washington, D.C.: American Psychiatric Association, 1980.

FINGARETTE, HERBERT, and HASSE, ANN FINGARETTE. *Mental Disabilities and Criminal Responsibility.* Berkeley: University of California Press, 1979.

HALL, JEROME. *General Principles of Criminal Law.* 2d ed. Indianapolis: Bobbs-Merrill, 1960.

HASSMAN, PHILLIP E. "Effect of Voluntary Drug Intoxication upon Criminal Responsibility." *American Law Reports*, vol. 73. 3d series. Rochester, N.Y.: Lawyers Co-operative, 1976, pp. 98–194.

———. "When Intoxication Deemed Involuntary So As To Constitute a Defense to Criminal Charge." *American Law Reports*, vol. 73. 3d series. Rochester, N.Y.: Lawyers Co-operative, 1976, pp. 195–243.

Home Office, Department of Health and Social Security. *Report of the Committee on Mentally Abnormal Offenders.* Cmnd. 6244. London: Her Majesty's Stationery Office, 1975.

MacANDREW, CRAIG, and EDGERTON, ROBERT B. *Drunken Comportment: A Social Explanation.* Hawthorne, N.Y.: Aldine, 1969.

ORCHARD, G. F. "Drunkenness, Drugs, and Manslaughter." *Criminal Law Review* (1970): 132–139, 211–218.

University of California at Berkeley, School of Public Health, Social Research Group. "Alcohol and Disinhibition: The Nature and Meaning of the Link." Workshop conference, 11–13 February 1980, at Berkeley/Oakland.

WILLIAMS, GLANVILLE. *Textbook of Criminal Law.* London: Stevens, 1978.

6.

SUPERIOR ORDERS

The defense of superior orders is an amalgam of several defenses: mistake of fact, mistake of law, and duress. Its clearest application is in military law, where a subordinate soldier acts in response to orders of his superior and the act is determined to have been a violation of the laws of war or military law. The defense was one of the issues in the trials of Nazi war criminals at Nuremberg after World War II and was prominent in the defense of the American soldiers involved in the My Lai massacre in Vietnam in 1968. It is also sometimes advanced by government officials who claim that superiors in the governmental hierarchy ordered them to engage in acts later determined to have been unlawful. Finally, it may be tendered by private persons, ordered by officials or by superiors in private institutions to engage in proscribed conduct. The validity of the defense varies significantly with the context.

Military orders. War consists mainly of acts that in peacetime would be criminal: killing, maiming, kidnapping, pillaging, arson, and theft. War reverses normal legal and moral principles and makes heroic that which ordinarily would deserve the severest sanctions. But not everything done in a state of war is excused. Some acts carried out by soldiers violate the laws of war, which are vague principles established by custom, treaties, and decisions of international tribunals and domestic courts. Some of these acts violate the military laws directly governing the soldier.

The vagueness of the boundaries of military immunity is compounded by the reluctance of nations in the modern world to admit that they are engaged in "war." Euphemisms abound. Nations prefer to engage in "police actions" or "reprisals." Although their soldiers may be fighting and dying in large numbers, nations often claim that they are merely rendering "logistic" or "technical" assistance to a warring country. Huge military organizations regularly employ force or the threat of force to "maintain the peace," and military activities are often conducted without the authorization of the domestic political body that has the power to declare war. Thus, the lawfulness of military operations is, in almost any instance, open to doubt.

A soldier in any society is subject to strict discipline. He is bound to obey any lawful order (and in some organizations, any order, legitimate or otherwise). Failure to follow orders on the field of combat often justifies immediate execution. Disobedience even in peacetime warrants severe discipline; in some systems, it results in capital punishment. Effective military operations require such obedience, and military training aims at producing it.

A soldier who receives orders to kill, kidnap, or destroy that are later determined to have been unlawful is faced with apparently conflicting obligations, both backed by severe sanctions. The sanctions for violating the order may be immediate or, at least, summarily imposed. One who complies with an order that is explicitly or implicitly supported by threat of severe, summary sanction will therefore often be supported by the defense of duress. However, even if all the conditions of duress do not exist, the excuse of superior orders may apply. It occupies much territory not inhabited by the duress defense.

Although a problem as old as war itself, the existence of a distinct defense of superior orders was in doubt in both the United States and Great Britain before the twentieth century. A number of earlier cases rejected the defense. After the Stuart restoration in 1660, the officer who had been commander of the guards at the 1649 trial of Charles I defended himself on the ground that "all [I] did was as a soldier, by the command of [my] superior officer whom [I] must obey or die." The court replied that "when the command is traitorous, then the obedience to that command is also traitorous" (*Axtell's Case*, 84 E.R. 1060 (para. 20) (c. 1661)). United States Chief Justice Roger Taney in 1851 declared: "It can never be maintained that a military officer can justify himself for doing an unlawful act, by producing the order of his superior" (*Mitchell v. Harmony*, 54 U.S. (13 Howard) 115, 137 (1851)).

Apparently the earliest statement of a general, governing rule appeared in Article 47 of the German Military Penal Code of 1872, which provided that "if execution of an order given in line of duty violates a statute of the penal code, the superior giving the order is alone responsible. However, the subordinate obeying the order is liable to punishment as an accomplice if . . . he knew that the order involved an act . . . which constituted a civil or military crime or offense." This provision remained in effect throughout World War II (Taylor, p. 47).

In 1914, both British and American military manuals exempted from liability those who violated the laws of war under orders of their government or commanders, while holding accountable those who originated the orders (Taylor, p. 47). A leading treatise on international law asserted the same point through five editions (Oppenheim, pp. 453–454). However, World War II called forth reconsideration of the issue. In 1944, both countries revised their military manuals, the British adopting essentially the German formulation of 1872 and the Americans recognizing that a superior order could be "taken into consideration in determining culpability" without suggesting how, why, or when (Taylor, pp. 48–49).

The matter received little clarification in the Nuremberg trials of 1945. Article 8 of the London Charter, promulgated by the victors in the war, rejected the defense of superior orders as such in advance of the trials, allowing the claim only in mitigation of punishment. However, as Glanville Williams noted, the "actual practice of the Allied tribunals was more enlightened than the instruments under which they acted" (p. 300). The defense was accepted in at least one case, where the claimed belief in the legality of the order was thought to have been reasonable.

The broadest form of the defense asserted at Nuremberg was "act of state." The claim was that an authorized act done on behalf of a state is imputed to the state, and only the state may be punished. The claims were flatly rejected at Nuremberg (McDougal and Feliciano, pp. 700–703). A more restrained version of the defense, as noted above, was treated ambiguously. After the Nuremberg judgments, the International Law Commission, at the request of the United Nations General Assembly, formulated the Principles of Nuremberg. Principle IV holds that a superior order "does not relieve [one] of responsibility under international law, provided a moral choice was in fact possible." No definition was given of "moral choice," but the concept was apparently intended to preserve only a defense of duress ("Decision and Judgment of the Tribunal," pp. 1176–1179).

It is doubtful that the Principles of Nuremberg was a correct statement of the law on this point (Redish). However, most of the orders in question at Nuremberg were so unconscionable that a more humane definition of the defense would have made no difference in the outcomes. Barring another Holocaust, the defense is available, regardless of "moral choice," for obedience to orders that the soldier reasonably believes to be lawful. As stated in the United States Army field manual, a superior order is a defense if the actor "did not know and could not reasonably have been expected to know that the act ordered was unlawful" (p. 182).

Even this formulation leaves many uncertainties and myriad problems of application. A major difficulty is determining whether there was a superior order for the conduct in question. Many military orders are oral, and often ambiguous. Even if the terminology is clear, its application to particular circumstances may not be. The order may be conditional upon future events, which must be evaluated by the subordinate. Circumstances on the battlefield change rapidly. When does an order expire? Presumably, the defense will be available whenever the subordinate who carries out the order (or conveys it to others) reasonably interprets it under all the circumstances, including the stress of the moment, the need for expedition, perceived military necessity, the actor's own knowledge of military law, and the practices he has observed in similar situations. If a soldier reasonably believes that he has received an order, it should not deprive him of the defense if it is later found that no order was in fact given.

Many of these problems are illustrated by prosecutions arising out of the participation of the United States military forces in the war between North and South Vietnam. After several years of increasingly unpopular American involvement in the undeclared war, the American press discovered and reported the My Lai massacre, one of many instances in which women and children in Vietnamese villages were killed by American forces. In *United States v. Calley*, 22 U.S.C.M.A. 534, 48 C.M.R. 19 (1973), Lieutenant William Calley, who had shot several women and children and ordered his subordinates to do the same, was convicted of murder. He claimed that his superior, Captain Ernest Medina, had told him in briefings before the invasion of the village that when they arrived no one but the enemy would be there and that it was essential to destroy everything in the village, including the inhabitants, who were enemies. Medina gave a different version of his directives. The trial judge instructed that Calley's orders to kill the inhabitants of the village, if he in fact did receive them, would be a defense unless the order was one "which a man of ordinary sense and understanding would, under the circumstances, know to be unlawful, or if the order . . . is actually known to the accused to be unlawful" (542, 27). The appellate court held that the burden was on the prosecution to disprove the defense beyond reasonable doubt, and that it had done so.

Military orders and domestic law. Generally, a defense of superior orders that will satisfy the criteria of the law of war or military law will also exculpate in a charge of violations of domestic law. That is, one who acts in obedience to an apparently lawful military order will receive immunity from all criminal prosecution—international, military, or domestic (*Montana v. Christopher*, 345 F. Supp. 60 (D. Mont. 1972)).

The American Law Institute's Model Penal Code carves out a defense to a domestic criminal prosecution which is even broader than that recognized in the law of war and military law. The Code asserts that it should be a defense to a domestic criminal prosecution that a member of the military acted in obedience to superior orders which he did not *know* to be unlawful (§ 2.10). Whether a soldier *should* have known the order to be unlawful, the Code's draftsmen state, is a matter best decided by military courts. There is much to be said for this position. Whether a soldier who did not know the order was unlawful *should* have known depends on the nature and quality of the instruction he received, the psychological stresses in the military situation, the practices he observed in combat, and military necessity. Such questions are not resolved efficiently or reliably by a domestic tribunal.

Domestic orders and domestic law. The application of the superior orders defense to purely domestic situations is less clear than in the military context. Authorities generally agree, however, that the principles are applicable if the circumstances are analogous (McDougal and Feliciano, p. 691). Where a domestic official issues an order to subordinates, as when a mayor orders policemen to "shoot all looters," the order lacks the coercive component inherent in many military orders. A domestic official who fails to carry out an order usually risks only his job; a soldier may risk his life and the lives of his fellow soldiers. Moreover, there is often time and opportunity for a domestic subordinate to question the order and to seek clarification or even legal advice. Still, in paramilitary organizations such as police forces, obedience is highly valued and carefully inculcated, emergency situations are common, and the superior often has express or implied authority to make interstitial law. The analogy to military conditions may be close. Where it is, a subordinate official who carries out the orders of his superior should be excused if he had a reasonable belief in the lawfulness of the order. At least in some contexts, as when a sheriff or executioner carries out an apparently lawful court order (Williams, p. 301; Model Penal Code § 3.03(3)(a)), this is clearly the case. With that exception, it appears to be the law in England that a superior order defense does not apply to a civil employee of the state (Williams, p. 301). The law in the United States is more hospitable to the defense.

In several prosecutions arising out of the Watergate scandal, such defenses were raised, with mixed results. There, members of a special investigations unit under the aegis of the White House were recruited by E. Howard Hunt, a former Central Intelligence Agency agent, under the supervision of John Ehrlichman, assistant to the President for domestic affairs. Hunt told his recruits that he was employed by the White House, wrote to them on White House stationery, and met with them in the Executive Office Building. He described his organization as "a sort of superstructure that was above the FBI and CIA" (*United States v. Barker*, 546 F.2d 940, 943 (D.C. Cir. 1976)) which had been formed "because the FBI was tied by Supreme Court decisions . . . and the [CIA] didn't have jurisdiction" (959). The job of the organization

was to conduct sensitive investigations involving "national security," "traitors," and "Soviet agents." Hunt then directed his recruits to burglarize the office of a psychiatrist in order to obtain "national security" information on a "traitor to this country" who was "passing . . . classified information to the Soviet Embassy" (943). Another burglary was carried out in the Democratic National Committee headquarters on Hunt's representation that the committee was receiving "money from Castroite sources in Cuba" (*United States v. Barker*, 514 F.2d 208, 217 (D.C. Cir. 1975)). The mission was to obtain proof thereof in the interest of "national security."

The defendants in the prosecutions arising out of the burglaries asserted apparent authority as a defense. Like soldiers in Vietnam, they claimed that they had accepted Hunt's representations because of their experience as CIA operatives, who were told only what they needed to know to carry out their tasks. Some judges of the Court of Appeals for the District of Columbia were of the opinion that the claims were legitimate under exceptions to the "mistake of law" defense; others thought the claims were plausible as "mistakes of fact." In the case involving the burglars of the psychiatrist's office, a majority of the court found the claim to be worthy of a jury's consideration (*United States v. Barker*, 546 F.2d 940). In other cases arising out of the burglaries, the defenses were rejected (*United States v. Barker*, 514 F.2d 208; *United States v. Ehrlichman*, 546 F.2d 910 (D.C. Cir. 1976)).

The Watergate burglars had some official or quasi-official connection to the government: they were recruited by a White House employee, with the approval of the President's chief domestic adviser. The difficulty the courts had with the superior orders defense in these cases may spring from a notion that persons who are acting in a governmental or quasi-governmental capacity have a higher burden than private citizens to ascertain that their acts are lawful. It is reasonably well settled, in the United States, that one who acts in reliance upon the order or permission of a government official may not be punished for that act, provided he neither knows nor has reason to know that the order or permission was unlawful (Model Penal Code § 2.04(3)(b)). Indeed, United States Supreme Court decisions hold that such punishment violates the due process clause of the Constitution (*Cox v. Louisiana*, 379 U.S. 559 (1965); *Raley v. Ohio*, 360 U.S. 423 (1959)).

Private orders. At the other end of the spectrum from military orders are orders from a private employer. A private individual or organization has no lawmaking power, nor any legitimate authority to employ force to obtain compliance with edicts. There is no strong public policy favoring obedience to private employers, and serious emergencies are uncommon. Accordingly, there is no recognized defense of superior orders in a purely private context (*United States v. Decker*, 304 F.2d 702, 705 (6th Cir. 1962)). A subordinate in a private organization who acts unlawfully in reliance upon an order or interpretation by a superior gains no immunity thereby; he must fit his defense into more conventional rubrics of mistake of fact or law or, rarely, of duress.

STEVEN DUKE

See also EXCUSE, *articles on* DURESS *and* THEORY; MILITARY JUSTICE, *articles on* COMPARATIVE ASPECTS *and* LEGAL ASPECTS; WAR CRIMES.

BIBLIOGRAPHY

American Law Institute. *Model Penal Code: Proposed Official Draft.* Philadelphia: ALI, 1962.

"Decision and Judgment of the Tribunal, Statement by Judge Herbert, and Sentences" [in "The I. G. Farben Case"]. *Trials of War Criminals before the Nuernberg Military Tribunals under Control Council Law No. 10, October 1946– April 1949*, vol. 8. Washington, D.C.: Government Printing Office, 1952, pp. 1081–1210.

GREEN, LESLIE C. *Superior Orders in National and International Law.* Leiden, Netherlands: Sijthoff, 1976.

McDOUGAL, MYRES S., and FELICIANO, FLORENTINO P. *Law and Minimum World Public Order: The Legal Regulation of International Coercion.* New Haven: Yale University Press, 1961.

OPPENHEIM, LASSA F. L. *International Law: A Treatise*, vol. 2. 5th ed. Edited by Hersh Lauterpacht. London: Longmans, Green, 1935.

REDISH, MARTIN. "Military Law: Nuremberg Rule of Superior Orders." *Harvard International Law Journal* 9 (1968): 169–181.

TAYLOR, TELFORD. *Nuremberg and Vietnam: An American Tragedy.* New York: Quadrangle, 1970.

U.S. Department of the Army. *The Law of Land Warfare.* Washington, D.C.: The Department, 1956.

WILLIAMS, GLANVILLE. *Criminal Law: The General Part.* 2d ed. London: Stevens, 1961.

EXECUTIONS

See CAPITAL PUNISHMENT; CRUEL AND UNUSUAL PUNISHMENT.

EXHIBITIONISM

See both articles under SEX OFFENSES.

EXILE

See BANISHMENT AND EXILE; CRIMINOLOGY: INTELLECTUAL HISTORY; PENAL COLONIES.

EXPERT TESTIMONY

See CRIMINALISTICS; MENTAL HEALTH EXPERT, ROLE OF THE; TRIAL, CRIMINAL.

EXTORTION

See BLACKMAIL AND EXTORTION.

EXTRADITION

See INTERNATIONAL CRIMINAL LAW; JURISDICTION; TERRORISM.

EYEWITNESS IDENTIFICATION

1. PSYCHOLOGICAL ASPECTS   A. Daniel Yarmey
2. CONSTITUTIONAL ASPECTS   Paul Marcus

1.
PSYCHOLOGICAL ASPECTS

Introduction and background

"I will never forget that face . . . I'm positive he is the man. . . ." On the basis of such eyewitness accounts, defendants can be convicted in some criminal courts without any corroborating evidence. Although the identification may be false and the testimony upon which it is based unreliable, judges and juries may believe reports of even a single eyewitness because he appears convincing (*Fry v. Commonwealth*, 259 Ky. 337, 82 S.W.2d 431 (1935); *Regina v. Corbett*, [1973] 11 C.C.C.(2d) 137 (B.C. Ct. App.), *aff'd*, 14 C.C.C.(2d) 385, 25 C.R.N.S. 296 (Can. S. Ct.) (1974)).

Jurists have long recognized that mistaken eyewitness identification is responsible for serious miscarriages of justice, more so, perhaps, than any other determining factor (Sobel). Courts are inclined to accept this error as an unavoidable product of human nature—the commonsense view of man as imperfect (*United States v. Amaral*, 488 F.2d 1148 (9th Cir. 1973)). Beliefs that perception and memory may be understood solely through personal experience promote such miscarriages of justice.

Eyewitness identification is frequently much less reliable than the courts would generally believe. However, it can often be facilitated and improved by minimizing faulty procedures and misleading questioning techniques. The major goal of eyewitness identification research is to provide the courts with scientifically established knowledge concerning the reliability of eyewitness identification. Information of this sort may minimize the risk of an erroneous conviction or acquittal.

Some of the earliest applications of psychology to law date back to the early twentieth century; a pioneer in the field was Hugo Münsterberg of Harvard University. One of Münsterberg's procedures was to stage a "mock crime" during a lecture to a group of students, lawyers, or judges. At a certain point, several persons would break into the hall, feign an assault or pull a gun and fire a shot, and then exit, all within a span of about twenty seconds. Münsterberg then asked his audience to describe the assailants and the events that had happened. His results, which have since been replicated in scores of lecture halls, indicated that the observers' reports of almost every incident, and their descriptions of the attackers' personal characteristics, contained numerous errors. Furthermore, Münsterberg showed that the mock crime did not have to be stressful in order to produce errors of perception and memory.

Another important pioneeer was William Stern. His investigations demonstrated that witnesses of all ages differ greatly in ability to recall details of crimes. Stern also showed that memory was adversely affected by imagination, by the influence of rumor, and by suggestive questions.

Psychological foundations

The term *eyewitness identification* refers to the process of a witness observing an incident or person(s), retaining that information in memory, and retrieving the information later when called to identify the suspect(s) or reconstruct the events. These perceptual and memory processes are divided into three cognitive stages: acquisition, retention, and retrieval.

Acquisition. The perception of an event involves the encoding of sensory information into memory codes. Perception entails more than a mere passive recording of an event: what witnesses observe depends on what they pay attention to. Attention is highly selective but is not always conscious. Factors determining attention include sudden changes in stimulation, the novelty and complexity of information, and the repetition and intensity of stimuli. Attention is also influenced by motivation, interest, and expectations.

What a witness perceives depends on the characteristics of the environment, the receptivity of his sensory system, his motivation, and his previous experiences in similar situations. Perception involves making sense of the stimuli activating the receptors. However, a person's interpretations may or may not be accurate. Perception will also be influenced by the observer's thoughts, feelings, and reactions during the perceived events, and, of course, defects of vision or hearing contribute to faulty perception. Because more information strikes the receptors than can be encoded, decisions must be made regarding which stimuli to encode and which to ignore. As a consequence, some important information may be excluded. Any perceptual gaps created by this selectivity tend to be filled through inference.

Retention. The encoding process prepares information for storage and also determines its accessibility at retrieval. Newly stored information may be changed by previously stored knowledge, labels, and images. Storage is selective since an individual may remember only highly salient, dynamic information. Information that is needed only for a few seconds, such as the time needed to dial an unfamiliar telephone number, is stored in short-term memory. This store has a limited capacity and can only retain approximately seven items of information at any one time before they are either forgotten or stored in long-term memory.

Long-term memory has an apparently infinite capacity to store information, some of which may be retained permanently. Although some information is nearly always accessible, such as knowing one's own name, other information, for example, where car keys were left, is accessible only some of the time. Furthermore, long-term memory is also constantly involved in encoding new material and recoding stored information into more meaningful units.

Stored information may remain in the memory relatively unchanged, but it may also be altered by information acquired from the questions of others, from newspaper accounts and television programs, or from overheard conversations. In other words, memory is an active, continuing process, not a fixed or static one.

Retrieval. Unlike the quick and automatic retrieval of information from the short-term store, retrieval from the long-term store is relatively complex. Two of the most common ways of testing memory are those of recall and recognition. A witness narrating his experiences utilizes recall memory. Such free reports tend to be highly accurate, but they may omit important details. A more difficult task is to recall information serially. Serial recall often shows good memory for information at the beginning and end of the sequence but poor recall for materials in the middle.

Memory is often facilitated by the use of cued recall, in which witnesses are asked such questions as "Can you state the suspect's age? Was he twenty-five, twenty-three, twenty-one, or nineteen?" Interrogation of this sort increases the completeness of witness reports, but accuracy is not as high as that in free recall.

Witnesses asked to identify a suspect from photographs or a lineup employ recognition memory. The individual compares the photograph or persons on display with stored information and makes a decision based upon a familiar or nonfamiliar match.

Errors in memory. Witnesses typically make two sorts of memory errors, those of omission and of commission. A failure to pay attention, or the decision to select some material over others, may mean that errors of omission will occur. Failure to retrieve may also result from poor memory organization: the needed information may be available but not readily accessible when the memory store is searched. With appropriate retrieval cues, information thought to be forgotten may be remembered.

Errors of commission refer to distortions and intrusions from associated memories being confused with the sought-after information. Moreover, decay of the memory trace over time can cause forgetting. Retrieval is also influenced by expectations and inference of what should have happened as opposed to what did happen. Other errors of commission are caused by alcohol and drug abuse, physical and emotional trauma, and such bodily changes as those associated with senility.

Memory is also a social process. People act and react toward others, and, as one would expect, perceptions and memory are influenced by the real or imagined presence and actions of others.

Thus, perception and memory are not automatic, mechanical processes that mirror reality in the same way that a camera or videotape gathers and stores information. Accordingly, eyewitness identifications that appear obvious and based on common sense may in fact be much more complex.

Applied research on eyewitness identification

An important question of legal concern is whether laboratory-derived findings and the theoretical relevance of attention, perception, and memory may be generalized to real-life situations. Actual crime-related situations tend to be unexpected, stressful, and confusing. In contrast, experimental subjects are usually aware that the crimes they are observing are simulated, that the people involved are not real criminals, and that a memory test will be given.

To take one example, researchers have extensively investigated the perception and memory of faces. What is the application of this work to the criminal identification of suspects through the viewing of mug shots, artists' drawings, commercial composites, and corporeal lineups? Laboratory studies have indicated that subjects asked to identify faces in a recognition memory test did so accurately in about 75 percent of their selections (Goldstein). Although these results should not be rejected because the studies were conducted under controlled, artificial conditions (*Ballew v. Georgia*, 435 U.S. 223 (1978)), such experimental investigations have to be critically evaluated for their scientific validity and reliability. Their results show what may be expected from witnesses under optimal viewing conditions; even under good conditions experimental subjects were wrong 25 percent of the time, and thus real-life recognition performance would undoubtedly be much poorer.

More significantly, research is increasingly being conducted outside the laboratory in more naturalistic settings, for example, testing persons who witnessed mock crimes performed in supermarkets and banks. Moreover, scientific investigators are no longer content with merely warning the police, lawyers, and judges of the dangers of eyewitness identification, as they did in the mid-1970s. Instead, researchers are concerned with making the process of identification more just and more reliable through an examination of the differences in the cognitive capacities and judgments of witnesses in relation to specific legal situations.

Gary Wells has suggested that research findings on eyewitness identification and testimony can be categorized into two functional classes. The first category, called *estimator* variables, consists of those events influencing the accuracy of identification that cannot be controlled by the criminal justice system. It includes such variables as the sex, age, personality, and race of the criminal or of the witness. Other such variables are witnesses' attitudes, prejudices, and stereotyped behavior; the physical nature of the criminal event, such as the amount of illumination and the duration and stress of the event; physical changes over time in the appearance of criminal suspects; and differences in artists' interpretations of witnesses' descriptions.

A second category of variables, which Wells calls *system* variables, can be controlled by the criminal justice system. It includes lineup procedures, delays in holding the lineup, tests with composite drawings and mug shots, and interrogation procedures. Understanding and control of these variables will not eliminate misidentifications, but taking cognizance of system variables may well lead the criminal justice system to a more reliable use of evidence.

Research evidence

A brief review of some of the more established findings on eyewitness identifications and testimony follows, beginning with estimator variables and proceeding to system variables.

Estimator variables: sex, age, and personality. In nonstressful laboratory conditions most studies indicate that females are superior to males in face recognition generally, and in recognizing faces of their own gender in particular. Evidence suggests that in crime-related situations women attend to and remember female-oriented materials, whereas men retain male-oriented details. Males and females do not differ in recall of facts from nonviolent incidents, and both sexes recall facts more clearly from nonviolent than from violent incidents. However, males are superior to females in recalling the details of violent events.

Research also suggests that men are more likely than women to be believed as witnesses. Men have more credibility because cultural stereotypes characterize them as independent, active, and self-confident. Women tend to be less believable because of their assumed lack of assertiveness. The speech manner of many women suggests a lack of confidence and greater suggestibility, and jurors have been shown to disbelieve witnesses who speak in such a manner.

The accuracy and credibility of eyewitnesses are also related to age. Children do not observe people or the environment as selectively and efficiently as do adults, and are inferior to adults in recall and recognition memory. The most serious problem in questioning children as eyewitnesses is their high susceptibility to suggestive or leading questions.

The elderly also present problems to the court as eyewitnesses. Evidence shows that healthy elderly witnesses are similar to young adults in identifying criminal suspects. However, the elderly make more false identifications of innocent people, are poorer in verbal recall of criminal events, and are less confident in their testimony. The elderly, unlike young adults, may misidentify an innocent bystander to a crime if the bystander looks like the stereotype of a criminal.

It should nevertheless be stressed that eyewitness self-confidence is not a valid predictor of performance accuracy, except under optimal conditions and when the person observed is very familiar to the witness. Nor does any evidence exist showing a relationship between personality factors and eyewitness identification.

Race. Most research on cross-racial identification indicates that individuals tend to be more accurate in recognizing faces of members of their own race; there is a high probability that suspects of other races will be falsely identified. Most such research has been conducted on blacks and whites, but similar results have been found with Japanese, Chinese, and other Asian subjects (*United States v. Watson*, 587 F.2d 365 (7th Cir. 1978)).

Social factors: conformity, attitudes, prejudices, and stereotypes. If a suspect is observed by more than one eyewitness and the witnesses have the opportunity to discuss the incident among themselves, some who were initially doubtful about their identification are likely to conform to the group opinion. A related problem is a tendency to conform to the suggestions of such authority figures as police officers. Witnesses may want to show the police that they are "good citizens" and are willing to do their duty even when this means disregarding their own judgment.

Newly acquired information is constantly being organized and reorganized to conform to already-existing knowledge and beliefs. Personal attitudes, prejudices, and stereotypes can distort perceptions of criminal events. In one study, observers who saw a white man holding a razor and standing next to a black man asserted later that the black man held the razor and was making threatening gestures with it. Society adheres to vivid stereotypes about physical appearance, and perceptions of demeanor may influence the identification of criminal suspects.

Illumination, duration, and emotionality of events. Eyewitnesses to a crime are rarely in a state of alertness. In addition, crimes frequently take place at night or in poor illumination. If a witness has good eyesight, his observations may be accurate. He must also know that a crime is being committed and must attach some significance to it. However, the crime's seriousness may not be known until after it is completed, and in such a case the probability of accurate identification is low. Moreover, many serious crimes are committed in a matter of seconds. Short observation periods obviously minimize the opportunity to encode and store information in long-term memory, particularly information that is complex and stressful.

Contrary to the belief of many judges, perception

and memory under extreme levels of stress are usually inaccurate (*People v. Johnson*, 38 Cal. App. 3d 1, 112 Cal. Rptr. 834 (1974)). When a witness is in a state of intense fear, attention may be focused on weapons or escape routes rather than on a criminal's face or physical characteristics.

Disguises. Even when the observation period has been relatively long, changes such as the removal of glasses, or alterations in hair style, can substantially retard recognition. The greatest loss in recognition accuracy results from changes in beards and moustaches.

Artists' impressions. Accuracy of artists' drawings of suspects' faces depends partly on accuracy of communication between eyewitnesses and artists and on the artists' ability. In addition to normal distortions of memory from biases and the passage of time, most witnesses have difficulty describing their visual memories.

System variables: lineup procedures. A lineup usually involves a single suspect standing among a group of individuals (foils) who are known to be innocent. If the witness identifies a foil as the guilty person, this discredits the value of his testimony. Lineup techniques would seem to be fair, but, as the United States Supreme Court acknowledges, "miscarriages of justice are related to the degree of suggestion inherent in the manner in which the prosecution presents the suspect to the witness for pretrial identification" (*United States v. Wade*, 388 U.S. 218 (1967); *Gilbert v. California*, 388 U.S. 263 (1967); *Stovall v. Denno*, 388 U.S. 293 (1967)). Furthermore, a jury may believe that a lineup identification is reliable because it was obtained by a procedure that is assumed to be fair (Wall).

Some of the estimator variables mentioned above can interfere with photographic and corporeal lineup identifications. However, controls over system variables can at least minimize suggestive influence. The possibilities of such influence are endless, ranging from the common presumption that the police would not arrange a lineup unless they had picked up the real criminal, to blatant differences in appearance between the foils as a group and the suspect. The reliability of a lineup identification also depends on the length of time between witnessing the criminal event and attempting to identify the suspect. Instructions should inform witnesses that the suspect may or may not be in the lineup. The common police practice of showing witnesses photographs of the suspect before conducting an actual lineup reduces reliability (*Bennett v. State*, 530 S.W.2d 511 (Tenn. 1975)). When a suspect's photograph has appeared in a photo dis-

play and that person is subsequently placed in a lineup, identification could depend on the familiarity deriving from the prior photo display. In the final analysis, identification of a suspect suggests solely that he is familiar to the witness for some reason, or that he resembles the criminal more than any of the foils.

Training in face recognition. Since facial recognition is of great importance for such persons as police officers, store detectives, and passport officers, training in this skill would seem to be valuable. Unfortunately, research indicates that facial recognition training is ineffective. Moreover, although the police, as well as lawyers, judges, and potential jurors, believe that police training and practical experience develop a superior ability to observe and remember details of criminal events, experimental evidence shows no differences in such ability between police and civilians. Police officers are also especially prone to perceive suspicious behavior as intent to commit crime, and may justify these perceptions by "remembering" events that have not happend.

Suggestive interrogation. The questions police ask also have an impact. Evidence shows that the phrasing of questions definitely can influence answers. In one study, for example, observers who were asked "How tall was the basketball player?" estimated that his height was about seventy-nine inches. Those asked "How short was the basketball player?" responded with an estimate of about sixty-nine inches.

Elizabeth Loftus has shown that post-event altering of information can influence recall. Witnesses who were asked "How fast were the cars going when they (hit) (bumped) (collided) (smashed) each other?" gave increasingly higher estimates of speed according to the increasing violence implied by the verb. In another experiment, subjects were asked either "Did you see *a* broken headlight?" or "Did you see *the* broken headlight?" one week after observing an unbroken headlight. Those queried with *the* answered in the affirmative twice as often as those queried with *a*. Other research indicates that misleading information has its greatest effect on memory if it is stored very soon after the initial perception of the critical event.

Obviously, the police and others need to be concerned with the manner in which questions are asked. To minimize the inadvertent biasing of memory, witnesses should give a free narration before being asked specific questions. Interrogation should also take place as soon as possible so that misleading information from various sources does not become part of the remembered event.

Hypnosis. Another system variable that can be controlled to assist interrogation is hypnosis. Forensic hypnosis, which differs from clinical hypnosis in that it involves establishing facts for judicial purposes as opposed to alleviating distress and pain, is valuable when it provides police officers with information that otherwise would not be remembered (*Harding v. State*, 5 Md. App. 230, 246 A.2d 302 (1968)). This information may lead to other competent evidence that can be independently corroborated. However, abuse is possible, as was recognized in *United States v. Adams*, 581 F.2d 193 (9th Cir. 1978): "We are concerned, however, that investigatory use of hypnosis on persons who may later be called upon to testify in court carries a dangerous potential for abuse. Great care must be exercised to insure that statements after hypnosis are the products of the subject's own recollections, rather than of recall tainted by suggestions received while under hypnosis" (198–199).

It must be emphasized that hypnotic memory, like other memory states, is susceptible to distortions and errors in recall. Furthermore, hypnosis cannot retrieve information that was not initially encoded. Hypnosis does not guarantee truth: individuals are able to simulate hypnotic traces that can deceive even highly experienced hypnotists; subjects can also willfully lie even when in deep hypnosis. However, willful lying is not the only major concern. Far more troublesome for the courts in cross-examination is the witness who believes that hypnosis reveals the truth, and is convinced that his memory now is accurate.

Hypnotized persons are hypersuggestible and hypercompliant, and they are consequently susceptible to leading questions and cues from police and other observers. Because of their wish to please the hypnotist and his associates, witnesses may create pseudomemories that are plausible but inaccurate. It is difficult to separate accurate recalled information from that which has been suggested or invented. For these reasons, most of the scientific community agrees that information gathered through hypnosis is not necessarily reliable. Unfortunately, in at least one case a defendant has been convicted primarily on hypnosis-based testimonial evidence (*Quaglino v. California*, Crim. No. 29766, Cal. App. 2d Dist., Sept. 20, 1977 (unrep.); Orne).

Earwitness identification. Witnesses can sometimes hear but not see their assailants because of darkness, the wearing of masks, or threats received by phone. Voice identification is often accepted by both law enforcement agencies and the courts (Tosi). However, the same problems inherent in eyewitness identification apply to earwitness identification. Errors result from the variability of the same speaker's voice on different occasions, the variability of voice quality in different speakers, the use of disguise, delay in testing, lack of attention and of intention to learn, age of the witnesses, and so on (Clifford).

Eyewitness identification and jury decisions. One field study of felony trials concluded that jurors attach little significance to eyewitness identifications (Myers). Contradictory legal observations indicate that jurors and court officers often place more faith in eyewitness testimony than any other type of evidence (*People v. Cashin*, 259 N.Y. 434, 182 N.E. 74 (1932); *Spires v. State*, 50 Fla. 121, 39 So. 181 (1905); *State v. Thomas*, 193 Iowa 1004, 188 N.W. 689 (1922)). The conclusions of both field and experimental research in this area have been inconsistent, thus emphasizing the complexity of the issues involved. Experimental evidence has shown, however, that mock jurors are highly influenced by the confidence that an eyewitness projects, regardless of the actual accuracy of his identification.

Conclusion

Many have argued that expert testimony relating to the quality of eyewitness identification has rational probative or evidential value (Clifford and Bull; Loftus; Loftus and Monahan; Sobel; Wall; Wells and Loftus; Woocher; Yarmey). Experimental evidence indicates that mock jurors deliberate longer on all the evidence after hearing such expert testimony. As indicated in *United States v. Brown*, 501 F.2d 146 (9th Cir. 1974), *rev'd on other grounds sub nom. United States v. Nobles*, 422 U.S. 225 (1975), it is now for the courts to decide whether expert testimony on eyewitness identification should be taken to assist the jury in understanding the evidence, or whether such testimony should be excluded on the ground that it invades the province of the jury.

A. DANIEL YARMEY

See also EYEWITNESS IDENTIFICATION: CONSTITUTIONAL ASPECTS.

BIBLIOGRAPHY

CLIFFORD, BRIAN R. "Voice Identification by Human Listeners: On Earwitness Reliability." *Law and Human Behavior* 4 (1980): 373–394.
———, and BULL, RAY. *The Psychology of Person Identification.* Boston: Routledge & Kegan Paul, 1978.
GOLDSTEIN, ALVIN G. "The Fallibility of the Eyewitness: Psychological Evidence." *Psychology in the Legal Process.* Edited by Bruce D. Sales. New York: Spectrum, 1977.
LOFTUS, ELIZABETH F. *Eyewitness Testimony.* Cambridge, Mass.: Harvard University Press, 1979.

——, and MONAHAN, JOHN. "Trial by Data: Psychological Research as Legal Evidence." *American Psychologist* 35 (1980): 270–283.

MÜNSTERBERG, HUGO. *On the Witness Stand: Essays on Psychology and Crime.* New York: Doubleday, Page, 1915.

MYERS, MARTHA A. "Rule Departures and Making Law: Juries and Their Verdicts." *Law and Society* 13 (1979): 781–797.

ORNE, MARTIN T. "The Use and Misuse of Hypnosis in Court." *International Journal of Clinical and Experimental Hypnosis* 27 (1979): 311–341.

SOBEL, NATHAN R. *Eye-witness Identification: Legal and Practical Problems.* New York: Boardman, 1972. (Supplement added, 1979.)

STERN, WILLIAM. "Abstracts of Lectures on the Psychology of Testimony and on the Study of Individuality." *American Journal of Psychology* 21 (1910): 270–282.

TOSI, OSCAR I. *Voice Identification: Theory and Legal Applications.* Baltimore: University Park Press, 1979.

WALL, PATRICK M. *Eyewitness Identification in Criminal Cases.* Springfield, Ill.: Thomas, 1965.

WELLS, GARY L. "Applied Eyewitness Testimony Research: System Variables and Estimator Variables." *Journal of Personality and Social Psychology* 36 (1978): 1546–1557.

——, and LOFTUS, ELIZABETH F., eds. *Eyewitness Testimony: Psychological Perspectives.* Cambridge, Mass.: Harvard University Press, 1982.

WOOCHER, FREDRIC D. "Did Your Eyes Deceive You? Expert Psychological Testimony on the Unreliability of Eyewitness Identification." *Stanford Law Review* 29 (1977): 969–1030.

YARMEY, A. DANIEL. *The Psychology of Eyewitness Testimony.* New York: Free Press, 1979.

2.

CONSTITUTIONAL ASPECTS

Eyewitness identifications by witnesses to a crime are often extremely important parts of the government's case against the defendant. One form of eyewitness identification takes place at trial when the victim of the crime for the first time states, "That's him; he is the one who robbed me." Traditionally, little question has been raised in connection with such an identification, so long as the witness was subject to cross-examination by the defendant's lawyer. More often, however, the initial identification by the witness takes place at a time before trial. At the time of trial, the witness then identifies the defendant again. In such a situation, the witness might simply state that he remembers the defendant as the robber, or might in addition refer to the pretrial identification. In the cases in which there has been a pretrial identification, the United States Supreme Court has been most con-cerned with possible violations of the defendant's constitutional rights.

Self-incrimination. Eyewitness identifications are not normally subject to serious challenge under the Fifth Amendment provision that "no person . . . shall be compelled in any criminal case to be a witness against himself." The Court has rejected the claim that the defendant is so compelled when he is required to participate in a lineup, dress the way the suspect was supposed to have dressed, or speak the words spoken at the time of the crime. "We have no doubt that compelling the accused merely to exhibit his person for observation by a prosecution witness prior to trial involves no compulsion of the accused to give evidence having testimonial significance." The Justices went on to explain that the important distinction under the privilege against self-incrimination is one between "an accused's 'communications' in whatever form, vocal or physical," which are protected, and "compulsion which makes a suspect or accused the source of real or physical evidence," which is permitted (*United States v. Wade*, 388 U.S. 218, 222–223 (1967)).

Due process. Although eyewitness identifications do not often run afoul of the privilege against self-incrimination, they do raise questions concerning the reliability of the procedure used by the government and the process needed to detect unreliability. The Supreme Court has provided answers to these questions in a series of cases beginning in 1967. That year, the Court decided that a defendant could successfully assert that the pretrial identification proceeding had been conducted so improperly as to violate his right to due process of law. It was not certain, however, what the basis of a due process challenge was to be. Some judges thought that the United States Constitution was violated if the proceeding was unnecessarily suggestive—that is, if it tended to show the witness which suspect was the "correct" one. The most prominent example of the unnecessarily suggestive procedure is the showup, where only the suspect is brought before the witness. Essentially, the witness is being asked, "This is the person who did it, isn't it?" Some judges found a violation of due process even if the identification was ultimately shown to be clearly correct, because of the government's unfair attempts to influence the witness when a more fair and reliable process could have been used. Other judges found a due process violation only if the proceeding was inherently unreliable—that is, if the validity of the identification was subject to real doubt, as where the witness had a limited opportunity to see the person and gave a very sketchy description. Still other judges looked to a combination of these two bases.

The due process issue was finally settled by the Supreme Court in *Manson v. Brathwaite*, 432 U.S. 98 (1977), a case in which the defendant was identified by an undercover police officer who purchased drugs from the defendant. The officer saw lying on his desk a single photograph of the defendant two days after the incident and said that the man in the photo was the same man from whom he had purchased drugs. The facts indicated without question that this procedure was suggestive, for the officer was given only one photograph to identify. Because the witness was a police officer and there was no emergency, it was also unnecessarily suggestive. The Court, however, declined to adopt a broad exclusionary rule to deter future identifications of that kind. Since the procedure for identification that had been followed was reliable under all the circumstances, the Court concluded that the identification testimony should be admissible at trial. The Court indicated that judges must look to numerous factors in determining whether the identification procedure was reliable, including the opportunity of the witness to view the defendant at the time of the incident, his degree of attention, the accuracy of his description, the witness's level of certainty, and the time between the alleged crime and the identification.

Fair trial. The case of *Wade* established the principle that the absence of a lawyer at a postindictment lineup could so affect the defendant's ability to receive a fair trial as to violate his constitutional rights. Although the government characterized the lineup as merely a preparatory step in the gathering of its evidence, at which the presence of a lawyer would be inappropriate, the Supreme Court disagreed. It concluded that the lineup was a significant and critical stage in the proceedings against the defendant, at which an attorney is needed to ensure that the risks of mistaken identification are kept to a minimum. The lawyer is necessary to preserve the defendant's basic right to a fair trail, specifically his right meaningfully to cross-examine the witnesses against him and to have effective assistance of counsel at the trial itself. The Court emphasized that the defendant, if unassisted by counsel at the lineup, would probably be unable to detect suggestive influences or to establish their existence by his own testimony at trial.

The Court in *Wade* also held that unless the defendant waives his right to a lawyer at the lineup, the government will not be allowed to offer at trial evidence regarding the lineup identification if counsel is not provided. As for in-court identification of the defendant, it is also impermissible—even if no reference at trial was made to the pretrial lineup—if the in-court identification was based on the unlawful pretrial procedure. For the in-court identification to be admissible, the trial judge would have to determine that it was based upon observations of the defendant other than at the lineup identification.

The most troublesome questions under the Supreme Court's *Wade* decision have never been adequately answered. The Court stated that the "presence of counsel itself can often avert prejudice and assure a meaningful confrontation at trial." Unfortunately, it never explained what function the attorney was to serve at the pretrial identification proceeding. Is he merely to act as an observer to detect suggestive techniques so that he may bring them out during his at-trial cross-examination? If this is his only role, one may well question whether attorneys are especially well trained as careful observers. If the lawyer determines that there is something suggestive about the proceeding, should he take the affirmative step of intervening and identifying such a proceeding for the government officials? If he fails to do so, is he foreclosed from objecting to the procedure at trial? Finally, and most troublesome of all, if the attorney does determine that some irregularity has occurred at some point during the proceeding, is he to be a witness at the trial when the identification proceeding is challenged? Such a function by the lawyer raises difficulty with respect to his usual role. The lawyer is employed as an advocate on behalf of his client, rather than as an unbiased witness.

The Supreme Court repeatedly emphasized in *Wade* that the lineup had taken place after the defendant was formally charged by means of an indictment. In *Kirby v. Illinois*, 406 U.S. 682 (1972), the in-court identification testimony was based upon a police-station view of the witness that took place before the defendant had been indicted or otherwise formally charged with any criminal offense. The suspect in *Kirby* had been identified the day he was brought in for questioning, some six weeks before he was indicted. The Court stated that the actions of the police constituted routine investigation techniques because no formal adversary criminal proceedings had yet been brought against the defendant. Until adversary criminal proceedings have been initiated against the defendant, the Court held in *Kirby*, there is no critical stage that would cause the Sixth Amendment right to counsel to be applicable. Therefore, the defendant was not entitled to a lawyer at this preindictment procedure. The Court went on to say in *Kirby* that adversary judicial criminal proceedings could be commenced "by way of formal charge, preliminary hearing, indictment, information, or arraignment." The lower courts are not in agreement as to whether the mere issuance of an arrest warrant will suffice.

The *Kirby* majority's interpretation of the holding in *Wade* is an exceptionally narrow one. It is true that the defendant in *Wade* had already been indicted, but that fact does not appear to form the chief basis for the Court's concerns in *Wade*. The author of the *Wade* opinion, Justice William Brennan, dissented from the ruling in *Kirby*, stating, "*Wade* did not require the presence of counsel at pretrial confrontations for identification purposes simply on the basis of an abstract consideration of the words 'criminal prosecutions' in the Sixth Amendment. Counsel is required at those confrontations because 'the dangers inherent in eyewitness identification and the suggestibility inherent in the context of the pretrial identification' mean that protection must be afforded to . . . '[the] right to a fair trial at which the witnesses against [the defendant] might be meaningfully cross-examined' " (*Kirby*, 696–697). Because these dangers are present whenever a lineup is held, whether before or after the issuance of an indictment, Justice Brennan, along with three other Justices, declined to vote with the majority in *Kirby*.

Perhaps the explanation for the Court's alteration of the basis for *Wade* was the fear that it would be impractical to require counsel at all police-arranged identification procedures, however early in the criminal investigation. This is a particularly interesting point to ponder in light of the congressional attempt to repeal the *Wade* holding. Title II of the Omnibus Crime Control and Safe Streets Act of 1968 provides: "The testimony of a witness that he saw the accused commit or participate in the commission of the crime for which the accused is being tried shall be admissible in evidence in a criminal prosecution in any trial court ordained and established under article III of the Constitution of the United States" (18 U.S.C. § 3502 (1976)). As noted by one federal judge, the courts have relied on the *Wade* holding rather than the statute, so that the statute "has proved to be meaningless" (McGowan, pp. 249–250).

Soon after the *Wade* decision, the Supreme Court was called upon to decide whether its right-to-counsel rule would apply to the situation in which the government conducted a postindictment photographic display containing a picture of the accused. In *United States v. Ash*, 413 U.S. 300 (1973), the witnesses were shown photographs to determine whether the defendant was the person they had viewed committing the crime. Several of them selected the defendant as the bank robber. The defendant unsuccessfully contended that he had a constitutional right to have his attorney present at the display. The Justices thought that counsel should only be present when the accused himself was confronted by the witnesses and the government officials, reasoning that the purpose of the right to counsel was to allow the defendant to have his lawyer assist him. If the defendant himself was not confronted by the government, there was no necessity for having the attorney present. Moreover, because identification proceedings such as photographic displays, blood testing, and handwriting sampling could be reproduced easily at trial, such proceedings could not be deemed critical under the Sixth Amendment.

The Court's position is difficult to understand. It is not at all clear why the presence of the defendant is necessarily linked to the presence of the attorney. Indeed, an effective argument could be made that there is more of a need for an attorney when the defendant is not present, because in that situation no one would be present to discover errors. Moreover, the fact that photographic displays can be reproduced at trial should hardly be dispositive. The comments and questions of the government officials will not necessarily be reproduced, nor will the comments and questions of the witness.

Conclusion. The Supreme Court has sought to establish minimal constitutional rules that apply to pretrial identification proceedings and to in-court testimony concerning such proceedings. It must be emphasized, however, that these are minimum rules. State courts are free, under their own state constitutions, to go beyond these rules, and some courts have done so. For example, some state judges have required the presence of counsel at lineups that take place prior to formal adversary judicial proceedings; other judges discourage the use of photographic identification proceedings when the defendant is in custody. This involvement by the state courts is desirable, for the Supreme Court appears to have answered the important questions touching on eyewitness identification in a very inconsistent fashion. In some cases, such as those involving postindictment lineups, the Court has firmly protected the defendant's right to a fair trial by providing counsel. In other cases, however, such as those involving photo displays or preindictment lineups, the Court has been unwilling to require the presence of counsel.

PAUL MARCUS

See also CRIMINAL PROCEDURE: CONSTITUTIONAL ASPECTS; EYEWITNESS IDENTIFICATION: PSYCHOLOGICAL ASPECTS.

BIBLIOGRAPHY

GRANO, JOSEPH D. *"Kirby, Biggers,* and *Ash:* Do Any Constitutional Safeguards Remain against the Danger of Convicting the Innocent?" *Michigan Law Review* 72 (1974): 717–798.

LEVINE, FELICE J., and TAPP, JEAN LOUIN. "The Psychology of Criminal Identification: The Gap from *Wade* to *Kirby.*" *University of Pennsylvania Law Review* 121 (1973): 1079–1131.

McGOWAN, CARL. "Constitutional Interpretation and Criminal Identification." *William and Mary Law Review* 12 (1970): 235–251.

POLSKY, LEON B.; UVILLER, H. RICHARD; ZICCARDI, VINCENT J.; and DAVIS, ALAN J. "The Role of the Defense Lawyer at a Lineup in Light of the *Wade, Gilbert,* and *Stoval* Decisions." *Criminal Law Bulletin* 4 (1968): 273–296.

PULASKI, CHARLES A. *"Neil v. Biggers:* The Supreme Court Dismantles the *Wade* Trilogy's Due Process Protection." *Stanford Law Review* 26 (1974): 1097–1121.

READ, FRANK T. "Lawyers at Lineups: Constitutional Necessity or Avoidable Extravagance?" *UCLA Law Review* 17 (1969): 339–407.

SOBEL, NATHAN R., and PRIDGEN, DEE. *Eyewitness Identification: Legal and Practical Problems.* 2d ed. New York: Clark, Boardman, 1981.

STEELE, WALTER W., JR. *"Kirby v. Illinois:* Counsel at Lineups." *Criminal Law Bulletin* 9 (1973): 49–58.

F

FAIR TRIAL, RIGHT TO

See Counsel: right to counsel; Criminal Procedure: constitutional aspects; Publicity in Criminal Cases; Trial, Criminal.

FALSE PRETENSE

See Theft.

FAMILY RELATIONSHIPS AND CRIME

"The most important part of education," said the Athenian in Plato's *Laws*, "is right training in the nursery" (643). Through acceptance of Freudian theory, this ancient belief gained new credibility during the first half of the twentieth century. According to Freudian theory, successful socialization begins with an early attachment to the mother, an attachment that must later be modified by a conscience, or "superego," that develops through identification with a parent of the child's own sex. In the case of a young boy, the theory continues, attachment to the mother leads to the boy's jealousy of his father, but fear of his father's anger and punishment forces the child to control his incestuous and antisocial desires. Since Freud argued that the development of one's conscience depends on attachment to the mother and identification with the father, psychoanalytic explanations of crime, developing from Freud's theory, have focused on paternal absence and maternal deprivation.

Toward the mid-twentieth century, two types of sociological theories became influential. First Charles Cooley and then George Herbert Mead proposed that people develop self-concepts which reflect how they believe they are perceived by "significant others." These self-concepts motivate a person's actions. The family acts as the first group of significant others from whom a child acquires a sense of identity. If the social role assigned by the parents is perceived by the child as one conducive to delinquent behavior, delinquency can be expected.

Edwin Sutherland suggested in the 1930s that both delinquent and nondelinquent behavior is learned from "differential associations" with others who have procriminal or anticriminal values. Children reared by families with "criminalistic" values would accept a criminal life-style as normal. Children neglected by their families would be more strongly influenced by nonfamilial associates, some of whom might be procriminal (Sutherland and Cressey).

The second half of the twentieth century witnessed the development of explanations for crime that took into account both psychological and sociological processes. Most popular among them are the "control theories," which assume that all people have urges to violate society's conduct norms and that people who abide by the norms do so because of internal and external controls. These controls can be traced to the family through "bonding" and discipline.

Control theories rest on an assumption that deviance is natural and that only conformity must be learned. "Social learning theories," on the other hand, assume that both prosocial and antisocial activities are learned. They claim that a desire for pleasure and for avoidance of pain motivates behavior, and hence they focus on rewards and punishments. Social-learning theories employ the notion of vicarious conditioning to explain how people learn by watching and listening, and direct attention toward the influence of parents as models for behavior and as agents for discipline.

Perhaps the most significant changes in thinking during the last third of the twentieth century have been methodological. Increasingly, social scientists have become aware of retrospective and expectational biases affecting data collection and interpretation. Their studies have provided a basis for reassessing theories about family relations and crime.

Broken homes and crime

Classical theories of personality endorsed the popular view that good child development requires the presence of two parents. This view seemed to have been corroborated by studies showing that the incidence of broken homes was higher among delinquents than among the nondelinquents with whom they were compared.

In line with the Freudian tradition, many believe that paternal absence leads to overidentification with the mother, resulting in compensatory masculine behavior in males. According to this viewpoint, delinquency is one symptom of compensatory masculine "acting-out." The theory purports to explain why delinquency is prevalent among blacks and the poor—groups with high rates of broken homes.

Anthropologists have used cross-cultural evidence to buttress these assumptions. Margaret Bacon, Irvin Child, and Herbert Barry, for example, garnered support for the masculinity thesis from ethnographies describing nonliterate cultures. Each culture was rated for frequency of criminality and for opportunities to develop identification with the father. Because cultures offering a relatively high opportunity for identification tended to have relatively little crime, the authors concluded that their analysis "supports the theory that lack of opportunity . . . to form a masculine identification is in itself an important antecedent of crime" (p. 229). However, some studies in the United States and in England have been less congenial to the masculinity thesis. Those studies that have made comparisons within a particular social class or among blacks have found that delinquency is not more prevalent among children from broken homes than among children from intact families.

If delinquency were a response to excessive maternal identification, the presence of a stepfather should reduce the criminogenic effects of paternal loss, but apparently this does not occur. Sheldon Glueck and Eleanor Glueck compared 500 male delinquents in Massachusetts reformatories with 500 nondelinquent boys of similar age, domicile, ethnic origin, and intelligence. Among the delinquents, 230 had lived with a substitute parent, usually a stepfather, and 72 had lived continuously with one parent, usually a mother; the corresponding figures for the nondelinquents were 60 and 111. Although a higher proportion of the delinquents came from broken homes, they were more likely than nondelinquents to have a father-figure at home. A substitute father rather than no father in the home correlated with high rates of delinquency among junior and senior high-school students as well. Travis Hirschi asked more than 4,000 students in Richmond, California, to describe their families and report on their own delinquent behavior. In this case, nearly identical rates of delinquency were reported by fatherless boys and by boys living with their natural fathers; these rates were lower than the rates of delinquency among boys living with stepfathers.

Evidence suggests that parental conflict may be responsible for the delinquency commonly attributed to broken homes. Michael Rutter was able to disentangle effects of parental absence and effects of parental discord in his study of children whose parents were patients in a London psychiatric clinic. Among those who had been separated from their parents, conduct disorders occurred only if the separations were the result of parental discord. In the case of those still living with both parents, such disorders occurred with the presence of parental conflict. It was further noted that the children's behavior improved when they were placed in tranquil homes.

Francis Ivan Nye found similar evidence among students in the Pacific Northwest. Nye asked high-school pupils to report the frequency of their delinquencies on a list that included driving without a license, defying parental authority, committing petty theft, and destroying property. The students also identified the parental figures with whom they lived, and classified the marriages of these parents as happy or unhappy. Youngsters reared in generally unhappy homes, albeit by their natural parents, reported committing delinquent acts with greater frequency than did those reared in generally happy, but reconstituted, homes. Thus, these data suggest that avoiding divorce does not prevent delinquency.

Domestic tranquillity, rather than presence of parents, may reduce the likelihood of delinquency. In tracing the lives of a group of men forty years after they had participated in a youth study, Joan McCord contrasted effects of conflict between parents with effects of parental absence. Compared with boys raised in quarrelsome but intact homes, boys reared by affectionate mothers in broken homes were half as likely to be convicted of serious crimes. For a boy with only one parent, whether or not that parent was affectionate appeared to have an important impact on whether the boy became a criminal. Criminality was no more common among those reared solely by affectionate mothers than among those reared by two parents in tranquil homes.

Parental relations and crime

The impact of family interaction on socialization has generally been considered a function of variations in parental affection and discipline. Conversely, both the absence of affection and inadequate discipline have been seen as sources of crime.

Parental affection. The view that maternal deprivation has dire effects on personality gained support from case histories documenting maternal rejection in the backgrounds of aggressive youngsters and from studies of children reared in orphanages, many of whom became delinquents. Indeed, John Bowlby suggested that the discovery of a need for maternal affection during early childhood paralleled the discovery of "the role of vitamins in physical health" (p. 59).

Critics of the conclusions reached in these studies noted the selective nature of retrospective histories and pointed out that institutionalized children not only lack maternal affection but also have been deprived of normal social stimulation. Such criticisms led to consideration of the impact of paternal as well as of maternal rejection.

The Gluecks gathered evidence about paternal rejection when they investigated why some boys became delinquent while other boys from the same neighborhoods did not. Psychiatrists, social workers, and social agencies collected information on the family interactions of nondelinquents and incarcerated delinquents. The Gluecks' study implied that the father's role can be an important one. From interviews with the parents, the Gluecks concluded that fewer than half the fathers of delinquents were sympathetic and affectionate toward their sons, whereas four out of five fathers of nondelinquents manifested these qualities. A majority of the mothers of both delinquents and nondelinquents seemed warm and affectionate, although more of the mothers of delinquents were hostile toward their sons. As part of the study, psychiatrists asked the boys how they perceived their parents. Just over half of the nondelinquents endorsed their fathers

as models, and almost two-thirds indicated affection for their fathers. By comparison, only a sixth of the delinquents endorsed their fathers as models, and fewer than one-third indicated affection for them.

Additional evidence that paternal as well as maternal rejection is linked to delinquency comes from the reports of high-school students studied by Nye. Those boys and girls who perceived mutual rejection between either their mothers and themselves or their fathers and themselves reported more delinquencies.

Hirschi compared the impact of paternal affection with that of maternal affection in his study of California students. Hirschi's analysis suggested that the two parents were equally important and, moreover, that attachment to one parent had as much beneficial influence on the child as attachment to both.

Thus, studies on emotional climate in the home present consistent results. Like parental conflict, negative parent-child relations enhance the probability of delinquency. Parental affection appears to reduce the probability of crime.

Variations in discipline. Psychoanalytic theory postulates that development of the superego depends on the "introjection" of a punitive father. This perspective generated research on successive training for control of oral, anal, and sexual drives and on techniques for curbing dependency and aggression. Although resultant studies failed to produce a coherent picture showing which disciplinary techniques promoted a strong conscience and which decreased antisocial behavior, they focused attention on the relationship between discipline and deviance.

In addition to considering specific disciplinary techniques, studies less closely tied to psychoanalytic theory have used such concepts as firmness, fairness, and consistency in analyzing relationships between discipline and crime. The Gluecks found that incarcerated delinquent boys rarely had had "firm but kindly" discipline from either parent, yet a majority of the nondelinquents with whom they were compared experienced this type of discipline. Parents of delinquents were more likely to use physical punishment and less likely to supervise their sons. The teenagers studied by Nye judged their parents' disciplinary practices in terms of fairness. These judgments indicated that adolescents who perceived their fathers as unfair tended to commit more offenses than those who judged their fathers to be fair; perceived fairness of the mother was unrelated to crime. Hirschi characterized discipline by asking if the parents punished by slapping or hitting, by removing privileges, and by nagging or scolding. He found that use of these types of discipline was related to delinquency, a conclusion which suggests that such punishments promoted the behaviors they were "designed to prevent" (p. 102).

Long-term studies. In studying the impact of family on delinquency, long-term studies are particularly helpful, providing information for judging whether parental rejection and unfair discipline precede or follow antisocial behavior. For two decades, David Farrington and Donald West traced the development of 411 working-class London boys born between 1951 and 1953. When the boys were between eight and ten years old, their teachers identified some as particularly difficult and aggressive. Social workers visited the boys' homes in 1961 and gathered information on the parents' attitudes toward their sons, disciplinary techniques used, and compatibility between the parents. In 1974, as the boys reached maturity, each was classified as noncriminal (if there were no convictions) or, according to his criminal record, as a violent or a nonviolent criminal. Farrington and West found that the families most likely to produce criminals had been quarrelsome, provided little supervision, and included a parent with a criminal record. Furthermore, boys whose parents had been harsh or cruel in 1961 were more likely than their classmates to acquire records for violent crimes. Parental cruelty was actually a more accurate selector of boys who would become violent criminals than was the child's early aggressiveness.

Other longitudinal studies show similar antecedents to aggression and antisocial behavior. McCord found that maternal rejection and lack of self-confidence, paternal alcoholism and criminality, lack of supervision, parental conflict, and parental aggressiveness permitted predictions of adult criminality that were more accurate than those based on a person's own juvenile offense record. In studying Swedish schoolboys, Dan Olweus found that ratings of maternal rejection, parental punitiveness, and absence of parental control predicted aggressiveness. Descriptions of the family had been obtained from interviews with the parents when the boys were sixth-graders, and aggressiveness was evaluated by the boy's classmates three years later. In her Finnish longitudinal study, Lea Pulkkinen discovered that lack of interest in and control of the fourteen-year-old child's activities, use of physical punishments, and inconsistency of discipline tended to lead to criminality by the age of twenty.

All of these studies suggest that delinquents have parents who act unfairly or who are too willing to inflict pain, whereas the parents of nondelinquents provide consistent and compassionate attention.

Siblings and crime

Studies of family relationships and crime have commonly centered on parent-child influence. Generally, if included at all, siblings are mentioned only in passing. Daniel Glaser, Bernard Lander, and William Abbott, however, focused on siblings when asking why some people become drug addicts. Three pairs of sisters and thirty-four pairs of brothers living in a slum area of New York City responded to questions asked in interviews by a former addict and a former gang leader. One member of each pair had never used heroin, whereas the other had been an addict. Results of this study suggested that the typical addict was about two years younger than the nonaddicted sibling, spent less time at home, left school at a younger age, and began having relationships with persons of the opposite sex when younger. The interviews did not yield evidence of systematic differences between addicts and their siblings regarding parental affection or expectations for success. Like the Finnish adolescents studied by Pulkkinen, and the British delinquents in the Farrington and West sample, the addicts appear to have had peers for their reference groups. Unfortunately, relatively little is known about why some children adopt peers instead of family as reference groups.

Differences in sex, intelligence, and physique provide partial answers to why one child in a family develops problems and another does not. In addition, several studies show that even after controlling for family size (delinquents tend to come from larger families), middle children are more likely to be delinquents than are their oldest or youngest siblings. Rutter suggests that parental actions could be the determinant, with delinquent children tending to be those who were singled out for abuse by quarreling parents.

Farrington and West analyzed criminal records among the families of the 411 London boys they studied. Having a criminal brother, they discovered, was approximately as criminogenic as having a criminal father. Data from Minnesota confirm the apparent criminogenic impact of sibling criminality. In 1974, Merrill Roff traced criminal records of approximately thirteen hundred sets of siblings born between 1950 and 1953. Males whose siblings had juvenile court records were about one and a half times as likely to have court records themselves as were those whose siblings did not have such records. Furthermore, those whose brothers had been juvenile delinquents were about twice as likely to have adult criminal convictions as those who were the only juvenile delinquents in the family.

Marriage and crime

Although crimes within the family typically go unrecorded, violence between husband and wife accounts for a significant proportion of recorded criminal assaults and homicides. Additionally, as has been noted above, criminal parents tend to rear delinquent children. Apart from these facts, relatively little is known about the relationship of crime to marriage.

Two links between crime and age of marriage have been forged in the literature. First, several studies suggest that delinquents marry at younger ages than do nondelinquents. Second, criminality tends to decline at about the time that marriage takes place. Perhaps because of the popular belief that marriage has a settling effect, researchers have sometimes concluded that marriage reduces crime. Yet at least three accounts of the relationship between marriage and crime can be given. Delinquents may turn to marriage when they are ready to settle down; or those delinquents who are less criminally inclined may be more likely to marry (with marriage marking no change in motivation); or marriage may provide the ground for change.

One of the few studies with information sufficient to test whether marriage has a palliative effect is that by Farrington and West. They compared men who married between the ages of eighteen and twenty-one with unmarried men at age twenty-one; the two groups had similar histories to the age of eighteen. These comparisons failed to support the view that marriage reduces delinquency.

Family intervention and crime

Because studies of the causes of crime have often implicated parents, treatment strategies have sometimes been aimed at changing parental behavior. If parents learn how to improve their socializing skills, programs aimed at changing patterns of family interaction can be expected to affect siblings as well as the delinquents whose problem behavior has been targeted for change. In fact, reduction in court appearances of siblings seems to have occurred as a result of a short-term family program reported on by Nanci Klein, James Alexander, and Bruce Parsons. In that project, the families of eighty-six juvenile delinquents were randomly assigned to one of four groups by the family clinic in Salt Lake County, Utah. The experimental program taught families to negotiate contracts in which the teenager would receive privileges as a reward for doing chores. The program also taught parents and children how to interrupt one another in order to clarify, inform, and provide feedback. A follow-up six to eighteen months after treatment had terminated showed that those assigned to the short-term intervention program had lower rates of recidivism than clients whose families had been assigned to client-centered group discussions, to a Mormon family-counseling program, or to a no-treatment control group. Between two and a half and three and a half years later, the siblings of the delinquents were traced through court records. Those whose families had been in the short-term intervention program showed fewer delinquencies than siblings of delinquents whose families had been assigned to one of the other groups.

As part of an ambitious family intervention program, Gerald Patterson studied the behavior of parents, siblings, and boys who had been classified as having severe conduct problems. Patterson hoped to change these problems through judicious use of rewards and punishments. He noted that when siblings first attempted to reduce the aggressive behavior of their brothers, their punitiveness increased hostile behavior. Evaluation of the effects of intervention showed that siblings had become more effective in controlling their brothers' hostility. The program has also tended to reduce the general deviance of siblings, and it appears to be a promising approach to reducing hostile behavior.

Interpreting the data

After World War II, scientists began to study socialization by producing in microcosm the conditions that seemed important for understanding personality development. Early studies had generally reflected the psychoanalytic perspective that characterized many ideas about family relations. Aggression was conceived of as instinctual, and the conscience was thought of as a "superego" that developed from identification with a parent. The pleasure principle was generally assumed to explain choice, and served as a foundation for studies of the effects of rewards and penalties on conduct. As Freudian influence declined, researchers began to consider aggression as acquired behavior, and altruism as an alternative to hedonistic motivation. Studies with these perspectives suggest new interpretations of relationships between family interaction and crime.

Laboratory experiments showing that the observing of aggression can produce aggressive behavior suggest why punitive parents may tend to have aggressive offspring. Imitation of aggression in the laboratory increases when aggression is described as justified.

Parents who justify their use of pain as punishment may foster the idea that inflicting pain is appropriate in other contexts.

Delinquency, as an extreme form of inconsiderate behavior, has as its antithesis altruistic behavior. Experimental studies of altruism suggest that conflict and rejection may tend to produce delinquency because the discomfort of living in the midst of conflict or among "enemies" minimizes the sense of well-being that tends to produce altruistic behavior.

Much effort has been expended in investigating the role played by rewards and punishments in teaching children how to act. Although it has been demonstrated that prompt feedback increases conformity to norms, some studies also show the paradoxical effects of rewards and punishments. Rewards sometimes decrease performance, and punishments sometimes increase forbidden actions. These studies suggest that use of rewards and punishments can create ambiguous messages. Similar ambiguities may affect parent-child relationships. Lax discipline and the absence of supervision, as well as parental conflict, could increase delinquency because they impede communication of the parents' socializing expectations.

By linking family relationships to crime, research provides support for Plato's view that training for citizenship should begin in the nursery.

JOAN MCCORD

See also ADULTERY AND FORNICATION; BIGAMY; CHILDREN, CRIMINAL ACTIVITIES OF; CONTRIBUTING TO THE DELINQUENCY OF MINORS; EDUCATION AND CRIME; HOMICIDE: BEHAVIORAL ASPECTS; INCEST; JUVENILE STATUS OFFENDERS; *articles on* VIOLENCE IN THE FAMILY.

BIBLIOGRAPHY

BACON, MARGARET K.; CHILD, IRVIN L.; and BARRY, HERBERT, III. "A Cross-cultural Study of Correlates of Crime." *Journal of Abnormal and Social Psychology* 66 (1963): 291–300.

BANDURA, ALBERT. *Aggression: A Social Learning Analysis.* Englewood Cliffs, N.J.: Prentice-Hall, 1973.

BOWLBY, JOHN. "Maternal Care and Mental Health." *Bulletin of the World Health Organization* 3 (1951): 355–533.

COOLEY, CHARLES H. *Human Nature and the Social Order* (1920). Introduction by Philip Rieff. Foreword by George Herbert Mead. New York: Schocken Books, 1964.

FARRINGTON, DAVID P., and WEST, DONALD J. "The Cambridge Study in Delinquent Development (United Kingdom)." *Prospective Longitudinal Research in Europe: An Empirical Basis for Primary Prevention of Psychosocial Disorders.* Edited by Sarnoff A. Mednick and Andre E. Baert. New York: Oxford University Press, 1981, pp. 137–145.

GLASER, DANIEL; LANDER, BERNARD; and ABBOTT, WILLIAM. "Opiate Addicted and Non-addicted Siblings in a Slum Area." *Social Problems* 18 (1971): 510–521.

GLUECK, SHELDON, and GLUECK, ELEANOR T. *Unraveling Juvenile Delinquency.* New York: Commonwealth Fund, 1950.

HIRSCHI, TRAVIS. *Causes of Delinquency.* Berkeley: University of California Press, 1969.

KLEIN, NANCI C.; ALEXANDER, JAMES F.; and PARSONS, BRUCE V. "Impact of Family Systems Intervention on Recidivism and Sibling Delinquency: A Model of Primary Prevention and Program Evaluation." *Journal of Consulting and Clinical Psychology* 45 (1977): 469–474.

MCCORD, JOAN. "A Longitudinal View of the Relationship between Paternal Absence and Crime." *Abnormal Offenders, Delinquency, and the Criminal Justice System.* Edited by John Gunn and David Farrington. New York: Wiley, 1982, pp. 113–128.

MEAD, GEORGE HERBERT. *Mind, Self, and Society from the Standpoint of a Social Behaviorist.* Edited with an introduction by Charles W. Morris. University of Chicago Press, 1962.

NYE, FRANCIS IVAN. *Family Relationships and Delinquent Behavior.* New York: Wiley, 1958.

OLWEUS, DAN. "Familial and Temperamental Determinants of Aggressive Behavior in Adolescent Boys: A Causal Analysis." *Developmental Psychology* 16 (1980): 644–660.

PATTERSON, GERALD R. "The Aggressive Child: Victim and Architect of a Coercive System." *Sixth Banff International Conference on Behavior Modification, 1974: Behavior Modification and Families.* Edited by Eric J. Mash, Leo A. Hamerlynck, and Lee C. Handy. New York: Brunner/Mazel, 1976, pp. 257–316.

PLATO. "Laws." *The Dialogues of Plato,* vol. 2. Translated by B. Jowett. New York: Random House, 1937, pp. 407–703.

PULKKINEN, LEA. "Search for Alternatives to Aggression in Finland." *Aggression in Global Perspective.* Edited by A. P. Goldstein and M. Segall. Elmsford, N.Y.: Pergamon Press, 1983, pp. 104–144.

ROFF, MERRILL. "Long-term Follow-up of Juvenile and Adult Delinquency with Samples Differing in Some Important Respects: Cross-validation within the Same Research Program." *The Origins and Course of Psychopathology.* Edited by John S. Strauss, Haroutun M. Babigian, and Merrill Roff. New York: Plenum, 1977, pp. 323–344.

RUTTER, MICHAEL. "Epidemiological Strategies and Psychiatric Concepts in Research on the Vulnerable Child." *The Child in His Family: Children at Psychiatric Risk.* International Yearbook for Child Psychiatry and Allied Disciplines, vol. 3. Edited by E. James Anthony and Cyrille Koupernik. New York: Wiley, 1974, pp. 167–179.

SUTHERLAND, EDWIN H., and CRESSEY, DONALD R. *Criminology* (1924). 10th ed. Philadelphia: Lippincott, 1978.

WEST, DONALD J., and FARRINGTON, DAVID P. *The Delinquent Way of Life: Third Report of the Cambridge Study in Delinquent Development.* London: Heinemann, 1977.

FEAR OF CRIME

Since the mid-1960s, fear of crime has emerged as a significant social issue, as demonstrated by national polls that have shown it to be increasing substantially in terms of public concern. Although changes in the wording of survey questions over the years make measurement of trends somewhat difficult, the responses suggest that the percentage of people who fear crime has increased from about 30 percent in the early 1960s to about 45 percent in the late 1970s. Victimization surveys since 1972 show that about 45 percent of the urban population feel "somewhat" or "very" unsafe or afraid to walk at night in their neighborhood (Skogan and Maxfield; Stinchcombe et al.).

Fear of crime tends to be defined as a psychological state of concern, worry, and anxiety about being victimized, which frequently involves such physiological concomitants as accelerated heart rate, pulse, and blood pressure. This emotional state is presumed to be evoked by the perception of a high risk of imminent danger. Some people experience these physiological components of fear regularly, perhaps daily. For others, perhaps most, fear is anticipatory or hypothetical; because of their concern and worry about being victimized, they avoid sites and times where the risk of danger is perceived to be high, such as their own neighborhood at night. As their coping behavior becomes routinized and habitual, they may rarely even worry about crime. Yet their fear is no less real than the fear of those who experience an accelerated heart rate, pulse, and blood pressure; it is real in its behavioral consequences.

Consequences of fear

Social critics have linked fear to various deleterious psychological states, such as anxiety, mistrust, alienation, dissatisfaction with life, and even mental disorders; and to various social states, such as the breakdown of social cohesion (Hartnagel). Although very little systematic research bears on these claims, two types of behavior have been studied: the avoidance of areas of the city associated with crime (avoidance behavior), and efforts to reduce the risk and cost of victimization in high- or low-risk areas (protective behavior).

Research shows that people who fear crime confine their activities to "safe" areas during "safe" times, avoiding certain urban areas and the restaurants, stores, jobs, and places of residence located in them (Garofalo). People unable to limit their behavior to

safe areas because of age or financial resources frequently become prisoners in their own homes, especially after dark (Skogan and Maxfield).

Findings on protective behavior are unclear. Surveys show that people purchase various aids for protecting themselves and their homes from crime, such as guns, additional locks, outside lighting, watchdogs, antiburglary equipment, and insurance; they also learn self-defense. However, those who fear crime the most are not necessarily the most self-protective (Skogan and Maxfield). One possible reason for this seeming anomaly is that fear motivates protective behavior, which in turn reduces fear, making the association between the two not readily evident. To estimate the effect of fear on protective behavior, researchers must control for the effect of protective behavior on fear. Additionally, those who fear crime the most—the poor—lack the financial resources to purchase protection for themselves and their homes.

Individual characteristics as causes of fear

Most research on fear of crime seeks to link it to the social and demographic characteristics of people, such as sex, age, income, education, and race, as well as to their victimization experience.

Victimization. Studies report that the relationship of fear of crime to victimization is stronger for serious than for nonserious crimes, but that this relationship is little affected by the number of victimizations (Garofalo; Skogan and Maxfield). The latter finding may result partly from studies generally asking people about their victimization experience over the previous year or six months, assuming that they are unable accurately to recall victimizations for a longer span of time. Yet most serious victimizations are experienced too infrequently to take place within the short period covered by such a study. By focusing only on recent victimizations in order to maximize reliability, these studies may underestimate the effect on fear of repeated victimization experiences.

Social characteristics as correlates of fear. Social class and race show a moderate relationship to fear. For example, James Garofalo has found that 54 percent of blacks and 41 percent of whites feel unsafe in their own neighborhoods at night, and that fear steadily increases as income decreases. Most researchers ascribe these relationships to the fact that nonwhites and low-income people experience and observe more crime in their homes and neighborhoods than do white and high-income people.

Perhaps the factors that are most correlated to fear are sex and age. Frank Clemente and Michael Kleiman have reported that 61 percent of females, but only 22 percent of males, fear walking alone at night. However, for reasons arising out of a need for a strong, masculine self-image, men may be less likely than women to acknowledge in a face-to-face or even a telephone interview that they are afraid to walk the streets at night in their own neighborhood. This is not to imply that there is no sex effect, but only that it may not be as strong as the research suggests.

The age effect appears to be curvilinear in that fear does not appreciably increase until about fifty years of age. According to Clemente and Kleiman, approximately 40 percent of people between the ages of eighteen and forty-nine, and 50 percent of those over fifty years of age, fear walking alone at night in their neighborhood; Garofalo, using a finer age gradation, holds that 63 percent of those over sixty-five express such feelings. Females and the elderly, who have less physical strength, may simply feel more vulnerable to victimization than do males and younger persons. In addition, females worry about rape, and the elderly are less able to replace stolen goods, thereby increasing the cost and danger to them of victimization.

One weakness of research on the correlates of fear is that it is somewhat atheoretical, relating fear only to social characteristics easy to measure in surveys. Explanations tend to be formulated ad hoc, with a few common threads leading to some seeming anomalies: those who are victimized least, the elderly and females, fear crime the most. Yet theoretically, this tendency might be expected if feelings of vulnerability cause fear, which leads to precautionary behavior and in turn reduces victimization.

A second weakness is that the data analysis is too simple, for it usually assumes that the causal effects are linear, unrelated, and unidirectional. Yet, as has been shown above, the effects of some variables, such as age and victimization, are nonlinear; hence, linear models underestimate these effects. Research also suggests that victimization experience and various social characteristics, such as age, race, and class, are interrelated; estimating their unique effects thus requires multivariate statistics. Clemente and Kleiman concluded from their statistics that only sex and city size have significant unique effects on fear, but that race, class, and age may be related to fear because nonwhites, the lower class, and the elderly tend to live in large cities—which is the underlying causal factor. Finally, although the causal effects are unidirectional for many unchangeable social statuses, such as age, sex, and race, they may be reciprocal for other statuses, such as income, and for victimization. Victimization can increase fear; but fear, through coping behavior, can decrease it. Hence, the net relationship between them may be weak, masking reciprocal causal effects.

Situational factors as causes of fear

People's sociodemographic characteristics are thought to correlate with fear because they influence perceptions of the danger of victimization. Fear is aroused when people find themselves in situations in which they perceive danger to be high, probable, and immediate. The direct study of such situations has been limited to examining the statistical distribution of fear among cities and among neighborhoods within a given city.

Crime rates. Perhaps the major situational characteristic regarded as explaining the distribution of fear among cities is the crime rate. People experience it directly through their own victimization and indirectly through hearing and reading of the victimization of others. Garofalo discerns a strong relationship between fear, as measured by survey reports, and crime rates, as measured by the Uniform Crime Reports (Federal Bureau of Investigation). Wesley Skogan and Michael Maxfield find some correlations between the fear of crime and crime rates in surveys comparing neighborhoods in Chicago. However, cities and neighborhoods with high crime rates differ from those with low crime rates in size, racial composition, and economic condition, factors that may influence the fear of crime. Indeed, Allen Liska, Joseph Lawrence, and Andrew Sanchirico report that the relationship between crime rates and fear is contingent on race and the type of crime; for the most part, it only seems to hold for whites and for robbery.

Mass media. The highly selective and systematic way in which the media treat crime-related topics suggests that there may be a close connection between the media and fear of crime, but results from the small amount of research that has been conducted on this topic thus far are mixed. Skogan and Maxfield, as well as Ranald Hansen and James Donoghue, find no relationship between fear and exposure to a variety of media. In contrast, George Gerbner and Larry Gross have revealed that frequent television viewers were more likely than occasional viewers to be fearful of crime and to envision themselves as potential victims of crime. Similarly, Anthony Doob and Glenn MacDonald have found that for people living in a high crime area there is a positive relationship between television viewing and fear. This inconsistency in the findings may reflect measurement problems, as well as the fact that research has only begun on this topic.

Other city characteristics. Since people tend to link dangerous street crime with strangers and large urban areas, it follows that city size will affect the fear of crime. Research tends to support this (Stinchcombe et al.; Clemente and Kleiman), but the relationship does not appear to be linear. Studies that include a very diverse sample of city sizes show a substantial city-size effect (Clemente and Kleiman), whereas those including only large cities show but a small effect (Garofalo). Hence, fear appears to increase with size until a certain point, perhaps one-fourth or one-third of a million, after which further increases in size have only minimal effects on fear.

Analyses of victimization survey data by Liska and his associates show that as the percentage of nonwhites in a city increases, so does fear of crime by both whites and nonwhites, but as racial segregation increases, the fear by nonwhites increases whereas the fear by whites decreases, independently of crime rates and city size. To explain these findings, they argue that both whites and nonwhites are influenced by cultural beliefs and stereotypes in the United States that associate crime with nonwhites. Hence, the presence of nonwhites, which is inversely related to the level of segregation for whites and directly related to the level of segregation for nonwhites, influences the fear of crime; indeed, cities and neighborhoods may develop a reputation for being unsafe to the extent to which they are predominantly nonwhite.

Skogan and Maxfield argue that because serious crime is a rare event, neither regularly experienced nor observed, most people tend to estimate their chances of being victimized from the presence of factors that they view as signs of disorder, such as teenagers, abandoned buildings, drugs, and vandalism. These authors show that such signs predict well the levels of fear in ten neighborhoods of three major cities. This finding may overestimate the causal effect of such signs on fear, for the research does not control for the objective crime rate, which is probably correlated to them.

Generally, research on the structural characteristics of cities and neighborhoods indicates that people estimate their chances of being victimized by the presence of variables associated with crime, such as teenagers, nonwhites, drugs, and abandoned buildings, as well as by the presence of crime itself. In fact, because serious crime is a rare event and is not simple to observe, it may be less important than the other variables. Liska, Lawrence, and Sanchirico have shown that for both whites and nonwhites the effect of the percentage of nonwhites on fear is considerably stronger than the effect of crime rates. Since these events and

social categories are unequally distributed across neighborhoods and cities, one would expect the fear of crime to be unequally distributed across them as well. Liska and his associates find that crime rates, city size, segregation, and the percentage of nonwhites in different cities collectively account for most of the variance in fear of crime for whites, but that these factors are slightly less influential for nonwhites. Garofalo and John Laub suggest that fear of crime is an expression of people's broader concerns over problems in contemporary urban life, among them the breakdown in family and primary relations, depersonalization, individualism, the changing social character of old neighborhoods, and the transformation or decline of moral values.

ALLEN E. LISKA
WILLIAM F. BACCAGLINI

See also AGE AND CRIME; CRIME PREVENTION: POLICE ROLE; MASS MEDIA AND CRIME; PUBLIC OPINION AND CRIME; VICTIMOLOGY.

BIBLIOGRAPHY

CLEMENTE, FRANK, and KLEIMAN, MICHAEL B. "Fear of Crime in the United States: A Multivariate Analysis." *Social Forces* 56 (1977): 519–531.

DOOB, ANTHONY N., and MACDONALD, GLENN E. "Television Viewing and Fear of Victimization: Is the Relationship Causal?" *Journal of Personality and Social Psychology* 37 (1978): 170–179.

Federal Bureau of Investigation. *Crime in the United States. Uniform Crime Reports for the United States.* Washington, D.C.: U.S. Department of Justice, FBI, annually.

GAROFALO, JAMES. "Victimization and the Fear of Crime." *Journal of Research in Crime and Delinquency* 16 (1979): 80–97.

———, and LAUB, JOHN. "The Fear of Crime: Broadening Our Perspective." *Victimology* 3 (1979): 242–253.

GERBNER, GEORGE, and GROSS, LARRY. "Living with Television: The Violence Profile." *Journal of Communication* 26 (1976): 173–199.

HANSEN, RANALD D., and DONOGHUE, JAMES M. "The Power of Consensus: Information Derived from One's Own and Others' Behavior." *Journal of Personality and Social Psychology* 35 (1977): 294–302.

HARTNAGEL, TIMOTHY F. "The Perception and Fear of Crime: Implications for Neighborhood Cohesion, Social Activity, and Community Affect." *Social Forces* 58 (1979): 176–193.

LISKA, ALLEN E.; LAWRENCE, JOSEPH J.; and SANCHIRICO, ANDREW. "Fear of Crime as a Social Fact." *Social Forces* 60 (1982): 760–770.

SKOGAN, WESLEY G., and MAXFIELD, MICHAEL G. *Coping with Crime: Individual and Neighborhood Reactions.* Beverly Hills, Calif.: Sage, 1981.

STINCHCOMBE, ARTHUR L.; ADAMS, REBECCA; HEIMER, CAROL A.; SCHEPPELE, KIM LANE; SMITH, TOM W.; and TAYLOR, D. GARTH. *Crime and Punishment: Changing Attitudes in America*. San Francisco: Jossey Bass, 1980.

FEDERAL BUREAU OF INVESTIGATION: HISTORY

Introduction. The development of the Federal Bureau of Investigation has been a twentieth-century phenomenon. At the time of the ratification of the United States Constitution, the police function was assumed to be quintessentially local. The kinds of laws to be enacted by the new national government would be enforced by customs agents, the federal courts, and their marshals: the need for a specialized federal mechanism to conduct criminal investigations was not foreseen. Even at the local level, police departments, in their recognizably modern form, did not develop until the mid-nineteenth century. By the 1880s, however, specialized detective forces were a feature of larger urban police forces. In Europe, where local detective forces had developed earlier, the middle of the century saw the emergence of organizations with some national investigative capacity, notably the Criminal Investigation Division (Scotland Yard) of the London Metropolitan Police in England and the Sûreté Générale in France.

During the Civil War, several American secret services were established, but with the coming of peace all were dismantled except for the unit serving the Treasury Department. Originally established to detect counterfeiting, the unit survives today as the United States Secret Service. In the last three decades of the nineteenth century a private-sector organization, the Pinkerton Detective Agency, was America's closest approximation to a national investigative mechanism. Pinkerton's could operate with ease across state lines, had a well-developed system of internal communication and record-keeping, and shared information with the investigative services of foreign nations.

But in the early twentieth century, in response to technological, economic, and demographic changes, with a more mobile population and jurisdictional boundaries more easily crossed, supralocal investigative mechanisms were created. First to emerge were state police forces, soon followed by a general-purpose national investigative organization.

Origins of the FBI. When the Justice Department was established in 1870, the authorizing legislation provided for the creation of an investigative service—which, however, did not occur until three decades later. During these years, attorneys general handled their investigative chores in an ad hoc fashion by hiring Pinkerton men or borrowing operatives from the Secret Service. In 1906, two members of Congress were indicted for federal land fraud. The investigation that led to the indictments had been conducted by the Justice Department, using borrowed Secret Service operatives. Congress evinced acute sensitivity to investigations directed at its members and, in 1908, prohibited the further employment of Secret Service operatives by other departments of the federal government. President Theodore Roosevelt reacted sharply, remarking that "it is not too much to say that [this prohibition] has been a benefit only to the criminal classes. . . . The chief argument in favor of the division was that congressmen did not themselves want to be investigated by Secret Service men" (Countryman, p. 51).

Taking the offensive, Roosevelt directed Attorney General Charles Bonaparte to develop an investigative capability within the Justice Department. The first appropriation for investigators restricted their activities to "detection and prosecution of crime against the United States." This 1909 provision was retained in successive years (28 U.S.C. § 533 (1976)). The bureaucratic beginnings were quite modest—twenty permanent and eighteen temporary investigators were hired. The new service was designated the Bureau of Investigation, and Congress, in 1935, renamed it the Federal Bureau of Investigation.

World War I: espionage and subversion. In its early years (1910–1916), the bureau did not involve itself with politically motivated crime. Its responsibilities for investigating "ordinary" crime were increasing rapidly with the passage of statutes prohibiting the interstate transportation of prostitutes, stolen goods, and obscene materials. By 1916 the bureau had grown to three hundred agents.

Even when concern over espionage and subversion developed after the outbreak of war in Europe, the Justice Department insisted that it had no authority to investigate either indigenous radicalism or the activities of German agents in America. In 1916, however, Attorney General Thomas Gregory successfully sought an addition to the language of his department's appropriations statute permitting the bureau to undertake "such other investigations regarding official matters under the control of the Department of Justice or the Department of State, as may be directed by the Attorney General" (28 U.S.C. § 533(3)). This was intended to provide for counterintelligence investigations (countering foreign intelligence services) on request of the State Department. The passage of the Immigration Act of 1917, ch. 29, 39 Stat. 874 (repealed) and of the Espionage Act of 1917, ch. 30, 40 Stat. 217 (codified in scattered sections of 18, 22, 50 U.S.C.) completed the legal foundation for counterintelligence and antiradical activity by the Justice Department, and the bureau was unleashed.

Gregory and Bruce Bielaski, director of the bureau, in addition to adding more agents, stimulated the development of a private but bureau-affiliated organization, the American Protective League. At its height in 1918, the league had 250,000 members nationwide, many of whom informed on persons they suspected of espionage or sedition and on suspected draft dodgers. After American entry into the war in 1917, the bureau conducted dragnet "slacker raids," rounding up men thought to be avoiding military service.

The coming of peace did not end this heightened bureau activity against supposedly dangerous subversives. In the spring of 1919 the country experienced a series of terrorist bombings, and as a result, Attorney General A. Mitchell Palmer set up the General Intelligence Division (GID) within the Justice Department to increase significantly the federal capacity for storing information on radicals and even those suspected of being soft on radicals (Irons, pp. 1206–1222). A young lawyer named John Edgar Hoover was assigned to head the GID. In 1921 the GID was integrated into the Bureau of Investigation, and Hoover became an assistant director of the bureau.

The bureau's largest antiradical raid occurred on January 2, 1920, when an estimated ten thousand people were arrested in thirty-three cities. Most were arrested without warrants, and many were not radicals at all. Despite the national concern over political violence and subversion, this second raid resulted in a political backlash against the bureau. Some of those arrested in Boston petitioned in the federal district court for habeas corpus, and the court ordered them released. The judge was sharply critical of the government's conduct (*Colyer v. Skeffington*, 265 F. 17 (D. Mass. 1920)). Even though reversed on appeal, this decision was a major setback to Hoover and Palmer.

In early 1921, the Senate Judiciary Committee held hearings on what had come to be known as the Palmer raids. The attorney general appeared along with Hoover and stoutly defended the conduct of his agents. The committee ultimately divided in its findings. This, the first congressional effort to examine the bureau, put both the bureau and the Justice Department on the defensive, and there was worse to come.

The bureau was thoroughly humbled in the scandals of the Harding administration. The new President named his longtime political associate Harry Daugherty attorney general, and through Daugherty, both the Justice Department and the bureau became implicated in the Teapot Dome affair and other illicit enterprises of the period.

Stone and Hoover: institutional rebuilding. With the death of Harding and the accession of Calvin Coolidge to the presidency in 1923, an early order of business was to restore confidence in the Justice Department and particularly in the Bureau of Investigation. Coolidge's prescription was the appointment of Harlan Fiske Stone, former dean of the Columbia University Law School, as attorney general. Stone's integrity was unquestioned, and he had been a public critic of the Palmer raids.

Among the new attorney general's first acts was to accept the resignation of the director of the bureau. On May 10, 1924, J. Edgar Hoover was summoned to the attorney general's office and offered the directorship on an acting basis. It has become part of FBI legend that Hoover agreed to accept on condition that the bureau be altogether removed from partisan politics. He was particularly insistent that appointment and promotion be made solely on merit and that the bureau be responsible only to the attorney general and to no other official within the executive branch. Stone concurred, and a memorandum of agreement and instruction was issued for the conduct of bureau affairs. It was only after Roger Baldwin, founder of the American Civil Liberties Union, sent a favorable recommendation to the attorney general that Stone made Hoover's appointment permanent.

In addition to insisting on professionalism, Stone's memorandum of instructions established a restriction on investigations: bureau activity would be limited to investigation of particular violations of federal law. This precluded general intelligence-gathering activity directed at political radicals. As a consequence of this "Stone line," the GID was disbanded. Although it is not clear whether all the material indexed by the GID on groups and individuals was destroyed, as of 1927 the bureau ceased its antiradical activities. The single exception involved Stone's recognition that investigations of Soviet and related Communist party activity could be undertaken at the request of the State Department.

The next decade brought much to occupy the bureau and its ambitious new director. The ever-increasing number of automobiles made it apparent that a central law enforcement mechanism was needed to deal with activities that were interstate in character, and consequently the bureau moved into new fields. The Dyer Act of 1919, ch. 89, 41 Stat. 324, as amended and codified, 18 U.S.C. §§ 2311–2313 (1976), for example, gave the bureau responsibility for policing the interstate transportation of motor vehicles. Prohibition and the concomitant rise of gangsterism focused national attention on the FBI. Congress bestowed new jurisdiction in dealing with kidnapping, bank robbery, and interstate fugitives. Hoover, as the bureau's reform-minded director, cut a dashing figure on the stage of the 1930s. The federalization of American law enforcement was in the spirit of the New Deal era, a period in which problems were perceived in national terms to a greater extent than ever before.

The bureau's famed crime laboratory was established in 1932 and was made available to local and state forces in need of sophisticated scientific analyses. In 1934, Hoover secured funding for a national fingerprint-identification service, taking this function over from the private International Association of Chiefs of Police. In 1930 the bureau had launched its series of Uniform Crime Reports, which Hoover advertised to Congress as meeting the demand for national crime statistics, and in 1934 the FBI's National Academy was established. This was, in effect, a national police training school for local officers, and evolved as a powerful part of the bureau's effort to establish itself as the coordinating agency of a national police system. Doubts were voiced by some about the steady expansion of the FBI, but they were ignored.

World War II and domestic intelligence. At the height of the bureau's glamorous gangster-fighting period, it again became involved with domestic security. With the rise of totalitarianism abroad, a new concern with internal enemies developed. On August 24, 1936, Hoover was requested by President Franklin D. Roosevelt to obtain more information on the domestic activities of Communists, right-wingers, and other subversive groups. The President's appetite for information had apparently been whetted by earlier, fragmentary reports concerning both foreign espionage and domestic organizations that might, if hostilities broke out, seek to subvert the national war effort.

After receiving the necessary authorization from Secretary of State Cordell Hull, Hoover informed FBI field offices that the bureau would seek "information concerning subversive activities being conducted in the United States by Communists, Fascists, and representatives or advocates of other organizations or groups advocating the overthrow or replacement of

the Government of the United States by illegal methods" (U.S. Congress, pp. 396–397).

In June 1939, Roosevelt issued a secret directive establishing the FBI as the coordinating agency for all domestic investigations under the espionage statute and for the collection of more-general domestic intelligence. Shortly after the outbreak of World War II, the President informed the nation that the FBI would "take charge of investigative work in matters relating to espionage, sabotage, and violations of neutrality regulations." In addition, and of significance for the future of FBI domestic intelligence operations, this statement exhorted "all police officers, sheriffs and other law enforcement officers in the United States [to] promptly turn over to the nearest representative of the Federal Bureau of Investigation any information obtained by them relating to espionage, counterespionage, sabotage, subversive activities, and violations of the neutrality laws" (U.S. Congress, p. 404). In later years the bureau looked to this statement as a charter for its domestic intelligence operations. On the basis of the June directive, Hoover entered into an agreement with army intelligence and navy intelligence delineating spheres of responsibility. Within the new FBI security division, files on potentially dangerous subversives were set up.

The war years provided the FBI with powerful reinforcement for monitoring political radicals. The federal statutory landscape was altered by the Smith Act of 1940, as amended, 18 U.S.C. §§ 2385, 2387 (1976), which made it a crime to advocate or conspire to advocate the forceful overthrow of the government and thus provided a statutory basis for FBI domestic security investigations where none had existed before. In the early 1940s the bureau began resorting to more intrusive investigative techniques. Until the spring of 1940, the Federal Communications Commission had resisted FBI suggestions that wiretapping by its agents was not illegal if the contents of the intercepted material were not disclosed. In May 1940, Roosevelt directed Attorney General Robert Jackson to authorize wiretaps to combat espionage and subversive activities. Some high officials of the Justice Department were deeply disturbed by the authorization for wiretapping, but the bureau resorted to it and to other intrusive techniques as well. Physical surveillance, elaborate record-keeping, mail openings, warrantless searches, and surreptitious entries ("black-bag jobs") were practiced by a whole generation of special agents who came to regard these methods as almost routine.

On balance, however, the bureau's performance in World War II was vastly superior to that in World War I. There was no vigilante activity comparable to that of the American Protective League, and Hoover, in fact, discouraged such impulses. Furthermore, with the exception of the internment of ethnic Japanese on the West Coast (which the FBI opposed), there was no general roundup of aliens or radicals in World War II, nor was there anything like the slacker raids of World War I. During World War II each draft-evasion case was investigated individually before any arrest was made.

Domestic Communism and McCarthyism. One of the principal issues that divides students of the FBI involves the relationship between J. Edgar Hoover and the group of congressmen and senators who, in the half-dozen years after World War II, politicized and distorted the problem of domestic Communism. Specifically, to what extent was Hoover simply following the direction of his political masters, and to what extent were these executive and congressional forces stimulated and fueled by Hoover and his bureau? The truth surely involves something of both, but regardless of what Hoover did to stimulate concern about domestic Communism behind the scenes, a series of legal initiatives were taken by elected officials to place the problem of domestic Communism high on the FBI agenda.

In 1947, the executive branch established the Federal Employee Loyalty-Security Program, which in its final form required that each federal agency conduct investigations of its personnel. If it were found that an employee might be subject to influence or pressure and thereby become a security risk, that information was to be forwarded to the FBI. The program also provided that the heads of the various federal agencies be furnished by the attorney general with the names of foreign and domestic organizations, associations, movements, or groups of persons which the attorney general "after appropriate investigation and determination" might designate as totalitarian fascist, Communist, or subversive (Executive Order 10450, 3 C.F.R. 936 (1953)), which resulted in the much-criticized "attorney general's list." If the attorney general was to make determinations after "appropriate investigation," it was obviously the FBI that must do the investigating. During these years security reviewing of prospective federal employees became a major task of the bureau.

In 1950, over President Harry Truman's veto, a new internal-security act was passed—the Subversive Activities Control Act (McCarran Act) of 1950, ch. 1024, 64 Stat. 987 (codified in scattered sections of 8, 18, 22, 50 U.S.C.). This law established the Subversive Activities Control Board (SACB), with which Communist organizations were required to register.

Although the registration provisions of the act were ultimately found unconstitutional, the very existence of the SACB resulted in a demand on the Justice Department, and on the bureau, for information. Of even greater importance was the portion of the McCarran Act that provided for the detention of dangerous, disloyal, or subversive persons in times of war or national emergency. The bureau had evolved the Custodial Detention Program on the eve of World War II and had established the Security Index of persons tentatively identified as dangerous. In 1943, Attorney General Francis Biddle ordered this program terminated, but the bureau quietly ignored the order. After the war, planning for emergency detention was revived around the surviving Security Index. Although neither the bureau nor the Justice Department made much effort to conform their evolving plans to the requirements of the detention portion of the McCarran Act, the act did further legitimate domestic intelligence collection.

For better or worse, little of this internal-security apparatus proved permanent. The SACB came to an end in 1973 after Congress declined to appropriate further funds for its useless operation. The attorney general's list had been discontinued even before the demise of the SACB, and 1973 also witnessed the disbanding of the Internal Security Division of the Justice Department and the return of its residual functions to the Criminal Division. By the end of the 1970s most of the preemployment investigating to determine "suitability" was being handled outside the bureau. Most important, the emergency detention provision of the McCarran Act was repealed in 1971.

Organized crime. The late 1950s saw a decreasing concern with domestic Communism and an increasing concern with organized crime. As early as 1951, Senator Estes Kefauver had presided over a highly publicized Senate investigation of organized crime. However, the event that focused public attention sharply on the problem was the discovery in 1957 of a gathering of major criminal figures at the home of gangster Joseph Barbara in Apalachin, New York. Senator John McClellan organized new Senate crime hearings; the counsel of his investigating committee and its principal interrogator was Robert F. Kennedy. With his brother's election to the presidency in 1960 and his own confirmation as attorney general in 1961, Kennedy was determined to increase law enforcement pressure on organized crime.

Hoover's FBI was, typically, slow to respond to outside efforts to change its priorities or investigative techniques, but Kennedy was in a political position not to be denied. Organized-crime matters were taken out of the bureau's GID and placed in the new Special Investigative Division, and wiretaps were used much more aggressively.

After Kennedy's resignation in 1964, the FBI organized-crime effort slackened briefly, and in 1965, President Lyndon Johnson ordered a halt to all electronic eavesdropping not related to national security. But interest in the area was resuscitated in 1967 by the report of the task force on organized crime of President Johnson's crime commission, and in 1968 Title III of the Omnibus Crime Control and Safe Streets Act of 1968 (part), 18 U.S.C. §§ 2510–2520 (1976 & Supp. III 1979) provided a means for the bureau to procure judicial warrants for electronic "searches."

The administration of Richard Nixon continued to press on the organized crime front, and in 1970, Congress enacted the most far-reaching law ever directed against organized criminality—the Organized Crime Control Act of 1970 (part), 18 U.S.C. § 1952 (1976). This statute authorized special grand juries to investigate organized crime and provided federal rules for granting witnesses immunity from the use of their testimony.

An important instrument in the federal effort against organized crime was the strike force, consisting of specially tailored teams of lawyers, investigators, and other specialists working under supervision of the Criminal Division of the Justice Department to focus on particular criminal enterprises. In the Hoover days, FBI cooperation in these matters was grudging, since the director did not want "his" agents to work under "outside" direction. Under Hoover's successors, however, performance was much improved. It is true that the bureau was late in making a commitment to fight organized crime, but considerable progress toward that end was made in the late 1960s and early 1970s.

Civil rights. On the subject of race, Hoover was very much a man of his generation. He reflected the attitudes and prejudices of the southern-dominated Washington, D.C., of his youth and of the Wilson administration, during which his governmental career was launched.

The absence of any instinctive sympathy for the plight of black Americans on the part of the director virtually guaranteed that the FBI would, at least initially, be on the wrong side of the modern civil rights movement. In the 1960s this mind-set of the director combined with bureaucratic motives to retard FBI involvement in defending the interests of civil rights protesters and of black Americans in the South. The bureaucratic motivation was the desire of the FBI field offices to protect their working relationships with local law enforcement agencies. To intervene on behalf of blacks or "outside agitators" when local police were looking the other way might generate ill will; in extreme cases, doing so would have involved FBI agents in investigating their local counterparts. Black leaders perceived this unwillingness to take their part and criticized the FBI and its director.

The turning point for the bureau came in 1964 after the nationally publicized disappearance in Mississippi of three civil rights workers. Bureau agents set out to identify and interview all Ku Klux Klan members in Mississippi and let it be known they would pay handsomely for information concerning the missing persons. The case was finally broken in August 1964, and the Justice Department eventually obtained convictions of six Mississippians for violation of the victims' civil rights.

From this point on, FBI agents throughout the South became increasingly involved in combating racist violence, and this involvement, in turn, gave rise to problems. Not only did special agents have to use a variety of dubious characters as informants, but the decision was made to utilize against organized racism a variety of tactics that heretofore had been reserved for use in counterintelligence operations or against domestic Communists. The first such counterintelligence program (Cointelpro) to be directed against non-Communist American targets was Cointelpro–White Hate Groups, established by William Sullivan, head of the Intelligence Division; it had the tacit backing of both Attorney General Kennedy and President Johnson.

Hoover, however, never relinquished his conviction that the civil rights movement had been subverted. He fixed particularly on Dr. Martin Luther King, Jr., demanding and receiving from his subordinates reassurance that King was a "dangerous man." As the *Church Committee Report* was later to reveal, King was made the subject of sustained surveillance, electronic eavesdropping, and Cointelpro-type activities.

Vietnam and the New Left. The Vietnam War and the student activism that it spawned became the occasion for further FBI overreaction. Hoover himself was never deeply concerned about antiwar activism, but Sullivan was. More important, so was the White House.

In June 1970, President Nixon created a working group of representatives from the FBI, the Central Intelligence Agency, the Defense Intelligence Agency, and the National Security Agency to consider the need for more extensive domestic intelligence activities in the light of the disorders taking place across the country. Hoover stood aloof from this process, and Sullivan represented the bureau. The group was coordinated by White House aide Tom Huston and ultimately recommended presidential approval of practices such as surreptitious entry, mail interception, and more-extensive electronic eavesdropping. Of course, the bureau had done such things in the past. But in the mid-1960s, Hoover, fearing adverse publicity, had placed restraints on these techniques, and Sullivan's Intelligence Division was chafing under these restrictions. The recommendations of the working group, which became known as the Huston Plan, were approved at the White House. Hoover, however, refused to go along, and most of the proposals were abandoned in the face of his opposition.

It was in part because of Hoover's perceived intransigence that the White House increased pressure on the CIA to become involved in domestic intelligence activity and formed its own "Plumbers group." What Hoover did agree to do for the White House was to install seventeen telephone taps on newsmen and White House employees suspected of receiving and leaking secret information. When this story was ultimately made public, it damaged the bureau far more than a few taps on political radicals could ever have done.

Upon Hoover's death in May 1972, L. Patrick Gray was appointed acting director. High-level officials at the bureau once again authorized warrantless entries and electronic surveillance in domestic-security cases. The extent to which Gray knew of, or approved the use of, these techniques is unclear. Even earlier, however, the events that were to humble the bureau before Congress and the national media were beginning to unfold. On March 9, 1971, a small group of radical activists broke into the FBI field office in Media, Pennsylvania, and made off with a number of documents. When published, these documents suggested a much more intrusive pattern of FBI surveillance of antiwar and New Left targets than had been known before.

The image of the FBI was further tarnished after it was disclosed that the acting director had destroyed documents as part of the Watergate cover-up. Gray failed to win confirmation and withdrew as acting director in 1973. With the Nixon administration crumbling under Watergate disclosures, William Ruckelshaus, a lawyer untainted by the scandals, was dispatched to the FBI in an attempt to restore confidence. During Ruckelshaus's seventy-day tenure as acting director, the FBI investigation of Watergate was pressed vigorously, but this gain for the bureau was more than offset when Ruckelshaus discovered that between 1969 and early 1970 the bureau had installed its seventeen wiretaps on employees and newsmen at the White House's behest.

A suit brought under the Freedom of Information Act by a television newsman, Carl Stern, resulted in the release of many Cointelpro files late in 1973. In March 1974, Attorney General William Saxbe released a report compiled by FBI agents and lawyers from the Criminal Division of the Justice Department that detailed many of the activities of Cointelpro. Saxbe's successor, Edward Levi, continued to make public the details of FBI abuses as he pressed for new guidelines to govern domestic-intelligence activity. Congress moved in early 1975 to establish two select committees to investigate the intelligence community.

During the course of the congressional hearings, the process of internal FBI reform was continued. In the spring of 1976 the new director, Clarence Kelley, simply closed down most domestic-security cases. The remaining cases were transferred to the GID except that of the Communist Party of the United States, which remained with the Intelligence Division because of its counterintelligence dimension.

Later in 1976, the Justice Department issued guidelines aimed at regulating future FBI domestic-intelligence activities. They restricted the circumstances under which domestic-security investigations could be begun, limited the techniques which might be used, and restrained the bureau in its use of informants. Justice Department oversight of the bureau (so often only token oversight in the past) was improved by the creation of the Investigative Review Unit and the Office of Professional Responsibility.

Attorneys general since Levi have accepted the desirability of a new legislative charter for the FBI that would dovetail the guidelines and provide a statutory basis for all the bureau's activity. Judge William Webster, who replaced Kelley as director in 1978, was also firmly committed to the need for a charter and succeeded in allaying the fears of many, if not all, congressional and media critics of the bureau.

Structure and functioning. The FBI moved from its offices in the main Justice Department building into the new J. Edgar Hoover Building in 1975. From this center are administered 59 field divisions based in major cities. They vary in size from the division in New York City, with a staff of more than fifteen hundred, to that in Anchorage, Alaska, with fewer than forty. In addition, there are 477 resident agencies in smaller cities, and 12 foreign liaison posts. It is in these offices that most of the actual investigative work of the FBI goes on. This is sometimes performed by individual agents and sometimes in cooperation with local police or with federal services such as the

Drug Enforcement Administration. In New York, for example, joint task forces have been established with the New York Police Department to deal with bank robberies and terrorism. The staffs of the foreign liaison posts interface with local law enforcement, with foreign intelligence services, and with the local components of the CIA and American military intelligence.

The bureau was frequently criticized during Hoover's later years for the ethnic homogeneity of the almost exclusively male special-agent force. By the 1980s, however, considerable progress had been made toward diversity. Out of 8,000 special agents in 1981, 543 were members of ethnic minorities and 328 were women.

Within the Washington headquarters, three major functional divisions direct investigative operations in the field. The GID handles most ordinary criminal matters, including civil rights violations and domestic-security cases. The Special Investigative Division, as noted above, has responsibility for organized crime. The Intelligence Division oversees the counterintelligence work of the bureau, the continuing investigation of the Communist Party of the United States, and the collection of some foreign intelligence within the United States.

In addition to these "line" divisions, there are several "staff," or service, divisions within the headquarters that are of importance, especially for the services they perform for local law enforcement. The Identification Division deals principally in fingerprints. The Training Division runs the bureau's Quantico, Virginia, facility and also prepares the bureau's internal manuals. The Laboratory Division devotes much of its effort to servicing local police.

The bureau's National Crime Information Center (NCIC), located within the Computer Systems Division, has emerged as a very significant and controversial component of the FBI. Begun in 1967, the NCIC computer contains files on stolen property, wanted persons, and missing persons, along with approximately 1.5 million computerized criminal histories. The NCIC is used by police in all states and by the Royal Canadian Mounted Police. The number of NCIC "hits," or matches of inquiries with information in the files, has risen year by year. Controversy has involved two concerns: that the system will become too good, and that in particular instances it will not be good enough. In the first case, the fear is that the NCIC will be able to make too much information available too quickly to local police. In the second case, the fear is that incorrect or out-of-date data may find their way into the system from one local police force and then be supplied to another halfway across the country. The bureau labors to maintain high standards of accuracy for input into NCIC, but doubts persist.

Conclusion. In the history of the FBI, two themes recur and intertwine. The first is the profound American ambivalence toward central policing. On the one hand, there have been vivid popular perceptions of growth in interstate crime and international espionage, and demands that the bureau respond. On the other hand, there have been persistent suspicion and hostility toward a "secret police" that collects too much information about citizens and is a potential instrument of tyranny. This ambivalence was manifest in Congress's nervousness about authorizing a national investigative service in the first place, and it continues in the debates over how much, and what kinds of, information the FBI should be authorized to maintain in its NCIC.

The second theme is the looseness of congressional and executive direction and supervision of the bureau. Again and again, statutes and presidential directives have spoken in broad, imprecise terms, or there was no formal direction at all. The bureau, and especially Hoover, encouraged and took advantage of this informality and lack of statutory and administrative standards. A consequence of this was the pattern of FBI surveillance and disruption practices revealed in the mid-1970s. The bureau did systematically conceal aspects of its activity from the Justice Department and Congress. But the bureau also received, especially during the early cold-war years, steady signals from successive administrations and power brokers on Capitol Hill which suggested that the bureau should closely monitor radicals and that its "masters" would just as soon not know the details.

There is, of course, nothing irrational about citizens wanting a national police mechanism sufficient to protect them, but not so powerful as to oppress them. But these objectives are in tension and in need of continuing balance and adjustment. Given the history of informal direction and loose supervision, and in spite of excesses and Hooverian eccentricities, the bureau has achieved a generally high level of professionalism.

RICHARD E. MORGAN

See also FEDERAL CRIMINAL JURISDICTION; FEDERAL CRIMINAL LAW ENFORCEMENT; INTERPOL; *both articles under* ORGANIZED CRIME; POLICE: HISTORY; SCOTLAND YARD.

BIBLIOGRAPHY

COBEN, STANLEY. *A. Mitchell Palmer: Politician.* New York: Columbia University Press, 1963.

COUNTRYMAN, VERN. "The History of the FBI: Democracy's

Development of a Secret Policy." *Investigating the FBI.* Edited by Pat Watters and Stephen Gillers. New York: Doubleday, 1973, pp. 33–63.

DONNER, FRANK J. *The Age of Surveillance: The Aims and Methods of the American Political Intelligence System.* New York: Knopf, 1980.

ELLIFF, JOHN T. *The Reform of FBI Intelligence Operations.* Princeton, N.J.: Princeton University Press, 1979.

Federal Bureau of Investigation. *Crime in the United States. Uniform Crime Reports for the United States.* Washington, D.C.: U.S. Department of Justice, FBI, annually.

GARROW, DAVID J. *The FBI and Martin Luther King, Jr.* New York: Norton, 1981.

HORAN, JAMES D. *The Pinkertons: The Detective Dynasty that Made History.* New York: Crown, 1968.

IRONS, PETER H. "'Fighting Fair': Zechariah Chafee, Jr., The Department of Justice, and the 'Trial at the Harvard Club.'" *Harvard Law Review* 94 (1981): 1205–1236.

JENSEN, JOAN M. *The Price of Vigilance.* Chicago: Rand McNally, 1969.

MORGAN, RICHARD E. *Domestic Intelligence: Monitoring Dissent in America.* Austin: University of Texas Press, 1980.

NAVASKY, VICTOR S. *Kennedy Justice.* New York: Atheneum, 1971.

PRESTON, WILLIAM, JR. *Aliens and Dissenters: Federal Suppression of Radicals, 1903–1933.* Cambridge, Mass.: Harvard University Press, 1963.

THEOHARIS, ATHAN. *Spying on Americans: Political Surveillance from Hoover to the Huston Plan.* Philadelphia: Temple University Press, 1978.

U.S. Congress, Senate, Select Committee to Study Governmental Operations with Respect to Intelligence Activities. *Final Report of the Select Committee to Study Governmental Operations with Respect to Intelligence Activities.* S. Rep. 94-755, 94th Cong., 2d sess. Washington, D.C.: Government Printing Office, 1976. Also cited as the *Church Committee Report.*

UNGAR, SANFORD J. *FBI.* Boston: Little, Brown, 1976.

WHITEHEAD, DON. *The FBI Story: A Report to the People.* Foreword by J. Edgar Hoover. New York: Random House, 1956.

WILSON, JAMES Q. *The Investigators: Managing FBI and Narcotics Agents.* New York: Basic Books, 1978.

FEDERAL COURTS

See COURTS, ORGANIZATION OF; *both articles under* CRIMINAL COURTS.

FEDERAL CRIMINAL JURISDICTION

Since the founding of the United States, the authority to define and punish crimes has been divided between the states and the federal government. Before the Civil War the United States exercised jurisdiction over only a narrow class of cases in which the federal interest was clearly dominant if not exclusive. Since the Civil War, federal criminal jurisdiction has been gradually expanding to subjects previously the exclusive province of the states. Because the bulk of these provisions have been intended to supplement state law and not to supersede it, the overlap between federal and state jurisdictions has been increasing.

Origins

The federal government has no general authority to define and prosecute crime. The Constitution created a federal government with only limited delegated powers; federal authority was confined to matters, such as foreign relations, that are not subject to effective governance by individual states. Any power not expressly granted to the central government was reserved to the states and to the people. General police powers and the bulk of criminal jurisdiction were not granted to the federal government, and accordingly were uniformly recognized to be reserved to the states.

The Constitution explicitly authorizes the federal government to prosecute only a handful of crimes: treason, counterfeiting, crimes against the law of nations, and crimes committed on the high seas, such as piracy. Each of these offenses involves a subject, such as foreign relations, over which the federal government has exclusive authority.

All other federal criminal jurisdiction rests on a less explicit but more flexible and expansive source of constitutional authority: the grant to Congress of power to pass legislation "necessary and proper" to the implementation of any enumerated federal power (art. 1, § 8). The First Congress clearly assumed that the necessary-and-proper clause authorized Congress to enact criminal sanctions to effectuate various enumerated federal powers. Indeed, the first general criminal legislation included a number of offenses clearly dependent upon the necessary-and-proper clause. For example, the Constitution empowers the federal government to raise and support an army, and the legislation established criminal penalties for such conduct as larceny of federal military property (An Act for the Punishment of certain Crimes against the United States, ch. 9, § 16, 1 Stat. 112 (1790)). Other sections of this legislation established penalties for conduct that would interfere with federal judicial proceedings, including perjury, bribery of a federal judge, and obstruction of federal process (§§ 18, 21, 22).

Several early decisions of the United States Supreme Court confirmed Congress's discretionary authority to define federal crimes not enumerated in the Constitution. Although the federal government had only the authority delegated to it in the Constitution, the Court's expansive construction of the necessary-and-proper clause in *McCulloch v. Maryland*, 17 U.S. (4 Wheat.) 316, 416–417 (1816) established that Congress has broad discretion to employ criminal sanctions when it deems them helpful or appropriate to the exercise of any federal power (Tribe, pp. 227–231). In *United States v. Hudson*, 11 U.S. (7 Cranch) 32 (1812) and *United States v. Coolidge*, 14 U.S. (1 Wheat.) 415 (1816), the Supreme Court held that Congress has the exclusive authority to define new federal crimes, and thus there are no federal common-law crimes (Conboy, pp. 306–308).

Before the Civil War there were few federal crimes and little overlap between federal and state criminal jurisdiction. Only the states exercised general police powers. Congress authorized federal criminal sanctions where necessary to prevent interference with, or injury to, the federal government. The principal antebellum federal crimes were (1) acts threatening the existence of the central government, such as treason; (2) misconduct by federal officers, such as acceptance of a bribe; (3) interference with the operation of the federal courts, such as perjury; and (4) interference with other governmental programs, including obstruction of the mails, theft of government property, revenue fraud, and bribery or obstruction of government personnel. These were matters of paramount, if not exclusive, federal concern. Since the federal government's programs and activities were relatively few, the last category of cases was correspondingly narrow. Federal law did not reach crimes against private individuals, which were the exclusive concern of the states. The only major exception to this pattern came in geographic areas under exclusive federal maritime or territorial jurisdiction, where Congress exercised general police powers because no state had jurisdiction. Only in those areas where federal jurisdiction was exclusive, as in the District of Columbia, did Congress adopt criminal penalties for antisocial conduct—such as murder or robbery of private individuals—that posed no direct threat to the central government.

The expansion of federal jurisdiction after the Civil War

After the Civil War, Congress significantly expanded the scope of federal criminal jurisdiction. For the first time Congress sought to extend the federal criminal law to a variety of subjects clearly within the scope of the state's general police powers. Although the Supreme Court's decisions rendered the civil rights legislation largely ineffective, the Court upheld the bulk of this new federal legislation, which was intended to complement existing state criminal laws.

Civil rights legislation. The most immediate consequence of the Civil War was the ratification of the Thirteenth, Fourteenth, and Fifteenth Amendments to the Constitution, which abolished slavery and forbade the states to deny to any citizen the right to vote, the privileges and immunities of federal citizenship, due process, and equal protection of the laws. Each amendment gave Congress enforcement authority, and Congress implemented them by passing a series of civil rights statutes between 1866 and 1875 (Bernard Schwartz, vol. 1, pp. 99–172, 443–791). The Reconstruction legislation, however, not only implemented the new prohibitions against unconstitutional state action, but also purported to extend federal jurisdiction to reach private conduct clearly within the realm of the states' traditional police powers. The Supreme Court promptly nullified many of the key provisions of the legislation, holding that the civil rights amendments had given Congress no new authority to criminalize the acts of one private citizen against another, and the provisions that were not invalidated or repealed remained "a dead letter on the statute book" for more than sixty years (Bernard Schwartz, vol. 1, p. 10). Not until the middle of the next century did decisions such as *United States v. Guest*, 383 U.S. 745 (1966) signal a greater willingness to uphold portions of the Reconstruction legislation proscribing private conspiracies to interfere with rights guaranteed by the Fourteenth Amendment.

Regulation of the mails and commerce. The most important post–Civil War development was the enactment of the first federal criminal penalties for the misuse of facilities under federal control in a manner that caused injury to private individuals, not to the government itself. The first significant step in this direction was the adoption of criminal penalties for the misuse of the mails—facilities provided by the government—to effectuate fraudulent schemes or to distribute lottery circulars and obscene publications (An Act relating to the postal Laws, ch. 89, § 16, 13 Stat. 504 (1865); An Act to revise, consolidate, and amend the Statutes relating to the Post-office Department, ch. 335, §§ 148–149, 300–301, 17 Stat. 283, 302, 323 (1872), commonly known as the Mail Fraud Act).

The next step was the adoption of penalties for misconduct involving the use of interstate facilities, uch as railroads, which are subject to federal regulation under the commerce clause. The scope of the earliest provisions was very narrow. For example, the interstate transportation of explosives and of cattle with contagious diseases was made criminal. Some of the later provisions were far broader. In 1887, Congress passed the Act to regulate Commerce, ch. 104, 24 Stat. 379 (1887), which established the Interstate Commerce Commission and authorized criminal penalties for willful violations. The Sherman Act of 1890, 15 U.S.C. §§ 1–7 (1976) outlawed attempts to monopolize and conspiracies to restrain interstate commerce. The Interstate Commerce Commission Act was particularly significant because it set the pattern for subsequent legislation that established a federal regulatory framework, an administrative agency, and a comprehensive scheme of civil and criminal sanctions.

No single factor explains the new congressional willingness to expand the scope of federal criminal jurisdiction. The unprecedented crisis of the Civil War had forced supporters of the Union to adopt a more flexible and expansive interpretation of the federal government's powers, and the expanded concept of federal power continued to influence the postwar Congress. In a few instances specific wartime precedents paved the way for postwar legislation. For example, the postmaster general had reported to Congress during the war that he was seizing incendiary, treasonous, and obscene publications; the first legislation regarding mail fraud and obscene mailings was adopted a few years later. Another factor that encouraged the passage of some of the postwar legislation was the growth of a strong and politically active antivice movement, which campaigned for legislation at the state level and then for complementary federal legislation. Anthony Comstock, a well-known proponent of antivice laws, played a leading role in the adoption of the federal laws forbidding the transportation of obscene publications in the mails and in interstate commerce.

But clearly the most significant factor influencing Congress was the dramatic postwar economic expansion and growth in interstate commerce, fueled by the development of a national rail system and, to a lesser extent, by the earlier development of the telegraph system and large waterways such as the Erie Canal. The unprecedented growth in interstate transportation and commerce created new national problems that demanded new national solutions (U.S. Congress, 1886, pp. 3–28, 175–181).

The constitutionality of many of the new criminal laws was challenged because they allowed federal prosecution of conduct—such as fraud—that was tra-

ditionally subject only to state regulation. The first case to reach the Supreme Court, *In re Rapier*, 143 U.S. 110 (1892), involved criminal penalties for misuse of the mails. Although the Court upheld federal authority to punish misuse of the mail facilities furnished by the government, that rationale did not apply to interstate commerce, which is regulated, but not created, by the federal government. The first decision sustaining federal criminal jurisdiction under the commerce clause came in the *Lottery Case* (*Champion v. Ames*), 188 U.S. 321 (1903), in which a sharply divided Court upheld the federal prohibition against transportation of lottery tickets across state lines. Since Congress, like the states, might deem wide-scale gambling by lottery to be injurious to public morals, the majority held that Congress should be able to employ its power over interstate commerce to assist the states in suppressing lotteries. The Court emphasized that the federal prohibition in question "supplemented the action" of the states which might otherwise be "overthrown or disregarded by the agency of interstate Commerce" (356–357).

In the two decades after the Supreme Court's decision in the *Lottery Case*, Congress enacted several more criminal prohibitions involving interstate commerce. The most important were the prohibition against the distribution in interstate commerce of adulterated or misbranded food or drugs (Federal Food, Drug, and Cosmetic Act of 1906, ch. 3915, 34 Stat. 768); the Mann Act of 1910, as amended, 18 U.S.C. §§ 2421–2424 (1976 & Supp. IV 1980), which prohibited the interstate transportation of women for immoral purposes; and the Dyer Act of 1919, ch. 89, 41 Stat. 324, as amended and codified, 18 U.S.C. §§ 2311–2313 (1976), which prohibited interstate transportation of stolen motor vehicles (Conboy, pp. 319–321).

The other significant legislation passed during this period was a comprehensive federal provision dealing with narcotics, the Harrison Act of 1914, ch. 1, 38 Stat. 785 (superseded by the Internal Revenue Code of 1939), which included criminal provisions. The Harrison Act's detailed regulatory scheme, including the criminal penalties, was upheld as a proper exercise of the power to tax, despite the fact that it was intended to accomplish a regulatory purpose in addition to raising revenue (*United States v. Doremus*, 249 U.S. 86 (1919)).

Prohibition. The effort to prohibit the sale and distribution of liquor culminated in 1919 with the ratification of the Eighteenth Amendment, which gave "concurrent" enforcement power to the states and the federal goverment. The express constitutional grant of concurrent jurisdiction was without precedent. In practice, the enforcement burden was borne largely by the federal government, and it resulted in a phenomenal increase in the number of federal prosecutions. Prohibition cases accounted for more than one-half of all federal prosecutions every year between 1922 and 1933. In 1932, the peak year, approximately sixty-six thousand of the ninety-two thousand federal criminal cases involved Prohibition (Rubin, p. 497). In December 1933, the Eighteenth Amendment was repealed, and the only new cases involved the federal provision prohibiting the importation of liquor into a state in violation of the state's laws.

The continuing expansion of federal jurisdiction after Prohibition

Federal jurisdiction never receded to its relatively narrow pre-Prohibition scope. In 1933, the Senate authorized a special committee to investigate racketeering, kidnapping, and other forms of crime; the committee reported that "the prevalence, atrocity and magnitude of the crimes then being committed and the apparent inability of the then existing agencies to cope with them, constituted the main reason" for congressional action in "a field which had, until then, been regarded as a matter primarily of local or State concern" (U.S. Congress, 1937, p. 38). By 1937, seventeen statutes proposed by the committee had been enacted, and the committee's work ultimately led to the adoption of federal criminal penalties for interstate transmission of extortionate communications, interstate flight to avoid prosecution, interstate transportation of stolen property, bank robbery, sale or receipt of stolen property with an interstate origin, and extortion or robbery affecting interstate commerce, as well as the first federal firearms legislation (pp. 40–54). The federal securities laws, including criminal as well as civil sanctions, were also enacted during this period.

Congress's authority to adopt criminal legislation under the commerce power was already well established, but the new legislation demonstrated Congress's growing willingness to assert jurisdiction over an increasingly broad range of conduct clearly within the states' traditional police powers. The proponents of the legislation candidly recognized that much, if not all, of the conduct involved was already prohibited by the criminal codes of most states, but they argued that the states' enforcement had been ineffective. The new federal criminal legislation was adopted during the same sessions in which Congress enacted a sweeping program under the commerce clause in an effort to combat the Depression.

In the decades after the 1930s the scope of the federal government's criminal jurisdiction continued to expand. The Mail Fraud Act and the prohibitions against extortion or robbery affecting interstate commerce were given particularly broad interpretations, and they proved to be adaptable to a wide range of conduct.

New legislation was also adopted. Of particular importance were the criminal provisions adopted to secure compliance with the expanding network of federal regulations. For example, beginning in 1935, Congress attempted the comprehensive regulation of national labor relations, and it subsequently established criminal penalties for conduct such as extortion or bribery of union officials and embezzlement or graft in connection with welfare and pension benefit funds. Similarly, criminal penalties were included in the regulatory schemes dealing with such matters as occupational health and safety, water pollution, and coal mine safety.

Nationwide concern with organized crime led to the adoption of several significant statutes between 1961 and 1970. The first provision, the Travel Act of 1961, 18 U.S.C. § 1952 (1976), authorized criminal penalties for interstate travel intended to facilitate gambling, narcotic traffic, prostitution, extortion, and bribery—illegal activities frequently associated with organized crime. In 1968, Congress authorized criminal penalties for extortionate credit transactions because loansharking was providing funds for organized crime. The Organized Crime Control Act of 1970, Pub. L. 91-452, 84 Stat. 922 (codified in scattered sections of U.S.C.) included provisions intended to help in the investigation of organized crime, and penalties for syndicated gambling; the most controversial portion of the bill was its Title IX, also called the Racketeer Influenced and Corrupt Organizations Act (RICO) of 1970, as amended, 18 U.S.C. §§ 1961–1968 (1976 & Supp. III 1979). In order to prevent organized crime from infiltrating legitimate businesses, RICO made it a federal offense to invest funds derived from racketeering activity into any enterprise in interstate commerce (Bradley, pp. 839–845).

In most instances the new federal criminal provisions were intended to supplement, not supplant, related state criminal provisions, and accordingly, in a growing number of cases the same conduct could be prosecuted under either state or federal law, at the prosecutors' discretion. Successive federal and state prosecutions were also permissible because the Supreme Court interpreted the double jeopardy clause as a bar only to reprosecution by the same sovereign (*Bartkus v. Illinois*, 359 U.S. 121 (1959)).

Conclusion

Despite the absence of any general police power, Congress has employed various federal powers—particularly the commerce clause, the power to tax, the postal power—to expand federal criminal jurisdiction dramatically. This development has been piecemeal, and concern has been expressed that federal jurisdiction extends to many cases where there is no significant federal interest (Friendly, pp. 55–61). The substantial overlap of federal and state law also permits the imposition of different sentences on persons who engage in the same conduct, depending upon whether they are prosecuted under state or federal law, leaving largely unfettered discretion in the hands of the federal prosecutors, who decide whether to bring federal charges (Ruff, pp. 1171–1174).

SARA SUN BEALE

See also BANK ROBBERY; COUNTERFEITING; ECONOMIC CRIME, *articles on* ANTITRUST OFFENSES *and* TAX OFFENSES; FEDERAL BUREAU OF INVESTIGATION: HISTORY; JURISDICTION; KIDNAPPING; MAIL: FEDERAL MAIL FRAUD ACT; MANN ACT; ORGANIZED CRIME: ENFORCEMENT STRATEGIES; SEDITION; TREASON.

BIBLIOGRAPHY

BRADLEY, CRAIG M. "Racketeers, Congress, and the Courts: An Analysis of RICO." *Iowa Law Review* 65 (1980): 837–897.
Comment. "Prosecution under the Hobbs Act and the Expansion of Federal Criminal Jurisdiction." *Journal of Criminal Law and Criminology* 66 (1975): 306–324.
CONBOY, MARTIN. "Federal Criminal Law." *Law: A Century of Progress, 1835–1935*, vol. 1. Edited by Alison Reppy. New York University Press, 1937, pp. 295–346.
FRIENDLY, HENRY J. *Federal Jurisdiction: A General View.* New York: Columbia University Press, 1973.
MILLSPAUGH, ARTHUR C. *Crime Control by the National Government.* Washington, D.C.: Brookings Institution, 1937.
RUBIN, EDWARD. "A Statistical Study of Federal Criminal Prosecution." *Law and Contemporary Problems* 1 (1934): 494–508.
RUFF, CHARLES F. C. "Federal Prosecution of Local Corruption: A Case Study in the Making of Law Enforcement Policy." *Georgetown Law Journal* 65 (1977): 1171–1228.
SCHWARTZ, BERNARD, ed. *Statutory History of the United States: Civil Rights.* 2 vols. New York: Chelsea House, 1970.
SCHWARTZ, L. B. "Federal Criminal Jurisdiction and Prosecutors' Discretion." *Law and Contemporary Problems* 13 (1948): 64–87.
STERN, ROBERT L. "The Commerce Clause Revisited: The Federalization of Intrastate Crime." *Arizona Law Review* 15 (1973): 271–285.
TRIBE, LAURENCE H. *American Constitutional Law.* Mineola, N.Y.: Foundation Press, 1978.
U.S. Congress, Senate, Committee on Commerce. *Crime and Criminal Practices.* S. Rep. No. 1189. 75th Cong., 1st sess. Washington, D.C.: Government Printing Office, 1937.
U.S. Congress, Senate, Select Committee on Interstate Commerce. *Report.* S. Rep. No. 46, Part 1. 49th Cong., 1st sess. Washington, D.C.: Government Printing Office, 1886.
WARREN, CHARLES. "Federal Criminal Laws and the State Courts." *Harvard Law Review* 38 (1925): 545–598.

FEDERAL CRIMINAL LAW ENFORCEMENT

Introduction

The federal criminal law enforcement system, because of its nationwide scope, visibility, and traditions, must be considered the most important enforcement system in the nation—the one that in many of its aspects serves as a model for all of the others. It is a system, however, with its own special problems.

Traditionally, the federal government has a secondary responsibility for overall criminal law enforcement in the United States. There is a strong commitment in this country to the notion that primary enforcement responsibility rests with the state and local governments. Accordingly, compared to state and local systems, the federal criminal law enforcement system is very small. More than nineteen thousand police agencies, employing perhaps half a million sworn officers, function at the state and local level. In excess of seven hundred thousand felony cases are filed each year in the state court systems. By contrast, only about fifty major law enforcement agencies are concerned with enforcement of the federal criminal laws. The total number of federal police is less than fifty thousand, and the average number of criminal cases filed in the federal courts (not including those filed in the District of Columbia) hovers around thirty-five thousand. The number of police officers employed by the New York City Police Department almost equals the total of federal law enforcement agents for the entire country.

A major component of the federal role in law enforcement is the protection of direct federal interests. Thus, federal criminal law enforcement efforts have always been aimed at crimes relating to fraud, embezzlement, or theft of federal monies or crimes involving damage to federal properties or injury to federal personnel. In protecting such interests, the federal system functions like any state or local system. But the federal government also performs another role. Since the 1870s, the federal government gradually has begun to assume an increasing responsibility for combating crime that does not offend against any direct federal interest, investigating and prosecuting crimes that historically were only within the province of state and local law enforcement. Many federal criminal statutes have been enacted that cover essentially the same ground as state crimes, and federal prosecutions increasingly have involved such crimes.

There are often special reasons for federal involvement in cases that do not involve a direct federal interest and that might otherwise have been pursued by state authorities. For example, in cases with multistate contacts the nationwide authority of federal agencies permits the federal government to do things that an individual state cannot easily do: conduct a coordinated investigation in several states at once, subpoena witnesses from different states into the jurisdiction of trial, and bring all of the defendants together. By means of interstate compacts and cooperation the states might be able to accomplish some of these things, but only through cumbersome procedures.

Federal investigation and prosecution of local crime may also be justified where special circumstances like political corruption are present, on the ground that such corruption may reflect a breakdown of local law enforcement or that it is easier for agencies not entrenched in local politics to handle the matter. A case can also be made that the federal government has a special responsibility for prosecuting organized crime because such crime is a national problem. A similar claim can be made in relation to the illegal traffic in drugs and guns. Federal involvement in those areas can also be justified on the ground that only a multistate approach can be effective and because of federal customs responsibilities and control over the international borders.

The increasing number of prosecutions by federal agencies of state-type cases has not been limited, however, to instances where there are such special reasons for federal involvement. In the context of such cases, concerns arise about the possible usurpation by the federal government of state and local government's traditional primary enforcement responsibilities, the problems associated with having two separate, overlapping criminal law enforcement systems operating side by side, and the difficulty of achieving a uniform national enforcement policy. Such concerns are best addressed by first examining the history and nature of the federal criminal law enforcement system.

History

The history of the federal criminal law enforcement system can be divided into four major periods. The first began on September 24, 1789, when Congress created the office of the attorney general of the United States and established United States attorneys for each federal judicial district. The first federal police agency, the Revenue Cutter Service, was established in 1789 to deal with smuggling. In the years that followed, federal criminal law enforcement was of limited scope and mainly concerned with protecting the integrity of federal activities such as the mails.

The second period began after the Civil War. In 1868, Congress authorized a federal detective force of twenty-five. In 1870 it established the Department of Justice, appropriating $50,000 for the detection and prosecution of crimes. In 1872 the original mail fraud statute (ch. 335, §§ 148–149, 300–301, 17 Stat. 283) was enacted, the first federal criminal statute of broad scope used extensively as a means of prosecuting criminal activity traditionally dealt with under state law. In the succeeding fifty years, a number of statutes of similar scope were enacted, including the Dyer Act of 1919, prohibiting the interstate transportation of stolen motor vehicles (18 U.S.C. § 2312); the White-Slave Traffic (Mann) Act of 1910, prohibiting interstate transportation of females for immoral purposes (18 U.S.C. §§ 2421–2424); and the Harrison Act of 1914, which imposed an occupational tax on those who deal in narcotic drugs (ch. 1, 38 Stat. 785). During this same period, about 1919, the Criminal Division was established within the Department of Justice, and five years later J. Edgar Hoover took over the Department's Bureau of Investigation, which later became the Federal Bureau of Investigation.

The third period, beginning in the 1930s in the aftermath of Prohibition and running through World War II, laid the foundation for the modern era in federal criminal law enforcement. The hallmark of the third period was a steady and rapid increase in the number and coverage of federal crimes. Between 1932 and 1935, thirteen major federal statutes in the field of criminal law and procedure were added to Title 18 of the United States Code. They included the Anti-Racketeering Act of 1934 (§ 1951), the Bank Robbery Act of 1934 (§ 2113), the Fugitive Felon Act of 1932 (§ 1073), and the Kidnapping Act of 1932 (§ 1201). During the 1930s, major federal gun control laws and additional narcotic tax laws were enacted as well.

The modern era of federal criminal law enforce

ment began in the 1950s. A new perception developed of crime as a national problem and of the federal government as having a responsibility for dealing with it, with special emphasis on the federal role in fighting organized crime. During this period, numerous new and innovative federal criminal statutes were enacted, and the personnel of many of the principal enforcement agencies was significantly increased.

The federal enforcement system

Police agencies. It is noteworthy that in common parlance no one refers to federal criminal law enforcement agencies as federal "police," perhaps in implicit recognition that they do not have the principal responsibility for maintenance of public order in the country in the manner of a local constabulary.

Three important investigative agencies are located in the Department of Justice—the FBI, the Drug Enforcement Administration (DEA), and the Immigration and Naturalization Service. The FBI is the largest federal criminal law enforcement agency (excluding the military services, of which mention will be made below). It has grown from approximately thirty-three hundred agents in 1948 to almost eight thousand. The FBI is the federal agency with a residual responsibility for enforcement of federal criminal laws not entrusted to specialized enforcement agencies. This gives it enforcement responsibility for a wide variety of criminal activities, ranging from organized crime, political corruption, and white-collar crime to foreign espionage. The FBI is organized regionally into 59 field divisions and 432 suboffices, all supervised from FBI headquarters in Washington.

The next largest agency with traditional criminal law enforcement responsibilities is the DEA. Previously called the Bureau of Narcotics and located in the Treasury, this agency was renamed and shifted to the Justice Department in 1973. The DEA has grown from fewer than two hundred agents in 1948 to approximately two thousand agents. The FBI, which had not previously conducted drug investigations, has been authorized to function in this investigative arena too. This has led to joint operations by the two agencies, and some proposals have been made to combine the DEA's two thousand agents with the FBI's staff of eight thousand.

A number of enforcement agencies are located in the Department of the Treasury: the Customs Service, which has grown from fewer than 150 agents in 1948 to more than 600; the Internal Revenue Service, whose 16,000 agents, special agents, and investigators (approximately 8,500 in 1948) have mainly civil but also some criminal law enforcement duties in the tax field; the Secret Service (some 300 agents in 1948 and about 1,550 agents in the early 1980s) with responsibility for presidential protection and similar duties, as well as counterfeiting and government check-forgery enforcement; and the Bureau of Alcohol, Tobacco, and Firearms (ATF) with approximately 2,000 agents, of whom about 1,200 have gun control, explosives, and arson responsibilities. Until 1972, the ATF was only a division within the Bureau of Internal Revenue, performing regulatory and criminal law enforcement functions. In that year the agency was upgraded to a separate bureau, still within the Treasury Department. Ten years later, under a reorganization plan submitted by the Reagan Administration, the ATF was to be phased out, its firearms and explosives enforcement functions and some 1,200 agents transferred to the Secret Service, and about 700 agents and employees with alcohol and tobacco enforcement functions handed over to the Customs Service.

Many other government departments and agencies also have investigatory personnel to deal with criminal violations arising out of the administration of their regulatory programs. These include criminal law enforcement personnel functioning within the Department of Agriculture, the Department of Labor, the Department of the Interior, the Securities and Exchange Commission (SEC), and the Food and Drug Administration.

The American tradition is that the military (with the exception of the Coast Guard, which plays an enforcement role in relation to smuggling) does not become involved in domestic civil law enforcement except in time of emergency and civil disorder. In 1981, however, the Attorney General's Task Force on Violent Crime recommended that the navy be called upon to assist in detecting illicit drugs being smuggled into the country by air and sea. But a report prepared by the task force's staff suggested that the use of a military arm for civil enforcement duties would create a dangerous precedent.

Prosecuting agencies. The great majority of federal prosecutions are handled by the ninety-five United States attorneys' offices, located within the ninety-five federal judicial districts in the fifty states and the United States territories and possessions. The United States attorneys, appointed by the President for four-year terms, are legally subject to the supervisory power of the attorney general, but in practice, many of their offices function with some degree of autonomy. Approximately two thousand assistant United

States attorneys, handling both civil and criminal matters, serve in these offices, whose staffs range from two assistants to more than a hundred. In most instances the decision whether to prosecute in an individual case is made by the assistant United States attorney in the field upon referral of a matter by a federal investigative agency. In a few areas, the investigative agency is required to refer the matter directly to the appropriate division in the Justice Department.

Several hundred federal prosecutors work in the Criminal Division of the Department of Justice, and lawyers in other divisions within the department, such as the Tax Division and the Civil Rights Division, may also be involved in criminal matters. Since the late 1960s, with mixed success, the Criminal Division has attempted to exercise greater supervisory control over decision-making by United States attorneys in the field, with a view to making federal prosecutive policy more uniform nationwide. The division also functions in an advisory capacity to the United States attorneys, providing technical assistance of various kinds, and attorneys, when needed, in the trial of particular cases.

Since 1966, Justice Department attorneys have also served in organized crime strike forces with special responsibility for investigating and prosecuting persons connected to organized crime. The strike forces are composed of government attorneys who report directly to the Justice Department, and of representatives from federal investigative agencies. Representatives from state agencies, although not formally part of the strike forces, may also be involved. At least eleven federal investigative agencies participate in the strike force program: the ATF, the Customs Service, the Department of Labor, the DEA, the FBI, the Immigration and Naturalization Service, the Internal Revenue Service, the SEC, the Postal Service, the United States Marshals Service, and the Secret Service. Strike forces operate in fourteen major cities, with suboffices located in a dozen other cities. The Justice Department attorneys investigate and prosecute matters viewed as related to organized crime that are referred to them by the other agencies. At times there have been jurisdictional disputes between the strike forces and the United States attorneys' offices, a fact symptomatic of the friction that occasionally develops between Justice Department attorneys in Washington and the United States attorneys in the field.

Statutory coverage. Since about 1950 there has been a significant increase in the number and substantive coverage of federal criminal law statutes. At an early date the constitutional foundation for a broad federal authority to criminalize conduct that does not threaten a direct federal interest was established,

based in the interstate commerce, taxing, or mails powers. Crimes founded in the commerce power typically are defined in terms of protecting the instrumentalities of commerce, transportation or movement across a state line, or activity that affects commerce; similarly, those based on Congress's power over the mails requires a use of the mails; and the taxing-power offenses typically involve violation of licensing-registration requirements incident to the collection of a tax.

In the 1950s, a wholesale expansion of federal criminal laws began. Some examples illustrate the broad range of subjects touched upon. Congress began to adopt a series of criminal provisions aimed at gambling (for example, 15 U.S.C. § 1176), and over the course of the next two decades a number of anti-gambling provisions were enacted (for example, 18 U.S.C. § 1953). In 1959, a new enactment made the embezzlement of labor union funds a federal crime (29 U.S.C. § 501). This was followed in 1962 by a similar provision relating to employee benefit plans (18 U.S.C. § 664). With the Gun Control Act of 1968, Congress extended the reach of federal gun control laws (18 U.S.C. §§ 921–928; 18 U.S.C. App. §§ 1201–1203). Provisions were also enacted relating to the illegal manufacture and distribution of explosives and the transportation of switchblade knives (18 U.S.C. §§ 841–848; 15 U.S.C. § 1242). In 1968, too, traveling across a state line with the purpose of inciting a riot became a federal crime (18 U.S.C. §§ 2101–2102). In 1978, legislation was enacted relating to the sexual exploitation of children (18 U.S.C. §§ 2251–2253). Additionally, since the 1950s new federal criminal statutes have been enacted in the fields of civil rights (for example, 18 U.S.C. § 245), consumer protection (15 U.S.C. 1264), occupational safety (29 U.S.C. § 666), and traffic in contraband commercial items such as cigarettes, fireworks, and counterfeit phonograph records (18 U.S.C. §§ 2341–2346; § 836; § 2318). It was during this period that Congress also substantially revised existing legislation relating to drugs, by enacting the Comprehensive Drug Abuse Prevention and Control Act of 1970 (21 U.S.C. §§ 801–965 *passim*).

Significantly, too, during this same period, Congress enacted several innovative statutes aimed particularly at organized crime, beginning with the Travel Act of 1961, which prohibited travel interstate to promote enterprises involving gambling, illegal liquor, narcotics, prostitution, extortion, bribery, or arson (18 U.S.C. § 1952). Another such law, making loan-sharking a federal crime, is found in the Consumer Credit Protection Act of 1968 (18 U.S.C. §§ 891–896).

The most significant of these laws is the Racketeer Influenced and Corrupt Organizations (RICO) Act of 1970, aimed at criminal activity that is operated as a business or that has an impact on legitimate business (18 U.S.C. §§ 1961–1968). RICO incorporates by reference eight major categories of state crime and most major federal offenses. It includes very stiff traditional penalties, and (unusual in a criminal context) it has provisions for forfeiture and civil remedies such as divestiture and corporate dissolution and reorganization. Two other similarly complex statutes enacted in 1970 were specifically aimed at large-scale illicit drug trafficking and illegal gambling (21 U.S.C. § 848; 18 U.S.C. § 1955).

Since the late 1960s efforts have also been made, beginning with the work of the National Commission on Reform of the Federal Criminal Laws, to reform and recodify the entire federal criminal code. Opposition to the various code reform proposals submitted to Congress in the 1970s came from both ends of the political spectrum, and the prospect that any substantial code reform will be achieved is not bright. Under any of these major code reform proposals, the substantial expansion of the coverage of the federal criminal laws already achieved would not be affected.

Case load. Despite an increase in the number of federal law enforcement personnel and the type and number of federal criminal statutes, the number of federal criminal prosecutions initiated annually has remained relatively constant since about 1930, averaging approximately thirty-five thousand cases. This striking statistic is probably accounted for, in large measure, by the government's increasing emphasis on the investigation and prosecution of major criminal cases, involving more persons, more individual crimes, and more complex facts. This has led to lengthier investigations and trials and more hours invested per case.

Assessment

The usurpation issue. The picture of federal investigative and prosecutorial agencies that emerges from the foregoing description can be summarized as follows. Although there has been a significant increase in the size of many of the agencies, they still remain small, particularly in relation to the geographic areas and population they cover. Yet, given the total number of federal enforcement personnel, the number of investigative agencies and prosecutorial offices is rather large. As a consequence, the federal criminal law enforcement operation is fragmented into many relatively small agencies and offices. In addition, on the prosecutorial side there is a large degree of decentralization, despite efforts to give Washington more control over the United States attorneys' offices and the development of the organized crime strike forces.

The combination of these characteristics—a relatively small, fragmented, and in part decentralized system—produces many inefficiencies in the federal criminal law enforcement operation. But it also serves to discourage a concentration of law enforcement power in any one agency or group of agencies that could lead to the development of a national police force and a possible shift in the traditional balance of law enforcement responsibilities.

Plans or proposals for the absorption of one agency and its functions by another, such as those described above in connection with the ATF and the DEA, or efforts to centralize authority over the United States attorneys, should be viewed against this background. They do not by themselves bespeak too great a concentration of federal criminal law enforcement power, and they may serve to make the federal operation more efficient and cost-effective. Only if they are harbingers of a new trend in the organization of federal enforcement agencies might there be cause for concern. Similarly, involving the United States Navy in anti-drug-smuggling operations should not by itself be viewed as a development that will upset the traditional balance in law enforcement. But it should be kept in mind that the involvement of the military more generally in domestic crime-fighting activities could, more than any other single step, quickly produce an enormous concentration of federal enforcement power and dramatically change the nature of the federal role.

As long as the resources available to federal criminal law enforcement remain limited, fragmented, and decentralized, there is little danger that the traditional primacy of state and local authorities will be usurped. The important issues lie elsewhere.

The rival systems issue. Generally, the federal, state, and local systems function reasonably well in parallel relation to one another. At the operational level, there is ordinarily cooperation between agents of state, local, and federal agencies. They often work together, share the results of investigations, or provide various kinds of mutual assistance. The issue of which jurisdiction prosecutes a particular offender often turns on which happens to apprehend him first, although that factor may not always be decisive. One jurisdiction may turn over a suspect to the custody of the other for trial because the case may not be viewed as appropriate for prosecution in the first jurisdiction. Or there may be special reasons for trying the case in the second jurisdiction, such as higher penalties or advantageous evidentiary or procedural rules. Occasionally, too, where prosecution has already occurred in one jurisdiction (whether successful or not), the other jurisdiction may also decide to prosecute for essentially the same conduct. Such duplicative prosecutions are permitted under existing federal constitutional doctrine, although barred in some jurisdictions by statute, state constitutional principles, or prosecutorial policy.

Occasional breakdowns in the operating relationships do, however, occur. The existence of a large number of federal criminal statutes that criminalize conduct subject to prosecution under state law makes possible wasteful competition, interference, and duplication of investigative efforts in federal, state, and local jurisdictions. For example, sometimes federal and state prosecutors dispute over which should have the first opportunity to try a particular individual; often such cases involve an element of notoriety. Complaints are also aired, on occasion, that one jurisdiction is not sharing the results of an investigation with the other, and there have even been rare instances of one jurisdiction seeking a court order to require the other to hand over a witness.

There is also the possibility that certain matters may not be prosecuted at all because one jurisdiction assumes that the other is handling the category of case in question. For example, when there were indications in 1978 that the federal government would deemphasize bank robbery investigations and prosecutions, it was not at all clear that local police and prosecutors were prepared—or had the resources—to pursue the cases that would no longer be handled on the federal level.

Overall, however, the degree of cooperation far outweighs the infrequent friction, and the extent to which prosecutions in one jurisdiction complement those in the other overshadows the few instances of cases that fall between the cracks. It is noteworthy that although state and local authorities sometimes complain about a lack of sufficient cooperation and coordination on the part of federal officials, they generally have not opposed increasing federal involvement in cases that do not protect a direct federal interest.

The national enforcement policy issue. The increased coverage of federal criminal statutes, however, does serve to exacerbate the case selection problem on the federal level. Deciding which cases to pursue—whether by way of investigation or prosecution—is difficult for criminal law enforcement agencies at all levels of government, but it has become especially complex for federal agencies. Although

these agencies have grown considerably, their limited resources make it possible to deal with only a very small fraction of the huge number of crimes committed each year across the nation that might be prosecuted by federal authorities. How does one select the relatively few cases to investigate and prosecute so as to focus the federal effort and make it reflect a consistent, rational policy?

Various methods are being used for this purpose. In the modern period, much use has been made of a federal "mission" approach, in which federal resources are channeled toward particular kinds of criminal activity. Of course, each of the specialized enforcement agencies has its own mission, but questions arise as to what proportion of the total resources available for law enforcement should go to these agencies. The largest agency, the FBI, has a very broad investigative authority and its mission or missions must be separately determined. Sometimes the government is said to "declare war" on a particular type of crime. Thus, in the 1960s it declared war on organized crime, and enforcement efforts directed against political corruption and drug trafficking were also emphasized. In the 1970s a federal war against white-collar crime was declared, and in the 1980s there has been much talk on the federal level of fighting violent crime, as well as an increased emphasis on combating the drug traffic.

A special way to focus the federal effort is to establish units charged with responsibility in a particular substantive area. The organized-crime strike forces described above, and the economic-crime enforcement units set up in 1979 within twenty-seven United States attorneys' offices, illustrate this approach.

Another approach involves the promulgation of prosecutorial guidelines or policy statements issued by the Department of Justice to the United States attorneys. In the past, such policy statements have been made with respect to particular crime categories, such as obscenity cases. In 1980 more general guidelines, entitled *Principles of Federal Prosecution*, were issued to the United States attorneys. Another variation involves the Justice Department's imposition of a requirement that before initiating prosecution in a particular category of case, the United States attorney's office must consult with or obtain approval from the Department. RICO prosecutions, for example, require such approval, and prosecutions for making false statements to a federal agency (prohibited by 18 U.S.C. § 1001) require prior consultation.

None of these methods for focusing federal criminal law enforcement efforts has been completely effective. The problem in part involves the inherent difficulty of making a decentralized and fragmented system of investigation and prosecution function in such a way that its various parts behave in a consistent manner. The problem, too, results from the fact that the federal role in law enforcement is still evolving with the passage of time and changes in administrations.

The nature of the federal criminal law enforcement role has not yet been clearly defined and settled by anyone in or outside of the government. Neither government officials nor legal scholars have as yet adequately addressed the issues involved. Insofar as the federal system has a significant responsibility for pursuing criminal activity that does not injure direct federal interests and that might as easily have been prosecuted by state and local authorities, it is still a system in search of a rationale.

NORMAN ABRAMS

See also DRUGS AND CRIME: LEGAL ASPECTS; ECONOMIC CRIME, *articles on* ANTITRUST OFFENSES *and* TAX OFFENSES; FEDERAL BUREAU OF INVESTIGATION: HISTORY; FEDERAL CRIMINAL JURISDICTION; KIDNAPPING; MAIL: FEDERAL MAIL FRAUD ACT; MANN ACT; *both articles under* ORGANIZED CRIME; PROSECUTION, *articles on* PROSECUTORIAL DISCRETION *and* UNITED STATES ATTORNEY.

BIBLIOGRAPHY

ABRAMS, NORMAN. "Assessing the Federal Government's 'War' on White Collar Crime." *Temple Law Quarterly* 53 (1980): 984–1008.
———. "Consultant's Report on Jurisdiction." *National Commission on Reform of Federal Criminal Laws: Working Papers,* vol. 1. Washington, D.C.: The Commission, 1970, pp. 33–66.
EISENSTEIN, JAMES. *Counsel for the United States: U.S. Attorneys in the Political and Legal Systems.* Baltimore: Johns Hopkins University Press, 1978.
FRIENDLY, HENRY J. *Federal Jurisdiction: A General View.* New York: Columbia University Press, 1973.
HUSTON, LUTHER A. *The Department of Justice.* New York: Praeger, 1967.
KAPLAN, JOHN. "The Prosecutorial Discretion: A Comment." *Northwestern University Law Review* 60 (1965): 174–193.
MILLSPAUGH, ARTHUR C. *Crime Control by the National Government.* Washington, D.C.: Brookings Institution, 1937.
RUFF, CHARLES F. C. "Federal Prosecution of Local Corruption: A Case Study in the Making of Law Enforcement Policy." *Georgetown Law Journal* 65 (1977): 1171–1228.
SCHWARTZ, LOUIS B. "Federal Criminal Jurisdiction and Prosecutors' Discretion." *Law and Contemporary Problems* 13 (1948): 64–87.
———. "Reform of the Federal Criminal Laws: Issues, Tactics, and Prospects." *Law and Contemporary Problems* 41 (1977): 1–62.
SEYMOUR, WHITNEY N., JR. *United States Attorney: An Inside View of "Justice" in America under the Nixon Administration.* New York: Morrow, 1975.
STERN, ROBERT L. "The Commerce Clause Revisited: The Federalization of Intrastate Crime." *Arizona Law Review* 15 (1973): 271–285.
"The Strike Force: Organized Law Enforcement v. Organized Crime." *Columbia Journal of Law and Social Problems* 6 (1970): 496–523.
U.S. Department of Justice. *Principles of Federal Prosecution.* Washington, D.C.: The Department, 1980.
———, Attorney General's Task Force on Violent Crime. *Final Report.* Washington, D.C.: The Department, 1981.
U.S. Department of Justice, Office of the Attorney General. *National Priorities for the Investigation and Prosecution of White Collar Crime: Report of the Attorney General.* Washington, D.C.: The Office, 1980.

FELONY

See CRIME: DEFINITION OF CRIME; CRIMINAL COURTS: FELONY DISPOSITIONS.

FELONY MURDER

See HOMICIDE: LEGAL ASPECTS.

FENCING AND RECEIVING STOLEN GOODS

1. THE PROFESSIONAL FENCE   Carl Klockars
2. LEGAL ASPECTS   Peter A. Bell

1.
THE PROFESSIONAL FENCE

There are many paths that stolen property may take from thieves to eventual consumers. In the simplest and shortest case, the thief himself is the ultimate consumer, using what he steals. Other paths are also relatively uncomplicated and involve only the thief or his agent selling stolen property to friends, neighbors, and acquaintances under the cover of friendly or neighborly privacy. Still others lead stolen property through sheltered markets such as bars, luncheonettes, beauty parlors, and auto service stations with the encouragement, if not the active participation, of their proprietors. Yet other paths, such as those involving the trade in stolen fine art, securities, and trade secrets, are at once more elaborate and technically sophisticated and require skilled direction by the successful dealer. With but few exceptions, adequate descriptions of these and other paths along which stolen property travels are lacking in the literature of criminology; no reliable information is available on the relative contribution of different patterns of sale, purchase, and distribution to the overall flow of stolen property from thieves to eventual consumers.

The concept of the professional fence

Despite the poverty of information on the overall traffic in stolen property and the role of the professional fence in it, it is certain that the professional fence has been an active, central figure in that traffic since at least the early seventeenth century. It was during this period that Mary Frith, alias Moll Cutpurse, organized the largest clearinghouse for stolen property in London. An outrageous woman who dressed in men's clothes and claimed to be the first woman to smoke tobacco, she is the character on whom Thomas Middleton and Thomas Dekker based their play *The Roaring Girle* (1610). The London underworld was dominated between 1715 and 1725 by Jonathan Wild, a professional fence who, according to Daniel Defoe, employed some seven thousand thieves. Although Defoe's estimate may be exaggerated, the definitive history of Wild's life and career by Gerald Howson suggests that Wild's operation may have been the largest organized criminal enterprise in English history. Wild, immortalized in John Gay's *The Beggar's Opera* (1728) and Henry Fielding's *The Life of Mr. Jonathan Wild The Great* (1743), enjoys a literary legacy second only to that of Charles Dickens's Fagin, a character based on the nineteenth-century London fence Ikey Solomon.

Such accounts demonstrate that the role of the professional fence is durable and establish unequivocally that certain fences have handled enormous quantities of stolen property over many years. It remains, however, impossible to assess with any precision what proportion of stolen property is handled by professional fences and what proportion follows other channels managed by other agents of distribution. In part, this is a problem of lack of information about the other channels, but it is also a question of how best to define the professional fence so as to distinguish him from other traffickers in stolen goods.

In the 1930s, Jerome Hall sought to distinguish what he called the "professional receiver" from the concept of the receiver of stolen goods embodied in traditional Anglo-American law. Traditional law, Hall argued, did not distinguish between the professional buyer of, and the ultimate consumer of, stolen property. Moreover, traditional law emphasized the receiving of stolen goods, whereas the most salient characteristics of the professional receiver were his delivery and distribution of stolen goods after they had been received. It was this activity, which traditional law failed to recognize, that caused Hall to define the professional receiver as a dealer in stolen property. Hall then went on to develop a simple typology, distinguishing his "professional receiver" dealer from both the "lay receiver," who knowingly bought stolen property for his own consumption, and the "occasional receiver," who bought stolen property for resale but only infrequently.

At least in part, Hall's redefinition of the professional receiver as a dealer and his break with the traditional legal image of the receiver were accepted by Carl Klockars. Klockars went farther than Hall: he abandoned the legal term *receiver* altogether and made use of the term *fence*, a concept meaningful in the vocabulary of the underworld for centuries. The fence was indeed a dealer in stolen property, not merely a thief selling his own stolen property or a member of a burglary gang charged with disposing of what the gang had stolen. Furthermore, the professional fence was not only a dealer but a successful dealer, buying and selling stolen property regularly and profitably for a considerable period of time, perhaps years. In addition, Klockars asserted, the professional fence was a public figure, in the sense that his continued performance as a successful dealer would gain him a reputation as a professional fence among lawbreakers, law enforcers, and others acquainted with the criminal community.

The career of the professional fence

The criminal careers of professional fences are as varied and diverse as the careers of any other entrepreneurs. They consist of individual solutions to the problems of becoming and being a dealer, successful, and public. In any professional fence's career the demands of all three of these problems press simultaneously for solution, but for descriptive purposes each may be considered separately in terms of the typical solutions it invites.

Becoming a dealer in stolen goods.

The problem of buying. The prospective dealer in stolen property must first learn how to buy it, and solving this problem is largely a matter of finding willing sellers. Many people in a variety of occupations and positions in society occasionally find themselves approached to buy stolen property. Persons engaged in such occupations as those of pawnbroker, jeweler, secondhand dealer, and auctioneer lend themselves to these invitations because of the similarity between the types of property commonly stolen and those routinely handled in their occupations. Other persons, for example, gamblers, bartenders, criminal lawyers, and policemen, are particularly likely to be invited to buy stolen property owing to the types of people they routinely meet.

The professional fence differs from such persons in that he must generate and maintain a steady clientele of willing sellers in order to buy stolen property regularly and routinely. The experience of numerous "stings," or undercover operations in which police pose as professional fences in order to trap thieves, suggests that creating a steady stream of willing sellers of stolen property is not difficult. In a famous sting operation described by *Washington Post* journalists Ron Shaffer, Kevin Klose, and Alfred Lewis, a group of undercover police managed to bring in dozens of thieves by identifying themselves as mafiosi who had come to take over the stolen-property business in the nation's capital. The fact that the police succeeded in building up their clientele of willing sellers of stolen property while introducing employees with such names as Rico Rigatoni and Angelo Lasagna indicates the level of sophistication of the criminal clientele they developed.

The problem of selling. The second skill to be mastered by the professional fence—how to sell the property he has bought—is more difficult and complicated. From the perspective of the thief, the fence provides at least three services as a buyer, each of which reflects the fence's ultimate abilities to sell it. First, the professional fence is able to buy and sell large quantities of stolen property. A thief who steals a trailer load of cigarettes may be able to peddle a few dozen cartons to friends, but if he wishes to sell the entire trailer load in one transaction, the professional fence can accommodate him. Second, the professional fence offers the thief access to markets for unique or unusual merchandise. An industrious thief may peddle an entire trailer load of cigarettes himself because smokers are easy to locate. But the thief who steals a computer, a rare manuscript, a case of dentist drills, or a trailer load of popsicle sticks may not know where to sell it. Finally, the professional fence offers the thief an opportunity to convert his stolen property into money rapidly, saving him the time and labor of selling large quantities of stolen merchandise in small units or searching out and developing difficult markets.

These three services bear witness to the fence's ready access to markets that are effectively closed to many, if not most, thieves. How, then, does the fence gain access to these markets when the thief cannot? One very general answer is that by virtue of a second, legitimate occupation the professional fence may be in those markets already. Thus, the art fence is likely to be a dealer in fine art, the fence for tobacco in the tobacco business, and the fence for dental supplies in the dental supply business.

This generalization is, however, limited by the size of the market for certain types of stolen property. Some professional fences are specialists dealing in only one or two product lines; others are generalists with abilities to buy and sell almost anything. In order for a professional fence to be a specialist, there has to be sufficient trade in a specialized type of stolen property to sustain him. There are specialist professional fences for such frequently stolen products as liquor, jewelry, tobacco, automobiles, and fine art, but a professional fencing specialty as narrow as dental supplies is doubtful, and one as narrow as popsicle sticks preposterous. If this sort of product is handled by a professional fence at all, it will be handled by a generalist who has developed a wide variety of markets.

Achieving success as a professional fence. Becoming a successful dealer in stolen property involves buying and selling profitably and continuing to do so without getting caught. The problem of making a profit in the stolen-property market must be understood in light of the fact that most stolen property is of necessity sold below legitimate market prices. A professional fence may be able to buy stolen property at a third of its legitimate market value, but if he is then able to sell that property at only one-half of its legitimate market value, he may well find it more profitable to remain in the legitimate market.

The professional fence's buying price is lower than the legitimate market price because it costs his suppliers less to steal property than it does for manufacturers to make it. Buyers of stolen property, in turn, would be foolish to assume the risks of purchasing stolen property if the fence's prices were not sufficiently below legal prices to warrant the additional risks and disadvantages. One may take civil action against a seller of defective goods if one is dealing in the legitimate market, but the courts will not enforce a similar claim in an illegal transaction.

The economics of the stolen-property market suggest that one of the most profitable strategies for the professional fence is to buy goods at stolen-property market prices and sell them at or near legitimate market prices. One of the ways of doing so is to maintain a legitimate business that carries the same products the fence purchases illegally. The legally and illegally purchased property can then be merged and sold at legitimate market prices.

This solution to the problem of making a profit in the stolen-property business also carries with it numerous advantages with respect to the professional fence's avoiding prosecution and conviction for his crime. In order to convict someone of the crime of receiving stolen property, it must be proved that the goods in question are stolen, that the person accused actually received them, and that the person who received the stolen goods had reasonable cause to believe they were stolen. Some examples of the ways in which the professional fence uses his legitimate business front as a shield against attempts to prove these evidentiary elements of the law of criminal receiving merit description.

Defenses against proof that goods are stolen. In order to prove that particular goods are stolen, the owner must be able to identify them, distinguishing them from other goods which may be similar in appearance. The fence's legitimate business front often permits the merging of stolen and legitimate stock to make them indistinguishable. Mass-produced name-brand products, foodstuffs, metals, loose precious and semiprecious stones, chemicals, and livestock are virtually indistinguishable as stolen once they are merged with quantities of similar products. Those products that bear uniquely identifying labels or characteristics can often be easily altered. Gold and silver jewelry can be melted down; consumer goods can be removed from their identifying cartons; labels can be cut from suits; jewels can be removed from their settings; stolen vehicles can be reduced to parts. Even if the professional fence does not in his front business have merchandise identical to the stolen property, he can often produce receipts from earlier purchases of identical property to offer as fraudulent evidence that the stolen goods are actually his.

Defenses against proof of possession. If the professional fence merges legitimate and stolen stock, removes labels and other identifying characteristics of stolen merchandise, and keeps a supply of purchase receipts of legitimate goods that cover purchase of similar stolen goods at a later date, he defends against proof of possession of stolen goods in the same stroke with which he frustrates proof that they are stolen. There are, moreover, further strategies that the professional fence may employ to guard against attempts to prove possession.

The most important of these strategies is probably the speed with which the fence can execute the complete transaction. If, for example, he can purchase stolen goods from a thief and distribute them to their ultimate consumers within a few hours, he greatly reduces the chance that the goods will be found in his possession. This strategy rests upon the reasonable assumption that there will be a delay between the time when the goods are stolen and the theft is discovered, reported, and investigated.

Defense against proof of possession may also be facilitated by a strategy known as the "drop." It involves instructing the thief to deposit ("drop") the stolen merchandise at a designated location where the professional fence, his agent, or the ultimate purchaser can take possession of it after it has been determined that the goods are not being kept under surveillance. In a functionally equivalent strategy, the thief maintains possession of the merchandise until the fence sells it on the basis of a sample; the thief thus assumes most of the risks of possession.

Defenses against proof of reasonable cause to believe goods are stolen. For the professional fence who maintains a legitimate business front, defense against proof that he had reasonable cause to believe goods he bought were stolen involves demonstrating that the illegal transaction could not be distinguished from normal, legitimate business practice. It is typically argued that something about the character of the goods, their price, or the person selling them should alert a reasonable person to the probability that they are stolen. If, for example, an unemployed laborer drives up in a car loaded with miscellaneous new merchandise that he offers to sell at a quarter of its legitimate market value, the law reasons that a normal person would have cause to believe the goods were stolen. Under such circumstances it is the professional fence's task to create a plausible alternative explanation.

The fence may, for example, argue that the thief represented himself as a friend or relative of someone who had had a legitimate business and that the business had failed and its merchandise was being sold at a discount to other dealers. Such a story might be accepted with regard to the seller and the merchandise, but it is somewhat strained with regard to the fence's purchase price.

To handle the problem of too low a purchase price, the professional fence may simply prepare a receipt for the goods which shows a higher price and also indicates that the higher purchase price was paid in cash. Alternatively, the professional fence may make out a check to the seller at a plausible purchase price, have the seller endorse it, and deposit the endorsed check in the business account. If questioned, the professional fence will then explain that he paid the seller the (reasonable) price shown on the check, but after doing so, the seller asked him to cash the check. The fence then claims that he agreed to do so and requested the seller to endorse the check; the fence then deposited the endorsed check in his business account. The story is of course untrue, but it gives the fence a receipt and a canceled check as evidence that a fair market price was paid for the goods.

The professional fence as a public dealer in stolen goods. The achievement of success by a professional fence carries in its wake a number of problems. Some are personal and may involve the reconciliation of the fence's wish for a positive self-concept with his actual career in crime. Accounts of the lives and characters of a number of famous fences, including Howson's study of Jonathan Wild, Herbert Asbury's sketch of the nineteenth-century New York fence "Ma" Mandelbaum, and Klockars's biography of the contemporary professional fence "Vincent Swaggi," suggest various ways in which this self-image problem can be handled.

The potential judicial consequences of a reputation as a successful dealer in stolen property are of a different order. The public professional fence, unlike the sporadic dealer who for years may keep his dealings private, must contend with the possibility of attracting aggressive enforcement efforts focused on him. In accounts of the lives of professional fences, two strategies of handling this problem predominate. One is to corrupt law enforcers with gifts or cash payments. The other is to play the role of informer: in return for being permitted to operate unmolested, the fence supplies criminal intelligence. He may agree to aid in the recovery of stolen property that police are under special pressure to recover, and he may arrange or facilitate the arrest of thieves or other criminals.

For the professional fence the advantages of the informer relationship are considerable, as are the risks. On the one hand, it offers a way of eliminating troublesome or dangerous thieves, sabotaging competition, and disposing of goods "too hot to handle" by returning them in exchange for protection. On the other hand, it risks the violent reaction of those whose criminal confidence the professional fence betrays, as well as of their friends and protectors.

In sum, the professional fence is a successful public dealer in stolen property. His role in the overall flow of stolen property from thieves to eventual consumers cannot be estimated, nor can it be said that enforcement efforts would be more rationally directed at him than at other agents in the traffic in stolen property: thieves, occasional dealers, or those to whom the professional fence sells. Further complexities include the problem of convicting the professional fence, and the issue of his services as an informant. Both the professional fence himself and the trade in stolen property merit much more research.

CARL KLOCKARS

See also CRIMINAL CAREERS: SPECIALIZED OFFENDERS; DELINQUENT AND CRIMINAL SUBCULTURES; FENCING AND RECEIVING STOLEN GOODS: LEGAL ASPECTS; *both articles under* PROFESSIONAL CRIMINAL; SHOPLIFTING: BEHAVIORAL AND ECONOMIC ASPECTS; THEFT.

BIBLIOGRAPHY

ASBURY, HERBERT. *The Gangs of New York: An Informal History of the Underworld.* New York: Knopf, 1928.

DEFOE, DANIEL. *The King of the Pirates, Being an Account of the Famous Enterprises of Captain Avery with Lives of Other Pirates and Robbers* (1725). The Works of Daniel Defoe in Sixteen Volumes, vol. 16. New York: Jenson Society, 1904.

FIELDING, HENRY. *The Life of Mr. Jonathan Wild the Great* (1743). London: Folio Society, 1966.

HALL, JEROME. *Theft, Law, and Society.* Indianapolis: Bobbs-Merrill, 1952.

HOWSON, GERALD. *Thief-taker General: The Rise and Fall of Jonathan Wild.* London: Hutchinson, 1970.

KLOCKARS, CARL. *The Professional Fence.* New York: Free Press, 1974.

SHAFFER, RON; KLOSE, KEVIN; and LEWIS, ALFRED E. *Surprise! Surprise! How the Lawmen Conned the Thieves.* New York: Viking Press, 1977.

WALSH, MARILYN. *The Fence: A New Look at the World of Property Theft.* Westport, Conn.: Greenwood Press, 1977.

2.
LEGAL ASPECTS

Introduction

Since the early days of the industrial age, observers of crime have emphasized that thieves would not steal if there were no one to buy their wares (Colquhoun, p. 289). That buyer, whose existence inspires 95 percent or more of the theft in America, is the receiver of stolen property. Once solely the jurisprudential stepchild of the thief, the criminal receiver increasingly is being recognized for what he is: not just the greedy consumer, hungry for bargains on "hot" items, but more importantly, the well-organized fence, master of the nation's burgeoning market for stolen goods. The story of the crime of receiving stolen property is the tale of the criminal law's attempt to cope with this sophisticated, well-hidden receiver while not simultaneously sweeping up the arguably innocent individual consumer of what turn out to be stolen goods.

Historical development

From its origins, the crime of receiving stolen property was merely theft's shadow. It did not even exist as a crime until 1691, when the first English statute addressing it provided that a person buying or receiving stolen goods, knowing them to be stolen, could be punished as an accessory after the fact to the theft (An act to take away clergy from some offenders, and to bring others to punishment, 3 & 4 W. & M., c. 9, s. 4 (1691) (England) (repealed)). It was not until 1827 that receiving was made an independent crime (An Act for consolidating and Amending the Laws in England relative to Larceny and other Offences connected therewith, 7 & 8 Geo. 4, c. 29, s. 54 (1827) (Great Britain) (repealed)).

In the period between the 1691 and 1827 statutes, there emerged in England an industrial society with a much greater supply and movement of identical goods. There also emerged the modern fence, the best-known example being Jonathan Wild (c. 1682–1725), who rose to wealth and position on the shoulders of London's thieves: they stole so that Wild could receive and redistribute. Wild in fact became too prominent, for he was hanged as a result of parliamentary legislation directed specifically against him (Klockars, pp. 1–28). His successes and demise provided lessons for his modern counterparts: that organization and control over thieves were critical to profitable fencing; that the fence could and should present to society the face of a legitimate entrepreneur; that self-interest would quell the inquisitiveness of those to whom he redistributed goods; and, finally, that notoriety was not to be sought. Simultaneously, Parliament's responses to Wild and to subsequent fences provided guides for modern efforts to combat the fence. Statutes criminalized certain activities, such as receiving stolen jewelry, and imposed requirements on certain classes of persons, such as pawnbrokers, in order to reach the most obvious areas of the stolen-property market. Procedural rules were altered to facilitate prosecutions; yet, the receiver was still punished less harshly than the thief (Hall, pp. 52–61, 70–76, 173–174).

Since 1827, the basic elements of the crime—"buying or receiving," "stolen property," and "knowing it to be stolen"—have remained largely the same in most American jurisdictions. As though engaged in a decades-long chess match, legislatures have made subtle procedural and substantive moves to facilitate the conviction of fences, and the fences have adjusted their practices or positions to check legislative efforts. Few fences are apprehended by the police. Of those charged with receiving stolen property, a consistently and notably low percentage are convicted (Hall, pp. 197–198; U.S. Congress, 1973, p. 3). There are indications of greater interest in dealing with the problems of the market for stolen goods. The Justice Department and Congress have given these problems more attention than they have received at any time in American history, and twenty-nine states amended their theft and receiving statutes between 1975 and 1980. For this new interest to effect change, however, courts and legislatures must come to grips with the societal and substantive legal problems that have plagued effective enforcement of the criminal law against the redistributors of stolen property.

Nature of the receiver

Little can be understood about the adequacy of legal rules concerning the crime of receiving stolen property without some understanding of the nature, significance, and practices of the criminal receiver. In fact, the criminal receiver is two persons. The receiver of stolen property is the bargain-hungry consumer, the "man of easy morals." This person does not commission the theft of property, and he probably would not steal it himself. However, he cannot resist the temptation to obtain a good deal on some property even if he believes it has been stolen (Williams, p. 828; Note, 1980, pp. 1225, 1241).

The fence. More significant is the other receiver, the fence. Theft is at least a $16 billion-a-year industry in the United States. Thieves have fences—or, more accurately, fences have thieves. Few thieves operate independently of some fencing network (Walsh, pp. 138–139). The theft industry's managers are not small men selling arms' lengths of wristwatches in Times Square: they are entrepreneurs directing sophisticated systems for the marketing of stolen goods. To understand the nature of the theft industry, it makes no more sense to focus attention on the thief or the ultimate consumer of stolen property than it does to focus on the assembly-line worker or the car buyer in order to understand the automobile industry (Walsh, pp. 138–146; Blakey and Goldsmith, pp. 1511, 1516–1520).

The fence—the theft industry manager—is typically a white, middle-aged legitimate businessman. He usually has never been arrested, or has been arrested only once. In about two-thirds of the cases, the businessman-fence buys from thieves solely the kinds of goods that he sells in his business, and he sells directly to the consumer. He generally pays the thief from 10 percent to 35 percent of the goods' wholesale price. No doubt because of the cushion built in by profits from his dealings in stolen property, this businessman tends to survive longer than most of his competitors. Because he is already dealing in goods of the sort he criminally receives, this fence can easily store large quantities of stolen goods and, with the use of false purchase documents, can easily merge his illegitimate goods with his legitimate stock (Walsh, pp. 41–42, 50–51, 71–73, 87–106).

Although not so numerous as the businessman-fence, there is another major kind of fence, often referred to as the "master" fence. The master fence is the broker. He has substantial contacts among thieves, so that he can arrange for a full range of thefts on demand, from simple home burglaries to complex cargo thefts. Similarly, he has substantial contacts with outlets for stolen goods, ranging from large legitimate businesses or other fences in distant cities to individual consumers. He has information about product demand and product availability, and the means by which theft can match that supply and demand. The master fence can move stolen goods swiftly through redistribution channels because he does not "order" from his thieves until a resale has been arranged. Most often the master fence never even sees the stolen goods: he uses the telephone to arrange the theft and delivery.

Both the businessman-fence and the master fence have generally good relations with the thieves with whom they deal. The fences provide the thieves not only with a necessary market for the goods they steal, but also with information about potential robberies and co-workers, financial assistance, and, in many instances, an important sense of community. Most thieves belong in one way or another to a network that revolves around a fence. Thus, the modern fence exercises many of the same aspects of control over "his" thieves that helped insulate Jonathan Wild from the law in early eighteenth-century London (Blakey and Goldsmith, pp. 1533–1538; Walsh, pp. 111–113, 135–136, 138–145).

The modern approach

Given the importance of the receiver of stolen property in encouraging increasingly intolerable levels of theft, it is not surprising that legislatures have been trying continually to devise rules which facilitate the successful prosecution of these receivers. Those efforts focus, as they have since the first English receiving statute of 1827, on the conduct of the defendant, the attendant circumstances, and the actor's mental state. Within each area, changes have been and can be made in the substantive and related procedural rules which will increase the probability of convicting fences, without creating substantial risks that innocent individual consumers of stolen goods will be swept into prison as well.

Conduct: "receiving." The 1691 English statute punished persons who bought or received stolen property. Under American law, some states, for example, South Carolina, punish no more than that (S.C. Code § 16-13-180 (1976)). Most states, however, have adopted some other formula, largely in response to situations in which the statute did not cover conduct that everyone agreed should be punished. For example, the master fence could argue that he had not bought or received anything, yet he was the linchpin of the entire theft operation. Some jurisdictions have attempted to close the loopholes by itemizing all the kinds of punishable conduct (Alaska Stat. § 11.46.190 (1980) (buying, receiving, retaining, concealing, disposing, and acquiring possession, control or title); Theft Act, 1968, c. 60 (Great Britain) (sixteen variations of conduct)). Other jurisdictions have recognized that the crux of the misconduct is the exercising of control over stolen property and have proscribed "possession" or "control" alone, with indications that the terms are to be construed broadly to cover the full range of criminal redistribution activities (N.Y. Penal Law (McKinney) §§ 165.40, 165.45, 165.50 (1975 & 1981–1982 Supp.)).

In line with the recognition that the receiver's redistribution is simply one of the integral parts of the process whereby property is illegally taken from people, a slight majority of jurisdictions have adopted consolidated theft statutes, under which one who receives stolen property will be convicted for theft, as will those who take property by embezzling, false pretenses, or extortion (Model Penal Code §§ 223.1–223.9). This consolidation has eliminated the theoretically awkward possibility that one charged with receiving stolen property would defend himself by claiming that he in fact stole it, a situation made more likely by the similarity of proof available to the prosecution in many cases of theft and of receiving.

Although it has been relatively easy for legislatures to define as criminal conduct that encompasses the activities of both fences and ultimate receivers, it has been more difficult to make allowance for the differences between the receiver-fence and the receiver-consumer. Most jurisdictions do not distinguish, in terms of conduct prohibited, the more seriously antisocial activities of the fence from those of the individual who buys a wristwatch from an arm of watches in Times Square, although a few describe separate receiving-type offenses on the basis of those differences, with an eye toward punishing the fence more harshly (Fla. Stat. Ann. § 812.019 (1981 Supp.); H.R. 6915, 96th Cong., 2d sess. § 2532 (1980) (proposed new federal criminal code)).

Circumstances: "stolen" property. With respect to the attendant circumstances required by most jurisdictions, that the property received be stolen, problems of proof and of apprehension methods dominate. A Senate committee has concluded that establishing the identity of property as "stolen" was the single evidentiary factor most inimical to the successful apprehension and prosecution of fences (U.S. Congress, 1974, p. 17). That difficulty exists because vast amounts of stolen goods are identical to nonstolen goods. One nineteen-inch Zenith color television set looks just like another. Neither manufacturers nor owners put serial numbers or other permanent identifying marks on these interchangeable goods, a fact making it difficult to prove beyond a reasonable doubt that a particular television set (or fur coat, or cassette player) in the possession of the defendant is one that has been stolen. This is particularly true for the businessman-fence, who usually has taken the precautions of preparing false purchase documents for the stolen goods he acquires and of having many identical legitimate goods on the premises at the same time. Manufacturers have resisted calls for product identification and record-keeping on the ground that such procedures would be prohibitively expensive (U.S. Congress, 1974, p. 18). Where some identifying name or number is affixed to a product, receivers can and do simply alter or obliterate the identification.

Also problematic is the effect on police tactics for apprehending fences of the requirement that the property be stolen. Courts have generally ruled that stolen property loses its "stolen" nature when the police recover it. Accordingly, if the police catch a thief, they cannot release him to deliver the property to his fence and then arrest the fence for receiving stolen property. Similarly, the police cannot use the relatively cheap and easy undercover techniques that have proved necessary to drug law enforcement. They cannot go to meet fences, bringing with them actually or purportedly stolen property, and hope to convict the fence of receiving, because the property is not "stolen" when it is in police hands.

Several approaches have been taken to minimize the fence-freeing implications of this traditional requirement. Police using the apprehension techniques described above have been able to charge the fence successfully with the crime of attempting to receive stolen property. Even this approach has run into some difficulty because courts have allowed the receiver in such cases the defense of "impossibility": he could not be guilty of attempt to commit a crime when the factual setting was such that it was impossible for him to commit the crime, since the property was not stolen (*People v. Jaffe*, 185 N.Y. 497, 78 N.E. 169 (1906)). The impossibility defense to attempt charges seems to have little vitality in the United States, but it flourishes in England and some other common-law countries (Elliott, pp. 110, 127–135; Blakey and Goldsmith, pp. 1553–1555).

Perhaps the more sensible approach is to abandon altogether the requirement that the property received be stolen property. The Model Penal Code (§ 223.6) makes such a suggestion by requiring only that the property received be that "of another" (cf. Colo. Rev. Stat. § 18-4-410 (1978) ("anything of value of another")). Any jurisdiction so doing would continue to require the prosecution to prove that the defendant received the property believing it to be stolen, so there is no increased danger of punishing persons society would not want to punish. Moreover, in any case where the defendant believes the goods to be stolen, the chances are very good that they are stolen, but because of the factors mentioned above, the prosecution simply cannot prove it. Abandoning the requirement that the received property be stolen would free the police to engage in the kind of apprehension techniques that they used in Portland, Oregon: there, an undercover policewoman offered to sell color television sets that she said were stolen to a range of apparently otherwise noncriminal persons (Note, 1980, p. 1241). Therefore, any legislature adopting the Model Penal Code's approach would want to ensure that a satisfactory entrapment defense existed to protect persons from police activity which encouraged them to commit crimes they would not otherwise have committed. That risk of police-inspired criminality might highlight again for a legislature the value of distinguishing between the receiver-fence and the receiver-consumer in making statutory changes.

Mental state: "knowing." As the above discussion suggests, it is the receiver's state of knowledge about the nature of the goods with which he is dealing that lies at the heart of why the criminal law wants to punish him. If a receiver has no reason to believe that goods are stolen, there is no point in punishing him: he is not blameworthy in any socially recognized sense, nor will he be deterred from buying stolen goods so long as he thinks them legitimate. However, once the receiver has reason to suspect that the property is stolen, he will be regarded as somewhat blameworthy for proceeding with the purchase, and he can be deterred from buying by the threat of punishment. On the other hand, outside the area of homicide, the criminal law rarely punishes persons directly for negligent acts.

The adherence of a plurality of jurisdictions to the requirement that the receiver "know" that the property was stolen demonstrates the unwillingness of the law to depart from punishing persons criminally only for knowing acts unless there is some good reason for that departure. This good reason in criminal receiving cases has been regarded as the difficulty of proving that the receiver had that knowledge.

Authorities find it difficult to obtain either direct or circumstantial evidence of what the receiver knew about the nature of the property he is charged with receiving. Direct evidence generally must come from the thief in return for immunity from prosecution. It is only useful in jurisdictions that do not regard the thief necessarily as the receiver's accomplice, since other jurisdictions do not permit an accomplice's uncorroborated testimony to sustain an element of the crime (Hall, pp. 176–185). Even then, prosecutors are reluctant to grant thieves immunity in order to reach receivers (Note, 1980, pp. 1230–1231), and thieves are reluctant to testify against their fences, who may control their future economic and physical well-being (Walsh, pp. 74, 138–146). The only other source of direct evidence about the receiver's state of mind is electronic surveillance, but constitutional, technical, and economic considerations have resulted in limited use of this often effective technique (Blakey and Goldsmith, pp. 1569–1572).

Prosecutorial reliance on circumstantial evidence encounters similar difficulties. The constant efforts of master fences and businessman-fences to legitimize their transactions undermine the efficacy of such evidence. In addition, many jurisdictions require that where the prosecution relies on circumstantial evidence, proof must exclude all reasonable hypotheses of innocence (Blakey and Goldsmith, pp. 1572–1575).

One approach to combating the weakness of available evidence about the receiver's mental state has been to make the receiver punishable for a more easily proved mental state. Many jurisdictions have required that the receiver need not "know" that the property was stolen but need only believe that it probably was stolen (Model Penal Code § 223.6). It is important to punish this sort of willful blindness about the nature of the property received, since both fences and consumers make it a point deliberately to avoid knowledge. About a third of American jurisdictions have reduced the mental element a step farther, requiring only that the defendant have "good reason to believe" or "reasonable cause to believe" that the property is stolen (Ark. Stat. Ann. § 41-2206 (1977); Ohio Rev. Code Ann. § 2913.51 (1982)). Although this change undoubtedly facilitates conviction for receiving (National Association of Attorneys General, p. 6), it also prescribes severe punishment for a defendant who may have been no worse than stupid with respect to the nature of the property he received. This concern could be allayed, and the conviction of sophisticated fences could be effected, if the reasonable-grounds-to-believe standard were applied only to persons in the business of buying or selling goods.

Presumptions. The approach of differentiating between consumers and dealers has been regularly used in the other main avenue for dealing with the problems of proof of mental state: that of presumptions. These are rules, usually set down in statutes, that push juries toward reaching certain conclusions about the defendant's mental state once the prosecution has proved certain underlying facts about his conduct. Traditionally, the most significant and widespread presumption has been that which presumes the defendant's knowledge or belief about the "stolen" nature of the property received from proof of unexplained possession of recently stolen property.

The more modern presumptions focus on the fence. For example, the influential Model Penal Code sets forth only three presumptions which will operate to lead the jury to conclude that the defendant had the requisite knowledge about the stolen character of the property received. All apply only to "dealers," persons in the business of buying and selling goods. The dealer's knowledge or belief is presumed from evidence about his possession or receipt of other stolen property or from the nature of his acquisition of the property in question (Model Penal Code § 223.6(2); Md. Code Ann. art. 27, § 342 (1982); N.M. Stat. Ann. § 30-16-11 (1978)). Other jurisdictions create presumptions of the requisite mental state from the purchase or sale of property by a dealer "out of the regular course of business" (Fla. Stat. Ann. § 812.022 (1981 Supp.)) or from a dealer's failure to inquire into the seller's legal right to sell the property he receives under certain circumstances (Cal. Penal Code § 496 (1982 Supp.)).

These presumption statutes represent a growing legislative recognition that the knowledge obtained through hearings and studies about criminal redistribution systems can be put to use to disrupt theft markets. Through presumptions, the legislature can force a jury to consider that certain provable facts may signify that a defendant had a less clearly provable state of mind.

The power of the legislatures in this area remains a limited one. Presumptions used in criminal cases will inevitably be subjected to close scrutiny for possible unconstitutionality (*People v. Stevenson*, 58 Cal. 2d 794, 376 P.2d 297 (1962)). The courts will examine the rationality of the connection between the proved fact and the fact presumed from it (Blakey and Goldsmith, pp. 1575–1589; Note, 1975, p. 1437). As increasing information is gathered about fences, legislatures should find it easier to articulate useful presumptions and to support those already articulated.

Sanctions. One final element is important in modern attempts to deal with the criminal receiver: the punishment meted out to him. Again, the distinction between the receiver-fence and the receiver-consumer is significant: if the legislature has drawn distinctions based on differences in conduct between the two kinds of receivers, then harsher penalties may be held out for the fence (H.R. 6915 (more severe penalty for "trafficking" than for "receiving")). The legislature might also consider setting minimum prison terms for persons convicted as fences (Tenn. Code Ann. § 39-4217 (1981 Supp.)), since judges and juries are notoriously lenient in their treatment of the apparently respectable citizens brought before them as fences (National Association of Attorneys General, pp. 1–2, 6; U.S. Congress, 1974, pp. 21–22). This is not to suggest that only minimal sanctions should be applied to the consumer-receiver. That individual may be more easily deterred from receiving than the fence, with his stronger economic motivation and greater sense of his own criminality. Deterrence of the ultimate consumption of stolen property will decrease the economic rewards throughout the redistribution system. However, if the sanction against the consumer, whom society condemns only half-heartedly, is too harsh, there will be a counterproductive reluctance to enforce the receiving law (Note, 1980, pp. 1227–1239).

Conclusion

The key figure in America's theft industry is the fence. Because of his position, techniques, and organization, he is one of the most difficult criminals to reach with the criminal law. However, society may be able to take steps that facilitate the conviction and deterrence of this crucial link in the chain of stolen-property redistribution without impinging on persons or behavior that is either innocent or a less serious thorn in society's side.

PETER A. BELL

See also CRIMINAL CAREERS: SPECIALIZED OFFENDERS; FENCING AND RECEIVING STOLEN GOODS: THE PROFESSIONAL FENCE; PROFESSIONAL CRIMINAL: PROFESSIONAL THIEF; THEFT.

BIBLIOGRAPHY

American Law Institute. *Model Penal Code and Commentaries: Official Draft and Revised Comments.* 3 vols. Philadelphia: ALI, 1980.

BLAKEY, G. ROBERT, and GOLDSMITH, MICHAEL. "Criminal Redistribution of Stolen Property: The Need for Law Reform." *Michigan Law Review* 74 (1976): 1512–1626.

COLQUHOUN, PATRICK. *A Treatise on the Police of the Metropolis, Containing a Detail of the Various Crimes and Misdemeanors by Which Public and Private Property and Security Are, at Present, Injured and Endangered: And Suggesting Remedies for Their Prevention* (1796). Reprint. Montclair, N.J.: Patterson Smith, 1969.

ELLIOTT, IAN D. "Theft and Related Problems: England, Australia, and the U.S.A. Compared." *International and Comparative Law Quarterly* 26 (1977): 110–149.

HALL, JEROME. *Theft, Law, and Society.* 2d ed. Indianapolis: Bobbs-Merrill, 1952.

KLOCKARS, CARL B. *The Professional Fence.* New York: Free Press, 1974.

National Association of Attorneys General, Committee on the Office of Attorney General. *Legislative Responses to Dealing in Stolen Goods.* Raleigh: The Committee, 1975.

Note. "Constitutionality of Presumptions on Receiving Stolen Property: Turning the Thumbscrew in Michigan and Other States." *Wayne Law Review* 21 (1975): 1437–1454.

Note. "Property Theft Enforcement and the Criminal Secondary Purchaser of Stolen Goods." *Yale Law Journal* 89 (1980): 1225–1241.

U.S. Congress, Senate. *Criminal Redistribution Systems and Their Economic Impact on Small Business, 1973: Hearings before the Select Committee on Small Business.* 93d Cong., 1st sess. on Criminal Redistribution (Fencing) Systems, pt. 1. Washington, D.C.: Government Printing Office, 1973.
———, Select Committee on Small Business. *The Impact of Crime on Small Business, Part VI (Criminal Redistribution (Fencing) Systems).* S. Rep. No. 1318. 93d Cong., 2d sess. Washington, D.C.: Government Printing Office, 1974.

WALSH, MARILYN E. *The Fence: A New Look at the World of Property Theft.* Westport, Conn.: Greenwood Press, 1976.

WILLIAMS, GLANVILLE. *Textbook of Criminal Law.* London: Stevens, 1978.

FINES

See articles under ECONOMIC CRIME; *articles under* SENTENCING; TRAFFIC OFFENSES.

FIREARMS

See GUNS, REGULATION OF.

FORENSIC PSYCHIATRY AND PSYCHOLOGY

See DIMINISHED CAPACITY; EXCUSE: INSANITY; MENTAL HEALTH EXPERT, ROLE OF THE; MENTALLY DISORDERED OFFENDERS.

FORENSIC SCIENCE

See CRIMINALISTICS.

FORGERY

The law against forgery is designed to protect society from the deceitful creation or alteration of writings on whose authenticity people depend in their important affairs. A person who, with the purpose of deceiving or injuring, makes or alters a writing in such a way as to convey a false impression concerning its authenticity is guilty of forgery in its contemporary sense.

History

The law of forgery may have originated with an early Roman law (c. 80 B.C.) that prohibited falsification of documents describing the passing on of land to heirs. The precise scope of what was considered forgery at common law is not universally agreed upon, but a statute passed in the time of Queen Elizabeth I (An Act against forgers of false deeds and writings, 5 Eliz. 1, c. 14 (1562) (England)) prohibited forgery of publicly recorded, officially sealed documents with the intent to affect the title to land, as well as the knowing use of such documents as evidence in court. In the first major expansion of the law's coverage, a 1726 decision declared that a false endorsement on an unsealed private document was indictable both under the Elizabethan statute and at common law (*Rex v. Ward*, 92 Eng. Rep. 451 (K.B. 1726)). Writing only half a century later, William Blackstone was able to declare, after referring to several contemporary statutes, that "there is now hardly a case possible to be conceived wherein forgery, that tends to defraud, whether in the name of a real or fictitious person, is not made a capital crime" (*250). Blackstone de-

fined common-law forgery, which he also called *crimen falsi*, as "the fraudulent making or altering of a writing to the prejudice of another man's right." Pillory, fines, and imprisonment were the penalties in those rare cases that were not subject to capital punishment (*247).

American law of forgery

As with their English antecedents, early American prohibitions of forgery focused more on the types of documents covered than on clarifying the definition of the crime itself. As a result, a rather technical body of case law developed. The most important effort to simplify and rationalize the law was the American Law Institute's Model Penal Code of 1962, variations of which were gradually adopted by the states. However, the principal federal forgery statute, which prohibits false making, forgery, or alteration of any writing for the purpose of obtaining or receiving any sum of money from the United States government, has remained virtually unchanged since its enactment (An Act for the punishment of frauds committed on the government of the United States, ch. 38, 3 Stat. 771 (1823)). This law, codified under 18 U.S.C. § 495 (1976), contains no definition of its central term, *forges*, and has been authoritatively interpreted by the United States Supreme Court to cover only that conduct which was understood as forgery in 1823 (*Gilbert v. United States*, 370 U.S. 650 (1962)). The definition of *forgery* applied in a state prosecution is determined by the statutes of that state and by state-court interpretation of those laws.

Interpretive issues. The problems of interpretation in forgery prosecutions may be grouped around the three key elements of the common-law offense: false making, writing, and intent to defraud.

Although a few jurisdictions have held to the contrary, the notion of false making in forgery generally refers only to a document's authenticity and not to the veracity of any factual assertions within it. A written statement may be full of lies and used to cheat, but this does not make it a forgery; on the other hand, an otherwise legitimate deed on which the date of filing has been altered, or the name of one person has been signed by another without permission, is a forgery. Similarly, a document with a genuine signature that has been procured by fraud or trickery is generally not considered a forgery, although a few jurisdictions have held that it is.

In the absence of a contrary statute, a writing is not considered forged unless it might deceive a person of ordinary observation or prudence. Moreover, unless the legislature has prescribed otherwise, the writing must have some apparent legal efficacy in terms of private or public rights; if it is completely innocuous or void on its face, it cannot be a forgery. For example, a check that requires two signatures but has only one cannot be a forgery, even if the one signature which appears is false. In addition, because only writings are covered, the fraudulent simulation of valuable objects, as in art forgery, is not within the traditional definition.

In forgery, the mens rea (culpable state of mind) is generally an intent to defraud, meaning a purpose to deceive or cheat another person or entity out of his or its legal due. There is no requirement that the intent involve a potential advantage to the forger, or that the fraudulent intention be successfully achieved.

Defenses and evidence. There are three principal defenses to charges of forgery. First, a person may have, or believe he has, the authority to sign another's name; or an alteration may be intended to correct what is genuinely believed to be an error in a document. In either event, there would be no intent to defraud, and probably no false making. Second, even if the document is clearly forged, the prosecution may not be able to prove by legally admissible evidence that the accused is the person who forged it. Finally, in a surprising number of cases, it is difficult to prove that the writing is not genuine. For example, the true payee often has a motive to deny receiving and cashing a check, so that a duplicate may be issued.

The testimony of a lay person is admissible evidence to identify handwriting with which he is familiar. However, where the issue is either the identity of the forger or the genuineness of the document, an expert questioned-document examiner will often have to make comparisons between the writing at issue and known exemplars of the handwriting of both the accused and the true payee. The techniques of scientific analysis sometimes do not provide a satisfactory answer, and the prosecution consequently fails.

Related offenses

The knowing use of forged writings has been prohibited as a separate offense at least since "uttering or publishing as true" certain forged writings was made a capital crime in 1729 (An Act for the more effectual preventing and further Punishment of Forgery, Perjury, and Subornation of Perjury, 2 Geo. 2, c. 25 (1729) (Great Britain) (repealed)). Under modern statutes, uttering is usually covered in the section dealing with forgery and carries the same maximum penalty as forgery itself. Mere possession of a forged instrument is generally not a crime until an attempt is made to use ("utter or publish") it. However, under federal law it is an offense knowingly and with fraudulent intent to transport a forged traveler's check or "security" (defined to include a check) in interstate commerce (18 U.S.C. § 2314 (1976)).

One who achieves a dishonest financial advantage by the use of a forged instrument may also be convicted of fraud, false pretenses, or theft by deception. But passing a worthless check, even when accompanied by misrepresentations or intent to defraud, is regarded only as a species of theft or false pretenses, not as uttering or forgery, so long as the checking account and signature are genuine. However, if the account does not exist or if the drawee bank or maker is fictitious, several states' laws treat the passing of the check as a separate offense or even as a form of forgery. Finally, it has often been pointed out that only a restrictive definition of *writing* permits any distinction to be drawn between forgery and counterfeiting.

The future of forgery laws

The highly influential Model Penal Code recommended that the technical restrictions on forgery laws be abolished and that both uttering and counterfeiting be consolidated with forgery (Model Penal Code, 1962, § 224.1; 1960, commentary on § 224.1). The Code defined *forgery* with specificity and included unauthorized alteration of a writing. It also included the making, completing, executing, authenticating, issuing, or transferring of a writing that misrepresents its time, place, or sequence of execution, or its authority, or that purports to be a copy of which there was no genuine original. *Writing* was defined broadly to include all forms of recording information, money, credit cards, trademarks, and "other symbols of value, right, privilege, or identification." The "purpose to defraud or injure anyone" was retained as an element. The offense would be graded: forgery of money, stamps, and other instruments issued by the government or representing interests in property would be a serious felony; forgery of a will, deed, contract, or other writing having legal efficacy would be a less serious felony; and any other type of forgery would be a misdemeanor. In a separate provision, the Code recommended punishing as a misdemeanor the fraudulent simulation of objects, such as art forgery, which creates a false appearance of "value because of antiquity, rarity, source, or authorship" (1962, § 224.2). The United States National Commission on Reform of Federal Criminal Laws made a similar set of recommendations in 1971 (§ 1751).

By 1980, at least twenty-three states had followed this lead in whole or in substantial part (Model Penal Code, 1980, commentary on § 224.1). Although some jurisdictions will undoubtedly retain a distinction between forgery and counterfeiting, more are likely to adopt the Model Penal Code's approach.

PETER GOLDBERGER

See also COUNTERFEITING.

BIBLIOGRAPHY

American Law Institute. *Model Penal Code and Commentaries: Official Draft and Revised Comments*, vol. 2. Philadelphia: ALI, 1980.
————. *Model Penal Code: Proposed Official Draft.* Philadelphia: ALI, 1962.
————. *Model Penal Code: Tentative Draft No. 11.* Philadelphia: ALI, 1960.
BLACKSTONE, WILLIAM. *Commentaries on the Laws of England* (1765–1769), vol. 4. Reprint. University of Chicago Press, 1979.
U.S. National Commission on Reform of Federal Criminal Laws. *Final Report.* Washington, D.C.: The Commission, 1971.
————. *Working Papers*, vol. 2. Washington, D.C.: The Commission, 1970.
WHARTON, FRANCIS. *A Treatise on the Criminal Law of the United States.* 2d ed. Philadelphia: James Kay, Jr. & Brother, 1852.

FORNICATION

See ADULTERY AND FORNICATION.

FRAUD

See CONSUMER FRAUD; MAIL: FEDERAL MAIL FRAUD ACT; THEFT.

FREE SPEECH

See LIBEL, CRIMINAL; OBSCENITY AND PORNOGRAPHY: LEGAL ASPECTS; PUBLICITY IN CRIMINAL CASES.

FREE WILL

See CRIMINOLOGY, *articles on* INTELLECTUAL HISTORY *and* MODERN CONTROVERSIES; EXCUSE: THEORY; GUILT; PSYCHOPATHY; PUNISHMENT.

FRISKING

See ARREST AND STOP; SEARCH AND SEIZURE.

FUNCTIONALISM

See DEVIANCE; HOMICIDE: BEHAVIORAL ASPECTS; WOMEN AND CRIME.

G

GAMBLING

Gambling can be defined broadly as participation in any risk-taking activity, from investing in stocks to planning nuclear weapons strategies to taking a lover. It can also be defined more narrowly as a bet or wager on the outcome of a probability game designed for risk-taking, or on a sporting event. This discussion concentrates upon the latter type of gambling, which historically and cross-culturally has been regulated or prohibited by law. Why this should be so is not entirely clear.

Gambling cannot by any stretch of the imagination be considered inherently evil (*malum in se*). Those who gamble do so voluntarily. Why, then, has gambling been given so much negative attention by governments? Why is betting—or accepting bets—sometimes viewed as a crime? Reasons that can be singled out are that gambling has been thought to be destructive of personality, to be fundamentally immoral, to invite fraud and deception, and to engender social decay.

Extent of gambling

The American public seems increasingly skeptical about the criminalization of gambling. Only a small minority of Americans see anything wrong with it. According to the 1976 report of the United States National Commission on the Review of the National Policy toward Gambling, 80 percent of Americans favor the legalization of some form of gambling, and two-thirds have actually gambled. The commission also estimated that $17.3 billion was wagered legally in 1975 on ten legal games, including horse racing, other sports, bingo, lotteries, and casino games (pp. 63, 69–70).

Clearly, the trend in the criminal law of gambling is away from strict prohibition, with distinctions made according to type and sponsorship of gambling activity. This is nothing new. Even at common law, gambling was not criminal if the game of chance was played privately. Only when conducted openly or notoriously, and where inexperienced persons were fleeced, was gambling a crime. Most gambling statutes impose minor misdemeanor penalties for public social gambling, with somewhat harsher penalties for gambling with a minor. By contrast, gambling by a professional player is often classified as a felony.

Macrostudies of gambling show that the United States criminal laws prohibiting gambling are more widely violated than any other type of prohibition. Gambling is, consequently, the quintessential victimless crime. Illegal gaming revenues have risen, while gambling arrests have declined. One study showed that during the fourteen years from 1960 to 1974, gambling arrests declined by 67.7 percent. In the same period, arrests for all offenses rose by 33 percent (U.S. National Commission, p. 35). The Federal Bureau of Investigation's Uniform Crime Reports show a similar rate of decline in gambling arrests (p. 194).

According to the Uniform Crime Reports, blacks are arrested for gambling at a substantially higher rate than whites or members of other races. In 1979, of all those arrested for gambling, 67 percent were black (p. 206). The high gambling arrest rate for blacks may be attributed partly to the urban residence patterns of blacks and partly to the priorities that seem to dominate gambling enforcement. The National Gambling Commission commented, with respect to the extraordinary black arrest rate, that "visibility, rather than race, is the basis for these arrests. Black participation in public social gambling (i.e., card or dice games) and numbers writing is high compared to the participation of whites" (pp. 37–38).

Thomas Mangione and Floyd Fowler studied the enforcement of antigambling laws in sixteen randomly selected American cities with populations in excess of 250,000. They identified four main targets of gambling laws and enforcement activities: (1) noncommercial social gambling in private places; (2) social gambling in public places; (3) direct participation in operating an illegal gambling operation for profit, such as taking bets on sporting events or horse races or running an illegal casino game; and (4) indirect participation in a commercial gambling operation. Mangione and Fowler found across the board that police officers in all sixteen departments considered gambling violations to be a low law enforcement priority. "Consistently," they wrote, "the resources devoted to gambling law enforcement were modest, averaging less than 1% of the police force" (p. 119). Nevertheless, about one-fifth of the departments they surveyed were committed to convincing citizens of police aggressiveness in the enforcement of gambling laws. The departments did this by making a large number of arrests for *public* social gambling. In addition, they arrested numbers writers or runners, but bookmakers were almost never arrested. Thus, such departments enforced the laws against visible, street-level gambling violations, but not those that took place behind closed doors. Urban blacks were probably the main targets of such law enforcement priorities.

According to the National Gambling Commission, public apathy is important in constraining most forms of gambling enforcement. The commission's nationwide survey of citizens found that there was widespread community feeling that gambling law enforcement was less important than law enforcement against crimes of violence or property crimes. Moreover, only one-fifth of the citizens surveyed thought that gambling law enforcement was more important than enforcement against such other vice offenses as narcotic trafficking or prostitution.

The National Gambling Commission cited corruption as yet another constraint on effective gambling enforcement. Any number of police departments, both large and small, have experienced gambling-related corruption. The most recent large-city examples of corruption have been those in Philadelphia and New York, where investigative commissions reported widespread and systematic payoffs by gambling operators to both plainclothes and uniformed police officers. New York City's Knapp Commission found corruption to be at its most sophisticated among plainclothesmen assigned to enforce gambling laws: those who participated in organized payoffs, called a pad, were collecting amounts ranging from $300 to $1,500 monthly. The Pennsylvania Crime Commission found similar sorts of corruption within the Philadelphia Police Department, and concluded that the "open and flagrant gambling operating . . . with no apparent interference from the police department" was attributable to police accepting protection money from gamblers (p. 168). Gambling corruption on a lesser scale has been found in such smaller cities as Carbondale and Reading, Pennsylvania; Syracuse and Schenectady, New York; and New Haven, Connecticut.

The use of arrest quotas also constrains effective gambling enforcement. Many police departments view gambling enforcement as a low-priority effort designed to produce symbolic gambling arrests to fulfill quota requirements, even though administrators and police officers well understand that these arrests will result neither in meaningful sentences nor in any significant reduction of illegal gambling.

The National Gambling Commission's surveys also showed that the police did not take gambling seriously. More than 70 percent of the officers surveyed agreed that the prosecutors would rather not be bothered with gambling cases. Criminal justice statistics indicate that such a perception is accurate. A substantial proportion of persons arrested for gambling either are not prosecuted, are prosecuted on reduced charges, are not convicted, or, if convicted, are given sentences that do not reflect the statutory provisions for gambling offenses. The commission concluded that the trend in local gambling enforcement has been toward lessened activity by municipal police departments, together with a somewhat increasing role for state authorities, and a significantly larger federal role.

Modern federal legislation outlawing certain gambling activities should be viewed as an increasing attempt by the federal government to interfere with illegal gambling activity conducted by organized crime. In 1948 the first major federal statute on the subject was enacted, prohibiting the operation of gambling ships off the coast of the United States (18 U.S.C. §§ 1081–1083 (1976)). After its enactment, casino ships disappeared from the California coast. Several ship operators, notably Benjamin ("Bugsy") Siegel, moved their gambling interests to Nevada.

The presence of Siegel and others like him in Nevada aroused the interest and antagonism of Senator Estes Kefauver, who in 1950 headed the Special Senate Committee to Investigate Organized Crime. The Kefauver Committee stopped in Las Vegas for one day in 1950 and found a "fantastic situation," with known hoodlums established as respectable Las Vegas proprietors. The committee was instrumental in the enactment of a group of statutes (known collectively as the Johnson Act) aimed at "nationwide crime syndicates" and prohibiting interstate transportation of gambling devices. Until the 1960s these statutes, together with the wagering excise tax and occupational stamp tax statutes, aimed at bookmakers, constituted the federal government's major substantive jurisdiction over gambling (15 U.S.C. §§ 1171–1178 (1976); I.R.C. §§ 4401–4405, 4411 (1982)).

President John Kennedy's administration undertook various legislative and executive efforts designed to curtail organized-crime revenue stemming from illegal gambling. Three federal statutes were passed in the 1960s to spur the antiracketeering effort. One prohibited the use of communication facilities to transmit wagering information or bets in interstate commerce. The act was not intended to be applied to the placing of social wagers over the telephone; its official purpose was to "assist the various states . . . in the enforcement of their [gambling] laws . . . and to aid in the suppression of *organized gambling activities* by prohibiting the use of wire communication facilities . . . for the transmission of bets or wagers and gambling information in interstate and foreign commerce" (18 U.S.C. § 1084 (1976)).

Two other statutes were passed by Congress, prohibiting interstate travel or the use of interstate facilities to promote illegal gambling, and extending existing prohibitions against interstate transportation of wagering paraphernalia (18 U.S.C. §§ 1952–1953 (1976 & Supp. IV 1980)). Congress felt that these antiracketeering statutes were necessary because, given the interstate nature of large gambling operations, no attack upon organized illegal gambling would be effective at the local level.

Federal jurisdiction was extended in 1970 with the passage of a statute known as the Organized Crime Control Act, which extended federal jurisdiction to cover intrastate gambling operations because these businesses were thought to have a deleterious effect on interstate commerce (18 U.S.C. § 1955 (1976)). Wiretaps have been widely used in gambling cases since 1968, when they were legalized under the provisions of Title III of the Omnibus Crime Control and Safe Streets Act (18 U.S.C. §§ 2510–2520 (1976 & Supp. IV 1980)). In actuality, 72 percent of all federal wiretaps have been made in connection with gambling investigations (U.S. National Commission, p. 25).

Federal criminal enforcement of gambling statutes has been effective against certain types of illegal gambling activities. For example, illegal casinos in such cities as Covington, Kentucky, and Hot Springs, Arkansas, presumably are no longer in existence. Illegal slot machines, once prevalent in many small communities, are now rare. Illegal horse-race wire rooms in many of the major interstate bookmaking operations appear to have ceased operation. Organized crime control of legalized casino gambling in Nevada and Atlantic City has been reduced, but not eliminated, as a result of federal government intervention. Nevertheless, federal efforts to curb intrastate gambling businesses, such as the numbers game or sports bookmaking, have not been successful. A federal official testified to the National Gambling Commission that judicial and public apathy are behind the lack of enforcement success in these areas. That testimony is quite consistent with the commission's findings that 80 percent of Americans approve of gambling.

It is impossible to estimate the illegal gambling "handle" with any degree of confidence, but knowledgeable observers agree that Americans gamble in excess of $50 billion annually. Most of this handle derives from sports betting, and is facilitated by the televising of major sporting events. Odds and "point spreads" on baseball, football, basketball, and boxing are freely quoted in daily newspapers. There can be no doubt that point spreads have generated tremendous interest in sports and betting. Football and basketball are ideally constructed for wagering. Even when teams lose or are well ahead in the fourth quarter or second half, bettors wait to see whether the point spread has made them winners or losers. As sporting events are increasingly broadcast on cable television, illegal gaming revenues will certainly rise.

The popularity of gambling among the public, as well as its seeming profitability to organized crime, has inspired a variety of legalized gambling forms. Twenty-one states now permit on-track racehorse betting; sixteen have lotteries and numbers games; thirteen allow dog racing; four have opened jai alai frontons; two have off-track betting schemes; and, with the addition of gambling in Atlantic City, two have casinos. Despite its reputation as a gambling mecca, Nevada ranked only fifth among the states in gambling revenues in 1978, behind New York, California, Florida, and Illinois, which derive such revenues mainly from racetrack betting.

Racing collected a diminishing share of gambling revenues from 1970 to 1980. In 1970, total legal gambling revenues amounted to $7.4 billion in the United States, 81 percent of it from racing. By 1980, racing revenues fell to 53 percent, or $17.5 billion. Casino and lottery revenues, however, have been rising. In 1980, for example, the two states with legalized casino gambling reported gross receipts of $3 billion, whereas legalized horse racing reported a combined handle of $11.2 billion—including revenues from off-track betting, as well as from harness, thoroughbred, and quarter-horse racing.

Gambling and personality

Fun, excitement, and the occasional thrill of winning seem to motivate most gamblers. Marvin Zuckerman contends that people who search out high sensation have a biological need for it. According to Zuckerman, fulfilling a general sensation need may depend on finding any of several "environmental possibilities" (p. 38). Gambling can be one, but the world is full of other risk opportunities. Whatever else may be said against it, gambling is not physically risky. Some psychologists even contend that gambling can be psychologically beneficial—some gamblers affirm their existence and worth through using skills in a risky setting. Whether a gambler's personality is healthy or pathological depends on his own self-perception (Kusyszyn). A 1978 review of the effects of gambling concluded that the evidence of the social and economic consequences of gambling fails "to confirm that moderate gambling is a significant source of harm, either to the gambler himself, those in his immediate environment, or to the community at large" (Cornish, p. 76).

But not all people who gamble do so moderately. There exists some research and serious analysis of the motives of those who gamble heavily. The Russian writer Fyodor Dostoyevsky captured the lure of roulette in his novel *The Gambler*, which he wrote to pay off his own gambling debts. A fascinating account of Dostoyevsky's working "under the lash" has been offered by the translator of an English edition of the novel (Dostoyevsky). The work inspired Freud's analysis of Dostoyevsky's heavy betting. For Dostoyevsky, gambling was a form of both self-punishment and self-actualization. His creativity was best stimulated when he had lost everything, pawned his last possession, and was forced to write.

Some psychiatrists compare the excitement of gambling to the intoxication of drugs. A psychologist who interviewed members of Gamblers Anonymous seems to agree: "The compulsive gambler continues to bet because the action has come to be a refuge from thought of the outside world. His anxieties associated with his wife, family, debts, or job disappear when he concentrates on money and action" (Livingston, p. 55).

There are no reliable statistics concerning the compulsive gambler, and attempts to characterize his personality have been inconclusive. Affluent gamblers may not be concerned over gambling losses, although for others, heavy gambling can prove disastrous. Since gambling does not produce classic health deficiencies such as those associated with chronic alcohol consumption, statistics with even the degree of objectivity of those for alcoholism do not exist. Furthermore, as with persons who use alcohol excessively, the difficulties that heavy gamblers experience in life situations might have arisen anyway. Is excessive gambling—or alcohol or drug abuse—the cause of personal maladjustment, or its consequence? Or, more likely, is it both cause and consequence?

History of gambling

English noblemen gambled often and heavily. It was as important for an English nobleman to know how to play cards or handle dice as it was to dance or ride a horse. Gentlemen set the style: as yeomen prospered, they took up the pastimes that gentlemen had so assiduously cultivated. Cockfighting and bull- and bearbaiting, with associated heavy betting, were popular in the yards of favorite village inns and alehouses. Eventually, apprentices and servants sought to emulate their social superiors.

To discourage heavy gambling, the Puritans enacted legislation in 1657 allowing losers in gambling transactions to sue for the recovery of twice the sum lost. If such a suit was successful, the loser and the Lord Protector would share in the recovery. The statute of 1657 also declared all gambling debts arising after 1647 to be "utterly void and of none effect." Upon restoration of the Stuart monarchy in 1660, however, all legislation enacted under the Puritan regime was apparently abrogated.

The 1660 Restoration also meant a return of permissible hedonism for the aristocracy. Charles II brought to England a taste for heavy gambling and a formidable reputation for sexual immorality acquired during his years of exile in France. His daughter, Queen Anne, continued in her father's tradition. According to George Trevelyan, both sexes gambled freely during Queen Anne's time. "The expenses of gambling burdened estates with mortgages which proved a heavy clog on agricultural improvement and domestic happiness. Immense sums of money changed hands over cards and dice" (p. 314). The Gaming Act of 1710 was intended to protect the landed aristocracy from consequences of heavy gambling (9 Anne, c. 19 (Great Britain)). Under its terms, "all Notes, Bills, Bonds, Judgments, Mortgages, or other Securities or Conveyances whatsoever" were to be unenforceable. William Hawkins, the English jurist, observed that "the vice of gaming may be ranked amongst the offences against the political economy of the state, inasmuch as it leads to ruin among the opulent . . . the love of gaming is frequently predominant with those men who have nothing to gain from success, and everything to lose from defeat" (p. 720).

As the King set the fashion for the aristocracy, the aristocracy set the fashion for the new merchant class. In emulation of the aristocracy, the merchant class also began to gamble in large numbers and for large stakes. By the nineteenth century many forms of gambling were to become democratized, particularly horse racing.

The historical lottery. Lotteries were popular—and remain so—because they present a rare opportunity to accumulate capital by luck alone. If high-stakes gambling suggests bets of such magnitude that a loss could dramatically undermine one's economic position in life, lotteries might be interpreted as gambling's counterpart of insurance. The difference is that instead of a large group insuring individuals against the risk of loss and hazard, the group pools its resources and, through chance, selects a beneficiary of good fortune.

The Puritans objected both to high-stakes gambling and to lotteries, precisely because of their social significance. Contrary to the general belief, the Puritans did not abhor games per se. So long as games did not lead to a waste of time but rather to a renewal of vigor, they were tolerated. But although gambling might be relaxing, it was considered wasteful and nonfunctional, and hence not an acceptable game or sport. Moreover, Puritanism and early capitalism found sudden wealth to be morally objectionable. Capitalism, at least in its early stages, was based on a theory of private saving, followed by private investment, and resulting in public productivity. God was believed to offer the rewards of wealth to the deserving, who by work, thrift, early rising, and prudent investment, come by it honestly. From the mid-seventeenth century onward, English society was in continuous conflict between the carefree and playful social values of the aristocracy and the sterner code prevailing in Puritan circles of widely varying social influence.

In the face of Puritan sentiment, Parliament authorized numerous lotteries between the sixteenth and nineteenth centuries. "By 1775," asserted the Royal Commission on Lotteries and Betting in 1933, "the lottery had become virtually an annual event. . . . First adopted as an expedient to meet some special need, and in particular as an inducement to assist in raising a loan, the state lottery became a regular financial instrument and ceased to be associated with loans" (p. 6).

The lottery made its entrance into American history for much the same reasons. The Virginia Company of London, after experiencing difficulty supporting its Jamestown settlement, petitioned the King for a new charter authorizing a lottery in order to further the process of colonization. During the fiscal year 1620–1621, out of Virginia's total operating budget of £17,000, lottery profits were to provide for £8,000. Lotteries, said one member of the company, were the "reall and substantiall food, by which Virginia hath been nourished" (Ezell, p. 8). No American governmental entity—with the exception of post–World War II Nevada or possibly nineteenth-century Louisiana—has ever been dependent upon gambling revenues for so large a proportion of its budget.

Not until the early nineteenth century, as the lottery became more widespread in England and dependence upon it increased, did its enemies gather enough influence to destroy it. "No mode of raising money," concluded a parliamentary committee appointed in 1805, "appears so burthensome, so pernicious and so unproductive" (Royal Commission on Lotteries and Betting, p. 174). Although the committee's report did not result in the immediate demise of the state lotteries, it contributed heavily to their downfall. England saw the last of its state lotteries in 1823.

England's Puritan opposition to lotteries reinforced America's opponents of gambling. Job Tyson, a prominent Philadelphia lawyer and Quaker, read an essay denouncing lotteries at a public meeting held on January 12, 1833. Five thousand copies of the influential essay were distributed throughout the United States. Subsequently, the rest of New England began to fall into line with puritanical sentiment in Pennsylvania. Antilottery forces gathered strength in Maine, Rhode Island, and Vermont. By the 1840s and 1850s, most of the South began to feel the pressure, and lotteries seem to have been more unpopular than popular by the time of the Civil War.

The Louisiana lottery was the most famous, or infamous, of the post–Civil War ventures. Its revenues were a carefully guarded secret, but it was no secret that 93 percent of those revenues came from out-of-state sales, thus openly flouting the antilottery laws of other states and drawing the wrath of a variety of opponents, of whom the most famous, persistent, and effective was the antivice crusader Anthony Comstock. When a bill was introduced into the House of Representatives in 1890 to ban from the mails all letters, postcards, circulars, newspapers, or pamphlets advertising lotteries, it met with no opposition, not even from Louisiana (Blakey, p. 71). In 1890 Congress made it illegal to transport lottery materials across state lines, and in 1895 it authorized postmasters to withhold delivery of lottery-related mail and to deny the use of the mails to any person acting as an agent for a lottery company. These laws finally prevented Louisiana from evading state and federal statutes directed at its lottery. National opposition to the lottery strengthened Louisiana's antilottery forces, and they captured the governor's office and a majority of the legislature. As a result, Louisiana discontinued its lottery. With the twentieth century approaching, lotteries vanished from the American scene.

The contemporary lottery

No state-sponsored lotteries appeared in the United States until 1964. In that year, supposedly conservative New Hampshire adopted a sweepstakes. The state had no sales or income tax, and already derived more than 60 percent of its revenues from "sin taxes" on horse racing, liquor, tobacco, and beer. Despite its rural Yankee and Puritan image, by 1960 New Hampshire was predominantly urban. Moreover, nearly one-third of its population was French-Canadian, and 37 percent was Roman Catholic. Thus, what had once been a value conflict over gambling between Puritans and aristocrats was now a conflict between the descendants of recent immigrants and older, rural Americans of Protestant background. The lottery, and other forms of legal gambling, could no longer stand or fall on the question of adherence to the Puritan and early capitalist ethic. Instead, debate over legalized gambling became less a question of the morality of private conduct than of the propriety of state conduct, involving an assessment of alternative tax sources, the social risks of legal gambling, and the capacity of the state to follow through on promises of control.

From 1960 onward, most states began to feel increasing pressure from taxpayers. In the search for revenue, gambling became a prime candidate, particularly through the lottery, off-track betting, and casino gambling. The attraction of all three lay in the fact that tax payments are made involuntarily, whereas gambling is a voluntary activity. Many politicians welcome legal gambling as a source of income that does not depend on the coercive power of the state for its success. Lottery revenues are often referred to as a "painless tax," although legislators recognize that the burden of providing such revenues falls upon identifiable groups.

It is not clear whether lottery revenues should always be regarded as a regressive form of public finance. Tax schemes are considered progressive if the tax rate increases with the amount of money earned; neutral if a percentage tax is placed on income; and regressive if the tax rate declines as income rises. Lottery revenues may be regressive when compared to an increase in the progressive income tax, but less regressive than a tax on food. In sum, considering the alternatives, as well as those from whom gambling revenues are obtained, such revenues might turn out to be regressive for some low-income groups, but not for others. (Aranson and Miller).

The lottery, however, is usually a regressive source of public revenue in that persons who occupy lower-income positions have the most incentive to purchase lottery tickets. That is, given a society of relatively wide disparity in the distribution of income, those on the lowest rung of the ladder have the most to gain in participating in the lottery. Some evidence suggests that state lottery revenues are drawn more regressively than state sales taxes, a finding that reformers have criticized precisely because of this regressiveness.

Wherever possible, politicians have tried to place lottery tax burdens on out-of-staters. For example, with only six hundred thousand inhabitants, New Hampshire expanded its lottery beyond the home market. In 1964, before Massachusetts, New York, and Connecticut introduced their own lotteries, 80 percent of the New Hampshire lottery tickets were sold to residents of those states. New York in 1967 became the second state to legalize a lottery, with monthly games, followed by New Jersey, which introduced weekly games in 1970. New Hampshire and New York then converted to the weekly lottery. Other states fell quickly into line—Connecticut, Massachusetts, Michigan, and Pennsylvania in 1972, Maryland in 1973, Illinois, Maine, Ohio, and Rhode Island in 1974, Vermont in 1978, and Arizona in 1981. By 1981, sixteen states and the District of Columbia had authorized lotteries (Burke).

Although the American Puritan tradition stands in opposition to the lottery, the nation's libertarian traditions encourage its acceptability as a revenue-raising device. The libertarian view justifies the lottery on the ground of its voluntariness. G. Robert Blakey has pointed out that voluntariness defines both the economic and the moral worth of the lottery. If the public participates in the lottery, that participation reflects the "collective conscience with respect to gambling" (p. 73). Several arguments may be adduced in favor of the lottery. It pleases voters who resist higher taxes, and it generates income without compulsion. Its revenues benefit worthwhile state projects and may also interfere with the profits of organized criminals. The lottery offers relatively harmless amusement and sometimes instant wealth to those who participate in it.

Opponents, however, charge that lottery revenues are drawn from the wrong sources, are not spent for promised purposes, and are costly to collect. The lottery is also a relatively expensive revenue-raising device. Most taxes cost the taxpayer about five cents for each dollar collected, but a lottery costs between fifteen and forty cents for each dollar. In addition, states sometimes earmark lottery profits for one purpose, but when faced with a budget crisis they may shift these profits into general funds. To give an example, this was done in 1968 in New York, where lottery profits had been designated for education but were shifted into the general fund. Lotteries have also been criticized as contributing relatively little to state financing. The National Gambling Commission found in 1976 that after all the promotion costs and payoffs to players were made, the twelve lotteries operating in 1975 returned only $277 million, or 0.3 percent of the $90 billion it cost to run local and state governments in those states (p. 147).

By 1980, however, lotteries returned around $2.4 billion in gross revenues and netted $1.4 billion for the state governments that ran them. In 1980, the state of Michigan alone grossed $501 million in lottery revenues, which returned $215 million to the state. The criticism that lotteries produce little revenue no longer seems valid. This increase is attributable partly to the expansion of the lottery and partly to its new technologies. The post-1980 lottery is far more attractive to players than was the lottery of 1964. The trend has been away from the traditional "sweepstakes" lottery operated once a year, and toward "instant" games and prizes. The popular three-digit daily numbers game is not very different from a slot machine in the type of gambling action it offers the bettor. Lottery authorities are considering installing video blackjack and poker in bars and hotels. Of the lottery revenues generated in 1980, more than 90 percent was derived from games, equipment, and technologies that were unavailable in 1964 (Burke, p. 63). Instant games are also said to appeal to higher-income groups.

Knowledgeable observers in the gambling industry see the lottery of the future as moving toward an ever-larger choice of games, especially those combining gambling with video technology. Depending upon whether one is for or against lotteries, new technologies will be interpreted as either appealing to or corrupting a younger, computer game–oriented generation.

Thus, the most fundamental criticism of the lottery, as well as of other forms of legal gambling, has to do with the government's role in promoting this "voluntary" activity. As more and more states compete with one another and with organized criminals for the lottery market, novel ways are invented to stimulate demand. States advertise and market the product with frequent drawings; inexpensive tickets; better chances of prize-winning; higher payout ratios; attractive prizes (including a larger first prize); simpler buying, drawing, and paying procedures; fast notice of results; and the opportunity for players to choose their own ticket numbers. States with large Hispanic populations have mounted entire lottery marketing campaigns in Spanish.

Given the entrepreneurial imperatives that have come to be associated with the lottery, the public policy issue may not rest on whether gambling as such is moral, but on whether the government ought to promote an activity that is, if not immoral, at least not exemplary. If government is, in Justice Louis D. Brandeis's dictum, "an omnipresent teacher," is promotion of the lottery an appropriate state activity, comparable to the promotion of education, public health, and other conventionally salutary activities?

Casino gambling

Of all forms of gambling, casino gambling is the most glamorous, the most difficult to understand and control, and apparently the most attractive to all social classes.

In the United States, the characteristic motive behind the legalization of gambling, including casino gambling, is the raising of revenue. In some states, legal gambling helps to alleviate fiscal problems. In Nevada, legal casino gambling more than helps—it is, in fact, essential for the state's economic survival. Casino gambling is the single largest industry in the state, employing nearly one-third of the work force. Forty-five percent of Nevada's fiscal 1981 budget of $347 million derived from taxes on casino gambling and entertainment. An additional factor to consider is that without legalized casino gambling, the state's sales-tax revenues would be reduced substantially. For example, the nongaming aspects of the casinos (hotel accommodations and sales of food and beverages) account for about half the sales tax. Moreover, since most of the sales of other goods and services are related to the presence of legalized casino gambling, tax revenues would be reduced still further by the absence of the gambling industry. As a result, to the extent that the welfare of the state depends upon the gambling industry, Nevada faces a continuing dilemma in its control structure. The capacity for control is relentlessly challenged, veering between the polarities of partnership and policing.

Even though gambling tables are taxed, casino gambling is not a major source of revenue for the British government. Thus, in contrast to Nevada, casino gambling in England is essentially a social issue. Casino gambling is legal, but there is a definite stigma attached to it. The official position of the government, under the Gaming Act of 1968, is that gambling is a social problem, to be suppressed as much as possible.

Gambling in England is controlled by the Gaming Board, which reports to the Home Office rather than to the Treasury, and the success of the Gaming Board is not measured by a rise in the popularity of gaming; on the contrary, if casino gambling were to disappear entirely from the British scene, the board would be congratulated.

Of all the factors that differentiate European and American attitudes toward gambling, none is more important than the "benevolent paternalism" inherent in British and European gambling policy. There is no question, for example, that European governments have traditionally relied on class segregation in framing casino gaming policy and law. Everywhere on the Continent, casino gambling is characteristically restricted to spas (such as Baden-Baden, for example), in effect excluding (and presumably protecting) the industrial working class from the temptations of casino gambling. In England, the attitude of the government toward the gambler in general, but particularly toward the working class "punter," is rather like that once displayed by benign colonial administrations: a combination of paternalism, benevolence, and sharp autocracy.

The same attitude is reflected in British licensing policies. The bettor, it is thought, must be protected from his own impulses. This attitude underlies a number of provisions in the 1968 Gaming Act. Casino gaming clubs, for example, are not permitted in working-class districts of London. Where gaming clubs do exist, as in the fashionable Mayfair residential district, they are designed to be exclusive, both by virtue of their location and by means of substantial membership fees that make them prohibitive for most British workers. Thus, the law does not prohibit the British worker from gambling; it simply puts the facilities out of reach.

American casinos, on the other hand, cater to whoever will play, and large numbers of people respond. When Atlantic City's Resorts International opened in the summer of 1978, it averaged a daily "win" of $759,208 during August. At the time, the most profitable Las Vegas casino, the MGM Grand, was winning about $200,000 a day. Nevada claims that casino gambling is a practically inflation- and depression-proof industry. Although that claim cannot be sustained year in and year out, it held remarkably true until the economic slump of 1982.

Several states are considering the legalization of casino gambling. Advocates of casino gambling lost a referendum in Florida in 1978, despite the appeal of Atlantic City's recent earnings. Opponents included a Baptist governor morally opposed to gambling, and major businesses that feared the decline of Florida's family-oriented tourist industry and also organized crime's interest in casino gambling; business leaders mounted an effective political campaign stressing that theme. Still, New Jersey advocates as well lost the first round of balloting, and the Florida advocates may eventually be successful, especially if tax cuts reduce the state's public services (Dombrink).

Other states are actively considering legalization. In 1981, New York City's mayor advocated legal casino gambling, whereas the state's governor opposed it. The legalization of casino gambling is invariably a major public issue, and gubernatorial backing would seem to be a prerequisite for further expansion in any given state. Of the currently available forms of gambling, casinos seem to be least favored by the voting public. When casino gambling was finally approved in New Jersey, voter approval was less than for any other type of gambling (Joyce, p. 159).

Nevertheless, casino gambling accessible to major population centers would be likely to attract a clientele among large groups of people, especially working people. The National Gambling Commission estimated that 9 percent of the population living within three hundred miles of Atlantic City will eventually become gamblers.

Casinos are very popular. No clocks are in evidence, illumination is the same both day and night, and there is no cash on the tables. All of these features are intended to offer psychological support to gambling. There also seems to be a relationship between crowds and gambling. Potential gamblers are put at ease by observing others gambling. For this reason, casinos try to appear as lively, festive places. Efforts are made to provide entertainment and beverage service so that players will feel that being in a casino is like being at a party—one that requires no special invitation.

Some commentators have argued that the very atmosphere of casinos is likely to produce more "tapped out" players (those who lose their bottom dollar) than lotteries or off-track betting produce. For example, a 1974 study of the impact of legalized lotteries and off-track betting by David Weinstein and Lillian Deitch found that lottery players place single, relatively small bets "in conjunction with purchases of other goods and services, in places such as newsstands, supermarkets and drugstores. There is nothing in these social situations to encourage excessive expenditures" (p. 134). Similarly, Weinstein and Deitch noted that even though off-track betting parlors offer only betting and therefore permit greater concentration on it than newsstands do, they are consciously designed to discourage socializing. By contrast, every effort is made to keep the casino gambler inside the casino by providing food, entertainment, and festivity.

Overgrowth, associated social problems, and difficulties of control are three major problems facing the casino gambling industry. Obviously, the eight operating casinos in Atlantic City cannot be as profitable as a single one would be. The more casino gambling expands in one area, the less likely is any given casino to be profitable. By 1981, Atlantic City faced a casino glut. Several investors postponed or canceled construction as they reviewed profit-and-loss statements showing that several casinos were having trouble breaking even.

The development of a casino gambling industry concentrated in one area may also generate unwelcome side effects. When land values soared in Atlantic City, so did the residential displacement of existing populations. Most casino jobs were filled by nonresidents of Atlantic City. Between July 1978 and July 1979, the unemployment rate in the city actually rose, from 8.4 percent to 10 percent (Michael Hawkins, p. 800).

The introduction of casino gambling may also invite a rise in street crime. Prostitutes as well are attracted to casinos, as they are to any place where men are likely to spend money freely. Casinos are designed to reduce inhibitions, and this can result in a generalized "shadiness." To guard against this, New Jersey instituted certain size and aesthetic requirements for casinos. Nevertheless, Atlantic City experienced a rise of approximately 25 percent in crimes of assault, car theft, prostitution, and larceny after Resorts International opened in May 1978 (Skolnick, 1979, p. 58).

As businesses, casinos are unusually tightly controlled, both internally by management and externally by government. Controls are essential to casino operation. Casinos, like banks, are subject to robbery and embezzlement. They must thwart armed robbery, employee embezzlement, and theft, as well as cheating by actual and potential schemers who possess extraordinary cunning and technical sophistication.

Organized crime and casino gambling. The Las Vegas casino gambling industry was begun and developed by well-known organized-crime figures. The legendary gangster "Bugsy" Siegel is generally recognized as the man who "invented" Las Vegas. His Flamingo Hotel, built in 1946, became the prototype for the contemporary Las Vegas casino. Siegel's ambition had been to build a luxurious complex offering gambling, recreation, entertainment, and other services catering to the area's increasing tourist trade. In 1947, when gross gaming revenues were $32 million, Siegel predicted that in ten years Nevada would be the largest gambling center in the world. His prediction came true in 1957, when the state's casinos grossed $132 million; in 1980, the gross was $2.4 billion. But 1957 also demonstrated the failure of the rudimentary administrative-law controls Nevada had instituted to screen hidden organized-crime interests in casinos. When gangster Frank Costello was shot in New York City that year, the daily gross revenue figures for the Tropicana Hotel were found in his jacket pocket.

Federal agencies thought that Las Vegas contributed to the spread of organized crime by offering gangsters a cloak of respectability, and major institutional lenders believed that Las Vegas casino operators lacked both business acumen and adequate internal controls to prevent "skimming." Thus, although the modern Las Vegas casino and the success of the gaming industry can be attributed to Siegel and others like him, so can the major control problems. The dilemma of control over the gaming industry has been posed by an inherent contradiction—the desire to maintain revenue sources originally developed by gangsters while at the same time dissociating the industry, and the states that legalize it, from the taint of organized crime (Skolnick, 1978, pp. 101–145).

The Nevada Gaming Commission was established in 1959 to change the disreputable image of the industry. The Nevada State Gaming Control Board was also established, as the working, professional arm of the commission. The board performed the three basic functions of governmental regulation of casino gambling: investigating applicants for licenses, policing the casino floor, and auditing to collect taxes.

The 1960s witnessed the first federal court victory for gaming control. In *Marshall v. Sawyer*, 301 F.2d 639 (9th Cir. 1962), a federal court upheld Nevada's right to maintain a list of "notorious and unsavory" persons who were not allowed to gamble or to occupy rooms in casinos. Most importantly, the court took judicial notice that the state was entitled to exercise strong controls over the gambling industry. "The problem of excluding hoodlums from gambling places," the court concluded, "can well be regarded by the state authorities as a matter of life or death" (652).

Despite the introduction of stricter controls, "grandfathering" led Attorney General Robert Kennedy and other federal authorities to regard Nevada gaming control as more symbolic than real. Without Kennedy's knowledge, the FBI had illegally installed listening devices in Las Vegas casinos and residences. These devices provided hard, but not legally usable, evidence of hidden ownership and skimming by organized-crime figures.

Because of the limitations of such illegally obtained evidence, the federal government was able to prove only one skimming case during the 1960s, in which several hotelmen pleaded guilty to concealing the gangster Meyer Lansky's financial interest in the Flamingo Hotel. Between 1960 and 1977, the hotelmen understated $36 million in casino receipts. Gamblers would repay IOUs that were never entered on casino records and therefore went unreported.

Compared to the gangsters, Howard Hughes was a highly reputable businessman. After his arrival in Las Vegas in 1966, he took control of the penthouse suite at the Desert Inn Hotel and proceeded to acquire seven casino properties formerly owned or controlled by reputed organized-crime figures. After Hughes's arrival, Las Vegas enjoyed a steady climb. A new era of respectability for Nevada and its much-maligned casino industry was signaled by the coming of Hughes and by the Nevada legislature's subsequent decision, with the passage of the Nevada Gaming Control Act (Nev. Rev. Stat. ch. 463 (1981)), to permit publicly traded corporations to operate casinos. It was thought that the presence of legitimate investors through the device of such corporations would ease federal pressure on the state. Publicly traded corporations were subject to Securities and Exchange Commission regulations, and thus offered an additional layer of control.

Some, probably most, of the casinos did cut ties with organized crime, but others retained them (*United States v. Polizzi*, 500 F.2d 856 (9th Cir. 1974)). Since it is in the nature of hidden interests to remain hidden, it would be difficult to say with any accuracy which casinos do and which do not retain such ties. As an illustration, the final report of the National Commission on the Review of the National Policy toward Gambling stated: "Although organized crime once was a significant factor in some Nevada casinos, its influence has declined considerably and consistently during the past ten years. In comparison with the situation 15 years ago, the presence of organized crime in Nevada today is negligible" (p. 78). The Commission's optimistic conclusions regarding the absence of organized crime in Nevada's gambling industry have since come to be widely questioned because of problems that arose in the years after the issuing of the report (Eadington, 1982, p. 18).

During the summer of 1979, several connections between casinos and organized crime were revealed. Acting upon the orders of the Nevada Gaming Commission, the Nevada State Gaming Control Board closed the casino of the $100-million Aladdin Hotel. The agents were making good on a promise by Nevada's governor to shut the Aladdin's casino unless its owners, who had been found guilty in a federal court of concealing hidden management by "unsavory" Detroit businessmen, found a suitable buyer. Closing the Aladdin casino was a historic event, since twenty-five hundred hotel employees were left unemployed. One member of the Nevada Gaming Commission explained that "where rot exists in a tissue, you have to cut it out to make it well."

At the beginning of June 1979, the FBI bureau in Kansas City released transcripts of wiretapped conversations between reputed Kansas City organized-crime figures and Las Vegas casino operators. One veteran Las Vegas casino executive was heard giving instructions on how to skim; an attorney for a hotel claimed to have influence over a major gaming official with regard to some crucial licensing and fine cases. A three-year investigation into a multimillion-dollar skimming scheme at a prominent Strip casino was completed, resulting in a $500,000 fine, the largest ever levied against a Nevada casino operator. In short, a new era of heightened federal investigative activity was resulting in disclosures of mob influence and in turn dealing a severe blow to the credibility of Nevada gaming control (Skolnick and Dombrink, p. 764).

New Jersey's gaming regulatory system has been modeled in most respects on Nevada's. This is apparent in the structure, duties, and powers of the New Jersey Casino Control Commission, its Division of Gaming Enforcement, and its licensing requirements. The New Jersey legislature has enacted an even more restrictive—some would say stifling—gaming control apparatus (N.J. Stat. Ann § 5:12-130.1 (1981–1982 Supp.)). Nevertheless, one leading commentator on gaming control, Alvin Hicks, has praised New Jersey's greater investigative authority, the increased responsibilities of the state prosecutor, and the state's strong antiracketeering provisions.

This is not to suggest that every casino has, or should even be thought to have, organized-crime connections or hidden interests. It ought to be recognized, however, that the organized-criminal roots of the casino business sometimes become a visible embarrassment when in-depth, historically oriented investigations are undertaken, as they have been by Nevada, New Jersey, and the federal government. This visibility, in turn, serves to reinforce public perceptions of the casino business as a pariah industry, and it will doubtless play a significant role in the question of whether casino gambling is to be more widely accepted throughout the United States.

JEROME H. SKOLNICK

See also ORGANIZED CRIME: OVERVIEW; POLICE: VICE SQUAD; VICTIMLESS CRIME.

BIBLIOGRAPHY

ARANSON, PETER H., and MILLER, ROGER LEROY. "Economic Aspects of Public Gaming." *Connecticut Law Review* 12 (1980): 822–853.

BLAKEY, G. ROBERT. "State Conducted Lotteries: History, Problems, and Promises." *Journal of Social Issues* 35, no. 3 (1979): 62–86.

——— et al. [Cornell Law Project]. *The Development of the Law of Gambling: 1776–1976.* Washington, D.C.: U.S. Department of Justice, Law Enforcement Assistance Administration, National Institute of Law Enforcement and Criminal Justice, 1977.

BURKE, DUANE V. "The Evolution of State Lotteries." *Public Gaming* 8 (1981): 62–63.

CORNISH, D. B. *Gambling: A Review of the Literature and Its Implications for Policy and Research.* Home Office Research Study No. 42. London: Her Majesty's Stationery Office, 1978.

DEVEREUX, EDWARD C., JR. *Gambling and the Social Structure: A Sociological Study of Lotteries and Horse Racing in Contemporary America.* 2 vols. Edited by Harriet Zuckerman and Robert K. Merton. New York: Arno Press, 1980.

DOMBRINK, JOHN. "Outlaw Businessmen: Organized Crime and the Legalization of Gambling." Ph.D. dissertation, University of California, 1981.

DOSTOYEVSKY, FYODOR M. "The Gambler." *The Gambler; Bobok; A Nasty Story.* Translated with an introduction by Jessie Coulson. Baltimore: Penguin Books, 1966.

DOWNES, D. M. et al. *Gambling, Work, and Leisure: A Study across Three Areas.* London: Routledge & Kegan Paul, 1976.

EADINGTON, WILLIAM R. "The Evolution of Corporate Gambling in Nevada." *Nevada Review of Business and Economics* 6 (1982): 13–22.

———, ed. *Gambling and Society: Interdisciplinary Studies on the Subject of Gambling.* Springfield, Ill.: Thomas, 1976.

EZELL, JOHN SAMUEL. *Fortune's Merry Wheel: The Lottery in America.* Cambridge, Mass.: Harvard University Press, 1960.

Federal Bureau of Investigation. *Crime in the United States, 1979.* Uniform Crime Reports for the United States. Washington, D.C.: U.S. Department of Justice, FBI, 1980.

FREUD, SIGMUND. "Dostoevsky and Parricide." *The Psychology of Gambling.* Edited by Jon Halliday and Peter Fuller. New York: Harper & Row, 1975, pp. 157–174.

Fund for the City of New York. *Legal Gambling in New York: A Discussion of Numbers and Sports Betting.* New York: The Fund, 1972.

———, and Twentieth Century Fund. *Easy Money: Report of the Task Force on Legalized Gambling.* Background paper by David Beale and Clifford Goldman. Millwood, N.Y.: Kraus Reprint, 1975.

GEERTZ, CLIFFORD. "Deep Play: Notes on the Balinese Cockfight." *The Interpretation of Cultures: Selected Essays.* New York: Basic Books, 1973, pp. 412–453.

GOFFMAN, ERVING. "Where the Action Is." *Interaction Ritual: Essays on Face-to-face Behavior.* Chicago: Aldine, 1967, pp. 142–270.

HALLIDAY, JON, and FULLER, PETER, eds. *The Psychology of Gambling.* New York: Harper & Row, 1975.

HAWKINS, MICHAEL. "Casinos and Land Use: Law and Public Policy." *Connecticut Law Review* 12 (1980): 785–808.

HAWKINS, WILLIAM. *A Treatise of the Pleas of the Crown, or a System of the Principal Matters Relating to That Subject, Digested under Their Proper Heads.* 5th ed. London: Worrall, 1771.

HICKS, ALVIN J. "No Longer the Only Game in Town: A Comparison of the Nevada and New Jersey Regulatory Systems of Gaming Control." *Southwestern University Law Review* 12 (1981): 583–626.

JOYCE, KATHLEEN M. "Public Opinion and the Politics of Gambling." *Journal of Social Issues* 35, no. 3 (1979): 144–165.

KALLICK-KAUFMANN, MAUREEN, and REUTER, PETER, eds. "Gambling in the U.S.: Public Finance or Public Problem." *Journal of Social Issues* 35 (1979): 1–182.

KAPLAN, H. ROY. *Lottery Winners: How They Won and How Winning Changed Their Lives.* New York: Harper & Row, 1978.

The Knapp Commission Report on Police Corruption. Report of the New York City Commission to Investigate Allegations of Police Corruption and the City's Anti-corruption Procedures. Foreword by Michael Armstrong. New York: Braziller, 1972.

Kusyszyn, Igor. " 'Compulsive' Gambling: The Problem of Definition." *The International Journal of the Addictions* 13 (1978): 1095–1101.

Livingston, Jay. "Compulsive Gamblers: A Culture of Losers." *Psychology Today*, March 1974, pp. 51–55.

Mangione, Thomas W., and Fowler, Floyd J., Jr. "Enforcing the Gambling Laws." *Journal of Social Issues* 35, no. 3 (1979): 115–128.

Pennsylvania Crime Commission. *Report on Police Corruption and the Quality of Law Enforcement in Philadelphia.* St. David's, Pa.: The Commission, 1974.

Royal Commission on Gambling. *Final Report.* Cmnd. 7200. London: Her Majesty's Stationery Office, 1978.

Royal Commission on Lotteries and Betting, 1932–1933. *Final Report.* Cmnd. 4341. London: His Majesty's Stationery Office, 1933.

Skolnick, Jerome H. *House of Cards: Legalization and Control of Casino Gambling.* Boston: Little, Brown, 1978.

——. "The Social Risks of Casino Gambling." *Psychology Today*, July 1979, pp. 52–58, 63–64.

——, and Dombrink, John. Symposium. "Legal Aspects of Public Gaming." *Connecticut Law Review* 12 (1980): 661–947.

Trevelyan, George Macauley. *English Social History: A Survey of Six Centuries, Chaucer to Queen Victoria.* 2d ed. London: Longmans, Green, 1946.

U.S. National Commission on the Review of the National Policy toward Gambling. *Gambling in America: Final Report.* Washington, D.C.: The Commission, 1976.

Weinstein, David, and Deitch, Lillian. *The Impact of Legalized Gambling: The Socio-economic Consequences of Lotteries and Off-track Betting.* New York: Praeger, 1974.

Zuckerman, Marvin. "The Search for High Sensation." *Psychology Today*, February 1978, pp. 38–43, 46, 96–97.

GANGS

See Crime Prevention: juveniles as potential offenders; Delinquent and Criminal Subcultures; Organized Crime: overview; Youth Gangs and Groups.

GENDER AND CRIME

See Prisons: prisons for women; *both articles under* Rape; Violence in the Family: wife beating; Women and Crime.

GENETICS AND CRIME

See Crime Causation: biological theories.

GENOCIDE

See International Crimes against the Peace; International Criminal Law; War Crimes.

GRAND JURY

The grand jury—typically composed of fourteen to twenty-three persons selected from the community—is an agency of the criminal justice process to which two important functions are assigned. First, the grand jury serves as a screening body; it reviews the evidence available to the prosecution and determines whether that evidence is strong enough to issue an indictment, the formal accusation necessary for prosecution. Second, in conjunction with the prosecutor, the grand jury utilizes its investigative authority to uncover evidence not previously available to the prosecution.

The two functions of the grand jury explain why it is commonly described as the "shield and sword" of the criminal justice process. In its role as a screening agency, the grand jury provides a shield against mistaken or vindictive prosecutions when it refuses to indict. In its role as an investigative agency, it provides the prosecution with a sword to combat crime. There are those who argue, however, that the true characterization of the grand jury should be quite different. As a screening agency, they contend, the grand jury actually serves as a rubber stamp of the prosecutor, rather than as a shield for the innocent. Looking to the grand jury as an investigative agency, they would characterize it as a "tool of inquisition" rather than as a legitimate weapon for combating crime.

One difficulty that arises in evaluating either criticism or praise of the grand jury is the tremendous diversity in the use of the institution among the fifty-one separate American legal jurisdictions, consisting of the fifty states and the federal system. Some jurisdictions use the grand jury as both a screening and investigative agency, others use it primarily for one function or the other, and a few rarely use it for either function. Moreover, different jurisdictions using the grand jury in the same role often subject its operation to considerably different legal controls.

History of the grand jury

The English origin of the grand jury is commonly traced to the jury created by the Assize of Clarendon, issued by Henry II in 1166. Prior to the issuing of this assize, the most common method of accusation was through a charge presented by the alleged victim, to which the accused responded either by presenting eleven compurgators (oath-takers) who swore to his innocence, or by submitting to trial by ordeal. The assize required that criminal accusations thereafter be "presented" by juries composed of twelve "good and lawful men" selected from the township. The new jury system replaced the compurgation stage of the old English procedure, with the defendant then being subjected to trial by ordeal. The Assize of Clarendon was designed to strengthen royal judicial authority at the expense of the judicial authority exercised by the feudal barons. The jurors were familiar with the local scene and could present charges that otherwise might not be known to the Crown's representatives. Jurors were required to accuse all whom they suspected and faced substantial fines if they failed to make appropriate accusations. In short, as originally designed, the grand jury was not intended to be the protector of the accused, but rather a body that would lend assistance to government officials in the apprehension of criminals.

By the end of the fourteenth century, the English criminal justice process had turned to trial by jury rather than by ordeal, and the original jury had been divided into two separate juries. The trial of guilt was before a twelve-person petit jury, and the accusatory jury was expanded to twenty-three persons, chosen from the entire county. This jury became known as *le grand inquest*, which probably explains its eventual title of grand jury. At this point, the grand jury remained essentially an accusatory body that assisted the Crown in ferreting out criminals. Accusations were either initiated by the jurors themselves, acting on the basis of their own knowledge, or were initiated by a representative of the Crown, often a justice of the peace, who supported his accusation with the testimony of witnesses who appeared before the grand jury. When the accusation was initiated by the jury itself, the jury issued a written charge, or "presentment," which it filed with the court. If the accusation was based on a case placed before the jury by the Crown's representative, the jury's charging document was called an "indictment." The Crown's representative ordinarily would place a proposed indictment before the grand jury, and if the jury found the Crown's evidence sufficient to proceed, it issued the indictment as a "true bill." If it found the evidence insufficient, it returned a finding of *ignoramus* ("we ignore it") or, in later years, "no bill."

It was not until the late seventeenth century that the grand jury, refusing to indict two prominent critics of the King, achieved its reputation as a safeguard against the oppression and despotism of the Crown. In the case of Stephen Colledge, charged with making treasonous remarks, the grand jury refused to indict, notwithstanding considerable pressure from the Lord Chief Justice. In the case brought against the Earl of Shaftesbury, the Crown's representative sought to place more pressure on the grand jury by presenting witnesses publicly rather than privately before the jurors alone, as had been past practice. The jurors nevertheless refused to indict. The Crown eventually succeeded in its attempt to stifle both Colledge and Shaftesbury. Colledge was subsequently indicted by a different grand jury, convicted, and executed, and the Earl of Shaftesbury fled the country to avoid a probable indictment by a new grand jury. The grand jury nevertheless had established its reputation as the protector of the individual against false accusations and as an independent screening agency capable of resisting the pressure of the Crown (Schwartz).

This view of the grand jury as the "people's panel" was reinforced in the American colonies, where grand juries refused to indict numerous opponents of the Crown. Thus, the infamous prosecution of John Peter Zenger for seditious libel was brought by prosecutor's information—a charging instrument issued by the prosecutor alone—because grand juries twice refused to issue indictments (Alexander, p. 19). It was with such cases in mind that those who drafted the Bill of Rights required grand jury review of prosecutions. The first clause of the Fifth Amendment prohibits prosecutions for all serious crimes "unless on a presentment or indictment of a Grand Jury."

Although it was the screening function of the grand jury that led to the prosecution-by-indictment requirement of the Fifth Amendment and to similar requirements in the early state constitutions, the grand jury continued to be recognized also as an important investigative body. Of course, with the development of the modern police department, the police assumed the primary investigative burden. The structure of the grand jury gave it an independence and range of authority, however, that remained especially useful in the investigation of certain types of crimes. Grand jury investigations of crimes of public corruption, for example, date back to colonial times. These investigations, along with investigations of other crimes that affected the community in general, such as fraudulent business practices, enhanced the grand jury's reputation as an effective weapon against those criminal forces that often evaded the reach of the police. Indeed, grand juries sometimes went beyond the investigation of crime to issue reports condemning inefficient government practices and suggesting civil reforms.

Structure

Certain elements of the legal structure of the grand jury relate primarily to either one or the other of its functions, but there are three basic structural features that influence both its screening and investigative roles—jury composition, jury independence, and the secrecy of jury proceedings.

Grand jury composition. In most jurisdictions grand jurors are drawn from the same constituency, and selected in the same manner, as the jury panel for petit jurors. The federal system and a majority of the states use what is commonly described as a random selection system. Jurors are selected at random from a voter registration list or similar list containing an extensive cross section of the community. A substantial minority of the states use a "discretionary" selection system, under which jurors are selected by local judges or jury commissioners, usually on the basis of recommendations by various community leaders. Both selection systems seek representation reflecting a cross section of the community, but the special requirements of grand jury service often result in the selection of a group that is less representative than the petit jury panel. Because grand jurors serve for much longer terms (at least several months), there is a tendency to be more lenient in excusing persons who claim they cannot afford to serve. As a result, in many jurisdictions the grand jury is likely to have a heavier concentration of affluent or retired persons than the petit jury.

In the past, it was quite common for jurisdictions to select a "blue ribbon" group of jurors for grand juries engaged primarily in investigations, as opposed to screening. The blue-ribbon group consisted of professionals and community leaders thought to have the education and sophistication needed for extensive investigations of such matters as government corruption.

For several reasons, blue-ribbon grand juries, although not unknown, are far less common today. First, selection of a blue-ribbon grand jury was dependent upon use of a discretionary selection system, and most jurisdictions have now turned to a random selection system. Second, most jurisdictions do not draw a sharp distinction between investigative and screening grand juries. In large urban communities, several grand juries may be used at the same time, and one or two may be assigned primarily to investigations while the others are engaged in screening. In most jurisdictions, however, a particular grand jury will spend part of its time screening cases ready for indictment, and part of its time conducting investigations. Finally, serious questions have been raised as to the legality of using a clearly nonrepresentative group of jurors even where the grand jury is concentrating primarily on investigations. Once the investigation is completed, the same grand jurors usually will then review the evidence and decide whether to indict. The United States Supreme Court has long held, however, that an indictment is constitutionally invalid if issued by a grand jury chosen through a racially discriminatory selection procedure. Many authorities conclude that the Court also would invalidate an indictment if the grand jury selection procedure failed to meet the other basic nondiscrimination requirement, that the jurors be drawn from a "fair cross section" of the community.

Grand jury independence.

Relationship to the prosecutor. Independence from the prosecutor is essential to the performance of both of the grand jury's functions. Grand jury independence is, of course, the basic premise underlying its shielding function. In investigation, although it is expected that the grand jury will work in cooperation with the prosecutor, some degree of independence is also assumed. As will be seen, the prosecutor is given, through the grand jury, investigative power far more extensive than that available to the police. This grant has been made partly because it is assumed the grand jury will restrain any overzealous prosecutor in the use of these powers. At the same time, it is also assumed that the grand jury, as a group removed from politics, will force a reluctant prosecutor to use these powers to investigate criminal activities that he might otherwise ignore for political reasons.

Although the grand jurors must be independent of the prosecutor, they also must be able, as a group of laymen, to make use of the professional expertise of the prosecutor. Accordingly, the legal structure governing the grand jury's relationship to the prosecutor seeks to maintain a balance that ensures grand jury independence yet facilitates use of the government resources available through the prosecutor. Typically, the grand jury is given the right to insist that the prosecutor assist it, while also given the authority to ignore such assistance. The prosecutor's position as the "legal adviser" to the grand jury illustrates this arrangement. The prosecutor serves as the primary source of advice on issues of law arising in grand jury proceedings, but the grand jury always retains the authority to seek further legal advice from the court. Similarly, although the prosecutor must be available to examine witnesses who testify before the grand jury, many jurisdictions also recognize a right of the grand jurors to exclude the prosecutor if they so desire.

The grand jury, at least theoretically, also has the final say on the evidence presented before it. Some jurisdictions require the grand jury to listen to any witnesses presented by the prosecutor, but others still recognize the common-law authority of the grand jury to refuse to hear such evidence. In all jurisdictions, the grand jury is free to consider additional evidence beyond that offered by the prosecutor. Jurors have authority to ask witnesses questions that go beyond the prosecutor's examination, and they also have authority to require the prosecutor to subpoena additional witnesses.

Available data indicate that grand juries only infrequently exercise their authority to override the prosecutor in determining the scope of their proceedings. Moreover, when that authority is exercised in a vigorous fashion, truly responsive assistance from the prosecutor is sometimes difficult to obtain. The ultimate power of the grand jury in such a situation is to petition the court for appointment of a special prosecutor. Many states grant the court broad discretion in ruling on such petitions. Although appointment of a special prosecutor is rare, some of the most famous grand jury investigations involved "runaway grand juries"—that is, grand juries that have pressed investigations over the regular prosecutor's opposition—assisted by special prosecutors. During the mid-1930s, the exploits of New York's famed "racket busting" grand juries, assisted by special prosecutor Thomas E. Dewey, inspired a series of runaway investigations throughout the country.

Relationship to the court. Although often characterized as an "independent body," the grand jury is also recognized to be an "arm of the court." The court cannot order the grand jury to indict or refuse to indict, but it can substantially influence what matters are considered by the grand jury. Initially, whether a grand jury is available to consider a particular matter may depend upon the discretion of the court. Many jurisdictions require that the court impanel at least one grand jury each term, but whether more than one grand jury exists often rests in the discretion of the court. In many jurisdictions, the court also can influence the allocation of grand jury resources by requiring the grand jury to undertake a particular investigation.

What evidence comes before the grand jury is also subject to judicial control. The court may, where necessary to prevent a miscarriage of justice, order that the grand jury be given certain evidence that may be exculpatory. More significantly, the prosecutor's authority to compel witnesses to testify before the grand jury rests on the use of judicially enforced subpoenas, and the court will refuse to enforce subpoenas if it determines that they are being misused. The judge who impaneled the grand jury ordinarily serves as the supervisory or presiding judge, with responsibility for ensuring that the grand jury and the prosecutor assisting it stay within legal limits. The supervisory judge is not present during the grand jury proceedings and ordinarily is unaware of the particulars of grand jury activity. However, the judge is available to hear any objections raised by witnesses or persons who are the subject of grand jury investigations. In addition to prohibiting particular misuses of the grand jury process, the judge may, in extreme cases, replace the prosecutor or even discharge the grand jury.

Grand jury secrecy. The requirement that the grand jury hear evidence in a closed proceeding grew out of the Crown's attempt to pressure the grand jury in the Earl of Shaftesbury's case by presenting its witnesses at a public hearing. By the time of the adoption of the Fifth Amendment, it was firmly established that all grand jury proceedings were to be secret, with only the final result, if an indictment, made known to the public. The secrecy of the proceedings no longer was designed simply to protect the jurors from improper pressures. As noted by the Supreme Court in *United States v. Procter and Gamble Co.,* 356 U.S. 677 (1958), grand jury secrecy came to be justified on several grounds:

(1) to prevent the escape of those whose indictment may be contemplated; (2) to insure the utmost freedom to the grand jury in its deliberations, and to prevent persons subject to indictment or their friends from importuning the grand jurors; (3) to prevent subornation of perjury or tampering with the witnesses who may testify before grand jury and later appear at the trial of those indicted by it; (4) to encourage free and untrammeled disclosures by persons who have information with respect to the commission of crimes; (5) to protect the innocent accused who is exonerated from disclosure of the fact that he has been under investigation, and from the expense of standing trial where there was no probability of guilt [681–682 n. 6].

Although the justifications for secrecy requirements continue to be accepted, there has been a gradual movement over the years toward narrowing those requirements. This movement has been supported by two lines of reasoning: (1) that the former, broader requirements often went beyond what was needed to serve the justifications for secrecy; and (2) that it was necessary to balance against those justifications other, equally important interests.

Perhaps the most significant loosening of secrecy requirements occurred in the exemption of the grand jury witness from the obligation of secrecy. In all jurisdictions, the prosecutor, grand jurors, and grand jury stenographer are prohibited from disclosing what happened before the grand jury, unless ordered to do so in a judicial proceeding. A few jurisdictions impose a similar obligation on grand jury witnesses, allowing them to discuss their testimony only with their counsel. In most jurisdictions, however, the witness no longer is sworn to secrecy. He is free to disclose what he wishes to whom he wishes. A major objective of grand jury secrecy is to keep a target from learning of the investigation, and thus to preclude his probable flight or attempt to tamper with witnesses. However, a witness questioned about another is now free to inform that person of the grand jury's interest in his activities.

The witness exemption was adopted partly because it was thought that requiring secrecy of the witness was unrealistic and unenforceable, particularly where the target is a relative or friend of the witness. Moreover, the exemption permits the witness to make a public statement concerning his grand jury appearance, which may be desirable in rebutting rumors concerning his testimony or in attracting public attention to what he views as grand jury abuses.

Another significant change in secrecy requirements has been the gradual expansion of the disclosure made to the indicted defendant. At one time, the defendant had no access to the testimony before the grand jury that led to his indictment. By the 1980s, however, in almost every jurisdiction, if a witness who testified before the grand jury later testified at trial, the defendant was given a transcript of that witness's grand jury testimony for possible impeachment use. Many jurisdictions also provide the defendant with a list of all persons who testified before the grand jury, whether or not they testify at trial. Several jurisdictions take the further step of providing the defendant with a complete transcript of all relevant testimony before the grand jury. Insofar as secrecy requirements encourage otherwise reluctant witnesses to assist the grand jury, that encouragement is likely to be lost through extensive postindictment disclosures. This is especially true of witnesses who are not likely to testify at trial and whose role therefore would not be known to the defendant except for the disclosure. On the other hand, full disclosure is said to be needed to ensure that a defendant has available all possible sources of information in preparing his defense.

Grand jury screening

The requirement of prosecution by indictment.

Federal prosecutions. The Fifth Amendment provides that except in certain military cases, "no person shall be held to answer for a capital, or otherwise infamous crime, unless on a presentment or indict-

ment of a Grand Jury." The net effect of this provision is to establish grand jury screening as the constitutional right of any person charged in a federal court with a felony offense. Although the amendment refers somewhat ambiguously to "otherwise infamous crimes," that term has been interpreted, in light of historical practice, as encompassing all felonies (offenses punishable by imprisonment for a term exceeding one year). Similarly, although the amendment does not state that a grand jury must review the prosecution's case against a defendant, that process is inherent in the issuance of an indictment. Since the Fifth Amendment is designed to protect the interests of the defendant, it does not require grand jury review when the defendant knowingly and voluntarily waives the use of an indictment. In such cases, and in prosecutions for misdemeanors, the federal prosecutor ordinarily will proceed by information, although he still has discretion to take the case before the grand jury.

State prosecutions. At the time of the adoption of the Fifth Amendment, all of the states also required that felony prosecutions be brought by indictment. This pattern continued until 1859, when the Michigan legislature, responding to criticism of grand jury practices, authorized prosecutors to bring felony prosecutions upon a prosecutor's information (Younger, pp. 68–69). Several states followed Michigan's lead, and in 1884, the constitutionality of this shift from indictment to information reached the Supreme Court in *Hurtado v. California,* 110 U.S. 516 (1884). Since it had long been held that the Bill of Rights applied only to the federal government, state prosecutions by information clearly did not violate the Fifth Amendment. State defendants argued, however, that such prosecutions violated the Fourteenth Amendment. The first section of that amendment provides that "no State shall . . . deprive any person of life, liberty, or property, without due process of law," and the defendants contended that the imposition of criminal penalties in felony cases prosecuted without grand jury review constituted a denial of liberty without due process. *Hurtado* rejected this claim.

The Supreme Court's *Hurtado* opinion stressed that due process requires the states only to adhere to those "fundamental principles of liberty and justice which lie at the base of all our civil and political institutions" (535). The emphasis, the Court noted, should be on "the substance" of those principles rather than their "forms and mode of attainment" in English common law. Under California law, a prosecutor's information could be issued only after a preliminary hearing at which a magistrate, upon examining the prosecution's witnesses and permitting cross-examination by defense counsel, certified the probable guilt of the defendant. This screening procedure, the Court concluded, fulfilled the substantive requirements of due process. In the years since *Hurtado*, the Supreme Court has found that various procedural requirements imposed on the federal government through the Bill of Rights reflect "fundamental principles of liberty" and therefore are required of the states by the Fourteenth Amendment's due process clause. It has continued to adhere, however, to the *Hurtado* ruling that prosecution by indictment is not such a requirement.

Following *Hurtado*, there was a gradual movement of the states to permit felony prosecutions by information where supported by a magistrate's finding of probable cause after a preliminary hearing. This movement probably reached its peak during the 1930s when England abolished the grand jury. Since then, only a handful of additional states have shifted to prosecution by information, but that was enough to make the practice the majority position. In the early 1980s only twenty states made grand jury indictment mandatory for all felony prosecutions, although several additional states required an indictment for capital offenses. In the remaining states, commonly called "information states," prosecution in felony cases ordinarily was brought by information.

It should be noted that the information states did not actually abolish the grand jury but simply gave the prosecutor the option of choosing between the information and indictment. Given that choice, prosecutors regularly prefer the information. Typically, indictments are used in information states only in rare cases, such as those in which the grand jury originally considered the case in an investigative capacity. However, some prosecutors in information states prefer grand jury review for certain types of crimes, such as homicide, and regularly use indictments in a substantial number of cases. It is only in the twenty states requiring prosecution by indictment, called the "indictment states," that grand jury review is the regular practice for all felonies. Moreover, even in those states, a substantial number of prosecutions may be by information, since defendants may waive the indictment requirement and agree to prosecution by information, a common practice where a defendant intends to plead guilty.

Screening procedures.

Presenting the prosecutor's case. The prosecutor's grand jury presentation ordinarily begins with an explanation of a proposed indictment and a summary of the evidence that will be offered to support it. The evidence is then presented through the testimony of witnesses or the introduction of documents. In many jurisdictions, the prosecutor has an obligation to produce, in addition to supporting evidence, any further evidence that he knows to be exculpatory. Thus, if a lineup produced conflicting eyewitness identifications, the prosecutor must make the jury aware of that conflict and not simply present the one eyewitness who identified the accused. The prosecutor's disclosure obligation is limited, however, to evidence obviously exculpatory and material. The prosecutor need not assume the role of a defense counsel and introduce all the evidence that a defense counsel might have wished to offer.

Although grand jury proceedings are secret, persons often are informed—for example, after being arrested—that charges against them will be presented to the grand jury. The grand jury proceeding is not an adversary proceeding, however, and those persons have no right to present their own evidence to that body. The potential defendant may write to the grand jury and ask it to consider certain evidence, but such communications are very rare. Another practice, only slightly less unusual, is to request the opportunity to testify before the grand jury. In most jurisdictions, the grand jury can reject or grant such a request at its discretion, but several states give the potential defendant a right to testify if he so chooses.

Evidentiary restrictions. Indictment jurisdictions differ substantially in their rules governing the type of evidence that may be presented to the grand jury. Several impose largely the same evidentiary rules as are applied at trial. They recognize, however, that in a nonadversary proceeding the prosecutor is more likely to present legally inadmissible evidence unintentionally. Accordingly, an indictment will not be invalidated if, after excluding any inadmissible testimony given to the grand jury, there remains sufficient admissible evidence to sustain the charge. Some other indictment jurisdictions generally favor application of the rules of evidence, but grant the prosecutor even more leeway. These jurisdictions recognize several broad exceptions to the rules, which are designed, in part, to cut down on defense opportunities for time-consuming pretrial challenges to indictments based on evidentiary rules.

Most indictment jurisdictions refuse to apply any rules of evidence to grand jury proceedings. In these jurisdictions, prosecutors may use any type of evidence without regard to whether it could be used at trial. Thus, prosecutors need not have key witnesses themselves testify, but may simply introduce statements the witnesses gave to the police, even though those statements would be inadmissible hearsay at trial. In *Costello v. United States*, 350 U.S. 359 (1956), the Supreme Court held that the prosecutorial practice of relying entirely on hearsay did not violate the Fifth Amendment. The Court stressed that historically, the grand jury was a "body of laymen" whose "work was not hampered by rigid procedural rules."

Standard for indictment. In many states the grand jury is directed to indict only if the evidence before it establishes probable cause to believe that the accused committed the felony charged; in others, it is directed to indict "when all the evidence taken together, if unexplained or uncontradicted, would warrant a conviction of the defendant" (Alaska Crim. R. 6(q) (1981)). The first standard is very much like that applied by a preliminary-hearing magistrate. The second is a somewhat more rigorous standard, being similar to the standard applied by a trial judge in ruling on a motion for directed acquittal. No matter which standard applies in the particular jurisdiction, the jurors need not be unanimous in their conclusion that it is met. At common law, a vote of a majority (twelve out of twenty-three jurors) was sufficient to indict. Many jurisdictions now permit smaller grand juries, but require a somewhat higher percentage of votes for indictment (for example, twelve out of sixteen).

In some jurisdictions, generally those applying the rules of evidence, a defendant may challenge an indictment as not supported by sufficient evidence. To sustain such a challenge, the court must find that the evidence before the grand jury, even if read in a light most favorable to the state, did not meet the applicable standard for indictment. Other jurisdictions refuse all challenges to the sufficiency of the evidence before the grand jury. They stand by the standard suggested in *Costello,* that "an indictment returned by a legally constituted and unbiased grand jury, . . . if valid on its face, is enough to call for a trial on the merits."

The debate. Few criminal justice issues have been the subject of such prolonged and heated debate as the comparative merits of prosecution by indictment and prosecution by information. Critics of prosecution by indictment tend to fall into two categories. First, there are those who see the screening grand jury as no more than a rubber stamp for the prosecutor. They point to states in which grand juries have refused to indict in less than 3 percent of their cases. They suggest that even those refusals probably represent situations in which the grand jury did what the prosecutor wanted it to do—cases in which the prosecutor preferred not to proceed but used the grand jury's "no-bill" as a buffer against potential public indignation. The legal structure of the grand jury, these critics argue, gives it only theoretical independence; in light of the prosecutor's ready access to investigative resources, his legal expertise, and his close working relationships with the grand jurors, it is inevitable that the grand jurors will follow his lead.

Supporters of grand jury screening claim that grand jury independence is more than an empty formalism. They acknowledge that the grand jury indicts in most of its cases, but contend that is because prosecutors, anticipating grand jury review, themselves eliminate the weaker cases. The success of grand jury screening, supporters argue, is evidenced by the high percentage of indictments that produce conviction and the very small percentage that result in dismissals for want of substantial evidence. Reference is also made to the experience in jurisdictions in which prosecutors do not screen so carefully and in which grand juries have refused to indict in as many as 15 percent of their cases.

A second group of critics acknowledge that the grand jury has some value as a screening agency, but believe that preliminary hearing is a better screening procedure. Although many indictment jurisdictions provide a preliminary hearing as well as grand jury screening, these critics see dual screening as too costly, and argue that only the better of the two procedures should be used. They contend that an independent magistrate, an adversary proceeding, and an open hearing clearly make the preliminary hearing the more effective procedure for eliminating unwarranted prosecutions. They also favor the preliminary hearing as more efficient, particularly in rural communities, where grand juries are not as readily available as magistrates.

Grand jury supporters respond that the grand jury is the better screening agency because its strength lies where screening is most needed—in those cases where special factors, such as the involvement of politics or racial animosity, will probably result in unjust accusations. Lay participation permits the grand jury to evaluate the prosecution's case in light of community notions of justice and fairness. Indeed, the grand jury has the recognized authority to "nullify" the law by refusing to indict, notwithstanding legally sufficient evidence. The grand jury's lay participation, supporters claim, is particularly important today, when so few cases go to trial.

Grand jury investigations

In contrast to their division in the use of the grand jury as a screening agency, both indictment and information jurisdictions use the grand jury as an investigative body. Although the extent of that use varies, the grand jury tends to be treated as a specialized investigative agency needed for a limited class of offenses. Compared to police investigations, grand jury investigations are expensive, time-consuming, and logistically cumbersome. However, the grand jury offers distinct investigative advantages where investigators must unravel a complex criminal structure, deal with victims reluctant to cooperate, or obtain information contained in extensive business records. Criminal activities presenting such investigative problems ordinarily relate to public corruption (for example, bribery), misuse of economic power (for example, price-fixing), widespread distribution of illegal services and goods by organized groups (for example, gambling syndicates), and threats of violence used by organized groups (for example, extortion schemes).

The subpoena to testify.

Significance. A major investigative advantage of the grand jury is its use of the subpoena ad testificandum, a court order directing a person to appear and testify before the grand jury. If the police wish to take a person into custody for questioning, they must have the probable cause required by the Fourth Amendment to justify the seizure of a person. Even then, the person has no duty to answer police questions. Moreover, if the person does answer and lies, his lying will not constitute a crime in most jurisdictions. If the prosecutor, on the other hand, wishes to question a person before the grand jury, he may simply utilize the subpoena to testify, which avoids all of these obstacles.

A subpoena to testify can be obtained without a showing of probable cause and, in most jurisdictions, without even a lesser showing that the person subpoenaed is likely to have relevant information. The compulsion of a subpoena to testify has long been held not to fall within the Fourth Amendment, since it does not involve taking a person into custody. Moreover, as various courts have noted, the grand jury (or the prosecutor acting on its behalf) may utilize subpoena authority on no more substantial grounds than "tips" or rumors. This enables the grand jury to serve as "a grand inquest, a body with powers of investigation and inquisition, the scope of whose inquiries is not limited narrowly by questions of propriety or forecasts of the probable result of the investigation" (*Blair v. United States*, 250 U.S. 273 (1919)).

Unlike the person questioned by a police officer, the subpoenaed person is compelled to answer questions before the grand jury unless he can claim an evidentiary privilege, such as the marital privilege or the privilege against self-incrimination. If the witness refuses to testify without such legal justification, he will be held in contempt and subjected to incarcera-

tion by the court issuing the subpoena. If the witness testifies and fails to tell the truth, he may be prosecuted for perjury since his testimony is given under oath.

The granting of broad investigative authority to grand juries through the subpoena to testify has been justified on two grounds. First, such authority is seen as an essential instrument of effective law enforcement. Adequate protection of society requires that there be some independent agency that can track down "every available clue" and examine "all witnesses . . . in every proper way to find if a crime has been committed." The general principle that "the public . . . has a right to every man's evidence" is said to be "particularly applicable to grand jury proceedings" (*Branzburg v. Hayes*, 408 U.S. 665 (1972)). Although the duty to testify "may on occasion be burdensome and even embarrassing," it is "so necessary to the administration of justice that the witness' personal interest in privacy must yield to the public's overriding interest in full disclosure" (*United States v. Calandra*, 414 U.S. 338 (1974)).

Safeguards. The granting of subpoena authority to grand juries also rests, in part, on the premise that extensive safeguards are available to prevent misuse of that authority. Judicial discussions of subpoena authority frequently note, for example, that the grand jury witness retains the same evidentiary privileges that would be available to a witness at trial. In particular, a witness who may be involved in a criminal enterprise can always exercise the privilege against self-incrimination, refusing to respond whenever his answer might provide "a link in the chain of evidence needed to prosecute" (*Hoffman v. United States*, 341 U.S. 479 (1951)). Indeed, if the witness is a potential target for indictment, the prosecutor may be required to inform the witness specifically, before he gives testimony, of his right to claim the privilege.

Courts also have stressed that the very presence of the grand jurors provides protection against misuse of the subpoena power. Thus, Justice Hugo Black noted in his dissent in *In re Groban*, 352 U.S. 330 (1957):

They [the grand jury] have no axes to grind and are not charged personally with the administration of the law. No one of them is a prosecuting attorney or law-enforcement officer ferreting out crime. It would be very difficult for officers of the state seriously to abuse or deceive a witness in the presence of the grand jury. Similarly the presence of the jurors offers a substantial safeguard against the officers' misrepresentation, unintentional or otherwise, of the witness' statements and conduct before the grand jury [347].

A final safeguard against misuse of the subpoena power lies in the supervisory authority of the court issuing the subpoena. As the Supreme Court has noted, the presiding judge has the continuing obligation, if other safeguards fail, to prevent "the transformation of the grand jury into an instrument of oppression" (*United States v. Dionisio,* 410 U.S. 1, 12 (1973)).

Critics of grand jury investigations maintain that its safeguards have failed. They contend that prosecutors have employed grand jury investigations to pry into beliefs and associations of dissident groups, have intimidated grand jury witnesses, and have sought to damage the reputation of individuals and businesses by conducting unwarranted investigations that were leaked to the press. Supporters of grand jury investigations do not deny that such abuses have occasionally occurred, but they contend that these are isolated practices which ordinarily are promptly terminated by the courts. Supporters note that grand jury investigations must of necessity constitute "fishing expeditions" that pry into a wide range of personal associations. In the end, much of the information sought may prove to be irrelevant, but disclosure has been made only to the grand jury. Secrecy requirements should prevent public disclosure of such information, unless the witness himself wishes to reveal his grand jury testimony.

Right to counsel. A primary legal reform urged by critics of grand jury investigations is the increased availability of counsel for witnesses. Except for a few jurisdictions, no provision is made for appointment of counsel for witnesses who are indigent. Even if a witness can afford to retain counsel, he normally cannot have counsel accompany him before the grand jury. Most jurisdictions take the position that the presence of the witness's counsel before the grand jury would be disruptive and inconsistent with grand jury secrecy. Those jurisdictions will, however, permit the witness to interrupt his testimony and leave the grand jury room for the purpose of consulting with his counsel just outside the grand jury room. Counsel for witnesses claim that this practice is not adequate, because witnesses do not always realize that they need legal advice in responding to a particular question. Moreover, witnesses often are fearful that they will appear to have "something to hide" if they too frequently leave the room to consult with counsel. A small group of states do permit witnesses to be assisted by counsel within the grand jury room. These jurisdictions strictly limit the lawyer to giving advice to the witness, thereby seeking to prevent him from turning the grand jury examination into an adversary proceeding by making arguments to the grand jury.

Subpoena duces tecum. The subpoena duces tecum (a court order directing a person to bring with him specified items in his possession) gives the grand jury the capacity to obtain physical evidence in a manner very similar to its capacity to obtain testimony. This subpoena is used primarily to obtain business records and other documents in investigations of white-collar crimes. However, it has also been used to require a suspect to provide such identification evidence as fingerprints or handwriting samples. A subpoena duces tecum, in contrast to a search warrant, does not require an advance showing of probable cause. Although the subpoena does direct the subpoenaed person to search his files and bring forth specified documents, it does not authorize the police or prosecutor themselves to search those files. The only Fourth Amendment limitation imposed upon the subpoena duces tecum relates to its breadth. A subpoena may not encompass such a wide range of material as to impose an unreasonable burden on the subpoenaed party. Whether the burden is too great depends on a variety of factors, including the relevancy of the documents, the capacity of the party to continue its business operations without the documents, and the time period over which the documents were prepared. Under appropriate circumstances, courts have upheld subpoenas directing companies to furnish even carloads of documents.

The safeguards applicable to the subpoena ad testificandum also apply to the subpoena duces tecum. However, the privilege against self-incrimination is far less likely to apply to a subpoena duces tecum. The privilege extends only to individuals, and therefore cannot be raised, notwithstanding potential incrimination, to subpoenas requiring production of documents belonging to corporations or similar entities. Moreover, even with respect to personal records, the privilege tends to be limited to private documents personally prepared by the subpoenaed individual. Since the privilege extends only to testimonial disclosures, it also cannot be raised in response to subpoenas requiring production of fingerprints or similar identification evidence.

Immunity grants. Perhaps the most significant advantage of the grand jury investigation is the availability of the immunity grant. An immunity grant is a court order that, in effect, supplants the witness's self-incrimination privilege. Since the privilege prohibits compelling a witness to give testimony that may be used against him in a criminal case, the privilege can be rendered inapplicable by precluding such use of the witness's compelled testimony. An immunity grant does exactly that. It directs the witness to testify and protects him against use of his testimony in any subsequent criminal prosecution.

The Supreme Court has held that to be effective, the immunity grant must guarantee against further use of both the witness's testimony and any evidence derived from that testimony (*Kastigar v. United States*, 406 U.S. 441 (1972)). Moreover, if a subsequent prosecution is brought, the prosecution bears the burden of establishing that all of its evidence was derived from a source independent of the immunized testimony. As a practical matter, unless the prosecution had a fully prepared case before the witness was granted immunity, it will be most difficult to prosecute successfully for a criminal activity discussed in immunized testimony. Many states simply grant the witness what is commonly called "transactional immunity." They bar any prosecution for a transaction discussed in the immunized testimony, without regard to the possible independent source of the prosecutor's evidence.

In taking away possible reliance on the privilege against self-incrimination, the immunity order often strips from the witness his last legal justification for refusing to give testimony before the grand jury. Recalcitrant witnesses granted immunity usually are forced to choose between answering the prosecutor's questions and being imprisoned for contempt. Many witnesses decide to testify, but others, sometimes fearing retaliation from their confederates, prefer contempt sanctions. Ordinarily, those sanctions can include imprisonment for several months or more.

Although immunity grants are issued by the court, the decision as to which witnesses shall be immunized lies largely in the prosecutor's discretion. The prosecutor must weigh the need for the witness's testimony against the probable consequence of relieving the witness of his criminal liability. Very often immunity is given to lower-level participants in organized crime in order to gain testimony against higher-level participants. Immunity is also frequently given to persons who probably are not themselves involved in criminal activities but nevertheless are relying on the privilege. Very often, these people are improperly using the privilege to protect others rather than to avoid self-incrimination, but such misuse of the privilege is so difficult to establish that it is simply easier to supplant the privilege with an immunity grant.

Grand jury reports. Although the grand jury's investigative authority is directed primarily at criminal activities, a substantial number of states permit grand juries to issue public reports on investigations that disclose noncriminal activities thought to merit public attention. Grand jury reports have focused on a variety of topics ranging from the low quality of public education to clearly fraudulent business practices that escaped criminality only because of inadequacies in the coverage of the criminal code. Some jurisdictions will not permit a report to contain derogatory information concerning an identifiable individual. They stress that the individual named in a report, unlike a person indicted, is not given the benefit of a trial in which the state must prove its charges. Other jurisdictions limit reports to specified subjects, usually relating to government operations. Several have provisions requiring court review of reports to ensure that they have some substantial basis in the evidence before the grand jury.

JEROLD H. ISRAEL

See also CHARGING; PRELIMINARY HEARING; PROSECUTION: PROSECUTORIAL DISCRETION.

BIBLIOGRAPHY

ALEXANDER, JAMES. *A Brief Narrative of the Case and Trial [in the Supreme Court of the Judicature of the Province of New York, 1735] of John Peter Zenger, Printer of the "New York Weekly Journal."* 2d ed. Edited by Stanley Nider Katz. Cambridge, Mass.: Harvard University Press, 1972.

ARENELLA, PETER. "Reforming the Federal Grand Jury and the State Preliminary Hearing to Prevent Conviction without Adjudication." *Michigan Law Review* 78 (1980): 463–585.

BRAUN, RICHARD L. "The Grand Jury: Spirit of the Community?" *Arizona Law Review* 15 (1973): 893–917.

CAMPBELL, WILLIAM J. "Eliminate the Grand Jury." *Journal of Criminal Law and Criminology* 64 (1973): 174–182.

CARP, ROBERT A. "The Harris County Grand Jury: A Case Study." *Houston Law Review* 12 (1974): 90–120.

CLARK, LEROY D. *The Grand Jury: The Use and Abuse of Political Power.* New York: Quadrangle, 1975.

DESSION, GEORGE H. "From Indictment to Information: Implications of the Shift." *Yale Law Journal* 42 (1932): 163–193.

FINE, DAVID J. "Federal Grand Jury Investigation of Political Dissidents." *Harvard Civil Rights–Civil Liberties Law Review* 7 (1972): 432–499.

FRANKEL, MARVIN E., and NAFTALIS, GARY P. *The Grand Jury: An Institution on Trial.* New York: Hill & Wang, 1977.

KEENEY, JOHN C., and WALSH, PAUL R. "The American Bar Association's Grand Jury Principles: A Critique from a Federal Criminal Justice Perspective." *Idaho Law Review* 14 (1978): 545–590.

National Lawyers Guild, Grand Jury Defense Office. *Representation of Witnesses before Federal Grand Juries.* 2d ed. New York: Boardman, 1976, with annual supplement.

SCHNEIDER, BRUCE H. "The Grand Jury: Powers, Procedures, and Problems." *Columbia Journal of Law and Social Problems* 9 (1973): 681–730.

SCHWARTZ, HELENE E. "Demythologizing the Historic Role of the Grand Jury." *American Criminal Law Review* 10 (1972): 701–770.

Symposium. "The Grand Jury." *American Criminal Law Review* 10 (1972): 671–878.

Symposium. "The Grand Jury." *Trial* 9, no. 1 (1973): 10–28.

Symposium. "The Granting of Witness Immunity." *Journal of Criminal Law and Criminology* 67 (1976): 129–180.

YOUNGER, RICHARD D. *The People's Panel: The Grand Jury in the United States, 1634–1941.* Providence: Brown University Press, 1963.

GUILT

Introduction

The drama of guilt is enacted upon a wider stage than that set by law. Betraying a friend, lying subtly to oneself, or perhaps even telling an injurious truth to another are among the many types of conduct that may give rise to some guilt—but not necessarily to legal guilt. The subject of this article is legal guilt. But because this legal concept is arguably weighted with moral significance, the relationship between it and moral guilt is also addressed.

The concept of legal guilt has a circumscribed role, not only within life but within the law itself. Judgments of guilt are neither to be identified with, nor implied by, judgments of invalidity or judgments of civil liability. A marriage or a will may be found invalid; this implies nothing about one's guilt in failing to satisfy the conditions required for a valid marriage or will. A judgment in a civil action in favor of a plaintiff and against a defendant does not by itself, even if the defendant has been found to be at fault, imply anything about the defendant's guilt. The legal concept of guilt is restricted to the criminal law, and it is within this area of law that verdicts of guilt are rendered. Consideration of this practice of rendering verdicts is essential if one is to grasp the nature of legal guilt.

The verdict of guilt

The verdicts of guilty and not guilty are legally significant acts that are embedded in a complex rule-defined practice in which charges are leveled, hearings held, and judgments rendered. What is a verdict? As distinguished from the factual assumptions underlying it, a verdict is not a statement of fact that one is or is not guilty as charged. Verdicts themselves are neither true nor false, but valid or invalid. If challenged, they may be "set aside," but not because they are false. It is an essential characteristic of verdicts that they make things happen rather than state what is so. If a verdict is valid a person becomes, by virtue of that fact, either guilty or not guilty before the law. This concept of legal guilt is referred to here as "legally operative guilt."

A number of issues related to the practice of rendering verdicts of guilt will be considered. First, what conditions must be satisfied if a verdict is to be valid? Second, what does it mean to be guilty in the legally operative sense? Third, what presuppositions underlie the legal practice of rendering verdicts of guilt? Fourth, what functions are served by this legal practice? Finally, is there a concept of legal guilt different from that of legally operative guilt, and if so, how are the different concepts related?

Validity conditions for verdicts. There is a common understanding as to what communicative behavior in what settings constitutes a verdict. Thus, for example, persons without legal authority may state their opinions about a defendant's guilt or reach moral judgments upon the matter, but without legal authority they cannot render legal verdicts. Only when a verdict has been rendered can its validity or invalidity be considered. Verdicts must be in compliance with rules that define the conditions to be satisfied if they are to be legally operative. These rules regulate such matters as the form and substance of the verdict, the conditions in which it is arrived at, and the setting in which it is delivered. Thus, a verdict may be set aside because of uncertainty in its formulation, as when it is unclear which of two defendants charged with an offense has been found guilty; because it has been announced in the absence of the defendant; because of misconduct by those charged with rendering it; or because of a lack of evidence to support it.

The meaning of legally operative guilt. What does it mean to be guilty before the law in the legally operative sense? The verdict itself is a formal pronouncement of condemnation by an authoritative social organ. In being declared guilty, one is branded. One's status is thereby transformed into that of the legally condemned. Being thus branded, one is set apart from others and placed in a condition that requires correction. Guilt, by its very nature, calls for something to be done. Further, being legally guilty in the operative sense implies that the guilty person is properly subject to punishment. Any legal practice restricted to establishing one's liability to make reparations or restitution, or restricted to providing compensation, would differ fundamentally from the legal practice of determining guilt. None of these alternative practices necessarily implies either condemnation or the idea of conduct causing injury to society, and thus of owing society something.

Presuppositions of the practice. A number of background conditions are presupposed by a legal practice embodying the concept of guilt. These are conditions whose presence makes intelligible the practice and whose absence would reasonably cause doubt about the existence of this particular practice.

First, a verdict of guilt presupposes the belief that there is a condition of guilt logically independent of the verdict. There are facts to be determined, and they relate, of course, to a person's being in fact guilty—what shall be referred to as "factual legal guilt." As a corollary, it is also presupposed that those charged with rendering verdicts will reflect on the evidence presented to them relating to the criminal charge and will not resort to such arbitrary devices for determining guilt as flipping coins.

Second, a verdict of guilt presupposes that the person adjudged guilty is the same person charged with having committed the offense. There would be an oddity, for example, in rendering a verdict against a person who at the time of conviction, because of severe amnesia, was believed to lack any sense of continuity with the person claimed to have committed the offense. Again, society could conceivably penalize close relatives of escaped felons in order to deter escapes, but in such a practice, verdicts of guilt would not be rendered against the unfortunate relatives. Liability to suffer penalties is not equivalent to being judged guilty.

Third, the practice presupposes that individuals adjudged guilty have the capacity to comprehend the significance of the verdict and of the punishment prescribed. Verdicts have a communicative function, and among the persons addressed are those convicted of crime. Verdicts would lose their point if they were addressed to individuals who did not comprehend their significance as condemnatory and who were at a loss to understand why suffering was to be imposed upon them.

A fourth consideration, connected with this last point, is more speculative: perhaps a general commitment throughout society to the norms established by law, to the values they support, and to the legitimacy of the practice that has been established is necessary in order to determine violations and guilt. Without these elements the legal practice of finding guilt would be transformed into one in which individuals with power merely enforced their will upon others. In such circumstances the normative basis of the practice would crumble, condemnation would inevitably fall upon deaf ears, and punishment would become merely a matter of making another suffer.

Finally, the social practice embodying guilt presupposes beliefs in an established order of things, in an imbalance to that order caused by wrongdoing, in the undesirability of alienation, and in the possibility of restoration. Unlike the concepts of pollution or shame, for example, the concept of guilt arises in a world in which people conceive of guilty wrongdoing as disrupting a valued order of things. This produces instability and sets the guilty person apart from others, but nevertheless also creates a situation that may be righted by sacrificial or punitive responses. Punishment, although it has other explanations as well, in this conception is a mode of righting imbalances through exaction of a debt owed by the guilty to society. The debt, once exacted, brings about rejoinder. Given this conception, the person branded as guilty is so branded because he has set himself apart by wrongdoing. "Guilt" then adheres to the guilty like a stain and weighs like a burden, and punishment serves both to purify and relieve. Punishment as a response to guilt is thus freighted with symbolic significance, and major shifts in how it is conceived would imply transformation in the legal practice of which it and guilt are now a part.

Functions served by the practice of rendering verdicts of guilt. Practices come into existence and persist for a variety of reasons. They may also, once in existence, serve interests that were not factors leading to their genesis. The universal fascination with crime and punishment strongly suggests that deep emotional needs may be gratified by the legal practice of rendering verdicts of guilt. It seems clear that these needs are better served by the drama of a public trial and conviction than by the growing phenomenon of the plea bargain.

Determinations of guilt and the infliction of punishment upon the guilty convey as nothing else can that there are indeed norms in effect in society and that they are to be taken seriously. Guilt determinations allay anxiety through reassurance that one's social world is orderly and not chaotic: it is a structured space in which not everything is permitted, where there are limits to conduct, and where retribution may be expected if these limits are breached. The practice also provides reinforcement for one's hope that in this world one is not merely a helpless victim, for guilt is founded upon the idea that individuals are responsible for what they do. Moreover, judging persons to be legally guilty permits a societally approved deflection of aggressive impulses. Punishment, like war, may allow for aggression without our suffering guilt as a consequence.

Finally, life outside the law, when issues of guilt and innocence arise, is filled with complexity, ambiguity, and irresolution. It is a virtue of law to make matters neater than they are outside the law, and to make smooth the rough edges of human interaction. The law presents a drama in which one is either guilty or not guilty and in which the guilty meet with their just deserts. Real life is, of course, quite different, but the law with its relative definiteness and its institutionalized means of retribution at least partially satisfies our longing for an ideal world.

Legally operative guilt and factual legal guilt. Some might argue that legally operative guilt is the entire substance of the concept of legal guilt, for, after all, what is more closely connected with legal guilt than liability to punishment? On the other hand, jurors are asked to consider whether a person is in fact guilty before they reach a verdict of guilt. What sometimes justifies setting aside a verdict is a judgment that the evidence of guilt—factual legal guilt— is insufficient to justify the verdict. This seems to establish that we possess a concept of legal guilt which is logically independent of a verdict of guilt, for it is a concept that guides those charged with reaching a verdict. Thus, it would seem wise to acknowledge the presence of two legal concepts of guilt and to address oneself to their relationship.

Factual legal guilt

We have seen that the norms governing the practice of rendering verdicts require that those charged with the responsibility consider the evidence relevant to factual legal guilt. In our own system of criminal law a verdict of guilt is to be returned only if it is believed beyond a reasonable doubt that the defendant is indeed guilty. Although the verdict is not a statement of fact, it presupposes beliefs about the facts. This brings us to a consideration of the nature of factual legal guilt. When is a person guilty in this sense?

First, conduct is normally a prerequisite for legal guilt. This means that a person must actually commit a certain act. It is not enough for him to merely think of doing it, nor is it enough for him simply to have a status of a certain kind, such as being a member of a certain race. Second, the conduct must normally be conscious. Individuals are not guilty for what they do while asleep. Third, there must be legal wrongdoing. Even the most egregious moral wrong does not occasion legal guilt unless the wrong is also a legal one. Fourth, one must have the capacity to appreciate the significance of the norms applicable to one. Animals and infants, for example, do not have the ability to experience guilt. Finally, it is normally a prerequisite for legal guilt that there be conscious fault or culpability with respect to wrongdoing, that is, there must be a "guilty mind" (mens rea). Whatever defeats one's fair opportunity to behave otherwise than he did—typically some reasonable ignorance of fact or limitation on his freedom of action—may excuse him.

These conditions are common to most legal systems. But how do they relate to the concept of legal guilt? Are there limitations on what legal systems can do with regard to specifying conditions for guilt? Here there are logical and, arguably, moral constraints on legal practice. The law could, imaginably, impose penalties upon individuals merely because of their race. In such a case, however, it would be odd to describe the defendant as having been found guilty. Some of the above criteria, then, may be essentially connected with the concept of legal guilt, in that failure to satisfy them would imply that the concept had no application.

The connection that factual legal guilt has with our moral conceptions of guilt is less clear: moral fault is not essential for legal guilt. Nevertheless, there may be a connection between legal guilt and moral fault that is more than merely accidental. As discussed above, the legal practice of rendering verdicts of guilt has special significance. Individuals who are guilty are viewed as justifiably condemned and as having set themselves apart from the community by disregarding its basic values. To this extent, a number of the conditions for being morally guilty—among them conditions related to a fair opportunity to behave otherwise than one did—are presuppositions of legal guilt as well. On this view, a system that allowed generally for a finding of guilt in conflict with certain moral constraints would be one that used existing institutions of the criminal law in a way fundamentally at odds with certain of its basic presuppositions. Prevention and social control would replace crime and punishment as these are now understood. Even today, when legal doctrine permits conviction of those without fault, it seems that something on the order of a lie is being perpetrated. This is because such convictions create the false impression that the guilty are insufficiently committed to the community's norms, whereas in the case of those not proved to be at fault this has not been established.

Moral and legal guilt

How are these concepts related beyond what has been suggested above? There can, of course, be moral guilt without legal guilt, legal guilt without moral guilt, and a range of instances in which the two overlap. Earlier, there were listed a number of examples of what might occasion moral guilt without legal guilt. To this list might be added those cases where compliance with evil laws creates moral guilt. Since it is sometimes morally right to violate an iniquitous law, it follows that there may be legal guilt without moral guilt. From a consideration of crimes such as murder, where generally those factually guilty are morally guilty as well, it is evident that the two overlap.

Moral and legal guilt may differ significantly. There is no concept in morality comparable to legally operative guilt; one is never morally guilty merely by virtue of being judged as such. Moral guilt is always factual guilt. Further, the law may specify in a relatively arbitrary way the norms that regulate conduct and the circumstances under which violation of these norms incurs guilt. But for moral guilt the norms and the conditions to be satisfied for incurring guilt are entirely immune from deliberate human modification.

Moreover, legal guilt is restricted to those situations in which a wrong is done to society. It is not enough that someone's personal rights have been violated. For the most part, however, moral wrongs that establish guilt arise in situations where another's rights have been violated; the guilt is not necessarily done to the society that conceives itself as threatened by the conduct. Thus, those in a position to condemn or forgive are those whose rights have been violated, and not some party that stands in an institutionally defined relationship to the wronged party.

Further, in being morally guilty there is no implication of being justifiably liable to punishment. There may be entitlement to criticize and to be resentful or indignant, but in a variety of situations where moral guilt arises, either the wrong done is not appropriately viewed as punishable, or the relationship (for example, between friends) is in no way seen as righted by punishment. What is essential for restoration in the moral sphere is such emotions and attitudes as guilt, contrition, and repentance. In addition, the objects of moral guilt differ from those generally of concern to the law. Maxims such as "the law aims at a minimum; morality at a maximum" and "the law is concerned with external conduct; morality with internal conduct" draw attention to the different emphases of law and morality. Finally, moral guilt may remain forever in doubt once all the facts are in. Moral reflection allows for the judgment that a person is and yet is not guilty; this depends on one's perspective, which is not precisely defined by any authoritative pronouncement. Thus, there is no need for moral reflection ever to come to rest.

The sense of guilt

What is the sense of guilt, and how is it related, if at all, to law? Guilt is a human sentiment that manifests itself in our inhibition from doing what we believe to be wrong and in our feeling guilty when we do what we believe to be wrong. Thus, it operates both in a forward- and a backward-looking manner. In this respect it resembles conscience, which "doth make cowards of us all" and which, when we disobey its dictates, makes us conscience-stricken. Guilt is the feeling most closely connected with wrongdoing, taking as its object belief in wrongdoing. What, more precisely, is it to feel guilt?

A person who feels guilt holds certain beliefs and is disposed to feel and act in certain specific ways. First, one is attached to avoiding wrong, and the mere fact that one has done wrong causes a feeling of pain. Second, just as there is a special satisfaction connected with thinking of oneself as the creator of what is valuable, so there is a special dissatisfaction that derives from the realization that one has been responsible for wrongdoing. This is partly because one sees oneself as a destroyer of value. Third, in feeling guilt one turns on oneself the criticism and hostility which, if another had acted in the same way, would have been directed at that person. Fourth, there is a sense of unease caused by one's feeling alienated from those to whom one is attached. Finally, the sense of unpleasantness associated with guilt is connected with carrying a burden from which one longs to be relieved. One feels obliged to confess, to make amends, to repair, and to restore. A further sense of unpleasantness is caused by one's resistance to do these things, owing to fear and perhaps pride, and the unease experienced until they are done.

How, if at all, is the human disposition to feel guilt related to the legal practice, described above? Individuals are often adjudged guilty and do not feel guilt. They may believe themselves innocent of the charge; they may believe that, although legally wrong, what they did was morally obligatory; or they may not have the requisite degree of internalization with regard to the law generally or to a particular law. Although all this is possible and no doubt even common, vulnerability to the feeling of guilt may be connected with the legal practice embodying the concept of guilt. For, as has been claimed, among the practice's presuppositions is a general acceptance of the authority of society's norms and of the institutions applying them. This seems to imply that individuals generally are liable, when violating the norms, to having their sense of guilt activated. If it were otherwise, condemnation and punishment would no longer have the significance that they do.

The future of guilt

From Ezekiel we learn:

The soul that sins shall die. The son shall not suffer for the iniquity of the father, nor the father suffer for the iniquity of the son; the righteousness of the righteous shall be upon himself, and the wickedness of the wicked shall be upon himself [18:20].

These words mark a dramatic change in prior practices related to guilt; it was individualized. With Christianity another dramatic change slowly came about: the inner life of the moral agent assumed an importance it earlier did not have. Our own age may now be witness to a drama of equal significance. Through a confluence of factors—philosophical determinism, the development of the behavioral sciences, the ideology of sickness and therapy, and utilitarianism—the very foundations of the concept of legal guilt have been placed in question.

The assault on guilt has moved along a number of parallel fronts. There are those who claim that the presuppositions upon which guilt depends are not in fact valid. Here one encounters either metaphysical lines of argument, or more empirically grounded theories asserting the existence of causative factors in every case that should exempt the wrongdoer from blame. This line of argumentation is evident in the modern tendency to see antisocial conduct as a matter for therapy, not punishment. Moreover, even if one were to acknowledge the reality of the conditions required for the appropriate application of the concept of guilt, it is sometimes claimed that we cannot have reasonable grounds for believing that these conditions are ever present. Skepticism of this kind may incline its adherents to urge foregoing concern with culpability at the time of the offense charged. Attention should focus rather upon what was in fact done—something observable—and, once this is determined, one should then concentrate on what would be the best disposition of the responsible party, given that party's condition at the time of trial. The orientation is almost entirely toward the future and away from the past.

Finally, some are prepared to say that the conditions

for guilt are valid, that we can know them, and yet that it is a mistake to continue the practice. Guilt and punishment are viewed by some as fundamentally irrational modes of viewing human conduct—relics from a superstitious past in which suffering is seen as magically erasing evil. From this perspective it is never a former evil that justifies infliction of present pain, only a future good to be realized.

These, then, are some of the strains of discontent with guilt. It is not always evident from a particular critique precisely what the implications are for customary ways of proceeding. For example, philosophical determinists do not customarily urge abandoning the criminal law. It remains unclear, too, whether the law, an institution intertwined so closely with our moral way of looking at things, could be fundamentally changed without a corresponding transformation in moral conceptions and in such moral feelings as guilt and indignation. Nonetheless, the above critiques may gradually modify morality as we have known it, and guilt may conceivably appear as strange to future generations as the world against which Ezekiel was rebelling appears to us.

Powerful assaults have been mounted upon guilt and punishment. They have not gone unanswered, and have in fact mobilized tenacious defenses of customary ways of thinking about human beings. Few ages in history have spoken to the issue of human responsibility with the power and force of our own. Some have insisted that humans are basically free, that they often choose their own enslavement, and that by taking their past wrongs seriously they can redeem themselves. For those of this persuasion the law, with all its imperfections, embodies recognition of the truth of human responsibility and daily reenacts the drama of human waywardness, of wrongdoing, and of its being righted.

HERBERT MORRIS

See also both articles under CRIME; EXCUSE: THEORY; JUSTIFICATION: THEORY; MENS REA; PUNISHMENT; *both articles under* STRICT LIABILITY; VICARIOUS LIABILITY.

BIBLIOGRAPHY

BRETT, PETER. *An Inquiry into Criminal Guilt.* London: Sweet & Maxwell, 1963.

DURKHEIM, EMILE. *The Division of Labor in Society.* Translated by George Simpson. New York: Free Press, 1947.

FEINBERG, JOEL. *Doing and Deserving: Essays in the Theory of Responsibility.* Princeton, N.J.: Princeton University Press, 1970.

FREUD, SIGMUND, *Civilization and Its Discontents* (1930). Translated by James Strachey. London: Hogarth Press, 1961.

HART, H. L. A. *The Concept of Law.* Oxford: Clarendon Press, 1961.

————. *Punishment and Responsibility: Essays in the Philosophy of Law.* Oxford: Clarendon Press, 1968.

LEWIS, H. D.; HARVEY, J. W.; and PAUL, G. A. "The Problem of Guilt" (Symposium). *Proceedings of the Aristotelian Society,* supp. vol. 21 (1947): 175–218.

MOBERLY, WALTER HAMILTON. *The Ethics of Punishment.* London: Faber & Faber, 1968.

MORRIS, HERBERT. *On Guilt and Innocence: Essays in Legal Philosophy and Moral Psychology.* Berkeley: University of California Press, 1976.

NIETZSCHE, FRIEDRICH. "On the Genealogy of Morals." *Basic Writings of Nietzsche.* Translated by Walter Kaufmann. New York: Random House, 1968.

PIERS, GERHARDT, and SINGER, MILTON B. *Shame and Guilt: A Psychoanalytic and a Cultural Study.* New York: Norton, 1971.

RAWLS, JOHN. *A Theory of Justice.* Cambridge, Mass.: Harvard University Press, Belknap Press, 1971.

RICOEUR, PAUL. *The Symbolism of Evil.* New York: Harper & Row, 1967.

ROSS, ALF. *On Guilt, Responsibility, and Punishment.* London: Stevens, 1975.

WOOTTON, BARBARA. *Crime and the Criminal Law.* London: Stevens, 1963.

GUILTY MIND

See CRIME: DEFINITION OF CRIME; *articles under* EXCUSE; GUILT; MENS REA; *both articles under* STRICT LIABILITY.

GUILTY PLEA

The article on ACCEPTING THE PLEA *considers the procedures followed at arraignment to ensure that the defendant's plea of guilty is voluntary and knowing and supported by a factual basis. The* PLEA BARGAINING *article, by contrast, describes current plea negotiation practices, involving prosecution or court tender of concessions to the defendant in an effort to induce him to plead guilty, and assesses their impact upon the criminal justice process.*

1. ACCEPTING THE PLEA Ronald N. Boyce
2. PLEA BARGAINING Albert W. Alschuler

1.
ACCEPTING THE PLEA

A large portion of the public harbors a mistaken assumption that criminal cases are resolved by attorneys battling over evidence and legal issues and a jury determining the guilt or innocence of the accused. In reality, depending on the jurisdiction and the crime charged, between 70 percent and 90 percent of serious criminal cases are resolved by pleas of guilty. The percentage may even be higher for petty offenses. In the majority of cases, the guilty plea process is the only procedure that focuses judicial attention on whether the accused is acting properly in conceding guilt. It may be the only time when a relatively unbiased evaluation is made as to whether an accused's conduct is criminally culpable. Consequently, the guilty plea process is one of the most significant procedures in the administration of criminal justice in the United States.

The adjudication of criminal guilt by the acceptance of a plea of guilty has been a part of the Anglo-American judicial system since the early common-law courts and has been readily accepted in the American judicial system (Alschuler). The number of criminal cases resolved by pleas of guilty has substantially increased over the years, and the guilty plea is now the most frequent method of determining guilt.

Arraignment

The arraignment is the beginning of the plea process. A defendant is formally arraigned when he is brought before a judicial officer having jurisdiction over the offense, advised of the charges against him, and called upon to plead (Fed. R. Crim. P. 10; *Garland v. Washington,* 232 U.S. 642 (1914)). At the point of arraignment, a defendant must assess whether he should pursue a trial or acknowledge guilt. Because special motions may be made or other relief requested during the arraignment process, it constitutes a critical stage in a criminal case (*Hamilton v. Alabama,* 368 U.S. 52 (1961)). Consequently, there are imposed on the guilty plea process constitutional requirements that must be complied with before such a plea may be accepted.

The plea

Depending upon the jurisdiction, a defendant may have several plea alternatives. He may plead not guilty, thereby forcing the prosecution to establish his guilt at trial. A plea of guilty, on the other hand, usually obviates any further need for the prosecution to offer evidence of the defendant's guilt and is itself a conviction sufficient for a judgment of guilt (*Kercheval v. United States,* 274 U.S. 220 (1927)).

In some jurisdictions an accused may plead not guilty by reason of insanity or mental illness (Cal. Penal Code § 1016 (1970)). In some jurisdictions such a plea may admit the commission of the offense but assert lack of culpability because of insanity or mental illness (*People v. Stewart*, 89 Cal. App. 3d 992, 153 Cal. Rptr. 242 (1979)). In other jurisdictions a plea of insanity is merely notice of the defense and admits nothing.

In most jurisdictions a defendant may also, under certain circumstances, enter a plea of nolo contendere, or no contest, to the charges against him (Fed. R. Crim. P. 11; Cal. Penal Code § 1016 (1970); Tex. Code Crim. P. § 27.02 (1980–1981 Supp.)). Such a plea cannot usually be entered without the court's approval. For example, Rule 11 of the Federal Rules of Criminal Procedure provides that a plea of nolo contendere may be made "only with consent of the court" and "only after consideration of the views of the parties and the interest of the public in the effective administration of justice." Similar provisions are found in state codes that authorize pleas of nolo contendere (Ariz. R. Crim. P. 17.1c (1981); Utah Code Ann. § 77-13-3 (1981 Supp.)). The main benefit to an accused in making such a plea may be psychological; he can then assert in public that such a plea was the expedient way of avoiding a long, complex, and expensive court battle. However, a plea of nolo contendere usually has the same legal effect as a plea of guilty. A conviction may be entered on such a plea and the defendant subjected to the same punishment as if he had pleaded guilty. In some jurisdictions a plea of nolo contendere is beneficial in that it may not be used as evidence of liability against the defendant in a subsequent civil action arising from the same facts (*United States v. Dorman*, 496 F.2d 438 (4th Cir. 1974)).

In a few jurisdictions a defendant may enter a "conditional plea of guilty." This plea acknowledges his guilt of the underlying substantive crime but preserves for final resolution, in an appellate court, matters of defense that would preclude a conviction (Wis. Stat. Ann. § 971.31(10) (1971)). In cases involving such a plea, issues as to the legality of a search or seizure, confession, or other contentions of a constitutional nature are reserved (Note, 1980a; *Lefkowitz v. Newsome*, 420 U.S. 283 (1975)). In most jurisdictions, however, a plea of guilty precludes later raising the constitutionality of any matter of evidence that might have been a defense if the defendant had elected to go to trial (*McMann v. Richardson*, 397 U.S. 759 (1970)).

Constitutional requirements for a guilty plea

The defendant facing a choice of plea must make his judgment in light of the charge, the facts and evidence relating to the case, and the legal principles that determine culpability. This decision is generally beyond the experience and expertise of lay persons; the economic and psychological impact of being charged with a crime can preclude reasoned judgment from even the most sophisticated defendants. The plea process involves critical considerations that require prudent guidance, assessment, and evaluation. In order to ensure that a plea of guilty is properly accepted, the United States Constitution requires specific procedures to be either followed or voluntarily and intelligently waived.

Right to counsel. Before entering a plea, the defendant generally needs the advice of counsel, to which he is constitutionally entitled (*Hamilton*). Although a defendant in a criminal case has a right of self-representation, courts are reluctant to allow him to waive the right to counsel and enter a plea of guilty, since it is recognized that such a judgment requires careful reflection and the evaluation of many factors. Most courts have required that in order for an accused to make valid waiver of counsel, he must at least be aware of his right to an attorney, at no cost to himself if he cannot afford one, and he must have some appreciation of the benefits of being represented by an attorney (*Gregory v. State*, 550 P.2d 374 (Alaska 1976); *Von Moltke v. Gillies*, 332 U.S. 708, 724 (1948)). A waiver of counsel will not be implied from the silence of a defendant, and an indigent must understand that he is entitled to representation by counsel even though he cannot afford to employ counsel (Fed. R. Crim. P. 11(c)(2)).

The role of defense counsel in the plea process is of the utmost significance. Although the decision to plead guilty must be the defendant's, when he acts upon the advice of reasonably competent counsel his plea is not likely to be subject to challenge on the basis of some constitutional deficiency. Thus, where a defendant acted on the advice of counsel and pleaded guilty to a murder charge in order to avoid the possibility of receiving a death sentence after a jury trial, the plea was upheld even though the fact that he could receive the death penalty only if he went to trial placed some compulsion upon the defendant to plead guilty (*Brady v. United States*, 397 U.S. 742 (1970)).

During the course of plea bargaining, a prosecutor may put strong pressure on a defendant to plead guilty. If the defendant is represented by competent counsel who can advise him as to the wisdom of accepting or rejecting such a plea offer, the presence of prosecutorial pressure does not necessarily make the plea process unconstitutional (*Bordenkircher v.*

Hayes, 434 U.S. 357 (1978)). Where counsel has fully advised a defendant as to the elements of an offense and what is admitted by pleading guilty, a subsequent voluntary plea of guilty may be constitutionally accepted as knowingly made even though during the plea process the court did not fully explore the defendant's understanding of the offense (*Henderson v. Morgan*, 426 U.S. 637 (1976)). Of course, reasonably competent counsel means counsel sufficiently acquainted with the relevant facts and law that he can provide prudent and informed advice, making possible an intelligent plea judgment by the defendant.

Understanding the consequences of the plea. When a defendant pleads guilty he usually gives up all the benefits that would be available to him if, instead, he were to contest the charges and go to trial. Is a guilty plea voluntarily made if a defendant does not realize the existing alternatives? The United States Supreme Court has determined that due process of law requires that a defendant be aware of the constitutional rights he is giving up before a conclusion can be made that he has voluntarily pleaded guilty. In *Boykin v. Alabama*, 395 U.S. 238 (1969), the Supreme Court required that before a guilty plea can be constitutionally accepted, the accused must be aware of three basic rights forfeited by such a plea: his privilege against self-incrimination, his right to trial by jury, and his right to confront his accusers. A waiver of these rights will not be presumed from the accused's silence (*Boykin*, 243).

Determining the voluntariness of the plea. A plea of guilty is constitutionally adequate only if it is voluntarily made, and the *Boykin* trilogy of advice is in part designed to ensure that when this plea is made, it is voluntary. A plea of guilty is involuntary if it is the product of incomprehension, terror, improper inducements, or threats (*Boykin*). The Supreme Court has determined that a guilty plea is improper if it is based on threats or false promises made by the prosecutor (*Machibroda v. United States*, 368 U.S. 487 (1962)). A guilty plea induced by an unkept promise of the prosecutor is involuntary (*Santobello v. New York*, 404 U.S. 257 (1971)), as is one induced by the prosecutor through a misrepresentation of the law (*Von Moltke*). A plea of guilty is not considered involuntary simply because it is entered to avoid the death penalty or because of pressure exerted by the prosecutor during plea bargaining, especially if the plea is based upon competent assessment by defense counsel of the facts and law applicable to the case (*Brady; Bordenkircher*). A plea of guilty may be voluntary even though the defendant continues to claim his innocence, if the plea is otherwise freely entered and insisted upon by the defendant (*North Carolina v. Alford*, 400 U.S. 25 (1970)).

A guilty plea is not voluntary if the defendant is mentally ill, under the influence of drugs or intoxicants, or misinformed to the extent that he cannot comprehend the consequences of his plea. No specific litany of requirements surrounds a plea of guilty beyond those in *Boykin*; however, most courts now make an extended inquiry to ensure that a plea of guilty is free of improper influences. Where a careful, on-the-record inquiry is made by the judge as to the voluntariness of the plea, it is less likely to be successfully challenged later (*Fontaine v. United States*, 411 U.S. 213 (1973)).

The accuracy of the plea. Before a plea of guilty can be accepted as constitutionally proper, the defendant must understand what he is admitting. If he is not aware of what conduct is required to constitute the offense with which he is charged, a plea of guilty is not properly made (*Henderson*). Consequently, to ensure that a plea is intelligently made and constitutionally valid, the judge should explain to the defendant the nature of the offense with which he is charged. When the defendant subsequently enters a plea of guilty, it is unlikely that he can afterward assert his ignorance of the standards required for criminal guilt of the offense charged.

There is no constitutional requirement that the record of a guilty plea contain an admission from a defendant of the facts constituting the offense. A defendant may still plead guilty to an offense of which he contends he is innocent and may do so to escape a more serious penalty (*Alford*), but the Supreme Court approved such a practice only where the record showed that the prosecution had a basis in fact for the charge and where the defendant was aware of what he was doing in making his plea of guilty.

Statutory standards for a guilty plea

The decisions of the Supreme Court specifying the constitutional standards for accepting guilty pleas are not comprehensive but merely sketch the broad parameters of the requirements of due process. However, most jurisdictions have by statute, rule, or court decision particularized the requirements for accepting a guilty plea. These requirements often exceed those of the Supreme Court for a constitutionally valid guilty plea.

Rule 11 of the Federal Rules of Criminal Procedure has been the model for several states as well as the federal standard governing the guilty plea process. According to this model, before a plea of guilty or nolo contendere may be accepted in most jurisdictions, the defendant must be advised by the court of the nature of the charge; of the minimum and maximum possible penalty; and of his right to court-appointed counsel, to plead not guilty, to undergo a jury trial, and to confront and cross-examine witnesses against him. The court is required to address the defendant in open court to determine that the "plea is voluntary and not the result of force or threats or of promise apart from a plea agreement" (Fed. R. Crim. P. 11(d)). The court must also determine that there is a factual basis for a plea of guilty (Fed. R. Crim. P. 11(f); *United States v. Montoya-Camacho*, 644 F.2d 480 (5th Cir. 1981)).

Plea bargaining, a common practice in the American criminal justice system, is lawful and not unconstitutional (*Bordenkircher*). However, a plea based on a plea bargain may be challenged if it was not made voluntarily and with understanding or if the bargain was not kept. Consequently, most jurisdictions now require that the fact and substance of any plea bargaining be stated before a plea is accepted, so as to make certain all parties are in agreement concerning the nature of the bargain (Fed. R. Crim. P. 11(e)(2)). The court may usually accept or reject the bargain. If it is rejected, the defendant's plea may be withdrawn (Fed. R. Crim. P. 11(e)(4)). In some jurisdictions, after the parties have reached a plea agreement, they may approach the judge for tentative approval. At the time of the arraignment and plea, the court may determine that the agreement should not be accepted. In this case, the court, if it has previously indicated approval of the bargain, must allow withdrawal of any plea made by the defendant based on the prior court approval (Ill. Ann. Stat. ch. 110A, § 402 (1976); Utah Code Ann. § 77-35-11 (1981 Supp.)). However, if the prosecutor complies with a bargain by recommending a sentence, the failure of the judge to give such a sentence is not a broken bargain.

The failure to follow statutes or rules governing the acceptance of a guilty plea will generally render the plea subject to challenge on appeal or by collateral process (*McCarthy v. United States*, 394 U.S. 459 (1969)). However, a minor or technical failure to comply with a statute or rule that is not prejudicial to a defendant will not invalidate an otherwise voluntary plea (*United States v. Timmreck*, 441 U.S. 780 (1979)).

Constitutional standards concerning guilty pleas and those contained in statutes and rules do not generally distinguish between felonies and misdemeanors; the same substantive standards are applicable to each class of crime, although the plea process may be less formal in misdemeanor cases (*Mills v. Municipal Court*, 10 Cal. 3d 288, 515 P.2d 273 (1973)). In practice, misdemeanor guilty pleas are often accepted through a less exacting process than that applied in felony cases.

In some jurisdictions the court can refuse a plea of guilty that it believes to be imprudent or contrary to the defendant's best interests. However, the court as a rule may not arbitrarily reject a plea bargain or guilty plea.

Withdrawal of a plea

Once a guilty plea has been accepted, it may still be withdrawn under some circumstances. In some jurisdictions a plea may be withdrawn only prior to sentencing; in others, it may be withdrawn even after judgment (Fed. R. Crim. P. 32(d)). In some jurisdictions, before sentencing, a guilty plea may be withdrawn for any just reason the trial judge believes proper. Withdrawal of a plea is within the court's discretion, and the court's judgment is set aside on appeal only for an abuse of discretion (*State v. Ellison*, 111 Ariz. 167, 526 P.2d 706 (1974); *State v. Haynie*, 607 P.2d 1128 (Mont. 1980)). After sentencing, most jurisdictions will allow a plea to be set aside only upon the defendant showing some special justification, such as a serious legal deficiency in making the plea.

Conclusion

The guilty plea process is less formal than a trial, but it involves compliance with significant constitutional, statutory, and rule provisions. Essentially it is designed to ensure that the plea is the product of a defendant's voluntary choice and is based on sound, rational judgment.

RONALD N. BOYCE

See also ARRAIGNMENT; *both articles under* COUNSEL; GUILTY PLEA: PLEA BARGAINING.

BIBLIOGRAPHY

ALSCHULER, ALBERT W. "Plea Bargaining and Its History." *Columbia Law Review* 79 (1979): 1–43.
American Bar Association. *Standards for Criminal Justice*. 2d ed. 4 vols. Prepared with the assistance of the American Bar Foundation. Boston: Little, Brown, 1980.
BOND, JAMES EDWARD. *Plea Bargaining and Guilty Pleas*. New York: Boardman, 1975.
COOK, JOSEPH G. *Constitutional Rights of the Accused: Pre-trial Rights*. Rochester, N.Y.: Lawyers Co-operative, 1972.

KAMISAR, YALE; LAFAVE, WAYNE R.; and ISRAEL, JEROLD H. *Modern Criminal Procedure: Cases, Comments, and Questions.* Supplement to 4th ed. St. Paul: West, 1980.

MOORE, JAMES WILLIAM. *Moore's Federal Practice.* 2d ed. Albany: Bender, 1980.

Note. "Conditional Guilty Pleas." *Harvard Law Review* 93 (1980a): 564–585.

Note. "Rule 11 of the Federal Rules of Criminal Procedure: The Case for Strict Compliance after *United States v. Dayton.*" *Virginia Law Review* 66 (1980b): 1169–1182.

Note. "Withdrawal of Guilty Pleas under Rule 32(d)." *Yale Law Journal* 64 (1955): 590–599.

SALTZBURG, STEPHEN A. "Pleas of Guilty and the Loss of Constitutional Rights: The Current Price of Pleading Guilty." *Michigan Law Review* 76 (1978): 1265–1341.

TORCIA, CHARLES E. *Wharton's Criminal Procedure*, vol. 2. 12th ed. Rochester, N.Y.: Lawyers Co-operative, 1975.

WHITEBREAD, CHARLES H. *Criminal Procedure: An Analysis of Constitutional Cases and Concepts.* Mineola, N.Y.: Foundation Press, 1980.

2.

PLEA BARGAINING

Definition and types of bargaining

The term *plea bargaining* is sometimes used informally to refer to every form of discussion between the prosecution and defense in a criminal case that might lead to disposition of the case without trial or to any sort of concession on the part of the defendant. For example, when a prosecutor offers favorable treatment to a defendant in exchange for his testimony against others, he may refer to this activity as plea bargaining; and a criminal defense attorney who approaches a prosecutor to seek a dismissal of the charges against his client may similarly refer to this activity as plea bargaining. Nevertheless, these usages seem imprecise, and the term is usually employed more narrowly. An unqualified dismissal of criminal charges involves neither a plea by the defendant nor an exchange, and although bargaining for testimony commonly will lead to an exchange, this exchange does not necessarily require the entry of a plea of guilty. As the language itself suggests, *plea bargaining* probably can best be defined as the exchange of any actual or apparent concession for a plea of guilty.

Under this definition, plea bargaining does not include pretrial diversion. Although diversion is often the result of a bargaining process and may be granted in exchange for concessions by a defendant (for example, his agreement to participate in a specified treatment program), it does not lead to the defendant's conviction on a plea of guilty. Instead, if the defendant complies with the required conditions, the charges against him are dismissed, and his case is thus "diverted" from any courtroom determination of guilt or innocence either by guilty plea or by trial.

It is common to distinguish between "express" and "implicit" plea bargaining. Express bargaining occurs when a defendant or his representative negotiates directly with a prosecutor, a trial judge, or very rarely some other official concerning the benefits that may follow his entry of a plea of guilty. Implicit bargaining, by contrast, occurs without face-to-face negotiations. Officials establish a pattern of treating defendants who plead guilty more leniently than those who exercise the right to trial, and individual defendants therefore may come to expect that the entry of guilty pleas will be rewarded. Of course, both implicit and explicit bargaining may influence a defendant to plead guilty in a single case.

The concessions that officials may offer for a plea of guilty are almost unlimited. Typically, a prosecutor may agree to reduce a single charge against a defendant to a less serious offense (perhaps from first-degree murder to manslaughter), to reduce the number of charges against a defendant (possibly dismissing four or five bad-check charges if the defendant pleads guilty to one), or to recommend a particular sentence to the court (one that the defendant may regard as more lenient than the sentence likely to be imposed after conviction at trial). Bargaining for a reduction in either the number or severity of criminal charges is commonly referred to as *charge bargaining*. Bargaining for a favorable prosecutorial sentence recommendation (or bargaining directly with a trial judge for a favorable sentence) is referred to as *sentence bargaining*. In cases of sentence bargaining, trial judges in a substantial number of jurisdictions either must impose sentences no more severe than those recommended by prosecutors or must afford defendants an opportunity to withdraw their guilty pleas. Even when trial judges are legally free to depart from bargained prosecutorial sentence recommendations, they tend to do so infrequently.

Although charge bargaining and sentence bargaining are the most common forms of plea bargaining, they are not the only ones. In exchange for a plea of guilty, a prosecutor may agree to provide leniency to a defendant's accomplices, withhold damaging information from the court, influence the date of a defendant's sentencing, arrange for a defendant to be sent to a particular correctional institution, or request that a defendant receive credit on his sentence for time served in jail awaiting trial. He may also agree to support a defendant's application for parole, attempt to have charges in other jurisdictions dismissed, arrange for sentencing in a particular court or by a particular judge, provide immunity for crimes not yet charged, or simply remain silent when his recommendation otherwise might be unfavorable.

The development of plea bargaining

A formal in-court acknowledgment of guilt has been regarded as a sufficient basis for criminal conviction from the earliest days of the common law. In this respect, common-law nations have departed from both ancient Roman law and the modern law of many jurisdictions on the Continent. In serious cases, most continental jurisdictions do not treat any form of confession as an adequate basis for dispensing with trial. When compared to the very long Anglo-American history of guilty pleas, however, the history of plea bargaining seems reasonably short.

In one sense, today's practice of plea bargaining does have "ancient antecedents" (Comment). The criminal justice system has long been characterized by broad discretion and has long rewarded some forms of cooperation by defendants—most notably, cooperation in procuring the conviction of other alleged offenders. Nevertheless, until well into the nineteenth century, Anglo-American courts seemed to discourage guilty pleas more than they encouraged them. Judges often advised defendants who offered to plead guilty to reconsider their decisions, and guilty pleas apparently accounted for a relatively small minority of convictions.

Plea bargaining emerged as a significant practice only after the American Civil War. It apparently became common at the turn of the twentieth century, a time when criminal trial courts were largely ignored by appellate courts, bar associations, and legal scholars. The practice first attracted significant attention as a result of crime commission studies conducted in the 1920s.

Among the historical developments that may have contributed to the growth of plea bargaining were (1) the increasing complexity of the trial process (which may have led to the greater use of nontrial procedures both for economic reasons and because officials sought to avoid the "technicalities" of trial); (2) expansion of the substantive criminal law (particularly the enactment of liquor-prohibition statutes); (3) increasing crime rates; (4) the frequent political corruption of urban criminal courts at and after the turn of the twentieth century; and (5) the greater use of professionals in the administration of criminal justice

(police, prosecution, and defense). Whatever the causes, it is commonly estimated that about 90 percent of all criminal convictions in the United States are by guilty plea rather than by trial (Alschuler, 1979).

A comparative perspective

Plea bargaining is not only a relatively recent development but also a peculiarly Anglo-American phenomenon. Despite occasional denials, there is ample evidence that plea bargaining does occur in England and most other nations in the British Commonwealth. The criminal procedure of most nations of the world, however, is patterned after that of continental Europe, and plea bargaining in any explicit form seems unknown in continental systems. Not only is the plea of guilty unrecognized in serious cases so that some sort of trial must occur even when a defendant confesses, but continental prosecutors and judges apparently do not promise or negotiate rewards for in-court confessions.

Some American scholars have suggested that continental judges do reward confessions informally by imposing less severe sentences when defendants acknowledge their guilt. Other scholars, however, have denied that any systematic "implicit bargaining" occurs (cf. Goldstein and Marcus; Langbein). Even if some implicit bargaining does occur on the Continent, it does not produce in-court confessions at nearly the same rate that plea bargaining produces guilty pleas in America. This fact seems ironic in view of the much greater doctrinal emphasis on the privilege against self-incrimination in America.

Operation of the plea bargaining system

As the following remarks may suggest, the day-to-day operation of the plea bargaining system cannot be neatly captured in a simple description.

In attending academic conferences on plea bargaining, I have been struck by the extent to which people who should understand this subject (and who, indeed, have written books about it) sound like the blind men describing the elephant. One scholar may begin by declaring that plea bargaining usually produces the same result as trial. When two experienced lawyers can use their expertise to predict the probable outcome of a trial, they are very likely to agree; and once this happens, there is no longer any need for the trial to be held. Another scholar then suggests that trial is often a capricious process whose results cannot be predicted. When a case goes to trial one either "wins big" or "loses big." The goal of plea bargaining is not to produce the same result as trial but to "vector" the risks of litigation and to reach a more sensible middle ground. Still another academic then contends that the object of plea bargaining is neither to produce the same results as trial nor to vector the risks of litigation. The goal is to escape altogether the irrationalities of an overly legalized trial system and . . . to achieve "substantive justice" without regard to technicalities. Then an older lawyer who has bargained more guilty pleas than everyone else in the room proclaims that all of this misses the point. A lawyer's object in plea bargaining is to take as much as possible from the other side by threat, bluster, charm, bluff, campaign contributions, personal appeals, friendship, or whatever else works. Finally some cynic . . . says that sometimes the dominant motivation is for lazy lawyers and judges to take the money and go home early. Of course, to some extent, all of these things are happening at the same time. The disagreement, if not wholly illusory, merely concerns the relative size of the trunk, tail, legs, ears, and side [Alschuler, 1981, p. 691 n. 103].

In view of the different forms that plea bargaining may take and the different considerations that may influence it, the efforts of some scholars to set forth mathematical and symbolic models of the plea negotiation process usually seem artificial to practicing lawyers. A few of the major operation issues, however, are discussed below.

The "sentence differential." Defendants in America plead guilty in overwhelming numbers partly because they believe that this action is likely to lead to more favorable treatment than conviction at trial. Whether this perception is justified is a matter of some controversy. Most empirical studies, such as that by Beverly Blair Cook, have concluded that a defendant's choice of plea is likely to make a substantial difference in his sentence. Nevertheless, a few studies, among them that by William Rhodes, have concluded that, at least in some crime categories, guilty pleas are not substantially rewarded.

Certainly, most prosecutors and defense attorneys can describe individual cases in which defendants rejected plea bargaining offers and then were sentenced much more severely after their convictions at trial. In *Bordenkircher v. Hayes*, 434 U.S. 357 (1978), for example, the United States Supreme Court upheld the conviction and sentence of a defendant who had rejected a prosecutor's offer to recommend a five-year sentence in exchange for a plea of guilty. The defendant then was charged by the prosecutor as a habitual offender and was sentenced to a mandatory life term after his conviction at trial. At the same time, there undoubtedly are cases in which a defendant's choice of plea does not significantly affect his sentence— cases, for example, in which a first offender who has committed a minor crime against property seems virtually certain to be sentenced to a short term of proba-

tion, regardless of the method of his conviction. Defendants may be influenced to plead guilty not only by accurate perceptions that more severe treatment will follow convictions at trial, but by inaccurate perceptions of this differential sentencing; by a desire to avoid the "process costs" of a trial—such burdens and expenses of the trial process as the loss of wages resulting from court appearances; by the lack of plausible defenses; and even, on some occasions, by remorse.

The significance of case load pressures. Especially during the 1960s, criminal case loads in America grew much more rapidly than the resources devoted to criminal courts, and it was commonly suggested that a practical inability to provide trials to more than a small minority of defendants accounted for the predominance of plea negotiation. Some scholars, such as Milton Heumann, have attempted to refute the "myth" that case load pressures "cause" plea bargaining. They emphasize that guilty-plea rates are often as high in rural and small-city jurisdictions and in jurisdictions with relatively small case loads as in the most overburdened urban areas. These scholars often have failed to consider the distinctive position of the part-time prosecutors who staff most of the courts with smaller case loads. A part-time prosecutor's salary ordinarily is unaffected by the time that he devotes to his prosecutorial responsibilities, and he therefore may sense some incentive to dispose of criminal cases expeditiously in order to devote greater time to his private law practice.

Certainly, financial pressure is not the only reason for plea bargaining, and the reduction or elimination of this pressure would not automatically bring plea bargaining to an end. Prosecutors would still have incentives to bargain in cases in which they doubted their ability to secure convictions at trial and in many other situations. At the same time, prosecutors and other officials regularly mention case load pressure as one important reason for plea bargaining practices. The best conclusion probably is that case load pressures are indeed a cause of plea bargaining, although they are not an indispensable cause.

The principal actors in the bargaining process

Prosecutors. In making plea agreements, prosecutors are influenced by a variety of concerns. As mentioned above, one important motivation is the perceived need to induce large numbers of guilty pleas in order to keep criminal case loads within manageable proportions. This administrative concern sometimes may lead prosecutors to offer greater concessions in complex cases, whose trials are likely to consume substantial amounts of time, than in more routine prosecutions.

In addition, prosecutors almost universally report that they consider the strength or weakness of the state's evidence an important bargaining consideration. On the theory that "half a loaf is better than none," they offer greater concessions to defendants who appear to have substantial chances of acquittal at trial than to defendants without plausible defenses. Indeed, in some situations, prosecutors may bluff defendants into pleas of guilty by concealing case weaknesses that would make convictions at trial impossible. The practice of "bargaining hardest when the case is weakest" suggests to some observers that "the greatest pressures to plead guilty are brought to bear on defendants who may be innocent" (Alschuler, 1968, p. 60).

Frequently, however, the issue compromised through plea bargaining is not whether the prosecutor has charged "the right person." Rather, the issue that the parties have compromised may be a legal issue, such as whether the undisputed circumstances under which evidence against the defendant was obtained rendered the seizure of this evidence unlawful. It also may be a mixed issue of fact and law, such as intention, causation, insanity, or self-defense. Some observers have suggested that the compromise of questions of identification should be distinguished from the compromise of issues that involve the passing of value judgments on the accused's conduct. Others, however, have maintained that all of these various forms of compromise raise similar issues of fairness and, in any event, that it would be difficult or impossible to distinguish among these various sorts of cases in an operational system of plea bargaining.

Prosecutors plainly are influenced by the equities of individual cases (the seriousness of the defendant's alleged crime, his prior criminal record, and so on). At times, they are influenced as well by their substantive views of the law that the defendant is accused of violating, offering substantial concessions in forgery cases, for example, but no concessions in rape prosecutions. Moreover, although it is commonly suggested that the victim of crime is the forgotten person in plea bargaining as in other phases of the criminal process, many prosecutors do give weight to the desires of victims and to those of police officers as well.

In most of the roles described above, prosecutors enter plea agreements primarily because these bargains seem to them to offer greater benefit to the state than the alternative of trial. On occasion, however, prosecutors bargain for more personal reasons.

Through plea bargaining, a prosecutor can avoid much of the hard work of preparing cases for trial and actually trying them. In addition, prosecutors can use plea bargaining to create seemingly impressive conviction records for political reasons (or perhaps because an individual prosecutor fears reassignment from a felony courtroom if he loses too many cases). The desire to be liked and to enjoy comfortable relationships with co-workers also may influence plea bargaining practices. Although most prosecutors probably do not deliberately sacrifice the public interest to their personal comfort or advancement, critics charge that the bargaining process is beset by conflicts of interest; it is often easy for prosecutors to rationalize decisions which serve their own interests rather than the interests of society.

One persistent issue is the extent to which prosecutors "overcharge" in the effort to induce pleas of guilty. Do they charge more-serious crimes than the circumstances of their cases seem to warrant, or a greater number of offenses than seem warranted, in an effort to induce defendants to plead guilty to the "proper" crimes? There is very little reason to believe that prosecutors often file fabricated charges to gain plea bargaining leverage. At the same time, both the likelihood of plea bargaining and other strategic concerns may lead prosecutors to construe the available evidence liberally and to file charges at the highest level that the evidence conceivably will permit. As the very concept of charge bargaining seems to imply, prosecutors often file charges that they intend to press to conviction only when defendants insist on standing trial.

Defense attorneys. Although bargaining with unrepresented defendants was once commonplace, it is now unusual except in prosecutions for traffic offenses and other minor crimes. In the main, defense attorneys seek to advance their clients' interests through plea bargaining in much the same way that prosecutors seek to advance the public interest. They recommend plea agreements to a client primarily when the concessions that the client has been offered seem to overbalance the client's chances of acquittal.

Again, however, there are allegations of conflict of interest. Private defense attorneys commonly are paid their fees in advance, and these fees usually do not vary with the pleas that their clients enter. Once an attorney has pocketed his fee, his personal interests may lie in disposing of a client's case as rapidly as possible—by entering a plea of guilty. Even conscientious attorneys may find their judgments colored to some extent by this circumstance, and not all defense attorneys are conscientious. "Cop-out lawyers"—

those who plead virtually all of their clients guilty—sometimes secure handsome incomes by representing large numbers of defendants for less than spectacular fees. Indeed, some of these lawyers have been known to deceive their clients in efforts to induce them to plead guilty.

Appointed attorneys may suffer a similar conflict of interest. The relatively small amount that an appointed attorney is likely to receive for representing an indigent defendant may seem inadequate compensation for a trial, but this amount may seem substantially less inadequate as a fee for negotiating a speedy plea of guilty.

Unlike private lawyers and other appointed attorneys, public defenders are salaried lawyers whose compensation does not vary with the time that their individual cases require. Nevertheless, public defenders are usually overworked, and some defenders seem to view plea bargaining in all but the most exceptional cases as necessary to the effective management of their case loads.

In theory, of course, the decision to enter a plea of guilty is the defendant's rather than his attorney's. Nevertheless, many defense attorneys speak of "client control" as an important phase of the plea negotiation process. When clients seem reluctant to follow their advice, these attorneys may use various forms of persuasion, including threats to discontinue their representation, in an effort to lead the clients to what the attorneys regard as a sensible course of conduct.

Too often, the serious problem of providing effective representation in the plea bargaining process has been neglected. It seems easy to assume that defense attorneys almost invariably will perform their intended role in the criminal justice system and therefore will advise a guilty plea only when it will advance a client's interests. It has been suggested, however, that this view of the defense attorney's role is more romanticized than real (Alschuler, 1975).

Trial judges. Although prosecutors and defense attorneys are the principal actors in the plea bargaining process, judicial participation in this process is far from rare. This participation may take various forms. In some courts, trial judges conduct in-chambers conferences and offer to impose specified sentences when defendants are willing to plead guilty. In others, judges offer suggestions to bargaining prosecutors and defense attorneys, and they may also offer less than definitive indications of the sentences that will follow pleas of guilty—for example, by describing how they have treated certain sorts of cases in the past or by indicating a probable range of sentences. At the same time, many judges do not participate in any form of explicit bargaining. These judges, however, may participate in implicit bargaining by taking a defendant's guilty plea into account in sentencing, and they may further the goals of plea bargaining by deferring routinely to prosecutorial plea bargaining decisions.

Primarily on the theory that judicial plea bargaining is more coercive than prosecutorial bargaining, some authorities have argued that judges should be prohibited from engaging in this practice, and this position has been adopted in court rules and appellate decisions in a number of jurisdictions. Recently, however, some scholars, including Norval Morris, have argued that plea bargaining tends to operate in a fairer and more rational fashion when judges take an active part.

Evaluations of plea bargaining

Prior to the mid-1960s, most courts and scholars tended to ignore plea bargaining, and the existing discussions of the practice were generally critical. The crime commissions of the 1920s, for example, generally described plea bargaining as a lazy form of prosecution that resulted in undue leniency for offenders. In 1967, however, both the American Bar Association and the President's Commission on Law Enforcement and Administration of Justice approved the concept of plea bargaining while recognizing a need for the reform of certain plea bargaining practices. Since then, other prestigious authorities have endorsed plea bargaining. The principal departure from the general pattern of approval was the 1973 report of the National Advisory Commission on Criminal Justice Standards and Goals, which recommended the abolition of all forms of plea bargaining. The burgeoning scholarly literature on plea negotiation also dates primarily from the mid-1960s. Like most of the national study groups and like virtually all American courts, most scholars have tended to approve of plea negotiation, at least in broad outline.

Plea negotiation obviously raises substantial legal and constitutional issues. For one thing, common-law courts traditionally treated a confession as involuntary when it had been induced by a promise of leniency from a person in authority. The application of this rule to plea bargaining would render all bargained guilty pleas invalid. In addition, the entry of a plea of guilty probably qualifies as a form of self-incrimination (perhaps, in fact, as the ultimate form of self-incrimination). The Supreme Court generally has treated incriminating statements as "compelled" when induced by promises of governmental benefit. Finally, a guilty plea waives the constitutional right to trial and subordinate trial rights such as the right to trial and subordinate trial rights such as the right to confront one's accusers. Under the "doctrine of unconstitutional conditions," waivers of constitutional rights are frequently held invalid when they have been required as a condition for receiving favorable governmental treatment.

Despite these substantial issues, the Supreme Court all but ignored plea bargaining during the period of its "due process revolution" under Chief Justice Earl Warren. One decision at the very end of the Warren Court era seemed to call certain plea bargaining practices into question (*United States v. Jackson*, 390 U.S. 570 (1968)). The Supreme Court did not pass directly upon the constitutionality of plea bargaining, however, until 1970 and 1971 when, in a series of cases, it forcefully approved the practice. The Court saw the presence of competent counsel as a significant safeguard of fairness in plea negotiation, and it emphasized that plea bargaining may result in a mutuality of advantage partly because the defendant limits his probable penalty while the state conserves scarce resources (*Brady v. United States*, 397 U.S. 742 (1970); *McMann v. Richardson*, 397 U.S. 759 (1970); *Santobello v. New York*, 404 U.S. 257 (1971)).

The Supreme Court has required that plea agreements be honored, and it has held that certain procedures must be followed in accepting pleas of guilty. The Court also has held that in some circumstances a trial judge constitutionally may accept a guilty plea submitted by a defendant who claims to be innocent (*North Carolina v. Alford*, 400 U.S. 25 (1970)).

Apart from the legal contentions noted above, critics of plea bargaining have advanced a number of objections to it. They have argued that plea bargaining subordinates the requirement of proof beyond a reasonable doubt to a practice that, in effect, renders defendants half-guilty, and that plea negotiation is substantially more likely than trial to result in the conviction of innocent defendants. Similarly, they have suggested that plea negotiation undercuts the effectiveness of various legal doctrines, such as the Fourth Amendment exclusionary rule. In addition, critics allege that plea bargaining is unfair as a sentencing policy in that it makes the defendant's fate depend on a single tactical decision, a decision irrelevant to any proper objective of criminal proceedings. Some critics also maintain that plea bargaining results in unwarranted leniency for offenders and that it promotes a cynical view of the legal process by encouraging defendants to believe that they have sold a commodity and that they have, in a sense, "gotten away" with something.

Critics of plea bargaining also object to the shift of power to prosecutors that plea bargaining has effected, arguing that the practice tends to reduce judges to figureheads who often do little more than ratify prosecutorial plea bargaining decisions. They maintain that, even more clearly, plea bargaining tends to make figureheads of the officials who prepare presentence reports after the effective determination of sentence through prosecutorial negotiations. Plea negotiation, they say, very frequently results in the imposition of sentence on the basis of incomplete information. In light of the conflicts of interest that may beset prosecutors, defense attorneys, and trial judges in bargaining, the critics sometimes contend that plea negotiation subordinates both the public's interest and the defendant's to the interests of criminal justice administrators. In their view, the practice also warps both the initial formulation of criminal charges and, as defendants plead guilty to crimes less serious than those that they apparently committed, the final judicial labeling of offenses. Finally, critics suggest that plea bargaining deprecates the value of human liberty and the purposes of the criminal sanction by viewing these things as commodities to be traded for economic savings.

Defenses of plea bargaining fall into three main categories. First, some defenders maintain that it is appropriate as a matter of sentencing policy to reward guilty defendants who acknowledge their guilt. They advance several arguments in support of this position—most notably, that a bargained guilty plea may manifest remorse or a willingness to enter the correctional system in a frame of mind that may afford hope for rehabilitation over a shorter period of time than otherwise would be necessary.

A second defense treats plea bargaining not primarily as a sentencing device but as a form of dispute resolution. Some plea bargaining advocates maintain that it is desirable to afford the defendant and the state the option of compromising factual and legal disputes. They reason that if a plea agreement did not improve the positions of both the defendant and the state, one party or the other would insist upon a trial.

Finally, some observers defend plea bargaining on grounds of economy or necessity. Viewing plea negotiation less as a sentencing device or a form of dispute resolution than as an administrative practice, they argue that society cannot afford to provide trials to all the defendants who would demand them if guilty pleas were not rewarded—or, at least, that there are more appropriate uses for the additional resources which an effective plea bargaining prohibition would require. Sometimes these defenders add that any attempt to prohibit plea bargaining would prove ineffective and would merely drive the practice underground.

Abolition and reform efforts

The claim that plea bargaining is a "practical necessity" derives support from the high percentage of criminal cases that are resolved by guilty pleas. A prohibition of plea negotiation might require a substantial increase in the resources devoted to criminal courts and to prosecutor and defender offices, and this prospect may seem unthinkable in political and economic terms. Nevertheless, opponents of plea bargaining sometimes maintain that the influx of resources necessary to provide trials to greatly increased numbers of defendants would appear terrifying only when viewed in percentage terms; when measured against other common social expenditures (for example, the amount spent on police), the necessary influx of resources would seem manageable.

Moreover, these plea bargaining opponents suggest that existing resources might be allocated more effectively by providing less elaborate trials to greater numbers of defendants. They point, for example, to the practices of Philadelphia, Pittsburgh, and Baltimore, where the frequent use of informal nonjury trials has resulted in guilty-plea rates far lower than those of most other urban jurisdictions. Finally, they suggest that it is difficult to know the extent to which trial rates would increase if plea bargaining were prohibited; a substantial number of defendants lacking plausible defenses might plead guilty without the inducements that plea bargaining now provides.

The most notable American effort to abolish plea bargaining began in Alaska in 1975. Attorney General Avrum Gross, the head of Alaska's statewide system of prosecution, ordered Alaskan prosecutors to refrain from bargaining in all cases filed after August 15 of that year. Five years later, a federally funded evaluation of this reform by the Alaska Judicial Council concluded that "the institution of plea bargaining was effectively curtailed, and . . . not replaced by implicit or covert forms of the same practice" (Rubinstein, Clarke, and White, p. vii). Nevertheless, Alaska's plea bargaining prohibition was not airtight. For example, the attorney general had no authority to control the sentencing practices of trial judges, and the Judicial Council did find evidence of "implicit bargaining" in some crime categories.

The Judicial Council concluded that Alaska's plea bargaining prohibition had led to a 30 percent increase in the number of trials. Nevertheless, a very substantial majority of convictions continued to be by guilty plea. Despite the increased number of trials, court delay was reduced, possibly because of a reduction in the dilatory tactics that plea bargaining had encouraged. The Judicial Council reported that the plea bargaining ban had led to very substantial increases in sentence severity in some crime categories but to no increases in others. Nevertheless, the finding that sentences became more severe in certain crime categories has been questioned (Alschuler, 1981, pp. 726–730).

Many observers regard the abolition of plea bargaining as an unrealistic objective and therefore focus more closely on proposals for the reform of plea negotiation practices. Indeed, one reform widely advocated in the late 1960s—that of placing plea agreements "on the record"—has been adopted in a substantial majority of American jurisdictions. In past decades, guilty-plea defendants usually were expected to (and did) declare that no promises had been made to induce their pleas. Today the practice of plea negotiation is generally avowed, and the terms of individual plea agreements are recorded when guilty pleas are accepted.

One common focus of reform efforts is the role of the trial judge. Some reformers advocate substantially less judicial involvement in plea negotiation, and others, substantially more. Some reformers also hope to limit the extent of the sentence differential between defendants who plead guilty and those who exercise the right to trial. They sometimes advocate the use of fixed discount rates administered by courts rather than prosecutors, in the hope that the rewards given defendants who plead guilty will become more uniform than they are today. Reformers sometimes also suggest that similarly situated defendants should be afforded equal opportunities to bargain, that more complete information should be made available to bargaining attorneys (for example, by preparing presentence reports before the bargaining process begins), and that negotiations should occur at a relatively early stage of the criminal process rather than on the eve of trial.

As part of the reform movement, some prosecutors' offices have formulated internal guidelines to regulate plea negotiation and other forms of discretionary decision-making. These guidelines have been designed both to reduce discretion and to afford office administrators greater control over their subordinates. Nevertheless, the variables that influence plea negotiation are so numerous and so complex that it usually seems difficult to reduce them to a formula. Many guidelines—for example, those promulgated by the Department of Justice in 1980—have been so general as to provide only minimal constraints on prosecutorial discretion. Moreover, even reasonably specific guidelines have sometimes proved delusive in practice. These guidelines generally have been subject to ill-defined exceptions for "weak cases"; some of them certainly have been intended more for political show than for implementation; and, at least in some places, individual prosecutors have tended to subvert guidelines by taking unofficial positions "off the record" and by agreeing not to oppose actions that they could not themselves recommend.

Conclusion

Plea negotiation probably will remain central to the American criminal justice system for the foreseeable future. Nevertheless, as the President's Commission on Law Enforcement and Administration of Justice observed in 1967, "Few practices in the system of criminal justice create a greater sense of unease and suspicion than the negotiated plea of guilty" (p. 9).

It has been suggested that continuing debate about the propriety of plea bargaining is unrealistic and that attention should focus exclusively on how the process best can operate. Nevertheless, the plea bargaining debate involves fundamental issues of sentencing policy, of the propriety of compromising questions of criminal guilt, and of the use of governmental inducements to secure waivers of constitutional rights. For these reasons, the debate seems likely to continue as long as the practice of plea bargaining persists.

ALBERT W. ALSCHULER

See also CHARGING; both articles under COUNSEL; CRIMINAL PROCEDURE: COMPARATIVE ASPECTS; GUILTY PLEA: ACCEPTING THE PLEA; INFORMAL DISPOSITION; PROSECUTION, articles on COMPARATIVE ASPECTS and PROSECUTORIAL DISCRETION.

BIBLIOGRAPHY

ALSCHULER, ALBERT W. "The Changing Plea Bargaining Debate." California Law Review 69 (1981): 652–730.
———. "The Defense Attorney's Role in Plea Bargaining." Yale Law Journal 84 (1975): 1179–1314.
———. "Plea Bargaining and Its History." Columbia Law Review 79 (1979): 1–43.
———. "The Prosecutor's Role in Plea Bargaining." University of Chicago Law Review 36 (1968): 50–112.
COMMENT. "The Plea Bargain in Historical Perspective." Buffalo Law Review 23 (1974): 499–527.
COOK, BEVERLY BLAIR. "Sentencing Behavior of Federal Judges: Draft Cases—1972." University of Cincinnati Law Review 42 (1973): 597–633.
EISENSTEIN, JAMES, and JACOB, HERBERT. Felony Justice: An Organizational Analysis of Criminal Courts. Boston: Little, Brown, 1977.
GOLDSTEIN, ABRAHAM S., and MARCUS, MARTIN. "The Myth of Judicial Supervision in Three 'Inquisitorial' Systems: France, Italy, and Germany." Yale Law Journal 87 (1977): 240–283.
HEUMANN, MILTON. Plea Bargaining: The Experiences of Prosecutors, Judges, and Defense Attorneys. University of Chicago Press, 1977.
LANGBEIN, JOHN H. "Land without Plea Bargaining: How the Germans Do It." Michigan Law Review 78 (1979): 204–225.
MORRIS, NORVAL. The Future of Imprisonment. University of Chicago Press, 1974.
President's Commission on Law Enforcement and Administration of Justice, Task Force on the Administration of Justice. Task Force Report: The Courts. Washington, D.C.: The Commission, 1967.
RHODES, WILLIAM. Plea Bargaining: Who Gains? Who Loses? Washington, D.C.: Institute of Law and Social Research, 1978.
ROSETT, ARTHUR I., and CRESSEY, DONALD R. Justice by Consent. Philadelphia: Lippincott, 1976.
RUBINSTEIN, MICHAEL L.; CLARKE, STEVENS H.; and WHITE, TERESA J. Alaska Bans Plea Bargaining. Washington, D.C.: U.S. Department of Justice, National Institute of Justice, 1980.
U.S. Department of Justice. Principles of Federal Prosecution. Washington, D.C.: The Department, 1980.
———, Law Enforcement Assistance Administration, National Advisory Commission on Criminal Justice Standards and Goals. Courts. Washington, D.C.: The Commission, 1973.
UTZ, PAMELA J. Settling the Facts: Discretion and Negotiation in Criminal Court. Lexington, Mass.: Heath, Lexington Books, 1978.

GUNS, REGULATION OF

Introduction

Americans own a greater number and variety of firearms than the citizens of any other Western democracy, and they also use their guns to assault, maim, and kill one another much more often. Thus violence in the United States is more serious, and a possible means of reducing that violence—gun control—is more difficult to achieve than in other industrialized countries. It is this special significance of firearms in American life that has led to the great gun control debate.

The debate over gun control is often a war of statistics, yet statistics do not answer most important policy questions. Common sense and ordinary reasoning are also necessary (Lindblom and Cohen). What makes the wide use of statistics even more puzzling is that both sides in the debate often invoke the same statistics. For example, there are now approximately 120 million guns in the United States. Opponents of gun control conclude from this that firearms are too numerous to be effectively controlled. Proponents of gun control, on the other hand, argue that the problem is so serious that stricter controls are necessary (Wright et al.).

Similarly, despite more than twenty thousand federal, state, and local gun laws, gun control has largely failed. Firearms continue to multiply, whereas deaths from guns have increased since the early 1960s to roughly thirty thousand per year. From the failure of gun control, its opponents conclude that controls cannot work, while its proponents declare that existing laws must be enforced or different kinds of controls tried. Whatever the proper interpretation of these facts, it is far from easy to pass and administer laws that promise to lessen the gun problem.

Firearms and violence

What exactly is the "gun problem"? Advocates of control begin by pointing out that more than 20 percent of all robberies and about 60 percent of all homicides are committed with firearms. Their opponents reply that the vast majority of the country's 120 million firearms are not involved in violence, and that crime rather than firearms is the real problem. "Guns don't kill people," they assert, "people kill people." In a trite sense, this reply is to the point: firearms would not contribute to the seriousness of the crime problem if there were no crime. But guns are not merely another weapon used in crime. Serious assault with a gun is, according to the best estimates, two and a half to five times as likely to cause death as a similar attack with a knife, the next most dangerous weapon (Zimring, 1968). And gun robberies are three to four times as likely to result in the death of a victim as are other kinds of robbery (Cook, 1979a; Newton and Zimring).

Thus far firearms have been discussed here as a general category, without distinguishing among handguns, rifles, and shotguns. In a sense that approach is appropriate, because a rifle or a shotgun, if used in an attack, is at least as dangerous as a handgun; but even a cursory study of statistics on firearms and violence suggests that the handgun is a special problem that merits a special set of solutions. The handgun—small, easy to conceal, and relatively unimportant in hunting—accounts for about one-fourth of the privately owned firearms in the country, but it is involved in three-fourths of all gun killings. In the big cities, handguns account for more than 80 percent of gun killings and virtually all gun robberies (Cook, 1976).

Even though the most common reason for owning a handgun is for household self-defense, studies suggest that loaded household handguns are more likely to kill family members than to save their lives. A Detroit study found that more people died in one year from handgun accidents alone than were killed by home-invading robbers or burglars in four and a half years (Newton and Zimring). The discovery that self-defense handguns are from this standpoint a poor investment—dismal though the news may be to the fearful urban dweller—does yield one promising conclusion: rejecting handgun ownership makes sense, even if other families retain their guns. But if unilateral disarmament is rational, why do people not give up their guns voluntarily, and why do handguns continue to proliferate in the cities?

To some extent, urban gun ownership results from misinformation about the risk of accidental death and the usefulness of guns in defense of the home. However, it is foolish to think that millions of American families keep handguns merely because they have not read the statistics, or to suppose that shipping them the latest gun control article will change their minds. The risk of accidental or homicidal death from a loaded gun in the home—although greater than the chance that the gun will save life—is nevertheless small. In the majority of homes with handguns, the only real use of the gun may be to make its owner feel less uneasy about the possibility that a hostile stranger will invade his home. This feeling of well-being is a statistical illusion but an emotional reality. People will fight the statistics that show otherwise because, even if their guns do not give them any real measure of protection, they have no other way to deal with their fears.

Gun control strategies

Simply because the problems are real does not mean that solutions are easy. Indeed, the extent of the gun problem in the United States should be a warning that reducing gun violence will be a difficult and expensive task. There are already more than twenty thousand gun laws in the nation to match the thousands of gun killings. Why should gun laws decrease the rate of criminal killings when criminals, by definition, do not obey laws? These sober reminders from the local rifle association should be a guide in reviewing a number of different types of gun control strategies. How are these various laws supposed to work, and is it likely that they will?

Place and manner restrictions. Most of the gun laws in the United States are place and manner restrictions. These laws attempt to separate illegitimate from legitimate gun use by regulating the place and manner in which firearms may be used. They prohibit the carrying of firearms within city limits or in a motor vehicle, the carrying of concealed weapons on one's person, or the discharging of a firearm in populated areas. Such laws attempt to reduce firearm violence by police intervention before violence or crime actually takes place. Since there are obvious limits to the police's ability to prevent firearm violence and to discover persons who violate place and manner laws, these laws may deter little violence.

Stiffer penalties for firearm violence. It is not true that the National Rifle Association opposes all laws intended to reduce firearm violence. In fact, the members of that organization have been among the most vocal supporters of laws that increase prison sentences or make them mandatory for persons committing crimes with guns. Such laws do not make it harder for potential criminals, or anyone else, to obtain guns. But the law is intended to reduce gun crime by making it so much costlier than crime without a gun that potential criminals either will commit the crime without a gun or will not commit the crime at all. More than half of the states have laws providing for longer sentences for criminals who carry or use a gun while committing a felony (Wright et al.).

In order to reduce the number of gun crimes, such laws would have to deter persons who would not be deterred by the already stiff penalties for gun crimes. Can the threat of additional punishment succeed? Despite the dearth of hard evidence, there is no reason to believe that such marginal deterrence is impossible. Perhaps the robber could be deterred from using a gun if the punishment for gun robbery were several times greater than that of nongun robbery. However, the problem is a complex one.

First, is it wise to make the punishment for gun robbery so harsh that the additional punishment the robber risks if he kills his victim seems relatively small? Second, it may be that the only way to make the distinction important is to reduce the punishment for nongun robbery. Third, punishment for robbery is already quite severe, at least as set forth in the statutes. How much more potential deterrence is left in the system?

The issue of additional deterrence is more complicated when the crime of gun assault, that is, an actual shooting, is discussed, because he who attacks with a gun is already risking the maximum punishment of the law if his victim dies. How much additional deterrence can come from making lesser penalties for nonfatal attack mandatory? Proponents of this approach suggest that although the penalties for crime seem severe, in reality light punishments are often given. Granting the truth of this observation leads, however, to the further question whether the same pressures might not undermine mandatory penalties for gun crime. One study conducted in Detroit suggests that just such an effect takes place for more serious felonies committed with a gun (Loftin and McDowall).

There may indeed be some hope of reducing gun crime by increasing the gap between the penalty for that crime and the penalty for other crimes. At the same time, it is difficult to believe that such a program will have a major effect on the rate of gun killings.

Prohibiting high-risk groups from owning guns. Another approach endorsed by opponents of more comprehensive gun control is to forbid certain high-risk groups from owning firearms. The groups usually covered include those with serious criminal records, the very young, alcoholics, drug addicts, and mental patients. Nearly every state, as well as the federal government, prohibits some type of high-risk ownership. Many of these laws do not go so far as to make a person prove his eligibility to own a gun; the ownership ban is supposed to be effective because the ineligible person will be subject to criminal penalties if he is caught possessing a firearm. That represents some improvement over simply passing stiffer penalties for gun crime, because the law attempts to separate the potential criminal from his gun before he commits a crime with it. If such laws could reduce the number of guns owned by people subject to the prohibition, they would indeed reduce gun violence. But trying to isolate a group of "bad guys" who cannot have guns from a larger group of "good guys" who will continue to own millions of them is neither easy nor very effective. It is not easy since if the purchaser does not have to prove that he is not in the prohibited class, the law is still trying to use the threat of future punishment as a substitute for a system that would make it physically more difficult for high-risk groups to obtain guns. It is not effective since most homicides are committed by "good guys," that is, by persons who would qualify for ownership under any prohibition that operated on only a minority of the population.

Permissive licensing. About half of the jurisdictions try to enforce the ban on gun ownership by high-risk groups through requiring that people must qualify before they can buy guns. This type of restriction takes one of two forms: a license to buy a gun, or an application to purchase coupled with a waiting period. Permissive licensing is thought to be an advantage over a simple ban on ownership because it makes a person prove that he is eligible to own a gun before he can obtain a license. Such a system no longer depends solely on the prudence of the people barred from ownership precisely because they are not thought to be good risks. However, proposing such a system is also precisely where what has been called the "gun lobby" draws the line and begins opposing controls because licensing imposes costs on all gun owners. Would licensing work, assuming that the opponents could be outvoted? Like ownership prohibitions, it would not prevent the majority of gun killings, which are committed by persons who qualify for ownership. But would it at least keep guns from high-risk groups? The problem with permissive licensing is that it leaves some 35 million handguns in circulation (Wright et al.). Half of all the handguns in the United States are acquired secondhand, and most of these are purchased from private parties, who may not ask to see licenses (Burr). Moreover, there are 35 million handguns available to steal. In short, it is extraordinarily difficult to let the "good guys" have all the firearms they want and at the same time to keep the "bad guys" unarmed. It does not appear that states with permissive licensing systems made much progress in reducing gun violence during all the years when the federal government failed to control interstate traffic in most firearms. With stronger federal aid, the potential of such laws is still limited, but it is not known to what extent.

Registration. This procedure records that a particular gun is the property of a particular licensed owner. Several states and cities have such registration laws, often coupled with other types of gun controls (Jones and Ray). Gun registration thus usually requires that the owner provide information about the guns he owns, in addition to the information about himself that is required to obtain a license. An analogy to the registration system for automobiles is often drawn by supporters of such controls.

For reasons that are at least partly obscure, registration is one of the most feared of all types of gun control laws, and the one that gun owners find hardest to understand. The fear is based in part on anxiety about "Big Brother" keeping information about details of personal life, and in part on the belief that registration is some kind of subversive plot to lower the nation's ability to resist invasion by a foreign power. The best argument against registration is clearly its cost, but the debate centers on the purpose of registration. If criminals—who, it must be remembered, do not obey the law—fail to register their guns, how can registration possibly reduce gun crime? The answer usually offered is that registration is designed only as a support to any system that seeks to allow some people, but not others, to own guns. If such a system is to prove workable, then some method must be found to keep guns where they are permitted by making each legitimate gun owner responsible for each gun he owns. After all, some of the "good guys" would otherwise pass on guns through the secondhand market to "bad guys" and thus frustrate permissive licensing systems. If registration helped to keep the "good guys" good, it could help prevent gun violence, even if not a single criminal were polite enough to register his gun.

There is also a theory that gun registration will deter the qualified owner from misusing his gun since it can be traced to him, but no one is quite sure how much prevention this technique will achieve. All in all, it is difficult to estimate how much additional prevention a licensing system obtains by requiring registration, but it seems perverse not to require registration of some kind in any system that seeks to prevent gun violence by barring certain groups from gun ownership.

Cutting down on the handgun. The most extreme solution that has been proposed in the gun control debate is a substantial reduction of the number of handguns owned by civilians. This proposal reacts to the frustrations of distinguishing the "good guys" from the "bad guys" by suggesting that no one should be permitted to own a handgun unless he has a special need for it. Two approaches have been enacted: restrictive licensing and handgun bans. Under a restrictive licensing system, a person who wants to own a gun must establish his need for it before he receives a license. Under a handgun ban, certain classes of persons (for example, police officers and members of gun clubs) are exempted from the operation of the law. Thus, a handgun ban is not necessarily a more restrictive control than restrictive licensing: whether it is depends on the classes allowed to possess guns. Moreover, handgun bans usually exert no direct control over the exempted classes, whereas a restrictive licensing system licenses those who would probably be exempted under a ban. A significant minority of American cities have experimented with either restrictive licensing or handgun bans.

Gun owners doubt that such plans will work because "when guns are criminal, only criminals will have guns." Moreover, if handguns are illegal, criminals will switch to other kinds of guns, a development that will not reduce gun crime but will spur efforts to confiscate all kinds of civilian firearms. Both of these arguments have some appeal, but both ignore important facts about the relationship between guns and violence in the United States. First, guns are more lethal than other weapons. Thus, substantially reducing the number of handguns should reduce the number of homicides resulting from accidental weapon use and the use of a weapon to settle an argument, even though some criminals will undoubtedly continue to use handguns. Second, it appears to be harder than one might suspect for the handgun robber or attacker to switch to a long gun. For this reason, the average handgun is many times more likely to kill than the average long gun. States that try to restrict handguns find that their major problem becomes not the long gun but the illegal handgun.

The real difficulty in restricting the handgun is whether any law can reduce the number of such guns in circulation enough to make headway against gun violence, and, if so, how long this will take and what its cost will be. It is possible, by law, to put a stop to the manufacture of handguns at any time, but even if this were done, some of the 35 million handguns in the civilian inventory would still be killing people in the twenty-first century. Under the best of conditions, collecting the vast arsenal of civilian handguns would be neither easy nor swift. Americans do not live under the best of conditions—the very crime rate that makes many people want gun control also makes gun control extremely difficult to achieve. How many citizens would turn in their guns when the law took effect? How long would it take to remove the guns from the streets, where they do the most harm? Should urban households be left fearfully defenseless? Is it desirable to add yet another victimless and unenforceable crime—possession of a handgun—to the depressingly long list of such crimes that have already accumulated? These are not easy questions to answer.

National controls. The primary federal gun control law is the Gun Control Act of 1968, Pub. L. 90-618, 82 Stat. 1213 (codified in scattered sections of 18, 18 App. 26 U.S.C.). Its main purposes were (1) to prohibit gun sales to high-risk groups; (2) to prohibit interstate traffic in guns; and (3) to prohibit imports of guns not designed for sporting use (Zimring, 1975). The Gun Control Act has had only limited

success in all three areas; even the import restrictions have been avoided. Gun importers have simply moved their gun manufacturing plants to the United States or have imported foreign parts to be assembled in American plants (Cook, 1979b).

Whatever gun control strategies are tried, it seems that local initiatives must have state and national support if they hope to achieve their goals. When jurisdictions pass strict laws against certain kinds of gun sales and resales, guns leak in from other jurisdictions that do not have the same controls. Moreover, the existing federal law designed to assist states and localities has not been adequately enforced.

Any gun control policy, even one that attempts to cut down drastically on the number of handguns on a nationwide basis, will be something of an experiment in the coming years. It is not known how effective any law can be when there are so many guns in circulation and so much pressure to keep them there.

JAMES LINDGREN
FRANKLIN E. ZIMRING

See also CRIME PREVENTION: ENVIRONMENTAL AND TECHNOLOGICAL STRATEGIES; FEAR OF CRIME; HOMICIDE: BEHAVIORAL ASPECTS; PUBLIC OPINION AND CRIME; VIOLENCE.

BIBLIOGRAPHY

BURR, D. E. S. *Handgun Regulation.* Orlando: Florida Bureau of Criminal Justice Planning and Assistance, 1977.

COOK, PHILIP J. "The Effect of Gun Availability on Robbery and Robbery Murder: A Cross-section Study of Fifty Cities." *Hearings before the Subcommittee on Crime of the Committee on the Judiciary, House of Representatives.* 95th Cong., 2d sess., 4 and 18 May 1978. Washington, D.C.: Government Printing Office, 1979a, pp. 281–311.

———. "The Saturday Night Special: An Assessment of Alternative Definitions from a Policy Perspective." Mimeographed. Durham, N.C.: Duke University, Center for the Study of Policy Analysis, 1979b.

———. "A Strategic Choice Analysis of Robbery." *Sample Surveys of the Victims of Crime.* Edited by Wesley G. Skogan. Cambridge, Mass.: Ballinger, 1976, pp. 173–187.

———, and BLOSE, JAMES. "State Programs for Screening Handgun Buyers." *Annals of the American Academy of Political and Social Science* 455 (1981): 80–91.

JONES, EDWARD D., III. "The District of Columbia's 'Firearms Control Regulations Act of 1975': The Toughest Handgun Control Law in the United States—Or Is It?" *Annals of the American Academy of Political and Social Science* 455 (1981): 138–149.

———, and RAY, MARLA WILSON. "Handgun Control: Strategies, Enforcement, and Effectiveness." Mimeographed. Washington, D.C.: U.S. Department of Justice, 1980.

KAPLAN, JOHN. "The Wisdom of Gun Prohibition." *Annals of the American Academy of Political and Social Science* 455 (1981): 11–23.

LINDBLOM, CHARLES E., and COHEN, DAVID K. *Usable Knowledge: Social Science and Social Problem Solving.* New Haven: Yale University Press, 1979.

LOFTIN, COLIN, and McDOWALL, DAVID. " 'One with a Gun Gets You Two': Mandatory Sentencing and Firearms Violence in Detroit." *Annals of the American Academy of Political and Social Science* 455 (1981): 150–167.

NEWTON, GEORGE D., JR., and ZIMRING, FRANKLIN E. *Firearms and Violence in American Life: A Staff Report Submitted to the National Commission on the Causes and Prevention of Violence.* Washington, D.C.: National Commission on the Causes and Prevention of Violence, 1969.

WRIGHT, JAMES D.; ROSSI, PETER H.; DALY, KATHLEEN; PEREIRA, JOSEPH; and CHEN, HUEY-TSYH. *Weapons, Crime, and Violence in America: A Literature Review and Research Agenda.* Washington, D.C.: U.S. Department of Justice, 1982.

ZIMRING, FRANKLIN E. "Firearms and Federal Law: The Gun Control Act of 1968." *Journal of Legal Studies* 4 (1975): 133–198.

———. "Is Gun Control Likely to Reduce Violent Killings?" *University of Chicago Law Review* 35 (1968): 721–737.

H

HABEAS CORPUS

Habeas corpus, a common-law writ of medieval origin, commands a person who has custody of a prisoner to produce the body of the prisoner before a judge. The writ's best-known function is that of permitting the judge to decide whether the custodian is authorized by law to detain his prisoner. If the judge holds that the detention is unlawful, the prisoner is immediately released. For this reason, the writ of habeas corpus has been celebrated for centuries as the Great Writ of Freedom. In Latin, the language of medieval English courts, the Great Writ is termed *habeas corpus ad subjiciendum.*

In other settings, the writ of habeas corpus may not free a prisoner, but instead may cause him to be transferred to a new scene. Thus, the writ may be used to obtain testimony from a person held in confinement. The court may issue a writ of habeas corpus *ad testificandum* directing the custodian to bring the prisoner to court to testify, or a confined person's presence may be required because he is a party to a pending case, as plaintiff or defendant. In criminal prosecutions, a defendant has a constitutional right to be present. To enable a person to prosecute a claim or to defend himself, a writ of habeas corpus *ad prosequendum, ad respondendum,* or *ad deliberandum* commands a custodian to produce a prisoner so that the judicial proceeding may go forward. Thus, a federal court in California that intends to try an indictment returned in that court against a defendant confined in New York City has authority to order state prison officials in New York to deliver their prisoner to the California court for trial (*Carbo v. United States,* 364 U.S. 611 (1961)). These forms of the writ of habeas corpus have been and remain a necessary part of judicial practice in the United States.

In its function of securing freedom for persons illegally confined, habeas corpus is largely related to criminal prosecutions, but it also has significant application in other cases. Patients involuntarily committed to institutions for the mentally ill may seek habeas corpus relief, and aliens arrested to be deported by immigration officers may obtain judicial rulings on the validity of the deportation proceedings. Virtually any kind of detention can be challenged for illegality through the writ of habeas corpus.

Criminal cases, however, provide the majority of occasions for habeas corpus litigation. A person suspected of having committed a crime can be held only briefly on the authority of arresting police officers; our system of justice requires that a judicial determination be made promptly as to the legality of the confinement and its terms, including possible release on bail. In the absence of a valid judicial order of commitment, a writ of habeas corpus will result in release of the prisoner. Similarly, a person arrested for purposes of extradition or rendition to face criminal charges pending in another jurisdiction may obtain judicial determination of the validity of his arrest and possible transfer by a writ of habeas corpus.

Habeas corpus functions also to determine whether judicially ordered commitments are valid. Over time this has come to include not only pretrial orders, but even final judgments sentencing convicted defendants to prison terms.

Historical antecedents

The origins of habeas corpus are still obscure. Employment of the writ may antedate the Magna Charta, issued by King John in 1215. In the seventeenth century, habeas corpus played a central role in political and constitutional struggles over the royal prerogative. When Charles I (1625–1649) tried to raise money by demanding "forced loans" from his subjects without the consent of Parliament, some who refused were summarily imprisoned by warrants of the Privy Council. In 1627 the Privy Council denied habeas corpus relief (*Darnel's Case* (Proceedings on the Habeas Corpus) [K.B. 1627], 3 T.B. Howell, State Trials 1 (London, 1816)), thereby creating one of the major grievances for which Parliament sought redress in the Petition of Right, to which Charles I reluctantly assented in 1628.

Thereafter, however, Charles governed without Parliament for eleven years, a period notorious for deprivations of the civil and religious liberty of English citizens. Eventually Charles was compelled to reconvene Parliament, which promptly enacted a statute declaring that any person imprisoned by command of the king or his privy council was entitled to release on writ of habeas corpus (An act for regulating the Privy Council and abolishing the court of Star Chamber, 16 Car. 1, c. 10, § 8 (1640) (England)).

The last great step in the development of habeas corpus was taken during the reign of Charles II (1660–1685). The judges had concluded that they lacked authority to issue writs of habeas corpus when the courts were in vacation, so that it was possible for a person to be imprisoned for a substantial period, until the next regular term of court. After their arrest, some prisoners had been hurriedly transported out of England and thus placed beyond the reach of writs of habeas corpus. The Habeas Corpus Act, 1679, 31 Car. 2, c. 2 (England) authorized judges to issue writs of habeas corpus without regard to the normal calendars of the courts. It established severe penalties for judges who refused without good cause to entertain petitions for writs of habeas corpus and for officers who refused to comply with writs when issued, and it also declared that arrested persons were not to be sent beyond the seas. The Habeas Corpus Act is widely celebrated as the culmination in England of the struggle for recognition of the principle that no person may be denied liberty without due process of law.

After the American Revolution, most states enacted statutes closely modeled on the act of 1679, and several of the new state constitutions guaranteed the right to habeas corpus. The United States Constitution included among a number of restrictions upon the powers of the new national government a provision that "the Privilege of the Writ of Habeas Corpus shall not be suspended, unless when in Cases of Rebellion or Invasion the public Safety may require it" (art. 1, § 9). The Judiciary Act of 1789, ch. 20, § 14, 1 Stat. 73 authorized federal courts to issue writs of habeas corpus for prisoners in custody by authority of the United States. Later, the jurisdiction of federal courts to entertain habeas corpus petitions was expanded by subsequent statutes, of particular note the Habeas Corpus Act of 1867, ch. 27, 14 Stat. 385, which authorized federal courts to grant habeas corpus to anyone imprisoned under the authority of a state if that imprisonment was in violation of the Constitution, laws, or treaties of the United States.

On one occasion at the outbreak of the Civil War, President Abraham Lincoln suspended the right of habeas corpus and ignored Chief Justice Roger Taney's ringing opinion denouncing this action (*Ex parte Merryman*, 17 F. Cas. 144 (C.C.D. Md. 1861) (No. 9487)). Two years later, Congress enacted legislation justifying Lincoln's order (An Act relating to Habeas Corpus and regulating Judicial Proceedings in Certain Cases, ch. 81, 12 Stat. 755 (1863)). Habeas corpus was also suspended in South Carolina in 1871 in an effort to combat the Ku Klux Klan, as well as in the Philippines during the Spanish-American War and in Hawaii during World War II.

Postconviction review of lower federal court decisions

The federal judicial system created in 1789 provided that trial court judgments in major criminal cases were not subject to review. The right of convicted defendants to appeal, which has come to be regarded as a normal aspect of criminal procedure, dates from 1891, when the United States courts of appeals were created. Similar patterns existed in state court systems, as well as in Great Britain, until the turn of the twentieth century.

Habeas corpus in lieu of appeal. Federal judiciary acts, dating from 1789, empowered all federal courts, including the United States Supreme Court, to issue writs of habeas corpus. Several persons who had been convicted in federal prosecutions sought habeas corpus relief in the Supreme Court, and issuance of the writ led to a kind of appellate review of the conviction. For many years, however, the Court held that habeas corpus relief would be granted only if the petitioner had been confined pursuant to the judgment of a court that lacked jurisdiction, as in *Ex parte Kearny*, 20 U.S. (7 Wheat.) 38 (1822).

Before the Civil War, the Supreme Court's inquiry into matters of jurisdiction was narrow and formal. In the latter part of the nineteenth century, for reasons yet to be fully examined by legal historians, the Supreme Court began a long process of expanding the concept of "lack of jurisdiction." One significant dictum declared that a trial court would lack jurisdiction if the statute defining the offense was unconstitutional (*Ex parte Siebold*, 100 U.S. 371 (1879)). A decade later, the Supreme Court stated that it could not see why punishment under an unconstitutional statute would violate a person's constitutional rights more than would a conviction under a valid statute if the proceedings were otherwise constitutionally flawed (*Hans Nielsen, Petitioner*, 131 U.S. 176 (1889)). This decision opened a way for possible review by means of habeas corpus of a wide range of procedural issues in criminal trials if the contentions were capable of being framed as constitutional violations.

The Supreme Court's expansion of the scope of habeas corpus slowed down at this time, probably because convicted defendants obtained the right to appeal to the new United States courts of appeals. The broad scope of appeal would encompass most, but not all, of the issues cognizable in habeas corpus. In 1938, the Supreme Court held that the Sixth Amendment guaranteed assistance of counsel to all persons accused of crime in federal courts, unless the right to counsel was knowingly and intelligently waived. Defendants convicted without counsel were likely also to have forfeited their statutory right of appeal by failure to proceed within the prescribed time. This had occurred in a landmark case in which the Supreme Court enunciated the principle of right to counsel (*Johnson v. Zerbst*, 304 U.S. 458 (1938)). The case was, therefore, a habeas corpus proceeding, originating in the lower federal courts and appealed to the Supreme Court.

Inquiry into facts outside the record. Another development of the greatest importance to habeas corpus practice was the granting of power to conduct factual inquiries. Historically, a writ of habeas corpus did not authorize a trial court to determine issues of fact. A writ was discharged—that is, the case was terminated—if the answer of the custodian disclosed a proper basis for confinement of the petitioner, normally the judgment or order of a court. In 1867, however, Congress authorized federal courts, in habeas corpus, to summarily hear and determine the facts of the cases and to dispose of them as law and justice required.

The power to determine facts in federal cases remained dormant until court decisions in the twentieth century enlarged constitutional safeguards of criminal defendants on matters taking place outside the courtroom. Since ordinary direct appeals are confined to the records compiled in trial courts, habeas corpus was necessary to deal with claims of this kind. An early example was an attack on a conviction following a guilty plea, on the ground that the defendant had been coerced into entering the plea by threats or pressures exerted prior to his appearance in the courtroom (*Waley v. Johnston*, 316 U.S. 101 (1942)).

Since 1948, persons confined in federal custody have had a statutory remedy that is intended to fulfill more expeditiously the essential role of habeas corpus. The statute permits a prisoner to ask the court to vacate, set aside, or correct a sentence if it "was imposed in violation of the Constitution or laws of the United States" (28 U.S.C. § 2255 (1976 & Supp. III 1979)). The literal breadth of the remedy has been narrowed by the Supreme Court's conclusion that some questions, including the makeup of a grand jury, are deemed waived unless raised at the outset of a prosecution (*Davis v. United States*, 411 U.S. 233 (1973)). The Supreme Court has not yet settled the scope of issues not based on the Constitution that may be raised under the Section 2255 provision allowing relief when a conviction is in violation of federal law. The Court has considered whether an administrative agency's regulation, on which prosecution had been based, was invalid on the ground that the agency had exceeded the authorization of the governing statute (*Davis v. United States*, 417 U.S. 333 (1974)).

Federal postconviction litigation became the laboratory for the development of modern postconviction remedies. In 1976, procedural rules specially designed for this kind of litigation were issued by the Supreme Court. As modified by Congress, they provide for expeditious processing of these cases.

Federalism and habeas corpus

The distribution of powers between state governments and the federal government is a fundamental aspect of the American federal system. As the several governments act in what they regard as their proper spheres, collisions occur. Over time the resolution of those conflicts results in new power distributions. When this process concerns liberty of persons, as it often does, habeas corpus litigation emerges as the focus for resolving the controversies.

The Habeas Corpus Act of 1867. The major expansion of the statutory base of federal power through habeas corpus came after the Civil War. Fearing that Southern state governments might interfere with reconstruction, Congress in 1867 authorized federal courts to grant habeas corpus to anyone in state custody. The grounds for relief were stated very broadly: anyone held "in violation of the Constitution or laws or treaties of the United States" was to be set free (28 U.S.C. § 2241(c) (1976)). As noted above, this statute also expanded the power of the federal courts to make factual determinations.

Exhaustion of state remedies. In the first decision by the Supreme Court under the act of 1867, the Court construed the act to require state prisoners to exhaust any available state remedies (*Ex parte Royall*, 117 U.S. 241 (1886)). This judicial gloss on the statute assured that state courts would be the principal forums for litigation of the federal claims of state criminal defendants. The exhaustion requirement was later codified in a federal statute (28 U.S.C. § 2254(b) (1976 & Supp. III 1979)).

When state remedies have been exhausted, the federal habeas corpus forum becomes available (*Brown v. Allen*, 344 U.S. 443 (1953)). Such sequential state-federal litigation is without parallel in the federal system. In areas other than criminal prosecutions, state courts must frequently adjudicate issues arising under federal law, including federal constitutional law. Subject to possible review by the United States Supreme Court, the judgments of the state courts are final and binding on the parties to such cases. Only in federal habeas corpus litigation do lower federal courts have the authority and the responsibility to reexamine the decisions of state courts on matters of federal law. Although a federal order granting habeas corpus relief only frees a prisoner from custody and technically does not disturb the state court's judgment, the effect is tantamount to a reversal of that judgment.

Federal courts exercise independent judgment on the ultimate questions of federal law arising in habeas corpus proceedings, but they are influenced by the analyses and conclusions of the state courts that have already ruled on matters presented. Factual findings made by the state courts must be given greater deference than are legal conclusions (28 U.S.C. § 2254(d); *Sumner v. Mata*, 449 U.S. 539 (1981)). Since the distinction between issues of fact and conclusions of law is intrinsically hazy, there will no doubt be future occasions for federal courts to elaborate on the appropriate standards of finality to govern federal habeas corpus litigation.

Fourteenth Amendment rights of state criminal defendants. The primary set of federal constitutional rights arising in habeas corpus litigation derives from the Fourteenth Amendment's command that no state shall "deprive any person of life, liberty, or property, without due process of law." As the Supreme Court has translated the broad principle of the due process clause into the specifics of the criminal process, federal habeas corpus litigation involving state prisoners has grown. Although both the Fourteenth Amendment and the Habeas Corpus Act were enacted immediately after the Civil War, their impact on state criminal prosecutions did not become manifest until well into the twentieth century.

The Supreme Court, whose views of the Fourteenth Amendment are authoritative, has jurisdiction to review judgments of state courts. Many of the Fourteenth Amendment cases came directly to the Supreme Court after a state's highest court had upheld a conviction or after a lower state court had passed judgment in a postconviction proceeding. Other cases reached the Supreme Court as federal habeas corpus cases. Because the Supreme Court is able to review only a few cases, the federal habeas corpus jurisdiction of lower federal courts is important for the nationwide implementation of emerging constitutional norms.

The early twentieth-century decisions involved matters that could be labeled as procedural, but the issues were generally of considerable importance to the outcome of prosecutions. The first case in the series, a 1923 federal habeas corpus case, overrode a prior judgment of the Arkansas supreme court and upset the convictions of five men sentenced to death, on the ground that the trial had been mob-dominated (*Moore v. Dempsey*, 261 U.S. 86 (1923)). Other early decisions found that convictions based on use by the prosecution of perjured testimony or on confessions coerced from suspects by the police violated the Fourteenth Amendment.

The pace of such decisions quickened in the 1950s and 1960s, as the Supreme Court gave an increasingly broad reading to the due process clause. The procedures that the Court found unconstitutional were in general closely related to the concern not to convict innocent persons: lack of defense counsel, prosecution failure to reveal exculpatory evidence, suggestive out-of-court identification of suspects, and improper inducement of guilty pleas.

New Fourteenth Amendment rights tended to be defined as a result of the discovery of unacceptable conduct by public officials in the course of prosecutions. Although such acts or omissions did not necessarily result in the conviction of innocent defendants, the circumstances gave rise to serious doubts. Thus, defendants tried without counsel might have been found guilty even with counsel representing them. Coerced confessions might well be true confessions. However, these matters of procedure are closely related to the truthfulness of the outcome.

On a number of important and recurring issues, the Supreme Court adopted a course of action that avoided the necessity of difficult case-by-case analysis of possible prejudicial injury suffered by particular defendants as a result of unacceptable actions by public officials: it began instead to issue positive mandates defining acceptable behavior by criminal justice officials. Thus, an absolute right to court-appointed counsel for indigent defendants replaced examination of how, in a given trial, lack of counsel may have harmed a particular defendant. The effect was to impose a duty on trial judges to advise unrepresented defendants of their right to counsel and to appoint counsel for those unable to retain attorneys. Similarly, confessions were ruled inadmissible if they had been obtained in circumstances deemed inherently coercive, whether or not a particular suspect's will had been overborne when he made an incriminating statement. Police were required to advise arrested persons of a set of rights, including the right to remain silent and the right to have counsel prior to any interrogation, a requirement commonly referred to as the *Miranda* warnings.

On another very important issue concerning behavior by government officials, the Supreme Court held that state courts must not allow the prosecution to use any evidence obtained by police in the course of an unreasonable search and seizure (*Mapp v. Ohio*, 367 U.S. 643 (1961)). This exclusionary rule, as it is commonly called, in barring the use of evidence that unquestionably proved guilt, placed concern for the integrity of public officials' performance squarely in opposition to concern for the verity of guilt determinations.

These Supreme Court rulings led some to question the use of federal habeas corpus to enforce constitutional norms that were not directly related to truth-seeking in the determination of guilt. The Supreme Court has responded in regard to the exclusionary rule. The Court held that federal habeas corpus courts may not entertain claims that a state criminal court had admitted evidence obtained by an unconstitutional search and seizure when there had been full and fair opportunity to litigate those claims in the

state courts (*Stone v. Powell*, 428 U.S. 465 (1976)). It is doubtful that the Court will treat other Fourteenth Amendment claims in the same way. After the 1976 decision, the Court upheld federal habeas corpus consideration of a claim that racial discrimination had taken place in the selection of the grand jury (*Rose v. Mitchell*, 443 U.S. 545 (1979)), a matter remote from the process for determining guilt or innocence.

While federal habeas corpus is usually applied to circumstances in which a public official has erred on a serious issue, a line of cases has developed in which no such question is presented. The Supreme Court has held that the Fourteenth Amendment is violated if a verdict of guilty is not based on evidence sufficient to support that finding beyond a reasonable doubt (*Jackson v. Virginia*, 443 U.S. 307 (1979)). Moreover, ruled the Court, this claim is cognizable in a federal habeas corpus proceeding. The possible implications of this decision are extremely broad.

Inadequate or abortive state proceedings. In theory, every claim presented in federal habeas corpus cases might have been determined in a prior state proceeding, but this theory has not always been reflected in practice. One reason, now largely overcome, was the serious inadequacy of state postconviction procedures. States generally began to establish modern postconviction procedures after federal habeas corpus litigation indicated that they were needed in order to deal with the developing constitutional law, particularly with claims requiring consideration of issues outside the record of the original prosecution. For a time, however, the federal remedy was in practice the only one available for prisoners in many states. Accordingly, major law reform efforts were addressed to overcoming the problems of states' antiquated systems (American Bar Association). These efforts were largely successful by the late 1970s. An important contribution to the reform of state laws was made by the Uniform Postconviction Procedure Act (1980) (National Conference of Commissioners on Uniform State Laws).

A second explanation for the lack of state court adjudication is failure by the state prisoner to present or to pursue fully the constitutional claim in the state courts. Whether this failure should foreclose federal courts, in subsequent federal habeas corpus proceedings, from determining the merits of the claims has posed an extraordinarily complex set of doctrinal questions. A satisfactorily principled resolution of the issues is still being sought.

If a constitutionally based claim lies close to the core of guilt determination, federal courts tend to exercise habeas corpus jurisdiction to hear the claim on its merits unless the prisoner is shown to have deliberately bypassed the state courts without excuse. In a leading case (*Fay v. Noia*, 372 U.S. 391 (1963)), a brutally coerced confession had been used to convict a defendant of murder; the defendant, having been sentenced to life imprisonment, elected to forego appeal for fear that retrial could lead to a death sentence. When a later change of law precluded a death sentence on retrial, the prisoner sought federal habeas corpus relief. Counsel for the state conceded that the confession had been elicited by police coercion. The Supreme Court held that the defendant's decision not to appeal from conviction was excusable since he then faced a "grisly choice," and it then proceeded to conclude that the prisoner was entitled to relief.

On the other hand, if the asserted constitutional right is more remote from the guilt determination process, a federal habeas corpus applicant is much less likely to prevail. The leading case of this kind also involved a claim of an inadmissible confession. The constitutional standard invoked was not coercion but the newer requirement that arrested suspects must be informed promptly of certain rights, failing which any later confession cannot be admitted into evidence. Although the police had fully met this requirement, the postconviction applicant contended he had not understood what the police had said. The claim had not been advanced either at trial or on appeal in the state courts. In a federal habeas corpus proceeding, the Supreme Court held that the applicant must not only explain satisfactorily why the issue had not been raised in the original trial, but further must show that admission of the confession had caused a miscarriage of justice. The court concluded that these requirements had not been met (*Wainwright v. Sykes*, 433 U.S. 72 (1977)).

By the beginning of the 1980s, the Supreme Court had not yet indicated which sets of constitutional claims would be governed by *Fay* and which by *Wainwright*. The most apparent distinction, based upon the question of whether the underlying right is important to the accuracy of guilt determination, may be criticized on the ground that all constitutional rights do not fit neatly into such categories. More fundamentally, constitutional rights have symbolic qualities that transcend narrow functional analysis of the accuracy of guilt determinations. Such rights may articulate a deep interest in personal privacy and autonomy, limits on the powers of government officials, and concern for fair and balanced processes that are separate from furtherance of truth-seeking in criminal trials. To the extent that constitutional rights are forfeited as a result of abortive state proceedings, these additional values are diminished.

Clarification of the distinction between *Fay* and *Wainwright* may prove unnecessary, owing to the emerging view of the right to effective assistance of counsel. Procedural errors and omissions of the kind that result in abortive state proceedings are commonly the result of choices made by defendants' attorneys, rather than by defendants themselves. Supreme Court opinions have sometimes mentioned supposedly shrewd defense counsel's tactics as a reason for holding that the defendant should be bound by his lawyer's decision and debarred from federal habeas corpus relief.

On the other hand, widespread concern has been voiced over the low quality of the work of much of the trial bar. Chief Justice Warren Burger, one of the most influential persons to address this question publicly, has declared that a large number of trial lawyers are not minimally competent. Forfeiture of a defendant's valuable constitutional right caused by the ignorance, carelessness, or simple mistake of his lawyer raises a serious question about the effectiveness of assistance of counsel. Claims alleging denial of effective assistance of counsel are being presented with growing frequency in state and federal courts, and a strong trend toward demanding a higher standard of professional competence is evident. Persons who challenge their convictions on the basis of ineffective assistance of counsel achieve substantially the same consideration that would have resulted from determination of the merits of the underlying constitutional issues.

Due process of law

Litigation that takes place through habeas corpus and its modern procedural counterparts demands a continuing search for understanding, at the most essential level, of the meaning of due process of law. Law is not a simple concept. It may be said to consist of rules distributing authority to make decisions, as well as rules that govern the decisions to be made. Both kinds of issues arise in habeas corpus cases and, for the most part, the source of the law to be applied is the Constitution. Embedded in the Constitution are fundamental determinations of the distribution of authority—between the states and the federal government, and, through the doctrines of the separation of powers, among the branches of the federal government. Also enshrined in the Constitution are living principles of limited government and individual rights that undergird and constrain all exercise of official power. Questions so basic to the structure and dynamics of the commonweal have no ultimate and certain solutions. It is the inevitable role of habeas corpus to reflect the movement and clash of those quintessential issues as they touch upon the liberty of persons. The Great Writ of Freedom has been and will continue to be a measure of our society's reconciliation of its most cherished values.

CURTIS R. REITZ

See also CRIMINAL PROCEDURE: CONSTITUTIONAL ASPECTS; PRISONERS, LEGAL RIGHTS OF.

BIBLIOGRAPHY

American Bar Association. "Postconviction Remedies." *Standards for Criminal Justice,* vol. 4. 2d ed. Edited by the ABA. Prepared with the assistance of the American Bar Foundation. Boston: Little, Brown, 1980, chap. 22.

AMSTERDAM, ANTHONY G. "Search, Seizure and Section 2255: A Comment." *University of Pennsylvania Law Review* 112 (1964): 378–392.

BATOR, PAUL M. "Finality in Criminal Law and Federal Habeas Corpus for State Prisoners." *Harvard Law Review* 76 (1963): 441–528.

COVER, ROBERT M., and ALEINIKOFF, T. ALEXANDER. "Dialectical Federalism: Habeas Corpus and the Court." *Yale Law Journal* 86 (1977): 1035–1102.

"Developments in the Law: Federal Habeas Corpus." *Harvard Law Review* 83 (1970): 1038–1280.

DUKER, WILLIAM F. "The English Origins of the Writ of Habeas Corpus: A Peculiar Path to Fame." *New York University Law Review* 53 (1978): 983–1054.

FRIENDLY, HENRY J. "Is Innocence Irrelevant? Collateral Attack on Criminal Judgments." *University of Chicago Law Review* 38 (1970): 142–172.

HART, HENRY M., JR. "The Supreme Court 1958 Term: The Time Chart of the Justices." *Harvard Law Review* 73 (1959): 84–125.

Marshall-Wythe School of Law, National Center for State Courts, Symposium. "State Courts and Federalism in the 1980s." *William and Mary Law Review* 22 (1981): 599–846.

National Conference of Commissioners on Uniform State Laws. "Uniform Postconviction Procedure Act (1980)." *Uniform Laws Annotated: Master Edition,* vol. 11, 1981 Supp. St. Paul: West, 1974, pp. 114–123.

OAKS, DALLIN H. "Habeas Corpus in the States: 1776–1865." *University of Chicago Law Review* 32 (1965): 243–288.

———. "The 'Original' Writ of Habeas Corpus in the Supreme Court." *The Supreme Court Review 1962.* Edited by Philip B. Kurland. University of Chicago Press, 1962, pp. 153–211.

REITZ, CURTIS R. "Federal Habeas Corpus: Impact of an Abortive State Proceeding." *Harvard Law Review* 74 (1961): 1315–1373.

———. "Federal Habeas Corpus: Postconviction Remedy for State Prisoners." *University of Pennsylvania Law Review* 108 (1960): 461–532.

SCHAEFER, WALTER V. "Federalism and State Criminal Procedure." *Harvard Law Review* 70 (1956): 1–26.

STRAZZELLA, JAMES A. "Ineffective Assistance of Counsel Claims: New Uses, New Problems." *Arizona Law Review* 19 (1977): 443–484.

HABITUAL OFFENDER

See PREDICTION OF CRIME AND RECIDIVISM; *articles under* SENTENCING.

HANDGUNS

See GUNS, REGULATION OF.

HEREDITY AND CRIME

See CRIME CAUSATION: BIOLOGICAL THEORIES.

HIJACKING

See INTERNATIONAL CRIMINAL LAW; KIDNAPPING; TERRORISM.

HOMICIDE

1. BEHAVIORAL ASPECTS   Marvin E. Wolfgang
    Margaret A. Zahn
2. LEGAL ASPECTS   Lloyd L. Weinreb

1.
BEHAVIORAL ASPECTS

Homicide is the killing of one human being by another. As a legal category, it can be criminal or noncriminal. Criminal homicides are generally considered first-degree murder, when one person causes the death of another with premeditation and intent, or second-degree murder, when the death is with malice and intent but is not premeditated. Voluntary manslaughter usually involves intent to inflict bodily injury without deliberate intent to kill; involuntary manslaughter is negligent or reckless killing without intent to harm.

Noncriminal forms include excusable homicide, usually in self-defense, and justifiable homicide, as when a police officer kills a felon or when a convicted offender is executed by the state. The classification of any homicide as either criminal or noncriminal, or of a death as either a homicide, an accident, or a natural death, is not uniform across all time periods or across legal jurisdictions. What is considered a homicide death varies over time by the legal code of given jurisdictions and by the interpretations and practices of agencies responsible for reporting deaths. When cars were first introduced into the United States, for example, deaths resulting from them were classified by some coroners as homicides, although now they are generally labeled accidental deaths unless caused by negligence. An abortion may be considered a criminal homicide or the exercise of women's reproductive choice. Homicide statistics, like those of many other crimes, reflect definitions and legal interpretations that vary over time and space.

Agencies responsible for reporting deaths influence how a death is reported. Roger Lane describes, for example, that coroners in early twentieth-century America were paid to determine the cause of death on a fee-for-service basis. The same fee was paid no matter how difficult the case, and in some cases, the fee was collected from the convicted offender. In difficult cases or those for which the coroner might not expect payment, as when a newborn was killed by an indigent woman, the cause of death might be reported as suffocation of the infant rather than as a homicide. Criminal homicide reflects the political processes that affect all definitions of crime.

Sources of data on homicide

Homicide data generally derive from either health or police agencies. There are two major sources of international data, one compiled by the United Nations in *World Health Statistics Annual* and the other by the International Criminal Police Organization (Interpol), which was established in 1950. In addition, the national police agency of each country reports the number of that country's homicides for every two-year period. *World Health Statistics Annual* publishes the causes of death, including homicide, for each reporting country. These statistics, which have been collected since 1939, are the joint product of the health and statistical administration of many countries and the office of the United Nations and the World Health Organization. Problems in the use of these sources include lack of consistent definitions and interpretations across jurisdictions and lack of consistent reporting by all countries. Some countries, including many Communist ones, do not routinely report.

Within the United States there are two major na-

tional sources of data on homicide: the National Center for Health Statistics (NCHS) and the Federal Bureau of Investigation's *Crime in the United States* (known as the Uniform Crime Reports and published annually). The NCHS data derive from coroners and medical examiners, who forward death certificates to the center's Division of Vital Statistics. These data focus solely on the homicide victim and generally include information on the cause of death and the age, race, and sex of the victim. Data about offenders, victim-offender relationships, and motives are not included. The various states entered this national reporting system at different times. Prior to the 1930s, when the system became fully national, the data available depended on which states and cities were included. Boston was the first entrant, and in general, there were data from East Coast cities very early. Boston had death data in 1880, Pennsylvania in 1906, and Washington, D.C. in 1880. Other states, such as Georgia and Texas, entered the registry much later—in 1922 and 1933, respectively. In establishing trends, then, there is difficulty in obtaining national data before 1930.

The Uniform Crime Reports, a voluntary national data-collection effort, began in 1930 and gradually accumulated reporting police districts. Homicide reports are detailed and include information on both victims and offenders and, since the 1970s, on victim-offender relationships. This system is the only national one with information on homicide offenders and includes information on crimes classified by size of population, state, county, and Standard Metropolitan Statistical Area. Although there are some problems with the use of the Uniform Crime Reports data, they are commonly used in studies of homicide.

Besides these national sources, researchers have used records of specific homicide cases, available either at medical examiners' offices or at police departments (Wolfgang, 1966; Block). These records are richer in detail than those at the national and international levels and provide more specific evidence on time and location of homicides, alcohol and drug involvement, sequence of events leading to victim-offender confrontations, and the like. Locally based data can be used to augment those compiled nationally and are useful for describing homicide events in detail. Because they are locally based, however, they may not be generalizable to all populations or cities.

Cross-national patterns of criminal homicide

Although there are problems in using international crime statistics because of differing definitions and methods in classifying the phenomenon, both Interpol and United Nations data nonetheless offer useful information on homicide rates in different countries. Of the two, data from the United Nations are more frequently used for cross-national studies. Marvin Wolfgang and Franco Ferracuti, for example, used these data in their discussion of the subcultural determinants of homicide (pp. 273–275). Basing their study on data from the late 1950s and early 1960s, they found that in general, the highest rates of homicide were in Latin America and the Caribbean. Among the fifteen countries and legal dependencies constituting the top quartile, ten were Latin American; the top three were Colombia, Mexico, and Nicaragua. The lowest rates were found in northern and western European countries. Nine northern and western countries were found in the bottom quartile.

Wolfgang and Ferracuti hypothesized that the relatively high homicide rates in Latin American and Caribbean countries, as well as in urban communities and southern states in the United States, are related to subcultural values supporting violence as a means of interpersonal dispute resolution (pp. 275–279). In countries with relatively weak normative supports for the resolution of violent disputes—as in many northern European, western European, and Asiatic countries—low homicide rates are found. These findings are reported for sixty-one countries and do not include many Islamic, African, and Communist countries. The last have not provided, or do not have, reportable data; hence, comparative findings reflect a select set of countries.

Marshall Clinard and Daniel Abbott, using United Nations data, presented international homicide rates for the late 1960s. Of twenty-five countries examined, nine of the thirteen highest were Hispanic; of the five lowest, three were northern or eastern European. Clinard and Abbott explained this observed variation by means of different theories of homicide. Subcultural theory was used to explain homicides in Hispanic countries that result from personal insult and extramarital involvements (p. 59). Homicides resulting from long-standing interfamilial or intertribal disputes were explained primarily as a function of normative or power conflicts. The authors applied this perspective to homicide in India, Ceylon, and sections of Africa (p. 61), introducing the concepts of tradition, obligation, and responsibility. Their formulation was used to account for certain kinds of homicide observed in tradition-bound sectors of African society—for example, those that are the outcome of failure to pay the bride-price attached to the ritual marriage contract.

Dane Archer and Rosemary Gartner compared selected cross-national homicide rates drawn from their comparative crime data file of 110 nations. Their data confirmed previous findings: Latin American and Caribbean countries are represented among the high-rate countries, and European countries are among the low-rate ones. Of the ten high-rate countries, five are Latin American, Caribbean, or Hispanic; of the ten low-rate countries, eight are northern, eastern or western European.

Insufficient cross-national data exist on the basic demographics of criminal homicide—that is, age, sex, race, and socioeconomic distributions. The existing data, however, suggest that criminal homicide is more prevalent among the young, among males, and among racial, ethnic, and religious minorities (Connor). The United States scores substantially higher than European countries, but lower than most Latin American ones, in the rate of criminal homicide. The rate in the United States is relatively high, especially when compared to other countries of similar levels of development, affluence, and cultural heritage.

Patterns of criminal homicide in the United States

Comparative studies have focused on the broad question of rates of homicide, but studies in the United States are more detailed. They show how the rate changes through time, which groups and regions are affected, the relationships between victims and offenders, and the like. Trend studies in the United States (Klebba; Farley) and comparative analyses in different time periods (Zahn) reveal that the overall homicide rate increased from 1900 to the early 1930s. The rate declined slowly after 1933 and was low in the 1940s and 1950s. Homicide in the United States was at a minimum in the 1950s (Farley) but was followed by a modest rise and then a steep rise from 1963 through the late 1970s. The pattern held for blacks and whites and for males and females, although homicide has always been much more common among blacks and males. Reynolds Farley has reported that age-adjusted homicide rates are about six times greater for nonwhites than for whites, and four times higher for men than for women. Homicide victimization rates are highest for young adults: the highest rates generally occur between the ages of twenty-five and thirty-five. Homicide is the leading cause of death among nonwhites between twenty and thirty years of age, and is the second most common cause of mortality for white men of these ages (Farley).

There are consistent differences between males and females, blacks and whites, and young and old in the rate of homicide victimization. There are also differences in geographic patternings of homicide, with higher rates of violence in the South. These differences have led some to posit a regional pattern of violence (Hackney; Gastil) according to which the South is characterized by a historic tradition of violence. That tradition, which defines the environment as hostile, was created by the perceived need for protection from threats originating outside the region. The southern identity has been linked to a "siege mentality," which denies individual responsibility; threats to the region come from outside the region, and threats to the person from outside the self. High rates of gun ownership reflect this mentality. Raymond Gastil developed further Sheldon Hackney's notion of southern culture, noting that the South remained a frontier society for a longer time than the North. Until the Civil War, many parts of the settled South were wilderness. Distances made schools harder to support and reach, and made the frontier skills with rifle and knife much more vital, generation after generation, than in the North. This tradition still exists.

Victim-offender relationships. Literature on homicide since the 1960s has attempted to describe the relationship between the victim and offender and the motive for the slaying. Although many relationships occur in human affairs, only some seem to be persistently associated with homicide. Seldom, for example, is an employee-employer relationship associated with homicide, but frequently a husband-wife relationship is. It is less common for a patron to kill a bartender than another person, even though they are all in the same social situation and may all have the same demographic characteristics.

Each homicide event can be characterized by motive. The descriptions of the motive or of the events by the participants may differ from those of official agencies or of researchers. Definitions used by some researchers for *friends, acquaintances,* or *strangers* are sometimes not specified, thus making it difficult to compare various studies of victim-offender relationships. Such comparisons show that in early American history the major type of homicide in both the North (Lane) and the South was that of a male killing another male with whom he was acquainted, while they were in a nonwork setting. In the 1920s and 1930s, criminal homicides became more prominent with bootlegging (Boudouris; Lashly). In the 1940s and 1950s, the percentage of homicides between husbands and wives was more pronounced, although homicides between two males known to one another as friends and acquaintances were still significant. In the late 1960s and the 1970s, victims who were strangers to the offenders, or victims killed by offenders who were unknown to the police, appeared to be more prevalent than in the past.

Numerous studies have examined the relative distribution of types of victim-offender relations, fewer have looked at characteristics that distinguish one type of homicide relationship from another, and fewer yet have studied the causal processes that may explain the differences. Wolfgang's initial study of Philadelphia (1958) confirmed some differences between types. An analysis of homicides in eight American cities (Zahn and Riedel) attempted to establish significant differences between murders of family members, friends, acquaintances, and strangers. The findings indicated that these types differ from one another in important ways. Domestic homicide involves both men and women; if a woman is killed or kills, she is most likely to be part of a family context. Offenders in domestic homicides tend to be older: the median age is the low to middle thirties. Although there is variation by city, family homicides involve more diverse use of weapons, such as knives, than do other types of homicides, in which guns are used in approximately two-thirds of the cases.

Homicides between two friends or acquaintances—the largest category in all cities—usually involve a male killing another male within the same racial group. Males tend to be close to the same age, generally in the early thirties, with the victim slightly older than the offender. Such homicides are likely to be witnessed, and guns are generally used. Seldom is the event related to another felony, such as robbery.

The killing of strangers is a distinct type, accounting for approximately one-fourth of the homicides in the eight cities studied in 1978. Stranger-to-stranger killings generally occur on the street or in commercial establishments. The victim is uniformly older than the assailant, and the disparity in ages is greater for such homicides than for others. Although stranger-to-stranger killings are usually intraracial, there is a higher percentage of interracial homicides, especially those with black offenders and white victims, in this category than in other types. The majority of the killings are committed with handguns, and in southern cities the percentage killed by guns is generally higher than in other cities. Unlike most other criminal homicides, stranger-to-stranger killings are often linked to other felonies. About 57 percent of these homicides are felony-linked, usually with robbery (Zahn and Riedel).

Some studies show an overall pattern in non-felony-related deaths. Richard Gelles examined intrafamily violence and found that violence emerges from a series of provoking arguments that escalate to the point of homicide. The arguments are often threats to identity and self-esteem, and sexual identity is often salient.

In a study of seventy cases of killings involving intimates, David Luckenbill concluded that criminal homicide begins when a victim engages in some "insulting" behavior that is interpreted as an offense to "face." The offender decides to restore face through a retaliatory move, the most common being the issuing of an ultimatum. The victim then escalates the interaction by accepting the ultimatum as legitimate, and establishes a working agreement that violence is appropriate to the situation. Involvement in battle is enhanced by the availability of weapons, and homicide is the result.

Whether these processes are the same in stranger-to-stranger killings is relatively unknown. Richard Block attempted to study this phenomenon by examining robbery-related injuries in Chicago and found that the process is affected by the victim's resistance and by the presence of a weapon. The robber's reaction to resistance is the use of force, which commonly results in injury to the victim.

The technology of homicide. Homicide is also characterized by technology, which includes implements used to kill (guns, knives, and clubs) and substances (drugs and alcohol) that may cause or contribute to the crime. Most studies show that a gun is the weapon of choice in the United States, although there is some variation depending on the victim-offender relationship, the region of the country, and even specific time periods. Guns are seldom used in the killing of an infant by a parent, but are frequently used in the killing of a victim by a stranger. A high percentage of homicide deaths in the South involve guns. The extent to which gun control would affect the rate of homicide remains an issue of continuing debate. Although some researchers suggest that the ready availability of guns in the United States may be related to the nation's high rates of criminal violence, others suggest that factors associated with the willingness to use guns are also of importance.

There have been attempts to explore the relationship between homicide and the use of alcohol and drugs. Studies that examine alcohol use and homicide commonly examine the percentage of victims, offenders, or both who were drinking at the time of the fatal attack. Wolfgang's study (1966), for example, found that in 64 percent of the homicides in Philadelphia, alcohol had been consumed by either the victim or the offender. Other studies find different percentages (Greenberg). Although much of the literature

shows some association between alcohol and homicide, the means by which this association occurs remains problematic. Wolfgang's 1967 report and the report of the National Commission on the Causes and Prevention of Violence (Mulvihill, Tumin, and Curtis) caution that there is no direct causal connection between alcohol and homicide. The link may be the result of weakened behavioral controls, or, as Gelles has suggested, people learn that drunken behavior is a "time out" from the norms and demands of civilized interaction.

The relationship between drugs other than alcohol and homicide poses many of the same problems. Paul Goldstein has suggested that drugs may be associated with homicide in one of three ways. First, drug use by offenders or victims may alter behavior and increase the likelihood of violence or of victimization. Second, some drug users may engage in violent crime accidentally while committing relatively nonviolent crimes aimed at securing money to buy drugs. Third, homicide may be systematically related to the use of illegal substances in that it may involve conflicts between rival drug dealers over territory, settlement for "bad debts" or for "bad drugs," and the like. Studies dealing with the impact of each of these problems have been made, although which, if any, of the three contributes most to the drug-homicide relationship is unknown. Some researchers (Goldstein) suggest that systematically related violence is the most frequent, although there are only limited data to support this contention.

Sociological explanations of violence

There are three sociological approaches to explaining homicide: the cultural-subcultural, the structural, and the interactional. Cultural theorists explain homicide as resulting from learned, shared values and behavior specific to a given group. The basic causes are in the norms and values, transmitted across generations, that are learned by members of a group. Certain subgroups exhibit higher rates of homicide because they are participants in a subculture that has violence as a norm. First developed by Wolfgang in 1958 and later expanded by Wolfgang and Ferracuti in 1967, this position asserts that there is a subculture of violence—that is, a subculture with a cluster of values that support and encourage the overt use of force in interpersonal relations and group interactions. The subculture is reflected in the psychological and behavioral traits of its participants. Ready access to weapons and the carrying of weapons are symbols indicating a willingness to participate in violence and to expect and be ready for retaliation. The development of favorable attitudes toward the use of violence in a subculture involves learned behavior and a process of differential association or identification. Because the use of violence is not necessarily viewed as illicit, the users do not have feelings of guilt about their behavior. In general, violence is a learned, shared mode of adaptation for specific groups of people (Wolfgang and Ferracuti).

Some critics take issue with the subcultural approach, stating that it fails to explain how or why the subculture emerged and why some who are exposed to it become violent but others similarly exposed do not. Data on individual males in low-status groups do not confirm that members of these groups necessarily condone violence any more readily than do other groups (Ball-Rokeach; Erlanger). However, these studies have been severely criticized on methodological grounds. Colin Loftin and Robert Hill, in examining rates of southern violence, suggested that structural indicators, such as poverty, may explain the correlation. According to them, there is strong evidence that socioeconomic variables are closely associated with homicide rates and that these variables are directly related to the maintenance of high levels of interpersonal violence in the South (p. 722).

These theoretical and empirical critiques lead to two alternative explanations for criminal homicide: the structuralist and the interactionist. The structuralist position, more amorphous than the subcultural approach, asserts that broad-scale social forces such as lack of opportunity, institutional racism, persistent poverty, demographic transitions, and population density determine homicide rates. These forces operate independently of human cognition and do not require individual learning to explain their impact. One illustration of this approach is the work of Richard Cloward and Lloyd Ohlin, who related opportunity and control structures to conflict gangs. Another is that of Pierre Van Den Berghe, who argued that resource competition leads to aggression: when population needs increase, competition for resources increases, and unless this competition is checked by attempts to monopolize or regulate the distribution of resources, homicide rates increase. In general, structural explanations suggest variables that influence homicide rates. They do not specify, however, the conditions under which these variables lead to homicide rather than to other possible outcomes, such as passivity. With few exceptions, the explanations fail to examine whether structural forces work the same way for rates of family, friend, and stranger-to-stranger killings. One study suggests that poverty

may be related to homicides within the family or among friends but not to nonprimary homicide (Parker and Smith).

Interaction theory focuses on the character of relationships that escalate into homicide. Interaction theorists see homicide as resulting from the interaction process itself; they examine how the act of a participant precipitates the acts of another and how escalating conflict culminates in homicide. Both Gelles and Luckenbill represent this viewpoint.

Each of these approaches provides some insights into homicide. Gelles and Murray Straus have attempted to blend the two approaches in the area of family violence, and Lynn Curtis has attempted such a synthesis for homicides and violence committed by blacks in the United States. According to Curtis, culture is an intervening interpretative variable between structural determinants and violent outcomes. The structural determinants of economic marginality and institutional racism are filtered through a series of subcultural values and behavior. When coupled with weapons possession and alcohol and drug consumption, such values lead to lethal conflict.

How effectively these integrated approaches can be researched has yet to be determined. Their inclusiveness, however, is both suggestive and appealing. Additional attempts at theoretical integration between these approaches would seem to be the next important step in the study of criminal homicide.

MARVIN E. WOLFGANG
MARGARET A. ZAHN

See also ASSASSINATION; GUNS, REGULATION OF; HOMICIDE: LEGAL ASPECTS; SUICIDE: BEHAVIORAL ASPECTS; TERRORISM; VIOLENCE; WAR AND VIOLENT CRIME.

BIBLIOGRAPHY

ARCHER, DANE, and GARTNER, ROSEMARY. "Homicide in 110 Nations: The Development of the Comparative Crime Data File." *International Annals of Criminology* 16 (1977): 109–139.

BALL-ROKEACH, SANDRA J. "Values and Violence: A Test of the Subculture of Violence Thesis." *American Sociological Review* 38, no. 6 (1973): 736–749.

BLOCK, RICHARD. *Violent Crime: Environment, Interaction, and Death.* Lexington, Mass.: Heath, Lexington Books, 1977.

BOUDOURIS, JAMES. "Trends in Homicide, Detroit 1926–1968." Ph.D. dissertation, Wayne State University, 1970.

CLINARD, MARSHALL B., and ABBOTT, DANIEL J. *Crime in Developing Countries: A Comparative Perspective.* New York: Wiley, 1973.

CLOWARD, RICHARD A., and OHLIN, LLOYD E. *Delinquency and Opportunity: A Theory of Delinquent Gangs.* New York: Free Press, 1960.

CONNOR, WALTER D. "Criminal Homicide, USSR/USA: Reflections on Soviet Data in a Comparative Framework." *Journal of Criminal Law and Criminology* 64 (1973): 111–117.

CURTIS, LYNN A. *Violence, Race, and Culture.* Lexington, Mass.: Heath, Lexington Books, 1975.

ERLANGER, HOWARD S. "The Empirical Status of the Subculture of Violence Thesis." *Social Problems* 22 (1974): 280–292.

FARLEY, REYNOLDS. "Homicide Trends in the United States." *Demography* 17 (1980): 177–188.

Federal Bureau of Investigation. *Crime in the United States.* Uniform Crime Reports for the United States. Washington, D.C.: U.S. Department of Justice, FBI, annually.

GASTIL, RAYMOND. "Homicide and a Regional Culture of Violence." *American Sociological Review* 36 (1971): 412–427.

GELLES, RICHARD J. *The Violent Home: A Study of Physical Aggression between Husbands and Wives.* Beverly Hills, Calif.: Sage, 1972.

———, and STRAUS, MURRAY A. "Determinants of Violence in the Family: Toward a Theoretical Integration." *Contemporary Theories about the Family,* vol. 1. Edited by Wesley R. Burr, Ruben Hill, F. Ivan Nye, and Ira L. Reiss. New York: Free Press, 1979, pp. 549–581.

GOLDSTEIN, PAUL J. "Drugs and Violent Behavior." Paper presented to the Academy of Criminal Justice Sciences, Louisville, Ky., March 1982.

GREENBERG, STEPHANIE W. "Alcohol and Crime: A Methodological Critique of the Literature." *Research on the Relationship between Alcohol and Crime: Perspectives on the Relationships between Alcohol Consumption and Criminal Behavior.* Edited by James J. Collins, Jr. New York and London: Guilford Press, 1981, pp. 70–109.

HACKNEY, SHELDON. "Southern Violence." *The History of Violence in America: Historical and Comparative Perspectives—A Report Submitted to the National Commission on the Causes and Prevention of Violence.* Edited by Hugh D. Graham and Ted R. Gurr. Introduction by John Herbers. New York: Bantam Books, 1969, pp. 505–527.

HEPBURN, JOHN R. "Subcultures, Violence, and the Subculture of Violence: An Old Rut or a New Road?" *Criminology* 9 (1971): 87–98.

International Criminal Police Organization. *Statistiques criminelles internationales.* St. Cloud, France: INTERPOL, biennially.

KLEBBA, A. JOAN. "Homicide Trends in the United States, 1900–1974." *U.S. Public Health Service Public Health Reports* 90 (1975): 195–204.

LANE, ROGER. *Violent Death in the City: Suicide, Accident, and Murder in Nineteenth-century Philadelphia.* Cambridge, Mass.: Harvard University Press, 1979.

LASHLY, ARTHUR V. "Homicide in Cook County." *The Illinois Crime Survey.* Chicago: Illinois Association for Criminal Justice, 1929, chap. 13.

LOFTIN, COLIN, and HILL, ROBERT H. "Regional Subculture and Homicide: An Examination of the Gastil-Hackney Thesis." *American Sociological Review* 39 (1974): 714–724.

LUCKENBILL, DAVID F. "Criminal Homicide as a Situated Transaction." *Social Problems* 25 (1977): 176–186.

MULVIHILL, DONALD J.; TUMIN, MELVIN H.; and CURTIS, LYNN A. *Crimes of Violence: A Staff Report Submitted to the National Commission on the Causes and Prevention of Violence.* 3 vols. Washington, D.C.: The Commission, 1969.

PARKER, ROBERT NASH, and SMITH, M. DWAYNE. "Deterrence, Poverty, and Type of Homicide." *American Journal of Sociology* 85 (1979): 614–624.

United Nations, World Health Organization. *World Health Statistics Annual.* New York: WHO, annually.

VAN DEN BERGHE, PIERRE L. "Bringing Beasts Back In: Toward a Biosocial Theory of Aggression." *American Sociological Review* 39 (1974): 777–788.

WOLFGANG, MARVIN E. *Crimes of Violence: Report Submitted to the President's Commission on Law Enforcement and Administration of Justice.* Washington, D.C.: The Commission, 1967.

———. *Patterns in Criminal Homicide* (1958). Reprint. New York: Wiley, 1966.

———, and FERRACUTI, FRANCO. *The Subculture of Violence: Towards an Integrated Theory in Criminology.* Translated from the Italian. London: Tavistock, 1967.

ZAHN, MARGARET A. "Homicide in the Twentieth-century United States." *History and Crime.* Edited by James A. Inciardi and Charles E. Faupel. Beverly Hills, Calif.: Sage, 1980, pp. 111–131.

———, and RIEDEL, MARC. "Homicide in Eight American Cities." Unpublished book manuscript, 1982.

2.
LEGAL ASPECTS

Introduction

The central theme of the law of homicide is the unique value of human life. While danger to life is an element of many other crimes as well, the law of homicide focuses on it directly, by declaring criminal a wide range of conduct that actually causes a death. Because life is valued so highly, such conduct is prohibited much more generally than conduct causing other kinds of harm. Whereas the criminal law for the most part is concerned with intentional harms, criminal homicide includes not only intentional killing but also a broad range of conduct from which death results unintentionally.

Homicide is the killing of a human being by another human being. (Suicide, insofar as the criminal law deals with it, is treated separately.) A question occasionally arises whether a death satisfies this definition, either because it is not clear whether the victim was a "human being" for this purpose or because it is not clear whether another person's conduct caused the death. Most often, the fact of homicide is not an issue. The difficult questions are whether the homicide is criminal or noncriminal and, if the first, in which category of criminal homicide it belongs.

The victim a human being. When homicide is the issue, the law makes no distinctions among human beings as victims. It is human life as such that is protected, and none of the criteria of worth by which we may classify persons for other purposes is material. Death is the more or less remote end for us all, but it is no less homicide that the life cut short would soon have ended anyway, because of age, ill health, or any other reason.

No question has arisen in any adjudicated case as to whether a living creature who is the victim of a homicide was a human being or belonged to some other species. A problem of definition sometimes arises because it is necessary to determine when, in the process of prenatal or postnatal development, life as a separate human being begins or when, in the process of dying, life as a human being ends. The usual rule is that the victim of a homicide must have been "born alive." The older law required that the fetus have been fully separated from the mother and have a separate existence, including an independent circulatory system; it was sometimes also required that the umbilical cord have been cut. There has been some modification of the requirement of full separation, probably in recognition of the easier and safer conditions of ordinary childbirth. It is still generally the law that the victim must have been born alive, which means at least that there were signs of separate existence and that the birth was far enough advanced so that it would ordinarily have been completed successfully. The destruction of a fetus before it has reached this stage of development is covered by statutes dealing specifically with abortion or the killing of a fetus.

At the other end of a life, the availability of heroic medical techniques to sustain some of the body's vital functions, including circulation and respiration, after other functions have stopped has raised the question of when life ends. The question may be critical if an organ transplant is contemplated, because it is homicide if a human being, however near death, is killed; a successful transplant requires that the organ be removed before necrosis of the tissue sets in. There is scant law to answer the question. In ordinary cases, death is deemed to have occurred when there is absence of a heartbeat and respiration. It has also been urged that irreversible coma or cortical brain death, which involves destruction of the cognitive faculties, is enough to constitute legal death, even if circulatory and respiratory action continue.

Action causing death. If someone acts with the intention to kill another person and the death occurs as he intended, there is no difficulty in establishing that his conduct is the cause of death. If he acts without intending to kill or if he has such intent but the death occurs in an unanticipated way, it may not be obvious whether his conduct or some other contributing factor for which someone else or no one is criminally responsible should be regarded as the cause of death. Efforts to define more precisely the element of causation in homicide have not taken the law beyond what the concept of causation itself conveys. The matter is left to the trier of fact, who must decide on the basis of common sense and ordinary experience whether to attribute causal responsibility.

Since homicide is constituted by a result rather than a particular kind of action, one can commit homicide by an omission or failure to act, if the omission is the cause of death. In many situations, more than one person has an opportunity to take action that would avert death; it would be an extravagant extension of the notion of causation to say that the failure of each caused the death. Furthermore, the criminal law does not generally impose a duty to aid another, even if aid would avoid serious injury to the other and could easily and safely be given. Accordingly, criminal liability for homicide based on an omission is limited to failure to perform an act that one is otherwise legally required to perform. Liability is not based only on a moral obligation, however plain, arising from the danger to life or any other circumstance.

The most common example of such liability is the death of a dependent child resulting from a parent's failure to provide the ordinary care required by law. The relationship of marriage also imposes on each spouse a duty to care for the other that will sustain liability for homicide. Other relationships, like the employer-employee relationship or the ship's captain-seaman relationship, may also provide a basis for liability; the increasing impersonality of such relationships makes liability doubtful if there is not also some other basis of liability. A legal duty to act may be prescribed by a statute or regulation or may arise from a specific contractual undertaking or a voluntary undertaking that places the other person in one's care. Even if there was a legal duty to act, a death resulting from an omission is not a criminal homicide unless all the elements of the offense, discussed below, are also present. If a person's omission to perform a legal duty was not intentional or negligent, we should probably not describe it as having caused the death; but in any case, in the absence of the required culpability, the omission would not constitute a crime. Convictions of manslaughter by omission are not as rare as convictions of murder by omission; the latter are not, however, unknown, the most common example being a parent's failure to care for an infant who is intentionally left to die.

When the failure to perform a legal duty manifests the same culpability that establishes liability for an act that causes death, liability for the omission, if death results, is unproblematic. One whose grossly negligent failure to act causes a death is not less guilty than one whose grossly negligent act causes a death. Similarly, if a person's legal duty to act has the effect that no one else will probably act in his place, his deliberate nonperformance with the intent to cause death is not very different from a deliberate act. It may not, however, always be possible to establish a close equivalence between acts and omissions. Doubts of this kind, if they arise, are resolved as part of the requirement that the omission in question be the cause of death.

The notion of causation is usually used disjunctively. Ordinarily, a conclusion that one person has killed another precludes a conclusion that another person's separate conduct has brought about the same death. Provided that the element of causing the death of another is satisfied in each case, there is no rule prohibiting more than one person from being criminally liable for the same death. If both parents of a child, each acting independently, failed to give him adequate care and the child died as a result, they might both be guilty of homicide. Similarly, in theory two persons whose independent acts were each the cause of another's death might both be liable.

Most American jurisdictions have preserved a common-law rule that a person cannot be convicted of homicide unless the death occurs within a year and a day after the conduct alleged to have caused the death. The purpose of the rule is to avoid a conviction if the passage of time has rendered the element of causation uncertain. Taking account of advances in medical science, the Model Penal Code and the law of some states have abandoned the rule.

Noncriminal and criminal homicide. Despite the value of life, the law recognizes that in some circumstances other values prevail. The official carrying out of a sentence of death, for example, is a deliberate, carefully planned homicide pursuant to the authority of the state. Killing an enemy in battle during war is another example of justifiable homicide, which the state not only permits but approves. There are in addition a number of situations in which the use of deadly force is permitted even though there is no official purpose to take life. In certain circumstances, deadly force can be used to defend oneself or others against the threat of death or serious injury or to prevent commission of a felony or the escape of a felon. The combination of another strongly supported value and the unavoidable necessity of risking life to protect that value excuses the homicide. If life is not taken intentionally, there is no criminal liability unless the actor's conduct is culpable to the extent specified by the categories of unintentional criminal homicide, the least of which requires substantial negligence. Many unforeseen deaths that can be traced causally to the conduct of a particular person occur simply as accidents for which no one is criminally responsible.

Criminal homicide is everywhere divided into categories that reflect the historical distinction in English law between murder and manslaughter. American statutory formulations have varied the terminology and the precise classifications; many statutes create more than two forms of criminal homicide, for purposes of definition and/or punishment. These variations notwithstanding, it is usually possible to discern a category that corresponds to the common-law crime of murder, the paradigm of which is a deliberate killing without legal justification or excuse, and a category that corresponds to the common-law crime of manslaughter and comprises killings that either are committed in circumstances which substantially mitigate their intentional aspect or are not intentional. In common speech as well as in the law, *murder* refers to the most serious criminal homicides, and *manslaughter* to those that may be serious crimes for which a substantial penalty is imposed but lack the special gravity of murder.

Murder

The traditional definition of *murder* is that it is a homicide committed with "malice aforethought." That phrase, as it developed in English law, was a technical term referring to the mental state of the actor or to the other equivalent circumstances that qualified a homicide as murder. It did not invariably require malice or forethought. While it is still common to use the phrase in connection with murder, it has no independent descriptive significance. In the common law, there was malice aforethought if the homicide was accompanied by (1) intention to kill; (2) intention to cause serious injury; (3) extreme recklessness or disregard of a very substantial risk of causing death; (4) commission or attempted commission of a felony; or (5) according to some authorities, resistance to a lawful arrest. Modern definitions of murder have clarified and in some respects limited these as elements of the crime of murder. In general, the distinguishing feature of the crime is an intent to kill or a disregard of so plain a risk of death to another that it is treated as the equivalent of an intent to kill.

Intention to kill. All jurisdictions place the intentional killing of another without justification, excuse, or mitigating circumstances within the category of murder, as the most serious form of criminal homicide. While intentional killings may be classified further into subcategories of greater or lesser gravity, there is no controversy about their general classification as murder. Intent to kill has nothing to do with motive as such. While the circumstances that give rise to the intent may mitigate culpability, the law makes no differentiation between a killing with a benevolent motive, like euthanasia, and any other intentional killing.

Ambiguities in the general use of the concept of "intention" to describe conduct have caused trouble in its use to define murder. If the actor's very purpose is to kill, there is no difficulty. It may be, however, that the death of another is an apparently necessary means to the accomplishment of his purpose but that he would be just as satisfied if it were achieved otherwise. Or, he may be aware that a death is a substantially certain consequence of his conduct, without wanting or trying to bring it about. Courts have wrestled with the distinctions among such states of mind and sometimes offer elaborate analyses of them in the context of particular facts. While such efforts may help to explain the result based on those facts, they do not yield generalizations beyond the ordinary open use of the concept of intention. In general, if the actor is aware that the likelihood of a death resulting from his conduct goes beyond the level of risk to the level of certainty or near-certainty, the element of intent is satisfied. The availability of another category of murder based on extreme recklessness instead of intent helps to ease the burden of decision in borderline cases.

Since persons who intend to kill unlawfully are not likely to proclaim their intention, murder must often be established without explicit proof of intent to kill. The use of a deadly weapon is ordinarily sufficient to establish that element of the crime. While this result may be based on a "presumption" arising from use of a deadly weapon, the presumption amounts only to the usual inference that a person intends the ordinary and probable consequences of his actions. A killing may be murder even though the actor intended to kill someone other than the person who was the actual victim. Although the killing of that person was not intentional, it is enough that the actor acted with the intent to kill. His intent is sometimes said to be "transferred" to the actual killing.

As one of the most serious crimes, murder has historically been a capital offense. All cases of murder were capital offenses under the common law, which remained unchanged in England until 1957, when the class of capital murders was sharply limited; before then, capital punishment could be avoided only by the exercise of executive discretion to commute the sentence of death. In the United States, the Pennsylvania legislature in 1794 limited capital punishment by distinguishing between intentional killings that are "willful, deliberate or premeditated" and those that are not (Pa. Act of April 22, 1794, ch. 257, § 2, 3 Dallas 599). (The formula was later changed to "willful, deliberate and premeditated.") The former, along with a restricted category of felony murder, discussed below, and killing by poison or lying in wait, were labeled murder in the first degree and remained punishable by death. All other kinds of murder were designated murder in the second degree and were not capital offenses. This distinction and the "degree" labels were adopted elsewhere and continue to be widely used. While the term *willful* by itself does not add to the requirement of intent, the deliberation-premeditation formula calls attention to the difference between someone who kills "in cold blood," fully aware of what he is doing and determined to bring about the result, and someone who acts intentionally but impulsively, without having turned the plan over in his mind. Courts have repeatedly observed that deliberation and premeditation require no particular period of reflection; a very short time before the plan is formed and, once formed, executed, is enough. For this reason and because it is so unclear what kind or quality of deliberation and premeditation is required, the formula has been criticized for giving juries power to dispense verdicts of different severity without any workable standard to guide them. As much criticized as it has been, and difficult as it has been to apply in close cases, the formula reflects a perceived difference of culpability in the paradigms.

Intention to injure seriously. The intention to injure that constituted one of the common law's categories of malice aforethought was an intention to cause serious physical injury, stopping short of death itself. Provided that the intended injury is truly serious, so that an accidental death from an ordinary assault is not included, few homicides that fall within this category would not also fall within one of the other categories of murder. Death having in fact been the result, in most cases in which a jury is able to find the necessary intent to injure it will be able to find either an intent to kill or extreme disregard of a risk to life. One of the functions of this category of malice aforethought may indeed have been to relieve somewhat the burden of finding an intent specifically to kill rather than to inflict a serious injury.

The Model Penal Code eliminates intent to injure as a separate basis of liability for murder. The drafters concluded that proper cases for liability of this type will be included without it. The only clear case of murder under the common law that is excluded under the Code is one in which the actor inflicts serious injury while taking express precautions not to kill his victim, and the victim dies anyway. Such a case would in any event fall within some category of criminal homicide—manslaughter, if not murder. On the other hand, retention of the common-law classification leaves the possibility that unless the degree of seriousness of the intended injury is emphasized, an unintentional killing not accompanied by the same culpability as an intentional killing will be treated in the same way. Some jurisdictions follow the lead of the Model Penal Code; many others retain this category of murder.

Extreme recklessness. The common law recognized as the equivalent of an intent to kill an attitude of extreme recklessness toward the life of others. One whose conduct displayed plain disregard for a substantial, unjustified risk to human life was guilty of murder if his conduct caused a death. Various formulas have been used to describe this category of malice aforethought, including phrases such as "a depraved mind regardless of human life," "an abandoned and malignant heart," and "a heart regardless of social duty and fatally bent on mischief." Whatever formula is used, the key elements are that the actor's conduct perceptibly creates a very large risk that someone will be killed, which he ignores without adequate justification. The risk must be large, and it must be evident; there must also not be circumstances that make it reasonable to impose such risk on others. It is not necessary that the actor be aware of the identity of the person or persons whose life he endangers or that he have any desire that they be killed. The Model Penal Code sums this up in a requirement of recklessness "under circumstances manifesting extreme indifference to the value of human life" (§ 210.2(1)(b)).

The scope of this category of murder evidently depends considerably on how "extreme" the actor's conduct has to be. Properly limited, the category includes only conduct about which it might fairly be said that the actor "as good as" intended to kill his victim and

displayed the same unwillingness to prefer the life of another person to his own objectives. Examples of such conduct, which have been the basis of convictions for murder, are firing a gun into a moving vehicle or an occupied house, firing in the direction of a group of persons, and failing to feed an infant while knowing that it was starving to death. Expanded much beyond cases of this kind, the category might include conduct involving a high degree of carelessness or recklessness that is nevertheless distinct from an intent to kill and more properly included within some lesser category of homicide.

The question is occasionally raised whether the actor must be aware of the risk he creates, if it would be plain to an ordinary reasonable person. Unless the actor is subject to some personal disability that accounts for his lack of awareness, it is most unlikely that he will be unaware of, rather than simply indifferent to, a plain risk so extreme that murder is in issue. In such a case, the resolution will probably depend on the jurisdiction's treatment of that kind of disability generally. If the disability is accepted as a defense or mitigation generally, then it will avoid the charge of murder; otherwise, the actor's lack of awareness will not help him. Thus, for example, while the Model Penal Code's formulation requires conscious disregard of the risk of death, one who was unaware of the risk because he was drunk could nevertheless be found guilty of murder, because the Code elsewhere provides that self-induced intoxication does not avoid a charge of recklessness as an element of an offense. Aside from special cases of this kind, it is probably safe to conclude that the extreme recklessness which characterizes this category of murder includes a realization of the risk. A lesser degree of risk, of which the actor might be unaware, would suffice for manslaughter but not murder.

Felony murder. The common-law crime of murder included a homicide committed by a person in the course of committing (or attempting to commit) a felony. The felon—and, according to the rules of accomplice liability, his accomplices—was guilty of murder even if he had no intent to kill or injure anyone and committed no act manifesting extreme recklessness toward human life. The origin of this doctrine may reflect the difficulty of proving specifically an intent to kill, in circumstances in which the intent to commit a felony may suggest a willingness to kill if necessary and other proof either way is lacking. Felonies under early English law were mostly violent crimes and were in any case punishable by death. An attempt to commit a felony was only a misdemeanor, however; the felony-murder doctrine, which also applied to uncompleted felonies, did change the outcome if a homicide was committed during an unsuccessful attempt.

The number of felonies has increased dramatically under modern law. Statutory felonies include a large number of offenses that, however serious on other grounds, do not ordinarily pose great danger to life. Application of the felony-murder doctrine to them distorts the concept of murder as a crime involving a serious direct attack on the value of human life. The explanation that the intent to commit the felony "supplies" the malice aforethought merely states the conclusion. So also, stretched to its logical limits, the felony-murder doctrine would make a felon guilty of murder even if the victim were killed by someone else trying to prevent the felony, provided it were found that the commission of the felony caused the death. In this way, it was occasionally held that when a policeman fired at felons and the bullet struck and killed a bystander, the felons were guilty of murder.

Far as such a death is from the intentional killing that is the paradigm of murder, one can perhaps understand the attitude which leads to the conclusion that the felon should be liable. If not for the felon's conduct—the commission of the felony—the victim would not be dead, accidentally or not. Since in that sense the commission of the felony is the cause of death and the felon has in any case engaged in criminal conduct, it is easy to hold him responsible for the death as well. Even so, it is not appropriate to describe his conduct as murder if he has not engaged in conduct that seriously endangers life. Murder is not simply homicide, but homicide of a particularly culpable nature because it is accompanied by defined mental states; although willingness to commit a felony is itself culpable, it is not the same as, or equivalent to, the culpability that qualifies a homicide as murder.

While the doctrine of felony murder has sometimes been extended to cases very remote from an intentional killing, the courts and legislatures have quite generally adopted rules to restrict its scope. One restriction that responds to the large number of nonviolent statutory felonies is that the doctrine is applicable only if the underlying felony involves violence or danger to life. Sometimes it is required that the *type* of the underlying felony meet this requirement; or it may be enough if the commission of the felony in the particular circumstances is violent or dangerous. The first approach retains the felony-murder doctrine on its own terms but confines it to a more limited group of felonies; to the same general effect are requirements that the felony have been a felony at common law or that it be *malum in se*. The second approach

may create liability in a case not covered by the first; it looks in the direction of a displacement of felony murder by a different rationale based directly on the dangerousness of the actor's conduct.

In many states that have more than one category of murder, the more serious category includes homicides committed in the course of one of a short list of particularly dangerous felonies: usually arson, rape, robbery, and burglary; commonly kidnapping; and sometimes one or two others. All other felony murders are in the less serious category. The Pennsylvania degree statute of 1794, referred to above, made this distinction; only homicides committed in the course of the first four mentioned crimes were murder in the first degree.

The nature of the underlying felony is restricted also by the requirement that it be "independent" of the homicide. Otherwise, every felonious assault from which death results might be prosecuted as murder, by operation of the felony-murder doctrine. Such an outcome would obliterate the common-law difference between murder and manslaughter and would treat alike homicides of very different character and culpability. Even so, the requirement of independence has been rejected in a few jurisdictions, which presumably leave it to the good sense of the prosecutor not to reach an inappropriate result. The requirement does not apply if the person who is killed is someone other than the victim of the assault.

Another way of restricting felony murder places strong weight on the element of causation. Mere temporal conjunction of the felony and death has never been sufficient for felony murder; it is necessary at least that the death would not have occurred but for the felony. Some courts have explicitly required more than "but for" causation; the death must be a reasonably foreseeable, or natural and probable, consequence of the felony and must not be attributable primarily to a separable, intervening cause. Various ad hoc rules rejecting felony murder when someone other than the felon or an accomplice actually commits the homicide or when an accomplice is killed take a similar approach, although they refer to the party who kills or is killed rather than to causation as such.

The duration of the period during which the felony-murder doctrine applies is not uniformly defined. Once the felony is in progress, the doctrine certainly applies, but it is possible to end its application sooner or later after the felony is complete or has been abandoned, to include or exclude, in particular, flight from the scene of the felony. Some statutes explicitly include the period of flight. There is no clear general rule; the doctrine usually is applicable if the flight is continuous with the commission of the felony and if it cannot yet be said that the felony has succeeded or failed.

A more general attack on felony murder rejects it entirely and subsumes appropriate cases of homicide in the course of a felony under another category of murder. If a felon acting either with intent to kill or with extreme recklessness commits a homicide, then he is guilty of murder on that basis; the fact that the acts were committed in furtherance of a felony obviously does not count against liability. Reflecting the conclusion that if no element of that kind is present, then the felon's liability for murder is gratuitous, the Model Penal Code and the statutes of a few states have eliminated the felony-murder doctrine. Elsewhere, there has been a partial displacement of the strict doctrine by allowance of an affirmative defense if the felon's own conduct was not intended to and did not in any way endanger life. Of course, if the commission of a felony is itself deemed sufficient to satisfy the requirement of extreme recklessness (on the ground that a felony of that nature is always extremely dangerous to life), the concept of felony murder is reintroduced with the pretense of a different rationale. The Model Penal Code, for example, notwithstanding its strong criticism of the felony-murder doctrine, provides that recklessness and extreme indifference to the value of human life, which support liability for murder, are presumed if the actor is committing, or is in flight after committing, one of half a dozen named violent felonies (§ 210.2(1)(b)). Some courts occasionally criticize the doctrine but preserve its force in particular cases by tenuous application of an alternative basis of liability to the specific facts. England, where the doctrine originated, abolished it by statute in 1957 (Homicide Act of 1957, 5 & 6 Eliz. 2, c. 11, § 1).

The uneven record of legislative and judicial efforts to limit or eliminate the felony-murder doctrine suggests strongly the central themes of the law of criminal homicide. When a death occurs and its occurrence can be attributed to the conduct of an identifiable person who is not blameless, there is a strong impulse to hold that person liable for the death, even if, from his point of view, the death should be viewed as accidental. The law not only reflects considered judgments about culpability; it also reflects an unconsidered effort to find an explanation and assign responsibility for an occurrence as disturbing to our sense of order as an unnatural death.

Resistance to a lawful arrest. Some of the older accounts of murder under the common law include resistance to a lawful arrest as a category of malice aforethought. Such a rule would impose strict liability for murder on a person whose resistance to a lawful arrest caused a death, even if it were accidental. It is now generally agreed that there is no such independent category of murder, although a statutory provision reflecting the traditional rule survives in a few states. A lawful arrest does not mitigate or excuse conduct in opposition to it, as might an unlawful application of similar physical force. Otherwise, homicide resulting from resistance to a lawful arrest is not treated differently from other homicide. Even in those states that have a special statutory provision, it is doubtful whether a wholly accidental death would be treated as murder if it did not also satisfy some other category of the crime. (England explicitly abolished this category of murder along with felony murder by means of the Homicide Act of 1957.)

Degrees of murder. The distinction between first-degree and second-degree murder that the Pennsylvania legislature adopted in 1794 applied to intentional killings and felony murder. The statute referred explicitly to killings "by means of poison, or by lying in wait"; but these were evidently intended simply as examples of "willful, deliberate, or premeditated killing." Statutory provisions differentiating types of murder were subsequently enacted in other states. They typically followed the Pennsylvania formula (including references to poison and lying in wait, which sometimes took on a significance of their own) and occasionally made additional distinctions. As in Pennsylvania, the dominant purpose has been to restrict the imposition of the most severe penalty, whether capital punishment or the longest period of imprisonment. Among the other circumstances that may qualify a homicide as first-degree, or capital, murder are the use of torture, destruction of or interference with the operation of a public conveyance, use of an explosive, murder for hire, and killing a public official or someone engaged in law enforcement.

Another approach is taken by the Model Penal Code, which rejects further classification of murder but specifies "aggravating circumstances" and "mitigating circumstances" to be taken into account in the determination of whether to impose capital punishment (§ 210.6). The aggravating circumstances include ones that have been used in statutory degree provisions, such as commission of specified violent felonies. They also include others which reflect a judgment that the special deterrent or preventive effect of the death penalty or an extreme measure of retribution is appropriate, as in the case of a defendant under sentence of imprisonment or previously convicted of murder or a violent felony, or where there has been more than one victim. Mitigating circumstances include aspects of the crime that lessen the defendant's culpability as well as factors about the defendant himself, including his youth and lack of a criminal history. Capital punishment can be imposed only if at least one aggravating circumstance, and no mitigating circumstance, is present. Decisions of the Supreme Court have imposed constitutional limitations on capital punishment, which appear to require an exercise of discretion in each case pursuant to legislatively prescribed standards. The approach of the Model Penal Code, which meets this test, has been widely adopted. The degree formula is still used to distinguish noncapital murders of unequal culpability; most often, as in the original Pennsylvania statute, the circumstances of first-degree murder are prescribed and other cases are grouped generally as second-degree murder.

Manslaughter

As the common law developed, manslaughter became a residual category that included homicides lacking the very high degree of culpability which characterized the capital offense of murder but not so lacking in culpability as to be noncriminal altogether. The need for an intermediate category of this kind reflects the special significance given to the taking of human life; whereas the criminal law might disregard other kinds of harm that was not fully intentional, it could not disregard a homicide accompanied by any substantial degree of fault.

Two general groupings of manslaughter are distinguishable in the common law, although they were treated as a single crime and were punishable similarly. They can be described generally as voluntary manslaughter and involuntary manslaughter, labels that are sometimes used in statutes to refer to separate crimes carrying different penalties, with voluntary manslaughter as the more serious offense. There is considerable variation among current statutory formulas, some of which continue to rely on the understandings of the common law and refer simply to manslaughter without defining it. It is still convenient to consider the crime according to the groupings of voluntary and involuntary manslaughter, those terms being used descriptively, whether or not there is explicit statutory differentiation.

Voluntary manslaughter. The principal category of murder refers simply to a homicide committed with intent to kill, without taking account of circumstances that might mitigate culpability because they explain, and in some measure excuse, the actor's state of mind. Voluntary manslaughter is an intentional homicide that would be murder but for the existence of such mitigating circumstances. It is commonly described as an intentional killing accompanied by additional factors that negate malice aforethought. Occasionally, voluntary manslaughter is described as a homicide committed in circumstances that overcome and eliminate an intention to kill. Such statements rely on a concept of intention that includes a measure of reflection; they should not be understood to require that the killing be unintentional in the ordinary sense.

Most often, the factor that reduces homicide from murder to voluntary manslaughter is some act of the victim that prompts the intent to kill. The usual rule is that an intentional homicide is manslaughter if the actor was provoked to kill by an adequate provocation and acted while provoked, before sufficient time had passed for a reasonable person to have "cooled off." It is not the provocative acts of the victim as such that reduce murder to manslaughter, but their effect on the actor. The most extreme provocation does not affect the result if it does not deprive the actor of self-control; one who responds to a provocation by coolly killing the person who provoked him is guilty of murder, not manslaughter.

Insisting that conduct be judged by the standard of a reasonable person, the law tended to develop rather rigid rules about the kinds of provocative act that were adequate; a violent battery by the victim and discovery of the victim committing adultery with one's spouse were the paradigms of adequate provocation. Abuse by means of "mere words" was the paradigm of inadequate provocation. Other, less certain, categories were assault or a threat of assault on oneself or a battery or assault on a near relative. Whatever the nature of the provocation, it was not adequate if the actor responded by intentionally killing someone other than the source of the provocation. If, on the other hand, he directed his response against one whom he mistakenly believed to be the source of the provocation, or if accidentally or negligently he killed someone other than his intended victim, the provocation might be allowed. Rules of this kind are sometimes expressed as a general requirement that the homicidal response be reasonably related to the nature and source of the provocation.

The cooling-off doctrine, as it is sometimes called, is yet another aspect of the requirement that provocation be adequate. A person is expected to regain control of himself within a reasonable period. Courts have sometimes applied this rule strictly and held that rage prolonged or renewed after enough time to cool off has elapsed does not reduce murder to manslaughter, whatever the actual provocation. Despite the argument that the passage of time and brooding over an injury might reduce rather than increase self-control, which may then be swept away by a slight reminder of the original injury, the evident judgment of the law was that only a sudden provocation adequate in itself should be taken into account.

The current direction of the law is to eliminate categorical restrictions of the provocation that may be adequate. The Model Penal Code eliminates all such restrictions and substitutes a general provision classifying as manslaughter "a homicide which would otherwise be murder [that] is committed under the influence of extreme mental or emotional disturbance for which there is reasonable explanation or excuse" (§ 210.3(1)(b)). This provision leaves it to the trier of fact to determine whether the actor's loss of self-control is reasonably comprehensible, without prescribing in advance what sorts of provocation in what circumstances may meet that standard. A number of jurisdictions have adopted such an approach in whole or in part, either by statute or judicial decision.

A distinct but related issue is whether the adequacy of provocation should be measured from the point of view of an "ordinary reasonable person" or from the point of view of the actor, taking into account any idiosyncratic features he possesses. A defendant has sometimes claimed that provocation which would have been inadequate for an ordinary person was adequate in his case because of some factor peculiar to himself that made the provocative act unusually disturbing. Once again, the law has tended to relax its earlier insistence on an objective standard—without, however, eliminating entirely the requirement that the actor's behavior be objectively comprehensible. The Model Penal Code, for example, provides that the reasonableness of the actor's explanation or excuse for his disturbance "shall be determined from the viewpoint of a person in the actor's situation" (§ 210.3(1)(b)). The commentary to this provision explains that the actor's physical handicaps are surely part of his "situation" but that idiosyncratic moral values are not; for the rest, the commentary observes, the reference to the actor's situation is deliberately ambiguous and leaves the issue to the common sense of the finder of fact.

A provoked intentional killing is the most common example of voluntary manslaughter. There are a number of other situations in which an intentional killing is not altogether excused but the circumstances diminish culpability enough to remove it from the category of murder. In general, such situations are those in which a recognized basis for excusing the killing fails to apply fully because one of its elements is absent; nevertheless, the partial applicability of the excuse mitigates the killing. Thus, for example, a person who kills another in what he believes is necessary self-defense against a threat of death or serious injury is excused entirely if his belief is reasonable. If his belief is unreasonable, the defense of self-defense is not available. Even so, the fact that he acted in response to what he believed was a deadly threat distinguishes the crime from an intentional killing not prompted by such fear. His fear seems as appropriate a basis for mitigation as passion or rage caused by provocation.

Similarly, one who uses deadly force in defense against an actual threat of death or serious injury may not be excused entirely if he provoked the attack or if he did not retreat as required before using deadly force. One may use deadly force to protect another person or to prevent commission of a felony, in circumstances that make these defenses not fully available. In these and similar cases of an imperfect excuse, the intention to kill is in a significant sense responsive rather than original with the actor. That element contradicts the extreme denial of the value of human life that characterizes murder. England and a few jurisdictions in the United States have recognized the possibility that a person's capacity to reflect and weigh the consequences of his conduct may be significantly less than normal, without being so abnormal that the defense of insanity is available. His "diminished capacity" may then provide a basis for reducing an intentional killing from murder to manslaughter. Even where this defense is recognized, it is allowed infrequently and in special circumstances only, lest all objective elements of the distinction between murder and voluntary manslaughter be swept away and replaced by an assessment of the actor's subjective culpability.

Involuntary manslaughter. As the name suggests, involuntary manslaughter comprises homicides that are not intentional and lack the special elements of culpability which qualify certain unintentional killings as murder but are nevertheless deemed too culpable to be excused entirely. The crime is recognized in all states in a variety of statutory formulations, which generally follow the common-law pattern and may rely wholly on the common-law definition. Whether or not it is explicitly differentiated from voluntary manslaughter by statute, involuntary manslaughter is regarded as a less serious offense and usually punished less severely.

A person whose criminal negligence causes the death of another is guilty of involuntary manslaughter. It is generally agreed that negligence sufficient for liability is considerably greater than what would suffice for civil tort liability. Such negligence may be characterized simply as "criminal," "gross," or "culpable" negligence; as "recklessness"; or as "reckless" or "wanton" carelessness. The central element is unjustified creation of a substantial risk of serious injury or death. Sometimes it is also required that the actor be aware of and disregard the risk, in which case the standard of culpability is more aptly described as recklessness than as negligence. The standard is measurably lower than the extreme recklessness that suffices for murder.

An alternative basis of liability for involuntary manslaughter under the common law and most statutory provisions is commission of an unlawful act or an unlawful omission from which death results. Although the unlawfulness of the conduct may be indicative of negligence, under this theory it is the unlawfulness, rather than the nature of the risk created by the conduct, that establishes liability. In principle, liability might extend to conduct that is unlawful but not criminal, but in practice, liability is usually restricted to conduct that is criminal (but not a felony that will support felony murder). Where vehicular homicide has not been made a separate offense, violation of a traffic regulation is a common example.

Frequently described as misdemeanor manslaughter, this form of criminal homicide has been criticized on the same grounds as felony murder and limited along the same lines. Paralleling the restriction of felony murder to violent felonies, misdemeanor manslaughter is sometimes limited to offenses that are *malum in se*, lest liability be extended to all the conduct that has been made a misdemeanor by statute. Moreover, the requirement of causation has been applied strictly, courts distinguishing between the illegal aspect of the conduct as a causal factor in the homicide, and merely an attendant circumstance of an accidental death. The tendency of the law, not always stated explicitly in the cases, is to confine misdemeanor manslaughter to situations in which the actor's negligence provides a basis for liability, the illegal act having only evidentiary significance on that issue. Such a development reflects the same analysis that has led to the restriction or elimination of felony murder as a distinct category of that crime.

A homicide resulting from an unlawful battery or assault on the victim without intent to kill or injure seriously may be treated as manslaughter without express reliance on the misdemeanor manslaughter rule.

The intention to injure the victim and the commission of an act to that end are evidently perceived, like criminal negligence, as a sufficient basis for liability if death results, without special emphasis on the illegality of the conduct. Since an unjustified attack is always at least a misdemeanor *(malum in se)*, such cases might also be regarded as straightforward examples of misdemeanor manslaughter. (Even if, because of aggravating circumstances, the battery were felonious, the "independence" requirement would preclude application of the felony-murder doctrine.) The Model Penal Code, which rejects the misdemeanor manslaughter rule entirely, eliminates liability for manslaughter when death results accidentally from a battery.

Negligent or vehicular homicide. In much the way that the Pennsylvania degree formula differentiated types of murder in order to limit application of the death penalty, statutes in many jurisdictions provide for a lesser category of involuntary criminal homicide. Commonly called negligent homicide or something similar and treated as a separate offense, the category may also be distinguished simply as a lesser degree of manslaughter. A lower standard of culpability applies than that for manslaughter. In particular, recklessness or conscious disregard of the danger to others is not required. While negligence suffices, it is still more than is needed for civil liability. The precise standard of culpability both as set forth in a statute and as elaborated by the courts is likely to depend significantly on the formula used to define involuntary manslaughter, with which it must be contrasted.

In some states, the lesser offense is made specifically applicable to motor-vehicle accidents and labeled "vehicular homicide." Even when a high degree of negligence can be established, juries have frequently been unwilling to convict a driver of manslaughter. The large number of traffic fatalities, often occurring in accidents for which liability is uncertain, has evidently made it easier to perceive such deaths as an ordinary, random incident of driving and has diminished the need to resort to the criminal law for explanation. Reduction of the criminality and the penalty attached to the offense acknowledges these changed attitudes and has made application of some criminal sanction more likely.

Penalties

The decision of the Supreme Court in *Coker v. Georgia*, 433 U.S. 584 (1977) raised considerable doubt as to whether capital punishment is constitutionally permitted for any crime other than homicide. Those jurisdictions that retain capital punishment always include among capital crimes a category of murder, which may be narrowly restricted. The Supreme Court has indicated that, except perhaps in very special circumstances, the Constitution prohibits mandatory imposition of the death sentence. The decision whether to impose sentence of death is made by the judge and/or jury, pursuant to various statutory procedures that generally provide for full consideration of aggravating and mitigating factors.

Whether or not capital punishment is retained, murder is always regarded as one of the most serious offenses, for which (or for the most serious category of which) the law's maximum penalty can be imposed. Most jurisdictions authorize a sentence for murder ranging up to life imprisonment, and a minimum sentence of imprisonment for a substantial number of years, commonly as many as ten or twenty. For the most serious category of murder, some jurisdictions provide a mandatory sentence of life imprisonment. Penalties for manslaughter vary widely. The maximum penalty may be as high as ten or twenty years' imprisonment, and the minimum as little as one or two. If involuntary manslaughter is treated separately, the maximum penalty is less—usually not more than five years' imprisonment. The penalty for negligent homicide or vehicular homicide usually does not exceed three years' imprisonment.

The sentencing provisions of the Model Penal Code are representative of this general pattern. Murder, a felony of the first degree (§ 210.2(2)), is punishable (capital punishment aside) by imprisonment for a minimum of not less than one nor more than ten years and for a maximum of life. Manslaughter, a felony of the second degree (§ 210.3(2)), is punishable by imprisonment for a minimum of not less than one nor more than three years and for a maximum of ten years. Negligent homicide, a felony of the third degree (§ 210.4(2)), is punishable by imprisonment for a minimum of not less than one nor more than two years and for a maximum of five years.

Conclusion

The extent to which criminal homicide can be characterized as a single crime or family of crimes is indicated by the fact that the less serious categories are treated as lesser included offenses within the more serious. In a prosecution for first-degree murder, for example, the jury is likely to be instructed on second-degree murder, as well as voluntary manslaughter and even involuntary manslaughter, if any view of the evidence would support those verdicts. The taking of human life, as the harm to be avoided, rather than a common type or measure of culpability, is what binds the whole together.

That element has been critical in efforts to reform or rationalize homicide offenses according to general principles of the criminal law. Although criminal responsibility is thought not to be properly based on fortuities, whether or not death results from an act is often fortuitous from the point of view of the actor and may have large consequences because the severity of the penalty increases so dramatically if death does result. When the circumstances of a death do not allow one to regard it as an ordinary event in human experience, the need for explanation is strong and includes the assignment of blame if that is plausible.

The replacement of strict rules and categories, such as those that characterized voluntary manslaughter, with more general and open principles that refer directly to our primary concerns, may not further the purpose of rationalizing the law of homicide as much as we should like. The exercise of judgment or discretion is, in the end, guided by the same basic impulses as those that led to the more rigid structure. Thus, for example, despite insistence that the doctrine of felony murder is not consistent with basic premises about criminal responsibility, it persists in one form or another. Perhaps the most significant and constant thread in the long development of the law of homicide has been the progressive narrowing of the application of capital punishment. That has not been the product of greater understanding of the bases of liability for homicide so much as a drawing away from capital punishment as such.

LLOYD L. WEINREB

See also ABORTION; ASSASSINATION; CAPITAL PUNISHMENT; CORONER, ROLE OF THE; EUTHANASIA; SUICIDE: LEGAL ASPECTS.

BIBLIOGRAPHY

American Law Institute. *Model Penal Code and Commentaries: Official Draft and Revised Comments.* Philadelphia: ALI, 1980.
DEVINE, PHILIP E. *The Ethics of Homicide.* Ithaca, N.Y.: Cornell University Press, 1978.
DUFF, R. A. "Implied and Constructive Malice in Murder." *Law Quarterly Review* 95 (1979): 418–444.
GEGAN, BERNARD E. "A Case of Depraved Mind Murder." *St. John's Law Review* 49 (1974): 417–459.
HART, H. L. A., and HONORÉ, ANTONY M. *Causation in the Law.* New York: Oxford University Press, 1959.
HOLLIS, CHRISTOPHER. *The Homicide Act.* Foreword by Gerald Gardiner. London: Victor Gollancz, 1964.

HUGHES, GRAHAM. "Criminal Omissions." *Yale Law Journal* 67 (1958): 590–637.

KADISH, SANFORD H. "Respect for Life and Regard for Rights in the Criminal Law." *California Law Review* 64 (1976): 871–901.

Law Commission. *Imputed Criminal Intent (Director of Public Prosecutions v. Smith)*. London: Her Majesty's Stationery Office, 1967.

MORELAND, ROY. *The Law of Homicide*. Indianapolis: Bobbs-Merrill, 1952.

MORRIS, NORVAL. "The Felon's Responsibility for the Lethal Acts of Others." *University of Pennsylvania Law Review* 105 (1956): 50–81.

———, and HOWARD, COLIN. *Studies in Criminal Law*. Oxford: Oxford University Press, Clarendon Press, 1964.

MORRIS, TERENCE, and BLOM-COOPER, LOUIS. *A Calendar of Murder: Criminal Homicide in England since 1957*. London: Michael Joseph, 1964.

Royal Commission on Capital Punishment (1949–1953). *Report*. Cmd. 8932. London: Her Majesty's Stationery Office, 1953.

SELLIN, THORSTEN, ed. "Murder and the Penalty of Death." *Annals of the American Academy of Political and Social Science* 284 (1952): 1–166.

WECHSLER, HERBERT, and MICHAEL, JEROME. "A Rationale of the Law of Homicide." *Columbia Law Review* 37 (1937): 701–761, 1261–1325.

WILLIAMS, GLANVILLE. *The Sanctity of Life and the Criminal Law*. Foreword by William C. Warren. New York: Knopf, 1957.

WOLFGANG, MARVIN E. *Patterns in Criminal Homicide*. Reprint. Criminology, Law Enforcement, and Social Problems Series 211. Montclair, N.J.: Patterson Smith, 1975.

HOMOSEXUALITY AND CRIME

Homosexual behavior is here defined as sexual behavior between persons of the same sex. Homosexuality is viewed as a characterological matter, related to a person's orientation. *Gay* and *lesbian* are used to denote persons who are not only homosexually oriented but also form an identity around that orientation and affiliate with a community of homosexually identified persons.

History of criminal sanctions

With the establishment of Christianity as the Roman state religion in the fourth century A.D., homosexual behavior began to be defined as illegal under Roman statutes, in which homosexual marriages were specifically proscribed (Boswell, p. 123). In 390, the three emperors then reigning jointly, Theodosius, Valentinian II, and Arcadus, outlawed anal sex. However, taxes on male prostitution were collected until the sixth century (Bullough, p. 31). The sixth-century emperor Justinian was clearly influenced by the Judeo-Christian Scriptures in compiling the *Corpus Juris Civilis*. For example, he used the term *sodomy* as a general category into which any sexual behavior other than heterosexual coitus could be placed.

By the early Middle Ages, all nonheterosexual behavior was considered *contra naturam* ("against nature"). The issue of "nature" came to dominate questions of sexuality for centuries. Civil law was generally more tolerant of homosexuality than canon law, although civil authorities used the Scriptures to justify their repressive actions. In the late eleventh and early twelfth centuries, a gay culture nevertheless arose, the likes of which had not existed since the height of Greek civilization. It was reflected in the writings of both clerics and laymen that were drawn from the high medieval equivalent of the popular culture (Boswell, p. 243).

Under the Church's influence in the thirteenth century, however, more anti-homosexual laws were enacted. St. Thomas Aquinas argued that homosexuality is "against nature," a view that, in conjunction with translations of Scripture that emphasize an anti-homosexual bias, still underpins religious and legal sanctions against homosexuality.

Beginning in 1533, anti-homosexual laws were enacted in Great Britain. "Buggery" laws forbade homosexual acts, anal sex, and later, solicitation for sex. These statutes were not revised until after the publication in 1956 of the Wolfenden Committee's report, which recommended the decriminalization of sodomy.

In North America, penalties for sodomy have been enacted since 1637. As with British law, American anti-homosexual laws have been plagued by ambiguities surrounding the definitions of the terms *sodomy* and *crimes against nature*.

Homosexual behavior was thus initially defined as sinful. As the power of the secular state rose and ecclesiastical power declined, however, homosexual acts were redefined as criminal. This religious and legal influence continues to be found in the wording of some legal proscriptions against homosexual behavior.

In the nineteenth century, religious and legal condemnation were joined by medical strictures. Homosexual "sins" and "crimes" came to be seen as illnesses. The religious, legal, and medical establishments combined interests to suppress homosexual expression.

Contemporary legal issues

Most American states have statutes against consensual sodomy. Currently, there is a trend to decriminalize consensual sex acts between adults, but homosexuals are still discriminated against by civil laws and regulations. The armed forces, for example, retain the right to discharge persons on the basis of their sexual orientation, and known homosexuals are barred from immigration. But progress has been made in more than fifty American municipalities, which have enacted rulings that protect homosexuals in such areas as housing, employment, public services, education, and credit. Many corporations, including a majority of the one hundred largest firms, have instituted policies banning discrimination in hiring or advancement based on affectional or sexual orientation. Among these firms are IBM, Exxon, General Electric, General Foods, Ford, DuPont, American Telephone and Telegraph, Bank of America, and Xerox (Voeller).

Although criminal laws against homosexuality are unevenly enforced in the United States, these laws have three main consequences: (1) they make possible the constant threat of criminal prosecution; (2) they support secondary legal sanctions against lesbians and gays, as in immigration and military policies; (3) they maintain the anti-gay climate for private physical and verbal attacks against homosexuals (Slovenko).

In fact, the majority of the states retain sodomy statutes that subject the estimated 10 percent of the population that is lesbian and gay to possible criminal prosecution for engaging in sexual acts that are consensual and between adults. These laws have been extended to heterosexual acts involving oral or anal intercourse. However, when invoked, they are generally applied only to homosexuals. Possible penalties for these felonies range from life imprisonment to several years in prison. Because they are vaguely worded, seldom enforced, and applied primarily to a special class of citizens, the laws are frequently challenged in the courts.

There have been few rulings by the United States Supreme Court relevant to the concerns of homosexual men and women. However, because of its impact on future rulings regarding the homosexual issue, special attention should be given to the 1976 decision in *Doe v. Commonwealth's Attorney for the City of Richmond*, 403 F. Supp. 1199 (E.D. Va. 1975), *aff'd*, 425 U.S. 901 (1976). In this ruling, the Supreme Court affirmed the decision of a three-judge district court, which had held that Virginia's crimes-against-nature statute was not unconstitutional as applied to private, consensual homosexual relations between adult males. Further,

the lower court had held that it is not necessary "to show that moral delinquency actually results from homosexuality"; rather, it suffices "that the conduct is likely to end in a contribution to moral delinquency" (1202). Finally, the court took note of the age of the sodomy statute, stating that it had an "ancestry going back to Judaic and Christian law" (1202) and citing in this connection Old Testament prohibitions.

Thus, the Supreme Court affirmed the majority opinion in *Doe* that alleged unnatural acts, even between consenting adults in the privacy of their own home (as was the case in *Doe*), are outside the protection of the constitutional right to privacy. It also preserved the standard which reasons in a circular fashion that homosexuality is immoral and that prohibiting it is accordingly moral (Richards).

Public-order crime

More frequently enforced against gay people are the many state and local ordinances against public-order crimes. Gay communities are chiefly affected by sanctions against prostitution and sexual acts in public places.

Prostitution. Researchers agree that only a minority of male street prostitutes identify themselves as homosexual in orientation, most presenting themselves as bisexual or heterosexual. Those involved in call services, however, generally consider themselves homosexual and are more likely to identify with the gay community. The customers of both groups, on the other hand, are almost exclusively homosexual. Homosexual prostitution, or hustling, although a male phenomenon, includes solicitation by male transvestites posing as heterosexual prostitutes. In these latter instances, the customers are usually heterosexual.

Like their female counterparts, male prostitutes generally enter the world of commercial sex after rejection by parents and because of pressing financial need. The majority have been arrested for petty crimes or drug offenses, as well as for prostitution, and one-fourth of them have also been arrested for crimes of violence. Although male hustlers rarely work for pimps, they do operate in a subculture from which they gain mutual support, a distinctive argot and set of norms and rationalizations, and training in the special skills needed in their work. The abuse of alcohol and other drugs is also facilitated and encouraged by the hustling subculture (Furnald).

Because the life of the street hustler is plagued by arrest and imprisonment, multiple drug use, and violence, male prostitutes seldom remain on the street beyond the age of thirty. Although a few runaways begin hustling at age fourteen or earlier, the median age of male prostitutes is in the early twenties. As with heterosexual prostitutes, youthful attractiveness and marketability decrease with age.

Both residents and merchants in areas frequented by street hustlers tend to file frequent complaints and apply pressure to police for "crackdowns" on commercial sex activity. Street "sweeps" and plainclothes decoy operations by police are seldom effective in suppressing such activity. Harassment and arrests in one area usually succeed only in relocating male prostitutes to another street or neighborhood. A policy of containment, coupled with foot patrol by officers who develop informants among the street hustlers, is often more effective in controlling the secondary crime that accompanies hustling.

Solicitation and public sex. In a study of nearly one thousand homosexual men and women in the San Francisco area, Alan Bell and Martin Weinberg found that cruising (seeking contact for sexual liaisons) was infrequent among lesbians. Although most homosexual men seek sexual partners in bars and bathhouses and on the streets, only a minority report cruising in public rest rooms, movie theaters, or parks, where the danger of being arrested or physically assaulted is greater. In their study, conducted under the auspices of the Institute of Sex Research, Bell and Weinberg found that most homosexual men "conduct their sexual activity in the privacy of their own home" (p. 79).

Solicitation statutes in all the states and the District of Columbia criminalize behavior that is seen as offending the public morality or constituting "lewd and lascivious conduct." Requests for sex, which would not be punishable if they took place between heterosexuals, are criminalized when made by homosexuals. Although courts have held that heterosexual solicitation does not constitute outrage of public decency, there is "harm in asking" among homosexuals.

Even in states that have repealed sodomy statutes, solicitation for homosexual acts remains illegal. These proscriptions provide the basis for a variety of law enforcement activities directed against the popular locales for male homosexual cruising. In cities such as New York, Los Angeles, and San Francisco, where gays have achieved a degree of political power, police forays into gay bars and baths are rare. Cruising in more public settings, such as parks, movie theaters, adult bookstores, and rest rooms, however, subjects homosexual men to the constant possibility of arrest by plainclothes decoys.

Typical of such vice squad activity is the use of police decoys in public rest rooms ("tearooms," in the argot of the gay community). Plainclothes officers are assigned to loiter in the rest facilities of parks and department stores, using a urinal or commode, washing their hands, or engaging men in conversation. One study found that participation of officers in such structured cruising often amounted to entrapment and frequently led to blackmail and other forms of police corruption (Humphreys).

Although some states, such as California, require registration of tearoom offenders as "mentally disordered sex offenders," convictions for public homosexual solicitation seldom result in imprisonment. Generally, the most serious consequence of tearoom arrests takes the form of public exposure in the news media. Since the late 1960s, for example, the careers of a presidential assistant, a nominee for the Supreme Court, a leading conservative congressman, and a number of eminent educators, clergymen, and business leaders, as well as other politicians, have been jeopardized by the activities of plainclothes officers operating in public rest rooms.

The majority of men who cruise in rest rooms are married, and few manifest a gay identity. Exposure through arrest is likely to result in the collapse of marriages or the loss of employment. In the Los Angeles area alone, thousands of men are apprehended each year in these facilities. Because the arresting officers tend to rely on "boiler plate" accounts that have previously held up in court, those prosecuted also lose confidence in the entire criminal justice system.

Crimes against persons

Traditionally, homosexuals have been accused of disproportionate committing of child molestation, prison rape, and homicide. Although there is some involvement by homosexually oriented men in all three of these criminal categories, the evidence clearly indicates that it is no greater than similar involvement by their heterosexual counterparts.

Homosexual men are particularly stigmatized by the myth that they are apt to molest young boys. A ten-year study of several hundred incarcerated sex offenders arrived at conclusions that differed sharply from this myth. "The adult heterosexual male constitutes a greater sexual risk to underage children than does the adult homosexual male" (Groth and Birnbaum, p. 181).

Although rape of male inmates in detention facilities is homosexual activity characterized by anal penetration, it is also usually committed by heterosexually identified males. The victims of these offenses are generally stigmatized as "punks" or "queens," although many of them have no homosexual identity. Prison rape follows the dynamics of heterosexual rape outside the penal institution. It does not result from a lack of sexual outlet; rather, it is a power relationship in which sexual force is employed in an act of hostility (Wooden and Parker, p. 33).

Homosexual elements in multiple homicides have received extensive publicity as the result of several notorious cases since the mid-1970s. Dean Corll, John Gacy, and William Bonin were mass murderers who killed a total of between sixty and one hundred young men in Houston, Chicago, and Los Angeles, respectively. Some of the victims were male prostitutes, others were runaways or hitchhikers, but all were sexually violated by their killers.

There can be no doubt that Corll, Gacy, and Bonin had strong homosexual components in their sadistic drives, but none was gay in identity or had any affiliation with the gay community. Both Corll and Bonin were engaged to be married and made only negative comments on the homosexual community. Gacy had been twice married in his compulsion to escape a gay identity. All such mass murderers are marginal to the gay world and manifest intense hostility toward homosexuality in themselves and others.

Absence of subcultural support

Apart from the rare criminalization of consensual homosexual relations through the chance application of sodomy statutes, crimes associated with homosexuality are almost totally without gay subcultural support. The exception to this rule is the activity of male hustlers, who do act in a subcultural context. Yet even that subculture is peripheral to the gay culture as a whole. The subculture of male prostitutes is a bisexual one involving many women, some of whom cohabitate with the hustlers. Additionally, the hustlers are more likely to identify themselves as bisexual than as homosexual. The satellite culture called the gay world tends to dissociate itself from the hustling subculture.

The scenes of public-order offenses—rest rooms, theaters, and bookstores—are distinctive in their lack of subcultural support. The majority of men who seek impersonal sex in public places do so with the purpose of avoiding the subcultural cruising spots where they might be identified as gay. Married men who are homosexual lack resources for countering exposure through arrest, largely because their compartmentalized marriages prevent involvement with the openly gay world. Gay subcultures not only provide skills and information sources that are protective, but pressure their participants into less highly stigmatized and criminalized settings and behavior.

Secondary crime

Victimless crimes inevitably produce secondary forms of crime. The criminalization of homosexual behavior encourages such illegal activities as blackmail, extortion, murder, robbery, "gay bashing," entrapment, and police corruption.

Blackmail. As a result of the differential enforcement of laws and the stigma attached to homosexuality, homosexual men and women are made vulnerable to blackmail. Persons apprehended for same-sex offenses in public or private fear publicity that would endanger their jobs, their relationships with family and friends, and, if they are seeking American citizenship, loss of their immigrant status (Rivera, pp. 139–140).

For those who are open about their sexual preference, discovery or loss of reputation is not a threat; but most homosexuals conceal their sexual orientation for fear of discrimination in employment, housing, or loss of family or friends. Homosexual persons are placed in a double bind—either they must be candid and risk discrimination, or remain "in the closet" and risk blackmail.

Murder victims. Closet gays are more likely to be crime victims than are gays who are open about their homosexuality. Homosexual marginals—those who operate only at the periphery of the gay community and are precluded by their marital status or fear of exposure from involvement in the gay culture—tend to interact with other social marginals such as hustlers and drug abusers. A victimization study by Brian Miller and Laud Humphreys found that 64 percent of the studied group of murdered homosexual marginals were killed by pickups or hitchhikers, most of whom were male prostitutes.

Limited to furtive sexual encounters with dangerous persons in unprotected settings, homosexual marginals are open to attack by exploitative criminal opportunists. The movement of homosexual marginals into openly gay life-styles decreases their vulnerability to violent crime.

Gay-bashing. Although lovers' quarrels are seldom responsible for murders in the gay world, openly homosexual men and women are sometimes attacked by "gay bashers." Encouraged by the "outlaw" status of homosexuals, gangs of youths engage in attacks on them ranging from verbal intimidation to homicide. As members of a stigmatized category, homosexual men and women are thereby "dehumanized," making them easy marks in a homophobic society. Juveniles often prowl gay ghettos and cruising areas to taunt or assault lesbians and gay men. Many of these gay-bashers are themselves sexually ambivalent. The psychological projection of their sexual feelings is relative to the degree of repression of their own homosexual inclinations.

Gay couples with dual incomes invest in property near the centers of large cities, renovating low-cost housing in the process of gentrification. In communities where gentrification forces ethnic minority groups out of their neighborhoods, reaction to the gay renovators may be hostile and violent. Gay-bashing also results from the perceived effeminacy of the stereotypical homosexual. Viewing the violation of gender-role stereotypes as a threat to social values, some juveniles attack the despised out-group.

Gay and lesbian targets are victimized not only by their assailants but also by a perceived lack of legal recourse and law enforcement protection. Homosexuals are aware that prosecution of assailants might lead to the loss of employment, family, and friends. Like other minority groups, they tend to see the police as enemies rather than protectors.

The police are often quick to pursue homosexuals and to use derogatory names when addressing them, but they are seldom available for protection when needed. The prevention and solution of anti-gay crimes are impeded by the mutual distrust between police and members of the gay and lesbian communities. However, large cities are appointing officers to serve as liaison agents with these communities in order to correct a long-standing history of antagonistic relations.

From criminal to victim

Although isolated homophile organizations were founded in both England and Germany at the end of the nineteenth century, the oldest continuing organizations in the Netherlands and the United States date from the period after World War II. The homophile movement began, slowly at first, not only to change the negative self-perception of homosexual men and women, but to educate the public and to effect reforms in laws regarding homosexual behavior. The Mattachine Society, established in 1950, and ONE, Inc., begun two years later and still in existence, founded journals of scholarly and literary merit.

Research by Alfred Kinsey, Evelyn Hooker, and others helped alter the view of homosexuals as isolated, pathological individuals into a recognition of them as a maligned segment of the population. McCarthy-

ism gave impetus to the formation of mutual support groups, particularly in Los Angeles.

In June 1969, responding to a police raid on the Stonewall Inn in New York City, gay people rioted and began to use the slogans of Gay Pride and Gay Power. Support for homosexual rights became a leading social movement in the 1970s, and a distinctive gay culture began to emerge, creating its own increasingly diverse subcultures. Lesbian and gay professional organizations, community services centers, newspapers, churches, and other institutions arose within the gay culture.

During the same period, substantial gains were made in legal reform, and openly lesbian and gay persons were elected and appointed to public office. In 1977, a nationwide survey by the research firm of Yankelovich, Skelly and White, Inc., found that public opinion was being transformed. Although 47 percent of the sample thought that sex between consenting homosexuals was morally wrong, 56 percent said they would vote for legislation guaranteeing civil rights for homosexuals and 70 percent said they subscribed to a statement that there should be no laws regulating sexual practices ("The New Morality").

Religious and medical opinion. Just as the emergence of negative sanctions against homosexual behavior was fueled by religious and, later, by medical condemnation, so legal reform in the area has been accompanied by changing attitudes on the part of churches and the psychiatric profession.

Changes in nomenclature. In general, psychiatrists once viewed homosexuality as an illness resulting from arrested psychosexual development, and both in practice and in case studies they concentrated on finding causes and cures for homosexuality. But in 1973 the board of trustees of the American Psychiatric Association voted to delete the word *homosexuality* from the second edition of their *Diagnostic and Statistical Manual of Mental Disorders,* thus removing the label of mental illness from homosexuality. In its place the term *sexual orientation disorder* was used, a term that applies only to those homosexuals who are distressed by, or in conflict with, their sexual orientation.

Following the lead of the psychiatrists, the American Psychological Association, the American Medical Association, and the American Bar Association also began to reform both terminology and policies. These changes were spurred by gay caucuses and by task forces of physicians, psychologists, sociologists, and other professional groups.

Easing of religious sanctions. Although slower to respond to the new liberation movement, some church groups have eased their condemnation of homosexuals as persons. The Episcopal Church has ordained openly gay and lesbian priests, and Presbyterians, Unitarians, and Methodists allow openly gay ministers. Active organizations of homosexuals now operate within the Roman Catholic and many Greek Orthodox, Anglican, and Protestant denominations, and gay and lesbian Jewish congregations have been formed. The Metropolitan Community Church, a body of homosexual believers, has hundreds of functioning congregations.

Backlash and defeats. Although gains have been made both in securing legal reform and in changing public and institutional opinion, there have also been defeats. In a few states, solicitation and even sodomy statutes were reinstated after having been repealed. Gay-rights ordinances were overturned in a few cities, notably Miami. New anti-homosexual laws were also passed, as in Oklahoma, where known homosexuals were denied the right of employment as public-school teachers.

The resurgence of right-wing fundamentalist Christianity resulted in attacks on homosexual rights in the late 1970s and early 1980s. An attempt to forbid employment of homosexuals in California public schools (Proposition 6) was defeated in a public referendum only after an intense campaign on the part of lesbian and gay activists, operating in conjunction with civil libertarians. This backlash against the lesbian and gay liberation movement also resulted in an increase of criminal victimization of homosexuals. Serious attacks by gay-bashing gangs and mentally disturbed individuals erupted in New York, San Francisco, Los Angeles, and some gay coastal resorts.

Conclusions

Although legal proscriptions against homosexual behavior proliferated in response to certain anti-homosexual themes in medieval Christianity, the resulting oppression of homosexuals formed the basis for the rise of a gay and lesbian liberation movement and the emergence of a homophile culture. Since 1950, the work of scholars and of gay and lesbian activists has modified anti-gay public opinion. Large communities of homosexuals have coalesced in major American cities, resulting in sharply increased visibility and the growth of lesbian and gay political power. Not only has the political and economic influence of homosexuals produced an easing of legal sanctions against consensual homosexual behavior, but it has also affected the operation of law enforcement agencies. Police increasingly recognize the importance of communication and cooperation with the growing homosexual communities.

In recent decades, the view of homosexuals as sinners and criminals has given way to concern about homosexuals as victims of crime. Increasingly firm evidence shows that such proscribed behaviors as male prostitution, sex in public places, and secondary crimes occur at the margins, not the center, of the gay culture.

Crime control and effective law enforcement are aided by the development of strong communities of proud and self-confident gay men and lesbians. As homosexually oriented people are integrated into a culture with its own literary heritage and successful role models, their behavior will be increasingly influenced by the gay culture's normative system and institutions.

Violence, extortion, commercialized vice, drug abuse, and a variety of publicly offensive acts tend to cluster around the margins of every cultural entity. This principle applies to ethnic and racial satellite cultures, as well as to the gay culture. Integration into the central stream of a minority culture lessens the risk that its members will be either victims or offenders in a crime. Decreasing the legal sanctions and criminal stigma directed against homosexuals as a group strengthens the protective community and enables gays and lesbians to cooperate more fully in law enforcement.

ANTHONY RUSSO
LAUD HUMPHREYS

See also CRIMINALIZATION AND DECRIMINALIZATION; PRISONS, *articles on* PRISONS FOR WOMEN *and* PRISON SUBCULTURE; PROSTITUTION AND COMMERCIALIZED VICE: SOCIAL AND ORGANIZATIONAL ASPECTS; VICTIMLESS CRIME.

BIBLIOGRAPHY

BELL, ALAN P., and WEINBERG, MARTIN S. *Homosexualities: A Study of Diversity among Men and Women.* New York: Simon & Schuster, 1978.

BOSWELL, JOHN. *Christianity, Social Tolerance, and Homosexuality: Gay People in Western Europe from the Beginning of the Christian Era to the Fourteenth Century.* University of Chicago Press, 1980.

BULLOUGH, VERN L. *Homosexuality: A History.* New York: New American Library, 1979.

FURNALD, RODMAN. "An Exploratory Study of Male Hustlers in Hollywood." Master's thesis, University of Southern California, 1978.

GROTH, NICHOLAS, and BIRNBAUM, JEAN. "Adult Sexual Orientation and Attraction to Underage Persons." *Archives of Sexual Behavior* 7 (1978): 175–181.

HUMPHREYS, LAUD. *Tearoom Trade: Impersonal Sex in Public Places.* Chicago: Aldine, 1970.

MILLER, BRIAN, and HUMPHREYS, LAUD. "Lifestyles and Violence: Homosexual Victims of Assault and Murder." *Qualitative Sociology* 3 (1980): 169–185.

"The New Morality." *Time Magazine*, 21 November 1977, pp. 111–118.

RICHARDS, DAVID A. J. "Unnatural Acts and the Constitutional Right to Privacy: A Moral Theory." *Fordham Law Review* 45 (1977): 1281–1348.

RIVERA, RHONDA R. "Our Straight-laced Judges: The Legal Position of Homosexual Persons in the United States." *Hastings Law Journal* 30 (1979): 799–955.

SLOVENKO, RALPH. "Homosexuality and the Law: From Condemnation to Celebration." *Homosexual Behavior: A Modern Reappraisal.* Edited by Judd Marmor. New York: Basic Books, 1980, pp. 194–218.

VOELLER, BRUCE. "Society and the Gay Movement." *Homosexual Behavior: A Modern Reappraisal.* Edited by Judd Marmor. New York: Basic Books, 1980, pp. 232–252.

The Wolfenden Report: Report of the Committee on Homosexual Offenses and Prostitution. Authorized American edition. Introduction by Karl Menninger, M.D. New York: Stein & Day, 1963.

WOODEN, WAYNE S., and PARKER, JAY. *Men behind Bars: Sexual Exploitation in Prison.* New York: Plenum, 1982.

HOT PURSUIT

See ARREST AND STOP; SEARCH AND SEIZURE.

HOUSEBREAKING

See BURGLARY.

HUMAN RIGHTS

See CORPORAL PUNISHMENT; CRIMINAL PROCEDURE: CONSTITUTIONAL ASPECTS; CRUEL AND UNUSUAL PUNISHMENT; INTERNATIONAL CRIMES AGAINST THE PEACE; INTERNATIONAL CRIMINAL LAW; TORTURE; WAR CRIMES.